PRINCIPLES OF MARKETING MANAGEMENT

EPIGRAPH

Whatever be the detail with which you cram your student, the chance of his meeting in after-life exactly that detail is almost infinitesimal; and if he does meet it, he will probably have forgotten what you taught him about it. The really useful training yields a comprehension of a few general principles with a thorough grounding in the way they apply to a variety of concrete details. In subsequent practice the [students] will have forgotten your particular details; but they will remember by an unconscious common sense how to apply principles to immediate circumstances.

——Alfred North Whitehead
(1861–1947)

PRINCIPLES

OF

MARKETING

MANAGEMENT

Richard P. Bagozzi
Stanford University

SCIENCE RESEARCH ASSOCIATES, INC.
Chicago, Henley-on-Thames, Sydney, Toronto
A Subsidiary of IBM

Acquisition Editor	Roger Ross
Project Editor	Geof Garvey
Text Design	Lee Madden
Cover Design/Production Administrator	Steve Leonardo
Composition	Allservice Phototypesetting Co.
Illustrations	House of Graphics

Library of Congress Cataloging in Publication Data

Bagozzi, Richard P.
Principles of marketing management.

Bibliography: p.
Includes index.
1. Marketing—Management.   I. Title.
HF5415.13.B34   1986   658.8   85-2203
ISBN 0-574-19335-9

Printed in the United States of America.

10 9 8 7 6 5 4 3 2 1

to Beverly, Benjamin, and Anna

ABOUT THE AUTHOR

Richard P. Bagozzi is a professor of marketing at the Graduate School of Business of Stanford University, in Stanford, California. Prior to this he was on the faculties of the University of California at Berkeley and the Massachusetts Institute of Technology. He holds undergraduate and advanced degrees in engineering and mathematics and an MBA in general business. His Ph.D. is from Northwestern University, where he specialized in behavioral sciences and statistics in management.

Before turning to a career in education, Professor Bagozzi worked as a project engineer for the Pontiac Motors Division of General Motors, where he was engaged in the design, development, and testing of new automobiles. He has continued his contact with industry through executive teaching and through occasionally advising companies, nonprofit organizations, and government agencies on management practices.

Dr. Bagozzi has done extensive research into customer behavior, sales force behavior, marketing communication, and research methodology. He is the author of Causal Models in Marketing *(John Wiley & Sons) and has authored and coauthored more than seventy-five articles in professional and scholarly journals. In 1982, an article he wrote for the May 1977* Journal of Marketing Research *was given the O'Dell Award for the piece making the most lasting contribution in the five years after its publication. In 1985, an article he wrote earned the Maynard Award as the most significant contribution to marketing theory and thought in the 1984 volume of the* Journal of Marketing.

Among other honors, Dr. Bagozzi has received the American Marketing Association's first-place award for his doctoral dissertation, a Senior Fulbright Research Grant to do research in Europe, the School of Business Administration (Berkeley) Outstanding Teaching Prize, and the Campuswide (Berkeley) Distinguished Teaching Award. Professor Bagozzi has served on the editorial boards of the Journal of Marketing, Journal of Marketing Research, Marketing Science, Journal of Consumer Research, Journal of Economic Psychology, Social Psychology Quarterly, *and* Journal of Personality and Social Psychology.

CONTENTS

PREFACE

In 1983, U.S. Secretary of Education Terrel Bell described higher education in America as a "tide of mediocrity." Compared to the conclusions drawn by the National Institute of Education in the following year, this was a flattering characterization. The NIE found that the quality of university education has fallen dramatically in recent years and that student interest and performance have never been at a lower point.

Such assessments obviously do not apply to every university or college or to every subject area. But over the years, I have been especially bothered by the state of marketing education at the universities with which I have had direct experience.

How is the field of marketing viewed in your college or university? Among nonmarketing faculty, my experience has been that marketing is all too often regarded as less fundamental or noble than other fields of study. Some even see it as an immoral activity. When passing students in the hallway or at the bookstore, I frequently hear how "easy" marketing courses are or, alternatively, how the field comes across as a confusing amalgam of ideas with no underlying core. Faculty and students tolerate marketing as a necessary part of the curriculum but do not seem to respect it.

Contrast these reactions to the attitudes held by most marketing professors and professionals. Among colleagues and friends, I have always marveled at the level of pride and commitment to the field of marketing. Marketers clearly believe strongly in the importance of what they are doing.

What, then, accounts for the diverging viewpoints of nonmarketing faculty and students on the one hand and marketers on the other? I believe that the divergence lies, in part, in fundamental ambivalences toward buying and selling. From Aristotle, to preachings in the Bible, through the Middle Ages, and up until the present, the role of the merchant has typically been disparaged and stigmatized. Although such prejudices are slowly breaking down, there seems to be an inherent wariness in all of us toward giving and receiving in general and marketing in particular. We regard buying as necessary and at times fun; but selling is construed in less favorable terms. Yet both must occur if human needs are to be fully satisfied. Our preconceptions and reactions to marketing are thus mixed in a way that the study of chemistry, literature, and the social sciences is not.

In the short run at least, there is little that we can do to overcome deep-seated attitudes toward marketing, for these are rooted in cultural, psychological, and social processes. But what we can do is strive to impart valid knowledge, enthusiasm, and respect for marketing.

It is my belief that what we do in the classroom has a direct bearing on how students conceive of marketing. Indeed, the materials we use and what we teach tend to have a self-fulfilling prophecy. If we approach our subject matter with high ideals, high expectations, and pride in the field, students will respond in a like manner. But if we feed into existing attitudes and expectations for mediocrity, we will have thwarted the education process and perpetuated a misleading image of marketing.

Principles of Marketing Management was written to provide a comprehensive, current introduction to the science, art, and management of marketing. It is designed to convey a deep *understanding* of the dynamics of marketing phenomena and to enhance one's *intuition* for approaching marketing problems. At the same time, it is intended to stimulate *excitement* in, and a sense of *respect* for, the field.

A Note to Instructors

Principles of Marketing Management is not intended as a me-too product for the mass market. Rather, it is designed to fill a gap in needs not now satisfied by current offerings.

We seem to have a choice in introductory textbooks between one of two extremes. On the one hand are a few so-called "high-level" textbooks aimed primarily at the MBA course. These books profess rigor and allegedly achieve it through injection of models, mathematics, and other quantitative material. At the other extreme are the many principles texts directed largely at the first marketing course for undergraduates. These books are marked by an encyclopedic approach with much color and fanfare. Neither alternative seems to meet the needs of some faculty and students for a truly valid window into marketing behavior and marketing management.

The typical MBA text has at least three shortcomings. First, its content misleads readers about its thoroughness. Quantitative content is presented more as a façade than a foundation for the field. Equations and models are typically noted so elliptically, without interpretation, that most students simply do not grasp their meaning and significance. Perhaps this reflects author ambivalence in that an argument can be made that the place for quantitative content is in advanced marketing management, models, or other specialty courses. The second problem with MBA texts is that, in an attempt to appear managerial, they have omitted much descriptive material. Yet most students in an introductory course need a certain amount of description to get a sense of what marketing is all about. Finally, MBA texts all too often make assertions and offer prescriptions that are presented as truth when in fact they should be qualified or noted as mere speculation.

Similarly, most principles texts suffer from three drawbacks. In the first place, they espouse simple answers to problems that are not simple. Much of marketing is too complex, too dynamic, for the sweeping generalizations and pat answers that one so frequently hears. Second, principles texts are generally not selective enough in their coverage and simply overload the student with trivial "facts" best left to the gameboard. At the same time, there is a general neglect of conceptual thinking that is needed to stretch the mind. Creative performance in the real world rests on what one expert in the area terms the "magic synthesis" of abstract "dreams" with concrete experiences.* Principles texts neglect the former and trivialize the latter. Finally, as with introductory MBA books, principles texts do not clearly enough distinguish knowledge from conjecture and in the process mislead the reader.

In *Principles of Marketing Management*, I have aimed at a niche in the market consisting of those people seeking a thoughtful, yet readable, first approach to the subject matter. My style of writing is somewhat more narrative than the overly structured and "listy" styles of most MBA texts. By the same token, I have introduced considerably more descriptive material than that found in the typical MBA book yet have avoided the simplistic treatment of principles texts. Indeed, rather than doing 25 or so surface chapters into every topic of the field, I have chosen to do 16 in-depth chapters into the most fundamental and timely areas. Nevertheless, there is ample material even for the lengthy semester courses found in some schools.

Although greater attention is paid to conceptual content than is found in principles texts, this is done in a more accessible, yet more comprehensive, way than currently exists in MBA books. I try to provide a sense of history and extended discussions of concepts, principles, and examples. Considerable use of visual materials is made to complement analytical concepts, and this is integrated into the flow of the text, not merely appended to it. In addition, I have purposely avoided presentation of mathematical material in most instances with the thought that it can be reserved for subsequent courses, additional readings, or instructor presentation, if desired.

Overall, the effect is to help the reader think more deeply about marketing phenomena, to gain skills in problem analysis, and to extend these mental tools into the implementation aspects of marketing. The emphasis throughout is upon knowledge, theories, research findings, and the conduct of marketing.

Principles of Marketing Management is primarily targeted at two audiences. One is the principles of marketing course found in upper-level undergraduate programs. Most juniors and seniors enrolled in business schools will find it enlightening and well within their abilities. A second audience is the introductory MBA marketing management course found in some colleges and universities. Specifically, instructors who desire a less quantitative but more descriptive approach than currently available will find this book useful. In addition, the book is especially appropriate for marketing courses in night MBA programs because it is so thorough in the fundamentals and promotes self-learning when class sessions are few in number. As secondary audiences, the book may appeal to certain undergraduate marketing management courses, the capstone undergraduate marketing seminar, or executive teaching programs where a comprehensive, descriptive, and challenging text is needed to complement cases or course projects. It should be noted that because the text combines some of the descriptive content of principles texts with some of the marketing management content of MBA courses, it will not short-change the nonmarketing major who may never be exposed further to marketing courses.

---

*Silvano Arieti, *Creativity: The Magic Synthesis* (New York: Basic Books, 1976).

A number of special features in the text are worth noting. I have attempted to draw material from the behavioral sciences wherever appropriate. For too long, basic texts have ignored subject matters from related fields such as psychology, sociology, organizational behavior, and communication science. The reader will find that many marketing principles are more easily comprehended and take on new meaning when shown to reflect everyday aspects of individual and social behavior. At the same time, I should note that, as I did research to enrich the behavioral content of the text, I discovered that a number of new insights arose. Thus, some original material can be found throughout the text and especially in the chapters on individual consumer behavior (Chapter 2), social dimensions of consumer behavior (Chapter 3), product (Chapters 4 and 5), marketing communication (Chapter 8), advertising (Chapter 9), and personal selling (Chapters 10 and 11). In addition, most chapters contain original frameworks for viewing selected subareas of marketing. These can be seen in key diagrams and the surrounding discussions.

Another feature of the text is the threefold approach taken in each chapter or in pairs of related chapters. Specifically, I have chosen to begin discussion of most topics from the micro (i.e., individual consumer) viewpoint. This perspective is the one students can identify with, and I find that it prepares them better for the second and third perspectives. The second viewpoint is the macro (i.e., economic, social, and/or legal). Along with the first, it serves as the primary means to convey descriptive content. The third viewpoint, which is sometimes broken out as a separate chapter, is the managerial perspective. By looking at marketing from micro, macro, and managerial vantage points, we come to better see how marketing functions and what we can do to make it function better

yet. I believe that, to fully teach and understand marketing, one must see it as an individual participant, a social actor, and a manager, and this philosophy is carried throughout the text.

Still another innovation of sorts is the final chapter. Here I have attempted to prepare a lively, self-contained overview of marketing management in general and the book in particular. Because the chapter can stand on its own, some instructors may prefer to use it as the first assignment to provide a foreshadowing of things to come.

By way of pedagogical elements, I have included the following:

Chapter Outlines to sketch the topics to follow and provide perspective.

Lead-off Quotes to stimulate thinking and set a tone of scholarship. Note that many chapters include provocative quotes from noted authorities, yet take opposite stances. This should loosen prejudices, open one's mind, and arouse interest.

Chapter Vignettes by Leaders in Field to communicate where the particular subfield of marketing stands today and where it will be going tomorrow. This also serves to increase legitimacy of the chapter and provide role models.

Italic Type to identify key concepts and theories.

Note to Students, Prologue, and Epilogue to help the student approach the learning experience with a useful frame of mind.

Tables, Figures, and Exhibits to provide a visual complement to verbal ideas, expand understanding, and introduce new ideas and/or examples.

Chapter Summaries to capture the key ideas of the chapter by way of summation. Note that the summaries are usually long and comprehensive and not of the token type frequently found in some texts.

Notes to direct the reader to further research and supporting or opposing viewpoints. Note that the references are more extensive than what is commonly found in texts; yet they do not include superficial or redundant citations. Rather, only classic and fundamental contemporary references are included.

Glossaries to help the reader grasp and retain key concepts and ideas. These appear at the end of each chapter, are cross-referenced where appropriate, and go into more detail than definitions found in many other texts.

Chapter Questions and Points for Discussion to help the reader push his or her thinking in new directions as well as to reinforce the material learned.

The following supplemental materials are made available as well:

Instructor's Manual includes chapter overviews, instructional suggestions, recommended cases, and answers to end-of-chapter questions. In addition, a special point is made to provide ideas and examples for classroom presentation and discussion. Most of these do not appear directly in the text. Hence, the opportunity is provided for expansion and enrichment of the learning experience. Indeed, enough material is suggested so that the instructor preferring never to review points directly from the text can introduce new examples and new material into the lecture or discussion.

Experiential Notebook and Study Guide includes exercises to involve the student actively in testing and extending knowledge.

Test Bank with approximately 1000 questions suitable for either quizzes or exams.

A Note to the Student

There is no one correct way to study from any textbook. Everyone has his or her own style for studying. If you are comfortable with the way you approach your work, then it is probably best to stick with it. As a point of reference, however, I would like to make some suggestions that have worked for me and for some of my students over the years.

It might be helpful to begin study of any particular chapter with a quick reading to get a feeling for the gist and scope of coverage. Focus should be placed on a few key concepts, the central theme or themes, and the significance of examples. Because the chapter summaries are comprehensive, yet relatively short, some people will find these a useful place to start. Don't worry at this point about understanding every idea or comprehending the details of every argument. Rather, merely try to get a feeling for the subject matter in a general sense.

Your main reading of the chapter should be done slowly and with a deep understanding as the goal. Begin with a study of the chapter-opening quotes. These were selected with a specific purpose in mind and relate to the content of the chapter and its implications. Although sometimes subtle, the quotes point to long-standing, fundamental issues. They usually express deep-seated values and prejudices and should lead you to think of the subject matter as you read it in somewhat broader and more novel ways than is normal.

As you read a chapter, underline key concepts and ideas. Write notes or questions in the margin for later review or investigation. Do not accept things at face value, but at the same time do not get bogged down at this point with excessive skepticism or disagreement. Reserve these reactions for further consideration after you are certain that you have grasped the depth and breadth of the subject matter.

When you feel that you have mastered the message, turn to a deeper probing and questioning. Go beyond what was said to think about the origins and validity of ideas, about how things might otherwise have been, and about the consequences of what you have learned for marketing and society in general. The questions at the end of each chapter might help you get started along these lines.

Throughout the term and at least once a week, you should reread your underlinings and the chapter summaries of previously read chapters. This will provide you with sufficient preparation for any examinations and will give you a solid perspective on the field after the course has ended.

You should give special attention to the diagrams and figures in each chapter. They are included to complement the verbal content and to expand your comprehension. If you work to understand each exhibit and to visualize its message, you will find that your understanding of the subject matter will deepen and your intuitive faculties will enlarge beyond that possible with only verbal learning.

Acknowledgments

I wish to express my gratitude to the many individuals who supported me in writing this text. Special thanks go to Roger Ross of SRA, who was the first person to encourage me to write this book and who, along with Dave McEttrick, had the courage to recommend publication despite its market-niche focus. Thanks go also to Geof Garvey, who edited the book throughout production, and to Rich Hagle, who copyedited the manuscript, and to Ann Tomchek for her helpful corrections and suggestions on galleys. My appreciation extends, too, to Lee Madden, who was responsible for overall design of the book, and to Alex Teshin for preparation of graphic illustrations.

I am indebted to my friend and colleague, Professor Lynn W. Phillips of Stanford University, who has unselfishly shared his wealth of knowledge with me and whose ideas can be seen especially throughout Chapter 16. Special thanks go to John C. Boyle for his critical comments on an earlier draft of the chapter and to John Hendry for his many substantive and editorial suggestions on the chapter's final draft.

I wish to acknowledge thanks to the following people, who—among others not revealed to me—provided valuable suggestions on parts or on the entire manuscript: Raj Arora (Bradley University), Marion Burke (Duke University), Ed Cundiff (Emory University), Ruby Roy Dholakia (University of Rhode Island), Eric Berkowitz (University of Massachusetts), Mike Mokwa (Arizona State University), Kent Monroe (Virginia Polytechnic Institute and State University), Chuck Gouldner (University of Colorado), Robert Spekman (University of Maryland), Mary Gilly (University of California, Irvine), John Graham (University of Southern California), Lynn Phillips (Stanford University), George Brooker (Puget Sound University), John Gwin (University of Virginia), William B. Locander (University of Tennessee), and Jerry Conover (University of Arizona). In addition, I am most grateful to the people who wrote the vignettes appearing throughout the text and to Kam Hon Lee (Chinese University of Hong Kong) for preparation of the chapter on international marketing (Chapter 15).

I am also grateful to the many people who helped type the final manuscript: Debra DiFiore, Diane Smith, Ligia Domingo, Betsy Friebel, and Renee Vogt. And to Brian Wansink for preparation of the answers to end-of-chapter questions.

Finally, I would like to thank my family for the love and support provided as I worked to finish this book.

Richard P. Bagozzi
Stanford University
April 1985

PROLOGUE: WHY STUDY MARKETING?

It is a general human weakness to allow things, uncertain and unknown, to set us up in hope, or plunge us into fear.
—— *Gaius Julius Caesar (102?–44 B.C.)*

Before we begin our excursion into the subject matter of marketing, we should ask ourselves why it is important to study marketing in the first place. At one level, you surely are aware that marketing constantly touches our lives and is an important economic, management, and social force in society. But if you are new to the study of marketing, you may not have thought very deeply about what marketing is and how it produces the effects it does. In general, we might think of four benefits that the study of marketing can have for us: (1) intellectual value, (2) practical utility, (3) social significance, and (4) career import.

Intellectual Value

The subject matter of marketing is inherently interesting. Unlike many subject matters that place primary emphasis on abstract ideas, numbers, or objects, marketing places the person and his or her feelings, impulses, and decision-making processes at the center of inquiry. We are fascinated by the reasons people behave as they do, and the study of people in their everyday activities of consumption is a central theme in marketing. The other side of marketing is the manager. Managers, too, are obviously people with behavioral characteristics that are just as complex and interesting as those of consumers. If you are a person who is curious about the subtleties and dynamics of how the marketplace works, and you are excited by the thought of learning new things about the world around you, then you should find the study of marketing an absorbing, pleasurable experience.

Practical Utility

Because each of us is a consumer, the study of marketing can have a direct impact on us. It can help us make better consumption decisions, deal more effectively with sellers, and generally communicate more effectively with others in our everyday activities. If we are engaged in business, government, or nonprofit organizations, the study of marketing can help us execute our managerial responsibilities. Indeed, a large part of marketing is concerned with how people and organizations can and should go about satisfying their own and the organization's needs.

Social Significance

Through markets and the institutions that arise to provide goods and services to the public, marketing plays a profound role in society. On the one hand, it plays a facilitating role allowing people and organizations the opportunity to fulfill their needs. On the other hand, it is an instrument for change, influencing values, attitudes, and behaviors. As with any technology, marketing tools can have productive or destructive effects, depending on how they are used. To understand such phenomena as inflation, the distribution of wealth, economic efficiency, socialization, and the quality of life, we need to examine the functions of marketing in society. In fact, as we shall discover throughout the text, the consequences of marketing do not stop with business and economic institutions and their effects on us. Rather, marketing activities go on in all organizations and groups, such as the Red Cross, the Democratic Party, the Lutheran Church, and the Metropolitan Museum of Art. We do not normally think of marketing activities as occurring in these organizations, but they do in disguised forms and with different labels attached to them. An understanding of marketing can help all organizations and institutions perform better.

Career Import

It is obvious that if one wants to work in advertising, retailing, sales, purchasing, or product research, the study of marketing is essential. Yet not so obvious is the fact that the study of marketing has benefits for persons working in nonmarketing functions as well. People concerned with accounting, financial matters, production, personnel, and other staff functions both affect and are affected by marketing decisions. Thus, from the perspective of a firm's productivity, all employees need to know something about marketing in order to integrate better their activities with others. Moreover, because most organizations engage in exchange relations with suppliers and consumers, both at home and abroad, the study of marketing has value as a source of knowledge about how to relate to other institutions in more effective ways. As you investigate marketing in this text, we hope you will learn what marketing careers are available or how marketing can help you professionally in a nonmarketing career.

Overall, the study of marketing can be a rewarding experience giving educational as well as pragmatic value. Our goal in this text is to provide you with a deep look into marketing and to help you gain a better understanding of yourself as a consumer and your potential as a manager in today's complex, fast-paced world.

CHAPTER ONE

The most difficult thing in science, as in other fields, is to shake off accepted views, to observe with one's own eyes, and think with one's own brains.
— George Sarton (1884–1956)

Be favorable to bold beginnings.
— Virgil (70–19 B.C.)

MARKETING:
THE INDIVIDUAL, THE ORGANIZATION, AND SOCIETY

What Is Marketing?

Marketing means different things to different people. Before we examine what it means to scholars and managers, take a moment to think about what it means to you. What are the first things to pop into your mind when you hear the word *marketing*?

If you are similar to most people new to the study of marketing, you might see images of advertisements in magazines or on television, a salesperson pushing products, department stores, delivery trucks, and flashy packages in the supermarket. These are, indeed, visible signs of modern marketing, but it involves many more complex phenomena that are less well known but no less important.

Marketing is so much a part of modern life that most of us tend to take it for granted. In our everyday activities, we become accustomed to our environment and filter out much of the stimulation. For instance, research shows that the average person is exposed to about 300 ads per day and perhaps remembers approximately 40 of them when pressed.[1] When we realize that advertising is but a small part of marketing, we can see that our image of marketing is a highly selective and incomplete one.

Some Early Definitions

One popular definition among some people is that *marketing is what marketers do*. This is an appealing definition, for it is simple and has the ring of truth to it. However, it begs the question: before it can be applied, we must define what a marketer is and to do so implies that we already know what marketing is. In other words, it lacks sufficient content to tell us anything about marketing.

To provide a formal, content-based definition of marketing, a group of practitioners and scholars proposed the following definition, which is the official one accepted by the American Marketing Association (AMA):

marketing is the performance of business activities that direct the flow of goods and services from producer to consumer or user.[2]

Let us examine this definition in greater detail. Notice that marketing is considered a business activity. This conforms to the origins of marketing, the layperson's concept of marketing, and the reality that all business firms perform marketing activities in one form or another. What are the activities? The definition specifies them as anything done to "direct the flow of goods and services." Traditionally, this includes activities concerned with the stimulation of demand and the delivery of goods. Packaging, promotion, personal selling, advertising, and wholesale and retail functions are the most common examples. Finally, the definition indicates to whom the goods and services are delivered, namely, the "consumer or user."

The AMA definition provides some insight into the meaning of marketing, but it has several shortcomings. One weakness is that it neglects, or at least deemphasizes, the marketer and the consumer. Figure 1-1A is a representation of the AMA definition. This definition focuses mostly on what goes on *between* marketer and consumer. It omits many things done by marketing managers (e.g., product design and market research), and it overlooks the decision processes and other behaviors of consumers. The dashed lines of the two circles indicate that the marketer and the consumer are deemphasized. A second limitation of the definition is that it overly restricts marketing to business firms. In reality, marketing functions are performed by government agencies, nonprofit organizations, unincorporated groups, and private citizens, as well as by business firms. We will have more to say about the universality of marketing throughout this text.[3]

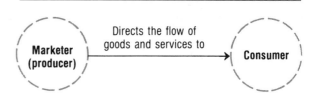

A. American Marketing Association definition of marketing (circa 1960–1980)

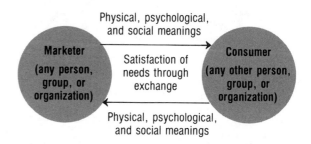

B. Marketing as exchange (circa 1980 to present)

Figure 1-1. A pictorial summary of two leading definitions of marketing

The most important drawback of the AMA definition is that it takes a simplistic and incomplete view of the marketing process. Notice in Figure 1-1A that marketing is construed to occur *from* marketer *to* consumer. The flow is in one direction. Such a viewpoint overlooks how marketing actually occurs in the real world. The process is not limited to a one-way flow or sequence from marketer to consumer. Rather, the vast majority of marketing activities involves interaction between seller and buyer. As a consequence, a number of marketers now view marketing in terms of *exchange relationships.*[4]

A Modern Definition of Marketing

We can think of marketing in two senses: (1) marketing as a *phenomenon for study* and (2) marketing as a *field of study.* Let us define both.

As a phenomenon for study,

marketing is the set of individual and social activities concerned with the initiation, resolution, and/or avoidance of exchange relationships.

We will have much more to say about this definition later in this chapter and throughout the book. For now, however, let us briefly define some of the terms and sketch this meaning. Notice first that marketing consists of individual and social activities. That is, any person, organization, or social entity can engage in exchange relationships with any other person, organization, or social entity. The activities performed by these parties are designed to create a new exchange relationship, resolve an ongoing one (e.g., complete a transaction, change the terms of a long-term contract, or dissolve a relation), and/or prevent the occurrence of an exchange. The activities might comprise offers and counteroffers, the mediation of rewards or punishments, power, or a whole host of other acts performed by the parties or manifest in their social relations. The ultimate aim of engaging in exchanges or avoiding them is to satisfy one's needs. Needs can be individualistic and selfish, group-based and altruistic, or both. A central theme of this text is that one cannot fully comprehend marketing or fruitfully conduct marketing operations without a thorough understanding of the behavior of the parties to an exchange. We will thus devote a considerable amount of effort to analyzing both consumer behavior and manager behavior in this text. Notice further that the flow is not one way: the parties to an exchange communicate with each other. Further, this two-way flow consists of the transfer of *shared meanings*. These entail physical (e.g., a product, money), psychological (e.g., ideas, affect), and social (e.g., prestige, status) meanings. Figure 1-1B summarizes the intent of this exchange-based conception of marketing. The marketer and consumer are encircled by solid lines to suggest the importance of the parties in an exchange as a means for understanding marketing.

As a *field of study*, marketing attempts to answer three questions:

1 Why do people and organizations engage in exchange relationships?

2 How are exchanges created, resolved, or avoided?

3 How should exchanges be created, resolved, or avoided?[5]

The first two questions address the science of marketing and require that we search for theories and data explaining marketing phenomena. The third question addresses the art and ethics of marketing and suggests that we consider managerial, moral, and social dimensions of marketing. On many occasions in upcoming chapters, we will address all three questions.

The field of marketing is quite broad in scope and both overlaps with and draws upon many related subject areas. As we shall discover in later chapters, marketers continually borrow concepts and methods from psychology, sociology, organization behavior, anthropology, and political science, as well as from the traditional disciplines of economics, mathematics, operations research, and management science. To gain an understanding of behavior in the marketplace, we shall find it necessary to take a strong interdisciplinary approach throughout the book. At the same time, marketers have made unique contributions to theory, method, and practice. These, too, will be highlighted in the pages ahead.

The Dimensions of Marketing

Marketing Systems

Figure 1-2 displays the general form of most marketing systems. At the top is the person or organization that initiates the exchange process. This person or organization has something of value desired by another person or organization and at the same time desires resources from that other person or organization. For example, the owner of a restaurant provides various meals that, hopefully, are attractive to others and anticipates receiving enough money to pay for costs and, perhaps, contribute to a profit. The final recipient of the person's or organization's offering is the *consumer* or *client*.

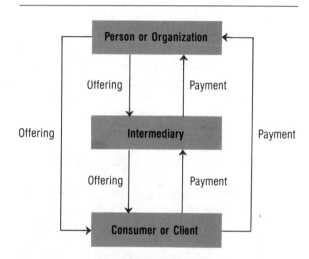

Figure 1-2. A simple marketing system

Sometimes the initiating person or organization will make the offering directly to the consumer and receive payment directly from him or her. In other instances, it is more customary or efficient or practical to deal through an intermediary. For instance, it is not feasible or economical for Procter & Gamble and other makers of toothpaste to deliver their wares directly to every family. Instead, they sell to independent wholesalers and retailers who serve as links between producers and consumers. The *intermediary* plays a facilitating role and receives payment for its services.

Presumably, the marketing system exists and continues to function because it meets the needs of all parties involved to one degree or another. We will explore the psychological, social, and economic forces that lead to functional and dysfunctional exchanges in later chapters. For now we should note that marketing consists of more than isolated exchanges between buyers and sellers. Rather, the marketplace is laced with networks of marketing systems. And to a certain extent, marketing systems are intertwined into still larger megasystems in society through the social glue of laws, norms, contracts, and mores.

Marketing from the Perspective of the Marketer

Two Generic Marketing Goals. All organizations have broad *objectives* that serve as ends it would like to achieve. Businesses, for example, might strive for certain levels of profits or return on investment, or nonprofit organizations such as welfare agencies might aim for a certain number of clients to be served. Each subarea or subdepartment in the organization then sets *goals* designed to serve as intermediate or facilitating steps enroute to the broader organizational objectives. For example, financial departments set goals for investment and cost management, and production departments set goals for manufacturing, assembly, and quality control.

As business areas within the organization, marketing departments also set goals. At the highest level, we can identify two marketing goals that function as guiding principles throughout marketing subareas. The first goal is the *satisfaction of consumer needs*. No organization can survive for long without meeting consumer needs. People will simply not purchase a product or service that they do not need. Thus, any organization, if it is to be successful, must proceed from the goal of customer satisfaction and adjust its programs to deliver an offering meeting consumer needs. However, this is not sufficient. Even if a product meets needs, people might not buy it if better or cheaper alternatives exist. Hence, the second fundamental marketing goal is the *attainment of a competitive advantage* over rivals. In sum, effective marketing begins with two activities: customer analysis and competitive analysis. Let us briefly describe each, because an understanding of their meaning is essential for grasping what marketing is all about.

Customer analysis refers to the marketing activities of the firm concerned with research into the behavior of consumers. Before one can design a product desired by consumers, it is necessary to learn how the product meets psychological and social needs of the consumer. From a psychological perspective, marketers study how consumers process information about products. This involves examination of perceptual, memory, evaluative, and mental decision-making activities. Marketers also scrutinize the emotional reactions consumers have to products and how prior learning and current motives influence choices. From a social standpoint, marketers investigate the role of interpersonal influence, family decision making, small group dynamics, mass communication and culture, and other collective phenomena in consumption. The study of consumer psychological and social needs is performed through marketing research, an activity that we will describe in depth in later chapters. The following two chapters lay the theoretical groundwork for understanding the elements of consumer behavior. Subsequent chapters show how this knowledge is then translated into action programs. Figure 1-3 presents a summary of the parts of customer analysis. Notice that what we learn from customer analysis influences how we implement marketing programs, which generally entail the design and development of the product, the estimation of demand, the communication of the product to consumers, and distribution.

Competitive analysis is a necessary complement to customer analysis. Following Porter,[6] we can identify five competitive forces impinging on any marketing effort:

1 Supplier power

2 Consumer power

3 Product substitutability

4 The threat of new entrants into the market

5 Rivalry among existing competitors

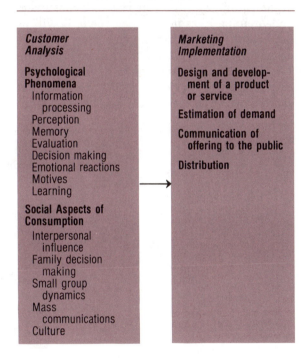

Figure 1-3. Customer analysis and its impact on other marketing programs

Supplier organizations affect the ability of a focal organization to market its wares. *Supplier organizations* are those institutions or groups that provide materials, component parts, people, money, services, and other resources needed by an organization to fulfill its mission. The balance of power between suppliers and the organizations that are their customers will determine the quality and production cost of a product or service and thus indirectly influence the ability of an initiating organization to meet its customer needs and attain a competitive advantage. Consumers, too, can be thought to interact with an organization and apply or be subject to varying degrees of power. For example, some buyers purchase so much that the threat of losing them can produce price concessions on the part of a seller.

To the extent that the organization can resist the power of consumers and/or impose its needs upon them, it will be better able to face threats emerging from the other competitive forces indicated in Figure 1-4. One class of threats is substitutability. Any product or service will satisfy a need that can be met at least partially by different kinds of products or services available in the marketplace. In a sense, candy bars compete with cookies, potato chips, and even soft drinks because each product form satisfies a hunger need for sugar or snacks. Similarly, threats arise from the possibility that new organizations might enter the market and sell the same product or service but perhaps at a lower price or of a higher quality. The candy bar market, for example, faces a continual influx of new producers because of the size of the market and the relative ease with which sweets can be produced and marketed. Finally, perhaps the most common and intuitively understood threat occurs as rivalry among existing organizations providing the same product. For instance, in the fast-food business, McDonald's, Burger King, A&W, and Wendy's each vies for a share of the prepared hamburger market. This represents competition among ongoing concerns selling similar products.

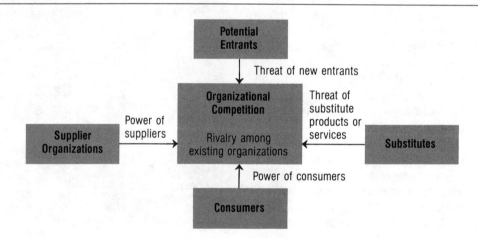

Figure 1-4. Five dominant forces in competitive analysis

SOURCE: Adopted with alterations from Michael E. Porter, *Competitive Strategy: Techniques for Analyzing Industries and Competitors* (New York: The Free Press, 1980), p. 4. Reprinted with the permission of The Free Press, a Division of Macmillan, Inc. Copyright © 1980, Macmillan, Inc.

To reiterate, marketers must address two goals if they are to be successful. First, they must design and develop a product that meets consumer needs. Second, they must adjust their entire marketing effort (products, communication programs, distribution, etc.) to fight off the potential competitive inroads made by five forces: suppliers, consumers, substitutes, new entrants, and existing rivals. Marketers have developed an elaborate body of knowledge and set of techniques for the conduct of marketing, and the remainder of the text describes these in considerable detail. As a caveat, it should be remembered that both marketing goals and their derivative strategies are subject to larger organizational objectives for service, profitability, or other aims. Further, we should stress that competition and power represent only one facet of an organization's relationships. Cooperation in formal and informal ways is central, too, as we shall see later in the book.

Three Marketing Strategies. Marketers utilize many different strategies to achieve the goals of consumer satisfaction and competitive advantage. *Marketing strategy* is how the organization chooses to allocate its resources to meet consumer needs and achieve a competitive advantage. This is done primarily through product design, development, and management; target market selection; and brand positioning and management. Communication, pricing, and distribution also play a role. We will examine three of the most widely used strategies here.[7]

Product Differentiation. The strategy of product differentiation aims to market a product or service that is perceived by consumers to be unique in some way. The hope is that people will find one's product not only need-satisfying but special. Over time, it is anticipated that consumers may become *brand loyal.* That is, they will consistently act with a strong preference for the differentiated brand and ignore other somewhat similar offerings or those products serving as close substitutes for the need being met. In essence, the marketer hopes that consumers will come to buy the brand out of habit or be less susceptible to price and other forms of inducement offered by the competition. Indeed, it has been argued that a product differentiation strategy insulates the marketer to a certain degree from each of the competitive threats.[8]

Organizations use a number of different tactics to accomplish product differentiation. One is to create a product with superior attributes. For example, some marketers attempt to incorporate superior quality or functionality into their products, usually through the addition of features not contained in rival brands. A second tactic is to provide customer services not offered by the competition. For instance, some supermarkets provide phone-in ordering, home delivery, and even baby-sitting. Still another tactic is based on psychological principles. Many firms use advertising, packages, and slogans to create a *brand image* unique to their products or services. The goal is to encourage consumers to specifically associate certain positive attributes with the product. These attributes may be relatively concrete and objective (e.g., high quality) or abstract and subjective (e.g., sensuality). The key point here is the consumer's perception. We do not have to look far to recognize the value and impact of brand images. Consider what images come to your mind from such well-known brand names as Jell-O desserts, Sear's Craftsman tools, Life Savers candies, Pepperidge Farm cookies and pastries, Thunderbird cars, Coca-Cola, and IBM computers. Each of these has a particular audio and visual appeal and suggests images of quality, workmanship, sensual attractiveness, or other positively evaluated characteristics.

Finally, product differentiation can be accomplished through the use of distinctive distribution networks. Rather than operating through mass wholesale distributors, for example, some wineries market directly to select retailers or even sell to final consumers through exclusive merchandise catalogs. Many distribution options are available to organizations, and each can be viewed as a differentiation strategy as well as a means for getting the product to the consumer. As an example, Figure 1-5 illustrates the options facing a small California wine producer. Notice that the winery has seven possible routes to reach the final consumer. Given its small size and desire to market a high-quality wine to the discriminating consumer, it chose to sell through its on-site wine shop and also through wine agents (i.e., independent salespeople who sell to select retailers and handle the transactions for many small wineries). These two channels permitted the seller to achieve a unique product image and differentiate itself from mass sellers such as Gallo and Inglenook. Gallo distributes much of its wine through its own distri-

butors, whereas Inglenook (United Vintners) tends to use independent wholesale distributors. Both attempt to reach the mass market through as many outlets (supermarkets, restaurants, taverns, liquor stores, etc.) as possible. Trentini Brothers (name disguised) produces a higher-quality wine and sells through only a handful of exclusive wine stores.

Before we discuss another marketing strategy, we should note that firms often combine several bases of differentiation. Thus, it is not uncommon to see an organization develop unique product attributes and reinforce the uniqueness through advertising, service, and distribution programs.

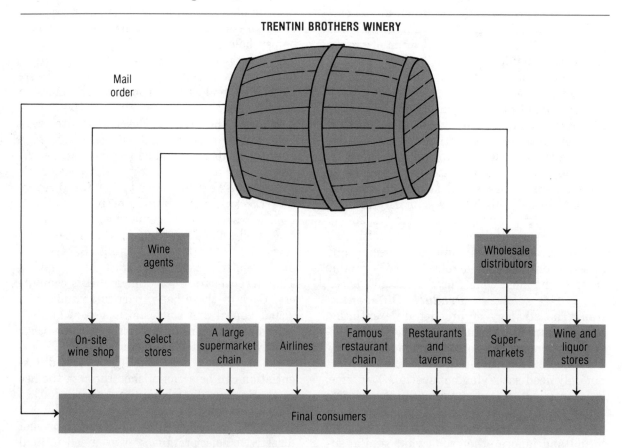

TRENTINI BROTHERS WINERY

Mail order

Wine agents

Wholesale distributors

On-site wine shop | Select stores | A large supermarket chain | Airlines | Famous restaurant chain | Restaurants and taverns | Super-markets | Wine and liquor stores

Final consumers

Figure 1-5. Alternative distribution channels for a small winery

Overall Cost Leadership. Although all firms try to keep costs to a minimum, not everyone makes it a top priority. Other strategies sometimes take precedence. For example, certain companies that choose a differentiation strategy find that they must invest in research to improve their products as well as spend extra money on advertising or promotion. These firms obviously have spending limits, but differentiation objectives are met first. In contrast, when an organization makes cost cutting its primary goal, we may call this *overall cost leadership.*

The purpose of overall cost leadership is to generate as great a profit margin as possible through high sales volume and low per-unit profit and to reinvest as much as possible in equipment and programs designed to maintain and improve efficiency. As Porter notes, "cost leadership requires aggressive construction of efficient-scale facilities, vigorous pursuit of cost reductions from experience, tight cost and overhead control, avoidance of marginal customer accounts, and cost minimization in areas like R&D, service, sales force, advertising, and so on."[9] Such a strategy permits one to compete effectively with existing rivals and at the same time bargain from strength with suppliers and customers. It also serves to discourage the entry of new competitors because of the relatively low profit margins that characterize competition based on price. In addition, it is believed that the successful execution of an overall cost leadership strategy requires that an organization possess an edge in terms of favored access to raw materials or a high relative market share. The former insures low costs for materials used in production, whereas the latter allows for certain economies of scale to be achieved, including the creation of customer loyalty.

Overall cost leadership and product differentiation tend to be mutually exclusive strategies because accomplishment of the latter entails relatively high expenditures, whereas the former tries to pare expenditures. This especially is the case for mass marketing firms, which attempt to appeal to as wide a market as possible. However, for smaller firms or for firms following a strategy of pursuit of limited segments of a market, it is possible to employ still a third strategy: market focus.

Market Focus. This strategy aims to concentrate on a particular subdivision (or segment) of the market, such as a specific geographic region or type of consumer. There are many ways to define market segments, and we will devote an entire chapter to the ideas and methods behind what has been called *market segmentation.* For now, we simply wish to note that firms find it necessary or advantageous to pursue select segments rather than an entire market. Sometimes they lack the resources to mass market. At other times, it is more profitable or less competitive to focus on portions of the market. Overall, the goal of market focus is to discover a segment (or small numbers of segments) and dominate and defend it against competitive threats.

Firms usually utilize either a product-differentiation or a low-cost approach to successfully employ a market focus strategy. Either orientation permits one to achieve a differential advantage over competitive forces. Occasionally, organizations attempt to use both product differentiation and low cost strategies when pursuing specific market segments. However, this is generally done when the firm has multiple segments and can use either a product-differentiation or low-cost approach in particular segments. Although it is possible to achieve a high market share within particular segments, the market focus strategy generally results in lower levels of overall sales volume compared to less focused strategies. Nevertheless, a focused strategy can yield high profits to the extent that its differentiation or cost practices produce a competitive advantage.

Figure 1-6 is a diagram summarizing the three approaches to marketing strategy. The area represented by 1 depicts the product differentiation strategy aimed at the mass market. Two leading practitioners of this approach are Coleman in camping equipment and Caterpillar Tractor in construction equipment. Market focus through product differentiation is shown as area 2 in Figure 1-6. Here the organization attempts to capture one or a few market segments with a unique product offering. Mercedes Benz in the automobile market is a good example. Market focus through both product differentiation and cost management (area 3) is represented by the strategy of California Canners and Growers (CCG). CCG markets a relatively high-priced line of diet canned fruits to the health-conscious market yet sells low-priced canned fruits in bulk to institutional and foreign markets. The fourth strategy (area 4), market focus through cost management, is practiced by the Fort Howard Paper Company, which markets industrial-grade paper products rather than higher-costing (and higher-priced) consumer or specialty paper products. Finally, area 5 signifies the overall cost leadership strategy targeted to the mass market. DuPont and Texas Instruments roughly follow this approach.

We should note in passing that the strategies outlined in Figure 1-6 are not the only paths that firms follow. Indeed, some organizations fail to follow any strategy or pursue ill-defined ones. Others attempt to have the best of all worlds and institute contradictory policies. Porter uses the phrase "stuck in the middle" to characterize the firm that chooses not to pursue either a product differentiation, or an overall cost leadership, or a market focus strategy: "This firm lacks the market share, captial investment, and resolve to play the low-cost game, the industry-wide differentiation necessary to obviate the need for a low-cost position, or the focus to create differentiation or a low-cost position in a more limited sphere."[10]

It is believed that the firm stuck in the middle will experience low profits because too many customers will seek lower priced or alternatively more differentiated products from other sellers. The former tend to be high-volume shoppers, whereas the latter tend to pay a premium for unique goods. The remainder of the market is less profitable because the seller's volume is relatively depressed and prices must be set lower than they otherwise could be. Thus, the firm stuck in the middle is left with the less desirable parts of the market.

Marketing Tools (The 4 Ps). Organizations use four generic *tools* to execute marketing strategies. These have come to be known as the 4 Ps—product, place, promotion, and price—and are sometimes referred to as the *marketing mix variables*. The four marketing mix variables constitute the primary means by

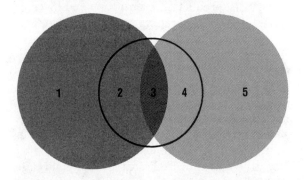

Figure 1-6. Three marketing strategies

1 Product differentiation—industry-wide market

2 Market focus through product differentiation—market segments

3 Market focus through product differentiation and cost management—market segments

4 Market focus through cost management—market segments

5 Overall cost leadership—industry-wide market

which organizations adapt to and/or influence responses in the marketplace. By skillfully varying the design of products, distribution (i.e., "place"), promotion, and prices, firms are able to provide offerings that meet consumer needs and achieve a competitive advantage. Although we will address the marketing mix variables in considerable detail throughout the remainder of the book, let us briefly define them here.

Product. By *product,* we mean any offering desired by a target person or organization. We usually think of products in physical terms, and, indeed, the physical characteristics or attributes of products are a major reason why people buy them. Soft drinks are cool and refreshing. Lawn mowers cut easily, are light, are easy to maintain, and so forth. By the same token, physical attributes will have no utility, no value, unless they are translated into subjective meanings by the consumer. Moreover, products possess intangible, symbolic attributes over and above the tangible ones and perform psychological and social functions. For example, an automobile is not merely a means of transportation. For some people, it represents a means of expressing pride, power, and social standing. Further, some things now commonly classified as "products," such as ideas, political candidates, and personal services, are nearly totally nonphysical in their meaning for the consumer.[11] As we shall see in upcoming chapters, marketers have developed an elaborate set of methodologies for measuring how consumers react to products, and we have learned much about how to efficiently and effectively design, develop, and implement new products in competitive environments.

Place. The channel of distribution between manufacturer and final consumer is not merely a means for the physical transport of goods. Rather, it is a tactic for accomplishing strategic objectives in its own right. In addition to providing the means for the physical consummation of an exchange, channels of distribution provide time utility.

Each channel option offers a different level of temporal value, ranging from fast deliveries by plane or the computer to slower modes such as boat, truck, or train. In addition, the attractiveness of a product can be enhanced through the provision of storage, credit, display, assortment, parts, service, and other place-related functions. Managers use these, along with variations in product features, to stimulate demand for their products.

Promotion. An organization can produce and distribute the best product in the world but fail to make a sale if no one knows about it. The function of promotion is to *inform* people about a product, its features, its availability, its price, and so on. Further, because many products are complex and differ in subtle ways from others, it is sometimes necessary to convince or *persuade* potential buyers of the advantages that one's product offers. Promotion tactics take many forms. Advertising in newspapers and magazines or on the radio, television, or billboards is perhaps the most common mode. But promotion also occurs through coupons, leaflets, in-store displays, phone calls, and face-to-face selling, to name a few options. As you might imagine, promotion plays an important communication role, giving the firm the opportunity not only to reach its customers but also to differentiate its products and services and thereby hopefully to match its offerings better to the needs of its clients and achieve a differential advantage over competitors.

Price. Pricing, too, is an important managerial tool. For most consumers most of the time, a price is perhaps a simple measure of a product's value—a signal of how much one will have to give up in order to obtain something else of value. For other consumers, a price is sometimes a signal of quality or exclusivity. Managers set prices, in part, as a stimulus for sales. This means setting some prices low as an inducement to the cost-conscious consumer and others high as a symbol to the image-oriented or status-seeking person. Of course, the firm's own costs must be taken into account, and the materials or labor put into a product will be selected with both the tastes and price sensitivities of the consumer in mind. By the same token, price is a competitive lever allowing firms the opportunity to meet or beat the competition.

We can readily appreciate that the marketing manager's task is a difficult one. He or she must skillfully blend product design, distribution, promotion, and pricing options into an overall program that not only meets customer needs and overcomes competitive threats but that also generates enough resources for the firm to survive and innovate in the future. Figure 1-7 summarizes the steps that occur between the relatively abstract and general organization objectives set by corporate managers and the more concrete, everyday actions taken by marketing managers and other marketing employees nearer the bottom of the organizational hierarchy. Notice that we have added *marketing tactics* to the topics we have already discussed. Marketing tactics consist of specific forms of tools employed, the way they are implemented, and the mix among tools chosen. Although not shown in Figure 1-7, we could have drawn separate sequences of steps from organizational objectives through goals, strategies, tools, and tactics for each function in the organization. For example, finance, accounting, personnel, production, and public relations departments each begin with the guidelines provided by organizational objectives and then translate these into workable policies and programs. Much of the remainder of the text focuses on how marketing is used to accomplish organization objectives and other goals.

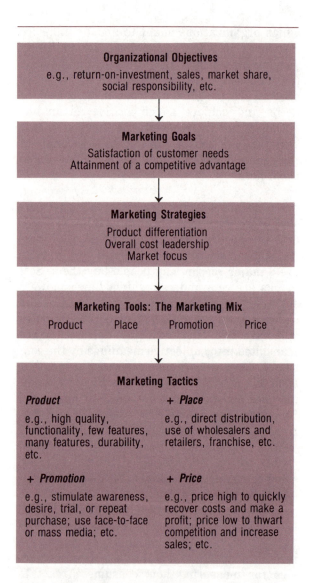

Figure 1-7. The translation of organizational objectives into action

The Origins and Functions of Marketing

Now that we have provided a capsule view of marketing, it is useful for our understanding of marketing to consider its evolution and functions in society.

The Need for Marketing

Marketing arose as a response to the needs of buyers and sellers. Imagine how people satisfied their needs in prehistoric times. To survive, individuals gathered nuts and berries, captured small animals, caught fish, and occasionally ate the remains of dead game left by predators. As time passed, people learned how to grow their own vegetables and grain, and they raised some of their own animals for food as well. Whether as hunters, grazers, or farmers, primitive peoples survived largely through their wits and cunning and self-produced their own food, clothing, tools, and weapons.

Self-production, however, has its limits. Not everyone is skilled in all the tasks necessary for survival. Not every geographical region is endowed with the game needed for food, the climate required for growing, or the mineral and other resources suitable for making essential tools. And time itself prevents people from doing all that one would like to do as one's tastes and desires expand. In short, scarcity places restrictions on how well one can survive through self-production.

At the same time, our early ancestors quickly learned that much is to be gained through cooperation with others. Hunting became more successful when done in groups. Survival against the elements was enhanced when people banded together and shared or divided tasks. People skilled at one activity, such as constructing a fishing net, found that they could *trade* their creations for goods not readily available to them, such as fruits and furs from faraway places.

Early trade was thus an outgrowth of the development of individual skills and needs coupled with the emergence of simple social relations that fostered mutual enhancement of those skills and needs. However, early trade tended to be conducted between two parties. A hunter traded pelts to a craftsman for a spear. A farmer exchanged wheat for an urn made by a potter. And so on. Figure 1-8A shows this early form of exchange.

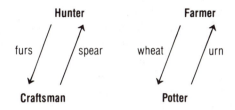

A. Simple two-person exchanges

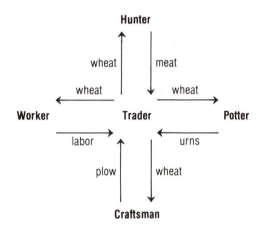

B. Emergence of a trader as a nucleus for two-person exchanges

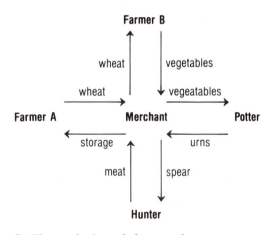

C. The evolution of the merchant

Figure 1-8. The evolution of marketing

After a while, much as people developed skills in self-production, certain individuals became astute traders and found that it was more efficient to bargain with more than one person at one or a few locations. Rather than traveling to each trading partner, the trader found that others came to him or her. This led to the formation of the *skilled trader* who offered a single commodity to many individuals who, in turn, exchanged different goods for the commodity. Figure 1-8B depicts this situation, a primitive form of organized marketing.

With increased experience, the trader soon learned how to set the terms for trade efficiently and gained knowledge of the worth and demand for a wide variety of goods that began to accumulate. Buyers, too, learned that the trader had many attractive wares and could save them time and effort if they dealt with a single trader rather than with many individual producers. The result was the evolution of a *merchant*, a person well known even in early biblical times. Of course, the evolution from simple exchange to skilled trader to merchant took many generations, if not centuries, to occur.

Merchants performed many complex transactions. They not only traded goods for other goods but also supplied services. Farmers received storage privileges, for example, and gave the merchant portions of their crops as payment. Soon the merchant found a need to keep records, extend credit, expand facilities, and hire additional help. This was made possible by the accumulation of profits or the desire to take risks. Over time, the merchant's business tended to take on an identity of its own and achieved a quasi-independent existence. Some merchants specialized, others diversified. A new language of transactions emerged, norms and laws evolved to regulate trade, and rudimentary forms of money came about. Further, *formal markets* developed to meet the needs of merchants and consumers alike. The time arose when the merchant became a central impetus to economic and social growth.

As merchants grew in power and as formal and informal relations among merchants and between merchants and government developed, the institution of business took shape. This institution came to take on a life of its own and legally achieved status as a person before the law, a development that guaranteed its existence, more or less, in perpetuity. Today, business is one of a number of institutions essential to society. Yet, its functions can have positive or negative effects on our lives, depending on how well it performs its role. In any event, although the form and actions of business institutions are sure to change, the functions it performs will continue because people and other institutions depend on it for survival. Most recently, we see a blurring of distinctions between business and other organizations, and many concepts and technologies originally thought to be strictly business related or nonbusiness related are now universally found in different degrees in all organizations. All societies—primitive, planned, and unplanned—face the need to produce and distribute goods and services to their populaces, and marketing is a key role in the process.

Marketing in the Twentieth Century

Modern organizations have tended to evolve through well-defined stages in their approach to marketing. Let us briefly describe these stages and the growth of marketing in this century.

The Inward Focus. In the early part of this century, business firms gave little thought to marketing. Rather, they focused on internal operations with particular emphasis given to organizational goals, production processes, labor problems, and financial constraints. If marketing was performed at all, it was given lower priority. Even then, it was limited to product design from a technological perspective (production-related concerns) and price setting to cover costs plus a desired margin (finance-related concerns). Very little effort was expended to research the market or to efficiently communicate and distribute one's wares.

The inward focus is still characteristic of some organizations even today, although most business firms now assume one of the two postures that we will describe shortly. New business organizations frequently take an inward focus because a great amount of energy and resources is needed to start operations and gain sophistication and knowledge about the market. In the public sector, government and other nonprofit organizations tend to emphasize the rules and procedures under which they must operate and the activities they must perform to deliver services. Often, this is done at the expense of marketing programs such as client need analysis, demand forecasting, new service development, outreach activities, and other innovations in the communication of services. Finally, some firms practicing an overall cost leadership strategy, others dealing in commodities, and public utilities have all been relatively more inward focused than marketing focused.

The inward focus works satisfactorily, if not optimally, under certain conditions. First, if demand for one's goods or services outstrips the supply, then marketing is less necessary. Assuming that one's product or service meets needs and has few competitors, about all that is required is an adequate distribution, communication, and pricing program. Even here, neither the product nor the marketing effort need be optimal, though some minimal thresholds must be surpassed. Second, the inward focus works moderately well when the product or service requires a very large capital and research investment and/or the cost to produce the product or service is very high. Under these conditions, the seller needs some assurance of a market that is large enough to take advantage of economies of scale and provide a price that is low enough to stimulate demand. Yet, even these firms cannot neglect marketing. The failure to meet consumer needs and perform effectively under the specter of the five competitive threats noted earlier in this chapter is an open invitation to

business disaster. In fact, as a general rule, we might speculate that an inward focus will result in less consumer satisfaction and less efficiency when compared to the other two orientations we turn to now.

The Outward Focus. A number of environmental realities have led some organizations to respond with an outward focus. By outward focus, we mean an emphasis on convincing consumers to try one's product and ensuring that the product is available when and where people desire it. Typically, the outward focus places a relatively great stress on personal selling, promotion, advertising, distribution, and retailing. Either the remaining market functions (e.g., product design) are neglected or else they have been fulfilled earlier.

The most important environmental forces precipitating an outward focus are competition and consumer reactions in the aggregate. As new firms become established and as old firms with new products gain experience, competitive threats tend to grow. No longer can the firm rely solely on its own uniqueness and the novelty of its products. Competition forces it to reach out and demonstrate why its wares are better than the seemingly indistinguishable offerings of rivals. At the same time, the pool of potential consumers begins to dry up. Most people with a strong need will have tried the firm's brand. If it is a durable good, these people will not be in the market again for some time. If it is a frequently purchased product, a portion of those who once tried it will not repurchase it because of disappointment with the product's performance or features or because of a relatively stronger preference for something else. Also, as time passes, the remainder of the market will contain a relatively high percentage of people who either have no need for the product or who will require greater selling efforts to get them to buy the product. All of these factors put pressures on the firm to attempt to stimulate demand directly and to consider competitive threats head-on. A final environmental force calling for an outward focus is the changing complexion of consumers. As consumers become more educated and their intellectual, financial, and temporal resources expand, they demand higher-quality, safer, and more varied goods and services. To meet these needs in an ever-increasing competitive environment, the firm must aggressively seek out its market.

The Holistic Focus. The inward focus is basically product, technology, or cost oriented, whereas the outward focus is primarily market or customer oriented. Obviously, all firms do a little of both. However, not every firm achieves an optimal balance or emphasizes each to the proper extent. When a firm balances its internal needs and constraints with its external demands and opportunities, and in so doing meets its own goals, satisfies consumers, and fulfills social responsibilities, we may say that it follows a holistic focus. This, of course, is an ideal that few organizations meet in an absolute sense. Nevertheless, it serves as a standard or philosophical perspective that has come to be known popularly as the *marketing concept.*

In practice, organizations attempt to achieve a holistic focus through a number of programs. We will address these in considerable detail throughout the text. For now, we should note that success hinges on blending activities that serve *integrative functions* with activities that generate *innovative outcomes.* The former attempts to coordinate the operations of the organization so as to better achieve objectives for sales, growth, market share, return on investment, and so on. This entails the effective implementation of organization design; the recruitment, training, motivation, and compensation of employees; management of relations with suppliers and customers; estimation of demand; scheduling of production; and, in general, planning, evaluation, and control of all the functional areas within the firm, including marketing. Innovative activities strive to inject new ideas and methods into the organization so as to overcome shortages of materials, increases in costs, encroachment by competitors,

and changing consumer tastes. This is accomplished through basic and applied research; new product design, development, and testing; market studies; the implementation of information generation and management systems; the skillful selection of target markets; brand and product positioning; and design of communication, pricing, and distribution systems. As we shall discover, marketing goes on throughout, or at least influences, all the facets of the integrative and innovative activities of the firm. The task for society in general and managers in particular is to combine both functions so that the organization can creatively adapt to and/or change its environment to the advantage of all.

The Universality of Marketing

It may not seem obvious to you, but marketing goes on in all organizations and in all societies. This is because all people and social entities have needs, and to satisfy these needs they must purposefully engage in exchange relations with others.

Marketing is an essential force in both the so-called free-enterprise and planned economies. In the former, marketing concerns tend to be privately owned, whereas in the latter, they generally are state owned. Yet, in both systems, many of the same marketing functions are performed, but perhaps in different forms or with different emphases. For example, both systems must estimate demand, design products, set prices, distribute goods, display them in retail stores, and inform the public of their availability. The processes of decision making might differ, the prices and assortment of goods might vary, and the degree of independence or control of the parties might diverge, but the general activities and many outcomes are remarkably similar. In fact, from a marketing standpoint, the systems can be seen to overlap in the sense that all free-enterprise economies exhibit some degree of centralization through government regulation and support, whereas all planned economies contain some independent entrepreneurs and a certain degree of decentralization of decisions.

To take a specific example, consider the idea of *competition*, which is generally considered to be confined to free-enterprise economies. Competition occurs even in the most totally planned societies. For instance, even if one has only a single store to go to, a number of goods or services will vie for the consumer's scarce money. And for many choices (e.g., where to get a haircut, which restaurant to attend, or which museum to visit), competition occurs in a more-or-less traditional sense. Although brand choice may be limited or nonexistent, shoppers in planned economies sometimes use the factory designation or date of manufacture within the month as a symbol of quality in much the same way that people in other systems use the brand name. Further, many planned societies permit farmers and skilled workers the opportunity to sell a portion of the fruits of their labor on the open market, thus competing with the state. When one adds in black market operations that pervade most of these, and indeed all, societies, one can see that competition is not limited to free-enterprise systems.

Today, throughout the world, we are experiencing a blending of institutional types. In planned societies, we see at least some relaxation of centralized control. Managers are given greater flexibility to set production quotas and decide what to produce, how to price their goods, and so on. In free-enterprise countries, we see the growth of firms through acquisition, through vertical integration,[12] and through increased cooperation among management, labor, and government bodies. Moreover, many hybrid institutions have arisen that are neither strictly independent nor government based. These hybrids are especially prevalent in the mixed social economies such as Sweden, Italy, and Yugoslavia, but they occur in the free-enterprise and planned economies as well. These are natural developments that have arisen to meet the needs of society, and marketing activities continue to play a key role in meeting human needs in virtually all sociopolitical systems.

There is another sense in which we might think of marketing as a universal phenomenon. In our everyday lives, we constantly engage in exchanges. Some of these are practical and involve the give-and-take of tangible entities: for example, money for milk. However, perhaps our most numerous exchanges are not practical and involve intangible entities and symbolic gestures. Indeed, in the course of a day, we participate in a myriad of exchanges with family members, friends, co-workers, and strangers. Here our transactions are typically performed unconsciously or with only a partial sense of what is going on and why. Nevertheless, these exchanges bear witness to the transfer and sharing of complex bundles of ideas and feelings, as well as material things on occasion. Because the nature, antecedents, and implications of these exchanges share much in common—in function, form, and process—with so-called marketing exchanges, it is difficult if not arbitrary to draw boundaries around them, at least in terms of their real properties. As a consequence, we see a blurring among the different types of exchange. Marketing principles related to the study and influence of exchanges thus have a generic quality to them at this level of abstraction and exist in all societies and all time periods.

Marketing Management: A Strategic Planning Model

Introduction

A useful starting point for the study of marketing is consideration of the management process. Marketing management serves as a central link between marketing at the societal level and everyday consumption by the general public. It thus provides an effective window on the many facets of marketing.

One way to view the marketing management process is to see it as a strategic planning model designed to accomplish the organization's mission. At the top, organization objectives set the tone. They function as guiding principles for the activities of the firm much as the values of an individual, the creed of a religion, or the laws of a society shape human social action. We have listed example objectives for organizations in Figure 1-9 (e.g., return on investment, employee welfare, social responsibility), but it should be stressed that each organization will have its own unique objectives and emphasize these in different degrees. Organization objectives are broad, general ends toward which the enterprise strives. They may be selected by the board of directors or managers of a firm, or they may be mandated by a parent organization, a government body, or the social system within which the organization exists. Organizational objectives are abstract and often ideal and must be translated into more concrete operational goals. These are translated and implemented by the marketing function, but every functional and staff area within the firm has its own way of operationalizing organization goals. A central problem for management is to coordinate and manage the intermediate goals of all areas so as to insure that the organization objectives are met in the most effective and efficient way.

The External and Internal Environments

Before we discuss the strategic marketing planning process, we should consider the role of the environments external and internal to the firm. These environments determine, or at least influence, the objectives of the organization, and the environments, in turn, affect virtually all phases of the marketing management process.

In general, the *external environment* shapes the organization in one of two ways. One is through the effect that the general environment has on the firm, and a second is through the influence that specific external organizations have on the firm. Let us briefly sketch these forces.

The general external environment affects the organization through the opportunities and constraints it places on the firm's ability to acquire resources, act to convert these into a market offering, and, in general, function as a social entity in an interdependent world. Economic conditions affect the costs of needed resources, the ability of people and organizations to acquire a firm's offerings, and the viability of competition. Legal conditions in the form of federal, state, and local laws and regulations influence how one must deal with customers and suppliers, what ingredients can and cannot be included in a product, what can and must be said about one's wares, what one's responsibilities are to consumers and the environment, and so on. Political conditions through lobbying and party interests informally pressure firms to act in certain ways, in addition to the formal influence they have through the legal system. Social conditions shape the organization through the expectations placed on the firm. Much of this is subtle and unplanned such as is reflected in cultural values; racial, religious, and ethnic variations; social and physical mobility; and local customs. Some of it springs from a partisan sense of urgency and is purposeful, such as is exhibited in the protest of special interest groups. A final influence from the general external environment stems from physical conditions. Climate, geography, natural resources, and the nature and availability of technology in society very much affect the organization along with the economic, legal, political, and social environment.

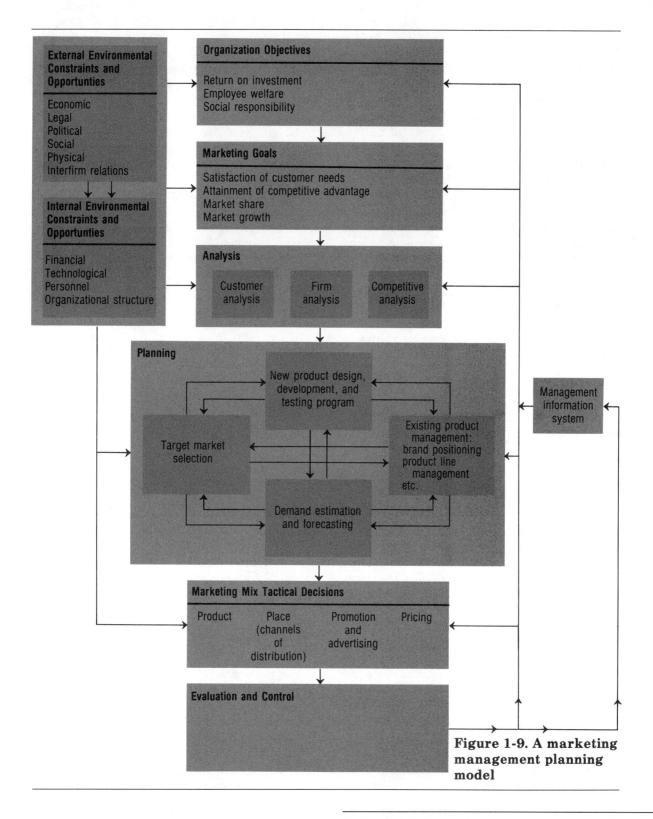

External Environmental Constraints and Opportunties

Economic
Legal
Political
Social
Physical
Interfirm relations

Internal Environmental Constraints and Opportunties

Financial
Technological
Personnel
Organizational structure

Organization Objectives

Return on investment
Employee welfare
Social responsibility

Marketing Goals

Satisfaction of customer needs
Attainment of competitive advantage
Market share
Market growth

Analysis

Customer analysis

Firm analysis

Competitive analysis

Planning

New product design, development, and testing program

Target market selection

Existing product management: brand positioning product line management etc.

Demand estimation and forecasting

Management information system

Marketing Mix Tactical Decisions

Product   Place (channels of distribution)   Promotion and advertising   Pricing

Evaluation and Control

Figure 1-9. A marketing management planning model

Parallel to the general external environment are the specific demands and possibilities arising from interactions with particular organizations. Any organization will be involved in a set of interactions with many other organizations. Some of these will be suppliers of needed resources, others will be formal customer groups or will be involved in cooperative or joint programs, and still others will be government, professional, and related bodies with an interest in or influence on the focal organization. Interorganization relations not only shape the objectives and goals of an organization, but they also influence its actions and well-being. One may study interorganization relations in terms of formal and informal exchanges, conflict, cooperation, and power. Although this is more the subject of sociology and the managerial subfield of organization behavior, we will have a number of things to say about such relationships and their effects on the organization and on marketing performance in general at various points in the text.[13]

The *internal environment* interacts with the external environment, and, just as important for our purposes, it influences the organization's objective- and goal-setting processes.[14] It also affects the remainder of the marketing management process. One way the internal environment functions is through the constraints it imposes on decision making, resource allocation, and everyday activities in the firm. The most important constraints in this respect are financial, technological, and personnel related. The organization structure, another aspect of the internal environment, exerts a direct impact on the functioning of the firm. This structure includes hierarchical lines of authority, rules and procedures, communication patterns, the degree of differentiation of tasks (i.e., organization complexity), and the distribution of power (i.e., centralization of authority). These factors affect how the organization adapts to its environment and how it implements the activities leading to goal attainment. More specifically, structure influences leadership, decision making, goal setting, planning, task execution, and

control. At the same time, vested interests, power, conflict, and cooperation among people and groups within the organization are thwarted, resolved, or fostered, depending on how the organization structure is designed and managed. We will have much to say about this role of the internal environment in forthcoming chapters. We will also mention how the organization acts upon and shapes its environment.

Marketing Management

The marketing management process can be viewed as an integrated sequence of five steps with feedback (Figure 1-9). In abbreviated form, the process can be written as:

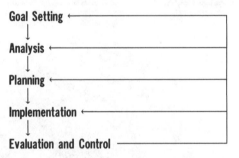

Let us outline the steps here as a prelude to the full development and description contained in subsequent chapters.

The marketing management process begins with *goal setting*. Management sets goals that serve as intermediate steps in the pursuit of the organization's mission. Marketing goals also function as measures of the firm's performance. The goals then become operational standards guiding the analysis, planning, implementation, and evaluation and control activities of the organization.

Analysis constitutes an important early step in the process. *Customer analysis* addresses the needs of consumers, which current products satisfy or fail to satisfy those needs, why those products succeed or fail, what kinds of products might be required to satisfy needs, how consumers go about satisfying needs and making decisions, and what the overall market(s) of consumers looks like.

Firm analysis considers the ability of the organization to meet the needs of consumers. This entails assessment of one's own current products, the potential for developing new products, the financial and production capabilities of the firm, the availability of needed inputs, public policy considerations, and the opportunity for effective communication and distribution of the product. *Competitive analysis* constitutes an assessment of existing or potential rivalry among firms selling the same product, the power dependence relations of the firm with customers and others, and the role of alternative sources of satisfaction as a competitive threat. All three forms of analysis—customer, firm, and competitive—are performed through research and managerial decision making, topics we will consider throughout the book.

Following analysis, four *planning processes* come to the fore. The first—*new product design, development, and testing*—is a crucial activity for the firm. It is here that the organization generates innovations and translates them into need-satisfying products. Most firms have special departments and people who perform these new product functions, and we will devote two chapters to their description. A second, related planning process is *existing product management*. Obviously, after a new product becomes established, the need for sound management does not end. Decisions must be made about the brand's current position, the need to add new features or models, and the need to eliminate some features or models. *Demand estimation and forecasting* comprise still a third essential planning activity. Indeed, the livelihood of the firm itself depends on how well it predicts demand. Finally, because it is both impractical and inefficient to capture all markets, strategic choices must be made in *target market selection*. These four planning processes are interactive, not static. For example, one cannot estimate demand without knowing the target market, and the selection of the target market depends on potential demand.

The strategic plans must next be *implemented*. This is accomplished through tactical choices among the marketing mix. Different levels and combinations of products, channels of distribution, promotion, and prices are the tools used to stimulate and meet demand.

Finally, the marketing management process ends, temporarily, with *evaluation and control* programs and *feedback* on the goal setting, analysis, planning, and implementation processes. Throughout the remainder of this text, we will elaborate on and illustrate the processes outlined above.

The Plan of the Book

The purpose of this book is (1) to help you better understand how and why marketing operates the way it does, (2) to help you gain skills in marketing management (e.g., goal setting, analysis, planning, tactical implementation, and evaluation and control), and (3) to help you think critically and creatively in your studies and in your approach to work and life in general.

To this end, an attempt is made to present marketing from three points of view. We will look first at marketing from the perspective of *the individual consumer*. This will help us to better understand what marketing means to us personally and how the manager must scrutinize marketing if he or she is to be successful. Second, we will examine marketing at *the societal level*. Marketing not only receives its mandate and authority from society-at-large, but it has a profound impact on the physical environment, culture, and institutional relations. Third, we will devote an extensive part of the book to *marketing management*. After all, much of what we mean by marketing is what marketers do. Indeed, we might argue that the degree to which individual consumer and broader societal needs are met depends fundamentally on the nature and efficiency of the marketing management activities performed by organizations.

Most of the following chapters are organized around the tripartite topics of the meaning of marketing to individual people, society, and managers. We hope that this book enriches your knowledge of marketing and helps you think with greater insight and intuition into the complex forces underlying life in the marketplace.

Summary

In this chapter, we have tried to introduce you to the subject matter of marketing. We began with some early definitions of marketing, but found these lacking. As a working definition, we prefer the following modern construal of marketing:

marketing is the set of individual and social activities concerned with the initiation, resolution, and/or avoidance of exchange relationships.

To be sure, this is a broad definition. But it reflects both a consensus among marketing scholars and how and where marketing is performed in the real world.

Next we turned to a description of *marketing systems*. We might think of marketing in terms of patterns of interconnected exchanges or networks of exchange relationships. Figure 1-2 showed a simple example wherein a producer was linked to customers not only directly but indirectly through intermediaries.

The discussion then focused on a characterization of marketing from the viewpoint of the marketer. We saw that organization objectives become translated into two *marketing goals: satisfaction of consumer needs* and *attainment of a competitive advantage.* The former is approached through customer analysis of psychological and social needs. The latter is attacked through competitive analysis. In particular, five competitive threats to any organization were identified (Figure 1-4):

1 Supplier power

2 Consumer power

3 Product substitutability

4 The threat of new entrants into the market

5 Rivalry among existing competitors

To operationalize the dual marketing goals of customer satisfaction and competitive advantage, firms generally employ one of three *strategies. Product differentiation* is the strategy of marketing a product or service that is perceived by consumers as being unique. It may possess attributes not contained in competitors' offerings, superior quality, or other advantages. *Overall cost leadership* is an alternative strategy that aims to achieve a competitive edge by maximizing sales volume and minimizing costs. The first two strategies tend to focus on an entire market or else strive for as much of the market as possible. The third one, *market focus,* is the strategy of concentrating on a portion or *segment* of a market.

Strategies are implemented and fine-tuned through *tactics.* Marketers generally employ one or more of four tactics, the 4 Ps of the marketing mix as they are more commonly known: *product, place, promotion,* and *price.* Much of the book is organized around these four topics.

We also saw that marketing is a fundamental human activity that owes its origins to basic needs and the development of social relations among people. As a matter of fact, marketing has gone on since early times and has been a central force in modernization and the improvement in the quality of life. By the same token, marketing as a technology has sometimes been abused or has at least had unintended negative effects.

In the twentieth century, one finds that marketing has progressed through three phases. The first might be termed the *inward focus* to indicate that firms emphasized internal operations (e.g., production, accounting, finance) relatively more than marketing. This was followed by a transition to the *outward focus*, where stress was placed on selling, consumers, distribution, and display of goods. Finally, in recent times we see the emergence of a *holistic focus.* Here the organization strives to obtain a balance between its internal needs and constraints and the external demands and opportunities afforded by its customers and other environmental forces. To the extent that a firm satisfies its own, consumers', and society's needs, we might say that it follows the so-called *marketing concept.*

We closed this introductory chapter with a strategic planning model of marketing. Figure 1-9 summarizes its parts which serve as subject areas for much of the remainder of the book. At this time, you might take another minute to look at this figure and mentally go over each box and process. Notice how organization objectives, shaped by the external and internal environments, determine marketing goals. These are, in turn, refined through analysis of the market, the firm's situation, and competitive conditions. Next, planning of the marketing effort is conducted, and the marketing mix implemented. Finally, evaluation and control functions are performed to regulate the marketing management process and ensure that it is proceeding on course.

We turn now to two chapters on consumer behavior which will give you the background needed to better comprehend the steps in marketing management outlined in Figure 1-9. The latter are developed in detail in Chapters 4–15. Chapter 16 provides a capstone summary of the book and at the same time extends discussion into the future.

Questions and Problems for Discussion

1 In your own words, define marketing. Interpret your definition.

2 Briefly trace the evolution of marketing from antiquity until earliest recorded history. Why is marketing needed?

3 In the twentieth century, marketing has progressed through three stages. State and describe these.

4 What two fundamental goals guide virtually every marketing effort? Briefly describe these.

5 Organizations tend to employ well-defined marketing strategies to reach corporate goals. Typically, one of the following strategies is used: product differentiation, overall cost leadership, or special market focus. Describe these. Is it possible to pursue both a product differentiation and overall cost leadership strategy for the same brand? Why or why not?

6 What are the 4 Ps (i.e., the marketing mix tools) and what role do they play in modern marketing management?

7 Does marketing occur in all societies and economic systems? Defend your answer.

8 Briefly discuss the marketing management planning model presented in the chapter.

NOTES

1. One study estimated that the average family of four sees or hears 1,518 advertisements per day; see Edwin W. Ebel, "Do We Advertise Goods . . . Or Do We Sell Them?" Paper delivered at the West Coast meeting of the Association of National Advertisers, May 8–10, 1957, p. 4. Another found that the average male is exposed to 285 ads per day, whereas the average female is exposed to 305 ads per day; see Steuart Henderson Britt, Stephen C. Adams, and Allan S. Miller, "How Many Advertising Exposures Per Day?" *Journal of Advertising Research* 12 (December 1972). A more conservative estimate of ad exposure is 38 per day; see Raymond A. Bauer and Stephen A. Greyser, *Advertising in America: The Consumer View* (Boston: Harvard University, Graduate School of Business Administration, Division of Research, 1968).

2. *Marketing Definitions: A Glossary of Marketing Terms* (Chicago: American Marketing Association, 1960), p. 15.

   In early 1985, the Board of Directors of the American Marketing Association met and proposed the following as the new official definition of marketing:

   Marketing is the process of planning and executing the conception, pricing, promotion, and distribution of ideas, goods, and services to create exchanges that satisfy individual and organization objectives—*Marketing News* 19 (March 1, 1985): 1.

   Notice how closely this definition corresponds to the modern definition proposed in this chapter.

3. For an introduction to marketing in nontraditional business enterprises, see Philip Kotler, "Strategies for Introducing Marketing into Nonprofit Organizations," *Journal of Marketing* 43 (January 1979): 37–44.

4. See, for example, Richard P. Bagozzi, "Marketing as an Organized Behavioral System of Exchange," *Journal of Marketing* 38 (October 1974): 77–81. Bagozzi, "Marketing as Exchange," *Journal of Marketing* 39 (October 1975): 32–39; Bagozzi, "Social Exchange in Marketing," *Journal of the Academy of Marketing Science* 3 (Fall 1975): 586-92. Bagozzi, "Science, Politics, and the Social Construction of Marketing," in K. L. Bernhardt, ed., *Marketing: 1776–1976 and Beyond* (Chicago: American Marketing Association, 1976), pp. 586–92; Bagozzi, "Is All Social Exchange Marketing?: A Reply," *Journal of the Academy of Marketing Science* 5 (Fall 1977): 315-26; Bagozzi, "Marketing as Exchange: A Theory of Transactions in the Market Place," *American Behavioral Scientist* 21 (March–April 1978): 535-56; and Bagozzi, "Toward a Formal Theory of Marketing Exchanges," in O. C. Ferrell, S. W. Brown, C. W. Lamb, Jr., eds., *Conceptual and Theoretical Developments in Marketing* (Chicago: American Marketing Association, 1979), pp. 431–47.

5. See Bagozzi, "Marketing as Exchange," 1978; Bagozzi, "Toward a Formal Theory of Marketing Exchanges," 1979. See also footnote 2.

6. Michael E. Porter, *Competitive Strategy: Techniques for Analyzing Industries and Competitors* (New York: The Free Press, 1980).

7. See Porter, *Competitive Strategy*, 1980, Chapter 2.

8. Porter, *Competitive Strategy*, 1980, pp. 37–38.

9. Porter, *Competitive Strategy*, 1980, p. 35.

10. Porter, *Competitive Strategy*, 1980, p. 41.

11. For a classic statement on an expanded conceptualization of products, see Philip Kotler and Sydney J. Levy, "Broadening the Concept of Marketing," *Journal of Marketing* 33 (January 1969): 10-15.

12. Vertical integration is a term used to characterize the practice of an enterprise expanding out from its primary function to perform other functions previously conducted by other institutions. For example, producers who originally sold their wares to independent wholesalers sometimes find it advantageous to set up or acquire their own wholesaling operations to distribute their goods. Occasionally, a retailer or wholesaler will expand outward and manufacture its own goods. Vertical integration ensures sources of supply, reduces costs, and provides more control over the selling process, among other reasons.

13. For research into the organization-environment interface, see William H. Starbuck, "Organizations and Their Environments," in Marvin D. Dunnette, ed., *Handbook of Industrial and Organizational Psychology* (Chicago: Rand McNally & Co., 1976); Howard E. Aldrich and Jeffrey Pfeffer, "Environments of Organizations," *The Annual Review of Sociology* 2 (Palo Alto: Annual Reviews, 1976). Jeffrey Pfeffer and Gerald R. Salancik, *The External Control of Organizations* (New York: Harper & Row, 1978); and Howard Aldrich, *Organizations and Environments* (Englewood Cliffs, N.J.: Prentice-Hall, 1979).

    For research into interorganization relations, see J. Kenneth Benson, "The Interorganizational Network as a Political Economy," *Administrative Science Quarterly* 20 (June 1975): 229–49; William M. Evan, "Toward a Theory of Inter-Organizational Relations," *Management Science* 11 (August 1965): B217–30; and Louis W. Stern and Torger Reve, "Distribution Channels as Political Economies: A Framework for Comparative Analysis," *Journal of Marketing* 44 (Summer 1980): 52–64.

14. For research into the internal structure and dynamics of organizations, see Richard H. Hall, *Organizations: Structure and Process*, 2nd ed. (Englewood Cliffs, N.J.: Prentice-Hall, 1977); and Jeffrey Pfeffer, *Organizational Design* (Arlington Heights, Ill.: AHM Publishing Corporation, 1978).

GLOSSARY

Brand Image. The thoughts and feelings a brand, its name, advertising, etc. engender in a consumer. These may be functional, nonfunctional, utilitarian, nonutilitarian (e.g., symbolic), or combinations of these.

Competitive Analysis. Assessment of (a) existing or potential rivalry among firms selling the same or similar products, (b) power dependence relations of one's own firm with suppliers, customers, and others, and (c) the role of alternative sources of satisfaction for suppliers and customers.

Customer Analysis. Research into the behavior of customers. Customer analysis strives to discover the needs of consumers, how consumers go about satisfying needs and making decisions, which current products and brands satisfy or fail to satisfy needs, and what new products might be required to satisfy old or emerging needs. It also is concerned with what the overall aggregate market of consumers looks like and what changes and trends can be forecasted.

Firm Analysis. Evaluation of the ability of the firm to meet consumer needs and demands, face competitive threats, and generally function in the larger sociopolitical and economic environments. Involves analysis of current products, the ability to develop new products, financial resources, production capability, public policy constraints, labor and capital needs, and the opportunity for effective communication and distribution of one's wares.

Marketing. The set of individual and social activities concerned with the initiation, resolution, and/or avoidance of exchange relationships.

Marketing Concept. The ideal standard or philosophical perspective wherein a firm attempts to balance its internal needs and constraints with its external demands and opportunities and in so doing meet its own goals, satisfy consumers, and fulfill social responsibilities. Such an approach is holistic as opposed to less optimal (from society's standpoint) atomistic approaches (e.g., focus only on technology, customers, or other isolated aspects of a firm's business).

Marketing Mix (the 4 Ps). Generic tools or tactics marketers can use to adapt to and/or influence responses in the marketplace. The four tools are product, place, promotion, and price:

Product. Any offering actually or potentially desired by a target person or organization. A product might be a physical object, an intangible service, an idea (e.g., abortion), person (e.g., a political candidate), or place (e.g., Florida). Products typically have physical and/or subjective attributes. They satisfy physiological, psychological, or social needs.

Place (channel of distribution). The existing set of institutions and functions that facilitate the exchange between marketer and customer. Examples of institutions include retailers, wholesalers, distributors, brokers, auctioneers, cooperatives, and organized markets (e.g., stock exchanges). Common functions entail storage, delivery, selling, display, assortment, service, parts, and provision of credit.

Promotion. Communication of a product, its price, availability, features and benefits, etc., to consumers. The objective is to inform and/or persuade. Promotions generally take the form of advertising, face-to-face selling, coupons, leaflets, in-store displays, phone calls, and other tactics.

Price. The cost of a product or service to the consumer. Price is usually expressed in monetary terms but can also encompass lost time, opportunity costs, psychic costs, and social costs. Price is most often viewed by the consumer as a sign of how much must be given up to acquire something of value. Occasionally, price is a signal of quality, prestige, or other unique value.

Marketing Strategy. How the organization chooses to allocate resources to meet or stimulate consumer needs and achieve a competitive advantage. In its broadest sense, it entails goal setting; customer, firm, and competitive analysis; new product development, target market selection, product management, and demand estimation; and implementation and management of the marketing mix. More narrowly, marketing strategy is characterized by a focus on product differentiation, overall cost leadership, or market focus (also termed *market segmentation*).

Product Differentiation. Marketing a product or service that is perceived in some way to be unique by consumers.

Overall Cost Leadership. Achieving the lowest costs through economies of scale, control of expenses, efficient buying, and other programs and actions.

Market Focus. Concentration on a particular segment of the market, i.e., on a specific geographic region or type of consumer (e.g., men vs. women; young vs. old; married vs. unmarried; high, middle, or low income; introvert vs. extrovert).

Commentary on Modern Marketing

Theodore Levitt
Graduate School of
Business Administration
Harvard University

"Prepare a short statement of where the field of marketing is today and where it will be tomorrow."

That has been my assignment—the answer intended for bright, first-time marketing students in MBA or better undergraduate programs. I will tell you my problem with the assignment. It presumes a common understanding as to what "the field" is, what "marketing" is, what "where" means, what "will" means, and when "tomorrow" is.

I don't intend this as an essay in epistemology, but consider your reaction if, in the assigned sentence quoted above, you substituted for *marketing* the word *sex*. You'd have the same problem as I. Are we talking about theory or practice, about older people (big old companies) or younger people (small young companies)? And, if young people (young companies), how young—barely pubescent teenagers or experienced college types? Are we talking about the U.S.A. or about Saudi Arabia, about Southern California or Northern Maine? Does it matter? You bet. Then how do you do the assignment? See my problem? Would you answer it differently if you were, say, a college professor of sexology with a Ph.D. or an active practitioner with a subscription to *Hustler;* a professor of marketing or a practitioner of marketing?

Consider in my assignment the term *the field.* Does it, when referring to marketing, include also the simultaneous design and manufacturing of products—which is certainly the case in customized

marketing of, say, corporate financing packages by investment bankers and commercial bankers, of much of what advertising agencies do in account solicitation, and of much of what architects do on speculation? Does it include market research and marketing decision support systems? Or, consider *marketing.* Does it include public relations? Are securities brokers considered to be doing marketing—even when they only execute orders? Suppose it's a "buy" order? Does that make them buyers, in which case they are acting as customers, but acting as sellers when it's a "sell" order? When IT&T gets a $900 million contract to build the telephone system for a Middle Eastern country, is it thought to have been doing marketing, designing, bidding, negotiating, contracting, or what? Gillette's Vice President of Business Relations, who has among his major duties (separate from the sales organization—he never asks for or takes an order), the cultivation of Gillette's relationships with major retailers and distributors. He does it via a vast array of ceremonial activities, ranging from hosting cocktail parties, dinners, and entertainments at twelve trade association conventions annually. He arranges for major accounts to get tickets for and V.I.P. treatment at the All Star baseball game, the World Series, the Superbowl, and the NCAA basketball playoffs. He attends charitable dinners that honor high officers of key accounts who are active in those charities. Is that "marketing"?

Or, consider the part of the question that asks "where marketing is today." Are we talking here about "where" in the organization chart of large corporations? Or of small ones? Or in consumer package goods companies like General Foods versus, say, banks, steel companies, or hospital management companies? Or do we mean "where in the organization's power structure"—that is, who calls the tune in this company—marketing, finance, manufacturing, distribution? Is distribution part of marketing at, say, McDonald's in the same way as at Interstate Trucking? Or, by "where marketing is today," do we mean in the Academy relative to, say, Finance or Computer Sciences? Or do we mean by that, "What's the state of marketing theory today relative to yesterday, or relative to economic theory, or relative to marketing practice?"

Regarding "tomorrow," do we mean next year, next decade, or next century? Would the answers be the same as between the U.S.A., the U.S.S.R., and the United Arab Emirates?

It isn't that I'm confused, only that there can be no single answer to any of the many and ambiguous questions buried inside this simple assignment. (This alone tells you something about marketing. It may not be an exact science, but it requires a lot of exactitude when you talk about it.) Nor is there likely to be a single answer, even if there were only a single clear question. The closest we can come to it is to make large generalizations that somehow give us a sense of the general drift of things, knowing that in the end it is up to each of us individually to employ that sense, along with whatever else we know and can learn, to help us understand things in the context of what, specifically, concerns us at any time and what, with high specificity, we are asked to do or must do. Newton's Universal Law of Gravitation is nice, except that it's not universal. Ask any astronaut. Nor does it much help Mr. Jim Palmer to know in exquisite intricacy exactly how his every pitch is affected by the powerful forces Newton described.

The best way to get a sense of what marketing is and does is to contrast it with something we've all encountered—selling. Marketing and selling are not the same thing. Selling is concerned with trying to get people to want what you have. *Marketing is concerned with trying to have what people will want.* Selling starts with taking to the marketplace what comes out of the factory. Marketing starts with trying to make in the factory what will sell in the marketplace. Marketing starts with trying to understand what people want and value, looking at the choices and resources (like money, time, etc.) available to them, and then designing products, delivery systems, sales programs, communications, price, and a lot of other things appropriate to what you've found out about those people. (When I say "products," I mean tangible products like bricks and Jell-O, and intangible products like appendectomies, auto repairs, and checking accounts.)

Marketing in this sense will be no different "tomorrow" than "today," and it makes no difference whether we're talking about General Motors or the general store, about the Intergallactic Bank and Trust Company or the internist at General Hospital, or about the Republican National Committee, the Salvation Army, or the Right Reverend Mr. Billy Graham's Crusade for Christ. A customer is somebody who willingly exchanges something that's his for something that's yours—whether it's his machine tools or his ideology, or your money, your time, or your belief system. Marketing is concerned with doing all the big things and all the little things which will cause people to prefer your offering over those of all others—or over doing nothing at all. To do that you have to know the prospective customers in and out, including all their options.

If marketing therefore starts with what the customer wants, not with what the factory has, it also becomes quickly obvious that the purpose of a business is not as simple as is often thought. Making money is certainly not the purpose of a business—certainly not in any sensibly prescriptive sense. Making money is no more the purpose of a business than eating is the purpose of life. Eating is a requisite, not a purpose, of life. Without it life cannot be sustained. Similarly, making money is not the purpose of business. It is a requisite of business. Without it business cannot be sustained. That's true even in the Soviet Union. Why? Because the process of producing things is a process also of wearing out the capacity to produce them. Milling machines wear out, typewriters wear out, people wear out. You have to make a surplus to replace them; otherwise, you go out of business. The economic machine grinds to a halt. And you have to make a surplus to finance the R&D necessary to replace the obsoleting things you produce. That surplus is called "making money." Obviously, making money is a necessity, not a purpose of business—capitalist business, socialist business, utopian business, government business, ecclesiastical business, educational business, eleemosynary business, all businesses. This is not a matter of opinion. It is a palpable and unyielding fact.

The operational definition of the purpose of a business is this: to get and keep a customer. Without a customer there is no business. A product is something people buy. If they don't buy it it's not a product; it's an artifact, not even a museum piece.

Marketing will be, and must do, in the future the same as it is and does today. Things change, as they always do; and the more they change, the more they remain the same. The reason this old aphorism is old is that it's been true so long. The reason it's true is that certain things abide through thick and thin. What looks like change to the unpracticed eye is often only activity. A pot of boiling water has lots of activity, but not much change, especially if it has a good lid. The "good lid" in society is something about the way people behave and about what they want and value. It may be PacMan today, but that's not much different from what they wanted and how they behaved as spectators in the Roman Colosseum, or as participants in the ghoulish games of the Druids—from which, incidentally, descended modern-day football. Their "ball" was the skull of a cannibalized enemy.

New technologies now suddenly tumble out at us in massive proportions, transforming the means by which we do things. They also transform how we study, understand, and respond to customers and competitors. But the objectives of their use in these respects are the same as all times before. Whether we will be able to understand the world better, develop better theory to guide our understanding and actions—this is unknown. This is a matter of some controversy among both scholars and practitioners. What is not controversial is that the quest for better theory, better understanding, and better action should continue. The trick is only to find out what "better" really means. There is no objective test, not even regarding "betterness" in respect to "action." Who is to say that when we succeed totally in perfecting our marketing actions, that this will, by some other standards, be viewed as "good" or "better." We will still be faced with having to answer Socrates' question as to who is happier, the pig wallowing in the gutter or the philosopher contemplating virtue.

As long as there are substantial numbers of people who define "good" and "better" in terms of whether these lead to happiness or virtue, we cannot escape that question.

Meanwhile, all people everywhere seem to want the world to do the world's work. In the entire history of recorded time, people have wanted some sort of transcendence, but also alleviation, ease, comfort, society, challenge, and security. And they've always everywhere been ready to pay for these, even resolute modern utopians who pay with their labors in special places they've set up for their ease, and those now-gone hippies who proclaimed with unctuous self-righteousness that "less is more." They too wanted more—their kind of more, for which they paid in their special ways in communes, or by begging for money (marketing themselves?) from honest workers on the streets. And as long as that's the condition of the world—people wanting more than what they come to this earth with on the day of their birth—as long as that's the case, there will be marketing. In its essential elements it will be the same in the future as it is today. We all market something, even if only ourselves. That requires finding out what other people want and value, and providing it in some way superior to others who seek to serve the same purpose.

CHAPTER
TWO

All human actions have one or more of these seven causes: chance, nature, compulsions, habit, reason, passion, desire.
——Aristotle (384–322 B.C.)

Human nature is not a machine to be built after a model, and set to do exactly the work prescribed for it, but a tree, which requires to grow and develop itself on all sides, according to the tendency of the inward forces which make it a living thing.
——John Stuart Mill (1806–1873)

In the popular language we may say that the ego stands for reason and sanity; in contrast to the id which contains untamed passions.
——Sigmund Freud (1856–1939)

CONSUMER BEHAVIOR: THE INDIVIDUAL DECISION MAKER

Introduction

Why do people buy what they buy? Why does person A purchase brand X rather than brand Y? How do people go about making decisions and choices in the marketplace?

These are questions that marketing scholars have been trying to answer for many years. They are also questions that practitioners constantly face in their everyday decision-making activities. For example, the brand manager[1] of Kellogg's Raisin Bran needs to know how people make decisions with respect to the breakfast meal. Do consumers weigh convenience, price, nutrition, and taste in equal proportions, or do they have other perhaps more complex criteria for making a decision? The brand manager must study the motivation and purchase patterns of consumers in order to optimally design the product ingredients, the package, the delivery system to market the product, and the communication program to inform and persuade people to try it. Similarly, the sales clerk in a department store, the manager of a museum, and the administrator of a social service such as the Red Cross all need to know how people react to their products or services so that they can better meet the public's needs. Government officials in the Federal Trade Commission and other agencies also study consumption so that they can more effectively administer programs that either affect, or are affected by, the demand for goods and services. And, of course, we all must study consumer behavior if we are to gain a better understanding of how the marketplace works.

In this chapter, we will examine a number of determinants of consumer behavior. The focus will be on the decisions and choices of *individual decision makers*. Indeed, we will peer deeply into the minds of consumers to see how they process information, respond emotionally, and proceed to act.

The examination of the social and cultural determinants of consumption will be presented in the following chapter where the focus will be on *group-based decisions*.

A Historical Look at Three Basic Models of Consumer Behavior

It is very difficult to identify the causes of consumer behavior. People buy things for many reasons, they seldom are aware of all their feelings and thought processes concerning purchases, and many external forces, such as economic and social conditions, constrain their behavior. Moreover, our scientific knowledge is limited, our methodologies are imperfect, and our ability to study consumer behavior is constrained by practical, moral, and ethical considerations. As a consequence, scholars in marketing and the behavioral sciences have attempted to search for simplified, yet fundamental, aspects of consumption in order to better understand and predict at least a portion of behavior in the marketplace. Three outstanding models underlie most of the theories that scholars have advanced: *the economic model, the stimulus-response model*, and *the stimulus-organism-response model*.

The Economic Model

Economists were perhaps the first to propose a formal theory of consumer behavior. Their model has led to the so-called vision of *economic man*,[2] which basically builds on the following premises:

1 Men and women are rational in their behavior.

2 They attempt to maximize their satisfaction in exchanges.

3 They have complete information on alternatives available to them in exchanges.

4 These exchanges are relatively free from external influence.

The goal of the economic model is to represent fundamental, general rules people follow in their everyday choices. The first premise merely asserts that people are assumed to follow criteria or rules when they decide to act. To be rational means, roughly, to be consistent in one's assessment and application of criteria to decision making. For example, if a consumer stated that he or she preferred apples to oranges and oranges to grapes, then we might expect him or her to prefer apples to grapes when faced with a decision between the two. At least, we would predict, given the expressed preference ordering among the three fruits, that he or she would choose apples over grapes in most situations. It would be somewhat irrational or at least nonrational for the person to choose grapes over apples. He or she would have to change preference ordering to do so. Another perhaps oversimplified rule might be "buy only brand names." Actually, all of us follow many rules that imply this kind of predictability.

The second premise of the economic model states that people are motivated to maximize the satisfaction they anticipate they will receive from goods and services. Given that people have limited resources and must therefore choose from among all possible combinations of offerings, they are believed to do so in accordance with the goal of personal utility maximization. In other words, people buy goods and services that best meet their needs and wants. Being rational serves as a means to achieve this goal.

The third premise is that people make their choices from among goods and services they are aware of. Although the information they have may be invalid or incomplete, they nevertheless are presumed to make their choices on the basis of the information that they perceive to be true.

The fourth premise is that economic choices are not determined by outside compulsion.[3] Rather, "economic man" is believed to have the ability to choose freely among alternative courses of action.

Actually, not every approach in economics takes all four premises as its starting point. Samuelson, for example, proposed a model of consumer choice not predicated on assumptions of mental processes such as utility maximization or rationality.[4] Rather, he built his *revealed preference theory* on the observable choices of the individual decision maker. Thus, with the premises that people will prefer more goods to fewer and will be able to rank-order their preferences among alternatives in a uniform and consistent way, Samuelson derived the classic implications of microeconomics that people will buy more of a good when their income rises and/or prices of the good fall. Similarly, Simon and others have proposed that satisficing (i.e., settling for satisfactory gains) and other decision rules can replace the often restrictive and unrealistic premise of maximization.[5]

Despite the attempts to modify economic man, the central premises remain as a basis for the neoclassical economic theory of consumer behavior that is a dominant viewpoint even today.[6] First, it is assumed that the consumption of goods and services is motivated by the utility (i.e., basic human satisfaction) that these goods and services can provide. Formally, we may write this as

$$U = u\,(x_1, x_2, \ldots, x_n), \qquad \text{2-1}$$

where U is utility; $x_1, x_2, \ldots, x_n$ stand for n different goods or services a person might desire; and $u\,(x_1, x_2, \ldots, x_n)$ is read "a function of $x_1, x_2, \ldots, x_n$." In words, equation 2-1 asserts that a consumer's utility is a function of the n types of goods he or she perceives to be available from the marketplace. It is assumed that the consumer attempts to choose those goods that will maximize his or her utility. This will depend on the consumer's tastes and preferences among the n goods.

Second, it is assumed that the choices of the consumer will be constrained by his or her resources. This may be expressed as

$$I = \sum_{i=1}^{n} x_i\, p_i, \qquad \text{2-2}$$

where I is the consumer's money income; p_i is the price of good i; and x_i, for $i = 1, 2, \ldots, n$, is as defined above. In words, equation 2-2 states that the total amount of money that a consumer spends on goods equals his or her income. Equation 2-2 is sometimes called the budget constraint.

Taking equations 2-1 and 2-2 and using certain mathematical procedures, economists have shown that the demand for any good, x_i, can be expressed by the following demand function:

$$x_i = d_i \left(\frac{I}{p}, \frac{p_i}{p}, \frac{p_j}{p}, T \right), \qquad \text{2-3}$$

for $i \neq j$ and where p is the price index, T stands for tastes, and the remaining symbols are as defined above. In words, equation 2-3 says that the quantity demanded for good x_i is determined by the amount of income one has, the price of the good, the prices of other goods, and one's tastes. Later in the chapter, we will have more to say about tastes, because its inclusion in the demand equation is a controversial issue among economists.

Figure 2-1 is a representation of the meaning of the demand equation. The dependent variable is the quantity demanded of good x, and the predicted directions of effects from the independent variables are shown as a plus (+) or minus (−) alongside the respective arrows. It is important to recognize that the predicted effect for a change in any one of the independent variables is made assuming that all other variables and unmeasured determinants are held constant. This is the well-known *ceteris paribus* (other things being equal) criterion. For example, as income rises for a consumer, the demand equation predicts that he or she will consume more of x, ceteris paribus. This results from the increased resources available to the consumer and the fact that tastes and prices remain constant.

However, as the price of x rises, less will be consumed because, given a fixed income, fewer resources will be at the disposal of the consumer. Similarly, as the price of a complement, y, increases, less will be demanded of x. For example, if x is coffee and y is cream, a consumer with tastes for both will purchase less coffee when the price of cream rises, ceteris paribus. Alternatively, if the price of tea, a regularly used substitute for coffee, rises, then more coffee will be demanded because tea is relatively more expensive and poses too heavy a burden on one's budget.

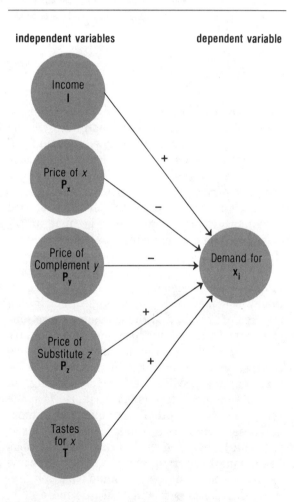

independent variables   **dependent variable**

Figure 2-1. The neoclassical economic model of consumer behavior

Finally, Figure 2-1 shows that the purchase of x is also a function of tastes. A large enough change in tastes, ceteris paribus, will produce a different ordering of preferences for a consumer among all desired goods. If one's taste for coffee increases sufficiently, for instance, then more coffee will be consumed *and* less will be demanded of at least one other good. Given fixed prices and fixed income, the increase in the consumption of coffee must result in less consumption of one or more other goods. The particular good or goods for which less will be demanded will depend on the new preference ordering resulting from the change in tastes and also on price and income constraints. Conversely, if one's taste for coffee decreases sufficiently, then less coffee will be consumed and more will be demanded of at least one other good. The smaller amount of coffee purchased allows the consumer to obtain more of other desired goods, ceteris paribus.

As a point of interpretation, notice that the economic model hypothesizes that demand (an observable phenomenon) will be a function of income, prices, and tastes (which, with the possible exception of tastes, are also observable). The mechanism or theory behind the prediction lies in the implied decision process [7] represented in equations 2-1 and 2-2. That is, it is assumed that the consumer attempts to maximize his or her utility, subject to budget constraints. Unlike the observed changes represented in Figure 2-1, however, utility maximization is believed to be unobservable. Although one can "test" the theory indirectly by observing the implications of the assumed maximization process (e.g., by examining how well changes in income predict demand), economists believe that the decision process itself is unobservable. As a consequence, they have concentrated primarily on the relationship of easily measured variables, such as income, on demand and have not systematically explored the decision criteria consumers might use to make choices.

Overall, the economic model has several attractive features. On the positive side, it has proven to be an important descriptive tool. For example, it provides an answer to questions of why people buy what they buy (i.e., they consume to achieve utility) and how they make decisions (i.e., they choose those goods that are perceived to satisfy their needs and fall within the resources of their budget constraints). The economic model provides answers that are mathematically rigorous, yet simple and intuitive. These characteristics have proven helpful in the teaching of economics and consumer behavior, as well as in the planning of corporate and governmental programs. Furthermore, as a predictive tool, the economic model has aided in the forecast of demand. This has permitted managers to more efficiently produce and price their wares.

On the other hand, the economic model of consumption suffers from a number of drawbacks. In the first place, it is oversimplified. It fails to consider many very real psychological, social, and cultural determinants of demand. Some work is being done to broaden the model in this regard, but such efforts have been at the fringe of the discipline and have not yet received wide acceptance by economists.[8] Second, the model provides only limited guidance for managers. The variables it models (e.g., income) are often too removed from the real processes governing choice and managers' potential leverage regarding these processes. For example, marketers know that, in addition to income and prices, advertising, promotion, product characteristics, and distribution policies influence consumption, but the economic model provides little guidance in this regard.[9] Finally, the economic model has been criticized as being nonscientific. The arguments are too complex to discuss here, but the charge has been made that the economic theory of consumption is both inadequately formulated and untestable in principle. These allegations have been made by economists and noneconomists alike.[10]

Before we examine alternatives to the economic view of consumption, it will prove useful to briefly discuss the meaning of two components of the model that have not received much attention by economists but that provide the major subject matter for consumer behavior researchers in marketing. The two components are the principles of utility maximization and tastes. Utility maximization, subject to budget constraints, implies that a consumer weighs the costs of obtaining goods against his or her other resources and at the same time attempts to obtain goods producing the highest level of satisfaction. These activities obviously involve mental decision processes. However, the economic model takes the processes as a given. Although consequences of the assumptions are examined, the internal dynamics are not. As we will see later in the chapter, marketers have attempted to explore the structure and processes of decision making in order to better understand and predict behavior. The activities they have studied have been labeled *information processing* to indicate that consumers perceive and evaluate data from their environment and from their memory to make decisions.

Tastes are another facet of the economic model toward which economists have been ambivalent. Generally, economists have ignored them. One school of thought even believes that tastes play no or at most a very minor role in consumption because they are "stable over time and similar among people." Economists such as Stigler and Becker feel that changes in income and prices are sufficient to explain the demand for goods and services.[11] As we shall see later in this chapter, and as common sense might indicate, people's tastes often change over time and differ widely across the population. Further, tastes have been identified as important causes of consumer behavior.

In general, economists leave "tastes" undefined or else regard them as a residual determinant of consumption (i.e., the unexplained portion of consumer behavior not accounted for by price and income effects). Marketers and other behavioral scientists regard tastes in a much different light. Roughly, what the economist and the layperson refer to as tastes, the marketer sees as a large number of distinct, yet similar, aspects of human psychology. For example, needs, wants, motivation, affect, emotions, values, and goals are some of the variables that marketers study as determinants of consumption and that express somewhat similar meanings as contained in the term *tastes*. We will explore what these variables are and how they influence consumer behavior shortly. Along with thought processes or "cognitions," tastes comprise the major determinants of consumer choice.

The Stimulus-Response Model

Managers have found the economic model particularly lacking in its ability to suggest specific actions for influencing consumption or for anticipating specific demands of consumers. Most firms require guidelines that will indicate how their actions actually influence trial and repeat purchases by consumers. A firm or organization is limited in its repertoire to changes it can make in the marketing mix. These changes, however, can be quite effective and extensive in their impact. For instance, a firm can vary prices, discounts, allowances, product characteristics, packaging, shipping practices, storage facilities, wholesale and retail locations, copy in advertisements, media placement of ads, the extent of personal contact by sales representatives, and a whole host of other tactics. These comprise the stimuli the manager has at his or her disposal to induce a response in the marketplace. The stimuli are sometimes referred to as *marketing policy variables.*

Individual marketing mix variables can influence more than one response on the part of a consumer with varying degrees of success. Typically, consumers' actions or their reactions to marketing mix stimuli include increased awareness of, interest in, and desire for a product, in addition to actual purchase of the product. Stimuli are assumed to operate through or upon unknown consumer processes represented in Figure 2-2 as a "black box" (i.e., unmodeled intervening processes). The processes in the black box are regarded as being unknown—no attempt is made to model their nature in the stimulus-response model. Rather, only their outcomes are monitored. Further, the marketing mix variables are not the only stimuli producing a response on the part of the consumer. Many forces not under the direct control of firms also influence consumer behavior. These are labeled environmental factors and include economic conditions, social determinants, and cultural influences, for example inflation, family pressure, and religious practices. Marketers have little or no control over these, but they do try to anticipate and forecast their effects.

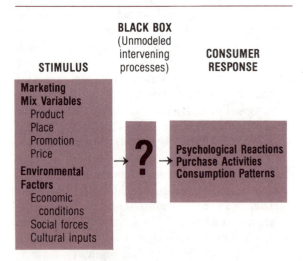

Figure 2-2. The stimulus-response model of consumer behavior

The stimulus-response model is used to represent and predict consumer behavior in many ways. At the level of the individual consumer, for example, a marketer might model the response to varying levels of a product's ingredients. Imagine that a manufacturer wishes to discover how a consumer reacts to the amount of an expensive spice in a packaged food product. Figure 2-3 shows a hypothetical "response function" illustrating how a customer's liking for the product varies as the amount of spice in the food increases. With no spice included in the product, the consumer actually expresses dislike for it. As the level of spices rises from zero to about .3 percent or .4 percent, liking increases to a maximum and remains there until the percentage of spices reaches approximately .6 percent. Beyond this point, liking decreases, although it is still positive. In this example, the level of spices is a physical stimulus for the consumer, and his or her felt degree of liking for the food product is the response.

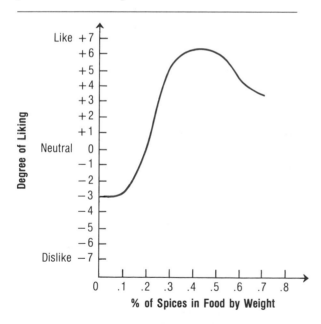

Figure 2-3. A response function for a consumer's reaction to the amount of spice in a packaged food product

By use of a stimulus-response approach, marketers can discover the reactions of consumers to different advertising appeals (e.g., emotional messages vs. rational-cost approaches), package designs, and prices, to name a few stimuli. Further, the responses of a consumer need not be limited to psychological reactions such as liking/disliking or attitudes but can encompass physiological responses such as increased heart rate or behavioral reactions such as the frequency of purchases actually made or amount of product actually purchased. Some marketers, for example, study the brand loyalty of toothpaste purchasers by recording which brands they purchase over time, how many of each brand they buy, when they switch brands, and so on. By observing how these actual behaviors vary with changes in advertising expenditures, prices, and coupon deals, marketers gain insight into which marketing policy variables are the most effective strategies to employ.

The stimulus-response model is perhaps most frequently used by management to depict the responses of groups of consumers rather than individuals. For example, a firm might want to model the level of total sales in California, the market share of brand X across the U.S., or the probability of purchase of brand Y for men as a function of advertising. One possible functional form for the advertising–sales–response relationship is the modified exponential curve (Figure 2-4). As advertising increases, sales increase. However, sales increase at a decreasing rate and approach a maximum or saturation level, s^*. Unlike the example for spices, which represented the response of a single consumer to different amounts of the spice, Figure 2-4 depicts the change in sales for a group of consumers (e.g., total sales for all customers in California) as a function of different potential levels of advertising. The sales and advertising relationship might be examined at the level of a firm or an industry. Of course, many different functional forms are possible, depending on the circumstances, and, as we shall see in later chapters, other functional relations are possible such as the Gomperz or logistic models.[12]

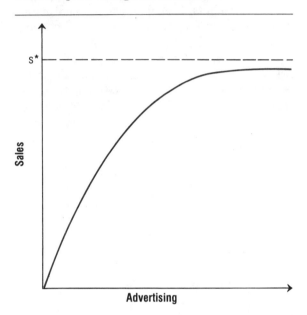

Figure 2-4. A hypothetical advertising-sales response function

The stimulus-response model has also been studied by psychologists. By varying the magnitude and timing of physical and social stimuli directed toward people, psychologists have been able to learn how we acquire emotional reactions and retain factual information. This research also serves as the basis for some practices in advertising and personal selling strategies, and similar research has been done in classical and operant conditioning and in memory processes.

Overall, the stimulus-response model is an appealing theory. First of all, it is simple, which makes it easy to understand and communicate to others. It also reduces the chances for error in its use as compared to more complex approaches. Second, the stimulus-response model is a highly useful managerial tool: the real-world actions available to the firm and the empirical responses most desired from the marketplace are easily represented. Third, the stimulus-response model is valued highly because it has been found to work well in the past. At least it has been found to sometimes provide accurate representations of the impact of marketing mix variables on sales and market share and other aggregate responses.

On the other hand, the stimulus-response model falls short on one very important and far reaching criterion: it omits the processes through which stimuli induce responses. Marketers need to know *how* their actions bring about responses so that they can more effectively and efficiently design and target their stimuli. Figure 2-5 illustrates a stimulus-response model, but it also includes three possible intervening processes. If all that a marketer were concerned with was the relationship between dollars spent on advertising and subsequent sales, he or she would miss the sequence of intervening processes. To stimulate a sale, an advertisement must first make the consumer aware of the product and then contain information creating a desire for the product. Next, the consumer must intend to buy it before a sale is made. Each of the linkages between advertising and final sale involves a different impact and probability of occurrence. Some people are never exposed to an ad and never become aware of it. Others who become aware may or may not develop a desire to try the product. Even some of those who desire the product may not intend to buy it. And so on.

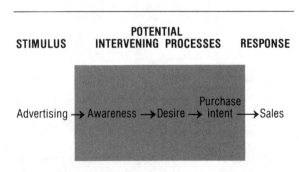

Figure 2-5. A stimulus-response model with intervening processes

Table 2-1 illustrates the shortcomings of the stimulus-response model if one fails to take into account the intervening processes. In Case 1, the response of sales to advertising is shown as a linear relation. For every $10,000 of advertising, 5 units are sold. This is represented as k, the slope of the response function. Hence, with an advertising expenditure, A, of $50,000, the manager expects to sell 25 units. However, the pure stimulus-response model fails to indicate *how* advertising generates these sales.

In Case 2, the sequential effects that the ad has on awareness, desire, and intentions to buy are shown as k_1, k_2, k_3 respectively. For every $1,000 spent on advertising, 1.25 people on the average are aware of the product. Eight of 10 of these have a desire for it, while 5 of 10 of those who desire it intend to and do buy it. Thus, when the ratios are multiplied by $50,000 in advertising, 25 units are again sold. By comparison, Case 3 shows that another ad, producing 4 times the level of awareness but only .25 of the degree of desire, will generate the same level of sales. Nevertheless, the process is quite different. In Case 2, the $50,000 ad was relatively less efficient at generating awareness but was considerably more effective at stimulating desire than the different $50,000 ad represented in Case 3.

TABLE 2-1
An Analysis of the Response of Advertising to Sales

Case #1: The Pure Stimulus-Response Model

$$\text{Sales} = kA = \left(\frac{5 \text{ units sold}}{\$10,000 \text{ advertising}} \right) \left(\$50,000 \text{ advertising} \right) = 25 \text{ units}$$

Case #2: Intervening Processes — low awareness, high desire, moderate intent

$$\text{Sales} = k_1 k_2 k_3 \, A = \left(\frac{1.25 \text{ aware}}{\$1,000 \text{ advertising}} \right) \left(\frac{8 \text{ desire}}{10 \text{ aware}} \right) \left(\frac{5 \text{ units sold}}{10 \text{ desire}} \right) \left(\$50,000 \text{ advertising} \right) = 25 \text{ units}$$

Case #3: Intervening Processes — high awareness, low desire, and moderate intent

$$\text{Sales} = k_1 k_2 k_3 \, A = \left(\frac{5 \text{ aware}}{\$1,000 \text{ advertising}} \right) \left(\frac{2 \text{ desire}}{10 \text{ aware}} \right) \left(\frac{5 \text{ units sold}}{10 \text{ desire}} \right) \left(\$50,000 \text{ advertising} \right) = 25 \text{ units}$$

The stimulus-response model would predict the same outcome in both instances but would not reveal the differential reactions consumers have. The addition of the intervening processes allows the marketer to perform a more detailed analysis of the impact of advertising and to design the stimulus more effectively. For example, without even necessarily changing the amount spent on advertising, one could judicially design an ad to produce awareness and desire for the product in the most effective way. This might entail varying the copy of the ad, which media it is placed in, or how often it is shown. In any case, to produce an optimal response, managers need to know how their advertising stimuli generate sales so that they can better fine-tune their policy variables.

A final limitation of the stimulus-response model is that it fails to allow for the possibility that some purchase behaviors are self-generated and that external stimuli have little, if any, influence. The stimulus-response model, by definition, ignores the internal origin and determination of buying intentions. People are represented as being buffeted by stimuli rather than freely discovering their needs and choosing among alternatives. Consumers, of course, make purchases in both ways, depending on the circumstances, and marketers need a theory rich enough to capture the dynamics.

The Stimulus-Organism-Response Model *Human Factors*

Recognizing the need to examine how stimuli actually influence responses, marketers have increasingly turned to approaches representing the physiological and psychological processes governing behavior. Figure 2-6 illustrates the general form that these efforts take. Consumer behavior is depicted as a stimulus-organism-response system where *organism* stands for a constellation of internal processes and structures intervening between stimuli external to the person and the final actions, reactions, or responses emitted. Notice that the intervening processes and structures consist of perceptual, physiological, feeling, and thinking activities. Obviously, these are complex, multifaceted aspects of human behavior, yet, as we will see shortly, a small number of fundamental processes and structures can be identified and their interrelationships specified. Indeed, the rest of this chapter provides a detailed analysis and expansion of these intervening mechanisms.

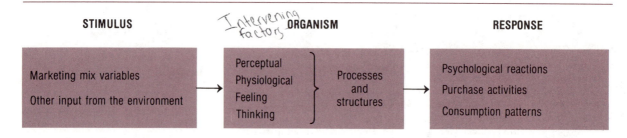

Figure 2-6. Consumer behavior as a stimulus-organism-response process

However, before we present these mechanisms, it will prove useful to define certain key concepts and identify general characteristics of the stimulus-organism-response model. The first concept we need to define is *structure*. By structure we mean a set of variables or entities and the relationships among them. Figure 2-7 shows a structure of thoughts or beliefs that a group of people revealed when they were asked to express their reactions toward the act of giving blood.[13] As shown enclosed in circles, the people formed three reactions: concepts of immediate physical pain, immediate internal sickness, and delayed costs. Moreover, as represented by the curved line segments connecting the circles, the abstract concepts were found to be positively associated in the memories of the respondents. For example, the stronger one perceived that giving blood would be physically painful, the stronger he or she believed that internal sickness and other delayed costs would occur. The statements indicated at the end of the straight line segments constitute the concrete measurement items appearing on a questionnaire and used to infer the abstract mental images people formed. A statistical procedure known as confirmatory factor analysis was used to represent the mental structure people had as to the believed costs of giving blood. Their responses to the seven items on the questionnaire were found to reflect three underlying and interrelated thoughts. Much of the information people store in their minds (i.e., interconnected ideas) about products and services can be represented through structures.

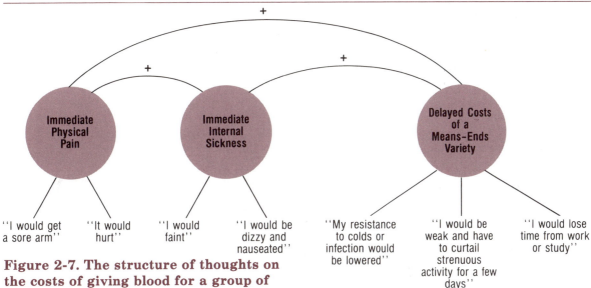

Figure 2-7. The structure of thoughts on the costs of giving blood for a group of consumers

Marketers study the structure of people's thoughts and feelings in order to get a better indication of what factors are important to them in decision making. Imagine that the Red Cross believes that people have invalid and exaggerated perceptions of the costs of giving blood. The Red Cross would like to use advertising to inform people of the true costs and convince them that they are not as bad as they may seem. The first question the Red Cross might need answered would concern those costs that people are most concerned about. It would be too expensive to focus the ad campaign on every possible cost, and, furthermore, it would be inefficient because some costs are not important. Therefore, it would be advantageous to perform a study of the structure of people's thoughts about the act of giving blood in order to identify salient beliefs. Findings could provide the basis for the design of messages to be used in ads. Other information would be of use to the Red Cross—such as the relative importance of each perceived cost as a criterion in actual decision making—but these and other topics are reserved for later discussion.

A second concept used extensively in the stimulus-organism-response model is the notion of *process*. By process we mean either (a) the sequence of steps or stages one goes through in decision making or (b) the cause-and-effect relationships in decision making. An example of the former is shown in Figure 2-8.[14] The series of steps taken by two women, A and B, as they decide on what type of dress to buy, are shown at the left. Person A begins the process first by looking for her size, then verifying whether the price is within an acceptable range or not, next searching for an appropriate color, etc. Person B also begins with a search for her size but then attempts to find a dress with long sleeves, a particular collar style, etc. The points to notice here are that each person uses many criteria to choose a dress and that a specific sequence of judgments was followed until an acceptable dress was found. Different people will often use different criteria and pass through different stages, although the objective of consumer research is to find a small number of frequently used sequences. Except for perhaps impulse or habitual purchases, most real consumer decision processes can be described as sequences of stages not unlike those shown by this model.

2. Do I need this type of item?
3. Do I have this type of item, color included, already in my wardrobe?
4. Is the item practical—in style, in fabric—i.e., will it be comfortable to wear and easy to care for?
   a) Is it a dress I could not make?
   b) Is it well made?
   c) Can I wear it in many situations?
5. Is the item on sale?
6. Is my size available?
7. Is the item within the price range I can afford?
8. Does the item fit in hips, thighs, rear, and at the waist?
9. Does the item fit at the neckline, shoulders, and bustline?
10. Color
    a) Is it black?
    b) Is it yellow or blue?
    c) Is it red with white flowers?
    d) Are the colors not too bright?
    e) Green, cranberry, or butterscotch print?
11. Is the item worth the price?
12. Do I like the item in general?
    a) Does it have large, rounded, glossy buttons?
    b) Does it have short cap sleeves?
    c) Is it a shirtwaist, or does it accent the waist?
    d) Does it have long sleeves?
    e) Is it youthful and/or innocent and demure?
    f) Is the skirt straight?
    g) Is the skirt pleated?
    h) Is it not polka dot or clashing patterns?
    i) Round or roll (cowl) collar?
    j) Cotton or synthetic mixture?
    k) Cotton pique?
    l) Arnel knit?
13. Do I like it better than other dresses considered?
14. Is it a known and favored brand?
15. Length
    a) Is it too long?
    b) Is it too short?
    c) Can the length be easily adjusted?

Figure 2-8. The decision processes of two shoppers (A and B) for women's dresses

SOURCE: From James R. Bettman, *An Information Processing Theory of Consumer Choice* (Reading, Mass.: Addison-Wesley, 1979), as adapted from Marcus Alexis, George H. Haines, and Leonard Simon, "Consumer Information Processing: The Case of Women's Clothing," Fall Educator's Conference, American Marketing Assn., Chicago 1968. Reprinted with the permission of the American Marketing Association.

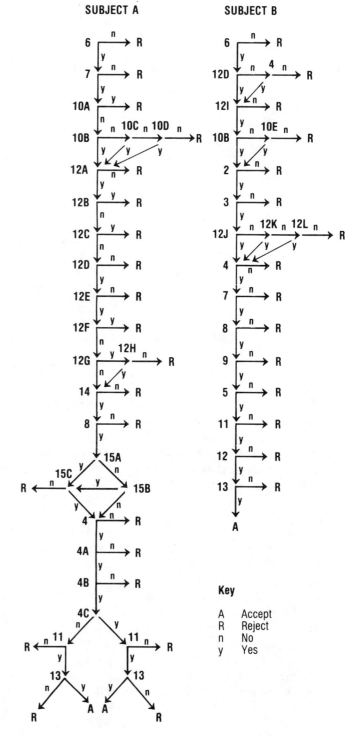

Marketers study sequences of purchase decisions for many reasons. Such information might be helpful to a retailer for deciding the color, style, and material of dresses to order. It might also help salespeople identify key needs in customers and provide them guidance on what to say to customers, when to be helpful, when to remain silent, and so on.

An example of the second type of process is displayed in Figure 2-9, where the causes of the purchase of a color television are represented for a particular person (or group of persons). The process begins when the person is exposed to stimuli from three sources of influence. First, exposure to advertisements conveys information as to the cost, availability, reliability, picture quality, etc., of particular brands of color televisions. This helps to shape the person's beliefs about the nature and quality of physical and subjective characteristics of TVs. Second, the chance viewing of a color TV in a friend's home serves to provide additional information about picture quality, reliability, etc., and to perhaps build a favorable attitude toward and desire for a color TV. The latter might result from the enhanced aesthetic pleasure attributable to color viewing. Third, the person's own children might also influence his or her attitudes toward color TVs, if only through their expressed requests for one. After one forms an attitude toward color TVs in general (and perhaps specific brands in particular), then an intention to buy may be formed. This, in turn, may lead to a visit to a retail store and subsequent purchase.

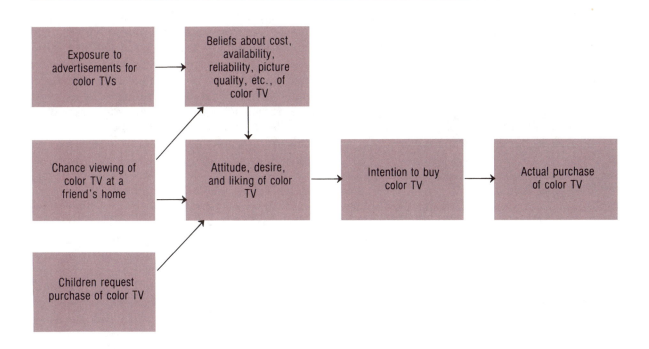

Figure 2-9. A causal diagram of processes determining the purchase of a color television

The processes illuminated by causal diagrams yield many useful insights for marketing managers. By studying which features of a TV that consumers value, for example, a brand manager can learn how to design the product to better appeal to consumers. Some people might be influenced more than others by the style and craftsmanship of the TV cabinet, the availability of an optional service plan, or the number of auxiliary features provided. Similarly, advertisers study different types of persuasive messages, alternative spokespersons, and optional media for ad placements as they impact upon the beliefs, attitudes, intentions, and purchase behaviors of consumers. A causal map helps the consumer researcher identify which variables affect people and how important each product attribute is. This is essential if the marketer is to efficiently allocate scarce resources to marketing mix stimuli. Further, through statistical and other procedures, researchers attempt to ascertain the relative impact of different stimuli on attitudes, intentions, and choice. This involves estimation of the magnitude or intensity of causal relations.

A General Model of Consumer Behavior

Introduction to the Model

In reality, consumer decision-making processes are quite complex and are influenced by many forces both within and without the individual. Yet, if we are to understand why and how people make choices and if managers are to effectively adjust their offerings in order to both respond to and stimulate the demand for goods by consumers, then we must attempt to represent the dynamics of those consumer actions.

Fortunately, it is possible to identify a relatively small number of elements common to most everyday consumption decisions.[15] Figure 2-10 is one example. Notice that consumer behavior is represented as a system, with special emphasis placed on the internal structures and processes occurring within the organism (i.e., the person). The elements of the model (i.e., arousal, information processing, etc.) represent functions (some psychological, others physiological) within the person. We do not actually see the functions. Rather, we infer their existence by observing and measuring people's thoughts, feelings, bodily states, and overt actions. For example, when asked, "What would be the better buy, two pounds of hamburger for $3.60 or one pound for $1.90?" a consumer might answer, "Two pounds for $3.60." If so, we might infer that the consumer computed a per-pound cost of $1.80 for the first option and compared this to the $1.90 per-pound cost for the second option. In other words, the consumer went through the information-processing stage of decision making.

The functions of this model are interconnected in many ways. For now, it should be noted that the model in Figure 2-10 represents a compromise between the many atomistic frameworks in the literature that explain very specific acts with highly specialized theories and the grand approaches that, through complex flow diagrams, attempt to capture the entirety of consumption in all its complexity.[16] As such, it attempts to point out a few of the more fundamental antecedents of consumption.

As we look more closely at the model and its functioning, let us begin with an overview of its parts and their relationships.[17] The consumption process appears to begin with an external stimulus striking the consumer's perceptual and sensing processes. In reality, there are at least three ways an act of consumption is initiated: (1) an external stimulus (e.g., an advertisement) is detected and acted upon; (2) a physiological agitation within the consumer presses for equilibrium; or (3) a psychological imbalance strives for resolution.

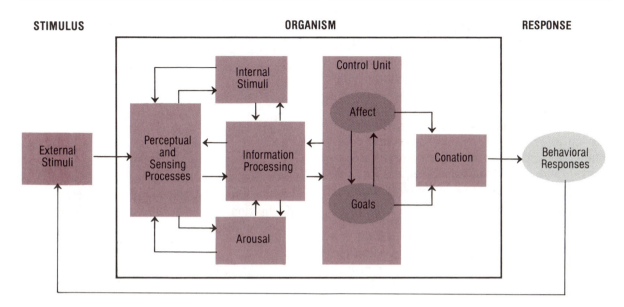

STIMULUS   **ORGANISM**   **RESPONSE**

Figure 2-10. A model of consumer behavior

External stimuli refer to any changes in the environment that can be potentially perceived or sensed. Changes in the physical attributes of products, package design, price, advertisements, promotion tactics, and persuasive appeals by a salesperson represent common marketing examples. A whole science has grown around the strategic use of stimuli in marketing, and we will elaborate on the tactics further in the chapters on product design, communication, advertising, personal selling, and channels of distribution.

Although exposure to an advertisement, an appealing package, or a sales pitch of a seller will often motivate one to purchase a product, the actual purchase behavior may spring from *internal forces*. For example, if a person has not eaten for an extended period of time, this will produce chemical and hormonal imbalances that will be experienced as hunger pains. This physiological tension may function as an internal stimulus to heighten one's perceptual readiness to see a restaurant or fast-food store. Thus, the direction of the motivation to purchase goes from internal stimuli to perceptual and sensing processes. If the hunger is strong enough, a person might even go out of his or her way to search for a restaurant, in which case the force of the motivation might continue from perceptual and sensing processing to pursuit of external stimuli. See Figure 2-10.

Although the need for food, water, warmth, and sex are powerful and pervasive factors shaping our actions, *physiological changes* are not the only internal stimuli. Our *thoughts* and *feelings* also give rise to consumption-related activities, often without external stimulation. For instance, a desire for novelty, intellectual stimulation, or solitude can lead one to attend an amusement park, purchase a best selling nonfiction book, or rent a cottage in the wild. These and other similar consumption activities often have their roots in *psychological tensions* within us.

Perceptual and Sensing Processes

The role of *perceptual and sensing processes* is an important one, for it serves as our conduit to the outside world. We experience the world through one of the five senses: seeing, hearing, touching, smelling, and tasting. The senses are at the periphery of our autonomic nervous system (ANS). They pick up information from our immediate environment and transfer it, via nerves, to various mental and/or physiological centers in the body. Sometimes sensations activate arousal mechanisms in the subcortex (i.e., the lower reaches of the brain such as the limbic system where some of our emotional and sexual responses are believed to be housed). At other times, they will stimulate a particular neural response that is ultimately connected to a gland or other organ deep in the ANS. The direction of stimulation is from perceptual and sensing processes to internal stimuli, while the former is from perceptual and sensing processes to arousal. More often than not, our perceptions will be acted upon cognitively in an activity called *information processing*. For example, an alluring end-of-aisle display for cheese and paté in a supermarket might stimulate thoughts about new ways to prepare hors d'oeuvres.

Perceptual and sensing processes can be further broken down into their component parts, as shown in Figure 2-11. External stimuli are initially monitored by perceptual and sensing processes in a stage termed the *sensory register* (also called a *buffer*). Its function is to briefly hold information from the external environment until it can be processed further. The sensory register is believed to store information in veridical form, that is, as it is represented physically as a visual, auditory, etc., stimulus. Later, this veridical information may be transformed and recoded to a form more easily stored and manipulated by other parts of the mind that are, in turn, housed in the information-processing stage. Information from stimuli are stored very briefly in the sensory register. For example, visual information is thought to be stored in the sensory register for less than one second. In fact, much of it may have decayed or been erased after about 0.3 of a second or so. The short life of information storage in our sensory register actually serves an important purpose. We are continually bombarded by so much external stimulation at any one point in time that it would be physically and psychologically overwhelming to cope with all of it at once. Only so much information can be monitored; hence, the rapid decay in the sensory register prevents a bottleneck and overload from occurring. In a sense, it also serves to prevent new information from overlapping with the old. As stimuli impinge on the sensory register, some is transferred to other stages for further processing (or for long-term storage), and some is merely erased and forgotten. This permits one to be able to accept new information on an ongoing basis.

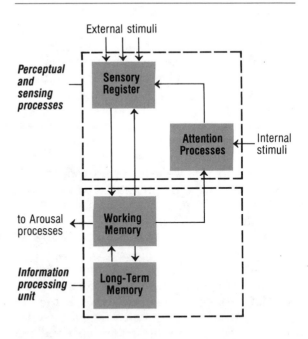

Figure 2-11. The perceptual and sensing system and its interface with external stimuli and information processing

A couple of other points need to be stressed about the sensory register. Although psychologists are not absolutely sure, there may be not one but many sensory registers. That is, we may all have a sensory register for visual stimuli, one for auditory, one for olfactory, and so on. Finally, for purposes of analysis, the term *sensory register* refers only to the monitoring and storage of stimuli for very short times and to encompass processes that are basically pre-attentive and precategorical. The sensory register is pre-attentive in the sense that we are not consciously aware of information it receives and stores. Rather, awareness occurs in other stages (e.g., through attentive processes and in working memory). The sensory register is precategorical: it neither stores specific information nor performs operations on the meaning of stimuli for the person. Rather, it stores information in a global, concrete way based on the physical characteristics of the stimulus. Abstract meaning of a stimulus occurs deeper in the information-processing and control units. However, it should be emphasized that our preconceptions do influence the sensory register as shown by an arrow from working memory to the sensory register in Figure 2-11. Figure 2-11 is a subset of the entire model of consumer behavior shown in Figure 2-10. The two dashed boxes in Figure 2-11—i.e., the perceptual and sensing processes and the information processing unit—correspond to the respective boxes shown in Figure 2-10.

Some of the information reaching the sensory register is stored and transferred to *working (short-term) memory* for further processing. Working memory has both conscious and unconscious aspects to it. At the conscious level, we thoughtfully act upon the information entering working memory. For example, we might try to remember a phone number presented at the end of an advertisement by repeating it over and over. This is known as the process of rehearsal, and it serves to transfer conscious and temporary storage of the phone number to more or less unconcious *permanent (long-term) memory.*

Other conscious processes performed in working memory include the use of mnemonics and other tactics to organize information such as chunking, where facts are grouped in clumps to make them easier to remember. An example of the former is the use of rhymes such as "Thirty days has September . . ." to remember the number of days in the month, while an instance of the latter would be the grouping of digits in a phone number for ease of memorization: 253-7160.

Working memory also encompasses conscious activation of our attention processes or the selection of pertinent information and occurs, for example, when we hurriedly pass through the supermarket looking for a particular brand of cereal on the shelf. It is not clear whether working memory can unconsciously act upon information. If it does, unconscious processing in working memory might be limited to comparisons or matching of information from the sensory register to stored representations from long-term memory. For example, as a consumer glances at the nutritional information on a package while passing a shelf in the supermarket, he or she might unconsciously compare the information to a preconceived set of important purchasing criteria: low sugar and high protein. Although the consumer would be consciously aware of seeing most of the nutritional information on the package, an integration of the thinking and motor reactions required to stop and grab the package might not be triggered until the cues of low sugar and high protein have been unconsciously interpreted and compared to personal requirements stored in long-term memory. Of course, the whole process often occurs for some people entirely at a conscious level, as when a health-food connoisseur meticulously examines product labels to find a satisfactory offering.

Working memory is also characterized by the amount of information it can handle, the length of time it can store information, and how it can store information. Generally, a person's short-term memory can process only about 7 pieces of information at any one point in time. The sensory register, on the other hand, is believed to be capable of handling 15 or more items of information. Working memory stores the information for longer periods of time than does the sensory register, however. Depending on whether one looks at visual or auditory information, it is believed that working memory lasts about 15 to 30 seconds as opposed to less than 1 second for the sensory register. Information can be retained indefinitely in working memory only through rehearsal. Finally, it is believed that working memory stores information in recoded form, as opposed to the veridical storage of the sensory register. The exact nature of this new code is little understood except that it is abstract and can entail verbal and visual images as well as semantic meaning.

The final component of perceptual and sensing processes is called *attention processes*.[18] Attention is the conscious allocation of processing capacity to information in the sensory register. Whether one will attend to information or not depends on (a) the number and strength of environmental stimuli competing with the attended input for attention, (b) internal stimuli, and (c) certain inputs from memory. The first constraint operates as follows. Whenever one or more pieces of information in the sensory register become objects of attention, the quality and amount of the input attended to (as well as transferred to working memory) will be affected by background noise (distraction). The attention processes allocate the limited amount of human capacity for monitoring information; but background noise continually disrupts this process if it breaks through a threshold level. Internal stimuli influence the process, too; physiological and psychological imbalances and needs stimulate one's attention to seek a means of correcting those imbalances and satisfying needs. Similarly, stored information in memory, such as one's intentions or goals, influences how one allocates his or her attention. As we discuss in later chapters, marketers design advertisements to exploit these aspects of human attention processes. One example of this is the rule-of-thumb practiced by some advertisers that a television commercial must mention and show the product within the first 10 seconds of an ad to attract attention and have the desired effect on brand remembrance.

Information Processing

An important stage of consumer behavior is information processing. As indicated in Figure 2-11, information processing consists of two components: working memory and long-term memory. Because we have already described working memory, discussion now will focus on long-term memory.[19] From the viewpoint of marketing, long-term memory consists of three classes of phenomena: (1) memory or storage, (2) judgment processes, and (3) control processes and conation (Figure 2-12).

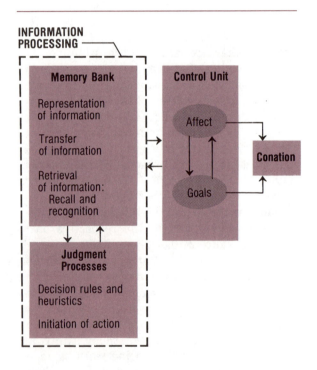

Figure 2-12. The components of long-term memory

All that we know or experience is stored in our brain as coded information in a *memory bank*. Typically, information is of one of two sorts. The temporal and spatial parts of our experience that occur as events and personal happenings are stored in *episodic memory*. Our memory of the layout and placement of foods in our favorite supermarket is an example. In contrast, our knowledge of words, symbols, their meanings, and the rules and relations among them are stored in *semantic memory*. For instance, when we operate an automatic bank teller machine or a mass transit ticket dispenser, we employ many symbols, rules, and procedures to obtain a meaningful output from the machine. This primarily requires information from semantic memory.

The actual representation of information in memory differs for episodic and semantic content. Recall the steps that the women shoppers went through in the purchase of a dress (Figure 2-8). The chronological list of actions represents episodic content from the memory of the shoppers. In contrast, Figure 2-13 shows one way to represent a consumer's semantic memory associated with the concept *coffee*. Notice that coffee is associated with many attributes (e.g., expensive), many effects (e.g., quenches thirst, causes nervousness), and is a subset or superset of other concepts (e.g., drink, Brand A). The beliefs about the consequences of giving blood shown in Figure 2-7 represent another example of semantic memory.

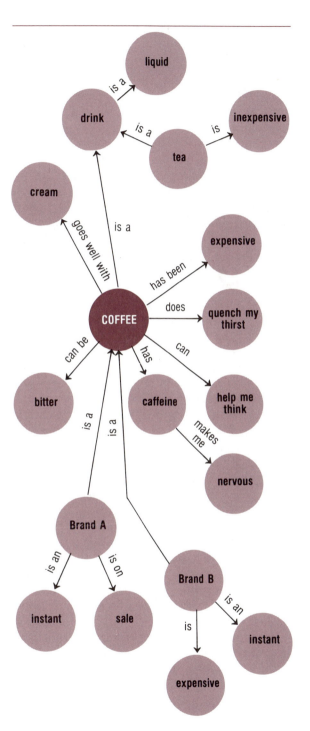

Figure 2-13. A portion of one consumer's semantic memory as activated by the word *coffee*

Information must be transferred from the memory bank to other stages of the model if it is to be useful. This is a little understood and very difficult process to study, but two phenomena, recall and recognition, have been thoroughly studied and are very important to a basic understanding of consumer behavior. Indeed, advertisers rely heavily on data on how well consumers recall and recognize ads in order to measure the effectiveness of the ads. We will have more to say about this later in the chapter on advertising. For now, it should be noted that recall involves producing information from memory with no or few cues. Recognition entails comparing a cue to a representation in memory and indicating whether one has seen or heard a particular stimulus. For instance, if a consumer were asked if he or she had seen an advertisement for radial tires on the television within the past two days and, if so, to identify its sponsor and major selling point, then this would require the (aided) recall of information. On the other hand, if a person were shown a television commercial with all brand name identification eliminated and asked to identify the brand, he or she would be engaged in a (masked) recognition activity. This entails matching the just-viewed commercial to information in memory and noting whether one had seen it before or not.

Information is mentally acted upon in the information-processing stage through *judgment processes* (Figure 2-12). To be useful in decision making, the coded information in episodic and semantic memory must be combined into a more condensed and meaningful (from the consumer's standpoint) representation. This might include an ordering and/or weighting scheme applied to the information. Imagine, for example, that a consumer uses information about price, nutrition, texture, and taste to select a breakfast cereal. How is he or she to assess many brands on these criteria and use the information? Table 2-2 lists five brands of cereal that the consumer is considering and how each brand scores on the criteria. The numbers in the table represent the consumer's subjective beliefs about how each brand scores on each criterion on a scale from 1 to 10, with the higher numbers indicating that the respective brand scores well on the corresponding criterion. For example, Brand A scores better than any other brand on nutrition but worse than any other brand on price. Given the information in the table, how can we predict which brand the consumer will purchase? Clearly, we need to know how the consumer uses and weighs the information. But how does he or she do this?

TABLE 2-2

Subjective Judgments of a Consumer on Four Criteria Applied to Five Brands of Cereal*

Brand	Price	Nutrition	Texture	Taste
A	5	10	6	5
B	8	6	6	8
C	7	6	8	9
D	7	7	8	7
E	6	8	7	4

*The higher the number, the better the respective brand scores on the criterion.

Psychologists and consumer researchers have discovered that people use one or more of a number of *decision rules* to make a choice when confronted with a task such as that depicted in Table 2-2. For example, some consumers might simply add up the judgments of each brand on all criteria (attributes) to arrive at a single overall rating. Thus, for the consumer's responses in Table 2-2, the overall ratings for Brands A–E might be the following:

- $R_{1A} = 26$

- $R_{1B} = 28$

- $R_{1C} = 30$

- $R_{1D} = 29$

- $R_{1E} = 25,$

where R_{ij} is person i's rating of Brand j. Presumably, if the consumer follows this simple adding rule, then he or she should select Brand C. We can write this rule in general form as

$$R_{ij} = \sum_{k=1}^{n} B_{ijk},$$ 2-4

where B_{ijk} is consumer i's belief as to how well Brand j scores on criterion k, and $n =$ number of criteria. In Table 2-2, i = 1 since it reflects one person's judgments; j = 1, 2, 3, 4, 5 for the five brands, and $n = 4$ for the four criteria. Equation 2-4 is really a special case of a somewhat more general rule called the *linear compensatory model*, which can be expressed as follows:

$$LCM_{ij} = \sum_{k=1}^{n} B_{ijk} V_{ik},$$ 2-5

where V_{ik} is person i's value (or importance) of criterion k and the remaining symbols are defined as for equation 2-4. In other words, the linear compensatory model implies that a consumer (1) forms beliefs about how each brand in his or her decision set scores on each of a set of criteria, (2) weighs those beliefs by the personal value or importance of the criteria, and (3) arrives at an overall attitude or judgment, LCM_{ij}. Notice that the model of equation 2-4, R_{ij}, assumes that each criterion is equally valued or equally important. The weight of unity is implicitly assigned to each criterion (i.e., V_{ik} = 1, for all i and k in equation 2-4). In equation 2-5, one's beliefs are in a sense weighted by one's values or importances for the criteria.

As an example of the linear compensatory model applied to the data of Table 2-2, imagine that the consumer expressed his or her importances for the criteria as follows:

	very unimportant									very important
	1	2	3	4	5	6	7	8	9	10
price		✔								
nutrition									✔	
texture							✔			
taste			✔							

This might be a typical profile for certain health-conscious consumers who at the same time are less concerned with price and taste. With the above importances, we can now compute the linear compensatory model judgment:

$LCM_{11} = 5(2) + 10(9) + 6(7) + 5(3) = 157$
$LCM_{12} = 8(2) + 6(9) + 6(7) + 8(3) = 136$
$LCM_{13} = 7(2) + 6(9) + 8(7) + 9(3) = 151$
$LCM_{14} = 7(2) + 7(9) + 8(7) + 7(3) = 154$
$LCM_{15} = 6(2) + 8(9) + 7(7) + 4(3) = 145$

As a consequence, by the linear compensatory model, the consumer prefers Brand A. Note that, instead of importances, evaluations of attributes might constitute the appropriate value weights.

Many other rules can of course be followed in decision making. Some of the more common include *affect referral, general information integration, conjunctive, disjunctive, lexicographic, sequential elimination, elimination by aspects, lexicographic semi-order,* and *additive difference* rules.[20] We briefly describe only one of these here: the lexicographic rule. Under a lexicographic judgment rule, a consumer first ranks criteria or attributes in order of importance. Next, all brand or choice alternatives are compared on the most important criterion. If one brand scores higher on the most important criterion than any other brand, then it is chosen. If not (e.g., suppose it is tied with two others), then the inferior brands are eliminated and comparisons are made among the tied brands using the second most important criterion. The procedure is continued until a final superior brand remains to be chosen or until no further brands can be eliminated. For example, suppose the consumer whose beliefs are listed in Table 2-2 ranks the criteria in the following order of importance (from highest to lowest): texture, price, nutrition, and taste. Given this ordering and the data of Table 2-2, which cereal brand would he or she choose, if any? If the consumer followed the lexicographic rule, he or she would choose Brand D. The logic is as follows. Brands C and D are tied on the most important criterion, texture, so Brands A, B, and E can be eliminated. But Brands C and D are also tied on the second most important criterion, price. Hence, we must examine the third most important criterion. Because Brand D is higher than Brand C on nutrition, the consumer chooses it as the most preferred cereal (according to the lexicographic rule). Notice that the lexicographic rule results in a different choice than either the linear compensatory model or its equal weighted version in this particular example.

Several assumptions underlying human judgment by rules deserve mention. First, most people are not consciously aware of the particular rule that they may be employing in any decision-making situation. Our mental processes occur too rapidly and below the threshold of awareness for this to happen. Of course, some people might purposely decide to use a linear compensatory model before shopping and then gather information and plug the numbers representing their beliefs and values into the formula. However, this is the exception, not the rule. Rather, we as consumers generally take in a wealth of information and then later make a decision without knowing exactly how it was made.

A second point to note is that the various decision rules that researchers investigate are not necessarily meant to correspond perfectly to the rules actually used by the consumers under study. Rather, the rules are models or simplified representations of complex, unobservable processes, and we hope that they will capture enough of actual consumer decision making to yield accurate predictions in the marketplace. Third, it should be stressed that the rules mentioned above probably represent only a portion of the rules that people implicitly follow. Indeed, even the small number of rules that have been investigated to date are not employed by everyone. Furthermore, it may be possible that some rules are context-specific or are a function of the mental capacities, learning experiences, or personalities of individual people. An example of the context-specific nature of rules can be seen in decision situations where time pressures exist. Here people may use expedient or "fuzzy" rules to simplify their decision problems. For instance, a consumer with an upset stomach might stop in a drugstore and purchase the first brand that is perceived to be adequate to relieve the discomfort. An extended comparison of the prices and features of each competing brand would be unnecessary and prolong the agony.

A fourth assumption to note with respect to the use of decision rules by consumers is that people are presumed to see product and brand alternatives as multi-attribute offerings. To the consumer, a car is not merely a "car." Rather, it is a bundle of benefits consisting of styling, handling, purchase price, miles per gallon, aesthetic appeal, feelings of pride, and so on. Similarly, a trip on an airplane is not merely "transportation" but rather a collection of experiences and feelings related to safety, departure/arrival time, convenience, price, and amenities. People make decisions based on the attributes associated with a product or service and the implications these attributes have for them.

Finally, it should be noted that decision rules are but one of a number of factors determining consumers' choices. Internal feelings, fears, and hopes, for example, sometimes override or interact with the rational evaluations that people make; and external forces such as social pressure constrain choices as well.

The Elements of the Control Unit and Their Impact on Behavior

Whether a favorable evaluation of information will result in initiation of actions leading to purchase will often depend on further mental activities related to one's affect toward a product/brand and one's goals (see the control unit in Figures 2-10 and 2-12). Consider first affect and its role in decision making.

Affect refers to the emotional or feeling component of a consumer's psychological reactions. Generally, five aspects of affect differentiate it from *cognitions* or beliefs, which, in turn, are the basic units of thought in information processing (Figure 2-14). First, affect possesses a polarity. One may feel positively or negatively toward a product or service, for example. Cognitions do not have a polarity in this sense. Second, affect may vary in intensity in that one experiences positive or negative feelings, attraction or repulsion, liking or disliking, etc., as a matter of degree. We may like a brand a small amount, a moderate amount, or very much, for instance. In contrast, although our confidence in beliefs may vary, the beliefs themselves do not have an intensity associated with them. Third, affect is typically a relational concept connecting a person to another person, product, or thing. We do not see affect, per se, but rather infer it from the behavior of a consumer in relation to a product or service. Cognitions, in contrast, are property concepts referring not to the relationship between a person and a product but rather to either a believed factual aspect of the product (e.g., "this wallpaper is washable") or what consequences a product can lead to (e.g.,

"if I buy this wallpaper, it will brighten the drab dining room in our house considerably and lead to a faster sale of the house when we put it on the market"). Fourth, an affective reaction toward a product implies a felt urge to act on the part of the person holding the feeling. All things constant, if a person feels positive toward a particular brand of cereal and has the need and means to acquire it, then he or she will do so. Cognitions do not necessarily imply an action on the part of the person holding one and are said to be action-neutral. Finally, affect is relatively more person-centered and subjective, while cognitions are relatively more product-centered and objective. Our beliefs, for example, can be proven true or false in principle because they refer to matters of fact. Affect does not have this property and is neither true nor false. Rather, our emotions toward products are experiences we have and, while influenced by factual content to a certain extent, are not based upon them by definition.

Affect influences decision making in a number of ways. One is that our feelings can lead us to weight product characteristics according to the meaning or implications of those characteristics for us. When the expressed importances or values of a consumer are used as weights in the linear compensatory model, they, in effect, serve as proxies for the consumer's affective reactions toward product attributes. A somewhat similar approach is taken in the expectancy-value attitude model, which we will discuss at the end of the chapter. A second way affect might enter the decision process is as a direct constraint or influence on the judgments one makes. For instance, our feelings can cause us to overlook some product attributes or misperceive others. Still another way that affect can influence decision making is as a parallel cause of actual choices, along with rational evaluations in information processing. In this sense, judgments and feelings do not interact but have independent impacts on choice. Finally, it is believed by some marketers[21] that the most common sequence in consumer behavior is judgments or beliefs → affect → purchase behavior. Thus, it is maintained that cognitive judgments of a brand are formed first; this leads, in turn, to emotional reactions toward the brand; and then actual choice behavior follows. We will provide the results of a study designed to test this sequence at the end of the chapter. The above sequence and alternatives will be considered in the chapter on communication.

The second major part of the control unit is the goals one has (see Figure 2-10). *Goals* are desired end states in relation to which an individual seeks information, evaluates alternative courses of action, and makes choices. They are largely cognitive in content and operate both at the conscious and unconscious level of awareness. Indeed, it is possible to conceive of goals along a continuum. At one end are the relatively subconscious goals people use to organize their actions. These include norms, values, and other internalized guidelines derived from socialization processes or the expectations of specific individuals, groups, or society-at-large. At this end of the spectrum, the goals function largely automatically with little or no prethought or awareness. Some forms of conspicuous consumption fall within this category, as when people buy "to keep up with the Joneses." Similarly, purchases made in response to social or peer pressure or as a function of tradition often stem from the influence of unconscious goals. At the other extreme are well-developed plans, rules, and procedures that one consciously follows. These may be internally developed through considerable effort and even years of trial and error. They may also be externally imposed such as is done in the use of checklists prescribed for buyers within an organization. More often than not, goals are socially negotiated and represent a joint decision between two or more people. For example, some husbands and wives construct elaborate budgets to manage their consumption. Overall, goals serve as a means for the self-regulation of one's behavior.

Goals interact with affect and judgment processes to influence choices in a variety of ways. For instance, goals may determine what information is to be gathered and how it is to be evaluated. Or we may develop feelings toward a product, brand, or its features as a function of how well it promises to fulfill our goals. Alternatively, goals may serve as independent determinants of choice in some situations, along with affect and rational judgment processes.

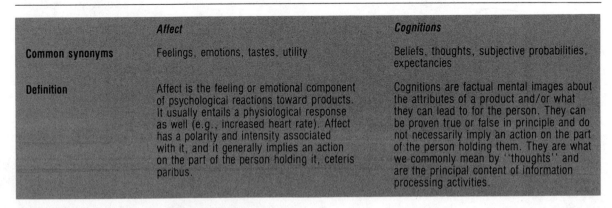

	Affect	Cognitions
Common synonyms	Feelings, emotions, tastes, utility	Beliefs, thoughts, subjective probabilities, expectancies
Definition	Affect is the feeling or emotional component of psychological reactions toward products. It usually entails a physiological response as well (e.g., increased heart rate). Affect has a polarity and intensity associated with it, and it generally implies an action on the part of the person holding it, ceteris paribus.	Cognitions are factual mental images about the attributes of a product and/or what they can lead to for the person. They can be proven true or false in principle and do not necessarily imply an action on the part of the person holding them. They are what we commonly mean by "thoughts" and are the principal content of information processing activities.

Figure 2-14. Affect and cognitions: two fundamental concepts in consumer decision making

The final component of the general model of consumer behavior is *conations*. Conations are specific intentions to act in a particular way. For example, if after reading an advertisement for an instant camera, a person thinks to himself, "I will go and buy this camera at store X," then he is experiencing a conation—i.e., an intention to purchase the camera. Although not all purchase behaviors are preceded by conations, they occur with sufficient frequency to warrant their inclusion in the model. In one sense, conations represent a mental stage at an intermediate level of abstraction. Information processing, decision rules, affect, and goals are all highly abstract mental events. Actual purchase behaviors, however, are concrete, observable happenings. Conations are less abstract than most mental events but are not as concrete as purchase behaviors. They function as a bridge between the conceptual and real worlds. As such, they help to channel our psychic energies into physical actions functional for the person. Marketers have long hoped that the measurement of intentions can serve as valid indicators or at least relatively accurate predictions of future behavior.[22] The success to date can best be described as mixed, but the search goes on.

Three Fundamental Kinds of Consumption

The general model of consumer behavior is an abstraction designed to symbolically represent most of the major elements and processes in all consumer choice decisions. As you might suspect, not every element or process within the model comes into play in every real-world decision. At this time in the development of our knowledge of consumer behavior, three frequently occurring subprocesses in Figure 2-10 can be identified: impulse buying, habitual purchasing, and consumption problem solving. Each will be illustrated through scenarios.

Impulse Buying

We are all familiar with the impulse buying situation but probably have not thought much about what actually goes on within the mind of the consumer. Let us consider first the outward, easily observed manifestations of impulse buying:

Frank Bollo, a husband with traditional sex-role values, is forced to do the weekly family shopping for food. Normally his wife does this, but this week she is recovering from a bout with the flu. Although Frank is not very familiar with the layout of the supermarket, his shopping proceeds uneventfully, largely due to the detailed list of groceries provided by his wife. Indeed, the entire process goes very smoothly, albeit at a slower than normal pace, and within 45 minutes Frank has successfully obtained every item on the list. As he approaches the checkout counter with his cart of groceries, however, something unusual and unplanned occurs. His eye catches a large, colorful display of wines, cheeses, and crackers located strategically a few yards from the cash registers. Frank is generally a beer drinker, but for some reason he can't resist the imported bottles of Valpolicella. Quickly, and apparently without thought, he grabs a bottle with his free hand and pushes the cart up to an open register.

Why did Frank purchase the wine and how did he make the decision? If we asked Frank directly, he might simply answer, "I don't know" or "It looked good, so I thought I might try it." We know from the scenario that "wine" was not on the list and that he normally did not drink wine. So this gives us some evidence to rule out both prior planning and habit as causes. Most likely, Frank was not aware of the reasons for his behavior at the time. We might say that he purchased the wine "out of impulse." But what does this mean in terms of the general model? Surely, some mental activities took place, however hidden these may be to Frank and to us as observers.

Impulse buying does encompass some of the phenomena and processes outlined in the general model. If we had an insider's view of Frank's mental activities, the processes might appear something like the following. As Frank passed the display, the bright colors, size of the display, and cheese odors were initial external stimuli picked up by perceptual and sensing processes (see Figure 2-15, Stage 1). The olfactory responses to the cheese odors then stimulate early food-related reactions, such as salivation and gastric juice pro-duction in the stomach. Similarly, the colors of the display and its physical size and shape create an orientation reaction consisting of visual sensing processes and resulting in turning of the head and related motor responses.

Next, in Stage 2, the physiological and orientation reactions lead to very brief and, probably, unconscious information processing. The motivation for the information processing might be merely to find out what is causing the physiological disequilib-rium and psychological tension. Thus, atten-

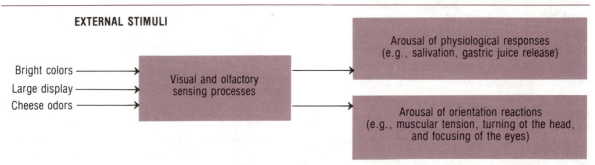

Stage 1. Initial stimulation of senses and arousal with early involuntary bodily reactions

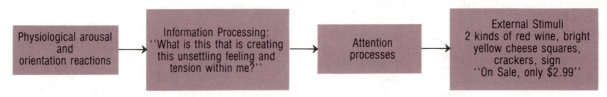

Stage 2. Further focus of attention and perception of global cues in display

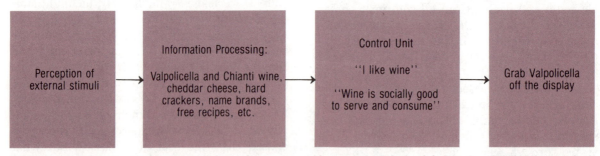

Stage 3. Brief information processing of more specific cues coupled with low-level affective and social reactions leading to purchase

Figure 2-15. Impulse buying of wine in the supermarket

tion might be allocated to global stimuli in the display such as the two types of wine (red and white), the presence of cheese, and a sign indicating "On Sale, Only $2.99."

In Stage 3, information processing of the stimuli might proceed somewhat further to the extent that notice is made of two kinds of red wine, cheddar cheese, hard crackers, "name brands," and free recipes. The processes in the control unit might then come into play. Even though Frank is not a regular wine drinker, he is a second generation Italian-American, and his experiences while growing up had instilled a positive feeling for wine as well as the realization that wine is a symbol of friendship and family ties. The former functions as affect, while the latter is a type of goal related to the unconscious pull of tradition. In any case, the processing up to this point was sufficient to lead Frank to reach for the bottle of wine. Most of the processes outlined in Figure 2-15 probably occurred below Frank's level of awareness at the time. Frank made an impulse purchase.

Habitual Purchase Behavior

Perhaps even more common than impulse buying is the so-called purchase by habit. The following scenario is typical of many of these instances of consumer choice (see Figure 2-16):

Sonja Bender is driving home from work and remembers suddenly that she drank the last of the milk remaining in the refrigerator earlier this morning. Her first decision is to search for a supermarket because it has greater variety and lower prices. If she finds a supermarket, she then looks for one-quart sizes, because she lives alone and any larger container tends to result in spoilage. Her decision sequence from this point on in the supermarket is to determine that her favorite brand is available, the price is reasonable, and the milk is fresh (as indicated by the date stamped on the container). If quart sizes are not available and/or any one of the other criteria is not satisfied, then she considers

a half gallon. Her logic is that, should an acceptable half-gallon be available, it is probably cheaper in the long run to purchase it rather than waste time and gasoline (and possibly a higher price) driving to another store. On the other hand, if half gallons are not available in the supermarket (or no supermarkets are found nearby), then she will consider a specialty or "mom-and-pop" store. If one of these is handy, then she applies the same ordered criteria as employed in the supermarket. If no stores are available, then she decides to wait until tomorrow when her regular shopping for the week is scheduled.

Habitual purchase behaviors have a number of features that deserve mention. First, the process begins with the stimulation of a need. Sonja recalled her need, thus the need resulted from internal forces. It would have been possible, of course, for her need to have arisen also as a function of an external stimulus such as a billboard advertisement for milk. In either case, the perceived need then leads to a well-structured process. Second, notice that a specific set of criteria was employed: supermarket availability, size of carton, favorite brand, price, etc. Presumably these have been learned through (a) many previous experiences in shopping and consumption and (b) the development of decision rules reflective of Sonja's biological needs, feelings, thoughts, and goals. Third, notice that the criteria were applied in a particular order. This, too, is most likely a consequence of prior learning, and the order of attribute consideration is probably one of decreasing importance. A fourth point to stress is that the criteria are simple in structure and content. Rather than applying many finely coded criteria, Sonja applied a small number of binary requirements. The price was reasonable or not, the milk was fresh or not, and so on. It is just not feasible or worth one's while to do an elaborate cost/benefit analysis for so inexpensive and readily available a product. In many habitual purchase situations, consumers will employ only one or two decision criteria. In fact, "one's favorite brand" is the only requirement needed for some consumption decisions. In others, the consumer uses his or her favorite brand as the most important cue in a lexicographic ordering, but will accept other "brand names" or "dealer brands," if necessary.

In summary, habitual purchase decisions are generally made purposefully but with little thought. Memory, affect, and goals play a dominant role, while information processing is of a shallow and brief nature. In one sense, the decision has been "worked out" in the past and stored in memory. It is reactivated each time a need for the product is triggered as when Sonja remembered she was "out of milk."

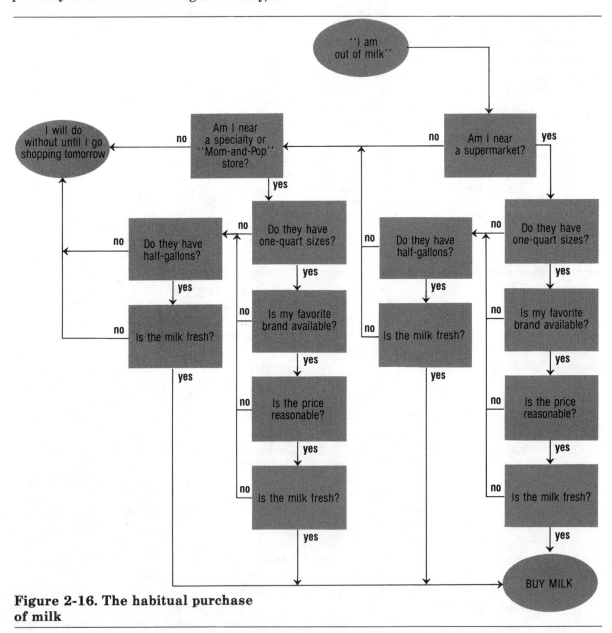

Figure 2-16. The habitual purchase of milk

Consumption Problem Solving

Many consumer choice situations are neither impulsive nor habitual. Rather, they involve complex decision making with an extensive amount of information processing and interaction with elements of the control unit. Let us look at one person's decision to purchase an automobile:

Carl Sanchez, a recent college graduate, has decided to buy a new car. Although he has bought a used car before, the cost of a new one is so great and the options to consider are so numerous that he decides to be systematic in his decision making. Carl begins by thumbing through magazines and looking for attractive ads. His goal is to get some idea of the styles and range of options available. He hopes also to narrow down the potential manufacturers to two or three, since he plans to visit only a small number of dealers. The net result of Carl's preliminary search is that he desires a sporty, but economical, foreign car. The three brands he will consider are Toyota, Datsun, and Fiat. Because he can spend about $10,000 to $11,000, the most attractive models for him are the Celica GT, 200SX, and Super Brava, respectively.

Carl intends to get price quotes from at least two dealers of each brand, but before he does this he believes that more information from disinterested sources would reduce the risk of too hasty a purchase. He remembers that Ted Stern, a colleague at work, owns a Super Brava and makes a point to plan to talk to Ted tomorrow at lunch. In the meantime, Carl decides to go to the local library to study what Consumer Reports—*an independent magazine that rates cars and other products—has to say. This turned out to be an eye-opener, for* Consumer Reports *evaluated each of the three cars on many product attributes. For example, the magazine presented a helpful summary table comparing the cars on such criteria as gasoline consumption, fuel tank capacity, ease of maintenance, costs of repair, ride and handling, passenger and luggage room, and overall comfort. Although Carl still feels far from a final decision, the information in* Consumer Reports *led him to remove the 200SX from his list of considerations (his "evoked set") because it had too little luggage capacity and too small a rear seat for his needs. His study of the information in the magazine also suggested that he should consider ease of maintenance and frequency of breakdowns as decision criteria, in addition to the ones he already believed to be important (i.e., styling, economy, ride and handling, and roominess for passengers and luggage).*

The activities of the next day added still further information and helped Carl crystallize his decision. His conversation with Ted reinforced his prior judgments about, and attraction for, the Super Brava. Similarly, his once-over of a Celica GT parked in the employee lot confirmed his beliefs about, and liking for, this car. He felt ready to examine new cars at the dealers and take test rides. Later that day and on each of the following two evenings, Carl carefully appraised the cars on each of his decision criteria. He recorded this information on a note pad along with price quotes from the salesmen.

On the fourth day, and after considerable stewing and pressure from the salesmen, Carl sat down to summarize his thoughts and feelings before making a final decision. He constructed the following table to represent his beliefs as to how each car scored on the product attributes he was considering:

	PRODUCT ATTRIBUTES					
Brand	Styling	Econ-omy	R&H	Roomi-ness	Mainte-nance	Break-down
Celica GT	9	9	6	8	7	6
Super Brava	8	7	8	9	5	8

Carl had no particular weighting or order of importance among the criteria. Moreover, his construction of the table represented the extent of his formal decision making activities. Rather than consciously applying some decision rule, Carl simply internalized the information and subjectively selected one of the two cars. The only other major determinant in the process was his belief that whatever choice he did make should "feel right."

Carl decided to purchase the Celica GT and somewhat nervously proceeded to the dealer offering the lowest price.

Carl Sanchez's decision to buy the Celica GT is an example of *consumption problem solving (CPS)*. Several features of CPS differentiate it from impulse buying and habitual purchases. First, it is obvious that CPS is a *lengthy* process. It often takes days to make a decision, with the time spent to gather and evaluate information and discover what one really wants. Second, CPS usually concerns products that are important to a person and/or are expensive. The elements of personal and financial *risk* are typically factors. Third, the process is made up of both *conscious and unconscious activities*. Carl Sanchez's decision making, for example, involved a number of planned, purposeful acts as well as subjective evaluations of which he was largely unaware. A fourth point to note is that CPS generally *proceeds in stages* marked by initial searches of information in memory or externally, followed by information integration and evaluation, followed by further information gathering, then evaluation, and so on. Fifth, CPS typically begins with a *need* and its arousing effects. Although perhaps not apparent from the above scenario, Carl Sanchez's motivation for the new car was a complex mix of transportation, personality, and social needs. Further, the needs are typically of a higher magnitude than those associated with impulse and habitual purchases. Finally, CPS is invariably a *complex* activity. Many product attributes must be assessed; the attributes often occur as shades of fine gradation; many brands sometimes enter

consideration; and the interactions of affect and goals with information processing can be quite intricate.

In sum, CPS is an important class of decision making. We might view it as a continuum of consumption instances varying from relatively simple problem solving such as found in the purchase of a winter coat to more involved decision making such as is exemplified in the purchase of a new home. With impulse and habitual purchasing, CPS covers most of the real world cases of buying.

Representing Consumption Problem Solving: The Case of the Attitude Model

Basics

As you might well imagine, there are many ways to operationalize CPS. Perhaps the most extensively studied and applied approach, however, is the attitude model (AM). In symbolic form, the AM can be expressed as follows:

$$PB = f(BI) \qquad \text{2-6}$$
$$BI = f(A) \qquad \text{2-7}$$

where PB = purchase behavior, BI = behavioral intention, and A = attitude. In words, equation 2-6 reads, "purchase behavior is a function of behavioral intentions." Similarly, equation 2-7 reads, "behavioral intentions are a function of attitudes." We can represent the relationships implied by equations 2-6 and 2-7 through the following causal diagram:

where β_1 and β_2 are parameters indicating the strength and direction of the relationships connecting A and BI, and BI and PB, respectively.

Assuming linear relationships, the cause-and-effect relationships can be written in equation form as

$$PB = \beta_2 BI$$
$$BI = \beta_1 A$$

where β_2 and β_1 are hypothesized to be positive.

As an example of how the attitude model might be used in practice, consider the problem faced by the Red Cross. The Red Cross would like to know why people do or do not donate blood. One dependent variable that they would like to predict and explain is the donation behavior of people at a particular blood drive. For instance, the Red Cross might desire to predict whether particular individuals will or will not give blood at a local drive. This dependent variable is analagous to purchase behavior (e.g., whether people will or will not buy brand X in week Y). A reasonable hypothesis is that the greater the probability of intentions to donate blood, the higher the probability of doing so. Equation 2-6 depicts this proposition. Moreover, another hypothesis might be, the more favorable the attitude toward the act of giving blood, the higher the probability of intending to do so. An actual study of donation behavior might begin by first measuring the attitudes and intentions of a sample of people and then recording whether individuals do donate or not in the upcoming drive. Statistical models could then be used to estimate and test the validity of the relationship between intentions and behavior and the relationship between attitudes and intentions. Attitudes might be measured with the following item:

For me, donating blood next week at center Z would be (check one box):

pleasant __ __ __ __ __ __ __ unpleasant
          1   2   3   4   5   6   7

Behavioral intentions might be measured with this item:

☐ definitely intend   ☐ probably intend   ☐ probably not intend   ☐ definitely not intend

An Extension of the Attitude Model: Case 1

The attitude model represented by equations 2-6 and 2-7 is probably too simplistic to give accurate predictions. A researcher would like additionally to know (a) what are the determinants of attitudes (especially those determinants under the control of management); and (b) what other factors influence intentions and thus, indirectly, behavior. We might answer the first question by representing attitudes as a function of beliefs as to the consequences of giving blood and how affectively charged these consequences are to potential donors. That is,

$$A = f(B, a), \qquad \text{2-8}$$

where B = one's beliefs and a = one's importances. The salient beliefs might include the perceived probabilities that giving blood would be physically painful, cause nausea, force one to lose time from work, and make one feel socially responsible. Each of these consequences would have a level of affect associated with it, depending on the emotional reactions of the individual person. The hypotheses implied by equation 2-8 are that (a) the lower the probability of perceived negative consequences and the higher the probability of perceived positive consequences, the more favorable the attitude to give blood and (b) the less noxious the perceived negative consequences and the more attractive the perceived positive consequences, the more favorable the attitude. Further, one might hypothesize that one's beliefs about the consequences of giving blood would be affected by characteristics of the Red Cross and general donating situation (e.g., pleasantness of recruiters, nurses, and others):

$$B = f(PSA),\qquad\text{2-9}$$

where PSA = product/service attributes. Management can influence the perception of PSA through advertising and actual changes in the PSAs.

To answer the second question posed above (i.e., what are other factors that influence intentions?), one might introduce two additional independent variables: personal normative beliefs (NB_p) and social normative beliefs (NB_s). The determinants of intentions can thus be written as

$$BI = f(A, NB_p, NB_s)\qquad\text{2-10}$$

Personal normative beliefs represent how strongly one feels that he or she ought to donate blood, while NB_s represents how strongly one feels that others whose opinions are valued feel that he or she ought to donate blood. Figure 2-17 summarizes the relationships hypothesized in equations 2-6 through 2-10. Marketers attempt, through surveys and experiments, to ascertain the relative magnitude of the causal paths depicted in Figure 2-17.

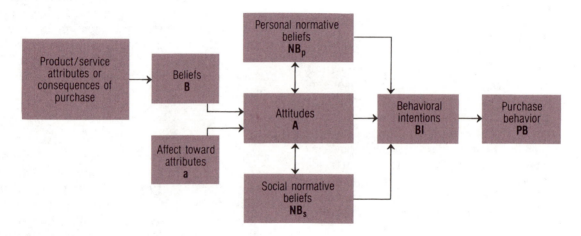

Figure 2-17. An extended attitude model, case 1

An Extension of the Attitude Model: Case 2

To provide an even more complete explanation for blood donation behavior, we might expand the model shown in Figure 2-17 to encompass the effects of advertising and other forms of communication, cultural norms and values, needs and motives, personality and lifestyle factors, and direct social influence from family, friends, and significant others. Figure 2-18 symbolically captures these interactions. In the following chapter, we will focus more on the external determinants of consumer choice with special emphasis devoted to group and social forces.

Summary

In this chapter, we have attempted to describe the psychological and physiological processes governing choices of individual consumers.

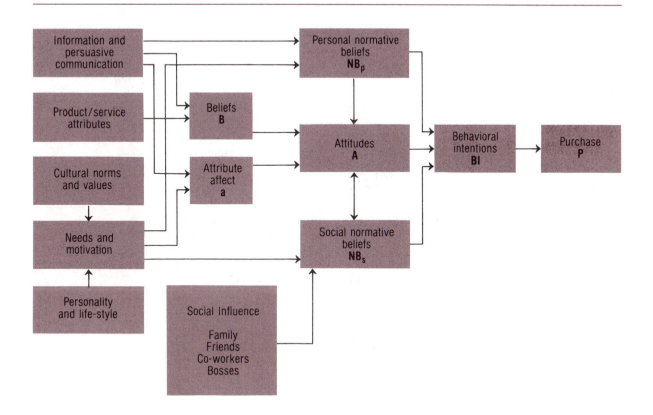

Figure 2-18. An extended attitude model, case 2

Traditionally, three models have been used to explain consumer behavior: the *economic model*, the *stimulus-response model*, and the *stimulus-organism-response model.* The economic model has the longest history and is the simplest and most mathematically rigorous. It postulates that consumers purchase in response to changes in price, income, and tastes (Figure 2-1). The major shortcomings of the economic model are that it fails to consider key psychological processes actually experienced by consumers, while at the same time omitting key determinants of consumption under the influence of managers. The stimulus-response model (Figure 2-2) overcomes the latter problem in that it places considerable emphasis on marketing mix elements and the effects they have on consumer actions. However, the stimulus-response model does not specify how the marketing mix produces responses. This results in a rather coarse-grained explanation of consumption and hampers its usefulness in practice. The stimulus-organism-response model, in contrast, strives to delineate the structures and processes internal to the consumer which actually regulate choices (see Figures 2-5 and 2-6).

The chapter then turned to an elaboration of the stimulus-organism-response model. As shown in Figure 2-10, the central variables in the model are perceptual processes, internal and external stimuli, arousal, information processing (e.g., abstraction, integration, and evaluation), affect and goal constraints, conations (i.e., intention formation), and behavior.

Consumer behavior in the stimulus-organism-response sense typically occurs as either *impulse buying, habitual purchase behavior*, or *consumption problem solving*. When we buy things on impulse, it is generally because an external (e.g., advertisement) or internal (e.g., deprivation) stimulus has caught our attention, and the product is easy to acquire. Very little thought occurs. Rather, emotional or motivational processes are primarily at work. These, however, may occur below the level of self-awareness. Under habitual purchase behavior, prior learning is crucial. Although needs usually initiate the purchase in such instances, cognitive processes predominate and include the execution of action sequences and the evaluation of limited decision criteria. Consumption problem solving involves extensive search, processing of infor-

mation, and interaction with the control unit. Cognitive processes and affective responses may both play important roles in consumption problem solving. The chapter presented examples of the three kinds of consumption.

The final topic discussed was the *attitude model*, which is a frequently applied subcase of the stimulus-organism-response model. The attitude model hypothesizes that the consumer's beliefs about product attributes or the consequences of product use coupled with the importances of affective content of the attributes or consequences of product use determine one's intentions to purchase or not. Figures 2-17 and 2-18 show how the attitude model can be expanded to incorporate other determinants of consumer behavior. In the next chapter, we will explore the social side of consumer behavior. Indeed, the psychological picture we presented in the present chapter should be regarded as only a partial explanation of the real causes of consumer behavior.

Questions and Problems for Discussion

1 How does economic theory explain consumer behavior? What are its strengths and weaknesses?

2 Describe the basic parts of stimulus-response models of consumer behavior. Point out their assets and liabilities.

3 Describe the general structure of stimulus-organism-response models of consumer behavior. What advantages do they yield over economic and stimulus-response approaches?

4 Define what the concepts *structure* and *process* mean. Give a brief example of each in the consumer behavior context.

5 Three key components of the general stimulus-organism-response model of consumer behavior (Figure 2-10) are (a) perceptual and sensing processes, (b) information processing, and (c)

the control unit (i.e., affect and goals). Briefly describe the parts and functions of these components.

6 How do decision rules operate in consumer information processing and choice?

7 Three broad classes of consumption include impulse buying, habitual purchase behavior, and problem solving. Compare and contrast these and give an example of each.

8 What is the attitude model and how does it function? What are its implications for marketing managers?

9 Interpret the operation of the extended attitude model shown in Figure 2-18.

10 Describe the process you went through for your last decision to go to the cinema. Do the same for your last purchase of an expensive product.

NOTES

1. The brand manager is responsible for the entire marketing program for a product. He or she sets overall product goals, creates the marketing strategies to meet the goals, and implements the strategies. This typically involves work in product design, marketing research, packaging, pricing, distribution, and promotion and advertising. The brand manager is sometimes called the product manager in some firms. He or she is basically a general manager in the broadest sense of the term.

2. For one description of economic man, see Harold K. Schneider, *Economic Man* (New York: The Free Press, 1974).

3. *Ibid.*

4. See, for example, Paul A. Samuelson, *Foundations of Economic Analysis* (Cambridge, Mass.: Harvard University Press, 1948).

5. Herbert A. Simon, "Rational Decision Making in Business Organizations," *American Economic Review* 69 (September 1979): 493–513.

6. An early statement of the neoclassical theory of consumer behavior can be found in J. R. Hicks, *Value and Capital*, 2nd ed. (Oxford: Oxford University Press, 1946).

7. Some economists believe that an actual decision process need not take place but rather that the consumer act as if he or she followed the rule entailed by Equations 2-1 and 2-2.

8. See, for example, Harvey Leibenstein, *Beyond Economic Man* (Cambridge, Mass.: Harvard University Press, 1976); Richard A. Easterlin, Robert A. Pollak, and Michael L. Wachter, "Toward a More General Economic Model of Fertility Determination: Endogenous Preferences and Natural Fertility," in Richard A. Easterlin (ed.), *Population and Economic Changes in Developing Countries* (Chicago: University of Chicago Press, 1980); and Gary S. Becker, "A Theory of Social Interactions," *Journal of Political Economy* 82 (November/December 1974): 1063–93.

9. A few economists have attempted to explore some of these other determinants of consumption within the context of economic theory. See, for example, R. Schmalensee, "A Model of Advertising and Product Quality," *Journal of Political Economy* 86 (June 1978): 483–504.

10. Mark Blaug, *The Methodology of Economics* (Cambridge, England: Cambridge University Press, 1980).

11. George J. Stigler and Gary S. Becker, "De Gustibus Non Est Disputandum," *American Economic Review* 67 (March 1977): 76–90.

12. For a description of some of the many response functions studied by marketers, see Phillippe A. Naert and Peter S. H. Leeflang, *Building Implementable Marketing Models* (Hingham, Mass.: Kluwer Nijhoff, 1978).

13. See Richard P. Bagozzi, "An Examination of the Validity of Two Models of Attitude," *Multivariate Behavior Research* 16 (July 1981): 323–59; Bagozzi, "A Field Investigation of Causal Relations among Cognitions, Affect, Intentions, and Behavior," *Journal of Marketing Research* 19 (November 1982): 562–84; Bagozzi, "Attitudes, Intentions, and Behavior: A Test of Some Key Hypotheses," *Journal of Personality and Social Psychology* 41 (October 1981): 607–27; and Bagozzi, "A Holistic Methodology for Modeling Consumer Response to Innovation," *Operations Research* 31 (January/February 1983): 128–76.

14. This example is an adaptation of research reported in Marcus Alexis, George H. Haines, and Leonard Simon, "Consumer Information Processing: The Case of Women's Clothing," in *Marketing and the New Science of Planning* (Chicago: American Marketing Association, 1968), pp. 197–205, and presented in James R. Bettman, *An Information Processing Theory of Consumer Choice* (Reading, Mass.: Addison-Wesley, 1979), pp. 236–37.

15. A number of excellent consumer behavior texts exist, including James R. Bettman, *An Information Processing Theory of Consumer Choice;* James F. Engel, Roger D. Blackwell, and David T. Kollat, *Consumer Behavior*, 3rd ed. (New York: Holt, Rinehart & Winston, 1978); John A. Howard, *Consumer Behavior: Application of Theory* (New York: McGraw-Hill, 1977); John A. Howard and Jagdish N. Sheth, *The Theory of Consumer Behavior* (New York: Wiley, 1969); and Francesco M. Nicosia, *Consumer Decision Processes: Marketing and Advertising Implications* (Englewood Cliffs, N.J.: Prentice-Hall, 1966).

16. The atomistic orientations are perhaps best represented in the work of authors focusing on narrow, well-defined aspects of consumer decision making such as are found in Peter Wright, "Consumer Choice Strategies: Simplifying versus Optimizing," *Journal of Marketing Research* 12 (February 1975): 60–67; or Jacob Jacoby, "Information Load and Decision Quality: Some Contested Issues," *Journal of Marketing Research* 14 (November 1977): 569–73. The grand approaches are exemplified by the work (referenced in note 15) of Bettman; Engel, Blackwell, and Kollat; Howard and Sheth; and Nicosia. Bettman has also done considerable research at the atomistic level.

17. The following discussion attempts to integrate some of our current knowledge about human information processing and decision-making activities into the model shown in Figure 2-10. For introductory reviews in the psychology literature, see Arnold L. Glass, Keith J. Holyoak, and John L. Santa, *Cognition* (Reading, Mass.: Addison-Wesley, 1979); and R. Lachman, J. Mistler-Lachman, and E. C. Butterfield, *Cognitive Psychology* (Hillsdale, N.J.: Lawrence Erlbaum Assoc., 1979). For recent treatments in the marketing literature, see J. R. Bettman, *An Information Processing Theory of Consumer Choice;* J. A. Howard, *Consumer Behavior: Application of Theory;* and W. Kroeber-Riel, "Activation Research: Psychobiological Approaches in Consumer Research," *Journal of Consumer Research* 5 (March 1979): 240–50.

18. See D. Kahneman, *Attention and Effort* (Englewood Cliffs, N.J.: Prentice-Hall, 1973); Glass, et al., *Cognition.*

19. Some theorists no longer claim that separate short- and long-term memories exist. Rather, it is believed that a single memory exists and that information is acted upon through operations, rules, or other forms of active processing (see Lachman et al., *Cognitive Psychology*, Ch. 8). The model of Figure 2-10 attempts to integrate some of this thinking while retaining the working memory/long-term memory distinction for pedagogical reasons. It may well be that working memory and long-term memory are at opposite ends of the same continuum.

20. Bettman, *Information Processing Theory of Consumer Choice*, pp. 176–203, defines these rules, which he terms "heuristics," and discusses their measurement and limitations.

21. See Howard, *Consumer Behavior: Application of Theory.*

22. Donald G. Morrison, "Purchase Intentions and Purchase Behavior," *Journal of Marketing* 43 (Spring 1979): 65–74; Manohar U. Kalwani and Alvin J. Silk, "On the Reliability and Predictive Validity of Purchase Intention Measures," *Marketing Science* 1 (Summer 1982): 243–86.

GLOSSARY

Affect. The feeling or emotional component of psychological reactions toward objects or actions. It usually entails a physiological response as well (e.g., increased heart rate). Affect can be positive (e.g., liking) or negative (e.g., disliking) and can vary in intensity. It generally has an emotive aspect to it. Needs, wants, and desires are basically affective in content.

Cognitions. Factual mental images about product attributes or the consequences of product use/ownership. Cognitions are what we typically mean by "thoughts." Beliefs, expectancies, and subjective probabilities are types of cognitions.

Conations. Specific intentions to act in a particular way. This is the volitional part of consumer behavior.

Consumption Problem Solving. The decision processes consumers go through in the acquisition of new or higher-cost, higher-risk products. Involves extensive search for information and evaluation of product attributes and alternative brands. Consumption problem solving usually involves relatively high levels of both affect and cognitive processes.

Decision Rules. Heuristics or guidelines implicitly or explicitly used by consumers to combine or simplify information, evaluate the information, and make choices among alternatives.

The Economic Model. A theory of consumption maintaining that people attempt to maximize their utility subject to their income and tastes and the prices of goods and services. Aside from the presumed maximization process, the economic model makes no statements about internal processes within the mind or body of consumers. In this sense, it is similar to the stimulus-response model. The economic model asserts that prices and income determine demand.

Episodic Memory. The stored temporal and spatial aspects of our past personal experiences, events, and happenings.

Goals. Desired ends in relation to which an individual seeks information, evaluates alternative courses of actions, and makes choices.

Habitual Purchasing. The acquisition of products as a result of predominantly automatic learned reactions. Little information processing is involved, although the action is often preplanned. Although purchases stem from needs, affect plays less of an overt role than in consumption problem solving. Habitual purchases most often occur for lower-cost, everyday products.

Impulse Buying. Purchases that arise primarily as a result of curiosity or emotional arousal, but typically of a low magnitude. Either the product or brand has not been purchased before, past purchases occurred much earlier, or no prior planning is the rule. In addition, the cost or risk of a purchase is relatively low, and very little information processing occurs prior to purchase.

Information Processing. The mental activity wherein stored thoughts or external and/or internal stimuli are acted upon. Information processing typically involves recall, recognition, abstraction, inference, integration, or other thinking activities. The basic units of analysis are cognitions and propositions.

Marketing Policy Variables. Stimuli such as prices, discounts, allowances, product characteristics, packaging, etc., that a manager has at his or her disposal to induce a response in the marketplace. Also known as the marketing mix or the 4 Ps (i.e., product, place, promotion, and price).

Organism. A constellation of internal processes and structures interacting between stimuli external to the person and the final actions, reactions, or responses emitted. These intervening processes and structures consist of perceptual, psychological, and physiological activities.

Process. The sequence of steps or stages one goes through in decision making or the cause-and-effect relations in decision making.

Recall. Producing from memory information previously learned and doing this with no or few cues.

Recognition. Entails comparing a cue to a representation in memory and indicating whether one has seen or heard a particular stimulus before.

Semantic Memory. Stored knowledge of words, symbols, their meanings, and the rules and relations among them used to form sentences, equations, and other representations.

The Stimulus-Organism-Response Model. A theory of behavior that hypothesizes that stimuli (e.g., perceived rewards or punishments) have well-defined effects on internal psychological and physiological processes and these, in turn, influence specific choices and actions on the part of the consumers.

The Stimulus-Response Model. A theory of behavior that maintains that actions of consumers can be explained by the effects of punishing or rewarding stimuli. The stimulus-response model makes no statements about the internal dynamics of consumers. In this sense, it is a "black box" theory. The model is predicated on the assumption that common stimuli will invariably lead to predictable reactions in consumers. Its tenets lie in the behaviorism of B. F. Skinner, a leading theorist in psychology. Classical conditioning theory also applies in some instances. Many management science theories of consumption and most aggregate models (e.g., advertising-sales response functions) are based on stimulus-response ideas.

Structure. A set of variables or entities and the relationship among them.

Tastes. A term used by economists and meaning roughly the same as affect. Although undefined by economists, "tastes" are a subject matter of psychologists and consumer researchers. Tastes influence choices.

Consumer Behavior: Past, Present, and Future

Richard J. Lutz
Professor of Marketing
University of Florida

The study of consumer behavior has been perhaps the dominant research topic within the field of marketing over the past three decades. Due to the origin of marketing as a subfield of economics, early studies of consumer behavior adopted a classical economics perspective. In the early 1950s, however, George Katona and his colleagues introduced the notion of *psychological economics,* which explicitly considered consumers' *willingness* as well as *ability* to buy.

With the emergence of the modern marketing concept and its inherent consumer orientation, increasing attention was devoted to understanding consumer behavior—i.e., why and how people buy. Initially, the goal of understanding consumer behavior gave rise to much rather indiscriminate borrowing of concepts and methodologies from social sciences other than economics, most notably psychology. The rationalistic economic model was rejected as too mechanistic, and consumer behavior researchers turned to personality theory, reference group influence, the theory of cognitive dissonance, and a host of other concepts as holding the key to consumer behavior.

Over the years, this borrowing of theories from other more basic disciplines has persisted, but it has become more selective and sophisticated. Consumer behavior research, as a subfield of research on marketing phenomena, has matured rather rapidly. As a descriptive science within what is essentially a heavily normative discipline, the subfield of consumer behavior has served as an oasis for those marketing scholars who are interested in knowledge for the sake of knowledge alone, rather than for its potential managerial implications. It is safe to say that consumer behavior researchers, as a group, are more excited about questions which ask why some phenomenon occurs than they are by questions about how to perform some marketing task more efficiently or effectively. As a result, consumer behavior researchers increasingly over the years lost touch with the parent discipline (i.e., marketing) and its inherent focus on consumer behavior as an important input to managerial decision making.

Eventually, consumer behavior researchers within marketing united with social science researchers in other disciplines who were also interested in consumer behavior to form a new multidisciplinary Association for Consumer Research. Since its inception in 1969, ACR has served to legitimize the study of consumer behavior in its own right, with no necessary linkage to marketing or managerial implications. While the membership of ACR is heavily dominated by marketing academics, the focus is nevertheless much more on theory-driven research rather than on problem-driven research. A preponderance of the studies that would be considered among the most influential in the field are noticeably sophisticated in their treatment of important theoretical issues; unfortunately, however, many of these studies seemingly have little to do with real-world consumer behavior. Researchers have been quick to adopt a theory designed to explain some behavioral phenomenon with little regard to whether or not that phenomenon is exhibited with the domain of consumer behavior. The theory as an end in itself is what is of major interest, rather than the theory as a means to the end of explaining some consumer behavior. Thus, the subfield of marketing called consumer behavior has, in large measure, evolved into a discipline of its own, albeit a discipline that has difficulty retaining its focus on the domain of behaviors it was originally intended to explain. As a result, consumer behavior research has failed to make many significant contributions to the broader field of marketing and its attendant managerial decision-making technologies.

The present state of the art in consumer behavior can be characterized as being overly concerned with explanation at the expense of descriptive research. That is, for explanatory, theory-driven research to make its maximum contribution, and indeed to make any contribution at all, a sufficient foundation of descriptive findings with respect to real-world consumer behavior must be in place.

Consumer Behavior at the Crossroads

Recent developments in the technology of marketing and marketing research present a simultaneous threat and opportunity to consumer behavior research as it is conducted today. The diffusion of Universal Product Code (UPC) scanners into supermarkets and chain stores throughout the U.S., coupled with the emergence of cable television (CATV) as a major media force, has already begun to have a significant impact on the nature and quality of data regarding consumer purchase behavior. Several research firms have established consumer panels wherein purchase data accumulated via UPC scanners are automatically recorded each time a member of a panel household makes a purchase at a supermarket. The cooperating panel households also periodically complete questionnaires assessing a variety of socioeconomic and psychographic variables. All this information is stored in a computer, forming large descriptive data bases. Some observers have stated that marketing (and especially consumer behavior) researchers will soon have at their disposal, as a result of the advent of UPC panels, the best descriptive data of any of the social sciences. The actual, computer-recorded purchases of literally thousands of households over a year or more will form not only very extensive, but also highly accurate, portrayals of consumer purchase behavior with respect to a plethora of consumer package goods.

In addition to these massive data banks, some market research firms are offering advertising pretesting services via CATV systems. In a typical system, several hundred households are recruited to become UPC panel members, and thus agree to have all their purchases recorded and stored. Additionally, the panel members agree to participate in a CATV arrangement whereby actual field tests of commercials are conducted.

For example, half of the panel members may see a particular test ad twenty times a week in their normal viewing pattern, while the other half is exposed to the ad only ten times. This is accomplished through a split cable system. The computer records which households were exposed to the different media weights and then monitors subsequent purchase behavior via the UPC portion of the system. Hence, an advertiser can test the direct effects of media weight on actual purchase behavior. This example is obviously only one type of test that might be conducted. The possibilities are virtually limitless.

Several of the research firms involved in these UPC/CATV operations have offered their data bases (once they are too "old" to be of further proprietary use in marketing decision making but still current enough to be useful in a scientific sense) to marketing academicians for research purposes. It is very likely that these data will give rise to an entirely new form of consumer behavior research that emphasizes accurate description of purchase patterns and rather straightforward "stimulus-response" (S-R) analyses of consumer response to marketing variables such as price and advertising. Both of these kinds of research have been sorely lacking in the consumer behavior literature, and the broader field of marketing will readily embrace this new research as being "real consumer behavior" research. Theoretically driven research that fails to address meaningful consumer behavior phenomena will be scorned as irrelevant. Herein lies the threat/opportunity for today's consumer behavior researchers.

The obvious threat is to theory-driven consumer behavior research as it is generally conducted today. Many of the studies are too narrow and too many steps removed from the reality of the marketplace. They have been conducted without sufficient consideration of the phenomena of real interest. In the future, this type of study will be increasingly rebuked for failing to address the real issue of concern, i.e., *consumer* behavior. Part of this lack of attention to real-world consumer behavior, however, may be attributable to the relative unavailability of adequate descriptive studies documenting the existence of interesting phenomena. Good descriptive data are difficult and costly to acquire, and most academic researchers have not had such data at their disposal.

Hence, the UPC/CATV data bases present a real opportunity for consumer behavior scientists to sharpen their focus on the phenomena of interest. As the descriptive findings accumulate, the need to explain these findings will become apparent. New research questions requiring sophisticated behavioral theories will emerge. For the first time in years, the bulk of consumer behavior research will have as its starting point real-world consumer behavior phenomena. There will be a surge of inductive theory building as sophisticated researchers turn their attention to deriving explanations for various patterns of consumer behavior observations. In short, consumer behavior research will blend its traditionally strong theoretical orientation with a renewed focus on managerially relevant consumer behavior issues, resulting in a reconciliation of marketing and its prodigal subfield.

Consumer behavior, as a discipline, will not be compromised under the latter scenario. It will remain a vital and growing scientific domain all the more robust and exciting as a result of its renewed focus on the phenomena which initially gave rise to its birth several decades earlier.

CHAPTER THREE

All for one, one for all.
—— *Alexandre Dumas,* The Three Musketeers

Men exist for the sake of one another.
—— *Marcus Aurelius Antoninus (121–180 A.D.)*

Everyone must form himself as a particular being, seeking, however, to attain that general idea of which all mankind are constituents.
—— *Goethe (1749–1832)*

So in every individual the two trends, one towards personal happiness and the other towards unity with the rest of humanity, must contend with each other.
—— *Sigmund Freud (1856–1939)*

CONSUMER BEHAVIOR: SOCIAL DECISION MAKING

Introduction

Chapter 2 examined consumer behavior as psychological and physiological phenomena. We peered deeply into the mind and body of the consumer to see how he or she makes consumption decisions. In the present chapter, we will investigate consumer behavior as a social phenomenon. That is, consumption will be viewed as an instance of interactional, group, and collective phenomena. We will begin with a discussion of the concept of a social unit and its meaning for the study of consumption. Various social theories will be discussed as they relate to marketing. Next, we will introduce the notion of the diffusion of innovation, which represents one way to look at the aggregate side of consumer behavior. Then, purchases of goods and services by the family will be considered. Finally, we will take stock of research into organizational marketing with particular emphasis placed on industrial buying behavior.

The Concept of Social Analysis and Some Leading Theories

It is quite natural for us to think of consumer behavior in an individualistic sense. After all, each of us is a consumer and has access to his or her own thoughts and feelings. And it is nearly as easy to infer what the thoughts and feelings of other consumers are, based on their words and deeds. But to comprehend the social side of consumption is not as natural for us and requires a change in our mind set. We do not normally "see" social phenomena because they are external to us and at a higher level of abstraction than our personal sensations and ideas. To grasp the social dimensions of consumption, we must break out of our egocentric way of looking at the world and attempt to understand the forces that bind individuals into a social network. In this section of the chapter, we will introduce some of the classic theories that help us to better interpret the social nature of consumption.[1]

Society, Groups, and the Individual

One form that social behavior takes is the interaction between an individual and a social unit, where the latter might be construed as an organization, an institution, a group, or society at large. Two general cases are worth considering. First, we can think of a social unit influencing or constraining the behavior of an individual:

social unit $\longrightarrow$ person

This is what sociologists and anthropologists mean when they say, "Society is coercive on the individual." At the most aggregate level, this happens when we act in response to norms, laws, or mores. At a less aggregate level, this also happens when our family or a work or reference group shapes our values and choices.

The second general category of social unit–person interactions occurs in the other direction, i.e., when an individual has an impact on the social unit:

person $\longrightarrow$ social unit

This occasionally takes place at the most aggregate level, for instance, when a person is able to get government or an organization to do something it had not intended to do. It occurs more frequently at less aggregate social levels, such as when a leader or a charismatic person influences the actions of a group. We will present examples of person–social unit interactions below when we discuss specific theories at this level of social inquiry. The four theories we will consider are social comparison processes, relative deprivation theory, equity theory, and role theory.

Social Comparison Processes. We are always making comparisons between ourselves and others. Sometimes we do this consciously. After an examination has been graded and returned or at the end of a course, how often have you felt the urge to discover how your friends have performed? Or in the early stages of information gathering and decision making, how many times have you sought the opinions and experiences of another who had already passed through a similar process?

Often we make personal comparisons with others without being fully aware of the act and its consequences for us until after its performance. Have you ever engaged in a conversation with another and found yourself using a new mannerism, a word, phrase, idea, slang, or other nuance borrowed from the person spoken to or from another acquaintance? Implicit comparisons with others occur frequently with respect to clothing such that our tastes are shaped partly by social comparison to others. Everyone is influenced to some different degree by subtle symbols communicated nonverbally by those close to us.

Social comparison processes are even occasionally institutionalized. Many firms, for example, regularly post lists of the rankings of their salespeople because they know that salespeople continually compare themselves to their peers and attempt to outdo each other. In short, social comparisons are part and parcel of our everyday world of experiences.

In general, we tend to compare one or more of three things: our beliefs, our feelings, or our personal experiences and outcomes. The impetus for social comparisons comes from within or without. Early theories represented social comparison processes as stemming from forces inside the person doing the comparison. Each person was thought to have a need or drive to evaluate his or her own beliefs, feelings, or experiences.[2] This is especially so for those things related to one's own personal worth. Social comparisons are made more frequently when we lack objective criteria for judging the full extent of our abilities and performance. Thus, social comparison processes are strategies for information acquisition about ourselves. Notice that the sequence of events according to the theory is clear: it begins with the needs of the individual and then leads to a comparison to others. We might also speculate that social comparisons do not always arise as a drive for comparison per se, yet still originate from within the person. For example, maintenance of one's own self-esteem[3] or a competitive orientation may require social comparisons over and above a need to evaluate one's abilities.

At the same time, the causal mechanism leading to social comparisons might, on occasion, spring from external forces. A good example of this occurs when advertisers include scenes that implicitly encourage us to "keep up with the Joneses." The portrayal serves as a model, and we find ourselves influenced through observational learning.[4] The ad stimulates us to make similar comparisons and to examine our own outcomes, attributes, or self-worth. This generally occurs below the level of self-consciousness, although we are sometimes aware of the process at a global level.

The theory of social comparison processes specifies that the comparison person one chooses will typically be similar to oneself. A similar other is more accessible, realistic, and personally relevant. Imagine, as an example, that you had recently taken up the game of golf. In order to assess how well you were doing, you would most likely compare yourself with someone much like yourself (a beginner of roughly the same age, physical characteristics, previous experience, etc.) rather than with a pro such as Tom Watson. And to a certain degree, the same principle applies to our consumption of goods and services. Where we shop and the things we buy are to a certain extent influenced by comparisons made with those around us. But we make more comparisons to persons with similar characteristics, and these have greater import than comparisons made with others very far above or below us in ability, wealth, or other relevant "social" dimensions.

The idea of social comparison processes is an important one in marketing. It forces us to look beyond the attributes of products and the psychology of consumers to explain consumption choices. We are led to the conclusion that the arousal of our needs for products and the decisions we make among alternatives are under the influence of meaningful comparisons to others. Indeed, some research even indicates that what we label our emotions to be depends on both our own psychological state and our interpretation of the reactions of people around us.[5] We compare our own appraisal of our feelings to that made by those in contact with us to interpret and define our emotions. As we shall see, the theory of social comparison processes provides the foundation for a number of other social theories in marketing.

On the negative side, the theory of social comparison processes has some limitations. In the first place, it does not fully explain what effects comparisons have on us. It implies that favorable comparisons enhance and unfavorable comparisons degrade our evaluations of self-worth. But what happens next? In the former case, the drive to compare will be reduced, and one will presumably achieve equilibrium. In the latter case, we would feel dissatisfied or threatened and would either change our self-image or attempt to act to change our performance or outcomes to a higher level. Which of the two alternatives we would choose and how either would be carried out are not clear from the theory. Similarly, some people may repress the drive for comparisons and avoid making them at times. But the theory does not specify how or when this might happen.

A second problem with the theory of social comparison processes is that the person or persons chosen for comparison may not be similar to the comparer. Indeed, people might seek others with different characteristics. We might consciously or unconsciously compare ourselves to others slightly better off than we are as a strategy for self-motivation, for instance. Other comparisons to differing referents are possible as well. Also, because people have so many attributes, it is likely that they will be similar in some ways and different in others. Hence, any theory must come to grips with the sense of similarity that is important in any comparison. The theory of social comparison processes does not go this far and fails to explain how comparison referents are chosen.

A third shortcoming of the theory is that it tends to neglect the larger social setting. Social influence from groups and normative influences in the social milieu are not treated at all. We turn now to theories that attempt to go beyond social comparison processes as construed above.

Relative Deprivation.[6] The theory of relative deprivation builds upon and is somewhat similar to the theory of social comparison processes, but it goes further. The theory hypothesizes that whenever we receive a reward or outcome in life, we compare the level of the reward or outcome to a standard of comparison. The standard of comparison is the reward or outcome received by the mode of a reference group or a particular member of the reference group we select as the standard. If our reward or outcome is similar to the referent's, we feel satisfied or at least do not feel dissatisfied. However, if our reward or outcome is inferior to the referent's, we feel dissatisfied. Hence the label "relative deprivation."

The theory further stipulates that dissatisfaction will lead to action. The action might consist of more effort expended in the pursuit of greater rewards or outcomes. It might also consist of responses of protest, anger, or aggression. Or it might be directed inward in the form of depression, self-abuse, or withdrawal. Sections A and B of Figure 3-1 summarize the theories of social comparison processes and relative deprivation, respectively.

The theory of relative deprivation places particular emphasis on *social* processes and their implications. Although psychological reactions play a role (e.g., in cognitive assessments and affective responses), the absolute level of our rewards or outcomes and their meaning to us are not the central mechanisms in the theory. It is the *relative* difference between what we obtain and what we expect to get as a function of relevant others that is important. Indeed, according to the theory, one can feel deprived even if he or she receives very high rewards if the level is below what a reference group receives. Similarly, if one receives very low rewards, he or she may feel satisfied if relevant others receive similar outcomes. Psychological arguments, such as provided by adaption level theory, hypothesize that the absolute level of rewards is important.[7] We are satisfied by rewards or not, it is believed, because of their ability to fulfill needs and our degree of habituation to them. It was out of the inability of psychological theories such as adaption level theory to fully explain behavior that social theories have arisen.

To illustrate the theory of relative deprivation, consider the salary negotiations that go on from time to time in professional sports. Football players, for example, earn on average over $150,000 per year, with a number of stars receiving $700,000 per year or more. When contract time arrives, who does the Players' Association use as its standard of comparison? It certainly does not use the income of the average wage earner or even the salary of the typical college graduate. Rather, the players choose the salaries earned by athletes in professional basketball or baseball as their reference point. It might seem incongruous and even unfair to hear players complain that their salaries are "so low," for in an absolute sense quite the contrary is true. But in a relative sense, the players feel "deprived." Notice that in order to explain the behavior of football players at contract time, we must resort to a social theory.

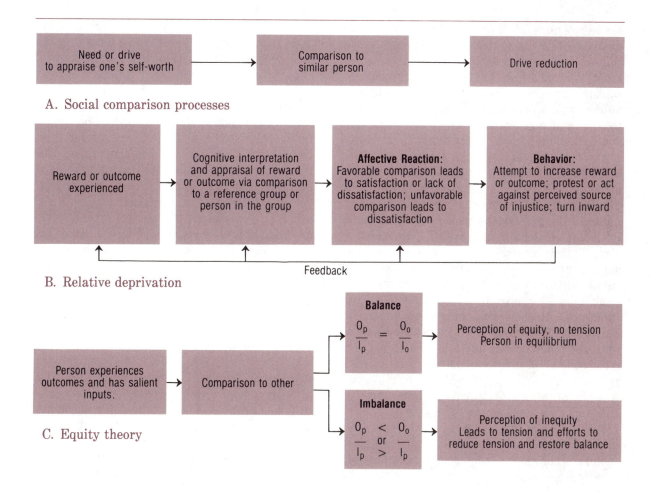

A. Social comparison processes

B. Relative deprivation

Feedback

C. Equity theory

Balance

$$\frac{O_p}{I_p} = \frac{O_o}{I_o}$$

Perception of equity, no tension
Person in equilibrium

Imbalance

$$\frac{O_p}{I_p} < \frac{O_o}{I_o} \text{ or } \frac{O_p}{I_p} > \frac{O_o}{I_o}$$

Perception of inequity
Leads to tension and efforts to
reduce tension and restore balance

Figure 3-1. Three simple social theories

The majority of research in marketing on group influence has focused on reference or peer groups. One stream of research has investigated the effect of group discussion among peers on the willingness to take risks. Although early studies tended to find that group discussion led to more willingness to accept risks in purchase decisions,[8] later studies found that risk taking as a function of group discussion depended on the product.[9] Group discussion leads to greater willingness to accept risk for low-risk products (e.g., facial tissue) and less willingness to accept risk for high-risk products (e.g., cold remedies). Another stream of research has found that group pressure influences brand choice behavior.[10] The rationale is that groups exert subtle pressures for conformity.

Equity Theory.[11] Equity theory provides an explicit social explanation for how people make comparisons and what they do as a result of these comparisons. The theory hypothesizes that a person compares the ratio of his or her outcomes to inputs to the ratio of the outcomes to inputs of a relevant other. If the ratios are equal, then balance or equity exists in the mind of the comparer. If the ratios are unequal, then an imbalance or inequity exists. The perception of inequity is believed to result in tension and dissatisfaction. The greater the perceived imbalance, the greater the tension. This, in turn, is thought to lead to efforts to reduce the tension. Tension is reduced by restoring balance: somehow the unequal ratios must be made equal. This can be accomplished by changing one's inputs or outcomes, altering the other's inputs or outcomes, switching the comparison person, or distorting one's perceptions of inputs and outcomes for any or all concerned. Inputs consist of any attribute or action of a person, such as age, education, intelligence, wealth, or effort. Outcomes include rewards that one receives such as money, gifts, status, prestige, or psychic benefits. It is conceivable that outcomes could consist also of negative factors, such as punishment or losses, but this possibility has not been developed within the context of the theory.

A final point to note with respect to equity theory is that a person can compare one's ratio of outcomes to inputs directly to a person with whom one interacts or indirectly to a person who interacts with a common other but not oneself. The former occurs when we make comparisons directly to a person as we meet with him or her face to face. The latter happens when we wish to see how well we have fared dealing with, say, a professor, supervisor, or department store when compared to known others who have similarly dealt with these entities. Section C in Figure 3-1 summarizes the propositions of equity theory. Notice how it is both similar to and different from social comparison processes and relative deprivation arguments.

Equity theory has not been applied as yet in marketing to any significant degree, so let us illustrate the theory with two hypothetical examples. Suppose you enter a restaurant, sit down at a table, and begin to scan the menu. After a while, you notice that the waiter is not paying much attention to you. Instead, he seems to be lavishly attending to the needs of others at a nearby table. The longer the waiter avoids your eye and the more he takes care of the other guests, the angrier you get. Finally, after what seems to be many minutes, you cannot control your resentment any longer, and, enraged, you storm out of the restaurant. While walking down the street after a cooling-off period, your partner expresses sympathy but notes that only five minutes elapsed between the initial sitting and the hasty exit.

What then accounts for such a strong reaction to the behavior of the waiter? Objectively, the time interval itself was not the cause of your response. You probably have waited much longer than five minutes to be waited upon without feeling angry. Perhaps a clue lies in the waiter's fawning over the other guests. You came to the restaurant with as much self-esteem and resources as anyone else. Thus, you perceive your inputs to be equal to the other guests' and expect that you will be treated as well as anyone else. But the seemingly extravagant treatment of the other guests and simultaneous neglect of you produced an imbalanced ratio of outcomes to inputs. Therefore, you in effect changed your comparison group and "punished" the waiter with the dramatic exit. Notice here that the original equity comparison was not with another person or group with which you were in direct interaction. Rather, you and the comparison group were "related" through your common connection to the waiter and restaurant.

As an example of equity in a face-to-face encounter, consider Salesperson R at the XYZ insurance company. R has not been meeting management's expectations. To find out what is wrong, Manager G accompanied R on her sales calls. G notices that R is a "hot-and-cold" seller. In some interactions, R and the customers hit it off exceedingly well, and sales are made with ease. But in other interactions, there appears to be tension, lack of effective communication, and few sales. We might say that the outcomes in the former were high, whereas those in the latter were low. After further study, G discovers that, in the successful sales dyads, both R and the customer were alike. Both were about the same age, had similar education levels, liked the same things, and so on. On the other hand, in the unsuccessful dyads, R and the customer differed in one or more attributes. For example, R was young, the customer old; R smoked, whereas the customer did not; R had a college education, the customer did not. Thus, R and the customer had similar inputs in the successful dyads but not the unsuccessful ones.

In essence, then, successful selling occurred when the relationships were balanced. If the ratio of outcomes (e.g., pleasant exchanges, expected mutual gain through purchase of an insurance policy) to inputs (e.g., similarity in characteristics) were equal between R and the customer, then a sale tended to occur. If the ratios were unequal, then it did not. Social equity was a necessary prerequisite to consummation of a sale. G noticed this and later redesigned the assignment of salespeople to territories to maximize the match in personal characteristics between salespeople and their customers.

Role Theory.[12] Role theory represents another body of ideas designed to relate the individual to specific social groups and the larger society. It goes further than the approaches discussed thus far in that it develops the nature of social influences in more detail. To see this, look at Section A at the top of Figure 3-2.

Here we see that any person can be thought to be influenced by two forces: the greater social context and the particular role or roles within which he or she functions. These forces are indicated as solid arrows a and b, respectively. The idea is that human action can be conceived largely as a response to social forces.

To understand what we mean by social context and role and their effects, let us take two examples. In Figure 3-2B we see the situation for Person C in his or her role as a buyer in an organization. Many organizations have specialized jobs for individuals whose primary responsibility is to act as agents for the firm and procure needed goods and services. Depending on the firm, the people who fulfill this role are known variously as buyers, purchasing agents, or materials managers. In any case, Person C is influenced by the social context (represented in part by organizational goals and policies) and his or her role as buyer. The buyer role consists of a set of expectations shared by the Purchasing Department, its head, and Person C. By expectations we mean the responsibilities, duties, and understandings held by members of the Purchasing Department of themselves and each other and in relation to the functions of the department. Expectations might be codified, such as occurs in the policies and procedures manuals of some purchasing departments. Or it might simply consist of spoken and unspoken agreements and understandings. In either case, the influence resulting from expectations is shown as arrow b in Figure 3-2B. Person C is further influenced by broader and more removed organizational goals and policies that serve as part of the social context for his or her actions. For example, most organizations have explicit and implicit rules of conduct regarding dress, demeanor, and office decor. These rules and other organizational norms and imperatives shape Person C's behavior, in addition to specific role prescriptions.

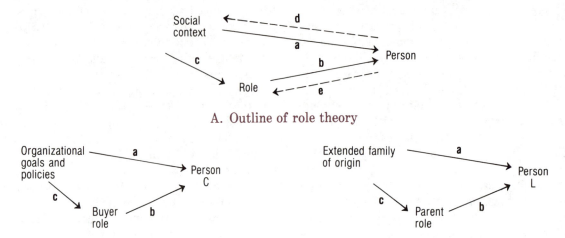

A. Outline of role theory

B. The role of a buyer in an organization

C. The role of a parent

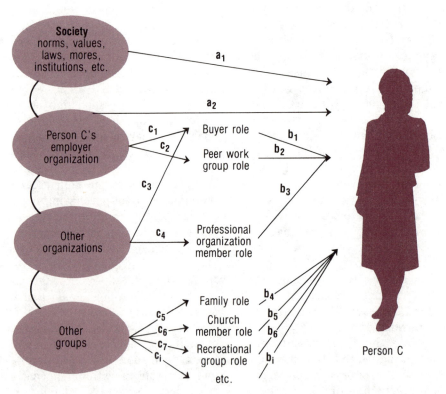

D. The multiple roles of a person and some of the social contextual forces

Figure 3-2. Role theory and some examples

At the same time, note in Figure 3-2B that the social context impinges directly upon roles. It does this in the organizational context, for instance, by specifying what the Purchasing Department should buy, how much freedom it has in its role, in what way goals for return on investment should be taken into account, and so on. The internal organizational context shapes the nature of particular roles.

As another example, Figure 3-2C shows role theory applied to the family. Here Person L serves in a parent role with all its expectations and prescriptions. The latter are represented in path b in Figure 3-2C. Person L's extended family of origin continues to influence L in a direct manner, too (path a in Figure 3-2C). For example, L might feel the need to participate in ceremonies and rituals with his or her extended family of origin. He or she continues to give and receive gifts at birthdays and holidays, attend weddings and funerals, and so on. The extended family of origin was, and continues to be, the primary mechanism defining what a parent role should be for Person L (path c in Figure 3-2C). This is done through example, socialization, consultation, and even overt supervision. Legal and other social forces shape the parent role, too.

The diagrams presented in Figure 3-2A–C only capture a part of the picture, of course. Each person is simultaneously in many roles. We have shown some of the many roles that Person C, the buyer, occupies in Figure 3-2D. Person C is at the same time a buyer, a colleague in a peer group, a family member, a partner on a bowling team in a weekly recreational league, and so on. The entire collection of meaningful roles for Person C is known as a *role set*. Notice further that society with its norms and institutions, as well as various organizations and groups, affect Person C directly and indirectly through their role-shaping functions. We have only represented a small number of the many possible sources of influence and their linkages.

To return briefly to Figure 3-2A, it can be seen that the person is also conceived as an influencer of the social context and his or her roles. We have drawn these as dashed arrows to indicate that the connections (d and e) are typically less frequent and forceful than the primary paths (a, b, and c). Society shapes the individual to a greater extent than the reverse. Another point to note is that each role will generally involve a number of interactions with many people. Person C, for example, will see numerous vendors and have frequent interactions with his or her supervisor and others affected by the purchase decision. Later in the chapter, we will discuss family and organizational buying in greater detail, for they constitute two of the most important social instances of consumption.

Social Exchange Theory in Marketing

There are many ways to study consumer behavior. We have seen that it is useful to look at consumption as a physiological, psychological, economic, and social phenomenon, depending on our point of view. Each perspective has something to offer and provides us with insight into why people buy what they buy. At the same time, each approach gives something up when compared to the others and paints only part of the picture. The physiological, psychological, and economic theories present a rich description of the role of the individual in decision making but neglect the social side of consumption. The social theories discussed up to this point capture the influence of the group but tend to underemphasize the individual.

None of the approaches considered thus far directly addresses the dynamics of face-to-face interactions that are so much a part of everyday consumption activities. We do not merely process information, make mental decisions, and then act on our decisions. Similarly, we do not act solely out of a social response to pressures. Rather, most of our consumption activities also involve considerable give-and-take and communication with numerous people enroute to the final act of consumption. It is this *interactive process* between a buyer and other individuals that allows our needs and rational decisions to be fulfilled and our social constraints worked out. But physiological, psychological, economic, and social theories only tangentially address the processes involved. We need a framework that depicts consumer behavior in all its complexity. Consumption is in part an individual phenomenon and in part a social phenomenon with both played out in a world of face-to-face encounters.

Social exchange theory represents one way to conceptualize the dynamics in this regard.[13] In Chapter 1, we introduced the notion of exchange and suggested that it serves as the fundamental subject matter of marketing.[14] We outlined the basic dimensions of any exchange and sketched a few general cases. Now we will delve deeper into exchange and relate it to the study of consumption.[15] Later chapters elaborate further on the process.

The Exchange Relationship. Our starting point is a definition of exchange itself. Figure 3-3A presents the common-sense notion of exchange. Two actors, A and B, conduct a transfer of entities, X and Y. A gives up X and receives Y; B gives up Y and receives X. Actually, this is an oversimplification, and some exchanges do not involve a two-way transfer at all.[16] However, because many if not most exchanges exhibit such transfers, we will begin with this conceptualization to keep the presentation simple.

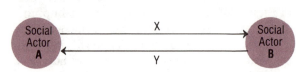

A. Common sense idea of exchange: a transfer of entities, X and Y

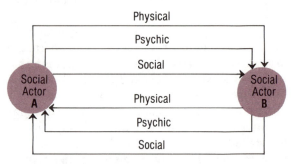

B. Exchanges involving the communication or transfer of physical, psychic, or social entities

C. The meaning of exchange: the phenomena to be explained

Figure 3-3. The elements of exchange

We normally think of the entities that are the objects of exchange in physical terms. Indeed, our automatic reaction might be to jump to the conclusion that X and Y stand for money and a physical product, respectively. Although such things are often the media of exchange, much more "changes hands" than money and a product. As shown in Figure 3-3B, we might think of the things being exchanged in three senses: physical, psychic, and social entities. Money and products are the best examples of physical entities, but physical abuse or affection are examples as well. Psychic entities encompass thoughts, feelings, or moral beliefs. We both give and receive factual information, praise, and ethical directives in our everyday exchanges, for instance. Social entities constitute group phenomena such as power, status, or authority. Something is gained or lost in their transfer with the value resulting from or defined in terms of one's relationship to another.

Overall, we can view exchanges as multifaceted transfers of tangible and intangible entities. Sometimes the transaction involves bundles of physical attributes, psychic experiences, and social consequences. A single entity, such as a product, often exhibits this complexity. At other times, the entities transferred achieve a relative independence or separability, such as occurs when a salesperson provides a physical product, reasons why the product can lead to various benefits, a warranty, an owner's manual, etc. Most entities exchanged have specific implications for the giver and receiver. The things exchanged will be rewarding or punishing to different degrees to the parties. The values of the things exchanged may be sought as ends in themselves or as means to ends. Of course, the parties to any exchange are typically only partially aware of the dimensions of the objects exchanged, their own motives, and the dynamics of the give-and-take.

To develop a theory of marketing in general and consumption in particular based on exchange, we must somehow specify the phenomenon to be explained in a way that lends itself to study and control. Figure 3-3C summarizes one way to conceptualize any exchange relationship as a dependent or endogenous variable. At any point in time, we propose that the process of exchange can be conceived as possessing three descriptors: *outcomes, experiences,* and *actions.* Each of these descriptors refers to states or conditions that can occur to the actors as individuals, as members of a group, or both. Let us explain what we mean by these descriptors.

Outcomes in an exchange refer to physical, social, or symbolic objects or events gained by the actors as a consequence of their relationship. Each person might receive separate outcomes such as a buyer and seller obtain in a consummated exchange. Or the parties might achieve mutual, shared rewards, as well as individual gains. The increase in sales connected to a new promotion campaign and resulting from give-and-take between the marketing and sales departments would be an example of joint outcomes for both. Individuals in both departments might share in the direct profit and social prestige of the successful campaign, as well as the salary regularly earmarked for them for performing their respective roles. In any event, outcomes in an exchange refer to the things the actors get, either as individuals, a unit, or both.

Another important variable representing an exchange is the experiences the actors feel. Experiences are psychological states and consist of affective, cognitive, or moral dimensions. They typically are conveyed symbolically through the objects exchanged, the functions performed by the exchange, or the meaning attributed to the exchange. Again, experiences can be felt by each actor individually, as well as jointly. Joint experiences entail what sociologists term *social constructions* in that both actors in the exchange are thought to produce a mutual, shared understanding as a consequence of their interchanges. The common joy or feeling of accomplishment felt by a husband and wife as they interact in a consumer decision-making process would be an example of a joint experience in this sense.

The final variable with which to represent an exchange is the actions performed by the actors as a product of their interchange. Actions might represent individual choices and responses or joint commitments. Examples include the degree of cooperation, competition, or conflict in the dyad; and the intensity, duration, and timing of actions. For instance, one measure of the degree of conflict in an exchange between a salesperson and customer might be the number of threats transmitted between them in a period of time.

The goal of conceptualizing exchanges as specific outcomes, experiences, or actions is to provide a set of dependent or endogenous variables for study. These are phenomena we hope to understand, explain, predict, and even, at times, control. With these as the subject matter of marketing, efforts can be made to specify explanatory variables (that is, independent variables, determinants, or antecedents that help us understand, explain, predict, or control outcomes, experiences, or actions of parties in an exchange) and relate these to exchange in an overall theory.

The Antecedents to Exchange. To explain exchange (i.e., variation in individual or joint outcomes, experiences, or actions), we will hypothesize four classes of determinants: social influence, social actor characteristics, third-party effects, and situational contingencies (see Figure 3-4). Each is briefly described below.

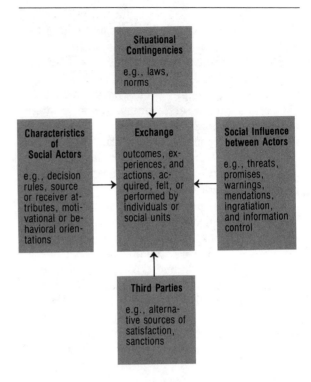

Figure 3-4. The determinants of exchange

Social Influence between the Actors. The parties to an exchange satisfy individual needs and reach mutual accommodations through a process of social negotiation. This process involves a give-and-take; the parties communicate their desires, intentions, and purposes; and adjustments in offers, counteroffers, and standards of acceptability are made throughout the process until an agreement to exchange or not is made. The process occurs both covertly and overtly, and the parties may or may not be fully aware of its dynamics or their role and outcomes during the negotiations.

The process of social negotiation involves a communication of rewarding or punishing stimuli through one or more of four modes of influence: threats, promises, warnings, or mendations.[17] A *threat* is made when one social actor sends a message conveying a punishment to the other social actor and the message is conveyed under conditions wherein the sender can actually mediate the punishment and no attempt is made to conceal the influence. For example, if a manufacturer were to state in a communication to a retail customer, "If you reduce the shelf space devoted to Brand X, then we will discontinue our promotion credit to you," then he or she would be employing a threat mode of influence. In contrast, a *promise* is made when one social actor sends a rewarding message to another such that the sender actually mediates the reward and no attempt is made to conceal the influence. The statement by a manufacturer, "We will give you a promotion credit of 5 percent of sales," would be an example of a promise in the above sense.

Threats and promises (and all modes of social influence) can be contingent/noncontingent, request-specific/nonspecific, and consequences-specific/nonspecific. A contingent message uses the if-then form to specify what will happen to the receiver of the message under certain conditions. The noncontingent message omits the conditions and relies solely on an assertion of intent or opinion on the part of the sender. The threat example in the previous paragraph is a contingent one, while the promise example is noncontingent. Further, the threat example is relatively specific as to its request and consequences.

A *warning* is said to occur when a sender communicates that a punishment will befall a target under certain conditions. The sender does not attempt to conceal his or her influence attempt under this mode; however, unlike the threatener, the sender of a warning does not directly mediate the punishing stimulus. Rather, either an external agent is involved and/or the punishment is contingent on the action or inaction of the target. The use of fear advertisements by the American Heart Association is perhaps the best example of a warning in the sense defined here.

A *mendation* is said to occur when a sender implies that a reward will accrue to a target should he or she act or fail to act. Again, the sender does not attempt to conceal his or her influence attempt; however, unlike the promiser, the sender of a mendation does not directly mediate the reward, but a third party and/or the target does. An example of the mendation mode of influence might be the following statement made by a salesperson to a potential customer: "If you buy machine Y before July 1, when the law changes, then you will be able to realize the special income tax credit."

Threats and promises usually imply the potential for the exercise of power by one actor over another. Warnings and mendations, in contrast, are perhaps best exemplified by the general mode of influence termed *persuasion*, where the element of force or coercion is presumed absent and the ideal of "free choice" is approached. Behavior in the marketplace is, of course, characterized by all four modes in varying degrees. These modes share the attribute that influence attempts are not concealed.

Influence can also be employed when the source of communication desires to hide his or her attempts. Under these conditions, the clandestine influence takes on a distinct manipulatory flavor. Reinforcement control, information control, and ingratiation are three types of influence in this sense. In later chapters, we will develop the processes of social influence in marketing in greater detail. A final point to note with respect to the use of social influence between actors in an exchange is that the impact of any mode depends on the characteristics of the social actors as well as the situation surrounding the exchange. It is to these that we now turn.

Characteristics of the Social Actors. The starting point for any exchange is the needs of the individual actors, the values of things that can be exchanged, and the give-and-take reflected in the social influence comprising the negotiations. The exact course of any exchange, including its final outcome, will depend, in part, on the unique interface of the characteristics of the actors (see Figure 3-4).

Two kinds of characteristics seem salient. The first is termed *source/receiver characteristics* and has been studied extensively by communication researchers.[18] Source characteristics include such variables as attraction, expertise, credibility, prestige, trustworthiness, or status. Receiver characteristics comprise such variables as self-confidence, background attributes, cognitive styles, and certain personality traits. In general, source and receiver characteristics influence exchanges through their ability to authenticate or deauthenticate the subjective expected utility associated with communicated threats, promises, warnings, or mendations.[19] For example, one study indicates that the greater the perceived similarity of a salesperson (a source characteristic akin to attraction), the greater the probability of purchase.[20] The premise is that promises or mendations from a similar salesperson were believed more, while those from the dissimilar salesperson were discounted. In a parallel manner, other source/receiver characteristics interact with the modes of social influence to affect evaluative behavior and compliance.

A second kind of social actor characteristic influencing exchanges is the interpersonal orientation of the actors. *Interpersonal orientations* refer to the degree of motivational predispositions or behavioral tendencies the actors bring to an exchange. Research in bargaining and negotiation suggests that the conduct and outcomes of the exchange depend on the degree to which the parties (1) have a positive interest in the welfare of the other as well as one's own welfare; and (2) are oriented toward equitable or joint gain as opposed to doing better than the other or maximizing individual gain, regardless of what or how the other does; and/or (3) are sensitive to interpersonal aspects of relationships with the other.[21]

Some individuals come to an exchange with cooperative, competitive, malevolent, rigid, responsive, etc., orientations, and these dispositions constrain the course of give-and-take by dictating the conditions for trade. One way in which interpersonal orientations are manifest is through the decision rules followed independently or jointly by the actors. Decision rules include, among others, maximize one's own gain; maximize the gain of the other; maximize the joint gain; take from each according to ability, give to each according to need; and balance outcomes over inputs (equity). A second way interpersonal orientations function is through affective processes such as is reflected in empathy-, altruism-, and charity-motivated decisions. Later chapters will consider further how the characteristics of actors affect face-to-face and mass-market exchanges.

Third-Party Effects. Exchanges are also influenced by the constraints or opportunities afforded by third parties, i.e., social actors outside an exchange but with an actual or potential interest in activities or outcomes of the exchange (see Figure 3-4). Following Thibaut and Kelley,[22] two standards held by the actors in an exchange seem salient. First, the parties to an exchange evaluate potential offers in light of their comparison level (CL), which represents the degree of satisfaction required or desired by the parties. The CL will be a function of the needs of the actors; their history of reinforcement, satiation, or deprivation; and their expectations tempered by the rewards that relevant others receive. Although the CL indicates the amount of benefits the parties would like to obtain in an exchange relationship, the acceptable amount may be less than this, particularly if the rewards available from other sources of satisfaction are lower yet. Thus, each party to an exchange also has a comparison level for alternatives (CL_{alt}), which represents the amount of rewards potentially accessible from a third party. The hypothesis is that, if the level of outcomes actually received by an exchange partner is below one's CL_{alt}, then he or she will leave the relationship for the more satisfying alternative.

Third parties also influence exchanges in two other respects. First, through social comparison processes with third parties, the actors in an exchange arrive at standards of equity with which they evaluate their actual and anticipated outcomes. Second, third parties use social influence (e.g., persuasion, coercion) to affect the outcome of exchanges. Over the years, for example, the executive branch of the federal government has used moral persuasion to induce manufacturers to limit their price increases. Similarly, environmentalists use influence tactics to alter the exchange relationship between polluters and consumers.

Situational Contingencies. Situational contingencies represent another class of determinants facilitating or constraining exchanges (see Figure 3-4). Four categories may be identified: the physical environment, the psychological climate, the social milieu, and the legal setting. The physical environment places limitations on the actions the parties to an exchange can make. Time pressures; the structure and content of issues, alternatives, and actions; and the quantity and quality of lighting, air, and noise are all instances of physical environment constraints affecting exchanges. Closely related to this factor is the psychological environment, which encompasses the level of emotional (e.g., anxiety provoking) and cognitive (e.g., informational) stimuli surrounding an exchange and potentially disrupting it. The social milieu also influences exchanges and includes social class, peer group, and reference group pressures.

This aspect of situational contingencies differs from third-party influences in that the former deals with generalized expectancies that the parties feel and do not necessarily attribute to specific social actors, whereas the latter refers to relatively specific, felt pressures identified with particular social actors (i.e., the third party). Further, the social milieu typically entails internalized compulsions in the form of norms, morals, or ethics, whereas third party influences are more external and tied to the actions of others. Nevertheless, the force of the social milieu is backed often by incentives or sanctions, should one stray from social expectations. Finally, the legal setting constitutes a particularly potent type of influence on exchange. Laws govern, in part, how, when, where, what, and why parties engage in exchange. Regulations function similarly.

Systems of Exchanges. Now that we have an idea of what individual exchanges look like, we can gain a picture of marketing and consumption in a larger sense by tying together two-party exchanges. In principle, it is possible to represent most forms of social behavior as networks or systems of exchanges. Social actors might be individual organizations, groups, institutions, or any aggregate or collective social entity. Of course, social actors can also be people performing individually or in roles. We can study the properties of interconnected actors through the use of exchange and systems concepts. To date, however, marketing scholars have not developed the systems notion of exchange in much depth.[23] We turn now to general systems theory that might serve as a basis for extending the exchange concept to group, organization, and macro social marketing phenomena.

General Systems Theory[24]

Recall from the previous chapter that "process" and "structure" are two important concepts with which we might fruitfully describe any phenomenon. A *process* is either (a) a sequence of steps or stages something passes through or (b) the cause-and-effect relationships producing change in something. A *structure* is a set of entities and the relationships among them at any one point in time. We used the concepts of process and structure to describe individual decision making, but they are general enough to serve as the basis for developing a social theory of marketing and consumption as well. Indeed, the notions of process and structure form the foundation of what we mean by the term *system*. Let us explore the meaning of system and systems theory in greater depth.

Figure 3-5 presents our interpretation of the ideas behind systems theory. Notice first in the center of the diagram that the focal point of systems theory is a system, that is, *a set of processes and the structure that facilitates and constrains those processes.* The processes and structure are shown to be circumscribed by a *system boundary.*

The system boundary is arbitrary, and it is relative to the needs and purposes of the system being considered. For example, when studying the internal operation of a firm, we might define (a) its activities (i.e., its processes) and (b) its rules, procedures, and authority relations (i.e., its internal structure) to be the system of interest and define its boundaries as the physical, legal, or perceived extremities of its operations. However, if we were studying the firm's relationships with its customers, we might define the channel of distribution as the relevant system. This system would be different from that used to describe internal operations and would consist of the sequence of exchange relationships from firm to wholesaler to retailer. The processes involved might include bargaining and negotiation, cooperative acts such as shared research and promotion, and everyday management of the flow

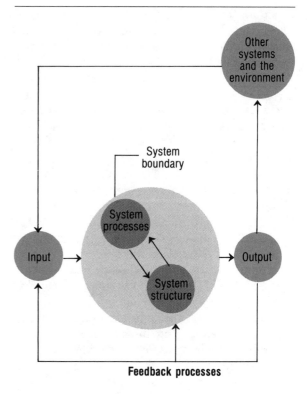

Figure 3-5. An outline of a social system

of physical goods, title, and remuneration. The structure would be defined as the contractual stipulations, informal understandings, and other social constraints particular to the organizations in the channel. The boundary of the channel system would be an imaginary one comprised of each organization and the relationships connecting them. For example, in simplified form, the system and its boundary could be represented by the following diagram:

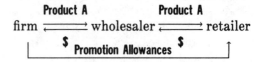

where we have left off the details of the processes and structural relations for clarity. The concept of a system can also be used to describe both larger and smaller social entities than the firm or its channel of distribution. We might, for example, define an industry or market, as well as a family or buying group within an organization, in system terms.

The focal system in Figure 3-5 interfaces with a number of other entities. *Input* to the system represents one important class of stimuli. This may consist of people, material, or information in one form or another. Input is processed within the system and perhaps becomes transformed or discarded. The entire operations performed on input are sometimes called *throughout processes* in the literature. The processes are governed, or at least influenced, by the internal structure of the system. Inputs are combined with matter, time, energy, knowledge, and other activities within the system to produce an *output.* This, too, may be a physical entity such as a product and/or it may be nonphysical such as is found in ideas, knowledge, symbols, and services.

Notice that this system is not a closed one. Rather, it is an *open system* both receiving from and delivering things to its environment. In the process, the possibility exists for the system or its environment or both to change.

In general, the output of the system can have two effects (see Figure 3-5). One is that it can result in *feedback*, which alters either the subsequent input to the system or the processes or structure within the system. For example, a firm might regularly monitor its output (e.g., sales orders) in order to adjust its input (e.g., procurement of raw materials needed to produce sales at current demand). The feedback from output to input is known as an *adjustment feedback process*, which attempts to achieve a desired performance output of the firm through fine-tuning of inputs. Another type of feedback is known as an *adaptive feedback process.* Here information from output is used as a basis for altering the structure and/or processes of the system in order to control future output at a desired level. For instance, a firm might survey the reactions of consumers to its products, find that its products are not living up to quality expectations, and then decide to redesign the product, change quality control operations, and advertise its new product.

The second general effect that the output of a system has is upon other systems or elements in the environment. Any output of a system may function as an input—reward or punishment, promise or threat, liberator or restrainer—for another system. By the same token, other systems can aid or inhibit the operations of the focal system. In general, purposeful systems have the opportunity to act on their environments in order to change them to advantage. But they are at the same time subject to pressures from the environment attempting to change them. We are thus led to a view of the world as one filled with many interdependent systems all of which function in physical, economic, legal, and social environments. At points in the remainder of the chapter and throughout the text, we will have numerous occasions to apply principles from system theory to help us better understand the workings of the marketplace.

Other Social Theories

Although many social theories are relevant to the study of consumption, the following is limited to the most important ones. However, some alternatives might someday deserve further consideration. At the most macro level, structuralism and functionalism offer ways to represent the relationships among large-scale and abstract social entities such as institutions (in the social sense of very broad societal functions). The economy, polity, and cultural value system in any society are examples. Theories of social power and conflict also represent potentially interesting ways to study consumption. Indeed, in later chapters we will consider how these social processes touch our lives through advertising, personal selling, interrelations among firms, and other ways. However, it will be more useful to incorporate processes of power and conflict within role, exchange, and systems theories and the other approaches discussed previously. An eclectic approach such as exchange theory that integrates different explanations of marketing behavior may prove more valid and useful.[25]

Now we turn to a description of knowledge in three areas of marketing dealing with social aspects of consumption: the diffusion of innovations, family decision making, and industrial buyer behavior. As we shall see, each area has been influenced in varying degrees by the social theories we have discussed thus far.

The Diffusion of Innovation

Research into the diffusion of innovations in society was first performed by sociologists and others outside of marketing but has since proved to be a valuable way to view the purchase of products.[26] It is one of the few theories to take into account the behavior of individual decision makers and social influences and at the same time provide a basis for aggregate predictions. We will begin with a description of the theory as it applies to the processes that people go through when deciding to adopt or purchase an innovation or new product. This micro theory incorporates social factors as well. Then we will turn to a macro theory of diffusion that serves as the basis for aggregate predictions of sales over time.

A Micro Model of Diffusion

It is useful to divide the decision process one passes through en route to a final purchase into stages. From the viewpoint of the decision maker, it is possible to think of the stages as follows:[27]

awareness → interest → evaluation → trial → adoption

A person must first be exposed to an innovation in order to become aware of its existence.

Next, assuming that initial perceptions stimulate one's curiosity or arouse one's needs in some way, he or she will develop an interest in the innovation and seek additional information. This will be followed by an assessment of the information to evaluate its need-satisfying potential and other implications for the would-be adopter. A favorable evaluation then leads to trial, and if one's expectations are confirmed, final adoption ensues.

This model provides a nice representation of how people react to an innovation. But researchers have found it lacking in a number of respects.[28] First, it neglects the possibility that a potential adopter might initiate the process rather than become aware solely through external communication. For example, a consumer might have a strong need, and the recognition of a problem could lead to a search for innovations. Second, the possibility and consequences of rejection of an innovation are not considered in the model. Rather, all the model implies is that, if one stage is not fulfilled, the process stops. Rejection prior to or after trial might constitute an important process for study. Third, the model tends to compartmentalize the stages. Evaluation, for instance, does not merely occur at one point in time. Rather, to a certain extent, it occurs on-and-off throughout the process. Fourth, only one sequence is considered, and it is understood to be largely immutable. In reality, some people might dwell on one stage more than on others, certain steps might be conducted automatically or even skipped, and activities other than those shown might be important. An example of the latter is the influence of the opinion of a friend or other knowledgeable person on decision making. Finally, the simple model presented above neglects postadoption consequences such as are exemplified in consumer satisfaction/dissatisfaction reactions.

For these reasons and others, researchers have revised and refined the micro diffusion model along the following lines.[29] As shown in Figure 3-6, the initial stage begins with either problem recognition by a consumer or external communication by a seller or independent source. If the consumer first recognizes a need, then he or she searches for an existing innovation or attempts to persuade a firm to develop and produce the innovation (represented as arrow a). Assuming that the consumer finds a suitable innovation, he or she then develops a deeper awareness of the innovation, gaining knowledge about its characteristics and uses (arrow b). This is not a one-way process. Rather, the consumer will typically interact with various sources of information (arrow c). The sources might be salespersons, third parties such as independent consumer rating organizations or government agencies, or friends and opinion leaders. On the other hand, a consumer will often first learn about an innovation from others. This can happen in one of two ways. One is for a salesperson, third party, friend, or opinion leader to convince the consumer that he or she has a problem (arrow a) and inform him or her of an innovation (arrow e). Again, this will generally involve a back-and-forth interchange, rather than a one-way flow of information (hence, the addition of path f in Figure 3-6).

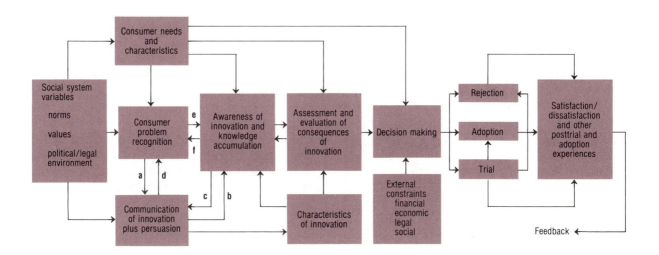

Figure 3-6. The diffusion of innovations: a micro model

The process that is represented in paths d, e, and f is part informational and part persuasional in content. The second way for a consumer to learn of an innovation is through mass communication. For example, an advertisement in a magazine, a brochure, a billboard, or a letter from a seller might serve as a source of awareness. Thus, arrow b also stands for mass communication in addition to face-to-face contact.

Notice that the early stages of processing are influenced by both social system variables and the characteristics of the consumer. The former entail societal-wide norms, values, and political/legal forces. For instance, governmental rules, regulations, tax policies, etc., can aid or inhibit the development of innovations. Personal characteristics of consumers that thwart or facilitate the adoption process include attitudes toward change, venturesomeness, education, contact with sources of information, motivation, risk proneness, and so on.

After one becomes aware of an innovation and gains knowledge about it, an information-processing and evaluation stage operates. Here innovation attributes are assessed for their need-fulfilling qualities, and consequences of adoption are appraised. Actually, evaluations of one sort or another occur throughout the process as the arrows to and from the Assessment and Evaluation box in Figure 3-6 indicate. Notice, too, that the characteristics of the innovation are shown as a separate box influencing the awareness and knowledge-acquisition stages as well as the assessment and evaluation phases. Product attributes represent one of the most important levers of management for influencing adoption, and we will devote the next four chapters to describe how they are designed and how they produce their effects.

Once a person has evaluated an innovation, he or she is in a position to make a decision. The process here follows many of the same activities that we outlined in the previous chapter. Various rules are applied to the information and evaluations made up to this point. In addition, specific external constraints often become important. For example, given a favorable evaluation of a new tractor and sower, a farmer would still have to see if banks would provide credit, if the forecast for demand and economic conditions supported a new purchase, and so on.

Three general decisions might be made. The consumer can reject the innovation outright. Similarly, the consumer might decide to adopt it outright. Or he or she may decide to give it a test and go through a trial period. This, of course, is only possible or appropriate for some products. The outcome of a trial can then lead to either rejection or adoption. In any case, whether an innovation has been rejected, adopted, or is in the trial stage, the consumer will experience different degrees of satisfaction/dissatisfaction with the overall innovation, its features, its performance, and so on. Finally, the outcomes of the process feed back on various stages producing change or reinforcing equilibrium.

Throughout the process of the diffusion of innovation at the micro level, social comparison processes are conducted. A consumer will make comparisons early on to others who have made a purchase he or she is considering. After purchase, comparisons will be made to those who have failed to make a purchase, who have purchased the same product, or who have purchased a competitor's product. Feelings of relative deprivation and/or equity might arouse one's curiosity about an innovation early on and/or lead to a motivation to adopt one later on. Many social exchanges will occur prior to, during, and after the decision process. In a sense, the diffusion of innovations at the micro level can be conceived as a complex individual and social system of relationships. There are many inputs, throughputs, outputs, feedback processes, and interchanges among systems and with the environment. In later chapters, we will elaborate on many of the processes and phenomena outlined in Figure 3-6. We turn now to ways to represent the process at the aggregate level.

A Macro Model of Diffusion

Managers are most interested in the total or aggregate level of adoption of their products over time. Information about the rate and total level of sales are needed to forecast subsequent demand, evaluate how well firm goals are being met and will continue to be met, estimate how much should be spent on advertising and promotion, and so forth.

The diffusion of most products into a market follows a particular pattern. Not everyone purchases the product when it is first made available. Indeed, not everyone is aware of it, some of those who are aware take a wait-and-see attitude, the product may not be available in every location, people might be deciding between the firm's product and a competitor's, some individuals need more time to make a decision, etc. As a consequence, when we look at adoption (i.e., sales) over time, we typically see an S-shaped curve such as that shown in Figure 3-7. As time progresses, sales start slowly, then begin to accelerate, and finally taper off. They may even decline after an initial peak. Considerable empirical evidence supports the S-shaped curve.[30] It should be noted that the S-shaped curve shown in Figure 3-7 is for industry or market sales, not the sales of one firm's product. In later chapters, we will explore the causes, nature, and implications of changing sales over time in greater detail.

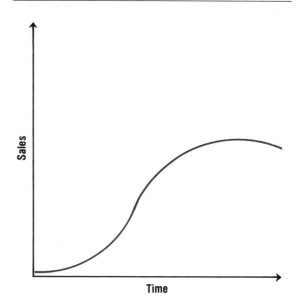

Figure 3-7. The diffusion of an innovation over time: an aggregate response curve

Bass has shown that sales (S) at any one point in time for an S-shaped curve can be computed from the following equation:[31]

$$S_t = pm + (q - p) \, y_t - \left(\frac{q}{m}\right) y^2, \qquad 3\text{-}1$$

where S_t is sales at time t, p is the initial probability of trial, m is the number of potential buyers of the product, q is the rate of diffusion that can be estimated from data, and y_t is the total number of people who have ever bought up to time t. Let us look at each term in the above equation to interpret its meaning. The first term represents the portion of sales due to the innovators who are first to purchase. The second term reflects the additional people who purchase as time goes on. These later adopters might be stimulated to buy as a consequence of word-of-mouth communication they experience in speaking with previous adopters. The final term in the equation might be thought of as a component needed to capture the declining proportion of the market available for sales as time passes. Overall, the market sales generated from the equation can be used as a basis for evaluating demand. We will show how to do this in a subsequent chapter.

To extend the concept of the diffusion of innovation at the aggregate level, we can study the characteristics of adopters to see if classes of consumers exist. The idea is that, whereas it might be impossible or impractical to know how each individual consumer will respond, we might find that a small number of relatively homogeneous groups of consumers exist. Figure 3-8 shows how we might classify adopters into five categories according to when they first try the product.[32] The first persons to adopt a new product are called *innovators*. About 2.5 percent of adopters might be considered innovators, although this and subsequent percentages vary from product to product. Next, a larger group, *early adopters*, tries the product. This might consist of about 13.5 percent of adopters. Then, the majority of adopters enter the market. The *early majority* and *late majority* perhaps comprise 34 percent of adopters each. Finally, much later after introduction of the product, a group termed *laggards* makes its first purchase. This group consists of about 16 percent of all adopters. We should note that Figure 3-8 is a classification of adopters only. As shown in Figure 3-6, the category of nonadopters (i.e., those who reject a product) represents an important group of people for study, too.

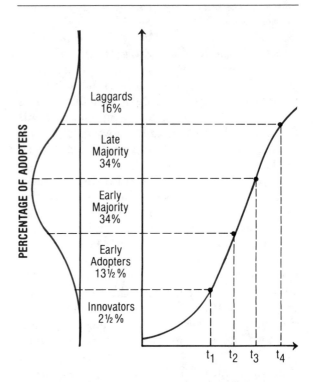

Figure 3-8. The percentage of adopters by category and their contribution to sales over time

What exactly do we know about the characteristics of innovators, later adopters, and nonadopters? Fortunately, quite a bit of research exists.[33] In general, our knowledge to date can be summarized as follows. Innovators (as opposed to noninnovators or nonadopters) tend to perceive less risk in new products and are more intrigued by and interested in them; they are less brand loyal and more easily influenced by deals (e.g., by two-for-one offers, cents-off coupons, free samples); they generally have more contact and exposure to mass media and individuals and are more selective in media choices such as special interest magazines; and they are more integrated socially, belong to more formal and informal groups, and are somewhat more disposed to social mobility upward. At the same time, on average, innovators are younger and have higher incomes, education, and occupational status. Finally, innovators tend to be more inner-directed, to see things in less black-and-white but more discriminating ways, and to act more as opinion leaders or role models for others than noninnovators.

In later chapters, we will consider in more depth the effects of opinion leadership and other forms of personal influence, as well as mass media effects. Also, in later chapters, we will discuss how aggregate and social concepts associated with the characteristics of innovators and noninnovators can be used to identify markets in a procedure known as market segmentation and how one might better forecast demand on their basis.

Family Decision Making

One of the most important determinants of consumption is the family. Family influence on consumption occurs through power relationships among family members, role specialization, exchange and decision-making processes, and subtle socialization processes. Moreover, the family serves as the most immediate social context for making choices and fulfilling one's needs. At the same time, the family is itself a social unit with characteristics and dynamics unique from the individual actions of its members and others in contact with it. A growing body of research exists examining the role of the family in consumer behavior.[34] We will examine three aspects of this research herein: the family life cycle, family decision-making processes, and family unit–family member interactions.

The Concept of a Family Life Cycle[35]

One way to describe a family is in terms of the persons in it and their relationships to each other. The persons will consist of one or more adults, natural parents or otherwise, and one or more dependents. Relationships will entail those associated with kinship and partnership, including the everyday and long-run expectations and behaviors made in relation to each other. This represents a relatively static definition of a family.

A more dynamic description can be achieved through specification of the stages the family and its members go through as time passes. These stages include changes in physical, psychological, economic, and social conditions in the family as it "ages."

Table 3-1 presents one popular model of the family life cycle used in marketing. For convenience, nine more-or-less sequential stages are identified. In the Bachelor Stage, young single people set up their own households. Relative to later stages, men and women in this first stage lead a relatively care-free life and pursue a basically hedonistic life style.

After marriage, men and women enter stage 2, Newly Married Couples. Here the couple continues the pursuit of pleasure but now works out joint activities attempting to arrive at mutual satisfaction. Some of the most important expenditures that the family will ever make are initiated in this stage. Decisions must be made for planned family size, housing, automobiles, durable goods, continued schooling of the adults, and leisure activities.

In stage 3, Full Nest I, the couple has its first child and perhaps adds one or two additional children in the immediate years ahead. Day-to-day expenses skyrocket, very little time for leisure is available, and most products and services purchased are for child care or home maintenance.

TABLE 3-1
A Model of the Family Life Cycle

Stage in Life Cycle	Important Life & Consumption Activities
1. Bachelor stage: Young single people not living at home	Few financial burdens. Fashion opinion leaders. Recreation-oriented. Buy: basic kitchen equipment, basic furniture, cars, equipment for the mating game, vacations.
2. Newly married couples: Young, no children	Better off financially than they will be in the near future. Highest purchase rate and highest average purchase of durables. Buy: cars, refrigerators, stoves, sensible and durable furniture, vacations.
3. Full nest I: Youngest child under six	Home purchasing at peak. Liquid assets low. Dissatisfied with financial position and amount of money saved. Interested in new products. Like advertised products. Buy: washers, dryers, TV, baby food, chest rubs and cough medicines, vitamins, dolls, wagons, sleds, skates.
4. Full nest II: Youngest child six or over	Financial position better. Some wives work. Less influenced by advertising. Buy larger-sized packages, multiple-unit deals. Buy: many foods, cleaning materials, bicycles, music lessons, pianos.
5. Full nest III: Older married couples with dependent children	Financial position still better. More wives work. Some children get jobs. Hard to influence with advertising. High average purchase of durables. Buy: new, more tasteful furniture, auto travel, nonnecessary appliances, boats, dental services, magazines.
6. Empty nest I: Older married couples, no children living with them, head in labor force	Home ownership at peak. Most satisfied with financial position and money saved. Interested in travel, recreation, self-education. Make gifts and contributions. Not interested in new products. Buy: vacations, luxuries, home improvements.
7. Empty nest II: Older married couples, no children living at home, head retired	Drastic cut in income. Keep home. Buy: medical appliances, medical care products that aid health, sleep, and digestion.
8. Solitary survivor, in labor force	Income still good but likely to sell home.
9. Solitary survivor, retired	Same medical and product needs as other retired group; drastic cut in income. Special need for attention, affection, and security.

SOURCE: William D. Wells and George Gubar, ''Life Cycle Concept in Marketing Research,'' *Journal of Marketing Research* 3 (November 1966): 362.
Reprinted with the permission of the American Marketing Association.

The Full Nest II stage, where children are over 6 years old but under about 13, shows a continuation of a life style dominated by the needs of children. Some increase in financial position occurs with a small improvement in discretionary spending. A few women return to the labor force.

In the Full Nest III stage, children are older, and the family has the need and resources to replace durable goods and consider spending on items heretofore not within its budget (e.g., expensive recreation equipment). Still more women return to the labor force as children approach college age and can take care of themselves. Pressures for possible college attendance by children in the years ahead, however, may put financial strains on some families.

Next, children reach the age of 18 or older, and the family enters the Empty Nest I stage. Here, especially for those families for which college expenses are nonexistent or not much of a burden, the family is at the height of its wealth. Money is spent on new cars, luxury goods, or extended vacations. For those families supporting college-bound children, the situation is less fluid, and discretionary expenditures are more like the previous stage.

The Empty Nest II stage is characterized by retirement. Much more money and mental energy is devoted to entertainment and personal health care. Although the family must watch expenditures and hold to a budget, it is perhaps best described as comfortable. The final two stages— Solitary Survivor, in labor force, and Solitary Survivor, retired—show further declines in health and wealth.

The concept of a family life cycle presents an important description of the major constraints and changes undergone by the family as it ages. However, a number of shortcomings should be noted. Most of these stem from the fact that, in the course of attempting to describe generalities, the family life cycle concept has neglected less common, but very real, family occurrences. For example, people who never marry and remain single or single-parent families are not represented in the model. Similarly, sometimes the patterns are not followed as outlined in Table 3-1. The death of a spouse prior to retirement, people who marry late, divorces and remarriages, very large families, births over an extended period of time, and extended and nontraditional family life styles are not taken into account. Perhaps this is to be expected because no model can be perfect. Nevertheless, people who fall outside the bounds of the family life cycle experience different needs and constraints on their consumption activities. And because they comprise large segments of the population, marketers must study their characteristics, if they hope to market effectively to them.

Some research exists employing the family life cycle concept in marketing. Roscoe and Sheth, for example, used the family life cycle concept to segment the market for long-distance telephoning.[36] They found that families consisting of relatively newly married couples or older single individuals spent less than average; families with young children, families with older children, and older couples spent about average; and families with teenagers spent more than average on long-distance calls. Young single individuals in their own households spent considerably less than any of the other family categories. This information was used by the American Telephone and Telegraph Company to design their products, services, and advertisements. In another study, it was found that the overall satisfaction of women engaged in activities associated with the consumption of food varied widely with stage in the life cycle.[37] The middle stages experienced the most dissatisfaction, whereas the early and later stages showed the greatest satisfaction. It appears that the combination of financial and time constraints coupled with the conflicting demands of multiple family members make the task of the meal preparer a difficult one. Marketers must incorporate such findings into their operations by designing products, packages, ads, etc. to better meet the needs of people in each stage in the life cycle.

Family Decision-Making Processes

Consumption by the family can be divided into three phases. The first concerns the processes leading up to actual choices and is termed *product decision making*. This involves the working out of individual preferences, the formation of mutual goals, and joint implementation of action in one form or another. The second phase of consumption refers to the activities undergone in the use of the product and is called *product enactment*. Here the functions of a product are fulfilled, whether this be eating it, in some other way using it up, or merely displaying the product as a symbol. Finally, consumption "ends" with repair, disposal, replacement, or other *post-use feedback* processes. Generally, this entails evaluation and expression of satisfaction/dissatisfaction with the product and its use by family members, as well as initiation of decision making and plans for the future in its regard.

In reality, it is difficult and somewhat artificial to divide consumption into neat phases. Indeed, we might view consumption as an intricate pattern of multiple decisions and family interactions. In the process of working out its needs, the family undergoes an open-ended and continuing integration of consumption with its other activities. The study of separate phases is done as a matter of convenience and as a method for gaining both understanding and a means to influence and anticipate changing consumption patterns.

Sheth has developed a theory of family consumption that goes far in identifying many of the individual and social forces involved.[38] We will focus on two aspects of his theory. First, he finds it useful to categorize consumption into (1) products used by individual family members (e.g., beer and razor blades by the husband; cosmetics by the wife); (2) products used directly by two or more family members (e.g., food products, toiletries, television); and (3) products used indirectly by the household as a unit (e.g., a lawnmower, carpeting, adornments). Each of these categories involves different degrees of interest and involvement on the part of family members. Different constraints and decision processes are associated with each category, too.

Sheth further identifies seven determinants that affect consumption. One's *social class* influences the style of decision making, among other things. Lower and working classes tend to segregate decision making, relying on a division of labor and more-or-less autonomous choices by husband or wife, depending on the product. Higher social classes tend to use more joint decision making, although some specialization still occurs. The *life style* of the family is a second determinant. Tastes in leisure activities play an important role in consumption by directing the allocation of time and money resources. A third influence is the *role orientation* of individual family members. To the extent that individuals see themselves in well-defined roles (e.g., mother makes the meals, father cuts the grass and disciplines the children, children wash dishes, etc.), decision making will tend to be less shared with respect to consumption for goods in general and goods related to one's roles in particular. Role specialization has the effect of creating both experts in an area and vested interests. The fourth determinant of consumption is the *family life cycle*, which we already have discussed. Fifth, the *perceived risk* that individual family members experience in consumption decisions is a constraint on choices. Riskier decisions are usually made jointly more often than nonrisky ones. Similarly, *product importance* is a factor. Decisions that concern only one family member or are of minor importance to all are made more frequently by one member, whereas decisions of a high saliency for all are made jointly more often. Finally, *time* is a constraint on consumption. Things that must be decided quickly are more frequently made by a single decision maker.

In the same way that Sheth's work delineates the *structure* of family decision making, Davis's research and the research of others present a picture of the *processes*.[39] What are the processes? An important one has to do with who makes consumption decisions. As we might expect, the husband makes some decisions, the wife others, and a few are made jointly. At least early studies indicated such a differentiation.[40] However, as we look deeper into the processes, we find that things are not so simple. Ferber and Lee found, for example, that the husband and wife shared family financial management decisions at the outset of marriage, but as time progressed, the wife more and more became responsible for payment of bills and other everyday money management activities.[41] Even with respect to shopping for everyday products which is largely conducted by the wife, the husband has been found to have a direct or indirect influence on many choices.[42] And in decision making for vacations involving the use of airplanes, it has been found that the degree of involvement of husband and wife depends on subissues within the overall decision.[43] For example, the husband tended to originate the idea of a trip, to suggest destinations, and to select the airline. But the actual choice of a final place to go was a shared decision. In his review of nine commercial studies, Davis observes:

> [T]he studies do dispel some of the conventional wisdom that views the world of supermarket purchases to be the exclusive domain of women. Husbands are involved in actual purchasing, although wives clearly predominate. Husbands are aware of brands in many product categories and express brand preferences on questionnaires.[44]

At the opposite end of the product spectrum to supermarket goods are durable goods. Here it has been generally found that a greater degree of joint decision making occurs.[45] Yet, the degree of mutuality varies with the steps in the decision process. In the purchase of automobiles, for instance, husbands and wives shop together, but the husband has the greatest say in the brand choice and has successively diminishing dominance over model and color decisions.[46] Similarly, Davis and Rigaux found that the husband tended to be the most influential in the early phases of decision making for purchase of an automobile.[47] The husband recognized the need for an automobile and thus initiated the decision process. He also had the lion's share of influence over the acquisition of information and choice of manufacturers to consider. However, at the point of choice of automobile features and selection of alternatives, both spouses shared in the decision.

In sum, we see that the family decision-making process depends on the product being considered (e.g., cost, perceived risk, importance, features) and the stage the couple is in with respect to the decision (e.g., problem recognition, information search, evaluation, choice). We know very little about the dynamics of the process, however. That is, how the couple actually comes to an accommodation and achieves mutual satisfaction is little understood. Part of the process is one of interaction, and it is to this that we now turn.

Family Unit–Family Member Interactions

One way to view the family is as a social system comprised of at least three key patterns of interaction. Perhaps the most powerful, yet difficult to study, interaction is the effect of the family on children. The processes involved have been considered under the general subfield of *socialization*.[48] A second fundamental interaction in the family is the effect that children have on the household unit.[49] Finally, the third interaction pattern is one of interpersonal influence consisting of power, conflict, bargaining, cooperation, and other dyadic and small group processes.[50] We will briefly consider research in each area.

Socialization is the process whereby people, and especially children, acquire knowledge, values, goals, attitudes, and skills. Consumer socialization is a special case related to specific knowledge, values, goals, attitudes, and skills in consumption. For example, knowledge about how to shop and the meaning of the price/quality relation are two common instances. In some societies, bargaining skills represent another skill learned through socialization. The processes that lead to this acquisition are thought to arise through interactions children have with parents, siblings, peers, teachers, and the mass media. Learning occurs through modeling, operant conditioning, and even classical conditioning.

Moreover, the processes are often subtle and require years of contact to induce learning. We are only now beginning to learn about the scope of socialization as a force in shaping cognitive, affective, moral, and social development.

The flow of influence in the household is not only one-way. Children also have an effect on the family. We do not have to look far to see the subtle and clever ways that children attempt to get parents to do their bidding. This occurs most frequently perhaps for consumption of candy, breakfast cereals, television programs, and other products with a component of immediate gratification. But it also occurs to a lesser extent in the consumption of everyday household items, durables, and recreation choices. Most studies have focused on the influence of children on the mother. However, we might expect that children also affect the father and siblings. Further, children have a general influence on the family through their access to new ideas and knowledge and their grass roots exposure to changing values, fads, and fashions. These impacts are little understood but represent interesting areas for future research.

The final aspect of family life that deserves consideration, but to date has received little attention, is the role of social interaction processes in family consumption decisions. Power, for example, might reside primarily with one person such that family decisions and outcomes are under the powerholder's control. The bases for power can be thought to reside in the powerholder's ability to reward or coerce or in his or her expertise, attractiveness, authority, or legitimacy.[51] In other instances, family decisions might entail relatively egalitarian encounters where decisions and outcomes are joint products under the influence of all.

Other possibilities exist as well. For instance, implicit or explicit bargains might be struck such that physical, social, and psychic rewards and punishments are exchanged in give-and-take processes in order to achieve desired goods and services. Or the family might develop rules and procedures, role relationships, and authority and responsibility patterns to guide consumption much as formal organizations do. The family represents one of the smallest social systems, and we have much to learn about how it goes about its everyday activities.

Industrial Buyer Behavior[52]

Industrial buying, or institutional or organizational buying as it is sometimes called, may be defined as

the decision-making process by which formal organizations establish the need for purchased products and services, and identify, evaluate, and choose among alternative brands and suppliers.[53]

Industrial buying is both similar to and different from purchasing performed by final consumers. Both involve decision making by one or more people. Both imply psychological and social processes of one form or another. And both are constrained by economic and environmental forces such as costs, market prices, and legal and ethical considerations. However, compared to purchasing by the final consumer, industrial buying exhibits a number of differences. It is performed more for others than for oneself. The process is relatively more formal, tends to contain more participants, and is driven more by functional and economic motives of a larger social entity as opposed to symbolic and personal needs of an individual and his or her partner or dependents. In addition, group processes of power, authority, and consensus tend to be more accentuated and salient in industrial buying.

The discussion of industrial buying will center on four topics. First, we will consider a number of *descriptive frameworks* that provide us with a picture of industrial buying. Second, we will address *individual difference models* that serve as one means to explain industrial buying. Next, *social interaction models* will be scrutinized. Finally, the discussion will close with *macro models.*

Descriptive Frameworks

A number of descriptive frameworks provide rich details of some of the important elements of industrial buying. Let us consider a sample of these.

Task Descriptions. Robinson, Faris, and Wind have identified three classes of tasks performed in industrial buying: *the new task, modified rebuy,* and *straight rebuy.*[54] In the new task circumstance, the organization faces a need or problem with which it has had little or no experience. Therefore, it must seek considerable information about product attributes, prices, alternative vendors, and other issues. The modified rebuy situation is one in which an existing product or service must be replaced and new information about the item of purchase, terms of sale, or sellers is desired. In the straight rebuy case, the organization merely reorders a product or service from an existing supplier or close substitute. The reorder is typically performed routinely or automatically with little additional effort or search for information. Figure 3-9 illustrates the three buying tasks and how they might occur within a single firm for the purchase of drills.

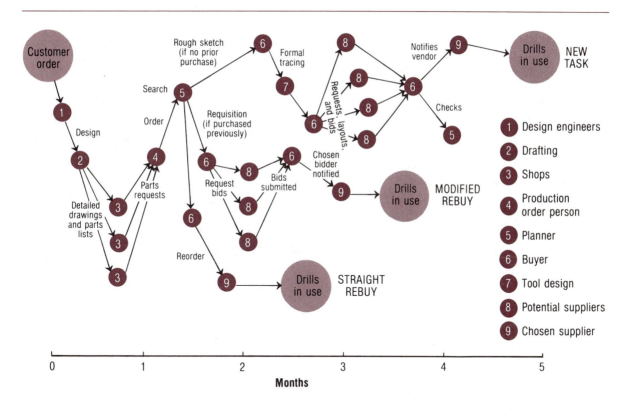

Figure 3-9. A decision-making network for the purchase of industrial drills

SOURCE: Patrick J. Robinson, Charles W. Faris, and Yaram Wind, *Industrial Buying and Creative Marketing* (Boston: Allyn & Bacon, Inc., 1967), p. 33.

The task descriptions provided by Robinson et al. show us that industrial buying is more than the clerical function that many authors had earlier regarded it. However, it neglects to include such issues as the magnitude or importance of the purchase to the buyer, the complexity of the product or service, and the relationship between buyer and seller (e.g., the experience, dependency, and size of parties). These issues influence the process of buying and need to be incorporated into any comprehensive description of tasks. To date, no framework incorporates all of the above elements.

A related issue concerns the decision maker. Exactly who is the decision maker? In some instances, a single individual such as the purchasing agent, buyer, or materials manager will make the decision. But in others, many people may be involved. Buzzell, for example, discovered that 14 people were involved in the purchase of an air compressor.[55] Figure 3-10 shows the decision-making network for the purchase of a test stand for automotive engines. Notice that 5 different people were involved in the decision within the firm: the product research supervisor, the section head of the mechanical division, the group head of the mechanical division, the technical buyer, and the business manager. In contrast to the situation of the purchase of drills shown in Figure 3-9, where the buyer acted relatively alone after a need was recognized in the firm, the purchase of the test stand involved more emphasis on group decision making among the technical buyer, group head of the mechanical division, and others. One can imagine that for very costly, complex, and essential goods and services, many people might be involved, and the process could be quite intricate and time consuming.

The above examples point to the need to study the stages or processes in industrial buying in order to gain a valid picture of how decisions are actually made. Let us turn to the literature in this regard.

Process Descriptions. Perhaps the earliest statement on the stages that transpire in industrial buying was provided by Cyert, Simon, and Trow.[56] These authors identified three primary processes in industrial buying: common processes (i.e., the routine, recurring activities that pervade one or more stages in decision making), communication processes (i.e., information transfer and flow among people and groups), and problem-solving processes (i.e., search and evaluation of alternatives potentially fulfilling a need). Webster went further and proposed more stages, integrating them somewhat more fully than Cyert et al.[57] His model suggested four activities: problem recognition, assignment of responsibilities for purchase tasks, information processing including search and evaluation of alternative products and vendors, and choice procedures among alternatives.

One of the most fully developed models of the steps in industrial buying is the eight-phase BUYGRID model of Robinson et al.:

1 Anticipation or recognition of a problem and general solution

2 Determination of desired attributes of product or service potentially solving problem

3 Further description of product/service attributes and quantity needed

4 Search for potential sources of supply and preliminary evaluation of their suitability

5 Acquisition and initial analysis of offerings from suppliers

6 Evaluation of offerings and selection of supplier(s)

7 Selection of an order routine

8 Performance feedback and evaluation.[58]

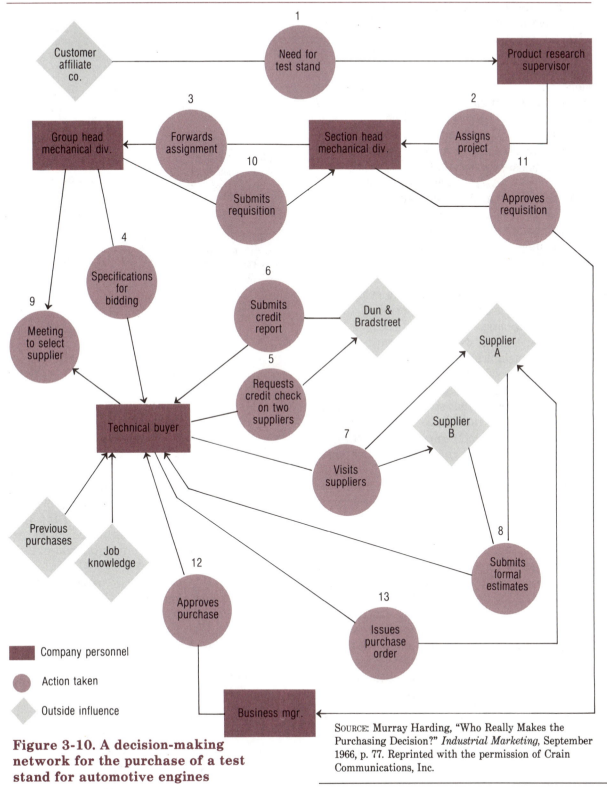

Figure 3-10. A decision-making network for the purchase of a test stand for automotive engines

Legend:
- Company personnel
- Action taken
- Outside influence

Diagram labels:
- Customer affiliate co.
- 1 Need for test stand
- Product research supervisor
- 2 Assigns project
- Section head mechanical div.
- 3 Forwards assignment
- Group head mechanical div.
- 10 Submits requisition
- 11 Approves requisition
- 4 Specifications for bidding
- 9 Meeting to select supplier
- 6 Submits credit report
- Dun & Bradstreet
- Supplier A
- 5 Requests credit check on two suppliers
- Technical buyer
- Supplier B
- 7 Visits suppliers
- Previous purchases
- Job knowledge
- 8 Submits formal estimates
- 12 Approves purchase
- 13 Issues purchase order
- Business mgr.

SOURCE: Murray Harding, "Who Really Makes the Purchasing Decision?" *Industrial Marketing*, September 1966, p. 77. Reprinted with the permission of Crain Communications, Inc.

It is hypothesized that the importance of each step and the time spent executing it will vary with the type of decision faced by a firm. For example, the new-task situation will generally encompass all or most of the stages and require more time per stage than other tasks. The straight rebuy might involve only a few stages and demand relatively less time per stage. Backhaus and Gunter propose an even more complex process model with 12 phases, but we will not discuss its details here.[59]

The description of tasks tells us what decision makers do; the description of the decision makers involved shows us who makes the decisions; and the description of stages or processes indicates how the decisions are made. However, none of the research described heretofore provides an explanation of why organizations buy what they buy. What is needed is a description of the forces that constrain and shape decision tasks and stages. That is, we need to identify the independent variables.

Descriptions of Independent Variables. One of the most thorough descriptions of the factors influencing industrial buying is provided by Webster and Wind.[60] These researchers have developed a framework consisting of four major determinants of organizational buying: the environment, the internal structure of the organization, the network of interpersonal relationships among people in the organization, and the psychology of the individual decision makers. Figure 3-11 summarizes these forces on buying. Notice that the set of individuals engaged in organizational buying is known as the *buying center*. The buying process and its outcomes are believed to be a function of social interactions among buying center members who act according to their own roles as constrained by organizational and task expectations. The actions of buying center members is further influenced by environmental contingencies and their own needs, skills, and effort.

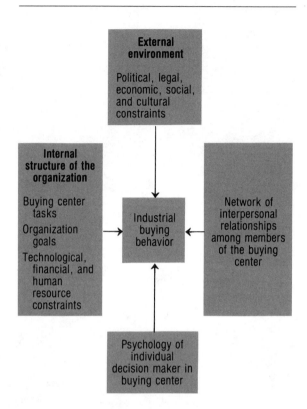

Figure 3-11. A summary of some of the determinants of organizational buying identified by Webster and Wind

Ultimately, Webster and Wind seem to take the position that organizational buying may be reducible to a theory of the actions of individual buying center members as played out in the organizational and environmental context at hand.

The Webster and Wind perspective has done much to help us understand the elements and structure of organizational buying. But as with any pioneering work, much of the detail about cause-and-effect mechanisms has been left out. We turn now to other contributions, which provide some of the details.

Individual Difference Models

Given that it is people who make decisions, it should come as no surprise that many authors have attempted to develop theories of industrial buying predicated on the characteristics of the buyer(s). The earliest explanations of buying saw it as a rational activity motivated by the goal of minimizing price. Later, rational models added quality, services, delivery arrangements, and assurance of supply to the list of motives shaping purchase choices. The decision maker was viewed as an information processor who weighed input from persons in the firm, salespeople, and catalogs to arrive at a final decision. The buyer was portrayed in a rather passive sense, however.

As researchers began to study industrial buying, they discovered that the process was active and involved nonrational and even emotional processes, as well as rational decision making.[61] For example, the fear of making an error, purchasing an inferior product, or looking foolish is sometimes a reaction that buyers have. Similarly, because every product or service entails trade-offs and lost opportunities, most decisions may involve an element of perceived risk along with the recognition of benefits. We thus see that the perception of rewards and costs by the individual decision maker is a key determinant of industrial buying.

Sheth has developed an intricate model of industrial buying based on the individual characteristics of buyers and the stimuli facilitating and constraining their choices.[62] The central element of the model lies in the expectations of people involved in the purchase. Sheth defines expectations as "the *perceived* potential of alternative suppliers and brands to satisfy a number of explicit objectives in any particular buying decision."[63] One's expectations are influenced by one's background (e.g., education, role, life style) and the feedback received from previous purchases.

Perceptual distortion of information might also play a role. The expectations then serve as input to the buying process along with product-specific factors (e.g., time pressure, type of purchase, perceived risk) and company-specific factors (e.g., organization size, orientation, and centralization). Sheth views the buying process itself as either an autonomous or joint decision, where the latter encompasses conflict resolution. Finally, the choice of a brand or supplier is thought to be additionally influenced by situational factors such as economic conditions (e.g., recession), strikes, organizational realignments, price changes, and new product introductions.

Although the model of industrial buying proposed by Sheth is based primarily on the psychology of the buyer, it does point the way for the need to take into account interpersonal relations and the effect that the social environment has on decision making. We turn now to a discussion of each topic in turn.

Social Interaction Models

Recently, authors have argued that it may be shortsighted to rely on theories of buying based only on the characteristics of decision makers or on the steps they go through enroute to a choice.[64] Instead, to fully account for why people buy what they buy, it is claimed that one must examine the social relationships within which buyers are engaged. This involves examination of the exchange relationships the buyer is a part of, including those with sellers, supervisors, peers, members of the buying center, and others within the organization. Exchanges might involve elements of cooperation, conflict, power, bargaining, and so on. This approach to the study of industrial buying is a relatively new one, and very little research to date exists. We will mention some of the studies touching upon this social exchange view of industrial buying.

In a study of the purchase of a large computer, Pettigrew found that the process was a political one in the sense that some members of the buying center acted as gatekeepers controlling information access, and the process involved different degrees of power and influence among actors.[65] Further insight into the interactive processes that people experience within the organization can be found in Patchen.[66] He found that it is difficult to describe the bases of power in terms of reward, expert, referent, coercive, and other common types of power. Rather, he discovered that subjective judgments by a panel of experts was a better means to assess the relative power of people in the purchasing decision. Lehmann and O'Shaughnessy present further evidence, albeit indirect, that political processes are a factor in at least some purchasing decisions within firms.[67]

When we turn to interactions between salespeople and buyers, a somewhat different picture emerges. Busch and Wilson found that the referent power of a salesperson led to influence over customers, whereas expert power was a stronger determinant of perceived trust by the customer.[68] Presumably, trust will lead to greater influence. The authors defined referent power as perceived attraction between salesperson and customer and expert power as perceived knowledge, information, and skill of the salesperson.

All of the interaction studies cited thus far use psychological processes to explain the social relationships. That is, they are not true social theories but rather reduce the social dimensions to the psychology of the actors involved. One study that examined the social aspects of organizational buying was conducted by Kiser, Rao, and Rao,[69] who found that buyers and sellers achieved the greatest outcomes when both parties focused on the relation as one of mutual gain rather than conflict or a win-lose encounter. This finding that an orientation of mutuality leads to greater joint rewards than one of individuality is a common one in the social psychology literature.[70] In later chapters, we will consider the salesperson-customer relation and other social interactions in greater detail. For now, we wish only to note that a social interaction approach is a fruitful way to study organization buying processes.

Macro Models[71]

We have seen that industrial buying can be usefully described in terms of the number of decision makers, the tasks they perform, the sequence of steps they go through as they perform their tasks, and the constraints that shape the conduct of those steps. At the same time, we found that it is helpful to construe industrial buying from the perspective of the psychological characteristics of the decision maker (e.g., motives, information processing) and the social interactions in which they engage (e.g., in terms of interpersonal exchange, conflict, and power). All of these points of view take a relatively micro orientation. We turn now to a more macro analysis that considers the effects of the environment and organization structure on industrial buying.

Johnston has developed a model of industrial buying based on the buying center as the unit of analysis and its relationship to the larger organization in which it is situated.[72] Figure 3-12 presents an outline of the central components in Johnston's model. Let us begin our description of his model with a consideration of the buying center in the middle. Johnston asks us to think of the buying center as a communication network linking all the individuals in the firm concerned with the purchase of goods and services. He represents the dynamics of buying through five constructs: vertical involvement, lateral involvement, integrative complexity, task differentiation, and centrality of purchasing manager.

Figure 3-12. The central variables in Johnston's model of industrial buying behavior

Vertical involvement refers to the number of levels in the organization communicating with or exerting influence upon members of the buying center. In some organizations or for some decisions in most firms, only one or two levels are involved in any particular decision. For instance, the purchase of a new desk might involve only an executive and a purchasing agent. On the other hand, the purchase of a computer might involve the chief executive officer, top management, policy level managers, and operating level managers, as well as the purchasing managers.

Lateral involvement concerns the number of departments and divisions in communication with or exerting influence upon members of the buying center. These departments and divisions can be at any level in the organization. Whereas vertical involvement provides an indication of the degree of hierarchical-authority participation in buying, lateral involvement reflects the diversity of total participation.

Integrative complexity, in contrast, is the amount of interconnection among members of the buying center. It is measured as the number of actual communication links in a buying center to the total possible and thus is a number varying from 0 to 1

with 0 indicating lack of complexity and 1 indicating maximum complexity. For example, Figure 3-13 shows two four-person buying center networks. In Figure 3-13A, integrative complexity is low: $4 \div 12 = .33$; in Figure 3-13B, it is high: $8 \div 12 = .67$. One expects communication and the diffusion of ideas to increase as the integrative complexity of the buying center increases.

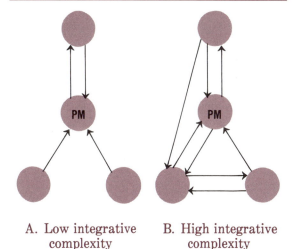

A. Low integrative complexity   B. High integrative complexity

Figure 3-13. Integrative complexity in a four-person buying center

PM = Purchasing Manager

The fourth buying center descriptor is *task differentiation*. This is simply the total number of people involved in the buying decision process. Finally, we may characterize the buying center in terms of the *centrality of the purchasing manager*. This is measured by the amount of communication the purchasing manager sends and receives. In Figure 3-13A, the purchase manager (PM) is more central than the PM in Figure 3-13B, although the difference is slight.

Johnston used the five buying center constructs as dependent variables in order to obtain insight into how the buying center is structured and how it responds to organizational and purchase-situational forces. He was interested in the effects of organization structure and the characteristics of the purchase context on the number of people involved in buying, the functions they perform, and how they are organized. As shown in Figure 3-12, four structural aspects of the firm and the three attributes of the purchase situation are hypothesized to influence the buying center.

Looking first at the impact of *organization structure*, Johnston discovered the relationships summarized in Figure 3-14. For capital-equipment purchases, only size of the firm and formalization have a statistically significant effect on the buying center (indicated with solid lines in Figure 3-14A). The larger the firm, the greater the integrative complexity. That is, large firms led to less interconnectiveness among buying center members—opposite to that suggested by theory. Perhaps large firms pursue greater specialization with respect to the purchase of capital equipment. Figure 3-14A also shows that the greater the formalization in the firm (i.e., the greater the use of written communication versus verbal), the less the vertical involvement of multiple levels in the purchasing decision. In effect, written forms of communication reflect the input and sanctions of management and thereby reduce the need for their direct involvement in purchasing decisions. Three of the arrows drawn in Figure 3-14A are shown as

dashed lines to indicate that, although Johnston found some evidence for the relationships, they were not statistically significant at the proper level to provide a definitive conclusion.

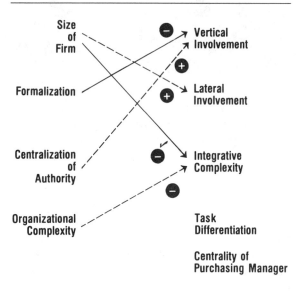

A. Capital-equipment purchases

Figure 3-14. The results of Johnston's investigation of the effects of organizational structure on the buying center

For industrial-services purchases, more relations were statistically significant (see solid lines in Figure 3-14B). Notice first that, as the size of the firm increases, the number of people involved in the decision process (i.e., task differentiation) increases. Next, as formalization increases, vertical involvement decreases. Centralization of authority (i.e., the degree to which power is centralized in the firm) and complexity (i.e., the number of separate departments and divisions) both positively influence vertical involvement. Finally, organizational complexity is shown to have a positive effect on lateral involvement.

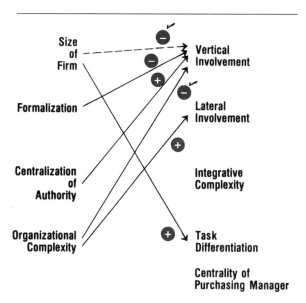

B. Industrial services purchases

Key
+ = positive effect
− = negative effect
↙ = opposite to hypothesis

complexity (see Figure 3-15A). Similarly, the novelty of the capital equipment purchase was shown to positively affect integrative complexity and task differentiation. Finally, the complexity of the purchase was found also to positively influence integrative complexity. For industrial-services purchases (see Figure 3-15B), purchase novelty was found to positively affect vertical involvement, integrative complexity, and task differentiation. Purchase complexity positively influenced lateral involvement and task differentiation.

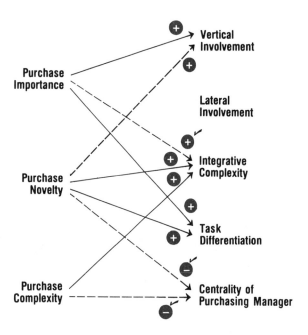

A. Capital-equipment purchases

Figure 3-15. The results of Johnston's investigation of the effects of purchase situation attributes on the buying center

The impact of *purchase situation attributes* on industrial buying can be seen in Figure 3-15. For capital equipment purchases, the importance of the purchase relative to other purchases was found to positively affect both vertical involvement and integrative

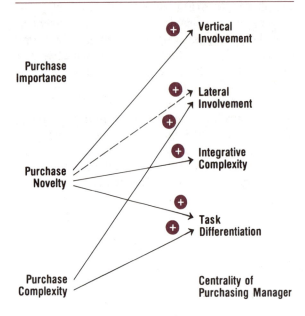

B. Industrial services purchases

Key
+ = *positive effect*
− = *negative effect*
✔ = *opposite to hypothesis*

Figure 3-15 cont.

Johnston's study helps us understand how macro phenomena influence the structure of the industrial buying process. It thus complements the individual difference and social interaction approaches that focus more on the activities that make up the process. Other studies that examine the effects of the environment on industrial buying can be identified but will not be discussed in this text.[73]

Summary

Consumer behavior is a highly complex phenomenon, and there is no single or correct way to study it. Rather, as the previous chapter and the present one demonstrate, we must examine consumption as both an individual, psychological process and a social one. Only in this way can we begin to grasp why and how people and organizations purchase and consume what they do.

In this chapter, we considered a number of ways in which consumption is influenced by social forces. We began with four means of describing how group influences affect the individual: social comparison processes, relative deprivation, equity theory, and role theory (see Figure 3-1). The theory of *social comparison processes* suggests that we have a need to compare our abilities, attributes, and outcomes to others' and that favorable comparisons are comforting whereas unfavorable ones are discomforting. In a somewhat similar manner, but in greater detail, the theory of *relative deprivation* maintains that unfavorable comparisons to others (or a reference group or norm) leads to efforts to increase our abilities, outcomes, protest activities, or self-criticism. *Equity theory* further proposes that we compare the ratio of our outcomes to inputs to the ratio of outcomes to inputs for a relevant other. If the ratios are equal, we perceive an equity balance and experience no tension. If the ratios are unequal, we perceive inequity, experience tension, and attempt to restore balance. The latter is done through efforts to increase our inputs or outputs, through cognitive distortion or reinterpretations, or through other actions. *Role theory* goes one step further than the previous three theories in that greater emphasis is placed on the relationships a person has in his or her social network. These relationships are represented as the expectations a person has of his or her own behavior relative to specific others and the expectations these others have of the person. As shown in Figure 3-2, a person typically has many roles originating from multiple individuals, groups, and organizations. The roles, in turn, influence how the person behaves.

A somewhat more active way to think of the social aspects of consumption is through *exchange theory.* We saw that our social relations with others involve the mutual transfer of physical, psychic, and social entities (see Figure 3-3). Indeed, our relationships can be described in terms of the shared meanings of the parties. These consist of outcomes, experiences, and actions acquired, felt, or performed by the individuals in an exchange or as represented through the social unit formed by the transaction. The shared meanings in the exchange were shown, in turn, to be affected by situational contingencies, third parties, social influence between the actors in the exchange, and their personal characteristics (see Figure 3-4).

Next, we introduced the notion of *general systems theory.* As shown in Figure 3-5, any system can be characterized through its internal structure and processes, the input that impacts on the structure and processes, the output that is produced, the feedback that is monitored, and other systems and environments that impinge upon the system. In later chapters, we will use the systems concept to represent product planning, channels of distribution, and other marketing phenomena.

The chapter turned then to an aggregate representation of consumption known as the *diffusion of innovation.* At the micro level, the diffusion of innovation begins with the recognition of a problem or need by a consumer (see Figure 3-6). This recognition might originate internally from the decision-making activities of a consumer or externally from a seller of innovations, contact with users, publicity in a magazine, and so on. Problem recognition is followed, in turn, by awareness, knowledge accumulation, assessment of innovations, decision making, trial, adoption or rejection, and finally satisfaction or dissatisfaction and its feedback. At the macro level, the adoption (i.e., sales) of innovations can be represented through mathematical models, and aggregates of adopters and non-

adopters can be divided into meaningful classes. This, in turn, provides a basis for forecasting and planning, as we shall see in subsequent chapters.

Family decision making was the topic of the next section of the chapter. We began by describing the stages that families typically pass through as they age. This was called the *family life cycle.* As detailed in Table 3-1, nine stages can be identified, ranging from young singles, through married couples with and without children, all the way to sole survivor in the final years of one's life. Among other uses, marketers employ the concept of the family life cycle to identify groups of consumers with different needs. A second topic under family consumption was *decision-making processes.* Here we pointed out the phases family members go through when solving consumption problems. Then we turned to the *interactions* family members undergo in decision making. The central topics considered were socialization, the effect of children on the household, and interpersonal influence processes such as power, conflict, bargaining, and cooperation.

The chapter closed with a consideration of *industrial buying behavior.* We discovered that organizations make consumption decisions, too, but in a manner different than final consumers. The process involves many individuals, is partly rational and partly nonrational, undergoes many steps, is influenced by the psychology of decision makers in interaction with each other and sellers, and is subject to organizational structure and environmental constraints.

Now that we have presented the major ideas and research findings in consumer behavior, we are in a position to turn to the activities that managers pursue to translate theories into practice. In the next two chapters, we will concentrate on how products are designed and developed to satisfy consumer needs. Then each succeeding chapter will address further marketing practices related to the four Ps: product, promotion, pricing, and place (i.e., distribution).

Questions and Problems for Discussion

1 What is a *social theory* of consumer behavior and what special problems does it pose?

2 Briefly describe the elements and operations of the theories of social comparison processes, relative deprivation, equity, and role relations. How do they function in consumer behavior?

3 Most social theories tend to emphasize either the individual or the social context. A few, such as *exchange theory*, attempt to focus on the *interactions* between people. Describe the general structure of any exchange and the determinants shaping exchanges.

4 What is *general systems theory* and how does it relate to marketing?

5 Discuss the operation of the micro model of the diffusion of innovations. What are the macro implications of the diffusion of innovations?

6 What is the concept of a *family life cycle* and how might a marketing manager use it?

7 Discuss the processes and peculiarities of family decision making.

8 How does industrial (or organizational) buying behavior differ from consumer buying behavior?

9 Describe the elements and functioning of industrial (or organizational) buying behavior in greater detail.

NOTES

1. The following discussion only briefly touches on the social theories dealing with the effects of mass and face-to-face communication on consumer behavior. These topics are covered in greater depth in later chapters. Also, the most abstract and grand social theories are not dealt with here. Although offering promise for the study of consumer behavior, they lack sufficient development to warrant their inclusion at this time. We will, however, introduce macro social concepts to a limited extent whenever appropriate in this chapter and later in the text. Readers interested in macromarketing, as this area of the field has come to be known, should consult the *Journal of Macromarketing* and the yearly proceedings of the macromarketing conference published by the University of Colorado, School of Business Administration.

2. Leon Festinger, "A Theory of Social Comparison Processes," *Human Relations* 7 (March 1954): 117-40; and J. Suls and R. Miller, *Social Comparison Processes* (Washington, D.C.: Hemisphere, 1977).

3. S. Morse and K. J. Gergen, "Social Comparison, Self-Consistency, and the Concept of Self," *Journal of Personality and Social Psychology* 16 (1970): 148-56, and S. R. Wilson and L. A. Brenner, "The Effects of Self-Esteem and Situation upon Comparison Choices during Ability Evaluation," *Sociometry* 34 (1971): 381-97.

4. A. Bandura and R. Walters, *Social Learning and Personality Development* (New York: Holt, Rinehart & Winston, 1963); M. Deutsch and R. M. Krauss, *Theories in Social Psychology* (New York: Basic Books, 1965), p. 67; A. Bandura, *Principles of Behavior Modification* (New York: Holt, Rinehart & Winston, 1969); and A. Bandura, *Social Learning Theory* (Englewood Cliffs, N.J.: Prentice-Hall, 1977).

5. S. Schachter and J. E. Singer, "Cognitive, Social, and Physiological Determinants of Emotional State," *Psychological Review* 69 (1962): 379-99.

6. For an introduction to relative deprivation theory, see S. Stouffer, et al., *The American Soldier* (Princeton, N.J.: Princeton University Press, 1949); W. Runciman, *Relative Deprivation and Social Justice* (London: Routledge and Kegan Paul, 1966); T. Pettigrew, "Social Evaluation Theory: Convergence and Applications," in D. Levine, ed., *Nebraska Symposium on Motivation* (Lincoln: Univ. of Nebraska Press, 1967), pp. 241-318; R. M. Williams, "Relative Deprivation," in L. Coser, ed., *The Idea of Social Structure* (New York: Harcourt Brace Jovanovich, 1975); T. D. Cook, F. Crosby, and K. Hennigan, "The Construct Validity of Relative Deprivation," in J. Suls and R. Miller, eds., *Social Comparison Processes* (Washington, D.C.: Hemisphere, 1977), pp. 307-34.

7. H. Helson, *Adaption-Level Theory* (New York: Harper & Row, 1964).

8. Arch G. Woodside, "Informal Group Influence on Risk Taking," *Journal of Marketing Research* 9 (May 1972): 223-25.

9. Daniel L. Johnson and I. Robert Andrews, "Risky-shift Phenomenon as Tested with Consumer Products as Stimuli," *Journal of Personality and Social Psychology* 20 (August 1971): 328-35, and Arch G. Woodside, "Is There a Generalized Risky Shift Phenomenon in Consumer Behavior?" *Journal of Marketing Research* 2 (May 1974): 225-26.

10. M. Venkatesan, "Experimental Study of Consumer Behavior Conformity and Independence," *Journal of Marketing Research* 3 (November 1966): 385; James E. Stafford, "Effects of Group Influence on Consumer Brand Preferences," *Journal of Marketing Research* 3 (February 1966): 68-75; Robert E. Witt, "Informal Social Group Influence on Consumer Brand Choice," *Journal of Marketing Research* 6 (November 1969): 473-76; and Robert E. Witt and Grady D. Bruce, "Purchase Decisions and Group Influence," *Journal of Marketing Research* 7 (November 1970): 533-35.

11. See, for example, J. S. Adams, "Toward an Understanding of Inequity," *Journal of Abnormal and Social Psychology* 67 (1963): 422-36; Adams, "Inequity in Social Exchange," in L. Berkowitz, ed., *Advances in Experimental Social Psychology* (New York: Academic Press, 1965). E. Walster, E. Bersheid, and G. Walster, "New Directions in Equity Research," *Journal of Personality and Social Psychology* 25 (1973): 151-76; L. Berkowitz and E. Walster, *Advances in Experimental Social Psychology* 9 (New York: Academic Press, 1976). A theory somewhat similar to equity theory is distributive justice within exchange theory. The theory of distributive justice asserts that people in exchange with others expect their profits (rewards minus costs) to be proportional to their investments or inputs. For a description of this theory, see George C. Homans, *Social Behavior: Its Elementary Forms*, rev. ed. (New York: Harcourt Brace Jovanovich, 1974); Karen Cook, "Expectations, Evaluations, and Equity," *American Sociological Review* 40 (1975): 372-88; and G. S. Leventhal, "The Distribution of Rewards and Resources in Groups and Organizations," in L. Berkowitz and E. Walster, eds., *Advances in Experimental Social Psychology*.

12. For an introduction to role theory, see Bruce J. Biddle, *Role Theory: Expectations, Identities, and Behaviors* (New York: Academic Press, 1979). A historical perspective and critique of the theory can be found in Jonathan H. Turner, *The Structure of Sociological Theory*, rev. ed. (Homewood, Ill.: Dorsey Press, 1978).

13. For introductions to social exchange theory, see Claude Levi-Strauss, *The Elementary Structures of Kinship* (Boston: Beacon Press, 1969); Peter M. Blau, *Exchange and Power in Social Life* (New York: Wiley, 1964); George C. Homans, *Social Behavior* (1974); Peter P. Ekeh, *Social Exchange Theory: The Two Traditions* (Cambridge, Mass.: Harvard University Press, 1974); R. M. Emerson, "Exchange Theory, Part I: A Psychological Basis for Social Exchange," and "Exchange Theory, Part II: Exchange Relations and Networks," in J. Berger, M. Zelditch, Jr., and B. Anderson, eds., *Sociological Theories in Progress* 2 (Boston: Houghton Mifflin, 1972); R. M. Emerson, "Social Exchange Theory," in A. Inkeles, J. Coleman, and N. Smelser, eds., *Annual Review of Sociology* 2 (Palo Alto, Calif.: Annual Reviews, 1976); J. K. Chadwick-Jones, *Social Exchange Theory: Its Structure and Influence in Social Psychology* (New York: Academic Press, 1976); J. W. Thibaut and H. H. Kelley, *The Social Psychology of Groups* (New York: Wiley, 1959); H. H. Kelley and J. W. Thibaut, *Interpersonal Relations: A Theory of Interdependence* (New York: Wiley, 1978); and Kenneth J. Gergen, Martin S. Greenberg, and Richard H. Willis, *Social Exchange: Advances in Theory and Research* (New York: Plenum Press, 1980).

14. The marketing perspective on exchange can be found in Philip Kotler, "A Generic Concept of Marketing," *Journal of Marketing* 36 (April 1972): 46–54; Richard P. Bagozzi, "Marketing as an Organized Behavioral System of Exchange," *Journal of Marketing* 38 (October 1974): 77–81; Bagozzi, "Marketing as Exchange," *Journal of Marketing* 39 (October 1975): 32–39; Bagozzi, "Social Exchange in Marketing," Journal of the *Academy of Marketing Science* 3 (Fall 1975): 314–27; Bagozzi, "Science, Politics, and the Social Construction of Marketing," in K. L. Bernhardt, ed., *Marketing: 1776–1976 and Beyond* (Chicago: American Marketing Association, 1976), pp. 586–92; Bagozzi, "Marketing as Exchange: A Theory of Transactions in the Marketplace," *American Behavioral Scientist* 21 (March/April 1978): 535–56; and Bagozzi, "Toward a Formal Theory of Marketing Exchanges," in O. C. Ferrell, S. W. Brown, and C. W. Lamb, Jr., eds., *Conceptual and Theoretical Developments in Marketing* (Chicago: American Marketing Association, 1979), pp. 431–47.

15. The theory presented in this chapter is developed in greater depth in Bagozzi, "Marketing as Exchange: A Theory of Transactions in the Marketplace" (1978) and "Toward a Formal Theory of Marketing Exchanges" (1979).

16. For a discussion of the many forms of exchange, see Bagozzi, "Marketing as Exchange" (1975).

17. James T. Tedeschi, Barry R. Schlenker, and Thomas V. Bonoma, *Conflict, Power, and Games* (Chicago: Aldine, 1973).

18. William J. McGuire, "The Nature of Attitudes and Attitude Change," in G. L. Lindzey and E. Aronson, eds., *Handbook of Social Psychology* 1 (Reading, Mass.: Addison-Wesley, 1969), pp. 136–314; and McGuire, "Attitude Change: The Information-Processing Paradigm," in C. G. McClintock, ed., *Experimental Social Psychology* (New York: Holt, Rinehart & Winston, 1972), pp. 108–41.

19. See Tedeschi et al., *Conflict, Power, and Games,* pp. 65–83.

20. Timothy C. Brock, "Communicator-Recipient Similarity and Decision Change," *Journal of Personality and Social Psychology* 1 (1965): 650–54.

21. Jeffrey Z. Rubin and Bert R. Brown, *The Social Psychology of Bargaining and Negotiation* (New York: Academic Press, 1975).

22. Thibaut and Kelley, *The Social Psychology of Groups.*

23. T. V. Bonoma, R. P. Bagozzi, and G. Zaltman, "The Dyadic Paradigm in Marketing Thought with Specific Application Toward Industrial Marketing," in T. V. Bonoma and G. Zaltman, eds., *Organizational Buying Behavior* (Chicago: American Marketing Association, 1978), pp. 49–66.

24. An introduction to general systems theory can be found in L. von Bertalanffy, *General System Theory* (New York: Braziller, 1968); von Bertalanffy, *Perspectives on General System Theory* (New York: Braziller, 1975); and E. Laszlo, *The Relevance of General Systems* (New York: Braziller, 1972). Systems theory is not the only way to extend the exchange concept to larger social entities. We might use other macrosociological frameworks, such as structuralism, functionalism, or conflict theory. For an early attempt to use what is essentially a structural approach to extend exchange, see Blau, *Exchange and Power in Social Life.* For an economic theory of exchange among organizations linked in a vertical marketing system, see O. E. Williamson, *Markets and Hierarchies: Analysis and Antitrust Implications* (New York: The Free Press, 1975).

25. For discussions of the assumptions of different social theories as well as their assets and liabilities, see Turner, *The Structure of Sociological Theory.* See also Randall Collins, *Sociology Since Midcentury* (New York: Academic Press, 1981).

26. Useful introductions to the diffusion of innovation can be found in Everett M. Rogers and F. Floyd Shoemaker, *Communication of Innovations*, 2nd ed. (New York: The Free Press, 1971); and Everett M. Rogers, *Diffusion of Innovations* (New York: The Free Press, 1962); Thomas S. Robertson, *Innovative Behavior and Communication* (New York: Holt, Rinehart & Winston, 1971). Everett M. Rogers, "New Product Adoption and Diffusion," *Journal of Consumer Research* 2 (March 1976): 290–301; James H. Donnelly, Jr., and John M. Ivancevich, "A Methodology for Identifying Innovator Characteristics of New Brand Purchases," *Journal of Marketing Research* 2 (August 1974): 331–34; Gerald Zaltman and Ronald Stiff, "Theories of Diffusion," in S. Ward and T. S. Robertson, eds., *Consumer Behavior: Theoretical Sources* (Englewood Cliffs, N.J.: Prentice-Hall, 1973), pp. 416–68; Lawrence P. Feldman and Gary M. Armstrong, "Identifying Buyers of a Major Automotive Innovation," *Journal of Marketing* 39 (January 1975): 47–53.

For more mathematical treatments of diffusion, see Frank M. Bass, "A New Product Growth Model for Consumer Durables," *Management Science* 15 (January 1969): 215–27; J. A. Dodson and E. Muller, "Models of New Product Diffusion through Advertising and Word of Mouth," *Management Science* 15 (November 1978): 1568–78; V. Mahajan and E. Muller, "Innovation Diffusion and New Product Growth Models in Marketing," *Journal of Marketing* 43 (Fall 1979): 55–68; A. Hurter and A. Rubenstein, "Market Penetration by New Innovations: The Technological Literature," *Technological Forecasting* 2 (1978): 197–221; S. B. Lawton and W. H. Lawton, "An Autocatalytic Model for the Diffusion of Educational Innovations," *Educational Administrative Quarterly* 15 (Winter 1979): 19–46.

One model of diffusion is the spread of diseases throughout a population. An introduction to the model can be found in N. T. J. Bailey, *The Mathematical Theory of Infectious Diseases and Its Applications*, 2nd ed. (New York: Homer, 1975).

27. Rogers, *Diffusion of Innovation*, pp. 81–86.

28. Rogers and Shoemaker, *Communication of Innovations*, pp. 104–5.

29. See Robertson, *Innovative Behavior and Communication;* Rogers and Shoemaker, *Communication of Innovations;* Rogers, "New Product Adoption and Diffusion"; Zaltman and Stiff, "Theories of Diffusion"; and Eric A. Von Hippel, "Successful Industrial Products from Customer Ideas," *Journal of Marketing* 42 (January 1978): 39–49. A micro and macro model can be found in D. Midgley, *Innovation and New Product Marketing* (London: Croom Helm, 1977).

30. Bass, "A New Product Growth Model for Consumer Durables"; and J. C. Fisher and R. H. Pry, "A Simple Substitution Model of Technological Change," *Technological Forecasting and Social Change* 3 (1971): 75–88.

31. Bass, "New Product Growth Model for Consumer Durables."

32. The categorization is from Rogers, *Diffusion of Innovations*. For a recent study questioning the usefulness of the categorization, see Richard W. Olshavsky, "Time and the Rate of Adoption of Innovations," *Journal of Consumer Research* 6 (March 1980): 425–28.

33. For research in consumer markets, see Feldman and Armstrong, "Identifying Buyers of a Major Automotive Innovation"; Donnelly and Ivancevich, "Methodology for Identifying Innovator Characteristics of New Brand Purchases"; John O. Summers, "Generalized Change Agents and Innovativeness," *Journal of Marketing Research* 8 (August 1971): 313–16; Kenneth Uhl, Roman Andrus, and Lance Poulsen, "How Are Laggards Different? An Empirical Inquiry," *Journal of Marketing Research* 7 (February 1970): 51–54; William R. Darden and Fred D. Reynolds, "Backward Profiling of Male Innovators," *Journal of Marketing Research* 9 (February 1974): 79–85; Louis E. Boone, "The Search for the Consumer Innovator," *Journal of Business* 43 (April 1970): 135–40; David B. Montgomery, "Consumer Characteristics Associated with Dealing: An Empirical Example," *Journal of Marketing Research* 8 (February 1971): 118–20; James H. Donnelly, Jr., Michael J. Etzel, and Scott Roeth, "The Relationship between Consumer's Category and Trial of New Products," *Journal of Applied Psychology* 57 (May 1973): 335–38; Jacob Jacoby, "Personality and Innovativeness Proneness," *Journal of Marketing Research* 8 (May 1971): 224–47; Donald T. Popierlarz, "An Exploration of Perceived Risk and Willingness to Try New Products," *Journal of Marketing Research* 4 (November 1967): 365–72; Kenneth A. Coney, "Dogmatism and Innovation: A Replication," *Journal of Marketing Research* 9 (November 1972): 453–55; Johan Arndt, "Role of Product-related Conversations in the Diffusion of a New Product," *Journal of Marketing Research* 4 (August 1967): 291–95; Thomas S. Robertson, "Purchase Sequence Responses: Innovators versus Noninnovators," *Journal of Advertising Research* 8 (March 1968): 47–52; James F. Engel, Robert J. Kegerreis, and Roger D. Blackwell, "Word-of-Mouth Communication by Innovator," *Journal of Marketing* 33 (July 1969): 15–19; J. M. McAurg and I. R. Andrews, "A Consumer Profile Analysis of the Self-Service Gasoline Customer," *Journal of Applied Psychology* 59 (February 1974): 119–21; James H. Donnelly, Jr., "Social Character and Acceptance of New Products," *Journal of Marketing Research* 7 (February 1970): 111–13;

Peter C. Wilton and Edgar A. Pessemier, "Forecasting the Ultimate Acceptance of an Innovation: The Effects of Information," *Journal of Consumer Research* 8 (September 1981): 162–71.

For research in industrial and institutional markets, see Frederick E. Webster, Jr., "Informal Communication In Industrial Markets," *Journal of Marketing Research* 7 (May 1970): 186–90; John A. Martilla, "Word-of-Mouth Communication in the Industrial Adoption Process," *Journal of Marketing Research* 8 (May 1971): 173–78; John A. Czepiel, "Word-of-Mouth Processes in the Diffusion of a Major Technological Innovation," *Journal of Marketing Research* 2 (May 1974): 172–80; Leon G. Schiffman and Vincent Gaccione, "Opinion Leaders in Industrial Markets," *Journal of Marketing* 38 (April 1974): 49–53; Vijay Mahajan and Milton E. G. Schoeman, "The Use of Computers in Hospitals: An Analysis of Adopters and Nonadopters," *Interfaces* 7 (May 1977): 95–107; Thomas S. Robertson and Yoram Wind, "Organizational Psychographics and Innovativeness," *Journal of Consumer Research* 7 (June 1980): 24–31.

34. For reviews of the literature, see Harry L. Davis, "Decision Making within the Household," *Journal of Consumer Research* 2 (March 1976): 241–60; and Robert Ferber, "Family Decision Making and Economic Behavior: A Review," in E. B. Sheldon, ed., *Family Economic Behavior: Problems and Prospects* (Philadelphia: Lippincott, 1973), pp. 29–61.

35. For a sociological conceptualization of the family life cycle concept, see John B. Lansing and Leslie Kish, "Family Life Cycle as an Independent Variable," *American Sociological Review* 32 (October 1957): 512–19; Arthur Norton, "The Family Life Cycle Updated: Components and Uses," in Robert F. Winch and Graham B. Spanier, eds., *Selected Studies in Marriage and the Family*, 4th ed. (New York: Holt, Rinehart & Winston, 1974), pp. 162–70.

A marketing perspective can be found in William D. Wells and George Gubar, "Life Cycle Concept in Marketing Research," *Journal of Marketing Research* 3 (November 1966): 355–63. See also Patrick E. Murphy and William A. Staples, "A Modernized Family Life Cycle," *Journal of Consumer Research* 6 (June 1979): 12–22. An eclectic view of the life cycle can be found in Chad Gordon, Charles M. Gaitz, and Judith Scott, "Leisure and Lives: Personal Expressivity across the Life Span," in Robert H. Binstock and Ethel Shanas, eds., *Handbook of Aging and the Social Sciences* (New York: Van Nostrand Reinhold, 1976), pp. 310–41, especially pp. 316–25.

36. A. Marvin Roscoe, Jr., and Jagdish N. Sheth, "Demographic Segmentation of Long Distance Behavior: Data Analysis and Inductive Model Building," in M. Venkatesan, ed., *Third Annual Conference of the Association for Consumer Research* (Ann Arbor, Michigan: Association for Consumer Research, 1972), pp. 258–78.

37. C. Milton Coughenour, "Functional Aspects of Food Consumption Activity and Family Life Cycle Stages," *Journal of Marriage and the Family* 34 (November 1972): 656–64.

38. Jagdish N. Sheth, "A Theory of Family Buying Decisions," in Jagdish N. Sheth, ed., *Models of Buyer Behavior: Conceptual, Quantitative, and Empirical* (New York: Harper & Row, 1974), pp. 17–33.

39. Harry L. Davis, "Dimensions of Marital Roles in Consumer Decision Making," *Journal of Marketing Research* 7 (May 1970): 168–77; Davis, "Measurement of Husband-Wife Influence in Consumer Purchase Decisions," *Journal of Marketing Research* 8 (August 1971): 305–12; Harry L. Davis and Benny P. Rigaux, "Perception of Marital Roles in Decision Processes," *Journal of Consumer Research* 1 (June 1974): 51–62. Davis, "Decision Making within the Household"; Isabella C. M. Cunningham and Robert T. Green, "Purchasing Roles in the U.S. Family, 1955 and 1973," *Journal of Marketing* 30 (October 1974): 61–64; Robert Ferber and Lucy Chao Lee, "Husband-Wife Influence in Family Purchasing Behavior," *Journal of Consumer Research* 1 (June 1974): 43–50; E. P. Cox, "Family Purchase Decision Making and the Process of Adjustment," *Journal of Marketing Research* 12 (May 1975): 189–95; and G. M. Munsinger, J. E. Weber, R. W. Hansen, "Joint Home Purchasing Decisions by Husbands and Wives," *Journal of Consumer Research* 1 (March 1975): 60–66.

40. Elizabeth H. Wolgast, "Do Husbands or Wives Make the Purchase Decisions?" *Journal of Marketing* 23 (October 1958): 151–58.

41. Ferber and Lee, "Husband-Wife Influence in Family Purchasing Behavior."

42. Haley, Overholser and Associates, Inc. *Purchase Influence: Measures of Husband/Wife Influence on Buying Decisions*, 1975. Referenced in Davis, "Decision Making within the Household," p. 258.

43. Travel Research, Inc. *A Study of the Role of Husband and Wife in Air Travel Decisions*, September 1968. Referenced in Davis, "Decision Making within the Household," p. 260.

44. Davis, "Decision Making within the Household," p. 244.

45. Cunningham and Green, "Purchasing Roles in the U.S. Family, 1955 and 1973"; Davis and Rigaux, "Perception of Marital Roles in Decision Processes."

46. Davis, "Dimensions of Marital Roles in Consumer Decision Making."

47. Davis and Rigaux, "Perception of Marital Roles in Decision Processes."

48. Scott Ward, "Consumer Socialization," *Journal of Consumer Research* 1 (September 1974): 1-14; Gilbert A. Churchill, Jr., and George P. Moschis, "Television and Interpersonal Influences on Adolescent Consumer Learning," *Journal of Consumer Research* 6 (June 1979): 23-35; George P. Moschis and Gilbert A. Churchill, Jr., "Consumer Socialization: A Theoretical and Empirical Analysis," *Journal of Marketing Research* 15 (November 1978): 599-609; Scott L. Ward, Daniel Wackman, and Ellen Wartella, *How Children Learn to Buy* (Beverly Hills, Calif.: Sage, 1977); George P. Moschis and Roy L. Moore, "Decision Making among the Young: A Socialization Perspective," *Journal of Consumer Research* 6 (September 1979): 101-12.

49. Lewis A. Berey and Richard W. Pollay, "The Influencing Role of the Child in Family Decision Making," *Journal of Marketing Research* 5 (February 1968): 70-72; and Scott Ward and Daniel Wackman, "Purchase Influence Attempts and Parental Yielding," *Journal of Marketing Research* 9 (August 1972): 316-19.

50. Very little research has been conducted into family interactions at the interpersonal level with respect to consumer behavior. For introductions in the sociology literature, see Constantina Safilios-Rothchild, "The Study of Family Power Structure: A Review," *Journal of Marriage and the Family* 32 (November, 1970); R. H. Turner, *Family Interaction* (New York: Wiley, 1970); Gerald R. Leslie, *The Family in Social Context*, 5th ed. (New York: Oxford Univ. Press, 1982); and Bert N. Adams, *The Family: A Sociological Interpretation*, 3rd ed. (Boston: Houghton Mifflin, 1980).

51. J. R. P. French, Jr., and B. Raven, "The Bases of Social Power," in D. Cartwright, ed., *Studies in Social Power* (Ann Arbor, Mich.: Institute for Social Research, 1959), pp. 150-57.

52. For an introduction to research into industrial buying and exposure to different theoretical viewpoints, see Jean-Marie Choffray and Gary L. Lilien, *Market Planning for New Industrial Products* (New York: Ronald Press, 1980); E. R. Corey, *Industrial Marketing: Cases and Concepts*, 2nd ed. (Englewood Cliffs, N.J.: Prentice-Hall, 1976); R. M. Cyert and J. G. March, *A Behavioral Theory of the Firm* (Englewood Cliffs, N.J.: Prentice-Hall, 1963); R. Haas, *Industrial Marketing Management* (New York: Petrocelli/Charter, 1976); Wesley J. Johnston, *Patterns in Industrial Buying Behavior* (New York: Praeger, 1981); John A. Howard and W. M. Morgenroth, "Information Processing Model of Executive Decision," *Management Science* 14 (March 1968): 416-28; James G. March and Herbert A. Simon, *Organizations* (New York: John Wiley & Sons, 1958); Franco Nicosia and Yoram Wind, "Behavioral Models of Organization Buying Processes," in Franco Nicosia and Yoram Wind, *Behavioral Models for Market Analysis: Foundations of Marketing Action* (Hinsdale, Ill.: Dryden Press, 1977), pp. 96-120; E. M. Rogers and A. R. Rogers, *Communication in Organizations* (New York: Free Press, 1976); Jagdish N. Sheth, "A Model of Industrial Buyer Behavior," *Journal of Marketing* 37 (October 1973): 50-56; Sheth, "Recent Developments in Organizational Buying Behavior," in J. N. Sheth, A. G. Woodside, and P. D. Bennett, eds., *Consumer and Industrial Buying Behavior* (New York: American Elsevier–North Holland, 1977), pp. 17-34; F. E. Webster, Jr., and Yoram Wind, *Organizational Buying Behavior* (Englewood Cliffs, N.J.: Prentice-Hall, 1972); David T. Wilson, "Industrial Buyer's Decision-Making Styles," *Journal of Marketing Research* 8 (November 1971): 433-36; Yoram Wind, "Organizational Buying Behavior," in G. Zaltman and T. V. Bonoma, eds., *Review of Marketing* (Chicago: American Marketing Association, 1978), pp. 160-93; and R. M. Hill, R. S. Alexander, and J. S. Cross, *Industrial Marketing*, 4th ed. (Homewood, Ill.: Richard D. Irwin, 1975).

53. Webster and Wind, *Organizational Buying Behavior*, p. 2.

54. P. J. Robinson, C. W. Faris, and Y. Wind, *Industrial Buying and Creative Marketing* (Boston: Allyn and Bacon, 1967).

55. Robert D. Buzzell, et al., *Marketing—A Contemporary Analysis* (Homewood, Ill: Richard D. Irwin, 1964), pp. 206-25.

56. R. M. Cyert, H. A. Simon, and D. B. Trow, "Observation of a Business Decision," *Journal of Business* 29 (October 1956): 237–48.

57. F. E. Webster, Jr., "Modeling the Industrial Buying Process," *Journal of Marketing Research* 2 (November 1965): 370–76.

58. Robinson, Faris, Wind, *Industrial Buying and Creative Marketing*, p. 14.

59. K. Backhaus and B. Gunter, "A Phase-Differentiated Interaction Approach to Industrial Marketing Decisions," *Industrial Marketing Management* 5 (October 1976): 255–70.

60. Webster and Wind, *Organizational Buying Behavior.*

61. H. Lazo, "Emotional Aspects of Industrial Buying," in R. S. Hancock, ed., *Dynamic Marketing for a Changing World* (Chicago: American Marketing Association, 1960), pp. 258–65; W. Feldman and R. Cardozo, "The Industrial Revolution and Models of Buyer Behavior," *Journal of Purchasing* 5 (November 1969): 77–88; and Robert F. Shoaf, ed., *Emotional Factors Underlying Industrial Purchasing* (Cleveland, Ohio: Penton Pub., 1959).

62. Sheth, "A Model of Industrial Buying Behavior," and "Recent Developments in Organizational Buying Behavior."

63. Sheth, "Model of Industrial Buying Behavior," p. 52.

64. T. V. Bonoma, R. P. Bagozzi, and G. Zaltman, "The Dyadic Paradigm with Specific Application toward Industrial Marketing," in T. V. Bonoma and G. Zaltman, ed., *Organizational Buying Behavior* (Chicago: American Marketing Association, 1978), pp. 49–66.

65. A. M. Pettigrew, "The Industrial Purchasing Decision as a Political Process," *European Journal of Marketing* 9 (Spring 1975): 4–19.

66. M. Patchen, "The Locus and Basis of Influence on Organizational Decisions," *Organizational Behavior and Human Performance* 2 (April 1975): 195–221.

67. Donald R. Lehmann and John O'Shaughnessy, "Difference in Attribute Importance for Different Industrial Products," *Journal of Marketing* 38 (April 1974): 36–42.

68. P. Busch and D. T. Wilson, "An Experimental Analysis of a Salesman's Expert and Referent Bases of Social Power in the Buyer-Seller Dyad," *Journal of Marketing Research* 13 (February 1976): 3–11.

69. G. E. Kiser, C. P. Rao, and S. R. G. Rao, "Vendor Attribute Evaluations of Buying Center Members Other than Purchasing Executives," *Industrial Marketing Management* 4 (March 1975): 45–54.

70. Rubin and Brown, *The Social Psychology of Bargaining and Negotiation* (1975).

71. Johnston, *Patterns in Industrial Buying Behavior.* See also Robert E. Spekman, "A Macro-Sociological Examination of the Industrial Buying Center: Promise or Problems?" in S. C. Jain, ed., *Research Frontiers in Marketing: Dialogues and Directions* (Chicago: American Marketing Association, 1978), pp. 111–15; Robert E. Spekman and Gary T. Ford, "Perceptions of Uncertainty within a Buying Group," *Industrial Marketing Management* 6 (December 1977): 395–403; and Robert E. Spekman and Louis W. Stern, "Environmental Uncertainties and Buying Group Structure: An Empirical Investigation," *Journal of Marketing* 43 (Spring 1979): 54–64.

72. Johnston, *Patterns in Industrial Buying Behavior.*

73. Spekman, "Macro-Sociological Examination of the Industrial Buying Center"; Spekman and Ford, "Perceptions of Uncertainty within a Buying Group"; and Spekman and Stern, "Environmental Uncertainties and Buying Group Structure."

GLOSSARY

Action. The physical movements people perform *and* the subjective experiences (e.g., meaning, affect) that precede, accompany, and/or follow such movements. The defining quality that separates action from behavior (i.e., the physical movements performed by a person) is the meaning, purpose, or intentionality that is associated with the physical movement by the person performing the behavior. *Individual action* refers to the physical movements and accompanying internal psychological processes performed by a person. When such actions also encompass a subjective taking account of the behavior and/or action of other people, we term them *social actions*. The majority of human actions are probably social in this sense.

Adaptive Feedback Process. Activities performed within a system whereby information from the monitoring of the output of the system is used as a basis for altering the internal structure and/or processes of the system. This is done in order to control the output to a desired level.

Adjustment Feedback Process. Activities performed within a system in order to purposefully achieve an output. This is accomplished through the regulation or fine-tuning of inputs.

Behavior. The physical movements or changes exhibited by a person, organization, or the characteristics of a person (e.g., consumption amount) or organization (e.g., sales). *See* action.

Buying Center. The collection of people who formally or informally influence purchase decisions in the firm. For example, purchasing agents, production engineers, design personnel, and cost accountants comprise a buying center in some firms.

Centrality of Purchasing Manager. The degree to which the purchasing manager interacts with others in the buying center. It is typically measured by the amount of communication (e.g., number of messages, conversations, letters, memos, etc.) sent and received by the manager. It may also entail the amount of influence or power wielded by the manager, although researchers have not investigated this dimension extensively.

Characteristics of Social Actors. Individual attributes of the parties to an exchange that either (or both) lead to an exchange or influence its course and outcomes. One class of attributes includes the needs, motives, and behavioral orientations of the actors. Another encompasses physical characteristics, decision rules, information-processing styles, personality, and other psychological characteristics that influence interpersonal communication and exchanges. See Figure 3-4.

Communication Processes. Information transfer and social influences among people, groups, and organizations.

Diffusion of Innovations. The processes whereby new products, technologies, ideas, etc., are adopted by people or organizations. We may study these processes at the micro (i.e., individual consumer) or macro (i.e., aggregate) levels.

Early Adopters. A category of people who are among the early persons, but not the first, to try a new product or innovation. The first people to try a new product or innovation are termed *innovators*. Early adopters are believed to typically encompass about 13.5 percent of all adopters. However, the percentage is likely to vary considerably, depending on the product or innovation, economic conditions, marketing programs, and characteristics of potential adopters. See Figure 3-8.

Early Majority. A large segment of the population that adopts a product or innovation somewhat later than both innovators or early adopters. It is believed that about 34 percent of all adopters belong to the early majority, but this percentage is sure to vary considerably, depending on many factors. *See* early adopters and Figure 3-8.

Equity Theory. A theory of human behavior that hypothesizes that a person compares the ratio of his or her outcomes to inputs to the ratio of the outcomes to inputs of a relevant other. If the ratios are equal, then balance exists in the mind of the comparer and no actions are undertaken. If the ratios are unequal, then imbalance exists, and the comparer will attempt to rectify the tension resulting from the perceived imbalance. Efforts to reduce tension include changing one's inputs and/or outcomes, altering the inputs and/or outcomes of another, switching the comparison person, or distorting one's perceptions of inputs and outcomes. See Figure 3-1.

Exchange Theory. A theory of human and organizational interaction explaining why and how two or more actors engage or fail to engage in the transfer of material, psychological, or social entities. See Figures 3-3 and 3-4.

Expectations. An anticipation or judgment that some event or state of affairs will come to fruition. Sometimes expressed as subjective probabilities.

Experiences. One category of events characterizing an exchange. Experiences are the thoughts, feelings, expectations, rules, ideologies, etc., felt by the parties to an exchange. These may be held individually or jointly.

Expert Power. A basis for influence residing in a power holder as perceived by another under his or her influence. Expert power consists of the degree of perceived knowledge or skill possessed by the power holder.

Family Decision Making. The processes underlying choices made by the family as a unit or by individuals acting in behalf of or in relation to the family or its members. These processes generally involve give-and-take, consensus, power, and social influence.

Family Life Cycle. The stages that a family and its members pass through as time goes on. The stages involve physiological, psychological, social, economic, and family-size changes. Each stage has different implications for consumption, media habits, activities of family members, and other behaviors and actions.

Feedback. Information, energy, or changes in physical outputs (e.g., rises or falls in sales) that are monitored by a system and used as input for control, adjustment, or adaptive purposes within the system.

General Systems Theory. A broad approach to the study of human behavior and social action that maintains that explanation can be achieved through the use of a small number of general concepts and principles. Perhaps the simplest applications of general systems theory involve the specification of inputs and outputs, system boundaries, feedback mechanisms, and throughput processes. Sometimes internal structures, environmental forces, and intersystemic relations will be specified as well. See Figure 3-5.

Industrial Buying. The decision-making processes whereby organizations or groups or individuals within organizations respond to or determine their needs for products, services, and materials. This generally entails the identification, evaluation, and selection of alternative suppliers and brands. Often, this is a group-based decision performed by a collection of people in the organization called the *buying center*. Three common tasks performed in industrial buying are

Straight Rebuy. The reordering of an existing product or service from a present supplier or close substitute.

Modified Rebuy. The purchase of a replacement for an existing product or service wherein a relatively large amount of new information is required as to product/service attributes, prices, alternative vendors, etc.

New Task Purchase. Purchases wherein a firm faces a new need or new problem requiring new products and/or services.

Innovators. The first people to adopt a new product or innovation. A considerable body of research exists investigating the characteristics of innovators. Among other characteristics, innovators generally have more contact with the mass media and other people, have higher education and incomes, and are less risk averse. Only a small proportion of the population is in this group—perhaps 2 or 3 percent or less. See Figure 3-8.

Integrative Complexity. The amount of interconnectedness among all members of the buying center. One operationalization is the number of actual communication links in the buying center to the total number of possible links.

Laggards. The final group of consumers to adopt an innovation. About 16 percent of all adopters fall into this category. See Figure 3-8.

Late Majority. Adopters of innovations who try the product or service relatively late after introduction and after many others have already tried it. Approximately 34 percent of all adopters are believed to be in this category. See Figure 3-8.

Lateral Involvement. The number of departments and divisions in communication with or exerting influence upon members of the buying center.

Life Style. A cluster of attributes of individual consumers or groups of consumers characterized by a distinctive pattern of attitudes, interests, opinions, and activities. Some research shows that life-style influences or is at least associated with consumption, media exposure, shopping habits, etc.

Macro Model of Diffusion. The rate and pattern of sales or product adoptions over time by aggregates of consumers. Diffusion in the macro sense can be represented mathematically as an S-shaped or similar curve. It is used to predict sales of product classes and occasionally brands for entire markets or meaningful subsets. See also "Demand Estimation" in Chapter 7.

Micro Model of Diffusion. The stages individual consumers go through from exposure or search for an innovation to final adoption. One frequently employed model is the following:

awareness ⟶ interest ⟶ evaluation ⟶ trial ⟶ adoption

For a fuller, revised micro model of diffusion, see Figure 3-6 and related discussion. It should be noted that the micro model has been incorporated into new product planning and other managerial models and is a basis for aggregation, too.

Outcomes. Within the context of exchange theory, outcomes refer to physical, social, or symbolic objects or events accruing to the actors as a consequence of their relationship. The outcomes might occur for one or both of the parties as individuals or jointly in a shared sense. Within the context of general systems theory, outcomes (or outputs) are things produced by the system, or more generally, effects or consequences of the system for people, other systems, or the environment.

Perceived Risk. The judged costs, losses, or possible negative consequences associated with a consumption problem or decision by the decision maker.

Problem-Solving Processes. As applied to groups or organizations, the purposeful activities surrounding search, evaluation, decision making, and choices in route to the pursuit of specific goals. A similar concept applies to individual decision making. See Chapter 2.

Process. (A) the sequence of steps or stages something (e.g., a person, organization) passes through or (B) the cause-and-effect relationships producing change in something.

Product Decision Making (by groups). The working out of individual preferences by group members, formation of mutual goals, and the joint implementation of action(s). The concept can be applied to families, buying centers, and other collectivities.

Referent Power. Perceived attractiveness of a power holder by another. It may involve identification processes as well.

Relative Deprivation Theory. A theory of human behavior that hypothesizes that whenever a person receives a reward or experiences an outcome, he or she compares the level of the reward or outcome to a standard of comparison. The standard of comparison is the reward or outcome received by the mode of a reference group or a particular member of the reference group chosen for comparison. If the reward or outcome is similar to the referent's, one feels satisfied or at least does not feel dissatisfied. If the reward or outcome is inferior to the referent's, one feels dissatisfied. Dissatisfaction, in turn, leads to action(s) to achieve equilibrium. The action might consist of more effort expended in the pursuit of greater rewards or outcomes. It might also consist of responses of protest, anger, or aggression. Or it might be directed inward in the form of depression, self-abuse, or withdrawal. See Figure 3-1.

Role Theory. A theory that maintains that people act in relation to others as a function of their own and the others' expectations. By expectations we mean the responsibilities, duties, and understandings shared by the person in the role and the others connected to the role person. Common examples include the parent role, the role of buyer in an organization, and the salesperson role. In one sense, roles are similar to the positions occupied by actors and actresses in a play or movie. Instead of exclusively following a formal script, however, people acting in roles "perform" according to informal and sometimes ambiguous expectations, as well as formal ones. Role theory posits that people act in response to social pressures embodied in their roles. See Figure 3-2.

Situational Contingencies. A class of constraints or facilitators influencing exchanges. Four categories may be identified: the physical environment, the psychological climate, the social milieu, and the legal setting. Some common environmental facilitators/constraints include time pressures; the structure and content of issues, alternatives, and actions; and the quantity and quality of lighting, air, and noise. The psychological climate encompasses the level of emotional (e.g., anxiety-provoking) and cognitive (e.g., informational) stimuli surrounding an exchange. The social milieu entails role, social class, peer, and reference group pressures. The legal setting consists of laws, regulations, and directives from a governmental body. See Figure 3-4.

Social Class. A categorization of people in groups on the basis of their education, income, occupation, and other ascribed or achieved attributes. Early social class categories were basically discontinuous and ranged from lower to upper classes. More recent versions are more or less continuous and include many categories. Also known as *social stratification.*

Social Comparison Processes. An activity wherein people compare their own beliefs, feelings, or personal experiences and outcomes with the beliefs, feelings, or personal experiences and outcomes of a relevant other(s). People are believed to choose as relevant others those who are similar to them. It is further believed that a need or drive exists to appraise one's self-worth. This is the impetus for making social comparisons; favorable comparisons lead to a strengthening or reaffirmation of one's self-worth, whereas unfavorable comparisons lead to a devaluation. The former results in equilibrium. The latter leads to dissatisfaction and either a change in one's self-image or efforts to change one's outcomes. See Figure 3-1.

Social Influence. The communication of punishing and/or rewarding stimuli to another with the purpose of achieving a desired response. Social influence typically occurs as threats, promises, warnings, and/or mendations. Ingratiation and information control are sometimes also used as modes of influence. Social influence is one of the most important and pervasive determinants of exchange behavior and outcomes. See Figure 3-4 and surrounding discussion.

Socialization. The process whereby people, and especially children, acquire knowledge, values, goals, attitudes, and skills. This is accomplished through social interaction, role modeling, and observational learning. Everyday consumption and proper behavior in organizations are two activities shaped by socialization processes.

Source/Receiver Characteristics. Attributes of people in interactions that shape the nature and course of the exchange. Source characteristics include such variables as attraction, expertise, credibility, prestige, trustworthiness, and status. Receiver characteristics comprise such variables as self-confidence, background attributes, cognitive styles, and certain personality styles. In general, source and receiver characteristics influence exchanges through their ability to authenticate or de-authenticate the subjective expected utility associated with communicated threats, promises, warnings, or mendations. See *social influence* and Figure 3-4. In later chapters when we consider advertising and communication processes, we shall discover that the nature and impact of source and receiver characteristics is more complicated than outlined in this chapter.

Structure. A set of entities and the relationships among them at any particular point in time. Entities might include such things as people, organizations, groups, roles, emotions, mental events, or any other physical, psychological, or social thing. Relationships might entail temporal, cause-and-effect, spatial, functional, or other types of associations. Thus, for example, we might speak of social structures, mental structures, attitude structures, role structures, rule structures, etc.

System. A set of processes and the structures that facilitate and constrain them.

Task Differentiation. The total number of people involved in an organizational unit or decision-making endeavor. Occasionally, task differentiation is defined in terms of the number of separate roles found in an organizational unit.

Third-Party Effects. Influence on an exchange originating from people, roles, or organizations outside the exchange proper. Third-party effects occur as sanctions or rewards. They also exist as implicit, potential, or anticipated sanctions or rewards. Alternative sources of satisfaction for either or both parties in an exchange comprise one important instance. See Figure 3-4.

Vertical Involvement. The number of levels in an organization communicating with or exerting influence upon members or decision makers in the organization.

CHAPTER
FOUR

How much there is in the world I do not want.

——Socrates (469?–399 B.C.)
(on seeing articles
of luxury for sale)

The possession of goods, whether acquired aggressively by one's own exertion or passively by transmission through inheritance from others, becomes a conventional basis of reputability.... In order to gain and to hold the esteem of men it is not sufficient merely to possess wealth or power. The wealth or power must be put in evidence, for esteem is awarded only on evidence.

——Thorstein Veblen (1857–1929)

He who is plenteously provided for from within, needs but little from without.

——Goethe (1749–1832)

Give us the luxuries of life, and we will dispense with its necessities.

——J. L. Motley (1814–1877)

PRODUCT:
MICRO AND MACRO PERSPECTIVES

Introduction

Perhaps the most visible aspect of marketing transactions is the *product* that changes hands. As noted earlier, we might think of two manifestations of products: the physical product and the psychosocial product. The former is exemplified by objects (e.g., a copy machine), places (e.g., a vacation site), or services (e.g., dry cleaning). The latter consists of knowledge (e.g., Brand X is durable), feelings (e.g., Candidate Y is attractive), or moral imperatives (e.g., donating blood is good). Notice that "products" can be persons, places, things, ideas, or activities. Thus, in one sense, the president, the Getty Museum, Stroh's Beer, the notion of détente between East and West, and legal services are all products. Each has a seller, whether we call him or her a campaign director, a curator, a bartender, the secretary of state, or a lawyer. Each has something to offer in the form of leadership, services, a physical product, peace of mind, or advice. And each has at least one buyer who "pays" in votes, money, or verbal support. We normally do not think of products in this broadened sense, but all human exchanges involve a transfer of tangible or intangible "products" between parties and thus share some common elements with everyday marketing transactions. The ideas and principles discussed below therefore apply to the marketing of products in the traditional as well as broader senses.

In this chapter, we will delve deeper into the meaning of a product. Our goal will be to examine its significance from two points of view. We will begin with an analysis at the micro level. That is, we will probe into the nature of a product from the perspective of the individual consumer. Next, our vantage point will shift to the macro level. Here we will examine economic, public policy, and sociological dimensions of products. In the following chapter, the managerial elements of products will be scrutinized. Emphasis will be upon strategies for new product development and ongoing product management decisions.

The Product and the Individual Consumer

When people think of products, they usually imagine them as physical entities. At least, this is the immediate, conscious reaction that we have toward products. If we look deeper into the meaning of products, however, we will see that they are complex, multifaceted things with tangible and intangible aspects. Let us begin our analysis of products from a philosophical perspective.

Figure 4-1 illustrates how we might think of a product in terms of its generic elements and their interrelationships. Here we see that products typically consist of three elements: the physical product, the words or symbols used to represent the product, and the meaning of the product for the individual. The simplicity of this scheme belies its importance, for it shows in a diagram what loosely occurs in the mind of the consumer in both conscious and nonconscious ways. Each circle represents an idea or feeling (or bundle of ideas or feelings) in the consumer's mind. Every product's physical characteristics, name, and meaning project images to the person experiencing it. Moreover, each circle corresponds to, or has a referent in, the outer physical world. The relationships between this "real" physical world and its experience as represented in the internal mental world determine what actions a person will take in relation to the product, if any.

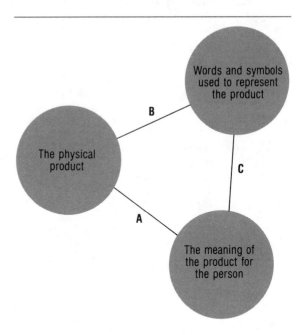

Figure 4-1. A conceptualization of the meaning of a product

Within the mind of the consumer, we might think of each product as having a representation such as shown in Figure 4-1. At any one point in time, the representation is fixed in content and achieves a temporary cognitive and emotional equilibrium. As soon as an external stimulus changes (e.g., a new physical attribute is added to an old product or a message is used to transmit a new meaning of the product), then the internal equilibrium of the mental representation will be upset.[1] This may result in a change in the way some or all of the elements of the product are perceived (e.g., shifting from liking to disliking the product), or it might stimulate action to relieve the imbalance (e.g., product trial). Of course, an existing product representation might also change through internal physiological, emotional, or cognitive processes, as noted in Chapter 2. The important point to recognize is that the internal mental representation of a product intervenes between external or internal stimuli, on the one hand, and actions in relation to the product, on the other hand. Marketers try to adjust their product offerings, messages, prices, and so on, to have a specific impact on the mental and feeling processes of consumers and ultimately on behavior. Before we examine managerial aspects of products more fully, let us look at the three elements in Figure 4-1 in greater detail.

The Physical Product

What Is a Product?

A product is a bundle of characteristics offered by one party, the seller, to another party, the buyer. The offering has tangible and intangible dimensions (see Figure 4-2). The tangible are the most apparent, but notice that they appear in many forms with each form varying as a matter of degree at many possible levels. You might think of the manager's task as one of deciding what combination of tangible characteristics to build into

his or her product. Thus, the manager faces a product size and shape decision, a product color decision, a product durability decision, and so on. He or she must also decide on a set of intangible characteristics, which consist of such elements as style, quality, and brand name, to "build" into the product. They are less physical than the tangible characteristics and perhaps are even nonphysical in some instances. Nevertheless, they are, in part, determined by the tangible characteristics. In one sense, the manager produces an aesthetic, prestigious, or utilitarian product by skillfully combining the tangible elements into a successful product offering. The other side of the process, of course, rests with the consumer. That is, the consumer's task, so to speak, is to decide on what combination of tangible and intangible characteristics to choose in order to "produce" personal satisfaction. We will have more to say about consumer decision making with respect to products in a moment.

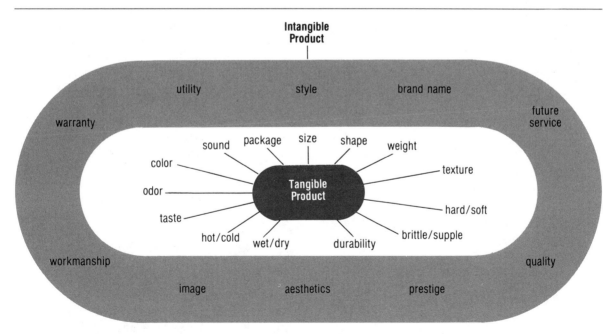

Figure 4-2. Tangible and intangible characteristics of products

To reiterate a central theme throughout this text, successful marketing in general and successful products in particular are achieved through two subgoals. One is that the marketer must begin with the needs of the consumer and design the product to meet those needs. To do otherwise is to risk having products sit on store shelves due to lack of consumer interest. A second objective is to design a product that will have a differential advantage over the competition. Because firms compete among themselves and, moreover, product forms and alternative activities compete for the consumer's scarce resources, a product must outperform its rivals in order to succeed. Both objectives are accomplished, in part, through product differentiation.

Product differentiation is the establishment of perceptible distinctions among product offerings in the mind of the consumer. As shown in Figure 4-3, this is done not only through the design of the physical product but also through the orchestration of marketing mix inputs. The output is a differentiated marketing offering. Let us turn to an analysis of some important characteristics of products that facilitate product differentiation.

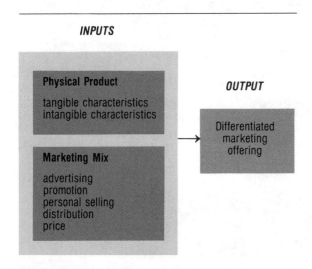

INPUTS

Physical Product
tangible characteristics
intangible characteristics

Marketing Mix
advertising
promotion
personal selling
distribution
price

OUTPUT

Differentiated marketing offering

Figure 4-3. Product differentiation

Some Central Product Stimuli

Managers use products' tangible and intangible characteristics to obtain desired responses from the marketplace. Yet, to have a practical impact on consumers, they must translate the physical characteristics of products into concrete *attributes* with demonstrable benefits, sometimes termed "selling propositions" by advertising and brand managers. For example, consider the case of a headache remedy. The physical ingredients might be aspirin, an antacid chemical, and a small amount of sweetener. These physical characteristics are too far removed in the minds of consumers, however, from the real attributes or benefits consumers seek. Rather, a consumer looks for such attributes as "fast acting," "no upset stomach," "effective even for the most severe headaches," "tastes good," and so on. These are the real pieces of information that the marketer desires to communicate. Indeed, a majority of advertising campaigns focus on only a few such attributes, known as the "core selling proposition," because they believe that consumers view products in relatively simple terms and have limited information processing capabilities. For many years the core selling proposition of the pain reliever Tylenol, for instance, was "effective but will not upset the stomach."

The attributes of products and services are thus key product stimuli influencing consumer choices. Indeed, the attributes become stored in the consumer's mind, are compared with rival brands, and are evaluated and related to needs as central parts of any decision-making process. It is not possible to overemphasize the role that product attributes play in marketing exchanges.

Nevertheless, the role of product attributes in decision making varies with the stage in the decision process, and other stimuli have equal, if not more important, effects at times. Consider the case of shopping in the supermarket. For some purchases, the consumer will have developed a set of beliefs and evaluations of product attributes even before entering the store. Yet, he or she might not have formed a preference for a particular brand. The stimuli at the point of sale then become important determinants of choice. One of the most effective in this regard is the *package*. In fact, the package is typically the final stimulus before actual purchase. It serves as a bridge between product attributes and their meaning on the one hand, and preference and intention to purchase on the other hand. The package can be a triggering mechanism for purchase, for relatively complex purchases such as new products as well as for habitual and impulse buying.

Package design (and product design) has a variety of effects. It attracts and holds one's attention. It conveys product information about the attributes, use, and consequences of a product. It stimulates the formation of an attitude, the development of an emotional reaction, and the emergence of a preference and intention. Finally, it induces trial and repeat purchase.

Although we are only now beginning to understand how a package produces these effects,[2] the effects of packages (and products) can be explained in two ways: *verbal effects* and *nonverbal* (e.g., image) *effects*. The verbal effects of a package occur through the brand name, logo, product description, typefaces, and so on, appearing on the surface of the package or product. We will have more to say about the literal and symbolic aspects of this communication when we discuss the words and symbols used to represent the product (see Figure 4-1). The nonverbal effects of packages and products are transmitted primarily through the shapes and colors used. Odors and physical sensations associated with taste, touch, and hearing are sometimes central as well. Shapes, colors, and other physical sensations communicate at both a nonconscious and a conscious level. We perceive these stimuli as wholes in the form of images, global feelings, and general impressions. Often they instill subconscious levels of arousal, cognitive

and affective dissonance, and approach/avoidance tendencies. They thus avoid counterarguments and other forms of overt resistance associated with verbal stimuli in persuasive communication.

The stimuli that are most effective consist of all-encompassing combinations of product attributes, package designs, and verbal elements. In other words, package colors, forms, and verbal cues work best when they mutually reinforce one another and highlight the product's attributes and benefits. We know very little about why and how they achieve their effects, however, and their skillful incorporation in a product offering is part art and part science.

Although we will focus more on product attributes than on package-related stimuli in this text, it is important to recognize that the latter often play an important role. Indeed, supermarkets are filled with many excellent examples of packages that serve as an essential stimulus in product sales. L'eggs pantyhose, for instance, successfully gained inroads in the market for stockings for women by rejecting the flat cardboard and transparent wrappings used by the competition. Instead, they used a three-dimensional plastic container in the shape of an egg to hold the stockings. Procter & Gamble's skin-conditioning lotion, Wondra, achieved an early foothold in the market, in part, on the basis of its package. In place of the traditional upright dispenser that is slow to pour as the contents are used up, Procter & Gamble marketed an upside-down container in which the contents are always ready to be used.

The crucial point to remember about any package is that it serves as a functional and/or symbolic extension of the product. Anyone who has ever shopped in Europe knows that the "external wrappings" are an indispensable part of the sale. The purchase of pastry in shops in France, for example, is accompanied by an elaborate ritual in which the proprietor artistically wraps the product and presents it with such style and ceremony that one feels that the product, and by implication the purchaser, is something special. The layout and selection of goods in the Ka De We department store in Berlin are arranged so skillfully and elegantly that one almost enjoys the process of shopping more than the purchase or product itself. Similarly, window displays in shops throughout Italy are done so creatively and tastefully that the aesthetic side of the experience becomes as important as the functional side. The point to be stressed here is that products are much more than utilitarian objects. The symbolic meaning of the product, its package, and the activities leading up to its purchase, as well as its use and ownership, are inseparable parts of the product. These factors need to be communicated through the stimuli selected by the marketer in the design of the product itself.

Classification of Products

Over the years, scholars have developed classifications to help us understand the many kinds of products in existence. Economists, for example, tend to classify products into durable goods, nondurable goods, and services. *Durable goods* are products that have an extended life. They might encompass relatively inexpensive items, such as a book or umbrella, or they might consist of expensive purchases, such as a television or automobile. *Nondurable goods* are products that are destroyed or transformed in a relatively short period of time or after a few uses. For example, bread, milk, toothpaste, or a newspaper fall within this category. Finally, *services* are time or activities that one purchases from another party. They cover such instances as hair styling, financial planning, and lawn care.

Why do people bother to classify products in the first place? One reason is that it supplies government planners with a convenient scheme for monitoring the progress of the economy. By tracking the production and sales of durable goods, nondurable goods, and services over time, we can gain an indication of the health of the economy and changing economic forces. Perhaps of greater utility is the use of the framework as a starting point in economic analysis and forecasting. Economists have found that the production and consumption of durables, nondurables, and services follow somewhat different economic laws. Indeed, they have developed unique theories and models for each type of product and have used these to predict the supply and demand for the goods as well as make policy decisions to influence production, consumption, and governmental programs. In one sense, classifications have stimulated the development of a more valid explanation of economic behavior than had existed before products were conceived as heterogeneous commodities. We will have more to say about this later in the chapter.

Marketers have proposed even more complex classifications of products.[3] Generally, these typically apply to either *consumer goods* (i.e., those purchased by the public for their own final use) or *industrial goods* (i.e., those purchased by organizations to become a part of, or to help them produce, their market offerings). Let us look first at a popular classification of consumer goods.

In general, all consumer goods can be classified as convenience, shopping, or specialty goods. *Convenience goods* are products one buys out of habit, impulse, or, on occasion, even urgency. For example, the purchase of coffee at work or school is generally done as a matter of habit, but to buy a pretzel from a vendor on the street is typically an impulsive act. And to search for the most convenient gasoline station, after discovering that one's tank is nearly empty, is a relatively urgent decision. The purchase of convenience goods such as these is usually done with little preplanning, effort, and time expended. In addition, the purchase price is most often low and/or the risk to the consumer in terms of the product is minimal. Indeed, the decision process for convenience goods is a limited one, encompassing few criteria, few product attributes, few or no comparisons to competitive brands, and simple decision rules. For example, a consumer's decision rule for the purchase of milk during the weekly shopping trip might be: "buy brand A, the top of the line, if available and under x dollars; otherwise, buy the store brand." Notice that the consumer applies only two criteria—price and availability—and simple rules are used (e.g., under x dollars, look for two brands only). This is typical for convenience goods. To take another example, imagine that you pass a boutique and a brightly colored scarf catches your eye. You might then enter the store, ask for the scarf, and after noting that it is reasonably priced, matches your wardrobe, and is a "designer brand," purchase it. Here, presumably, only three product attributes played a central role: price, physical attractiveness, and the prestige of the brand.

Shopping goods are products for which the customer goes through considerable effort to obtain "the best buy." This involves examination of products on many attributes, use of many criteria, and application of relatively complex rules for decision making. Moreover, the consumer will often compare prices, styles, workmanship, and so on, among competing brands and across different grades of products within the same brand or product line. Examples of products in this categorization include clothing, stereo systems, oriental rugs, automobiles, watches, and sporting equipment. Purchases of these types of products entail shopping in the common-sense usage of the term. A typical example might be captured in the following scenario.

Tom Jones decides he wants to buy a stereo system for his apartment. After talking with friends and reading advertising and independent evaluations in the literature, he decides that a moderately priced system that is small enough to fit in his cramped apartment, yet rich enough in sound quality, represents the kind of stereo he wants. Moreover, to make the decision process manageable, he defines his evoked set to include SONY, Kenwood, Marantz, and Panasonic. At least each of these manufacturers has a system appealing to his initial subjective criteria for aesthetic visual appeal and the other attributes noted above.

Tom's first visit to a specialty shop leads him to eliminate the Marantz brand because it is too expensive for his budget; and, to his evoked set, he adds a system by SANYO and leaves open the possibility that his needs might be satisfied by mixing components from different manufacturers. Further, the salesperson convinces him that he should also examine such esoteric criteria as power, resolution, speaker range and quality, and the opportunity to add components to his system in the future. Needless to say, his decision is complex; many brands and many criteria are involved. Yet, he feels the need to somehow cope with the abundant information and make a decision soon. Despite pressure from the salesperson, Tom decides to visit another store in the area and then return home "to think about it" for a few days.

Over the weekend, he collects ads from many stores advertising in the Sunday newspapers. This allows him to eliminate a few brands from his evoked set and to narrow his shopping to two discount stores— one a large local retailer, the second a chain selling nationally. He has decided on two possibilities. System A consists of a SONY receiver, Kenwood speakers, and a Girard turntable. System B is comprised of a SANYO receiver, Kenwood speakers, and a Panasonic turntable.

Table 4-1 depicts his evaluations up to this point. Notice that neither system scores the highest on all criteria. Also, Tom is uncertain about the final prices because each store allows some flexibility. Nevertheless, both systems are relatively close in the attributes noted in Table 4-1, and both satisfy Tom's need for a system that will fit in his apartment. After visiting the two most promising stores, he discovers that the local retailer offers the best prices over the chain store, and he decides on System A. The prices were as follows: Store P: System A = $700, System B = $820. Store Q: System A = $740, System B = $825.

TABLE 4-1

Tom Jones's Assessment of Two Stereo Systems Prior to His Second Shopping Trip

	EVALUATION OF PRODUCT ATTRIBUTES[a]			
	Sound Quality	Visual/ Aesthetic Appeal	Service and Warranty Provisions	Price
System A	8	7	10	?
System B	9	8	8	?

[a]On a 1–10 point scale with 10 representing the highest score.

This example illustrates a number of elements characteristic of purchases of shopping goods. First, unlike convenience goods, shopping goods involve many product attributes. Over the course of his decision making, Tom considered about ten different attributes. Shopping goods are simply more complex. Second, because the price and risk associated with a purchase are high, Tom compared many brands and did so at a number of stores. Third, the process involves an extensive search for information from numerous sources. Tom relied on friends, advertisements, salespeople, independent evaluations, as well as his own inspections and judgments. Fourth, the process was an evolutionary one with many steps. Tom continually updated his knowledge, discarded facts, changed his mind, and generally proceeded through a series of decision stages. This was necessary to develop a set of meaningful product attributes and potential brands to consider and to evaluate these brands on the attributes.

Finally, although not discussed in the scenario, decision making for shopping goods usually involves the application of complex rules. These are generally implicit and nonconscious but nevertheless represent how one arrives at a final choice.[4] We touched upon some of these rules in the chapter on consumer behavior. Decision rules govern how information should be weighted and combined and under what conditions actions should be taken, if any. For instance, Tom's decision rule might have been, "Score each system on the four product attributes on a scale of 1 to 10, weight each attribute equally, sum the scores across systems, and choose the system with the highest score."

Specialty goods possess such unique attributes that consumers make special efforts to secure them. In fact, it is not so much the class of goods itself, as it is the manufacturer or brand, that defines a specialty good. People want or prefer such goods to the extent that they will incur considerable expense or inconvenience to obtain them. Price and comparison shopping are not central criteria in the decision process. Rather, quality, styling, aesthetic appeal, or prestigious image are the key attributes. For example, some wealthy individuals insist on Gucci clothes and accessories, vacations in Tahiti, or Lamborghini sports cars, despite the fact that other products with essentially similar attributes exist. It should be noted that specialty goods are not limited to expensive items. For some of us, a special restaurant, hair stylist, musical performer, or local tavern constitute specialty goods. That is, we seek them because they are unique in some way.

Industrial goods, too, can be usefully classified. One way to do this is to classify them into raw materials, component parts, capital goods, supplies, and services. *Raw materials* are the basic ingredients used to produce a finished product. They usually exist as natural minerals, foodstuffs, or processed or partially processed chemicals. A ready-to-eat cereal might consist of wheat, vitamin additives, sugar, salt, and a preservative. A motorbike contains aluminum, steel, rubber, plastic, and chemicals such as oil and paint, among other ingredients. *Component parts* are finished or partially finished goods that go into the final product. For example, a motorbike is assembled with wheels, tires, a gas tank, seat, chassis, engine block, and other finished components. *Capital goods* are products that are used to produce finished goods or services but are not a physical part of the final product. They generally have a long life. For instance, buildings, machinery, lighting, office equipment, and computers are essential capital goods used in the production of other products. *Supplies* are also products used to produce finished goods without becoming a part of them. However, unlike capital goods, supplies have a relatively short life in that they are consumed or transformed quickly in the production process. Common examples include gas, oil, business forms, light bulbs, janitorial supplies, typewriter ribbons, and ballpoint pens. Finally, *services* are activities provided by others because they facilitate the functioning of the organization. These including accounting, legal, construction, maintenance, manpower, and other services.

Unlike the economic classification scheme for goods described above, the consumer and industrial goods categories have had somewhat less of an impact on the science and practice of marketing. At the end of the chapter we will discuss how these latter classifications have been used to predict and influence marketing activities.

The Product Line

A *product line* is the list of all the products a particular firm sells within a particular category of goods. The definition of a category might be any of the ones discussed above, or, more frequently (because some firms sell many products), more refined categories are needed. Therefore, the criteria used to specify a category are usually based on some common characteristic that is shared by all products lumped into the product-line grouping. The most frequently employed criteria for defining product lines are based on the physical characteristics, use, purchaser, price range, or distribution channel of the products. For example, Procter & Gamble has eight brands in its detergent line: Bold, Bonus, Cheer, Dash, Duz, Gain, Oxydol, and Tide. General Foods sells five brands in its coffee line: Maxwell House, Maxim, Brim, Sanka, and Yuban. Supermarkets, because they typically market between 10,000 and 12,000 items, need broader category labels such as canned goods, fruits and vegetables, dairy products, jars and bottles, and case goods. These, in turn, are broken down into subcategories such as bar soap, detergents, sugar, flour, cereal, and cake mixes. Each subgroup will have a number of national and dealer (i.e., store) brands under it.

We may further describe product lines in terms of their width and depth. For a given firm, the *width* of its offerings refers to the number of product lines it sells. The more product lines it sells, the wider its offerings. *Depth* connotes the number of different items sold within a particular product line. The more items, the deeper the line. Figure 4-4 illustrates the concept of product line for a small travel agency. Notice that three product lines are provided: transportation arrangements, travel packages, and auxiliary services. These three lines constitute the agency's width of offerings. The depth of each product line can be seen to vary from four items for transportation arrangements to two items for auxiliary services. A larger, full-service travel agency might offer both wider and deeper services. For instance, it might also provide credit, foreign money exchange, escort services, tickets to the theater or sporting events, mail and message services, rental of equipment, and travel insurance. It should be stressed that the concepts of width and depth apply to any organization's product lines. The width of Procter & Gamble's lines is represented by such items as coffee, toothpaste, shampoo, soap, detergents, and disposable diapers. Its depth in detergents consists of eight brands; in toothpaste, there are two: Crest Plus and Gleem II.

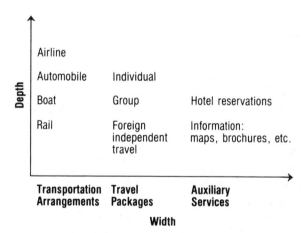

Figure 4-4. The concepts of product-line width and depth applied to a small travel agency

Actually, product lines sometimes are so extensive that they must be described by more than width and depth. We might think of a firm's product line in terms of a multidimensional space. For example, Table 4-2 shows part of the product line space for a supermarket. Here three dimensions are important: width, depth, and length. Table 4-2 lists only a portion of the possibilities under each. For firms such as Sears or General Electric, whose product offerings might number in the hundreds of thousands, even more complicated product line breakdowns are required.

TABLE 4-2
A Portion of the Product Line Space for a Supermarket

Width	Depth	Length
Canned Goods	Fruit	Nescafé
	Vegetables	Tasters Choice
		Folgers
	Coffee	Hills Brothers
		High Point
	•	Maxwell House
	•	Sanka
	•	•
		•
Jars and Bottles	Baby Food	Pepsi-Cola
		Coca-Cola
	Soft Drinks	7-Up
		Canada Dry
	Ketchup	Hires Root Beer
	•	Vernor's Ginger Ale
	•	•
	•	•
	•	•
Case Goods	Detergents	All
		Cheer
		Dash
	Bar Soap	Fab
		Tide
	Cereal	Dealer Brands
	•	•
	•	•
	•	•
	•	•
•	•	•
•	•	•
•	•	•

Still another way to describe a firm's product line is in terms of homogeneity. The many varieties of soups sold by Campbell constitute a relatively homogeneous product line. General Foods, in contrast, has a relatively heterogeneous product line. Among other offerings, it sells dog food, desserts, cereals, coffee, and candy.

From the consumer's perspective, product lines have a number of important implications. On the one hand, wider and deeper product lines provide a greater range of choice and allow consumers the opportunity to fine-tune their purchases of goods and services. Presumably, this results in increased satisfaction. During wartime or depressions, and in both lesser developed or overly planned economies, shortages of goods and services often occur; and even in the best of times, product lines are narrow and short. In normal periods or in free enterprise of mixed economies, product lines are relatively fuller. On the other hand, the proliferation of products poses an information-processing problem for consumers. Full satisfaction requires accurate and efficient coping with information. The sheer variety offered and the advertising clutter caused by many competing sponsors of rival product lines can work against this. From society's standpoint, too many product lines could lead to inefficiency with respect to productive and allocative efficiency. However, it is difficult to determine when or if this point has been reached. Very little research, if any, has addressed this issue.

From the firm's perspective, product lines have a number of consequences. Most of these stem from the fact that the use of product lines is a tool for product differentiation. In addition, product lines allow the firm to capitalize on economies of scale in production and marketing. They also provide a means to generate greater revenues and profits, if used skillfully. Finally, product lines are potentially effective competitive levers for increasing or maintaining market share. We will have more to say about the managerial dimensions of product lines in the following chapter.

The Concept of a Product Life Cycle (PLC)[5]

An Early Definition. Drawing upon an analogy from biology (i.e., birth → growth → decline → death), marketers have proposed that products also pass through well-defined stages from their inception until their withdrawal from the marketplace. Figure 4-5 shows a common representation of the PLC concept. Notice that dollar sales and profits are plotted against time in years. Looking first at sales, we see that in the *introduction stage* increases are slow. That is, the curve is relatively flat. Many people are not aware of the product, and some of those who are aware might be reluctant to make a purchase. The task of the marketer is to build awareness and confidence through promotion and advertising, gain acceptance by retailers, and gear up production to meet anticipated demand.

Once the product is evaluated favorably and people try it, sales increase more rapidly. Thus, the *growth stage* shows a relatively steep slope. Here the task of the marketer is to adjust production, distribution, advertising, and pricing to meet demand and stave off competitors. This might mean expanding production still further, reaching out to new markets, maintaining relatively high advertising levels, and lowering prices somewhat.

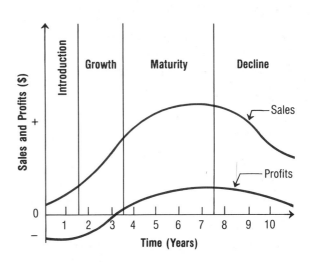

Figure 4-5. The concept of the Product Life Cycle

After a while, the market gets saturated and/or competitors make large inroads. Sales increases slow and perhaps sales even flatten out. This stage is termed *maturity.* Competition among firms for sales reaches its peak during this stage. Firms either take defensive actions such as cost-cutting programs, further searches for new markets, or promotional deals, or else they assume an aggressive posture encompassing increased advertising, improvements in the product, and price decreases. Occasionally, marketing strategies will involve both defensive and offensive tactics during the maturity stage.

In the final stage, *decline*, sales begin a downward trend. Sometimes the descent is gradual, occurring over many years. At other times, consumer tastes change quickly and/or competitors gain dramatically in strength, with the result that sales dip abruptly. The end result is often removal of the product from the marketplace. If the demise of the product is irreversible, then marketers will typically lower their advertising and promotion budgets to reduce expenses, stop research and development work on the product, and curtail overall marketing support.

A final point to note about the traditional PLC concept shown in Figure 4-5 is that profits also tend to follow a regular pattern of growth, saturation, and decline. However, notice that profits lag sales in terms of the beginning point of rapid growth. Also, in the beginning, there may well be losses, with profits emerging only years after product introduction. Profits are believed to peak at the end of the growth stage or the beginning of maturity.

Refinements in the PLC Concept. You might have noticed that the length of each stage in the PLC varied. The introduction stage was the shortest; growth was somewhat longer. Maturity was longer yet. And decline was about as long as maturity, although it can be shorter or longer than that shown, depending on market conditions and the actions of the firm. This raises an interesting question: How do we know when any product is in a particular stage of the PLC? The answer is difficult to ascertain because the transition from one stage to another is not necessarily inevitable or deterministic.

Indeed, the evidence for the existence of PLCs in the real world is mixed. Dhalla and Yuspeh,[6] for example, could not find any products that definitely went through the four stages. On the other hand, others have found that some products do roughly follow the PLC curve.[7] But even for those products that do appear to follow the PLC, the duration of stages varies widely and/or the overall shapes deviate from the neat S-shaped curve of Figure 4-5. For example, in Buzzell's study of instant coffee and frozen orange juice, the time from the beginning of growth to maturity was about 12 years.[8] In contrast, Cunningham found that the five industrial goods he examined varied from 3 to 10 years between growth and maturity.[9] Other products do not exhibit the S-shape at all but show rising, falling, flat, or widely fluctuating patterns.[10] Thus, one or more of the stages shown in Figure 4-5 has been known to be omitted in reality, depending on the product.

At least five issues have implications for the validity of the PLC curve. The first concerns the *definition* and *measurement* of sales.[11] Sales might be measured as units sold, total dollar value, total dollar value corrected for inflation or seasonality, sales in regions or territories, sales by customer groupings, sales per unit of time, and so on. No fool-proof rules exist for preferring one measure over another in every situation. Yet, the choice of measurement is obviously crucial to the shape of the PLC curve. Until a sound rationale and research reveal the best measure or measures, one might examine a number of alternatives to see the implications. In any event, previous failures to observe a PLC curve may have stemmed from improper or fallible measures.

A second issue concerns the choice of *level of aggregation* to use for the sales variable. Table 4-3 shows some possibilities. Notice that one might model the life cycle of products all the way from generic product classes to individual brands embedded within those classes. For example, we might plot sales of alcoholic and nonalcoholic drinks over time to see how consumption of these two *generic product classes* have changed. In one sense, all drinks compete among one another because they satisfy the general need for a thirst quencher or a social beverage. At the next level of specificity, we might examine the sales of a homogeneous product class within the generic category. A *homogeneous product class* is one that can be considered more or less a direct substitute for another. Some homogeneous product classes under the category of drinks might be coffee, tea, soft drinks, or juices. Loosely speaking, each of these competes with the other when we are thirsty, and it is possible to plot a PLC for each. Homogeneous product classes, in turn, can be subdivided into product forms. *Product forms* are variations of the homogeneous product satisfying the same general need as the latter plus a more specific subneed. For instance, the need for coffee is stimulated in part by the general thirst drive plus a specific preference or craving for coffee. The latter might consist of a learned need, physiological dependence on caffeine, or other factors. In any case, product forms for coffee include grounds, caffeinated instant, and decaffeinated instant. One might graph a PLC for each.

TABLE 4-3
Levels of Aggregation of Sales for the Product Life Cycle (PLC)

PHENOMENON TO BE REPRESENTED			
Generic Product Class	*Homogeneous Product Class*	*Product Form*	*Brand*
Drinks	Coffee	Instant Coffee	Brim Instant
Transportation	Automobiles	Sports Car	Porsche
Educational/ Entertainment/ Activities	Museums	Art Museums	National Gallery

Finally, each product form will consist of a number of *competing brands*. Among ground coffees, for example, Maxwell House, Folger's, Hills Brothers, Chock Full O' Nuts, and numerous store brands vie for the consumer's dollar. In Table 4-3, we have listed Brim Instant, a freeze-dried decaffeinated instant coffee, as an example of one brand. The PLC concept can be applied to individual brands as well as the aggregate product categories. In fact, we might even examine the PLC for subgroupings of individual brands such as sales of Brim Instant in the midwestern United States or purchases by a particular ethnic group. Table 4-3 also presents two other examples: transportation and educational/entertainment activities.

Table 4-3 suggests that the PLC concept can be applied at many levels of aggregation. But to which, if any, does the PLC concept apply in reality? Although the evidence is not all in, it appears that product forms conform the closest to fitting a PLC. Individual brands fluctuate greatly and frequently deviate from the idealistic PLC shape.

Similarly, broad and generic product classes often follow longer time frames and are subject to more forces, making analysis difficult. Thus, at the present, it seems that the PLC works best with respect to industry sales of product forms. For example, it would apply better to sales of electric lawn mowers than to all lawn mower types or to a Sears Craftsman Electric Mower. However, as we look deeper into the phenomena in the future and learn more about measurement and the dynamics involved, we may well discover that the PLC has utility at both broader and more specific levels of analysis.[12]

Still another issue with respect to the PLC concept is that dealing with *timing*. How long is each stage? How does one define the specific dimensions of a stage? What accounts for variations in the length of a stage over time and across products? One way to ascertain the length of stages is to plot changes over time and then, when a transition occurs, call it the end of one stage and the beginning of another. This is a subjective procedure but may yield satisfactory results if the data are well-behaved and roughly follow an S-shape. A somewhat better method is to set norms that generalize to at least a relatively broad class of products. For example, some authors have specified the transition from introduction to growth and from growth to maturity for 37 selected household appliances as follows:

The beginning of the growth stage is defined as the first two successive years of sales growth rate of 5 percent or greater following introduction. The end of the growth stage is signaled by a yearly rate of growth (percentage change in sales) equal to or less than the growth rate in consumer expenditures for all household products.[13]

These norms offer the advantages of being explicit, having some face validity, and allowing testability and replication. However, it should be recognized that there is still some element of arbitrariness in any rule-of-thumb. Also, products may still vary widely, depending on the circumstances. It was found that the duration of periods for the 37 household appliances noted above varied from 0 to 18 years for the introduction stage and from 3 to 44 years for the growth stage.[14] With such a large variation even for similar types of products, it is no wonder that generalizations and predictions from PLC theory are difficult to make. Moreover, it is probably even more difficult to set realistic norms for the transition from maturity to decline, because sales sometimes decrease, then increase, and then decrease many times before reaching a constant pattern.

Nevertheless, research continues into the study of PLC timing issues. There is some evidence that the introduction and growth stages have been decreasing for new product entrants over the years. As Table 4-4 shows, the length of time from introduction to maturity has shortened from about 46 years on average for household appliances introduced in 1922–1942, to 26.5 years for the period 1945–1964, and less than 9 years for 1965–1979.[15] The truncation of the PLC is most likely due to an acceleration in technological change, competition, and the increased education and sophistication of consumers.

TABLE 4-4

Average Duration of Introduction and Growth Stages for Selected Household Appliances

Product Groups	Introductory Stage Duration (years)	Growth Stage Duration (years)
12 Household Appliances Introduced 1922–1942	12.5	33.8
16 Household Appliances Introduced 1945–1964	7.0	19.5
9 Household Appliances Introduced 1965–1979	2.0	6.8

A fourth issue concerns the overall *pattern of consumer purchases* with respect to first-time sales, repeat sales, and total sales. Some products such as toothpaste or office supplies have a relatively short life, and the opportunity exists for considerable repeat sales by the same consumers. If we were to plot only total sales, we could miss the dynamics of consumer behavior reflected in the receptivity of the product. Figure 4-6 shows two PLC curves for similar products where the total sales for each is roughly equal. However, notice that for Case A total sales are composed of the sum of trial plus repeat sales, where trial rises moderately quickly and then stagnates and repeat sales begin a somewhat similar ascent and also then level off. In contrast, Case B produces similar sales with quite different levels for trial and repeat purchases. Trial is quite good, reaching higher levels than Case A. Nevertheless, due to very poor repeat sales, Case B is not able to surpass the sales of Case A.

Had we only focused on total sales, we would have concluded that the products were identical. Yet, as the curves reveal, Case A has not achieved the initial acceptance by the market it could have achieved (perhaps advertising is inferior or insufficient, or distribution is inadequate); and Case B, while generating amazing first-time purchases, fails to appeal sufficiently to the public to generate acceptable repeat purchases (perhaps the product fails to meet expectations communicated in advertising, or competitors have a differential advantage). The point is that we can gain a better understanding of PLC behavior by decomposing sales into its parts. Notice that total sales for Cases A and B and trial for Case A tend to follow the classic S-shaped PLC curve, while repeat sales for Case B is far from the expected form. A final point not revealed in Figure 4-6 is that the trial and repeat curves often cross. We have not extended the curves long enough in time to show this.

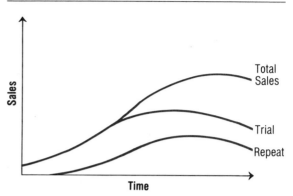

Case A. Good trial, average repeat

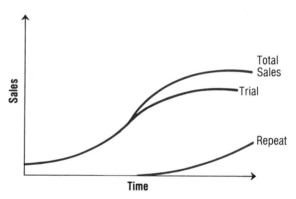

Case B. Very good trial, poor repeat

Figure 4-6. Two typical patterns for first-time (trial), repeat, and total sales over time

The last refinement in the PLC concept that we need to discuss concerns the *determinants of the curve* (e.g., the causes of sales). So far we have discussed the PLC largely as a descriptive phenomenon. The plot of sales over time merely describes the state or level of sales. It does not address the forces that produce sales. Yet this omission can create a false impression as to the inevitability of sales growth and decline. The PLC concept fails to note that sales are under the influence of many factors and can be controlled to a certain extent by management.

A classic example of this is provided by Procter & Gamble's detergent, Tide.[16] Tide was introduced in 1947 and has not at all followed the classic PLC curve. In fact, since its introduction, it might be still considered in the growth stage. It has not reached maturity in nearly four decades. What accounts for this unusual longevity and vitality? Well, the manufacturer has incorporated no fewer than 55 major improvements in the product over the years. Presumably, these improvements have stimulated demand both in terms of first-time purchases and repeat purchases. The actions of management have been successful in winning the battle, too, against competitors. In short, Procter & Gamble has been able to circumvent the forces that tend to produce a full PLC from birth to death.

Levitt has termed this an exploitation or extension of the PLC by the firm.[17] The idea is depicted graphically in Figure 4-7. At time 0, the firm introduces the product, and it grows along a PLC curve (I) until it reaches point x in time. If the firm were to do little in terms of new marketing activities, then sales might well flatten out and begin a decline towards point A. The curve from 0 to A represents the expected path under "normal" marketing expenditures and competitive pressures. However, if at time x the firm finds a new geographical market, a new use for the product, or in some other way stimulates sales (e.g., through a major redesign of the product, more advertising, a price drop, and so on), then the "life" of the product might be renewed along curve II. At point Y in time, a potential decline toward B is again possible. This might also be avoided through the development of new markets or new marketing programs, producing an increase in sales along curve III, and so on. The points to stress are that the rise and fall of products are not certain events, at least in the short- or mid-term, and that management can influence the shape of the PLC for its products. The presentation in the next chapter suggests ways in which this can be done.

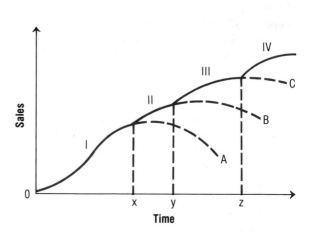

Figure 4-7. The extension of the PLC

By now, it should be obvious that the PLC concept is an oversimplification. Nevertheless, it harbors enough truth and serves as a guide in many firms for strategic planning and implementation of the marketing mix that it deserves our scrutiny. Instead of the idealistic shape and sequences represented in Figure 4-5, it is perhaps more realistic to develop models allowing more complex patterns and stages. Hopefully, we will learn more about the causes of the PLC and develop a small number of fundamental forms. One direction for research is to develop contingency theories. That is, the shape and sequences might depend on particular consumer groups, product technologies or functions, geographical or other segments, and so on. In reality, we may someday find a set of sequences such as the one shown in Figure 4-8.

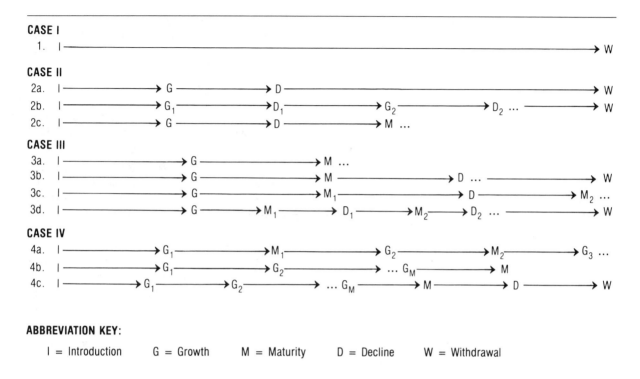

CASE I

1. I ——→ W

CASE II

2a. I ——————→ G ——————→ D ————————————————————————→ W

2b. I ——————→ G₁——————→D₁——————→ G₂——————→ D₂ ... ——————→ W

2c. I ——————→ G ——————→ D ——————→ M ...

CASE III

3a. I ——————————→ G ——————————→ M ...

3b. I ——————————→ G ——————————→ M ——————→ D ... ——————→ W

3c. I ——————————→ G ——————————→ M₁——————→ D ——————→ M₂ ...

3d. I ——————————→ G ——→ M₁ ——→ D₁ ——→M₂——→ D₂ ... ——————→ W

CASE IV

4a. I ——————→ G₁——————→M₁——————→ G₂——————→M₂——————→ G₃ ...

4b. I ——————→ G₁——————→ G₂——————→ ... Gₘ——————→ M

4c. I ——————→ G₁——————→ G₂——————→ ... Gₘ——————→ M ——————→ D ——————→ W

ABBREVIATION KEY:

I = Introduction   G = Growth   M = Maturity   D = Decline   W = Withdrawal

Figure 4-8. Some possible Product Life Cycle sequences

For Case I, a new product is introduced to the market but quickly fails and is withdrawn. As we shall see in the following chapter, this is a more frequent occurrence than one might think. Case II shows the situation where a new product at least achieves some early growth. In 2a, sales grow but then decline and never recover. Perhaps advertising has stimulated people to try the product, but it subsequently fails to live up to expectations and repeat purchases never materialize. In 2b, a series of growth-decline cycles follows product introduction, but sales never reach acceptable levels and the product is discontinued. In 2c, introduction and growth are again followed by decline. However, the drop in sales is arrested, and a satisfactory saturation level is reached to enable the product to survive. Case III illustrates instances approaching the classic PLC pattern. In 3a, sales grow and reach maturity for an indeterminant period.

Example 3b is exactly the classic PLC shown in Figure 4-5. In 3c, the initial decline has ended—either through management actions, market forces, or both—and a second lower level of maturity is reached. In 3d, a new period of decline follows the second saturation level and ultimately results in withdrawal. Case IV shows the situation where decline and, to a certain extent, even maturity have been overcome or at least postponed. Examples 4a or 4b would seem to fit the pattern followed by Tide. In sum, Figure 4-8 points the way to better descriptions of the PLC. However, ultimately, we must search for ways to model the effects that price, advertising, and other variables have on sales, if we are to develop a meaningful PLC framework for management.[18]

A New Direction. As a final comment on the PLC as a description of the physical product, we should note that theories of evolution, natural selection, and adaptation and change offer promising frameworks for study.[19] Just as biologists study the evolution of the species or social scientists study the development of systems, so too might marketers investigate the evolutionary processes of product growth. Although very little work has been done in this regard, the years ahead are sure to show a greater emphasis placed on evolutionary perspectives. We turn now from analysis of dimensions of the physical product to discussion of some nonphysical apsects of products and their relation to consumer behavior.

The Words and Symbols Used to Represent the Product

As we saw in Figures 4-1 and 4-2, a unique part of any product is its image. The most direct and lasting way that this imagery is communicated is through the words, terms, ideas, and other distinctive symbols used to signify the product. Indeed, some symbols are so powerful that they instill immediate recognition of the product and perhaps a special idea or feeling about it. Sometimes the symbol exists as letters standing for a corporate name, such as IBM or A&P. Or a number is added to the name to give it uniqueness and an identity: Mobil 1, Chanel No. 5, Phillips 66. If the marketer is clever enough, he or she may choose words to convey an idea about the quality or function of the product: Sears Craftsman tools, Spic and Span all-purpose cleaner, Sea & Ski sun tanning and skin-care products. Other words are created anew but achieve a familiarity transcending their artificial origins: Jell-O, Kleenex, Xerox. Animals are used on occasion, perhaps to create an image of humor, warmth, or "social distinctiveness": Smokey the Bear, Charlie Tuna, the Lacoste Alligator. People are used in at least two senses. One is as a spokesperson that the public knows well or identifies with: Karl Malden for American Express, Bill Cosby for Coke or Texas Instruments Computers. A second use of people is in a caricature or to evoke nostalgia or fantasy: Colonel Sanders for Kentucky Fried Chicken, the Marlboro Man, Charlie cosmetics.

Of course, symbols are fickle and can backfire, as the Florida Citrus Commission discovered when their spokesperson, Anita Bryant, became involved in a public controversy with homosexual groups. Similarly, most powerful symbols are two-edged swords. Charmin's Mr. Whipple is readily identified by the public, but some people are offended by his seemingly demeaning attitude toward women. Nevertheless, the fickle and double-edged aspects of symbols prove the point: namely, products are more than their physical characteristics. The name or symbol is just as much a part of the product as is its shape, color, or durability.

Figure 4-9 illustrates many of the forms that symbols take when used as part of a product. We might think of all of these as producing a *brand image*.[20] That is, the image (i.e., thoughts, feelings, moral reactions) arising from a product are a complex function of the brand name, product jingle, spokesperson, and so on attached to the product. Also, as stressed in the chapters on consumer behavior, the brand image is a function of the person's prior learning, needs, motivation, and expectations. We construct our image of a brand by combining the things that we perceive with our individual psychological makeup.

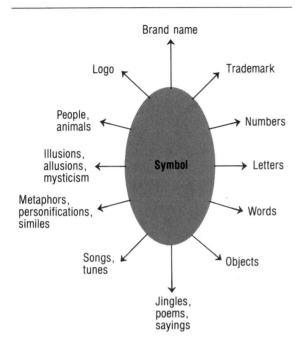

Figure 4-9. How symbols are manifested in products and services

In general, product symbols have three characteristics. First, they are *a means of communication*. They convey factual information, confidence in the seller, emotional content, and social meaning. For example, some people see the Golden Arches of McDonald's as a symbol of a place (1) to get a relatively good quality meal quickly and at a low price, (2) to meet with friends or make new acquaintances, and (3) to have a good time or break the monotony of work or school. These reactions and others are perhaps frequently below the level of self-awareness, but they are nevertheless associated with the symbol. McDonald's and other restaurants are more than merely places to eat. They are settings for the fulfillment of basic needs and the realization of higher-order needs. Of course, not everyone experiences symbols and the product or service in this way. But this is another way of saying that people differ and that marketers need to discover and cater to market segments. The communication aspect of symbols is perhaps the most obvious, managerially employed, and publicly acceptable property of them.

A second characteristic of symbols is that they serve as *a means of influence and control*. That is, they are used to initiate, coerce, or force action. For instance, a package display for candy can stimulate impulse buying as a function of its power to tie in with a hunger drive, or a sexually arousing ad for a movie might influence patronage due to its powers. Sometimes symbols work the other way around and block usage of the product. Presumably, for at least a small number of people, the Surgeon General's warning on cigarette packs has scared them sufficiently to reduce consumption. In any event, symbols can occasionally go beyond informational input and cause people to act in particular ways. However, this aspect of symbols is perhaps less frequent in marketing and requires a relatively powerful stimulus and/or strong emotional or physiological involvement on the part of the consumer.

The final dimension of symbols is less purposeful than the first two. Symbols now and then stem from *a need for self-expression* on the part of the seller. Without necessarily intending to inform the public or produce a sale, marketers will go to great ends to display their wares. Small shopkeepers or restaurateurs, for example, have been known to grossly "overspend" on furnishings, displays, and signs. Although not strictly necessary from an utilitarian standpoint, the expenditures serve as an expression of the person's self-image, aesthetics, or personal pride. This attribute of symbols is probably the least frequent, given the profit motive, but it occurs more often than one might think. It can influence others as well.

A final point to stress about the words and symbols used to represent a product is that their effects, if any, are usually indirect. We are not usually aware of the impact of the symbols on us. Rather, they relate to us and shape our behavior through largely nonconscious processes. This occurs primarily through their ability to trigger biological and physiological reactions, to conjure up images and stored feelings in memory, and to suggest new information which becomes fuel for the psychological construction of reality. Because symbols are somewhat vague and ambiguous, they are ripe for the perceiver to interpret them from one's own needs and wants. There are many managerial decisions that must be made in regard to the words and symbols used to represent products (e.g., whether to brand or not, how to implement an effective brand strategy), but these topics are reserved for the following chapter.[21]

The Meaning of Products for Consumers

We have examined the physical dimensions of products and touched upon their significance for the consumer. However, we have said little as to the mental and feeling *processes* that consumers pass through as they evaluate products. Figure 4-10 outlines the processes.[22] Notice first that there are many stimuli. In addition to the physical product and all its features and the many ways that the product communicates symbolically, various stimuli from the marketing mix and from the social and political environment impinge upon the consumer. Out of this maze of information, the consumer perceives some subset. A few product attributes, the brand name, an advertisement, the expectations of family members, and other stimuli might fill this subset at any one point in time.

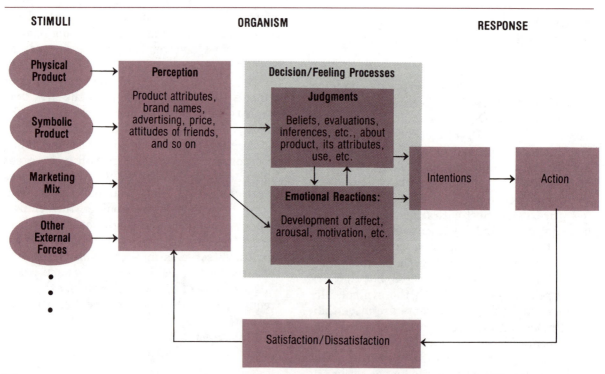

Figure 4-10. An outline of the consumer's response to product-related and other stimuli

Product: Micro and Macro Perspectives

The interpretation of one' perceptions and construction of one's psychological reality occur in the stage labeled *decision/feeling processes.* Two subprocesses are most important here. First, the information perceived is acted upon psychologically. Judgments are made through the formation of beliefs about product attributes, evaluations of these attributes, inferences, and other thinking processes. These processes are roughly what we mean by rational decision making and information processing. Nonrational processes occur, too, as emotional reactions. After exposure to a stimulus or cue, affective responses are developed or activated, physiological arousal may occur, and one's needs and motives are brought into play. Notice that judgments and emotional reactions are shown to interact in Figure 4-10. Not shown in the figure is how information and feelings are integrated. We know very little about these processes, but we have touched upon them in the first chapter on consumer behavior when we discussed attitude formation, information processing, and decision rules.

The outcomes of decision/feeling processes may instill an intention to act on the part of the consumer. Intentions, in turn, might influence actual behavior; i.e., the actions one takes (e.g., shopping). In Figure 4-10, notice further that outcomes from our actions (e.g., experience with the product) feed back upon both our perceptions and our judgments and emotions. This occurs partly through the development of reactions of satisfaction/dissatisfaction toward the product, its attributes, use, and so on. Satisfaction/ dissatisfaction reactions are themselves comprised of cognitive responses (e.g., expectations, comparisons of expected to obtained outcomes) and affective responses (e.g., disappointment, anger, pleasure).

Although Figure 4-10 presents some of the processes involved in consumer responses to products, it does not indicate the type of content manifest in these. As an example of content, Figure 4-11 illustrates one consumer's (partial) mental map of the Volkswagen (VW) Golf. Let us begin with an examination of the person's cognitive structure in the top half of the figure. Notice that the VW Golf is represented as a circle and is connected to many other circles. You might think of each circle as representing a concept in the mind of the consumer. These might be concepts of objects, people, abstract ideas, actions, and so on. One set of associations that the VW Golf has is with bicycles, trains, buses, and planes. That is, these are all modes of transportation and share this common content. The lines connecting concepts represent mental associations in memory. The longer the line, the farther away the concepts are at either end of the line in the consumer's mind. Also, concepts that are indirectly linked to a focal concept only through a common intermediary concept are farther away from each other than directly linked concepts. We have chosen to present only a small portion of the consumer's cognitive structure and to focus on the concepts associated most with the VW Golf. Thus, for example, we have omitted some concepts farther removed from the VW Golf but tied to one of the concepts that are connected to the VW Golf: e.g., blue-sky, blue-bird, blue-uniform, blue-sad, etc. Further, note that the different modes of transportation are farther from the VW Golf than the Mazda GLC, which is a somewhat similar automobile. Therefore, in Figure 4-11, the VW Golf and Mazda GLC are directly connected by a relatively short line to indicate this psychological proximity.

A. Cognitive structure

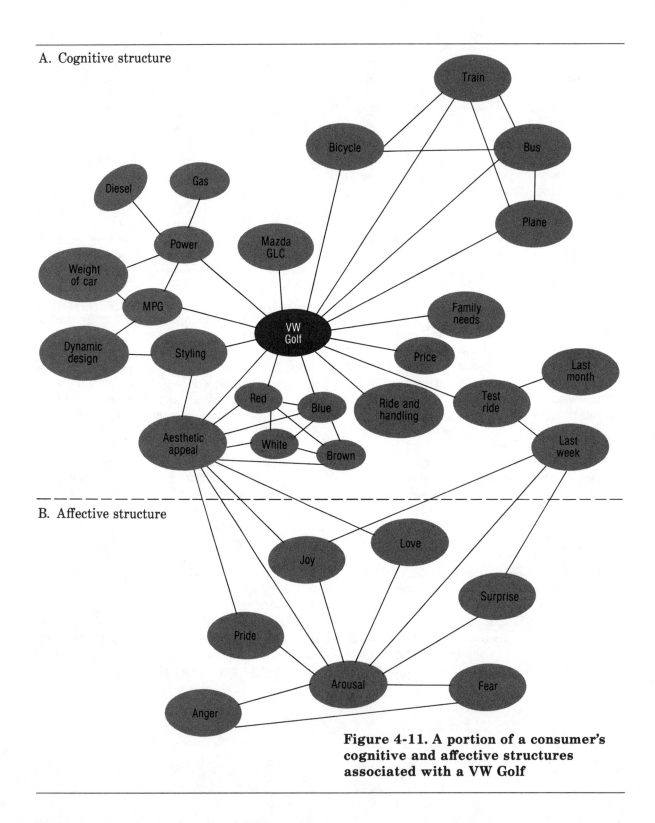

B. Affective structure

Figure 4-11. A portion of a consumer's cognitive and affective structures associated with a VW Golf

Another property to note in the top of Figure 4-11 is that many attributes of the VW Golf are directly and indirectly connected to it. In the consumer's mind, the VW Golf is, in part, a bundle of attributes: power, miles per gallon (mpg), styling, aesthetic appeal, color, ride and handling, price, and fill-ups. Also, some of these attributes are mutually related to each other through other attributes: mpg and styling are connected to each other through aerodynamic design (as well as through the VW Golf); weight of the car is connected to power and mpg. The VW Golf might also be connected to social concepts such as the felt needs of family members or expectations of society for an economical, pollution-free automobile. Still another type of concept is less semantic and more episodic (e.g., a test ride last week; see Figure 4-11). By episodic, we mean the recording or remembrance of a specific personal event in time. Our memory for meaning (i.e., semantic content), while connected to episodic concepts, is less temporally and spatially dependent. The cognitive structure contains representations of both types of concepts.

In the bottom half of Figure 4-11, we can see the consumer's emotional structure as exists in the mind. Here again, the closeness of emotional states is represented by the length of line used. In addition, the larger the circle, the stronger the emotion. The cognitive and affective structures are interconnected. For example, the idea of aesthetic appeal for the particular consumer shown in Figure 4-11 is linked to feelings of pride, joy, love, and overall arousal. The person's experiences in the previous week's test drive is connected to joy, arousal, and surprise. Psychologists are only now beginning to study these linkages, and we know very little about the processes involved. Nevertheless, the cognitive/affective structure is a central force guiding behavior.

One way that marketers might use the notions depicted in the Figure 4-11 is as follows. A marketer might wish to change the conceptualization of the VW Golf held by a group of consumers. He or she could consider the following alternative tactics:

1 change the meaning of an existing product attribute (e.g., by redesigning the advertising).

2 introduce a new product attribute not considered before by the consumer.

3 change the consumer's interpretation or evaluation of either a competitor's product or alternative ways to satisfy the basic need satisfied by the product (e.g., by persuading the consumer that the Mazda GLC is less satisfying than the VW Golf or that mass transit is less desirable).

4 alter the role of other criteria (e.g., family pressure) through persuasion to make non-attribute concepts more salient.

5 increase the positive affective associations to the product or its attributes and decrease the negative (e.g., through advertising).

In these ways, one gains access to the cognitive and affective structures, and the changes or additions made influence the consumer's conceptualizations and feelings. We might think of the entire network shown in Figure 4-11 as being analogous to a pinball machine. When a new concept is added or a change is made in an existing one, the result is similar to the release of a pinball and its subsequent activation of many lights, buzzers, and so on. Just as the path of the pinball spreads its influence throughout the gameboard, so too will a new concept or change in an old one influence many other concepts in the consumer's mind. The ultimate objective of the marketer, of course, is to stimulate intentions and choice behavior. Exactly how this works is not well understood but is subject for future study.

This concludes our discussion of the product and the individual consumer. In upcoming chapters, we will investigate how consumers structure their perceptions, cognitions, and feelings and how marketers can measure these and use them to advantage in decision making. We turn now to some more global issues concerned with products.

Products from a Macro Viewpoint

At the macro level, we may look at products in three senses: aggregate descriptive, economic, and public policy. The macro view of products complements the micro perspective assumed in the first part of the chapter and helps describe the environment, constraints, and opportunities shaping managerial decisions, which are, in turn, presented in the following chapter. Let us now look at each of the facets of products at a macro level.

An Aggregate Description of Products[23]

The PLC concept is in one sense a macro description of the sales of products as they pass through time. But it does not go very far. To gain a deeper understanding of products at the macro level, we can also look at them in terms of three dimensions: the cost, timing, and expected risk/benefit associated with new product development.[24]

Beginning with *cost considerations*, let us examine the cases of consumer and industrial goods. New product development involves such activities as idea generation, market identification, consumer measurement, sales forecasting, business analysis, product design, marketing planning, test marketing, and product introduction (including advertising, sales force, promotion, and distribution programs). Each of these incurs different costs. Mansfield and Rapoport studied the costs involved for product innovation in the chemical industry. Column 1 in Table 4-5 summarizes their findings for this relatively representative "industrial good." Notice that

development costs averaged $960,000, while introduction costs averaged $1,270,000, for a total of $2,230,000. Hauser and Urban provide a similar breakdown of estimated costs for consumer goods (see column 2 in Table 4-5). Consumer goods undergo about $1,350,000 for development, on average, whereas $5,000,000 is spent on introduction activities.

TABLE 4-5

Average Costs of New Product Introduction for Industrial[a] and Consumer Goods[b]

Industrial Goods	Consumer Goods
Development (e.g., research, prototype/pilot plant, etc.):	Development (e.g., market identification, design, testing):
$ 960,000	$1,350,000
Introduction (e.g., tooling and manufacturing, marketing start-up, etc.):	Introduction (e.g., advertising, sales force, promotion, distribution, etc.):
$1,270,000	$5,000,000
TOTAL $2,230,000	$6,350,000

[a]In the chemical industry. Adapted from E. Mansfield and J. Rapoport, "The Costs of Industrial Product Innovation," *Management Science* 21 (August 1975): 1382.

[b]Adapted from G. L. Urban and J. R. Hauser, *Design and Marketing of New Products* (Englewood Cliffs, N.J.: Prentice-Hall, 1980), p. 48.

A few points are worth noticing in Table 4-5. First, the overall costs of the average consumer good are considerably higher than the total costs of the average industrial good. Second, although introduction costs are somewhat greater than developmental costs for industrial goods, such costs are grossly more expensive for consumer goods. Among nonbusiness people, it is not generally recognized that so much money is needed to develop and launch a new product. Third, the vast sums of money involved, coupled with the timing and risk considerations discussed below, suggest that a formal, well-thought-out decision process is needed to effectively and efficiently manage new product introductions. We will develop an outline of such a decision model in the next chapter.

Timing is also a key variable in new product development. The PLC curve shown in Figure 4-5 begins with introduction, but obviously many activities occur before this. A company must invent a new idea. The idea must be realized in a form that can be tested in order to see consumer reactions. Production and marketing activities must be planned and brought to fruition. And so on. Adler studied the elapsed time from idea generation, to test market, to introduction for more than 39 products. A few of these appear in Table 4-6. It can be seen that products such as Marlboro filter cigarettes or Flav-R-Straws took only a total of two or three years from idea generation to market introduction, whereas other products such as Crest toothpaste or the Polaroid Color Camera took 10 to 15 years or more. Further, notice that, while the lag between test market and introduction is typically only one year (and sometimes less), the time between idea generation and test market covers many years. Although Table 4-6 lists only consumer goods, it is important to stress that timing considerations for industrial and consumer goods are generally different. As Urban and Hauser[25] note:

For a typical industrial production, five years is a reasonable estimate of time for design, testing, and setup of manufacturing. In the case of consumer products, the time is about two to two-and-a-half years, if the product is successful at each phase and if no major R&D work is required.

In sum, we see that new product development results in a considerable investment in time. Given that people's needs change, that competitors may also enter the market at any time, and that economic and financial conditions continually shift, one can see the need for a well-planned new product development process.

TABLE 4-6

Time from Idea Generation to Test Market to Introduction for Nine Products

Brand/Product	Idea First Conceived	Test Market	Intro- duction	Total Years
Ban (roll-on deodorant)	1948	1954	1955	6
Crest (fluoride toothpaste)	1945	1955	1956	10
Flav-R-Straws	1953	1956	1957	3
Johnson liquid shoe polish	1957	1960	1961	3
Lustre Creme (liquid shampoo)	1950	—[a]	1958	8
Marlboro (filter cigarettes)	1953	1955	—	2
Maxim (freeze-dried instant coffee)	1954	1964	—	10
Purina Dog Chow	1951	1955	1957	4
Polaroid Color Camera	1948	1963	1963	15+

[a]Data not available.

SOURCE: Adapted from L. Adler, ''Time Lag in New Product Development,'' *Journal of Marketing Research* 3 (January 1966): 18–20.

The final way we might describe products at the aggregate level is in terms of the *risk and benefits* involved. We know that all products do not succeed. But what percentage do succeed, what are the uncertainties, and what can we expect to achieve taking into account the uncertainties? Figure 4-12 shows the outcomes of the pruning process that occurs from idea generation until commercialization.[26] On the y-axis is plotted the number of ideas surviving at each of the stages in new product development (i.e., in screening, business analysis, development, test marketing, commercialization). The x-axis shows the cumulative time from idea generation to commercialization. The figure shows that there is a rapid fall off from many ideas to the one remaining at commercialization. In 1968, Booz, Allen, and Hamilton studied 51 companies and found that, for every successful idea brought to commercialization, 58 ideas were generated, on average. Only about 12 of these passed the screening stage, and 6 more were pruned out through a business analysis examining the potential revenues and costs. About 3 or 4 ideas failed to make it through the development process itself (i.e., product engineering, consumer measurement, etc.). Testing eliminated about one or two ideas, so that only one made it through the gauntlet to commercialization. By 1981, the picture changed radically but still reveals considerable risk. Now 7 new ideas must be generated for every success. When we couple the pruning process prior to commercialization with the vicissitudes stemming from competitive battles and other forces after introduction, it is little wonder that business is such a risky endeavor.

For industrial products, Mansfield and Wagner estimated that probabilities of technical completion, commercialization (given technical completion), and economic success (given commercialization) are .57, .65, and .74, respectively.[27] This yields an overall probability of success of .27 (i.e., the multiplicative product of the three stages).

Failures tend to be more a result of commercial problems (e.g., lack of a viable market, competition, inadequate marketing) than technical shortcomings.[28]

For consumer products, Urban and Hauser estimate that the probabilities of a successful design, test market (given design), and market success (given successful test market) are .50, .45, and .85, respectively. This gives an overall probability of success of .19. Hence, consumer goods are considered riskier than industrial goods. Notice that the biggest difference occurs during test marketing. Consumer goods are particularly vulnerable in this stage. On the other hand, once the product passes the test phase successfully, consumer goods have a higher chance of success than industrial goods. Overall, however, the launch of a new consumer good is riskier than the launch of an industrial good.

We can combine the estimates of probability of success with cost estimates to determine the benefit of conducting each stage in the new product development process. For example, Table 4-7 illustrates the gain achieved by testing the product before introduction. In the top half of the figure, we see that the expected cost for one success is $26,316,000 = $5,000,000 \times (1/0.190)$, if we save development (i.e., design and testing) costs. That is, to produce one success, on average, the firm must market about 5.26 products $= 1/0.190$. In the bottom half of Table 4-7, we see the effect of saving only design costs. The probability of success for testing without design is $0.225 = 0.450 \times 0.500$. To produce one success from test marketing, about $4.44 = 1/0.225$ products must be tested; and to produce one successful product, about $1.18 = 1/0.850$ test market successes are required. Therefore, the total expected cost of test marketing is $1,000,000 \times 1/(0.225 \times 0.850) = $5,228,000$; and the expected cost of introduction is $5,000,000 \times 1/0.850 = $5,882,000$. The total for the two activities is $11,110,000. To determine the total benefit of testing, we subtract this total from the total at the top of Table 4-7 to

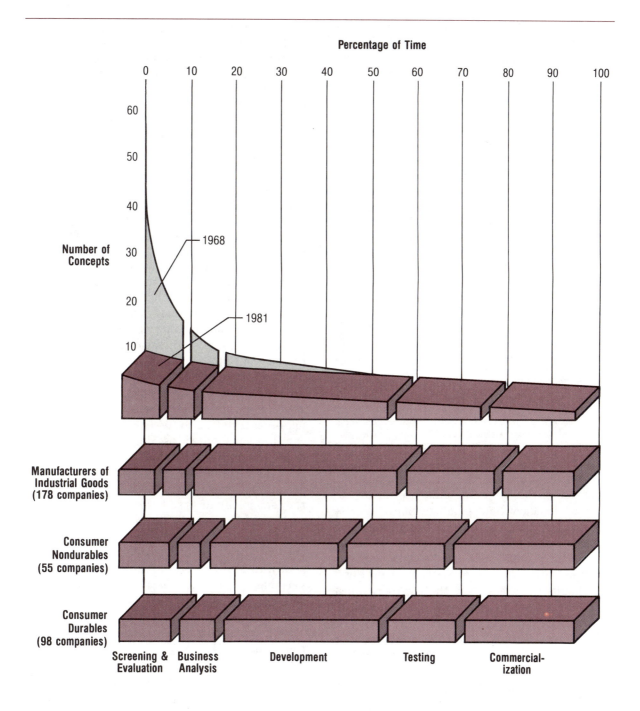

Figure 4-12. The new product gauntlet

SOURCE: *New Products Management for the 1980s* (Booz, Allen & Hamilton, Inc. New York: 1982).

arrive at $15,206,000. Urban and Hauser present other examples of savings due to investment in design and other activities.[29] The procedures used to calculate these savings are similar to the ones illustrated in Table 4-7 but will not be presented herein.

TABLE 4-7

Expected Gain If Firm Uses Test Marketing Procedures

	Average Cost	Probability of Success	Expected Cost
"Save Development Costs" (Design and Testing)			
Introduction	$5,000,000	0.190	$26,316,000
"Save Design Costs"			
Test Market	$1,000,000	0.225	$ 5,228,000
Introduction	5,000,000	0.850	5,882,000
Total Expected Investment			$11,110,000

Net Benefit of Test Marketing = $26,316,000 − $11,110,000
= $15,206,000

Source: Reproduced from G. L. Urban and J. R. Hauser, *Design and Marketing of New Products* (Englewood Cliffs, N.J.: Prentice-Hall, 1980): p. 55. ©1980, Prentice-Hall. Reprinted by permission of the publisher.

In sum, we have attempted to show how products might be described at an aggregate level. There are other ways to do this, but examination of cost, timing, and expected risks and benefits provides an informative picture of product "behavior." We should note, however, that the examples used herein are very rough ones. For one thing, most of the numbers are averages. As you know, averages are imperfect summaries of phenomena. They do not reveal the range and dispersion of numbers, which could have been considerable in each of the earlier examples. In addition, some of the above analyses were based on subjective estimates. These, too, can vary widely depending on the type of product, market, or time period examined. Hence, we should regard the previous examples as general tendencies. Finally, still another way to construe products at the aggregate level is as an adoption and diffusion process. We have already described this process in the preceding chapter. Recall that the purchases of new products occur at different times depending on the number of consumers and whether one is an innovator, early adopter, late adopter, or laggard.

Economic Views of Products

Economists have a well-developed theory of products based upon the concept of *product differentiation*. We have already touched upon product differentiation in Figure 4-3 where it was suggested that marketers produce a differentiated product by (a) varying the tangible and intangible characteristics related to the physical product and (b) introducing unique inputs from the marketing mix, such as advertising or distribution practices. In this section of the chapter, we will focus on the implications of differentiated products on market structure and market conduct. To build upon a model from industrial organization theory, the major relationships of product differentiation to forces in the marketplace can be represented as illustrated in Figure 4-13.[30] Basic market conditions impinge upon the market structure to constrain or facilitate certain patterns of relationships. For example, the technology of production and economies of scale might shape the physical characteristics of a product and how many versions might be efficiently produced. Product differentiation is shown in Figure 4-13 to influence a number of variables. It creates barriers to entry. It is sometimes made in response to competitive pressures as well as consumer needs; yet if successful in making sales, it can draw in other competitors. Hence, arrows connect product differentiation to the number of buyers and sellers in two directions. Further, product differentiation is accomplished through advertising, distribution, etc., and can produce more freedom in pricing. These conduct variables, in turn, influence economic performance and feed back upon market structure. We will have more to say on the relationship of product differentiation to market conduct, performance, and structure in later chapters on advertising, channels of distribution, and pricing. But for now, we will focus briefly on the role of product differentiation in market power.

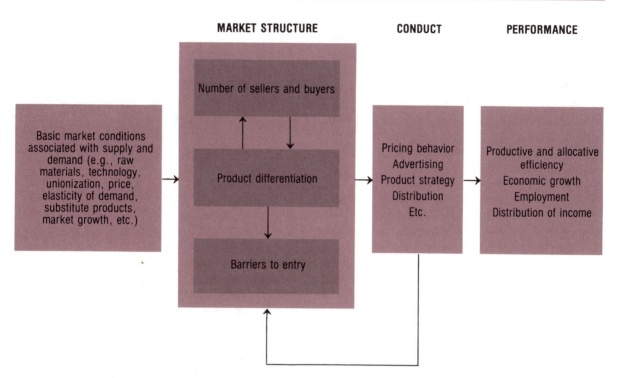

MARKET STRUCTURE

Number of sellers and buyers

Product differentiation

Barriers to entry

Basic market conditions associated with supply and demand (e.g., raw materials, technology, unionization, price, elasticity of demand, substitute products, market growth, etc.)

CONDUCT

Pricing behavior
Advertising
Product strategy
Distribution
Etc.

PERFORMANCE

Productive and allocative efficiency
Economic growth
Employment
Distribution of income

Figure 4-13. The role of product differentiation as revealed in an industrial organization model from economics

Economists tend to view product differentiation through its ability to achieve cost and price advantages over rivals.[31] Although this might occur through the orchestration of any one or more of the inputs shown in Figure 4-3, two cases seem to be the most frequent. One of these occurs as a consequence of *physical differentiation* of the product. The seller simply varies the ingredients, workmanship, or functioning of the product to achieve a differential competitive advantage. If done effectively in relation to the needs and demand of consumers, the result will be a weak form of monopoly in that no strong substitutes will exist for the product. Thus, the seller may be able to charge a higher price than if more directly competitive rivals existed. Recognizing that physical product differentiation (and the similar type arising from convenient distribution locations) can satisfy consumer needs, economists ask the question of how much differentiation is dysfunctional for the consumer, the firm, and general market performance. For physical product (and distributional) differentiation, they typically conclude that it is functional to the extent that product quality is high, prices are not too high, sellers can produce large volumes and thus incur economies of scale, and profits are generated and subsequently feed back into the economy as new investment and greater employment. Perhaps because physical differences in products are easily measured, whereas the value judgments of consumers' preferences for these differences are not, economists have tended to give higher marks to this type of differentiation. As one economist summarizes it,

Much and perhaps most of the product differentiation effort observed in a modern private enterprise economy represents little more than a natural and healthy response to legitimate demands. People's wants are diverse, and consumers plainly desire a varied menu of consumption opportunities. It is a rare consumer who doesn't value convenience in the location of suppliers, and many will pay a price premium for a certain amount of locational convenience. Nearly every consumer prefers good service over poor, though the prices individuals are willing to pay for extra services vary widely. The diversity of preferences for physical design and performance characteristics is especially great.[32]

However, the question remains as to when monopoly power resulting from such differentiation is too great from an economic performance standpoint. The conditions when this will happen are little understood in practice. Nevertheless, economic theory predicts that under monopolistic competition (where many sellers market differentiated products) high prices and excessive profits may not be the rule.[33] The latter are likely to occur only under pure monopoly and differentiated oligopoly conditions.

A second type of product differentiation is due to *advertising*. Here economists acknowledge some social benefits but generally emphasize the social costs. Their arguments apply most to products relatively similar in physical characteristics, so we will limit discussion to these. Basically, it is argued that advertising creates a false image of differentiation among products that are essentially identical in attributes and makeup. The ability to differentiate then creates monopoly power and permits the firm to charge higher prices than justified under undifferentiated competition. The processes that create monopoly power are little understood for the most part. One argument asserts that advertising leads to differentiation, which in turn stimulates brand loyalty. When consumers purchase in a brand-loyal way, they do so out of habit or through learning and at the same time fail to examine competitive offerings carefully. In fact, the seller achieves a monopoly of sorts. So far, evidence supporting this hypothesis is weak or nonexistent.[34] Another argument alleges that the image built up through advertising constitutes barriers to entry for potential rivals. New competitors must spend disproportionately more to overcome the image advantage of entrenched firms. Porter lists this form of differentiation as a barrier to entry, but again, little research exists on the issue.[35] Yet another rationale is that neither advertising alone nor product innovation alone can produce differentiation. Rather, both are needed at the same time. Limited evidence for this argument can be found in the drug industry.[36]

An often cited finding suggesting that advertising does create image differentiation, and this in turn results in excessive prices, as in the ReaLemon case.[37] In 1973, ReaLemon reconstituted lemon juice sold for $.62 in the supermarket and cornered 80 percent of the market. Yet the price of a leading competitor selling essentially the same physical product was about $.47. The seller's own marketing plan describes the situation as follows:

Although reconstituted lemon juice is virtually indistinguishable one brand from another, heavy emphasis on the ReaLemon brand through its media effort should create such memorability for the brand, that an almost imaginary superiority would exist in the mind of the consumer, a justification for paying the higher price we are asking.[38]

Despite instances such as this, it is very difficult to prove that the price differentials do not reflect cost and/or quality differences. Scherer maintains that differentiation through image advertising does "work" under three conditions. First, image advertising works best when products are indistinguishable and/or are difficult to evaluate. The advertisements provide the persuasion leading to the sale compared to the condition where no rationale exists for choice among essentially identical products with no advertising. Second, it is effective also for products that have strong intangible characteristics such as prestige or social status. The public nature of the advertising reinforces the social image or subjective value of the product. Finally, image advertising is more effective the greater the risk associated with the product. Presumably, this is why so many consumers pay high prices for ethical drugs when essentially the same generic drugs are available at much lower prices. They pay a premium for the perceived higher quality control presumably practiced by the firm with a well-known reputation.

In sum, the economist takes an ambivalent stance toward product differentiation. On the one hand, product differentiation is acknowledged to satisfy heterogeneous needs in consumers, provide cost savings and competitive advantages for firms, and sometimes stimulate a healthy economy. On the other hand, it is criticized for its role in creating monopolies, high prices, barriers to entry, resource misallocation, poor quality products, media clutter, and other social costs. Much opportunity exists for the researcher desiring to find the truth of product differentiation effects, for currently little is known in this regard.

Public Policy Aspects of Products

Public policy issues related to products occur in three areas. One concerns antitrust problems and is dealt with in later chapters (e.g., advertising and pricing) where the Antitrust Division, the Federal Trade Commission, and the president are discussed as they relate to marketing practices. The second area concerns the physical product and its implications for the consumer. The third examines aspects of packaging and the law. Let us look at the latter two areas in more detail.

The Physical Product. A number of laws address product ingredients and product safety. The earliest of these arose out of public horror toward practices of food processors and drug manufacturers revealed in the early 1900s. Upton Sinclair and others published exposés detailing the adulteration and occasional outright use of poison chemicals in foods. Drugs, too, commonly contained harmful ingredients or too often failed to contain anything more potent than colored water, sugar, or flour, despite their claims. In any event, the Federal Food, Drug, and Cosmetic Act now protects consumers against specific harmful ingredients used in the past. Moreover, certain types of fillers and other adulterators are forbidden or controlled. Related to this, legislation exists setting sanitation standards in restaurants, hospitals, and certain food processing plants, among other locations. Whether these restrictions go far enough or too far is a matter of debate.

In 1972, the Consumer Product Safety Act was passed with a provision establishing a Consumer Product Safety Commission. This was an outgrowth of the high incidence of accidents consumers experienced in the use of products. The Consumer Product Safety Commission examines products for safety hazards and can forbid the sale of products and invoke penalties in certain instances. Often, firms are asked to withdraw their products from the marketplace and voluntarily comply. Over the years, many unsafe products have been identified and either altered to make them safer or else withdrawn completely. This has frequently happened with toys (e.g., a toy dart gun) and child care products (e.g., unsafe baby cribs). But other products such as tools, household items, clothing, and appliances come under scrutiny as well.

Finally, products are protected by patent and trademark laws in the case of physical products or copyright laws in the case of literary works. These prevent others from directly reproducing one's ideas, although today's products are so complex and so many design and technological alternatives exist that enforcement is sometimes difficult. Nevertheless, firms are quick to exercise their rights. Consider the case of Lacoste and its familiar alligator logo found on shirts and other products, and sold throughout the world.[40] In 1982, a one-man company, Mad Dog Productions, Inc., headed by Barry Gottlieb, decided to take on the giant in the shirt business. As a spoof, Gottlieb named his shirt the Croc O' Shirt and chose as his logo a dead-looking upside-down crocodile with its tongue sticking out. Says Gottlieb, "[The shirts] make a satirical statement. The Croc O' Shirt is a humorous symbol for the growing counter-preppy movement." The latter statement refers to the prep school and post-prep school segment of the market who allegedly represent the primary purchasers of Lacoste shirts. Lacoste sued Mad Dog for trademark infringement of its presumed claim to "all 'lizard-like' creatures." The seemingly harmless association to a simple symbol by a fledgling company has obviously been taken seriously by the manufacturer. Legal battles such as these reveal the importance of intangibles in the marketplace and the thoroughness and intensity of competitive rivalry.

Packages, Labels, and Warranties. Public policy issues apply not only to the physical product but also to the packages, labels, and warranties closely attached to them. In 1967, for example, the Fair Packaging and Labeling Act was passed providing for labeling standards and labeling requirements on products.

Among other provisions, the act requires that package sizes be standardized and meet certain regulations. Laws govern that the name of the manufacturer must appear on products; that information must be provided as to food additives, ingredients, and weight; that products such as pillows, bedding, and children's pajamas must meet flammability standards; and so on. Finally, in 1975, warranties were covered under the Magnuson-Moss Warranty Improvement Act. This provided rules requiring that repairs under full warranties (as opposed to limited warranties) must be conducted within a specified period of time without charge, among other regulations.

In sum, public policy issues touch many aspects of products. One goal of public policy measures is to protect the consumer from abuses. A second is to provide the consumer with information so that he or she can make better decisions. A third is to promote competition and reduce the costs associated with restraint of trade. Finally, public policy is designed to enhance the entire performance of the economy through its regulation of the practices and structure of business. Later chapters elaborate more on these goals and the extent of their realization as they relate to marketing.

Summary

This chapter has focused on the notion of a product from the viewpoint of the consumer and society. Construed broadly, a product is any person, place, thing, idea, or activity desired by one party and offered by another. Products and money serve as the media of exchange and in so doing define a market. At the same time, we must remember that the physical transfer of a product for money is but a small part of any transaction. Indeed, a whole host of intangible and tangible economic, psychological, and social factors accompany any exchange. The manager attempts to understand these forces and both adjusts to them and influences them to a certain extent. These topics will be covered later.

At the micro consumer level, we saw that consumers respond to product attributes and the consequences of product ownership and use. This is in part a rational process where judgments are made as to the nature of products (e.g., perceived product attributes) and their implications and in part an emotional and social process where feelings and constraints from the outside are taken into account. The physical product, too, can be construed in a micro sense. Products can be classified in many ways according to their physical properties, use, end users, or other criteria. We presented a number of the more popular classificatory schemes. In addition, products proceed through stages or a life cycle of sorts such that sales rise and fall over time with important implications for consumers and managers alike. You might view Figure 4-8 at this time.

At the macro social level, products can be fruitfully described as aggregate entities. This helps us in the study of larger economic and societal patterns such as is reflected in cost, timing, risk, and innovative trends. Further, product differentiation at the macro level was seen to have positive and negative effects on consumers, business, and the economy. And public policy issues concerning product ingredients and safety, the rights of consumers and sellers, packaging and warranties, etc., took center stage.

Now that we have acquired a perspective on what a product means for the consumer and on what consequences it has for society, we are in a better position to examine the managerial aspects of products. The following chapter elaborates on new product development and product management issues.

Questions and Problems for Discussion

1 What is a product? Discuss its meaning from the perspective of the buyer and from that of the seller.

2 In what ways might products be classified? What use can such classifications serve?

3 Define a product line and discuss how it might be described.

4 What is the concept of a product life cycle? What implication does the PLC have for management?

5 Discuss the role of symbols in product design and consumption and in marketing in general.

6 Describe what a customer's cognitive and affective mental structure for soft drinks might look like. How might a brand manager use such information?

7 From the perspective of consumers and management, discuss the advantages and disadvantages of full versus limited product lines.

8 New product development was said to be associated with certain issues of cost, timing, and risk/benefit. Briefly discuss these.

9 How do economists tend to view products?

10 Discuss the public policy aspects of products.

NOTES

1. For a description of the dynamics of the attitude formation and attitude change processes, see Richard P. Bagozzi, "A Field Investigation of Causal Relations among Cognitions, Affect, Intentions, and Behavior," *Journal of Marketing Research* 19 (November 1982): 562–84.

2. For numerous findings and rules of thumb from practitioners, see, for example, Walter Stern, ed., *Handbook of Package Design Research* (New York: John Wiley & Sons, 1981).

3. See, for example, Leo V. Aspinwall, "The Characteristics of Goods Theory," in W. Lazer and E. J. Kelley, eds., *Managerial Marketing: Perspectives and Viewpoints*, rev. ed. (Homewood, Ill.: Richard D. Irwin, 1962), pp. 633–43; Louis P. Bucklin, "Retail Strategy and the Classification of Consumer Goods," *Journal of Marketing* 28 (January 1963): 50–55; Richard H. Holton, "The Distinction between Convenience Goods, Shopping Goods, and Specialty Goods," *Journal of Marketing* 23 (July 1958): 53–56.

4. The issue of consciousness is a complex one and is mixed up with ideas of introspection and intentionality. For some interesting discussions of these issues, see R. E. Nisbett and T. D. Wilson, "Telling More Than We Can Know: Verbal Reports on Mental Processes," *Psychological Review* 84 (1977): 231–59; P. Morris, "The Cognitive Psychology of Self-Reports," in C. Antaki, ed., *The Psychology of Ordinary Explanations of Social Behavior* (London: Academic Press, 1981), pp. 183–203; Peter Wright and Peter D. Rip, "Retrospective Reports on the Causes of Decisions," *Journal of Personality and Social Psychology* 40 (1981): 601–14. Although the evidence is far from complete, it is believed that one's knowledge of the processes of decision making are largely nonexistent. Nevertheless, the products of decision making are available to self-awareness, as are possibly some higher-order executive cognitive processes.

5. For a recent review of the literature on the PLC concept, see David R. Rink and John E. Swan, "Product Life Cycle Research: A Literature Review," *Journal of Business Research* 7 (September 1979): 219–42. See also Yoram Wind, *Product Policy: Concepts, Methods, and Strategy* (Reading, Mass.: Addison-Wesley, 1982); and George S. Day, "The Product Life Cycle: Analysis and Applications Issues," *Journal of Marketing* 45 (Fall 1981): 60–67.

6. Nariman K. Dhalla and Sonia Yuspeh, "Forget the Product Life Cycle Concept!" *Harvard Business Review* 54 (January–February 1976): 102–12.

7. Robert D. Buzzell, "Competitive Behavior and Product Life Cycles," in J. S. Wright and J. L. Goldstucker, eds., *New Ideas for Successful Marketing* (Chicago: American Marketing Association, 1966), pp. 46–48; William E. Cox, Jr., "Product Life Cycles as Marketing Models," *Journal of Business* 40 (October 1967): 375–84; Rolando Polli and Victor Cook, "Validity of the Product Life Cycle," *Journal of Business* 42 (October 1962): 385–400; and Frank M. Bass, "A New Product Growth Model for Consumer Durables," *Management Science* 15 (January 1969): 215–17.

8. Buzzell, "Competitive Behavior and Product Life Cycles."

9. M. T. Cunningham, "The Application of Product Life Cycles to Corporate Strategy: Some Research Findings," *British Journal of Marketing* 33 (Spring 1969): 32–44.

10. Cox, "Product Life Cycles as Marketing Models"; Buzzell, "Competitive Behavior and Product Life Cycles"; and Rink and Swan, "Product Life Cycle Research."

11. See Wind, *Product Policy*, for a discussion of some of these issues.

12. One new direction of research in this regard concerns work across firms in industrial, consumer, and other industries. Preliminary work with the PIMS data shows that the PLC concept has wide generalizability and interacts in predictable ways with market structure, performance, and strategic marketing decision variables. See, for example, Hans B. Thorelli and Stephen C. Burnett, "The Nature of Product Life Cycles for Industrial Goods Businesses," *Journal of Marketing* 45 (Fall 1981): 76–80.

13. William Qualls, Richard W. Olshavsky, and Ronald E. Michaels, "Shortening of the PLC—An Empirical Test," *Journal of Marketing* 45 (Fall 1981): 76–80.

14. Qualls, Olshavsky, and Michaels, "Shortening of the PLC."

15. Adapted from data appearing in Qualls, Olshavsky, and Michaels, "Shortening of the PLC."

16. For a discussion of the Tide situation, see David S. Hopkins, *Business Strategies for Problem Products* (New York: Conference Board, 1977).

17. Theodore Levitt, "Exploit the Product Life Cycle," *Harvard Business Review* 43 (November–December 1965): 81–94.

18. Frank M. Bass, "The Relationship between Diffusion Rates, Experience Curves, and Demand Elasticities for Consumer Durable Technological Innovations," *Journal of*

Business 53 (1980): 551–67; Robert J. Dolan and Abel P. Jeuland, "Experience Curves and Dynamic Demand Models: Implications for Optimal Pricing Strategies," *Journal of Marketing* 45 (Winter 1981): 52–73.

19. See, for example, Gerard J. Tellis and C. Merle Crawford, "An Evolutionary Approach to Product Growth Theory," *Journal of Marketing* 45 (Fall 1981): 125–32.

20. For a classic discussion of the concept of a brand image and its relation to the physical product, see Burleigh Gardner and Sydney J. Levy, "The Product and the Brand," *Harvard Business Review* (March–April 1955).

21. Further treatment of symbols can be found in Sydney J. Levy, "Symbols for Sale," *Harvard Business Review* 37 (July–August 1959): 116–22; Sydney J. Levy, "Symbolism and Life Style," in S. A. Greyser, ed., *Toward Scientific Marketing* (Chicago: American Marketing Association, 1964), pp. 140–50.

22. For an outline of some of the different processes and sequences occurring in Figure 4-9, including development of a statistical model to measure these, see Richard P. Bagozzi, "A Holistic Methodology for Modeling Consumer Response to Innovation," *Operations Research* 31 (January–February 1983): 128–75.

23. Many of the ideas and data presented in this section can be found in L. Adler, "Time Lag in New Product Development," *Journal of Marketing Research* 3 (January 1966): 17–21; E. Mansfield and S. Wagner, "Organizational and Strategic Factors Associated with Probabilities of Success in Industrial R and D," *Journal of Business* (April 1975); Glenn L. Urban and John R. Hauser, *Design and Marketing of New Products* (Englewood Cliffs, N.J.: Prentice-Hall, 1980), pp. 46–59; E. Mansfield and J. Rapoport, "The Costs of Industrial Product Innovation," *Management Science* 21 (August 1975): 1380–86.

24. See Urban and Hauser, *Design and Marketing of New Products*, pp. 46–59, from which parts of the following discussion were drawn.

25. Urban and Hauser, *Design and Marketing of New Products*, p. 53.

26. The figure is based on a similar diagram found in *Management of New Products*, 4th ed. (New York: Booz, Allen, and Hamilton, 1982), p. 9.

27. Mansfield and Wagner, "Organizational and Strategic Factors Associated with Probabilities of Success in Industrial R and D," p. 181.

28. Mansfield and Wagner, "Organizational and Strategic Factors . . . and Industrial R and D." See also A. Gerstenfeld, *Effective Management of Research and Development* (Reading, Mass.: Addison-Wesley, 1970).

29. Urban and Hauser, *Design and Marketing of New Products*, pp. 55–59.

30. Figure 4-12 is an adaptation and partial rendition of a well-known model found in economics. For one recent version of the entire model, see F. M. Scherer, *Industrial Market Structure and Economic Performance*, 2nd ed. (Chicago: Rand McNally, 1980), pp. 3–6.

31. See Scherer, *Industrial Market Structure and Economic Performance;* and Joe S. Bain, *Barriers to New Competition* (Cambridge, Mass.: Harvard University Press, 1956).

32. Scherer, *Industrial Market Structure and Economic Performance*, pp. 376–77.

33. See Scherer, *Industrial Market Structure and Economic Performance*, pp. 12–21, 152–64, 387–88.

34. See, for example, J. J. Lambin, *Advertising, Competition, and Market Conduct in Oligopoly over Time* (Amsterdam, Netherlands: Elsevier/North Holland, 1976).

35. Michael E. Porter, *Competitive Strategy: Techniques for Analyzing Industries and Competitors* (New York: The Free Press, 1980), p. 9.

36. Ronald S. Bond and David F. Lean, *Sales, Promotion, and Product Differentiation in Two Prescription Drug Markets* (Federal Trade Commission Staff Report, Washington, D.C.: U.S. Government Printing Office, February 1977).

37. This example is taken from Scherer, *Industrial Market Structure and Economic Performance*, p. 382.

38. Quoted in Scherer, *Industrial Market Structure and Economic Performance*, p. 382, from *In the Matter of Borden, Inc.*, Federal Trade Commission Complaint, docket no. 8978, para. 83.

39. Scherer, *Industrial Market Structure and Economic Performance*, pp. 382–83.

40. *Newsweek*, International Edition, May 3, 1982, p. 51.

GLOSSARY

Brand Image. The thoughts and feelings a brand, its name, advertising, etc., engender in a consumer. The brand image is a function of prior learning, needs, expectations, and social forces. We construct our image of a brand by combining the things we perceive in it with our psychological makeup.

Classification of Goods or Products

Consumer Goods. Products purchased by the general public for their own final use.

Convenience Goods. Products one purchases out of habit, impulse, or, on occasion, even urgency.

Durable Goods. Products that have an extended life.

Industrial Goods. Products purchased by organizations to become a part of, or help produce, market offerings. These are generally classified as raw materials, component parts, capital goods, supplies, or services.

Nondurable Goods. Products that are destroyed or transformed in a relatively short period of time or after a few uses.

Services. Time or activities one purchases from another party.

Shopping Goods. Products for which the customer goes through considerable effort to obtain "the best buy." Typically, this involves examination of a number of brands on many attributes, use of many decision criteria, and the application of relatively complex rules for decision making.

Specialty Goods. Products possessing such unique attributes that consumers make special efforts to secure them. The consumer typically prefers a single brand, and price and comparison shopping are not central criteria in the decision process.

Homogeneous Product Class. Products that can be considered more-or-less direct substitutes for one another.

Product. Any offering actually or potentially desired by a target person or organization. A product might be a physical object (e.g., brand X beer), an intangible service (e.g., home protection), an idea (e.g., "smoking is hazardous to one's health"), a person (e.g., a pop singer), or a place (e.g., the Grand Canyon). Products typically have physical and/or subjective attributes. They satisfy physiological, psychological, or social needs.

Product Attributes. Characteristics of a product. These might entail physical features or the functions or consequences of product ownership, use, and disposal.

Product Differentiation. Marketing a product or service that is perceived in some way to be unique by consumers. This is accomplished through product design, advertising, and in certain instances distributional and selling practices. Product differentiation is a strategy used to achieve an advantage over competitors. However, its effects in a larger sense on consumers, competitors, and the economy are little known.

Product Form. A variation in a product within a product class wherein the product satisfies the same general need as all products in the class but in addition satisfies a more specified subneed. For example, instant, regular, decaffeinated, and freeze-dried coffees are product forms of the product class of coffee.

Product Life Cycle. The stages that products pass through over time. The classic definition specifies four stages:
introduction → growth → maturity → decline
The classic definition has been modified to take into account other patterns and the influence of managerial decisions (see text).

Product Line. The list of all products a particular firm sells within a particular category of goods.

Product Line Depth. The number of different items sold within a particular product line.

Product Line Width. The number of different product lines a firm sells.

A Day in the Life of a Product Manager

C. Merle Crawford
Graduate School of
Business Administration
University of Michigan

This is a story about a friend of mine. It speaks to the question of just what product management and, particularly, new products management is all about. The names and places have been changed to protect....

As Hadl Stevens slipped down the entry ramp and swung onto the Interstate for his Monday morning trip to the office, he found himself in a reflective mood. He recently had been promoted and had spent most of the weekend thinking about the implications of his new position. Hadl worked for a large food company for about eight years. He had started as a marketing assistant, then assistant product manager, then product manager. His assignments have put him on some seven different products.

About three months ago he had been transferred to new products and was assigned to help in the launching of a new lemonade. It had now gone to market, successfully, and had just last week been turned over to the regular product management department to continue marketing it. Hadl was now to begin work on a very important new line—frozen cake mixes.

He knew basically what his job was—to direct the activities of the firm as they related to the new mixes, coordinating and integrating them so as to maximize the profit from the line. He competed with all of the other product managers (new and established) for the attention and resources of the firm, and he loved it. Major responsibility, quick payoffs to the individual, every day a new set of situations, excitement, lots of attention from top management, great experience, and accomplishment.

But he also knew frustrations. Some of those other product managers had been around longer than he had, and they all had friends in key places around the firm. Sometimes people in manufacturing or laboratory research or finance were uncooperative—almost antagonistic. They made jokes about incompetent product managers, and how only their egos were bigger than their inflated job descriptions.

And persons outside the firm were sometimes even worse—government regulators seemed to actually be against innovation, for example, and retailers acted like they owned the consumer. Competitors also had product managers and new products of their own. They also spent advertising money like they printed it themselves.

He also wondered from time to time why his job differed so much from what he knew to be the practice in nonfood firms—e.g., General Electric or Steelcase or IBM. Those firms also used product managers, sometimes, but not with the authority or responsibility he had. They stressed what they called functions, such as research, sales, manufacturing, etc. They typically used a committee approach to new products and often had marketing planners to handle the ongoing marketing. Hadl, on the other hand, was supposed to represent the whole company, and he knew that everyone would look to him for guidance on the new cake mixes.

Anyway, the week ahead would be a busy one. He knew that. First, he had to complete the transfer of the lemonade product to another manager. Next, and most critical, he had to assess the team which had been gathered to work on the new frozen cake mixes. There was a nutritional chemist from research, a manufacturing engineer, an analyst from finance, a marketing researcher, and himself. Other people, such as those from packaging, sales promotion, and legal joined the team from time to time for short periods. Some of the team members were experienced veterans, others were not. His boss and other bosses up the line also made themselves members of his team, whether Hadl wanted them or not.

Third, he had to develop a rough schedule of events for the cake mixes because integrating and coordinating properly was a key task of the new products manager.

But he knew that the really tough task ahead, besides getting the team to work together like a small company within the company, was concept and product evaluation. The firm's new product strategy was clear—there would be innovation, and new products would be significant improvements on what was already in the market. No me-too's.

R&D had already developed prototypes . . . the new process would work. But would the cakes be any good? Who would like them? What flavors would they want? Who would actually prepare the cakes, and what mistakes would they make? Would the new cakes be preferred over competition? Which competition? What would sitting around in retail frozen food compartments do to the taste? And so on.

And along the way, every product-use test would have to be converted into estimated shares of market, and then projected out as sales, costs, and profits. Millions of dollars were at stake. There could be no errors.

He began to wonder whether he was better, or worse, off than Ann Lagoni, whom he had met at the party Saturday night. Ann was also a marketer, but she worked for a high-tech firm that was new in the fiber optics business. In her firm, there was just one new products manager . . . the president. Her job in marketing was to open conversation with the market—the users. See that the firm's technical people (including their president, an engineer who started the firm four years ago and whom Ann called a technocrat) knew what the users wanted and needed. Hadl found it interesting that Ann, as a marketing person, had to force user attitudes onto the technical people developing the new products. He certainly didn't.

Ann's other task was to plan the marketing of the new products. She had discussed trade shows, some technical advertising, training salespeople and distributors, building service capability. Ann had to fight, too, but it was a fight against technical people and against the idea that scientists knew what the user needed. They called her a peddler and joked about how they had managed to market their first product without a marketer. Still, they knew they needed her and supported the market research she did, so long as it didn't show them wrong. Hadl knew he would have a lot to learn if he took a job out there.

Thinking of high-tech products reminded him of the speech given at a recent new products conference by a top new products consultant. The expert had painted quite a different picture for new products management in the future, and Hadl wondered if he was really correct. For example, were firms like Ann's and his actually coming together in their management styles, as each adopted more of the ways of the other? He saw that Ann's scientists were adopting marketing, and suddenly he realized that his cake mix scientists were displaying some of the attitudes of those optics engineers. The firm had never before bet so much on technology.

And was the expert right when he said many larger firms not in packaged goods (and thus not using the product manager approach) were actually fragmenting into smaller companies? Not actually breaking up, of course, but putting new products work into teams, and letting the teams become quite independent of the ongoing firm. He said the IBM-PC was developed by a team of people transferred from Armonk, New York, to Boca Raton, Florida. The PC products are still marketed from there.

Hadl agreed with another forecast—that the information explosion would continue. He knew there would be more and better market research data, especially from new services such as BASES and BehaviorScan. And that the management scientists would continue their attack on intuitive decision making by providing new decision models and other systematic methods of analysis. Forecasting sales volume (outside of people management) was perhaps the toughest part of Hadl's job and he welcomed forecasting models of all types.

And he agreed with the expert in predicting a continuation of social pressures on "worthless" products (even though cake mixes were often cited), on marketing which only confused people, on products which were simply not safe to use, and on products which failed to work as promised.

But he wondered about some of the other forecasts—e.g., that many firms in the future would continue with old products or just copying the products of others, that products would fail at about the same rate as in the past, that test marketing would fade away as newer methods of market testing replaced it, that the life cycle of new products would continue to shorten even as the development cycle continued to lengthen, and that profits and losses from new products would continue to increase.

Most of these forecasts just increased the demands on people like Hadl. There would be more frustrations and disappointments. And yet, he realized that these demanding situations were exactly what made his job important. He took pride in getting the lemonade product to market successfully, but he wondered how he would handle failure when it came. For it almost certainly would come. Ann Lagoni had experienced it, and she said it hurt, personally.

As Hadl pulled into the company parking lot, he returned to the reality of today. He began to think about the list of 18 people he knew he had to contact today, and the meeting in the lab where the team scientist would demonstrate a new consistency in the dough. The new consistency would obsolete all of the product test data to date, but they said it would work just as well and have a longer shelf life too. Maybe.

Yes, his truly was an integrative function, heavily keyed to involvement with people, and yet almost totally dependent on careful analysis of data. It was an impossible job, yet absolutely essential. Sometime soon he wanted to get a good book on the subject and see what others had to say about it.

CHAPTER
FIVE

There is one thing stronger than all the armies in the world: and that is an idea whose time has come.
——Victor Hugo (1802–1885)

Necessity is the mother of invention.
—— Plato (428?–347 B.C.)

Invention is the mother of necessity.
—— Thorstein Veblen (1857–1929)

He had been eight years upon a project for extracting sunbeams out of cucumbers, which were to be put into phials and hermetically sealed, and let out to warm the air in raw inclement summers.
——Jonathan Swift (1667–1745)

PRODUCT: MANAGERIAL DECISIONS

Introduction

Up to this point, we have examined the meaning of products at the micro level (i.e., as the consumer experiences products) and at the macro level (i.e., at the level of society as reflected in aggregate, economic, and public policy views). We have discussed the managerial aspects of products only as they have directly helped to explicate the micro and macro analyses. Now we will develop the meaning of products more fully from the perspective of the organization. In a sense, the managerial viewpoint is an intermediate one bridging the micro and macro. The successful functioning of any organization depends on how well it interprets the needs of its customers and adjusts the operations of the firm to meet those needs. At the same time, it must do this within the context of the larger social and economic environment that shapes its actions. Significantly, modern organizations have developed sophisticated procedures for coping with the opportunities and constraints they face.

In this regard, let us look more deeply into that aspect of the organization concerned with product decisions. Figure 5-1 shows the central components and their interrelationships. Notice first that product decisions begin with the *overall organization goals*. These are the ultimate ends and objectives necessary for the survival of the firm and the effective implementation of its mission. The goals are typically formulated as targets related to profitability, return on investment, meeting customer needs, being socially responsible in terms of employment and pollution practices, and so on. The important point to note is that these central goals influence and constrain the means required to meet those goals. Broadly speaking, the means encompass production, personnel, marketing, R&D, financial, accounting, and other programs. Each of these has its own subgoals, which we term objectives.

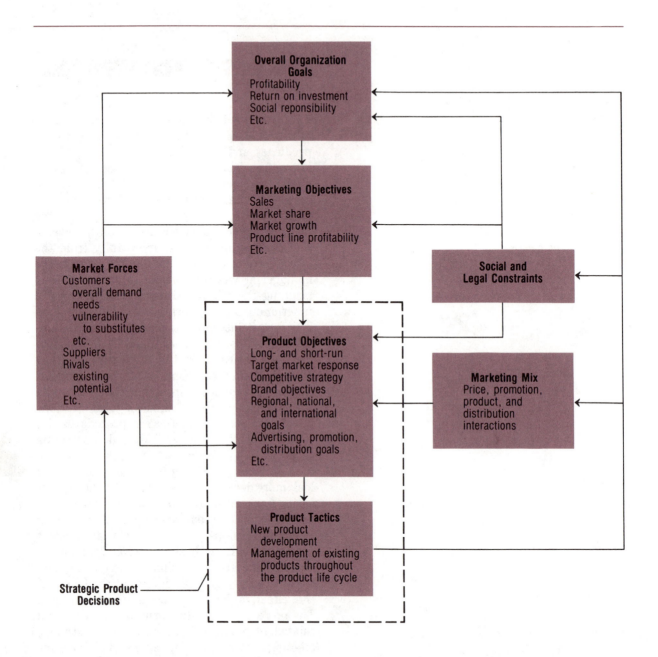

Figure 5-1. A framework for formulating product decisions

Only *marketing objectives* are displayed in Figure 5-1, but it should be remembered that the objectives of the other programs interact with them. Marketing objectives reflect goals for sales, market share, market growth, product-line interactions, profitability, brand image, and so on. Although the line between marketing objectives and the goals of the firm is often a fine one, the former are usually derived from the latter and are more specific and/or serve as intermediate steps in the pursuit of broader organization goals. Similarly, *product objectives* are even more specific and focused than marketing objectives. They typically serve as substeps needed to achieve the broader marketing objectives.

Ansoff has proposed a framework that places product objectives (and other marketing mix objectives) in a useful light.[1] Figure 5-2 presents his matrix, which is designed to define four different types of growth faced by any firm. *Market penetration* is the strategy of gaining a greater share of sales in an existing market with one's existing products. The battle between Bic's cigarette lighter and Gillette's Cricket lighter had largely been one for market share in this sense during the early 1980s. Market penetration en-

compasses mostly a strategy of aggressive advertising and promotion, rather than product changes, per se.

A second growth strategy (i.e., *market expansion*) occurs when a firm markets existing products in new markets. As sales taper off in old markets, either due to maturation or competitive inroads, marketers often devote more effort to finding new markets because this tends to be the least expensive alternative. This strategy has especially been the direction taken by French, German, and Italian wine producers, who have found their home markets to be saturated, whereas the U.S. wine market is in the growth stage but perhaps rapidly approaching maturity. The most common tactics practiced in the market expansion strategy include research to identify markets and forecast demand, advertising, promotion, and distribution to enter the new market.

There comes a time, however, when marketing one's existing products is no longer viable or at least must be given lower priority. Rather, through *new product development*, one attempts to secure another foothold in existing markets. Indeed, in today's volatile, competitive world, most successful companies rely on this strategy as part of their overall corporate policy. Without continual innovation, firms simply cannot respond to the changing needs of consumers and to competitive threats.

Finally, to market new products in new markets, the firm practices a *diversification* strategy. This involves the most comprehensive marketing program, including new product development, extensive market research and forecasting, and a full implementation of the marketing mix. We see firms increasingly turning to this strategy as they seek to grow and keep one step ahead of the competition. For example, Easton Corporation, a manufacturer of automotive repair parts, recently began diversification through a new venture into auto repair outlets. A final point to note about Ansoff's framework is that it omits one very important alternative. Namely,

PRODUCTS

		Existing	New
MARKETS	Existing	1. Market penetration	3. New product development
	New	2. Market expansion	4. Diversification

Figure 5-2. Ansoff's market matrix

SOURCE: H. I. Ansoff, *Corporate Strategy* (New York: McGraw-Hill, 1965), p. 109. Reprinted with the permission of the publisher.

firms sometimes find it advantageous to acquire entirely new businesses such as Philip Morris did by buying Miller beer. Thus, *acquisition* can be a new product strategy too.

Returning to Figure 5-1, we can thus see that product objectives are a function of what market response the firm desires from whom and when. The firm must set objectives to answer such questions as: What is the target market? How big is it? How does it behave? Who are the existing competitors? What response does the market make to what product strategy? Other essential, but somewhat less fundamental, goals relate to brand objectives, product line objectives (e.g., cannibalization), and advertising/promotion/distribution goals connected to the product.

An important point to emphasize in Figure 5-1 is that product objectives are not merely derivatives of marketing objectives and organizational goals. In fact, product objectives are also strongly influenced by market forces, social and legal constraints, and marketing mix considerations. Consider first the role of *market forces*. Product objectives depend very much on consumer behavior. The design of product attributes, packages, the brand name and logo, and so on must all take into account consumer perceptions, judgments, and emotions. Suppliers play a role, too, in terms of the materials they provide, the prices they charge, and, in general, the bargaining power they have over the firm. Existing and potential rivals must be scrutinized to ensure that the firm has a product with a competitive advantage. Next, as we described in the previous chapter, *social and legal constraints* provide direct guidelines shaping product design and the brand name. Finally, *marketing mix* considerations influence product objectives. Each of the marketing mix stimuli has the potential to complement or interfere with the others, depending on the circumstances. For instance, as we develop in a later chapter on pricing, consumers sometimes derive their image of product quality as a function of price.

The higher the price, the greater the perceived product quality. In sum, the organization must thoughtfully coordinate all of the marketing mix objectives if it is to obtain the desired response.

After a firm has set sound product objectives, it is in a position to implement them through *product tactics*. Product tactics refer to the specific actions the firm takes as reflected in its commitment to (a) new product development (e.g., R&D, test marketing) and (b) management of products throughout the PLC (e.g., branding, product-line pruning, product extension). The particular product tactics that are implemented feed back upon market forces, the marketing mix, social and legal constraints, marketing objectives, and goals of the firm. It is through the skillful use of tactics, for example, that the firm achieves its goals. This is a grass roots implementation problem.

The remainder of the chapter is organized around the two broad product tactics: new product development and management of products throughout the PLC. Also included in the discussion is an integration of the role played by product objectives and strategy.

New Product Development[2]

The need for new product development is especially acute in today's world. Consumers are more discriminating and prone to seek change than they have ever been. Competition among firms is fierce. Technological growth is accelerating. The economies of most nations are volatile. Fluctuating interest rates and material shortages, coupled with alternating periods of inflation and recession, put added pressure on firms. All of these factors make it essential that organizations purposefully conduct ongoing new product development programs.[3]

A Natural Selection Model

Before we discuss new product development programs, it is useful to place the process within the context of theories from organization behavior. In this regard, the natural selection model is quite applicable.[4] Figure 5-3 presents an outline of this model applied to the new product development process. The overall process begins with *variation and change in the environment.* Consumer needs change, rivals continually introduce new innovations, and the economic and social environments evolve rapidly in unique and often unpredictable ways. The outcomes of these changes (indicated as O_1 and O_2 in Figure 5-3) consist of new demands on the part of consumers, new ideas for products and how to produce and market them, new threats from competitors, and new constraints and opportunities from the legal/social system. This information and more must be continually monitored from the environment. Indeed, this is one motivation for maintaining research departments, management information systems, and the purchase of information from professional services.

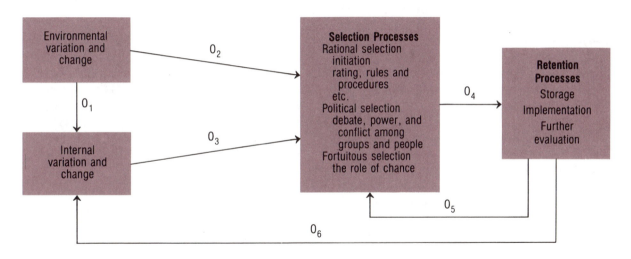

Figure 5-3. The natural selection model applied to new product development

Outcomes

O_1, O_2, O_3 *New ideas absorbed and generated; modifications in old ideas; synthesis of old ideas, etc.*

O_4 *Some ideas are rejected, some accepted, and some modified, added to, etc.*

O_5, O_6 *Feedback indicating (a) when satisfactory ideas have been temporarily accepted or at least stored, and therefore some processes of idea generation and evaluation can be curtailed or (b) when ideas are insufficient and new generation and selection are needed*

Yet an organization cannot rely entirely on information from the outside for its innovations. As shown in Figure 5-3, the organization must also act as its own generator of ideas to produce *internal variation and change*. The generation of ideas is stimulated by input from the environment, but more often than not, the firm creates its own output. Organization theorists call this the *enactment process*. That is, the organization socially constructs new concepts to be evaluated and implemented later.

The next step in new product development is termed *selection*. The goal of innovative firms is to enhance the volume of new ideas generated in the environmental monitoring and enactment phases (i.e., increase the low of O_1, O_2, and O_3), and the objective of selection is to prune inferior ideas and end up with a few manageable, fruitful concepts. The outcomes of selection (O_4) result in some ideas rejected, some accepted, some modified, some added to, and so on.

Three types of selection processes typically occur in most firms. One is *rational selection*. Here new product ideas are evaluated according to formal organization rules and procedures. A simple rule applied by some firms is to "imitate the successes of the competition." Of course, this is usually not a viable long-run strategy. More often, firms rate new ideas in terms of their ability to stimulate demand, to be manufactured efficiently, to gain a competitive advantage over similar products, to make a profit, and so on. The ratings might consist of checklists that management applies to each new idea. Other rational schemes might involve formal models, computer simulation, and other guidelines. Another form of selection is *political selection*. Political selection involves the social processes of debate, conflict, negotiation, and power occurring among groups and individuals within the organization. These processes are often informal in contrast to the formal rules of rational selection. Nevertheless, political processes are very real and pervasive activities influencing selection. Another process is termed *fortuitous selection* to indicate that uncertainty and change shape idea evaluation and choice. Seldom is a firm absolutely certain of the quality of a new idea. In fact, successful firms sometimes institute official risk-taking policies as a counterbalance to excessive structure and rationality in the selection process. Both Procter & Gamble and General Foods, for example, require that new product ideas not excessively threaten existing products in the firm, yet some overlap is encouraged, allegedly to stimulate internal competition and ensure that established products do not stagnate and new ideas are not prematurely discarded.

Another natural selection process is called *retention*. New ideas are stored, at least temporarily, and translated into final form as a new product. The new product might also proceed further along the evaluation process, such as involved in a market test prior to implementation. Retention also encompasses new product introduction, or roll-out as it is sometimes termed in the trade. Further, as the product enters the market, its performance is continually evaluated. The outcomes of retention (O_5 and O_6 in Figure 5-3) influence enactment and selection processes. If the new product is a success, then certain aspects of idea generation and selection might be curtailed, resources might be redirected toward monitoring consumer needs or forecasting economic trends, and R&D might shift somewhat to more basic research. If, on the other hand, the new product falters in some way, then perhaps new ideas must be generated, modified, and selected. The overall process, then, is a continuous one with some opportunity for self-correcting feedback. Let us turn now to a more detailed and expanded new product model.

A Managerial Model

Figure 5-4 is a new product development model that integrates many of the concepts and research described up to this point. Notice that the model follows the natural selection process in terms of the general activities performed and the outcomes at each stage (see Figure 5-3). Notice further that the overall process is influenced by strategic considerations. These have already been introduced and illustrated in Figures 5-1 and 5-2. We begin now with a description of the components in the new product development model.

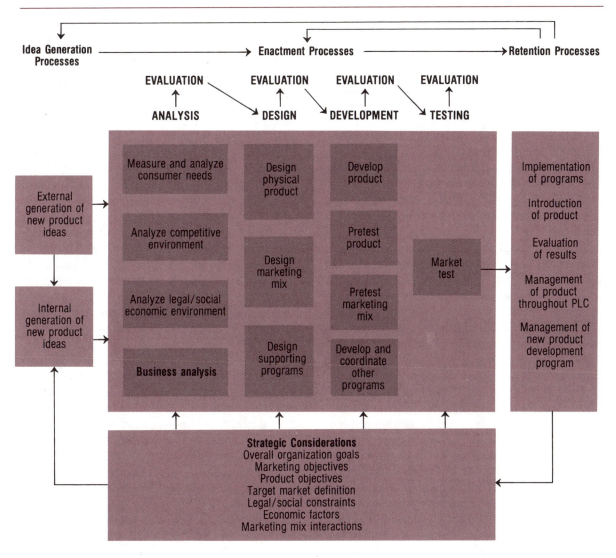

Figure 5-4. An outline of the new product development process

Idea Generation Processes. Organizations and people tend to become set in their ways. The status quo evolves to thwart efforts at change. Organization functions, rules, and procedures tend to solidify. Individuals become accustomed to the immediate world as it exists around them. Groups, managers, and employees develop vested interests. In short, change is often seen as a threat, or at least one becomes numb to certain changes.

In some respects, this is a natural outcome. A person cannot hope to deal with all stimuli impinging on him or her at once and develops ways of coping with it. Similarly, organizations selectively focus on those activities they deem most important.

However, too much selectivity and a resistance to change weakens the organization's ability to adjust and survive. Indeed, one way for firms to break out of the lethargy of selectivity biases is to maintain a healthy variation-seeking system. This means that the flow of new ideas from without the organization and the generation of new ideas from within must be fostered. The greater the ability of the firm to acquire and produce new ideas, the greater the probability that the enactment and retention processes will produce a winner, all things being equal. Organizations need to encourage exploration and change in order not to stagnate and become vulnerable to erosive forces in the marketplace.

Successful firms employ a number of approaches to generate new ideas. Sources outside the organization are regularly monitored and consulted. For example, ongoing panels, surveys, or focus groups are used to track consumer reactions and discover changes in tastes. The actions of competitors, especially with respect to new product designs or improvements, are followed closely. Trade shows are attended to pick up new ideas and tidbits of things to come. Governmental publications, the popular press, and academic and professional journals are studied. Professional services, such as provided by marketing research firms, ad agencies, and new product consultants, are used. Occasionally, new ideas are found in universities, through licensing arrangements with other firms, as a result of unsolicited proposals by inventors, or simply through library searches. A primary conduit to those outside sources of information is the *marketing information system* department that many firms now employ. This is a group of data collection, analysis, storage, and dissemination personnel who perform an important role in research, forecasting, and advising. We will explore the functions of marketing information systems in the following chapter.

Sources inside the organization are also essential generators of new ideas. Brand managers, for instance, are perhaps the most eclectic and knowledgeable people with respect to consumer needs, competitive offerings, and new developments. Therefore their views are regularly sought. Salespeople, too, are often sources of ideas, as they are in direct contact with customers and the vagaries of the marketplace. Managers participate actively in producing new ideas either as individuals or as members of committees or new venture teams. Employees-at-large are frequently contacted for their ideas, and some companies have formal programs to encourage and reward suggestions made from workers who are seemingly removed from product management. Finally, groups and departments within the firm are assigned special responsibility for generating new ideas. This is typically housed in a number of places including the R&D department, product engineering, marketing research, or various new product development groups.

It should be stressed in Figure 5-4 that strategic considerations in general and product objectives in particular have an influence on the idea-generation process. Strategies provide focus and structure, guiding the search for, and formulation of, ideas. For example, Gillette and other firms reject ideas from outsiders unless they are already patented, presumably to avoid legal complications.[5] Other firms narrowly define their overall business mission, target market, or product forms to hold the number of new ideas to manageable levels; and still other companies face potential antitrust actions if they enter one new market or else risk competitive retaliation or public resistance if they enter another. Moreover, at the micro level, firms with extensive product lines face cannibalization issues where the potential introduction of new products might adversely "eat into" sales for established ones. Thus, they are wary of devoting too much development effort that might be counterproductive. In short, many strategic issues often influence where and how firms go about generating new product ideas.

There is a danger, however, of imposing too much control on the idea-generation process. It is perhaps obvious that too restrictive a search and brainstorming process risks eliminating potentially good ideas prematurely. But perhaps not so obvious is the functional linkage between idea-generation and enactment processes. The selection process depends directly on the input of ideas because the number or quality of new ideas affects the outcome of selection to a great extent. If not enough new ideas are generated and/or the selection process is too discriminating, for example, then missed opportunities could result. On the other hand, too many ideas and/or too loose a selection process can drain resources and allow poor products to reach the market. This possibility is less likely in practice, however, since there rarely are too many good ideas. Because the enactment process naturally functions best when it is thorough, its successful functioning is enhanced still further by providing it with as many ideas as possible. Hence, too much control at this point through strategic and other considerations should be avoided, because these tend to reduce variation (i.e., the number of good and bad ideas) and introduce pre-evaluation biases. We turn now to enactment processes and its subprocesses.

Enactment Processes. Enactment processes serve a screening function. Enactment consists of five broad subprocesses: analysis, design, development, testing, and evaluation (see Figure 5-4). Each of these, in turn, interacts with the others and is comprised further of a number of interrelated subactivities. Let us examine some of these.

Once a sufficient number of ideas has been generated, they are ready for *analysis*, the first enactment process. Generally, firms conduct four types of analyses (refer back to Figure 5-4). A very important one is the *measurement of consumer needs*. We will have much more to say about this topic in Chapter 6. For now, let us illustrate one class of consumer measurement procedures frequently used in practice: namely, the measurement of consumer perceptions.

Imagine that a small brewery located in Saginaw, Michigan, is contemplating entering the Detroit-area beer market. The owner and brewmaster, Fritz Neibecker, knows that the Saginaw market cannot absorb any more of his beer, and this prevents him from operating his plant at full capacity. He sees the Detroit market as a potentially lucrative area for selling beer and fulfilling his long-run aspirations for expanding his facilities and entering the elite club of medium-size beer producers. Over the past 50 years or so, economies of scale associated with brewing beer, combined with relatively high budgets needed to advertise beer effectively, have forced the closing of most small breweries, because they could not make a profit. Fritz Neibecker viewed Detroit and its suburbs as an opportunity to forestall a creeping threat to his business.

At the same time, Detroit is already a highly competitive market for beer with over nine major producers vying for the trade. On the surface at least, it would seem that Fritz Neibecker should think twice before entering this market. Indeed, he had early on decided that, if he were to succeed, he could not merely sell his existing brand, Old German Gold, in Detroit, but he would have to develop a new brand with a differential advantage over the competition. Old German Gold was much like the leading competitors in taste. The questions he needed to answer were: What are the major attributes in beer that Detroiters seek? How do they perceive the existing beers to score on these attributes? Are there unfilled market niches in the sense of groups of consumers seeking attributes in a beer that no existing producers satisfy well? Can his company brew and market a beer to satisfy this niche if it exists? Will other companies later introduce a similar beer?

To answer these questions, Fritz Neibecker hired a group of marketing students at a nearby university to do a survey of Detroit beer drinkers. Using various statistical and measurement procedures, the researchers found that two basic attributes are sought in a beer: heaviness vs. lightness and mildness vs. bitterness. Figure 5-5 presents a perceptual map of the average Detroit beer drinker. That is, the perceptual map represents how the beer drinker perceives each of the brands to score on the two taste dimensions. For example, notice that Blatz is perceived to be very bitter but in the middle with respect to heavy/light. Miller, in contrast, is perceived to be very mild and also near the middle on the heavy/light dimension. From past studies, Fritz Neibecker knew that Old German Gold was perceived to be slightly mild and neither heavy nor light (see the X in Figure 5-5). Thus, his suspicions were verified about Old German Gold's similar positioning as existing beers in the Detroit market. In this case, Hamm's and Stroh's, two established brands, are very close in taste to Old German Gold; and Schlitz, Car-

ling's, and Canadian imports also are not too far away. If Fritz Neibecker is to enter the Detroit market with any chance of success, he would do well to introduce a new beer in areas of the perceptual map where no current beers are dominant. We should note that people have different taste preferences in beer. Some prefer heavy beers, others light, others mild, and still others bitter.

Fritz Neibecker decided to market two new beers in the Detroit market (see the two check marks in Figure 5-5). One beer was to be moderately heavy but largely in the middle with respect to bitter/mild. He felt that this beer woud capture those preferring a heavy beer, since no beer would be as heavy as the new one. Yet, it is not so heavy that it would not appeal to those already drinking Schlitz, for instance. At the same time, the new beer is in a presumably acceptable range on the bitter/mild dimension. The other new beer was also planned to be in the center on bitter/mild but was designed to be moderately light. In fact, it was hoped that it would be as light or lighter than Miller Lite, a leader on this attribute. Fritz Neibecker felt that his new beers would appeal roughly to anyone's preferences falling within the respective circles drawn with dashed lines in Figure 5-5.

Given the picture of the market and Fritz Neibecker's plans for two new beers, a number of other issues must be dealt with before one could recommend that he enter the market. An important question to answer is whether there are enough people located in the circles in terms of their preferences. Hence, an estimate of the market sizes for the new beers must be made. This topic will be described in the chapter on demand estimation. Second, the willingness of people in the market to try the product and repeat purchase must be made. This topic is discussed in the following chapter. Third, Fritz Neibecker must have the technology and ability to produce the products. Through a blending of ingredients and adjust-

ments in the brewing process, he might be able to alter the present beer, since it currently is not too far from the new proposals. Discussion of production and engineering topics such as these is beyond the scope of this book. Finally, somehow Fritz Neibecker must get retailers to *stock the beer and inform and persuade consumers to try it. These issues are dealt with in later chapters. In sum, the use of perceptual maps is one procedure for measuring and analyzing consumer needs. It serves as an early step in the new product development process.*[6]

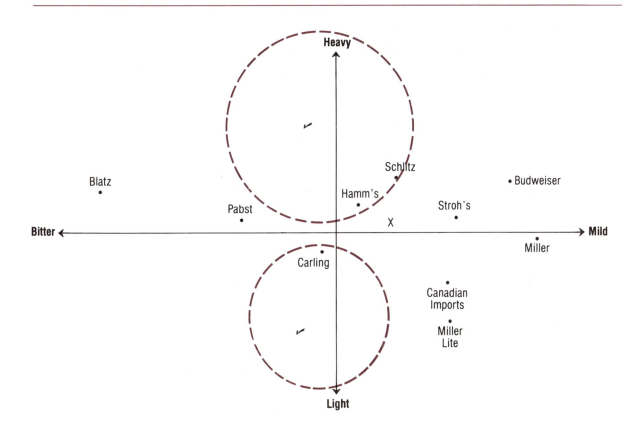

Figure 5-5. A perceptual map of beer drinkers

A second type of analysis that can be performed is a *competitive analysis*. Notice that the use of perceptual maps brings in competitive considerations and integrates them with consumer psychology. Porter provides a framework for analyzing the competition in still further ways.[7] For example, in addition to rivalry among firms within an industry, the firm's livelihood depends on the availability of substitute products for one's wares, the bargaining power of suppliers, the bargaining power of buyers, and the threat of new entrants in the industry. Porter presents a methodology for analyzing these forces and describes strategies for combating them. We will elaborate on some of his suggestions and others in later chapters.

The third analysis performed in the enactment phase is of the constraints arising from the *legal/social/economic environment*. Legal issues to be concerned with include those related to patents or licensing, product ingredients and general safety, and governmental regulations on packaging, labels, warranties, and other aspects of the new product decision. Social considerations overlap with the legal but go further in that many consequences of marketing go beyond that codified in the law. For instance, some products might be potentially harmful to certain people or the environment; or full disclosure of product ingredients, unit prices, product grade or quality, and open dating of perishables might help consumers make better decisions. The actions of any organization have wide-ranging implications for social welfare, and a firm that formally considers these in its new product decision processes is not only socially responsible but may be wise in that customer goodwill increases and costly legal entanglements may be avoided. Similarly, analysis of the economic environment is essential in terms of trends in consumer income and spending, the availability of raw materials and labor resources, the costs of borrowing, and so on. A potentially profitable idea must be translatable into a physical product that can be produced, marketed, and sold; and the resources of a whole host of economic and financial institutions are needed along with a hospitable overall economic climate.

The final analysis in enactment, and an important one, is termed *business analysis* in Figure 5-4. Any new idea must be evaluated in terms of its ability to meet larger corporate and marketing goals for profitability, return on investment, growth, and market share, among others. This means making forecasts of sales, estimates of costs, and determinations of potential profits or losses. It is in this stage of enactment that past experience must be welded with uncertainty and guesswork to produce meaningful predictions. The inputs of accounting, finance, production, design, and marketing personnel must be combined effectively to accomplish this. In later chapters (e.g., on pricing), we elaborate and illustrate typical business analyses.

It should be noted in Figure 5-4 that the outputs of analysis are evaluated according to rules and standards set by management. For example, the perceptions and attitudes of consumers must reach certain levels of favorability to justify a positive evaluation and further consideration in the new product development process. Potential sales and profits of minimal levels must be forthcoming to warrant further analysis. And so on. As one example of how evaluations might be quantified, consider Table 5-1. The firm makes an early assessment of new product concepts and evaluates each on criteria of market performance, competitive advantages related to the product and the potential marketing mix programs, and internal operations. Each new product alternative would be evaluated on each criterion on a scale, for example, of 1 to 10. A 1 indicates "product concept is very poor on the criterion," a 10 indicates "product concept is very good on the criterion," and a 5 or 6 indicates "neither poor nor good, i.e., neutral." The persons doing the ratings might be a committee of managers from R&D, marketing research, product management, etc.

TABLE 5-1
An Example of a New Product Evaluation Form

Criterion	1	2	3	4	5	6	7	8	9	10	Importance of Criterion	Rating	Subtotal
Market and Performance Criteria													
Overall Sales Level					✔						.20	1.00	
Growth Potential			✔								.30	.90	
Market Share						✔					.30	1.80	
Profitability							✔				.20	1.40	5.10
Competitive Advantages													
Product Quality								✔			.20	1.60	
Price		✔									.30	.60	
Advertising				✔							.20	1.00	
Sales Force			✔								.05	.15	
Promotion							✔				.05	.35	
Distribution									✔		.20	1.80	5.50
Internal Operations													
Supply Considerations	✔										.30	.30	
Financial Issues			✔								.30	.90	
Production Issues								✔			.25	2.00	
Personnel				✔							.10	.40	
Shipping					✔						.05	.25	3.85
												TOTAL	14.45

Table 5-1 shows the scores for one hypothetical product. In addition to the subjective scores on the criteria, each criterion within each of the three categories of criteria might be given a relative rating in terms of importance. The new product rating is then computed as the product of subjective evaluation times importance. Importance weights might be set in accordance with company norms and discussion among the key managers in the firm. Table 5-1 presents one "decision rule," but of course, many others might be applied in terms of the list of criteria, the scoring of products on the criteria, and the formula used to weight and combine weighted scores into a total overall index. For whatever rule is used, each new product alternative can be compared to each other to choose the one with the highest score and presumably greatest chance for success.

A successful evaluation of the four types of analyses leads to the *design phase* of enactment. As was indicated in Figure 5-4, three design activities are crucial: design of the physical product, design of the marketing mix, and design of support programs within the organization. We briefly consider these below.

The *design of the physical product* involves a translation of the new product idea into a form that will be manufactured efficiently, satisfy consumer needs, gain a differential advantage over the competition, and earn a profit. Somehow management must find a compromise between the ideal and the possible. A useful beginning in the design phase is to start with consumer needs and perceptions as gathered through research. To the extent that the firm can realize product attributes that genuinely satisfy needs, it will have overcome a fundamental obstacle to success. And if it can either introduce new attributes that satisfy needs but are not fielded by the competition or else improve on old attributes, it will gain an edge over rivals. There are many technological, engineering, and stylistic design decisions that must be made, and most organizations have specialists in each area. The design of the physical product is part science and part art. The firm begins with more or less abstract ideas and incomplete information but must fashion a concrete product early on in order to provide an evaluation of the product's potential receptivity in the market. From an organizational standpoint, this entails coordination of creative personnel and activities with technical and pragmatic concerns. The process is very much one that sociologists term "the social construction of reality." It is a rational, political, and fortuitous process.

Early decisions must also be made with respect to the *design of the marketing mix*, i.e., promotion, product, place (physical distribution), and price. It makes little sense to design the best physical product in the world but fail to make it available to the public through retailers, to inform consumers of the offering and persuade them to try it, and to price it attractively and competitively. The marketing mix is so intimately intertwined with the product and its meaning for the consumer that effective marketing demands that the processes be coordinated. Once the product concept has been decided upon and perhaps a picture, mockup, or prototype designed, work can begin on development of a core selling proposition, the brand name, copy design for advertisements, promotional materials, sales presentations, and alternative plans for distribution. These activities often take so much time to perform that they must be begun well before market introduction. Of course, along the way, management might decide to scrap the product at any time. But such are the risks associated with any business venture.

The final design decision is the *design of supporting programs* within the firm. Production must begin planning for a potential new product, particularly with respect to tooling. Financial plans must be made to acquire the needed investment and operating capital. The personnel department must anticipate labor needs. And so on. These topics are better treated in other texts but deserve mention because all of the firm's activities must be planned in an integrative way to bring a product successfully to market.

Returning to Figure 5-4, we can see that the output of the design processes must again be evaluated vis-à-vis organization standards and goals. If the design decisions pass critical scrutiny here (e.g., through a formal evaluation), then the third enactment process can begin: *development.*

The output of design must be coupled with information discovered in analysis to generate a physical form of the product. This is a formative process whereby criteria learned earlier are applied, assessed, adjusted, and readjusted until a physical product with a reasonable chance of success emerges. As with so many of the steps in the new product development process, *product development* consists of a blending of ideas, research findings, and managerial judgment with the practicalities of technological limitations.

Once the physical product has been developed and a prototype built, it is ready for *pretesting.*[8] Actually, firms will often construct a number of design variations to test in the hope of finding the right product to market. One commonly-used procedure for pretesting—especially for products with strong personal and subjective dimensions—is *expert judgment.* For example, producers of beer, soft drinks, tea, and coffee rely heavily on the opinions of expert tasters. These are people who, through years of apprenticeship and trial and error, have acquired a sensitivity to the ingredients of products and their subtle variations and effects.

A second pretesting method is to use *employee evaluations.* Manufacturers of soaps and detergents, for instance, will regularly provide their product free to their employees and ask them for their assessments. Producers of snacks, beverages, and other foods often maintain kitchens and testing rooms on their premises to obtain feedback from employees. Although disadvantages arise with employee evaluations (e.g., biased responses, nonrepresentativeness of the final market), the benefits of early testing frequently outweigh the limitations. Some companies even use a combination of expert judgments and employee evaluations. Procter & Gamble, for instance, gives its employees its mouthwash and deodorant products and allegedly monitors their effectiveness through professional breath and armpit sniffers!

A third pretesting method is *laboratory testing.* This commonly employed procedure is particularly suited to the testing of the reliability and durability of products and their component parts. Laboratory tests offer the advantage of providing accurate, controllable simulations of product usage. Indeed, such tests are used in conjunction with the design stage to simulate usage under heavy and even extreme conditions. A disadvantage of this approach is that it is not always possible to simulate all usage conditions. Not only do people use products differently, but many dimensions of product usage are subjective and difficult to measure and forecast. Nevertheless, firms go through considerable effort to duplicate consumer usage as closely as possible through *field testing.* A good example is afforded by the automotive industry. Cars are pretested under realistic conditions ranging from highway and backroad conditions to mountain and desert driving. Most auto firms also maintain elaborate "proving grounds" with cement, asphalt, brick, and dirt roads. This semirealistic testing is combined with numerous laboratory tests of individual components, systems of components (e.g., the radio, engine), and the entire car itself. Sometimes police forces and taxi companies also are used as testing grounds. All of the pretesting procedures noted here are preparatory to market testing.

Marketing mix pretests are often conducted, too, to gain a preliminary indication of their effectiveness. Advertising copy, personal selling presentations, promotion deals, and distribution alternatives are scrutinized by experts and evaluated in mathematical and simulation models. Some of this work is conducted by specialists in the home company, some by personnel in advertising agencies, and some by private consultants outside the firm. We will discuss the developmental work done in pretesting the marketing mix in later chapters in the book.

The final area for development is that related to the *coordination of other operations* of the firm. To bring a new product idea and design to fruition requires the orchestration of production, quality control, purchasing, finance, shipping, legal, and other functions, along with marketing operations. Not only must each functional area of the firm design and plan ahead for the activities it performs in relation to new product development, but it must operationalize its ideas and plans in concert with the evolving product. This requires that critical path scheduling be implemented and, in general, that a whole host of procedures and operations is set in motion, pretested, and refined. This, too, is an evolutionary process that management must continually monitor, evaluate, and control.

As with all the subprocesses under enactment, an evaluation of the development outcomes and their pretests is essential. Sometimes the evaluation is subjective, relying upon the voting of management. Often rules-of-thumb or formal standards are used to assess a new product's performance. Typically, these are based on the demands of consumers and a performance comparison to competitors' products if these exist. For example, some firms require that pretests of their new products be perceived to be significantly more attractive than the leading products of competitors. Consumer products firms often use rules such as, "a new detergent will not be evaluated favorably and given the go-ahead for market test and introduction unless (a) consumers in a pretest rate it 50 percent more effective than the market leader, brand X, (b) a majority indicates a preference for the new brand over all leading brands, and (c) 75 percent express an intention to try it." Every firm will have different rules for each of its new products. An unfavorable evaluation in the development stage might lead to abandonment of the new product or possibly a return to an earlier stage such as redesign. A favorable evaluation at least temporarily permits the new product development process to continue.

As illustrated in Figure 5-4, the enactment process ends with an actual *market test* of the new product and its evaluation. Actually, all firms do not necessarily perform market tests in every situation. Indeed, at least two criteria are usually employed before deciding to test market or not. The first requirement is that an estimate of the costs of test marketing must be examined and evaluated in relation to the expected gains and losses. Test markets for frequently purchased consumer goods found in the supermarket, for example, can cost from $1,000,000 to $2,000,000 for each city in which the product is tested. Obviously, undertaking such an endeavor requires that expected revenues and profits after subsequent product introduction will recoup the test market costs as well as the normal costs associated with producing and marketing the product. Every firm will have a different expected payback period, but seldom will firms support a losing proposition for more than three or four years.

A second criterion that is often applied to test marketing concerns the reaction of the competition. One drawback with test marketing is that it can provide rivals with information on product innovations, planned marketing strategies, and so on. In some situations, it might be prudent to forgo a market test to avoid giving competitors the extra time to learn from one's new ideas. Because test markets often take from six months to a year to complete, rivals could gain valuable time in their efforts to respond to the potential competitive threat. By skipping test marketing, one can often get a head start that could prove crucial in the long run. In addition, test marketing is often vulnerable to sabotage by the competition. Through their pricing, promotion, and advertising policies, competitors sometimes positively or negatively influence the test market results of a potential new rival. If they feel that a new rival might eventually eat into their sales, they might drop their prices, increase advertising, introduce a new deal, etc., to hamper the sales in the competitor's test market. Or even if competitors do not necessarily fear a new product entry, they might raise prices and reduce promotion support to make a new product test of a competitor perform at a high but artificially inflated level. That is, if competitors believe the rival's new product is inferior, a successful market test might stimulate the rival to introduce the product and thus subsequently incur a loss to the benefit of the competition. Firms also have been alleged to randomly change marketing mix variables to disrupt the test market results of rivals. Fortunately, however, from the new product marketer's standpoint, the gains from test marketing often outweigh the losses.

Assuming the firm believes that something is to be gained through market tests, it must then choose a test market strategy. One or more of three options are typically practiced: representative introductions, natural field experiments, or controlled field experiments. In the representative introduction, one or more cities are chosen as test cities. For example, some firms choose Peoria, Illinois; Fresno, California; or Syracuse, New York, because these cities are representative of the entire country in terms of sociodemographic characteristics and are not so large in size as to make a test cost prohibitive. It is important to realize that "representativeness" is a relative term referring to one's target market. Syracuse might be representative of the target market if one is testing a new toothpaste for the "average" consumer, but it might be a poor choice if one is testing a new food product targeted to Mexican Americans. Denver, Phoenix, or Austin might be more representative test markets for the latter. In the representative introduction, an attempt is made to test a product under as realistic conditions as possible. Product characteristics are held constant (i.e., the new product is tested as designed), and no unusual levels of advertising, promotion, etc., are conducted, nor will large variations in these be examined in various cities. Advertising, for example, might be set as a percentage of planned total advertising as a function of the size of the city. At the end of the test market and at key points throughout, sales will be monitored. This might be done by recording the sales in each store, the amount shipped from the home firm to retailers and wholesalers, or the amount shipped from wholesalers to retailers.

In a natural field experiment, the firm attempts to see the responses of consumers to different prices, advertising levels, promotions, and so on. However, rather than setting these before the fact, it offers one product at one uniform price and promotion schedule to retailers who, in turn, set their own prices, decide to adopt promotions or not, control shelf space allocated to the new product, and so on. The firm then studies sales as a function of the naturally varying in-store stimuli. The advantage of the approach is that a deeper analysis is performed than in the representative introduction (i.e., rather than looking at only total sales, one examines the response of sales to variations in the marketing mix). A disadvantage is that little or no control is imposed on the marketing mix variations, thus making analysis difficult and preventing a full examination of ranges of effects.

The controlled field experiment consists of manipulation of product design, prices, advertising, and other stimuli in different markets in order to observe the optimal marketing mix along with the overall receptivity of the product. Here it is possible to more validly infer the connection between each change in product design, price level, etc., on the one hand, and actual sales, on the other. However, the greater degree of information provided comes at a higher cost because coordination and measurement procedures are complex. Moreover, experiments are difficult to design and are subject to contamination.

Test marketing ends with an evaluation of the results. The overall objective is to project the rate of product trial and repeat sales and the total level of sales and revenue over time. Later chapters present a methodology for accomplishing this. This must then be compared to costs and a decision made as to *product introduction,* an early step in the retention process. We turn now to the final activities in the new product development process.

Retention Processes. The new product development process "ends" with product introduction, the implementation of marketing mix and other programs, and a continuous monitoring, assessment, and control of the marketing program (refer back to Figure 5-4). Because later chapters expand on marketing mix considerations, we will only briefly discuss three central retention processes here: new product introduction, product strategy decisions, and management of the product throughout its life cycle.

New product introduction (also known as commercialization or product launch) is an especially uncertain and expensive undertaking. Consider the following, for example:

. . . in 1977 S. C. Johnson spent over $7 million on television and magazine advertising, along with a $7 million sampling campaign to introduce Agree Creme Rinse and Hair Conditioner. Then in 1978 they launched Agree Shampoo with a $30 million campaign. During the same period Gillette planned to spend about $15 million to get buyers to try its Ultra Max shampoo; in the same year Gillette spent over $8 million to introduce Atra automatic tracking razors.[9]

Despite all of the studies and plans one makes, one never knows for sure whether a new product will be accepted. There are simply too many uncertainties, and consumer needs, competitive responses, and economic conditions may change unpredictably.

To cut down on the uncertainty, management can do a number of things. First, a careful plan and scheduling of activities must be performed. Schemes such as PERT (program evaluation and review technique) or CPM (critical path method) might prove helpful in planning. Second, the firm must decide when and where to begin introduction. Timing is crucial to get a head start on the competition. Wide distribution in a relative sense is important in order to take maximum advantage of consumer demand. Yet, to be too early and reach too far can also pose problems. For example, initial advertising and promotion for the Kodak Instamatic Camera was so successful that people flocked to stores to purchase it. However, in the beginning, the manufacturer was unable to meet the demand, and many stores ran out quickly. The result was that some customers were highly disappointed and reacted angrily toward retailers and Kodak. Moreover, some consumers, looking for a way to retaliate, purposely purchased other brands. Thus, a hastily or poorly planned introduction can result in lost sales. Third, the related issue of target markets must be addressed. As we saw in the chapter on macro consumer behavior, some people are more innovative or less risk-prone than others and will try a product with little deliberation and resistance. Others require considerable time, are risk-averse, and rely on the experiences and opinions of early adopters. Hence, firms often need to target their introduction campaigns to innovators and early adopters so as to reach the most responsive market first. Later, prices, advertising, promotion, and distribution can be adjusted to reach the later adopters.

A key element in the retention process is the firm's *new product strategy*. In this regard, let us consider first the concept of a *product portfolio*. Figure 5-6 shows a summary of the idea of a product portfolio and is adapted from a publication by the Boston Consulting Group.[10] Managers believe that the health of any firm can be meaningfully summarized through a description of the firm's relative market share and market growth. As shown in Figure 5-6, we might classify any firm depending on whether it has a high or low relative market share and whether the market growth rate is high or low. The idea is that profitability and return on investment are thought to be intimately linked to these variables. A high growth rate implies larger sales volume and, consequently, lower costs and greater price flexibility. The low costs are a result of economies of scale and experience curve effects. Similarly, high market share implies additional cost savings and pricing and other advantages.[11] The combination of a favorable market growth and market share leads to high profitability.

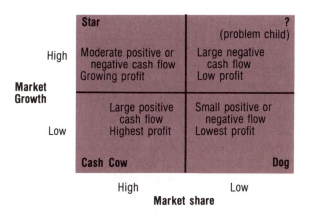

	High market share	Low market share
High Market Growth	**Star** Moderate positive or negative cash flow Growing profit	**?** (problem child) Large negative cash flow Low profit
Low Market Growth	**Cash Cow** Large positive cash flow Highest profit	**Dog** Small positive or negative flow Lowest profit

Market share

Figure 5-6. The concept of a product portfolio

However, a firm's optimum profitability is thought to depend also on the achievement of a balance between cash flow and new product investment opportunities.[12] Notice in Figure 5-6 that the combinations of high and low market share with high and low growth lead to different levels and directions of cash flow. A positive cash flow means the firm has generated a large amount of revenue from sales relative to investment requirements, whereas a negative cash flow means that more is spent on investment than is derived from sales. When both market share and market growth are low, the cash flow is small but can be either positive or negative, depending on the balance between sales revenue and investment.

This situation is termed "a dog" by the Boston Consulting Group, and profits are typically very low, other things being equal. When market share is low but the market is growing, cash outflow is large because the firm must invest in distribution, promotion, and advertising to reach new customers and maintain market share. This situation is termed "a question mark" or "problem child" because profits are generally low and if new investments are not made, the danger exists that the product will become a dog with very low profits or even losses. Sufficient investment in a question-mark product, however, can lead to an increase in market share with a concomitant relative rise in cash flow and increased profitability. This situation is called "a star" for obvious reasons. When market growth is low, but market share is high, the firm is in the enviable position of having a positive and even large cash flow and high profits. This situation is appropriately labeled "a cash cow." Because a cash cow generates considerable revenue, the optimum strategy for a firm is often to put this money to best use, such as investing in new product development or converting a question mark to a star. Hence, we see that market share, market growth, and investment tactics interact. To maximize profits, a firm must adjust its investments (e.g., R&D, advertising, promotion, etc.) according to the location of the products in the product portfolio.

The picture is not as simple as the product portfolio concept indicates, however. Sometimes other criteria such as product quality and product differentiation must be taken into account. For example, it is conceivable that some firms might profit most when market share and growth are low, the so-called dog condition. Small firms often cannot hope to compete on price because they are unable to achieve economies of scale or to afford high levels of advertising. As a consequence, they create a distinctive product and pursue a special market segment that values the product and is even willing to pay a premium for it. We will have more to say about the role of market segmentation in the following chapter. For now, we wish to stress that while market share, growth, and cash flow are important, other considerations such as firm size, market opportunities, product differentiation, etc., also may play an important role in some instances.

A second strategic concept is the *product line strategy*. We have already discussed how the product line can vary in width, depth, length, and other dimensions. Management must decide whether it should market a single product, a full line of products, or a limited line of products. In addition, it must decide on how many variations, options, accessories, etc., to offer within each brand, product type, or product line. A number of alternatives may be identified in these respects. One tactic is to avoid full product lines and, instead, concentrate on single products or limited product lines in markets. A firm might choose to do this because it is small in size, has a small market share and confronts larger, more efficient competitors. By focusing its efforts on a small number of market segments, it presumably can achieve a profitable foothold in part of the market. Another tactic is to offer a product in every market segment possible. Obviously this approach is available only to larger firms with relatively higher market shares and greater resources. The extent of a product line to market depends on the firm's goals with respect to return on investment, sales, and market share. Also, one limiting factor is the degree of competition and cannibalization among one's own product lines. General Foods faced a critical decision after it developed Maxim, a freeze-dried coffee. Would consumers perceive it as just another coffee and either reject it outright or merely substitute another General Foods brand for it? Or would a new market segment be tapped? Apparently, a little of both happened.

Firms attempt to support as many profitable product lines as they can afford. One reason for this is the increased economies of scale, learning curve effects, and technology/management transfers that can occur across product lines. On the other hand, given that the sales of products in a product line will rise and fall at different times and that it is difficult to ascertain at what stage in the PLC each product is in, firms will sometimes prematurely or belatedly prune less profitable products and reduce the product line. Unfortunately, very little is known about how to form and maintain an optimal product line.

The final strategic decision is the *brand strategy*. Here the firm must decide first whether to use a brand name for its products or to sell them unbranded. On the one hand, to use a brand name offers definite advantages. For the consumer, a brand name can make shopping faster and less risky. It is faster because the consumer may use the brand name as a cue to avoid wasteful searches and comparisons. It is less risky because the brand name may serve as a symbol of quality, value, or some other sought-after asset. For the seller, a brand name can serve as a means of influencing behavior. Consumers who have not tried a new product may see the brand name as a positive enticement. The reputation of the manufacturer generalizes or "rubs off" on all its brands. Consumers who have purchased the brand often may continue to do so without much deliberation and with essentially no comparisons to other offerings. This is a consequence of both learning through habitual behavior and the tendency to mentally associate the frequently purchased brand with one's needs and decision rules at a stronger level than other brands. Hence, from the firm's viewpoint, a brand can be both a promotional device and a competitive lever.

However, the use of a brand sometimes poses costs. For the consumer, one can become too habitual if in so doing cheaper and/or better quality brands exist but are unknown. For the seller, branding incurs certain expenses associated with the need for special packages, promotion, and advertising. Also, the firm is especially vulnerable if the brand should, rightly or wrongly, get a bad name. Firestone tires, for example, experienced serious safety and legal problems with one of its lines of tires a few years ago. The publicity was so negative that people avoided the Firestone brands and sales of the entire company suffered. Among other measures to correct this negative image, the company spent a large amount on television advertising and selected James Stewart, the well-known actor, as a spokesperson. A brand image is a fickle, yet important and powerful, asset for any firm.

The alternative to branding is to sell *private* or *dealer brands*. The manufacturer markets the same or similar products but puts the label of the retailer on it. Most supermarket chains, for instance, have their own private label brands, which they sell along with the well-known brands. Manufacturers find the dealer brand opportunity a chance to sell more volume than they might strictly through their regular branded marketing. This permits better scheduling of production, economies of scale, higher total sales, and so on. Consumers sometimes prefer private brands because they are cheaper and generally of a high or at least adequate quality. One drawback for the manufacturer is that profit margins on private brands are typically lower. Also, sales tend to fluctuate more and make the seller relatively more vulnerable. This is a consequence of the greater price competition among sellers resulting, in turn, from the relatively more standardized private brand. Private brands tend also to pose somewhat more uncertainty and shopping effort for consumers when compared to well-known brands. The manufacturer of branded goods is motivated more to maintain product quality.

Given that the firm decides to employ a brand strategy, additional issues must be addressed. An important one is whether to use individual brands for each product or a *family brand*. For example, General Foods uses the former strategy. More people are aware of Jell-O, Maxwell House Coffee, Log Cabin Syrup, and Sanka than they are of the manufacturer, General Foods. In contrast, Kellogg's and General Mills employ the family brand strategy by attaching their name as an umbrella for each brand they sell. Another issue is the particular brand name to use. We have already discussed the effect of brand names on consumers. From the seller's standpoint, one must select a new brand name with a forceful symbolic impact and/or use an existing name. Occasionally, new spinoffs of an old name are used such as General Foods did with Maxim. A third brand-related issue concerns where to market (e.g., what market segment to pursue, to market internationally, etc.), and a fourth relates to marketing mix interactions—price, advertising, distribution, etc. We will have more to say about these in later chapters.

The final element in the retention process is *management of the product throughout the life cycle*.[13] Figure 5-7 summarizes marketing conditions (i.e., "characteristics") that change throughout the PLC and appropriate managerial responses to them. Let us begin with a look at the introduction stage. Many consumers are perhaps not aware of the product class, and even fewer are aware of the brand. Distribution is "patchy" in that relatively few retailers stock the product. Hence, sales are low, profits negligible, and cash flow negative. Competition, however, is weakest in this stage. The task for the marketer is to increase consumer awareness (e.g., through heavy informational advertising) and gain acceptance by the retail trade (e.g., by providing promotional deals as incentives).

These goals obviously require large expenditures on advertising, promotional incentives, sales force efforts, and so on. This, then, accounts for the large cash outflow and negligible profits. Because early purchases are made disproportionately by innovators and early adopters, special targeting must be directed toward them. For example, this might mean selective use of certain media and advertising copy that informs as well as instills a desire to try the brand. The product itself is rather "basic" in the sense that its design is based on consumer needs as they now exist and on managerial/technical constraints. Price is a particularly difficult variable to set. On the one hand, a relatively low price might be preferred to entice customers and discourage competitors from entering the market. Yet, on the other hand, because startup expenditures are large, volume is low, costs are high, and prices also need to be high to support further expansion into the market and make a profit. Although striking a balance depends on the particular firm's objectives and market forces, prices tend to be relatively higher for most firms in the introduction stage.

CHARACTERISTICS	Introduction	Growth	Maturity	Decline
Sales	Low	Fast growth	Slow growth	Decline
Profits	Negligible	Peak levels	Declining	Low or zero
Cash flow	Negative	Moderate	High	Low
Customers	Innovative	Mass market	Mass market	Laggards
Competitors	Few	Growing	Many rivals	Declining number
RESPONSES	Introduction	Growth	Maturity	Decline
Strategic focus	Expand market	Market penetration	Defend share	Productivity
Mkg. expenditures	High	High (declining %)	Falling	Low
Mkg. emphasis	Product awareness	Brand preference	Brand loyalty	Selective
Distribution	Patchy	Intensive	Intensive	Selective
Price	High	Lower	Lowest	Rising
Product	Basic	Improved	Differentiated	Rationalized

Figure 5-7. Management considerations throughout the stages of the product life

SOURCE: Peter Doyle, "The Realities of the Product Life Cycle," *Quarterly Review of Marketing* 2 (Summer 1976), p. 5. Reprinted with the permission of the publisher.

In the growth stage, sales accelerate, cash flow turns positive and reaches moderate levels, and profits increase. However, competition also increases with the effect that profits tend to peak near the end of the growth stage. The type of consumer making purchases changes, too. Most purchases are now made by late adopters. This necessitates the use of new advertising media, changes in copy to build preference and instill repeat purchase, and a reduction in price to combat the competition and at the same time attract additional price-sensitive consumers. Further, as a result of changing consumer needs and product quality assaults by competitors, the product itself might have to be improved. Overall, total marketing expenditures (advertising, distribution, sales, etc.) are high but perhaps lower than in the introduction stage. The goal in the growth stage is to reach out to more consumer markets, achieve greater acceptance by more retailers, and generally expand operations to flow with the tide.

At some point, everything begins to slow down. Sales rise very slowly or even stagnate; profits remain positive but decline; and pressures for relatively more cash outflow begin. Part of the reason for these effects is greater competition, but part of it is also due to saturation in the market. Fewer and fewer new people are around to try the product. Indeed, management might well infer that the product is in the maturity phase. However, as we indicated earlier, it is very difficult to determine that maturity has been reached, and maturity is not inevitable, at least not in the short and medium run. Moreover, through its use of the marketing mix, management can renew the product life cycle. Hence, while many firms may well take a defensive strategy to defend market share and shift marketing expenditures around accordingly, as Doyle hypothesizes in Figure 5-7, some firms might assume an aggressive posture. This could include increased expenditures, a search for new markets, further improvement in the product, the development of a differentiated line of products, dropping the price in saturated, competitive markets, but maintaining a higher price in new markets, comparative advertising, and so on.

Somewhere down the road, most firms can expect to see their products enter the decline stage. Although some old customers continue repeat purchasing and a few laggards purchase for the first time, sales simply reach a level where profits drop precipitously or even disappear. Here again the firm must make a crucial decision. Should it reduce marketing support to cut down on expenditures or should it attempt to rejuvenate the product to turn it around or at least prolong its life?

The dilemma is that whatever action the firm takes can have a self-fulfilling prophecy. Withdrawing support can accelerate or even cause a premature death, and increasing support can give the product new life. Yet the prospect always exists that the market forces are stronger than the marketer's levers, and decline will continue unabated. We know very little about how to identify weak products or when to increase or decrease support. About all one can say at this point is that it is important to monitor sales, consumer feedback, competitive actions, and market conditions and evaluate how much influence the firm has at its disposal. This means establishing a market information system, doing simulations and market response studies, and in general melding research with managerial analysis, know-how, and guesswork.

As a brief illustration of the concept of the management of a product throughout its life cycle, consider Figure 5-8, which shows the changes made in the marketing mix over time for a brand of toothpaste. In the introduction stage (called "entry" by the authors), the firm tries to establish a foothold in the market. Considerable effort is placed on product quality and achievement of a real advantage over the competition. Advertising and promotion strive to primarily build awareness and secondarily induce trial. Special effort is devoted to persuade retailers to stock the brand and give it maximum shelf space. Price is set as the sum of costs plus a sought-after margin based perhaps on expected sales and a return-on-investment norm. As the market grows and competition strengthens, the goal shifts from market penetration to maintenance of market share (the "maintenance" stage in Figure 5-8). Research is conducted to identify product weaknesses for future changes. Advertising stresses product advantages in order to build brand loyalty. An attempt is made to gain a rapport with retailers, perhaps through providing more service. Prices are set in relation to the competition. In the proliferation stage (i.e., maturity), sales stagnate. The firm

PRODUCT LIFE CYCLE STAGE				
Strategy consideration	Entry	Maintenance	Proliferation	Exit/decline
Objective	Establish market position	Stabilize market share	Secure new market segments	Prepare for re-entry
Product design	Assure high quality	Identify weaknesses	Adjust size, color, package; add flavor	Modify weak features
Promotion	Build brand awareness	Stress favorable evaluation	Communicate new features	Educate on re-entry features
Distribution	Build distribution network	Solidify channel relationships	Deliver all versions	Smooth re-entry features
Pricing	Use cost-plus	Price with competition	Use price deals	Reduce price to clear stock

Figure 5-8. Product life cycle strategies for a brand of toothpaste

SOURCE: Ben M. Enis, Raymond La Grace, and Arthur E. Prell, "Extending the Product Life Cycle," *Business Horizons* 20 (June 1977): 53. Reprinted with the permission of the publisher.

responds by searching for new geographical markets. But this is not enough. It recognizes the need to change the product and introduces an "improved" version of the old product. This might entail changing ingredients, package, sizes, and so on. Advertising copy adjusts accordingly, and retailers must be informed and won over with respect to the need to stock the new product versions. This is done through price and other deals. Finally, decline arrives, and the firm must decide whether to modify the product as a "new improved" offering and/or introduce a new toothpaste entirely. Procter & Gamble, for example, has done both with its earlier Crest and Gleem brands which now are called Crest Plus and Gleem II. New flavors have been introduced as well.

A temptation of sellers is to rely more on cosmetic product changes and advertising/promotion when an established product falters. For example, although introduced as a dandruff shampoo, Procter & Gamble's Head and Shoulders quickly achieved

acceptance by consumers and eventually became the country's best selling shampoo. However, after a while, Johnson's Baby Shampoo and others made competitive inroads, and took leadership away from Head and Shoulders. The relative decline of Head and Shoulders was also blamed on consumer perceptions that the product was harsh on hair, particularly for everyday use, as was the cultural custom embodied in "the dry look" of the day. However, Procter & Gamble had research evidence showing that their product was not significantly harsher than other shampoos. They attempted to counter such "false" attributions through a change in advertising. In effect, their ads stressed the ability of the product to leave one's hair soft and manageable even after frequent washings. The campaign failed to return the product to its prior leadership role, and further consumer research was conducted. The research showed that, despite advertising claims to the contrary, people still perceived the product as too harsh on hair. Further, the consumer's perception was discovered to be based on the product fragrance, which at that time was highly medicinal. Consumers, therefore, developed a product attribute inference of harshness from the fragrance, and this influenced their behavior accordingly. To counteract this, Procter & Gamble changed the fragrance and advertised the new improved product. The subsequent success of the product over the years has been attributed, in part, to this change. The moral of the story is that one must often make a physical change in the product and not merely rely on advertising. The example also shows the role and value of consumer research. And it illustrates again the fact that people buy things not so much for so-called objective criteria but rather based on their subjective evaluations and judgments. A successful marketer of new products must study and understand the psychology of the consumer and how it relates to the product, the competition, and other socioeconomic forces.

Summary

This chapter considered products from the manager's perspective. The new product development process was described in detail. Managerial strategies and decisions related to products in all stages of the life cycle were also scrutinized. Overall, we can see that the idea of a product is a complex, yet crucial, concept in marketing. We might think of a product first as the bridge that links the world of the consumer to the world of the manager and second as the glue that, through the mechanism of markets, holds together social and economic institutions in one form or another. Subsequent chapters elaborate further on the idea of a product and relate it to the actions that firms might take in its promotion, i.e., through the orchestration of the marketing mix.

Figure 5-1 presents a description of the elements of the product decision process. Notice that the general organization goals determine more specific marketing objectives, and these in turn lead to still more specific product objectives. We might think of the product objectives as intermediate steps needed to achieve the more general goals of the organization. Product objectives are specifically concerned with implementation strategies. Figure 5-1 also points out the two tactical activities used to implement the product objectives. These are new product development and the management of existing products throughout the product life cycle. Finally, notice that market forces, social/legal constraints, and interactions with pricing, promotion, and distribution decisions enter the overall product decision process.

We then turned to a consideration of new product development. We began the discussion by placing new product development into the framework of the natural selection model (see Figures 5-3 and 5-4). New ideas are generated within the firm as well as from the outside. Successful firms attempt to stimulate the flow of new ideas with as little external constraint imposed on the process as possible. Emphasis is upon creativity and not necessarily practicality at this stage in the new product development process. Next, ideas are selected and evaluated in a complex stage known as *enactment*. As we saw in Figure 5-4, consumer needs are measured, the competitive and legal/social environment are assessed, a business analysis is made, the physical product is designed and refined, product and market tests are conducted if necessary, and the product is integrated with the marketing mix decisions and other programs within the firm. Finally, the last stage in new product development is the *retention* process. Here, the programs chosen under enactment are implemented, the new product is introduced, and the results are monitored with any necessary corrections made periodically.

This chapter also introduced the notion of a *perceptual map*. A perceptual map is a geometric representation of the perceived attributes or characteristics of a set of competing brands (see Figure 5-5 for an example applied to the beer market). Although we will explore the use of perceptual maps in greater depth in the next chapter, we should note here that it is an effective tool for discovering what are the important characteristics consumers desire in one's product and how each competitor stacks up on these characteristics.

Still another important concept introduced in the chapter was the idea of the *product portfolio*. A number of product portfolio schemes exist, but in this chapter we chose to present only one: the Boston Consulting Group Framework (see Figure 5-6). Briefly, the BCG model is based on the premise that survival and profitability depend on the attainment of two goals: market growth and market share. By examining a firm's products and assessing their individual growth and market share characteristics, one may make certain recommendations to maintain and/or enhance the health of the firm.

The chapter closed with a description of product management throughout the life cycle. We noted that support for a brand depends on its stage in the life cycle. One must continually examine the market in terms of consumer knowledge and acceptance and competitive conditions and then adjust the marketing mix accordingly (see Figure 5-7). An example was illustrated for the management of a brand of toothpaste throughout its life cycle.

We now turn to a more detailed consideration of market segmentation and positioning—two central product-related strategies.

Questions and Problems for Discussion

1 Name and discuss the five generic marketing strategies related to product management.

2 Describe the overall new product development process from the perspective of organizational natural selection. Why is new product development needed?

3 What are the central elements in the enactment phase of new product development?

4 What is idea generation and what role does it play in new product development?

5 Name the key activities in the retention phase of new product development and describe how they function.

6 Pretesting and market testing of products are sometimes performed in new product development programs. Briefly discuss why these activities might be undertaken and point out any drawbacks.

7 What is a product portfolio and how does it enter product decisions?

8 Discuss the concepts of product line strategy, brand strategy, private branding, and family brands.

9 Products must be managed throughout their life cycles. Elaborate upon this assertion.

10 Evaluaton is a key management function throughout the new product development and product management processes. How can new product ideas and new products be evaluated?

NOTES

1. H. I. Ansoff, *Corporate Strategy: An Analytical Approach to Business Policy for Growth and Expansion* (New York: McGraw-Hill, 1965).

2. For excellent treatments of new product development and the topic of the following section (i.e., management of products throughout the PLC), see Glenn L. Urban and John R. Hauser, *Design and Marketing of New Products* (Englewood Cliffs, N.J.: Prentice-Hall, 1980); Yoram Wind, *Product Policy: Concepts, Methods, and Strategy* (Reading, Mass.: Addison-Wesley, 1982); D. F. Midgley, *Innovation and New Product Marketing* (New York: John Wiley & Sons, 1977); Edgar A. Pessemier, *New Product Decisions: An Analytical Approach* (New York: McGraw-Hill, 1966); and Edgar A. Pessemier, *Product Management: Strategy and Organization* (New York: John Wiley & Sons, 1977).

3. The issue of what constitutes a new product is a difficult one. From the firm's perspective, any product with which it decides to consider marketing but with which it has no experience is new. But from the customer's standpoint, a new product is one he or she had no knowledge of. Moreover, we might speak further as to the kind and degree of newness. For example, a product might be entirely new (i.e., new in concept, design, and realization) or it might be partially new (e.g., new in form, size, attributes, functions, and so on). In this section of the chapter, we primarily emphasize newness from the firm's viewpoint. Thus, a new product is one the firm has no experience with but is considering marketing. That product could be an existing one or an entirely new one from the consumer's vantage point. However, with respect to the framework for new product development presented below, we should note that all steps are performed in their totality only when the product is new from both the firm's and the customer's perspective.

4. For a description of the natural selection model applied to organizations, see Karl E. Weick, *The Social Psychology of Organizing*, 2nd ed. (Reading, Mass.: Addison-Wesley, 1979). See also Donald T. Campbell, "Evolutionary Epistemology," in P. A. Schlipp, ed., *The Philosophy of Karl R. Popper*, vol. 2 (La Salle, Ill.: Open Court, 1974) pp. 413-63.

5. Urban and Hauser, *Design and Marketing of New Products*, p. 125.

6. We discuss perceptual maps in greater detail in Chapter 6. For an example in the beer market, see Richard M. Johnson, "Market Segmentation: A Strategic Management Tool," *Journal of Marketing Research* 8 (February 1971): 13-18.

7. Michael E. Porter, *Competitive Strategy: Techniques for Analyzing Industries and Competitors* (New York: The Free Press, 1980).

8. For a quantitative, managerial-based model of pretesting, see Alvin J. Silk and Glenn L. Urban, "Pretest Market Evaluation of New Packaged Goods: A Model and Measurement Methodology," *Journal of Marketing Research* 15 (May 1978): 171-91.

9. Urban and Hauser, *Design and Marketing of New Products*, p. 463.

10. "The Product Portfolio," Perspectives No. 66, Boston: The Boston Consulting Group, 1970.

11. Robert D. Buzzell, Bradley T. Gale, and Ralph G. M. Sultan, "Market Share—A Key to Profitability," *Harvard Business Review* 53 (January–February 1975): 97-106.

12. George S. Day, "Diagnosing the Product Portfolio," *Journal of Marketing* 41 (April 1977): 29-38. See also D. F. Abell and J. S. Hammond, *Strategic Market Planning* (Englewood Cliffs, N.J.: Prentice-Hall, 1979), pp. 173-94.

13. For discussions of the issues involved, see Peter Doyle, "The Realities of the Product Life Cycle," *Quarterly Review of Marketing* 2 (Summer 1976): 1-6; Ben M. Enis, Raymond LaGrace, and Arthur E. Prell, "Extending the Product Life Cycle," *Business Horizons* 20 (June 1977): 46-56.

GLOSSARY

Acquisition. A type of growth pursued by firms and consisting of the purchase of entirely new businesses. *See also* diversification strategy, market expansion, market penetration.

Brand Strategy. The decision to use a unique name (i.e., the brand name) for one's product so that it has a specific identity in and of itself or as a result of its association with the manufacturer or seller. A nonbrand or unbranded strategy is one alternative (e.g., the so-called "no-name" brands found in some supermarkets). A special case of the brand strategy is the dealer brand or store brand. Here the retail seller uses its own name and competes with national manufacturer brands.

Business Analysis. A set of procedures performed during new product development and designed to evaluate a potential product in terms of its ability to meet such organizational goals as break-even, profitability, return on investment, sales, market share, etc. The procedures encompass estimates of costs, forecasts of sales, prediction of economic conditions, and so on.

Competitive Analysis. Evaluation of (1) rivalry among firms selling the same or similar products, (2) probability that consumers can satisfy needs with different types of products, (3) ability and power of suppliers vis-à-vis focal firm, (4) potential for new entrants in market, and (5) the legal environment with respect to selling practices.

Diversification Strategy. A growth strategy marked by the introduction of new products in new markets (in contrast to the new product development strategy narrowly defined by Ansoff to consist of the introduction of new products in existing markets). *See also* market expansion, market penetration.

Enactment Processes. A set of assessments and evaluations performed during new product development and consisting of (1) consumer, competitive, legal/social, and business analyses, (2) physical product, marketing mix, and supporting program design, (3) product development and pretests, marketing mix pretests, and auxiliary program development, and (4) market tests. *See also* retention processes, selection processes.

Market Expansion. The growth strategy characterized by the marketing of existing products in new markets. *See also* acquisition, diversification strategy, market penetration.

Market Information System. A group of people and programs within the organization concerned with data collection, data analysis, storage, and dissemination as a service to decision making. A fuller definition and description is provided in Chapter 7.

Marketing Objectives. Goals for sales, market growth, market share, profitability, product line performance, cannibalization, brand image, etc. These are usually derived from broader organizational objectives or serve as intermediate steps in their pursuit. Informal, implicit marketing objectives may exist as well.

Market Penetration. The growth strategy aimed at getting a larger share of sales in an existing market. *See also* acquisition, diversification strategy, market expansion.

Overall Organization Goals. The ultimate ends and objectives of the firm, sometimes denoted as the fundamental values of the firm. Typical examples include sales growth, overall profitability, return on investment, social responsibility, concern for employee health and welfare, and so on. Most organizations also have informal, implicit goals as well.

Product Line Strategy. The product decisions concerned with the width, depth, and length of product lines. Should the firm market a single product, a full product line, or a limited product line? How many versions or variations in each product should be sold? When should an existing product be dropped or a new one added? What profitability is desired? How much cannibalization can be tolerated? etc.

Product Objectives. Specific goals with respect to new or existing products either derived from or necessary to achieve marketing objectives. For instance, long- and short-run profit expectations, target market responses, brand awareness, product line performance, interactions, durability, and reliability are important product objectives.

Product Portfolio. A multifaceted description of a firm's performance of its product(s). One framework—that used by the Boston Consulting Group—focuses on market growth and market share. High growth and a strong market share are believed essential for high profitability and high return on investment. Other factors sometimes considered are relative costs to produce the product, degree of product differentiation, research and development expenditures, and so on.

Product Tactics. Specific actions taken to implement product plans and achieve product objectives. The two most important consist of new product development and ongoing management of the product throughout its life cycle.

Retention Processes. The third and final stage in the natural selection model of new product development. In this stage the product is introduced (i.e., "rolled out"), marketing mix and other programs are implemented, and a continuous process of monitoring, assessment, and control is instituted, followed by appropriate feedback if necessary. See also enactment processes and selection processes.

Selection Processes. The general processes whereby an organization prunes inferior new product ideas to end up with a few manageable, fruitful concepts. Selection processes are used interchangeably with enactment processes but usually are used in somewhat looser, less specific senses. Three types of selection processes are:

Rational Selection. The evaluation of new product ideas according to specific organization rules, procedures, and standards.

Political Selection. Social processes of debate, conflict, negotiation, and power occurring among groups and individuals within the organization in relation to new ideas.

Fortuitous Selection. The influence of random and systematic external risk and uncertainty over and above the rational and political selection processes.

New Product Management: A Look at the Present and a Forecast of the Future

C. Merle Crawford
Graduate School of
Business Administration
University of Michigan

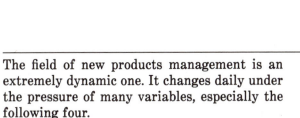

The field of new products management is an extremely dynamic one. It changes daily under the pressure of many variables, especially the following four.

The High Cost of Failures

Every new product seems to cost more than the previous one. There is more competition, population and income growth have made for much larger markets, and there are many more things to be done in the development process. For most firms, marketing a new product today costs a great deal more than it did just 10 years ago. This means that greater returns are necessary. But the leverage of greater returns also works the other way. Whereas there was a time when a company could almost sneak a new product into the market and lose very little if it flopped, losses today are counted in the millions. Some people think one of the car firms recently lost over a billion dollars on one flop.

Longer Lead Times

For many reasons, it now takes much longer to prepare a new item for launch. Government regulations, for example, more difficult R&D, stretched-out developments designed to reduce the strain on cash flow, more preemptions by competitors that send us back to GO without collecting $200, and the longer periods required for thorough product-use testing.

Part of this is deliberate, reflecting the higher cost of failure, for example. But most is due to changing times, about which managements can do very little. This means that when a new product is marketed, important decisions were made about it a long time ago—usually several years. This increases the risks. Many times the product being marketed is not what the firm would like to market, but there wasn't time to go back and make changes.

Technology

The third pressure is technology. It is not new and has been going on for a century. But it continues to grow, and it will grow more. Fiber optics, computers, lasers, biogenetics, ceramics that carry electrical current, new alloys from the space program, new chemicals almost beyond listing let alone understanding, and on and on. Even the simple potato chip is now a technological marvel of sound waves, chemistry, genetics, and scientific production.

Mature industries such as steel, tires, and machinery have made heavy commitments to technical R&D with amazing consequences. People now say there may be mature managements, but no mature industries. So-called high technology has no monopoly on technological breakthroughs any more.

Every single phase of the new product process is being affected by technology. R&D, obviously. But production as well. New product managers, for example, are encouraged to come up with products which can be manufactured under the most advanced processes. And they do daily battle beside (or against) optical scanners in food markets, complex distribution systems electronically designed and controlled, cable TV systems, electronic mail, video conferencing, and scores more. Even the clearly creative process of concept generation now uses morphological matrices, focus groups, right-brain/left-brain systems, conjoint measurement, and more.

Need for New Products

As if those problems of greater costs of failure, longer development times, and technological complexity weren't enough, managements now want new products more than ever. They need them and, indeed, must have them. That is, if they are to grow and hold their positions in dynamic markets.

The typical new products manager hears management say, "Yeah, but what have you done for us recently?" And they mean very recently. So we now develop new businesses, not just new products. That is, when a product is announced, you can assume that three or four line extensions are on their way down the chute right behind it. It has to be that way because competitors will market those other items if the innovator firm doesn't.

No one can sit still today, not without great risk. It used to be that a really profitable new product launch gave some coasting time—like getting into orbit. But the leaders don't coast today. They can't afford to. Some managements even have new product strategies which call for finding firms, or even whole industries, where there is coasting. They hit such markets with immense innovative force and literally take them over.

Annual reports reflect the intensity. Poor earnings are usually cited as due to (1) competitive innovative encroachments, (2) new product failures, or (3) the high costs of developments which are under way but are still not on the market. Future improvements are almost invariably predicated on future new product successes.

The consequences of these strong forces are many. There is excitement and change in the land of new product management. Let's look first at the changes which have come about recently, and then at the changes we see coming in the future.

Strategy

Most successful firms are now operating under precise and restrictive new product strategies. They have picked the markets for which they want new products—Gerber for babies, Pepsi for younger people, Toro for the lawns and sidewalks, Wang for the office.

And they have decided which technologies they will bet on, which departments of the business are most critical, and how innovative they will be. Harris Corporation, for example, has a strategy of reacting rapidly to breakthroughs of others, while Merck is committed to being first if at all possible.

Nevertheless, strategies change, some are more successful than others, and even in the best firms some managers work hard at trying to escape the restrictions. In fact, we actually encourage people to fight for what they believe. To push for it almost beyond reason. We call these people product champions, and they are children of this era. In other firms, there are actually funds available against which scientists may draw when they want to push for something that seems unlikely or goes against strategy. But these are planned exceptions—to planned strategies. Strategies help firms compete in games where they can most clearly expect to be winners—competing today is tough, so it's better to pick the arenas deliberately.

Organization

Innovation has also hit corporate organization. Like with the product champions just mentioned. But there have been other innovations as well, the most valuable of which appears to be the new product team.

We've had teams for many years, but today's teams are different. Formerly they were really just small committees, where people from R&D sat with people from production, marketing, etc., to discuss how things were going. If the firm was small, the group was actually the management committee, and it worked well, but if the firm was large, the committee was about as ineffective as committees have always been.

So today's team is an intense group of people, totally dedicated to the product under development. The production engineer is much more a team member than a production department staffer. Ditto the other team members. And there is a leader, usually the new products manager. The team has just one purpose, and that purpose is fulfilled when the new item is successfully launched. The team may then become the new product's ongoing management, or its members may phase back into the new product stream and start over.

Great publicity has been given to the team which developed the IBM-PC, and how they were relocated from Armonk, New York, to Boca Raton, Florida, to guarantee freedom of action. But 3M has been using such teams for years, and now many firms are adopting the practice.

One of the major advantages of the team is that it tends to overcome the natural frictions of competition which exist between departments of a firm. The Mktg/R&D/Mfg interfaces. Other changes have addressed this critical problem.

Idea Generation

Creating new ideas was a hot topic during the 1940s, 1950s, and 1960s, but of late it has been rather quiet. Today it is alive again. New techniques are appearing weekly, companies are turning to consultants to help them ideate, and the concept-generating function once again occupies the attention of key new product people. This is timely because we still need great ideas and there are many great ideas waiting to be found.

Product Evaluation

Once we have an idea, it begins a long trip down the road of evaluation. First as a concept, then as a prototype, then in usable form, then in final form, then as a marketable product, etc. These evaluations used to be few and rather informal. The firm would survey some market users about the idea (maybe), then have some people (often just employees) try out the product when it was ready, and then perhaps test market the finished product if there were ample time and money.

Today, things could not be more different. Concept evaluation alone now gets more attention than all evaluation used to. Prototype testing and finished-product use testing are complex sciences, requiring data appropriate to the very complex mathematical systems which are used to analyze them.

Equally advanced systems are used to evaluate the communications side of the development—the advertising, the personal selling materials, the packaging, the branding, and so on. Even the financial plan itself is the consequence of extensive testing and analysis, far different than the simplistic methods formerly used to set marketing budgets for new products.

And evaluation today does not end with marketing. More and more we see post-launch tracking plans, designed after the tracking plans used by NASA for guided missiles. Such plans give in-flight feedback which then permits corrections to keep the new product under "control" as it speeds toward its sales and profit goals.

Managerial Styles

These new intensities, technologies, methodologies, strategies, etc., have changed the managerial task of new products people. The field is more exciting than ever and certainly more dynamic. There is opportunity for quick gain (winners get prompt and challenging promotions), failures are usually seen as a cost of progress without direct personal harm, managing a new product is comparable to running a firm, and each day brings a new set of surprises. New product managers get the attention of top management, and the experience is outstanding.

Successful new product people today are using the most advanced principles of human resource management; they have to be very clever at managing people because they rarely have line authority to order anyone to do anything. Yet they must get the job done, bring a new product to market successfully, and in such a way that it stays there.

The Future

We cannot forecast the future of new product management any differently than we forecast everything else—we extrapolate. More companies will adopt the practices that the leaders are proving today. And the leaders will come up with further modifications on their recent advances.

Certainly there will be improvements in organization. The team approach works well, but not in all situations. We still need ways of getting the equivalent of an independent team in a setting which cannot handle several independent groups seeming to run amok.

There will be still more methods of ideation. And here we can expect some discontinuities—methods we now know nothing about. But the biggest change will be the acceptance of ideation as a process, carefully constructed for each situation, utilizing many of the common techniques of creativity as parts of a systematic whole. In other words, it too will be managed.

And we will continue the recent surge in new methodologies for evaluating ideas. Product-use testing needs them, and so does market testing. The traditional test-marketing method has become too expensive and too time-consuming for most firms.

Lastly, marketing will continue to gain stature in new product management, and to lose it. Firms which still let R&D control the process will move this control to marketing. So will firms which have been using committees headed by coordinators. Marketing assures orientation to the attitudes, practices, and needs of the intended consumer.

But marketing will also lose, as managements continue to recognize that the focus on new products is necessarily general management. Just as the product manager for established products is really a surrogate or proxy general manager (without the power of an office), so too is the new product manager. So in consumer packaged firms the responsibility will remain in the product management departments, but in other firms it will move to general staff. Corporate directors of new products will be the common mode.

New products which result from all this will be unique, life-saving, foolish, fascinating, trivial, profitable, unprofitable, fun, frustrating, useful. . . .

CHAPTER
SIX

All mankind is divided into three classes: those that are immovable, those that are movable, and those that move.
——Arab proverb

What is food to one man is bitter poison to others.
——Lucretius (90–55 B.C.)

MARKET SEGMENTATION AND POSITIONING

Introduction

The long-run success of any organization depends on its ability to understand the needs of its customers and to deliver a product that not only meets those needs but does so better than the competition. We might think of the firm's task in this regard as a search for the optimal intersection of three phenomena: the design of superior product characteristics, maximization of consumer satisfaction, and attainment of a competitive advantage. The Venn diagram in Figure 6-1 shows the desired outcome and six less satisfactory alternatives. Only in sector 7 are all three goals realized. The other sectors, 1 through 6, result in either inferior product characteristics, consumer dissatisfaction, and/or competitive disadvantages.

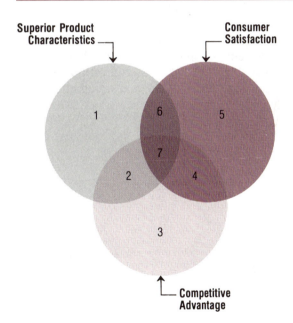

Figure 6-1. Marketing success as an intersection of three desired outcomes

How can a firm go about achieving the optimal outcome illustrated in Figure 6-1? The answer to this is difficult to ascertain. A firm must plan and coordinate many complex activities associated with the marketing mix and do so in an atmosphere of environmental uncertainty. Yet the process must begin somewhere. Generally, most firms approach the problem in the early stages by performing three interrelated activities: (1) product decision making, (2) market segmentation and positioning, and (3) demand estimation and forecasting. These activities are shown connected with double-headed arrows in Figure 6-2 to stress that each is intimately intertwined with the others. We have already discussed product decisions in the previous two chapters where the foundation was laid for viewing consumer, macro, and managerial aspects of products. The present chapter will begin where the previous one ended. We will delve still deeper into product design and its relationship to consumer needs and competitive reactions. Then, in Chapter 7, the ideas and principles will be extended further as input and constraints to the demand estimation and forecasting phases of the marketing effort.

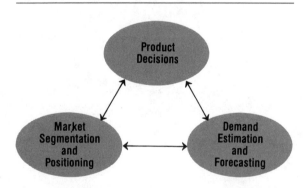

Figure 6-2. Three interrelated decisions early in the strategic planning process

Before we begin our discussion of market segmentation and positioning, we should emphasize two points to place things in perspective. First, it should be stressed that our sequential presentation of the topics of product design, market segmentation, and demand estimation and forecasting is done for pedagogical convenience only. In reality, the activities are generally carried out simultaneously with considerable mutual adjustments made among them along the way. Second, the decisions illustrated in Figure 6-2 represent only one part of the marketing mix. In later chapters, we will develop the ideas and principles concerned with promotion (i.e., mass and direct face-to-face communication), distribution, and pricing. These topics obviously interact with product-related decisions but must be reserved until later. This should be kept in mind as one reads the following.

Basic Definitions

Market segmentation is the classification of consumers, products, or markets into groups on the basis of their characteristics. Although we will have more to say about the methods and varieties of segmentation shortly, let us illustrate the concept with an example. Imagine that we were asked to segment consumers, products, and markets for beer. Table 6-1 presents one way to do this. Notice first that consumers are divided into three groups: nondrinkers, drinkers who switch brands, and drinkers who are loyal to any one brand. Many other ways are available to classify consumers such as by income, consumption volume (e.g., light, moderate, or heavy drinkers), or personality type. Product characteristics or forms constitute a second broad way to perform segmentation. As shown in Table 6-1, we might think of beer in four forms: low-priced, premium, super-premium, and light beers. Another example of segmentation by product types might be pilsner, ale, bock, and dark beers. Finally, we might segment the beer market itself into Western, Southern, Midwestern, and Eastern regions. Consumer needs and the consumption of beer have been found to vary by geographical market. Or at a higher level of generality, one might divide the market for alcoholic consumption into beer, wine, and liquor. Many other forms of segmentation are possible.

TABLE 6-1

Example Segmentations for Consumers, Products, and Markets: The Case of Beer

Object of Segmentation	Example
Consumers	nondrinkers
	switchers
	brand loyals
Products	low priced
	premium
	super premium
	light beers
Markets	Western
	Southern
	Midwestern
	Eastern

Why do firms bother to segment consumers, products, and markets? At least two reasons can be identified. First, and most obviously, firms use segmentation to organize their tasks and to cope with the demands of the marketplace. It is just not physically possible to meet everyone's needs and reach out to the entire marketplace. A balance must be reached between what a firm might like to achieve under ideal conditions and what it is able to deliver under real-world constraints.

Second, firms employ market segmentation as a strategic tool. Indeed, we might picture the *strategic design process* as a three-step process (see Figure 6-3). In the first stage, the manager discovers what the market segments are and examines their potential according to criteria such as size, buyer preferences, intentions, or choice. This involves market segmentation plus examination of each segment according to the chosen criteria. To take an example, let us imagine that a brewery finds its sales to be lagging. Assuming that it segments potential consumers as shown in Table 6-1—as nondrinkers, switchers, and brand loyals—it might consider three options. One way to increase sales is to get nondrinkers to try its brand. Normally this is difficult to do, for most nondrinkers have strong reasons for not drinking beer. However, as people reach drinking age, a percentage of them will try beer and enter the drinker segment. Thus, it behooves the producer to think of nondrinkers as part of its market when designing programs. Another way for the producer to increase sales is to win a larger share of people who have no particular favorite brand and who switch from one brand to another. This might be done with specials, coupons, or other incentives. The last strategy for a producer to increase sales is to more aggressively pursue drinkers who are loyal to one brand. This means inducing people loyal to other brands to try the producer's brand and getting those loyal to the producer's brand to purchase in greater quantities. The latter might be achieved by persuading people to drink beer on more occasions (e.g., holidays), to serve beer more often to friends and guests, and perhaps to drink more at each sitting. Michelob has recently pursued a campaign to win women drinkers, and other sellers have pushed beer drinking in traditional "cocktail" settings. (There are, of course, ethical and moral concerns surrounding alcoholism, drunk driving, and other issues, that must be taken into account in any responsible marketing program. An increased consumption program might be more justifiable for a marketer of exercise equipment or health foods.) In any event, the first step in the strategic design process is completed with an assessment of each segment according to the number of potential customers, their preferences for one's products versus another's, their intentions to try one's product, their past behavior, etc.

Step 1: Market Segmentation
Subdivide consumers, products, and/or markets into meaningful groups.
Examine each segment with respect to criteria of interest (e.g., size, preferences, intentions, choice).

↓

Step 2: Target Marketing and Product Positioning
Evaluate and rank each segment according to normative criteria addressing organization goals, consumer needs, environmental constraints, and competitive forces.
Select a target segment or segments and adjust the product to fit that segment or segments.

↓

Step 3: Design of Remainder of the Marketing Mix
Communication, distribution, and pricing.

Figure 6-3. Three early steps in the strategic marketing program design process

The purpose of *step 1, market segmentation,* is fact finding. No judgments are imposed beforehand as to what constitutes a "good" segment. Rather, it is in *step 2, target marketing and product positioning,* that normative criteria come to the fore (see Figure 6-3). The initial analysis in step 2 is to evaluate each segment found in step 1 and arrive at ratings or a ranking according to agreed upon standards. For instance, a firm might decide to pursue the segments with the greatest number of potential buyers, the one with the highest purchasing power, or the one with the highest percentage of people indicating an intention to try the brand. As reasonable as this strategy might seem, it is important to note that such a plan might not always be the best one. Under some conditions, the largest segment might be the most competitive, be the least profitable, or offer poor growth potential. Hence, it would not be wise to select this segment for a target without considering other factors. The tendency to select the largest segment irrespective of taking into account competitive and other market factors has been termed the "majority fallacy" by marketers.[1] We will describe ways that organization goals, consumer needs, environmental constraints, and competitive forces can be taken into account later in the chapter. For now, we should emphasize that firms often find it more advantageous to enter smaller market niches. The next activity that is taken in step 2 is the selection of one or more segments and the adjustment of the product to fit these segments. This activity is known as product or brand positioning.

The final step in the design of the strategic marketing program, *step 3,* involves fashioning the remainder of the *marketing mix.* These other components must be integrated with product decisions and other business activities of the firm in order to achieve a reasonable degree of success. We will develop the concepts and issues involved in these activities in the remaining chapters of the text.

Market Segmentation in Practice

Taking a descriptive viewpoint, we can categorize market segmentation strategies practiced by firms on the basis of whether or not they differentiate their products and to what extent they purposefully subdivide their market(s). Table 6-2 presents the six possible strategies based upon these distinctions. Case I describes the situation where a firm neither differentiates its product nor segments the market. Rather, it simply attempts to sell the same product to as many consumers as possible. Either the firm assumes a production focus and ignores consumer differences or else it explicitly designs a product that it hopes will appeal to broad or even universal needs. The market is seen as an undifferentiated or homogeneous aggregate. The Case I strategy is sometimes practiced by the sellers of basic commodities, such as coal or oil, and is often the approach taken by fledgling firms in other industries. However, as markets become saturated, competition increases, or consumer needs change, the Case I strategy becomes less viable.

TABLE 6-2
Six Market Segmentation Strategies

	MARKET SEGMENTATION		
PRODUCT DIFFERENTIATION	No Segments	One Segment	Many
No	Case I	Case II	Case III
Yes	Case IV	Case V	Case VI

In the Case II strategy, the firm markets an undifferentiated product in a single market. Presumably, it survives on the basis of logistical advantages arising from geographical proximity to its customers or a monopoly of sorts on raw materials or workmanship. For example, many very small "job shops" exist in industrial areas and manufacture single products as component parts or as tools for use by a larger firm.

The Case III strategy, in contrast, consists of marketing an undifferentiated product to many segments. Unlike Case I, where no particular segment is pursued, the Case III strategy depends on the ability of the marketer to select fruitful customer groups from among the many in the mass market. This requires a relatively more outward market focus in that measurement and analysis of customers must be performed and special efforts to reach them undertaken. In Germany, for example, many very small breweries market a single brand of beer to a few customers (select stores, factories, beer gardens). A similar situation exists in the United States for some small producers of potato chips.

Cases I–III occur frequently in lesser developed countries, where little or no product differentiation is practiced. They are less common in modern societies. More frequent are instances of product differentiation. In Case IV, the firm differentiates its offering but sees its market as a homogeneous aggregate. This is perhaps most commonly practiced by small retailers such as drugstores, mom-and-pop grocery stores, and carry-out restaurants. A quite different strategy can be found in Case V. Here a firm tailors its offering to the needs of a special client. For example, large companies in Sweden have pioneered "systems selling," where they design, manufacture, and deliver entire factories. In the past, the companies found it increasingly difficult to compete effectively in selling machinery and other capital goods because other countries with lower labor costs could underprice them. By capitalizing on their scientific and technological advantages, they shifted competition to a higher plane and are presently quite successful. Case V is of course practiced by small firms, too, such as when artisans or specialists design a product or service on demand.

By far the most common and important market segmentation strategy in modern societies occurs in Case VI, where product differentiation is practiced in multiple market segments. Case VI is an inevitable outgrowth of increasing complexity in human needs and competition among firms coupled with the advantages of economies of scale and broad-based business operations. Yet, we should stress that the Case VI strategy is applied frequently to advantage by small- and medium-size firms and is definitely not the sole purview of the largest enterprises. The key to its success lies in the relative advantages firms have, based on their ability to design products that satisfy diverse needs and generate enough sales to make a profit in the face of competition. Often this requires a mass market orientation, but if a firm can find a relatively unfulfilled need in the market, it can operate profitably on a smaller scale.

The rest of the chapter presents three broad methods for conducting market segmentation, target marketing, and positioning: i.e., logical, empirical, and hybrid procedures. Although the ideas have been developed most for Case VI situations, it should be stressed that some of the principles apply to the other cases as well.

Logic-Based Market Segmentation

Classification-of-Goods Theory[2]

The simplest and earliest method of segmentation is known as the *classification-of-goods theory*. Products are subdivided on the basis of their physical characteristics and/or consumer behavior. We have already discussed various classifications in Chapter 4. A widely accepted summary categorization appears in Figure 6-4. The first distinction among all goods occurs between industrial and consumer goods and is based, presumably, on the end-user. Although we would like our categories to be mutually exclusive in any classification, we should acknowledge that the industrial/consumer good dichotomy is not a clean one: some goods are consumed by both users at least some of the time (e.g., paper, pencils, hand soap). Next, industrial and consumer goods may be further subdivided. The most common industrial categorization is the Standard Industrial Classification (SIC) system performed by the Office of Statistical Standards of the United States Department of Commerce. This results in a classification of 450 manufacturing industries based on the type of products produced or operations performed. For each of the industries in each of a number of geographical territories, data are available on annual sales, number of firms, number of employees, value added, and other information.

The other method of industrial goods classification shown in Figure 6-4 is input/output analysis and is drawn from economic theory. Goods are classified on the basis of their similarity in the input/output matrix. This method is used less frequently than the SIC method and will be discussed sparingly in this text.

Consumer goods are classified in four categories in Figure 6-4: convenience, shopping, specialty, and preference goods. The first three categories have been developed by Holton[3] and Bucklin[4] and were described in Chapter 4. The addition of the preference good category is due to Holbrook and Howard.[5] A preference good is one that is low in clarity with respect to product characteristics and at the same time scores low in terms of the magnitude (e.g., importance) of purchase. In addition, the consumer experiences low ego involvement, is perhaps low in product-specific self-confidence, and devotes some mental effort prior to shopping in information search but little physical effort in actual shopping behavior. A good example of a preference good might be the restaurant a family "spontaneously" chooses while engaged in daily activities at home. The consequences of the choice are relatively low as is the ego involvement. Moreover, about the only information search performed is typically a check to see family member preferences and if the restaurant is open or not.

In contrast, the decision to patronize a new restaurant or to celebrate an important occasion at a restaurant is more ego involving with greater implications. Hence, a choice of restaurant here would be either a shopping or specialty good, depending on the extent to which restaurant attributes and extent of information processing played a role.

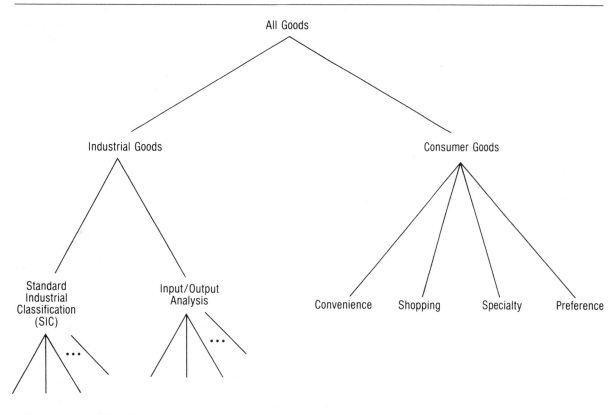

Figure 6-4. Classification-of-goods theory

Notice that the product class of "restaurant" could be put into more than one category. Indeed, a trip to a fast-food restaurant is often a convenience good. We thus see that the classification of any physical product depends crucially on its psychological and social meaning for a consumer and that generalities are difficult to make with respect to any product. Further, consumer needs and perceptions are so volatile that any classification system will be imprecise at best.

The ambiguity of various classification-of-goods schemes has limited their use as a guide for marketing strategy. About the only research to draw firm generalizations have been the PIMS studies.[6] But even here, the findings have been limited to differences at gross levels of generality such as between consumer and industrial firms. As a consequence, we will not discuss the classification-of-goods approach further but rather will focus on more fruitful procedures actually used in practice.

Hierarchical Market Definitions

A new approach that is gaining many adherents is the *hierarchical market definition* method. In this approach, product forms and brands are organized by similarity and ordered on the basis of a criterion or criteria. Figure 6-5 illustrates alternative hierarchies for the beer market. In Figure 6-5A, the ordering criterion is by product form with brands then displayed for each product form. We have chosen only one possible product form categorization (i.e., low-priced, premium, super-premium, light, and low-alcohol beers), and only a few leading brands are shown for simplicity. Notice that there are several competing brands under each product form and that some manufacturers have an entry under each form, whereas others market only a few forms. Figure 6-5B shows a hierarchy ordered first by producer and then product forms are listed under each producer. Notice that Schlitz (now owned by Stroh's), Budweiser, and Stroh's each have an entry under each product form (except, at present, low-alcohol) but Miller only sells premium, super-premium, and light beers. Some domestic producers now even market dark beers as another product form not shown in Figure 6-5.

Although not shown in Figure 6-5, there are at least two other ways to organize a market in a hierarchy. One is first by brands and then by product forms. For instance, some deodorant manufacturers use a single brand name for multiple product forms (e.g., for roll-on, stick, cream, and aerosol forms). Another way to organize a hierarchy is through a combination of product forms and brands. That is, the initial organizing criterion might consist of either or both product forms and brands, and then further breakdowns by product subforms or other criteria could be used. Alternatively, just about any meaningful criterion can be used at each level of a hierarchy. For instance, it might be useful in some situations to use geographical distinctions ordered by increasing degrees of specificity or product attributes in conjunction with brands and product forms. The opportunities for the hierarchical segmentation of markets are nearly unlimited.

Now that we have defined a hierarchical definition of a market, we can address the issues of what uses it provides for marketers and what advantages it offers over the older classification-of-goods approaches. The most obvious benefit of a hierarchical definition of the market is that it allows the marketer the chance to better manipulate product characteristics with competitive considerations. At a glance, we can see what product forms, manufacturers, and brands vie in a particular market. The classification-of-goods approaches tend to be tied too closely to product characteristics, to underrepresent consumer behavior, and to neglect competitive conditions. Thus, a market hierarchy yields favorable descriptive attributes.

More important, the hierarchical approach provides managerial guidelines. To see this, imagine that the hierarchy shown in Figure 6-5A closely resembles how people actually purchase beer. Specifically, this description of the market assumes that consumers first decide on what type of beer they desire when they initiate the purchase process. Only after they determine which form of beer they want do they begin to examine and evaluate the opportunities available under that form. The process ends with a choice of a particular brand. Given that Figure 6-5A represents the consumer decision process, management can learn a number of things. First, to take the perspective of Miller, the market definition suggests that it is missing an opportunity to sell to one segment: low-priced buyers. No matter how well Miller does in the premium, super-premium, and light segments, it will have lost sales because there are consumers with needs that differ from what Miller provides. Of course, the decision to enter the low-priced segment will depend on (1) its ability to produce and market appropriate products; (2) the size, purchasing power, needs, etc., of the market for this type of beer; (3) the receptivity of retailers (e.g., some stores, bars, and restaurants might have exclusive contracts with competitors or simply have no room to stock another beer); and (4) the strength of the competitors' brands.

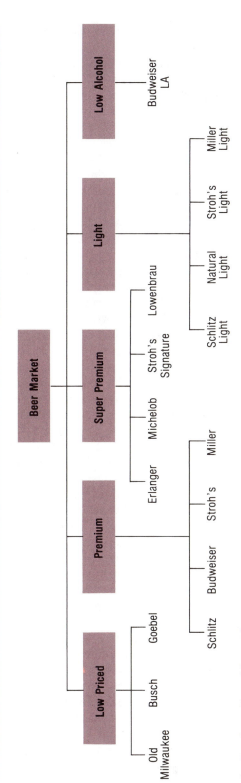

A. Product form hierarchy

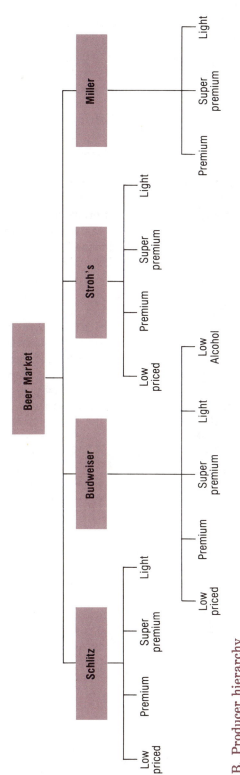

B. Producer hierarchy

Figure 6-5. Hierarchical market definitions for a portion of the beer market

A second managerial implication revealed by the hierarchy shown in Figure 6-5A is the potential opportunity afforded by the introduction of a new product form. Given the hierarchy, a manager should ask whether there are nondrinkers of beer who fail to drink because the existing forms are undesirable and also whether current drinkers would prefer a form other than that available. Perhaps there is room in the market for a heavy beer to satisfy the drinker who seeks a full-bodied beer and is not concerned about calories, or for a nonalcoholic but otherwise "true" beer for those who enjoy the taste of beer but who do not want the alcoholic side-effects.

On the other hand, if consumers see the beer market as shown in Figure 6-5B, then new managerial implications arise. Consumers first select a producer or brand and then decide on the exact form of beer they desire. In this situation, we discover that the firm's decisions are quite different than those shown in Figure 6-5A. Under these circumstances, introduction of a low-priced beer by Miller must be regarded with new caution in that each product form of a producer competes with another form from that same producer. This is known as cannibalization. Miller must weigh the anticipated gain in sales and profits through a new introduction against the probable loss in sales for its existing brands. General Foods faced a similar dilemma when it first considered introducing Maxim, its freeze-dried coffee, a few years ago. Although it ultimately decided that cannibalization of sales from its regular and instant coffees would be small, it is not clear that this was true and that Maxim could achieve a strong independent position over the years. Indeed, Maxim's share of the instant market has dwindled from a high of nearly 12 percent to 2 or 3 percent. Similarly, Diet Coke's success in the mid-1980s came at the expense of Coca-Cola.

Up to this point, we have defined hierarchies that use intuition and logic as criteria. They are based largely on established conventions suggested by the characteristics of products, markets, and/or manufacturers. The advantages of such approaches are that they are relatively easy to execute and offer a certain degree of face validity. The major disadvantages of the approaches lie in the limitations of managerial judgments and the omission of empirical criteria based on how the real world actually works. We intuitively know that some consumers select beers first by product form and then by brand, but that others choose the brand first and then the product form. But what are the actual percentages of consumers in each category? Only empirical measurements can tell us this. Further, logic-based hierarchies do not tell us whether some consumers are indifferent to one or more stages in a hierarchy. Some purchasers might choose by product form but not favor any particular brand. Other buyers might be concerned only with the brand and not consider product forms. People might focus on other attributes such as body, calories, or foaminess. In addition, some consumers will be brand loyal, others producer loyal, and still others product form loyal. And, as indicated earlier, some people will switch brands continually. All of these possibilities suggest the need to go out into the real world and record *how* people actually buy beer.

These issues have led to the development of hierarchical market segmentation with the injection of a certain amount of empirical information. The best known empirical approach, the *Hendry Model* (also sometimes called "market partitioning"), was developed by practitioners.[7] The Hendry Model attempts to develop a hierarchy such as shown in Figure 6-5 by examining actual data on how many people switch from one brand to another in a unit of time. Because of the assumptions of the model and the estimation procedures used, the approach works best with frequently purchased consumer goods (e.g., toothpaste, facial tissue, snack foods). The most common means of data collection is through either panels and diaries, where consumer purchase behaviors are recorded over time, or surveys, where consumers are asked to indicate the previous brand of a product class purchased, the brand bought prior to that, and so on. These responses are totaled, and partitions in a hierarchy are defined on the basis of the rate of switching. Low switching between entities (e.g., product forms, brands, or producers) defines separate branches in a hierarchy, whereas high switching between entities defines within branch subcategories.

The Hendry and other market-partitioning methods go further than classification-of-goods and logic-based hierarchical approaches in that they combine managerial judgment with actual measurements of consumer behavior. Moreover, they tend to use rigorous principles of mathematical modeling and to employ powerful statistical techniques such as cluster analysis. However, as with any methodology, some things are given up, and certain shortcomings should be noted. Although the procedures are based on real behavior, they do not go very far in terms of content. That is, all that is measured is whether one switches or not. Other behaviors related to consumption are not part of the model. In this respect, we should note that the work of Bettman and others (see Chapter 2) provides a richer recording of the entire process consumers go through.[8] If the market-partitioning models could incorporate more of the sequence of behaviors that consumers take and choice criteria applied in decision making, the resulting hierarchies would have more validity. Another limitation of the partitioning approaches is that although some limited modeling of *how* consumers behave is taken into account, they do not explain *why* consumers switch brands or buy what they buy. In other words, the determinants of choice—psychological antecedents (e.g., motivation, emotions, cognitive processes), social forces (e.g., norms, small-group pressure), environment constraints (e.g., income, economic conditions), or managerial stimuli (e.g., price, promotion, specific product attributes)—are omitted. We turn now to another general segmentation approach that attempts to address the process and causes of consumer choice in somewhat greater depth.

Empirically Based Market Segmentation

Demand Elasticity and Market Response Approaches

Economists and management scientists have developed somewhat similar methods for market segmentation, the *demand elasticity* and *market response* methods.

The demand elasticity segmentation method is based on the presumed effects of product differentiation on consumers' willingness to purchase the product. Neoclassical economic theory assumes that consumers buy in terms of a single demand function. Demand elasticity, on the other hand, assumes that consumers often have multiple demand functions, depending on the basis for differentiation. A product might be differentiated through a combination of distinctions in price, product attributes, distribution, and so on. The most common situation is depicted in Figure 6-6A. Two demand functions are shown for two segments, x and y, respectively. The segments might be individual consumers or homogeneous groups of consumers. Each segment exhibits a different price elasticity of demand, which defines the segments. This difference might occur for the same product or for different products. To carry the role of elasticity one step further, we can also define market segments through the cross-price elasticities of demand between products. That is, to the extent that a price change in one product affects the demand for another product, the products may be considered substitutes. By examining the cross-elasticities between different products and selecting suitable cutoffs, it is possible, in theory, to identify different markets.

This has proven to be difficult in practice, however, due to data limitations. Nevertheless, recent developments in the retail trade, with scanners and the Universal Product Code (UPC), should help to overcome these problems.

In the market response method, consumers are segmented on the basis of the actions they take as a function of marketing mix stimuli under the manager's control.[9] As illustrated in Figure 6-6B, we can think of different groups or segments of consumers as defined by their different responses to a managerial control variable. For example, sales might reach a level r_1 for segment A when advertising is at level mcv_1 but attain only level r_2 for segment B. In this way, it is possible to map the responses of different groups of consumers to combinations of marketing mix stimuli under the manager's control. One advantage the market response method has over most other methodologies is that it incorporates dynamic effects in that the changes of consumer reactions to varying stimuli are represented. Furthermore, by selection of responses of strategic interest to management (e.g., sales, market share, return on investment), it is possible to identify the most fruitful segments and better implement the marketing effort.[10] The primary shortcoming of the market response method is that it is difficult to obtain empirical data to support the response functions, and considerable measurement problems often arise. As a consequence, the procedures have not as yet received much study or use in practice.

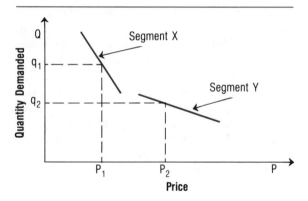

A. Price elasticity of demand in segmented markets

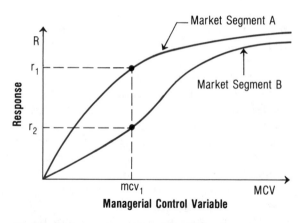

B. Market response as a function of managerial controllable variables

Figure 6-6. Demand elasticity and market response methods of segmentation

Traditional Empirically Based Methods for Consumer Segmentation[11]

The most widely used procedures for market segmentation have been developed by marketers. Before we outline the variables employed in traditional segmentation methods, however, let us begin by discussing the objectives of the approach and how it is used in practice.

We might think of the objective of traditional market segmentation as a two-pronged goal. First, the objective is to predict a criterion (i.e., a dependent variable) on the basis of one or more segmentation variables (i.e., independent variables). For example, we might want to predict intentions to buy a product as a function of education. Are people who intend to purchase more or less educated? If we discover a relationship between education and intentions, then this could have managerial implications.

This brings us to the second goal of traditional market segmentation. Given that we have discovered an independent variable that relates to a desired dependent variable, what consequences could this have for decision making? For instance, if we found that intentions were highly related to education with those intending to buy possessing the lowest educational level, then this allows us to identify and predict potential users, and it also might suggest where, when, and how to reach these prospects. Knowledge of educational levels of users might provide guidance in the design of products, the design of advertising messages, placement of advertising, use of distribution methods, and so on. The absence of an intention by those high in education might lead to research to discover why. Perhaps highly educated people are not aware of the product or where to obtain it. In sum, traditional market segmentation has two purposes: the first is to discover correlates, predictors, or causes of outcomes desired by the firm (e.g., intentions to buy, purchase frequency, or brand loyalty); a second is to draw managerial implications so as to better design one's marketing program. Of course, implicit in the pursuit of both goals is the understanding that any independent variable related to a desired outcome criterion has a sound theoretical rationale behind it. In general, those variables connected to criteria through causal or functional mechanisms will provide the best results. Variables that are merely correlated or fortuitously associated are less desirable.

Figure 6-7 provides a pictorial representation of the goals of traditional market segmentation applied to the choice of a new bicycle. The first goal of segmentation is to focus on a single product attribute in the market. The filled-in circles in Figure 6-7A represent the position of a person with respect to his or her perceived reliability and overall attitude. There are 10 people plotted in the figure. For example, person 5 perceives the brand to have a low reliability and has a highly unfavorable attitude. Person 7 perceives a high reliability and has a highly favorable attitude. The slope of the straight line fitted through the filled-in circles shows the degree of relationship between reliability and attitude. Apparently, for the 10 people surveyed, perceived reliability in Brand A is positively related to their attitude toward the brand. The greater their perception of strong reliability, the more favorable their attitude. In fact, the slope is about .8. For an increase in perceived reliability of .8 of a unit, attitude increased 1.0 unit.

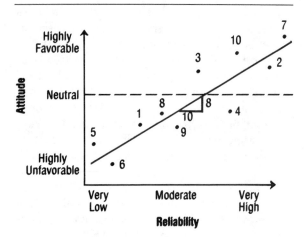

A. Simple segmentation of potential bicycle purchasers based on perceived reliability and its ability to predict attitude

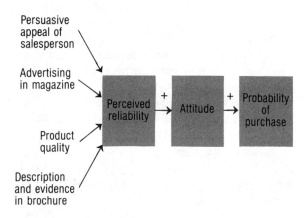

B. Relation of outcome of segmentation to managerial criteria

Figure 6-7. An example of market segmentation based on a product attribute and its ability to predict attitude

Given the positive relationship between perceived reliability and attitude, one can explore the second purpose of traditional market segmentation: derivation of managerial implications. Figure 6-7B presents a pictorial representation of one possible set of implications. Notice first that attitude is related to probability of purchase. Actually, this is something we would want to test on real consumers. After all, even though perceived reliability might lead to a favorable attitude, this would not be very promising if attitude, in turn, did not stimulate purchase. Thus, one implication of our finding illustrated in Figure 6-7A is that further research is needed to discover the impact of attitude on behavior, if any. Second, as shown at the left of Figure 6-7B, we must devise ways to influence perceived reliability, given this is an indirect determinant of purchase probability.[12] Four things to consider are the use of persuasive appeals by a salesperson, arguments to include in advertisements, particular features to design into the bicycle, and descriptive content in a brochure.

The example shown in Figure 6-7 is only one particular and oversimplified instance of how a traditional market segmentation might be performed. Let us extend the example slightly to better show the use of market segmentation. In Figure 6-8, we see again that perceived reliability is used to predict attitude. However, one additional predictor is used: place of residence. For residences of central cities, perceived reliability does not significantly predict attitude at all. Perhaps people in cities are concerned with product attributes other than reliability. On the other hand, people in rural and urban areas show a positive relation between perceived reliability and attitude. A similar finding results for residents of college towns. Indeed, there is less variability around the line that is fit to the college town sample than the urban and rural sample. This might reflect a greater need for reliability, greater consumer confidence in judgments, or other factors. In any case, the example shows that more than one segmentation variable is often necessary and that some variables and/or criteria may not lead to a meaningful segmentation of the market.

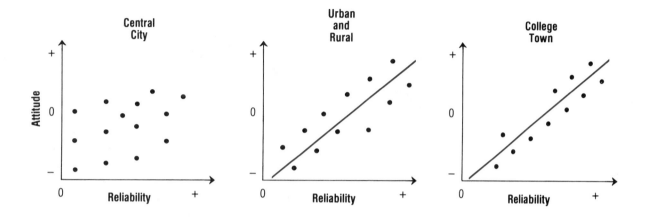

Figure 6-8. Market segmentation with two independent variables (reliability and place of residence) and one criterion (attitude)

To extend the example still further, Figure 6-9 illustrates a somewhat different way to perform a segmentation. In Figure 6-9A, the responses of 40 consumers are plotted for two desired attributes of bicycles: performance and reliability. Next, based on how close together different consumer's desired attributes are, three groups are formed: A, B, and C. The grouping can be accomplished formally with statistical procedures such as cluster analysis. Group A desires high performance but is not too concerned with reliability. Perhaps people in Group A are professional racers interested primarily in very lightweight bicycles. Group C, on the other hand, is very much concerned with reliability but desires little in performance capabilities. This might encompass consumers interested in a sturdy, three-speed bike to be used in leisure cycling over varied terrain. Group B prefers a moderate amount of performance and reliability and might represent those using a bicycle as a regular mode of transportation on paved streets. Ten people, indicated with plus signs in Figure 6-9A, cannot be classified in Groups A, B, or C. Notice that the grouping of consumers into segments in Figure 6-9A is based solely on desired product attributes, and no dependent variable criterion is employed such as is exhibited in Figures 6-7 or 6-8. We might term the former *similarity segmentation* and the latter *criterion segmentation*.

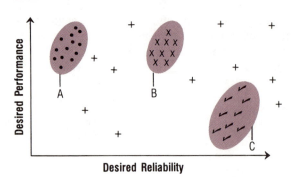

A. Segmentation on the basis of two product attributes

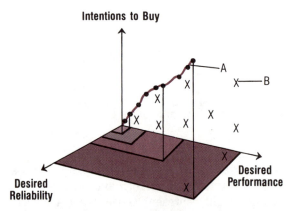

B. Relation of desired attributes to intentions to purchase for groups A and B

Key
• = group A
X = group B

Figure 6-9. A more complicated, two-step market segmentation

The next step is to investigate whether the segments formed in Figure 6-9A relate meaningfully to a criterion or criteria of interest. Figure 6-9B, an attempt to relate desired performance and reliability to intentions, shows one possibility. Only Groups A and B are displayed to keep the diagram simple. Notice that the desires of consumers in

Group A are related to their intentions to purchase. As their desires for performance and reliability increase, so do their intentions. However, no discernible relation exists for Group B (represented as x's). Thus for Group A, management has some basis for incorporating performance and reliability into product design, advertising, and promotion. The task is to determine the optimal level of product attributes and how to reach and communicate to these particular consumers. We will have more to say about these problems later in the chapter and in subsequent chapters.

For Group B, management should address a number of issues. One question to ask is whether people in Group B prefer different attributes. Perhaps price or aesthetic appeal are more important for them than performance or reliability. Alternatively, one or more other variables might be used to further segment consumers in Group B. For example, suppose we suspect that the choices of people who seek moderate amounts of performance and reliability depend on whether they have owned a bicycle before or not. Figure 6-10 shows a plot of consumers in Group B, further

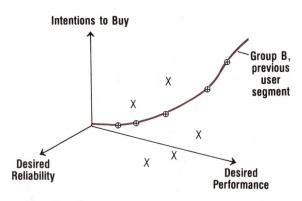

Key
⊕ = previous user
X = never used

Figure 6-10. An extension of the market segmentation example of Figure 6-9

TABLE 6-3

Classical Bases for Market Segmentation *(continued on page 232)*

Criterion	Example	Criterion	Example	Criterion	Example
DEMOGRAPHIC		Income	Less than $5,000	Occupation	Unemployed
Population size	Less than 20,000		$ 5,000– 9,999		Household and service workers
	20,000– 99,999		$10,000–14,999		Unskilled workers
	100,000– 249,999		$15,000–19,999		Semiskilled workers
	250,000– 499,999		$20,000–24,999		Skilled laborers
	500,000– 749,999		$25,000–29,999		Clerical and sales
	750,000– 999,999		$30,000–34,999		Managers and proprietors
	1,000,000–2,499,999		$35,000 and over		Professionals
	2,500,000–3,999,999				
	4,000,000+	Wife's labor force behavior	Unemployed	Religion	None
Age	Less than 6		Part-time		Catholic
	6–10		Full-time		Moslem
	11–15		(noncareer-oriented)		Protestant
	16–20		Full-time		Jewish
	21–25		(career-oriented)		Other
	26–34				
	35–44	National origin	China	*GEOGRAPHIC*	
	45–54		France	Residence	Rural
	55–64		Germany		Urban
	65 and older		Great Britain		(Central city)
Sex	Male		Greece	Region	New England
	Female		India		Mid-Atlantic
Number of children	0, 1, 2, 3, 4, 5,		Italy		Southeast
	6 or more		Japan		East Central
Marital status	Never married; Married;		Latin America		West Central
	Separated; Divorced;		Poland		Southwest
	Widowed		Sweden		West
			etc.		Pacific

segmented by prior usage: never used and previous uses. We have circled those respondents who were previous users of bicycles. Notice now that a relationship exists between desired product attributes and intentions for this subsegment of Group B. This illustration shows that market segmentation is a complex process and often involves many steps.

A final point to note concerns the criteria we have used. All have been continuous (i.e., interval or ratio scaled) variables. That is, attitude, intentions, and probability of purchase can be measured on graduated scales. However, it should be noted that criteria can also be represented as nominal (e.g., buy or do not buy) or ordinal (e.g., prefer A to B and B to C) variables. We have used continuous variables in our examples be-

cause they occur frequently, have desirable statistical implications, and are easy to comprehend. Nevertheless, nominal and ordinal criteria are frequently used in practice, too, and there are methodologies for their use.

We are now in a position to describe the most commonly used market segmentation variables in greater depth. Table 6-3 lists the most common variables used as a basis of segmentation and includes examples of each. We have already mentioned some of these in the preceding discussion. Similarly, Table 6-4 presents common criteria used in segmentation studies. Let us now describe some of the more important variables.

Demographic Segmentation. Demography is the statistical study of the patterns of characteristics of populations that might define

TABLE 6-3 (Continued)

Criterion	Example	Criterion	Example	Criterion	Example
SOCIAL UNIT		*PSYCHOGRAPHIC*		Usage rate	Light
Family life cycle	Young, single	Life style	Activities		Moderate
	Young, married, no children		Interests		Heavy
	Young, married, children under 6		Opinions toward work	Benefit sought	Performance
	Married, children 6–18		leisure		Economy
	Married, children over 18 and in college		consumption		Prestige
			politics		Esthetic
	Older, married, no dependent children		etc.	Loyalty status	Switcher
	Older, married, retired	Need level	Orientation to psychological		random
	Older, single or widowed		safety/security		variation-seeker
Social class	Upper		family		marketing-stimulus-responder
	Old rich		esteem		Brand loyal
	New rich		self-actualization		Producer loyal
	College-educated professional	Personality	Introvert/extrovert		Store loyal
	Middle		Ego strength		
	Comfortable living standard		Androgeny	Trial/repeat purchase class	Unaware
	Just getting along		Achievement motivation		Aware
	Lower		Self-confidence		intend not to try
	Poor but working				intend to try
	Poor without employment	*BEHAVIORAL BASED*			Try
		User Status	Nonuser, never tried		do not repeat
			Nonuser, tried before		repeat only once
			Current user		repeat intermittently
					repeat often
					Etc.

these populations in greater detail. In Table 6-3, we have listed 12 common breakdowns investigated by demographers and frequently used by marketers. Each breakdown has been found at one time or another to provide valid predictions of a criterion of interest.

Demographic variables are used in segmentation in many ways. One is to better predict attitudes, intentions, or product choice and usage. Either a demographic breakdown itself will be related to a criterion or else another independent variable will relate better to a criterion, depending on the value of a particular demographic variable examined. A second way demographic variables are used are as strategic guidelines. Target markets are selected on the basis of demographic variables, and then marketing mix stimuli are adjusted

accordingly. Let us look at some examples of how demographic variables are used.

Some insurance companies segment their markets by education level. A typical breakdown is by no high school diploma, high school diploma, undergraduate college degree, and graduate degree. Once prospects have been identified and their education level determined, sales agents are assigned to potential clients on the basis of their own education level. The goal is to have a reasonably close match in education between prospect and salesperson. The rationale for this strategy is based on the theory that a match in education will accompany other similarities and that similarity will lead to interpersonal attraction, enhanced rapport, and overall effective communication. This, in turn, should produce more

TABLE 6-4
Common Criteria in Market Segmentation Studies

Psychological	Awareness	Interest	Confidence
	Beliefs	Intention	Recall
	Evaluations	Preference	Recognition
	Affect	Attitude	Satisfaction
Behavioral	Buy/do not buy	Frequency of purchase	
	Amount of purchase	Choices among alternatives	

sales. Some research supports this theory.[13] This example again emphasizes the point that segmentation is not merely a search for associations between demographic (or other) variables and a criterion. Rather, one should also have a theory and supporting research, if possible, to back up any presumed associations.

Another demographic variable frequently used in segmentation research is sex. Examples are legion. A quick glance at hair care products, magazines, and boutiques will show the impact of sex on segmentation. We frequently see separate products, brands, and even stores for men and women. The assumption is that men and women differ on at least some needs and preferences. Some of these might be biological. More often they probably stem from different socialization. In any case, marketers attempt to provide different products to satisfy these different needs and to advertise and distribute their wares accordingly.

We should note, however, that exceptions and opportunities exist in an opposite sense. Some marketers attempt to broaden the appeal of their product to both sexes. We see this in the development of unisex shops. Another example is Michelob's effort to win the female market (see Figure 6-11). Is it wise to attempt to persuade women to drink beer? After all, few women presently drink beer. Only time will tell. There do not appear to be any fundamental stumbling blocks—women in Germany and elsewhere constitute large segments of the beer market. If nothing else,

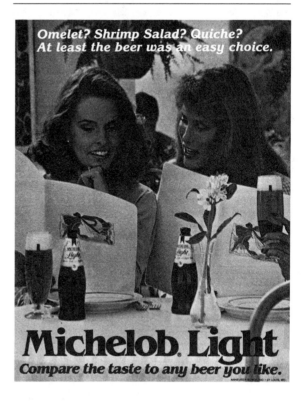

Figure 6-11. An appeal to a nontraditional market

© Copyright 1980, Anheuser-Busch, Inc. Reprinted with permission.

women comprise a large segment of buyers, if not consumers, in the United States.

A classic example of sex segmentation and the power of marketing can be seen in the case of Marlboro cigarettes. The majority of Marlboro smokers are men, but this has not always been so. Indeed, prior to the early 1950s, Marlboro was advertised as a women's cigarette, and few men smoked it. Faced with a very small share of the market and little prospect for growth (due in part to the fact that women tended to smoke much less than men), the manufacturer reversed image and advertised its product with a distinctly masculine theme. In the ensuing years, Marlboro not only did very well but became the leading selling cigarette and remains at the top even today with a market share of about 21 percent. The fact that essentially the same physical product can at one point in time appeal largely to women while at another point in time appeal primarily to men shows the influence of marketing on behavior. It also demonstrates that market segments can be fickle.

Several other demographic variables, including population size, age, number of children, income, occupation, wife's labor force behavior, race, religion, and nationality, can be used in market segmentation. The primary advantage provided by demographic variables is that they are relatively easy to employ because data are readily available. However, although they have sometimes correlated with important criteria, demographic variables have fared poorly, at least as predictors of individual behavior. On the other hand, predictions of groups of households with similar characteristics have achieved greater success.[14]

Geographic Segmentation. Consumer needs and behavior differ by geographic region. Marketers attempt to capitalize on these differences whenever they can. The two most common geographical distinctions are made by region of the country or place of residence (see Table 6-3). The example shown in Figure 6-8 illustrated one way that place of residence can be used as a segmentation variable. Geographical distinctions are crucial, too. For instance, oil companies adjust their products to fit climatic conditions, coffee is blended differently to suit regional variations in taste, and advertisers use different messages and spokespeople to fit geographical idiosyncracies. A good example of the sensitivity of consumer behavior to regions of the country was an earlier ad campaign for Bic pens. Mel Brooks, the well-known comedian, performed a commercial skit for the Bic Banana. The ad did quite well in New York but less well in the Midwest and other regions.

Geographic segmentation takes on special significance when a firm decides to market its products across national boundaries. Many pitfalls face the multinational marketer since consumer needs, institutional relationships (e.g., distribution, retailing), legal regulations, and the mass media differ fundamentally from one country to another. Moreover, hidden cultural factors surrounding language differences, customs, and norms (e.g., those concerning bribery and gift giving) can affect one's marketing program dramatically.

Social Unit Segmentation. A more eclectic way to segment a market is on the basis of the social unit(s) to which one belongs. The two most widely used bases for segmentation in this regard are family life cycle and social class segmentation (see Table 6-3).

The idea behind *family life cycle* behavior as a basis for segmentation is that, as a family ages, (1) its income typically increases and then later decreases; (2) children are born, grow, and eventually leave the family; and (3) many other economic, social, and psychological changes take place in a more or less regular way. These changes, in turn, serve as constraints, facilitators, and motivation for certain types of consumption. For example, newly married couples tend to purchase consumer durables at higher rates than families at other stages in the life cycle. Families with children over 6 years of age but under 18 tend to be more economy minded (and therefore sensitive to price appeals and coupons), consume more "child services" (which occurs at disproportionately higher rates as relative income rises), and generally focus relatively more on in-home activities (e.g., watching cable or video TV programs) relative to families in other stages. Many other differences in consumption needs, media habits, and shopping behaviors exist as one moves from newly married to retired families.[15] To better design products and reach the submarkets implied, marketers must understand the changes that take place as the family ages.

Social class, or social stratification as it is sometimes called, represents another way to subdivide people on the basis of social attributes.[16] The idea here is that social position shapes one's tastes, desires, and behavior. To live in the upper, middle, or lower classes also implies variation in experiences and differential access to resources, opportunities, and information. All of these factors are thought to lead to differences in consumption patterns. Part of the mechanism producing these differences stems from social comparison processes. To different degrees all of us compare ourselves to others and arrive at evaluations of how well off we are and what we "should" or "should not" have, do, and be.

Marketers attempt to predict consumer needs and choices on the basis of one's social class position. A common procedure is to use one's education level, income, and occupation as predictors. Coleman and Lee have developed simple equations to classify people into social classes on the basis of their education, income, and occupation.[17] This can be used to predict consumption. For discussions of the use of social class in market segmentation, see Carman [18] and Jain.[19]

Psychographic Segmentation.[20] As the name implies, psychographic segmentation attempts to divide people into meaningful groups on the basis of psychological variables. The most commonly applied procedure is known as *life-style segmentation*.[21] In this approach, people are asked to express their activities, interests, and opinions (i.e., AIO). Together with demographic background data, a person's scores on an AIO inventory are then used to group people in clusters and/or predict a relevant criterion (e.g., purchase intentions, actual choices). Often, further segmentations on the basis of previous usage or specific product classes are used in conjunction with an AIO analysis. Table 6-5 presents a list of typical variables employed in a life-style segmentation. Notice that the variables cover a wide spectrum of a person's life and can provide a detailed picture of consumer characteristics. Furthermore, this information is particularly valuable in product and advertising design decisions because it closely relates to the needs, motives, preferences, and experiences of potential customers.[22] In this way, the marketer has more specific and useful guidelines to prepare advertising copy and implement other everyday marketing decisions. Overall, life-style segmentation has been applied quite frequently in many areas of marketing with some success.[23]

TABLE 6-5
Some Life-Style Dimensions

Activities	Interests	Opinions	Demographics
Work	Family	Themselves	Age
Hobbies	Home	Social issues	Education
Social events	Job	Politics	Income
Vacations	Community	Business	Occupation
Entertainment	Recreation	Economics	Family size
Club membership	Fashion	Education	Dwelling
Community	Food	Products	Geographic
Shopping	Media	Future	City size
Sports	Achievements	Culture	Stage of life cycle

SOURCE: Joseph T. Plummer, "Applications of Life Style Research to the Creation of Advertising Campaigns," in *Life Style and Psychographics*, ed. William Wells (Chicago: American Marketing Association, 1974), p. 160. Reprinted with the permission of the publisher.

Two other means of psychographic segmentation—by need level and by personality—have proved less fruitful. One way to perform segmentation by need is on the basis of Maslow's hierarchy of needs.[24] Abraham Maslow hypothesized that needs can be arranged in a sequence ranging from the most fundamental or primary needs to higher-order needs (see Table 6-3). At any point in one's life, only one need is important, and a person is not motivated much by needs above that need in the hierarchy. Thus, for example, if a person is most concerned with safety and security, he or she will not strive for esteem or self-actualization until the lower-order needs are satisfied. The implications for market segmentation are that (1) people can be subdivided on the bases of their needs and (2) the product, advertising, etc., should be adjusted to these specific needs. The difficulty lies in identifying people at particular need levels and efficiently reaching them with one's messages. Moreover, people tend to have multiple needs and to jump from one need, or level, to another rapidly. So, in practice, Maslow's hierarchy of needs is a rough guideline at best.

One further difficulty with using needs as a segmentation variable is that it is based on an incomplete theory. Traditionally, our theories assume that needs have an independent existence of their own and that, as a given, they determine behavior. That is, a particular one-way sequence is assumed:

consumer has needs ⟶ marketer identifies needs and designs product to correspond to these needs ⟶ consumer buys product matching his or her needs

In reality, the process is often a two-way flow: needs are "constructed" through an interaction between marketer and consumer. As a person matures within a particular society and as a society evolves over time, needs become differentiated and refined. Our primitive needs for physiological maintenance are transformed into secondary needs and new higher-order needs arise as well. The process involves an individual psychological construction as well as a social construction. This makes it very difficult to predict needs, however, because the construction of needs is little understood. Many new product successes thus have an element of chance involved. Nevertheless, marketers do study needs and attempt to segment the market accordingly. Indeed, the marketer will often be aware of a need long before it is technologically or economically possible to fulfill. It was not until 1982, for example, that Coca-Cola and Pepsi-Cola introduced caffeine-free colas. The need existed long before this, but manufacturers either felt that not enough people would purchase the product to make it profitable or else that negative publicity about colas would be harmful to that huge market if caffeine were made a public issue.

Personality segmentation has generally been disappointing,[25] despite some early apparent successes.[26] It appears that personality is either a minor determinant of behavior, difficult to measure, or incompletely conceptualized.[27] It remains to be shown that personality variables can provide a fruitful mode of segmentation.

Behavior Based Segmentation. One of the most successful procedures has been to divide consumers into groups on the basis of the actual actions, choices, or behavior they exhibit in relation to a product class or a particular brand. As shown in Table 6-3, common bases include user status, usage rate, benefit sought, loyalty status, or trial/repeat purchase class.

Consider segmentation by *user status*. A typical breakdown might be into nonuser, never tried product (or brand) before; nonuser, tried before; and current user. By segmenting the market into these categories, the marketer hopes to gain a number of benefits. First, one can learn why some people never buy one's brand and why others who bought it before no longer buy it. Perhaps the people in the first category are not aware of the product or where to buy it. Those in the second category may have been disappointed in a particular feature of the product or perhaps found competitors' brands more attractive. Second, the marketer can learn more about who buys his or her products and why. This, in turn, might lead one to focus resources on target markets with the greatest potential for a sale. At a minimum, the firm could gain a better understanding of its market and obtain guidelines of what to say in communications and where to say it.

The decision on how to allocate marketing resources to different user-status segments depends on a number of factors. One factor, of course, is a firm's resources. Small firms usually do not have the luxury of pursuing all segments. They must select one or two and generally will choose the current user segment. Larger firms tend to consider all segments, although a ranking of priorities is usually made. A second factor is the competition. To gain a competitive advantage over rivals, firms must leave no stone unturned. By regularly monitoring the characteristics and purchase patterns of consumers in each user-status segment, the firm is provided with information necessary to better design its product and other marketing mix stimuli. Finally, market growth is a factor. Each user-status segment grows or declines at a different rate. Each offers a different potential for sales. A firm must take this into account in its market segmentation and product portfolio decisions.

Usage rate or "volume" segmentation is another popular means of partitioning markets.[28] The method is applied along the following lines. First, consumers of specific product classes (or brands) are divided into nonusers and users. Second, users are then divided into a "light half" (i.e., the first 50 percent of all users by volume) and a "heavy half" (i.e., the second 50 percent of all users by volume). Finally, marketing resources are allocated accordingly. For example, some firms might decide to direct 100 percent of advertising at the heavy half because these people are most likely to buy. Other firms might use another rule such as 80 percent marketing effort for the heavy half, 10 percent to the light half, and 10 percent to nonusers. The appeal of *"heavy half theory"* is that companies generally have the data to make the appropriate analysis. The data can be derived either from firm records (e.g., banks have records on usage rates of its customers), panel studies or surveys, or sources such as charge accounts.

To better see the idea behind usage segmentation, look at Figure 6-12, which represents the findings from a panel study of *Chicago Tribune* subscribers. Notice that 22 percent of households are nonusers of colas, and 78 percent are users. Interestingly, the heavy half of cola consumers, which constitutes 39 percent of all households (i.e., 50 percent of 78 percent), comprises 90 percent of all cola sales. Beer consumption is even more lopsided: 17 percent of the population consumes 88 percent of all sales. We thus see that heavy users may comprise numerically a small fraction of a market but account for much of the consumption. Figure 6-12 illustrates also that some products are consumed by nearly all people (e.g., soaps and detergents), whereas others (e.g., beer, dog food) are consumed by less than 33 percent of the total population. The task for the marketer is to measure demographic, geographic, social unit, and/or psychographic variables in the nonuser, light half, and heavy half segments and investigate meaningful hypotheses in order to better design the marketing mix.

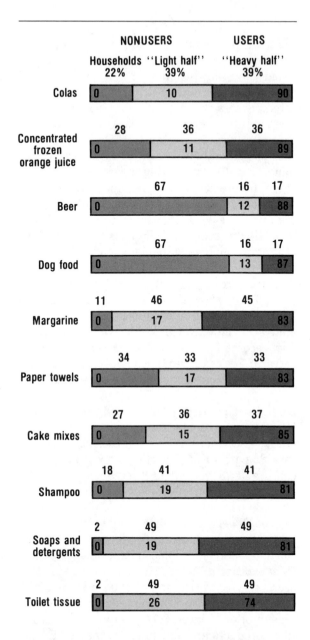

Figure 6-12. A nonuser/user/heavy-half analysis for several product classes

SOURCE: Adapted from Dick Warren Twedt, "How Important to Marketing Strategy Is the 'Heavy'?" *Journal of Marketing* 28 (January 1964): 72. Reprinted with the permission of the American Marketing Association.

Still another method for partitioning the market is known as *benefit segmentation.*[29] In this approach, buyers or potential buyers are divided according to the benefits they seek in a product class or specific brand. The benefits might be with respect to product attributes. For example, some consumers buy mouthwash on the basis of taste and price, whereas others are more concerned with germ-killing properties. Benefits might also consist of consequences resulting from the ownership or use of a product or service. Thus, most people may purchase mouthwashes for their medicinal function, but a few may be after sex appeal or a desire not to offend others.

A classic example of benefit segmentation applied to the toothpaste market is shown in Table 6-6 and is due to Haley. Notice that there are four benefit segments: the sensory segment, the sociables, the worriers, and the independent segment. These labels are subjectively drawn from the measured benefits and other characteristics noted under each column. Let us briefly look at one segment, the sociables. This group primarily uses toothpaste because of its "brightness of teeth" consequences. Teens and young people make up the largest part of the segment. Moreover, members of the segment tend to smoke more, score higher on sociability (a personality trait), and exhibit an active life style. As a group, they use Macleans, Plus White, or Ultra Brite. The remaining segments are motivated more by taste, decay prevention, or economic attributes. The three segments seeking these benefits tend to favor Colgate or Stripe, Crest, or brands on sale, respectively.

TABLE 6-6

An Example of Benefit Segmentation:
The Toothpaste Market

	SEGMENT NAME			
	The Sensory Segment	The Sociables	The Worriers	The Independent Segment
Principal Benefit Sought	Flavor, product appearance	Brightness of teeth	Decay prevention	Price
Demographic Strengths	Children	Teens, young people	Large families	Men
Special Behavior Characteristics	Users of spearmint-flavored toothpaste	Smokers	Heavy users	Heavy users
Brands Disproportionately Favored	Colgate, Stripe	Macleans, Plus White, Ultra Brite	Crest	Brands on sale
Personality Characteristics	High self-involvement	High sociability	High hypochondriasis	High autonomy
Life-style Characteristics	Hedonistic	Active	Conservative	Value oriented

Source: Russel I. Haley, ''Benefit Segmentation: A Decision-oriented Research Tool,'' *Journal of Marketing* 32 (July 1968): 33. Reprinted with the permission of the publisher.

Managers can use benefit segmentation in a number of ways. Most obviously, benefit segmentation provides a relatively detailed and multifaceted picture of consumer needs and other descriptive characteristics. This can be used in product design, advertising, pricing, and distribution decisions to better reach the market. At the same time, the method can be used to compare competing brands in terms of consumer profiles. A firm, then, can gain an indication of where it is strong or weak and make needed changes. It may also suggest new marketing opportunities in terms of a new product, new advertising, and so on.

If we know what brands people purchase and if we monitor their purchases over time, segmentation can also be performed on the basis of *loyalty status*.[30] In general, we might define six categories of loyalty:

• *Random Switcher.* The random switcher purchases brands strictly by chance. No discrimination among brands is made. Every brand has an equal probability of being chosen. This is the situation wherein no deterministic factors are present. Neither individual characteristics of consumers nor marketing stimuli play much of a role. The consumer is not loyal to any brand. Indeed, brands are not a motivating force in consumption. Only the product class is.

• *Variation-Seeking Switcher.* The variation seeker may also purchase at random, but unlike the random switcher, he or she is motivated by a need or drive to seek variation in brands. Brands are discriminated, and each one has a probability of purchase which can be, but is not necessarily, equal to the others. In the pure random case, the consumer seeks complete variability and purchases at random. In the modified random case, the consumer tries one brand for one or more purchases and then purchases another to seek variety. The one chosen may or may not have a probability of choice equal to any other. After consumption of the second brand on one or more occasions, the consumer then seeks a third to achieve variety. And so on.

- *Market Stimulus Switcher.* Here the consumer switches brands as a function of the appeal of one or more marketing mix stimuli. For example, a consumer might regularly purchase one brand of detergent but switch whenever a new brand comes on the market or whenever other brands lower their prices by a sufficient amount. Another consumer might purchase whatever brand is on sale or whenever he or she receives a coupon. Of course, switching can be induced by any one or more of many marketing stimuli such as price, promotion, product attribute, or distribution factors.

- *Brand Loyal Buyers.* The brand loyal buyer purchases a favorite brand on every or nearly every occasion. He or she will switch only when his or her brand is unavailable. It should be recognized that some consumers might be loyal to one, two, or a small number of brands. Thus, one might purchase either brand X or Y on any occasion, depending on availability, one's preferences of the day, changing marketing mix factors, or combinations of these. We would treat X and Y as a brand loyal "class" for this consumer.

- *Producer Loyal Buyer.* The producer loyal buyer is motivated by manufacturer. He or she purchases the brands from a particular manufacturer whenever possible.

- *Store Loyal Buyer.* People may also patronize a particular store in a regular way similar to the brand or producer loyal cases.

Once markets have been segmented by loyalty status, the information can be used in a number of ways. One is in planning and prediction. A firm can get a rough indication of the effectiveness of its marketing effort through the distribution of customers by loyalty type. It also can use the information in conjunction with data gathered on competitors to compute market share and thereby monitor the health of the firm. Another way to use loyalty status is to perform further segmentation on demographic, geographic, social unit, and/or psychographic bases in order to gain an understanding of why people are loyal or why they switch. This, in turn, can be used to design the marketing mix stimuli.

The final behaviorally based segmentation procedure is termed *trial/repeat purchase class* segmentation. We can classify potential buyers and actual buyers according to the psychological and behavioral stage they are in at any one point in time or the stages they pass through over time. For example, Figure 6-13 shows one simple sequence of stages. The first stage is unawareness of the product or brand under consideration. Of all those unaware, some will become aware but not intend to buy, whereas others will become aware and intend to buy. Some people who eventually try the product or brand will not repeat purchase, others will repeat a number of times but then discontinue, while still others will more or less continue to purchase regularly. A segmentation based on the classes shown in Figure 6-13 can be used to direct the marketing effort. For example, if many people are unaware of one's brand, then informational advertising might be required. Or if people are aware but fail to try the product, then persuasive advertising, price changes, or coupons might be required. Furthermore, given the stages people are in, the marketer can measure other characteristics of people to search for correlates or determinants of their level of awareness, strength of intentions, and choices.

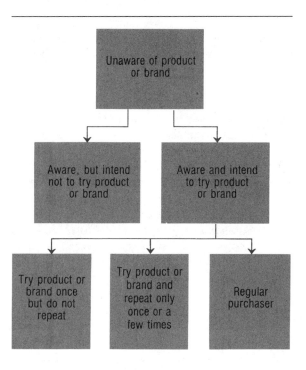

Figure 6-13. Some meaningful trial/repeat purchase classes

Final Comments on Consumer Segmentation. Before we discuss industrial buyer segmentation procedures, three points need to be made. First, we should stress that segmentation is usually best employed in a hybrid manner. Some combination of bases listed in Table 6-3 often needs to be considered in order to produce meaningful results. The particular set of factors chosen depends on the setting one is investigating and at the same time is something of an art. Second, segmentation works best when sound theoretical thinking supports the choice of variables included in an application. One should endeavor to provide a rationale why a particular independent variable should serve as a suitable predictor. This can, in turn, be derived from research in psychology, sociology, demography, economics, or other fields. The marketing literature, too,

needs to be regularly consulted, as new developments continually arise. Finally, although beyond the scope of this text, we should note that successful segmentation depends also on the use of rigorous statistical methodologies. Among others, these include regression, cluster, factor, causal, and componential analysis.[31]

Methods for Industrial Buyer Segmentation[32]

The sellers of industrial and institutional goods and services also use market segmentation. The industrial marketer's planning task is a two-step process. In the first step, total market demand for a product class must be estimated. In the second step, company demand as a percentage of market demand must be forecast. The following chapter addresses both of these problems in considerable detail. An important input to the second step is the selection of particular customers to approach. Let us examine how this might be done.

According to Wind and Cardozo, firms typically use one or more of three bases to segment industrial markets (see Table 6-7).[33] Consider first product characteristics. A seller might segment the market by *end use*. For example, a manufacturer of tractors might divide buyers into general farm use, road construction, house construction, and large building and bridge construction. Each of these segments has different product attribute needs and requires different financing, warranty, and repair services. Another product characteristic basis for segmentation is size of purchase. Marketers of basic commodities often segment their markets either by the dollar value or weight of purchases. Finally, segmentation on such product attributes as cost or durability might be followed. Segmentation based on product characteristics is often difficult to implement and/or least appropriate as a valid predictor of sales. For this reason, some firms segment by *organizational characteristics* because this is perhaps the easiest mode of operation. For instance, a manufacturer of large drill bits might segment the market into metal mining, anthracite mining, bituminous and lignite mining, oil and gas mining, and mining or quarrying of nonmetallic minerals except fuels. This is an example of segmentation by industry type. Other bases for partitioning by organizational characteristics include size of firm and organization structure. The disadvantage of segmentation by organizational characteristics is that it often is only moderately able to predict meaningful criteria such as sales. Nevertheless, it is probably the most widely employed procedure because of its ease of use.

TABLE 6-7

Three Bases of Industrial Market Segmentation and Some Examples

Product Characteristics	Organizational Characteristics	Decision Making Unit Characteristics
End use	Industry type	Source loyalty
Size of purchase	Size of firm	Buyer characteristics
Benefits, cost, durability, etc., of product	Structure of firm	Buying center and buyer-seller exchanges

---

Segmentation by *decision-making unit characteristics* is perhaps the most theoretically justified method. These characteristics are the attributes of the people making purchase decisions, their actions, and the processes (e.g., cooperative, conflict, power) involved. Included in the processes are interactions between buyers and sellers as well as among buyers. This segmentation procedure is theoretically desirable because it aims to base groupings on the actual determinants of purchases. However, this method is the most difficult to implement.

Choffray and Lilien propose a four-step procedure for implementing a decision-making unit segmentation (see Figure 6-14):

First, the pattern of involvement in the purchasing process is measured within a sample of firms in the macrosegment (i.e., industry or market) selected as target. Administration of the decision matrix (a procedure for categorizing decision makers in each phase of decision making by buyers) calls for a two-stage sampling procedure. In each firm, a senior management member is identified first. He is asked to name those people in his organization who would be most likely to participate in the decision to purchase a product in the class investigated. Only those individuals identified are contacted and provide the measurements.

Second, we define an index of interorganizational similarity in participants' involvement. This index relies only on the involvement (or noninvolvement) of each category of participants in every phase of the decision process.

Third, we identify groups of organizations homogeneous in the structure of their purchasing decision process. Cluster analytic methods are used for this purpose.

Fourth, we describe each microsegment in the purchasing process.[34]

In this way, the firm can identify unique customer groups, discover their needs, and adjust the product and communication program to the individual groups. Choffray and Lilien present an extended example of the approach applied to the marketing of industrial air-conditioning.[35]

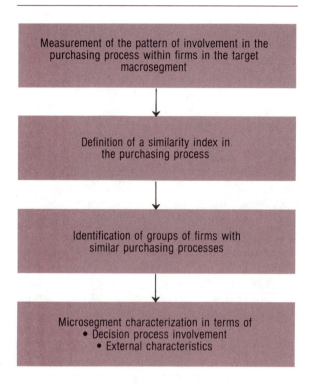

Figure 6-14 flow chart:

Measurement of the pattern of involvement in the purchasing process within firms in the target macrosegment

↓

Definition of a similarity index in the purchasing process

↓

Identification of groups of firms with similar purchasing processes

↓

Microsegment characterization in terms of
• Decision process involvement
• External characteristics

Figure 6-14. Industrial market segmentation on the basis of the decision-making unit

SOURCE: Jean-Marie Choffray and Gary L. Lilien, *Market Planning for New Industrial Products* (New York: Ronald Press, 1980): 83. Reprinted with the permission of the publisher.

One final point about industrial marketing segmentation should be made. In the everyday use of segmentation, marketers often combine two or more of the bases listed in Table 6-7. An excellent example is provided by a market segmentation performed by an aluminum company.[36] As shown in Figure 6-15, the aluminum market was first segmented on the basis of industry type into automobile, residential, and beverage container manufacturers. Next, given that the residential market seemed most promising, a second segmentation was performed on the basis of end

use. This resulted in three subsegments: semi-finished material, building components, and mobile homes. The firm then segmented this submarket on the basis of customer size into small, medium, and large. Finally, purchasers in the large segment, determined to be the best one, were found to seek one of three benefits: low price, high quality, or good service. The firm decided to pursue the service segment because this seemed the best match between its strengths and market demand.

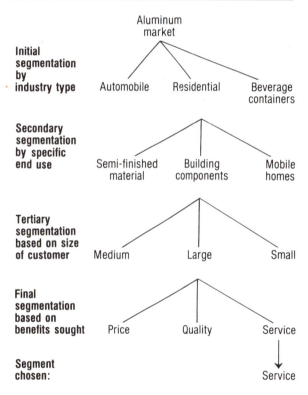

Figure 6-15. An example segmentation of the aluminum market

SOURCE: Derived from E. Raymond Corey, "Key Options in Market Selection and Product Planning," *Harvard Business Review* 53 (September–October 1975): 119–28.

Perceptual Mapping and Product Positioning

Perceptual Mapping

Most products and services consist of many physical and intangible attributes with many consequences for the would-be purchaser. An automobile is not merely "an automobile." Rather, it is a bundle of characteristics (e.g., color, size, ease of handling, smoothness of ride, roominess, miles per gallon, price, etc.) and consequences (e.g., feelings of pride, power, and prestige). The marketer's task is to decide how many attributes to build into the product, how much quality to include in each attribute, and how to combine the attributes to gain a competitive advantage.

The consumer's behavior will be complex and variable, for he or she must decide which attributes to seek and which of numerous offerings is the most attractive. This complicates matters, since the firm must start with an understanding of the needs of consumers. The marketer must first study consumer behavior and translate that knowledge of consumer needs and buying motivations into a finished product.

Due largely to the implicit coping strategies employed by consumers in decision making, only a few product attributes are important in any choice process. Furthermore, marketers have developed a methodology (known as "perceptual mapping") that can be used to measure the consumer's reactions to important attributes of competing brands or products.[37] We can identify two categories of consumer reactions to the psychological products. One concerns *perceptual/cognitive responses*, and the other deals with *preference/affective responses*. The first is a sensory and thinking reaction; the second is largely emotional in content. We might think of the consumer as forming a unique perceptual/cognitive *and* preference/affective image for each product or brand he or she encounters.

Thus, each product or brand occupies a separate "position" in the mind of the consumer. The differences and similarities among products and brands form a multidimensional image space, which we term a *perceptual map*.

To better understand the concept of a perceptual map, let us look at an example. Imagine that we asked an experienced beer drinker for his or her perceptions of the beers with which he or she is familiar. There are at least two ways to do this: (1) by use of multidimensional scaling (a procedure that uses only a consumer's judgments about how similar beers are) or (2) through factor analysis (a method that examines the associations among beliefs about each of a number of beers). We will not concern ourselves here about the mechanics of applying these statistical procedures.[38] Rather, we will focus on the output produced by the procedures.

Figure 6-16 shows one person's perceptions or judgments of the Northern California beer market where he lives. This person had images of 20 different brands. Some are light beers, some premium, and some super-premium. A few are foreign beers (e.g., from the Philippines, Japan, Germany, Denmark, and Mexico), but most are domestic. Notice that the beer drinker tends to see beers in two dimensions: heavy/light and bitter/mild. For example, Anchor Steam beer is perceived to be very heavy and relatively bitter. Coors, on the other hand, is perceived to be relatively mild and light. Carta Blanca is near the middle on these attributes. Other beer drinkers might perceive different attributes. For example, color, calories, price, and gaseousness might be important attributes for some people. It should also be noted that some beer drinkers will feel that only one attribute is essential in a beer, whereas others will desire three or more. Research using perceptual maps for a wide variety of everyday products, however, has generally found that possession of two or three attribute dimensions will give the product a strong appeal for most consumers. As products become more complex and/or the consumer's experiences and information-processing capabilities expand, more attributes may be take into account in decision making.

A number of interesting ideas emerge from a simple perceptual map such as shown in Figure 6-16. First, a perceptual map indicates what are the most important attributes in consumer decision making. These attributes should become the focal ones in product design and advertising decisions. Second, a perceptual map shows where one's own product and those of the competition score on each salient product attribute. Management thus gets an indication of its strengths and weaknesses and its primary rivals in the minds of consumers. A third by-product of a perceptual map is that it suggests possible opportunities in the market. In Figure 6-16, for example, we see that no beer is perceived to be in the bitter and light quadrant. This might represent a potential entry point for a new product. Of course, whether the unfulfilled niche is really a viable market or not will depend on (a) the firm's ability to produce and market a light, bitter beer and (b) the number of people preferring such a beer and willing to try it. A number of other implications can be drawn from perceptual maps, but before we can discuss these, a few other concepts must be introduced.

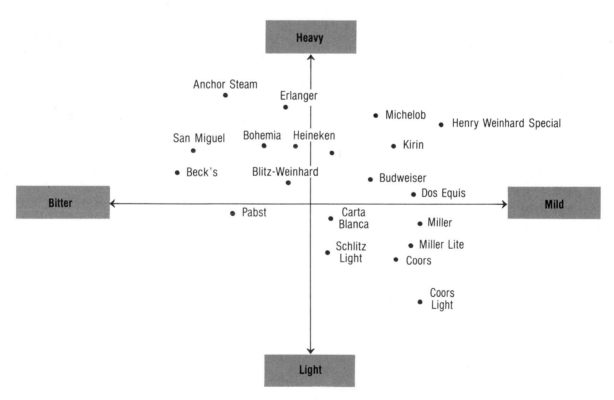

Figure 6-16. A perceptual map of the beer market in Northern California as seen by one beer drinker

Figure 6-16 illustrates only one facet of perceptual maps: namely, the perceptual/cognitive responses of the consumer. To gain a more complete picture of consumer responses, we need also to look at preference/affective reactions. In this respect, there are two issues to consider. One is the desired combination of attributes a consumer seeks, termed the *ideal point*. A second is the distribution of people preferring different combinations of attributes in a particular market or market segment. Figure 6-17 introduces these two concepts.

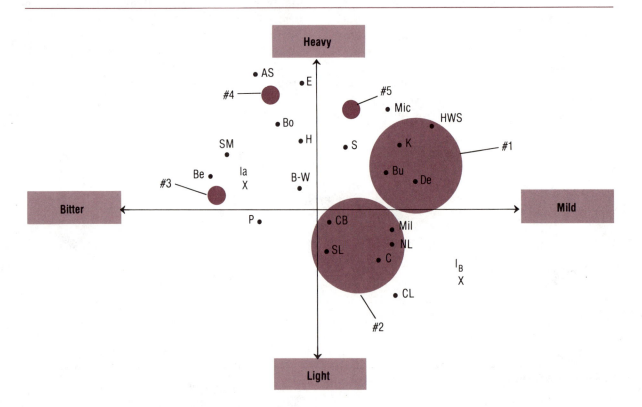

Figure 6-17. A perceptual map of the Northern California beer market: ideal points and market preferences

An *ideal point* can be loosely interpreted as the preferred combination of attributes desired by a person (or a group of people treated as an aggregate). In Figure 6-17, we have represented the ideal points for two consumers, A and B, and these are indicated with *x*'s. Notice that Consumer A's ideal (I_A) is represented by a somewhat bitter and somewhat heavy beer. Which beer will Person A choose? Given he or she has preference, I_A, and perceives the market as shown in Figure 6-17, Person A will most likely choose the beer closest to his or her ideal. Thus, Becks, San Miguel, Bohemia, Heineken, Blitz-Weinhard, and Pabst would each appear to have about an equal chance of selection. The actual choice will, of course, also depend on the person's past behavior, the availability of alternatives at the time of consumption, and other factors. In contrast, Person B prefers a mild, light beer (I_B). Presumably, Person B's most likely choice will be Coors Light (or possibly Coors' Regular or Miller Lite).

Figure 6-17 also shows the distribution of preferences for beer for five groups of drinkers. The average preferences for these groups are shown as circles in the figure. The larger the circle, the more people there are that have a preference in the range encompassed by the circle. We might think of the center of each circle as constituting the mean preference value (i.e., ideal point) for a group of people. The circumference would represent the boundary for a locus of points based on a distribution. For instance, a circle might represent all people in a group showing a preference within plus or minus one standard deviation of the mean preference value. In Figure 6-17, notice that groups 1 and 2 contain the greatest number of people. Most drinkers apparently prefer a somewhat mild and either slightly light or slightly heavy beer. Few people prefer a bitter beer (group 3) or a heavy beer (groups 4 and 5).

Product/Brand Positioning[39]

Let us consider some further managerial implications of perceptual maps. For purposes of discussion, we will take the perspective of an existing producer, Pabst. Notice Pabst's current location on the perceptual map shown in Figure 6-17. It is largely by itself, being perceived as a somewhat bitter, but neither light nor heavy, beer. Let us additionally assume that Pabst is losing sales and market share and that something must be done. What options does Pabst have? The perceptual map shows that Pabst is relatively far away from any preference group. It could, therefore, attempt to aggressively seek customers from either group 2 or 3. How might it do this? One way would be to change the advertising. If Pabst wanted to appeal to people in group 2, it could advertise itself as a somewhat

mild beer. However, given that Miller, Coors, and others are also vying for people in this group, Pabst should weigh the strength of competition versus the likely demand for its beer by these people. On the other hand, Pabst could go after group 3 by advertising itself as a bitter beer. Again, whether this would be a viable strategy or not would depend on the number of beer drinkers in group 3, their receptivity to Pabst, and the degree of competition.

It may not be desirable for Pabst to attempt to draw customers merely with a change in advertising. After all, consumers base their judgments on actual taste, not only on advertising. As a result, Pabst could change its ingredients to either make its beer more or less bitter, depending on its estimate of market demand and competitive conditions. Generally, to change the position of a product, some combination of physical alterations and communication modifications must be made.

Another use of perceptual maps is in tracking consumer beliefs and feelings over time. Consumer markets are not static. People's perceptions, needs, and preferences change over time. Sometimes new product attributes become salient in decision making, requiring the addition of a new dimension to a perceptual map. Sometimes tastes change, and existing preference clusters shrink or grow or else new ones need to be added to a map. Or a new brand will enter a market to change the equilibrium. Given the many possible changes, it behooves the marketer to monitor the evolution of the market over time so as to better anticipate and respond to volatile market forces. Many a firm blindly followed the status quo only to later find that consumer needs had changed or that the market took on a different complexity over time. The U.S. automakers found themselves in this position throughout the 1970s and into the 1980s.

Perceptual maps are used in both product positioning and brand positioning situations. Figures 6-16 and 6-17 illustrated the concept of brand positioning where similar products from different manufacturers vie for the consumer's scarce resources. Product positioning applies when different products roughly satisfying similar needs are in competition. For example, Figure 6-18 shows a map for beverages as perceived by one consumer. Thirteen beverages that loosely act as substitutes when one is thirsty are plotted. The particular consumer represented by Figure 6-18 sees drinks along two attribute dimensions: side-effects and taste. Water has few or no side-effects, but tastes poorly. Coffee tastes good but has side-effects (caffeine-related nervousness, acid stomach). Whole milk tastes better than average and has few side-effects (except perhaps some cholesterol). A product map can be used to study competition among generic substitutes and to perhaps discover unfulfilled needs. Apple juice, orange juice, and lemonade compete fairly closely. No drink scores well on both taste and lack of side-effects. Perhaps an opportunity exists here. At least more research might be warranted in this regard.

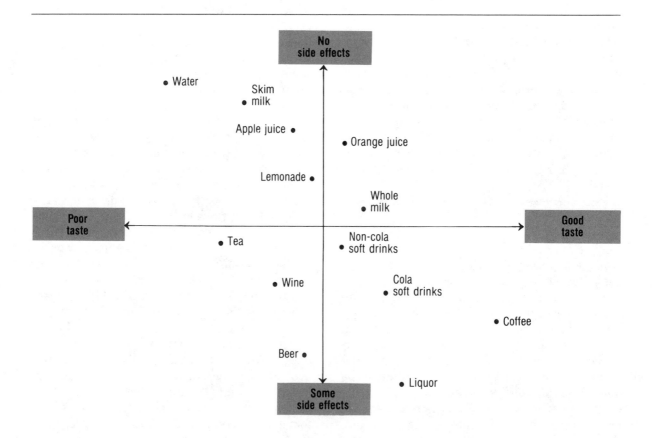

Figure 6-18. A perceptual map of the beverage market

Still another use of perceptual maps is in segmentation. Indeed, an emerging marketing strategy tool is to employ perceptual maps in conjunction with hierarchical market partitioning. Figure 6-19 shows one possibility applied to the beer market. Here we have combined a product form hierarchy with a two-dimensional perceptual map for each product form. The dimensions are again heavy/light (H/L) and bitter/mild (B/M). We have plotted only a few brands to keep the diagram simple. By performing a separate perceptual map for each product form, one can gain a finer picture of where brands score on product attributes, what the competition is, and which new product opportunities are available. One could also develop perceptual maps for different geographic, demographic, psychographic, or other bases of segmentation.

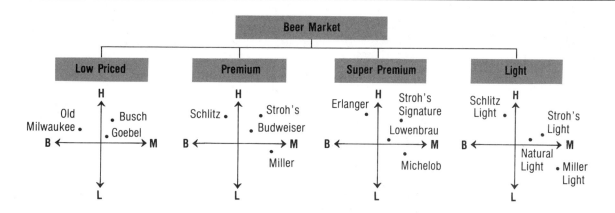

Figure 6-19. Combining perceptual maps and hierarchical market partitions in market segmentation

Clustering procedures are used to define meaningful groups of brands or products on perceptual maps.[40] Figure 6-20 shows an example of clustering applied to the beer market map originally illustrated in Figure 6-16. Again, we will not concern ourselves with the statistical details of clustering but will focus only on the results. The clustering methodology forms groups of brands or products based on important similarities among them. In Figure 6-20, we see that eight separate groups emerge from the clustering procedures. Representative descriptive labels are placed next to each cluster. For example, Anchor Steam beer and Erlanger form one grouping that might be considered a "high calorie, filling" cluster. Michelob and Henry Weinhard Special form a "high-quality, special occasion" cluster. Carta Blanca is off by itself and does not appear to be similar to any beer in any other cluster. We term this a "nondescript" cluster because the brand is in the center on product attributes.

The information provided by clustering and a perceptual map provides a more detailed picture of how consumers conceive of different brands and their attributes. Imagine, for instance, that a producer is considering putting a new beer on the market.

One strategy would be to select a segment where enough people express a preference and few competitors are clustered. A possibility is to introduce a relatively heavy, yet mild, beer to compete with Michelob and Henry Weinhard Special. The new brand, N, is shown in Figure 6-20 with an x in the top right quadrant. This might be a good strategy since only two competitors appear presently located in the high-quality, special occasion cluster. A better alternative, A, which still fits in the cluster but is somewhat milder and lighter, is shown by a check mark in Figure 6-20. More people would presumably prefer this beer. The task for the marketer is to create an image of high quality,

lightness, and mildness, and to differentiate the beer from the "solid quality premium" market. Had we not performed a cluster analysis, we might not have discovered the unique groups in the upper right quadrant of Figure 6-20.

Perceptual maps can be used with attitude-type scales to more explicitly measure consumer perceptions of product attributes for competing brands.[41] Perceptual maps can be combined with questionnaire data on attitudes, opinions, or other information obtained from people regarding their personal feelings, beliefs, or experiences. Figure 6-21

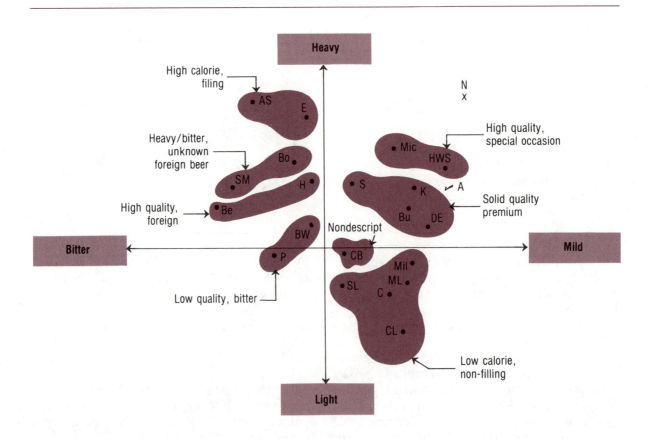

Figure 6-20. A perceptual map of the beer market with brand clusters

presents an example applied to the beer market. Each arrow represents one attitude or personal characteristic for consumers. Think of the tail of each arrow as being extended backwards from the arrowhead and through the perceptual map. We have done this for the attribute "filling" but avoided extending the other arrows to keep the figure simple. Each arrow represents a vector of attitudinal intensity. The farther one goes in the direction of the arrow, the stronger the attitude. The way to determine where a beer scores on an attitude

attribute in the mind of the consumer is as follows. For filling, for example, we should drop a perpendicular line from a beer of interest to the extended arrow. This is done for Erlanger (E) and Coors (C). The person's attitude, then, for Erlanger is that it is perceived to be filling and Coors is perceived to be unfilling. Similar evaluations of each beer on each attribute can be made. Also, many other attributes than those shown can be investigated, but we have omitted them from the diagram for the sake of simplicity.

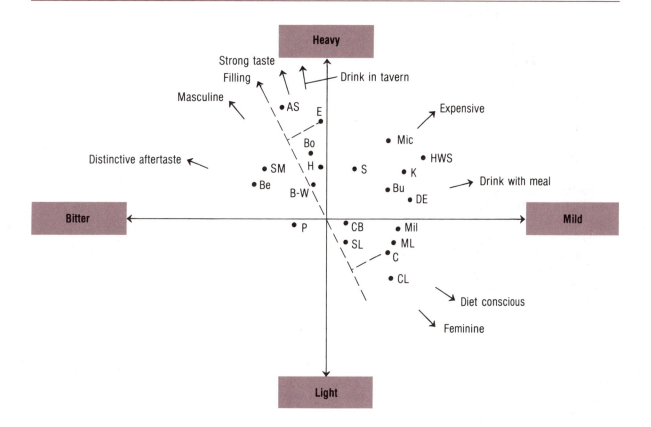

Figure 6-21. A perceptual map of the beer market with attitude vectors

Conjoint Analysis[42]

Imagine that you are a brand manager for a carpet cleaner and are confronted with the following decision. You are to select a final design for the carpet cleaner based on five product attributes: package design, brand name, price, quality (represented by using the Good Housekeeping seal of approval), and dependability (a money-back guarantee). Figure 6-22 displays the five attributes and the possible alternatives from which to choose. This is an actual decision faced by a brand manager and is typical of many real-world product design problems. Management must make a commitment on a final design. A number of product attributes and alternatives for each is to be considered. The choice of any final design will involve trade-offs for the firm based on cost considerations on the one hand and the likely ability of different designs for stimulating demand on the other. For example, implementing a money-back guarantee policy will cost the firm money, but it may influence more people to try the product. Some design alternatives are relatively objective in their form and impact (price), while others are more subjective (brand name) or both subjective and objective (package design, Good Housekeeping seal, money-back guarantee). The decision process is thus a complex one (108 possible combinations of attribute alternatives are to be considered) and is filled with uncertainty. A quantitative methodology, termed conjoint analysis, is sometimes used to yield consumer-based decisions.

Conjoint analysis is used to elicit a consumer's utility for different levels or forms of product attributes. A consumer is asked to express his or her evaluation of or preference for different combinations of product attributes. For instance, a consumer might be asked to evaluate package design A with the K2R brand name priced at $1.39 and

1. Package design:

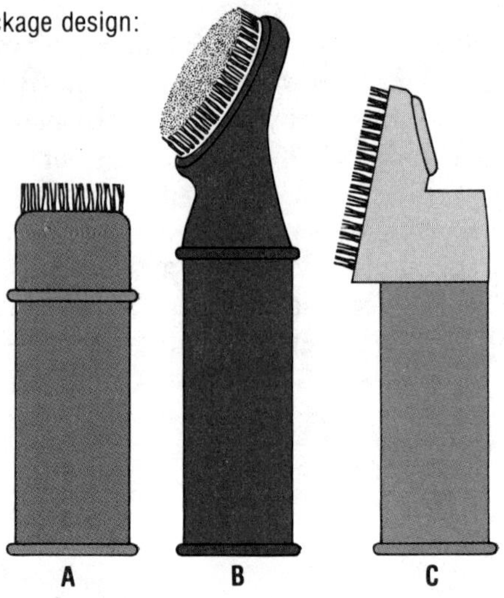

2. Brand name: K2R, Glory, or Bissell
3. Price: $1.19, $1.39, or $1.59
4. Good Housekeeping seal: yes or no
5. Money-back guarantee: yes or no

Figure 6-22. Five product attributes for a floor cleaner and potential design alternatives for each

Source: Adapted from Paul E. Green and Yoram Wind, "New Way to Measure Consumers' Judgments," *Harvard Business Review* 53 (July–August 1975): 108. Copyright © 1975, by the President and Fellows of Harvard College; all rights reserved.

without either a Good Housekeeping seal or a money-back guarantee. This combination of attributes would be ranked with other combinations. Then the rank order of combinations for each attribute alternative would be calculated.

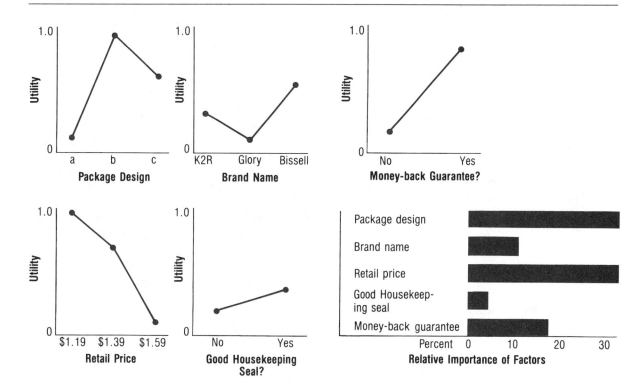

Figure 6-23. Utility levels for product attribute alternatives for one consumer

Figure 6-23 shows the output of utilities for one consumer's evaluations of alternative combinations of attributes. Notice that the package design B had the highest utility (U ≃ 1.0), whereas design A (U ≃ .1) and design C (U ≃ .6) are less valued. Overall, the combination of attribute alternatives most highly valued by the consumer are design B, Bissell, $1.19, and inclusion of both a Good Housekeeping seal and a money-back guarantee. The bar graph at the bottom of Figure 6-23 illustrates the relative importance of attribute alternatives. We see that package design and retail price are most important while the Good Housekeeping Seal is much less important and

the brand name and money-guarantee are of intermediate importance. Depending on the costs involved, it appears that management should make an effort to implement package design B and keep the price low. The other alternatives are less of a concern and might be chosen on the basis of cost considerations. We have oversimplified the problem by neglecting goals for return on investment, likely demand under each combination of attribute alternatives, and other factors, but the example illustrates how conjoint analysis can provide management with information for product design decisions.

Positioning Strategies

The final topic we wish to discuss is the choice of alternative positioning strategies by a firm. Ideally, an organization should strive to position its products so that attributes or criteria will satisfy consumer needs and do so with a competitive edge. This is best done for each of the market segments chosen by the firm.

In general, there are six frequently applied bases for positioning.[43] Each is discussed below.

The most obvious basis for positioning is on specific *product attributes*. The firm attempts to emphasize one or a small number of strongly demanded product features, and the feature or features chosen should exhibit a certain degree of uniqueness if possible. A good example of positioning by product attributes is Crest toothpaste. Crest was the first brand to focus on the inclusion of fluoride, a decay-prevention ingredient. Its early advertising almost entirely stressed this feature. In recent years, other manufacturers have brought out fluoride toothpastes (e.g., Lever Brothers' Aim) or emphasized other product attributes such as low price or taste.

A closely related basis for positioning is by *product benefits*. Actually, the line between product attribute and product benefit positioning is a fuzzy one. After all, people seek attributes for the benefits they provide. Thus, Crest's emphasis on fluoride is just as much an appeal to its decay preventive features. Some benefits are less firmly linked to particular product attributes. Sex appeal or anti-bad breath benefits of some toothpastes fall under this category.

Positioning for specific *usage occasions* or *functions* is a third possibility. Arm and Hammer Baking Soda is marketed as a deodorant for refrigerators and cat litter boxes, as well as for cooking. Michelob is positioned as a special occasion beer: "Weekends are made for Michelob." And A-1 steak sauce is now pushed as an ingredient topping for hamburger in addition to its earlier special positioning as a steak flavor enhancer.

A fourth strategy is to position by *user category*. Marlboro, Camel, and Winston cigarettes are positioned as masculine products, whereas Virginia Slims is decidedly feminine. Dog food is marketed in adult and puppy varieties. Restaurants sometimes have separate English and Spanish menus or separate adult and child menus to appeal to the different clientele.

Still another positioning strategy is to portray one's product *relative to the competition*. Sometimes the particular competitor is not identified, such as occurs with "Brand X" comparisons or when some caffeine-free soft drink brands mention their "caffeine" competitors. Lately, sellers have been more explicit and have identified their rivals directly, hoping to draw customers away from them. Pepsi seems to have had some success in this regard positioning itself as a more popular alternative to Coke, whereas Schlitz appears to have fared less well in its head-on taste comparison with Budweiser and others. Occasionally, a producer need not even mention a competitor directly or indirectly to make comparisons. B. F. Goodrich, the tire manufacturer, has developed humorous commercials playing on its similarity in name to Goodyear. However, rather than mentioning Goodyear, it draws an implicit association through reference to the Goodyear blimp in its commercials.

Whether this actually enhances Goodrich's position, as opposed to creating confusion, remains to be seen. The classic example of relative positioning to the competition is Seven-Up's Un-Cola campaign in the early 1970s. Seven-Up successfully marketed itself as an alternative to colas to be drunk in heretofore cola contexts (i.e., with a hamburger, alone as a thirst quencher, at meals, when friends visit, etc.). Prior to its campaign, Seven-Up was perceived as a special purpose drink (e.g., a mixer) and not so much as a soft drink.

The final strategy is to position on a *hybrid* basis. The hybrid strategy combines two or more of the bases noted above. The firm either comes out with multiple brands wherein each is based on a different level of a single basis (or on completely different bases) or else a single brand is positioned on two or more bases. An example of the former is provided by Heublein, Inc., which has three brands of vodka: a top-of-the-line (Smirnoff), a middle-of-the-road (Relska), and a cheap brand (Popov). An example of positioning on multiple bases can be found in the Kitchen Aid food preparer. Kitchen Aid positions its products on the basis of superior quality and extensive features. As with food processors (a generic competitor), the Kitchen Aid food preparer kneads dough, mixes pastry, beats, creams, slices, shreds, purees, and makes pasta. Unlike food processors, it also stuffs sausage, mills grain, opens cans, grinds, and buffs silver. However, it does not grate, mince, or chop as a food processor does. It is also considerably more expensive than most food processors. Overall, it offers more advantages, with fewer disadvantages and, at the same time, is in a somewhat higher-quality position than the food processor option. Its high price and heavy metal construction reinforce this image. Customers must choose between one or the other on the basis of price/quality and benefits desired. Recently, Kitchen Aid has introduced a food processor, perhaps reflecting the existence of a market segment not viewing the food processor as a substitute for the food preparer.

Summary

This chapter has addressed additional issues in product design and the interface between the consumer and the firm. Two central concepts were discussed: market segmentation and positioning. *Market segmentation* is defined as the classification of consumers, products, or markets into groups on the basis of their characteristics. It is done primarily to better identify consumer needs and enhance the match between the firm's offerings and those needs. As such, market segmentation is a strategic tool for more effective marketing. *Product or brand positioning* is the choice of a particular niche in the market based on the characteristics of the product and brand or the consequences they have for consumers. The specific product or brand characteristics and consequences used in positioning are drawn from actual consumer perceptions/cognitions and preference/affect. The methodology used to accomplish this is known as *perceptual mapping*. Overall, the objective of positioning is to choose a sector of the market that both meets consumer needs and achieves a differential advantage over the competition.

We discussed two broad approaches to market segmentation. *Logic-based market segmentation* proceeds from preconceived definitions of the product and market. In the *classification-of-goods theory*, products are subdivided on the basis of their physical attributes and/or consumer reactions as perceived by the firm. The approach is driven more by the firm's needs than the actual needs of consumers and for this reason is not as effective as other procedures. Nevertheless, for industrial goods, it has proven an inexpensive and useful technique. We will discuss its use in this regard in Chapter 7 when we consider the SIC system in greater detail. Another logic-based procedure, the *hierarchical market definition* method, is on sounder footing. In this procedure, product forms and brands are organized by their similarity and are ordered on a criterion such as producer, product subform, product attributes, or geographical area. The primary advantage of a hierarchical market definition is that is provides a meaningful description of markets and suggests managerial guidelines related to product design, new entry possibilities, and the status of the competition. To the extent that hierarchies can be found that correspond to how the consumer really sees the market and makes decisions, the approach offers promise.

Perhaps the most widely used and ultimately most valid approach is *empirically based market segmentation.* We discussed three classes in this respect: (1) demand elasticity and market response methods, (2) traditional statistical approaches for consumer segmentation, and (3) industrial buyer segmentation. Each of these procedures is based on the premise that natural segments exist in the market and the best way to find out how consumers or buyers behave differently from one segment to another is to measure their actual behavior.

In consumer segmentation, we attempt to predict a criterion (e.g., purchase intentions, actual product choice) on the basis of meaningful independent variables (e.g., beliefs and evaluations of product attributes, social standing, or sex). Further, to enhance our predictions, we search for groups of consumers that are relatively homogeneous in some dimensions. For example, we might find that attitudes will predict brand choice only for a particular age group, education level, or degree of familiarity with the product class. Table 6-3 lists many commonly used bases for segmentation. Many examples were presented in the chapter.

For industrial market segmentation, a number of options were considered. However, segmentation by decision-making unit was felt to be the most theoretically justified because it strives to arrive at buyer groupings based on the actual determinants of purchases. A four-step procedure was outlined and is summarized in Figure 6-14.

Finally, the chapter closed with a discussion of perceptual mapping and product positioning. Significantly, the ideas reflect the philosophy that the road to success begins with an assessment of consumer needs and adjustment of one's product to both meet those needs and gain a competitive advantage over rivals. Subsequent chapters present in-depth discussions on how marketers attempt to accomplish these goals through orchestration of the marketing mix.

Questions and Problems for Discussion

1 Name the three grassroots activities that should be performed in any strategic marketing planning process. Briefly describe each.

2 Define market segmentation and comment on why firms engage in it.

3 What is the classification-of-goods theory and how might it be used? What are its strengths and weaknesses?

4 Discuss the hierarchical market definition procedure and point out its pros and cons.

5 Prepare a hierarchical market definition for coffee.

6 Describe the demand elasticity and the market response methods of market segmentation.

7 Name the traditional methods for market segmentation. How are they used and what criteria are used to evaluate their effectiveness?

8 What is benefit segmentation and how is it used?

9 Briefly comment on industrial market segmentation. How does it differ from consumer market segmentation?

10 Define and describe the concepts of perceptual mapping and product positioning.

11 What is conjoint analysis and how is it used in product management?

12 What product/brand positioning strategies are open to management? Elaborate on these.

NOTES

1. Alfred A. Kuehn and Ralph L. Day, "Strategy of Product Quality," *Harvard Business Review* 40 (November-December 1962): 100–110.

2. For a review of classification-of-goods theories, see Yoram J. Wind, *Product Policy: Concepts, Methods, and Strategy* (Reading, Mass.: Addison-Wesley, 1982): pp. 67–74.

3. Richard H. Holton. "The Distinction between Convenience Goods, Shopping Goods, and Specialty Goods," *Journal of Marketing* 22 (July 1958): 53–56.

4. Louis P. Bucklin, "Retail Strategy and the Classification of Consumer Goods," *Journal of Marketing* 27 (January 1963): 50–55.

5. Morris B. Holbrook and John A. Howard, "Consumer Research on Frequently Purchased Nondurables and Services: A Review," (Washington, D.C.: Project on Synthesis of Knowledge of Consumer Behavior, RANN Program, National Science Foundation, April 1975).

6. Reinhard Angelmar and Richard P. Bagozzi, "Typical Marketing Behavior over the Product Life Cycle," unpublished working paper, Massachusetts Institute of Technology, 1983.

7. See D. H. Butler, "Development of Statistical Marketing Models," in *Speaking of Hendry* (Croton-on-Hudson, N.Y.: Hendry Corporation, 1976), pp. 125–45; M. U. Kalwani and D. Morrison, "A Parsimonious Description of the Hendry System," *Management Science* 23 (January 1977): 467–77. For a new, more advanced approach that integrates logical and empirical content, see the Prodigy Model of G. L. Urban, P. Johnson, and R. Brudnick, "Market Entry Strategy Formulation: A Hierarchical Model and Consumer Measurement Approach," working paper, Sloan School of Management, M.I.T., Cambridge, Mass., 1979.

8. See James R. Bettman, "The Structure of Consumer Choice Processes," *Journal of Marketing Research* 8 (November 1971): 465–61, and chapter 2 of this text.

9. Early work on response methods to segmentation can be found in Glenn L. Urban, "A Mathematical Modeling Approach to Product Line Decisions," *Journal of Marketing Research* 6 (February 1969): 40–47; Henry Assael, "Segmenting Markets by Response Elasticity," *Journal of Advertising Research* 16 (April 1976): 27–35; Parker Lessig and John O. Tollefson, "Market Segmentation through Numerical Taxonomy," *Journal of Marketing Research* 8 (November 1971): 480–87; John O. Tollefson and V. Parker Lessig, "Aggregation Criteria in Normative Market Segmentation Theory," *Journal of Marketing Research* 15 (August 1978): 346–55.

10. Vijay Mahajan and Arun K. Jain, "An Approach to Normative Segmentation," *Journal of Marketing Research* 15 (August 1978): 338–45.

11. For introductions to traditional market segmentation, see Henry J. Claycamp and William F. Massy, "A Theory of Market Segmentation," *Journal of Marketing Research* 5 (November 1968): 388–94; Frank M. Bass, Douglas J. Tigert, and Ronald T. Lonsdale, "Market Segmentation: Group versus Individual Behavior," *Journal of Marketing Research* 5 (August 1968): 264–70; Ronald Frank, William Massy, and Yoram Wind, *Market Segmentation* (Englewood Cliffs, N.J.: Prentice-Hall, 1972). Yoram Wind and Richard Cardozo, "Industrial Market Segmentation," *Industrial Marketing Management* 3 (1974): 153–66; Henry Assael and A. M. Roscoe, Jr., "Approaches to Market Segmentation Analysis," *Journal of Marketing* 40 (October 1976): 67–76. New developments in market segmentation are discussed in Yoram Wind, "Issues and Advances in Segmentation Research," *Journal of Marketing Research* 15 (August 1978): 318–37.

12. For a more comprehensive development of a consumer behavior model relating managerial and psychological variables to actual choice, see Richard P. Bagozzi, "A Holistic Methodology for Modeling Consumer Response to Innovation," *Operations Research* 31 (January–February 1983): 128–76.

13. See, for example, Franklin B. Evans, "Selling as a Dyadic Relationship—A New Approach," *American Behavioral Scientist* 6 (May 1963): 76–79.

14. Bass, Tigert, and Lonsdale, "Market Segmentation."

15. For an early statement on the family life cycle concept applied in marketing, see William D. Wells and George Gubar, "Life Cycle Concept in Marketing Research," *Journal of Marketing Research* 3 (August 1968): 355–63.

16. For a new treatment of social class, see Ricard P. Coleman and Lee Rainwater, *Social Standing in America* (New York: Basic Books, 1978).

17. Coleman and Rainwater, *Social Standing in America.*

18. James M. Carman, *The Application of Social Class in Market Segmentation* (Berkeley, Calif.: Institute of Business and Economic Research, University of California, 1965).

19. Arun K. Jain, "A Method for Investigating and Representing an Implicit Theory of Social Class," *Journal of Consumer Research* 1 (June 1975): 53–59.

20. For an introduction and review of the area, see William D. Wells, "Psychographics: A Critical Review," *Journal of Marketing Research* 12 (May 1975): 196–213.

21. The theory of life-style segmentation is presented in Yoram Wind, "Life Style Analysis: A New Approach," in Fred C. Allvine, ed., *Proceedings of the American Marketing Association Annual Educators' Conference* (Chicago: American Marketing Association, 1971), pp. 302–5; Joseph T. Plummer, "The Concept and Application of Life Style Segmentation," *Journal of Marketing* 38 (January 1974): 33–37; and William D. Wells and Douglas J. Tigert, "Activities, Interests, and Opinions," in James F. Engel et al., eds., *Market Segmentation* (New York: Holt, Rinehart & Winston, 1972).

22. Examples can be found in L. Percy, "How Market Segmentation Guides Advertising Strategy," *Journal of Advertising Research* (October 1976): 11–26.

23. Ruth Ziff, "Psychographics for Market Segmentation," *Journal of Advertising Research* (April 1971): 3–9; Elizabeth A. Richards and Stephen S. Sturman, "Lifestyle Segmentation in Apparel Marketing," *Journal of Marketing* 41 (October 1977): 89–91.

24. Abraham H. Maslow, *Motivation and Personality*, 2nd ed. (New York: Harper & Row, 1970). B. Curtiss Hamm and Edward W. Cundiff, "Self-Actualization and Product Perception," *Journal of Marketing Research* 6 (November 1969): 470–72; Edward M. Tauber, "Reduce New Product Failures: Measure Needs as Well as Purchase Intention," *Journal of Marketing* 37 (July 1973): 61–64.

25. Franklin B. Evans, "Psychological and Objective Factors in the Prediction of Brand Choice; Ford versus Chevrolet," *Journal of Business* (October 1959): 340–69; W. T. Tucker and John J. Painter, "Personality and Product Use," *Journal of Applied Psychology* (October 1961): 325–29.

26. Ralph Westfall, "Psychological Factors in Predicting Product Choice," *Journal of Marketing* 26 (April 1962): 34–40.

27. Walter Mischel, *Personality and Assessment* (New York: John Wiley & Sons, 1968). For a review in marketing, see Harold H. Kassarjian, "Personality and Consumer Behavior: A Review," *Journal of Marketing Research* 8 (November 1971): 409–18.

28. Dik W. Twedt, "How Important to Marketing Strategy Is the 'Heavy User'?" *Journal of Marketing* 28 (January 1964): 71–72; S. M. Barker and J. F. Trost, "Cultivate the High-Volume Consumer," *Harvard Business Review* (March–April 1973): 118–22.

29. Daniel Yankelovich, "New Criteria for Market Segmentation," *Harvard Business Review* (March–April 1964): 83–90; Russell I. Haley, "Benefit Segmentation: A Decision-Oriented Research Tool," *Journal of Marketing* 32 (July 1968): 30–35; James H. Myers, "Benefit Structure Analysis: A New Tool for Product Planning," *Journal of Marketing* 41 (October 1976): 23–32; Roger J. Calantone and Alan G. Sawyer, "The Stability of Benefit Segments," *Journal of Marketing Research* 16 (August 1978): 395–404.

30. Jacob Jacoby and David B. Dyner, "Brand Loyalty versus Repeat Purchasing Behavior," *Journal of Marketing Research* 10 (February 1973): 1–9; Ronald W. Frank, "Is Brand Loyalty a Useful Basis for Market Segmentation?" *Journal of Advertising Research* (June 1967): 27–33; Jacob Jacoby, "Model of Multi-Brand Loyalty," *Journal of Advertising Research* 11 (June 1971): 25–31; A. S. C. Ehrenberg, *Repeat Buying* (Amsterdam: Elsevier/North Holland, 1971); Frank M. Bass, "The Theory of Stochastic Preference and Brand Switching," *Journal of Marketing Research* 11 (February 1974): 1–20; Robert C. Blattberg and Subrata K. Sen, "Market Segmentation Using Models of Multidimensional Purchasing Behavior," *Journal of Marketing* 38 (October 1974): 17–28.

31. Paul E. Green, "A New Approach to Market Segmentation," *Business Horizons* 20 (February 1977): 61–73; Richard P. Bagozzi, "A Holistic Methodology for Modeling Consumer Response to Innovation"; Ronald Frank, William Massy, and Yoram Wind, *Market Segmentation* (Englewood Cliffs, N.J.: Prentice-Hall, 1972); Paul E. Green and Donald S. Tull, *Research for Marketing Decisions*, 4th ed. (Englewood Cliffs, N.J.: Prentice-Hall, 1978).

32. The discussion in this section is drawn in part from Jean-Marie Choffray and Gary L. Lilien, *Market Planning for New Industrial Products* (New York: Ronald Press, 1980), Chapters 3 and 4.

33. Yoram Wind and Richard Cardozo, "Industrial Market Segmentation," *Industrial Marketing Management* 3 (1974): 153–66.

34. Choffray and Lilien, *Market Planning for New Industrial Products*, pp. 83–84.

35. Choffray and Lilien, *Market Planning for New Industrial Products*, pp. 83–90.

36. E. Raymond Corey, "Key Options in Market Selection and Product Planning," *Harvard Business Review* 53 (September–October 1975): 119–28.

37. For an introduction to perceptual mapping, including illustrations, see Paul E. Green and Vithala R. Rao, *Applied Multidimensional Scaling* (New York: Holt, Rinehart & Winston, 1972); Yoram Wind and P. J. Robinson, "Product Positioning: An Application of Multidimensional Scaling," in R. I. Haley, ed., *Attitude Research in Transition* (Chicago: American Marketing Association, 1972); Richard M. Johnson, "Market Segmentation: A Strategic Management Tool," *Journal of Marketing Research* 8 (February 1971): 13–18. An alternative to the use of multidimensional scaling for deriving perceptual maps is factor analysis and is discussed in Glen L. Urban and John R. Hauser, *Design and Marketing of New Products* (Englewood Cliffs, N.J.: Prentice-Hall, 1980), Chapter 9.

38. See Green and Tull, *Research for Marketing Decisions*; Urban and Hauser, *Design and Marketing of New Products*.

39. Henry Assael, "Perceptual Mapping to Reposition Brands," *Journal of Advertising Research* 2 (February 1971): 39–42.

40. For a description of the procedures with illustrations, see Green and Tull, *Research for Marketing Decisions*.

41. Green and Tull, *Research for Marketing Decisions*.

42. Paul E. Green and Yoram Wind, "New Way to Measure Consumer's Judgments," *Harvard Business Review* 53 (July–August 1975): 107–17; Paul E. Green and V. Srinivasan, "Conjoint Analysis in Consumer Research: Issues and Outlook," *Journal of Consumer Research* 5 (September 1978): 103–23.

43. The six bases were suggested by Wind, *Product Policy: Concepts, Methods, and Strategy*, pp. 79–81.

GLOSSARY

Benefit Segmentation. The identification of groups of consumers as potential buyers, based upon similarities in needs or product attributes desired.

Brand (or Product) Positioning. The design and execution of a marketing program to create a particular image of a product somewhere within the confines of a perceptual map. This might involve changing the perceived image of an established brand (termed "repositioning") or introducing a new brand in a new sector of a perceptual map (termed "brand extension"). Repositioning and brand extension are accomplished through product design, advertising, promotion, packaging, etc.

Classification-of-Goods Theory. The subdivision of products on the basis of their physical characteristics and/or consumer behavior. As shown in Figure 6-4, all goods can be categorized first as either industrial or consumer goods. Two popular subdivisions of industrial goods can be made on the basis of either the standard industrial classification system or input/output analysis. Consumer goods can be classified into convenience, shopping, specialty, and preference goods. Further insight into the classification of goods can be found in the preceding two and the following chapter. A major drawback of the approach is that it does not incorporate empirical content and thus fails to represent how behavior actually occurs in the marketplace.

Conjoint Analysis. An analytical procedure that yields utilities for different levels of product attributes. The technique translates actual preferences of consumers into implied utilities. Conjoint analysis is used in product design decisions.

Demand Elasticity Method of Market Segmentation. The sales responses of different groups of consumers to price are used to choose market segments. Examination of cross elasticities for different products can be used to define markets.

Empirically Based Market Segmentation. The use of data, measurements, and models for dividing markets into meaningful groups that are based on how and why consumers actually make decisions and choices. Three broad types of empirical procedures were discussed: demand elasticity, market response, and traditional methods.

Hendry Model (market positioning). An analytical procedure for defining markets and based on consumer brand-switching data. This is a type of hierarchical market definition.

Hierarchical Market Definition. The organization of product forms and brands on the basis of similarity and construction of some kind of ordering on the basis of a criterion or criteria (see Figure 6-5). Two common hierarchical market definitions are (1) organization by product form first, then ordering by brand for each product form and (2) organization by producer first, then ordering by product forms for each producer. An advantage of the approach is that it allows the marketer the chance to integrate product characteristics with competitive considerations. It also provides managerial guidelines (see discussion in chapter). The major disadvantage of the approach is that it is not tied closely enough to how consumers actually make decisions and choices. Market-partitioning approaches such as the Hendry model introduce some empirical content but do not go very far. Hierarchical market definitions comprise a category of logical brand market segmentation methods. The Hendry and similar market partitioning approaches introduce some empirical content, but not as much as the empirically based market segmentation procedures discussed in the chapter.

Ideal Point. A concept used in conjunction with perceptual maps. The ideal point represents the consumer's most preferred combination of product attributes. Sometimes the consumer will prefer as much of an attribute as possible (e.g., the greater the economical performance of a car, the better). Alternatively, an intermediate amount of an attribute might be desired such as moderate sweetness in a beverage.

Life-style Segmentation. The identification of groups of consumers as potential buyers and based upon an inventory of their activities, interests, and opinions.

Logic-Based Market Segmentation. The use of pre-determined criteria or rules to divide a market into meaningful groups. The two types discussed were the classification of goods theory and hierarchical market definitions. A general shortcoming of all logic-based approaches is that they are not necessarily rooted in how consumers actually make decisions and choices and may deviate from reality to a considerable degree.

Market Response Method of Market Segmentation. Here the responses of different groups of consumers to various levels of marketing stimuli (e.g., advertising, distribution coverage, etc.) are examined to discover the most fruitful market segments. The responses monitored might be sales, awareness of brand, recall of ads, attitude, intentions, and so forth.

Market Segmentation. The classification of consumers, products, or markets into groups on the basis of their characteristics. There are three broad types of market segmentation: logic based, empirically based, and hybrid approaches (i.e., mixtures of logical and empirical).

Perceptual Map. A mathematical and/or geometric representation of a consumer's (or group of consumers') perceptions or beliefs regarding salient product attributes and where each of a number of brands score on such attributes (see Figure 6-16). Either multidimensional scaling or factor analysis is used to construct perceptual maps (based on consumer responses to certain questions). Perceptual maps are used by management to identify key product attributes desired by consumers, to see where one's brand scores on the attributes in the mind of the consumer, to see where one's brand and the competition lie in relation to each other in the mind of the consumer, and to discover unmet market niches. The information so gleaned can be used to guide product design, pricing, advertising, promotion, and distribution decisions.

Strategic Design Process (for market segmentation). A three-step procedure consisting of

Market Segmentation. Subdivision of consumers, products, and/or markets into meaningful groups and relating the groups to a criterion of interest.

Target Marketing and Product/Brand Positioning. Evaluation of each segment with respect to normative criteria—e.g., organization goals, environmental constraints, competitive forces.

Design of Remainder of Marketing Mix. Communication, pricing, and distribution. See Figure 6-3.

Traditional Methods of Market Segmentation. Examination of individuals and groups of consumers on various variables with the hope of discovering potential purchasers of one's product. Factors used to identify potential users include demographic, geographic, social unit, psychographic, and behavioral variables (see Table 6-3). Often, the segmentation variables will be used to predict psychological and/or action responses as criteria (see Table 6-4). For instance, age, income, social class, and past purchases might be used to predict future intentions to purchase and actual choices made.

CHAPTER
SEVEN

Everywhere chance reigns, just cast out your line and where you least expect it, there waits a fish in the swirling waters.
——Ovid (43 B.C.–17 A.D.)

Men occasionally stumble over the truth, but most of them pick themselves up and hurry on as if nothing happened.
—— Winston Churchill (1874–1965)

He uses statistics as a drunken man uses lamp-posts—for support rather than illumination.
——Andrew Lang (1844–1912)

Do not confuse the finger pointing at the moon with the moon.
——Chinese proverb

Knowledge is of two kinds. We know a subject ourselves, or we know where we can find information upon it.
——Dr. Samuel Johnson (1709–1784)

MARKETING MEASUREMENT: INFORMATION MANAGEMENT AND DEMAND ESTIMATION

Acquiring knowledge and translating it into action is a key to success in the marketplace. The person, organization, or society that better understands the world and is able to change it to its advantage will be the one that accrues superior outcomes. Marketing research is one way to obtain knowledge needed to make effective decisions.

In this chapter, we will examine how firms look at, adapt to, and influence their environments. We will begin with a description of the idea of information and the concept of a *marketing information system* (MIS). The MIS is to the firm as the brain and central nervous system are to the human body. That is, it enables the organization to monitor interpret, adapt to, and control its environment. Next we will outline a number of techniques used to estimate demand for one's products or services. Demand estimation is a pivotal activity in the firm's planning process. It allows management to optimally design production and marketing mix programs, as well as to estimate how well organization goals will be achieved.

Information Management

The Need for Information

A Definition. Information may be defined as *factual knowledge about the characteristics, actions, antecedents, or consequences of (1) social actors outside or inside the firm and (2) the environments within which they operate. Social actors* are consumers, competitors, employees, and institutions (e.g., suppliers, wholesalers, retailers, nonprofit organizations, and government bodies) and their agents. *Environments* are the physical, technological, economic, legal, and social conditions that constrain or facilitate the behavior or function of social actors.

Why is information so important to the marketing function? Basically, ==information is the input to decision making.== The quality and nature of information will affect the efficiency, effectiveness, and relevance of decisions. This, in turn, will determine the ability of the firm to implement its planning, evaluation, and control processes in an expedient way. The latter processes, of course, are important tools for achieving overall firm goals. Figure 7-1 symbolically depicts the dependence of the firm on information.

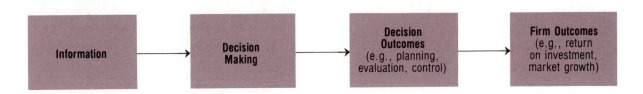

Figure 7-1. The central role of information in decision making and the achievement of organizational goals

==**What Information Is Needed?**== All organizations need accurate, detailed information about their environments and about their ability to respond to and affect those environments. This information includes the environment itself, some aspects of the firm, and some of their relationships.

==*Consumer Behavior.*== First and foremost, the firm needs to know ==who its customers are.== This means doing research to measure consumer attitudes about products and their attributes. Market segments must be identified. Intentions to purchase as well as postpurchase behavior must be assessed, and additional data must be collected on other relevant psychological, social, or economic dimensions of consumers.

What are the needs of our customers? Why do people buy our brands and how do they go about making their decisions? Why do people fail to buy the product class we sell? Why do some people purchase from the competition and not us? How often do people buy our product and how do they use and dispose of it? These are some of the questions firms need to ask about consumers.

==*Aggregate Demand.*== For purposes of planning, the firm needs to know its ==overall sales potential.== The firm needs to estimate demand at the macro level, that is, groups, collections, or aggregates of individual consumers.

Key questions to ask are the following. What is our rate of growth? What market share do we have? How do sales vary by meaningful segments or groups such as geographical region, age of consumer, sex, social class, or life cycle? Do sales fluctuate over time? Does that fluctuation reveal a pattern? Does that pattern indicate a trend, or does it relate to seasonality, periodic cycles, or other regularities? What causes sales? What portion of the market is unaware, aware, shows positive affect or preference, intends to buy, has bought before, etc.? Are there groups of consumers with unmet needs to whom we are not marketing? And so on.

==*The Competition.*== A firm cannot hope to survive without an adequate understanding of its rivals. It needs this information to know where to position its products and how to design its marketing mix to achieve a superior position in the market. The types of questions it must answer are the following.

Who are the market leaders and where does the firm stand in relation to them? At what levels do its products compete? That is, to what extent is competition at the level of (1) generic needs across products, (2) product form variations, and (3) firm rivalry for specific product forms? Does the firm have the resources to take on competitors directly or should it attempt to differentiate itself significantly from competitors and perhaps pursue less competitive markets? Should the firm compete on the basis of price, product attributes, service, or other factors? What are the chances of new rivals entering the market? What are the conditions (economic and otherwise) in the firm, industry, and environment favoring one competitive strategy over another? And so on. Porter considers some of these and other factors in his analysis of competitive strategies.[1]

Political / Legal / Social Environment.

Any action a firm might take, whether this consists of new product introduction, advertising, or whatever, will be constrained or facilitated by the environment in which it operates. Political forces involving the threat or actual use of power must be continually monitored and dealt with one way or the other. Legal restrictions must be heeded. And social demands in the form of ethical, moral, and normative imperatives must be taken into account.

Many questions must be addressed. What special interest groups or publics are affected by or affect our organization, either directly or indirectly? What is the nature of our relationships with suppliers and intermediary firms? What is the balance of power, the opportunity for alternative sources of satisfaction, the degree of mutuality and conflict of interest, etc.? Which laws and regulations affect us? How well are we meeting our social responsibilities to our customers, our competitors, and the general public? How is the organization perceived by the outside world? And so on.

The questions dealing with consumer behavior, aggregate demand, the competition, and the political/legal/social environment are primarily *external* to the firm and are only partially and indirectly under its control. Information needs do not stop here, of course. Much must be learned about the activities, resources, and constraints *within* the organization if an effective marketing program is to be realized. Moreover, much must be learned about the relationships and linkages to the outside world. How effective are the actions that the firm takes or might take in obtaining desired responses from customers and other social actors? The following is a sampling of the information needs of any organization in these senses.

Product Considerations.

We have already detailed the needs of firms with respect to the physical, psychological, and social aspects of products in previous chapters. Basically, the firm must determine what needs its products satisfy, what attributes to build into the product to satisfy these needs, what the level of quality of those attributes should be, how to effectively and efficiently produce the product, when to add or drop a brand or product line, and so on. It must also make decisions with respect to the brand name, logo, warranty, and package. To address these issues, the firm needs information from inside and outside the firm. It obtains this information through market research: laboratory and field tests, surveys, experiments, focus groups, and other techniques that we will discuss later in this chapter.

Distribution Questions.

There are many ways to bring a product to market. The firm must consider all of its options and discover which is most cost effective. It needs information on the benefits and drawbacks of direct marketing (i.e., using company-paid salespersons to sell directly to final customers) versus indirect marketing (i.e., working through intermediaries, such as independent sales representatives or wholesalers). If it decides on the former, then the firm must consider the merits and shortcomings of using its own sales force, mail order, mass media (e.g., television, radio, magazine, newspaper), or the telephone as direct approaches. On the other hand, if it decides to use intermediaries, then it must consider the pros and cons of which type (e.g., agents, brokers, distributors, wholesalers, retailers) and how many to work through. The firm often needs to consider whether to deal with intermediaries on a contractual basis, acquire its own intermediaries, or create its own through internal development or franchise relationships. To evaluate any of the above options, the firm needs information on likely costs, sales volume, the services required to market effectively (e.g., provision of credit, storage, delivery, insurance), and the degree of control and cooperation required to coordinate activities. We will consider distribution issues in much more detail later in the text.

Pricing Considerations. Many things need to be learned about pricing. One is the effect that prices have on the individual consumer and on aggregate demand. Another is the relationship of costs to pricing in terms of breaking even and making a profit. Still another consideration is the legal restrictions on pricing. These and other issues can be addressed through historical analyses and other forms of research, such as surveys or experiments, which investigate the effect of different levels of price on consumption. Pricing issues will also be examined later in the book.

Communication Issues. How can an organization communicate most effectively with its customers and others? To determine this, firms need information on advertising, promotion, and personal selling. They need to know what to say, how to say it, where, and when. Specific questions—about advertising copy, media selection, message repetition, and personnel issues related to the recruitment, selection, training, and management of salespersons—must be addressed. The firm must weigh the effects of advertising versus face-to-face communication versus the use of coupons and other promotional deals. As with all of its information needs, the best way

to gain knowledge is through market research. Communication will be a major topic for discussion throughout the remaining chapters of the book.

Organization Behavior. A final area that firms must consider in their information planning is the internal dynamics among people, groups, and departments throughout the organization. The relationships between social actors within the firm and across departmental lines are central elements determining goal setting, budget allocations, performance evaluations, and everyday decision-making activities. Although the processes involved are in part rational, involving formalization and rules, they are also sometimes "nonrational," encompassing conflict, power, and even randomness. Marketers need to understand the formal and informal side of the organization in order to better achieve their goals. This means being concerned with the design of groups and tasks; the use of persuasion, incentives, and negotiation; and the general management of conflicts of interest and power disparities in productive ways. It is a difficult task to coordinate marketing with production, purchasing, personnel, finance, and other functions. But this must be done to meet consumer needs and compete effectively. The management of the internal affairs of the organization depends heavily on the gathering and use of information. Let us turn now to a central component in this process: the marketing information system.

The Marketing Information System (MIS)

Introduction. A marketing information system is *a collection of equipment, people, and programs in the organization whose function is to monitor, gather, analyze, evaluate, store, and disseminate knowledge.* The hope is that the MIS will better enable the organization to adapt to and/or influence its environment to its advantage. The knowledge generated by an MIS is used directly in decision making and problem solving to help the organization better reach its goals. Although the concept of an MIS is a relatively new one,[2] it has been estimated that 77 percent of major corporations in the United States employ formal MIS's in their operations.[3] Those companies that fail to have a formal MIS generally hire consultants to perform information services and/or have a partial MIS in place.

Figure 7-2 presents an outline of a typical MIS. Before we describe its parts, it is helpful to think of the MIS and its role in the organization in terms of systems theory. That is, we can view the overall operation of the MIS as follows:

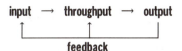

Input in the form of information is selected and acted upon in a throughput system. The throughput system gathers, analyzes, interprets, and stores data. Its output becomes the input to decision making and problem solving and ultimately feeds back to subprocesses within the input and throughput systems. Let us examine the details.

Input. Information arises from the internal and external environments of the organization (see Figure 7-2). In general, information takes either one of two forms. *Evaluative information* has positive or negative consequences for the firm. It might consist of opportunities for the firm to consider or dangers to avoid. The evaluative information might originate from

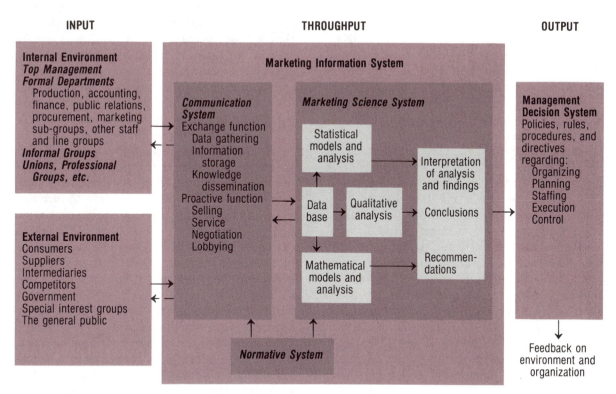

Figure 7-2. A schematic of a marketing information system and its interfaces, inputs, outputs, and feedback

an identifiable source that could directly reward or punish the firm or else it might not be directly mediated by any party, per se, but nevertheless have favorable or unfavorable implications. One example of the former would be a price cut by a competitior designed to take away business from the firm. An example of the latter would be a favorable change in the general economic climate. Most information sought by the firm is evaluative to one degree or another. *Nonevaluative information* consists of factual knowledge with no discernible positive or negative consequences for the firm. Organizations receive considerable amounts of nonevaluative information in their everyday operations and must filter it out. For example, other companies continually attempt to sell products or services to the firm that are not needed, and much available economic data are not essential to the firm's operations.

Table 7-1 summarizes many of the sources of environmental information available to the firm from *outside providers*. We have classified them into two categories: secondary sources and subscription and contractual sources. *Secondary sources* are information compilations formed with no particular user in mind. Rather, they consist of data gathered in a regular way and general enough to be of use to many potential users. The cost to the user is minimal. Indeed, they can be found in most libraries or obtained from their sources at nominal costs. Government publications, directories, indices, journals, and other publications are typical examples. *Subscription and contract sources* are information services operated by research firms for particular users and special purposes and are available for a fee. The cost to the user can be considerable, yet it is less than the cost of the third category of information, primary research. Audits, consumer panels, advertising effectiveness studies, and semistandardized and custom research are the major kinds of subscription and contract sources. The third source of information is *primary research*. It consists of information gathering, analysis, and interpretation performed by the firm itself in order to answer particular questions and solve problems. We will describe some of the ways that this is done shortly, but first we must discuss some of the components of the MIS.

The Communication System. The communication system is the MIS's and firm's conduit to the outside world (see Figure 7-2). It serves as a transfer mechanism receiving information from the internal and external environments, storing selected information for future use, and disseminating information back to the outer world as well as within the organization. These activities are termed the *exchange function* in Figure 7-2 to indicate the interorganizational and intraorganizational contact operations served by the communication system. The activities performed in the exchange function represent back-and-forth transfers of information without necessarily attempting to induce specific responses from the exchange partners. However, as shown in Figure 7-2, the communication system also serves as a means of influence. We have termed this the *proactive function*. Firms are not merely responsive or adaptive to their environments but also attempt to shape and change them. They do this through the provision of attractive and unique product offerings, through persuasive and other influential techniques in face-to-face and mass media selling, and through negotiation and lobbying with their publics. Throughout the remainder of the text, we will find occasion to elaborate on both the exchange and proactive functions performed by marketing organizations. The activities performed in the communication system are most often located in different departments of the firm, although their operations are closely coordinated. Thus, for example, information gathering is done primarily by the market research department and secondarily by virtually all other departments; information storage is performed by the data-processing department as well as other groups; and proactive functions are housed in public relations, sales, distribution and logistics, and advertising sections of the firm.

TABLE 7-1
External Sources of Information Frequently Used by Firms to Gain Knowledge about the Environment

Item	Source	Description
A. Secondary Sources		
1. Survey of Buying Power	Published yearly by *Sales and Marketing Management*, a professional magazine.	Data provided on state, county, and city population, income, and other information that can be used to predict sales
2. U.S. Census of Manufacturers	Published by United States Department of Commerce about every five years.	Data on number of establishments of specific types, number of employees, value added, capital expenditures, etc., by state, county. Useful in estimating demand for industrial goods
3. U.S. Annual Survey of Manufacturers, U.S. Industrial Outlook; County Business Patterns; and numerous other publications	United States Department of Commerce, Washington, D.C.	Further information on markets
4. Private Directories Register of Corporations Million Dollar Directory; Middle Market Directory	Standard and Poor's, published annually Dun and Bradstreet, published annually	Data on specific companies Data on specific companies
5. Statistical Yearbook, and numerous other publications	United Nations, New York	Data on income, population trends, education, gross national product, manufacturing, consumption, etc., for countries throughout the world
6. International Directory of Published Market Research	Undine Corporation, New York City	Listing of over 4,000 published research reports
7. Ulrich's International Periodicals Directory	R. R. Bowker, New York City	Listing of over 60,000 journals, trade publications, etc.
8. Guide to American Directories	Klein Publications, Coral Springs, Florida	Listing of contents of over 6,000 directories
9. Professional and Academic Journals and Newspapers	*Journal of Marketing, Journal of Marketing Research, Marketing Science, Journal of Consumer Research, Journal of Retailing, Journal of Advertising Research, Management Science, Operations Research, Harvard Business Review, Business Horizons, Business Week, Fortune, Wall Street Journal,* etc.	Research on various marketing topics
10. Trade and Professional Associations	Various	Detailed information on products, marketing approaches, etc.
11. Guides, Indexes, and Reference Works	Various libraries	Important sources include: *Business Periodicals Index, Marketing Information Guide, Encyclopedia of Business Information Sources, Data Sources for Business and Market Analysis, Public Affairs Information Service, Handbook of Modern Marketing,* etc.
12. Marketing in Europe: Special Reports	The Economist Intelligence Unit, Ltd., London	Market information on industries and sectors in Europe
13. (a) European Companies: A Guide to Sources of Information;	Beckenham, Kent, England: CBD Research, Ltd.	(a) Market information on business in Europe
(b) Statistics Europe: Sources for Social, Economic, and Market Research;		(b) Lists organizations providing statistical information in Europe
(c) Directory of European Associations		(c) Lists trade, professional, and scientific associations in Europe

(cont.)

TABLE 7-1 (Continued)

Item	Source	Description
14. (a) *European Free Trade Association;*	(a) 1211 Geneva, Switzerland	(a) Information on six European countries
(b) *European Economic Community*	(b) 1049 Brussels, Belgium	(b) Information on nine other European countries
15. *United Nations Educational, Scientific, and Cultural Organization (UNESCO) Publications*	75700 Paris, France	Information and statistics on social and economic conditions around the world
B. Subscription and Contractual Sources		
1. Audits		
(a) *A. C. Nielsen's Retail Index*	(a) Northbrook, Illinois	(a) Audits of drugstores, supermarkets, and mass merchandisers to determine sales, prices, promotion, and advertising at retail level
(b) *Audits and Surveys Product Audit, Inc.*	(b) 1 Park Avenue, New York	(b) Audits of products sold at retail to determine sales, inventory, and distributors
(c) *SAMI Reports*	(c) Selling Areas—Marketing, Inc.	(c) Audits of sales measured by warehouse withdrawal
2. Consumer Panels		
(a) *MRCA Panel*	(a) Market Research Corporation of America	(a) Weekly diary of consumption of goods and services by 7,500 housewives
(b) *Chicago Tribune Panel*	(b) Chicago, Illinois	(b) Panel diary of consumption of everyday products
3. Advertising Effectiveness Services		
(a) *Starch Advertisement Readership Service*	(a) Daniel Starch and staff	(a) Readership of magazines and newspapers through personal interviews
(b) *A. C. Nielsen Television Index*	(b) Northbrook, Illinois	(b) Measurement of size and nature of television audiences for individual TV programs
(c) *Simmons Media/Marketing Service*	(c) W. R. Simmons & Associates Research, New York	(c) Survey of media exposure and product use behavior of consumers
(d) *Burke Scores*	(d) Burke Research, Cincinnati, Ohio	(d) Measurement of day-after recall of advertisements and other consumer reactions
4. Semi-standardized Services		
(a) *National Family Opinion Surveys*	(a) National Family Opinion, Toledo, Ohio	(a) Mail surveys of families tailored to user needs
(b) *Consumer Mail Panel*	(b) Market Facts, Inc., Chicago	(b) Mail survey of consumers
5. Custom Designed Research	More than 400 market research firms in U.S. Many of these are listed in Ernest S. Bradford, *Bradford's Directory of Marketing Research Agencies and Management Consultants in the United States and World*, Middlebury, Vermont: Bradford Co.	Depth interviews, surveys, experiments, focus groups, simulations, etc., specifically designed to answer problems of individual firms

The Normative System. An important, but not often recognized, part of the MIS is the normative system. The normative system is to the MIS as the superego is to the individual or laws and values are to society. The normative system shapes judgments of what is good or bad, what is important or unimportant, and what actions should or should not be taken in the MIS. The normative system translates organizational goals into subgoals, policies, and standards in the MIS. Part of this translation is a formal process sanctioned by the organization. Part of it is an implicit shaping by informal processes of power within the firm.

As shown in Figure 7-2, the normative system influences the communication and the marketing science systems in the MIS in two ways. First, it has all of the implications of the natural selection model (see Chapter 6): the quality and quantity of information entering the organization's decision processes are first dependent on *enactment* operations. The better the organization is able to monitor external variation and generate internal variation, the better the information obtained. Next, information is *selected* on the basis of rational, political, and partly fortuitous processes. Rules, procedures, conflicts of interest, chance, and other factors influence what information is gathered and how well it is selected. The information selected is then evaluated, stored, and implemented in *retention* processes. For details and examples of the natural selection model in marketing, the reader is urged to review the discussion in the previous chapter. The second influence of the normative system on the communication system is to dictate which actions are appropriate to take in the proactive function. This entails evaluating alternative courses for action in terms of organizational goals. It also entails the incorporation of ethical and moral criteria related to what actions are socially acceptable or not.

The normative system also influences the marketing science system by specifying what variables should be studied, what models and methodologies should be employed, what criteria should be used to evaluate the results of research, and what should be done with the findings and conclusions once we have them. Marketers often are unaware of or take for granted the normative forces that shape their research. This is unfortunate, for normative forces are conventions that harbor biases of one form or another. Statistical, mathematical, and data-gathering procedures are not infallible and introduce random and systematic errors into research. The researcher must be aware that any approach chosen to do research has flaws and that other approaches have advantages and disadvantages. While we might not be able to conduct value free research, we should, at a minimum, be aware of our values and their effects and attempt to mitigate their negative impact.

The Marketing Science System. The central element in the MIS is the marketing science system (see Figure 7-2). It receives information from the communication system, processes that information, and produces output needed for decision making. There are five components to the marketing science system: (1) the data base; (2) the statistical models and analysis; (3) the mathematical models and analysis; (4) qualitative analysis; and (5) the products of analysis, including interpretation, conclusions, and recommendations. Let us look at each.

Data Bases. The data base is the information about the environment that the firm needs in its decision-making activities. An organization's analysis and decisions can be no better than the data with which it has to work. We have already noted the important role of enactment, selection, and retention processes in this regard. In addition, we should stress the function of scientific criteria[4] such as reliability and validity, and managerial criteria such as robustness and ease of use. The nature and quality of data are issues to be reckoned with if the firm is to interpret and respond to its environment effectively.

Much of a firm's data base is collected from secondary sources and from subscription and contractual services; some of it comes from the firm's own primary research; and some of it comes from within the firm in the form of "residuals"—the learned experiences, shared wisdom, and culture of the organization.

Organizations attempt to construct formal, readily accessible data bases (e.g., computer systems), and in fact some of the residuals can be codified and incorporated into such objective records. Nevertheless, much of it remains subjectively housed in the minds of managers and elsewhere in the firm's social system in the form of subjective understandings, rules-of-thumb, myths, and the like. It should be remembered that the data base for analysis consists of subjective residuals as well as the objective records.

Statistical Models and Analysis. One way to process and use data is in statistical models. Statistics is a branch of applied mathematics and attempts to achieve three goals: description, evaluation, and hypothesis testing and prediction. A statistical model is a procedure or method for accomplishing these goals. If we want to describe a phenomenon in summary form, we may use descriptive statistics. For example, to describe the attitudes of a group of people toward a new product, we could use the mean (average) score on a seven-point attitude scale and its variation around the mean as a summary of the responses of the group. A nonstatistical way to look at the attitudes would be to write down the score for each person surveyed and use this as our measure of attitudes. But as more and more people are surveyed, it will become increasingly difficult to get an overview because of the proliferation of numbers. Summary descriptive statistics provide a cogent (e.g., two meaningful numbers) indication of attitudes without all the confusion.

Statistics are useful, too, as tools for evaluation. That is, they help us to compare different phenomena and judge which is higher/lower, better/worse, etc., than others. For instance, suppose we suspect that our brand is doing poorly because we have measures indicating people have more positive attitudes toward the competitor's brand than ours. Or suppose that we wanted to evaluate which of two segments to market to and the only data we had concerned the probability of purchase for our brand by individual people in each segment. Statistics could help us in both situations. For the first, we could compare (a) attitudes toward the competition for buyers versus nonbuyers of the competitor's brand, (b) attitudes toward our brand for buyers versus nonbuyers of it, and (c) attitudes of buyers of the competition versus attitudes of buyers of our own brand. The first two comparisons might tell us whether attitudes are possible determinants of purchase of the competitor's brand and of our brand, respectively. The third comparison might help us discover whether people are more satisfied with the competition than with our brand. For the comparison of people in the two market segments, statistics could tell us which of the two groups has a higher probability of purchase, if any. In all of the above examples, the mean and standard deviation of consumer responses for the groups in question are all the information that would be required to perform the comparison. A statistical formula especially designed to make the comparisons would then be applied to the summary statistics (e.g., a t-test or analysis of variance).

A final use of statistics is in hypothesis testing and prediction. Statistical models can be used to estimate the relationships or degree of association between variables and to predict the level of a dependent variable based on independent variables. For example, we might want to discover if there is a relationship between attitudes of consumers and sales and use this information to predict future sales. Statistics provides a method for doing this. Many statistical models are available for analysis. Some of these include correlation, cross-tabulation, regression, discriminant, factor, and cluster analyses.

Mathematical Models and Analysis. Mathematical models are frequently used to examine data in two ways. One, models are constructed to represent marketing phenomena or managerial decisions, and a computer is used to derive the ideal levels or combinations of variables or parameters within the models. These are called optimization models. For example, the following equations represent a simple model for determining the optimal marketing mix of personal selling (PS), advertising (A), and pricing (P):

$$S = k_1(PS)^\alpha A^\beta P^\gamma$$
$$C = k_2 S$$
$$\Pi = (P - C)S - (PS) - A$$

where S = sales, C = cost, Π = profits, k_1 and k_2 are constants, and α, β, and γ are parameters representing the effects of the respective marketing mix variables on sales. Researchers use optimization procedures like the preceding to determine the levels of (PS), A, and P required to maximize Π.[6] The construction of a mathematical model is largely a theoretical and intuitive exercise with the choice of variables to include in the model dictated by normative criteria (e.g., variables under the control of managers are chosen for study). For discussions on how actual empirical findings can be taken account in these models, see Naert and Leeflang[7] and Parsons and Schultz.[8]

A second use of mathematical models is through simulation. Marketing phenomena or decisions are represented mathematically as imperfect models of reality. Instead of attempting to determine an ideal situation according to an objective such as profit maximization, different combinations of levels of variables are manipulated to see their effects. As a result, the outputs one obtains need not necessarily, and often are not, the best. Nevertheless, one can obtain a relatively realistic picture of the effects of changes in independent variables such as advertising or prices upon a dependent variable such as sales.

The following is a simple way to draw the distinction between the two types of mathematical models: optimization depicts events as management would like them to be, and simulation depicts those events as they are more likely to be. Mathematical models offer the advantage of precision, given their assumptions. However, they generally are not as valid as statistical models in terms of their correspondence to the real world. We will discuss some of the leading models at points throughout the remainder of this book.

Qualitative Analysis. Often the firm will not have the data and/ or methodological know-how to perform statistical or mathematical analyses, and sometimes the problems faced by the firm do not lend themselves to quantitative analysis. As an alternative, qualitative approaches—the broad class of methodologies based on observational, subjective, or intuitive skills of the researcher—are used. Examples include depth interviews, participant observation, focus groups, and projective techniques.[9] Qualitative approaches are less structured than quantitative procedures but often address deeper problems and provide richer analyses. However, they are sometimes difficult to use effectively and are best left to persons with considerable experience.

Products of Analysis. The outputs of analysis are results (see Figure 7-2). To be useful, results require interpretation and translation into conclusions and recommendations. Management must relate the meaning of the findings to the needs, goals, and constraints of the organization. In so doing, the influence of the normative system and its specification of research objectives and imperatives must be taken into account. The conclusions and recommendations then serve as input to the managerial decision system (see Figure 7-2).

One final point about the marketing science system deserves mention. Notice in Figure 7-2 that the marketing science system affects the communication system as well as being affected by it. Its impact on the communication system is felt primarily in terms of what information is sought and also what information is communicated to outsiders. Consequently, the models that are used in statistical, mathematical, and qualitative analyses impose restrictions on the communication system. This is not generally recognized by managers, but one analyst nicely identified the interaction a number of years ago in a pioneering book: "One cannot specify what information is needed for decision making until an explanatory model of the decision process and the system involved in it has been constructed and tested."[10] We will describe many of the leading explanatory models used by managers throughout the remainder of the book.

Output. The conclusions and recommendations reached by the MIS through research shape the form and content of decision making throughout the firm. As shown in the right-hand portion of Figure 7-2, the organization constructs policies, rules, procedures, and directives to coordinate and manage the activities of the firm. This occurs through the general functions of organizing, planning, staffing, execution, and control. These functions, in turn, are performed both at the very top of the organization and throughout the subgroups in the firm. We will describe the specific managerial processes when we discuss advertising, promotion, personal selling, channels of distribution, and pricing in later chapters. A final point to note in Figure 7-2 is that the managerial decisions and their effects feed back upon both the environments and organization. The firm is very much an open system evolving in response to internal and external pressures.

The Research Process[11]

A Definition. We may define *marketing research* as the formal process of knowledge generation, discovery, and use. The objective of marketing research is to support decision making and problem solving within the organization. Figure 7-3 presents an outline of the steps taken in the typical research process as seen from the viewpoint of the individual researcher.

The research process begins with a definition of the problem. Here questions are asked, anomalies detected, and new frontiers probed. The researcher asks "why" and "how" questions about the marketplace and/or his or her operations. Why are sales declining? How do consumers make decisions when buying our product? And so on. Objectives are formed as to what needs to be learned. The problem definition is in part guided by the organizational decision that is to be addressed and in part by previous research into similar problems and the creative thinking of both the researcher and management.

Once the problem has been defined, one of two general approaches or research styles might be followed: a deductive track or an inductive track (see Figure 7-3). Actually, in any real research endeavor both deductive and inductive processes will occur in different degrees. Because individual firms and researchers tend to adopt one or the other, we have shown them as separate paths in Figure 7-3. Nevertheless, we should note that, within each path, deductive and inductive thinking may interact, even though one form or the other may predominate.

In the deductive track, problem definition leads to theory formulation. Concepts are specified in the form of independent, intervening, and dependent variables; the concepts are employed in statements in order to construct hypotheses; and hypotheses are arranged and ordered to arrive at formal models of the phenomena to be studied. Overall, the concepts, hypotheses, and models constitute a

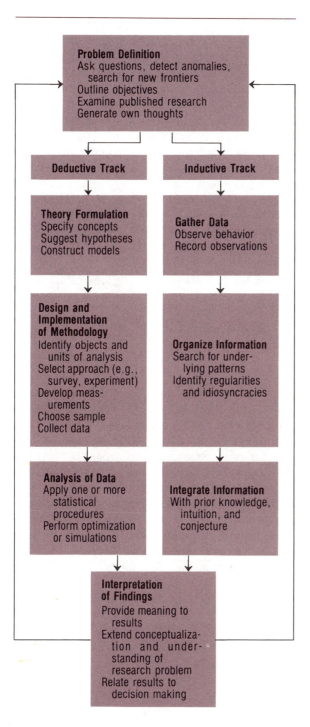

Problem Definition
Ask questions, detect anomalies, search for new frontiers
Outline objectives
Examine published research
Generate own thoughts

Deductive Track

Inductive Track

Theory Formulation
Specify concepts
Suggest hypotheses
Construct models

Gather Data
Observe behavior
Record observations

Design and Implementation of Methodology
Identify objects and units of analysis
Select approach (e.g., survey, experiment)
Develop measurements
Choose sample
Collect data

Organize Information
Search for underlying patterns
Identify regularities and idiosyncracies

Analysis of Data
Apply one or more statistical procedures
Perform optimization or simulations

Integrate Information
With prior knowledge, intuition, and conjecture

Interpretation of Findings
Provide meaning to results
Extend conceptualization and understanding of research problem
Relate results to decision making

Figure 7-3. The process of marketing research

theory to be investigated. The next step in the deductive track is to design a methodology and implement it. This means identifying the objects and unit of analysis for study. For example, do we want to learn about individual consumers, groups of consumers, organizational buyers, societal patterns, or some other level of analysis? A specific research method must then be chosen such as a survey or an experiment. After a research method is chosen, measurements must be developed, a sample chosen, and the data collected. Data analysis is then performed. One might apply one or more of the many available statistical procedures to the data or else perform optimization or simulations in a mathematical model. Finally, the results are interpreted in a form that will produce a deeper understanding of the research problem and suggest solutions and new ideas. Thus, we see a feedback path from interpretation to problem definition in Figure 7-3.

In the inductive track, problem definition leads to data gathering. Data gathering in the inductive track is conducted in a looser, unstructured way and earlier in the process than is true for the deductive track. The focus is on exploration and discovery of meaningful hypotheses rather than testing existing theories. Data are typically gathered through observation (e.g., visually by the researcher, on videotape, through depth interviews, by a tape recorder, etc.). After the data have been recorded, they are ready for scrutiny. An early step in this regard is an attempt at a loose organization of the data. The researcher will review the data and search for patterns, recurring themes and regularities, as well as idiosyncracies and unusual occurrences. Next, the information learned through examination of the data is combined with prior knowledge and intuition and conjectures. Needless to say, this is very much a subjective process, and considerable skill and ingenuity are demanded. The inductive track ends with interpretation of the findings and use of the information to make a decision. It is important to remember that the research process is a continuous one, with an ongoing cycle of conjecture, discovery, further conjecture, etc.

Marketing research is an indispensable part of the functioning of any organization. Sometimes the firm does little research itself but rather relies on outsiders to provide it. More often than not, however, firms conduct many research activities on their own. Indeed, over 73 percent of all large business concerns have separate marketing research groups, and individual units within most firms conduct research on their own as well as through their research departments.[12] In a survey of 798 companies, for example, it was found that 93 percent measure market potentials, 85 percent perform market forecasts, 67 percent study the effectiveness of their ads, 85 percent conduct competitive product studies, 81 percent study the effects of prices, 50 percent conduct consumer panels, and 52 percent perform promotional studies of the impact of premiums, coupons, sampling, and deals.[13] These represent only a portion of the research activities that firms perform.

Three Research Methods. Organizations use many different methods to conduct research. The following briefly describes the three most frequently practiced orientations: surveys, experiments, and open-ended explorations.

Survey Research.

survey research, people are asked to express their ideas, thoughts, beliefs, feelings, intentions, and other responses. For example, a consumer might be asked to indicate his or her degree of liking for a brand of product and intention to purchase it. Usually, this is done through the medium of a questionnaire, which might be administered face-to-face by the researcher, by phone, by mail, or on a computer terminal. The purpose of a survey is generally to learn something about individuals or groups of individuals. Once the data are collected, either descriptive statistics will be used to summarize characteristics of people (e.g., the average stated preference for Deodorant X by men)

or else hypotheses will be tested (e.g., whether attitudes relate to intentions) or predictions will be made (e.g., a forecast of sales based on intentions). The information sought and the questions asked in a survey are relatively structured. A researcher will have a general idea of the kinds of variables to measure and, perhaps, specific hypotheses to test as well. Occasionally, questions from standardized personality and other inventories will be used. Many other issues concerning sample size and selection, questionnaire content, administration procedures, coding, and analysis must be addressed. But these are beyond the scope of this text, and the reader is referred to books on research methods. In this text, focus will be placed on the research questions firms must address and on the knowledge we have to date with respect to these questions. The mechanics of how to conduct research is best left for specialized treatments.

Survey research is an effective and efficient way to gather data. Its major drawback is that statements relating to cause and effect cannot be made with assurance because relationships observed in the survey might be based on spurious associations. For example, we might find a positive correlation between consumers' attitudes toward the decor of a restaurant and their behavior. We might infer, based on the correlation, that people liked the decor and chose the restaurant on this basis. However, causality could have been absent or the direction could have run the other way (e.g., people might have tried the restaurant for no particular reason, and when later asked for their attitude, said they were favorable, not on the basis of their attitude toward the decor, but for other reasons or merely to give a rationale for why they chose the restaurant). If this reverse causal sequence were the true one, then management would be mistaken to spend scarce funds advertising the decor. There are methodological and statistical safeguards that can be employed to improve survey research, but you should be aware that assumptions about causality are often problematic.

Experimental Research. An experiment consists of the manipulation of one or more independent variables (e.g., price or advertising) and the observation of their effects on one or more dependent variables (e.g., sales). In the *true experiment*, people are randomly assigned to treatment and control groups; those in the former are exposed to an independent variable whereas those in the latter are not. Random assignment controls are used to neutralize the effects of extraneous factors that could influence the dependent variable. If a difference should exist between the experimental and control groups on the dependent variable, then we can be confident that it was due to the independent variable and not other factors. True experiments are usually conducted in a laboratory where maximum control of experimental stimuli is possible and external biases can be eliminated. Firms use true experiments in many ways to test product ingredients, package designs, advertising messages, sales presentations, and other aspects of marketing.

A *field experiment* is similar to a true experiment, but rather than occurring in a lab, it is conducted in the real world. As with the true experiment, independent variables are manipulated to determine their effects on a dependent variable of interest. Random assignment to treatment and control groups is done whenever possible. However, less control is feasible in the field experiment with the consequence that extraneous, unknown forces might be at play. Yet, the field experiment offers the advantage of being performed in a realistic setting and thus overcomes the artificiality of the lab setting. Firms use field experiments primarily to test new products, prices, or advertisements. True and field experiments allow the researcher the opportunity to discover causal relations more easily and validly than survey designs. On the other hand, the conduct of experiments is often more difficult and narrower in scope than a survey.

A compromise that is sometimes possible is the *quasi experiment.*[14] An independent variable of interest is found to naturally vary in the field and the opportunity exists to monitor a dependent variable. Quasi-experiments score high in realism and moderately well in their ability to detect causality. The major difficulty is in conducting them since it is not easy to discover or anticipate their occurrence.

Open-ended Explorations. Survey research is a moderately structured approach, and experiments are highly structured. Their strengths lie in their ability to test hypotheses. However, both approaches can obscure more subtle phenomena in the marketplace. What is needed sometimes is an approach that is more sensitive to discovery than to formal hypothesis testing. Fortunately, such approaches exist, and for lack of a better term we call them *open-ended explorations* to describe the collection of largely inductive research methods known variously as focus groups, depth interviews, participant observation, projective techniques, and other names.[15]

The *focus group interview* consists of a small number of people (typically, 6 to 12 persons) gathered together and asked to express their thoughts and feelings on an issue, product, or some other subject. The "interview" is conducted in an unstructured way under the loose guidance of a moderator. The moderator's task is to keep people talking about the subject at hand, to draw out shy or nonverbal people, and to occasionally channel the discussions in fruitful directions through questions or comments. However, the tone of a focus group is decidedly nondirective. People are allowed free reign to express whatever reaction comes to mind, and discussions are permitted to proceed in any direction even tangential to the topic of the session. It is hoped that the free environment and relatively long period of the interview (about 1½ to 2½ hours) will reveal deep consumer needs, motives, beliefs, values, and feelings not easily learned from other methods. To aid in the discovery, the focus group session is usually tape recorded (and sometimes videotaped) for later analysis. Also, researchers or clients will occasionally observe the group from behind two-way mirrors recording verbal and nonverbal responses of group members. Focus groups are used in new product development, product testing, package design, brand name selection, advertising copy, and promotion research. A firm may conduct many focus groups as part of any study. People are chosen for the groups on the basis of their characteristics and membership in a target group. They are generally given a gift or cash award at the end of the session for their cooperation.

Depth interviews are somewhat similar in purpose and form to focus group interviews but are conducted by an interviewer on a one-on-one basis. The objective is to induce the interviewee (usually a typical consumer) to express his or her thoughts, emotions, and values. The target of the questions will consist of both general and specific issues related to the person, a product, or something else. The interviewer will generally ask relatively vague, open-ended questions. This is done so that the interviewee responds on the basis of his or her own psychological makeup and not so much on what he or she thinks the interviewer is looking for. As the interviewee answers questions, the interviewer will either write down every word spoken and other reactions or else record them on a tape recorder. Later, the interviewer or an analyst will analyze the interviews to search for patterns or clues to the interviewee's motives and needs. The interviewer's questionnaire form will leave about one blank page for each question, and the interview will typically take an hour or so. For married couples, separate interviews are sometimes attempted simultaneously in different rooms by different interviewers. The overriding goal of a depth interview is to obtain a rich picture of the underlying forces guiding people's choices and behavior.

Projective techniques are used to detect deep-seated psychological forces in consumers. In the normal application, a vague or ambiguous stimulus is shown to a subject, and he or she is asked to describe what it is, suggests, or means to him or her. The stimulus might be a word, statement, object, or picture. The most frequently used projective techniques are word association, sentence completion, picture drawing, and picture interpretation methods. As with focus group and depth interviews, analysts perform detailed studies and interpretations of a person's responses to projective stimuli in the hope of discovering the underlying causes of behavior.

Open-ended exploratory techniques provide insights into human behavior not easily detected by other, more structured methods. However, they are time intensive, require highly skilled personnel to conduct the research, and are generally regarded as less reliable and valid than some quantitative methodologies. However, because of the limitations inherent in all approaches to marketing research, organizations often use more than one method to provide as rich and detailed a picture as possible.

Demand Estimation

Up to this point, we have discussed the needs of the firm for information and how, in general, the firm might satisfy its needs through measurement and research. The MIS plays a central role in this respect. Now we turn to the issue of demand estimation, one of a number of specific activities performed by the MIS. In later chapters, we will highlight other important research functions that the MIS fulfills.

All organizations face the problem of estimating the demand for their goods and services. Indeed, accurate demand forecasts are required for planning throughout the areas of the firm. The production department uses forecasts to time the scheduling of inputs and outputs and anticipate breakdown and maintenance contingencies. The personnel department needs forecasts to efficiently manage the work force. The procurement and the shipping and receiving departments require demand forecasts to effectively perform their functions. Finance and accounting departments employ forecasts to set budgets and estimate cash flows. Top management desires forecasts to better form strategies and plan, evaluate, and control the overall performance of the firm. And of course, various marketing groups apply forecasts when designing products, setting prices, choosing distribution channels, determining advertising budgets, and conducting other activities associated with the management of the marketing function.

In the remaining part of this chapter, we will discuss how firms estimate demand. We begin with an analysis of the concept of demand. Then we address, in turn, heuristic, subjective, and objective procedures for demand estimation.

The Concept of Demand

At its simplest level, demand for a product or service is the quantity sold. Figure 7-4 shows three ways in which demand might be depicted. Figure 7-4A shows demand (sales) varying with time. As time increases, so do sales. This is perhaps the simplest way to characterize demand, but it does not tell us very much. About all we learn from such a description is how sales have varied in the past and where they are today. Nevertheless, if the forces producing sales follow regular patterns, we may be able to predict, within reasonable tolerances, what subsequent sales will be, merely on the basis of historical data on sales. We will describe the procedures that can be used to accomplish such a forecast shortly. For now, we should note that predictions based solely on past performance have severe data requirements, make strong assumptions, and sometimes are too imprecise to be of real use in planning. The reasons for this are complex and varied but largely stem from the failure to take into account the causes of sales. By not examining the causes, one must rely more on guesswork and also be vulnerable to unexpected changes in existing determinants of sales and the possible emergence of new, latent causes.

Ideally, we would like to model the degree of dependence of sales on its causes so that as the causes vary over time we will be able to estimate how sales might respond. Figure 7-4B depicts this objective. Notice that sales rise as the level of cause C_i increases. We would like to measure C_i at one point in time and perhaps monitor its time path, too. The association between sales and different levels of C_i would then serve as a more sound criterion for prediction than basing one's forecasts on time alone. To use such an approach requires data on at least two variables: sales plus one or more of its causes. Thus, in practice, we can improve predictions if we examine all or most of the important causes of sales. A multidimensional approach would then be required, with each dimension beyond sales consisting of an appropriate cause, C_i. Later in the chapter, we will describe procedures for accomplishing this.

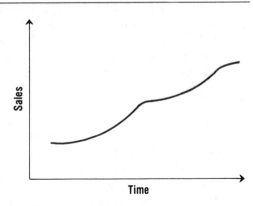

A. Demand (sales) over time

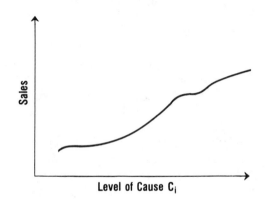

B. Demand as a function of its causes

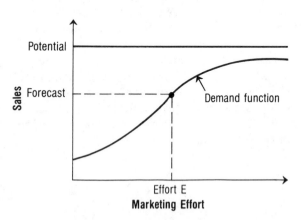

C. Demand as a function of marketing effort

Figure 7-4. Three ways to look at demand

The causes of sales are, in general, twofold. One type is termed *external* or *uncontrollable causes* to indicate that they originate outside the firm and are largely beyond the influence of management. These include such forces as economic conditions (e.g., inflation, disposable income), cultural values, fundamental tastes, the physical environment, government actions, and so on. The firm has no direct control over these, yet they often influence sales. Occasionally, firms are indirectly able to influence the external causes, but their power is limited, and most changes occur slowly if at all. Most of the firm's efforts, therefore, are directed toward the anticipation of changes in the environment or else are focused on the things that they can do to more directly influence sales. In this regard, the *internal* or *controllable causes* take center stage. These are the marketing mix variables (i.e., product design, distribution, communication programs, and pricing strategies)—the stimuli the firm uses to obtain desired responses from the marketplace.

Figure 7-4C presents one way to view the relationship between sales and the variables under the firm's control. We have used the general label *marketing effort* in the figure to point out that the firm can influence sales by varying the amount and nature of one or more of the marketing mix variables at its disposal. The easiest way to measure marketing effort is through expenditures that the firm incurs. For example, we might vary total marketing expenditures to see how sales change, or we might take a portion of total marketing expenditures to see how sales move in response to different advertising or price levels. We would expect that marketing effort is connected ultimately to consumer behavior and that as expenditures rise so will sales. Figure 7-4C shows the relationship as an S-shaped curve to indicate that sales rise first at an increasing, then a decreasing rate before ultimately leveling off. This is a reasonable assumption that meets our understanding of consumer behavior, markets, and past research. The exact shape of the S-curve will vary from industry to industry, firm to firm, and time period to time period because the forces linking the marketing mix variables to sales vary with these factors. In addition, environmental conditions will influence the shape of the S-curve. For example, when the economy is booming, the S-curve will rise quickly, reflecting a high sensitivity of people and markets to marketing stimuli, whereas during times of economic trouble, the S-curve will be flatter and less responsive to marketing stimuli. People simply have more resources and confidence in the former situation than in the latter.

Some additional ideas deserve mention in Figure 7-4C. Notice that the response of sales to marketing effort (which is called a *demand function*) crosses the y-axis at a positive value and reaches an asymptote. This simply reflects the fact that some sales are expected at no or low levels of marketing effort, whereas at very high levels the market will eventually become saturated. The saturation level is termed *potential*, in Figure 7-4C. Another point to note is that, at any one specific level of marketing effort (e.g., effort E in Figure 7-4C), there will be a *forecast* of demand based upon the curve.

It is important to distinguish between industry demand and firm demand. Figure 7-5 illustrates the two concepts. *Industry demand* refers to sales for all firms in a particular industry. The total possible sales for all these firms is called the *market potential*. For a given level of *industry effort* (e.g., E_I in Figure 7-5), one can make a *market forecast* (F_M). Industry effort consists of the sum of efforts from all firms in the industry.

The response of industry sales to industry effort is termed a *market demand function*. Any single firm in the industry will only sell a portion of the market potential, known as *firm demand*. Given its products and managerial know-how, any firm will have a possibility of sales, termed the *firm potential* (see Figure 7-5). The response of firm sales to firm marketing effort is called the *firm demand function*. For both the market and firm demand functions, companies often select three or so levels of effort as forecasts of demand. We have shown three such levels for the firm's demand only in Figure 7-5 to keep the diagram simple. The levels of *firm effort*—E_{f1}, E_{f2}, E_{f3}—might be the lowest, average, and highest amounts of expenditures, respectively, that the firm could contemplate at one particular point in time. Given the firm demand function, these three alternatives would then yield *firm forecasts* of F_{f1}, F_{f2}, and F_{f3}, respectively, representing low, medium, and high predictions. Notice that these predictions are based on *different* possible levels of marketing effort. Another concept to note in Figure 7-5 is that, at any *one* level, the firm will face a range of possible sales forecasts. The range will be a consequence of uncertainty and/or measurement error if based on empirical data. Hence, around the firm demand function, we have drawn an upper bound (U_F) and lower bound (L_F) for forecasting. This simply reflects a range of tolerances for one's predictions. The less the uncertainty and/or the measurement error, the closer U_F and L_F will converge to the firm demand function. Ranges could also have been provided for the market demand function but were omitted for simplicity in Figure 7-5.

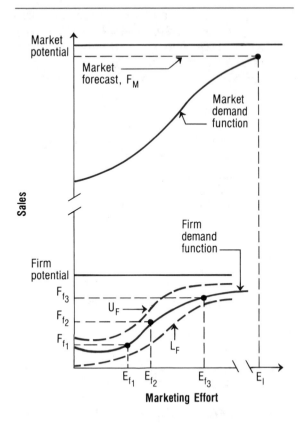

Figure 7-5. Industry and firm demand functions

Before discussing how demand is estimated, the final concept we wish to introduce is *timing*. Firms have different needs for demand estimation, depending on what stage in the life cycle their products are. In new product development, consumer demand is particularly problematic. The firm might draw upon past experience with similar products as a basis for line extensions—products that are "new" in minor ways. But for truly new and distinctive products, demand is especially difficult to estimate. This is largely a consequence of the uncertainty surrounding the consumer's integration of the product concept and its consequences into his or her belief

and affective systems. It takes time, mental effort, and social validation for consumers to become aware of a product, process its features, comprehend its significance, and generally interpret its meaning and decide to purchase it or not. The newer the product, the more difficult and time intensive the process. Also, the newer the product, the less one is able to generalize from past experience. Hence, the learning and interpretation of what a new product is and means for the consumer are very much psychological and social constructions of reality. The paths and outcomes of these processes are difficult to forecast. As a result, demand estimation procedures tend to be highly subjective and rely heavily on qualitative methodologies and managerial judgments. Focus groups and depth interviews are central tools in the decision process. A panel study where employees or possibly a small group of selected consumers are asked to try the product in realistic settings may also prove informative. A small-scale market test might also be employed to gain knowledge about the product's potential acceptability. To forecast demand, management might use the Delphi Method or other expert opinion approaches that will be described later.

During new product introduction, the opportunity for valid feedback is enhanced. Hence, firms might conduct interviews with early adopters or even perform surveys. The idea is to track the responses of consumers in order to detect signs of problems or missed opportunities. The information learned in the introduction stage must then be integrated and used to forecast demand. As in the new product development phase, objective models are lacking and subjective methods based on managerial judgments are most useful.

In the growth, maturity, and decline stages of the product life cycle, more data are available and quantitative techniques can be employed. Some of the ones we will discuss include cross-sectional regression models, time series models, and various other approaches. For a summary of techniques commonly used in practice, see Chambers et al. and Makridakis and Wheelwright.[16]

Heuristic Methods of Demand Estimation

The ultimate aim of forecasting is to arrive at an estimate of firm demand. One way to estimate firm demand is to project market demand and then gauge what portion of the market the firm can hope to win. Three heuristic approaches are frequently used to do this: (1) the chain ratio method, (2) the SIC procedure, and (3) the Index of Buying Power forecast.

The Chain Ratio Method. The Chain Ratio Method is used to predict the demand for a firm's brand and is based on a hierarchical model of interconnected estimates of demand for each of a series of levels in the hierarchy.[17] The idea is that one can begin with an estimate of total potential demand for a product class in a market and then through successive subdivisions move to the demand for a particular brand in that market. An example follows.

Imagine that we desired to estimate the demand for a new heavy beer designed to appeal to two distinct market segments: (1) working and middle class drinkers who seek a hearty "he-man's" beer and (2) sophisticated connoisseurs who want a full-bodied beer, yet one worthy of their cosmopolitan self-image. Company X, the developer of the new heavy beer, feels that a market for each exists but needs to know if potential demand will make entry worthwhile. The firm has already decided to market two separate brands to the segments and has named them "Paul Bunyan Brew" and "European Export,"

respectively. The names were based on research showing that some outdoors-oriented working and middle class beer drinkers preferred heavier beers, and some upper class beer drinkers preferred heavier beers as well. Yet, no domestic beer and few imports fit their needs.

There are two ways to apply the Chain Ratio Method. One is to begin with the entire population in a region as the potential market and then begin to break this down into submarkets until one is left with the market available to the firm. For example, the following provides an abbreviated illustration for the two brands of heavy beer for Company X:

40,000,000	Population in Midwest (Company X's market area)
× $40.00	Per capita expenditures on alcoholic beverages
$1,600,000,000	Total expenditures on alcoholic beverages per year
× .4	Percentage spent on beer
$640,000,000	Expenditures for beer per year
× .05	Estimated percentage that will be spent on heavy beer
$32,000,000	Total expenditures on heavy beer
× .80	Estimated share by Paul Bunyan Brew
$25,600,000	Total potential expenditures on Paul Bunyan Brew
$6,400,000	Total potential expenditures on European Export

These totals represent estimates of sales assuming no competition. Possible competitive entries must be taken into account along with production and marketing costs to assess whether Company X should market the new beers.

The second way to use the Chain Ratio Method is to begin with total industry sales for a product class and refine the sales estimate through various assumptions. To illustrate:

$600,000,000	Total sales of beer in Midwest market
× .30	Percentage of all beer drinkers who consume specialty beer
$180,000,000	Total expenditures on specialty beer
× .60	Percentage of specialty beer drinkers who might try heavy beer
$108,000,000	Potential expenditures if all who try become regular purchasers
× .20	Percentage who try who do become regular drinkers
$21,600,000	Potential expenditures on heavy beer
× .80	Estimated share by Paul Bunyan Brew
$17,280,000	Total potential expenditures on Paul Bunyan Brew
$4,320,000	Total potential expenditures on European Export

Notice that the two implementations of the Chain Ratio Method in our example yield different estimates of demand. Why the discrepancy? At least two shortcomings of the Chain Ratio Method can be identified. One problem concerns the choice of multipliers. Many different multipliers may be chosen. Yet, we are generally lacking criteria to guide such a choice. In other words, little is known about the validity of one multiplier or another. Second, for whatever multipliers one chooses, measurement error is sure to exist, given the high level of abstraction of the concepts and fallibility of observations. Moreover, error in any one multiplier will carry throughout the analysis, given the dependency of each level in the hierarchy on preceding levels. For these reasons, use of the Chain Ratio Method must be regarded with caution. Perhaps different sequences should be pursued to obtain a convergence. And efforts should be made to give a sound rationale for any multipliers used and to use good measurements. Finally, it is probably best to employ other procedures along with the Chain Ratio Method as complementary analyses.

One of the weakest links in the Chain Ratio Method is the estimation procedure used to compute a firm's potential sales as a fraction of the forecast sales for a market. In the above examples, 5 percent of all expenditures for beer and 20 percent of all those specialty beer drinkers who would try heavy beer were predicted to be the two estimates of demand for the firm's beer, respectively. The problem with these estimates is that they do not directly take into account competitive conditions or specific marketing mix efforts used. One way to do this is to use a multiplier to represent the ratio of specific marketing expenditures to the expenditures of all firms in a market. For example, the following multiplier might be used:

$$ms_i = \frac{A_i^{e_{a_i}} P_i^{-e_{p_i}}}{\Sigma (A_i^{e_{a_i}} P_i^{-e_{p_i}})}$$

where ms_i is Firm i's share of the market, A_i is Firm i's expenditures on advertising, P_i is Firm i's price for the product in question, and e_{ai} and e_{pi} are the elasticities of advertising and price, respectively, for Firm i. The elasticities express the percent change in demand for a 1 percent change in the appropriate marketing mix variable. The equation expresses the hypothesis that the effectiveness of Firm i in stimulating demand will be in proportion to its marketing expenditures relative to all competing firms. More complicated formulae for computing market share can be formed that take into account all marketing mix stimuli, the differential effectiveness of each firm, and so on. But discussion of these is beyond the scope of this text.[18]

The SIC Method. A common procedure used to estimate demand for industrial goods and services is the Standard Industrial Classification (SIC) Method.[19] In this approach, demand for particular geographical regions (e.g., sections of the country, states, counties, standard metropolitan statistical areas, cities) is estimated on the basis of number of establishments, employees, value of production (or in some cases sales or payroll), and other factors.

Table 7-2 presents an outline of the SIC system and some of its categories. As shown at the left of the table, there are 11 principal divisions under which establishments are classified. The basis of classification is by the type of activity with which the establishment is engaged. An establishment is defined as "an economic unit, generally at a single physical location where business is conducted or where services or industrial operations are performed."[20] Notice that an establishment differs from an enterprise or company. The latter are broader categories and may consist of more than one establishment. Also notice in Table 7-2 that each of the 11 principal divisions can be further subdivided into major group numbers. We have taken the manufacturing category and listed the 20 major groups underneath it as an illustration. It should be kept in mind that each principal division in the SIC system has many major subgroups. Next, note that each major group can be partitioned into subgroups. We have shown the subgroups for Major Group 20, Food and Kindred Products. There are 9 subgroups under this major group. Finally, each subgroup can be segmented into clusters of industries with each given an industry number. Table 7-2 shows the 6 industry clusters under Subgroup Number 208, Beverages. Although we have not shown it in Table 7-2, it is possible to even obtain a more detailed classification than by the four-digit industry number. In fact, the Bureau of the Census provides a seven-digit code consisting of three numbers past the standard SIC code. The fifth digit represents product class, the sixth and seventh individual products. For example, 35331 signifies screens, tubing, and catchers for rotary oilfield and gasfield drilling machinery and equipment. Thus, you can see that very many detailed classifications exist for industrial products.

What good is the SIC system? Its primary use is by firms marketing industrial products. The best way to grasp its value and use is through an example. Imagine that you are a manufacturer of a new bottle filling and sealing device (BFSD) and wish to estimate demand for your product. The initial

TABLE 7-2

Summary of the Standard Industrial Classification (SIC) System

Principal Divisions in SIC	Major Group Number	Subgroup Number	Industry Number
01–09 Agriculture, Forestry, & Fishing	20 Food and Kindred Products	201 Meat Products	2082 Malt Beverages
10–14 Mining	21 Tobacco Manufacturers	202 Dairy Products	2083 Malt
15–17 Construction	22 Textile Mill Products	203 Canned and Preserved Fruits and Vegetables	2084 Wines, Brandy, and Brandy Spirits
20–39 Manufacturing	23 Apparel Products	204 Grain Mill Products	2085 Distilled, Rectified, and Blended Liquors
40–49 Transportation, Communications, Electric, Gas, & Sanitary Services	24 Lumber and Wood Products, except Furniture	205 Bakery Products	2086 Bottled and Canned Soft Drinks and Carbonated Water
50–51 Wholesale Trade	25 Furniture and Fixtures	206 Sugar & Confectionery Products	2087 Flavoring Extracts and Flavoring Syrups, Not Elsewhere Classified
52–59 Retail Trade	26 Paper and Allied Products	207 Fats and Oils	
60–67 Finance, Insurance, & Real Estate	27 Printing, Publishing, and Allied Industries	208 Beverages	
70–89 Services	28 Chemicals and Allied Products	209 Miscellaneous Food Preparation and Kindred Products	
91–97 Public Administration	29 Petroleum Refining and Allied Industries		
99 Nonclassifiable Establishments	30 Rubber & Miscellaneous Plastic Products		
	31 Leather & Leather Products		
	32 Stone, Clay, Glass, & Concrete Products		
	33 Primary Metal Industries		
	34 Fabricated Metal Products, except Machinery & Transportation		
	35 Machinery, except Electrical		
	36 Electrical and Electronic		
	37 Transportation		
	38 Measuring, Photographic, Medical, Optical, Watches, etc.		
	39 Miscellaneous Manufacturing Industries		

Source: Standard Industrial Classification Manual, Washington, D.C.: Office of Management and Budget, 1972.

step is to identify all potential users of your BFSD. We might begin by selecting all SIC industry codes that could employ a BFSD in their operations. How does one know which industries use BFSDs? We could check our existing customers and see which industry clusters they fall into. In addition, we might solicit the opinions of our sales force because they know the industry. Finally, we might perform phone surveys, conduct studies of the literature, search through the SIC manual, and choose potential customers based on intuition or even hire outside consultants.

Suppose the firm decides that manufacturers of malt beverages (2082), fluid milk (2026), bottled and canned soft drinks and carbonated water (2086), and groceries and related products, not elsewhere classified (5149), are its most likely prospects. (The SIC code 5149 was considered because it covers bottling of natural spring and mineral waters.) Then the firm's next task is to choose

a criterion for estimating the number of BFSDs that will be sold to each type of industry. In Table 7-3, we have listed two SIC industry clusters to show how one might estimate demand. Column 1 shows four sizes of malt beverage producers and five sizes of fluid milk producers, respectively. The size of each producer is based on the number of employees for each. Column 2 shows the number of firms at each size. The data in columns 1 and 2 are available from the *Census of Manufacturers*. To forecast market potential for the BFSD, the manufacturer must estimate the number of units used by each size firm (column 3) and the percentage of these that might require replacing in any year (column 4). The data for columns 3 and 4 might be obtained from past experience or by surveying the potential buyers. To estimate market potential, one simply multiplies columns 2, 3, and 4 and sums the results. Performing these operations yields about 93 BFSDs needed for replacement each year.

TABLE 7-3
Estimation of Market Demand for the New Bottle Filling and Sealing Device

SIC Industry Number	Industry Name	1 Size of Firm (# of Employees)	2 Number of Firms	3 Estimate of Number of Units Used for Each Size	4 Percentage of Firms Needing Service during Any Year	Market Potential $2 \times 3 \times 4$
2082	Malt Beverages	1–9	25	1	.01	.25
		10–99	47	2	.01	.94
		100–499	71	4	.02	5.68
		500+	24	5	.03	3.60
2026	Fluid Milk	1–4	657	1	.005	3.28
		5–19	563	2	.01	11.26
		20–49	499	3	.01	14.97
		50–99	405	4	.01	16.20
		100+	373	5	.02	37.30
						≈ 93

SOURCE: 1972 Census of Manufacturers

An estimate of market potential does not complete the manufacturer's task. One must take into account the competition and estimate market share. One must also consider demand arising from overall growth in the GNP and not merely replacement sales. Finally, the manufacturer must identify specific firms so that it can contact them to make a sale. *Dun's Market Identifiers* or other publications might be an aid in this regard.

One final point to note is that any real use of the SIC method would generally be more detailed than we described here. The example in Table 7-3 is based on data for the entire country and includes only two of a number of possible industry clusters. In a more typical usage, market potential would be estimated separately for each of a number of geographical areas and for all potential industry clusters within these areas. One could then add up the market potential for each area to hopefully obtain a more valid estimate of total market demand. It is also important to stress the need for research into the determination of estimates of usage and demand at the level of each size of firm for each industry cluster.

The Index of Buying Power Method. A useful procedure for estimating the demand for consumer goods is the Index of Buying Power Method. This is a simple mathematical formula that can be used to compute the market's ability to buy on the basis of a weighted average of the population, income, and retail sales in that market. The Buying Power Index (BPI) is published by *Sales & Marketing Management* magazine in July of each year and is prepared for geographical regions in both the United States and Canada. Specifically, for the United States, data are provided on individual states, counties, consolidated metropolitan areas, and cities. For Canada, the breakdown is by province, counties, metropolitan areas, and cities.

Table 7-4 presents sample data on population, retail sales, and effective buying income for Detroit and the surrounding metropolitan area. In addition to the *Survey of Buying Power, Sales & Marketing Management* also publishes data on retail sales by product category in metropolitan markets, newspaper market reach, television market reach, and other information.

The BPI for a particular geographical area is computed as

$$BPI_i = .5I_i + .3R_i + .2P_i$$

where I_i is the percentage of Effective Buying Income (EBI) in area i, R_i is the percentage of net retail sales, and P_i is the percentage of national population in area i. The EBI is further defined as personal income less personal tax and nontax payments. The coefficients or weights in the BPI equation (i.e., .5, .3, and .2) were derived from empirical data and regression analyses.

To take an example, suppose that we wanted to estimate the potential sales for an electric shaver. The first step is to compute the BPI for a target area. Suppose that one target area is the Detroit suburban area. Then the BPI for the Detroit suburban area can be computed as

$$BPI_D = .5(1.7170) + .3(1.8682) + .2(1.3852)$$
$$= 1.6962$$

where P is read directly from Table 7-4 and I and R are calculated respectively as the ratios of the Detroit suburban total to the U.S. total. As a consequence, we conclude that about 1.70 percent of the total U.S. retail sales potential resides in the suburban Detroit area. The next step to estimate potential sales for the electric shaver is to multiply the BPI by the nationwide sales of the firm's electric shavers. For instance, if national sales were $50 million, then one would expect sales in suburban Detroit to amount to $848,100 (i.e., $50,000,000 × 0.016962).

TABLE 7-4
Representative Data for Index of Buying Power Method of Demand Estimation

MICHIGAN

MICH. SMM ESTIMATES — METRO AREA / County / City	Total Population (Thousands)	% of U.S.	Median Age of Pop.	% of Population by Age Group 18–24 Years	25–34 Years	35–49 Years	50 & Over	Households (Thousands)	Total Retail Sales ($000)	Food ($000)	Eating & Drinking Places ($000)	General Mdse. ($000)	Furniture/ Furnish./ Appliance ($000)	Auto-motive ($000)	Drug ($000)
DETROIT	4,345.0	1.9016	29.8	12.7	16.8	17.2	24.1	1,523.2	20,786,278	4,411,732	1,969,436	2,760,804	1,010,971	3,775,952	943,536
Lapeer	72.0	.0315	27.8	11.7	17.9	15.7	21.4	22.0	225,009	63,393	19,705	8,216	7,704	44,731	15,496
Livingston	103.7	.0454	28.7	10.9	18.4	16.2	22.3	32.6	354,663	88,402	37,495	30,719	13,198	48,891	19,067
Macomb	699.1	.3059	28.6	12.2	19.8	19.0	18.4	235.0	3,685,942	891,687	304,048	445,268	203,530	726,476	169,242
East Detroit	37.6	.0165	33.1	12.3	13.1	20.1	27.4	13.3	300,305	65,298	14,844	2,543	14,804	123,513	17,864
Roseville	53.6	.0235	27.2	14.8	19.9	17.7	16.7	18.1	311,059	73,989	27,928	91,954	13,237	23,978	14,934
St. Clair Shores	75.0	.0328	30.8	10.9	15.9	21.8	21.5	26.0	295,382	75,009	40,340	25,903	12,280	40,386	19,593
Sterling Heights	110.7	.0484	26.3	10.1	21.6	17.8	13.5	33.6	787,583	157,771	42,705	163,860	36,148	179,840	20,630
Warren	159.0	.0696	28.7	11.0	20.8	20.2	16.7	53.7	804,699	254,925	81,415	70,508	45,265	116,391	28,845
Oakland	1,019.5	.4462	29.7	12.4	17.4	18.4	22.4	363.2	5,976,644	1,133,217	591,045	828,721	344,734	1,027,383	247,788
Pontiac	76.1	.0333	28.1	15.8	17.8	14.1	23.5	26.8	337,223	52,273	25,645	53,620	12,566	79,446	13,315
Royal Oak	70.0	.0306	31.1	12.9	17.7	17.5	25.6	27.7	421,357	60,513	43,105	21,704	24,106	109,010	13,118
Southfield	75.9	.0332	32.8	10.7	14.6	20.4	26.3	28.2	1,115,533	122,594	125,711	277,880	72,075	152,515	34,590
St. Clair	140.3	.0614	30.1	12.0	15.1	15.6	27.0	48.2	534,727	125,652	60,328	51,539	23,976	73,875	26,882
Wayne	2,310.4	1.0112	30.5	13.2	15.5	16.4	26.6	822.2	10,009,293	2,109,381	956,815	1,396,341	417,829	1,854,596	465,061
Allen Park	33.7	.0147	31.9	11.4	13.2	21.0	24.9	11.5	120,392	36,795	19,726	8,807	8,307	7,983	10,481
Dearborn	89.5	.0392	36.1	12.2	12.7	17.2	34.2	34.3	1,228,882	98,111	110,022	208,423	75,943	312,465	56,635
Dearborn Heights	66.7	.0292	29.0	11.0	17.1	19.3	19.9	22.2	257,973	80,737	43,537	1,678	6,967	14,685	8,475
• Detroit	1,180.0	.5164	31.8	13.5	14.8	15.0	30.2	448.3	2,743,764	632,520	320,378	182,482	94,240	590,411	132,678
Garden City	35.2	.0154	25.8	11.2	17.7	20.2	13.6	10.9	182,858	11,986	21,289	6,526	3,008	78,464	2,249
Lincoln Park	44.4	.0194	29.6	14.9	14.7	19.2	22.8	15.5	263,586	73,335	15,335	46,124	10,259	22,223	15,609
Livonia	104.2	.0456	27.9	8.5	17.2	21.9	15.9	30.2	872,639	182,835	56,325	145,929	74,556	107,732	44,941
Taylor	78.1	.0342	25.4	13.1	21.2	17.2	12.5	23.8	585,807	117,260	39,432	156,223	13,564	92,122	20,390
Westland	84.3	.0369	26.4	12.4	22.8	16.7	13.7	26.8	502,436	127,710	37,124	109,294	10,222	71,049	21,844
Wyandotte	33.5	.0147	30.7	13.9	14.0	16.1	27.9	12.2	60,677	12,006	10,172	4,584	8,172	5,521	4,966
SUBURBAN TOTAL	3,165.0	1.3852	29.2	12.4	17.6	18.0	21.9	1,074.9	18,042,514	3,779,212	1,649,058	2,578,322	916,731	3,185,541	810,858
TOTAL U.S.	228,497.1														

MICH. (cont.) SMM ESTIMATES — METRO AREA / County / City	Total EBI ($000)	Median Hsld. EBI	% of Hslds. by EBI Group (A) $8,000–$9,999	(B) $10,000–$14,999	(C) $15,000–$24,999	(D) $25,000 & Over	Buying Power Index
• Detroit	9,704,728	19,440	4.7	11.8	27.8	34.5	.4560
Garden City	316,972	28,414	1.8	4.8	24.1	63.7	.0175
Lincoln Park	414,841	25,816	2.9	6.8	26.7	53.1	.0235
Livonia	1,044,613	32,836	1.2	3.2	16.9	74.6	.0650
Taylor	634,028	25,950	2.0	6.1	31.7	53.9	.0425
Westland	751,438	26,974	1.8	6.3	28.9	57.7	.0437
Wyandotte	290,873	22,933	3.3	8.7	30.4	42.8	.0128
SUBURBAN TOTAL	31,149,816	26,379	2.7	7.4	25.4	54.3	1.6962
TOTAL U.S.	1,814,106,815						

Notice that suburban Detroit, with about 1.38 percent of the U.S. population, is expected to account for 1.70 percent of potential sales. This might indicate that people from outside suburban Detroit account for some of the extra expected sales. Therefore, the manufacturer must keep in mind that his or her advertising and promotion programs will probably have to reach beyond suburban Detroit. In any event, the BPI can be used as a rough guide in planning. For example, some firms use it to allocate their advertising, promotion, and personal selling efforts. The most typical rule is to devote a percentage of the total budget in proportion to the BPI for the area. Thus, in suburban Detroit, the manufacturer of the electric shaver might apportion 1.70 percent of his or her national budget for advertising to this area. Of course, other factors might be taken into account, such as the need to cover a wider area if buyers from outside the area regularly shop there or the desire to meet competition. Thus, firms might allocate more or less than the BPI, depending on other strategic goals.

According to *Sales & Marketing Management*, the "BPI . . . is most useful in estimating the potential for mass products sold at popular prices. The further a product is removed from the mass market, the greater the need for a BPI modified by more discriminating factors—income, age, sex, etc."[21] Notice, therefore, that the methodology applies more to moderately priced goods than to very low-priced (e.g., food products) or very high-priced goods (e.g., automobiles). Notice further that the model is regarded as a rather crude predictor and that other factors—sociodemographic, psychological, etc.—might be important to consider. Firms often find it advantageous to develop more complex models tailored to their specific products and markets than is provided by the BPI. Also, note that the BPI is a means for estimating total potential and does not really indicate what marketing mix variables will influence sales. Other approaches and criteria are needed to provide managers guidance on how marketing mix stimuli will influence sales in an uncertain, competitive environment. We will mention some of these later.

Subjective Methods of Demand Estimation

Heuristic methods of demand estimation are intended primarily for determining market potential. They are rules-of-thumb loosely based on empirical data and are designed to have wide applicability for many products in many markets. As such, they are sometimes too general and too abstract to be of much service for particular applications. Another weak point with heuristic approaches is that the estimation of firm demand as a fraction of market potential lacks a sound rationale and at the same time builds upon an often fallible market potential estimate. On the positive side, heuristic methods provide a useful starting point in demand estimation.

We turn now to subjective methods that are both more empirically based and closer to the demand situations of specific firms. These approaches are designed to provide more direct estimates of firm demand. They are subjective to the extent that they rest on the judgments of either managers or consumers, yet in recent years, efforts have been made to quantify them. Furthermore, as we learn more about how managers and consumers actually make judgments, we should be able to improve upon these approaches. The three subjective methods most often used[22] are the jury of executive opinion, the sales force composite, and the intention to buy survey methods. We will briefly describe these below.

The Jury of Executive Opinion. Perhaps the simplest procedure for making forecasts is to ask managers for their best guesses. This can be done in a number of ways. One is to have a panel of managers meet face-to-face, discuss possible forecasts, and then reach a consensus estimate. Research in organization behavior suggests that such group-based judgments are better than individual decision making, decision making by individual vote, or the decision constructed from the average votes of all individuals in a group.[23] However, the social visibility and status and personality differences among participants can bias the final judgment in adverse ways.[24]

A somewhat better way to arrive at subjective estimates is by use of the Delphi Method.[25] Under this procedure, the judgments of individuals in a group of experts are solicited anonymously (usually by questionnaire). Then the median judgment is computed and communicated to the individuals in the group who are again asked to make a new judgment. In practice, it has been found that such a procedure quickly leads to a consensus, typically within two rounds. The premise is that a consensus so reached will be close to the true demand to be estimated. At least it is believed that the Delphi Method will be more valid than individual judgments or other group-based decisions.

The Delphi Method has been applied in marketing with some success.[26] It appears to be most reliable when about 5 to 10 group members are used and when the members are experts as opposed to nonexperts—that is, people who know the market and the business, as opposed to those less knowledgeable. In addition, the approach represents an easily implemented procedure that quickly provides estimates. Its major drawback lies in the biasing influence of group feedback, which, while less troublesome for face-to-face feedback, might still produce invalid judgments. Moreover, because the approach is predicated on judgments made by individuals, it contains all the limitations common to human judgment.[27] Despite these limitations, it can be a useful adjunct to decision making.

The Sales Force Composite Method. Many firms selling industrial products and some selling consumer goods solicit opinions from their sales forces as to potential demand for their goods. The simplest way this is done is to ask salespeople for overall sales estimates in their territories. They are generally asked to do this by each product in their respective product lines. Management then adds up the estimates of its sales force to arrive at a total for the company. The logic behind the sales force composite method is that salespeople should be very knowledgeable about future potential sales to existing customers and can provide valid estimates also of undeveloped potential in their territories and the chances of taking business away from the competition. The shortcoming of the approach is that salespeople may systematically underestimate sales in order to keep their quotas low and subsequently appear to be high sales performers. To counteract this tendency somewhat, management sometimes allocates sales support, promotional, and advertising budgets on the basis of the salesperson's estimates.

A number of things can be done to improve estimates based on salespeople's judgments. One is to ask salespeople for their degree of uncertainty (or their confidence) in their estimates. This can then be used to weight or discount their estimates. Another tactic is to combine each salesperson's estimate with estimates provided by the district and regional sales managers. A third possibility is to apply a correction factor to each person's estimate based on his or her history of over- or underreporting. Finally, subjective judgments might be combined with objective estimates such as those generated by surveys of buyers or quantitative forecasts.

A final point to note is that the judgments of salespeople are liable to the same problems plaguing all human judgment methods.[28] Unfortunately, we know very little about the empirical adequacy of the sales force composite approach, and much more research is needed.[29]

Demand Estimation through Buyer Intentions. The jury of executive opinion and and sales force composite methods rely on the subjective judgments of managers; that is, the sellers. One may also estimate demand on the basis of the stated intentions to purchase as provided by buyers. In the typical application, buyers are surveyed by phone, mail, or personal interview and are asked to express their intentions to purchase a product class and/or brand, among other queries. Usually, they are able to express their intentions to purchase as a matter of degree and with respect to a particular time horizon (say, six months or a year). The responses of buyers are then added up and used to generate potential market estimates and brand shares. The approach has been found to be of limited success for forecasting consumer durables and industrial goods and gaining an indication of the potential of new products. A typical intention question follows:

What is the probability that you will purchase a television within the next year? (Circle the appropriate probability)

No chance				50-50				Certain		
0	.1	.2	.3	.4	.5	.6	.7	.8	.9	1.0

Intentions are not always related strongly to behavior. One reason is that people's needs, judgments, and evaluations change between the time of measurement of their intentions and the opportunity to act. Further, events change, economic conditions fluctuate, competitors come and go, prices jump up or down, and so on. Hence, we might not expect intentions to be strong predictors of behavior as time passes. Another problem concerns the measurement of intentions. It is important to measure intentions at the same level of specificity as the behavior to be predicted. For example, if we want to learn if people plan to attend a particular concert, we should ask their intentions to attend that concert and not merely their intentions to attend concerts at an unspecified time in the future. In general, intentions and behavior can correspond according to action, target, context, and time. There have been a number of recent developments in the measurement of intentions and the prediction of behavior, but they are too complex to discuss here.[30]

Objective Methods of Demand Estimation

Forecasting Based on Past Sales. Perhaps the simplest forecasting approach is to make predictions of future sales on the basis of past sales. We will discuss a number of procedures that work on this principle, but first let us define some useful concepts.

If we look at the pattern of sales for typical firms over time, it is possible to identify a number of underlying "forces" behind the observed sales. Figure 7-6 presents sales for Firm X for each quarter over a three-year period (1982-85). Notice that actual sales fluctuate from quarter to quarter but generally increase over the long run, as shown by the straight line running through the actual data. A more or less constant rise or fall in sales over time is termed a *trend*. A closer look at the pattern of actual sales, however, reveals that sales rise by a relatively constant amount for the first two quarters of each year but jump sharply in the third quarter before again falling to a level indicative of the overall trend. The jumps are marked with S's in Figure 7-6. Unusual rises or falls in sales that occur periodically over short periods of time (within a year) are called *seasonal* fluctuations. Seasonal fluctuations might be caused by such forces as legal restrictions, holiday spending habits, religious practices, weather, salary and payroll disbursement customs, labor force practices, manufacturer constraints, conventions in wholesale or retail trade, or particular cultural rituals. The third quarter jump in sales for Firm X might reflect advance orders made by wholesalers and retailers in anticipation of the Christmas rush. Trend patterns reflect longer-term forces than do seasonal changes. For example, a trend may be in response to a gradual fall or rise in disposable income, population, inflation, or innovation in a society. It might also be a consequence of basic changes within an industry or the firm itself over an extended period of time (say, 5 to 10 years).

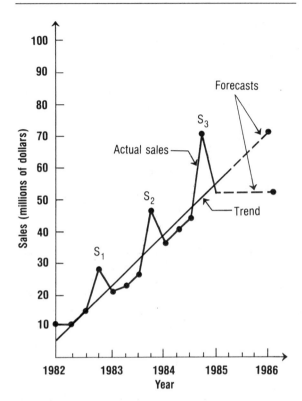

Figure 7-6. Sales for Firm X over a three-year period (1982–85) illustrating the concepts of trend and seasonality

Although not shown in Figure 7-6, three other temporal forces deserve mention. One is changes due to *cycles*, recurring and very long-run (every 10 to 25 years or more) changes in sales. The most well known in this regard is the *business cycle*. Economists believe that a very long-run cyclical change in the economy underlies most societies and that this change is independent of shorter-run forces such as associated with trends, seasons, wars, recessions, and other factors. Depending on the theorist, peaks of great prosperity and severe depressions are thought to occur about every 40 to 75 years. In the years in between, we see a very gradual, but steady, rise and fall.

Because sales for individual firms are so idiosyncratic to the practices of that firm and the industry and target market characteristics within which it operates, most data on long-run business cycles are not very meaningful to the firm's operations. The most relevant cycles to consider are those associated with a firm (e.g., the product life cycle), industry (e.g., competitive cycles), or the economy in the medium run. Unfortunately, except for the product life cycle, we know very little about the forces underlying the cycles and their effects.

Another factor to consider is *random error*. Any measurement of sales will contain an element of "noise" manifest as irregular over- or underestimates of the true level of sales. Random error is caused by many sources, some of which include imprecise measurement instruments, poor recordkeeping, and other haphazard or nonuniform disturbances impinging on sales. Generally, random error is small in magnitude.

The final factor affecting sales is termed *systematic error*. Systematic error occurs as a regular or steady influence on sales. We differentiate systematic error from trend or seasonality, which are also regular, in the following way. Trend and seasonality are global or summary effects produced by one or many largely unidentified sources. Systematic error is that part of trend or seasonality that either can be (eventually) identified and separated from the latter or else is not highly correlated with it. One example of a systematic error effect might be an action by a competitor such as a price cut. Another might be the influence a firm has over its own sales when it increases advertising. Forecasts based on past sales do not explicitly take into account systematic error, and when it is uncorrelated with trend or seasonal effects, it makes such forecasts less useful. Under these conditions, the theory-based forecasting methods we discuss at the end of the chapter become advantageous.

In summary, the observed pattern of sales for a firm can be broken down into five parts. Namely, actual sales can be construed as the sum of trend, seasonal, cyclic, random error, and systematic error components. We might view the task of demand estimation as one of identifying each component and projecting it into the future. Let us turn to the procedures based on past sales, which attempt to model, control, or correct for one or more of the components of sales.

Naive Methods. The most basic procedures simply extend the past into the future on the basis of rules-of-thumb. Imagine that we are at the end of 1985 and wish to forecast sales for 1986. A simple rule might be to predict that sales will be an average of sales in the past year, or we might simply forecast that sales in the fourth quarter of 1986 will be the same as in 1985. This is shown as a dashed horizontal line in Figure 7-6. Another rule might be to extend the trend line and use this to forecast sales (see Figure 7-6). Notice that the predictions from these differ by about $10 million in sales or by an amount nearly as great as 20 percent of total sales in the fourth quarter of 1985. Also note that both methods are predicated on the assumption that whatever forces produced sales in the past will be at work in the future and will have effects similar to the past. Further, it is presumed that no new determinants of sales will emerge such as a new competitor, shortages in supplies or raw material, market saturation, changing consumer needs, or other forces. Overall, the naive approach is simple but fraught with errors and shortcomings.

Correction for Seasonality. Because sales over a few periods of years will often contain regular seasonal fluctuations, it is helpful to adjust for these effects before making forecasts based on sales in the past. The best way to see this is through an example. Table 7-5 presents quarterly sales data for a firm, Company K, over a seven-year period. Notice that sales during any one year are relatively equal in quarters 1, 2, and 4 but jump in quarter 3. In addition, sales tend to rise from 1977 to 1983.

To remove the seasonal effect and arrive at an adjusted data set, the following procedure can be used. First, for the period under study, sales should be averaged separately across each quarter. Next, an average of sales per quarter should be computed. Third, a seasonal index should be calculated for each quarter consisting of the average sales for that quarter divided by the average sales for all quarters. Finally, to determine the seasonally adjusted sales, one should divide each record of actual sales in a quarter by its appropriate seasonal index. The top half of Table 7-6 shows the computations, and the bottom half displays the sales data corrected for seasonality. We have only used the data from the first six years in order to be able to forecast to the seventh year in later examples.

Two points should be noted. First, although our example is done for quarterly data, the approach applies to seasonal effects appearing in any data set (e.g., monthly, bimonthly, semi-annual, etc., data). Second, the reason for adjusting for seasonality is to put the data in a form available for further analysis by other forecasting procedures. When using data corrected for seasonality, one should multiply by the seasonal index for the period in question to make comparisons between forecasted and actual sales. Let us turn to two frequently used procedures building on seasonally adjusted data.

TABLE 7-5

Historical Record of Sales
(in millions of dollars)
for Company K — Raw, Unadjusted Data

QUARTER	1977	1978	1979	1980	1981	1982	1983
1	95	96	102	110	113	118	124
2	101	111	115	117	125	127	133
3	115	127	127	135	149	152	163
4	102	104	110	111	115	117	123
TOTAL	413	438	454	473	502	514	543

(Column group header: YEAR)

TABLE 7-6

Correcting for Seasonality

Computations (Data from Table 7-5)

1. Quarterly Average (1977 to 1982 only):
   95 + 96 + 102 + 110 + 113 + 118 = 634 ÷ 6 = 105.7
   101 + 111 + 115 + 117 + 125 + 127 = 696 ÷ 6 = 116.0
   115 + 127 + 127 + 135 + 149 + 152 = 805 ÷ 6 = 134.2
   102 + 104 + 110 + 111 + 115 + 117 = 659 ÷ 6 = 109.8

2. Average per Quarter:
   95 + 101 + ... + 123 = 2,794 ÷ 24 = 116.4

3. Seasonal Index:
   Quarter 1 = 105.7/116.4 = .908
   Quarter 2 = 116.0/116.4 = .997
   Quarter 3 = 134.2/116.4 = 1.153
   Quarter 4 = 109.8/116.4 = .943

Seasonally Adjusted Data

QUARTER	1977	1978	1979	1980	1981	1982
1	105	106	112	121	124	130
2	101	111	115	117	125	127
3	100	110	110	117	129	132
4	108	110	117	118	122	124

(Column group header: YEAR)

The Method of Moving Averages. This approach forecasts sales as an average of a number of periods in the past. The general formula for computing sales in the next period is

$$S_{t+1} = \frac{S_t + S_{t-1} + \cdots + S_{t-n+1}}{n},$$

where S_{t+1} is forecast sales, S_t is sales for the current year, S_{t-n+1} is sales in previous years, and n is the number of periods considered. This formula simply averages sales in the past n periods and uses this as the forecast. As an example, suppose that we wished to predict sales in the first quarter of 1983 based on the data shown in Table 7-6.

With $n = 6$, the moving average forecast is

$$S_{1983,\,Q1}$$
$$= \frac{105 + 106 + 112 + 121 + 124 + 130}{6}$$
$$\times 1.057$$
$$= \$123 \text{ million,}$$

where we have included the seasonal index for the first quarter as a multiplier. Notice that this slightly underestimates the actual sales of $124 million shown in Table 7-5. The error of forecasting can be computed as

$$\text{Forecasting Error} = \frac{|123 - 124|}{124} \times 100$$
$$= 0.81\%.$$

Before we make more detailed comparisons among various time-based forecasting techniques, let us examine another approach.

Exponential Smoothing. Exponential smoothing, a frequently applied procedure, is defined by the following equation:

$$\overline{S}_t = \alpha S_t + (1 - \alpha)\, \overline{S}_{t-1},$$

where $\bar{S}_t$ is the smoothed sales for the current period, t, S_t is the actual or seasonally adjusted sales in t, $\bar{S}_{t-1}$ is the smoothed sales as computed in period $t-1$, and α is a smoothing constant. The smoothing constant is a number between 0 and 1 and must be selected by the researcher. Low values for α (e.g., .1 or .2) are appropriate when sales change slowly, whereas high values (e.g., .8, or .9) are relevant for rapid changes in sales. One way to choose α is by trial and error on historical data.

As an example of exponential smoothing, let us again predict the first quarter sales for 1983 for the situation shown in Table 7-6. To perform the calculations, we must begin with data from 1980 and 1981. The first set of calculations are, using $\alpha = .1$,

$$\bar{S}_{1981} = (.1)(124) + (.9)(121) = 121.3$$
$$\frac{1982}{\text{Forecast}} = (1.057)(121.3) = 128.2,$$

where seasonally adjusted sales for 1980 have been used for the smoothed sales because the latter are not available when one begins exponential smoothing. Next, for 1982, we make the following computations:

$$\bar{S}_{1982} = (.1)(130) + (.9)(121.3)$$
$$= 122.3$$
$$\frac{1983}{\text{Forecast}} = (1.057)(122.2) = 129.2.$$

The error of forecast is 4.19 percent.

Analysis and Comparison of Methods. Forecasting based on past sales offers a number of advantages and disadvantages. On the plus side, they are easy to use, data are readily available, and as shown above, they often give reasonably accurate forecasts. On the negative side, because they fail to explicitly model the true causes of sales as predictors, they can give poor forecasts if the determinants of sales vary in random or unexpected ways. Fortunately, since the causes of sales tend to operate in a regular manner and are usually correlated across time, the use of previous sales levels as predictors of future levels often works satisfactorily.

Within the class of methods based on past sales, a number of differences can be identified. Naive forecasts are typically the most erroneous. To forecast sales next year as the same as sales in the current year is to assume that all causes of sales will be constant. Given all the different forces in the environment and the impact of the marketing mix on sales, we would seldom expect such a forecast to work well. Similarly, to simply extend the trend into the future is to presume that the sum of effects will increase or accelerate at the same rate as in the past. This, too, is generally too imprecise for the needs of management. The naive approaches are especially poor for predicting changes in sales, such as a sharp rise or increase due to seasonality or other forces.

The moving average and exponential smoothing methods offer improvements over the naive approaches. Nevertheless, they have their limitations. Moving average forecasts tend to lag behind actual sales when there is a strong trend one way or the other. The problem with the approach is that all periods included in a moving average are weighted equally. Exponential smoothing overcomes this limitation to the extent that sales in periods prior to the most recent period are weighted the most heavily. However, if the most recent period is exceptional, then the approach can be quite inaccurate. Moreover, as with the naive and moving average procedures, exponential smoothing is not at all accurate in the prediction of turning points in sales.

Two approaches to forecasting based on past sales that are fairly accurate with respect to both trend and turning point predictions are the Box-Jenkins and related time series techniques.[31] Discussion of the approaches is beyond the scope of this text.

Three drawbacks with the approaches are that they are relatively costly to use, demand a high level of technical expertise, and require data for at least 40 to 60 periods.

Before we explore alternatives to forecasts based on past sales, let us compare the methods so far discussed. Figure 7-7 shows the results of forecasts for sales in 1983 using data from 1977 to 1982 (see Table 7-5). Notice that the simple trend forecast is the best, whereas the moving average method is the worst. The naive forecast and exponential smoothing with $\alpha = .8$ are about equal and in the middle. Exponential smoothing with $\alpha = .1$ is nearly as bad as the moving average method. We have used the raw sales data for simplicity, as the seasonal effects are minimal. Table 7-7 presents the error in forecasting for each method.

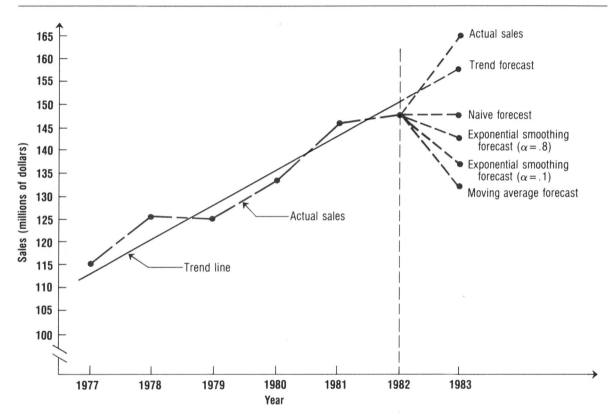

Figure 7-7. A comparison of sales forecasts by various methods—unseasonalized data

The findings in Figure 7-7 should not lull us into thinking that a trend projection will necessarily be better than more complex approaches in all situations. For one thing, had we based our trend projection on only two years of data (i.e., 1981 and 1982), we would have forecast sales of $152 million and had a prediction nearly as inaccurate as the naive forecast. Thus, trend forecasts are highly dependent on the number of years included in the analysis. Also, had sales fallen in 1983 to $145 million, say, then the exponential smoothing and naive methods would have been better predictors. This brings us to an important consideration. Trend forecasts work fine when the data are well behaved such as shown in Figure 7-7. Here, despite some fluctuations from year to year, sales rise in a relatively steady manner. But what happens when sales fluctuate—when they rise and fall a number of times over a few years' period or from month to month?

TABLE 7-7

Forecasting Error for Various Approaches Applied to the Data of Table 7-5, Third Quarter 1977–1982, and Shown in Figure 7-7 (in millions of dollars)

Method	Forecast	Actual	Error
Trend	160	163	1.84%
Naive	152	163	6.75%
Exponential Smoothing (α = .1)	138	163	15.33%
Exponential Smoothing (α = .8)	151	163	7.36%
Moving Average	134.2	163	17.67%

Figure 7-8 illustrates this situation. Now we see that the trend and naive forecasts miss the mark by the widest margins, whereas the moving average and exponential methods are much better forecasters. Indeed, although no exponential smoothing constant would lead to an adequate forecast of sales for the data displayed in Figure 7-7, we find that the exponential smoothing method, with α somewhat greater than .1, would yield a near-perfect prediction for the data shown in Figure 7-8. Table 7-8 presents the forecast errors for each approach.

Theory-Based Forecasts. The methods of demand estimation that are based entirely on past sales are a theoretical in the sense that the determinants of sales are not modeled as predictors. To achieve the most accurate and meaningful estimates of demand, we must

TABLE 7-8

Forecasting Error for Various Approaches Applied to the Data of Figure 7-8 (in millions of dollars)

Method	Forecast	Actual	Error
Trend	145	127.5	13.73%
Naive	145	127.5	13.73%
Exponential Smoothing (a = .1)	124.4	127.5	2.43%
Exponential Smoothing (a = .8)	141.6	127.5	11.06%
Moving Average	130.8	127.5	2.59%

strive to identify the uncontrollable and controllable causes and use these as predictors. One methodology particularly applicable in this regard is multiple regression.[32] Although discussion of the details of the method is beyond the scope of this book, it is helpful to present the structure of the procedure and provide an illustration.

To estimate demand, the general form of the multiple regression equation can be written as

$$S = \alpha + \beta_1 X_1 + \beta_2 X_2 + \cdots + \beta_k X_k + \epsilon$$

where S is sales, α is an intercept parameter showing the level of sales when the independent variables are fixed at zero, $X_1, X_2, \ldots, X_k$ are k independent variables (i.e., predictors or causes of sales), and ϵ is a disturbance term representing random error.

The best way to grasp the meaning of the demand equation shown above is with an example. The following represents an equation that was used to estimate the sales for a vegetable compound:[33]

$$S = -3649 + .665X_1 + 1180 \log X_2 + 774X_3 + 32X_4 - 2.83X_5 + \epsilon,$$

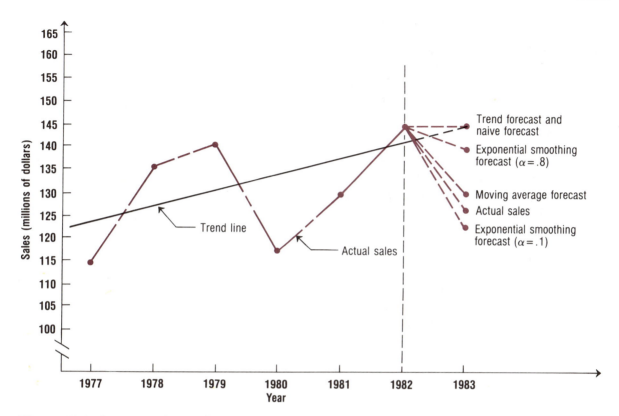

Figure 7-8. A comparison of sales forecasts by various methods— unseasonalized data for company Y

where S is the yearly sales in thousands of dollars, X_1 is sales in the previous year in thousands of dollars, X_2 is the amount spent on advertising for the year in thousands of dollars, X_3 is a dummy variable that takes on a value of 1 for the first 18 years of sales and a value of 0 for the next 35 years, X_4 is an index taking on, in succession, 0-52 for the 53 years under study (and 53 on up in the future), and X_5 is disposable personal income in billions of current dollars. The way the equation is used is to replace the X's with appropriate values for the period we desire to forecast. For example, suppose that $X_1 = 12,000$, $X_2 = 500$, $X_3 = 0$, $X_4 = 53$, and $X_5 = 400$. Then, our forecast of sales for next year would be

$$S_F = -3,649 + 7,980 + 3,185 + 0$$
$$+ 1,696 - 1,132$$
$$= \$8,080 \text{ thousands or } \$8,080,000.$$

The most difficult part of using multiple regression approaches to predict sales is the selection of relevant independent variables. As a general rule, we would anticipate that the most valid and successful predictions will result when a strong rationale exists for relating independent variables to sales. Variables that have a causal impact on sales are to be preferred. Because sales will be a function of the actions of the firm and the constraints or facilitators in the environment, as many of these as possible should be modeled.

Among the most important variables under the firm's control are advertising, promotion, personal selling, pricing, and distribution expenditures. Of course, for new products, it is very difficult to forecast the effects of these variables. Other methods such as simulations, subjective or heuristic approaches, or market tests might be required. The most important variables in the environment that affect sales are competitors' advertising and pricing practices, consumer needs and the ability to purchase, and socioeconomic constraints. Any firm needs to continually conduct research, propose models, check its forecasts against reality, and update its models if it is to compete effectively. An ongoing program involving multiple regression and other forecasting techniques is essential. An MIS can be put to advantage here, too.

Final Comment on Demand Estimation. There are so many methods available for conducting forecasts that a firm needs to evaluate the assumptions, appropriateness, costs, and benefits of each if it is to make wise choices. We have only touched upon some of the approaches and some of the issues related to their use in marketing. For fuller discussions, the reader is referred to Wheelwright and Makridakis[34] and other basic works on forecasting.

A useful goal in any demand estimation program is to pursue a strategy of *method convergence*. Rather than relying on only one approach, the firm should strive to obtain forecasts using different methods, perhaps even based on different data sets. In this way, management can have confidence in its forecasts to the extent that they converge. At the same time, the firm should avoid the pitfalls associated with confirmation biases. That is, research should also be subjected to questioning in the form of rival hypotheses.[35] And, indeed, we should develop hypotheses and seek data to disconfirm those hypotheses we have confirmed in the past. Only in this way can we cut down on being misled by spurious forces in the environment and our own reasoning limitations. Only in this way can we approach more valid theory-based forecasts.

Summary

This chapter has addressed the organization's need for, acquisition of, and use of information. It has done this from the viewpoint of the marketing function. To market effectively, the firm must purposely consider its dependency on knowledge. Indeed, the success of any organization's planning, implementation, and control programs depends directly on the quality and quantity of the information it has at its disposal and its ability to interpret and utilize this information expediently.

The *marketing information system* (MIS) is the primary mechanism for knowledge acquisition, generation, and utilization. It has five major components (see Figure 7-2): input, the communication system, the normative system, the marketing science system, and output. *Input* in the form of information from the internal and external environments of the organization constitutes the initial impetus to the MIS. The *communication system* acts upon the information, preprocessing it for transfer to other parts of the MIS and the firm as a whole. It also serves a proactive role in the sense of transmitting information to specific targets, on occasion, for the purpose of stimulating a desired response from them. The *normative system* provides a guidance function in the MIS. It dictates what information the firm should search for and value, and it shapes the methods, analysis, and interpretation of knowledge as well. The *marketing science system* is the core of the MIS, functioning much like the brain and central nervous system operate in the human body. It is here that data are analyzed via statistical, mathematical, or qualitative methodologies. And it is here that the findings are interpreted and conclusions and recommendations are made. The final component of the MIS, *output*, consists of specific policies, rules, procedures, and directives shaping decision making and problem solving in the firm. The outputs are coordinated and integrated with goals from top management and, in turn, serve to constrain and influence organizing, planning, staffing, execution, and control functions in the firm.

The chapter also provided an outline of the research process itself. It was shown that problem definition plays a pivotal and initiating role and that both inductive and deductive approaches are essential. Three broad research methodologies were described: survey research, experimental research, and open-ended explorations. To be innovative, organizations must learn how to effectively employ each from time to time.

Finally, the chapter closed with a discussion and analysis of demand estimation. We began with the concept of demand and pointed out three senses in which we might construe it: sales over time, sales as a function of all its determinants, and sales in response to the factors under the control of the firm. Demand was further broken into industry and firm demand with a discussion of a number of important dimensions of each that one must keep in mind when forecasting sales. We then closed the chapter with an introduction to the three major forms of demand estimation techniques: heuristic, subjective, and objective methods of demand estimation. Figure 7-9 provides a summary of these.

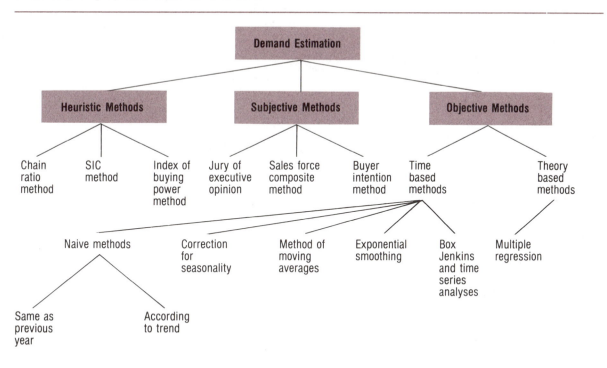

Figure 7-9. A summary of major demand estimation techniques discussed in Chapter 7

Questions and Problems for Discussion

1 Briefly define information and describe the central kinds of information needed by modern marketing organizations.

2 What is a marketing information system (MIS)? Briefly describe its six major components and draw a diagram indicating their interrelations.

3 Define the three major sources of information and give an example of each.

4 What is the purpose of the communication subsystem of the MIS and what functions does it perform?

5 The heart of any MIS is the marketing science system. Describe its five components and note the interrelations among them.

6 Discuss the marketing research process and contrast the two alternatives generally employed in the conduct of research.

7 Three broad classes of research methods are typically used by marketers. Describe and contrast these.

8 Suppose you are the director of new product development at the XYZ Company. In what way might you use marketing research as input to the decision to develop and market a new product? How could an MIS be used to aid decision making?

9 Three heuristic methods of demand estimation are the Chain Ratio Method, the SIC Method, and the Index of Buying Power Method. Briefly describe and compare these and note their strong points and limitations.

10 Common subjective methods of demand estimation include the jury of executive opinion, the sales force composite method, and surveys of buyers' intentions. Describe how these are conducted and point out their strengths and weaknesses.

11 The so-called objective methods of demand estimations fall under two categories: forecasts based on past sales and theory-based forecasts. Discuss the various versions under each category and consider their pros and cons.

12 Suppose you are the vice-president of marketing for a large corporation. Given the need to forecast demand for its toothpaste brand in a section of the country not marketed in before, how would you go about doing this? How would you estimate demand for a new dental floss and revolutionary container-applicator?

NOTES

1. Michael E. Porter, *Competitive Strategy: Techniques for Analyzing Industries and Competitors* (New York: The Free Press, 1980).

2. Chris Argyris, "Management Information Systems: The Challenge to Rationality and Emotionality," *Management Science* 17 (February 1971): B257–B292; J. Dearden, "MIS Is a Mirage," *Harvard Business Review* (January–February 1972): 90–99; David B. Montgomery, "The Outlook for MIS," *Journal of Advertising Research* 13 (June 1973): 5–11; David B. Montgomery and Glenn L. Urban, *Management Science in Marketing* (Englewood Cliffs, N.J.: Prentice-Hall, 1969); David B. Montgomery and Charles B. Weinberg, "Toward Strategic Intelligence Systems," *Journal of Marketing* 43 (Fall 1979): 41–52.

3. Richard H. Brien, "Marketing Information Systems: The State of the Art," *Proceedings of the American Marketing Association* (Chicago: American Marketing Association, 1973), p. 20.

4. Richard P. Bagozzi, *Causal Models in Marketing* (New York: John Wiley & Sons, 1980).

5. P. A. Naert and P. S. H. Leeflang, *Building Implementable Models* (Boston: Martinus Nijhoff/Leiden, 1978).

6. For a discussion of optimization in marketing, see Montgomery and Urban, 1969. An extended example can be found in John D. C. Little, "BRANDAID: A Marketing Mix Model, Structure, Implementation, Calibration, and Case Study," *Operations Research* 23 (July–August 1975): 628–73.

7. Naert and Leeflang, *Building Implementable Models.*

8. L. J. Parsons and R. L. Schultz, *Marketing Models and Econometric Research* (New York: American Elsevier/North Holland, 1976).

9. R. Bogdan and S. J. Taylor, *Introduction to Qualitative Research Methods* (New York: John Wiley & Sons, 1975); Bobby J. Calder, "Focus Groups and the Nature of Qualitative Marketing Research," *Journal of Marketing Research* 14 (August 1977): 353–64.

10. Russell L. Ackoff, *A Concept of Corporate Planning* (New York: Wiley Interscience, 1970), p. 116.

11. For descriptions of the nature of research, its antecedents, structure, and purposes, see Gerald Zaltman, Christian R. A. Pinson, and Reinhard Angelmar, *Metatheory in Consumer Research* (New York: Holt, Rinehart & Winston, 1973); Shelby D. Hunt, *Marketing Theory: Conceptual Foundations of Research* (Columbus, Ohio: Grid, 1976); Richard P. Bagozzi, *Causal Models in Marketing* (New York: John Wiley & Sons, 1980); Gerald Zaltman, Karen LeMasters, and Michael Heffring, *Theory Construction in Marketing: Some Thoughts on Thinking* (New York: John Wiley & Sons, 1982). For treatments of how to conduct research, see Gilbert H. Churchill, Jr., *Marketing Research: Methodological Foundations* (Hinsdale, Ill.: Dryden Press, 1976); Paul E. Green and Donald S. Tull, *Research for Marketing Decisions*, 4th ed. (Englewood Cliffs, N.J.: Prentice-Hall, 1978).

12. Dick Warren Twedt, ed., *1978 Survey of Marketing Research* (Chicago: American Marketing Association, 1978).

13. Twedt, *1978 Survey of Marketing Research.*

14. Thomas D. Cook and Donald T. Campbell, *Quasi-Experimentation: Design and Analysis Issues for Field Settings* (Chicago: Rand McNally, 1979).

15. See Peter Sampson, "Qualitative Research and Motivational Research," in R. M. Worcester, ed., *Consumer Market Research Handbook* (London: McGraw-Hill, 1972); Danny N. Ballenger, Kenneth L. Bernhardt, and Jack L. Goldstucker, *Qualitative Research in Marketing* (Chicago: American Marketing Association, 1975); Bogdan and Taylor, *Introduction to Qualitative Research Methods;* Calder, "Focus Groups and the Nature of Qualitative Research"; Harold Kassarjian, "Content Analysis in Consumer Research," *Journal of Consumer Research* 4 (June 1977): 8–18.

16. J. C. Chambers, S. K. Mullick, and D. D. Smith, *An Executive's Guide to Forecasting* (New York: John Wiley & Sons, 1974); Spyros Makridakis and Steven C. Wheelwright, *Forecasting: Methods and Applications* (New York: John Wiley & Sons, 1978). Vithala R. Rao and James E. Cox, Jr., *Sales Forecasting Methods: A Survey of Recent Developments*, Report No. 78-119 (Cambridge, Mass.: Marketing Science Institute, December, 1978); J. Scott Armstrong, *Long-Range Forecasting: From Crystal Ball to Computer* (New York: Ronald Press, 1977).

17. For some behavior support for the method, see J. Scott Armstrong, William B. Denniston, Jr., and Matt M. Gordon, "The Use of the Decomposition Principle in Making Judgments," *Organizational Behavior and Human Performance* 14 (1975): 257–63.

18. See Philip Kotler, *Marketing Decision Making: A Model-Building Approach* (New York: Holt, Rinehart & Winston, 1971).

19. For a description of the SIC system, see *Standard Industrial Classification Manual* (Washington, D.C.: United States Government Printing Office, 1982).

20. *Standard Industrial Classification Manual* (Washington, D.C.: Office of Management and Budget, 1972), p. 10. For further details on what constitutes an establishment, the reader is referred to the above publication.

21. *Sales and Marketing Management*, July, 27, 1981, p. A-37.

22. In his survey of 175 firms, Dalrymple found that 68 percent of the firms used the jury of executive opinion at least occasionally, 63 percent used the sales force composite method at least occasionally, and 32 percent used the buyer intention survey at least occasionally. Indeed, of all estimation procedures used, the first two were used the most often. See Douglas J. Dalrymple, "Sales Forecasting Methods and Accuracy," *Business Horizons* 18 (December 1975): 71.

23. See, for example, Charles Holloman and Harold Henrick, "Adequacy of Group Decisions as a Function of Decision-Making Process," *Academy of Management Journal* 15 (June 1972): 203–12.

24. See Solomon Asch, "Studies of Independence and Conformity: A Minority of One against a Unanimous Majority," *Psychological Monographs* 70 (1956): 68–70; Victor Vroom, Lester Grant, and Timothy Cotton, "The Consequences of Social Interaction in Group Problem Solving," *Organization Behavior and Human Performance* 4 (February 1969): 77–95.

25. Norman Dalkey, *The Delphi Method: An Experimental Study of Group Opinion* (Santa Monica, Cal.: The Rand Corporation, 1969); Norman Dalkey and Olaf Helmer, "An Experimental Application of Delphi Method to the Use of Experts," *Management Science* 9 (April 1963): 458–67.

26. Marvin Jolson and Gerald Rossow, "The Delphi Process in Marketing Decision Making," *Journal of Marketing Research* 8 (November 1971): 443–48; Roger J. Best, "An Experiment in Delphi Estimation in Marketing Decision Making," *Journal of Marketing Research* 11 (November 1973): 448–52.

27. Paul Slovic and Sarah Lichenstein, "Comparison of Bayesian and Regression Approaches to the Study of Information Processing in Judgment," *Organizational Behavior and Human Performance* 6 (November 1971), pp. 649–744. Amos Tversky and Daniel Kahneman, "Judgment under Uncertainty: Heuristic and Biases," *Science* 185 (1974): 1124–31; H. J. Einhorn and R. M. Hogarth, "Confidence in Judgment: Persistence of the Illusion of Validity," *Psychological Review* 85 (1978): 395–416; R. E. Nisbett and L. Ross, *Human Inference: Strategies and Shortcomings of Social Judgment* (Englewood Cliffs, N.J.: Prentice-Hall, 1980).

28. See references in footnote 27.

29. For exceptions, see Richard Staelin and Ronald E. Turner, "Error in Judgmental Sales Forecasts: Theory and Results," *Journal of Marketing Research* 10 (February 1973): 10–16; Jacob Gonik, "Tie Salesmen's Bonuses to Their Forecasts," *Harvard Business Review* 56 (May–June 1978): 116–23.

30. Donald G. Morrison, "Purchase Intentions and Purchase Behavior," *Journal of Marketing* 43 (Spring 1979): 65–74; Richard P. Bagozzi, "Attitudes, Intentions, and Behavior: A Test of Some Key Hypotheses," *Journal of Personality and Social Psychology* 41 (1982): 607–27.

31. George E. P. Box and Gwilym M. Jenkins, *Time Series Analysis: Forecasting and Control*, 2nd ed. (San Francisco: Holden-Day, 1976); Charles R. Nelson, *Applied Time Series Analysis for Managerial Forecasting* (San Francisco: Holden-Day, 1973). For a somewhat different, but nevertheless fruitful, approach to forecasting based on past sales, see Frank M. Bass, "A New Product Growth Model for Consumer Durables," *Management Science* 15 (January 1969): 215–227; W. Dodds, "Application of the Bass Model in Long-Term New Product Forecasting," *Journal of Marketing Research* 10 (August 1973): 308–11.

32. For an introduction and description of multiple regression, see Green and Tull, *Research for Marketing Decisions;* Parsons and Schultz, *Marketing Models and Econometric Research.*

33. Kristian S. Palda, *The Measurement of Cumulative Advertising Effects* (Englewood Cliffs, N.J.: Prentice-Hall, 1964).

34. Steven C. Wheelwright and Spyros Makridakis, *Forecasting Methods for Management*, 2nd ed. (New York: John Wiley & Sons, 1977). See also references in footnote 16.

35. For a perspective on research stressing the need to seek both confirming and disconfirming hypotheses and evidence in any rigorous research endeavor, see J. R. Platt, "Strong Inference," *Science* 146 (1964): 347–53. For an example of strong inference wherein multiple confirming and rival hypotheses are examined, see Richard P. Bagozzi, "An Examination of the Validity of Two Models of Attitude," *Multivariate Behavioral Research* 16 (1981): 323–59.

GLOSSARY

Chain Ratio Method of Demand Estimation. A heuristic procedure for forecasting demand that begins with total potential demand for a product class and then, through successive decompositions based on assumptions of the market and the firm's capabilities, moves toward the demand for a particular brand.

Communication System (in the MIS). The social actors and their policies and actions directed at the exchange and proactive behaviors. See Figure 7-2.

Data Base. The storehouse of knowledge needed by the firm in its decision-making activities.

Delphi Method. See the jury of executive opinion method of demand estimation.

Demand. The quantity of goods or services desired or actually purchased by consumers.

Demand Function. The relationship between causes of demand (e.g., product design, pricing, advertising, distribution) and actual or forecast sales.

Environmental Information. Information about the firm's environment. There are two sources.

Outside Providers: secondary sources (i.e., information compilations with no particular user in mind) and subscription sources (i.e., information services providing information research for particular users and special purposes for a fee).

Inside Providers: primary research performed by the firm itself to gather, analyze, and interpret information.

Environments. The physical, technological, economic, legal, and social conditions that constrain or facilitate the behavior or function of social actors, including a focal firm. See Figure 7-2.

Evaluative Information. Knowledge having either direct positive or direct negative consequences for a firm (e.g., opportunities or dangers). Most information is evaluative.

Exchange Function (in the MIS). The communication tasks in the MIS consisting of receipt of information from the internal and external environments, storage of selected information, and dissemination of information back to the outer environment as well as to parts of the internal organization. See Figure 7-2.

Experimental Research. The manipulation of one or more independent variables (e.g., price, advertising, product design) and observance of their effects on one or more dependent variables (e.g., sales, consumer satisfaction, buying intentions). Three types of experiments were described in the text: true, field, and quasi experiments.

External Environment. Consumers, suppliers, intermediaries, competitors, government, special interest groups, the general public, and other social entities outside the firm and potentially influencing its decisions. See Figure 7-2.

Heuristic Demand Estimation Methods. Projection of firm's sales based on a percentage of expected market sales. This might be termed an indirect method. Three heuristic approaches are frequently used: (1) the chain ratio method, (2) the standard industrial classification (SIC) procedure, and (3) the Index of Buying Power formula.

Index of Buying Power Method of Demand Estimation. A heuristic procedure for forecasting demand based on a weighted average of the population, income, and retail sales in a particular geographic area. Each July, *Sales & Marketing Management* magazine publishes data and an equation that can be applied to various geographic regions in the United States and Canada.

Industry Demand. Total sales for all firms in a particular industry.

Information. Factual knowledge about the characteristics of (1) social actors outside or inside the firm and (2) the environments within which they operate. Information serves as input to decision making processes and may take evaluative as well as nonevaluative forms.

Input. Information arising from the internal and external environments of the organization and ultimately influencing decision making. See Figure 7-2.

Intention to Buy Method of Demand Estimation. A subjective method for forecasting demand based on a survey of intentions to buy of consumers.

Internal Environment. Top management, formal departments in the firm, informal groups, unions, professional associations, and other social entities within the firm potentially influencing its decisions. See Figure 7-2.

Jury of Executive Opinion Method of Demand Estimation. A subjective method for forecasting demand based on judgments made by a group of experts. Judgments are solicited anonymously, and the median judgment is computed and communicated to the individuals in the group who are asked to make another forecast. The procedure is repeated until a consensus is reached.

Management Decision System. The part of the MIS concerned with the generation of policies, rules, procedures, and directives regarding organizing, planning, staffing, execution (i.e., implementation), and control. These decisions and resulting plans are based in part on input from the marketing science system and in part on managerial judgment and group decision making within the organization. The output consists of feedback to the internal and external environments. See Figure 7-2.

Marketing Effort. Demand stimulation tools under the control of management. For instance, advertising, promotion, publicity, product design, pricing, and distribution tactics are such tools.

Marketing Information System (MIS). The organization's collection of equipment, people, and programs, whose function is to monitor, gather, analyze, evaluate, store, and disseminate knowledge (i.e., information).

Marketing Research. The formal process of knowledge generation, discovery, and use performed by an organization as part of its decision making activities. See Figure 7-3.

Marketing Science System. That part of the MIS which receives information from the communication system, processes the information, and produces output needed in decision making. Its five components include (1) a data base; (2) statistical models and analysis; (3) mathematical and logical models and analysis; (4) qualitative analysis; and (5) the products or outputs of analysis (i.e., interpretation, conclusions, and recommendations). See Figure 7-2.

Mathematical Models and Analysis. Procedures used to optimize combinations of abstract variables or simulate their relationships as expressed in formulas. *See* marketing science system and Figure 7-2.

Nonevaluative Information. Knowledge with no discernible positive or negative consequences for the firm.

Normative System. The evaluative guidance mechanisms of an organization shaping judgments of what is good or bad, what is important or unimportant, and what actions should or should not be taken. This may reside in the values of individual actors (e.g., managers, employees) or formal rules, procedures, and policies. See Figure 7-2.

Objective Demand Estimation Methods. The prediction of future sales on the basis of past sales and other factors. Various statistical and curve fitting procedures are described in the text. *See also* heuristic demand estimation and subjective demand estimation.

Open-Ended Explorations. Unstructured or loosely structured data collection methods whose purpose is to collect information for evaluation rather than hypothesis testing. This is done typically through focus groups, depth interviews, projective techniques, or participant observation. *See* qualitative analysis.

Proactive Function (in the MIS). The influence of social actors within and without the organization. This is done through provision of attractive product offerings, the use of persuasion and power, bargaining, lobbying, negotiation, and other tactics. See Figure 7-2.

Qualitative Analysis. The use of unstructured methodologies (e.g., depth interviews, participant observation, focus groups, and projective techniques) to interpret data. *See* marketing science system and Figure 7-2.

Sales Force Composite Method of Demand Estimation. A subjective method for forecasting demand based on the judgments of a firm's salespeople.

Social Actors. Consumers, competitors, employees, institutions (e.g., suppliers, wholesalers, retailers, government bodies, nonprofit organizations), salespeople, or other individual persons or social entities capable of engaging purposefully in exchange relations.

Standard Industrial Classification (SIC) Method of Demand Estimation. A heuristic procedure for forecasting demand in a particular geographic region based on rules of thumb of likely demand. The rules of thumb are based, in turn, on the number of establishments, number of employees, value of production, sales, payroll, etc., of firms in the geographic area.

Statistical Models and Analysis. Procedures based on probability and used to summarize data, test hypotheses, and make predictions. *See* marketing science system and Figure 7-2.

Subjective Methods of Demand Estimation. Direct forecasts of firm sales based on judgments made by either consumers or managers. Three common procedures include the jury of executive opinion, the sales force composite, and the intention to buy survey methods. *See* heuristic demand estimation, objective demand estimation.

Survey Research. The collection of responses from people through a questionnaire administered face-to-face by a researcher, by phone, by mail, or by a computer terminal.

CHAPTER EIGHT

What you say is more important than how you say it.
—— *David Ogilvy (1911–   )*

Execution can become content, it can be just as important as what you say....
The facts are not enough...don't forget that.
Shakespeare used some pretty hackneyed plots, yet his message came through with great execution.
—— *William Bernbach (1911–1982)*

"The medium is the message" because it is the medium that shapes and controls the search and form of human associations and action.
—— *Marshall McLuhan (1911–1980)*

You'll never really know what I mean and I'll never know exactly what you mean.
—— *Mike Nichols (1931–   )*

MARKETING COMMUNICATION

Introduction

Up to this point, we have concentrated primarily on consumer behavior and marketer behavior. We have examined the psychological and social forces shaping why people and organizations buy what they buy, and we have considered how marketers design and develop products and services, segment the market, position their offerings, and estimate demand. Now we must address the linkages *between* marketer and customer in greater detail.

In this chapter, we shall investigate *marketing communication* processes and structures. Our focus will be upon the ways people and organizations impart information and/or influence other people and organizations. To this end, the chapter begins with a description of the classic source-message-media-receiver (SMMR) model of communication, which allows us to introduce many of the elements of the communication process that will be discussed in more depth later in this chapter and in other chapters. Next, we will treat the information-processing model of communication that dominates contemporary marketing thought and practice. Following this, two new alternatives will be developed: the cognitive response and affective response models. We will then close the chapter with an integration of the various perspectives on communication. This chapter sets the stage for the following three chapters on advertising, salesperson behavior, and sales force management, respectively.

A Classic Model of Communication[1]

Figure 8-1 presents an outline of the source-message-media-receiver (SMMR) model of communication. The basic skeleton of this model can be traced at least as far back as Aristotle. In the following pages, we will provide an updated rendition of the model because much of it is still valid today and it serves a useful pedagogical function for organizing the many fragmented areas of research relevant to the study of communication in marketing.

Before we examine the parts of the SMMR model, let us briefly describe it in global terms. Beginning at the left side we see that a *sender* or communicator desires to make contact with a potential receiver. This is done by preparing a *message*. A message is a set of symbols used to express meaning by one person in contact with another. As we shall discover, the decisions of what to say (i.e., message content) and how to say it (i.e.,

message structure) are complex ones with many parts and options. The message itself must then be conveyed in some way, and this involves choice of a *medium* or media. Two broad alternatives for conveying messages are personal (i.e., face-to-face) and nonpersonal (i.e., mass) channels of communication. Each of these media exhibits many variations and will be described later. The communication process "ends" with a *receiver* decoding, processing, and interpreting the message and reacting in some way. If the sender monitors and picks up a reaction on the part of the receiver, we say that *feedback* has occurred.

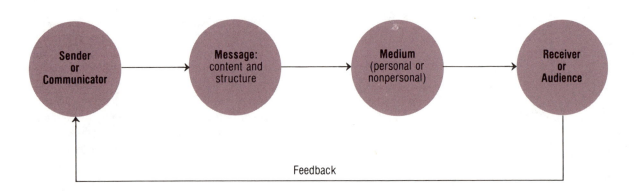

Figure 8-1. The classic source-message-media-receiver model of communication

Of course, communication is not restricted to a one-way flow of information with feedback. Rather, communication is very much a two-way process of give-and-take with sender and receiver constantly switching roles. Thus, marketers and consumers act as both senders and receivers in varying degrees, depending on the circumstances.

One final point to note is that it is very difficult, if not impossible, to separate the idea of *communication* from the

notion of *social influence*.[2] All influence requires certain forms of communication to execute it, and all communication is tinged with evaluation, action, and other implications for sender and receiver. Hence, in the vast majority of situations, communication and influence go hand in hand. To be sure, in some instances, communication will contain or imply only a small amount of influence from one party to another, but nevertheless, influence will almost always be present.

Figure 8-2 summarizes eight forms in which social influence and communication occur. We have listed them in a rough continuum with the top representing relatively unilateral and the bottom largely bilateral influence/communication modes. The middle categories—persuasion and education—are the most commonly applied communication tactics in marketing, yet the other categories occasionally occur. Let us briefly look at them.

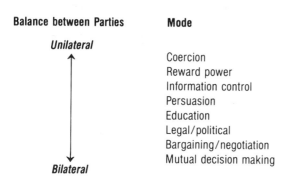

Balance between Parties

Unilateral

↑

↓

Bilateral

Mode

Coercion
Reward power
Information control
Persuasion
Education
Legal/political
Bargaining/negotiation
Mutual decision making

Figure 8-2. Eight modes of communication and influence

Under *coercion*, one party in a relation attempts to influence another through the application or threat of punishing stimuli or the deprivation of positively valued stimuli. Stimuli may have physical, psychological, or social significance. The use of coercion is infrequent and often regarded as immoral, unethical, or illegal, but it does occur in the marketplace in the form of strong-arm tactics by organized crime on retailers and violence and vandalism against businesses, among other instances. Protest activities such as boycotts, picketing, and civil disobedience represent relatively mild forms of coercion and are sometimes used by consumer groups.

Reward power is the application of pleasant stimulation as a means of influence. The inducement might be small (e.g., a free sample) or large (e.g., a rebate), legal (e.g., a contest) or illegal (e.g., a bribe). Under *information control*, one party attempts to withhold, distort, filter, regulate, or augment knowledge in order to influence another party to act in a particular way. This sometimes occurs in the form of false or deceptive advertising or manufacturer negligence with respect to product safety, to give two examples.

Persuasion is the attempt to influence another by the use of rational and/or emotional arguments. Under rational persuasion, the objective is to convince the receiver that it is in one's own best interests to act in a particular way. Under emotional persuasion, the aim is to appeal to feelings. These may be negative (e.g., our fears) or positive (e.g., our desires). A subtle feature that distinguishes persuasion from the previously discussed modes of influence is that the persuader does not directly control or administer rewards or punishments to the receiver. Rather, it is the actions of the receiver made under conditions of "free choice" that lead to any subsequent rewards or punishments. For example, sellers may promise benefits that are associated with their wares, but whether one will actually experience these depends on the choices made by the buyer. Contrast persuasion in this sense with coercion or reward power, where the coercer or power holder directly applies (or threatens or promises to apply) a punishment or reward, respectively. For instance, a bribe by a seller actually involves the seller giving a reward, the bribe, to a potential buyer. Perhaps because of its free choice property, as well as its effectiveness, persuasion is a frequently applied influence tactic in marketing.

Another popular influence tool in marketing is the *educative* tactic. Here a communicator presents information that still leaves the receiver free to reach his or her own conclusion and act accordingly. Unlike persuasion or information control, where the sender manipulates things in a selective and often self-serving way, educative tactics typically contain "full information." That is, they present both the pros and cons of an issue in as complete a manner as possible. Relative to persuasion, the needs of the receiver are given more weight under the educative tactic. Indeed, of all the influence tactics discussed so far, this is the most bilateral one. Many people feel that educative appeals are the only justifiable tactics that business or other institutions should employ. However, in practice, both in the business world and in our everyday relations with others, persuasion is an important force allowing us the opportunity to better meet our needs in a world often filled with scarcity, competition, and uncertainty.

The *legal/political* influence mode is even more bilateral than the educative mode. In this situation, a person or organization appeals to governmental or other social institutions to support and even enforce its will. The presumption is that society, through its laws and norms, will sanction certain behaviors. For example, consumers or businesses use the courts to redress breaches in contracts or gain compensation for injuries experienced in trade.

In *bargaining/negotiation*, the sender and receiver enter an exchange and agree to give and take until a joint solution to a shared problem arises. The parties are generally equal in power or at least possess enough power to reward and/or punish each other to a significant degree. *Mutual decision making* is quite similar to bargaining/negotiation except that the relationship between sender and receiver is even more bilateral. The interests of both parties in mutual decision making more closely coincide than in bargaining/negotia-tion, although the difference may be a slight one. Bargaining/negotiation goes on in bazaars, flea markets, and business-government exchanges. Mutual decision making occurs between organizations in the channel of distribution, as well as in family consumer decision making.

We are now in a position to discuss the elements of the SMMR model of Figure 8-1 in greater detail. We will begin with the sender and proceed from left to right until we cover all facets. As we discuss each element and the supporting research, you should keep in mind that each represents a unique determinant of the behavior (e.g., purchase of Brand X or not) of the receiver. Whether a person will make a purchase or not depends on the characteristics of the source, the nature of the message, the power of the media, and the attributes of receivers.[3]

The Sender

Three characteristics of the source appear to be critical factors in the communication process: credibility, attractiveness, and the mediation of rewards and punishments. Let us consider each.

Source Credibility.[4] Imagine that an advertiser of a new cold remedy has two options for a television spot. One consists of a relatively unknown announcer explaining what a new ingredient is and why cold sufferers should try the brand now containing it. The second employs exactly the same message but uses Robert Young to deliver it. Robert Young is a well-known actor familiar to millions for his successful role in the TV series, Dr. Welby, M.D. The advertiser, of course, wishes to use the most powerful ad execution possible at the least cost. We know that the ad with Robert Young as spokesperson would surely be more expensive, but would it be more effective? Intuitively, you might guess that the ad with Robert Young would be perceived as more credible than the one with an unknown announcer. And indeed, research indicates that source credibility often increases attitude change, persuasion, and even behavioral compliance. But what exactly is a credible source? Would the above ad for the brand of cold remedy have been even more "credible" had a Nobel Prize-winning medical researcher served as the spokesperson? To answer these questions, let us look at the meaning of credibility in more depth.

Source credibility is generally considered to have two parts: *source expertise* and *source trustworthiness.* A source will be perceived to be expert if he or she is believed to be highly educated, to have had considerable first-hand experience, or to be particularly competent in some way. We tend to believe the persuasive appeals of experts more than nonexperts, and this is especially true when the education, experience, and/or competency of the speaker is strongly related to the issue at hand. For example, most people would place more credence in the diagnosis of problems with their car made by a master mechanic than with an assessment made by their local pharmacist. But the master mechanic's opinion on the best medication for the one's skin problem would be less valued than the pharmacist's. Source expertise is also thought to be related to one's status (i.e., the higher the status, the higher the perceived expertise).[5]

Source trustworthiness refers to the audience's perception that the source is honest and sincere in his or her intentions.[6] Further, we generally attribute greater trustworthiness in a speaker if he or she is perceived not to have a vested interest in our acting in the particular way advocated in the message. This aspect of trustworthiness partly explains why advertisements and personal selling appeals have such a difficult time working. Because we usually perceive a seller as personally gaining from a sale, we tend to discount what he or she says. The trick is to use a credible source who does not appear to be acting solely out of self-interest. Another aspect of trustworthiness is consistency in the source. To the extent that a source is seen to exhibit the same behavior and advocate the same arguments over time, he or she is perceived as trustworthy. People who switch positions too often or do so for insufficient or self-serving reasons are viewed as less trustworthy.

Source credibility—that is, perceived expertise and trustworthiness—can be seen to have a number of effects. The most obvious is that credibility rubs off on the message content and increases our subjective judgment that the information contained in it is valid. A second effect might be that credible sources interact complexly with message, media, and receiver characteristics. We will consider these possibilities later in the chapter. Finally, as executed in the real world, source credibility might be confounded or associated with other subtle characteristics of the source where the unknown characteristics and not credibility, per se, produce attitude or behavior change in a receiver. For instance, most credible sources are physically attractive, command unusual respect or sympathy, or exude charisma. We turn now to another important source characteristic that is often confused with source credibility.

Source Attractiveness.[7] Common sense tells us that we communicate better with, and are more easily influenced by, people to whom we are attracted. Why is this so? One reason might be that we feel more comfortable and less threatened by someone we like or by someone with whom we are similar or familiar. Another reason might be that attraction itself, through emotional processes, produces attitude change, yielding, and behavioral compliance. Still another reason that a receiver might be influenced by an attractive source is that the former feels a need to identify with the latter. This is similar to the notion of referent power.[8] A more cognitive-based explanation is that an attractive source (relative to an unattractive one) causes a receiver to inflate the utility of a message from the source.[9] For example, it has been observed that the promises of an attractive source are believed more than the promises of an unattractive one; whereas the threats of the unattractive source are believed more than the threats of an attractive one. The implications of research on source attraction are that, to the extent that spokespersons in ads or salespeople in face-to-face encounters are personally attractive (physically, intellectually, socially, and otherwise), the higher the probability that communication and influence will be enhanced. However, one would not want the attraction to be so strong as to detract from the content of the message and the ability of the receiver to evaluate a brand, develop a positive attitude, and decide to act to buy the brand. Fortunately, one study indicates that even low levels of attraction between salesperson and customer (in this case operationalized as similarity) may be sufficient to produce a sale.[10]

Mediation of Rewards and Punishments by Source.[11] As noted earlier with respect to coercion and reward power, a source can achieve influence strictly through the stimuli at its disposal. Two factors need to be considered: capability and intentionality of the source. A necessary condition for influence through the use of rewards or punishments is that a source must have the capability to administer sanctions. This means that a source must control rewarding and/or punishing stimuli and be able to communicate and monitor the actions of the receiver. At the same time, it is not sufficient to merely possess the wherewithal to sanction. The source must be willing to use his or her resources, and the receiver must perceive that the source can and will do so under the appropriate conditions.

The potential to mediate rewards and/or punishments has a number of effects in the communication process. Perhaps the most obvious, but the least frequently observed, is the use of extreme amounts of reward or punishment as the sole means of influence. Here compliance is affected through the pleasure-seeking power of a reward or the pain avoidance power of a punishment rather than through rational choice and exchange associated with the product, service, or issue at hand. Somewhat more common in marketing is the parallel administration of a small reward or

punishment as an auxiliary to an exchange between a buyer and seller. For example, manufacturers provide small gifts, entertain, promise additional services, give cash discounts for prompt payment, etc., as part of the transaction process with industrial or retail buyers. This is in addition to the exchange of the product for money. Many other physical, psychic, and social rewards and punishments might accompany formal exchanges.

Final Comments on Sender. As a summary, Table 8-1 presents the source variables common to most communication/influence attempts. At this point, we should again stress that these represent only one of a number of possible determinants of receiver behavior. As shown in Figure 8-1, the message, media, and receiver characteristics also influence receiver behavior in addition to the source characteristics listed in Table 8-1.

TABLE 8-1
Summary of Source Characteristics in the Communication Process

Source Characteristic	Description
Credibility	*Source expertise:* perceived competence, education, experience, etc., of source by receiver. *Source trustworthiness:* perceived honesty, sincerity, accommodativeness, disinterest, and consistency of source by receiver.
Attractiveness	Perceived similarity, familiarity, liking, etc., of source by receiver.
Mediator of Rewards and/or Punishments	Perceived capability of source to reward or punish and willingness or intention to do so.

Furthermore, it should be noted that source characteristics and the other determinants can be thought to influence receiver behavior in two ways. One is that each cause has a direct effect on the receiver, independent of any of the other causes. Psychologists term this type of influence a *main effect.* For example, source credibility can influence purchase intentions of a receiver over and above what the message says, how it is said, where it is said, and what the personality of the receiver might be. A second way that the determinants shown in Figure 8-1 operate is as *interaction effects.* That is, some determinants will influence the receiver only in conjunction with other ones. For instance, research shows that fear appeals in a message only work, or at least work best, when the source is highly credible. When the source is very low in credibility, the use of fear in a persuasive argument lacks impact.[12] Let us continue our exploration of the elements in the classic SMMR model of Figure 8-1.

The Message

Compared to other aspects of the communication process, we know quite a bit more about the effects of message characteristics on the receiver. Table 8-2 lists the major options available when choosing a message. The labels "message content" and "message structure" are used to categorize the options. Each will be described below. Before doing this, we should note that the art of communication is reflected in the optimal combination of message content and structure. In the following chapter, we will describe how advertisers accomplish this. It turns out that each advertising agency has its own unique approach, its own general personality, which is reflected in the way message content and structure are executed. We term this the agency's "creative style." Message content and message structure go hand in hand, and we separate them here only for purposes of discussion.

TABLE 8-2

Key Message Variables in the Communication Process: What to Say (message content) and How to Say It (message structure)

Message Content	Message Structure
Rational Appeals 　Product attributes 　Consequences of use	One-sided versus Two-sided Appeals
Emotional Appeals 　Positive or negative mood 　Humor 　Fear	Order of Presentation of Arguments Amount of Information Repetition
Extraneous Factors 　Distraction and 　　counterargumentation 　Use of a foil	

Rational Appeals. One of the most frequently employed message content tactics is the use of rational arguments. In this approach, a set of facts is presented, perhaps with a conclusion stated, and an appeal to the receiver's capacity to reason is made. The content in the message is presented mainly in a dispassionate way and in a logical sequence. The objective is to speak to the receiver's thought processes.

In the typical marketing application, specific product attributes are described in a way suggesting benefits to the potential user, or the message will more directly focus on the positive consequences of using or owning the product. These might be utilitarian, physical, psychic, or social in nature.

Rational appeals are probably used most often by salespeople selling industrial products or consumer durables. Nevertheless, we often see rational appeals in ads for everyday products such as floor cleaners, detergents, and lawn care products. The rational appeal is especially useful when products have functional characteristics, are used to accomplish some goal, and/or result in a savings in time or money. A good example are the ads for Mobil 1 oil. Among other benefits, the ads stress increased mileage (up to 10 miles per tank), longer oil-change intervals, and better engine starting in hot and cold conditions. These are very much rational appeals.

One issue with regard to the use of rational appeals is whether or not to include a definite conclusion in the message. A considerable body of research indicates that messages that draw conclusions versus those that do not are more persuasive.[13] On the other hand, the danger exists that the audience receiving a definite conclusion will be insulted or in some other way turned off.[14] For instance, a communication that draws a conclusion too strongly or dogmatically can backfire by inducing counterarguments, disparaging thoughts, and other negative reactions in the receiver.

Rational appeals influence us in a particular way. They function as sources of information that we use to form beliefs. These, in turn, become integrated with our stored knowledge, values, and emotions and eventually influence our attitudes. If their effect is strong enough, they may ultimately produce an intention to act and instigate actual behavior changes (e.g., product trial). All along, given their noncoercive and relatively nonevaluative content, rational appeals tend to be given a special status in our minds. Any attitude change is attributed relatively more to ourselves than to the external influence—at least when compared to other, more compelling forms of influence such as reward power or coercion. We arrive at an attribution of free choice and the implicit thought that "since I drew the conclusion myself without external compulsion, I must really believe what was said, and it has valid meaning to me."

Emotional Appeals. Rational appeals work through our thought processes. Emotional appeals, in contrast, play on our feelings. The belief is that our feelings are motivational conduits to action.

An emotional message typically has one of two goals. On the one hand, it might strive to put the receiver or audience in a particular mood or affective state. The premise is that our mood will enhance our attention, facilitate the processing of rational content in the message, and/or rub off on the product or brand in the sense of producing liking through transference. On the other hand, an emotional message might be so compelling that it, in and of itself, stimulates us to act without necessarily processing and evaluating rational content in the message. Three ways in which emotional appeals are executed in marketing are positive/negative mood, humor, and fear appeals.

Positive/Negative Mood Appeals. Some communications, particularly those found in radio and television advertisements, attempt to place the audience in temporary positive or negative moods. This is done with music, words, pictures, and images designed to either conjure up old emotionally tinged memories or stimulate new feelings vicariously. By inducing feelings, it is hoped that an internal tension or dissonance will be created and that this, in turn, will produce drive reduction behaviors such as information seeking or product trial.

Positive moods are created through pleasant music, attractive scenes or spokespersons, associations made to fondly remembered events or places, and other pleasing stimuli. Usually, direct tie-ins to the senses are made through unusual or familiar tastes, aromas, sights, sounds, and physical sensations. Stimuli that invoke involuntary responses, biological and otherwise, are used, too: e.g., pictures of babies, animals, human nudity, food, etc. One way such positive stimuli operate is to attract and to arouse basic and learned needs in us. They also make the receiver more alert and motivated and thus enhance information processing. At the same time, the increased feelings of well-being and elation are believed to have the potential to generalize to the brand itself. If we feel fine and even euphoric, then this might lead to a positive evaluation and liking of Brand X.

Negative moods might also enhance communication and influence at times. How often have you been annoyed by unpleasant, abrasive ads on television addressing such issues as bad breath, clogged sinuses, excruciating headaches, loose dentures, ring around the collar, or spots on one's dishes and glasses? Advertisers believe that such ads not only attract attention but also help people confront "problems" they normally deny or repress. Of course, for people who do not recognize or accept these issues as problems, such ads miss the mark and even invoke bad will. Nevertheless, advertisers believe that some people will be reached, if only because these people see the ad as a sympathetic and public acknowledgment that their "problems" are real and worth addressing. In a sense, viewers are allowed to feel sorry for themselves and to feel that "at least someone cares about me and my problem." A question seldom addressed is whether such attempts at persuasion "create" problems that do not exist or play on people's vulnerabilities. Most ads probably do not go this far, but the line between persuasion and manipulation is a fine one.

Negative mood–inducing ads are thought to have still another effect. Intuitively, we all know that our memory for facts, places, and ads decays over time. But some things decay more quickly than others, and certain things do not decay much at all or do so very slowly. Imagine what happens when we watch the seemingly silly ad for Charmin with the equally abrasive Mr. Whipple as spokesperson. Immediately after viewing the ad, we might remember "Charmin bathroom tissue," "soft," and our general distaste for Mr. Whipple and the ad. However, as time passes, we might disassociate Mr. Whipple and his accompanying negative affect from "soft Charmin bathroom tissue." Then later, as we pass the shelf of bathroom tissue in the supermarket, our unconscious memory that Charmin is soft might be the trigger needed to induce us to reach for Charmin rather than the competition. To the extent that our negative images dissipate quicker than our remembrance of the

brand name and its attributes, the attention-getting and dissonance-arousing aspects of the ad might be beneficial. Unfortunately, from a scientific standpoint, it is not known how or if such "sleeper-like effects" do indeed work in marketing.[15]

Humor.[16] The use of humor in communication is a little-understood topic. Nowhere is this more apparent than in the advertising industry, where humor is a controversial issue. Some advertisers explicitly avoid humor because they believe that (1) it is often too subtle and will not be appreciated or understood by everyone, (2) it takes too long to develop in 30- or 60-second ads and therefore uses up too much valuable time, (3) it can be distracting by focusing attention away from the brand and its attributes and toward the humorous person or situation, (4) it is too ephemeral and will not be remembered as well as factual information, and (5) it is too expensive to produce. As a consequence, ad agencies such as Ted Bates and Ogilvy & Mather prefer rational appeals. On the other hand, some agencies employ humor in nearly all of their ads. Doyle Dane Bernbach and Leo Burnett are two leading examples. These agencies and others believe that humorous ads (1) attract *and* hold attention, (2) involve the audience with the ad and product in deeper cognitive and affective ways than thinking ads, (3) reward the audience and create a positive mood, thereby increasing liking for the brand, (4) communicate more effectively to all levels of social and intellectual development, because things difficult to put into words are more easily expressed in funny skits, (5) are almost the only way to advertise painful, sensitive, and embarrassing topics, and (6) are remembered better than factual ones.

What does research tell us? One pioneering analysis of the literature found that evidence is lacking to allow us to choose between humorous or serious message strategies. Still, the authors suggested that the following tentative conclusions were warranted:

1 Humorous messages attract attention.

2 Humorous messages may detrimentally affect comprehension of selling points.

3 Humor may distract the audience long enough to inhibit counterargumentation.

4 Humorous messages are persuasive but not necessarily greater than serious appeals.

5 Humor tends to enhance source credibility.

6 Audience effects may confound the effect of humor (e.g., the values or background of audience might interfere with humor).

7 A humorous context may increase liking for the source and in turn enhance persuasive effect of the rational part of the message.

8 Humor can function as a positive reinforcer and enhance the message.[17]

Clearly, the use of humor is an important topic for future research. We will have more to say about humor when we discuss the other models of communication later in the chapter and when we consider agency styles in the following chapter. The need to study humor to find out if it really is effective is apparent when one recognizes how frequently it is used in practice. One study found, for example, that 15 percent of television ads use humor.[18] With 30-second spots costing upwards to $300,000 or more to show once on national television, the need for greater understanding of humorous executions is evident.

Fear Appeals.[19] Marketers occasionally employ messages designed to arouse anxiety in the audience. At least two kinds of fear appeals have been used in this way. One type features the threat of *negative physical consequences.* For example, a communicator might stress the harm that would befall one if he or she did not adopt a certain practice (e.g., "You may get cavities and toothaches if you do not brush your teeth with Brand X") or refrain from doing something regularly done (e.g., "Stop smoking or you may get lung cancer, emphysema, or heart disease"). The second type of fear appeal dramatizes the threat of *social disapproval.* Here the communicator suggests that one will be shunned, disparaged, ridiculed, or in some other sense thought less well of as a person. For example, ads for mouthwashes, antiperspirants, deodorant soaps, car waxes, and lawn fertilizers often imply that if one does not use the appropriate product, others will surely develop a negative image of him or her. This type of fear appeal is aimed at a person's need for approval from others or the anxiety associated with shame, guilt, or embarrassment. Closely related to this are communications implying that one will not be loved unless he or she behaves in a particular way. Advertisements have been known to not-so-subtly imply that if a "housewife" does not cook with Brand Y, her husband and children will reject her. The fear of not being loved is frequently exploited this way in personal relations as well as the mass media.

Exactly how does a fear communication produce its effects? An obvious explanation is that fear arousal threatens the well-being of the individual and causes emotional and cognitive dissonance (i.e., "If I do not buy life insurance, my family may suffer"). To resolve the dissonance, the receiver can either reject the message, repress having seen it, or act to relieve the tension (e.g., by purchasing insurance from Firm Z).

From a managerial standpoint, two questions need to be asked: Should fear be used and, if so, how strong should the appeal be? No firm guidelines can be given to answer the first question. Fear appeals appear to be appropriate for insurance, medical, and personal care products. However, one must weigh ethical issues and the possibility that people may feel that they are being manipulated or taken advantage of. The second question is also difficult to answer. Given that a fear appeal is deemed appropriate, it might be thought that the greater the fear aroused in a communication, the greater the persuasion. This has been found to be true in some cases, but in other instances, as the level of fear rose, persuasion decreased.[20]

The upshot of current research is that the relationship between fear and persuasion is curvilinear (see Figure 8-3). With low levels of fear, persuasion increases as fear rises. Soon, however, fear becomes dysfunctional, and after peaking, persuasion actually declines as fear increases beyond a point. Why? One possibility is that fear has two opposing mental effects whose sum cancels each other out at low and high levels of fear.[21] When fear is low, arousal through the message and the chances that one will emotionally block it will be minimal. Hence, persuasion will be low. As fear rises, arousal tends to accentuate the importance of the message, but emotional blockage does not rise as quickly, with the net effect being an increase in persuasion. However, further increases in fear arousal produce greater blockage, with a slower rise in perception of the saliency of the message. Thus, when we combine the stronger force to block with the relatively weaker strength of the importance of the message, persuasion is seen to decline. Over all levels of fear, the relation to persuasion is curvilinear.

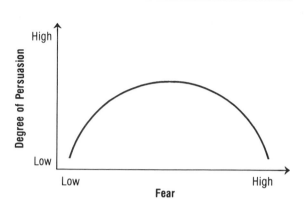

Figure 8-3. The curvilinear relationship between fear and persuasion

Extraneous Factors. When someone tells us something, a common reaction is to be skeptical and question it. This is especially true if we perceive that the speaker will in some way gain from our acceptance of the message. Further, it has been observed that people actually silently *counterargue* against attempts to change their attitudes or persuade them to do something. Given this natural reaction on the part of people, what can a communicator do to overcome it?

Strange as it might seem, it has been found that, by including *distracting elements* in a communication, persuasion can sometimes be enhanced.[22] The idea is that distractors inhibit counterargumentation on the part of the audience. Counterargumentation might have one or both of two effects. First, it competes with pro arguments for time to mentally process one's thoughts. Second, it enters the decision and evaluation process as negatively weighted information to be combined with pro arguments. In either case, counterarguments have the effect of diminishing persuasion. Hence, if distraction inhibits counterargumentation, persuasion should be increased. The danger is that distractors can potentially interfere with pro arguments as well.

Therefore, the trick is to target distractors only at counterargumentation and/or make sure that they are not so strong as to prevent pro arguments from getting through to the person.

How is this done? Normally, distractors consist of audio or visual elements incidental to the main content and point of a communication. For example, background music or extraneous noises are sometimes used in radio and television ads. Similarly, busy colors are used in print ads, or quick movements tangential to the primary action are employed in TV ads. Humor might also be used as a distractor.

Still another extraneous message factor is borrowed from drama and literature. Authors and playwrights have long known that if they hope to effectively "educate" their audiences, they can not directly "lecture" to them. Rather, they must use a *foil*, a character in the story or play who is educated by another character. The foil then becomes a vehicle for learning by the audience. The use of a foil avoids the teacher-pupil, master-servant, or parent-child connotations that frequently arise in us when people try to teach us something. In effect, the use of a foil cuts down on counterargumentation. The audience learns vicariously or through observational learning processes. Some psychological research supports the occurrence of greater persuasion under conditions where audiences overhear a person attempting to persuade another person rather than when audiences are confronted directly.[23] Although little or no research exists in marketing on this issue, television ads in particular occasionally show "secret" viewings of conversations between others (called "slice-of-life" commercials) wherein one or both parties extol the virtues of a product. Seemingly unplanned testimonials or "blind" supermarket tests surreptitiously monitored by a camera fall within this category of extraneous message content factors. Perhaps viewers believe such overheard encounters because of the absence of ulterior motives on the part of the participants. Messages sent by paid spokespersons are generally discounted or given less credibility.

One-Sided versus Two-Sided Appeals.[24] One decision facing a communicator concerns how he or she should structure a persuasive argument. Should one only mention positive attributes of a product, or should one also acknowledge any negative attributes? Should one present only favorable arguments supporting the adoption of one's product, or should unfavorable arguments also be included? The answers to these questions are not so obvious.

Classic research by Hovland and colleagues established the following generalizations.[25] A one-sided approach tends to work better when the audience is already favorable toward the arguments or issue and/or will not hear opposing arguments. Presumably, for these people, use of a two-sided appeal would needlessly raise doubts and produce less persuasion. A two-sided approach tends to work better when the audience is unfavorable to one's arguments, is better educated, or is likely to hear counterarguments.

What accounts for the superiority of two-sided arguments in the conditions noted above? One possibility is that mention of negative factors by a communicator "inoculates" the audience against potential counterclaims raised by competitors.[26] That is, if one acknowledges certain negative points about a product and then refutes or at least mitigates them, the receiver will not be surprised by a competitor's subsequent counterarguments. In fact, the receiver might well refute the counterarguments and thereby build a resistance to competitive threats. Another reason two-sided appeals might be more effective is that they enhance the credibility of the source and/or message.[27] When a speaker presents both sides of an issue, we respect and believe him or her more, and no matter on what side of the issue we decide upon, we more firmly hold to it because we feel we arrived at it relatively more ourselves.

How might one-sided and two-sided appeals be most effectively implemented? One option is to state a drawback as a minor one and emphasize the advantages to be gained by selecting the advocated alternative. For example, oil- and latex-based paints compete with each other for the exterior house-painting market. An advertiser of oil-based paints might say, "Sure, our oil-based paint is a little more difficult to apply than latex paints, but it looks better, allows the wood to breathe, and will last longer." This approach has been called a refutational appeal in the literature.

Another tactic is to use *comparison advertising*.[28] Comparison advertising may be defined as the practice of explicitly naming one or more competitors in an ad and making comparisons to one's own brand. The advertiser almost always asserts that the sponsor's brand is superior in some way. Superiority might be claimed on one or more important product attributes or in toto. As one might expect, consumers typically doubt the truthfulness of comparison ads.[29] As a consequence, advertisers often use independent research firms to make test comparisons and state this in their ads to build credibility. Comparison advertising is particularly effective for brand positioning to show competitive advantages. Presumably, it will work best to the extent that clear brand differences exist on important product attributes.

The evidence one way or the other on comparison advertising is mixed. One researcher discovered that viewers of comparison ads versus noncomparison ads seem to have greater recall of message content.[30] Another study found that comparison ads did not produce significantly higher believability, credibility, or purchase intentions than noncomparative ads.[31] Still other researchers have found that comparison messages mentioning the competition by name were more effective than noncomparison messages but were less effective than comparison messages mentioning only Brand X designations.[32] More research is needed; the issues are complex and most studies have examined only narrow topics in laboratory settings. It is not clear that comparison advertising will have a positive or negative effect. Some circumstantial evidence even exists suggesting that comparison ads made by Bayer and Anacin pain remedies with Tylenol helped the competition (i.e., Tylenol) more.[33]

A final point to consider on the topic of one-sided versus two-sided messages is the issue of *corrective advertising*.[34] Corrective advertising is the practice of requiring that certain product attributes or possible consequences of product use be explicitly disclosed through advertising. This was instituted by the Federal Trade Commission in order to remedy the effects of deceptive or false advertising. The warning placed on cigarette packages and in cigarette ads is a good example. Another is a corrective ad run by Ocean Spray a few years ago on television where they acknowledged that what they meant by "food energy" in earlier ads for cranberry juice was simply "calories." Corrective advertising is designed to benefit the public by presenting "the facts." In a sense, it represents a two-sided message when viewed in the context of the sponsor's history of communications. Whether corrective advertising will weaken or strengthen the credibility of the sponsor, in addition to informing the public, remains to be seen.

Order of Presentation of Arguments. An important message structure decision to make concerns order effects. Two issues must be considered. First is *within message order effects*. Given that one has multiple arguments or multiple product features to stress, in what order should one present the information? Should one place the most forceful arguments first, last, or in the middle of a message? Second, within a medium such as magazines or television, where should the message be placed? This is an *across message order effect* issue. Will communication be more effective in the beginning, end, or center of a magazine, television program, or sequence of ads?

There is surprisingly little research on these issues in the behavioral sciences and almost none in marketing.[35] Therefore, based on tangential research and common sense, we will only suggest some tentative conclusions and guidelines.

Research in human memory indicates that, given a series of things to remember, we generally remember things presented first and last better than those presented in the middle. As a result, one might conclude that the best arguments and the most salient product attributes should be presented early or late in a communication but not buried in the center. Memory research also tends to show that material presented last is somewhat better remembered than that presented first. On the other hand, we sometimes learn important material better if it is presented early. Hence, a trade-off exists, and until more is known, we might use trial and error or experimentation to determine which option (first or last) is best in any particular communication.

The above comments apply to the effect of order on memory. However, the audience's memory is not the only criterion or goal with which to assess the effectiveness of communication messages. With respect to receptivity, putting the most important or forceful content first would appear to offer the greatest possibility to attract attention and motivate the receiver to consider all arguments to follow. But if one desires to leave the audience in as positive a frame as possible, putting the best arguments at the end might be more effective because a progression in argumentation from weak to strong could build to a climax.

If one has pros and cons to present in a message, putting favorable information first might build an initial positive attitude, and the subsequent negative information might have less of an impact than if it had been presented first. On the other hand, if a person has a greater memory for later content, then the long-run attitude might be more negative than had a reverse sequence been presented.

We thus see that the issue of order of arguments is far from clear. For short communications such as 30-second advertisements on television, the position of arguments within the message might not be as crucial as other factors such as source, message content, or media effects. For longer communications, such as a salesperson-customer interaction that can go on for an hour or more, the order of arguments is more important. However, no research exists telling us what ordering is the most effective.

Similarly, we know little about the optimal order of messages within a medium. Magazines charge more for ads in the centerfold or inside or back covers. Presumably, these are viewed more often. Television ads tend to be viewed most in the center of programs and least at the ends. But these conclusions are largely hearsay, and no definitive research exists on the issue.

Amount of Information.[36] The decision about how much information to place in a single communication is in part a content and in part a structure decision. We intuitively know that we can only attend to and process a limited amount of information at any one point in time. As information content increases, it is believed that a point will be reached where our ability to handle it diminishes. Information "overload" is thought to occur when too much information is transmitted. It results in slower, less accurate, and inefficient processing. At the same time, it is believed that overload may produce feelings of confusion and frustration. Moreover, it is possible that too much information might cause receivers to cope by focusing on unimportant or misleading information and thus even develop a false sense of confidence and satisfaction with their decision because they feel they received "full information."

Research on these issues is not conclusive. As indicated in the first chapter on consumer behavior, we do know that decision makers cope with abundant information through simplifying strategies and rules. But the conditions under which this becomes dysfunctional are little understood. Recent research has focused on the design of information environments[37] and on consumer characteristics related to information processing and overload.[38] But discussion here is beyond the scope of this text.

Various rules-of-thumb have developed over the years with respect to the number of product attributes or arguments to include in marketing communications. For short messages, such as 30-second or 60-second ads, common wisdom suggests that no more than three selling points can be absorbed by consumers. Indeed, some advertisers believe that only a single selling point should be made in an ad, given the low involvement of audiences with the media, the relative unimportance of products, and the short time for processing. In other contexts, such as longer advertisements on television (e.g., 90-second ads), magazine ads, and customer-seller interactions, the magic number 7 plus or minus 2 is sometimes invoked.[39] That is, about 7 pieces of information are believed to be all that one can cope with in a message.

A final comment to note on information load is that some research exists about the type of information needed to make effective shopping decisions in the supermarket. Because of space limitations, we can only refer the reader to the literature on *open dating* (i.e., printing the perishable date on products),[40] *unit pricing* (i.e., presentation of the price per unit quantity of a good),[41] and *nutritional labeling.*[42]

Repetition.[43] The final message structure variable we will consider is repetition. Discussion here will be limited to the role of repetition in learning. Later in the chapter, we will consider the effects of repetition on information processing and other psychological processes. Also, the topic of repetition will be discussed again at considerable length when we cover the topic of advertising wearout in the next chapter.

Repetition can occur in two ways. Within a message, a brand name or product attribute can be repeated. Across time, the same message can be repeated. Thus, repeated exposure can occur as intra- and inter-stimulus effects.

A number of effects of repetition can be identified. First, some research suggests that we might develop a positive feeling for something solely through repeated exposure to it. This has been called the "mere exposure" effect, and it is believed to occur *without* awareness or learning.[44] Second, and more typically, repetition increases learning.[45] For example, repeated exposure of a "neutral" stimulus (such as an ad, product, or brand name) with a reward (such as pleasant sights, sounds, tastes, or other stimuli already viewed as rewarding in some way) can result in the development of an emotional reaction to the originally neutral stimulus. This is called classical conditioning. Instrumental learning occurs when a behavioral response is subsequently rewarded (reinforced) sufficiently and frequently enough. Cognitive learning occurs through observation of associations or inferred causal connections. Repetition of a neutral stimulus/ rewarding stimulus pairing, a response-reward sequence, or associations, respectively, increases the probability of learning. At least these are the effects of repetition on learning in theory.

What does research show us in practice? One study reveals that repetition does enhance recall.[46] As the number of repetitions in ads rose, recall increased but with diminishing returns. Higher levels of repetition increased recall but at relatively smaller rates than lower levels. Very small or no discernible effects of repetition were observed on attitudes, intentions, or behavior. In addition, the research showed that repetition works best with convenience as opposed to shopping goods. Apparently, the low interest and involvement with convenience goods requires repetition to build awareness, whereas shopping goods are salient enough already and people seek information on their own without the need for much advertising.

In the analysis of repetition effects, we should keep in mind that communication occurs at two levels: the micro or individual receiver level and the macro or aggregate level. At the micro level, repetition is needed to make individuals aware of products and their features. Because a number of ideas are often contained in an ad, we often need to be exposed to it a number of times to pick up all the information. Each exposure, up to a few, results in new information being transmitted. Also, we tend to forget what we have learned or at least become preoccupied with other matters so that products and their features are not always on our mind. Repetition increases memory, cuts down on decay, and keeps brands and product attributes on our mind closer to the point of actual decision making. Finally, to the extent that content in repetitive messages is positively reinforcing, repetition tends to build or at least maintain our liking for stimuli. A point might be reached where increased repetition at the micro level becomes too familiar and we then tune it out, reduce our attention, or counterargue. At the macro level, repetition is needed to reach larger and larger portions of a market who are unaware of the product or its attributes. In addition, portions of the market are continually wooed away by competitors and must be regained. This would seem to call for more repetition. However, given a relatively fixed size of any market and the fact that repetition reaches some who are already aware, one might expect diminishing returns to scale at the macro level. See the discussion on wearout in the following chapter.

The Medium

Up to this point, we have maintained that effective communication depends on the characteristics of the *source* (i.e., credibility, attractiveness, ability to mediate rewards and punishments) and the *message* (i.e., what is said—message content, and how it is said—message structure). Now we wish to explore still another variable influencing communication: the *medium* (see Figure 8-1).

Personal and Nonpersonal Media. Between any source and receiver, we can identify two types of media. With *personal media,* the "distance" between source and receiver is small. Both parties are in relatively direct contact, and verbal and nonverbal communication plays an important role. Moreover, feedback is instantaneous, and interactions go through a readily identifiable process from beginning to end. The source and receiver are aware of who each other is in personal media. Face-to-face contact between a salesperson and customer is perhaps the most common personal medium. But phone calls and letters can be personal media as well.

Nonpersonal media, in contrast, put more distance between source and receiver. Contact is indirect through one or more channels; feedback, if it occurs at all, is delayed; and the communication "process" is largely one way from source to receiver. In addition, source and receiver are generally unknown to each other as individuals. The source "sees" the receiver as a largely impersonal audience, whereas the receiver views the source as an impersonal institution or perhaps an agent for the institution. Radio, television, magazines, newspapers, fliers, and billboards represent the most frequently used nonpersonal media. Nonpersonal media are sometimes referred to as simply *mass media.* In this chapter, our discussion of media will be limited to consideration of the two-step flow model of communication, which represents a combination of personal and nonpersonal media and explains part of the process of social influence. We will explore other aspects of media in subsequent chapters.

The Two-Step Flow Model. Exactly how do mass communications influence the public? A classic study was performed over 40 years ago to answer the key questions and issues.[47] In particular, researchers were concerned with why people vote the way they do. Radio and print media were thought to influence voting, but no one seemed to know exactly how. The upshot of the study was surprising. Mass media were found to have a negligible impact on voting. At least, the mass media did not directly influence the public. Rather, the influence was found to be indirect. As represented in Figure 8-4, the mass media had the greatest impact on a small number of individuals, termed *opinion leaders*, and these people, in turn, influenced the general public. Step 1 in the model represents nonpersonal contact, whereas Step 2 constitutes direct, interpersonal contact. In sum, the mass media were found to work largely through intermediaries.

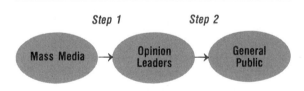

Figure 8-4. The classic two-step flow model of communication

The two-step model was an important revelation in the political arena as well as in marketing. It showed that the mass media had a smaller direct effect than commonly believed. After discovery of the two-step flow of influence, the practice of communication began to change drastically. Sources in ads were chosen from the ranks of opinion leaders. Messages were designed to reach opinion leaders more directly, and media were selected on the basis of which outlets were watched or read more by opinion leaders. And so on.

Research into the dynamics of communication continued with a number of new findings coming to light during the two decades following the original two-step flow model research.[48] Briefly, although the sequence shown in Figure 8-4 was often corroborated, other sequences were found to occur sometimes as well. In particular, as shown in Figure 8-5, three additional effects (drawn as solid lines) were observed. One of these was the observation that the general public did not always wait for opinion leaders to make pronouncements but rather often sought them out for information and advice. Hence, an arrow is also drawn from the general public to opinion leaders in Figure 8-5. A second finding was that the mass media often directly reach selected others and not only opinion leaders. Specifically, we can identify innovators and reference group members as people sometimes reached directly by the mass media. These people need not be, and often are not, opinion leaders. In Figure 8-5, solid arrows are drawn from the mass media to innovators and reference group members to reflect this additional direct influence. Third, and very important, it was discovered that a powerful means of influence occurs among peers, family members, co-workers, and others within the general public. Typically, this occurs as word-of-mouth communication,[49] and social comparison and other processes play an important role as well. We discussed many of these forces in the chapters on consumer behavior. The solid arrows from innovators and reference group members to the general public in Figure 8-5 capture these effects. A final point to note in Figure 8-5 is that a number of other flows occur but with somewhat less influence than those discussed heretofore. These are shown as dashed lines. Notice that the mass media directly affect the general public and that opinion leaders directly affect innovators and reference group members, too.

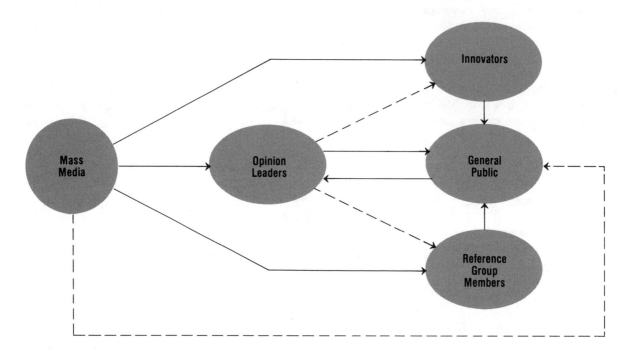

Figure 8-5. A modern rendition of the communication process: multidirectional flows

A considerable body of research exists in marketing identifying who opinion leaders typically tend to be[50] and how they influence others.[51] Also, quite a bit has been written on ways of measuring opinion leadership.[52] We will not discuss this research herein because of space limitations. However, we will close this section on media effects with a brief summary of how practitioners have tried to apply research based on the two-step and multidirectional flow models.

Communication strategies have attempted to reach, stimulate, and even create opinion leaders. Opinion leaders might be reached through personal contact, phone calls, personalized mail, or strategic selection of effective media. Research is needed to identify reading and viewing habits of opinion leaders, to find key mailing lists, to identify leaders in the community, and to generally understand the life-styles, psychographics, and activities of opinion leaders. Opinion leadership can sometimes be stimulated by hiring influential people to use a product or simply by providing highly visible people with the product free of charge. The Blitz-Weinhard Brewing Company once paid selected beer drinkers in cities to drink and advertise their beer in taverns. Sporting goods companies provide free tennis rackets and other equipment to professionals in the hope that incidental contact with amateurs will stimulate sales. Finally, opinion leaders can be created by selection of highly visible, respected, and influential people in groups or communities and then educating them, increasing their enthusiasm for a product, and so on.[53] At least such a tactic once worked for promoting record sales in high schools.

Another strategy building on recent research is to increase word-of-mouth communication. Advertisements, packages, slogans, and even products can be designed to stimulate word-of-mouth conversations. A recent Chex Cereal ad on television showed one family eating Chex; and they turned to pass the box to another family, presumably next door, followed by the second family trying the cereal, passing it on, and so forth. The power of word-of-mouth communication can be phenomenal, and it's free. However, sometimes word-of-mouth communication can hurt a product. For years, McDonald's has had to fight negative rumors about the use of digestible plastics in shakes and red worm meat in its hamburgers. The latter rumor alone is alleged to have lowered sales by as much as 30 percent in areas where the rumor was rampant.[54] For years, Procter & Gamble tried to counteract rumors that its logo represented a fiendish symbol of Satan, but by 1985, it gave up and changed the logo. So, ads that implore us to "tell your neighbor" or "pass it on" may constitute a double-edged sword.

The Receiver

In addition to the source, message, and medium, the *characteristics of the receiver* also determine the outcome of a communication attempt. In the next sections of this chapter, we will elaborate on the cognitive processes and affective responses receivers experience. In this section, we will focus on research into how the attributes of receivers influence communication.

Some research suggests that the personality of a receiver affects the communication process. For example, it has been found that those lower in self-esteem are more easily persuaded than those higher in self-esteem.[55] However, under conditions where a communication contains rewards or punishments, high self-esteem leads to greater compliance.[56] Presumably, people higher in self-esteem are less anxious and better able to rationally assess the meaning of the environment for them. Similarly, some research indicated that people who trust others more are also more easily persuaded.[57] High trusters, like those high in self-esteem, tend to view messages with greater believability and attribute higher credibility than low trusters and those low in self-esteem. In the next section of the chapter, we will use an information-processing theory to better interpret the effects of personality on persuasion.

Audiences also differ in their education levels, intelligence, patience, values, and attitudes. The same source, message, or medium will have different effects, depending on the audience's abilities, inclinations, prejudices, orientations, cognitive styles, and learning histories. However, probably the most important factors affecting the outcome of influence attempts are the mental and feeling processes people go through when processing information.

An Information-Processing Model of Communication[58]

The classic SMMR model of communication is an important one, but it tends to underemphasize what the receiver does when confronted by a persuasive appeal. That is, it fails to consider *how* receivers process information. Within the past decade or so, a considerable body of research has focused on these processes.

The Model

Figure 8-6 is an outline of an information-processing model of communication. It is intended to represent the mental stages one passes through from the point of initial reception of a communication until a final decision to act or not to act is made. There are five such stages.

Notice that, from the perspective of the receiver, the process begins with *exposure* to an ad, a pitch by a salesperson, or any other piece of information presented from the outside. The first reaction the receiver has is *perception* of the information. Awareness and attention processes are early reactions with roughly the same meaning as perception. Next, the perceived information is initially processed in order to gain *comprehension*. This is basically a "what is it" reaction. It is here that information is converted to understanding and knowledge. At this point, one or both of two things might happen. First, some or all of the knowledge might be transferred to *memory* for storage. Or, second, the knowledge might be further interpreted in an *information-integration* stage. Attitude formation is a special case of information integration. After integration, knowledge is assessed and evaluated in a *decision-making* stage. Here preferences develop, and one either yields to a communication or rejects it. A favorable decision or yielding then leads to an *intention* to act. Finally, the process ends with performance of a *behavior*, such as purchase.

The information-processing model is basically an SOR (stimulus-organism-response) model.[59] The five stages perform intervening or mediational roles between stimulus communications and behavioral responses. In a sense, we can think of the receiver as mentally acting upon the information presented to him or her. Before a communication can produce a behavioral response, each stage must occur in the order indicated. This might be called the closed form of the model because it does not allow for variability in the process. A less rigid version might be termed the open form of the model, which would permit certain stages to be skipped, to play less of a role, or even to occur out of sequence at times. Nevertheless, the basic information-processing model stipulates a particular sequence of psychological events: cognition $\longrightarrow$ affect $\longrightarrow$ behavior. In marketing, the information-processing model is also known as the learning-response model or the hierarchy-of-effects model.

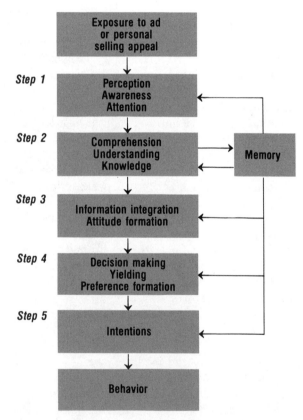

Figure 8-6. An information-processing model of communication

Assuming that the information-processing model is valid, we can gain an indication of how communication affects responses in a receiver as follows.[60] Let us assume that exposure and each stage have a probability of occurrence, that the probability of each stage is proportional to the joint probability that the previous stages have occurred, and that the stages are statistically independent. Finally, let us assume, for discussion purposes, that the probability of exposure is .9 and the probability of each of the remaining steps is .7. As a consequence, the probability of each stage can be computed as:

$$\text{probability of perception} = (.9)(.7) = .63$$
$$\text{probability of comprehension} = (.9)(.7)(.7) = .44$$
$$\text{probability of information integration} = (.9)(.7)(.7)(.7) = .31$$
$$\text{probability of yielding} = (.9)(.7)(.7)(.7)(.7) = .22$$
$$\text{probability of intentions} = (.9)(.7)(.7)(.7)(.7)(.7) = .15$$
$$\text{probability of behavior} = (.9)(.7)(.7)(.7)(.7)(.7)(.7) = .10$$

Thus we see that the chances of information getting through are systematically reduced as one passes through the stages. Even with relatively high probabilities for exposure and subsequent processing at each stage, the probability of a behavioral response is low.

As a consequence, one can readily appreciate the difficulty communicators face. The first task is to gain exposure, but not everyone can or will be reached by a communication effort. Even among those who become exposed, a systematic mental filtering process goes on. We should stress, however, that the stages in information processing do not merely filter and transfer information from one stage to another. Rather, as noted in the chapters on consumer behavior, construction processes occur as well. That is, information is added to, transformed, and generally interpreted according to the receiver's needs, values, prior learning, and expectations. Thus, knowledge is a two-way street. It reflects "objective" content inherent in the world outside the receiver. Yet, at the same time, it contains the unique "subjective" content that the receiver infuses into the information. This occurs in all stages of processing but especially in the first four. The arrows from memory to the stages in Figure 8-6 represent, in part, the constructive processes. A person's worldview, mind-set, expectations, predispositions, cognitive schemata, prejudices, etc., are examples.

Relation of the Information-Processing Model to Communication

The information-processing model can help us better understand how communication and social influence work.[61] We might think of each of the parts of the SMMR model as independent variables impinging on the information processing of a receiver. Source characteristics, message content and structure, media, and receiver attributes each influence information processing in different ways. As a matter of fact, it is useful to think of each of the independent variables as reaching into the depths of information processing with different degrees of success. Some of the SMMR variables we discussed are more effective than others in attracting attention, building comprehension, aiding information integration, influencing preferences, and so on. Certain SMMR variables work well in early stages of information processing but poorly in later ones, and vice versa. We therefore should realize that communicators face trade-offs in the design of persuasive attempts. The information-processing model can aid us in the managerial design process. To illustrate the principles involved, we will consider a number of SMMR variables: humor, fear, source credibility, and repetition.

Humor and Information Processing

How can we explain the effects of a humorous message through the information-processing model? Basically, humor affects the five stages differently and, when compared to other message strategies, offers advantages and disadvantages.

In Table 8-3 we see some possible effects of humor on each of the five stages in the information-processing model. Notice first that humor is particularly effective in attracting attention. Also, to the extent that it builds curiosity and is psychologically rewarding, it tends to hold attention. A related point is that, relative to rational appeals, it usually results in greater involvement with the message. This has the effect of raising arousal and stimulating later information-processing stages such as preference formation. Second, with respect to comprehension, humor helps to get across an intuitive sense of the point of a message. One obtains an overall gestalt. It can, however, detract from processing of rational product benefits because of the mental response competition that occurs between global processing (a largely right-brain function) and detailed, linear processing (a basically left-brain function). Third, in information integration, humor facilitates the organization of affective reactions but is not as well suited to helping a person structure cognitive responses. It can potentially function as a distraction and inhibit counterargumentation, however. Fourth, humor is particularly effective in inducing positive feelings for a brand or other global aspects of objects but not necessarily for developing feelings toward specific product attributes. Finally, humor might be powerful enough to stimulate intentions to try an impulse item but probably has no special powers for other products.

TABLE 8-3

The Differential Effects of Humor on the Stages of Information Processing

Stage of Processing	Effect of Humor
Perception	1. Attracts attention. May also serve to hold attention throughout the presentation of the communication.
↓	
Comprehension	2. Tends to detract from a literal understanding of rational product benefits. But gives a global, intuitive understanding. Overcomes resistance to sensitive personal issues.
↓	
Information Integration	3. Not well suited for cognitive content but can facilitate affective learning. May serve as a distractor to prevent counter-argumentation.
↓	
Yielding and Preference Formation	4. Helps develop positive feeling for overall brand if well focused. But not particularly suited to developing feelings toward specific product attributes. Involves audience with ad and product/ brand to high degree.
↓	
Intentions	5. For impulse items, may stimulate intentions to try product. But generally has no differential advantage or disadvantage on this stage.

As a manager designing persuasive messages, how can one put such ideas to use? First, for new products, humor is probably best used in ads to attract attention. This should be kept to a minimum, however, because one important purpose of ads for new products is to convey key product features and benefits. Therefore, in television or radio ads for new products, humor should most likely be restricted to either the first few seconds or else kept low-key in later portions of the ads. Perhaps one effective strategy for new products would be to use humor in ads to gain attention but then shift to a rational appeal.

Second, for established products or for products where people are familiar with brands and/or attributes, humor might be an effective tactic to build liking for a brand. However, when products are complex or when many arguments are necessary to convince consumers, humor is a less appropriate tactic.

Overall, when humor is used, an effort should be made to focus on product attributes as much as possible. The drawback with humor is that people often remember the funny spokesperson and the humor of the message but do not process the brand name, its features, and the selling propositions contained in the ad. Humor sometimes detracts from remembrance, too.

Fear and Information Processing

In Figure 8-3, we suggested that the relationship between the level of fear arousal and persuasion is curvilinear. Persuasion is low for low or high levels of arousal, but it is highest at some intermediate level of fear. We can use an information-processing argument to explain this. Figure 8-7 shows the processes and is based on the compensation hypothesis proposed by McGuire. Level of fear arousal is plotted on the x-axis, whereas persuasability is plotted on the y-axis. Notice first that as fear arousal increases, the probability of perception and comprehension decreases because fear arousal is threatening and is likely to interfere with the receiver's ability to attend to and concentrate on the message. Indeed, for high levels of fear, the receiver might entirely repress the message so that neither perception nor comprehension occur. On the other hand, fear arousal enhances yielding. This is largely a consequence of the ability of the arousing message to function as an anxiety cue and to evoke psychological responses that make the receiver subservient and susceptible to influence. In sum, notice that fear arousal has opposite effects on different stages of information processing. When we add the opposing tendencies together in Figure 8-7, we see that a curvilinear response is formed.

Intermediate levels of fear arousal produce the greatest amount of persuasability. It is at these levels that the message gets through with the most impact. The implication is that, given a choice of fear arousal for message contact, low and high levels are to be avoided. The exact level to use is perhaps best determined experimentally or by trial and error.

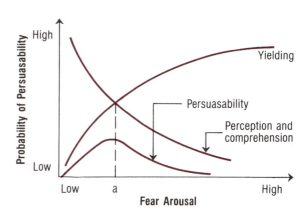

Figure 8-7. An information-processing-model explanation for the curvilinear relationship between fear, arousal, and persuasability

Before we leave the topic of fear arousal, we should note that McGuire's compensation hypothesis has even wider applicability. In particular, for personality characteristics of the receiver such as self-esteem, a curvilinear relationship to persuasibility is also predicted.[62] Figure 8-8 shows this relation which has an important difference to note from the relation of fear arousal to persuasion shown in Figure 8-7. As receiver self-esteem rises, attention and comprehension rise, too. Those higher in self-esteem tend to be more outgoing, to be exposed to more sources of information, to process information more accurately, and so on. By the same token, those high in self-esteem tend to know more pro and con arguments, to be more questioning, and to counterargue more. As a consequence, self-esteem is negatively related to yielding. Again, when we combine the opposing forces, we see a curvilinear relation. People with intermediate levels of self-esteem are persuaded more than those with low or high levels of self-esteem.

The important point to note about the compensation hypothesis is that message options and receiver characteristics have different effects on different stages of information processing. Further, to determine the ultimate effect of a communication effort, one must combine the differential impacts of the independent variables.

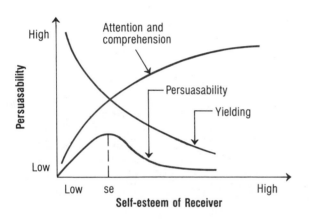

Figure 8-8. The relationship between source self-esteem and persuasibility

Source Credibility and Information Processing

The majority of research has either found a positive relation[63] between source credibility and persuasibility or no relation.[64] However, under some conditions, a recent study found that low-credibility sources can actually be more influential than high-credibility sources.[65] An information-processing analysis can account for this counterintuitive finding.

The conditions under which low credibility led to greater influence than high credibility were the following. The receiver read a persuasive communication (with either a high- or low-credibility source), signed a petition supporting the issue advocated in the communication, and then expressed his or her attitude toward the issue. Notice that the sequence here is cognitive processing (reading of communication) → behavior (signing of petition) → affect (expression of attitude). Source credibility was found to affect attitudes, with the low-credibility source producing more influence than the high-credibility one. Why? The authors argue that the receiver knows he or she behaved in a particular way (i.e., signed the petition) and that this information is processed in a particular way prior to attitude formation, depending on other cues in the persuasive appeal. If the source were highly credible, the receiver would have two possible explanations for his or her own petition-signing behavior: i.e., either the credibility of the source or one's own attitude could account for it. Thus, some uncertainty should exist in these subjects, and their assessment of their own attitudes should be relatively low. However, for those reading a message from a low-credibility source, the receiver realizes that he or she complied with the behavioral requests despite the lack of credibility and hence infers that he or she must have had a positive attitude. Therefore, these individuals should express a relatively stronger attitude toward the issue in the persuasive communication than those exposed to the high-credibility source.

Notice that, to explain persuasibility (in this case measured by the person's attitude), we have had to resort to an information-processing argument. Here what is processed is one's own attributions for the causes of prior behavior. Notice further that the greater influence of low source credibility over high source credibility applies to the case where behavior precedes attitude. The more common greater effect for high versus low source credibility in the literature occurred when attitude preceded behavior.[66]

Repetition and Information Processing

The effects of message repetition can be interpreted from an information-processing standpoint. Because we will consider the processes in some depth in the following chapter, comments here will be limited to an introduction to some of the issues involved.

We might begin by thinking of the effects of repetition at the macro (i.e., aggregate market) and micro (i.e., individual consumer) levels. At the macro level, repetition has the effect of reaching greater and greater proportions of a market. Not everyone will be aware of a brand, its price, product attributes, and so on. Presentation of an ad in the media for the first time will be viewed by only a portion of the market. Only a fraction will become aware. Repeated presentations will reach some of those people not reached by the first or early presentations. Thus, exposure to an ad for the market as a whole will be a function of the number of repetitions. Of course, we might expect the relationship to reflect diminishing marginal returns in that a point will be reached where each repetition brings fewer and fewer new people into the aware category. Nevertheless, repetition is needed to make people in the market aware of the brand.

Consider now what happens at the micro level to individual consumers. An initial exposure to an ad might have only the effect of making one vaguely aware of the advertised brand. Further processing in the hierarchy of responses shown in Figure 8-6 may not occur. Because people typically pay little attention to ads and because the importance of many products to people is low, this probably is a common reaction. However, the next time the person is exposed to the same ad, additional processing may take place. For example, the mention of the brand name might capture one's attention, and an effort to comprehend the selling points might transpire. Another repetition might lead to still deeper processing, including attitude formation, counterargumentation, and consideration of product trial. For people fully aware of a brand and who may have developed a favorable predisposition to it, repetition might serve still a further function. It might stimulate one to initiate a purchase trip or make a plan to purchase the advertised brand on one's next shopping trip. Further, repetition might produce what is known as top-of-the-mind awareness. As one passes a storefront display or a shelf of wares in the supermarket, recall or recognition of the advertised brand might induce one to try the product or trigger a previously stored plan to purchase it.

Back at the macro level, we can see that different proportions of people will be aware, have an understanding of the message, develop a favorable attitude, intend to buy, and so on. We can think of repetition as moving people from one stage in the hierarchy to another stage. In a sense, the number of people in each stage will be a function of repetition. In the next chapter, we will consider the effects of repetition on forgetting and other reactions consumers have as individuals and in the aggregate.

Cognitive Response and Affective Response Models of Communication

We turn now to two approaches that might be thought of as special cases of or refinements in the information-processing model of communication: the cognitive response and affective response models. In the cognitive response model, emphasis is placed on thought processes engendered by a communication. In the affective response model, stress is placed on the emotional and physiological reactions stimulated by a communication. However, as we shall discover, cognitive and affective reactions occur in both models. For the most part, only the degree of processing and possibly the sequences among reactions change.

The Cognitive Response Model[67]

A central part of the information-processing model is the message. The model hypothesizes that a person processes message content, gains an understanding of it, integrates this with prior knowledge, forms an attitude, and then decides to act or not. Without necessarily rejecting this sequence, the cognitive response model introduces an additional set of internal mediating processes. Specifically, it is hypothesized that a persuasive communication is not only processed for content and meaning, but it leads to or is accompanied by the generation of cognitions that may or may not be contained in the message itself. In other words, after reception of a message, a person is believed to produce various thinking responses. These might entail thoughts, ideas, inferences, and other mental reactions. Some of these might be contained in the message. However, cognitive responses frequently will be merely implied by the message or other cues in the communication setting, or they will be generated from expectations, stored information, or mental construction processes internal to the receiver and not arise directly from the message.

In general, the four most common cognitive responses are believed to be the following: counterarguments, support arguments, source derogation, and schemata processing. Each of these may occur at or below the level of awareness. Figure 8-9 shows an outline of the cognitive response model. Notice the central mediating role of the cognitive responses.

Before we describe how cognitive responses affect the persuasive communication process, let us briefly define the four types of reactions. A *counterargument* is a mental statement contradicting, disputing, or refuting a point made in a communication. For example, a person might see an ad on television asserting that regular use of Drain Cleaner X will keep one's drains unclogged for up to four weeks. The viewer, however, might silently (or verbally) react by thinking (or stating), "I used that drain cleaner before and it didn't even keep my drain clean for a week." A *support argument* is a mental assertion upholding, corroborating, or backing a point made in a communication. For instance, the viewer of the drain cleaner ad might think, "It seems to me I remember my neighbor saying that Drain Cleaner X performed well for him, especially on bathroom clogs." A *source derogation* is a mental attribution that the spokesperson or message is inferior, negatively evaluated, or in some other way disparaged in the mind of the receiver. For example, a viewer of the drain cleaner ad might feel that "the ad is stupid and insulting" or that "the spokesperson is not credible and is only delivering the message because he was paid to do so." Finally, a *schema*[68] is an organization or representation in memory of past experiences, judgments, or feelings that are used to categorize, define, or interpret new, usually more complex, information, stimuli, or experiences. In a sense, a schema is like a model or ideal construction of the world. New knowledge is thought to be processed and evaluated in relation to it. At a gross level, our prejudices and stereotypes function in this way. At deeper levels, we may have many schemata that function rather automatically and below levels of awareness in the interpretation of many stimuli. Some of us, for example, might develop patterned ways of classifying selling points in ads, construing how a product should be evaluated, or searching for foods in the supermarket. Presentation of a new ad, introduction of a new product, or the next trip to the supermarket will be affected by the schemata through which we look at the world.

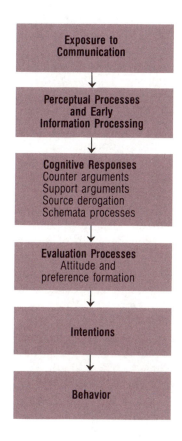

Figure 8-9. The cognitive response model

Returning to Figure 8-9, let us consider how information is processed and how cognitive responses might mediate the effects of a persuasive communication on behavior. The process again begins with exposure to information, and perceptual and interpretive cognitive activities occur. Next,

the person generates specific cognitive responses. These will be either favorable or unfavorable to the appeals in the message (on occasion, they may simply be irrelevant). In either case, the cognitive responses are then evaluated along with information in the message and prior knowledge in memory. Depending on how all favorable and unfavorable evaluations are integrated, the person may experience attitude change and form a preference or predisposition to act. This, in turn, leads to an intention to act or not, followed by potential choice-related behaviors.

The cognitive response model is very similar to the information-processing model. However, two differences should be noted. First, the former model places less emphasis on the effects of message comprehension, message information integration, and message yielding than the latter model. Whereas the information-processing model makes these stages a requirement and attributes causal primacy to them, the cognitive response model leaves open the possibility that decisions and choices may not be crucially affected by message content, per se, but rather may be accentuated or even overridden by self-generated cognitive reactions. Thus, a second difference in the models is the specification of particular mental processes in the cognitive response model that can influence attitudes, intentions, and behavior but are not contained explicitly in the information-processing model. Some new research supports the validity of the former model over the latter.[69] We turn now to a brief summary of how the cognitive response model can explain certain communication effects of source credibility, message content and structure, and receiver characteristics.

Source Credibility.[70] Whether or not source credibility will augment the effects of a persuasive message can be explained by the receiver's predisposition toward the message content and the cognitive responses engendered. Highly credible sources are expected to be *more* persuasive than less credible sources when the receiver is initially *unfavorable* toward a message. For these people, high credibility inhibits counterargumentation, whereas low or moderate credibility facilitates it. No change in support arguments is expected since these people are unfavorable at the start. As a consequence, those exposed to the less credible source will have more negative evaluations to integrate than those exposed to the highly credible source. Hence, high credibility is expected to result in more persuasability than low or moderate credibility for those negatively predisposed. On the other hand, highly credible sources are expected to be *less* persuasive than low or moderate credible sources when the receiver is initially *favorable* toward a message: low or moderate credibility leads to the generation of more support arguments than high credibility because low credibility threatens one's initial position. Because people are predisposed toward the message to begin with, however, no difference in counterargumentation is expected. As a result, those exposed to the less credible source will have more positive evaluations to integrate than those exposed to the highly credible source. Therefore, low or moderate credibility is expected to lead to greater persuasion than high credibility for those already positively predisposed. Receivers neither favorably nor unfavorably disposed to a message are not expected to be influenced by source credibility according to the cognitive response model.

Message Effects. *Distraction* in a message might be expected to have one of two effects. On the one hand, it might prevent counterargumentation. Yet, on the other hand, it might inhibit support argumentation as well. It is not clear when one or the other (or both) will occur. Perhaps the receiver's initial position on an issue is again a factor. If one is initially predisposed to a message, then distraction might inhibit generation or rehearsal of support arguments. Presumably, no or few counterarguments would be generated by those initially favorable. Thus, distraction for this audience would be counterproductive because of suppression of pro arguments. In contrast, if one is initially unfavorable, then distraction might prevent or limit counterargumentation. These people also would tend not to generate pro arguments. Overall, then, the initially unfavorable receiver would appear to be persuaded more, if distractors were administered. Of course, distraction should not be so great as to prevent reception of the message.

Repetition, too, can be interpreted from a cognitive response perspective.[71] Repetition of positive appeals tends, in the beginning, to facilitate comprehension and thwart counterargumentation. The receiver needs time to process the information in the positive appeal and form an evaluation. However, after a while, repetition becomes counterproductive because processing time shifts from consideration of positive appeals to boredom and then to consideration of negative aspects or implications of the message. Our thoughts drift and we search for disconfirming evidence with high levels of repetition. This phenomenon is known as *wearout*, and we will investigate it further in the next chapter.

Receiver Characteristics. The *self-esteem* of receivers might also augment or inhibit cognitive responses. Those high in self-esteem might generate both pro and con arguments in response to a message, whereas those low in self-esteem might tend to focus more on support arguments *or* counterarguments. The high self-esteem information processor is more accurate and balanced in his or her assessments of messages and has greater confidence in his or her judgments and cognitive responses. The low self-esteem processor is less accurate and confident and is driven more either by product risk aversion (resulting in more counterargumentation) or the need for approval or compliance (leading to more support argumentation). Risk aversion for the low self-esteem processor will lead to less persuasion than for the high self-esteem processor, whereas the need for approval or compliance in the low self-esteem receiver will lead to greater compliance than the high self-esteem receiver. Hence, to predict how self-esteem will moderate persuasion, we must also know the person's tendency toward risk aversion or the need for compliance, in addition to determination of the type of cognitive responses made. Presently, the above reasoning is speculative.

The Affective Response Model[72]

A communication will sometimes influence an affective or emotional state before any further psychological or behavioral response occurs (see Figure 8-10). That is, after one first experiences a communication, physiological and feeling states associated with an emotion might arise. The emotional reaction, then, may have a number of effects. One is that it might have an impact on perceptual and cognitive processes. For example, affective arousal might increase attention, enhance information processing, and improve memory retrieval. A second effect is that emotional reactions might lead to attitude change, preference formation, or the activation of a goal, rule, script, or schemata. Third, affect might—through prior learning, automatic (i.e., biological or reflexive) reactions, or curiosity urges—directly influence intentions and/or choice behaviors. Let us now briefly explore four ways in which affect might precede or occur without cognitive processes, before ultimately influencing behavior.

High-Pressure Communication. Sometimes consumers are confronted with a compelling communicator and message and, due to the dynamics of the situation, develop an initial liking for a product or brand. This will be likely to occur to the extent that no alternative brands are available (or none is considered at the time), a real need exists, and the seller presses for compliance. A door-to-door vacuum cleaner or encyclopedia salesperson might fit this scenario. Any cognitions in the brief sales encounter are likely to be confined to assessment of what one needs to do to buy the product. As a consequence, sales pressure quickly

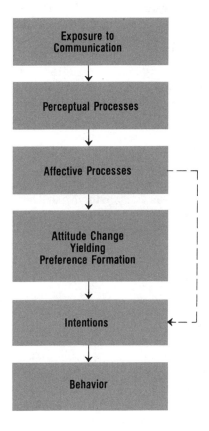

Figure 8-10. An outline of the affective response model

leads to positive affect toward the product and then acquiescence, with little information processing occurring along the way. Indeed, other needs and costs are temporarily bypassed. After the sale, of course, the consumer will process information associated with the original encounter, subsequent experience with the product, exposure to ads from rival brands, and so on. This, in turn, may lead to additional cognitive responses (e.g., "second thoughts"), affective reactions (e.g., anger), and intentions (e.g., asking for a refund). In any case, the process began with an emotional response to a persuasive appeal, as contrasted with the information-processing and cognitive response models that begin with a thinking response to communication.

Postcognitive Learning. After a person has been exposed to a communication, processed it, and developed an attitude or preference, a new affectively charged communication presented at a later time may have one of two effects. First, to the extent that prior learning had occurred (either through classical or operant conditioning) or stimulus generalization occurs with the new communication, an emotional reaction might be engendered without any or very little cognitive processing. Second, the new affectively charged communication might stimulate retrieval of stored evaluations from memory[73] or activate a schema[74] or script that then serves as a precursor to volitions or choice itself. Another way affective responses might constitute the initial reaction to a stimulus occurs as a consequence to prior learning. To the extent that previous exposure to ads or prior usage results in emotional reactions, subsequent presentation of cues tied to the learned emotions will induce affective responses followed by further processing and/or action. Classical conditioning and operant learning are two examples. Notice that thinking processes may, but need not, accompany such reactions.

Dissonance Attribution.[75] In dissonance attribution, a consumer first performs a behavior (e.g., purchase of Brand X) for whatever reason. Then he or she mentally reflects upon performance of the behavior and infers that he or she must have liked or been attracted to the object of the behavior to have acted accordingly. This, in turn, may lead to further thoughts, feelings, and plans. The behavior $\rightarrow$ affect $\rightarrow$ cognition sequence occurs most frequently or with the strongest impact when no or few extraneous determinants of the original act are perceived. The person must have an objective basis to conclude that it was his or her own internal states (e.g., liking of Brand X) that led to the act rather than coercion, habit, luck, or impulse. In a sense, performance of a behavior leads to attitude formation or change, and this leads to cognitive learning and subsequent volitions. You might recall seeing advertisements aimed at people who have already made a purchase. The ad might have shown an interview with a recent purchaser where he or she effusively extols the virtues of the brand. This ad has the purpose of bolstering or reinforcing the attitude of the receiver who also bought the brand. Such ads are sometimes designed additionally to reduce dissonance in people who have made a purchase but who may experience second thoughts or be exposed to ads from competitors. By helping people develop positive feelings after purchase, the sponsor hopes that they will speak well of the product to others, make future purchases of the same brand, and so on.

Intense Emotionality. A final example of affective response occurs when a stimulus of considerable positive or negative qualities gains one's attention. An intense stimulus might be perceived as potentially satisfying a particularly salient or deprived need (such as a drink would be to a very thirsty person). Alternatively, an intense negative stimulus might be perceived to be life threatening or dangerous in some way. In addition, the stimulus need not arise from external sources but may be internally generated. In any case, a person's first reaction is likely to be affective. It is interesting to observe that some instances of consumption fitting this case need not exhibit gross or readily visible signs of intense emotionality. Consumption characteristics of compulsive, neurotic, or paranoiac behaviors (e.g., excessive gambling, hoarding) fall into this category. Probably more typical examples, however, are purchases of items in once-a-year clearance sales that sometimes take place in atmospheres of frenzy and urgency. Although the trip to a clearance sale might be a rational preplanned affair, the choice of particular items amid a scene of chaos is often an intense emotional experience.

An Integration of the Various Communication Models[76]

As the foregoing presentation indicates, consumers react to communication appeals in many different ways. Nevertheless, for purposes of study and for decision-making purposes, we can identify a small number of sequences that capture the vast majority of reactions people have to persuasive and educative appeals. Figure 8-11 illustrates five generic responses to communication: the cognitive response, affective response, parallel response, low-involvement response, and social response models.

Communication ⟶ Cognitions ⟶ Affect ⟶ Intentions ⟶ Behavior

A. Cognitive response model

Communication ⟶ Affect ⟶ Cognitions ⟶ Intentions ⟶ Behavior

B. Affective response model

C. Parallel response model

Communication ⟶ Cognitions ⟶ Intentions ⟶ Behavior ⟶ Affect

D. Low-involvement response model

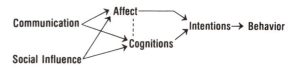

E. Social response model

Figure 8-11. Five generic communication response models

Cognitive Response Model

The cognitive response model has already been treated at length and is a special kind of information-processing model. A persuasive communication is thought to induce cognitive reactions at the outset, such as comprehension, information integration, and support or counterarguments. The cognitive response model is quite similar to the micro diffusion of innovation model we discussed in an earlier chapter. It has also been called the learning response model because thinking processes comprise its central features. Advertisers know it as the hierarchy-of-effects model, but because virtually all models rest on a hierarchy of one form or another, we will avoid this usage. As shown in Figure 8-11, the initial cognitive reactions are hypothesized to influence attitudes (i.e., affect) and ultimately influence intentions and behavior.

We would expect the cognitive response model to validly depict consumer reactions when the product is important to the consumer, when functional benefits are derived from it, when he or she is involved sufficiently with the message, and when clear differences (usually tangible ones) exist among competing brands. Under these circumstances, consumers typically pass through a cognitive response sequence. All of these conditions combine to require that thinking processes be applied before decisions are made and actions are taken.

Affective Response Model

This model, too, has been thoroughly considered in this chapter (see Figure 8-11). A persuasive communication is first believed to stimulate an emotional response, then thinking processes, and finally intentions and action. The affective response model, except for its dissonance attribution variant, has not been considered very much in marketing.

The conditions where it is most descriptive of consumers' responses to communication appeals are the following. First, the product must again be a salient one. In this case, its importance is more emotional than rational, although financial risks may also play a role. Second, the product has symbolic or social significance rather than functional utility. Third, the consumer must be involved with the message, or, if uninvolved, he or she must be aroused by physiological, emotional, or other attention-getting stimuli. The latter may operate below levels of awareness or at least with low levels of involvement. Finally, although clear, tangible differences do not have to exist among competing brands, intangible differences must be perceived. The latter will typically be based on emotional or social appeals.

Parallel Response Model

A new model, not considered previously, allows for the simultaneous occurrence of affect and cognitions (see Figure 8-11). Rather than requiring a series of steps between affect and cognitions, the model permits them to exist as parallel reactions. This possibility recognizes that human information processing can, under certain conditions, proceed through functionally autonomous actions in the central nervous systems. Since people respond in parallel affective/cognitive ways, a manager would want to fine-tune the stimuli under his or her control because these stimuli influence an individual consumer's psychological states differently, and the ultimate path and impact on behavior will depend on how the parallel responses operate on the stimulus information. For example, it would not be accurate to assume that one particular appeal (whether rational or emotional) would ultimately have the same effect regardless of the consumer's psychological processing structure. Such an approach might be suitable for the cognitive response or affective response models where a processing-in-series sequence is the rule. In these models, output from one stage serves as input to the next, and the overall effect on intentions or behavior is roughly equal, given that the stimulus has both cognitive and affective meaning. However, for parallel processing, the cognitive and affective content are acted on separately and will have independent effects not contaminated by sequential operations. Rejection or blockage at either the affective or cognitive stages in the cognitive response or affective response models precludes further processing. This is not necessarily the case in the parallel response model where, (a) if factual information is undecipherable, forgotten, or confusing, affective processing can continue to ultimately influence choice, or (b) if affective processing is thwarted, cognitive processing can continue, also with further effects on choice.

One might expect parallel responses under the following conditions. First, the stimulus communication must convey affective meaning and must have a moderate to high saliency to induce a response. Yet, that affective content should not be so high as to overwhelm cognitive information that is also a required part of the communication. Second, it is necessary, too, that sufficient prior experience has occurred with the product and/or the content of the message to the extent that distinct affective and cognitive representations exist in memory. Without sufficient prior content in both modes, one cannot expect much parallel processing because new material will require focused processing, which usually happens in one mode or the other or, if in both modes, occurs in sequence.

Low-Involvement Response Model[77]

Figure 8-11 displays still another sequence that consumers occasionally pass through in response to a communication: the low-involvement response model. In this case, the consumer is uninvolved with either the message or the product, and few differences exist among alternative brands. Thus, the initial reaction to a communication will be cognitive but at a low level (e.g., "Where can I buy Brand Y?"). Then, intentions are quickly formed and a purchase is made. Finally, product use leads to some affective development, but again at a relatively low level. Usually, the low-involvement response sequence occurs for frequently purchased products such as coffee or margarine. The low saliency of the product coupled with the habitual pattern of purchase typically undergone ensure that processing will be at a superficial level with little or no perceived affective arousal engendered prior to purchase. Stronger affect, if it does form, occurs after purchase but will persist at relatively low levels and/or dissipate after actual use.

Social Response Model

The final model we wish to consider in Figure 8-11 is the social response model. Up to this point, we have assumed that behavior change in a consumer is due to the influence of a persuasive communication. Now we must consider the possibility that behavior will also be influenced by other determinants, along with the effects of the communication. We have already considered social determinants in Chapter 3. These include such variables as normative beliefs, family pressure, and social comparison processes. We might also expand the social response model to include other stimuli such as economic constraints. Notice in Figure 8-11 that the social response model drawn is really the parallel response model plus social influence. We have presented the model in this way strictly for simplicity, as social influence can occur as an additional determinant for each of the models shown in Figure 8-11.

The five generic response models are not the only possibilities. They do suggest, however, a wide range of potentially useful models. Simpler representations are possible in the sense that certain stages might occasionally be skipped or at least play minor roles in certain choice situations. In many industrial buying contexts, the cognitive response model will be the rule, perhaps, with the affect stage dormant. For other settings, affect may be so powerful that cognitions fail to be a factor. And so on.

On the other hand, the five generic response models might point the way to more complex structures. For instance, it is important to realize that each variable in Figure 8-11 can represent a whole class of constructs and be manifest in complex structures and processes. For example, many cognitions and feelings might arise and be related among themselves in intricate ways. A final point to note is that different situations will be conducive to one response model or another. For contexts requiring extensive problem solving, the cognitive response model will be dominant. For impulse purchases, the low-involvement or parallel-response models may be more appropriate. And so on. Very little is known at this time when one model or the other will be descriptive of consumer responses to persuasive communications.

Summary

In this chapter, we have considered the role of communication in marketing. Without a doubt, organizations cannot function well or for long if they do not develop effective communication programs. Communication is needed not only to inform customers but also to convince them of the best brands to consider. As with all of the marketing mix tools, communication is an essential tactic for meeting consumer needs and achieving a competitive edge over rivals.

We began our discussion of marketing communication with a presentation of the classic *source-message-medium-receiver model* (Figure 8-1). This model stipulates that whether or not a communication will produce its intended effect depends on who says what, in which channel, and to whom. That is, influence depends on source characteristics, message content and structure, media selection, and receiver characteristics.

The key *source characteristics* are credibility (i.e., expertise, trustworthiness), attractiveness, and the ability and intention to mediate rewards or punishments. Each of these can be thought of as an independent variable influencing consumer behavior, over and above the other communication variables. *Message content* includes rational appeals, emotional appeals, distraction, and use of a foil. A rational appeal stresses beneficial product attributes or consequences of product use. An emotional appeal consists of mood messages, humor, or the use of fear. Distraction in a message is employed to prevent counterargumentation. A foil represents a dialogue within a communication designed to symbolically and indirectly educate an audience. Message content variables serve to convey meaning to a receiver.

Message structure refers to the form of the meaning communicated. We discussed four frequently employed options: one-sided versus two-sided appeals, order of presentation of arguments, information quantity, and repetition. Each structural option provides managers with tactical alternatives but entails trade-offs.

Next, we considered the communication *medium*, i.e., the channel used to send a message. Generally, personal (i.e., face-to-face) or nonpersonal (i.e., mass) channels are used. We discussed media effects in terms of the *two-step flow model* of communication. This model maintains that mass communication has a number of effects. Surprisingly, the most important is not necessarily the direct one from mass media to consumer. Rather, indirect effects are often crucial. For example, advertisements might reach *opinion leaders* who, in turn, influence consumers. Or ads might stimulate word-of-mouth communication among consumers. These and other indirect effects, including active solicitation of information by consumers, constitute key channels of communication. Nevertheless, we should not discount the direct impact of mass communication efforts.

The final variable in the SMMR model is the *receiver*. The central receiver variables include self-esteem, background characteristics, personality traits, and past learning experiences. Because communication effects are dependent on receiver characteristics, one must take these into account in the design of persuasive campaigns.

The chapter then turned to an *information-processing model* of communication. Whereas the SMMR model focuses primarily on things external to the receiver, the information-processing model examines the mental stages the receiver passes through from reception of the message until performance of a behavior. As shown in Figure 8-6, there are five such stages: perception, comprehension, information integration, decision making, and intentions. To understand how such strategic communication decisions as message design and media selection will impact on consumers, one must consider how the receiver processes the stimuli. Humor, fear appeals, repetition, source credibility, and other tactics impinge on each stage of information processing in unique ways.

Two new explanations of communication effects are the *cognitive response* and *affective response* models. These models describe the mental and feeling construction processes that go on after one receives a communication. In addition to processing messages for meaning, receivers generate thoughts and react with emotions that are sometimes connected and sometimes unconnected to the message, per se. The combination of responses so generated enter the information-integration and decision-making stages of information processing. It is important to consider these because they are real, they influence consumer choices, and they are not considered explicitly by earlier models.

The chapter closed with an outline of five generic sequences that consumers pass through after exposure to a communication attempt (Figure 8-11). Different products, because of their importance to the consumer and their complexity, and different communications, because of the stimuli used and the degree of involvement of the consumer with the medium, will imply different sequences. The five sequences can serve as a planning guide in the design of communications and a forecasting and research tool in the prediction of consumer responses. In the following chapter, we will consider behavioral, managerial, and social aspects of one specific, but important, form of communication: advertising.

Questions and Problems for Discussion

1 What is meant by communication? Compare and contrast communication to social influence.

2 Figure 8-1 presents the classic source-message-medium-receiver model of communication. Why is this model important and how can it be used in the design and execution of marketing communications?

3 Many people believe that marketing communication should be limited to providing factual information. What is your position on this issue? What consequences for any organization might ensue if its communication were limited to providing factual information?

4 Three characteristics of the sender of a message that influence audiences are: source credibility, attractiveness, and the mediation of rewards and punishments. Briefly describe what these are and how they function.

5 A basic decision in any communication program is whether to use rational or emotional appeals. Discuss the pros and cons of each.

6 What is the phenomenon of counterargumentation and how might it be reduced or overcome? To what does "use of a foil" refer in persuasive communications?

7 Discuss the central issues and choices concerning the design of message structures.

8 What is the two-step flow model of communication and why is it important?

9 How does the information-processing model of communication explain the operation of humor? fear? source credibility? and repetition in communication?

10 Describe and compare the cognitive response and the affective response models of communication. How might these models be of use to managers?

11 How would you design a communication program to attract blood donors?

12 How would you design a communication program for a chain of health food stores to market tofu-based ice-cream cones and packaged ice cream?

NOTES

1. An early synthesis of the classic view of communication can be found in Harold D. Lasswell, *Power and Personality* (New York: W. W. Norton & Co., 1948), pp. 37-51; 178-190. For an introduction to communication theory, see E. P. Bettinghaus, *Persuasive Communication*, 2d ed. (New York: Holt, Rinehart & Winston, 1973); S. Littlejohn, *Theories of Human Communication* (Columbus, Ohio: Charles Merrill, 1978). A comprehensive, modern treatment from a marketing perspective can be found in Michael L. Ray, *Advertising and Communication Management* (Englewood Cliffs, N.J.: Prentice-Hall, 1982).

2. For a treatment of social influence, see James T. Tedeschi, Barry R. Schlenker, and Thomas V. Bonoma, *Conflict, Power, and Games* (Chicago: Aldine, 1973).

3. A summary of the body of knowledge related to the classic communication model can be found in William J. McGuire, "The Nature of Attitudes and Attitude Change," in G. Lindzey and E. Aronson, eds., *The Handbook of Social Psychology*, 2d ed. (Cambridge, Mass.: Addison-Wesley, 1969), pp. 135-314. See also William J. McGuire, "Attitude Change: The Information-Processing Paradigm," in C. G. McClintock, ed., *Experimental Social Psychology* (New York: Holt, Rinehart & Winston, 1972), pp. 108-141.

4. Representative research on source credibility can be found in C. Hovland and W. Weiss, "The Influence of Source Credibility on Communication Effectiveness," *Public Opinion Quarterly* 15 (Winter 1951): 635-50. See also G. Miller and J. Baseheart, "Source Trustworthiness, Opinionated Statements, and Response to Persuasive Communication," *Speech Monographs* 36 (1969): 1-7. In marketing, see Robert B. Settle and Linda L. Golden, "Attribution Theory and Advertiser Credibility," *Journal of Marketing Research* 11 (May 1974): 181-85. A new perspective that we will discuss later in this chapter can be found in the work of Dholakia and Sternthal (e.g., Ruby R. Dholakia and Brian Sternthal, "Highly Credible Sources: Persuasive Facilitators or Persuasive Liabilities?" *Journal of Consumer Research* 3 [March 1977]: 223-32).

5. L. S. Harms, "Listener Judgments of Status Cues in Speech," *Quarterly Journal of Speech* 47 (April 1961): 164-68.

6. C. I. Hovland, I. L. Janis, and H. H. Kelley, *Communication and Persuasion* (New Haven: Yale University Press, 1953).

7. Classic treatments of attraction can be found in T. M. Newcomb, "The Prediction of Interpersonal Attraction," *American Psychologist* 11 (1956): 575-86; C. W. Backman and P. F. Secord, "The Effect of Liking on Interpersonal Attraction," *Human Relations* 12 (1959): 379-84; T. M. Newcomb, "Varieties of Interpersonal Attraction," in D. Cartwright and A. Zander, eds., *Group Dynamics*, 2d ed. (New York: Harper & Row, 1960); D. Byrne, "Attitudes and Attraction," in L. Berkowitz, ed., *Advances in Experimental Social Psychology*, vol. 4 (New York: Academic Press, 1969), pp. 35-89; R. F. Priest and J. Sawyer, "Proximity and Peership: Bases of Balance in Interpersonal Attraction," *American Journal of Sociology* 72 (1967): 633-49; D. Byrne, *The Attraction Paradigm* (New York: Academic Press, 1971); more recent discussions include C. A. Insko and M. Wilson, "Interpersonal Attraction as a Function of Social Interaction," *Journal of Personality and Social Psychology* 35 (1977): 903-11; G. Levinger and J. Snoek, *Attraction-in-Relationship: A New Look at Interpersonal Attraction* (New York: General Learning Press, 1972); T. L. Huston and G. Levinger, "Interpersonal Attraction and Relationships," in M. R. Rosenzweig and L. W. Porter, eds., *Annual Review of Psychology*, (Palo Alto, Cal.: Annual Reviews, 1978), pp. 115-56; H. T. Reis, J. Nezlek, and L. Wheeler, "Physical Attractiveness in Social Interactions," *Journal of Personality and Social Psychology* 38 (1980): 604-17; E. Berscheid and E. H. Walster, *Interpersonal Attraction*, 2d ed. (Reading, Mass.: Addison-Wesley, 1978); Michael J. Baker and Gilbert A. Churchill, Jr., "The Impact of Physically Attractive Models on Advertising Evaluation," *Journal of Marketing Research* 14 (November 1977): 538-55.

8. J. R. P. French, Jr. and B. Raven, "The Bases of Social Power," in D. Cartwright, ed., *Studies in Social Power* (Ann Arbor: Institute of Social Research, 1959), pp. 150-67.

9. Tedeschi, Schlenker, and Bonoma, *Conflict, Power, and Games*, pp. 66-69.

10. T. C. Brock, "Communicator-Recipient Similarity and Decision Change," *Journal of Personality and Social Psychology* 1 (1965): 640-54.

11. See French and Raven, "The Bases of Social Power"; Tedeschi, Schlenker, and Bonoma, *Conflict, Power, and Games*; J. D. Singer, "Interpersonal Influence: A Formal Model," *American Political Science Review* 57 (1963): 420-30. J. Z. Rubin and B. R. Brown, *The Social Psychology of Bargaining and Negotiation* (New York: Academic Press, 1975).

12. Brian Sternthal and C. Samuel Craig, "Fear Appeals: Revisited," *Journal of Consumer Research* 1 (December 1974): 22–34.

13. C. Hovland and W. Mandell, "An Experimental Comparison of Conclusion-Drawing by the Communicator and by the Audience," *Journal of Abnormal and Social Psychology* 47 (1952): 581–88; B. Fine, "Conclusion-Drawing, Communicator Credibility and Anxiety as Factors in Opinion Change," *Journal of Abnormal and Social Psychology* 54 (1957): 369–74.

14. See Jack W. Brehm, *A Theory for Psychological Reactance* (New York: Academic Press, 1966), especially Chapter 6.

15. See Noel Capon and James Hulbert, "The Sleeper Effect—An Awakening," *Public Opinion Quarterly* 37 (Fall 1973): 322–58.

16. For basic research into humor, see A. J. Chapman and H. C. Foot, eds., *Humor and Laughter: Theory, Research, and Applications* (London: John Wiley & Sons, 1976); A. J. Chapman and H. C. Foot, eds., *It's a Funny Thing, Humour* (Oxford: Pergamon, 1977); P. McGhee, *Humor: Its Origin and Development* (San Francisco: Freeman Press, 1979); Karen O'Quin and Joel Aronoff, "Humor as a Technique of Social Influence," *Social Psychology Quarterly* 44 (December 1981): 349–57. In marketing, see Brian Sternthal and C. Samuel Craig, "Humor in Advertising," *Journal of Marketing* 37 (October 1973): 12–18; J. Patrick Kelly and Paul J. Solomon, "Humor in Television Advertising," *Journal of Advertising* 4 (Summer 1975): 31–35; Mervin D. Lynch and Richard C. Hartman, "Dimensions of Humor in Advertising," *Journal of Advertising Research* 8 (December 1968): 39–45.

17. Sternthal and Craig, "Humor in Advertising," p. 17.

18. Kelly and Solomon, "Humor in Television Advertising."

19. The classic study investigating the effects of fear arousal was conducted by Irving L. Janis and Seymour Feshbach, "Effects of Fear-Arousing Communication," *Journal of Abnormal and Social Psychology* 48 (January 1953): 78–92. For a psychological perspective, see Harold Leventhal, "Findings and Theory in the Study of Fear Communications," in L. Berkowitz, ed., *Advances in Experimental Social Psychology*, vol. 5 (New York: Academic Press, 1970), pp. 119–86. For marketing viewpoints, see Michael L. Ray and William Wilkie, "Fear: The Potential of an Appeal Neglected by Marketing," *Journal of Marketing* 34 (January 1970): 54–62; Brian Sternthal and C. Samuel Craig, "Fear Appeals: Revisited and Revised," *Journal of Consumer Research* 1 (December 1974): 22–34; John J. Burnett and Richard L. Oliver, "Fear Appeal Effects in the Field: A Segmentation Approach," *Journal of Marketing Research* 16 (May 1979): 181–90.

20. See, for example, Leventhal, "Findings and Theory in the Study of Fear Communication"; Irving L. Janis, *The Contour of Fear*, (New York: Wiley, 1968). Sternthal and Craig, "Fear Appeals: Revisited and Revised."

21. William J. McGuire, "An Information-Processing Model of Advertising Effectiveness," unpublished working paper, Department of Psychology, Yale University, 1969.

22. J. Allyn and Leon Festinger, "The Effectiveness of Unanticipated Persuasive Communications," *Journal of Abnormal and Social Psychology* 62 (February 1961): 35–40; Leon Festinger and Nathan Maccoby, "On Resistance to Persuasive Communication," *Journal of Abnormal and Social Psychology* 68 (November 1964): 359–66; J. L. Freedman and D. O. Sears, "Warning, Distraction, and Resistance to Influence," *Journal of Personality and Social Psychology* 1 (1965): 262–66; Robert A. Osterhouse and Timothy C. Brock, "Distraction Increases Yielding to Propaganda by Inhibiting Counterarguing," *Journal of Personality and Social Psychology* 15 (August 1970): 344–58; David M. Gardner, "The Distraction Hypothesis in Marketing," *Journal of Advertising Research* 10 (December 1970): 25–30; M. Venkatesan and Gordon A. Haaland, "Divided Attention and Television Commercials: An Experimental Study," *Journal of Marketing Research* 5 (May 1968): 203–5. Stewart W. Bither, "Comments on Venkatesan and Haaland's Test of the Festinger-Maccoby Divided Attention Hypothesis," *Journal of Marketing Research* 6 (May 1969): 237–38.

23. Elaine Walster and Leon Festinger, "The Effectiveness of 'Overhead' Persuasive Communications," *Journal of Abnormal and Social Psychology* 65 (1962): 395–402.

24. Carl I. Hovland, Arthur A. Lumsdaine, and Fred D. Sheffield, *Experiments on Mass Communication* (New York: Wiley, 1949); Carl I. Hovland, *The Order of Presentation in Persuasion* (New Haven: Yale University Press, 1957); E. W. Faison, "Effectiveness of One-Sided and Two-Sided Mass Communications in Advertising," *Public Opinion Quarterly* 25 (1961): 468–69.

25. Hovland et al., *Experiments on Mass Communication.*

26. William J. McGuire, "Inducing Resistance to Persuasion: Some Contemporary Approaches," in L. Berkowitz, ed., *Advances in Experimental Social Psychology*, Vol. 1 (New York: Academic Press, 1964), pp. 191–229; George J. Szbillo and Richard Heslin, "Resistance to Persuasion: Inoculation Theory in a Marketing Concept," *Journal of Marketing Research* 10 (November 1973): 396–403.

27. E. Walster, E. Aronson, and D. Abrahams, "On Increasing the Persuasiveness of a Low Prestige Communicator," *Journal of Experimental Social Psychology* 2 (1966): 325–42; Settle and Golden, "Attribution Theory and Advertiser Credibility."

28. Stanley M. Ulanoff, *Comparative Advertising: A Historical Perspective* (Cambridge: Marketing Science Institute, 1975); William L. Wilkie and Paul W. Farris, "Comparison Advertising: Problems and Potential," *Journal of Marketing* 39 (November 1975), pp. 7–15; Kanti V. Prasad, "Communications Effectiveness of Comparative Advertising: A Laboratory Analysis," *Journal of Marketing Research* 13 (May 1976), pp. 128–37; Linda L. Golden, "Consumer Reactions to Explicit Brand Comparisons in Advertisements," *Journal of Marketing Research* 16 (November 1979): 517–32; Stephen Goodwin and Michael Etgar, "An Experimental Investigation of Comparative Advertising: Impact of Message Appeal, Information Load, and Utility of Product Class," *Journal of Marketing Research* 17 (May 1980): 187–202.

29. Thomas Barry and Roger Tremblay, "Comparative Advertising: Perspectives and Issues," *Journal of Advertising* 4 (Winter 1975): 15–20. In addition to discovering the perception of lack of truthfulness, these authors found that the consumers surveyed did not particularly like comparative ads. However, because the practice of comparison advertising was new at the time of the study, people may not have thought deeply about the issues.

30. Prasad, "Communications Effects of Comparative Advertising."

31. Golden, "Consumer Reactions to Explicit Brand Comparisons in Advertisements."

32. Goodwin and Etgar, "An Experimental Investigation of Comparative Advertising."

33. "A Pained Bayer Cries 'Foul'," *Business Week*, July 25, 1977, p. 142.

34. Michael B. Mazis and Janice E. Adkinson, "An Experimental Evaluation of a Proposed Corrective Advertising Remedy," *Journal of Marketing Research* 13 (May 1976): 178–83.

35. H. Gilkinson, S. Paulson, and D. Sikkink, "Effects of Order and Authority in an Argumentative Speech," *Quarterly Journal of Speech* 40 (1954): 183–92. Hovland, *The Order of Presentation in Persuasion.*

36. Jacob Jacoby, Donald Speller, and Carol Kohn, "Brand Choice Behavior as a Function of Information Load," *Journal of Marketing Research* 11 (February 1974): 63–69; Jacob Jacoby, Donald Speller, and Carol Kohn Berning, "Brand Choice Behavior as a Function of Information Load: Replication and Extension," *Journal of Consumer Research* 1 (June 1974): 33–42; J. Edward Russo, "More Information Is Better: A Reevaluation of Jacoby, Speller, and Kohn," *Journal of Consumer Research* 1 (December 1974): 68–72; Jacob Jocoby, "Information Load and Decision Quality: Some Contested Issues," *Journal of Marketing Research* 14 (November 1977): 569–73; John O. Summers, "Less Information Is Better?" *Journal of Marketing Research* 11 (November 1974): 467–68; William L. Wilkie, "Analysis of Effects of Information Load," *Journal of Marketing Research* 11 (November 1974): 462–66.

37. James R. Bettman, "Issues in Designing Consumer Information Environments," *Journal of Consumer Research* 2 (December 1975): 169–77; James R. Bettman and Pradeep Kakkar, "Effects of Information Presentation Format on Consumer Information Strategies," *Journal of Consumer Research* 3 (March 1977): 233–40; Valerie A. Zeithaml, "Consumer Response to In-store Price Information Environments," *Journal of Consumer Research* 8 (March 1982): 357–69.

38. Lawrence A. Crosby and James R. Taylor, "Effects of Consumer Information and Education on Cognition and Choice," *Journal of Consumer Research* 8 (June 1981): 43–56.

39. George A. Miller, "The Magical Number Seven, Plus or Minus Two: Some Limits on Our Capacity for Processing Information," *Psychological Review* 63 (1956): 81–97.

40. Prabhaker Nayak and Larry J. Rosenberg, "Does Open Dating of Food Products Benefit the Consumer?" *Journal of Retailing* 51 (Summer 1975): 10–20.

41. J. Edward Russo, "The Value of Unit Price Information," *Journal of Marketing Research* 14 (May 1977): 193–202; James M. Carman, "A Summary of Unit Pricing in Supermarkets," *Journal of Retailing* 48 (Winter 1972–73): 63–71; Zeithaml, "Consumer Response to In-Store Price Information Environments."

42. Edward H. Asam and Louis P. Bucklin, "Nutrition Labeling for Canned Goods: A Study of Consumer Response," *Journal of Marketing* 37 (April 1973): 32–37; Warren A. French and Hiram C. Barksdale, "Food Labeling Regulations: Efforts toward Full Disclosure," *Journal of Marketing* 38 (July 1974): 14–19.

43. Alan G. Sawyer, "The Effects of Repetition: Conclusions and Suggestions about Experimental Laboratory Research," in G. David Hughes and Michael L. Ray, eds., *Buyer/Consumer Information Processing* (Chapel Hill, N.C.: University of North Carolina Press, 1974), pp. 190–219; Alan G. Sawyer, "Repetition and Affect: Recent Empirical and Theoretical Developments," in A. G. Woodside, J. N. Sheth, and P. D. Bennett, eds., *Consumer and Industrial Buying Behavior* (New York: North-Holland, 1977); Alan G. Sawyer, "Repetition, Cognitive Responses, and Persuasion," in R. E. Petty, T. M. Ostrom, and T. C. Brock, eds., *Cognitive Responses to Persuasion* (Hillsdale, N.J.: Erlbaum, 1981).

44. Robert B. Zajonc, "Attitudinal Effects of Mere Exposure," *Journal of Personality and Social Psychology Monograph* 9 (1968): 1–28; William R. Wilson, "Feeling More than We Can Know: Exposure Effects without Learning," *Journal of Personality and Social Psychology* 37 (1979): 811–21.

45. Steuart Henderson Britt, "Applying Learning Principles to Marketing," *MSU Business Topics* 23 (Spring 1975): 5–12; Michael L. Ray, "Psychological Theories and Interpretations of Learning," in S. Ward and T. S. Robertson, eds., *Consumer Behavior: Theoretical Sources* (Englewood Cliffs, N.J.: Prentice-Hall, 1973), pp. 45–117.

46. Michael L. Ray and Alan G. Sawyer, "Repetition in Media Models: A Laboratory Technique," *Journal of Marketing Research* 8 (February 1971): 20–29.

47. Paul F. Lazarsfeld, Bernard Berelson, and Hazel Gaudet, *The People's Choice*, 2d ed. (New York: Columbia University Press, 1948).

48. Elihu Katz, "The Two-Step Flow of Communication: An Up-to-date Report on a Hypothesis," *Public Opinion Quarterly* 21 (Spring 1957): 61–78; Elihu Katz and Paul F. Lazarsfeld, *Personal Influence* (New York: The Free Press, 1955); Bernard Berelson and Gary A. Steiner, *Human Behavior: An Inventory of Scientific Findings* (New York: Harcourt, Brace & World, 1964).

49. William H. Whyte, Jr., "The Web of Word-of-Mouth," in L. H. Clark, ed., *The Life Cycle and Consumer Behavior* (New York: New York University Press, 1955), pp. 113–22; Ernest Dichter, "How Word of Mouth Advertising Works," *Harvard Business Review* 44 (November-December 1966): 147–66; Jagdish N. Sheth, "Word-of-Mouth in Low-Risk Innovations," *Journal of Advertising Research* 11 (June 1971): 15–18; Johan Arndt, "Selective Processes in Word-of-Mouth," *Journal of Advertising Research* 8 (June 1968): 19–22; James F. Engel, Robert J. Kegerreis, and Roger D. Blackwell, "Word-of-Mouth Communication by the Innovator," *Journal of Marketing* 33 (July 1969): 15–19.

50. Thomas S. Robertson and James H. Myers, "Personality Correlates of Opinion Leadership and Innovative Buying Behavior," *Journal of Marketing Research* 6 (May 1969): 164–68; Lawrence G. Corey, "People Who Claim to Be Opinion Leaders: Identifying Their Characteristics by Self-Report," *Journal of Marketing* 35 (October 1971): 48–53; James H. Myers and Thomas S. Robertson, "Dimensions of Opinion Leadership," *Journal of Marketing Research* 9 (February 1972): 41–46; William R. Darden and Fred D. Reynolds, "Predicting Opinion Leadership for Men's Apparel Fashions," *Journal of Marketing Research* 9 (August 1972): 324–28; John O. Summers, "The Identity of Women's Clothing Fashion Opinion Leaders," *Journal of Marketing Research* 7 (May 1970): 178–85; Stephen A. Baumgarten, "The Innovative Communicator in the Diffusion Process," *Journal of Marketing Research* 12 (February 1975): 12–18.

51. Katz and Lazarsfeld, *Personal Influence;* Alvin J. Silk, "Overlap across Self-designated Opinion Leaders: A Study of Selected Dental Products and Services," *Journal of Marketing Research* 3 (August 1966): 253–59; John G. Myers, "Patterns of Interpersonal Influence in the Adoption of New Products," in R. M. Haas, ed., *Proceedings of the American Marketing Association Educator's Conference* (Chicago: American Marketing Association, 1966), pp. 750–57; David B. Montgomery and Alvin J. Silk, "Clusters of Consumer Interests and Opinion Leaders' Spheres of Influence," *Journal of Marketing Research* 8 (August 1971): 317–21; Johan Arndt, "Role of Product-Related Conversations in the Diffusion of a New Product," *Journal of Marketing Research* 4 (August 1967): 291–95; Baumgarten, "The Communicator in the Diffusion Process"; Fred D. Reynolds and William R. Darden, "Mutually Adaptive Effects of Interpersonal Communication," *Journal of Marketing Research* 8 (November 1971): 449–454.

52. Everett M. Rogers and F. Floyd Shoemaker, *Communication of Innovations,* (New York: The Free Press, 1971); Michael J. Houston, "An Evaluation of Measures of Opinion Leadership," in K. L. Bernhardt, ed., *Marketing 1776–1976 and Beyond* (Chicago: American Marketing Association, 1976), pp. 564–71; Silk, "Overlap across Self-designated Opinion Leaders"; Arndt, "Role of Product-Related Conversations"; Myers, "Patterns of Influence in Adoption of New Products"; Summers, "Identity of Women's Clothing Fashion Opinion Leaders"; Reynolds and Darden, "Mutually Adaptive Effects of Interpersonal Communication."

53. Joseph R. Mancuso, "Why Not Create Opinion Leaders for New Product Introductions?" *Journal of Marketing* 33 (July 1969): 20–25.

54. Alice M. Tybout, Bobby J. Calder, and Brian Sternthal, "Using Information Processing Theory to Design Marketing Strategies," *Journal of Marketing Research* 18 (February 1981): 73–79.

55. I. L. Janis and P. B. Field, "A Behavior Assessment of Consistency of Individual Differences," in C. I. Hovland and I. L. Janis, eds., *Personality and Persuasibility* (New Haven, Conn.: Yale University Press, 1959): 29–54.

56. S. Lindskold and J. T. Tedeschi, "Self-Esteem and Sex as Factors Affecting Influenceability," *British Journal of Social and Clinical Psychology* 10 (1971): 114–22.

57. Tedeschi, Schlenker, and Bonoma, *Conflict, Power, and Games.*

58. McGuire, "Attitude Change: The Information-Processing Paradigm"; James R. Bettman, *An Information Processing Theory of Consumer Choice* (Reading, Mass.: Addison-Wesley, 1979); Robert J. Lavidge and Gary A. Steiner, "A Model for Predictive Measurements of Advertising Effectiveness," *Journal of Marketing* 25 (October 1961): 59–62.

59. Lavidge and Steiner, "Model for Predictive Measurements of Advertising Effectiveness"; Michael L. Ray, "Marketing Communication and the Hierarchy of Effects," in P. Clarke, ed., *New Models for Mass Communication Research* (Beverly Hills, Cal.: Russell Sage Foundation, 1973), pp. 147–76.

60. See McGuire, "Attitude Change: The Information-Processing Paradigm," p. 120.

61. McGuire, "Attitude Change: The Information-Processing Paradigm," pp. 123–31.

62. William J. McGuire, "Personality and Susceptibility to Social Influence," in E. F. Borgatta and W. W. Lambert, eds., *Handbook of Personality Theory and Research* (Chicago: Rand-McNally, 1968), pp. 140–62.

63. Hovland and Weiss, "The Influence of Source Credibility on Communication Effectiveness"; Miller and Basehart, "Source Trustworthiness, Opinionated Statements, and Response to Persuasive Communication."

64. H. Sigall and R. Helmreich, "Opinion Change as a Function of Stress and Communicator Credibility," *Journal of Experimental Social Psychology* 5 (1969): 70–78; A. Eagly and S. Chaiken, "An Attribution Analysis of the Effect of Communicator Characteristics on Opinion Change: The Case of Communicator Attractiveness," *Journal of Personality and Social Psychology* 32 (1975): 136–44; H. Johnson and R. Izzett, "The Effects of Source Identification on Attitude Change as a Function of the Type of Communication," *Journal of Social Psychology* 86 (1972): 81–87.

65. Dholakia and Sternthal, "Highly Credible Sources."

66. For other examples of attribution explanations of reactions to persuasive communications, see Alice M. Tybout, "The Relative Effectiveness of Three Behavioral Influence Strategies as Supplements to Persuasion in a Marketing Context," *Journal of Marketing Research* 15 (1978): 229–42; Carol Scott, "The Effects of Trial and Incentives on Repeat Purchase Behavior," *Journal of Marketing Research* 13 (1976): 263–69; Richard F. Yalch, "Pre-Election Interview Effects on Voter Turnout," *Public Opinion Quarterly* 40 (1976): 331–36.

67. D. F. Roberts and N. Maccoby, "Information Processing and Persuasion: Counterarguing Behavior," in P. Clarke, ed., *New Models for Communication Research* (Beverly Hills, Cal.: Russell Sage Foundation, 1973); Peter Wright, "The Cognitive Processes Mediating Acceptance of Advertising," *Journal of Marketing Research* 10 (February 1973): 53–62; Peter Wright, "Consumer Choice Strategies: Simplifying vs. Optimizing," *Journal of Marketing Research* 12 (February 1975): 60–67; Peter Wright, "Cognitive Responses to Mass Media Advocacy," in R. E. Petty, T. M. Ostrom, and T. C. Brock, eds., *Cognitive Responses to Persuasion* (Hillsdale, N.J.: Erlbaum, 1981); Bettman, *Information Processing Theory of Consumer Choice.*

68. See, for example, R. C. Schank and R. P. Abelson, *Scripts, Plans, Goals, and Understanding: An Inquiry into Human Knowledge Structure* (Hillsdale, N.J.: Erlbaum, 1977); P. W. Thorndyke and B. Hayes-Roth, "The Use of Schemata in the Acquisition and Transfer of Knowledge," *Cognitive Psychology* 11 (1979): 82–106.

69. R. E. Petty, T. M. Ostrom, and T. C. Brock, eds., *Cognitive Responses in Persuasion* (Hillsdale, N.J.: Erlbaum, 1981).

70. Brian Sternthal, Ruby Dholakia, and Clark Leavitt, "The Persuasive Effect of Source Credibility: Tests of Cognitive Response," *Journal of Consumer Research* 4 (March 1978): 252–60.

71. J. T. Cacioppo and R. E. Petty, "Effects of Message Repetition and Position on Cognitive Responses, Recall, and Persuasion," *Journal of Personality and Social Psychology* 37 (1979): 97–109.

72. Ray, "Psychological Theories and Interpretations of Learning"; Michael L. Ray and Rajeev Batra, "Emotion and Persuasion in Advertising: What We Do and Don't Know about Affect," in R. P. Bagozzi and A. M. Tybout, eds., *Advances in Consumer Research*, vol. 10 (Ann Arbor, Mich.: Association for Consumer Research, 1983); Richard P. Bagozzi, "A Holistic Methodology for Modeling Consumer Response to Innovation," *Operations Research* (January–February 1983); R. B. Zajonc, "Feeling and Thinking: Preferences Need No Inferences," *American Psychologist* 35 (February 1980): 151–75; for a criticism of the affective response model, see Richard S. Lazarus, "Thoughts on the Relations between Emotion and Cognition," *American Psychologist* 37 (September 1982): 1019–24.

73. This has been termed *affect referral* by Peter Wright, "Consumer Choice Strategies: Simplifying vs. Optimizing," *Journal of Marketing Research* 11 (February 1975): 60–67.

74. S. T. Fiske, "Schema-Triggered Affect: Application to Social Perception," in M. S. Clarke and S. T. Fiske, eds., *Affect and Cognition: the 17th Annual Carnegie Symposium on Cognition* (Hillsdale, N.J.: Erlbaum, 1982).

75. Ray, "Psychological Theory and Interpretations of Learning"; H. H. Kelley, "The Processes of Causal Attribution," *American Psychologist* 28 (1973): 107–28; D. J. Bem, "Self-Perception Theory," in L. Berkowitz, ed., *Advances in Experimental Social Psychology*, vol. 6 (New York: Academic Press, 1972).

76. Ray, "Psychological Theory and Interpretations of Learning"; Ray and Batra, "Emotion and Persuasion in Advertising"; Richard P. Bagozzi, "A Field Investigation of Causal Relations among Cognitions, Affect, Intentions, and Behavior," *Journal of Marketing Research* 19 (November 1982): 562–84. Some of the ideas discussed here were earlier treated in Bagozzi, "A Holistic Methodology for Modeling Consumer Response to Innovation."

77. H. E. Krugman, "The Impact of Television Advertising: Learning without Involvement," *Public Opinion Quarterly* 29 (1965): 349–56; Rajeev Batra and Michael L. Ray, "Operationalizing Involvement as Depth and Quality of Cognitive Response," in R. P. Bagozzi and A. M. Tybout, eds., *Advances in Consumer Research*, vol. 10 (Ann Arbor, Mich.: Association for Consumer Research, 1983).

GLOSSARY

Affective Response Model. A theory of communication which maintains that the first reaction to a message after perception consists of physiological and/or emotional responses. See Figure 8-10. Compare to the cognitive response model and the information-processing model of communication. At least four situations are indicative of the affective response model. *See* high-pressure communication, postcognitive learning, dissonance attribution, and intense emotionality responses.

Audience. *See* receiver.

Bargaining/Negotiation. A situation in which two or more parties in an exchange debate until reaching a joint solution to a shared problem. Although bilateral, the relationship is not quite as balanced or cooperative as in mutual decision making.

Classical Conditioning. Learning that occurs when a neutral stimulus (termed the *conditioned stimulus*) is repeatedly paired with a natural reward (termed the *unconditioned stimulus*) until eventually the neutral stimulus will elicit by itself the same response that the unconditioned stimulus alone naturally elicits. The response is termed an *unconditioned response*. It is believed that most emotional reactions to brands, products, or other stimuli are learned through some form of classical conditioning. Classical conditioning is sometimes referred to as *Pavlovian conditioning*, reflecting the person to first observe the phenomenon in dogs, Ivan Pavlov. *See* operant conditioning, cognitive learning, mere exposure effect.

Coercion. The attempt by one party to influence another party through the application or threat of punishing stimuli or the deprivation of positively valued stimuli.

Cognitive Learning. Learning that occurs when a person observes associations or causal connections and reasons as to the relationships between things. *See* mere exposure effect, classical conditioning, operant conditioning. Cognitive learning is sometimes termed *problem solving* or *decision making*.

Cognitive-Response Model of Communication. A special case of the information-processing theory of communication. As shown in Figure 8-9, four types of cognitive responses can be generated in reaction to a communication: counterarguments, support arguments, source derogation, and schemata processes. *See also* information processing model of communication.

Communication. The sending and receiving of information, affect, and/or influence from one party to another. Although communication can occur in one direction from sender to receiver, the most typical communication occurs in a bidirectional manner, where sender and receiver change roles and interact in a back-and-forth sense. The classic communication model is termed the source-message-media-receiver model and is shown in Figure 8-1.

Communicator. The person or party initiating a communication. Also termed the *sender* or *source*.

Comparison (Comparative) Advertising. The practice of explicitly naming one or more competitors in an ad and noting differences from one's own brand.

Corrective Advertising. The practice of requiring a sponsor to disclose certain product attributes or other aspects of the product or previous claims in order to set right misleading impressions. The FTC can require that an advertiser do this to remedy the effects of deceptive advertising. See Chapter 9.

Counterargumentation. A response in a receiver characterized by thoughts refuting the points in a message. Counterargumentation is typically silent and often below the level of awareness of the receiver. It not only has the effect of thwarting the communication of factual arguments but prevents the processing of other information as well. See support argumentation, source derogation, schemata processing, and cognitive response model.

Dissonance Attribution Responses. One of four situations common to the affective response model. In this case, a person first performs an action (e.g., purchase of Brand X), and then infers that he or she must have liked the brand, otherwise it would not have been purchased. This is a behavior $\longrightarrow$ affect sequence. The other three situations where the affective response model applies is the high-pressure communication, postcognitive learning, or intense emotionality cases. *See* affective response model.

Distraction (Distracting Elements in a Communication). Audio and/or visual content in a communication that is incidental to the intended or primary message content. It is sometimes purposefully included in ads because it is believed to inhibit counterargumentation. Too much distraction, however, can inhibit information processing and be counterproductive.

Education (or Educative Tactic). The presentation of information so that the recipient is free to reach his or her own conclusion and act accordingly. More than other modes of social influence, education involves "full information" in that pros and cons are communicated.

Emotional Appeals. The use of humor, fear appeals, or positive/negative mood appeals to influence feelings or one's attitude. Ultimately, the goal of the use of emotional appeals may be to influence intentions and induce action (e.g., product trial).

Emotional Persuasion. An appeal to feelings (e.g., one's fears or desires).

Fear Appeals. The use of messages designed to arouse anxiety and thereby increase the possibility that a particular action will be taken to reduce the anxiety. Fear appeals typically feature either the threat of negative physical consequences or social disapproval. The relationship between level of fear and persuasibility is believed to be curvilinear with intermediate levels of fear producing the maximum persuasion. See Figures 8-3 and 8-8.

High-Pressure Communication Responses. One of four situations common to the affective response model. In this case, a compelling communicator and/or message induces an affective response that in turn leads to action. One common situation is the face-to-face sales encounters of the door-to-door variety where a consumer has no opportunity to compare other brands and reflect on the decision. The other three situations where the affective response model occurs are termed postcognitive learning, dissonance attribution, and intense emotionality. *See* affective response model.

Humor (Humorous Appeals). The use of amusing, funny, or comical messages. The objective is to attract and hold attention, create a positive mood, or enhance the probability that the message will be processed in a favorable way.

Influence. *See* social influence.

Information Control. The withholding, distortion, filtering, regulating, or augmenting of knowledge in order to influence another party.

Information Load. The facts, knowledge, or data communicated to a consumer. It is not known with certainty how much information a consumer is capable of processing or whether too much is dysfunctional. Although people are capable of remembering and processing as much as seven or more pieces of information, ads generally communicate only one or two or on occasion three selling points. This is probably because ads are presented in relatively low involvement media and address products of relatively low salience to consumers.

Information-Processing Model of Communication. A theory of communication that represents the mental stages a person experiences when processing a message. As shown in Figure 8-6, exposure leads to perception, then comprehension, then information integration, then decision making, then intentions, and finally behavior. *See* source-message-medium-receiver model.

Instrumental Learning. *See* operant conditioning.

Intense Emotionality Responses. One of four situations common to the affective response model. In this case, a stimulus of considerable positive or negative qualities gains one's attention and induces an affective response. A positive stimulus is one perceived to potentially satisfy a particularly salient or deprived need. A negative stimulus is one perceived to be threatening or dangerous in some way. The other three situations where the affective response model is applicable is the high-pressure communication, postcognitive learning, or dissonance attribution cases. *See* affective response model.

Left-Brain Functions. A theory of human thinking which maintains that linear, rational, verbal, and cognitive processes are functionally performed in the left hemisphere of the brain for most right-handed people and the right hemisphere for most left-handed people. *See* right-brain functions.

Legal/Political Influence. The appeal by a party to a governmental or other social institution to support or enforce its will. Recourse through the courts is a common example. Governmental regulatory bodies, arbitration, and ombudsmen are also instances of legal/political influence.

Low-Involvement Response Model. A particular model of communication which claims that the first response to message is a cognitive one, followed then by intentions, then behavior, then affect. This is thought to occur when the product (or brand) and/or the media is of low salience, i.e., low involvement. See Figure 8-11. See also the discussion on affect, cognitions, and involvement in Chapter 9.

Mediation of Rewards and/or Punishments. Perceived capability of a source by a receiver to reward or punish one and the willingness or intention to do so.

Medium. The communication channel by or through which a message is conveyed. Two types of media can be identified: personal and nonpersonal.

Mere Exposure Effect. The development of positive feelings or a positive attitude toward a neutral stimulus solely through repeated exposure to the stimulus. The phenomenon is believed to occur without awareness or learning. The mere exposure effect is thought to be distinct from the three primary mechanisms of learning: classical conditioning, operant conditioning (i.e., instrumental learning), or cognitive learning. *See* repetition.

Message. The information or data conveyed in a communication and consisting of factual, affective, and/or influential symbols. As shown in Table 8-2, message content (i.e., rational appeals, emotional appeals, extraneous factors) and message structure (i.e., one versus two-sided appeals, order of presentation of arguments, information volume, repetition) constitute two dimensions of messages.

Mutual Decision Making. A process of social influence similar to bargaining/negotiation wherein two or more parties cooperate to solve a shared problem. Mutual decision making is somewhat more egalitarian and bilateral than bargaining/negotiation.

Nonpersonal Media. Indirect communication through a printed, recorded, or filmed intermediary such as a magazine, radio, or television ad. Also termed the *mass media*.

Nutritional Labeling. The practice of printing the vitamin, mineral, and other nutritional content of a product on a package.

One-Sided Appeals. The use of only positive arguments or product attributes in a message. One-sided appeals are believed to work best when an audience is already favorable toward an issue or brand and/or will not hear opposing arguments. *See* two-sided appeals.

Open Dating. The practice of printing the date on a product after which it will become spoiled or perishable. For instance, supermarkets or manufacturers stamp dates on milk, cereal, or medicinal products.

Operant Conditioning (Instrumental Learning). Learning that occurs when a behavioral response is followed by a reward (i.e., reinforcement) and thereby results in a higher probability that the behavior will occur again. The reward must be in some way (e.g., physiological, social) pleasing. *See* classical conditioning, cognitive learning, mere exposure effect.

Opinion Leaders. Individuals who are perceived by others as being more knowledgeable or expert and whom they rely for information or advice.

Order of Presentation of Arguments. The issue of where in a message or advertising campaign to place the most salient arguments or product attributes in order to enhance recall.

Parallel-Response Model. A particular model of communication which maintains that a communication might at times induce two parallel responses simultaneously: one cognitive, the other affective. These responses, in turn, influence intentions and, eventually, behavior. See Figure 8-1.

Personal Media. The use of a person to convey a message through face-to-face interaction. A salesperson-customer interaction is a typical example.

Persuasion. The attempt to influence another by use of rational and/or emotional arguments.

Postcognitive Learning Responses. One of four situations common to the affective response model. In this case, a person has already processed a communication and developed an attitude. Upon presentation of another exposure to the same or similar communication, the stored emotion previously learned is activated, and this affect, in turn, induces intentions and/or action. The other three situations where the affective response model is applicable is high-pressure communication, dissonance attribution, and intense emotionality cases. *See* affective response model.

Rational Appeals. The use of factual arguments in order to appeal to a receiver's capacity to reason. In marketing, this is typically done through emphasis of product attributes and/or the consequences of product use (e.g., product benefits). Rational appeals influence beliefs which in turn affect attitudes. If they are strong enough, they may ultimately influence intentions and even behavior (e.g., product trial).

Rational Persuasion. The attempt to convince another that it is in one's own best interests to act in a particular way.

Receiver. The person or party receiving a communication. Also termed the *audience* or *target.*

Receiver Self-Esteem. The degree of personal self-confidence in a recipient of a communication. It is believed that the relationship between self-esteem and persuasibility is curvilinear with intermediate levels of self-esteem yielding the highest amounts of persuasibility (see Figure 8-8).

Repetition. The repeated presentation of a single message or similar messages within an ad or across ads over time. Repetition is needed to create learning and to reach larger and larger portions of an audience. It is also believed to lead to favorable attitudes through the so-called "mere exposure effect." See Chapter 9, especially the concept of advertising wearout. *See also* mere exposure effect.

Reward Power. The application of pleasant stimulation by one party on another for the purpose of influence.

Right-Brain Functions. A theory of human thinking which maintains that musical, color, spatial, intuitive, and possibly evaluative processes are functionally performed in the right hemisphere of the brain for most right-handed people and the left hemisphere for most left-handed people. *See* left-brain functions.

Schemata Processing. A response in a receiver consisting of mental representation of past experiences, judgments, or feelings used to categorize, define, or interpret new, usually more complex, information or experiences. Schemata processing typically occurs more or less automatically and below the level of awareness. *See* cognitive response model, counterargumentation, support argumentation, and source derogation.

Sender. *See* communicator.

Social Influence. An attempt by one party to change the beliefs, attitudes, or behavior of another party. Social influence is accomplished through one or more of the following: coercion, reward power, information control, persuasion, education, legal/political maneuvers, bargaining/negotiation, or mutual decision making. The transfer of "neutral" information or the exchange of "neutral" information represents a type of social influence commonly labeled education. This is perhaps the most common type of communication along with the asking of questions. It is difficult to separate social influence from communication, however, as most information has evaluative or political overtones and all social influence involves communication of one form or another. See Figure 8-2.

Social Response Model. A particular model of communication which maintains that social influence either can act as an independent determinant of, or interact with, affect and cognitions to influence intentions and/or behavior. Social influence can be a component of the cognitive response, affective response, parallel response, or low-involvement response models. See Figure 8-11.

Source. *See* communicator.

Source Attractiveness. The degree of attractiveness of a source as perceived by a receiver. Source attractiveness may overlap with or be a function of perceived similarity, familiarity, or identification. Source attractiveness is thought to facilitate communication, increase the believability of a message, lead to a positive attitude toward the source and object of communication, and even induce action. Source attractiveness is similar to the concept of referent power.

Source Characteristics. An umbrella term used to describe source credibility, attractiveness, and the ability and intentions to mediate rewards or intentions. *See* source-message-medium-receiver model of communication.

Source Credibility. The degree of expertise and trustworthiness in a source as perceived by a receiver. Expertise is a function of education, experience, and/or competency. Trustworthiness is a function of honesty, sincerity, accommodative intentions, and/or a lack of self-interest. The higher the source credibility, the more that a message is believed. Source credibility might also increase the favorability of one's attitude toward a brand advocated in a communication or even induce action (e.g., product trial).

Source Derogation. A response in a receiver consisting of attributions that a spokesperson and/or message is inferior, negative, or in some other way to be disparaged. It may occur silently and below the level of awareness. It has the effect of diminishing the believability of a message or interfering with the processing of it. *See also* cognitive response model, counterargumentation, support argumentation, schemata processing.

Source Expertise. *See* source credibility.

Source-Message-Medium-Receiver Model of Communication. A classic representation of the communication process dating back to Aristotle. Communication consists of a sender who transmits a message through some medium to a receiver who, in turn, provides feedback of some sort. *See* information-processing model of communication and Figure 8-1.

Source Trustworthiness. *See* source credibility.

Support Argumentation. A response in a receiver consisting of thoughts upholding or corroborating a point made in a communication. Support argumentation is generally silent and often below the level of awareness of the receiver. It has the effect of enhancing the impact of a communication. *See also* counterargumentation, source derogation, schemata processing, cognitive response model.

Two-Sided Appeals. The use of both positive and negative arguments (or product attributes) in a message. Two-sided appeals are believed to work best when the audience is initially neutral or unfavorable toward one's arguments or brand, when the audience is high in education, or when the audience is likely to hear opposing views or negative information. In practice, only minor or small amounts of negative information are presented. The negative information is believed to "inoculate" the audience and create strong source credibility. *See* one-sided appeals.

Two-Step Flow Model. A theory of communication which maintains that messages transmitted through radio, print, TV, or other mass media influence receivers in the general public primarily through their intermediate impact on opinion leaders (see Figure 8-4). More recent research shows that receivers also at times solicit information from opinion leaders and are influenced by other actors under the influence of the mass media (e.g., innovators, reference groups). Moreover, receivers are sometimes directly influenced by the mass media. See Figure 8-5.

Unit Pricing. The practice of displaying the price for a product on a per unit or weight basis. For example, the price per ounce for detergent might be presented on a supermarket shelf as well as the total price. This facilitates brand comparisons and evaluations of product value.

The Present and Potential of Marketing Communication

Michael L. Ray
Stanford University

The need, both today and in the future, is for direct, simple, effective, and honest mass communication because the world is changing and we are changing more rapidly than ever. We are at the midpoint of a decade that seemed to have dawned just yesterday. A new century is approaching. The very basis of communication and society is being altered with every year. On the one hand, there is the possibility of technological breakthroughs that will allow us to continue to live in the amazing affluence of the last three decades. On the other hand, even with such breakthroughs, there is a trend in the world toward a questioning of affluence for its own sake.

In this setting it is significant to be studying ways of improving mass communication, particularly advertising. There is a need now, more than ever, for efficiency in communication. We know that the basis of advertising, personal selling, sales promotion, and publicity/public relations is communication. But there is confusion as to how these components of the communication mix can be put together to get to the right people, at the right time, with the right message, for the right response.

In the context of this critical need it is painful to see advertising that is irritating, useless, and unethical. At the same time, there is no doubt that advertising can be one of the most pleasurable, useful, and moral forms of communication confronting us.

Advertising is irritating, useless, and unethical when it too often reaches the wrong people with the wrong message at the wrong time.

Advertising is pleasurable, useful, and moral when it makes a meaningful communication with the people who need the message.

Obviously the purpose of this book and this chapter is to minimize the incidence of the first type of advertising and marketing communication and maximize the second. How well have marketers done in this regard? And what are the environmental conditions that will affect our ability to communicate now and in the future?

A useful way of looking at these questions is the right and left brain paradigm. Even though brain researchers will tell us that this split of brain functions is too simple, there is significant evidence that we have two sides to our nature as represented by the right and left hemispheres of the brain. In addition, there are events relating to the right and left sides of the brain which will have significant effects on all aspects of marketing communication—personal selling, advertising, sales promotion, and publicity/public relations—for years to come.

Simply put, the right-left brain distinction first developed by psychologist Roger Sperry (and for which he won a Nobel Prize) states that the left brain governs our verbal and analytical capabilities while the right brain is more visual, holistic, and intuitive in nature. When the implications of this research filtered into the public media in the 1970s, there was initially an outcry that our educational system emphasized and overstimulated left brain capabilities to the detriment of the creative and, possibly, more humanistic right-side capabilities.

In advertising, there was new definition put on the old controversy between those who advocated more emotional and image-laden advertising (right brain) as opposed to those who emphasized more rational, product-attribute, and perhaps hard-sell directions (left brain). This controversy extended into the types of advertising research that would be done, with the argument that, for instance, day-after-recall studies done by telephone were entirely verbal and missed the "right-brain" effects of television advertising.

Someone in marketing who wishes to communicate effectively—that is, get the right message, to the right people, at the right time, with the right response—would do well to pay attention to this right-left dichotomy in general, however incorrect it may be in the specifics of brain physiology. On the left side, for instance, there is the tremendous growth of technology for communication. As this is being written, approximately one-third of all American households are wired for cable TV. In some large cities cable subscribers can get over 50 channels of television. Those in all areas with satellite dishes can get literally hundreds of channels. This tremendous capability is being combined with personal computers and two-way communication to the point that the balance of power in marketing channels of communication is moving to the receiver or consumer rather than the sender or the marketer.

Whereas in the past, advertising and selling messages of all types were presented to consumers in an almost forced way, it is now possible for consumers to utilize this technology to make every decision—even those that now are simply repetitive ones—an informed decision with information on all product attributes. Thus even with a purchase of the proverbial can of peas, a consumer who wanted to could access a data bank that would indicate the best purchase in the peas category at that particular time. This would be in contrast to our usual haphazard and repetitive approach to buying in such convenience goods categories today.

One outcome of all of this technology is that the various aspects of marketing communication are becoming very similar. With many channels of information available and two-way communication within control of consumer, advertising could and is becoming very much like a personal selling message, and sales promotion and publicity/PR are becoming much more personally focused to the prospect. Already we see that direct mail retailing such as mail order and telephone order buying is growing at a much faster rate than shopping in stores. This means that consumers as a whole are getting more comfortable with doing their shopping at home with the information sources available to them.

But the left-brain technological balances should be seen in the enormous capacity humanity has for right brain-type activities. Books such as Alvin Toffler's *The Third Wave*, Marilyn Ferguson's *The Aquarian Conspiracy*, and John Naisbitt's *Megatrends* all point out that the technology will be fit in with and utilized only insofar as the consumer's intuitive and creative side is served. Already in the early 1980s there was evidence that consumers were not fully utilizing all the telecommunications available. And even though certain components of marketing communications such as sales promotion became more important, it was also recognized that sales promotion that simply lowered price was not reaching the hearts of the people in any long-term sense.

It probably is a decent summarizing remark to say that marketing communication recognizing and utilizing both sides of our nature is most likely to be effective. The exciting potential is that the technology for achieving this sort of synergistic balance is available today and will be even more so in the future.

CHAPTER
NINE

I do not read advertisements—I would spend all my time wanting things.
—— Archbishop of Canterbury

Advertisements contain the only truths to be relied on in a newspaper.
—— Thomas Jefferson (1743–1826)

Advertising is a valuable economic factor because it is the cheapest way of selling goods, particularly if the goods are worthless.
—— Sinclair Lewis (1885–1951)

If I were starting my life over again, I'm inclined to think I would go into the advertising business in preference to almost any other.
—— Franklin Delano Roosevelt (1882–1945)

ADVERTISING, SALES PROMOTION, AND PUBLICITY

Communication tactics are one of the most important and flexible links between an organization and its markets. Unlike product, price, and distribution, which are more difficult to change and remain relatively stable over time, communication is often the first and most effective lever an organization has to respond to or influence its markets.

As shown in Figure 9-1, the organization has control over four tools in the communication mix: advertising, promotion, publicity, and personal selling. These are defined in Table 9-1. As an indication of their relative importance, we might note that the following amounts of money were spent on each in 1980:

Advertising	$55 billion
Promotion	$40 billion
Publicity	$ 5 billion
Personal Selling	$80 billion[1]

In this chapter we will address the first three. Personal selling will be the subject of the following two chapters.

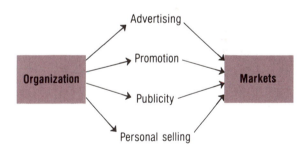

Figure 9-1. The communication mix: the organization's link to its markets

TABLE 9-1

Definitions and Examples of the Primary Tools in the Communication Mix

Communication Tool	Definition	Examples
Advertising	Any paid form of nonpersonal presentation of ideas, goods, and services by an identified sponsor.[a]	Television, radio, newspaper, magazine, direct mail, outdoor (e.g., billboard), specialty (e.g., embossed pens, calendars), and transit (e.g., bus and subway signs).
Promotion	Short-term incentives by an identified sponsor directed at final customers or intermediaries with the purpose of encouraging purchase or adoption of a product, practice, or activity.	Coupons, samples, price-off packages, contests, bonus packs, premiums, rebates, point-of-purchase materials, store demonstrations, trade shows and exhibits, trade allowances, and consumer education services.
Publicity	Any form of nonpaid, commercially significant news or editorial comment about ideas, products, or institutions.[b]	Conferences, press releases, newsletters, feature articles, photos, films, slides, tapes, annual reports, fund raising, special events, and public affairs.
Personal Selling	Oral presentation of ideas, goods, or services by a paid spokesperson directly to a prospective buyer or adopter.	Industrial salespeople, sales engineers, missionary salespeople, clerical salespeople, door-to-door salespeople, telephone sales, and team selling.

[a]Ralph S. Alexander and the Committee on Definitions, *Marketing Definitions* (Chicago: American Marketing Association, 1963), p.9.
[b]*Marketing Definitions: A Glossary of Marketing Terms* (Chicago: American Marketing Association), 1960.

Before we begin consideration of advertising, promotion, and publicity, we should point out two caveats. Although we will discuss these elements of the communication mix separately, this is done for presentational reasons only. You should realize that managers must consider when each tool is appropriate and what combination of tools is most desirable in any overall marketing program. Furthermore, it should again be stressed that communication is only one factor under the control of management and that product, price, and distribution programs must be integrated with communication options in any overall marketing effort.

Introduction to Advertising

Scope and Purpose of Advertising

Advertising is without question one of the most pervasive and least costly modes of communication available to a manager. We cannot escape exposure to ads. Indeed, it has been estimated that the average family sees or hears over 1,000 ads in a normal day,[2] yet the cost of an ad per 1,000 people reached is estimated to be only $1.20 in the *Good Housekeeping* magazine, for example.[3] And the use of radio, television, newspapers, and other media can be equally inexpensive on the basis of cost per thousand people reached.

In general, advertising and other communication tactics are designed to increase sales in one or more of five ways:

1 get new users who have never tried the product class (or brand)

2 get old users of the product class (or brand) who no longer purchase it

3 get users of the competitor's brands

4 get switchers who are not loyal to any brand

5 get increased consumption by current users.

Focus on any one of these will result in greater sales, but the objectives and effects of advertising are actually more complex than the five goals noted above. Sometimes advertising is targeted at a very specific group within the above categories such as "elderly purchasers of competitor Brand X." At other times, a market segment will cut across categories such as "all women aged 25–35, married with at least one child." Then, too, sales will sometimes not be the primary goal of an advertising campaign. For example, the objective may be merely to increase awareness of one's brand in Market Y from 10 percent to 35 percent. Indeed, any one or more of the psychological states in the hierarchy-of-effects model may be a goal in a specific ad campaign. Moreover, advertising may at times lack any particular objective relative to a target audience. It may, for instance, be designed merely to build a positive company image in the public at large or, occasionally, to serve simply as a means of expression or pride for the advertiser with no particular utilitarian goal in mind.

In this chapter, we will emphasize the purposeful side of marketing. Typically, marketers attempt to influence either psychological or behavioral variables. Psychological variables include, among others, brand awareness, knowledge of product attributes, beliefs about the consequences of product attributes, emotional reactions toward a brand (e.g., interest, liking), and intentions to purchase. Behavioral variables encompass, among others, trial purchase, brand loyalty, increased usage, switching, and overall sales.

Size of Advertising

Advertising is big business. It has to be an over-$55-billion-a-year industry in the U.S. alone. This means that about 2 percent of the U.S. gross national product—about $255 per person per year—is spent on advertising. To place this in perspective, Table 9-2 shows how 10 other countries around the world compare to the U.S. All told, the U.S. currently accounts for about half of the free world's expenditures on advertising.[4] Yet, even socialist countries (e.g., U.S.S.R., East Germany) advertise extensively, although we know little about their actual expenditures.[5]

TABLE 9-2

Comparison of Advertising Expenditures in the United States and Ten Other Countries

Country	Percentage of Gross National Product (1979)	Per Capita Expenditures in U.S. Dollars (1979)
United States	2.02	$224.37
Sweden	1.88	201.59
United Kingdom	1.74	91.87
Puerto Rico	1.59	46.32
Switzerland	1.59	200.79
Australia	1.37	115.17
Canada	1.32	122.04
Argentina	1.27	25.25
Ireland	1.02	37.90
Singapore	1.00	37.96
West Germany	1.00	102.14

SOURCE: *World Advertising Expenditures* (Mamaroneck, N.Y.: Starch INRA Hooper, 1980), pp. 7, 11. Reproduced with permission.

TABLE 9-3
The Top Ten Advertising Agencies in the United States Based on World Billings in 1984

Agency	Worldwide Ad Billings (in millions)	Gross Incomes (in millions)	Per Cent Gross Income in United States	Representative Accounts over the Years
1. Young & Rubicam	$3,202.1	$480.1	67.3%	Ford Motor, General Foods, Johnson & Johnson, Procter & Gamble
2. Ogilvy & Mather International	2,887.9	421.0	64.2	American Express, General Foods, Sears Roebuck, Shell Oil
3. Ted Bates & Co.	2,839.2	424.4	62.0	Brown & Williamson Tobacco, Colgate-Palmolive, ITT, Continental Baking, Mars
4. J. Walter Thompson	2,706.7	405.8	53.8	Burger King, Ford Motor, Kodak, Kraft
5. Saatchi & Saatchi Compton	2,301.7	337.5	46.6	Procter & Gamble, Playtex, Cunard, Nabisco
6. BBDO International	2,275.0	340.0	69.1	Delta Airlines, General Electric, Pepsi-Cola, R.J. Reynolds, Black & Decker
7. McCann-Erickson Worldwide	2,169.4	325.2	36.4	Coca-Cola, Exxon, General Motors, Miller Brewing
8. Foote, Cone & Belding	1,802.3	268.5	73.3	Clorox, Levi Strauss & Co., Hallmark Cards
9. Leo Burnett	1,734.8	253.5	64.4	Kellogg, Nestle, Philip Morris, Procter & Gamble
10. Doyle Dane Bernbach Intl.	1,510.6	218.3	69.2	Excedrin, Magnavox, Viceroy, Volkswagen, Alka-Seltzer

SOURCE: Based in part on material published in *Advertising Age,* March 28, 1985, p. 1. Reproduced with permission.

In the U.S., there are over 8,000 advertising agencies. Table 9-3 lists the top 10 in terms of world billings (i.e., total amount of money charged to clients for media, production, and other services), gross income, percentage of gross income in U.S., and representative client accounts. Notice that all the companies listed are billion-dollar operations, and the percent of business done in the U.S. varies from about 36 percent to 73 percent per firm. Table 9-4 presents the top twenty leading national advertisers. Notice that Procter & Gamble is the leading single advertiser. Three of the top 10 are consumer goods firms with many product lines; two are large retailers; two are diversified tobacco concerns; two are automobile companies; and one is a large utility.

Overall, more than 17,000 companies in the U.S. use advertising to sell their wares,[6] although less than 100 account for about 50 percent of all expenditures on national advertising.[7]

Advertising in Early Times

Throughout history, sellers have used one or another form of advertising to reach buyers. Primitive traders simply hung an animal carcass on a pole to announce their offerings. The Phoenicians painted messages on boulders and mountainsides along trade routes to inform and lure buyers. Craftsmen from Roman times and

TABLE 9-4
Twenty Leading Advertisers in 1983

Company	Advertising Expenditures (in millions)
1. Procter & Gamble Co.	$773.6
2. Sears, Roebuck & Co.	732.5
3. Beatrice Foods Co.	602.8
4. General Motors Corp.	595.1
5. R. J. Reynolds Industries, Inc.	593.4
6. Philip Morris, Inc.	527.5
7. Ford Motor Co.	479.1
8. AT&T	463.1
9. K Mart Corp.	400.0
10. General Foods Corp.	386.1
11. Nabisco Brands, Inc.	367.5
12. Pepsico, Inc.	356.4
13. Warner-Lambert Co.	343.6
14. American Home Products Corp.	333.5
15. Unilever U.S.	324.9
16. McDonald's Corp.	311.4
17. Johnson & Johnson	295.3
18. Mobil Corp.	294.9
19. J. C. Penney Co.	292.5
20. Anheuser-Busch, Inc.	290.6

SOURCE: *Advertising Age,* September 14, 1984, p. 1. Reproduced with permission.

Today, one way to characterize advertising is through the organizations that have evolved to create and produce it and the institutions that pay for and communicate it. Figure 9-2 presents a simple schematic of the key actors. The advertiser is, of course, the sponsoring firm that desires to reach the public with a message. The advertising agency is a specialized firm that designs, produces, and distributes the advertising message. The media are the organizations that actually communicate it (e.g., newspaper, magazine, television, and radio companies). At the right of Figure 9-2 are the people and institutions who interact with advertisers, agencies, and media. Let us take a closer look at the key actors.

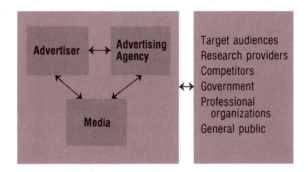

Figure 9-2. Primary actors in advertising

throughout the Middle Ages used special markings on their products and on the sides of their buildings to advertise themselves.

Of course, the growth of advertising closely paralleled the development of new technologies in communication. With the advent of the printing press, for example, advertising in the form of leaflets and in newspapers began in the early 1500s. Indeed, the practice quickly became so widespread that in 1759 Dr. Samuel Johnson noted, perhaps prematurely, that "[t]he trade of advertising is now so near perfection, it is not easy to propose any improvement."[8] But improve it did. As the telephone, radio, and television emerged, so too did new forms of advertising. New developments in computers and other electronic wonders are sure to stimulate ever-refined and creative ways to reach others.

The Advertiser. Advertising is sponsored by a wide assortment of institutions. Most consumer and industrial goods manufacturers advertise, as do the majority of retailing establishments. The government, too, is a heavy advertiser. In 1979, for example, the federal government spent $146.1 million, including $98.7 million for military recruiting, $9.2 million by the U.S. Postal Service, and $11.4 million by Amtrak.[9] Nonprofit organizations also find advertising indispensable, as witnessed by its frequent use by the Red Cross, March of Dimes, and churches, among others. Dentists, doctors, and lawyers have even joined the ranks of advertisers, although belatedly and with some controversy.

Nearly every organization has special people and arrangements for handling communication tasks. Let us focus for a moment on private companies, for these have the most elaborate communication systems. Typically, communication is under the leadership of an advertising director, the vice president of marketing, the head of public relations, or, on occasion, the vice president of sales. But companies employ different frameworks to accomplish this and other goals. Most firms are organized under either a *functional* or a *brand management* system.[10] Figure 9-3 illustrates a typical functional hierarchy. Notice that five central business functions are shown directly below the chief executive officer. One of these is marketing. Marketing itself is divided into five subfunctions: sales, advertising, marketing research, new product development, and distribution. For the example shown in Figure 9-3, communication is under the guidance of the advertising director. Three tasks are delineated: promotion planning, media planning, and advertising account management. The key attribute of a functional organization of marketing tasks is that no person or group is responsible for the entire design, development, and management of a specific product or brand. Rather, the tasks required to market brands are parcelled out to specialized subgroups under the vice president of marketing. The advertising subgroup handles communication issues for all brands but does not have responsibility for selling, marketing research, product development, or distribution. Separate groups exist for the latter tasks under a functional organization.

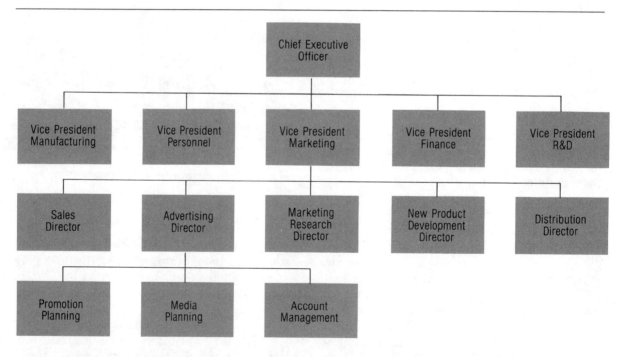

Figure 9-3. An example of a functional organizational hierarchy (partial rendition)

Contrast the functional arrangement to the brand management organization of marketing tasks (see Figure 9-4). Some functional specialization still exists for basic marketing tasks, but we see the further allocation of broad, general marketing responsibilities to brand managers. We have shown the brand managers under the advertising director, although they are sometimes situated under products managers or group product managers. The important point to note is that separate brand managers exist for each brand. Moreover, each brand manager (sometimes also called a product manager or marketing manager) is responsible for coordinating and administrating the entire marketing program for his or her brand. This means developing marketing strategies, plans, and forecasts; working with advertising agencies to develop ads; interacting with co-workers responsible for designing, making, selling, and distributing the product; participating in the pricing of the product; designing promotion; gathering and interpreting information on how well the product is doing after launch; initiating improvements and generally managing the product and its marketing throughout the life cycle.[11]

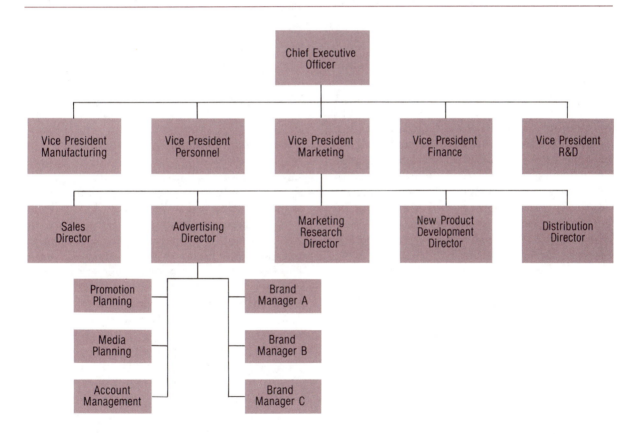

Figure 9-4. An example of a brand management organizational hierarchy (partial rendition)

Which organizational type is the best? There is no definitive answer to this question. Firms selling in the same general product category have found either approach to be successful. Many consumer goods firms employ a brand management arrangement. General Foods, for instance, uses the brand management organization in its cereal product group and in its coffee product group, among other places. Thus, separate brand managers exist for nutritional cereals, family cereals, and children's cereals, as well as for regular, instant caffeinated, and instant decaffeinated coffees. Procter & Gamble also uses a brand management system. On the other hand, Pepsi-Cola employs a functional organization.[12]

Although firm guidelines are not possible to state, we might speculate on possible pros and cons of the functional and brand management organizations. The primary advantage of the functional arrangement is that it is simple and at the same time tends to promote cross-fertilization among brands. The latter arises because one or more individuals are directly involved with multiple brands and can apply their learning and experiences to all brands. The principle disadvantages are that effort and resources will not always be optimally allocated among brands, and other marketing subfunctions (e.g., distribution) will compete for attention and resources as well. The former condition arises because managers either lack valid criteria to efficiently coordinate many brands or else they have vested interests or pet projects that run counter to the most effective allocation for all brands under their purview. The latter condition arises as a consequence of a relative lack of mutuality and communication when compared to the more centralized coordination of the brand management system. Indeed, the real advantage of the brand management arrangement lies in the assignment of overall responsibility to a single individual (or small number of individuals), which tends to result in strong motivation, the absence of neglect of some brands, and efficient coordination of manufacturing, design, and marketing activities related to the brand.

Moreover, the brand management system tends to respond faster than the functional system to changes in the market and environment, and it represents an effective means of training and developing managers with promise for future advancement. Finally, competition between brand managers can be a positive force within the company. For example, General Foods has many brands of coffee such as Sanka, Brim, Maxim, Yuban, and Maxwell House, which results in functional rivalries. Nevertheless, certain drawbacks need to be mentioned. The brand management system sometimes results in the emphasis of the short run at the expense of the long run. Due to its isolated nature, it fails to benefit as well from learning transfers from experiences with other brands. And it results in somewhat less effective market segmentation strategies than under the functional arrangement because it uses more of a bottom-up than top-down process for initiating and making many marketing decisions. Finally, brand competition can become dysfunctional if conflicts emerge within the firm and/or excessive cannibalization of sales across brands occurs.

Every firm handles its communication needs differently. At one time, many firms conducted advertising research, media planning, copy creation, production of ads, and purchasing of media time in-house. The Coors Brewing Company was one of these up until the late 1970s, and Quaker Oats, General Electric, and Scott Paper still do some of their own advertising. However, as the tasks associated with advertising proliferate and become more complex, difficult, and expensive to execute, most firms have found the need to hire advertising agencies to handle their communication needs. Firms still, of course, have internal people responsible for communication and the handling of contacts with ad agencies. Indeed, some companies retain certain advertising tasks in-house, while farming out others. Lipton, for example, often performs media planning and buying, but hires outside agencies to design and produce its ads. Whatever the arrangements, advertising agencies are an indispensable part of communication programs of most modern organizations.

The Advertising Agency. Advertising agencies plan, create, execute, and place advertisements in media for clients (i.e., for advertisers). Figure 9-5 presents a typical organizational structure for medium-sized ad agencies. Notice that the agency has four major components: administration, creative services, marketing services, and account services. *Administration* is concerned with the everyday management of financial, accounting, and personnel matters. We will have nothing more to say about these functions but will focus on the other three herein. *Creative services* consist of people concerned with the design, development, and production of the actual ads. These include artists, copywriters, photographers, television producers, designers, and other creative specialists. These people take the goals and plans formulated by advertisers and account people and translate them into real ads. Obviously, this is a highly subjective and nonlinear activity, as the name implies. *Marketing services* consist of technical support with special emphasis on marketing research, media planning, and sales promotion. Typically, behavioral scientists and statisticians comprise the researchers, operations researchers dominate media planning, and a mixture of specialists engage in sales promotion.

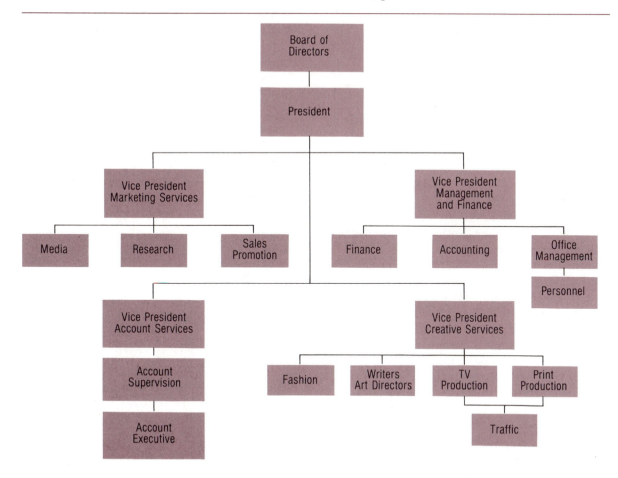

Figure 9-5. Organizational structure of medium-sized advertising agency

SOURCE: American Association of Advertising Agencies

The center of any advertising agency is the *account services* group. Each brand of a client will generally be handled by an account manager. He or she is the counterpart of the brand manager found in many client firms. The account manager interacts with the client firm and manages and coordinates all the activities needed to deliver an ad. For example, the account manager will work with the client to formulate an advertising strategy. This may include consideration of goals with respect to the hierarchy of effects, broad themes to stress in advertising copy, definition of the target market(s), and so on. The account manager will also administrate the advertising program within the advertising agency. This means working with people and problems surrounding marketing research, media, message design, production, and a whole host of other activities.

Advertising agencies are compensated in a variety of ways.[13] The most relevant is by commission. That is, the advertiser pays the media to run its ad, and for its services, the advertising agency receives a percentage (usually 15 percent) of the amount billed to the advertiser.[14] For example, an ad agency might produce a television ad and place it on the Super Bowl. The media billing of $1 million would result in compensation of $150,000 to the agency. Notice that the agency will receive a commission each time the ad is shown. Occasionally, advertising agencies are paid through a fee system. That is, at the outset, the client agrees to pay the agency's specific fee for services rendered. Still another source of compensation is a markup on materials used or actual payment of prespecified costs. Overall, the vast majority of advertiser-agency relationships involves some negotiation and combination of compensation schemes.

The Media. The media are channels of communication that carry messages from an advertiser to a target audience. The most common media used are radio, television, newspapers, magazines, outdoor (posters, billboards, painted bulletins), direct mail, and miscellaneous vehicles (e.g., the Yellow Pages, specialty items such as calendars and pens). In the United States and most nontotalitarian societies, the media are independent institutions, although they are frequently subject to some regulation by governments.

TABLE 9-5

A Comparison of Advertising Expenditures in Major Media in 1950, 1960, 1970, and 1980 (in millions of dollars)

Medium	1950	1960	1970	1980
Newspapers	2,070	3,681	5,704	15,615
National	518	778	891	2,335
Local	1,552	2,903	4,813	13,280
Magazines	478	909	1,292	3,225
Business Publications	251	609	740	1,695
Television	171	1,627	3,596	11,330
National	116	1,347	2,892	8,365
Local	55	280	704	2,965
Radio	605	693	1,308	3,690
National	332	265	427	935
Local	273	428	881	2,755
Direct Mail	803	1,830	2,766	7,655
Outdoor	142	203	234	610
Miscellaneous	1,122	2,342	3,848	10,795
Total				
National	3,260	7,305	11,350	30,435
Local	2,440	4,655	8,200	24,315
Grand Total	5,700	11,960	19,550	54,750

SOURCE: *Advertising Age,* April 30, 1980, Part 4; January 5, 1981; February 16, 1981. Reproduced with permission.

To get a picture of the relative use of the media and how this has changed over time, look at Table 9-5. Total expenditures have been allocated over various media for a 30-year period. Notice that the relative proportion of money spent on newspapers, magazines, business publications, radio, and outdoor has declined significantly over the period. Advertising expenditures on television, direct mail, and miscellaneous media have increased or remained the same as a proportion of total expenditures. We can observe further that the use of local television and local radio has increased dramatically, perhaps reflecting the need to reach specific market segments with custom-tailored ads. Finally, notice that newspaper advertising represents the single largest expenditure, although it has declined from about 36.3 percent in 1950 to 28.5 percent in 1980. Television advertising is the second largest category, whereas direct mail comes in third.

Which media are the most effective and efficient? The answer to this depends on what criteria one employs to measure effectiveness and efficiency. Table 9-6 on page 382 presents four frequently used media—TV, radio, magazines, and newspapers—and evaluates and compares them on 35 criteria. Notice that TV reaches the most people, radio costs the least on a 1,000 person-reached basis, magazines score high on sensory stimulation, humor is best executed on TV, newspapers facilitate selective ad positioning while TV does not, TV is best for brand name registration whereas magazines and newspapers are worst, and radio is the most consistently monitored medium across seasons but TV is the poorest. These and the other comparisons are, of course, gross generalizations and should be taken in only a suggestive way.

Behavioral Dimensions of Advertising

Advertising agencies draw heavily upon principles from the behavioral sciences in the design of ads. Much of this is done subjectively and is an outgrowth of the culture and philosophy of the advertising agency. Indeed, it is often possible to identify a unique advertising style running throughout an agency's ads. At the same time, objective findings from marketing and the behavioral sciences and from an agency's own research are frequently employed in ad design as well. In this part of the chapter, we will discuss both the art and science of advertising by focusing on creative styles and on behavioral research inputs to advertisements.

Ad Agency Creative Styles[15]

An advertising agency, like any company, has a personality that is reflected in its approach to business and its outputs. Often, the personality of an agency is closely tied to its leadership, particularly the influence of its current leaders and the charisma and creativity of its founders. We will consider four relatively distinct ad agencies, each of which owes its style to the inspiration of one or more people: the Leo Burnett agency (Leo Burnett), the Doyle Dane Bernbach agency (William Bernbach), the Ogilvy & Mather agency (David Ogilvy), and the Ted Bates agency (Rosser Reeves). Perhaps in no other area of marketing is success so dependent on intangible, subjective inputs as is the design and production of advertisements.

Leo Burnett. Leo Burnett has handled the advertising for a long list of clients, including Kellogg, Seven-Up, Nestle, Phillip Morris, Procter & Gamble, United Airlines, Maytag, Pillsbury, and Allstate Insurance. You probably recognize at least some of the following companies: "Me and my RC," "Fly the Friendly Skies of United," the Jolly Green Giant, Keebler Cookies and elves, the lonely Maytag repairman, Charlie the Tuna, "You're in good hands with Allstate," Morris the Cat, and the Pillsbury Dough Boy.

TABLE 9-6
A Comparison of Four Media on Thirty-five Criteria

Criterion	TV	Radio	Magazines	Newspapers
Total population reach (adults and children)	Very Strong	Good	Fair	Good
Selective upscale adult reach	Fair	Good	Very Strong	Good
Upscale adult selectivity (per ad exposure)	Poor	Fair	Very Strong	Good
Young adult selectivity (per ad exposure)	Fair	Very Strong	Very Strong	Fair
Cost per 1,000 ratios	Fair–Good	Very Strong	Strong	Good
National media availabilities and uniform coverage	Very Strong	Poor	Good	Poor
Local market selectivity	Good	Good	Poor	Very Strong
Ability to control frequency	Fair	Good	Good	Very Strong
Ability to pile frequency upon reach base	Very Strong	Very Strong	Good	Fair
Ability to exploit time of day factors (in scheduling)	Fair	Very Strong	Poor	Poor
Ability to exploit day of week factors (in scheduling)	Fair	Very Strong	Poor	Very Strong
Seasonal audience stability	Poor	Very Strong	Good	Good
Predictability of audience levels	Fair–Poor	Good	Good	Very Good
Depth of demographics in audience surveys	Poor	Poor	Very Strong	Fair–Good
Reliability and consistency of audience surveys	Fair–Good	Good	Fair–Good	Good
Ability to monitor schedules	Good	Poor	Very Strong	Very Strong
Ability to negotiate rates	Good	Fair	Poor	Poor
Fast closing and air dates	Fair	Good	Poor	Very Strong
Opportunity to exploit editorial ''compatibility''	Poor	Fair	Very Strong	Good
Selective ad positioning	Poor	Fair	Good	Very Strong
Advertising exposure	Good	Good	Good	Good
Advertising intrusiveness	Very Strong	Good	Fair	Poor
Audience concern over ad ''clutter''	Very High	High	Almost None	Almost None
Emotional stimulation	Very Strong	Fair	Fair	Poor
Sensory stimulation	Fair–Good	Fair	Very Strong	Fair
Brand name registration	Very Strong	Good	Fair	Fair
Product or efficacy demonstrations	Very Strong	Poor	Fair	Fair
Ability to exploit attention-getting devices	Very Strong	Poor	Very Strong	Good
Ability to use humor	Very Strong	Good	Poor	Poor
Ability to use slice-of-life approach	Very Strong	Good	Poor	Poor
Ability to convey detail and information	Fair	Fair	Very Strong	Very Strong
Ability to stimulate imagination	Fair–Good	Very Strong	Fair	Poor
Package identification	Good	Poor	Very Strong	Good
Prestige and respectability of the medium	Fair	Fair	Very Strong	Strong
Ability to talk person-to-person with audience	Fair–Good	Very Strong	Poor	Poor

SOURCE: *The Media Book* (New York: Min-Mid Publishing, 1978), pp. 433 and 436.

Ads for those companies and products have a number of common elements: many of the ads emphasize emotions and/or humor. At the same time, they typically focus on genuine product attributes in a realistic way. As a consequence, Leo Burnett's ads are often characterized by the words "warm and believable." They create pleasant feelings yet do so without excessive embellishment and without making false claims. A good example is provided in the "Fly the Friendly Skies of United" ads. Here a catchy phrase was put to music, and ads exuded a human quality highlighting pleasant airline personnel and pleased customers of all ages and backgrounds. The United Airlines ads also demonstrate another quality of Leo Burnett: namely, ads frequently center on ordinary, everyday people. They contain individuals with whom the viewer can readily identify. This aspect of Leo Burnett has been called "the common touch" and creates a wholesome image. Many of its ads for Procter & Gamble demonstrate this quality.

Occasionally, Leo Burnett has employed animation. Animated characters such as Charlie the Tuna, the Keebler Cookie Elves, the Jolly Green Giant, Tony the Tiger, and the Pillsbury Dough Boy supply an element of fantasy that entertains and delivers the message in a nonthreatening way. It is also thought to lead to enhanced remembrance of advertised brands and product attributes over time because of the presumed longevity that animated images convey. And animated characters are ideally suited for communicating warmth and humor. Finally, Leo Burnett uses animation dramatically to convey a story. In a typical application, one cartoon character will inform another of the benefits of a particular brand. Rather than lecturing the audience directly, the ad indirectly educates the consumer.

The tactic is a common one in literature, plays, and the movies and has been termed "use of a foil." Its effect is to reduce the skepticism and defenses that we all have towards others trying to directly persuade us to do something, and, in general, the tactic is consistent with theories of observational learning.[16] Closely related to this is Leo Burnett's frequent attempt to portray the "inherent drama" in a product:

Of course we . . . stress this so-called inherent drama of things because there is usually something there . . . [I]f you can find the thing about that product that keeps it in the marketplace . . . something about it that makes people continue to buy it . . . capturing that, and then taking that thing . . . and making the thing itself arresting. . . .[17]

Thus, although we might empathize with the lonely Maytag repairman, we get the point that the manufacturer's products are of a very high quality and are made to last. Each ad reenacts the repairman's search for someone who needs his services and will give him a purpose in life.

One of the most successful campaigns for Leo Burnett over the years has been for Marlboro Cigarettes. Up to about 1954, Marlboro was primarily purchased and smoked by women. It had minuscule sales compared to the market leaders and was not even distributed nationally. The cigarette could be bought with either an ivory tip or a red "beauty" tip, where the latter was designed to hide lipstick stains which were thought to be embarrassing. Studies showed that men viewed it as a "feminine/sissy" cigarette. Then Leo Burnett was asked to handle the advertising. Based in part on research indicating that heavy users of cigarettes were young to middle-aged men and blue collar workers, a decision was made to go after this market. No other brands were directed toward men at the time. Further, the men surveyed expressed a desire for "full, honest flavor" in their cigarettes.

Marlboro ads in the mid to late 1950s used the theme "delivers the goods on flavor." Ads stressed a strong-tasting cigarette, and masculine themes were introduced, especially in the print media. For example, fishermen, tennis players, and other sportsmen were featured. Often a tattoo on the back of the hand or arm was highlighted to symbolically convey an image of virility. Cowboy themes were tried, too, and by the early 1960s, the theme was changed to "You get a lot to like with a Marlboro—filter, flavor, flip-top box." By this time, the cowboy image was used almost exclusively. In 1972, the theme was changed again to "come to where the flavor is" and "come to Marlboro country," both of which are still used today. Throughout the ads, one can identify a strong aura of masculinity created through the use of rugged cowboys, spectacular scenery, cattle and horses, brown tones, and so on.

Leo Burnett was so successful that Marlboro soon became the leading selling cigarette in the United States. In 1980, Marlboro had about 17 percent of the market, followed by Winston (14 percent), and Kool (10 percent).

Most of Leo Burnett's ads employ a "soft sell" approach to advertising. The goal is not to be too offensive, pushy, or intrusive. An impact on the marketplace occurs subtly through positive affect and realism. Moreover, repetition of ads is felt to be important. Among all ad agencies, Leo Burnett seems to employ the most equal balance in its emphasis between message content and structure.

Doyle Dane Bernbach. Obviously, all ads have elements of both content and structure, but many agencies emphasize one or the other. Doyle Dane Bernbach concentrates heavily on message structure or, in the words of William Bernbach: "Execution can become content; it can be just as important as what you say."[18]

Many of DDB's ads seem to follow a philosophy of "how it is said is more important than what is said." The medium is the message.[19] Yet, as we will describe in a moment, humor and refutational arguments have been central to DDB's ads as well.

Let us look at some of the more successful DDB ads. While you might not have heard of DDB, you are certain to have been exposed to some of its ads. Doyle Dane Bernbach was the first agency to advertise Volkswagen in the United States. They handle the accounts of American Airlines, G.T.E., Polaroid, Stroh's Beer, and some of Procter & Gamble's products. You may remember the Avis "We're number two, we try harder" campaign. Or the Jack-in-the-Box warning, "Watch out, McDonald's!" Similarly, DDB was responsible for the recent series of ads on Mobil 1 Oil. Doyle Dane Bernbach has done ads for American Tourister luggage and Alka Seltzer, too. What things, themes, or formats can you identify in many of the foregoing ad executions?

One common thread is the use of humor. Humor is employed for a variety of reasons. It attracts and holds one's attention, and it rewards the audience. In a sense, if we see an ad and are pleased or entertained by it, we will be more inclined to look forward to the ad again and perhaps develop a positive attitude toward the brand. This sequence of viewing $\longrightarrow$ reward $\longrightarrow$ enhanced probability of viewing again and developing positive affect contains elements of operant conditioning. Humor also tends to stimulate involvement with an ad.

A second element of many DDB ads is the use of refutational arguments. The idea here is to acknowledge a drawback or shortcoming of a brand and then to turn it into an asset or selling point. This might be done by taking a client who is not the market leader and positioning the brand relative to the leader(s) in order to increase its visibility and enhance its image. Avis, for example, was successfully positioned in relation to Hertz, the number one company in rental cars.

The hope was that people would perceive Avis as a more accommodating firm in its drive to overtake Hertz. (However, it is believed that the Avis campaign did less to damage Hertz than it did to increase primary demand and take sales away from firms lower in market share.[20]) Another way that DDB uses a refutational approach is to pick one or more attributes of a brand that seem to be a problem and then turn them into an advantage for the seller. For instance, the Volkswagen "Bug" appeared to compare unfavorably to Detroit's line-up of fancy medium and full-sized cars. But DDB was able to use the seemingly ugly appearance and small size of the VW to advantage by stressing its low cost, economical performance, and homely attractiveness. Indeed, the loyalty of VW bug owners has assumed religious proportions. Doyle Dane Bernbach uses clever themes and hilarious executions to implement its refutational approach.

Still another tactic of DDB is to employ a storyline that contains "an unusual turn of events." For example, one classic ad for VW opens with a shot of the boots of a person walking through heavy snow in the early morning. The person enters his garage, starts the car, and drives to another garage. Up to this point no words are spoken, nothing is said about what the ad is about or who its sponsor is. Then at the second garage, the man enters a large snowplow and drives away with the following query ending the ad: "Have you ever wondered how the man who drives a snowplow drives to the snowplow? This one drives a Volkswagen. So you can stop wondering." The idea with building an ad around an unusual turn of events is that it injects an element of mystery or suspense into the ad. The curiosity so generated then leads the audience to rivet its attention on the ad. It also psychologically involves the viewer with the ad and increases the chance that the brand will be recognized, remembered later, and perhaps positively evaluated.

Doyle Dane Bernbach will sometimes put the brand of its client through "a tough test of the product." By subjecting a brand (and also occasionally its competitors) to a difficult test, it is believed that this will forcefully convey the superior functionality or durability of the focal brand. For example, one DDB ad for American Tourister luggage shows a huge gorilla savagely banging a suitcase against concrete and steel bars. Of course, the suitcase survives intact, implying that it will serve well even the most demanding customer.

A number of other principles are followed in DDB's ads.[21] An effort is made not to be condescending but rather to treat the audience with respect. Copy is factual and puffery avoided. Unlike Leo Burnett, less emphasis is placed on repetition. Rather than overplaying the same ad or always using the same theme, new executions are continually made. An attempt is made to develop a unique personality for the brand. The philosophy of DDB can be summed up through the following:

[T]he most important thing as far as I am concerned is to be fresh, to be original.... Because you can have all the right things in an ad, and if nobody is made to stop and listen to you, you have wasted it.[22]

In a word, *creativity* is the guiding principle of DDB.

Ogilvy & Mather. David Ogilvy, like Leo Burnett and William Bernbach, has had a major impact on how advertising is conducted. Among his most central directives are the following:

What you say is more important than how you say it.

Give the facts.

Be well-mannered, but don't clown.

If you are lucky enough to write a good advertisement, repeat it until it stops pulling.

Every advertisement should be thought of as a contribution to the complex symbol which is the brand image.

It is the total personality of a brand rather than any trivial product difference which decides its ultimate position in the market.[22]

Notice that one watchword of Ogilvy's approach is *rationality.* Ads are designed to appeal to the intellect and thinking side of human nature. The emotional, such as found in humor, is downplayed. This is in marked contrast to ads by Leo Burnett or Doyle Dane Bernbach. This philosophy can be found nearly universally throughout Ogilvy & Mather's ads for its clients: American Express, Hershey Chocolate, Sears Roebuck, Schaeffer Beer, General Foods (e.g., Maxim Coffee), and Unilever. Even its ads for Dove Soap are more cognitive than ads for Dove's competitors.

A second theme found in many of Ogilvy & Mather's ads is the importance of the brand image. This is believed especially important for marketing everyday products and as competition increases:

The greater the similarity between brands, the less part reason plays in brand selection. There isn't any significant difference between the various brands of whiskey, or cigarettes, or beer. They are all about the same. And so are the cake mixes and the detergents, and the margarines. The manufacturer who dedicates his advertising to building the most sharply defined personality for his brand will get the largest share of the market at the highest profit.[23]

Ads by Ogilvy & Mather do not neglect reason. Rather, they focus relatively less on product attributes and instead attempt to create an image for the brand. To create an image, ads will contain many thought-provoking themes, and famous personalities will frequently be highlighted. Helena Rubinstein has been used in ads for cosmetics,

and Ted Williams and Johnny Miller in ads for Sears, for example. At the same time, the creation of a brand image has been a central focus in Ogilvy & Mather's ads for luxury or exclusive products. For instance, themes of prestige or status have been used to sell Rolls-Royce cars ("At 60 miles an hour, the loudest noise in this Rolls-Royce comes from the electric clock"), travel, and Schweppes drinks. A more recent successful image campaign by Ogilvy & Mather is the Pepperidge Farm bread truck driven by a wizened New England baker.

A strong point of many Ogilvy & Mather ads has been its effective and creative copy. You may recall seeing its "Come to Shell for Answers" campaign in which an eight-page booklet was marketed as an educational promotion for consumers on driving techniques, proper care of automobiles, and other tips. This program not only increased customer awareness of Shell and built positive attitudes, but it generated general public acclaim and recognition by government officials for its excellence.[24]

Four final points to note with respect to Ogilvy & Mather concern repetition, comparative advertising, research, and a mellowing in strategy. The agency tends to use high rates of repetition of the same ads and in this sense is similar to Leo Burnett but differs from DDB. Second, Ogilvy & Mather avoids the use of comparative ads:

Our study of television commercials that name names suggests that there is little to be gained from this type of advertising for the advertising industry, the advertiser, or the consumer. The only one who may benefit is the competitor who is named in the advertising.[25]

This illustrates a third dimension of Ogilvy & Mather—the value placed on the amount of money spent on consumer research. Leo Burnett also conducts relatively high amounts of research. Doyle Dane Bernbach, however, is more intuitive in its approach and places less emphasis on research.

Finally, it should be noted that David Ogilvy recently softened his opposition to the use of humor somewhat and also now believes that the use of celebrities in ads should be reexamined, as they "are far below average in their power to sell."[26]

Ted Bates. Rosser Reeves helped make Ted Bates and Company one of the leading advertising agencies. Its accounts over the years have included Bufferin, Palmolive Soap, Colgate Toothpaste, Viceroy and Kool Cigarettes, Prudential Insurance, M&M Candy, Coors Beer, and Maybelline. You might remember some of their slogans: "It writes the first time, every time" (Bic pens), "They melt in your mouth, not in your hand" (M&M Candy), "Colgate cleans your breath as it cleans your teeth," and "How do you spell relief? R-O-L-A-I-D-S."

Ads from the Ted Bates agency have typically followed the Rosser Reeves philosophy.[27] A key idea of this philosophy is that the "hard sell" is more effective than the soft sell approach. The Ted Bates agency believes that more impact per ad will be achieved by a factual, forceful orientation than by humorous or so-called creative ads. The latter are thought simply to entertain or detract from the message. Ads are made forceful through the use of fear- or anxiety-provoking copy or else somewhat irritating or offensive executions. In addition, the impact is augmented through repetition—lots of it. One classic Reeves ad from the 1950s was for Anacin: a hammer banged on an anvil as a person winced with excruciating headache pain and the copy promised "Fast, Fast, Fast Relief." What many people might not realize is that one ad for Anacin ran for over 10 years without a change, and although it cost only $8,200 to make, it is reputed to have earned more money for the manufacturer than the film "Gone with the Wind" generated.[28]

Advertising from the Ted Bates agency is generally more factual, more cognitive than even ads from Ogilvy & Mather. The objective of a largely rational (as opposed to a lighter or emotional) perspective is nicely put in Rosser Reeves's "Unique Selling Proposition" (USP):

Each advertisement must make a proposition to the consumer, not just words, not just product puffery, not just show window advertising. Each advertisement must say to each reader: "Buy this product, and you will get this specific benefit."

The proposition must be one that the competitor either cannot, or does not, offer. It must be unique—either a uniqueness of the brand or a claim not otherwise made in that particular field of advertising.[29]

The USP chosen for a brand is often given a scientific character in an ad. Thus, Certs contains "a magic drop of Retsyn," Colgate has "MFP fluoride," and "only Viceroy gives you 20,000 filter traps in every filter tip." By focusing on a specific product benefit (hopefully a unique one), it is felt that the self-interest of the audience will be stimulated and serve as the primary moderator of sales.

Despite the emphasis on a factual, hard-sell pitch, however, the most effective ads for Ted Bates seem to be those that combine a USP with fear-arousing stimuli. These might be ones stressing physical consequences (e.g., cavities) or social embarrassment (e.g., bad breath).

Comments on Ad Agencies. In retrospect, we can see that the four advertising agencies chosen for examination are quite different in style. Which is the most effective? This is impossible to say with certainty. As Table 9-3 reveals, each agency is doing quite well. It seems that there are multiple routes to success. The creation and production of effective ads is a complex endeavor involving a combination of creativity, research skills, managerial know-how, and luck. Each agency must begin with its own skills and resources and construct its outputs in an evolutionary way. Because every agency begins with different inputs and because the process evolves nonlinearly, one should expect diverse approaches to similar problems. Perhaps nowhere else in marketing is the impact of organizational culture and the social construction of reality to be felt with such force as in the advertising agency and its products.

Many other agencies could also have been chosen to illustrate the art and diversity of advertising. For example, the approach of Young and Rubicam is summed up as follows:

It [i.e., the creative approach] must have the right strategy, be believable, have drama, make the product a hero, make a friend and build on and be consistent with the basic personality of the product.[30]

You probably have seen their ads for Kentucky Fried Chicken, Pabst Beer, Jell-O (with Bill Cosby), Dr. Pepper, Oil of Olay, and Eastern Airlines. N W Ayer, another leading advertiser, attempts to portray "human contact" in its ads. Thus, its ads for AT&T have successfully stimulated people to "reach out and touch someone" through long-distance phone calling, and its ads for Budweiser Light Beer have stressed emotional situations where athletes overcome adversity to perform splendidly. Still another ad agency, D'Arcy-MacManus & Masius, often uses celebrities "to cut through media clutter

and accomplish long-term goals"[31] for establishing a competitive edge, memorability, continuity, and a unique image. Nowhere is this more evident than in its ads for Florists' Transworld Delivery (FTD) where Merlin Olsen, a former all-pro football player (now commentator), is the spokesperson. Notice that this focus on celebrities in ads contradicts David Ogilvy's latest views. The vastly different styles and strategies in the advertising business illustrate the important role of subjective, creative input in managerial decisions. Before we turn to the managerial side of advertising, let us briefly consider how some findings from the behavioral sciences are reflected in contemporary advertising.

Behavioral Science Principles in Advertising

Repetition and Wearout.[32] Repetition of ads might be thought to be needed for a number of reasons. At the *micro level* of the psychology of the individual consumer, repetition is required to attract attention. Many ads and other stimuli compete for the consumer's scarce time. Moreover, given that people tend to tune out ads and to have "low involvement" with most ad-carrying media, repetition is needed to "break through" perceptual barriers. In addition, consumers forget information in ads and must be reminded periodically of their content. Finally, repetition might be thought to be necessary to reach deeper and deeper into the mind of the consumer. Persuasion sometimes requires more repetition than awareness, for example.

At the *macro level* of aggregates of consumers, repetition is needed to reach greater and greater percentages of the market unaware of the product, brand, or key selling points. Further, repetition is needed to "move" higher and higher percentages of the target audience through the stages in the hierarchy-of-effects models: that is, from awareness to interest to desire to action. Eventually, a point is reached where saturation occurs, and greater efforts to reach people lead to diminishing returns. Indeed, it is believed that the relationship between repetition and aggregate responses such as awareness, recall, attitude change, and sales is S-shaped (see Figure 9-6). Let us take a deeper look at the effects of repetition at both the micro and macro levels.

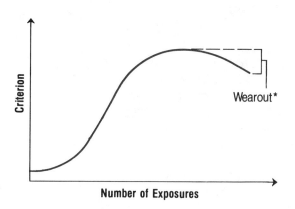

Figure 9-6. Advertising wearout

e.g., awareness, interest, believability, attitude, and sales

Micro Processes.
Krugman, a leading practitioner, asserts that three exposures are all that are needed to achieve the desired effects of advertising.[33] His argument is the following. The first exposure to an ad by an individual consumer is needed to attract attention. The consumer reacts primarily perceptually and secondarily cognitively with a "What is it?" response. A later, second exposure has two effects according to Krugman. One is the evaluative "What of it?" reaction, and the other is a recognition response of "Aha, I've seen this before!" Krugman believes that subsequent exposures lead to no deeper information processing. The third and each succeeding exposure are reminder ads calling up from memory that which is already known and has been learned. Krugman maintains that more than three exposures is not only wasteful but leads to disengagement of audience in-

terest. As a matter of fact, ads are thought to work powerfully "only when the...consumer...is interested."[34] A final point that Krugman makes is that people really forget very little in the sense that, although they may not recall ads very well, their recognition powers are very strong.[35]

Most of Krugman's hypotheses have not been directly tested, but other reasoning tends to support them. For example, most ads contain relatively simple messages, so it is not difficult to accept that one or two exposures will attract one's attention and lead to an evaluative (e.g., good/bad) reaction to the message, advertised brand, or overall ad execution. And all of us at one time or another have found ourselves tuning out ads after hearing or seeing the same ad on multiple occasions.

How, from a psychological standpoint, might repetition affect a consumer? Aside from the obvious effects of increasing the depth of our learning, providing reinforcement, and maintaining top-of-the-mind awareness, repetition has subtle and not always positive impacts. A common outcome is that our attitude toward a brand can level off and even decline after repeated exposure to an ad or similar ads. This is thought to occur because we either become bored with an ad and ignore its message, counterargue against the message, or else we become irritated with the ad and downgrade the advertiser. The observed decline in awareness or attitude has been termed *wearout*.

Psychologists offer varied interpretations of the effects of repetition. Perhaps the most common effects occur early in learning. Repeated exposure merely serves to aid in the transfer of information (e.g., the brand name or a key product attribute) from short-term memory to long-term memory. Through rehearsal (i.e., mentally repeating information), chunking (i.e., grouping of bits of information in sets), or the use of mnemonics (i.e., conscious word or picture associations made to the information), we can enhance the probability that information gets stored. Moreover, repetition in the early stages of exposure can maintain "top-of-the-mind" awareness, as well as aid in the retrieval of information from long-term memory. All of these outcomes are in addition to the possibility of classical conditioning or the mere exposure effect occurring.[36] In classical conditioning, repeated exposures of an arousing ad along with a brand name, say, may lead to the development of positive feelings, depending on the strength of the arousing stimulus, the number of repetitions, and other factors. The mere exposure effect also results in positive feelings and requires repeated exposures of a neutral stimulus (e.g., a brand name), but the exact psychological mechanisms are little understood.

In addition to these effects, social psychologists suggest that repetition may lead to certain "cognitive responses."[37] Repeated exposure may stimulate counterarguments, support arguments, source derogations, and/or particular schema (i.e., more-or-less automatic application of mental categories used to interpret ads). Although these responses can occur after a single exposure, multiple exposures may have additional special effects. For example, repetition might induce habituation to the message in an ad such that initially positive information becomes relatively less salient or arousing. In a sense, the person has a reaction similar to, "I've heard that before," and he or she loses interest. At the same time, the receiver might generate message-related thoughts detrimental to the brand; e.g., "Maybe Brands Y & Z are just as good as the advertised brand." Alternatively, repetition might eventually result in the generation of nonmessage-related thoughts. After exposure to repeated showings of a TV ad, for example, the receiver might find his or her mind drifting and followed by thoughts unrelated to the message, brand, or ad execution. This might lead to greater receptivity to appeals made by the competition, activities in generic competition with that required to acquire the focal brand in the ad or simply a disengagement from the focal brand.

A final point to note is that affective responses might be generated along with or independent of cognitive responses. Further, any response can be related to the message, the sponsor, the spokesperson, the overall ad execution, or acts or things entirely unrelated to these objects.

Macro Processes. Although empirical evidence confirms the existence of advertising wearout at the aggregate level, most managerial models have not taken this into account until recently.[38] Simon's ADPULS model does represent wearout, however, and further predicts different responses in the marketplace, depending on whether advertising is increased or decreased. His model also makes predictions as to the effects of constant advertising versus spaced (i.e., pulsed) advertising. The mathematical models for macro effects of repetition are too involved to present here, and the reader is referred to the literature for more details.

Solutions to Wearout. What can an advertiser do to forestall or overcome wearout? The easiest and perhaps most frequently used tactic is simply to change how the same message is delivered. For instance, if humor is a focal message tactic, when wearout occurs, one could try other humorous executions to emphasize the same selling points. Or one spokesperson could be substituted for another. To the extent that people "see through" this approach or again become indifferent to ads, such a tactic is often a short-run alternative at best. Somewhat more effective is to change from one message mode to another. For example, a repetition campaign based on humor might be changed to one predicated on testimonials or slice-of-life executions (i.e., where two "real" people argue about the merits of a brand). Still another possibility is to introduce additional material to process in an ad with the hope that people will be motivated to concentrate more closely as it plays.

This might be done by speeding up commercials electronically, adding background music, or introducing distracting sights or sounds. Finally, one might try new media. This should be particularly effective for compensating for wearout at the macro level.

All of the aforementioned tactics can be done during a campaign without necessarily changing the central content of the message. Nevertheless, if what is communicated is more important than how it is said, then these tactics might be suboptimal. For products with functional appeals or unique features, wearout might be reduced through the introduction of new brand attributes/benefits and/or selling appeals. Mobil Oil found this to be necessary in its Mobil 1 campaign, where it became efficacious to add the characteristic of long drain time (25,000 miles) to its two long-standing product benefits of saving up to 10 miles per tankful and providing operating efficiencies in very hot or very cold temperatures. The addition of this new product attribute was done late in the campaign only after various humorous executions that featured the original two product benefits had been tried. Notice that wearout often ultimately hinges on making actual changes in a product, not merely changing advertising executions or media.

Affect, Cognitions, and Consumer Involvement. In the previous chapter, we discussed how communication generally operates through two fundamental psychological states: affect (i.e., emotions) and cognitions (i.e., rational thoughts). We also examined various hierarchy-of-effects models which maintained that communications are processed through one or more sequences, depending on the circumstances and the experience of the consumer. We now want to discuss a planning model that combines the above ideas and is actually used by one advertising agency. Before we describe the model, however, we must briefly introduce another concept: involvement.

For purposes of discussion, we shall define two types of involvement: product involvement and media involvement.[39] *Product involvement* is the degree to which a person is motivated to purchase and/or use a product. It entails one's need for, or the importance of, the product. Perceived risk may also be a factor. For most people, the purchase of an automobile, stereo set, insurance, or wristwatch constitutes a high-involvement product acquisition. In contrast, the purchase of coffee, toothpaste, a hamburger, or a novel is a relatively low-involvement buying act. *Media involvement* refers to the degree of attention allocated to a particular mode of communication. A face-to-face interaction is generally a high-involvement medium, whereas television is a low-involvement medium. Magazines are somewhere in between these two, at least with respect to processing of ads.

Foote, Cone & Belding, a leading national advertiser, employs a conceptual model in its planning activities to better manage its clients' accounts.[40] As shown in Figure 9-7, this model combines product involvement, affect and cognitions, and hierarchy-of-effects sequences into a fourfold classification.

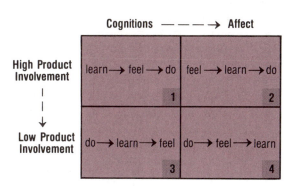

Figure 9-7. Planning model for Foote, Cone & Belding

Consider first cell 1. This applies to products high in involvement and high in cognitive demands. An example would be a personal computer for the first-time buyer. Involvement is high because of the unknown nature of the product, the expense involved, and the potential uses and benefits foreseen. Cognitive processing is high because of the complexity and scope of product attributes and the many steps needed to use the computer. In this situation, a person must first devote a considerable amount of time and mental effort to learn about computers, different brands, and uses (e.g., office and home management, recreational games, educational programs). After a learning period, the potential buyer develops preferences for features and brands and other feelings (e.g., "I really like computers"). This, in turn, leads to shopping behaviors and purchase (the "do" stage in Figure 9-7, cell 1).

Cell 2 might apply to the purchase of clothing. Here the consumer is highly involved, but affective reactions initiate (and perhaps dominate) the decision process, instead of cognitive processing. Hence, feelings develop first ("I love that coat"), then thinking states ("Will it go with my suit?"), and finally action ("I will go to another store to compare quality and prices").

The purchase of coffee at the supermarket might fit cell 3. Imagine that a consumer has used the last coffee in the jar on Wednesday morning. On his or her return home from work later that evening, a trip to the convenience store finds him or her "mindlessly" picking up milk, bread, coffee, and the daily newspaper. Notice that the purchase of coffee began with the act of purchase—perhaps out of habit and subject to the remembrance of running out nine hours earlier. Each subsequent use of the coffee in the morning may lead to reinforcement and further learning ("Boy, this is a great cup of coffee"). Over time, this should enhance one's feelings for the coffee.

Cell 4 is similar to cell 3 but here feelings follow action directly and then lead to thoughts. For example, at mid-morning, an unperceived or vaguely perceived hunger pang might stimulate purchase of a candy bar from a vending machine. While biting into the bar, the consumer experiences pleasurable feelings and then thinks about "how good a buy the candy is" and "I think I will have another."

Of course, we could have as easily chosen negative sequences for each of the above examples, though the results would be more complex. For instance, after biting into the candy bar and finding it stale and foul smelling, the consumer might feel angry and decide "never to buy this brand again."

A number of additional points should be made with respect to the Foote, Cone & Belding model shown in Figure 9-7. First, the dimensions are probably best regarded as end points on a continuum rather than mutually exclusive categories. Cognitions represent believed rational facts or perceived means-ends connections in their extreme form, and affect is purely emotional. But many mental states are mixtures of cognitions and affect. For instance, most evaluations (e.g., good/bad judgments) contain thinking and feeling elements. A second point to note is that, as time passes and consumers gain experience, some purchase events move from cell 1 to cells 2, 3, or 4, depending on the circumstances. For instance, although the first time you ever purchased coffee might have been relatively involved because of your lack of knowledge and the many brands available, later purchases most certainly occurred almost automatically, perhaps even habitually. This illustrates movement from cell 1 to cell 3. A similar movement occurs from cell 2 to cell 4, as in the purchase of cosmetics. Purchases based primarily on thinking activities sometimes also change over time and become more affective as one begins to feel deeper about a product or its use. We have shown the most common temporal shifts as dashed arrows in Figure 9-7. It should be acknowledged, however, that some changes may occur upward and to the left. For instance, an affectively based purchase of a fine wine, novel, or classical music recording might evolve into both deeper affective and cognitive appreciation over time. And an impulse or habitual purchase might be a trigger to greater involvement over time. Nevertheless, we would predict that these latter possibilities occur with less frequency than the downward and rightward movements.

Foote, Cone & Belding uses the planning model in at least three ways.[41] First, as a rough guide early in the planning process, a client's product is categorized into one of the four cells. If the product falls in cells 1 or 3 for example, then advertising copy will be developed to stress primarily rational appeals. If, on the other hand, the product falls into cells 2 or 4, emotional content will probably be emphasized. More specifically, Foote, Cone & Belding believes the following creative approaches best fit the respective cells:

- cell 1: demonstration of product use and benefits; considerable copy to convey information; detailed information.

- cell 2: emotional appeals to involve audience; use of ego or self-esteem appeals.

- cell 3: induce trial (e.g., through point-of-purchase displays, samples, coupons); reminder ad executions.

- cell 4: gain attention so as to arouse personal tastes; emphasize social connections.

A second use of the model is in the selection of media. Cell 1 products require more involving media such as magazines or direct mail. Larger ads are needed, too. Cell 2 products also require involving media but can additionally be reached through strong television executions because of their larger emotional components. Products in cell 3 can be effectively conveyed on radio, short TV spots, small print or poster ads, and point-of-purchase displays. Finally, cell 4 products demand media with greater attention-getting appeals: billboards, newspaper ads, and point-of-purchase displays. Of course, all of the aforementioned comments should be taken as loose guidelines, since any particular application may deviate from the norm.

A third use of the planning model of Figure 9-7 is in copy testing. As will be discussed later in this chapter, rational and emotional ads and high- and low-involvement products dictate different ad-effectiveness measurement procedures. Whereas recall measures might be adequate for cell 1 products, and actual purchase histories or aggregate sales might be sufficient for cells 3 and 4 products, those in cell 2 generally require either more visual (e.g., recognition) or deeper (e.g., arousal, attitude) indicators. We turn now to the problem of measuring advertising effects.

Measuring the Effectiveness of Advertising

Does it really pay to advertise? Organizations certainly believe so, or they would not pay so much money to do it. But does advertising really help the organization reach its goals?

Most executives maintain that the ultimate objective of advertising is to influence sales, either immediately or in the long run. Yet our knowledge of the effects of advertising on sales is sparse and incomplete. Some research shows a positive relationship between advertising and sales, but very little is known about whether the relationship is one of cause-and-effect or merely an empirical association.[42] Part of the difficulty lies in determining the forces affecting sales. Sales are a function of a variety of factors, each with a different magnitude of influence that varies from situation to situation and from time period to time period. For example, sales are under the influence of the prices of other products (substitutes and complements) as well as the price of the firm's own brand. Then, too, sales will be affected by product quality, packaging, distribution practices, promotions and deals, changing consumer tastes, and economic and social conditions. Advertising is probably a determinant, too, but to disentangle the relative role of each force is nearly an impossible task—at least researchers have met with little success to date. Nevertheless, the reality of the size of the monetary commitment made each year to advertising suggests that advertising plays a very large role.

Decisions must be made one way or the other on how much to spend on advertising, which media to advertise in, what messages to transmit, how to present the messages, and so forth. Although managers may not be able to directly link these controllable factors to actual sales responses in the market as a whole, they can obtain an indication of how effective advertising will be by examining the influence of particular ads on the psychological reactions and behavior of individual consumers or groups of consumers. This is done in the laboratory, through focus groups, in surveys, and in panels. In effect, managers make judgments on the efficacy of ads by ascertaining their impact on intervening variables between ad presentations and final sales. Some realism is given up in exchange for better control of extraneous factors and manageability of the research process.

Most often, the influence of ads is measured through people's brand name awareness, knowledge, recall, recognition, beliefs about product attributes, interest, attitudes, or intentions as a function of exposure to ads. The majority of tests of the effectiveness of ads is performed on TV ads, although considerable testing of magazine and radio ads is done as well. Typically, tests are conducted by independent research services hired by the sponsor of an ad. We will describe a sampling of leading companies and approaches below. The term *copy testing* is used as an umbrella description for most tests of advertising effectiveness at the level of people's psychological and choice responses.

Television Ad Copy Testing

Burke Marketing Research, Inc. Perhaps the most common method for measuring the effectiveness of ads is known as "day-after recall" and is performed by Burke, among others (e.g., Gallup & Robinson, Inc.). With minor variations, day-after recall testing is done in the following manner.

On the day following the showing of an ad on commercial television, telephone numbers in a target viewing area are drawn randomly and called. Respondents are asked if they watched the test program on the previous day. If they answer yes, then they are considered "program viewers." Next, the program viewers (usually a sample of 200) are asked if they were in the room during the entire program and were not asleep or changing channels. If they answer in the affirmative, then they are classified as a "commercial audience" (typically numbering about 140). People in the commercial audience are then asked further questions to determine the effect, if any, of viewing target ads. One or more of three ad effectiveness measures are taken: claimed recall, related recall, and actual ad content. In claimed recall, depending on the sponsor's desires, either the product category or both the brand and product category are mentioned to the respondent and he or she is asked if he or she recalls the ad. In related recall, correct details from the ad must be provided by the respondent as well (e.g., any audio or video content that "proves" the person saw the ad). The measures of claimed or related recall for an ad are simply the percentage of people so recalling the ad. This is called a "Burke score." Finally, measures of actual content recalled by each respondent might be recorded. For example, this might entail relating key selling points or specific descriptions of the ad, spokesperson, etc. Depending on the client's needs, day-after recall can be monitored in any one or more of 33 cities in the U.S.

A "good" Burke score depends on the audience (e.g., men or women, demographic profile) as well as product category. Burke has norms reflecting averages for product classes. For instance, a Burke score of 24 percent is considered the norm across a wide variety of product classes and audiences. If a sponsor ad scores above 24 percent, one generally considers the ad "effective." Although Burke disclaims that its measures show persuasiveness or propensity to buy, the implication is that recall scores represent a necessary indicator of effectiveness in the sense of reaching into the hierarchy-of-effects model. That is, because recall is believed to be a necessary state for progression through the hierarchy of effects, we have an indirect measure of or proxy for the impact of an ad.

Common wisdom suggests that Burke scores are directly proportional to the length of an ad; the frequency that a brand name is mentioned and/or shown; the earlier the brand is mentioned or shown in the ad; the use of animation (i.e., animation increases recall); the greater that an ad ties into past ads (e.g., through use of the same spokesperson over time); and more generally the cognitive information in an ad.

The advantages of day-after recall measures are that they are naturalistic (i.e., ads are tested "on-air"), relatively inexpensive, fast, and easily understood. In addition, it often allows the sponsor to obtain breakdowns by audience type and to ask other questions (at additional cost). The method seems to work best for new brands or products with at least a few clear attributes.

A major drawback with the procedure is that it does not go very far. That is, it may not be highly correlated with attitudes or intentions toward a brand.

Moreover, it has been criticized for overemphasizing cognitive content and overlooking emotional responses. Finally, one does not often know how much above the norm is needed to achieve advertising goals, and to get much above the norm is very difficult in any case. And the relation of recall to behavior is not a perfect one and is typically unknown.

Day-after recall is, of course, a postexposure measure of advertising effectiveness because the target ad has already been produced and shown to the public. Burke also uses a technique for measuring advertising effectiveness prior to exposure by the public. This is called the "Clucas Diagnostic Advertising Research Technique." Television ads in either rough or finished form are shown to viewers who are asked to write down any thoughts coming to mind *as they watch the commercial.* The data are collected in a test location. This procedure gets closer to the time that ads produce their effects and provides information useful in the design phase of advertising. It trades "on-air" realism for more diagnostics, while at the same time saving the expense of putting an ad on air prior to testing. Recently, there has been somewhat of a trend away from day-after recall and other postexposure measures to pre-exposure procedures such as the Clucas Technique. Whether this is a permanent or temporary shift in approach remains to be seen.

Bruzzone Research Company. Rather than using telephone interviews, Bruzzone employs a mail survey to measure the effects of TV ads. A random sample of 1,000 households is taken, and respondents are asked to comment on anywhere from 8 to 15 different commercials. Each commercial is presented in storyboard form (a pictorial summary of the ad) with the brand name removed. Typically, about 500 people return the questionnaire.

Four measures are obtained. One is an aided recall of the ad. A second is recognition of the brand name from a list of three choices. The third measures interest in the message. And the fourth includes a checklist of commercial characteristics (e.g., was the ad clever, silly, etc.?).

On the positive side, the Bruzzone method is somewhat cheaper than many other services, tests many ads, and at the same time yields large samples and representative U.S. samples, rather than specific cities only. On the negative side, some nonresponse biases are possible, the presentation is somewhat artificial, and some of the drawbacks of the Burke approach apply as well.

AdTel, Inc. AdTel uses a procedure that measures ad effectiveness in a naturalistic way and employs dependent variables relatively close to the ultimate goal of final sales. People living in one or more of three cities in the East, Midwest, or West see commercials on a dual cable CATV system. Some people may see test ads with one particular copy strategy while others see ads of another strategy or else act as a control group. In addition to the possibility of obtaining responses of people to questionnaires (e.g., attitudinal measures), actual purchases can be recorded through panel diaries in which respondents participate. The sample for each cable split numbers 1,000.

The advantages of AdTel include an ability to monitor effects over a long period of time, naturalistic viewing, control over extraneous factors such as distributional differences or the weather (since the location is the same for test and control samples), actual purchase dependent variables, and large samples. On the other hand, error may exist in the recording of purchase histories, and those participating might not be representative of the U.S. as a whole or desired target markets.

Communicus, Inc. Two different methods are used by Communicus to test TV ads. One consists of visits to homes or on-the-spot public solicitations where respondents are asked to watch ads on a portable 8mm film projector-viewer. The second is comprised of group viewing of videotapes on television. Typically, people are recruited in public places such as shopping malls. Unlike the procedures used by Burke or AdTel, however, people are asked to watch commercials in an unusual way. First, they observe segments of an ad. For example, a 30-second ad might be divided into three segments, each defined by the thoughts or ideas contained therein. At the end of each segment, the ad is stopped, and the viewer is asked about the segment, his or her comprehension of the selling points, and how important the information was to him or her. Next, the respondent is shown the entire ad in uninterrupted form, and questions are asked of the person's understanding of the ad and his or her intent to try the brand.

The primary advantage of this method is the quality and depth of information provided that can serve useful diagnostic purposes. The drawbacks with Communicus's procedure are the small sample sizes generally obtained, the potential for ambiguity in analysis of responses, and the artificiality of the viewing.

ASI Market Research, Inc. ASI uses still a different technique for measuring the effectiveness of TV ads. People in Los Angeles are recruited to view "television previews" in a theater setting. About 400 people are tested at a time. At the outset, respondents fill out a questionnaire that solicits background information and brand preferences for the product categories to be tested (usually four) and control categories. Following this, a sequence of TV pilot show, ads, questionnaire, TV pilot show, ads, and questionnaire is presented. A group discussion period is also included in the middle of the sequence. The key measurements taken include interest and involvement in the ad (measured via a hand dial throughout the viewing), brand recall, recall of ad content, preference change, and diagnostic feedback from the group discussions.

The major assets of the method are the large samples, the ability to test a number of ads, and the provision of cognitive and preference data, as well as qualitative information. On the minus side are the facts that the viewing is not representative of in-home viewing, the possibility exists for nonrepresentative samples, and the measures used may not be related to intentions and actual behavior.

Print Ad Copy Testing

Recall and recognition measures are the two most frequently applied indicators of print ad effectiveness. On occasion, measures are taken also of reader interest or like/dislike for an ad or brand, among others. We will briefly describe the recognition and recall procedures below.

Recall of Print Ads. The recall test procedures conducted by Audience Studies, Inc., are typical of those employed throughout the industry. On the day following exposure to a test magazine, readers are contacted and asked, "Do you recall seeing any advertisements in this issue of _____ (magazine) for _____ (product category)?" If the person replies in the affirmative, he or she is asked to identify the brand. If he or she identifies the brand correctly, then the person is asked to describe the ad. To be counted as a positive recaller, the person must mention a piece of information contained in the ad. However, this need not be very specific. The recall measure for an ad is the percentage of readers who so recall the ad. ASI also measures other responses such as product interest and ad-generated ideas and impressions.

A slightly different procedure is used by Gallup & Robinson to measure recall, which they term, "Proved Name Registration." A reader is first asked to recall and describe ads from a target magazine. The only cue given is the sponsor of the ad. To be counted as a recaller, some content of the ad must be identified. Gallup & Robinson also measure remembrance of selling points in an "Idea Playback Profile" and various attitude indicators in a "Favorable Buying Attitude" score.

Recognition of Print Ads. Starch Inra Hooper, Inc., measures recognition of print ads. First, a person is qualified as a reader of the focal magazine. Next, through a page-by-page search, each respondent is asked if he or she saw or read the ad(s) on each page. If the reader answers yes, he or she is asked to describe what was seen or read. Three measures are obtained. One is the percentage of readers who claim to have seen an ad before ("Noted"). A second is the percentage of readers claiming to have seen or read particular parts of the ad indicating the brand or advertiser ("Associated"). And a third is the percentage of readers who claim to have read 50 percent of the ad copy or more ("Read Most").

Recall and recognition entail somewhat different mental processes. In recall, the person is given a minimal cue and asked to generate from memory the target information. In recognition, the target is presented and the person is asked to acknowledge having seen it before or not. Recall is thus more difficult than recognition. Indeed, the scores for ads are generally much higher for recognition than for recall. Both measure aspects of memory, but it is not clear whether they measure unique or overlapping mental states.[43] Also, recognition scores are believed to carry considerable amounts of measurement error. To remedy this, researchers sometimes derive "proven recognition" scores. These consist of the difference in recognition scores between those previously exposed to an ad and those not exposed.

Masked recognition procedures are sometimes used as well. Here the name of the brand is covered or removed from an ad, and the reader is asked to identify the brand of an ad he or she has seen before. Notice that this task lies between the recall and pure recognition tasks described above.

As with the recall and/or recognition procedures used to test TV ads, we should reiterate that the tests of print ads may not adequately measure the affective impact of ads. Moreover, recall or recognition may be imperfect predictors of attitude, intentions, and actual behavior.

Copy Testing in Other Media

Copy testing is of course performed on ads in other advertising media such as radio or billboards. For purposes of brevity, we will not describe the procedures here. However, most of the techniques aim to measure recall, recognition, or on occasion attitudes (e.g., like/dislike). Radio ad copy testing shares many similarities to TV ad copy testing, and billboard ad copy testing is similar to print ad copy testing.

Final Comments on Copy Testing

A burning controversy in both the practitioner and academic spheres has been the adequacy of copy testing procedures.[44] Many authors believe that day-after recall and similar measures overemphasize the cognitive side of consumer behavior at the expense of the emotional. Foote, Cone & Belding has tested both TV and print ads using recall and masked recognition measures. They found that recall does tend to underrate "emotional" ads, whereas masked recognition appears suitable for both "rational" and "emotional" ads.[45] It is doubtful, however, whether either procedure adequately monitors the depth and breadth of cognitive or affective processes. Furthermore, the need still remains for testing procedures capable of accurately predicting intentions, trial, and repeat purchase behaviors.

Advertising Management

A Framework

Up to this point in the chapter, we have touched upon many facets of advertising and considered many of the decisions that must be made with respect to advertising (e.g., copy design and testing, organizational structure). The previous chapter introduced many of the options facing the advertising manager as well (e.g., message content, message structure, media choices, spokesperson effects, and audience characteristics). The decision elements are numerous and complex to say the least. And when it is remembered that advertising is but one of many issues to be resolved in any marketing program, the challenge and difficulty faced by a manager becomes readily apparent. In this section of the chapter, we will briefly outline a communication model useful in planning and controlling the advertising effort.

Figure 9-8 presents the model and is owed to Ray.[46] It is presented from the point of view of an organization confronted with communication decisions.

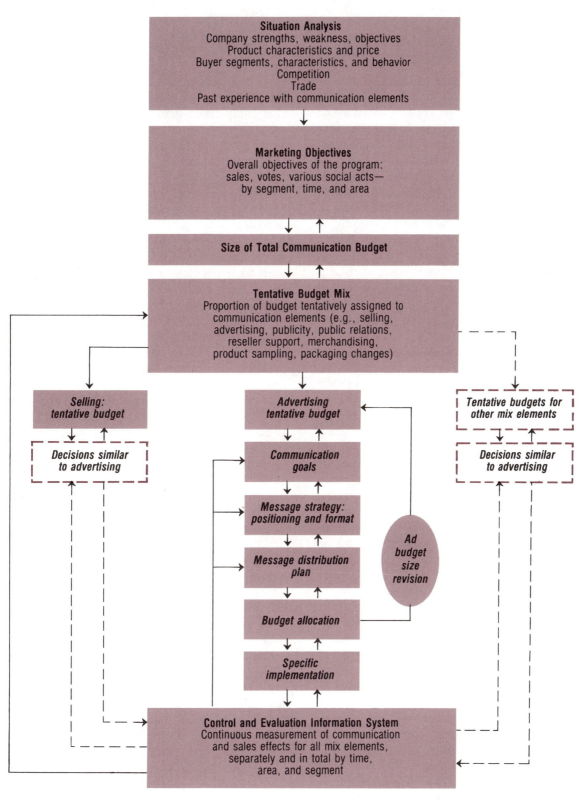

Figure 9-8. A communication planning model

SOURCE: Michael L. Ray, "A Decision Sequence Analysis of Developments in Marketing Communications," *Journal of Marketing* 37 (January 1973): 31. Reprinted with the permission of the publisher.

Notice that the process begins with a *situation analysis.* Company strengths and weaknesses are evaluated along with broader organization goals and the competition. Next, *marketing objectives* are assessed. These, in turn, constrain the *communication budget.* Indeed, the budget decision sets limits on the overall communication effort as well as on the mix of programs comprising it. Once goals are set and the budget determined, the final steps involve the allocation, design, monitoring, and management of the communication effort. Here *implementation* and *control and evaluation* constitute central elements of the communication decision process. We now consider some of the decision processes sketched in Figure 9-8.

Goals and Budgeting

As we indicated earlier, broad advertising goals are set with respect to inducing trial, switching, brand loyalty, and increased per capita consumption. At the same time, intermediate and operational goals are formulated. These might include objectives for producing specific levels of awareness, recall and recognition, knowledge of product attributes, interest, liking, intentions, etc., in particular markets and for specific market segments. Some firms use formal models such as DAGMAR (Defining Advertising Goals, Measuring Advertising Results) to aid in the planning of advertising programs, but discussion of the details is beyond the scope of this text.[47]

To achieve goals requires resources. Budgets have historically been set in many ways. An infrequent but sometimes used procedure is simply on the basis of *subjective judgments* of an executive or group of executives. More common is the use of rules of thumb based upon *percentage of sales.* Some fraction of the previous year's or expected sales (e.g., 2 percent) is used to set the budget for the following year. It has been estimated that between 50 and 70 percent of all firms set their advertising expenditures as a percentage of sales.[48] Still another tactic is to set the budget on the *basis of competition.* Either competition is matched (in total dollars or as a percentage of sales) or else an amount above or below the competition is set so as to beat or, alternatively, not threaten rivals.

Setting budgets by subjective judgments, percentage of sales, or competitor levels is a hit-or-miss affair. What is desirable is to set advertising budgets at levels needed to stimulate sales. Advertising is a controllable variable influencing sales, so a method more closely tied to the intended effects of ads will in the long run better achieve organization goals. The *objective and task* approach tries to do this. The organization first defines a specific goal to be achieved (e.g., "60 percent awareness by consumers of our new product within four months"). Then the tasks (e.g., number of ads to show, the media to show them in, etc.) are designed to reach the goal. The necessary budget is set on the basis of the tasks required. Usually, multiple goals, multiple tasks, and a number of alternative scenarios will be considered and weighed. The organization typically will work closely with the ad agency to arrive at a viable budget and advertising campaign.

The essence of the task and objective method is to discover the specific relationship between ad expenditures and consumer responses. One way to do this is through *experimentation.*[49] Different ads and varying the number and scheduling of ads could be tried in selected cities, for example, to see the differential response. Still another way to ascertain the response is through *statistical modeling,* where sales, say, are related to advertising expenditures.[50] Finally, some firms use a *normative approach* for discovering the relationship wherein managerial judgments are quantitatively used to predict responses.[51]

Media Selection[52]

There are three basic decisions regarding media choices: the general medium (e.g., magazines) or media to use, the specific vehicles (e.g., *Time* vs. *Sports Illustrated*) within media to employ, and the scheduling of ads within and across media. Let us briefly consider each.

Media Choices. What media should one choose when advertising? The primary options include television, radio, magazines, newspapers, billboards, direct mail, and/or the Yellow Pages. Among other criteria, the communication characteristics, audience reach, and cost must be taken into account.

Communication characteristics means the ability of the medium to convey information and influence the consumer. Some media are better than others for attracting attention, stimulating emotions, demonstrating product attributes or benefits, and achieving conviction and intent to try the product. Table 9-6 presented a comparison of four leading media on these and other characteristics. For example, magazines are very strong for conveying sensory stimulation, whereas radio is fair. Magazines convey humor poorly, but TV is especially effective in this respect. And so on. The task for the manager is to match the ability of the medium to the target consumer. This means research is needed into both the nature of people who are exposed to one medium or another and the characteristics of likely consumers. Demographic and psychographic profiles of audiences and target markets represent one type of information useful to the decision maker in this regard.

Audience reach, or the number of people exposed to particular media, is also important. Some media such as newspapers or television reach wide segments of the population. For example, about 80 percent of American adults read newspapers one or more times a week,[53] and nearly 60 percent of all American households watch television between 7 P.M. and 11 P.M. Indeed, the average household watches 6 hours and 26 minutes of television a day.[54] With 98 percent of all homes equipped with a television, one can readily appreciate the power of TV to reach the American public. On the other hand, other media are quite selective, reaching narrowly defined audiences. For instance, by advertising in *Car and Driver, Successful Farming,* or *Factory,* one may reach the automobile buff, farmers, and plant managers, respectively. Again, the characteristics of the consumer and his or her reading and viewing habits must be taken into account along with the distribution of media when choosing a communication channel.

The final criterion that must be considered in media choices is, of course, the cost. Table 9-7 presents some comparisons as a rough guide. One must weigh the desired audience reach with the cost when choosing a medium.

TABLE 9-7
An Indication of Comparative Costs of Selective Media

Medium	Costs
Television	Medium-sized market area = $150,000 for 30-second ad
	National market = $1,000,000 or more for a 30-second ad depending on program
Radio	About $50,000 for a typical ad in a large metropolitan area
	A few thousand dollars in smaller cities
Magazines	In 1975 (CPM = cost per thousand): *Good Housekeeping* = $1.20 CPM (total = $28,000) *Parents* = $3.16 CPM (total = $17,400)
Newspapers	¼ page ad in: major city = $5,000 to $25,000 small city = $500 to $1,000
Billboard	$1,000 to $25,000 per month depending on location
Direct Mail	About $500 to $700 per 1,000
Yellow Pages	$500 to $1,500 for a 2-inch column

Vehicle Choices. Once one has chosen a medium or media, the next decision is to select the specific entities to advertise in within a medium or media. Again, the characteristics of the vehicle, audience reach, and costs must be evaluated. Although the choices are complex and numerous, a number of paid research services provide data to help the decision maker. For instance, Arbitron, A.C. Nielsen, Leading National Advertisers, Inc., the Simmons Marketing Research Bureau, Media Records, Inc., Publishers Information Bureau, and Mediamark Research Inc. supply information on vehicle exposure data for television, radio, magazines, and/or newspapers.

The data provided by Mediamark Research Inc. is typical and consists of a sample of about 20,000 adults covering more than 40 product categories and broken down by over 18 demographic, 20 psychographic, and a number of usage segments, all for many vehicles. The information provided by various services might help a manager answer such questions as, What is the most efficient magazine to advertise in to reach male fisherman 18 to 35 years old? Which newspaper in city A reaches the most older adult women with incomes over $30,000 per year? What percentage of homes will watch "60 Minutes" on a Sunday evening?

Media Schedules. The choice of media and vehicles answers the question of where to advertise. But one must also decide when and how often. We have already touched upon the scheduling issue when we discussed repetition and wearout. The decision maker must decide how many exposures per person is desired, what proportion of the target audience should be reached at this repetition level, and when to place ads.

Basically, there are four generic strategies that one might follow. One is simply to maintain an even amount of ad expenditures (or size of ad) over time. An advertiser might do this if consumers purchase uniformly over time (i.e., no cyclical or seasonal buying is the rule). It is also a viable strategy if the brand is very well known and/or competitors also advertise uniformly and one does not want to risk open rivalry. However, the maintenance or level strategy as it is sometimes called is essentially a passive one in that the attempt to stimulate sales or act competitively is neither very aggressive nor tied to consumer or market forces.

A second option is to start a campaign at a high level and then decrease advertising (or ad size) over time to some maintenance level. This is a common ploy for new product introductions where one desires to build awareness early. Sometimes the approach is repeated periodically such that a general rise and fall strategy is manifested over time.

Still another strategy is to use an intermittent (pulse) strategy over time. For example, an advertiser might place an ad on the radio only on Mondays. Or alternatively, heavy media usage might occur for 10 days, followed by no advertising for a week, say, then resumption, then no advertising, etc. Of course, a pulse strategy might consist of heavy-light-heavy-light sequences as well, where at least a minimal amount of advertising is done at all times. The intermittent strategy is frequently done to concentrate expenditures in a way that will optimize consumer learning or reinforcement. It is also done to "stretch budgets" or to coincide with particular consumption patterns. An example of the latter is the absence of ads for snacks on TV at the dinner hour followed by increasing frequencies of such ads during the later evening hours. Similarly, ads for greeting cards appear just before Christmas, Valentine's Day, and Mother's Day, but usually not at other times.

The final scheduling strategy is to change ad exposures dynamically depending on the conditions. Changes in competitor moves, income, buyer preferences, or other factors typically dictate a fine tuning in scheduling over time.

Media Models. The ultimate choice of media, vehicles, and scheduling is probably more one of art than science. The wisdom of media planners and trial and error play a strong role. Nevertheless, management scientists have developed models to aid in the decision-making process. It is beyond the scope of this text to describe these models. And the reader is referred to the original presentations of two of them: MEDIAC and ADMOD.[55]

Concluding Comments on Advertising Management

In addition to setting goals, formulating a budget, and planning media strategies, managers must make many other advertising decisions. As Figure 9-8 showed, and as mentioned earlier in this chapter and in the preceding chapter, decisions on advertising copy must also be made. This entails making numerous message content, structure, and spokesperson choices. The integration of all these decisions into a coherent advertising program and into an overall marketing effort is no easy task. Organizations have found it necessary to hire and develop specialists in a wide variety of functional areas and to rely on outside providers of expertise to more effectively plan and execute the marketing effort. Hopefully, the discussion in this part of the chapter has given you a perspective on the kinds of activities that a modern organization must engage in to survive and flourish.

Social and Legal Aspects of Advertising

Advertising and Society

Advertising has a pervasive and potentially powerful influence on society. For purposes of discussion, let us examine its impact on individual consumers, economic conditions, and society as a whole.

The Effects of Ads on Individuals. A deep concern of many is whether advertising is used to manipulate the public. Over the years, advertisers have been accused of playing on the subconscious motives of people[56] and even of using such techniques as subliminal advertising.[57]

Do ads manipulate us? Are we induced to buy things we neither want nor need? Exactly what are the effects of ads on us?

Much of the research to date has been limited to an examination of the opinions of people toward advertising. Tables 9-8 and 9-9 summarize the findings of two studies. In general, it appears that most people are either positive or indifferent toward advertising, but a sizable minority appears to be negatively predisposed. What are the complaints?

One study found that 23 percent of ads categorized by respondents were labeled annoying (i.e., irritating), and 5 percent were termed offensive (i.e., vulgar, morally bad, or dishonest).[58] The rest (72 percent) were either informative or enjoyable. The most annoying ads were for soaps, detergents, dental supplies, mouthwashes, depilatories, and deodorants. The most offensive ads were for liquor, cigarettes, and beer. In another study, the most irritating TV ads were found to be for feminine hygiene products, women's undergarments, and hemorrhoid products.[59] Thus, certain ads appear to arouse strong negative reactions in at least some people.

But do the effects of ads go deeper than this? Do ads shape values, influence life-styles, and actually stimulate actions people would not normally take? If ads have these effects, it appears that they do so largely without working subliminally on the unwary consumer. Most of the research to date indicates that subliminal messages may arouse people but do not necessarily produce behavior changes.[60] Moreover, it has been argued that consumers typically react naturally to ads with reasoned judgments, healthy skepticism, critical appraisal, counterargumentation, and on occasion outright rejection.[61] This has been found to be true even in the case of children, who are generally believed to be especially vulnerable to the influence of advertising.[62]

On the other hand, through classical conditioning, cognitive learning, or the mere exposure effect, ads have the potential to influence our emotions in the short run and shape our values and beliefs in the long run.[63] However, the role of advertising as an agent of socialization is little studied and even less understood. Some evidence exists showing that stereotyping occurs with respect to the portrayal of blacks[64] and women[65] in ads. But we know little about exactly how and to what degree ads influence people over long periods of time. In the broadest sense, about all that one can say is that ads both reflect and influence the needs of individual consumers.

Although we may not know much about the long-run psychological effects of ads in a scientific sense, developments in the legal sphere have done much to clarify the issues. We will return to these after examining the economic and social impacts of advertising.

The Effects of Ads on the Economy. In contrast to our relative ignorance of the influence of ads in a long-run psychological sense, we know much more about the role of advertising in the economy.[66] As you might expect, both pro and con arguments can be made.

On the positive side, advertising is believed to provide financial support to the mass media, encourage economic growth, inform consumers about new products, and, in general, serve as a necessary tool of organizations for both responding to and influencing demand. In addition, it is maintained that advertising lowers prices[67] and enhances competition.[68]

On the negative side, economists sometimes charge that advertising creates false product differentiation, produces a barrier to market entry because of the high cost of advertising, and in general increases industry concentration and monopoly power and profits.[69] Indeed, recent research seems to suggest that advertising permits some manufacturers to charge a premium for their goods.[70]

In short, it is fair to say that advertising can have both positive and negative consequences for the economy and consumers. Some of the detrimental effects are counteracted by competition in the marketplace and by actions taken by the judicial and executive branches of government. Other negative consequences, such as excessive or

---

TABLE 9-8

Attitudes toward Advertising: The Bauer and Greyser Findings

ATTITUDE	PERCENTAGES	
	1964	1967
Favorable	41	49
Mixed	34	31
Indifferent	8	3
Unfavorable	14	15
Unclassifiable	3	2

Source: R. A. Bauer and S. A. Greyser, *Advertising in America: The Consumer View* (Boston: Division of Research, Graduate School of Business Administration, Harvard University, 1968), p. 393. Reprinted with the permission of the publisher.

TABLE 9-9

Attitudes toward Advertising: The Bartos and Dunn Findings

Attitude	Percentage
The Fans	23%
Skeptical Enthusiasts	22%
The Moderates	26%
Aesthetic Critics	17%
The Rejectors	12%

Source: R. Bartos and T. Dunn, *Advertising and Consumers* (New York: American Association of Advertising Agencies, 1976), pp. 68–69. Reprinted with the permission of the publisher.

false product differentiation, are difficult to define and prove one way or the other. Moreover, there is a delicate balance that must be maintained between the needs of special interest groups on the one hand and the freedom of individuals and firms on the other hand. Most societies attempt to arrive at some healthy balance of social equity and the need to encourage innovation and risk taking. Where the line should be drawn is difficult to say, and one way to ensure that imbalances will be addressed is to encourage and institutionalize debate and conflict among the players. This is exactly what has evolved in the modern American economy where consumer groups, companies, government bodies, and other groups interact to work out their needs for the common good. In Chapters 12 and 13, on pricing, we will discuss some of the results to date, which have been mixed.

The Effects of Ads on Society at Large. Advertisements have an effect on society, but the impact is complex and reciprocal. Consider the issue of materialism. Has advertising made society more materialistic? Certainly over the past century, nearly all societies have come to be users of more and more material goods and services. Did advertising produce materialism or did it follow materialism in the sense of permitting people to better meet their materialistic needs? The answer is probably a little of both. At times, advertising arouses needs in us; at other times, our needs already exist and advertising is one of a number of facilitators leading to need fulfillment. The question of which needs are "genuine" and which are "artificial" probably cannot be answered objectively or scientifically but rather fall within the realm of ethics and the law.

A recent qualitative study by a leading psychologist points up the difficult problem of studying the social effects of advertising and how many issues must be considered.[71] The study concerned the effects of advertising on the smoking behavior of women.

Prior to about 1920, very few American women smoked. Then advertisers began showing women in ads for cigarettes, not merely as incidental or decorative copy as previously, but actually smoking. This was done on billboards and in many print media. Also, some advertisers used various promotional tactics. For instance, attractive women were hired to "light up" in public places, such as New York's Waldorf-Astoria Hotel. Opinion leaders were provided free cigarettes and encouraged to smoke "for the liberation of women." Even debutantes in parades were used as promotional tools by advertisers. By 1935, about 18 percent of the female population smoked, and this increased to a peak of around 33 percent in the mid 1970s, after which smoking declined somewhat.

Advertisers employed a variety of techniques to persuade women to smoke throughout this period. Celebrities were used as spokespersons. Sexual and health claims were used freely, and principles of classical conditioning, psychoanalytic psychology, and communication theory were utilized subtly and no so subtly.

Can we say that advertising caused women to smoke? The answer seems to be maybe. Certainly, ads stimulated some women to try smoking for the first time, and they served as reinforcements for others to continue smoking once they began. Yet, did these women do so because of the ads or because they chose to do so? Did they have a need to smoke or was it created by advertising? Was the need a desire for pleasure, an addictive habit, or something else? Would women have eventually smoked anyway, even without advertising?

Another factor to consider is the social setting. Smoking occurred perhaps out of peer pressure or as a means to identify with or belong to a group. In addition to the effects of ads, one must consider word-of-mouth communication and social pressures to smoke. Perhaps the rate of growth of smoking was just as much a function of everyday social processes as it was due to the influence of advertisements. Socialization through paid advertisements, the movies, novels, role modeling by respected public figures, peer pressure and so on surely played a supportive part.

In any event, large numbers of women did not begin smoking overnight. If advertising played a role, its effects appear to have taken a long time to occur, perhaps decades. Although each single ad might arouse us emotionally or stimulate thoughts, the effects are generally short-lived and/or of a low magnitude. Repetition must occur typically over a long period of time for more permanent or deep-seated effects to arise. At the same time, many other forces in society interact with advertising. These are psychological (e.g., self-generated doubts, counterargumentation), social, cultural, and legal. It is no wonder that it is so difficult to discover the social effects of advertising and that so few have tried.

Nevertheless, marketers in general and advertisers in particular must consider the effects of their actions carefully. This means relying on personal morals and standards of conduct, as well as more formal codes of ethics prescribed by professional associations and organizations. It also means having thoughtful and fair legal and other governmental bodies that consider the needs of all parties, topics we will turn to shortly. It may not be possible to ascertain with certainty the hidden or long-run effects of advertising, but it is important that everyone involved—advertisers, ad agencies, and consumers—at least attempt to do so in order to reduce the number of negative implications. No one can say positively that advertising made women smoke and thus indirectly contributed to the incidence of lung cancer in women. Yet each individual person involved with advertising must face such questions and answer them to the best of his or her ability if one is to achieve self-respect and protect the interests of society.

Advertising and the Government[72]

The regulation of advertising in the U.S. is handled primarily by the Federal Trade Commission (FTC), an agency of the federal government created by Congress in 1914.[73] Since its creation, the powers and responsibilities by the FTC have been revised and in most cases expanded through the passage of key acts (e.g., the Wheeler-Lea Act of 1938 and the Magnuson-Moss Act of 1975) and the enforcement of laws in key court cases. Let us take a look at some of the important actions the FTC has taken to directly protect consumers. The FTC also might take action against firms if advertising in some way is construed to lessen competition or in some way constitute unfair practices. These latter issues will not be considered here but are similar to the unfair use of pricing as described later in Chapter 12.

Deceptive Advertising.[74] A primary responsibility of the FTC is to detect and remedy deceptive ads. One definition of deceptive advertising might be any advertisement that is factually false or misleading. However, this definition is too vague, and the ultimate test of what is or is not deceptive must often be determined through the courts. Since 1938, legislation and court decisions have used one or more of the following criteria to determine deception:

1 Untruthful aspects of ads

2 A failure to reveal facts, especially those potentially harmful

3 Consumers' net general impression of the ad, irrespective of its factual content.

4 Vague or ambiguous assertions interpretable in multiple ways where one or more interpretations involves a deceptive claim in one or more of the three senses listed above.

To prevent the incidence of deception, the FTC requires that advertisers provide documentation (e.g., a laboratory report or survey study) showing that any claim in the firm's ads is true and that the ad agency used said evidence in the preparation of ads. Further, the FTC encourages the use of comparative advertising of two or more brands by sponsors. This form of advertising has become popular in recent years.

In addition to demanding that false advertising be dropped or changed, the FTC can impose fines. It also can require the advertiser to perform corrective advertising. A well-known example of corrective advertising was Warner-Lambert's $10.2 million campaign that the FTC demanded be made to inform consumers that earlier assertions that Listerine Mouthwash prevented colds and sore throats were not true.

TABLE 9-10
Relative Percentage Use of Promotions by Method

Promotion Method	Relative Percentage
Premiums, incentives, specialties	25%
Business meetings, conventions	19%
Direct mail	15%
Trade shows, exhibits	15%
Point-of-sale displays	11%
Printing, production, audiovisual, fees, etc.	10%
Promotion, advertising space	5%
TOTAL:	100%

SOURCE: Derived from R. A. Strong, "Sales Promotion-Fast Growth, Faulty Management," *Harvard Business Review 54* (July–August 1976): 118.

Other FTC Actions. The FTC regulates the use of endorsements or testimonials by advertisers. If an endorser claims to use the brand in an ad, then he or she must actually do so. Also, an average consumer must be able to expect similar performance or benefits from use of the brand as the endorser claims to obtain.

Bait-and-switch advertising, where a brand is advertised at an unusually low price but the consumer discovers subsequently that the item is not available and sales personnel attempt to sell another item in its place, is also regulated by the FTC. Indeed, we might come to see FTC involvement in any advertising practice injuring consumers in some way.

Promotion and Publicity

Promotion[75]

Promotion is the use of incentives to encourage purchase or selling. Table 9-10 presents one estimate of the relative use of various modes of promotion in the U.S. Promotions are sponsored by the seller and are typically directed at consumers, dealers, or the sales force. Let us examine each type.

Consumer Promotions. Whereas the direct goal of most advertising is to induce a psychological response (e.g., awareness, interest, desire, preference, or intention) and only indirectly to stimulate behavior, the objective of consumer promotions is to produce an action response. To do this, marketers employ one or more of a variety of stimuli.

Coupons are given to consumers with the promise of a reduction in price or a mailed-in rebate. The coupons are printed in magazines or newspapers, put on or within packages, or mailed directly to consumers. Some supermarkets now have video display terminals that show available coupons and print out and dispense them on command. It has been estimated that more than 21 billion coupons are distributed each year and nearly 60 percent of all households use them.[76] Thus, coupons appear to be a popular incentive for consumers. On the other hand, the redemption rate of coupon usage can vary widely depending on product category, brand, and media used to communicate to consumers; and consumers may not return to the brand after redemption. Furthermore, retailers find the handling of coupons to be a nuisance, and manufacturers sometimes pay out large sums of money to fraudulent redeemers. Despite these shortcomings, couponing is used extensively.

Another popular consumer promotion is the use of *free samples*. A free sample might be sent in the mail, handed out on the street, delivered door to door, offered in a store display or demonstration, or found attached to another product. Sampling is an expensive way to promote, but it is quite an effective way to encourage trial. Often, free samples are produced in smaller or single-use sizes to reduce costs. However, to build a liking or preference for a new brand may require repeated use, so small sampling may not always be enough to accomplish one's goals.

Still another frequently used consumer promotion is the *premium*. A premium is a free or low-priced product given to the consumer in exchange for purchasing a brand at regular price or sending in a boxtop or brand identification mark from a previous purchase. The use of premiums is believed to cost the sponsor somewhat less than other promotions because the consumer makes a purchase first and a larger number of total sales typically result. In a sense, premiums are a reward following trial or regular usage and resemble operant conditioning or instrumental learning. That is, behavior occurs first (i.e., purchase and usage), followed by a reinforcement (i.e., the premium), which in turn increases the probability that another purchase of the brand will occur in the future. Trading stamps are another form of premiums.

Other forms of consumer promotions include *contests*, *games*, *prizes*, and *cents-off deals* (e.g., a price reduction put on the package label or near the packages on display). One of the more subtle types of promotion is the giving of free gifts, termed *specialty advertising*. Here a pen, calendar, coffee mug, playing cards, or other item is given to the consumer. The item will have the name of the seller, brand, and even address or telephone number displayed on it in a conspicuous manner so that the consumer is reminded of the seller. Specialty advertising is also used as a dealer promotion tool.

One major drawback with consumer promotions is that they sometimes do not build preference for a brand or encourage repeat sales. Rather they serve merely as a free gift or price reduction. Their effect may be short-lived as well. However, in the aggregate, if enough new purchasers can be enticed to try the product, it may generate more revenue than the costs. Experimentation is often needed to ascertain its value. Another danger with consumer premiums is that they may lower the quality image of the brand. The consumer might think, "If the brand is so good, why do they have to give me something else to try it?" Nevertheless, because some products are so low in involvement and because consumers may buy a competitor's brand without much thought or out of habit, consumer promotions are often the only way to overcome resistance and induce trial.

Dealer Promotions. Dealers, too, typically need incentives to carry and push a sponsor's brands. As firms become more competitive and brands proliferate and overlap in features and benefits, additional value may be required for a firm to break through the competition. This is especially true for low-involvement products and with increasing media clutter. Thus, dealers (e.g., retailers, wholesalers) are targeted for special promotional efforts.

Perhaps the most important dealer promotion, at least in the retail trade, is the *point-of-purchase display* (P-O-P).[77] Actually, this is just as much a consumer promotion as a dealer promotion. A P-O-P promotion consists of a sign, poster, or other attention-getting device either placed next to merchandise or else conspicuously presented along with merchandise but away from competitor's brands and other products. For example, supermarkets, drugstores, and liquor stores will position special displays of toothpaste, soaps, wines, canned goods, or other items at the ends of aisles or on colorful cardboard stands in the aisles. The manufacturer will typically provide the displays free of charge to the retailer. More complex and expensive displays may entail a sharing of expenses. In any case, the logic of P-O-P displays is that one desires to place communication stimuli as close as possible to the actual act of purchase. Because people either are indifferent to some purchases, have not fully made up their mind before shopping, or have not considered certain products or brands, it behooves the seller to utilize a stimulus as an instigator to purchase or a last-minute aid to the decision-making process.

A second commonly used dealer promotion is the *allowance*. Here a manufacturer will give a wholesaler or retailer free merchandise, actual cash awards, money for advertising, or discounts in exchange for buying goods for the first time or in greater quantity or for allocating special selling effort to one's wares.

Still other dealer promotions might consist of special *gifts, bonuses, contests, prizes,* free *training* or *business advice,* free *vacations,* and *specialty advertising items.* The value of such seemingly unimportant or gimmick-like appeals is that they are novel, even exciting, and provide rewards and recognition in addition to normal compensation. The *trade show* and *convention* are two additional forms of dealer promotions.

Sales Force Promotions. Firms often use incentives to motivate their own sales forces. These are in addition to one's salary, bonus, or commission and include *contests, prizes, free trips, gifts,* and other forms of reward. Some companies even provide catalogs of gifts and send them to the spouses of salespeople in the hope that family pressures will motivate sales. Because we will treat the personal selling function in more detail in the following two chapters, nothing more will be said here.

Final Comments on Promotion. It should be stressed that the effective use of promotions requires that the managers recognize their interdependence with other marketing mix stimuli and especially with advertising. Indeed, many promotions reach the consumer only through advertising. In addition, advertising and promotion can be mutually reinforcing. One study showed, for instance, that sales of coffee were .6 purchases per 100 shoppers when no advertising or P-O-P displays were used, 2.5 purchases per 100 when only displays were used, 1.9 purchases per 100 when only ads were used, but 8.1 purchases per 100 when *both* ads and displays were used.[78] The use of both tactics seems to have increased the impact of each other. This type of "interaction effect" has been found for snack foods, paper products, soft drinks, and many other everyday items.

The issue facing marketing managers is not so much whether to advertise *or* to promote. Rather, most marketing efforts will require both advertising and promotion. The question to answer then is what proportion of each to employ. In practice, a wide range of advertising to promotion budget ratios are used even within the same industry. A common ratio is 70:30 for everyday consumer goods. That is, of the total communication budget, 70 percent is spent on advertising and 30 percent on promotions. Other ratios are, of course, possible and in fact are used, depending on the circumstances.

Many factors enter the decision process on which ratio to use. We can only mention a few of these here. One consideration is buyer behavior. How do consumers make decisions? Ready-to-eat cereals are an example. Many consumers make lists of groceries to buy before they embark on the weekly shopping trip. This would seem to indicate that advertising is crucial, as people need to have the preferred brand(s) in mind before entering the store. Other consumers do not decide on a brand until they pass the shelves in the store. This tends to suggest the importance of in-store point-of-purchase displays, cents-off deals, and other promotion techniques. However, even those who make up their minds before shopping may be influenced by coupons or free samples sent by mail. And those who have not decided on a brand before shopping may be influenced by information seen in ads that ultimately yield high "top-of-the-mind awareness" while passing a display of cereal. Hence, for cereal at least, a large amount of advertising and promotion are needed. A reasonable advertising to promotion ratio might be 70:30 or 65:35, for example.

On the other hand, for headache or cold remedies, the ratio of advertising to promotion should be higher, perhaps 90:10. Here, consumers purchase either in urgent contexts or when they are about to run out of their medication. From the seller's viewpoint, consumers must be made aware of a brand and repeatedly reinforced through advertising. Few decisions are stimulated by point-of-purchase or other promotions. Yet, because sellers desire to get people to try a new brand or to switch from a competitor's brand, some promotion is needed, such as free sampling. Therefore, a high advertising to promotion ratio is dictated.

Another consideration when setting the advertising to promotion ratio is, of course, the degree and nature of competition. Imagine that you are the brand manager for Hires Root Beer, a soft drink with a very small market share. What advertising to promotion budget would you set? If Coca-Cola, Pepsico, Seven-Up, and the other leading companies used an 80:20 ratio, should you follow suit? Probably not. Although the same ratio would meet the competition in a relative sense, the other firms have such larger budgets overall that Hires would be "outshouted" in the marketplace so to speak, and no competitive advantage would be realized. A better strategy might be to use a 30:70 ratio, say, such that more emphasis is placed on consumer and dealer promotions. Hires's problem is (1) to get people to try its brand and switch brands (therefore suggesting couponing and P-O-P displays) and (2) to get stores and restaurants to stock it (suggesting allowances and free goods).

In addition to buyer behavior and competitive factors, a firm must consider the stage in the product life cycle when considering an advertising and promotion budget. Introduction and growth suggest advertising to gain awareness and retailer deals to gain acceptance in the store. Mature products require small changes and fine-tuning of tactics. The decline stage often demands withdrawal of advertising and promotion supports.

Direct Marketing. There is another marketing tactic that closely resembles promotion, although the fit is not perfect. This is *direct marketing*. In direct marketing, a firm communicates to potential customers, and they, in turn, buy directly from the firm. No intermediaries such as wholesalers or retailers are used. The most widely used means of communication is through the mail. However, the telephone is also used frequently. Typical examples of direct marketing include catalogue companies (e.g., Eddie Bauer, L. L. Bean, Sears), publishing houses, and book and record clubs. Financial service organizations now increasingly use direct marketing as well. Direct marketing is especially popular with people who do not have the time, ability, or inclination to travel to stores.

Publicity[79]

Publicity is "any form of nonpaid commercially significant news or editorial comment about ideas, products, or institutions."[80] It is usually conveyed under the sponsorship of a newspaper, TV or radio station, or magazine. Although publicity is not paid for by the firm whose product or service benefits from the coverage, the firm typically provides much if not most of the information through a news release or other document. Indeed, firms spend considerable time and money attempting to get stories placed in the news media. The major advantage of publicity, other than its free aspect, is that the public generally perceives the information more positively than if the firm were to advertise it. People perceive the media as impartial and may even see publicity as an endorsement. Advertisers, of course, are typically perceived as self-serving.

Organizations attempt to coordinate their advertising and promotion campaigns with publicity. Sometimes publicity will lead advertising, introducing the product to the public. Some advertisers will, of course, quote favorable publicity in their ads. But as you probably already guessed, publicity is a double-edged sword. Firms have no real control over what is said and how it is said, and negative publicity can be disastrous. For example, sales of the rotary engine Mazda were allegedly hurt by the Environmental Protection Agency's publication of its very low gas mileage. Magazines such as *Consumer Reports* can influence sales one way or the other, too, and firms have no input to their evaluations or its publication.

Public relations is not only targeted at the community at large. Specific consumer segments are sought through publicity in trade or special interest magazines. Also, lobbying might be regarded as one form of public relations.

Summary

Marketing communication is a complex yet essential function for any organization. It literally serves as the means to respond to or influence demand and other environmental forces. The four major communication tools include advertising, promotion, publicity, and personal selling. In the broadest sense, we might view the objectives of communication as increased sales through focus upon (1) new users who have never tried the brand or product class, (2) old users of the brand or product class who no longer purchase it, (3) users of the competitors' brands, (4) switchers who are loyal to no brand, and (5) current users who might consume more.

Advertising is perhaps the most far-reaching and on a per capita basis the least expensive communication tool. At the same time, its impact is not as strong or compelling as more direct modes of influence such as personal selling. Yet, advertising remains an essential managerial tool. Indeed, for everyday consumer products, it is perhaps the most important means of communication. For other products and services, it shares center stage with promotion, publicity, or personal selling.

We saw that the key actors in any advertising effort consist of the advertiser, the advertising agency, and the media. These independent institutions cooperate among themselves to transmit messages to the public at large or special target markets. Of course, it should be remembered that considerable competition exists among advertisers in the communication media, too. Effective marketing requires an unusual degree of coordination between firm and advertising agency. Special roles within each institution facilitate this. Figures 9-3 and 9-4 are sketches of two typical organizational structures used to manage things from the firm's side and Figure 9-5 shows the structure of a typical ad agency. The brand manager of the firm and the advertising account executive in the agency perform the facilitating exchanges between organizations.

We spent a considerable amount of time exploring behavioral science dimensions of advertising in this chapter. Recall first that advertising agencies were found to exhibit unique approaches which we termed *creative styles*. For example, the Leo Burnett agency typically uses humor or emotions. Their ads might be described as "warm and believable," and they sometimes use everyday people in the ads to convey a wholesome image and "the common touch." On occasion, animated characters are used to communicate a story (e.g., light drama), enhance remembrance, and in a nonthreatening way indirectly educate the consumer. Doyle Dane Bernbach rely relatively more on message structure and execution. Their ads also generally employ large amounts of humor to attract and hold one's attention. Sometimes they use refutational arguments, at other times a story line will present "an unusual turn of events." In still other DDB ads, the product will be put through an unusual test to dramatically show its utility. Ogilvy & Mather tend to emphasize the rational side of consumption. Special effort is given to the creation of a unique brand image as well. The Ted Bates agency, in contrast, is known for its hard sell. It typically emphasizes facts, a unique selling proposition, and on occasion fear appeals. Most other ad agencies express their own unique personalities through their ads.

Another aspect of behavioral science in advertising was discussed along with the phenomena of *repetition and wearout*. Over time, a decline in advertising effectiveness commonly occurs. At the micro level, this happens because people become bored with repeated messages and ignore it or else become irritated and counterargue against it or downgrade it. At the macro level, markets become saturated and a proportion of previously reached audiences either tune out, counterargue, or switch allegiances to competitors.

Wearout might be ameliorated through a variety of means. Ad structure might be changed. For example, a switch from factual to humorous executions might be attempted. Alternatively, ad copy might need alteration. For instance, new product attributes could be communicated. Finally, new advertising media can be tried. A switch from TV to radio might be called for.

The chapter then turned to a description of the Foote, Cone & Belding planning model (see Figure 9-7). Here brands are categorized in terms of *product involvement* (either high or low), the primary type of processing (cognitive or affective), and the order of processing (e.g., learn → feel → do or feel → learn → do). The model can be used as an aid in the design of copy, selection of media, and copy testing. The discussion of affect, cognitions, and consumer involvement integrates many of the principles discussed in this and the preceding chapter. The notion of media involvement was also discussed.

The measurement of *advertising effectiveness* was our next topic. We examined a number of commercially used techniques, most of which relied on measuring psychological responses such as recall, recognition, attitudes, or intentions as dependent variables. The advantages of these procedures lie in the ease of data collection and presentation of findings. Moreover, the things measured represent necessary changes in consumer responses that are, in turn, intermediate between exposure to an ad and actual purchase. At least, the responses are associated with processing of ads and serve as rough predictors of the likelihood of purchase. On the other hand, the measurement techniques can be highly inaccurate. Further, some procedures (e.g., recall) possibly overestimate cognitive responses and underestimate emotional aspects of ads. One must therefore have a clear idea of what response is desired and select a method accordingly. Even with the best of procedures, however, the question of validity must be faced, as psychological responses are often too far removed from the ultimate behavioral responses desired.

The chapter then turned to the general topic of *advertising management*. Figure 9-8 presented an overall framework for managing the communication function in general and advertising in particular. An important activity in this regard concerns *goal setting and budgeting*. Goals are set broadly in terms of ultimate organization ends and gross communication objectives (e.g., desired product trial). More specific goals with respect to awareness, recall, recognition, or intentions are also formulated.

Budgets are financial plans designed to aid goal attainment. They are set on the basis of a variety of criteria. Subjective judgments of managers are sometimes used as the criteria. Hopefully, such a method is based on real skills of decision makers who take into account the ability of advertising to produce sales. Another method is simply to use a rule-of-thumb, such as a fixed percentage of sales. On occasion, budgets are set to meet or overtake the competition (e.g., 120 percent of a competitor's budget). Perhaps the most justified and valid procedure is the objective and task method. Here the firm defines a specific goal and then sets a budget necessary to carry out the activities designed to accomplish the goal. Finally, some organizations use experimentation, statistical modeling, or normative mathematical modeling to estimate budgets.

Next we considered *media selection*. One decision point in this regard concerns which media to advertise through. The primary options include TV, radio, magazines, newspapers, billboards, direct mail, and/or the Yellow Pages. The choice of a medium is influenced by the number of people in the audience, their attributes, the cost of advertising there, and the ability of the medium for accomplishing desired goals such as product demonstration, conveying facts, or stimulating emotions.

A second media selection decision concerns which specific vehicle to use within each medium or media chosen. For instance, if magazines are chosen, a technical advertiser might select a professional magazine, whereas a mass marketer might opt for *Time*. The final media selection decision is scheduling. This is a timing issue of when and how often to advertise. We considered four generic options: a constant level, a high level followed by decline, pulsing, and responsive tactics.

The social and legal aspects of advertising were also scrutinized in this chapter. We began with a discussion of the effects of ads on people as individuals. These effects range from short-lived emotional or thinking stimulation to long-term accumulations of beliefs, values, and socialization. The annoying and offensive qualities of ads were examined, too, as well as the topics of manipulation and subliminal advertising. Next the effects of advertising on the economy were considered. Among other positive consequences, advertising is thought to serve an informative function for consumers in economic decision making, to financially support the mass media, to encourage economic growth, and to provide an essential linkage to consumers for strategy implementation by firms. On the other hand, negative implications were discussed, including higher prices, false product differentiation, the creation of barriers to entry, and promotion of market concentration and monopoly power.

Advertising also affects society at large. It has the potential for creating or contributing to social problems. And as with all of life's actions, it raises moral and ethical issues for individuals, institutions, and society. The choices are not unique to advertising, but they take on added importance given the power that advertising has.

Our discussion of advertising closed with the topic of regulation. We saw that self-regulation and especially the activities of the FTC have a strong influence on advertising practices. This is especially true with regard to deceptive advertising and the use of bait-and-switch tactics. Thus, the government has an impact on what is said in ads. Finally, the chapter ended with a look at *promotion* and *publicity.* We considered consumer promotions (e.g., couponing, sampling, the use of premiums), dealer promotions (e.g., point-of-purchase displays, allowances), and sales force promotions (e.g., contests). Each type of promotion is designed to provide an incentive to the respective audience. Moreover, the incentive is more directly action oriented than typical advertising appeals. However, it should be pointed out that many promotions are communicated through advertising. Also, the use of both promotions and advertising can achieve significantly more sales than the use of either one alone. Another topic we considered is what ratio of advertising to promotion to employ in any particular marketing effort. This is a strategic choice that must be based upon how consumers make decisions, what the resources of the firm are, what the competition is doing and is likely to do in the future, the stage in the product life cycle, and other factors. Publicity, too, is a useful communication mode. The trick is to influence in a positive way any information communicated by a firm or its products.

1 Broadly speaking, the ultimate goal of advertising is to increase sales. Name five senses in which sales might increase in response to advertising.

2 Firms typically organize their marketing tasks by functions or brands. Briefly describe and contrast these alternative forms of organization design.

3 Describe the structure and functions of modern advertising agencies. Upon whose shoulders does the advertiser-agency relationship rest?

4 Advertising agencies differ considerably in their underlying philosophies and creative styles. What implications does this have for advertisers in the selection of an agency and the management of everyday relations?

5 What is the phenomenon of advertising wearout and how can advertisers combat it?

6 Describe the advertising planning model of Foote, Cone & Belding. How might it be used in practice?

7 Discuss the issues surrounding the measurement of advertising effectiveness.

8 The heart of Ray's Communication Planning Model (see Figure 9-8) is the budgeting process. Describe how budgets are set in practice. What budgeting process would you recommend and why?

9 What are the key decisions that must be made in media selection and on what bases are they made?

10 Contrast the effects of ads on individuals, the economy, and society at large. Given the pros and cons, do you think advertising should be controlled more or less than it is now? What should the role of advertising be?

11 What is the purpose of promotions? Discuss the forms of promotions.

12 On what basis should the ratio of advertising to promotion budget be set?

NOTES

1. The advertising estimate is from *Advertising Age*, January 5, 1981. See also Robert J. Coen, "Vast U.S. and Worldwide Ad Expenditures Expected," *Advertising Age*, November 13, 1980, p. 10. The promotion estimate is from Louis J. Haugh, "Sales Promotion Grows to $40 Billion Status," *Advertising Age*, April 30, 1980, pp. 199ff. Another liberal estimate of promotion expenditures in the U.S. for 1983 was $71.7 billion. See Russell D. Bowman, "Sales Promotion: 1984 and Beyond," *Sales Promotion Monitor* 2 (September 1984): 69. The publicity estimate is simply a guess by this author, as no reliable data exists. For background, see John E. Marston, *Modern Public Relations* (New York: McGraw-Hill, 1979). The personal selling estimate is from Michael L. Ray, *Advertising and Communication Management* (Englewood Cliffs, N.J.: Prentice-Hall, 1982), p. 12. However, this number, too, is only a rough guess.

2. Steuart Henderson Britt, Stephen C. Adams, and Allan S. Miller, "How Many Advertising Exposures per Day?" *Journal of Advertising Research* (December 1972): 3–9.

3. "Numbers Aren't Everything," *Media Decisions*, June 10, 1975, p. 69.

4. Robert J. Coen, "Vast U.S. and Worldwide Ad Expenditures Expected," *Advertising Age*, November 13, 1980. In 1960, the U.S. accounted for about two-thirds of world expenditures on advertising, but is expected to comprise only about 40 percent by the year 2000.

5. Robert S. Trebus, "The Socialist Countries," in S. Watson Dunn and E. S. Lorimor, *International Advertising and Marketing* (Columbus, Ohio: Grid Publishing, Inc., 1979), pp. 349–60. See also Philip Hanson, *Advertising and Socialism* (White Plains, N.Y.: International Arts & Science Press, 1974).

6. *Standard Directory of Advertisers* (Skokie, Ill.: National Register Publishing Company, 1978).

7. *Advertising Age*, September 11, 1980, p. 1.

8. *The Works of Samuel Johnson, LL.D, IV* (Oxford: Talboys and Wheeler, 1825), p. 269.

9. David A. Aaker and John G. Myers, *Advertising Management*, 2nd ed. (Englewood Cliffs, N.J.: Prentice-Hall, 1982), p. 9.

10. Two other arrangements are the organization by geographical territory and the organization by end user. For purposes of brevity, these will not be discussed here. Also, it should be noted that combinations of the four types of organizations are sometimes employed. For instance, the brand management system is often embedded in a functional hierarchy.

11. For a discussion of the role of a brand manager in modern organizations, see Richard M. Clewett and Stanley F. Stasch, "Shifting Role of the Product Manager," *Harvard Business Review* (January–February 1975): 65–73; Ann M. Morrison, "The General Mills Brand Manager," *Fortune* 12 (1981): 99–107.

12. "The Brand Manager: No Longer King," *Business Week*, June 9, 1973.

13. See *Agency Compensation: A Guidebook* (New York: Association of National Advertisers, Inc., 1979).

14. Fifteen percent is the most common commission, but it can vary according to the medium or country advertised in. For example, outdoor ads typically have a 16 2/3 percent commission.

15. Portions of the following discussion on advertising agency styles are drawn from Aaker and Myers, *Advertising Management*, pp. 345–60 and Ray, 284–90. The author also wishes to thank Professors Brian Sternthal and Richard Yalch for ideas used herein.

16. Albert Bandura, *Social Learning Theory* (Englewood Cliffs, N.J.: Prentice-Hall, 1977).

17. Denis Higgens, *The Art of Writing Advertising* (Chicago: Advertising Publications, 1965), p. 44.

18. Quoted in Martin Mayer, *Madison Avenue, U.S.A.* (New York: Pocket Books, 1958), p. 64.

19. Marshall McLuhan, *The Medium Is the Message* (New York: Random House, 1967).

20. Jerry Della Femina, with Charles Spokin, ed., *From Those Wonderful Folks Who Gave You Pearl Harbor* (New York: Simon and Schuster, 1970), pp. 38–39.

21. Aaker and Myers, *Advertising Management*, pp. 349–50.

22. David Ogilvy, *Confessions of an Advertising Man* (New York: Atheneum Publishers, 1963), pp. 99–103.

23. Ogilvy, *Confessions of an Advertising Man*, p. 102.

24. Ogilvy and Mather, New York, "Come to Shell for Answers: Summary Report," September 4, 1978.

25. Philip Levine, "Commercials That Name Competing Brands," *Journal of Advertising Research* (December 1976): 14.

26. Thomas Watterson, "Top Ad Exec's Lament—TV Commercials 'Silly,' " *San Francisco Examiner*, November 13, 1983, D1–D3.

27. Rosser Reeves, *Reality in Advertising* (New York: Alfred A. Knopf, Inc., 1961).

28. Higgens, *The Art of Writing Advertising*, p. 124.

29. Reeves, *Reality in Advertising*, p. 47.

30. "Ayer, Y & R Share Agency of the Year Honors," *Advertising Age*, March 14, 1979, 1ff.

31. "Research Suggests Using Celebrity Spokesman as Focal Point for Floral Group's Consumer, Trade Ads," *Marketing News*, November 11, 1983.

32. Herman Simon, "ADPULS: An Advertising Model with Wearout and Pulsation," *Journal of Marketing Research* 19 (August 1982): 352–63; Bobby Calder and Brian Sternthal, "Television Commercial Wearout: An Information Processing View," *Journal of Marketing Research* 16 (May 1980): 173–86; George E. Belch, "The Effects of Television Commercial Repetition on Cognitive Response and Message Acceptance," *Journal of Consumer Research* 9 (June 1982): 56–65; C. Samuel Craig, Brian Sternthal, and Clark Leavitt, "Advertising Wearout: An Experimental Analysis," *Journal of Marketing Research* 13 (November 1976):365–72; Michael L. Ray and Alan G. Sawyer, "A Laboratory Technique for Estimating the Repetition Function for Advertising Media Models," *Journal of Marketing Research* 8 (February 1971): 20–29; Alan G. Sawyer, "Repetition and Affect: Recent Empirical and Theoretical Developments," in A. G. Woodside, J. N. Sheth, and P. D. Bennett, eds., *Foundations of Consumer and Industrial Buying Behavior* (New York: American Elsevier, 1977), pp. 229–42; Alan G. Sawyer and Scott Ward, "Carry-Over Effects in Advertising Communication," in J. N. Sheth, ed., *Research in Marketing*, vol. 2 (Greenwich, Conn.: JAI Press, 1979), pp. 259–314; Alan G. Sawyer, "Repetition, Cognitive Responses, and Persuasion," in R. E. Petty, T. M. Ostrom, and T. C. Brock, eds., *Cognitive Responses in Persuasion* (Hillsdale, N.J.: Lawrence Erlbaum Associates, 1981), pp. 237–61; John T. Cacioppo and Richard E. Petty, "Effects of Message Repetition and Position on Cognitive Response, Recall, and Persuasion," *Journal of Personality and Social Psychology* 37 (January 1979): 97–109.

33. Herbert E. Krugman, "Processes Underlying Exposure to Advertising," *American Psychologist* 23 (April 1968): 245–53; —— "Memory without Recall, Exposure without Perception," *Journal of Advertising Research* 17 (August 1977): 7–12; —— "Why Three Exposures May Be Enough," *Journal of Advertising Research* 12 (December 1972): 11–14; —— "What Makes Advertising Effective?" *Harvard Business Review* (March–April 1975): 96–103.

34. Krugman, "Why Three Exposures May Be Enough," p. 13.

35. Recent research supports this latter assertion. See Richard P. Bagozzi and Alvin J. Silk, "Recall, Recognition, and the Measurement of Memory for Print Advertisements," *Marketing Science* 2 (Spring 1983): 95–134. Although people as individuals tend to have stronger powers to recognize an ad than to recall it, aggregate measures across consumers and ads generally show that recognition and recall measures are both highly correlated and stable over at least short periods of time (e.g., three weeks).

36. R. B. Zajonc, H. Markus, and W. R. Wilson, "Exposure Effects and Associative Learning," *Journal of Experimental Social Psychology* 10 (1974): 248–63.

37. See discussion on cognitive response model in Chapter 8. See also Peter Wright, "Cognitive Responses to Mass Media Advocacy," in R. E. Petty, T. M. Ostrom, and T. C. Brock, eds., *Cognitive Responses to Persuasion* (Hillsdale, N.J.: Lawrence Erlbaum, 1981); Sawyer, "Repetition, Cognitive Responses, and Persuasion"; Cacioppo and Petty, "Effects of Message Repetition"; Belch, "Effects of Television Commercial Repetition"; and Calder and Sternthal, "Television Commercial Wearout."

38. Russell I. Haley, "Sales Effects of Media Weight," *Journal of Advertising Research* 18 (June 1978): 9–18; John D. C. Little, "Aggregate Advertising Models: The State of Art," *Operations Research* 27 (July–August 1979): 629–67; Hermann Simon, "ADPULS: An Advertising Model with Wearout and Pulsation," *Journal of Marketing Research* 19 (1982): 352–63.

39. See discussion on the low-involvement model in previous chapter. The notion of media involvement was first described in H. E. Krugman, "The Impact of Television Advertising: Learning without Involvement," *Public Opinion Quarterly* 29 (Fall 1965): 349–56. See also H. E. Krugman, "Memory without Recall, Exposure without Perception," *Journal of Advertising Research* 17 (August 1977): 7–12. See, in addition, Rajeev Batra and Michael L. Ray, "Operationalizing Involvement as Depth and Quality of Cognitive Response," in R. P. Bagozzi and A. M. Tybout, eds., *Advances in Consumer Research*, vol. 10 (Ann Arbor, Mich.: Association for Consumer Research, 1983).

40. David Berger, "The Consumer Mind: How to Tailor Ad Strategies," *Advertising Age*, June 9, 1980; "A Retrospective: FCB Recall Study," *Advertising Age*, October 26, 1981; Richard Vaughn, "How Advertising Works: A Planning Model," *Journal of Advertising Research* 20 (October 1980): 27–33.

41. Vaughn, "How Advertising Works: A Planning Model."

42. D. G. Clarke, "Econometric Measurement of the Duration of Advertising Effects of Sales," *Journal of Marketing Research* 13 (November 1976): 345–57; R. Ackoff and J. R. Ernshoff, "Advertising Research at Anheuser-Busch Inc. (1963–1968)," *Sloan Management Review* 16 (Spring 1975): 1–15.

43. Bagozzi and Silk, "Recall, Recognition, and the Measurement of Memory."

44. H. A. Zielske, "Does Day-After Recall Penalize 'Feeling Ads'?" *Journal of Advertising Research* 22 (February–March 1982): 19–22; Bagozzi and Silk, "Recall, Recognition, and the Measurement of Memory"; Krugman, "Why Three Exposures May Be Enough"; "Memory without Recall, Exposure without Perception."

45. Zielske, "Does Day-After Recall Penalize 'Feeling Ads'?"

46. Michael L. Ray, "A Decision Sequence Analysis of Developments in Marketing Communications," *Journal of Marketing* 37 (January 1973): 29–38.

47. R. Colley, *Defining Advertising Goals for Measured Advertising Results* (New York: Association of National Advertisers, 1961); D. C. Marschner, "DAGMAR Revisited—Eight Years Later," *Journal of Advertising Research* 2 (April 1971): 27–33. See also G. L. Lilien, A. J. Silk, J. J. Choffray, and M. Rao, "Industrial Advertising Effects and Budgeting Practices," *Journal of Marketing* 40 (January 1976): 16–24.

48. A. J. San Augustine and W. F. Foley, "How Large Advertisers Set Budgets," *Journal of Advertising Research* 15 (October 1975): 11–16; C. Gilligan, "How British Advertisers Set Budgets," *Journal of Advertising Research* 17 (February 1977): 47–49. See also N. K. Dhalla, "How to Set Advertising Budgets," *Journal of Advertising Research* 17 (October 1977): 11–17.

49. J. C. Becknell, Jr., and R. W. McIssac, "Test Marketing Cookware Coated with 'Teflon'," *Journal of Advertising Research* 3 (September 1963): 4–5. See also G. J. Eskin, "A Case for Test Market Experiments," *Journal of Advertising Research* 15 (April 1975): 27–33.

50. L. J. Parsons and F. M. Bass, "Optimal Advertising-Expenditure Implications of a Simultaneous-Equation Regression Analysis," *Operations Research* 19 (May–June 1971): 822–31.

51. J. D. C. Little, "A Model of Adaptive Control of Promotional Spending," *Operations Research* 14 (November–December 1966): 175–97; B. M. Enis, "Bayesian Approach to Ad Budgets," *Journal of Advertising Research* 12 (February 1972): 13–19.

52. H. Assael and H. Cannon, "Do Demographics Help in Media Selection?" *Journal of Advertising Research* 12 (December 1972): 7–11; J. D. McConnell, "Do Media Vary in Effectiveness?" *Journal of Advertising Research* 10 (October 1970): 19–22; J. Z. Sissors, "Matching Media with Markets," *Journal of Advertising Research* 11 (October 1971): 39–43; D. Gensch, *Advertising Planning* (New York: American Elsevier, 1978).

53. *Facts about 1980 Newspapers* (Washington, D.C.: American Newspaper Publishers Association).

54. *Nielsen Report on Television 1980* (Northbrook, Ill.: A. C. Nielsen Company).

55. J. D. C. Little and L. M. Lodish, "A Media Selection Model and Its Optimalization by Dynamic Programming," *Industrial Management Review* 8 (Fall 1966): 15-23; J. D. C. Little and L. M. Lodish, "A Media Planning Calculus," *Operations Research* 17 (January-February 1969): 1-35; D. A. Aaker, "ADMOD: An Advertising Decision Model," *Journal of Marketing Research* 13 (February 1975): 31-45. See also V. Srinivasan, "Decomposition of a Multiperiod Media Scheduling Model in Terms of Single Period Events," *Management Science* 23 (December 1976): 349-60.

56. V. Packard, *The Hidden Persuaders* (New York: Pocket Books, 1957).

57. W. B. Key, *Subliminal Seduction* (Englewood Cliffs, N.J.: Prentice-Hall, 1973): *Media Sexploitation* (Englewood Cliffs, N.J.: Prentice-Hall, 1976); and *The Clamplate Orgy* (Englewood Cliffs, N.J.: Prentice-Hall, 1980).

58. R. A. Bauer and S. A. Greyser, *Advertising in America: The Consumer View* (Boston, Mass.: Division of Research, Graduate School of Business, Harvard University, 1968), p. 183.

59. D. A. Aaker and D. Bruzzone, "Audience Reactions to Television Commercials," *Journal of Advertising Research* 21 (October 1981): 15-23.

60. T. E. Moore, "Subliminal Advertising: What You See Is What You Get," *Journal of Marketing* 46 (Spring 1982): 38-47; J. Saegert, "Another Look at Subliminal Perception," *Journal of Advertising Research* 19 (February 1979), 55-57.

61. F. M. Nicosia, *Advertising Management and Society* (New York: McGraw-Hill, 1974). Bauer and Greyser, *Advertising in America.*

62. S. Ward, "Children's Reactions to Commercials," *Journal of Advertising Research* 12 (April 1972): 37-45.

63. R. B. Zajonc, "Feeling and Thinking: Preferences Need No Inferences," *American Psychologist* 35 (February 1980): 151-75; A. Bandura, *Social Learning Theory* (Englewood Cliffs, N.J.: Prentice-Hall, 1977).

64. H. H. Kassarjian, "The Negro and American Advertising, 1946-65," *Journal of Marketing Research* 6 (February 1969): 29-39.

65. A. E. Courtney and S. W. Lockeretz, "A Woman's Place: An Analysis of the Roles Portrayed by Women in Magazine Advertisements," *Journal of Marketing Research* 8 (February 1971): 92-95; C. Scheibe, "Sex Roles in TV Commercials," *Journal of Advertising Research* 19 (February 1979): 23-27. See also A. E. Courtney and T. W. Whipple, "Sex Stereotyping in Advertising: An Annotated Bibliography," (Cambridge, Mass.: Marketing Science Institute, 1980); M. Butler and W. Paisley, *Women and the Mass Media* (New York: Human Science Press, 1980).

66. J. L. Simon, *Issues in the Economics of Advertising* (Urbana, Ill.: University of Illinois Press, 1970); M. Pearce, S. M. Cunningham, and A. Miller, *Appraising the Economic and Social Effects of Advertising* (Cambridge, Mass.: Marketing Science Institute, 1971); J.-J. Lambin, "What Is the Real Impact of Advertising?" *Harvard Business Review* May-June 1975: 139-47; J. M. Ferguson, *Advertising and Competition: Theory, Measurement, Fact* (Cambridge, Mass.: Ballinger, 1974); D. G. Tuerck, ed., *Issues in Advertising: The Economics of Persuasion* (Washington, D.C.: American Enterprise Institute, 1978); P. W. Farris and M. S. Albion, "The Impact of Advertising on the Price of Consumer Products," *Journal of Marketing* 44 (Summer 1980): 17-35; R. Schmalense, *The Economics of Advertising* (Amsterdam: Elsevier/North-Holland, 1972); P. N. Bloom, *Advertising, Competition, and Public Policy* (Cambridge, Mass.: Ballinger, 1976); Y. Brozen, ed., *Advertising and Society* (New York: New York University Press, 1974).

67. L. Benham, "The Effect of Advertising on the Price of Eyeglasses," *Journal of Law and Economics* 15 (October 1972): 337-51; R. L. Steiner, "Does Advertising Lower Consumer Prices?" *Journal of Marketing* 37 (October 1973): 19-26.

68. J. Backman, *Advertising and Competition* (New York: New York University Press, 1967).

69. See for example, Ferguson, *Advertising and Competition.*

70. Farris and Albion, "Impact of Advertising on the Price of Consumer Products."

71. S. Winokur, "Freud and Fashion: Tobacco Firm's Seduction of Women," *San Francisco Examiner and Chronicle,* August 21, 1983, A6-A7; S. Cunningham, "Not Such a Long Way, Baby: Women and Cigarette Ads," *Monitor* (American Psychological Association), November 1983, p. 15.

72. S. E. Cohen, "Advertising Regulation: Changing, Growing Area," *Advertising Age*, April 30, 1980; D. Cohen, "The FTC's Advertising Substantiation Program," *Journal of Marketing* 44 (Winter 1980): 26–35; R. F. Wilkes and J. B. Wilcox, "Recent FTC Actions: Implication for the Advertising Strategist," *Journal of Marketing* 38 (January 1974): 55–61; J. L. Welch, *Marketing Law* (Tulsa, Okla.: Petroleum Publishing Co., 1980); B. J. Katz, et al., eds., *Advertising and Government Regulation* (Cambridge, Mass.: Marketing Science Institute, 1979); Brozen, *Advertising and Society.*

73. A considerable amount of self-regulation occurs within the advertising industry, too. For example, the Council of Better Business Bureaus has a body of members (the National Advertising Division), which hears complaints. Unsatisfactory compliance with the National Advertising Division's mandates will lead to review by the National Advertising Review Board, a group of 50 people (40 advertising professionals and 10 public members). Failure to comply with this latter body's recommendations will result in referral to a government body such as the FTC. Still another self-regulatory mechanism is the Code Authority of the National Association of Broadcasters, which handles radio and TV ads. Members agree to abide by the Code, which supplies guidelines covering such areas as children's ads, ads for alcoholic beverages, and ads for personal care products. The American Association of Advertising Agencies and the Association of National Advertisers also have codes of conduct. Finally, it should be pointed out that state governments also regulate aspects of advertising such as bait-and-switch practices.

74. D. M. Gardner, "Deception in Advertising: A Conceptual Approach," *Journal of Marketing* 39 (January 1975): 40–46. M. T. Brandt and J. L. Preston, "The Federal Trade Commission's Use of Evidence to Determine Deception," *Journal of Marketing* 41 (January 1977): 54–62.

75. S. J. Levy, *Promotional Behavior* (Glenview, Ill.: Scott Foresman, 1971); M. Chevalier and R. Curhan, *Sales Promotion* (Cambridge, Mass.: Marketing Science Institute, 1975); O. Riso, ed., *Sales Promotion Handbook*, 7th ed. (Chicago: The Dartnell Corporation, 1979); R. A. Strang, *The Promotional Planning Process* (New York: Praeger, 1980); G. R. Smith, *Display and Promotion*, 2nd ed. (New York: McGraw-Hill, 1978); J. F. Engel, M. R. Warshaw, and T. C. Kinnear, *Promotional Strategy*, 4th ed. (Homewood, Ill.: Richard D. Irwin, Inc., 1979). R. M. Prentice, *Consumer Franchise Building* (Chicago: Commerce Communications, Inc., 1984).

76. E. Mahany, "Package Goods Clients Agree: Promotion Importance Will Grow," *Advertising Age*, April 14, 1975: 46–48. The number of coupons distributed is difficult to estimate. Some trade people claim that over 40 billion coupons are distributed each year, so the 21 billion estimate may even be low.

77. M. Chevalier, "Substitution Patterns as a Result of Display in the Product Category," *Journal of Retailing* (Winter 1975–76): 65–72; J. P. Kelly and E. D. Robinson, "Sales Effects of Point-of-Purchase In-Store Signing," *Journal of Retailing* (Summer 1981): 49–63.

78. Point-of-Purchase Advertising Institute, 1978, quoted in D. I. Hawkins, R. J. Best, and K. A. Coney, *Consumer Behavior: Implications For Marketing Strategy* (Plano, Tex.: Business Publications, 1983), p. 563.

79. J. E. Matson, *Modern Public Relations* (New York: McGraw-Hill, 1979); S. M. Cutlip and A. H. Center, *Effective Public Relations*, 5th ed., (Englewood Cliffs, N.J.: Prentice-Hall, 1978); H. F. Moore and B. R. Canfield, *Public Relations: Principles, Cases, and Problems*, 8th ed. (Homewood, Ill.: Richard D. Irwin, Inc., 1981).

80. "Marketing Definitions" (Chicago: American Marketing Association, 1960).

GLOSSARY

Account Executive (or Advertising Account Executive). The person in an advertising agency responsible for supervising the creation and production of an ad. He or she is the principal contact person with the advertiser. Within the agency, the account executive works with the creative group, research department, production, and media planning. The counterpart of the account executive in the advertiser's organization is typically the brand manager. The account executive is called the account supervisor in some agencies. The account executive is a general manager in the broadest sense of the term.

Advertiser. The sponsor of ads, usually a company, nonprofit organization, government institution, group, or private individual.

Advertising. Any paid form of nonpersonal presentation of ideas, goods, and services by an identified sponsor. The sponsor is termed an advertiser. Most ads are produced by advertising agencies.

Advertising Agency. The independent organization responsible for planning, executing, and placing ads in media for advertisers. See Figure 9-5.

Advertising Budget. The amount of money spent by an organization on advertising. The amount is set on the basis of executive subjective judgments, rules-of-thumb (e.g., a percentage of sales), to meet or break competition, or objectively according to specific goals and the tasks needed to accomplish those goals. Experimentation, statistical models, or normative models may be used as input to the latter approach.

Advertising Substantiation. A report providing evidence as to the validity of claims made in an ad and demonstrating that said proof was used in preparation of the ad. The FTC and some media vehicles (e.g., national TV networks) may request to see such documentation from the advertiser and/or ad agency.

Advertising to Promotion Ratio. The relative proportion of a communication budget allocated to advertising and promotion, typically expressed as numbers such as 60:40, which indicates 60 percent allocated to advertising and 40 percent allocated to promotion.

Allowances. A type of promotion directed at a dealer whereby the sponsor (e.g., manufacturer) gives a wholesaler or retailer free merchandise, actual cash awards, money for advertising, or discounts in exchange for buying goods for the first time or in greater quantities or for allocating special selling effort.

Audience Reach. The number of people exposed to an ad at least once during a specific time period (e.g., four weeks).

Bait-and-Switch. A selling ploy in which a very low price is offered to attract customers to a store whereupon the seller informs customers that the item is unavailable and attempts to sell them another item, usually at a higher price.

Brand Management System. See Figure 9-4. An arrangement of tasks and responsibilities in an organization such that responsibilities within marketing are divided by brand. *See* functional management system of organization.

Brand Manager (or Product or Market Manager). A person in an organization responsible for coordinating and administrating the entire marketing program for his or her brand. This includes developing marketing strategies, plans, and forecasts; working with advertising agencies to develop ads; interacting with coworkers responsible for the design, manufacture, distribution, and selling of the brand; participating in pricing; designing promotion; gathering and interpreting data on the market and marketing effort; and initiating improvements and managing the brand throughout its life cycle. The brand manager is typically a middle or lower-middle manager. See Chapters 4 and 5.

Cents-off Deals. Consumer promotions consisting of price reductions put on a package or near packages on display.

Comparative Advertising. Advertising showing two or more brands in a particular product class and making comparisons or contrasts of product attributes or benefits of usage.

Copy. The visual, verbal, and auditory elements contained in an ad.

Copy Decisions. The question of what to say (i.e., message content) and how to say it (i.e., message structure). See Chapter 8. Copy decisions must be made along with media selection, planning, and budgeting decisions.

Copy Testing. Measurement of the impact of an ad. The criterion might be a psychological state (e.g., awareness, recall, recognition, attitude, intentions) or actual behavior (e.g., trial, purchase frequency or amount). It is hoped that the measure will show the effectiveness of the ad.

Corrective Advertising. A type of advertising whereby the sponsor clarifies the intent or impression conveyed in earlier ads or admits misinforming the public. The FTC may order or request that a firm conduct corrective advertising. Over the years, this has been done by a number of advertisers such as Ocean Spray Cranberry Juice, which they originally said was high in "food energy" but for which they were later required to note that "food energy" meant nothing more than "calories."

Coupon or Couponing. A type of promotion directed at consumers wherein the consumer will be given a refund or reduction in the price of purchase upon presentation of the coupon to retailer or manufacturer. The manufacturer typically mails the coupon to consumers or places it on or in packages, magazines, or the newspaper.

Creative Style. The unique communication approach taken by an ad agency in its creation of ads. Each agency has a personality that becomes reflected in the content and/or form of its advertisements.

Direct Marketing. The solicitation and selling of goods and services by a firm directly (i.e., without use of intermediaries) to consumers. Usually this is done by mail or phone.

FTC (Federal Trade Commission). An agency of the federal government concerned with the regulation of advertising, competitive practices of firms, and other matters.

Functional Management System of Organization. See Figure 9-3. An arrangement of tasks and responsibilities in an organization by broad managerial functions. Marketing functions are divided similarly into subfunctions such that people generally have responsibilities cutting across brands. *See* brand management system of organization.

Media Involvement. The degree of attention allocated to a particular mode of communication. Face-to-face sales encounters are high-involvement media, whereas television is generally a low-involvement medium for ads. Magazines are somewhere in between. *See* product involvement.

Media Selection. A central decision in the advertising process consisting of the choice of modes of communication to use to reach target consumers. Generally, one must first select one or more media, then specific vehicles within media, and finally when and how often to advertise. The media selection decision is, of course, in addition to the planning, budgeting, and copy decisions.

Medium (Media). Any device, symbol system, or means used to convey communication. The most common advertising media include television, radio, magazines, newspapers, billboards, posters, sky writing, mail, telephone, and the Yellow Pages.

Point-of-Purchase Display. A promotional device consisting of posters, table-like displays, or other material placed next to merchandise or used to highlight merchandise such as at the end of an aisle in the supermarket.

Premium. A free or low-priced product given to the consumer in exchange for purchasing a brand at regular price or sending in a boxtop or brand identification mark from a previous purchase. The use of premiums is a type of consumer promotion.

Product Involvement. The degree to which a person is motivated to purchase and/or use a product. The salience of a product for a person. Often related to the perceived risk of a product, its cost, and/or the consumer's ego involvement with it. A consumer might also experience the similar phenomenon of brand involvement. *See also* media involvement.

Promotion. The use of incentives by a sponsor (e.g., manufacturer) to encourage purchase or selling efforts. Promotions are directed to consumers, dealers, or salespeople. Consumer promotions include couponing, premiums, free samples, contests, games, prizes, cents-off deals, and specialty items. Dealer promotions consist of point-of-purchase displays, allowances, special gifts, bonuses, contests, prizes, free training or business advice, free vacations, and specialty items. Sales force promotions encompass contests, prizes, free trips, gifts, and other special forms of reward.

Publicity. Any form of nonpaid commercially significant news or editorial comment about ideas, products, or institutions.

Reach. *See* audience reach.

Sampling. A type of consumer promotion whereby a brand is given to a consumer free of charge. The sample may be the normal size of the product as it is presented for sale or it might be a reduced portion. Samples are sent in the mail, handed out on the street, delivered door-to-door, offered in a store display, attached to another product, or dispensed from a machine.

Specialty Advertising. The use of free items (e.g., pens, coffee mugs, calendars, bottle openers) to provide a gift to a customer and serve as a reminder. The advertiser's name, telephone number, address, slogan, etc., are typically placed on the item.

Storyboard. A pictorial mockup of a television ad done before production. It consists of a number of hand drawn pictures arranged to communicate the intended content of the ad and it includes the announcer and/or spokesperson comments.

Subliminal Advertising. The practice of inserting visual or auditory stimuli within an advertisement where the stimuli are perceivable but below the level of awareness. Advertisers deny that this is done, and researchers have found that a subliminal effect is difficult to produce and is usually limited to the power of suggestion and does not influence attitudes or behavior. At least, the latter outcome has not been shown in research to date.

Unique Selling Proposition. The selling point or idea conveyed in an ad. The USP is typically a product attribute or benefit of product usage not shared by other brands. The Ted Bates agency was one of the earliest users of USP designation. Sometimes the USP is called the core selling proposition.

Wearout. The phenomenon commonly observed in practice where additional advertising exposures actually lead to a leveling off and eventual decline in advertising effectiveness (i.e., in awareness, recall, recognition, attitude, intention, or sales).

Advertising: Where Has It Been and Where Is It Going?

John G. Myers
University of California,
Berkeley

Many intelligent people think of advertising as a kind of environmental pollution. Although critics have identified advertising as a contributor to socially harmful things, such as air and water pollution, they have been more concerned in recent years with the role advertising plays in decreasing the quality of what gets into our heads and minds. Critics argue that advertising plays upon and essentially "teaches" the basest of human motivations and values. It surrounds us in a sea of trivia, pouring forth billions of sales pitches which bombard the population on a daily basis. Many of these messages appear premised on a kind of "I am better than you are!" law of competition noted for its selfishness, self-centeredness, and self-engrandisement. Such values are counter to pretty well everything taught in the classroom, home, or church, or so the argument goes. Advertising has been called mental pollution. It is not pollution of our air or water. It is not life threatening like nuclear waste dumps or pesticides, but pollution nevertheless. From this viewpoint, advertising is considered a negative rather than a positive force in socialization. Such reasoning often leads to the conclusion that consumers, particularly young ones, need protection from advertising. In the extreme case, it is argued that all forms of advertising should be banned or made illegal. Others would restrict various forms of advertising either by banning it in certain media such as television, or restricting the content of advertising messages.

Perhaps you think of advertising this way, or more as harmless puffery with no particular social significance. Regardless of your views, it is important to recognize that advertising is a complex, controversial, and fascinating subject and more than just a tool invented by business to sell products. The subject of the opening paragraph, for example, is really a subfield of advertising dealing with its social and economic effects and government regulation of business behavior and the law.

Where has advertising been? Advertising as we know it today is an aspect of each of the major mass media forms of newspapers, magazines, radio, and television. Advertisers have been defined as private or public-sector organizations that use mass media to accomplish an organizational objective.[1] Modern advertising is thus directly tied to the technological invention of each media form. Ancient advertising goes back to the first forms of bartering exchange and primitive markets.

An interesting question is why advertising has continued to exist and flourish against such an onslaught of sustained criticism by philosophers, religious leaders, political scientists, economists, political leaders, and some of the world's greatest thinkers and

---

1. David A. Aaker and John G. Myers, *Advertising Management* (Englewood Cliffs, N.J., 1982), 2nd ed., p. 3.

doers? One can safely say that there always have been and always will be those who believe there must be a better way to produce and distribute wealth, a better way to "run" society, and a better "system of exchange" than one premised on the existence of advertising. Perhaps the closest thing to a society which banned all advertising was China's experiment with its Cultural Revolution. Advertising, as you may have guessed, is not the only way to support mass media, and until recently has not been of significance in most socialist or communist countries where media are government supported and highly controlled. But why, in Western capitalist democracies, have powerful and influential people been unable to slow the growth of this thing called advertising?

First let me tell a story of when I was most impressed by this apparent paradox. Back in the early 1970s, a student of mine went to work for the Stanford Research Institute and was given the task of predicting the size of the advertising industry in the United States 10 years hence. He spent about six months on this project, interviewing national advertisers, agency, media, and research executives, and arrived at the then amazing conclusion that by the target year, 1984, the industry would double in size. About $20 billion was spent on advertising in the United States in the early 1970s. The forecast was that, by 1984, this figure would climb to about $40 billion. This prediction was made in a highly critical consumerism and environmental protection climate around the time and, for many people, was very difficult to believe.

Today, in 1984, it is evident that the student forecast was off the mark by a significant amount. He had not overestimated the growth in advertising, but actually underestimated it. Advertising surpassed the $40 billion mark in about 1978. Advertising volume in 1983 was $75.85 billion and was forecast to reach $86 billion in 1984.[2]

Why has advertising been so resilient? Why does the industry continue to grow at about the same rate as the national economy? What benefits does society gain for all this mental pollution? As a famous advertising researcher asks, "Is All This Advertising Necessary?"[3] You should read this article for the long answer to this question! The short answer is simply that advertising is what you get if you give business and increasingly nonbusiness organizations the freedom to compete. Advertising is on the one hand a tool which has been proven in many cases a more efficient tool than many other marketing tools for managing or building sales and profits. On the other, it is a mirror of "mass" society values in any particular time period. Many would argue that advertising determines basic mass society cultural values because it publicizes them so broadly and effectively on a day-to-day basis. A better statement is that advertising neither leads nor follows; it simply utilizes what is to communicate and persuade in the most effective way possible. What we see in the advertising mirror is a great variety of ways to communicate determined largely by the different segments to which appeals are directed. What you also see in large-scale mass media advertising is the copywriter's attempt for a common denominator that will reach at least some significant fraction of millions of viewers. With enough advertising dollars, it is technically possible to present a new product message to over 90 percent of all U.S. households in about four weeks.

---

2. Robert Coen, "Final Figures: Advertising Surged in '83," *Advertising Age*, May 14, 1984, p. 62ff. In this article, Coen makes the interesting observation that "the amounts spent for advertising may seem large but they are really very modest compared with the approximately $2.2 trillion consumers spent for the goods and services that these advertising budgets supported." Advertising has been slightly over 2 percent of the gross national product in recent years and since 1976 has been growing faster than both inflation and the national economy.

3. Leo Bogart, "Is All This Advertising Necessary?" *Journal of Advertising Research* 18 (October 1978): 17–26.

Advertising is a fascinating subject because of its symbolic value. It is perhaps the premiere and most highly visible symbol of what we know as Western capitalism. To truly understand this, one must understand that advertising is basic to many of the freedoms we take for granted. The press and mass communication and media systems as we know them, in the United States at least, would not exist without the support of advertising. A distinctive feature of Western capitalism is the value that is placed on understanding markets in general and "the consumer" in particular. This value is manifest in yet another industry—the industry of marketing research whose growth parallels advertising in many important respects. Advertising has created the industry of advertising agencies and employment for thousands of people who create and manage the dissemination of advertising. It is not often recognized that hundreds of companies in the business of production and publication of advertising materials derive their source of support from advertising. The point is that advertising reaches into an amazing number of corners of modern industrialized western society and its durability and stability is very much dependent on this simple fact.

What of the future? You may want to do your own forecast on the growth of advertising into the 1990s. What is highly likely is that, as in the past, it will be based on the growth of mass media and new forms of mass media such as teletext and videotex systems. The in-home computer revolution will surely affect advertising, but exactly in what ways remains to be seen. Ultimately, the future of advertising at the national level is determined by political actions and the future directions of the nation generally.

CHAPTER
TEN

Everyone lives by selling something.

—— Robert Louis Stevenson
(1850–1894)

BEHAVIORAL ASPECTS OF PERSONAL SELLING

Introduction

Personal selling is the marketing function dealing with customers on a direct or face-to-face basis. It is similar to advertising, promotion, and publicity in that it is designed to serve as a communication bridge between the organization and the outer world. However, unlike the other modes of communication, personal selling permits buyer and seller greater flexibility in expressing one's needs and adjusting offers and counteroffers.

In this chapter, we will examine the behavioral aspects of personal selling. We will begin with a description of the role of personal selling, the kinds of salespeople, and what salespeople do in their everyday activities. Next we will provide a general overview of the selling process. Finally, the chapter will close with a treatment of what we know about face-to-face interactions from the research literature. In the next chapter, we will deal with the issues surrounding the management of the sales force.

Overview of Personal Selling

The Role of Personal Selling

By any measure, personal selling is an important component in today's world. Nearly 10 percent of the labor force is engaged in sales, and more than $80 billion is spent each year on selling in the United States alone.

At the level of the individual firm, personal selling is equally important. Industrial and consumer goods firms find it necessary to give sales management equal status with such functions as manufacturing, marketing, and accounting/finance. Indeed, it is not unusual for personal selling to constitute the largest operating expense in many organizations.

Some firms are literally dominated by the personal selling function. Companies selling door-to-door, such as Avon, spend most of their promotion dollars on the sales force and are dependent on it in a fundamental way. Similarly, industrial firms rely heavily on the sales force in their marketing efforts and use other modes of communication such as advertising to a much lesser extent. Consumer goods firms, while depending greatly on advertising and promotion, still utilize the sales force to sell to wholesalers and retailers. Even government and nonprofit organizations do personal selling, but, instead of calling their agents *salespersons*, they use the terms *recruiters, representatives, agents, fund raisers,* or *development personnel.*

Figure 10-1 illustrates the role of personal selling in four common situations. In the first, a publisher of paperback books employs its own sales force to sell either to distributors or large chain bookstores. The distributors, in turn, sell to supermarkets, drugstores, chain bookstores, and small bookstores by use of their own sales forces (not shown). The retailers then sell directly to final consumers.

The small producer of premium wines pursues a different track. Too small to afford its own salespeople, it uses a manufacturer's representative as an independent agent acting on behalf of the seller. He or she generally handles the accounts for a number of sellers and may even do so for different product classes. In exchange for the services of the manufacturer's representative, the firm pays either a straight fee or a preestablished percentage of sales. For the small wine producer, the manufacturer's representative contacts wholesale distributors and large supermarkets, and if a sale is made, the producer ships the goods directly to the buyer. One producer in the Napa Valley, for example, sells most of its wine strictly in Southern California through a single manufacturer's agent.

A third situation is shown in Figure 10-1 for the manufacturer of personal computers. Here the manufacturer's own sales team sells either to retailers or corporate accounts. Finally, a manufacturer of nuts and bolts finds that, in order to cover the entire United States, it must use a combination of manufacturer's representatives and its own salespeople (see Figure 10-1).

Types of Salespeople

In general, we might identify seven fundamental types of salespeople:[1]

Account Representatives: salespeople working directly for a company and responsible for calling on established clients. Although they can generate new business, they are primarily responsible for maintaining ongoing relations. Account representatives can be found in such industries as packaged goods, apparel, foods, and textiles.

Detail Salespersons: salespeople whose function is to introduce new products, answer questions, educate clients, and in general build goodwill. Detail salespersons generally neither seek nor take orders. A typical example is the pharmaceutical detailer who calls on doctors, hospital administrators, and pharmacists. Customers place orders through a wholesaler, or in the case of patients, make a specific purchase at a prescription drugstore at the suggestion of a doctor. Sometimes the detail salesperson is known as a missionary seller. Textbook salespeople are missionary sellers since their function is largely to introduce teachers and professors to the books offered by their companies.

Sales Engineers: salespeople specializing in technical knowledge. Sales engineers can be found in the chemical, electronics, equipment, and machinery industries. They typically solicit new business as well as manage ongoing accounts.

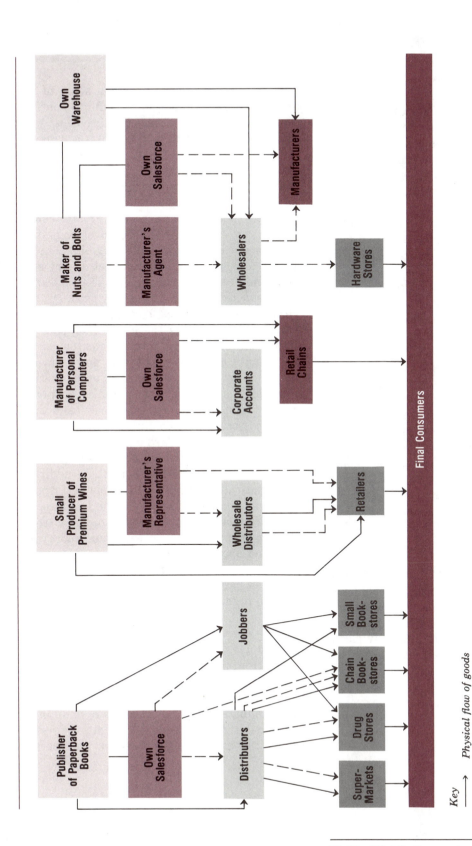

Key
→ Physical flow of goods
⇢ Contacts made by salespeople
— Internal linkage
  within one organization
--- Relationship between two organizations

Figure 10-1. The personal selling
function in four common situations

Nontechnical Indus-trial Products Salespersons: salespeople selling industrial products but not specially trained in a technical area. They can be found in industrial supply, office equipment, and certain materials industries. It is believed that interpersonal and general managerial skills are needed to sell effectively in these situations rather than any particular knowledge per se.

Service Salesper-sons: sales personnel selling intangible benefits as opposed to physical products. They may be found in the advertising, insurance, investment, and security fields.

Retail Salespersons: salespeople who sell directly to the final consumer. Each of the aforementioned salespeople sells primarily to organizations and institutions; because they operate away from the home organization, they are sometimes called *outside salespeople.* Retail salespeople typically operate within a retail store, although they may occasionally work on a door-to-door basis. The term *inside salesperson* is sometimes used for retail and other (e.g., phone) sales personnel working in an organization's office. Retail salespeople may be order takers, as in a fast-food restaurant, or (more generally) function as both order takers and order getters, such as a salesperson in a department store. The terms *retail clerk* and *sales clerk* are sometimes used to mean the same thing.

Agent Salespersons: salespeople working on a temporary or contractual basis. The manufacturer's representative is a common example. Although the sponsorship of the agent salesperson is usually clear, occasionally he or she is neither strictly an agent for the seller nor the buyer, but rather serves as a broker to bring about a meeting of the minds. In some states, the real estate broker roughly fits this category.

What Salespeople Do

To gain a sense of the role of the salesperson, it is useful to consider what they do in their everyday activities. A recent study of 25 companies across a wide assortment of industries found that the following general activities were performed: selling, maintenance of distribution relations, planning, decision making, and managing communication.[2] Let us look at these in greater detail.

Selling involves getting new business and servicing the old. Exactly how this is done depends on whether one sells consumer or industrial goods. The *consumer goods salesperson* introduces new products, discusses their attributes, compares them to the competition, explains the level of support the buyer can expect (e.g., promotions, deals, advertising), answers questions, and provides guidance on the order quantity, price, method of display, etc. He or she may also supply financial and other business advice and even help in stocking and maintaining the product on the shelf. The *industrial goods salesperson* also describes his or her product and provides reasons why it should be bought. In addition, he or she may serve a broader role performing business consultant services. For instance, an industrial salesperson must often demonstrate how one's product fits in with the product design and operational aspects of the customer's firm since the product he or she sells either becomes part of the customer's product or is used to produce it.

Maintenance of distribution relations is a second broad activity of salespeople. This means facilitating the flow of goods from manufacturer through wholesalers, distributors, and retailers. Problems may arise in delivery schedules, damaged goods, misunderstandings of the terms of trade or in one's responsibilities, and so on. In addition to solving these everyday problems, a salesperson may on occasion assume a broader role by helping an intermediary with its managerial problems. Finally, a salesperson responsible for selling to wholesalers may be expected to aid in the latter's selection of viable retailers.

Selling is more than what goes on in face-to-face contacts. Salespeople spend a considerable portion of their time in *planning* activities. A salesperson must decide on whom to call on, how often, and when to do so. This means scheduling visits to potential as well as existing clients in a way minimizing time and money costs while maximizing the generation of new accounts and the effective servicing of old ones. At the same time, salespeople are required to evaluate the potential for new business in their territories and to estimate the strength and moves of competitors. This means that the salesperson must perform the roles of analyst and strategist. He or she must also establish goals, develop budgets, monitor one's own and the company's performance, and coordinate one's activities with the broader goals and policies of the home firm. In short, the salesperson is a general manager of his or her territory.

Closely related to the above activities is a fourth one, *decision making*. Salespeople must make choices on the allocation of their time in the face of constraints and opportunities. Sometimes the more structured decisions are aided by the use of formal rules or models. For example, some firms have "call norms," which specify how frequently a salesperson should visit customers. One industrial company stipulates that "A" accounts (those customers buying more than $100,000 per year) should be visited at least six times per year, "B" accounts ($50,000–$99,999 per year) should be visited at least four times per year, and "C" accounts (less than $50,000 per year) should be visited at least twice per year. Mathematical models on the computer have been developed to schedule the call rate so as to maximize profits in some firms. We will have more to say about this and other managerial sides of sales force behavior in the following chapter. A final aspect of decision making concerns the unstructured or unexpected demands placed on salespeople. Problems in production or shipping, changing customer needs, competitive inroads, labor disputes, conflicting demands from multiple customers, and a whole host of other economic, political, or climatic factors require that the salesperson be prepared to make decisions quickly and with limited information.

The last broad activity performed by salespeople is the *management of communication*. The salesperson is both a conduit for information and an instrument for persuasion and influence. And this, of course, occurs in both directions: from home firm to customers and from customers to home firm.

A vast array of activities falls under the rubric of sales force communication. First of all, the salesperson can be thought of as part of a larger communication network bridging the home organization and customer organizations. A typical salesperson, of course, has contact with many people in the customer's organization who have decision-making responsibilities. These might consist of individual persons such as buyers, purchasing agents, or materials managers or groups of customers responsible for corporate purchases such as those found in the buying center. To get through to the decision makers, the salesperson must deal with receptionists, secretaries, phone operators, and other "gatekeepers" in the customer's organization. Additionally, before and after a sale, it is not unusual for the salesperson to have to deal frequently with accountants, clerks, shipping and storage personnel, production people, and others directly and remotely connected to the actual purchase. Similarly, in the home organization, the salesperson must deal with one's immediate supervisor, market researchers, accountants, shippers, and a whole host of other support people. When one realizes that most salespeople have many customers and make frequent calls on each prospect, we can see that the communication links are overwhelming in number.

As a communication link, the salesperson also must sometimes serve in the role of recruiter of new salespeople and trainer of new hires. He or she is expected also to respond to innumerable requests for information from customers and reams of paper work from the home office. Orders must be filled, expense reports documented, progress reports filed. Finally, the salesperson is required to actively convey a positive image of the company and its products and to aggressively convince others to buy from the company. It can be readily seen that the salesperson must be highly skilled in interpersonal communication.

The Selling Process

To understand the behavioral aspects of personal selling, it is helpful to conceptualize selling as a process. In this part of the chapter, we will look at the process from two vantage points: the process an individual salesperson goes through from beginning to end of a sale and the interpersonal process transpiring between salesperson and customer.

The Selling Process from the Salesperson's Perspective

There are many ways to think about the steps an individual salesperson goes through. Retail clerks go through perhaps the most varied steps, with some exchanges encompassing very short time intervals and others relatively long ones. For instance, a salesperson selling television sets may spend literally only one minute making a sale because the customer, prior to entering the store, had already thought about what he or she wanted, made comparisons of TV sets in newspaper ads, and decided that the set on sale in the salesperson's store was the one he or she definitely intended to purchase. All the salesperson might have to do in such a "presold" case is to confirm the availability of the set when the customer arrives and then fill out the sales slip. At the other extreme, the TV salesperson might occasionally interact with the same customer over and over again over a period of days and even weeks before a sale is made. The process might involve complex sequences of questions, answers, efforts to persuade, resistance to persuasion, heightened interest, waning interest, and so on. With the variety that human interactions can take, it would seem an impossible task to hope to ever describe the selling process in simple terms. Imagine describing the process involved in the sale of a mainframe computer to a university, a process that not only often takes a year or more of negotiations but can involve as many as 15 to 20 people or more.

Obviously, to get a sense of the selling process, we must simplify the description and focus on the important elements. From the perspective of the salesperson, we can list a sequence of the most fundamental steps in selling. Each firm in each situation would, of course, have its own unique steps. For example, the salesperson of Xerox photocopiers roughly follows five steps: approach, survey, demonstration, proposal, and close.[3]

Figure 10-2 shows one way to picture the selling process from the viewpoint of the seller in many contexts. Notice that for ease of explanation we can divide the process into three broad activities: preliminary activities, face-to-face selling activities, and follow-up activities.

The *preliminary activities* are designed to provide the salesperson with the tools needed to effectively complete a sale as well as to create the situation most conducive to meeting customer needs. One early task is to review current accounts to see who needs to be serviced next and who might either increase the quantity purchased of an ongoing order or buy different products carried by the seller for the first time. At the same time, the salesperson must survey his or her territory to identify possible new business from previous nonbuyers. On a regular basis as part of one's preliminary activities, time must be allocated

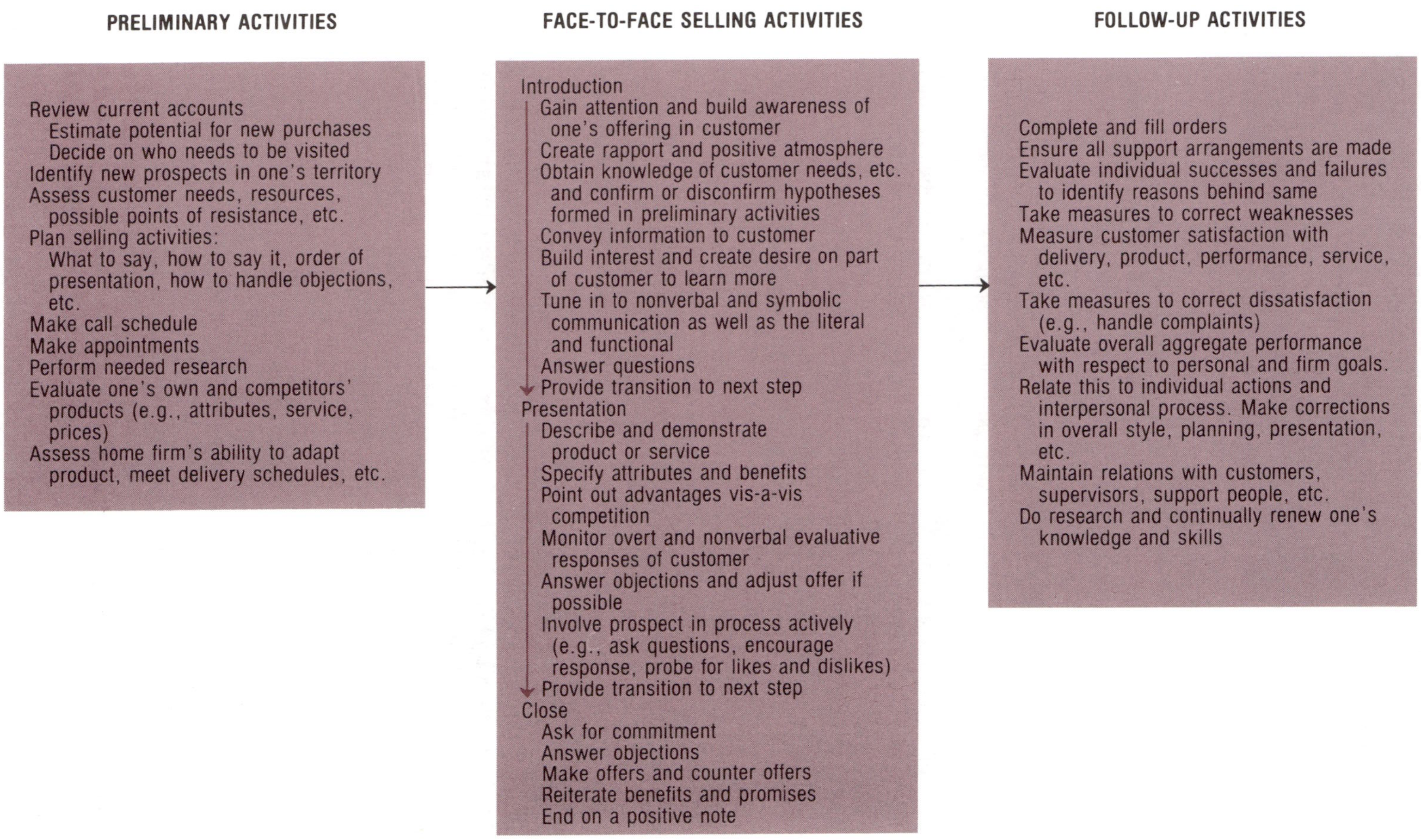

PRELIMINARY ACTIVITIES

Review current accounts
  Estimate potential for new purchases
  Decide on who needs to be visited
Identify new prospects in one's territory
Assess customer needs, resources,
  possible points of resistance, etc.
Plan selling activities:
  What to say, how to say it, order of
  presentation, how to handle objections,
  etc.
Make call schedule
Make appointments
Perform needed research
Evaluate one's own and competitors'
  products (e.g., attributes, service,
  prices)
Assess home firm's ability to adapt
  product, meet delivery schedules, etc.

FACE-TO-FACE SELLING ACTIVITIES

Introduction
  Gain attention and build awareness of
    one's offering in customer
  Create rapport and positive atmosphere
  Obtain knowledge of customer needs, etc.
    and confirm or disconfirm hypotheses
    formed in preliminary activities
  Convey information to customer
  Build interest and create desire on part
    of customer to learn more
  Tune in to nonverbal and symbolic
    communication as well as the literal
    and functional
  Answer questions
  Provide transition to next step
Presentation
  Describe and demonstrate
    product or service
  Specify attributes and benefits
  Point out advantages vis-a-vis
    competition
  Monitor overt and nonverbal evaluative
    responses of customer
  Answer objections and adjust offer if
    possible
  Involve prospect in process actively
    (e.g., ask questions, encourage
    response, probe for likes and dislikes)
  Provide transition to next step
Close
  Ask for commitment
  Answer objections
  Make offers and counter offers
  Reiterate benefits and promises
  End on a positive note

FOLLOW-UP ACTIVITIES

Complete and fill orders
Ensure all support arrangements are made
Evaluate individual successes and failures
  to identify reasons behind same
Take measures to correct weaknesses
Measure customer satisfaction with
  delivery, product, performance, service,
  etc.
Take measures to correct dissatisfaction
  (e.g., handle complaints)
Evaluate overall aggregate performance
  with respect to personal and firm goals.
Relate this to individual actions and
  interpersonal process. Make corrections
  in overall style, planning, presentation,
  etc.
Maintain relations with customers,
  supervisors, support people, etc.
Do research and continually renew one's
  knowledge and skills

Figure 10-2. An outline of the selling process from the salesperson's perspective

to a formal assessment of customer needs, resources, constraints, likely points of objection, and so on. This provides the salesperson with guidelines for making a presentation and knowing how to adjust one's selling points to the needs of the prospect as an exchange transpires. Next, the salesperson must make sure he or she is knowledgeable about one's own product and the firm's capabilities as well as the competitors'. With the aforementioned preliminaries taken into account, the salesperson can make a call schedule and appointments and plan the content and form of a rough face-to-face selling effort.

Notice in Figure 10-2 that the actual *face-to-face selling activities* are presented as a sequence of three main steps: introduction, presentation, and close. Actually, it is important to recognize that within each step a dynamic back-and-forth process goes on between buyer and seller.

In the *introduction*, the salesperson strives to capture the attention of the prospect, create a positive atmosphere, and build rapport. In addition, the salesperson must gain knowledge about the customer's needs and expectations in order to lay the groundwork for the upcoming presentation of main selling points. The exchanges occurring in the introduction typically involve a curious mixture of utilitarian and symbolic aspects. The former is marked by the giving and receiving of information and the discussion of the more-or-less concrete, rational parts of both parties' businesses. The latter is characterized by interchanges and sharing of feelings, most of which are transmitted nonverbally and often unintentionally. Personal needs meld together with organizational exigencies as the early parts of the encounter evolve toward the more formal transactional activities.

The *presentation* phase has an air of "getting down to business." Here the salesperson makes a special effort to portray the product or service in its most flattering light. Product features are described, benefits stated, and advantages vis-à-vis the competition noted. The alert salesperson continually tunes in to the prospect so as to pick up subtle and overt evaluative responses. A raising of the brows, twinkle in the eye, frown, or off-hand comment can signal not only whether the prospect is impressed or not but point to the relative importance of product attributes or some special concern.

Inevitably, the customer will raise points of information and/or objections related to the product itself or stumbling blocks within the customer's organization. Here the salesperson may succeed or fail on the basis of how well he or she has thought out possible responses. Moreover, objections can be overcome through strategic adjustments in product design or the design of an entire package offering. A salesperson must know how far he or she can bend and when to interject an offer or counteroffer. Throughout the process, the salesperson works to involve the prospect. This might mean stopping to ask if the customer has understood a point, probing for likes and dislikes, or in some other way engaging the customer. Overall, in the presentation phase, the salesperson aims to convince the customer that it is in his or her own best interests to purchase the product.

The final step in the face-to-face interaction is the *closing*. It is here that the salesperson explicitly asks for a formal commitment. Benefits and promises may be reiterated, final objections turned aside, and a last-ditch adjustment of the total package made to induce a sale. Whether successful or not, the salesperson generally tries to end on a positive note.

But the selling process really does not "end" with the closing. As shown in Figure 10-2, a whole host of *follow-up activities* continue. A successful sale requires that an order be completed and that all support arrangements (product design, credit, delivery, etc.) be resolved. After the sale, customer satisfaction must be measured and corrections made if necessary. The salesperson should reflect upon the process leading to a sale or failing to do so. He or she must identify the forces that caused or failed to bring about the sale. This entails a self as well as situation evaluation. Changes may have to be made in planning, attitude, motivation, selling technique, product offering, and so on. Follow-up activities also involve a conscious maintenance of relations with customers, supervisors, gatekeepers, support personnel, and everyone else connected to a sale. Finally, we must emphasize that the salesperson should be ever vigilant of changes in his or her environment and continually work to improve his or her skills and knowledge with respect to selling, the customer, one's own offerings, and the competition.

The Selling Process as an Interpersonal Phenomenon

Selling cannot be divorced from buying and vice versa. Indeed, we can view buying and selling as a complex interpersonal process. You probably noticed that our description of the selling process from the salesperson's perspective inevitably used terms and concepts applied to both seller and buyer. Now we wish to briefly outline a framework for viewing the selling process in more explicit interpersonal terms. Figure 10-3 shows a diagram of the central elements. Many of the concepts were introduced in Chapter 3 and will not be redefined here in the interest of brevity.

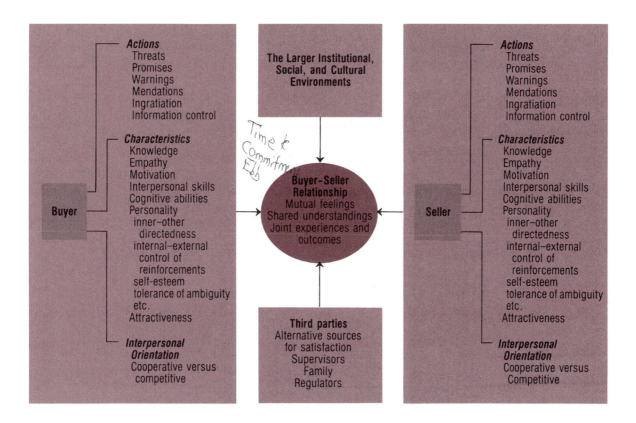

Figure 10-3. An outline of the selling process in an interpersonal sense

The dynamics of selling as an interpersonal process take place through the *buyer-seller relationship* (see center of Figure 10-3). It is here that the content of exchange is expressed in common meanings: mutual feelings, shared understandings, and joint experiences and outcomes. These common meanings, of course, emerge out of the communication process between buyer and seller. Each person shapes the relationship through the strategic use of one or more *actions* at his or her disposal. Generally, the actions include threats, promises, warnings, mendations, ingratiation, and information control (see Chapter 3 for definitions and discussion of these). These actions serve as conduits for the administration of rewarding or punishing stimuli or the use of persuasive and educative tactics.

The impact of the actions are regulated, in part, through the *characteristics* of the buyer and seller. For example, interpersonal attraction not only enhances the flow of communication, but it sometimes adds value to the transaction and even influences the evaluations and preferences of the actors in a positive direction. Similarly, the rewards or punishments transmitted through the six types of actions can be facilitated through greater knowledge, empathy, motivation, etc., on the parts of both buyer and seller. The research relating to these and other characteristics will be considered later in this chapter.

Notice further in Figure 10-3 that each person's *interpersonal orientation* is shown to affect the buyer-seller relationship. Interpersonal orientation includes the predispositions and expectations of buyer and seller for acting cooperatively or competitively. Selection of one orientation or the other not only induces a mutual response on the part of the other person in an exchange but can affect the magnitude of joint outcomes (e.g., profit).

A final point to note in Figure 10-3 is that the buyer-seller relationship is constrained and influenced by forces external to the face-to-face interaction. Constraints from the larger institutional, social, and cultural environments shape the buyer-seller relationship, as do identifiable third-party effects such as the availability of alternative sources of satisfaction.

Not reflected in Figure 10-3 but central to any interpersonal selling activity is the role of time and the concomitant ebb and flow of events marking the process. We sometimes think of time only in terms of constraints: we must accomplish some task by performing certain acts in x amount of time. Time pressure is a very real force affecting how buyer and seller react to each other. But it is important also to recognize that it is not time, per se, that is of interest. Rather, we must think about what things go on in time that make the selling process the phenomenon it is. We touched upon some of these things in Figures 10-2 and 10-3. However, we know very little about the natural course of buyer-seller encounters or the proper timing of actions throughout an exchange.

This especially is a problem in cross-cultural interactions. For example, Japanese-American business customs are quite different and pose problems for both parties. Americans generally try to get down to business early. They prefer a short introduction phase and jump quickly to the presentation and closing. Japanese businesspeople are accustomed to quite long introductions and protracted negotiations during the presentation phase. The closing is often a perfunctory capstone to the detailed negotiations preceding it. For many American salespeople, however, the closing is the climax where persuasive powers are brought to bear. You can well imagine the dissonance and misunderstandings that might arise when naive American and Japanese businesspersons get together and negotiate "out of phase." This is but one example of timing issues in the selling process.

Salesperson Behavior:
What We Know from the Research Literature

A vast literature exists on sales force behavior. To keep the treatment here manageable, we have chosen to begin the discussion with a description of one research program of an industrial sales force that brings together ideas from many researchers. Following this, a number of insights from other researchers dealing with different problems and sales forces will be presented. Finally, this chapter will close with new principles from research in social psychology that show promise for helping us understand the behavior of salespeople.

Contributions from Marketing

An In-depth Investigation of an Industrial Sales Force[4]

Background. Over the period of about two years, the author investigated an industrial sales force of 122 salespeople and 33 sales managers. The study entailed extensive interviewing of the salespeople, managers, and support personnel, as well as participant observation of many sales transactions and administration of a questionnaire to all relevant parties.

Before we present the findings, let us briefly describe the company, product, sales force, and situation. The salespeople sell steel and plastic straps used in shipping to secure boxes, crates, and packages. They also sell the seals used to bind the straps and small tools used to apply the seals. Each salesperson has an exclusive geographical territory. He or she sells typically to purchasing agents, materials managers, or, in the case of small concerns, owner-managers. Buyers come from a very wide assortment of industries such as manufacturers of steel, automobiles, appliances, packaged goods, and containers. Many small buyers exist, too, such as lumberyards, farmers, and job shops. Most salespeople sell to over one hundred customers in their territories.

Within each territory, about four or five competitors exist selling similar products. In addition, generic competition occurs from small sellers of wire, twine, rope, and other alternatives. Competition from the latter, however, is not extensive as they tend to constitute inferior substitutes (e.g., twine and wire become loose and fall off boxes in a short time). Most competition arises from the oligopolistic nature of the industry.

Company sales are very much a function of the efforts of the sales force. Indeed, other marketing mix factors play less of a role. For instance, price competition is a relatively minor factor because of the uniform cost of steel, which makes up the majority of sales. The products sold by all competitors are similar, and each seller employs a distribution network based on decentralized company-owned warehouses. Advertising is not a powerful stimulus, and it consists mostly of institutional-type ads. In short, the competing firms have no significant differential advantages in the marketing mix vis-à-vis each other. They depend heavily for their success or failure on the ability of the salespersons. Contrast this situation to the role of pharmaceutical detailers who have only a relatively small influence on sales in that advertising, brand names, and promotions often have stronger effects.

The Problem. Management desired to learn more about its sales force. One approach to the study of any sales force is the case method because it provides a rich picture of the dynamics of selling in a realistic, unobtrusive way.[5] In this sense, it goes deeper than and avoids the artificiality of such procedures as experiments or surveys. By necessity, most case studies of sales forces focus on only one or two salespeople.

There are two shortcomings that should be noted. First, findings from any case study tend to be idiosyncratic to the persons studied. Generalization is often difficult, and one often cannot rule out the suggestion that any results were a fluke. Second, it is not easy to gain quantitative insights. For example, although a case study might reveal that successful selling is a function of training, motivation, and self-confidence, it cannot tell us explicitly about the relative impact of each determinant on success. For these reasons, the author decided to employ a survey methodology on all persons in the sales force including their managers. Qualitative techniques were not abandoned, however, since extensive interviewing and observation over a period of months occurred in the field and within the sales and marketing departments prior to administration of the questionnaire.

In consultation with management, the author developed a rough conceptual model hypothesizing that salesperson outcomes (e.g., total sales) were a function of three forces: the salesperson (P), the interactions the salesperson has with key individuals (I), and the environment or situation within which the selling tasks occur (E). In equation form, this hypothesis can be expressed as

Job Outcomes = f(P,I,E)

Figure 10-4 summarizes the major elements that make up both job outcomes and the salesperson, interpersonal, and environmental variables. Notice that many job outcomes are listed. Although management is most concerned with performance (e.g., total sales per person, new business generated), it also takes an interest in the welfare of its employees and thus cares about job satisfaction, self-esteem, and morale. Of course, it has a utilitarian interest in the latter as well, since the possibility exists for these variables to feed back on performance.

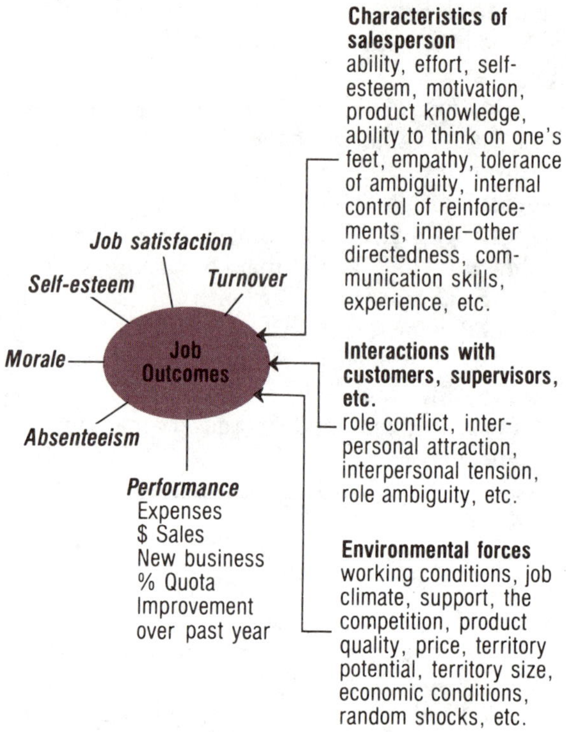

Figure 10-4. Job outcomes as a function of the salesperson, the interactions the salesperson has, and the environment

The model shown in Figure 10-4 suggests that job outcomes are first caused by the salesperson. How well one does on the job depends, in part, on how hard one works, on one's abilities, on one's motivation and self-confidence, and on a whole host of other psychological factors. We will have more to say about these shortly when we describe the specific studies. At the same time, a person's successes are not entirely a consequence of one's attributes, powers, and liabilities. Rather, the nature of the interpersonal relationships a salesperson experiences are also crucial to the generation of successful job outcomes (see Figure 10-4). For example, success depends, in part, on the course of role conflict

A. Performance (P) causes job satisfaction (S)

That is, as one's performance increases, greater job satisfaction results.

B. Job satisfaction causes performance

That is, as one's job satisfaction increases, subsequent performance increases.

C. Performance and job satisfaction influence each other

That is, increased performance results in greater job satisfaction, and greater job satisfaction leads to increased performance.

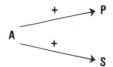

D. Performance and job satisfaction do not influence each other but are dependent on one or more common antecedents (A)

That is, as the antecedent increases, so do performance and job satisfaction, and hence their association.

Figure 10-5. Four possible accounts of the correlation between performance and job satisfaction

and strain, on the uncertainty or ambiguity of expectations that one and one's role partners experience, and on interpersonal attraction. These, too, will be considered subsequently when the studies are considered. Finally, how well one does on the job is a consequence of forces beyond the control of the individual. As shown in Figure 10-4, these encompass working conditions, marketing mix elements, territorial design and potential, economic factors, and competitive reactions.[6]

Study 1. The initial study focused upon *the relationship between performance and job satisfaction* and on certain psychological antecedents to both per-

formance and satisfaction. For decades, firms have observed a positive association between performance and satisfaction. The question is whether the association is causal or correlational. Four possibilities occur (see Figure 10-5): performance causes satisfaction, satisfaction causes performance, performance and satisfaction influence each other reciprocally, or performance and satisfaction are determined by common antecedents and do not interact causally at all. Any one of these would produce the observed positive correlation between performance and satisfaction.

Why would management be interested in the performance-job satisfaction relation? If satisfaction influenced performance, this would imply that the firm might consider the direct influence of satisfaction as a means for influencing performance. Management could influence satisfaction by strategically altering the managerial climate. For instance, the compensation program, span of control, salesperson-manager relationship, or formal feedback (e.g., praise) could be adjusted to enhance job satisfaction. On the other hand, if satisfaction were found not to be a cause of performance, the firm should question whether job enlargement or job enrichment programs are valuable from a utilitarian point of view. Similarly, if performance were found to be a cause of satisfaction and if management conceived of satisfaction as a goal in its own right, this would imply that the firm should consider shifting some resources away from making people directly happy to the creation of the conditions under which they would perform up to their capabilities. This would have the additional benefit of indirectly enhancing job satisfaction.

No previous studies have investigated performance/satisfaction in a sales force context. So we must turn to work done in other areas and to our own intuition to predict what to expect. Research in the organization behavior literature has found that performance influences satisfaction but not vice versa. A person first obtains outcomes from the job. In the selling situation, many of these are concrete (e.g., level of sales, bonuses received, percentage of quota attained). Next, the person makes an assessment—consciously or unconsciously—of the discrepancy between expected and actual outcomes. The greater the difference (actual is usually less than expected), the higher the dissatisfaction. Notice that two steps are involved: first a cognitive assessment; then an emotional reaction to the outcome of the assessment. This is, thus, one explanation for why performance might influence satisfaction.

Consider next the sequence from job satisfaction to performance. Here the connection is more difficult to justify. A person must not only be aware of his or her own feelings, which is a difficult thing to do deeply and consistently. But he or she must also attribute those feelings to specific aspects of the job and subsequently decide to act accordingly. For example, if satisfied, one must decide to work harder or more efficiently. Or if dissatisfied, one must decide to work less hard. Because one's feelings at any one point in time are typically the result of many forces, job related and otherwise, the association between current satisfaction with dimensions of the job and subsequent performance is not expected to be strong. Hence, job satisfaction is predicted to not be a cause of performance. At least, this is the prediction in the short run.

Figure 10-6 summarizes the hypothesized relations between performance and job satisfaction. In addition to these central variables, we have included three

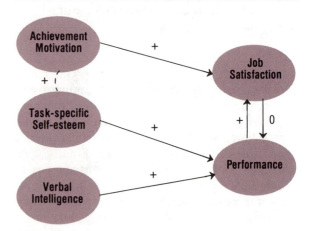

Key
+ = hypothesis of a causal relation.
0 = hypothesis of no causal relation.

Figure 10-6. A summary of variables and hypothesized relationships in study 1

antecedents in the figure: achievement motivation, task specific self-esteem, and verbal intelligence. Let us consider their role.

Achievement motivation is expected to affect job satisfaction directly and possibly performance indirectly through its impact on task specific self-esteem. We might construe motivation as a combination of the things people value and their perception that certain actions will lead to attainment of those valued things. The more one values certain rewards and at the same time perceives that particular acts will lead to those rewards, the more motivated one will be. Any sales job will have a set of intrinsic and extrinsic rewards (see Table 10-1). It is these that salespeople, in different degrees, will strive for. The greater the motivation, the greater the effort expended in goal directed activities and hence the higher the expected satisfaction and performance.

TABLE 10-1
Typical Intrinsic and Extrinsic Rewards Sought by Salespeople

Intrinsic Rewards	Extrinsic Rewards
Being the best	Salary
Personal growth	Bonuses
Feeling important and	Job security
needed	Work relationships
Self-respect	Recognition
Feeling involved, stimulated,	Office, automobile,
and challenged	expense account
A sense of freedom	Awards, prizes
A chance to be creative	
and innovative	
A chance to advance	

Task-specific self-esteem is also expected to directly affect performance (see Figure 10-6). By task-specific self-esteem we mean self-confidence with particular aspects of one's selling job such as achieving quota, quality of planning, potential to achieve the top 10 percent in sales, management of time and expenses, quality of customer relations, and knowledge of one's own and the competitors' products and company. It is hypothesized that the greater the task-specific self-esteem, the higher the level of performance. The rationale lies in the psychological theory of cognitive balance. To the extent that a salesperson's self-image concerning the job requires high performance to maintain a consistent view of the self, one will be motivated to do what it takes to perform well. Similar processes are expected to function at all levels of self-esteem. Notice further that motivation potentially works through self-esteem in route to its impact on performance.

The final antecedent shown in Figure 10-6 is *verbal intelligence*. Verbal intelligence is the cognitive ability to accurately and efficiently perceive, attend to, and process information related to the job. The salesperson deals with a wealth of data, directives, and inquiries from bosses, customers, and others. Moreover, face-to-face exchanges can be subtle and seemingly too fast to follow or control in all respects. It is expected that verbal intelligence will be correlated with effective planning and execution skills and the general ability to "think on one's feet." Hence, as shown in Figure 10-6, the greater the verbal intelligence, the higher the performance.

What were the findings? Figure 10-7 summarizes the results, where the number and sign accompanying each arrow indicates the outcomes. The numbers are standardized between -1 and $+1$ for ease of interpretation. Each number displayed in Figure 10-7 is statistically significant. Therefore, we may interpret the numbers as reflecting the degree of association between the variables linked by the respective arrows. For example, as hypothesized, performance influences job satisfaction ($+.31$) but not vice versa ($.00$). Apparently, feelings follow actual achievements but do not determine those achievements. At least this was found to be so in the short time period of the study. It is possible that, in the long run, job satisfaction can have an effect on performance.

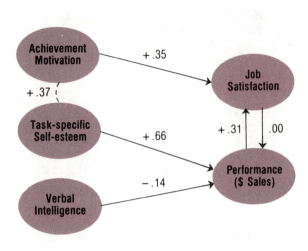

Figure 10-7. A summary of results for study 1

Another finding to note in Figure 10-7 is that achievement motivation positively affects job satisfaction (+.35), as predicted. Similarly, motivation is positively related to task-specific self-esteem (+.37), and self-esteem, in turn, positively influences performance (+.66). This again was according to hypotheses.

Contrary to hypotheses, verbal intelligence is negatively related to performance (see Figure 10-7). The higher the verbal intelligence, the lower the performance. What could account for this counterintuitive finding?

One possibility is that the match between customer and salesperson was dysfunctional. If customers perceived the more "intelligent" salespeople as being aloof or in some way dissimilar from themselves, this could introduce a barrier to communication and even result in negative evaluations of the product. Another possibility is that the more "intelligent" salespeople found the job boring or in some other way unchallenging. Finally, it must be acknowledged that the measure itself,

verbal intelligence, may be an unreliable or invalid indicator of the thinking, planning, and face-to-face abilities originally hoped for. In any event, verbal intelligence had only a small effect on performance.

On balance, however, Study 1 provides a number of insights into the relationship between performance and job satisfaction and some of the things causing these variables. Happiness is a function of performance outcomes and not the other way around. Task-specific self-esteem and achievement motivation are central determinants of performance and satisfaction. Verbal intelligence is a questionable factor but points to a need to match salesperson to customer and salesperson to the task at hand. Let us now turn to the study dealing with interpersonal variables.

Study 2. Two interpersonal variables are especially important in selling contexts: *role ambiguity* and *role strain.* Role ambiguity means the uncertainty a salesperson experiences regarding the expectations of customers, supervisors, and others. Role strain is tension and strain arising from interpersonal relations with customers, supervisors, and others. The latter is often manifest as conflict.

Although all members of organizations engage in numerous interpersonal exchanges, salespeople seem to face a set of interactions that differ in both kind and degree. In addition to normal encounters with supervisors and others in the home organization, salespeople must regularly deal with a large set of customers, gatekeepers, and support personnel who are outside the organization yet who are central to the selling job.

Moreover, for a variety of reasons, exchanges with customers are more intense and risky than the typical intrafirm encounter. First, the salesperson-customer exchange usually transpires away from the salesperson's organization. Physical separation lessens the direct scrutiny of supervisors, and it tends to weaken normative control resulting from informal group affiliation in the home organization. Second, even though the actions of the salesperson are relatively hidden from the supervisor, the performance outcomes, of course, are not. This condition, coupled with the fact that the salesperson's livelihood depends so directly on these outcomes, makes the salesperson vulnerable and dependent on the customer. Third, because of the functions performed by the salesperson and the scarcity of resources and competition in the environment, he or she will be confronted with a set of conflicting demands. Customers bring pressures to bear to lower prices, change product design, expedite shipments, and generally meet their needs; while management urges that sales expand, expenses decline, profits rise, and the company's needs be met.

Overall, the selling situation is one where uncertainty and interpersonal conflict are great, and demands for coping exceed the norm for most occupations. In one sense, a salesperson is similar to a diplomat or ambassador in a hostile land. He or she is pulled in various directions, and his or her degree of success depends on harmonizing these conflicting forces and demands.

Figure 10-8 shows the effects of role ambiguity and role strain on three key dependent variables: task-specific self-esteem, performance, and job satisfaction. Notice in each case that role ambiguity and role strain are hypothesized to negatively impact on the dependent variables. That is, the poorer the ability of the salesperson to cope with ambiguity and strain, the lower the self-esteem, performance, and satisfaction on the job.

Role ambiguity operates in the following manner. As uncertainty in expectations rise, a point is eventually reached where the ability of the salesperson to make accurate judgments decreases and risk increases. Further, high uncertainty induces confusion, frustration, and emotional conflict. The

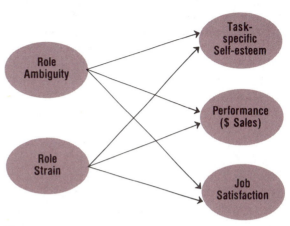

Key
Arrow indicates a hypothesis of a negative causal relation.

Figure 10-8. A summary of variables and hypothesized relationships in study 2

net effect is that mistakes are made more frequently, motivation is inhibited, the person feels less well about himself or herself and the job, and performance declines. Of course, some people are better able to cope with ambiguity than others and therefore do not experience the aforementioned effects as strongly or at all.

Role strain has somewhat different effects. Consider first its impact on task-specific self-esteem. As tension mounts, one's ability to cope lessens. At the same time, people identify personal competence with the self; the job is important for one's livelihood and family; and family, peers, and society expect success. Hence, excessive role strain threatens one's self-image if not coped with effectively. Role strain negatively affects performance, too, because of its tendency to draw attention away from planning and other job-related activities and its anxiety-provoking quality for disrupting the processing of information related to the job effort. Similarly, excessive role strain inversely interacts with job satisfaction in the sense that people are inclined to devalue and dislike things that make them uncomfortable or prevent them from achieving what they need and want.

Figure 10-9 summarizes the actual findings where again each number is a standardized, statistically significant coefficient reflecting the degree of association between the respective variables. We can see in each instance that the hypotheses are confirmed. The ability to cope with role ambiguity and role strain is an important determinant of one's task-specific self-esteem, performance, and job satisfaction.

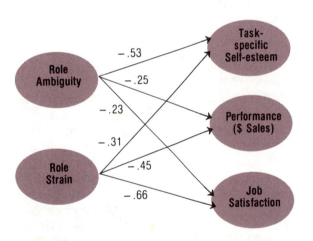

Figure 10-9. A summary of results for study 2

Study 3. The first two studies focused on the behavior and outcomes of salespeople. Now we wish to examine the behavior of sales managers and compare it to that of their subordinates. Such investigations are rare in marketing.

Study 3 began with an inquiry into how managers and subordinates differ as a group. The findings revealed that, in terms of their average characteristics, salespeople and their managers are remarkably similar. However, two differences should be noted. First, sales managers as a group tend to possess higher levels of job satisfaction than the salespeople working under them. Perhaps this is a function of the greater responsibility, higher salary, and more prestige given the sales managers. Second, sales managers as a group tend to be more internally controlled than their salespeople. That is, they believe that they have more control over their successes and outcomes in life than salespeople believe. This difference was observed on a psychological measure termed the *internal/external control of reinforcements* scale. The scale classifies people on a continuum marked on one end by those believing that they have the power to completely control their own life events and marked on the other end by those believing that it is luck or external factors that determine one's life events. Most people can be placed somewhere between the extreme end points. Apparently, sales managers approach their environments (e.g., their jobs) with an attitude of greater mastery and perceived efficacy than salespeople approach their environments.

Group differences are suggestive but can obscure subtle effects. As a consequence, the relationships between certain key independent variables and the following three dependent variables were investigated: performance, new business, and job satisfaction. Figures 10-10 and 10-11 present the key findings.

Figure 10-10 considers the relationships for salespeople and shows interesting results. Notice that task-specific self-esteem, role ambiguity, and role strain are the only variables influencing all three dependent variables. The higher the task-specific self-esteem and the greater the ability to cope with role ambiguity and role strain on the one hand, the higher the performance, new business generated, and job satisfaction on the other hand.[7] Motivation influences performance and job satisfaction but not new business. Perhaps the incentives for generating new business are lacking in this particular company. Generalized self-esteem—self-confidence in everyday situations—affects only performance and then at a level relatively smaller than the effect of task-specific self-esteem. It seems that self-confidence must be focused on the job at hand to be effective. We will have more to say about managerial implications in the following chapter.

A quite different picture emerges for sales managers (see Figure 10-11). Here we see first that the trait of *other directedness* is strongly and positively associated with performance. Other directedness refers to the degree that one relies on contemporaries for sources of personal direction. It appears that higher performing managers pay closer attention to the needs and cues of others around them. Notice next in Figure 10-11 that motivation leads to new business but not overall sales, a reversal from the salesperson findings. Now it seems that the incentives generate new customers but do not necessarily motivate vigilance in ongoing relations.

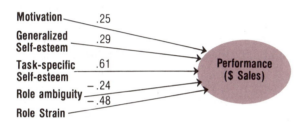

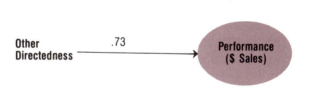

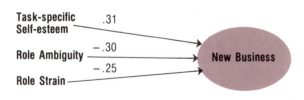

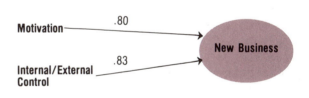

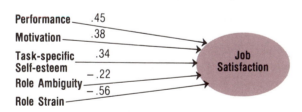

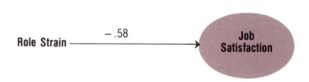

Figure 10-10. A summary of results for study 3 (salesforce sample)

Figure 10-11. A summary of results for study 3 (manager sample)

Sales managers high in internal control generate more new business (see Figure 10-11). A sense of personal efficacy thus appears necessary for successful generation of new business. Recall that internal/external control was not a factor for salespeople. Thus, in addition to other directedness, internal control might be a key factor differentiating promotable from nonpromotable salespeople. Finally, unlike salespeople, sales managers apparently have no problem coping with ambiguity and strain. At least performance and new business are not adversely affected by these variables. Nevertheless, role strain does negatively impact on job satisfaction. It appears that sales managers are bothered by role strain, but the effect stops there and does not lead to decreased productivity.

The picture emerging from Study 3 is a subtle one. Managers are perhaps more complex than people have imagined. One insight is that managers, as opposed to salespeople, have a stronger sense of themselves as acting as free agents. They view themselves as masters of their own fate in that they feel they have greater control over their outcomes. Indeed, managers with higher internal control generated more new business than managers with lower internal control. At the same time, managers coped with ambiguity and strain better than salespeople did, and they did not let ambiguity and strain negatively influence their actual job outcomes. Finally, it can be said that the more successful managers appear to be neither exclusively extroverts nor introverts. Rather, the manager possesses a strong internal sense of his or her own ability to change things to one's own advantage while at the same time being attuned to the needs and demands of others.

Findings from Other Studies

The Salesperson as Strategist.[8] One researcher hypothesizes that performance is a function of two key skills of salespeople: the ability to form impressions of the customer's decision processes and the ability to formulate strategies based on those impressions. With respect to impression formation, a salesperson can form judgments of the customer's beliefs as to product attributes, the importance of product attributes, and the susceptibility of change in the beliefs and importances. Findings from a study of industrial salespeople confirmed the effect on performance of inferred beliefs of customers. Importance and susceptibility were not predictors of performance in this study, however.

With respect to strategy formulation, a salesperson could strive to change perceptions of product attributes or increase or decrease the salience of certain attributes. Results from the same study noted in the previous paragraph showed that the salesperson's accuracy in assessing strategies was related to his or her successful performance.

One implication of the research is that salespeople should consider gathering information on the customer's decision criteria. Further, salespeople should be trained to use this information in their own assessment of customer decisions and in their strategic choices in the field. Shortly, we will suggest a number of other strategies that salespeople can use to stimulate sales more directly.

A Contingency Theory of Selling.[9] It has been proposed that the performance of salespeople is a function of salesperson behaviors (e.g., information gathering, adaptation to customers, and use of power), salesperson characteristics (e.g., knowledge, Machiavellianism,[10] and other directedness), and situational characteristics (e.g., relative power of customer and salesperson, level of conflict in interactions). We have already touched upon many of these variables in this chapter. Given the complexity of the selling situation and the unusual turns any interaction can take, one tactic for studying sales force behavior is to develop theories peculiar to specific situations or classes of situations. By tailoring our theories to particular contexts, we may be better able to explain and predict the course and outcomes of sales force behavior.

Emerging Contributions from Social Psychology

In the final part of this chapter, we will consider a number of possible strategies that salespeople could use to influence customers. Specifically, we will briefly treat the use of distraction, the foot-in-the-door tactic, and the door-in-the-face technique. Either technique may be appropriate, according to the circumstances. It should be stressed that the following entails speculation because the principles have not been verified in the selling context.

Distraction. We considered the phenomenon of distraction in Chapter 8, "Marketing Communication." Recall that it has been observed that, when people are exposed to persuasive communications, they silently counterargue and derogate the source, among other cognitive responses. To the extent that this happens, interference with message processing may occur, and the receiver may bolster his or her original position in opposition to the message or even develop negative evaluations toward the message, spokesperson, or sponsor. Thus, counterargumentation and source derogation function as mediators of attitude change and favorable action on the part of a receiver. Obviously, such processes occur in face-to-face encounters as well as mass media programs.

What a salesperson would like to do is prevent, inhibit, or at least delay counterargumentation and source derogation on the part of the customer. One way to do this is to strategically create distraction during the face-to-face presentation phase of the selling process. The proper amount of distraction can interfere with counterargumentation and source derogation. Let us consider some possible tactics.

Preconceived questions or volunteered information randomly leaked during the presentation by the salesperson might have a distracting effect. Similarly, the use of a rapid, and/or varied pace, multimedia support, and novel or surprising stimuli can promote distraction. A skillful communicator can get a customer to focus on physically attractive elements of the product, the salesperson, or the setting. If all else fails, sometimes positive ideas can distract.

Inevitably, some counterargumentation will arise and reach vocalization. When this happens, it is crucial for the salesperson to have compelling replies or at least push the issue aside or move on to positive material. Preplanning and practice are essential if one is to accomplish this.

The salesperson must shape the course and content of any transaction to his or her advantage. A negative first impression, an invalid inference early on, dislike for the salesperson, or simply irrelevant thoughts generated by something the salesperson says can poison an exchange. It should be stressed that it is not enough to have an attractive message and deliver it forcefully. One must actively work to thwart the customers' natural inclinations for skepticism and automatic tendencies to generate negative cognitive responses to any sales appeal.

The Foot-in-the-Door Tactic.[11] Social psychologists have discovered that people are more likely to comply to a large request after they have complied to a small request than when they are asked to comply directly to the large request only. The rationale is that compliance to the small request leads one to make a self-attribution that he or she must have a positive attitude toward the requester or more generally toward the idea of yielding to the persuasive imperatives of the situation at hand. Thus, the first request enhances the person's likelihood of compliance to the second request.

The foot-in-the-door tactic is a sequential strategy based on escalating commitment. A salesperson might attempt to get a prospect to acquiesce to a point, purchase a minor product, or agree to a demonstration or trial period. Then, sometime after the initial compliance, the salesperson can initiate the closing. In some situations, a seller may even find it efficacious to try a sequence of three or more escalating requests. Each request in any execution must result in both compliance and the generation of a self-attribution that one complied not out of coercion or external reward but as a consequence of one's own decision, needs, or motives.

The Door-in-the-Face Technique.[12] This tactic begins with a large request, indeed so large that it is invariably refused, and is then followed with a smaller request. It is, of course, the second request that is the object of the communicator's ploy. The rationale behind the technique is similar to the norm of reciprocity or the golden rule: do unto others as they do unto you. Because the first large request is turned down and then followed by a second smaller request, the receiver of the message perceives the latter as a concession. Hence, by the norm of reciprocity, another concession (i.e., compliance with the second request) is required.

An important point to note with respect to the first, large request is that it should be so large that one attributes his or her rejection to the unreasonableness of the request rather than one's own attitude. At the same time, the first request should not induce anger. Both conditions are necessary for one to act out of normative expectations rather than emotional or rational pressures.

In the selling context, the door-in-the-face technique might be used as follows. Starting with a large request, a salesperson could systematically reduce requests until either a sale is eventually made or one reaches the lowest possible terms of trade.

Summary

Personal selling is the marketing function dealing with customers on a direct or face-to-face basis. It plays a central role in marketing for service and consumer goods as well as for industrial goods.

Many organizations have their own sales forces. However, some firms, because of their small size or because it is more efficient to do so, rely on the sales forces of intermediaries or use independent agents (review Figure 10-1). Seven basic types of salespeople were identified: (1) account representatives, (2) detail salespersons, (3) sales engineers, (4) nontechnical industrial products salespersons, (5) service salespersons, (6) retail salespersons, and (7) agent salespersons.

Salespeople perform a number of essential activities. Part of their time is devoted to *selling* (i.e., getting new business and servicing old). We all have images of the salesperson describing his or her offerings, answering questions, and attempting to persuade prospects to make a purchase. But this is only part of the job. The salesperson must work actively to *maintain distribution relations.* This means facilitating the flow of goods from manufacturer through wholesalers and retailers. A considerable portion of the salesperson's time is spent also in *planning* on whom to call on, how often, when to do so, what to say, and so forth. A closely related activity is *decision making.* Here the salesperson must make choices on the allocation of his or her time in the face of constraints and competing opportunities. Rules of thumb, heuristics, and formal models aid this process. Finally, the salesperson *manages communication* linkages. This means performing the roles of order taker and order getter, recruiter, trainer, researcher, troubleshooter, and ongoing liaison between the firm and other organizations.

The chapter then gave a description of the *selling process*. From the perspective of the salesperson, we saw that three broad subprocesses are typically employed: preliminary activities, face-to-face selling activities, and follow-up activities (review Figure 10-2). Further, within the face-to-face selling phase, we saw that the subprocess goes through three stages: introduction, presentation, and closing. From the viewpoint of the buyer-seller interaction, we observed that each party to the exchange influences the relationship through his or her actions, characteristics, and orientations (see Figure 10-3). Through skillfully controlling what is communicated and how it is communicated, the parties shape the course of the interaction. All of this occurs, of course, within the confines of larger institutional and environmental constraints, the availability of alternative sources of satisfaction, and direct third-party influence such as from supervisors or regulators.

We next reviewed a series of studies of the behavior of an industrial sales force. Management was interested in learning what determined performance, job satisfaction, and other job outcomes. These were generally believed to be influenced by the efforts and characteristics of salespeople, the nature of the interactions they have with customers and relevant others, and the external environment in which the interactions are embedded.

In the first study, it was discovered that performance influences job satisfaction but not vice versa. Further, achievement motivation and task-specific self-esteem were found to be important determinants of performance and satisfaction. Verbal intelligence was negatively related to performance, contrary to predictions, but its impact was very small.

The effects of role ambiguity and role strain were investigated in Study 2. It was discovered that salespeople who were better able to cope with uncertainty and tension and strain had higher levels of self-esteem and satisfaction and performed better.

A third study compared salespeople to their sales managers. As a group, sales managers tended to be more satisfied with their jobs and to possess a higher level of internal control of reinforcements (i.e., they believed more than salespeople believed that they were the masters of their own fate). Additionally, sales managers tended not to allow ambiguity and strain on the job to negatively affect their performance. The sales manager, more than their salespeople, combined elements of extroversion and introversion in that they were both outwardly attuned to the needs of those around them and at the same time were inwardly focused and analytical. Such are the skills needed for effective management.

The chapter closed with consideration of three strategies drawn from research in social psychology: the use of distraction, the foot-in-the-door tactic, and the door-in-the-face technique. Distraction can be used to keep the sales prospect off-balance, yet focused on the salesperson's message. The idea is to inhibit source derogation and counter-argumentation. The foot-in-the-door tactic strives to get the customer to yield to an innocuous request and thereby become more vulnerable to a later focal request of a more demanding nature. The door-in-the-face technique attempts to induce concessionary reciprocity as a consequence of the salesperson's reduced request following the customer's refusal of a preliminary large request. All three tactics are speculative in that they have not been formally applied or studied in the selling context. In the next chapter, we will consider the managerial decisions faced in directing a sales force.

Questions and Problems for Discussion

1 One way to characterize personal selling is through the tasks that salespeople perform on the job. Describe the five central tasks.

2 Another way to characterize personal selling is as a process. Three subprocesses are involved: preliminary activities, face-to-face selling activities, and follow-up activities. Briefly describe these.

3 At the same time, selling is very much an interpersonal endeavor. What are the phenomena that characterize the buyer-seller relation and what forces shape it?

4 On what basis might the performance and productivity of the sales force be measured? What three general determinants should management consider in the prediction and influence of performance?

5 The individual characteristics of salespeople obviously affect performance. Discuss the central characteristics and how they function to affect performance. What are the implications for management?

6 What are the key interpersonal factors influencing performance and how should management endeavor to take them into account or control them?

7 How do salespeople and managers differ? What should one look for when considering the promotion of a salesperson to sales manager?

8 Discuss the tactics salespersons might use to stimulate sales as revealed in recent marketing studies and research in social psychology.

NOTES

1. The first five are those regularly employed by *Sales and Marketing Management:* e.g., Thayer C. Taylor, "A Letup in the Rise of Sales Call Costs," *Sales and Marketing Management,* February 25, 1980, pp. 24-30. The final two are added for completeness. For another classification of salespersons, see Robert N. McMurry, "The Mystique of Super-Salesmanship," *Harvard Business Review* 39 (March-April 1961): 114.

2. G. David Hughes and Charles H. Singler, *Strategic Sales Management* (Reading, Mass.: Addison-Wesley, 1983), pp. 59-68.

3. Hughes and Singler, *Strategic Sales Management,* p. 82.

4. The details of the study can be found in R. P. Bagozzi, "Salesforce Performance and Satisfaction as a Function of Individual Difference, Interpersonal, and Situational Factors," *Journal of Marketing Research* 15 (August 1978): 517-31; ———, "Performance and Satisfaction in an Industrial Sales Force: An Examination of Their Antecedents and Simultaneity," *Journal of Marketing* 44 (Spring 1980): 65-77; ———, "The Nature and Causes of Self-Esteem, Performance, and Satisfaction in the Sales Force: A Structural Equation Approach," *Journal of Business* 53 (July 1980): 315-31; ———, "Salespeople and Their Managers: An Exploratory Study of Some Similarities and Differences," *Sloan Management Review* 21 (1980): 15-26. Some of the research is based on earlier research: G. A. Churchill, Jr., N. M. Ford, and O. C. Walker, Jr., "Organizational Climate and Job Satisfaction in the Salesforce," *Journal of Marketing Research* 13 (November 1976): 323-32; N. M. Ford, O. C. Walker, Jr., and G. A. Churchill, Jr., "Expectation-Specific Measures of the Inter-Sender Conflict and Role Ambiguity Experienced by Industrial Salesmen," *Journal of Business Research* 3 (April 1975): 95-112; O. C. Walker, Jr., G. A. Churchill, Jr., and N. M. Ford, "Motivation and Performance in Industrial Selling: Present Knowledge and Needed Research," *Journal of Marketing Research* 14 (May 1977): 156-68.

5. For excellent examples, see Robert T. Davis, "Sales Management in the Field," *Harvard Business Review* 36 (January-February 1958): 91-98; ———, "A Sales Manager in Action," in H. W. Boyd, Jr., and Robert T. Davis, eds., *Readings in Sales Management* (Homewood, Il.: Richard D. Irwin, 1970), pp. 259-68. See also J. S. Livingston, "Pygmalion in Management," *Harvard Business Review* 47 (July-August, 1969): 81-89.

6. The environmental influences will not be discussed here. See Bagozzi, "Salesforce Performance and Satisfaction as a Function of Individual Difference, Interpersonal, and Situational Factors" for an investigation of the effects of territory potential on sales. See also H. C. Lucas, Jr., C. B. Weinberg, and K. W. Clowes, "Sales Response as a Function of Territory Potential and Sales Representative Workload," *Journal of Marketing Research* 12 (August 1975): 298-305.

7. We have drawn the effects of role ambiguity and role strain as negative arrows to be consistent with the previous figures. The negative effects mean that, as role ambiguity and role strain increase (i.e., the ability of the person to cope decreases), the performance, new business, and job satisfaction decrease. In the description given in the text, the effects of role ambiguity and role strain are presented in the positive sense.

8. Barton A. Weitz, "Relationship between Salesperson Performance and Understanding of Customer Decision Making," *Journal of Marketing Research* 15 (November 1978): pp. 501-16; Barton A. Weitz and Peter Wright, "The Salesperson as a Marketing Strategist: The Relationship between Field Sales Performance and Insight about One's Customers" (Cambridge, Mass.: Marketing Science Institute, Report No. 78-120); Barton A. Weitz, "Effectiveness in Sales Interactions: A Contingency Framework," *Journal of Marketing* 45 (Winter 1981): 85-103.

9. Barton A. Weitz, "A Critical Review of Personal Selling Research: The Need for Contingency Approaches," in Gerald Albaum and Gilbert A. Churchill, Jr., eds., *Critical Issues in Sales Management: State-of-the-Art and Future Needs* (Eugene: University of Oregon, 1979), pp. 76-126; reprinted in N. M. Ford, O. C. Walker, Jr., and G. A. Churchill, Jr., eds., *Research Perspectives on the Performance of Salespeople: Selected Readings* (Cambridge, Mass.: Marketing Science Institute, 1983). See also Adrian B. Ryans and Charles B. W. Weinberg, "Salesforce Management: Integrating Research Advances," *California Management Review* 24 (1981): 75-89.

10. Machiavellianism refers to "one who views and evaluates others impersonally and amorally in terms of their usefulness for his own purposes." See Richard Christie and Florence L. Geis, *Studies in Machiavellianism* (New York: Academic Press, 1970).

11. J. L. Freedman and S. C. Fraser, "Compliance without Pressure: The Foot in the Door Technique," *Journal of Personality and Social Psychology* 4 (1966): 195–202; P. Pliner, H. Hart, J. Kohl, and D. Saari, "Compliance without Pressure: Some Further Data on the Foot in the Door Technique," *Journal of Experimental Social Psychology* 10 (1974): 17–22; M. Snyder and M. R. Cunningham, "To Comply or Not Comply: Testing the Self-perception Explanation of the 'Foot-in-the-door' Phenomenon," *Journal of Personality and Social Psychology* 31 (1975): 64–67; C. Seligman, M. Bush, and K. Kirsch, "Relationship between Compliance in the Foot in the Door Paradigm and Size of First Request," *Journal of Personality and Social Psychology* 33 (1976): 517–20.

12. R. B. Cialdini, E. J. Vincent, K. S. Lewis, J. Catalan, D. Wheeler, and L. B. Darby, "Reciprocal Concessions Procedure for Inducing Compliance: The Door in the Face Technique," *Journal of Personality and Social Psychology* 31 (1975): 206–15; M. Even-Chen, Y. Yinon, and A. Bizman, "The Door in the Face Technique: Effects of the Size of the Initial Request," *European Journal of Social Psychology* 8 (1978): 135–40.

GLOSSARY

Account Representatives. Salespersons responsible primarily for maintaining ongoing relations with customers. Although they can seek out and take orders, they generally do not do so because they perform more of a support role.

Achievement Motivation. The psychological processes governing choices and consisting of two interacting components: a value component and an expectation component. The value component reflects the person's need or drive for particular intrinsic and extrinsic rewards on the job. The expectation component reflects the perceived connections between the performance of specific acts and attainment of the rewards. *See* extrinsic rewards, intrinsic rewards.

Actions (in a Buyer-Seller Relation). Threats, promises, warnings, mendations, ingratiation, or information control by one or both parties in an exchange relation. Actions are used to influence or persuade others.

Agent. A seller working on a contractual basis for a manufacturer. He or she is sometimes termed a manufacturer's agent or representative.

Buyer-Seller Relationship. The set of mutual feelings, shared understandings, and joint experiences and outcomes existing between a particular buyer and seller.

Closing. The set of activities near the end of a face-to-face exchange between buyer and seller whereby the salesperson asks for a commitment and generally brings closure to the meeting. *See* face-to-face selling activities, introduction, presentation.

Detail Salespersons. Salespersons whose function is to introduce new products, answer questions, educate clients, and, in general, build goodwill. They do not seek out or take orders. The detail salesperson is sometimes called a missionary seller. Pharmaceutical and textbook salespeople are common examples.

Distraction (Use of). A persuasive communication strategy whereby a person interjects or employs background disruption along with the delivery of a message so as to interfere with counterargumentation or source derogation effects.

Door-in-the-Face Technique. A persuasive communication strategy whereby a person begins with a very large request in the hope that when the anticipated refusal by the other person is followed by a smaller focal request there will be a greater probability of compliance than had only the focal request been made. *See* foot-in-the-door tactic.

Extrinsic Rewards. Tangible ends on the job for which a salesperson strives. Examples include salary, bonuses, job security, work relationships, recognition, awards, prizes, office, automobile, and expense account. *See* intrinsic rewards, achievement motivation.

Face-to-Face Selling Activities. The process transpiring between buyer and seller. From the salesperson's perspective, three broad steps occur: introduction, presentation, and closing. *See* preliminary activities, follow-up activities. See also Figure 10-2.

Follow-up Activities. The set of actions performed after face-to-face exchanges between buyer and seller whereby the salesperson completes and fills orders, makes support arrangements on customer's behalf, evaluates individual successes and failures and takes measures to correct same, measures customer satisfaction and institutes corrective procedures where called for, evaluates aggregate performance, maintains relations with key others, performs research, and maintains one's knowledge and skills. *See* preliminary activities, face-to-face activities. See also Figure 10-2.

Foot-in-the-Door Tactic. A persuasive communication strategy whereby a person makes a small request of another person in the hope that compliance to the small request will lead to a greater probability of compliance to a subsequent, larger focal request than had the original person only asked for compliance to the focal request. *See* door-in-the-face technique.

Gatekeeper. A person working in a customer organization through whom a salesperson must work to gain access to the decision maker(s). Secretaries, clerks, receptionists, and others perform this role.

Internal/External Control of Reinforcements. Degree to which a person perceives that rewards and other outcomes are contingent on one's own characteristics and behavior as opposed to being independent of them.

Interpersonal Orientation. A behavioral predisposition of one party toward another in a relationship consisting either of a cooperative or competitive attitude.

Intrinsic Rewards. Intangible ends on the job for which a salesperson strives. Examples include personal growth, being the best, feeling important and needed, self-respect, feeling involved and stimulated, a sense of freedom, a chance to be creative, and an opportunity for advancement. *See* extrinsic rewards, achievement motivation.

Introduction (in Face-to-Face Selling). The activities designed to gain attention, create rapport, build interest, stimulate desire, and generally set up the presentation phase of personal selling. It also entails answering questions and responding to the symbolic, nonverbal side of the relationship. *See* face-to-face selling activities, presentation, closing.

Job Outcomes. Experiences, behaviors, and consequences produced by salespersons and valued by management. Among others, these include turnover, morale, absenteeism, job satisfaction, self-esteem, and performance (i.e., expenses, dollar sales, new business, percent quota achieved, and improvement over past year or quarter).

Job Satisfaction. Degree of pleasure with aspects of the job such as level of compensation, promotion opportunities, relations with supervisor, support, job security, and opportunity to demonstrate ability and initiative.

Missionary Salespersons. *See* detail salespersons.

Motivation. *See* achievement motivation.

Nontechnical Industrial Products Salesperson. A seller of light industrial products who is not trained in a technical area. He or she can be found in industrial and office supplies, office equipment, and certain materials fields.

Other Directedness. Degree to which a person relies on contemporaries and others for sources of personal direction.

Performance. A job outcome consisting of expenses, dollar sales generated, new business, percent quota achieved, or improvement over past year or quarter. *See* job outcomes.

Personal Selling. The marketing function dealing with customers on a direct or face-to-face basis and consisting of efforts to persuade a customer to try or continue using one's product or service.

Preliminary Activities. The set of actions performed prior to face-to-face exchanges between buyer and seller whereby the salesperson reviews responsibilities and goals, identifies new prospects, plans selling activities, makes call schedules and sets appointments, performs research, and assesses one's own strengths and weaknesses as well as those of the customer and competition. *See* face-to-face selling activities, follow-up activities. See also Figure 10-2.

Presentation (in Face-to-Face Selling). The set of activities consisting of description and demonstration of a product or service. The salesperson makes a special effort to point out key product attributes and advantages vis-à-vis the competition. Objections are answered, adjustments made to the offering package where necessary, and active involvement of customer in the process is solicited. *See* face-to-face selling activities, preliminary activities, closing.

Retail Salesperson. Seller of products directly to final consumer. He or she works in a store or shop. Sometimes called a retail clerk, sales clerk, or, simply, a salesperson.

Role Ambiguity. The uncertainty a salesperson experiences as to what is expected of him or her by customers, supervisors, and others. It is believed that effective coping with role ambiguity is essential for success on the job and positive feelings of job satisfaction.

Role Strain. The tension and strain arising from interpersonal relations with customers, supervisors, and others. It is often accompanied by conflict. In addition, it is believed that effective coping with role strain is essential for success on the job and positive feelings of job satisfaction.

Sales Engineer. A salesperson specializing in technical knowledge associated with a product or service. He or she both solicits new business and manages ongoing accounts. The seller of electrical machinery, pumps, or cranes fits this category.

Service Salespersons. Sales personnel selling intangible benefits as opposed to physical products. For example, service salespersons can be found in the insurance, advertising, investment, and security fields.

Task-Specific Self-Esteem. Degree of self-confidence with respect to such things on the job as ability to reach quota, achieve top 10 percent of all salespersons, skill in planning and management of time, quality of customer relations, knowledge of own products and company and competitors' products, and ability to assess customer needs.

Verbal Intelligence. The cognitive ability to accurately and efficiently perceive, attend to, and process information related to the job. Believed to be correlated with planning and execution skills and the ability to "think on one's feet."

CHAPTER
ELEVEN

In the factory we make cosmetics.
In the store we sell hope.
——Charles Revson
President of Revlon, Inc.

SALES FORCE MANAGEMENT

The decision to use a sales force depends on the relative costs and effectiveness of personal selling vis-à-vis advertising, promotion, or marketing through intermediaries, such as wholesalers and retailers. Sometimes the choice is between use of one's own sales force or some other mode of marketing, such as direct sales, company owned stores, sales to distributors, or manufacturer's representatives. In other instances, organizations find it necessary to use combinations of approaches involving company sales forces, sales by mail or phone, and sales through intermediaries. We will discuss the rationale leading to one form of marketing system or another in Chapter 14, on channels of distribution. This chapter examines how the sales force can be managed.

The first part of the chapter is a discussion of the steps in sales force management and the forces constraining it. Next, structural aspects of the sales force are described including organizational design and size aspects. Issues related to the management of salespeople are then presented. Specifically, recruitment, selection, training, motivation, supervision, and performance evaluation are considered. Finally, the chapter closes with a treatment of topics related to the management of programs and activities. These encompass compensation, allocation of effort to products, and allocation of effort to customers and territories.

Overview of Sales Force Management

Figure 11-1 summarizes the central elements in the sales force management process and their interrelationships. Notice that organizational objectives influence marketing goals which, in turn, influence sales force goals and strategies.[1]

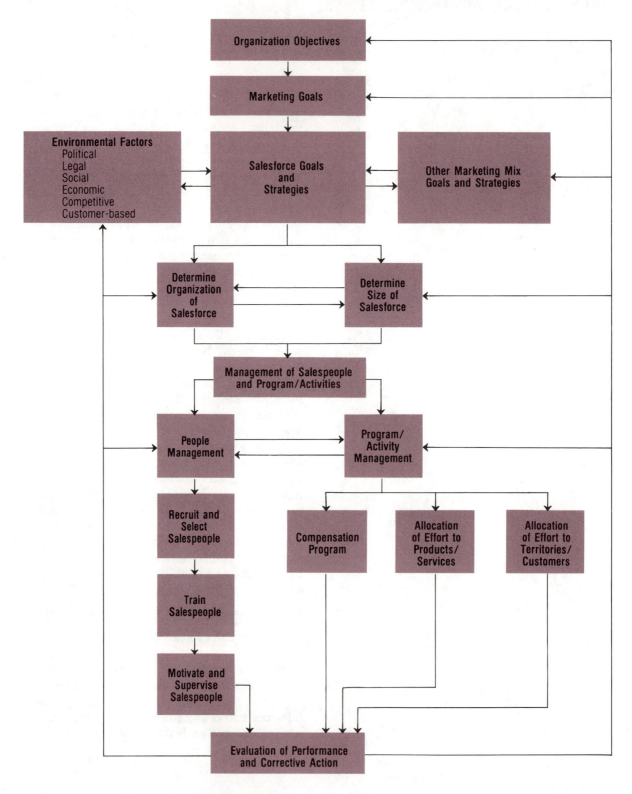

Figure 11-1. A framework for viewing the sales force management process

Sales force goals are specific ends that the sales force can produce. Salespeople directly generate revenue for the organization, and it is customary to subdivide revenue-related outcomes into finer categories and relate these to broader firm objectives. For example, sales force goals for dollar or unit sales might be linked to organization goals for growth; profitability by products or accounts might be connected to return on investment for the firm; and salesperson improvement over sales in the previous year or percent quota achieved might be associated with corporate market share objectives.

Sales force strategies are specific activities selected to serve as a means for achieving sales force goals. Through purposeful design of the sales force, management of personnel, and program execution, sales force goals are pursued. We will have more to say about these central activities shortly.

Notice further in Figure 11-1 that sales force goals and strategies are shown to interact with two general forces: one within the firm and the other without. That is, other *marketing mix goals and strategies* for the organization and *environmental forces* interact with sales force goals and strategies. Coordination with product design, advertising, promotion, pricing, and distribution policies and tactics is necessary to efficiently reach customers and attain an edge over the competition. For example, some firms use advertisements to build awareness and brand images, mail and phone contacts to screen prospects and set appointments, and face-to-face selling to demonstrate their products and close sales. Many environmental forces must be taken into account as well. Total market potential must be forecast, specific territory potential estimated, the strength of the competition assessed, and so on.

Once sales force goals and strategies have been determined and marketing mix and environmental constraints discerned, the tactical and implementation phases can begin. Two early steps in this process involve the determination of the *organization design* and the *size* of the sales force (see Figure 11-1). These decisions are obviously related and at the same time jointly influence how people and programs must be managed to achieve sales force goals.

As shown in Figure 11-1, a number of key decisions fall under the category of *people management*. Salespeople must be recruited, screened, and selected. Training in the product, customer characteristics, the competitive environment, and how to sell must be performed. Special consideration must be given to salesperson motivation and supervision, and this must be integrated into the everyday activities of managers. This means setting realistic goals, providing support and feedback, and paying attention to work load, work habits, expenses, human development, and leadership issues. Finally, performance must be evaluated for each individual salesperson as well as for products, customers, territories, and regions.

The other set of decisions shown in Figure 11-1 are *program/activity management* decisions. These obviously are closely related to people management issues and are given special distinction here for purposes of discussion. Compensation programs are necessary to attract, motivate, and retain effective salespeople. The selection of an appropriate compensation program is part art and part science and typically involves some combination of salary, commission, bonuses, and/or noncash incentives. Another key decision is the allocation of sales efforts to products. Because selling usually involves many products or at least different versions of the same product, decisions must be made on how much time, money, and effort to devote to each product or version. Management, for example, would like salespeople to emphasize products with higher potentials for profitability, and bonuses and commissions usually reflect this. Similarly, because a firm will generally have many customers located in dispersed areas, decisions must be made on the allocation of time, money, and effort to sales territories. Included in these decisions are the optimal size of territories and call norms. As with people management decisions, the management of programs and activities receives closure through performance evaluation and the institution of any needed corrective actions. Let us now turn to more detailed consideration of the strategic, tactical, and implementation issues outlined in Figure 11-1.

The Structure of the Sales Force

Organization Design[2]

An early decision that must be made is how to design the sales force and integrate it with the other activities in the organization. The goal is to define roles and responsibilities so as to make individual salespeople and the sales force as a whole as productive as possible. This means giving consideration to hierarchical and horizontal relationships in the firm.

Span of Control and Vertical Considerations. Any design decision will interact with the size of the sales force. Small firms can use a *line design*. Figure 11-2A shows a line design for a very small organization where the firm's three salespeople report directly to the president of the company. As sales expand and salespersons are added to the firm, a point will be reached where it is not efficient or practical for the president to manage the sales force. In this case, a sales manager may be added as shown in Figure 11-2B. The sales manager might be additionally responsible for recruiting, training, and sales forecasting, as well as managing six salespeople in this particular example.

A. A very small firm

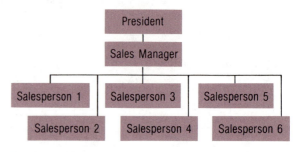

B. A small firm

Figure 11-2. Line organization designs for small companies

A limiting factor in any organization is the *span of control*. By span of control we mean the number of people reporting to a manager. In Figure 11-2A, the span of control is 3, while in Figure 11-2B, it is 6. Too small a span of control is obviously wasteful, but too large a span of control can lead to insufficient direction of salespeople. Management would like to have a span of control that permits the greatest amount of support and attention at the lowest possible cost.

At the same time, the optimum span of control will serve as a constraint on how many *vertical levels* an organization must have. Management would like to keep the number of vertical levels to a minimum in order to facilitate communication and reduce costs. But to have as small a span of control as is possible in order to accomplish direct supervision objectives means that more vertical levels are required. Therefore, it can be seen that a trade-off exists between span of control and vertical level decisions. To reduce the span of control may mean increasing the number of vertical levels.

Table 11-1 illustrates the trade-off. Five different spans of control and three organization levels are shown for simplicity. Management must first decide on what its optimum span of control is and on how many total salespeople are needed (i.e., the decision on the size of the sales force). In the next section of the chapter, we will describe how the sales force size decision might be approached. For now, let us assume that it has been determined that about 120 salespeople are needed for a particular company. Suppose further that the optimum span of control was determined to be 5. This might be based on how frequently and for how long sales managers must interact with salespeople on a regular basis. Given the required size and span of control, we can see from Table 11-1 that three vertical levels are needed to effectively manage this sales force.

TABLE 11-1

The Trade-off between Span of Control and Vertical-level Decisions in Organization Design

SPAN OF CONTROL	NUMBER OF SALESPEOPLE BY ORGANIZATION DESIGN			
	One Level	Two Levels	Three Levels	...
3	3	9	27	...
4	4	16	64	...
5	5	25	125	...
6	6	36	216	...
7	7	49	343	...
⋮	⋮	⋮	⋮	
⋮	⋮	⋮	⋮	

Figure 11-3 displays one possible configuration to accomplish this. Notice that the three vertical management levels consist of a vice president of sales, 5 regional sales managers, and 25 district sales managers (only the 5 district managers under the second regional manager are shown for simplicity). The 125 salespeople are then directly supervised by the 25 district managers. The maximum span of control is 5, and up to 125 salespeople can be accommodated by such a sales force design. Figure 11-3 illustrates a complex organization design known as a *line and geographic design.*

Complex Designs. In general, vertical levels for the structure of any sales force can be organized according to one or more of three criteria: geographic, product, or customer specialization. Let us briefly consider the rationale for these distinctions.

Geographic Specialization. Figure 11-3 is a typical design based on geographical considerations and is in practice one of the most frequently employed frameworks. The regions represent a division of the total area of company operations into mutually exclusive sections. Within each region are mutually exclusive subareas, termed districts. Salespeople will operate within a particular district and be given exclusive territories in which to sell.

The advantages of the geographical organization are manifold. Travel expenses tend to be minimized in comparison to other alternatives. Salespeople are provided with well-defined responsibilities and are given "protected" territories. As a consequence, feelings of fairness are high and motivation fostered. The salesperson knows he or she will be rewarded in direct proportion to his or her efforts, and commitment to the company and customers is enhanced. Coordination with other marketing mix programs is made easier, too. Finally, the geographical approach is flexible in that it is readily altered to take into account changing levels of sales, competition, and undeveloped potential.

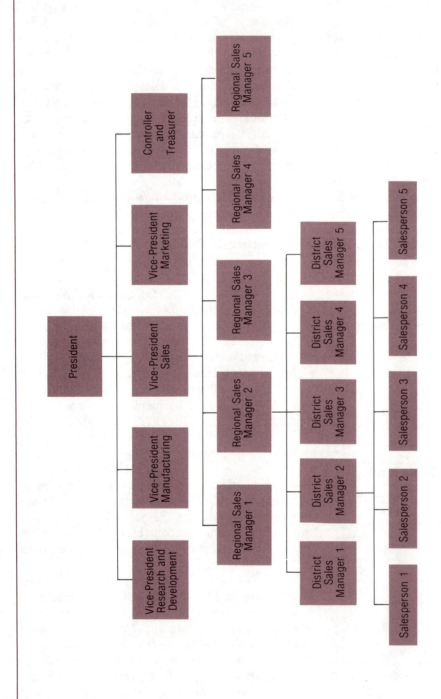

Figure 11-3. A 3-level, 125-person sales force organization

On the other hand, geographical specialization has drawbacks. If customers within a territory differ significantly in terms of sophistication and needs, a single salesperson may not be able to adequately service everyone. Similarly, as one's products increase in number and/or complexity, any particular salesperson may be unable to effectively sell all products. For these reasons, other forms of organization have been developed.

Product Specialization. Salespersons must know their product and its uses if they are to effectively persuade others to buy it. Obviously, this becomes difficult or even impossible as products become technologically sophisticated and/or the product line expands in width and depth. Some firms thus find it advantageous to organize the selling effort by product categories or even by models within a category. For example, many manufacturers of instrumentation typically use different salespeople to sell different instruments.

A shortcoming with product specialization is that a firm will sometimes send many salespersons to the same customer with each one selling something different. Several salespersons might even visit the customer on the same day. Thus, some inefficiencies can result in terms of added travel costs and duplication of effort. Organizations must weigh the pros and cons of product specialization versus other modes of organization.

Customer Specialization. Customers may differ to such an extent that it becomes necessary to have salespeople focus on only one class of buyers. This is especially so for products and services that must be custom designed or that require special training and installation. For a long time, the International Business Machines Corporation (IBM) structured its sales force by customer type. Its salespeople sold only to particular clients such as banks, insurance companies, wholesalers, re-tailers, manufacturers, and universities. Customer specialization is less viable for purchasers of small amounts or for those who are dispersed over wide geographic areas.

Hybrid Organizations. Many firms sell such a wide assortment of products to such a variety of customers in scattered areas that some combination of geographical, product, and customer organizations is required. Figure 11-4 presents a simplified example. Notice first in the left of the diagram that a geographical organization is used. Here all salespeople sell the same product line to all customers in their respective territories. The center of Figure 11-4 shows the organization for three different products sold by the company. Products A, B, and C are so unique that each salesperson sells only one. Nevertheless, he or she sells to all customers in his or her territory. A specialized product sales manager heads the sale of the three products, and within product categories a geographical organization is employed. Notice that the span of control for district managers is 3 and for regional managers is 5. For the product line shown at the left of Figure 11-4, which contains simpler products, the spans of control for district managers and regional managers are 5 and 6, respectively. Finally, at the right of Figure 11-4 a customer specialization form of organization is illustrated. Here salespeople sell either to chemical or electronics industries but have exclusive geographic territories.

Another point to note in the hybrid organization show in Figure 11-4 is the presence of staff specialization within the sales force hierarchy. Notice that a director of training and a director of sales planning and forecasting are included. As selling becomes more complex and/or sales expand, additional roles and increased specialization must occur.

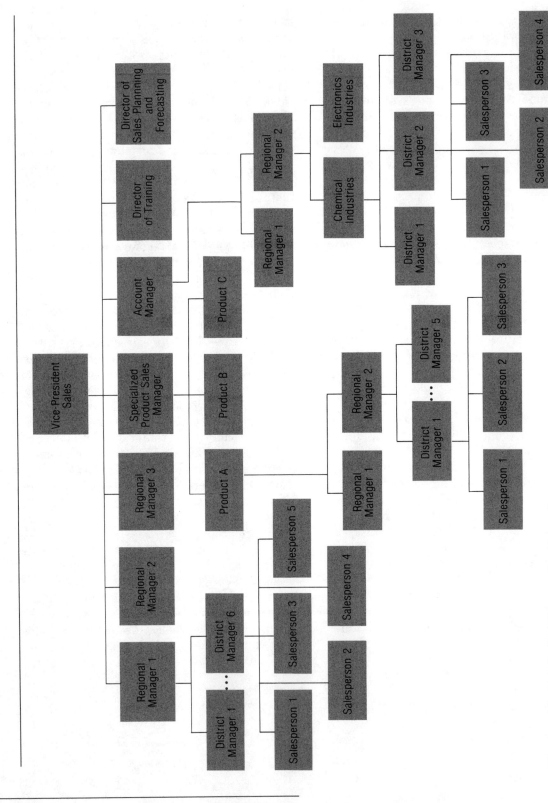

Figure 11-4. A hybrid organization of selling by geographical, product, and customer specialization

Sales Force Size

A central decision that has far-reaching consequences is how to determine the number of salespeople to utilize. Too few salespeople can lead to lost sales and an overworked sales force. Too many salespeople can waste resources. We saw in the previous section that the size of the sales force influences organization structure. But perhaps of even greater importance is the role of sales force size as a revenue generating tool. After all, the sales force is a marketing mix tactic directly influencing demand.

Many factors are relevant to the decision regarding the size of the sales force. Among others are the time needed to service customers, travel time, expenses, product complexity, customer needs, market potential, and sales goals. At least three approaches have been proposed to estimate sales force size requirements, each based on a subset of the aforementioned factors: the breakdown method, the workload method, and the sales potential method.[3]

The Breakdown Method. The objective in the breakdown method is to give each salesperson an equal potential to sell. The approach requires that estimates be made of total company sales and sales per salesperson. The number of salespeople required then is determined as $n = S \div s$ where n = number of salespeople, S = firm sales, s = sales per salesperson, and it is assumed each salesperson will sell the same amount. For example, if a firm forecasts yearly sales of $400 million and believes that a salesperson should be able to generate $10 million in revenue in a year, the number of salespeople needed is 40.

The breakdown method suffers on a number of accounts. It neglects the fact that salespeople can differ, perhaps drastically, in ability. If this is true and people are hired in numbers according to the formula, actual sales generated may deviate greatly from forecasts. At the same time, workloads may vary, compensation may be difficult to administer fairly, and employee morale may suffer.

Equally disconcerting is the fact that the method takes sales as a given. But in reality, sales are a function of the sales force, including its size. What one would like is a method taking into account the differential productivity of salespeople.

The Workload Method.[4] An improvement of sorts is to estimate sales force size as a ratio of the total effort in hours needed to sell the product to the time available to a salesperson for selling: $n = H \div h$ where H = hours per year needed to achieve a specific level of sales and h = hours per year available from a salesperson. Thus, to estimate n, we must have estimates of H and h.

The easiest quantity to obtain is perhaps h. For example, let us assume that a salesperson works 40 hours per week, 48 weeks in a year, and one third of the time actually selling (the remaining two thirds might constitute time devoted to paper work, meetings, etc.). Therefore, $h = 640$ hours in a year per salesperson.

To determine H, we need to estimate the total number of customers, the number of calls made on each customer in a year, and the time devoted to each call. For instance, Table 11-2 presents a case for an industrial firm. The customer classification is by sales volume with A accounts buying the most and D accounts the least. The number of customers must also be estimated. This might be done with one or more of the methods described in Chapter 7. The calls per year represent norms established on the basis of either assessments of travel and presentation time, past practice, or other criteria. Hours per call can be similarly ascertained. Overall, a total of $H = 33,450$ hours per year is needed to service accounts in this example.

As a result, the number of salespeople required for this company is $n = 33,450 \div 640 = 52$ salespeople. This solution yields the number of salespeople needed to adequately (and equally) cover estimated sales.

TABLE 11-2

Estimation of Total Hours per Year Required to Service Estimated Market Demand for a Firm Selling Industrial Products

Customer Account Classification	Number of Customers	Calls per Year	Hours per Call	Total Hours per Year
A	1,100	8	1.00	8,800
B	2,700	6	.75	12,150
C	3,500	4	.50	7,000
D	5,500	2	.50	5,500

A number of shortcomings with the approach should be noted. First, it assumes that territories can be designed with equal workloads or, if designs other than geographic ones are employed, that workloads will be equal across salespeople. The former may be difficult to achieve because of differences in competition, undeveloped potential, density of customers, topography, and other factors across territories. The latter may be problematic because of geographical constraints and changing responses across customers. Second, as with the breakdown method, the workload method fails to take into account that salespeople differ in ability and effort put forth. The quality of planning and interpersonal negotiations is as crucial as the time and frequency devoted to contacts. Third, the method is not based on sound demand stimulation knowledge, and it does not factor in profit considerations. For instance, the call norms may not be optimum and in any case do not allow for adjustment as a variable stimulus depending on the sensitivity of customers.

The Sales Potential Method.[5] It has been observed that salespeople in territories with higher sales potential sell more than those in territories with lower sales potential. However, the level of sales as a percentage of potential is typically lower for the high-potential than low-potential territories. The relationship is shown in Figure 11-5. As territory potential increases, the sales volume per 1 percent of potential decreases and in a nonlinear way.

This relationship can be used to determine the optimum size of a sales force as a function of productivity considerations. In any application, one can employ historical data on sales and potential sales to construct a graph similar to Figure 11-5. Barring this, best-guess estimates by management could be used.

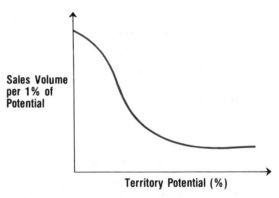

SOURCE: Based on W. J. Semlow, "How Many Salesmen Do You Need?" *Harvard Business Review* 37 (1959): 126–32.

Figure 11-5. The relationship between territory potential and sales volume per one percent of potential

TABLE 11-3

Example of the Sales Potential Method

Number of Salespeople	Estimated Firm Sales	Profit before Selling Costs	Selling Costs	Profit	Investment	Return on Investment
200	19,000	5,350	4,000	1,350	17,600	7.7
100	16,000	4,500	2,000	2,500	14,400	17.4
65	12,200	3,470	1,300	2,170	9,880	22.0
50	10,000	2,700	1,000	1,700	9,000	18.9
10	2,700	345	200	145	4,080	3.6

Table 11-3 displays data for one example.[6] Here information from a graph similar to Figure 11-5 was used. Notice that the optimum sales force size for maximizing return on investment is 65, whereas it is about 100 when the criterion is maximum profit.

The sales potential method has the virtue of relating sales force size to productivity. However, some flaws should be noted. First, the procedure assumes that sales territories can be constructed so as to be equal in potential. Although many firms attempt to do this in order to provide equitable opportunities for salespeople, it is difficult to operationalize and in practice introduces measurement error in any real world application. Second, across each territory it is assumed that competition and other exogenous factors are equal and that salespeople's efforts and abilities are about the same. Obviously, to the extent that these assumptions are violated, error will be injected in any analysis. Finally, the sales potential method can be criticized on the basis of circular reasoning. Because the variable, territory potential, appears on both sides of the equation implied by Figure 11-5, an element of tautological reasoning is introduced.[7] Despite the aforementioned shortcomings, the sales potential method may provide acceptable guidelines in certain uses.

Management of Salespeople

Recruitment and Selection

All companies must be concerned with the staffing function if they are to maintain effective performance, correct weaknesses, replace lost personnel, and in general renew and revitalize their organizations. We can look at the recruitment and selection process as shown in Figure 11-6. The organization has certain personnel needs that can be expressed through goals for new hires. These goals concern desired outcomes for performance, turnover, morale, and other factors related to productivity and employee welfare. In turn, the goals are achieved through the formulation of concrete decisions and tasks. These encompass the determination of the number of salespeople to hire, specification of job qualifications and desired employee characteristics, identification of sources for new hires, design of enticements (e.g., advertisements, bonuses), application of decision rules for selection among applicants, institution of ethical and affirmative-action guidelines, and evaluation of the overall recruitment and selection program. Let us examine the rationale behind the various elements of the recruitment and selection process and consider specific steps in its implementation.

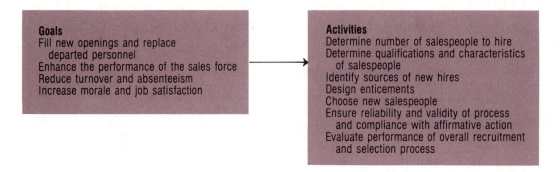

Goals	Activities
Fill new openings and replace departed personnel	Determine number of salespeople to hire
Enhance the performance of the sales force	Determine qualifications and characteristics of salespeople
Reduce turnover and absenteeism	Identify sources of new hires
Increase morale and job satisfaction	Design enticements
	Choose new salespeople
	Ensure reliability and validity of process and compliance with affirmative action
	Evaluate performance of overall recruitment and selection process

Figure 11-6. The elements of the recruitment and selection process

Quantity and Quality. The *number of salespeople* to recruit depends on a variety of factors. First, some people will be needed simply to replace salespersons lost to retirements, prolonged illness, unexpected death, promotions, resignations, or involuntary separations. For example, it is not unusual in the United States for turnover alone to account for a loss of more than 25 percent of the sales force in one year.[8] Second, changes in territory design, new product introductions, product life cycle evolution, competitive responses, economic conditions, and customer needs will necessitate adjustments in the size of the sales force. Management must somehow make estimates of the number of new people to hire. This is done in part as a function of sales forecasts, past outcomes, and managerial judgment. Decision calculus models on the computer and simulations may be employed to facilitate the decision process as well.

Closely related to the quantity issue is the timing problem. Because advertising, interviewing, and decision making take time, these factors must be incorporated into any recruitment plan. Moreover, the length of any training program and the anticipated startup time needed by a salesperson to "learn the ropes" once he or she begins selling must be considered. These factors affect how many recruits are sought and when.

The number of salespeople pursued is also influenced by the supply of viable candidates, the success rate at finding qualified people and persuading them to work for the company, and the attrition rate following hiring but occurring during and after training or in the early days on the job. These variables make the recruitment job more difficult yet must be factored into any program.

Specification of the *quality of salespeople* to hire is a very difficult undertaking. To be sure, management desires to obtain highly motivated and skilled professionals. But the identification of the key attributes of such individuals has so far eluded the experts.

A starting point is to perform a thorough analysis of the selling job itself in order to specify the responsibilities and activities required of any salesperson. Certain physical, health, education, and work experience characteristics may be necessary to perform required tasks. These then become screening criteria. Of course, it is essential to ensure that any such criteria are truly needed to perform the tasks. Most such screening criteria are generated from a job analysis and then instituted as "background information" on an employee application.[9]

Screening criteria of this sort do not go very far. It is common for many more people to pass the criteria than a firm can hire. How does one then select from among the many qualified applicants? Furthermore, seldom is it possible to know with a reasonable degree of certainty whether or to what extent a quantitative causal relationship exists between such criteria and success.

Some firms use additional, sometimes even more subjective, measures of people. For example, recommendations, interviews, self-statements, and psychological tests are employed to ascertain aptitude, motivation, and personality traits thought to be central to success. We have already touched upon some possibilities in this regard in the previous chapter. Recall that achievement motivation, task-specific self-esteem, and the ability to cope with ambiguity, tension, and strain were key factors found in a few studies. Many other personal characteristics have been suggested. Depending on the context, such attributes as analytical ability, energy level, empathy, ego drive, sensitivity, tenacity, aggressiveness, communication skills, and past achievements have been proposed as indicators of quality, among others.

The problem with psychological and related criteria to date is that they have not been measured very reliably. In addition, the validity of the measures must be addressed. One would like a valid relationship to exist between the scores on any measure used as a predictor of success and actual performance achieved. Also, as we note shortly, certain legal issues make the use of subjective measures hazardous, though perhaps not insurmountable.

The upshot of contemporary knowledge and practice is that universal or infallible characteristics cannot be identified in the specification of what it takes to define a quality salesperson on an a priori basis. As a consequence, organizations typically employ a qualitative procedure marked by informal weighting of background information, interview impressions, recommendations, and, on occasion, aptitude and personality testing.

Sources of Candidates. Recruitment is typically delegated to district managers, although in some firms, regional managers or even people within the home organization take primary responsibility. In any case, various tactics are followed. Advertisements in newspapers or professional magazines are frequently used. Customers and competitors occasionally provide leads. Teachers, professors, and college placement offices are important sources. Employment agencies are sometimes relied upon as well, and even the home organization can be used to advantage. For example, some people desire a change in jobs or a transfer in territories. Employees may know of likely prospects, too.

Whatever method is employed, and a combination of tactics is usually the rule, it is important to continually cultivate contacts and evaluate the success of sources over time.

Ethical and Legal Constraints. Every organization has a set of social policies it follows in the hiring of employees. With respect to the personal selling function, two related concerns deserve mention.

The first is *affirmative action.* The Equal Employment Opportunity Commission (EEOC) was created to administer Title VII of the Civil Rights Act of 1964. One consequence of this act is that firms must have an Affirmative Action Compliance Program and demonstrate that they do not discriminate in recruiting and hiring on the basis of race, sex, or ethnic group membership. For example, federal regulations require that inquiries made of candidates prior to employment mention only criteria that are "bona fide occupational qualifications." That is, any criterion must be necessary for performance of the job. Similarly, of those people actually selected by a firm after recruitment, it is stated that "a selection rate for any race, sex, or ethnic group which is less than four-fifths (or 80 percent) of the rate for the group with the highest rate will generally be regarded by the federal enforcement agencies as evidence of adverse impact, while a greater than four-fifths rate will generally not be regarded by federal enforcement agencies as evidence of adverse impact."[10]

The second issue relates to the use of background variables and psychological data in the selection of salespeople. Concern here is with what are known as *test bias* and *test validity*. Not only must criteria used in selection be shown not to discriminate on the basis of race, sex, or ethnic group in an absolute sense (the bias issue), but such criteria must be proven to truly predict performance and do so on data for the very company wanting to use such procedures (the validity issue). These are complex issues dealing with research methodology and legal concerns, and for further details, the reader is referred to the growing literature.[11]

Evaluation of the Recruitment and Selection Program. A number of procedures can be undertaken to evaluate the recruitment and selection process. A simple method is to monitor and keep records of the performance of salespersons over time classified by how they were hired. In this way, one can discover if a particular method of recruitment (e.g., advertising versus university interviewing versus personal references), a particular area of the country, or a particular recruiter has been more successful than other sources. An electrical products manufacturer used this method and found that the most successful salespeople were recruited through educational institutions, salespeople of competitors, and acquaintances of company executives. The least successful salespeople came from employment agencies, sales personnel from firms of noncompetitors, and employees of customers. Unsolicited applications and people recommended by the company's own salespeople were in the middle.[12]

A second, rather crude, measure of the performance of the recruitment and selection process is to simply observe the turnover rate over time. The problem with this approach is that turnover will in general be a function of many factors in addition to recruitment and selection policies. For example, turnover may also be caused by more attractive opportunities with competitors or outside the industry, poor compensation and promotion programs, conflict with supervisors, or changing interests on the part of salespeople.

Finally, the recruitment and selection program can be evaluated over time in terms of the effort, costs, and lost sales resulting from its implementation. For example, the time devoted to making inquiry calls, processing applications, writing letters, and performing interviews can be monitored. The percentage of offers accepted and the success in hiring people from target groups can be tracked as well. Still another issue to consider is the length of time that positions remain open.

Training[13]

Introduction to Training. Sales training is an essential activity that goes on not only when one first enters a company but continues throughout one's career. Figure 11-7 presents the central decision points in any sales training program. The first question to answer, of course, is: "Should the firm use a formal training program at all?" In other words, can the training objectives be achieved more efficiently through informal or on-the-job instructions? The answer to this will depend on how complex the selling job is and what broad goals the firm hopes to achieve. Training programs are needed to convey knowledge, impart the right frame of mind and level of motivation, develop selling and managerial skills, increase effectiveness, and decrease costs. In addition, a good training program can overcome some of the limitations of the recruitment and selection program, and at the same time, contribute to the efficiency of future supervision and job design programs.[14]

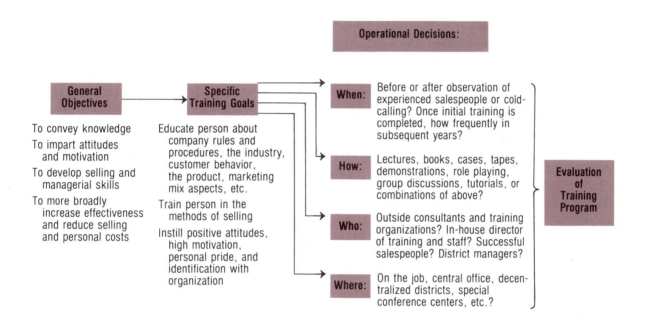

Figure 11-7. A summary of the rationale and decision issues in any sales training program

The Content of Training Programs. A number of specific goals for any sales training program can be identified (see Figure 11-7). One category concerns *knowledge*. Salespeople must be educated about the history of the firm, current rules and procedures, organization structure, product attributes, industry characteristics and the competition, customer needs and decision processes, legal constraints, moral and ethical expectations, territory peculiarities, unwritten rules and conventions, and social and cultural customs in the organization, the sales territory, and buyer organizations.

A second theme that must be conveyed through the training program is the recommended *method(s) for selling.*

Every firm will have at least a rough outline of the steps in selling, including guidelines for planning, approaching customers, conducting a transaction, closing, and followup. We described the process in the previous chapter, and you might want to review the discussion there at this time.

A useful way to divide the selling process into parts suitable for training purposes is *prospecting, approach, demonstration, handling objections, closing,* and *followup.*[15] It is crucial that salespeople be trained in the logic and methods for accomplishing these activities.

The third specific goal of training noted in Figure 11-7 is *inspirational*. Salespeople must be motivated, which means setting high expectations and creating enthusiasm. It also means clearly pointing out extrinsic and intrinsic rewards emanating from the particular job at hand and noting how performance of certain activities will lead to achievement of task goals and the rewards. Along with this, the training program should stress the need for pride in one's work, profession, and the company. In addition, salespeople must be taught how to develop a healthy self-concept with respect to performance of specific tasks, to handle ambiguity and role strain, and to deal effectively with people on a personal and professional level.

Some Operational Decisions. Once the general goals and specific content of the training program have been determined, it is necessary to consider four operational issues: when, how, who, and where to train (see Figure 11-7). The question of *when* to conduct training entails many options. Usually, the formal training program occurs at the beginning of one's employment or soon thereafter. Some firms expose new hires to selling before any formal training program is begun. This can be done by having new people accompany seasoned salespeople on calls. Alternatively, after a day or so of orientation, new hires can be sent out to sell on their own. This is termed *cold-calling*, and is typically done for a few weeks and then followed by a formal training program. The practice is more than a rite of passage and can function to weed out people not suited for the job.

Training does not end with the initial exposure and introductory training program. Salespeople receive constant on-the-job training in the form of seminars, sales meetings, programmed learning aids, regular publications, and periodic observation and feedback by supervisors. Further, many firms have refresher courses and specialized training

programs now and then throughout the salesperson's career. Continued training is needed to update salespeople on product changes, new product introductions, evolutions in the marketplace, new selling techniques, and so on.

How should training be conducted? Usually a combination of techniques is used and a variety of materials employed. Lectures are used to transmit information, demonstrations aid in observational learning, and cases and business and negotiation games help to fine-tune strategies and tactics. Role playing provides practice and a chance to receive constructive feedback. Group discussions allow one to raise questions and consider issues not always obvious to the individual. Observation of a new salesperson in the field by a peer or supervisor supplies still additional fine-tuning opportunities.

In addition to cases and games, audio and videotapes, books, programmed learning aids, and paper and pencil exercises are used in training. Sometimes testimonials from successful salespersons are used both as motivators and role models.

The question of *who* is to conduct training is also answered through a combination approach in most instances. Some training is performed by the training director and his or her staff. Regional or district managers may also contribute, and outside consultants are frequently solicited for their special expertise in particular areas. Some firms even hire outside firms to conduct the entire training program or parts of it.

The final operational decision concerns *where* to conduct training. As you undoubtedly have guessed, training goes on in various places: on the job, in a central office, at the regional or district levels, at special conference centers, in resort areas, and so on. Where training occurs depends, in part, on how long the program is to last, how convenient a location is needed, the costs involved, and the role that atmosphere is to play. Obviously, a one- or two-week training program faces different constraints than a 10- to 12-month undertaking. The average training periods for industrial, consumer products, and service firms have been estimated at 26, 19, and 12 weeks, respectively.[16]

Evaluation of the Training Program.[17] Ideally, we can measure the effectiveness of sales training programs by assessing how well they have achieved the goals noted in Figure 11-7. For example, management might run experiments to see the effects of training. Different training programs might be compared to each other and to a no-training control group. Additionally, evaluations of any training program could be performed by trainees, those conducting the training, and outside experts. Finally, videotapes of trainees role playing could be made prior to training, at some point in the training program, and immediately after training to see the actual impact of any program.

Motivation of Salespeople[18]

Salespeople are both less observable and more vulnerable than people in other occupations. They are less observable because they have considerable freedom and operate away from the home organization much of the time. This makes supervision difficult. But they are more vulnerable because the fruits of their efforts are quite visible to all, competition can be fierce, and the bargaining power of customers must be reckoned with. Somehow management must motivate salespeople at arm's length and in a climate rife with uncertainty, rejection, and disappointment.

In general, sales managers use a variety of social influence tactics to motivate their staffs. Later in this chapter we will discuss cash and noncash incentives as compensation issues. In this part of the chapter we will cover more subtle, nonmonetary, intangible motivation tactics. These include the use of inspirational leadership, positive affect, sanctions, persuasion, information, and performance goals.

Before discussion of these, however, it should be noted that motivation is both a personality trait that one brings to the job and a variable psychological state with attendant ups and downs. As a personality trait, motivation can be thought of as a baseline level of self-actuation determined largely by early life experiences in the family and school. Some people have stronger needs and drives than others, and one way to ensure that the desired levels of motivation are achieved in the sales force is to hire those with high levels at the outset. As a variable state, motivation can be considered a temporary psychological force at least in part under the influence of external forces. Motivation in this sense reinforces or is in addition to the basic drives that one develops in early life. We will use the terms *trait motivation* and *state motivation* to distinguish the two types. Achievement motivation is a combination of both. The tactics used by management to motivate salespeople are primarily directed at state motivation.

Inspirational Leadership. Inspirational leadership refers to influence through referent power, identification, or charismatic charm. The culture of personal selling is infused with images and expectations for extremes of effort, sacrifice, achievement, and in general "the right stuff." Management motivates through inspirational leadership when it selects managers on the basis of their ability to incite others to work at very high levels of performance. Inspirational leadership is also practiced through the use of professional speakers and special audiotapes and videotapes designed to arouse and stimulate people. Finally, by creating and perpetuating certain corporate myths and success stories, management indirectly motivates salespeople to perform at their best.

Positive Affect. The use of positive affect represents a second means to create high levels of motivation. The proper application of praise, positive feedback, and human warmth and understanding can impel others to perform up to their capabilities.

This must be done in a genuine way and not be perceived as overly self-serving. Another form of motivation through positive affect occurs via small group and peer relations. Friendship, support, and comradeship frequently serve as vehicles for creating positive feelings toward the company and job. They also function to promote social comparison processes and to motivate others to achieve at levels higher than their peers.

Sanctions. Sanctions are seldom used in any organization but may have a place in certain circumstances. They are designed to gently coerce better performance. For example, reprimands for violation of certain rules can be used to shape future behavior. Similarly, strong criticism at the proper moment can have a lasting impact. Many firms have formal self-examination interviews with supervisors and salespeople after a sale has been lost to a competitor. These sessions can be quite trying and involve pointed cross-examination and even verbal censure. Whether such negative feedback is the most effective means of supervision is debatable, but some managers claim that the motivational impact can be dramatic if handled well.

Persuasion. One of the more common, and recommended, forms for inducing high levels of motivation is through persuasion. Here managers use rational arguments to convince salespeople that it is in their own best interests to act in a preferred way. Persuasion has the advantage of getting people to infer that their actions were performed out of their own free will. This leads to higher levels of self-direction than reward or coercive modes of influence where one perceives he or she acts more as a function of external compulsion than internal volition.

Information. Information control is another mode of influence that management can use to motivate salespeople. By skillfully supplying or rationing information, management has the power to create enthusiasm and commitment at the proper moment. Memos, news clippings, journal articles, and other pieces of information serve an unobtrusive educative function and can reinforce desired behavior. Of course, this must not be done in a manipulative way if it is to lead salespeople to attribute their own reactions to the materials as one of free commitment and self-discovery.

Performance Goals. The final nonfinancial way to motivate is through goal setting. The establishment of *quotas* is perhaps the best example. Here salespeople and managers sit down and negotiate mutually acceptable performance goals for the next selling period. Quotas will be based typically on sales forecasts, desired profit, past performance, and other factors. Management desires to set quotas high enough to motivate salespeople but not so high as to be perceived as unreachable. Salary, bonuses, prizes, and/or commission will often be tied to the degree that the quota is achieved. Quotas are not only absolute goals for which salespeople strive, but they are relative goals. That is, salespeople attempt to improve upon their past quota performances and achieve at levels above their peers.

As you can well imagine, motivation is a key issue for salespeople and their managers. It propels people in the pursuit of excellence or whatever goals they value, and it is a managerial tool for organizational goal attainment as well. In addition, you may or may not be aware that motivation is at the very heart and survival of the firm. In most economies, differences between competing products increasingly disappear as firms innovate or imitate, and buyers find it difficult to make decisions strictly on the basis of "objective" distinctions. Take the computer field as an example. Technological and human performance differences among competing brands are often either too difficult to assess or too minor to worry about. With no overwhelming means to discriminate among brands on the basis of product attributes or services, the role of personal selling becomes quite decisive. Indeed, the firm with the most highly motivated sales force is often "the winner."

Supervision of Salespeople

A large part of management of the sales force is concerned with handling interpersonal relationships. In this regard, five activities must be performed: delegating, coordinating, managing conflict, coaching, and counseling.[19] Let us briefly look at these.

Delegating. Delegating consists of "assigning responsibility and authority to a subordinate and holding him or her accountable for results."[20] The objective of delegation is twofold. From one perspective, managers use delegation as a means to motivate and enrich the job for salespeople. Along with this, it is believed that proper delegation helps prepare salespeople for promotion and increases understanding and empathy between them and their managers. From another perspective, delegation increases the managerial productivity of the organization. It does this by giving more time to managers so that they can more effectively plan and make operational decisions.

Delegation can be accomplished in the sales force in a variety of ways. Salespeople can be given certain responsibilities for recruitment and training. They can be provided with freedom to manage their everyday sales activities in ways that they see fit, and they can be encouraged to gather information on competitors, undeveloped potential, and customer needs and complaints and to participate along with management on key tactical decisions at the grass roots level. All of this must be done, however, with an understanding of the rights and responsibilities for all concerned and the necessity for authority and hierarchical relationships. With increased responsibility comes a need for greater accountability.

Coordinating. Coordinating is an everyday supervisory activity concerned with the integration of planning and activities. Sales force goals must be compatible with larger organizational objectives, and activities must interface with the programs of the remainder of the marketing mix. Programs must be realistic and operate within the constraints of one's budget and environmental pressures. Efforts must be made to clearly communicate expectations and directives to salespeople. In general, the sales manager must see to it that the functioning of the sales force is in harmony with the rest of the organization.

Managing Conflict. Conflict is ever-present for most managers.[21] Conflicts occur between salesperson and customer, between customer and firm, among salespersons, between salesperson and manager, and between the sales force and other parts of the firm. One should not automatically assume that conflict is dysfunctional. Indeed, a certain amount of conflict can serve as a signal of a latent or impending problem. It can even act as a challenge, motivating people to strive for higher levels of achievement. Hence, not only might managers welcome a certain degree of conflict, but they may on occasion stimulate it. For example, a sales manager might inject a small element of ambiguity in his or her directives or slightly overload a salesperson with work. The temperament of certain salespeople may be such as to require aggressive, but friendly, teasing between salesperson and manager to bring out the best in effort. Other minor forms of conflict might have positive effects as well.

For example, minor conflicts between employees in routine decision making can serve as a *discovery procedure*. To belabor the obvious, the fact that everyone in the organization agrees on a new strategy does not mean the course of action proposed is the right one to take; and lack of debate can indicate a lack of careful consideration of alternatives. Within reason, considering more points of view before taking action increases the thoroughness of the decision-making process and the likelihood that a sound decision will be reached.

Minor conflict, as a source of "eustress," may itself improve performance. Research on stress has shown an "inverted U" relationship between stress and performance—that is, up to a certain point, the stressor intensity correlates positively with performance; beyond that point, stressor intensity and performance are negatively correlated.

Despite the positive aspects of conflict, it is probably true that most conflicts must be resolved or at least controlled. As we saw in the previous chapter, research shows that too much ambiguity and role tension and strain can actually depress performance and cause dissatisfaction. Management must either select people who can cope effectively with these forms of conflict or else structure the organization and provide guidance to reduce conflict and/or help people better cope with it. This means designing territories and workloads in an optimum way, providing the resources and support needed to carry out one's tasks, constructing mechanisms and outlets for the discussion of grievances and problems, eliminating most ambiguity in rules and procedures, and in general watching for the signs of conflict such as large drops in sales, absenteeism, changes in personality, and so on.

Coaching. Coaching consists of "observing skill performance, demonstrating means for improving these skills, providing an opportunity to practice the skills, and giving feedback."[22] In a sense, this is the teaching function of management. Supervisors must closely monitor the actions of salespeople but at the same time provide a certain degree of freedom. There is no "right way" to sell, and each individual must develop a process consistent with his or her own abilities and limitations, yet flexible enough to adjust to different customer needs and practices when the occasion dictates it. Coaching ensures that this is done in a way such that organizational goals are met. Often, it is carried out as part of a periodic training function.

Counseling. The final supervisory activity is counseling. This is perhaps the most subjective and personal activity and the one most difficult to execute. By counseling is meant the giving of professional and personal advice, the sharing of problems and experiences, the discussion of misunderstandings, and the communication of values. Counseling is largely an informal process but may need to be conducted at times in a formal manner because of ethical and social conventions. In any event, counseling is a necessary activity for making the organization a more human place within which to work.

Evaluation of Performance

Effective control of the selling effort requires the establishment and measurement of performance standards, but this is very difficult. Performance measures should be linked directly to the effort, ability, and efficiency of the individual salesperson, but in any real situation performance may well be the consequence of many external factors, unrelated to the salesperson. Figure 11-8 summarizes some of the forces affecting performance. Notice, too, that many measures of performance are suggested.

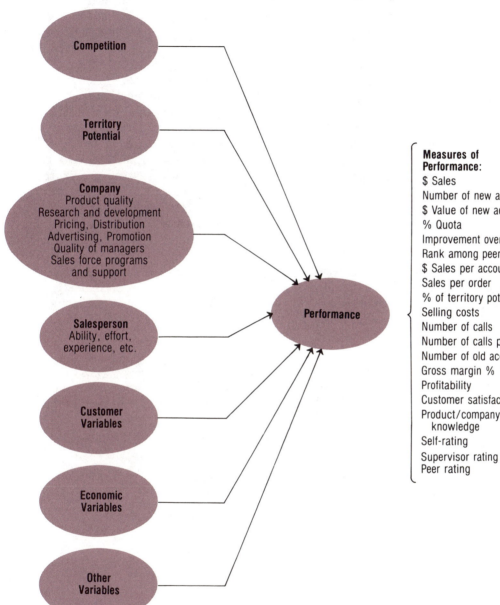

Measures of Performance:
$ Sales
Number of new accounts
$ Value of new accounts
% Quota
Improvement over past year
Rank among peers
$ Sales per account
Sales per order
% of territory potential
Selling costs
Number of calls
Number of calls per order
Number of old accounts lost
Gross margin %
Profitability
Customer satisfaction
Product/company/competitor
  knowledge
Self-rating
Supervisor rating
Peer rating

Figure 11-8. Some determinants of the performance of salespeople

One indication of performance is the *input* needed to produce a particular level of total sales and/or generate new business. Inputs include such factors as expenses, number of calls made, time spent in selling activities, and so on. The assumption is that output (e.g., sales) will be a function of inputs. In addition, salesperson efficiency and profitability will be affected by the use of inputs. Cost management, in particular, is an important activity to implement. For example, the average cost per call has been estimated at between $100 and $210.[23] These and other costs can be related to sales to determine a profit analysis of the personal selling effort if desired.

Outputs are probably the most frequently used measures of performance. In this respect, total sales and percent quota achieved are the dominant indicators. Total sales tends to obscure somewhat the individual salesperson's contribution in that it is a coarse-grained, overall measure of the result of all forces and not merely the effect of the salesperson. Nevertheless, because it is easily measured and is invariably correlated with actual effort and ability, it has a place in many performance evaluations. The percentage of quota achieved builds in more direct controls for the territory's opportunities and constraints, and reflects somewhat better the impact of the salesperson. It gives a more direct measurement of the salesperson's ability to generate revenue. Moreover, because it typically is reached through a mutual understanding between salesperson and manager, it is perceived to be a relatively equitable measure by the salesperson.

New business generated is important for the growth and survival of the firm. Therefore, it is a frequent adjunct to total sales or percent quota measures and is often tied to bonuses or other monetary rewards. Improvement over past year's sales is similarly a growth-oriented indicator and reflects in part the learning and/or increased effort of a salesperson.

Gross margin percentage can be an important measure of performance for some firms. It reflects how well the salesperson distributes his or her effort across products and at the same time watches costs.

Many of the other measures of performance noted in Figure 11-8 have a place in certain circumstances. In any setting, it is important that management continually monitor performance indicators and relate these to the determinants shown in Figure 11-8. For example, with multiple regression or other multivariate statistical procedures, it is possible to discover the relative impact on performance of such determinants as work load, territory potential, competitor effects, salesperson effort, and selling experience. Similarly, simulations or field experiments may be employed as research techniques in this regard. The objective is to obtain an indication of the salesperson's contribution to performance and to make any correction factors if warranted.

TABLE 11-4

Proportion of Consumer and Industrial Firms Using Various Compensation Programs

Compensation Program	Percentage of Firms
Straight Salary	24%
Commission Only	7%
Salary plus Bonus	33%
Salary plus Commission	27%
Salary plus Bonus plus Commission	9%
	100%

SOURCE: Drawn from *Sales & Marketing Management* 120 (February 27, 1978): 60

Management of Sales Force Programs and Activities

Closely related to the management of salespeople is the management of sales force programs and activities. Indeed, the two types of management interact and constitute the major controllable levers for affecting sales force performance. In this part of the chapter, we will consider three topics: compensation of salespeople, allocation of effort to products, and allocation of effort to territories or customers.

Compensation of Salespeople[24]

Many different methods are used to compensate salespeople. Among the most frequently employed alternatives are straight salary; commission only; salary plus bonus; salary plus commission; or salary plus bonus plus commission. Table 11-4 presents the percentage of consumer and industrial firms using one approach or the other.[25] In addition to these modes of financial compensation, such noncash incentives as contests, honors, and special recognition are used to reward high performance.

The objectives of any compensation program are complex. A central purpose is, of course, to motivate aggressive selling and high levels of exertion. Another aim is to channel efforts in particular directions. For example, bonuses or commissions might be higher for newer than older products or higher for high-profit items than less profitable ones. Less recognized among some firms is the need to integrate compensation programs with the entire selling effort. The proper compensation program can help in recruiting, training, and performance evaluation, for example.

Single-Method Plans

Straight Salary. Straight salary consists of a fixed payment for each pay period and is employed under a number of circumstances. Most of these occur when it is difficult to ascertain the salesperson's contribution to sales, when other factors such as advertising or promotions account for the bulk of sales, or when the salesperson plays predominantly a supportive role. Straight salary is also sometimes used when selling is performed by a team or when negotiations cover a wide spectrum in time and involve expensive products. Among other firms, pharmaceutical, chemical, petroleum, defense, steel, cement, aerospace, and service companies typically use straight salaries.

The advantages of using straight salaries are that they are easy to administer and are a fixed cost (i.e., they do not rise with increases in sales volume). A straight salary also minimizes jealousy and feelings of inequity between salespersons, and it gives management somewhat more control over salespeople than other methods. The primary disadvantage of the approach is that the connection between salary and effort on the one hand and performance on the other is relatively weaker than under other methods. Hence, straight salary may not be the most effective motivator and may lead salespeople to emphasize products that are less profitable or easier to sell.

Straight Commission. The straight commission is, in one sense, the polar opposite of the straight salary. Here the salesperson is paid a percentage of sales or of gross margin, usually 3 to 20 percent depending on the product. Most firms using a commission plan provide a draw against future commissions in order to give salespeople a minimum level of income to expect. Commission plans are used by door-to-door selling firms and in the furniture, automotive, and apparel industries, among other industries.

A straight commission plan has two advantages. First, it is probably the most powerful incentive system of all compensation schemes. Therefore, it is very effective as a motivator. Second, selling costs are generally low and predictable because costs are variable and tied to sales. When sales are low, so are selling costs.

But there are certain drawbacks. If sales are unpredictable or slow in coming, then a commission-only plan will result in erratic wages, which will tend to discourage salespeople. Further, commissioned salespersons tend to be more difficult to control and to resent paper work or any activities that cut into their selling time. As a consequence, management is less likely to get them to do research, to develop new customers, or to cooperate in training and other programs. The drawbacks probably account for the low percentage of firms using a straight commission program (i.e., about 7 percent). Nevertheless, the approach has its place for small firms, when working capital is low, or when very high motivation is required.

Combination Plans. As we saw in Table 11-4, most firms use a combination of financial incentives to compensate their sales forces, with the most popular plan being salary plus bonus. *Bonuses* are usually based on amounts sold over quota and/or on the amount of new business generated. They are paid as a single lump sum at the end of a sales period and typically amount to about 5 to 15 percent of total compensation.[26]

Because combination plans involve mixtures of salary, commission, and/or bonuses, they potentially share both the advantages and disadvantages of the approaches noted heretofore. The task for management is to skillfully blend the programs so as to accentuate the positives and downplay the negatives. One would like to achieve a compensation program with high levels of incentive, some degree of security for salespeople, and maximum control by management.

As an example, consider the following plan for an industrial sales force. Here, the base salary is $18,000 per year. In addition, if the salesperson sells between $300,000 and $400,000, he or she receives an additional 4 percent of the amount sold in this range. If he or she reaches the $400,000 level, a bonus of $3,000 is given. Sales beyond the $400,000 level result in an additional commission of 6 percent. Thus, if a person were to sell, say, $472,000 in goods, his or her payment for the year would amount to $29,320 (i.e., $18,000 + .04 × $100,000 + $3,000 + .06 × $72,000). This program provides a guaranteed salary, yet it includes certain incentives for effective performance.

In setting a compensation plan, management must consider additional factors. First, the rules must be easily understood. Second, salespeople must perceive that the goals implied by the incentives are both reachable and fair. Third, the compensation program should be easy to administer. Finally, the potential final payment achieved must not be too high in the sense of threatening to reach the compensation level of managers. Many firms try to keep total compensation of salespeople about 25 to 30 percent below that of their managers.

Noncash Incentives. Financial rewards are not the only means of compensation. Sometimes contests and prizes are given for particular accomplishments. For example, passing a particular milestone in sales, achieving a certain degree of longevity, or closing an unusually lucrative deal might warrant an additional form of compensation. Typically, paid vacations or pieces of merchandise such as color televisions or gold watches are given. Some firms use gift catalogues as incentives and distribute them to the salesperson's family. As the salesperson attains prespecified levels in sales or generates new accounts of a specified amount, he or she is eligible to receive an item of his or her choice from the catalog. By involving the entire family, an added pressure is brought to bear.

Special contests may be run periodically to serve as added incentives. This is often done in a competitive way so as to encourage peer comparisons.

Still another form of noncash incentive is the use of an automobile for both home and business after achievement of a particular level of sales. Or, if one already has a company car, it can be upgraded to a more luxurious or, in some other way, desirable vehicle. Some firms offer reduced prices on company stock, insurance, or other programs as well.

A powerful noncash incentive is recognition. Publicity surrounding individual achievements can be a source of pride and serve as a reward and motivator. Recognition is provided in published newspapers and salesperson rankings, at banquets, at sales meetings or training events, and on plaques. Whatever the medium, noncash incentives should be given rarely and for clear achievements so as to be viewed as special and desirable by salespersons. Noncash incentives work most effectively when integrated into the culture and rituals of the organization.

Allocation of Effort

Products. Most salespeople sell a range of products or multiple variations of the same product. Therefore, a problem arises for allocating salesperson time and effort across products. Three issues can be identified:

Firstly, there may be cost interdependencies—a change in the level of production of one product changes the cost of another. Secondly, there may be demand interdependencies, when a change in value of a marketing variable for one product affects the level of demand for the other; this is normally referred to as cross-elasticity of demand. Thirdly, these decisions must be carried out in the context of a constraint on the total effort available.[27]

As a consequence, the allocation of selling effort to products can directly affect the growth, profitability, and market share of the firm. Management's task is to devise a method for allocating this effort effectively.

A crude way to do this is to allocate effort in proportion to sales. Thus, the following formula might be used:

$$E_i = \frac{S_i}{\sum\limits_{j}^{n} S_j} E_t$$

where E_i = effort devoted to product i, S_i = sales of product i, E_t = total effort available, and n = number of products. This formula is easy to apply but assumes that all products are equally profitable and that sales for each will be equally responsive to effort put forth. Although it is possible to alter the formula to take into account the relative effectiveness of different levels or kinds of effort, it is too imprecise for fine-grained decisions. The formula is used only when nothing better exists to guide actions.

A more promising managerial allocation approach has been developed based on subjective and analytical considerations.[28] For lack of a better term, we will call it the *sales force product allocation approach.* The method follows the philosophy of Little's decision calculus, which strives to develop a "model based set of procedures for processing data and judgments to assist a manager in his decision making."[29] It is beyond the scope of this book to consider the details of this model, but we will note that the model employs an algorithm based on a heuristic and yields near-optimum allocation of a salesperson's time to products. The objective function of the model contains gross margin and sales.

Territories. A problem faced by many firms is to design the appropriate size of territories. Sometimes the firm is starting off and can design its territories from scratch. More often, the problem is to redesign existing territories.

Whatever the situation, at least four broad criteria can be identified for designing sales territories:

1 The territories should be roughly circular in shape and contain as dense or closely spaced a pattern of accounts as possible. This reduces travel time and costs and increases actual time in face-to-face exchanges.

2 Territory boundaries and assignment of accounts should be specified clearly.

3 Territories should permit a sound basis for the evaluation of salespersons.

4 Territories should be roughly equal in workload and potential. This promotes feelings of fairness and enhances motivation.[30]

Several mathematical models are available to aid in the design of sales territories. Most of these attempt to create equal workloads (i.e., time and effort) and/or sales potential territories.

A popular method for designing territories is by use of the computer and linear programming. The approach has been called the Geoline Model,[31] and its "objective is to group small geographic units into a prescribed number of sales territories such that the territories are equal with respect to the chosen activity measure and are also compact and contiguous."[32] The activity measure might be a measure of workload or sales potential. The Geoline Model has been applied to pharmaceutical and food firms, among others. It is a flexible, relatively easy-to-use procedure. One drawback is that it does not take into account call frequencies. Moreover, profit considerations are not directly accommodated.

Customers. Salespeople typically sell to many customers and approach numerous prospects. Needs and sales potential differ across customers and prospects as well. To approach selling with the maximum chance for success, effort must be allocated in a purposeful and efficient way. In general, the problem is to divide one's time and frequency of calling among existing customers and prospects. One must also decide upon a sequence of calls in order to minimize travel time and costs.

Lodish has developed an interactive computerized method for allocating selling time to customers.[33] The method is termed CALLPLAN. It yields a schedule of calls to make on customers, given limited time and a desire to maximize profits. Input to the model includes estimates of likely sales response to various call frequencies, travel time, time per call, and profitability per account. The model has been extended to handle both the call frequency problem and the territory design problem.[34] Further extensions to incorporate product and sales force size decisions have been made, too.[35]

The CALLPLAN model is best suited to selling situations where the salesperson must make many calls and sales are direct functions of interpersonal exchanges between salesperson and customer. It has the shortcoming of not taking into account the quality of interactions. Further, its validity depends on the ability of salespeople to estimate customer responses to calls.

The science of the management of sales force programs and activities has progressed very far. However, it is not possible to do the topic justice in this book. Therefore, it is recommended that you consult the suggested literature in the footnotes for details and applications.

Summary

This chapter considered managerial aspects of personal selling. It serves as a complement to the previous chapter, which focused on behavioral modalities in face-to-face selling.

The chapter began with an overview of the sales force management process. As shown in Figure 11-1, sales force goals and strategies determine a set of fundamental decisions that must be made in any selling situation. Two early decision points involve the *organization structure* and *size of the sales force*. We explored one simple design consisting of a direct line of authority from president or sales manager to sales representatives. Next, organization by geographic, product, and customer specializations was examined. The size decision was approached through three procedures: the breakdown, workload, or sales potential methods.

A central and ongoing problem concerns the *management of salespeople*. The activities here include recruitment and selection, training, motivation and supervision, and performance evaluation.

The organization renews itself primarily through its *recruitment and selection* programs. The direct goal is to fill new openings and replace departed personnel. The indirect goal is to reduce turnover and absenteeism, increase morale and job satisfaction, and, in general, enhance performance of salespeople. This is accomplished through the following activities: determination of number of people to hire, specification of qualifications of salespeople, identification of sources for new hires, design of enticements, choice among candidates, ongoing assessment and implementation of a fair and valid hiring program, and formal evaluation of accomplishment or performance goals and administration of corrections if warranted.

The *training program* is the first in a series of operational activities designed to help the organization adapt to and act upon customers, competitors, and other environmental forces. Motivation, supervision, and performance evaluation are the remaining adaptive and proactive operations. Training programs strive to convey knowledge, develop selling skills, and instill a spirit, sense of pride, and level of motivation thought to be necessary for effective selling. The main decision points here include determination of when, how, whom, and where to train, as well as formal implementation of an evaluation program of the training function. Training goes on shortly after one is hired as well as throughout one's career.

Motivation and supervision go hand in hand. Consider first motivation. Managers have a variety of nonmonetary, intangible motivation tactics from which to choose: inspirational leadership, application of positive affect, imposition of sanctions, use of persuasion, information control, and goal setting. The objective of any motivational program is to get people to put forth the effort needed to effectively reach customers, overcome any resistance, thwart the competition, and, in general, excel.

Motivation programs must be integrated with the everyday activities surrounding supervision. Five supervisory functions are performed in any selling organization: delegating, coordinating, managing conflict, coaching, and counseling. Each is needed to handle problems concerned with interpersonal relationships and the integration of the selling effort with other activities in the firm. The interface with larger organization objectives, planning, forecasting, product development and management, pricing programs, distribution policies, advertising and promotion goals, and other agendas requires special attention.

Performance evaluation is an essential activity but difficult to do well. Figure 11-8 presents a list of 20 performance measures that could be used to monitor the health of any selling effort. Management would like to learn what proportion of performance is due to salespeople and what proportion is due to external factors such as company policies, organization design, competitive and economic forces, territory potential, customer characteristics and practices, and so on. This information is needed if one is to apportion resources efficiently and make effective strategic changes in the selling effort.

The final set of topics addressed in the chapter concerned the *management of sales force programs and activities.* Three issues were examined: compensation of salespeople, allocation of effort to products, and allocation of effort to territories and customers.

Sales force compensation is designed to motivate aggressive selling and to channel efforts in directions most functional for the firm. At the same time, it is desirable that compensation programs be integrated with the recruiting, training, and performance evaluation activities, since it reinforces these and to a certain extent can correct weaknesses within them. The most frequently used compensation programs are salary plus bonus, salary plus commission, or straight salary. Commission-only programs are used only by a small percentage of firms. We discussed the pros and cons of these programs in the chapter, and you might want to reread the treatment therein. Noncash incentives such as contests, awards, and special recognition were also considered as forms of compensation.

Because of varying profit potentials across products and limitations in time, rules are needed for the *allocation of effort to products.* A formal model based on decision calculus and mathematics was briefly mentioned in the chapter.

Mathematical models also exist for the efficient *allocation of effort to territories.* A computer model, the Geoline Model, uses linear programming to design efficient sales territories.

Finally, the chapter closed with an introduction to the issue of *allocation of effort to customers.* This is the problem of how many calls to make on each customer and prospect and how to schedule the sequence of calls in the best way. Many mathematical decision models have been developed to solve this problem. The CALLPLAN model was one of the first and most successful in this regard.

Questions and Problems for Discussion

1 Describe the central elements of any sales force management process.

2 On what basis should one design a sales force organization? What alternative designs exist and what are their pros and cons?

3 How large should a sales force be? What methods are there for determining sales force size and what are their strengths and weaknesses?

4 What objectives should be taken into account in the recruitment and selection of salespersons and how might the recruitment and selection program be evaluated?

5 What activities should be performed in any sales force recruitment and selection program?

6 What are the objectives of any training program, how might training be conducted, and on what basis can the training program be evaluated?

7 How can management motivate salespeople?

8 What are the key tasks a sales manager must perform in the supervision of salespeople?

9 What criteria should be taken into account in the evaluation of the performance of salespeople? Consider measures of performance and their determinants.

10 Discuss the alternative modes of sales force compensation. What do you think the best mode would be for a pharmaceutical salesperson? a home solar heater salesperson? a machine tool salesperson?

11 Discuss the managerial problems surrounding the allocation of effort to products, territories, and customers.

NOTES

1. For a discussion of how sales force goals and strategies are related to broader organization objectives, see Porter Henry, "Manage Your Salesforce as a System," *Harvard Business Review* 53 (March–April 1975): 85–95.

2. For general background on organization design decisions, see J. R. Galbraith, *Designing Complex Organizations* (New York: Addison-Wesley, 1973); J. R. Galbraith and D. A. Nathanson, *Strategy Implementation: The Role of Structure and Process* (New York: West Publishing Co., 1978). For specific insights into the sales force, see G. David Hughes and Charles H. Singler, *Strategic Sales Management* (Reading, Mass.: Addison-Wesley, 1983), chapter 18.

3. For a detailed description of the methods, see Peter T. FitzRoy, *Analytical Methods for Marketing Management* (London: McGraw-Hill, 1976), pp. 198–202.

4. The workload method is sometimes also called the buildup method. For a complete description, see Hughes and Singler, *Strategic Sales Management*, pp. 539–41. See also W. J. Talley, Jr., "How to Design Sales Territories," *Journal of Marketing* 25 (1961): 7–12.

5. W. J. Semlow, "How Many Salesmen Do You Need?" *Harvard Business Review* 37 (May–June 1959): 126–32.

6. Semlow, "How Many Salesmen Do You Need?"

7. H. C. Lucas, Jr., C. B. Weinberg, and K. W. Clowes, "Sales Response as a Function of Territorial Potential and Sales Representative Workload," *Journal of Marketing Research* 12 (August 1975): 298–305.

8. For a background on turnover issues, see J. H. Dobbs, "Sales Force Turnover Can Make You—Or Break You," *Sales and Marketing Management*, May 14, 1979, pp. 53–58; The Conference Board, *Salesmen's Turnover in Early Employment* (New York: The Conference Board, 1972).

9. For an excellent example of an application blank, see Hughes and Singler, *Strategic Sales Management*, pp. 241–54.

10. "Testing and Selecting Employees' Guidelines," *Employment Practice Guide*, vol. II (Chicago: Commerce Clearing House, Inc., 1978), pp. 2223–24.

11. Jerome Siegel, *Personnel Testing under EEO* (New York: Amacom, 1980).

12. Richard R. Still, Edward W. Cundiff, and Norman A. P. Govoni, *Sales Management: Decisions, Policies, and Cases* (Englewood Cliffs, N.J.: Prentice-Hall, 1976), p. 237.

13. For background, research, and proscriptions on training, see Hughes and Singler, *Strategic Sales Management*, Chapter 10; J. J. Falvey, "Myths of Sales Training," *Sales and Marketing Management*, April 3, 1978, pp. 40–43; C. E. Harris, Jr., "Training the Sales Neophyte," *Training and Development Journal* 29 (February 1975): 46–51; J. F. Harrison, ed., *The Management of Sales Training* (Reading, Mass.: Addison-Wesley, 1977); D. S. Hopkins, *Training the Sales Force: A Progress Report* (New York: The Conference Board, 1978), Report No. 737.

14. C. E. Hayne, "How to Measure Results of Sales Training," *Training and Development Journal* 31 (November 1977): 3–7.

15. For a detailed presentation of these activities, see W. J. E. Crissy, William H. Cunningham, and Isabella C. M. Cunningham, *Selling: The Personal Force in Marketing* (New York: John Wiley & Sons, 1977), pp. 119–29.

16. Hughes and Singler, *Strategic Sales Management*, p. 280.

17. An introduction to evaluation of training programs can be found in C. E. Hayne, "How to Measure Results of Sales Training," *Training and Development Journal* 31 (November 1977): 3–7. See also Hughes and Singler, *Strategic Sales Management*, pp. 280–81.

18. For a background on the theory and management of motivation see F. Herzberg, "One More Time: How Do You Motivate Employees?" *Harvard Business Review* 46 (January–February 1968): 53–62; O. C. Walker, Jr., G. A. Churchill, Jr., and N. M. Ford, "Motivation and Performance in Industrial Selling: Present Knowledge and Needed Research," *Journal of Marketing Research* 14 (May 1977): 156–68; S. X. Doyle and B. P. Shapiro, "What Counts Most in Motivating Your Sales Force?" *Harvard Business Review* 58 (May–June 1980): 133–40.

19. Discussion of these five activities draws on ideas presented in Hughes and Singler, *Strategic Sales Management*, Chapters 12 and 13.

20. Hughes and Singler, *Strategic Sales Management*, p. 326.

21. See A. C. Filley, *Interpersonal Conflict Resolution* (Glenview, Ill.: Scott, Foresman and Co., 1975); E. Duffy, *Activation and Behavior* (New York: Wiley, 1962).

22. Hughes and Singler, *Strategic Sales Management*, p. 382.

23. In 1978, the average cost per personal sales call was estimated to be $97.67 (CARR Reports, Cahners Publishing Company. Cited in A. F. McGann and J. T. Russell, *Advertising Media: A Managerial Approach* [Homewood, Ill.: Richard D. Irwin, Inc., 1981], p. 218). In 1983, the average cost per call was estimated at about $210 (*USA Today*, July 12, 1984).

24. For background on compensation issues, see D. A. Welks, *Compensating Salesmen and Sales Executives* (New York: The Conference Board, 1972), Report No. 579; J. U. Farley, "An Optimal Plan for Salesmen's Compensation," *Journal of Marketing Research* 1 (1964): 39-43; J. P. Steinbrink, "How to Pay Your Sales Force," *Harvard Business Review* 56 (July-August 1978): 111-22; R. Y. Darmon, "Alternative Models of Salesmen's Response to Financial Incentives," *Operations Research Quarterly* 28 (1977): 37-49; V. Srinivasan, "An Investigation of the Equal Commission Rate Policy for a Multi-Product Salesforce," *Management Science* 27 (July 1981): 731-56.

25. For a somewhat different set of proportions, see "Managers on Compensation Plans," *Sales and Marketing Management*, November 12, 1979, pp. 41-43.

26. Hughes and Singler, *Strategic Sales Management*, p. 606.

27. FitzRoy, *Analytical Methods for Marketing Management*, p. 208.

28. D. B. Montgomery, A. J. Silk, and C. E. Zaragoza, "A Multiple-Product Sales Force Allocation Model," *Management Science* 18 (1971): 3-24.

29. J. D. C. Little, "Models and Managers: The Concept of a Decision Calculus," *Management Science* 16 (April 1970): B466-85.

30. FitzRoy, *Analytical Methods for Marketing Management*, p. 203.

31. See, for example, S. W. Hess, "Realigning Districts by Computer," *Wharton Quarterly* (Spring 1969): 25-30; S. W. Hess and S. A. Samuels, "Experiences with a Sales Districting Model: Criteria and Implementation," *Management Science* 18 (1971): 41-54.

32. FitzRoy, *Analytical Methods for Marketing Management*, p. 204.

33. L. M. Lodish, "CALLPLAN: An Interactive Salesman's Call Planning System," *Management Science* 18 (December 1971): 25-40; L. M. Lodish, "Vaguely Right Approach to Sales Force Allocations," *Harvard Business Review* 52 (January-February 1974): 119-24; W. K. Fudge and L. M. Lodish, "Evaluation of the Effectiveness of a Model-Based Salesman's Planning System by Field Experimentation," *Interfaces* 8 (November 1977): 97-106. For criticisms of CALLPLAN and an alternative, see A. A. Zoltners, P. Sinha, and P. S. C. Chong, "An Optimal Algorithm for Sales Representative Time Management," *Management Science* 25 (December 1979): 1197-1207.

34. L. M. Lodish, "Sales Territory Alignment to Maximize Profit," *Journal of Marketing Research* 12 (February 1975): 30-36.

35. L. M. Lodish, "A User-Oriented Model for Sales Force Size, Product, and Market Allocation Decisions," *Journal of Marketing* 44 (Summer 1980): 70-78.

GLOSSARY

Affirmative Action Compliance Program. Formal demonstration that firm does not discriminate in recruiting and hiring on the basis of race, sex, or ethnic group membership. *See* test bias, test validity.

Allocation of Effort to Customers. The design of efficient call frequencies to customers and sequences of calls. CALLPLAN, a computerized mathematical model, provides one way to design the most promising number of calls to make on customers.

Allocation of Effort to Products. The assignment of time and energy to one's products in order to efficiently achieve sales, gross margin, or other objectives. Mathematical models have been developed to aid in this process.

Allocation of Effort to Territories. The design of territory sizes in order to create equal workloads or sales potential across territories. The Geoline Model is a computer procedure designed to do this and uses linear programming.

Bona Fide Occupational Qualifications. Those requirements specifying personal characteristics for new hires that have been demonstrated to be necessary for the conduct of the job.

Bonuses. A form of financial compensation added to one's base salary or commission and based upon amounts sold over quota and/or the amount of new business generated. *See* compensation.

Breakdown Method. A procedure for determining sales force size based on the following formula: $n = S - s$ where $n =$ number of salespersons, $S =$ firm sales, $s =$ sales per salesperson, and it is assumed each salesperson generates an equal amount of revenue. *See* sales force size.

CALLPLAN. *See* allocation of effort to customers.

Coaching. The activity consisting of the giving of advice to salespersons on how to sell and manage their territories. *See* supervision.

Commission. Financial compensation consisting of a percentage of sales or of gross margin. If a commission is the only form of financial compensation made to a salesperson, the compensation plan is termed a *straight commission* plan. *See* compensation.

Compensation. Rewards given salespersons for specified performance. Although intangible rewards are often provided, the term *compensation* is usually reserved to refer to tangible rewards. Two types are *financial compensation* and *noncash incentives.* Salary, commission, and bonuses comprise the principal financial compensations, while contests, awards, and special recognition are the primary noncash incentives. Most firms use a combination compensation plan consisting of salary plus either bonus or commission.

Conflict Management. The resolution or control of interpersonal tension, strain, aggression, or misunderstandings among salespeople, between salespersons and customers, between salespersons and managers, or between salespeople and other agents in the home firm or customer firms. *See* supervision.

Coordination. The managerial activity concerned with the integration of plans and actions of salespeople and sales programs and policies with the larger organization. *See* supervision.

Counseling. The giving of professional or personal advice, the sharing of problems and experiences, the discussion of misunderstandings, and the communication of values. Counseling often is difficult to separate from and overlaps with other supervisory activities. *See* supervision.

Customer Specialization. A form of organization design wherein salespeople are assigned responsibility for selling to a particular customer or class of customers. *See* sales force design.

Delegation of Responsibility. The assignment of duties and authority to subordinates with the objective of creating motivation, enriching the job, preparing one for possible promotion, and freeing up managers' time. *See* supervision.

Geographic Specialization. A form of organization design wherein company sales operations are divided into mutually exclusive geographic regions and these, in turn, are subdivided still further into mutually exclusive subregions. A typical application will include regions, districts, and territories arranged in a hierarchy. Salespeople operate within a territory and are given exclusive responsibility for it. They generally sell a full range of products to all customers in their territory. *See* sales force design.

Geoline Model. *See* allocation of effort to territories.

Goal Setting. A form of influence used to motivate salespeople and based upon the establishment of specific objectives. *See* quotas.

Hierarchical Relations. Formal authority and responsibility linking people in roles and organized as a gradient from higher to lower. *See* vertical levels, horizontal relations.

Horizontal Relations. Interactions among people occupying roles within a particular level of the organization. The interactions might involve formal (i.e., codified) or informal contracts. *See* hierarchical relations, vertical levels.

Hybrid Organization Design. A form of organization design combining geographic, product, and/or customer specialization. *See* sales force design.

Information Control. A form of influence used to motivate salespeople and based upon the regulation of the flow of knowledge.

Inspirational Leadership. A form of influence used to motivate salespeople and based upon referent power, identification, or charismatic charm.

Line Organization Design. A simple hierarchical structure of the sales force based upon the reporting of all salespeople to a single manager. In very small firms, all salespeople may report directly to the president. In somewhat larger firms, a sales manager works between salespeople and the president. *See* sales force design.

Motivation. *See* achievement motivation, trait motivation, state motivation.

Persuasion. A form of influence used to motivate salespeople and based upon the use of rational arguments.

Positive Affect (use of). A form of influence used to motivate salespeople and based upon the application of praise, positive feedback, or human warmth and understanding.

Product Specialization. A form of organization design wherein salespeople are assigned responsibility for selling particular products, usually a single product category or small number of variations. Salespeople may or may not be assigned to geographic territories. But if they are, they will sell the limited line of products to everyone in their territories. *See* sales force design.

Quotas. Performance goals for salespeople to achieve. These are typically based on negotiation between salesperson and manager. They will be a function of past performance, forecasts, desired profits, and what is deemed acceptable and fair.

Recruitment. The search for and solicitation of people to fill new positions and/or replenish depleted ones.

Recruitment and Selection Program. The managerial function concerned with determination of number of new people to hire, specification of qualifications for new hires, identification of sources for candidates, choice among candidates, assessment and implementation of a fair and valid hiring program, and formal evaluation of achievement of sales force goals as a function of recruitment and selection.

Salary. A fixed financial payment for services rendered during a specific pay period. If a salary is the only form of financial compensation made to a salesperson, the compensation program is termed a *straight salary* plan. *See* compensation.

Sales Force Design. Specification of the roles and responsibilities for salespeople and managers as reflected in formal hierarchical (i.e., vertical) and horizontal relations in the firm. *See* line organization design; geographic, product, and customer specialization. *See also* hybrid organization design, sales force size.

Sales Force Goals. Specific ends that salespeople can generate such as dollar or unit sales, profitability, improvement over past performance, or percent quota achieved. Typically, these are related to broader marketing and organizational goals for growth, return on investment, market share, or other objectives. *See* sales force strategies.

Sales Force Size. The number of salespeople in the sales force. At least three methods can be used to determine the proper size: the breakdown method, the workload method, or the sales potential method. Because of trade-offs between span of control needs and vertical level requisites, the size of the sales force will affect the organization design decision. *See* sales force design.

Sales Force Strategies. Specific activities selected to serve as a means for achieving sales force goals. Among others, these include purposeful design of the sales force, management of personnel, and program execution. *See* sales force goals.

Sales Potential Method. A procedure for determining sales force size that takes into account productivity of salespeople and is based on the relation between sales volume in territories and territory potential. *See* sales force size.

Sanctions. A form of influence used to motivate salespeople and based upon mild punishments or coercion. Reprimands and strong criticism are examples. The appropriateness of this tactic is debatable and borders on the unethical.

Selection. The choice of people to hire from among those recruited.

Span of Control. The number of people reporting to a manager.

State Motivation. The variable form of human striving for rewards. It can be influenced through internal processes as well as external stimuli. *See* trait motivation, achievement motivation.

Straight Commission. *See* commission.

Straight Salary. *See* salary.

Supervision. The management activity consisting of delegation of responsibility, coordination of plans and actions, management of conflict, coaching, and counseling.

Test Bias. An aspect of the application of test procedures used in selection of people for hire that discriminates on the basis of race, sex, or ethnic group membership. *See* test validity, affirmative action compliance program.

Test Validity. In the use of tests for the selection of new hires, test validity refers to the veracity with which criteria predict performance. Test validity must be established before said tests can be used as a means for selection. It should be noted that a test procedure can be valid yet still be biased. In such cases, it is illegal to use the procedure. *See* test bias, affirmative action compliance program.

Training Program. The formal activity concerned with transmission of knowledge to new or existing salespeople, development of selling skills, socialization of values, and stimulation of personal pride and positive attitudes.

Trait Motivation. The more-or-less fixed or chronic level of drive that one brings to the job. It is gained early in life through experiences in school and the family. *See* state motivation.

Vertical Levels. Positions in an organization arranged in a hierarchy and based on formal authority and responsibilities. *See* hierarchical relations, horizontal relations.

Workload Method. A procedure for determining sales force size based on the following formula: $n = H - h$ where n = number of salespeople, H = hours per year needed to achieve a specific level of sales, and h = hours per year available from a salesperson. *See* sales force size.

Sales Management: Today and Tomorrow

G. David Hughes
Burlington Industries
Professor of Business
Administration
University of North
Carolina, Chapel Hill
and
Charles H. Singler,
Consultant
Vice President, Sales
(Retired)
Burroughs Wellcome Co.

Sales Management Today

Today, too much of sales managers' time is spent in reacting to situations rather than making events happen in their favor. If urged to take training in sales management, they would probably respond, "I'm not managing half as well as I already know how." Many recent changes in the selling and sales management environment have impeded more effective sales management. Some of these forces will be examined briefly.

Short-Term Results Orientation. Sales management evaluation, like much of corporate evaluation, has been reduced to a shorter and shorter time horizon. Meeting a quarterly or annual quota is rewarded. Building a sales organization for long-term corporate benefits is completely outside the evaluation system of most selling organizations. Thus, first-line and middle sales managers can be frustrated by the lack of job descriptions and performance standards that reflect their responsibilities for developing sales representatives and young managers.

First-line and second-line sales managers tend to receive training in "how-to" activities, such as recruiting and training. They receive little training in "why" these activities are performed. This weakness in training is unfortunate because it neglects an important dialogue between field sales managers and top management. This dialogue is necessary to keep the company informed about the rapidly changing demand and competitive conditions in the marketplace and to encourage the field sales manager's commitment to corporate objectives. The dialogue also helps top managers identify persons who have potential for higher levels of management. Young sales managers need to be exposed to the broad management process early so that they may learn how to manage and so that they may test their skills and decide how far they want to go in the management hierarchy.

Increasing Complexity. Many forces are making the sales management job more complex. The products are more complex, which requires continuous training sessions for all representatives. Buyers are becoming more sophisticated. Many of them have received training in negotiation skills, which means that sales representatives need to be trained in these skills. Buying is frequently done only at the central office, which greatly changes the role of the representative and the design of the sales organization. Many companies are using a national accounts management system in which a representative has responsibility for all sales to a single company. Team selling is frequently used when calling on a central headquarters. Training these teams in the skills of negotiation is an important sales management activity.

The information explosion has reached sales management. The first-line sales manager can have sophisticated computer printouts of sales potentials to areas as fine as a ZIP code. Sales, activity, and expense evaluations for each representative can be provided on a very frequent basis. Many sales managers are experiencing an information inundation, with no training in using quantitative data. Conversely, the computer programmer has little appreciation of the data needs of sales management, so that computer systems frequently do not meet its needs.

The social and legal environment adds complexities to sales management. A sales representative and a sales manager can be fined and jailed for violation of antitrust laws. A company can be held legally responsible if a representative misrepresents the benefits of a product. Recruiting, promoting, and compensating representatives must be equitable, without discrimination with regard to age, sex, race, or other factor.

In summary, the rapidly changing environment is accelerating the change in the role of the sales manager from that of a "super-salesperson" to that of a "supervisor of salespersons." Few field managers are adequately trained for this change in role. Even fewer managers are provided with an adequate job description and a performance evaluation system that will motivate and reward them in these expanded activities.

Sales Management Tomorrow

The practice of sales management tomorrow will reflect three environmental forces from today—the changing role of the representative, social changes, and the information revolution.

The Changing Role of the Representative. Relationships will shift from that of a buyer and a seller to that of a client and a consultant. The representative of the future will perform more of a consulting role by analyzing the needs of clients and linking his or her product/service offer to the strategic profit plan of the client. This expanded role will require the representative to engage in sophisticated financial analysis, using computers and management information systems at his or her company and the client's.

Sophisticated information systems make it possible to give the representative "bottom-line responsibility" for the territories or accounts that are managed. Thus, the new representative can be given goals in terms of contribution and return on investment. Accounts can be managed as though they were an investment portfolio. This financial responsibility at the territory level provides the young representative with early experience that will be invaluable when he or she is promoted to higher levels of sales management. These analytical skills will change the job description of many selling positions and consequently the recruiting, selection, training, and evaluation procedures.

Social Changes. As the average age of the population becomes older, sales managers will be faced with the question of how to motivate the older representative so as to prevent "mental retirement on the job." Federal and state legislation prevent forced retirement, so sales managers must find more creative solutions. Some companies are using older representatives in part-time roles in sparse territories where the company would have no coverage or would use distributors. If the older representative has the talents, he or she might be interested in a staff position such as in sales training, customer relations, government relations, or college recruiting.

Dual career couples will create problems when a spouse is promoted and the other spouse does not want to move. Sales managers may want to develop cooperative arrangements with other companies regarding dual moves. Some companies are providing career counseling sessions so that couples may develop plans for the time when they must consider a move.

Sales management has been more open to women than many careers; thus, we may expect to see more women in top sales management positions. Some of the older generation representatives may find the possibility of a woman boss difficult. General sales managers will need to provide training for new women sales managers, perhaps through the case method, to help them develop confidence in their management abilities. General managers may need to be especially supportive during the early months after a woman is promoted to management.

The legal dimensions of sales management will continue, but the emphasis will change. Equal employment opportunity cases will shift from cases of discrimination in hiring and selecting to discrimination in evaluating, compensating, and promoting. General sales managers will need to develop clearer performance standards and better evaluation procedures. They will also find it necessary to train field sales managers in applying evaluation procedures in order to defend themselves successfully in court when an employee brings a discrimination case. It is ironic that it has taken court proceedings to improve some weak areas of sales management.

The Information Revolution. The rapid development of computer technology will continue, and the computer will become part of the modern representative's tool kit. Needs analysis, proposals, letters, and reports will be done on microcomputers by the modern representative. First-line sales managers will analyze market potentials, design territories, maintain territory income statements, compute bonuses, maintain personnel records, plan, and complete reports using microcomputers. Electronic mail and electronic filing systems will greatly reduce these onerous tasks at all levels of sales management. These electronic wonders will increase the productivity of representatives, but there will also be a need for investment in microcomputers and in the training of persons to use them.[1]

As the costs of the sales calls increase, we may expect to see greater use of telephone selling. General managers will need to develop policies for products and situations when telephone selling is the best strategy. Some companies are using it to cover an open territory while recruiting a new representative or training an old one. Strategic choices must be made among alternatives such as a company salesperson, telephone selling, and the use of brokers. Thus, electronics are creating more alternatives for sales managers to consider as they develop strategies.

---

1. For a discussion of the application of microcomputers in sales management see G. David Hughes, "Computerized Sales Management," *Harvard Business Review* 61 (March–April 1983): 102–112; G. David Hughes and Charles H. Singler, *Strategic Sales Management* (Reading, Mass.: Addison-Wesley, 1983), chapters 5 and 13.

In summary, sales management tomorrow will reflect the continuing changes in the social, legal, and technical environment. These changes will require sales managers to recruit more analytical representatives, retrain present representatives, and promote to management positions candidates who are qualified to operate in this technical environment. The new complexity of the selling role will make the setting of performance standards and evaluation even more difficult. Thus, the future of sales management can be predicted by extrapolating the trends in the early 1980s.

Sales Management in Tomorrow's Tomorrow

One of the criticisms of present business practice has been the short time horizon, probably the result of return on investment as a driving criterion. Short horizons emphasize results, in contrast to developing people to achieve long-term organizational objectives. As senior executives recognize the need to shift to long-term objectives, we can expect a greater emphasis on developing representatives, field sales managers, and general sales managers. This emphasis will require better job descriptions, better performance standards and measures, and better training for management at all levels of sales management. In tomorrow's tomorrow we will see more emphasis of formal training for sales managers than is currently the practice. Some top managers have become so accustomed to short-term crisis management that they have not developed skills in the basic management functions of planning, organizing, staffing, directing, and controlling. It will be necessary to develop these skills in those persons who manage in tomorrow's tomorrow.

CHAPTER
TWELVE

At Rome, all things can be had at a price.
——Juvenal (60?–140 A.D.)

Remember that time is money.
—— Benjamin Franklin
(1706–1790)

The real price of everything, what every thing really costs to the man who wants to acquire it, is the toil and trouble of acquiring it.
—— Adam Smith (1723–1790)

PRICE: BEHAVIORAL AND MACRO DIMENSIONS

Introduction

Price can mean many things, depending on one's perspective. For the *consumer*, the price of a product or service represents the resources one must forgo to obtain something of value. For *society*, the prices of goods and services are the primary mechanisms whereby supply and demand are brought into equilibrium in the economy at large. And for the *manager*, price is a key decision variable affecting the performance of the organization.

In this chapter, we will look at the meaning of price from the viewpoint of the consumer and society. We will begin first with an examination of price as experienced by the individual person. Our focus will be on the various forms that prices take and how consumers respond psychologically to these. Next, we will investigate the role of price from a societal vantage point. Emphasis will be placed on the economist's macro representation of price as it applies to aggregates of consumers and on the public policy interpretation of price as a measure of social welfare. The topic of price from the manager's perspective will be reserved for the following chapter. It should be noted, however, that the three outlooks on price overlap somewhat and at the same time interact. This will be more apparent as the chapters unfold.

Price and the Individual Consumer: The Psychology of Price

When we examine the role of price in consumer decision making, it is important to remember that it is only one of a number of inputs. We might think of the final decision to purchase as an outcome dependent on four broad determinants: (1) brand-related criteria, (2) the resources and psychology of the decision maker, (3) other perceived offerings in the marketplace, and (4) social constraints and facilitators (see Figure 12-1). Brand-related criteria refer to the bundle of characteristics perceived in a particular brand. Any brand will possess a number of product attributes related to its physical characteristics (e.g., taste, durability) and the second-order consequences associated with its use and ownership (e.g., time savings, social prestige). Its desirability will further be augmented by the nature of the persuasive arguments or affect communicated in its promotion and by the availability and other aspects of place associated with its distribution.

Price is of course a factor but only one of four connected to a particular brand. Moreover, other factors external to the brand can influence the purchase decision, as shown in Figure 12-1. The resources (e.g., financial, time) of the consumer serve as a constraint on purchase as do one's needs, motives, and decision rules. Similarly, to the extent that complements and substitutes exist, the final decision to purchase will be affected. Finally, any decision is subject to the push and pull of social forces from family members, bosses, or reference groups, or from society at large, such as is reflected in laws, norms, or mores. Price, then, is but one of a number of forces shaping choice, albeit an important one.

The Stimulus-Response View

We know very little about the psychological reactions of consumers to prices, and much of what we do know is based on the shared wisdom of retailers and other practitioners. Despite the unfortunate lack of scientific evidence to support the implicit consumer model that retailers follow, their model is worth examination for two reasons. First, the model is perhaps more than minimally valid. Practitioners are astute observers, and it is to be expected that trial-and-error learning has resulted in at least a partial representation of reality. Second, even if their

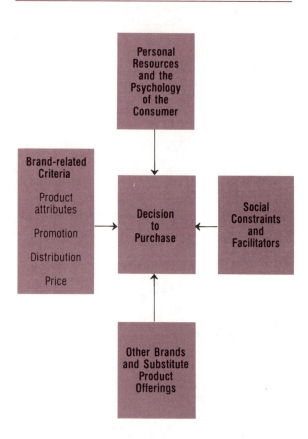

Figure 12-1. Some determinants of purchase decisions including price

judgments contain considerable error, practitioners (because of the uniformity of their behavior) sometimes have enough of an influence as a group to actually shape behavior in the long run. That is, people might not initially respond as the retailer envisions them to, but repeated exposures to a stimulus (price) lead consumers either to adapt to the stimulus and act without much thought or else to anticipate and mentally process prices according to past experience. Thus, the possibility exists for a self-fulfilling prophecy to the extent that pricing practices function as reinforcements, conditioned stimuli, or expected cues.

What is the model commonly held by many practitioners? Basically, it is a stimulus-response representation. Consumers are assumed to regard price largely in a negative way: the higher the price, the more costs a consumer must incur and/or the less other rewards the consumer might gain when meeting that price. As a consequence, the task of the marketer, when setting a price, is to either disguise its true level, cause it to be perceived less than what it is, or instill an image that the product is worth the price (e.g., because of its high quality). Five general tactics can be identified as representative of the folklore shared by practitioners: customary pricing, charm pricing, price lining, price reductions, and price/quality pricing.[1]

Customary Pricing. Customary pricing is the practice of using a single, well-known price for an extended period of time. Thus, for as long as possible, newspaper publishers have tried to maintain the price of a daily paper at 30¢, theaters have attempted to keep the price of movie tickets at about $5, and taverns have fought to hold the price of a beer at $1. Presumably, the logic of customary pricing is that consumers get used to paying a certain amount over time and, especially for frequently purchased products, might come to resent a price change. A customary price and frequent purchases leads consumers to take the costs of consumption for granted. But a price change would serve as a shock, making the cost of the product again salient. Moreover, from the retailer's perspective, the maintenance of prices tends to reduce administrative work associated with changing price tags, updating records, and other tasks. Because the costs to the seller frequently rise, however, some adjustments must be made. Typically, to maintain profits, and at the same time retain the customary price, the seller must reduce the size of the product or alter its ingredients in the face of cost increases. This has its own dangers and can only be done infrequently, however. For example, although candy bar producers are able to periodically shave an ounce or two off the "standard" size, they can only do this once or twice without reaching a point where people will no longer perceive the bar to be worth the price or to satisfy their cravings for a snack. In periods of rapid inflation with rising costs for raw materials and labor, manufacturers are often forced to make numerous adjustments in product size and quality. Indeed, the pressures are such as to ultimately require a price change, and a new customary price must be set, with the cycle beginning anew.

Charm Pricing. Sellers often set prices on the basis of the presumed psychological meaning of the numbers used to express the prices. In what might be termed the tactic of *conspicuous consumption pricing*, a high price is set with the hope that buyers will perceive the product to be unique, consist of special ingredients, or reflect exemplary workmanship. The thinking is also that people buy things not only for what the product is in a physical sense but also for what it means in broader psychological or social senses. A high price might even be sought by some potential purchasers as part of their need to express a particular life style or communicate their wealth and taste in a public way. Rather than reflecting the material costs of the products, per se, prices of goods and services in boutiques, specialty shops, and exclusive restaurants often stem from a conspicuous consumption pricing policy.

Another form of charm pricing is called *odd-or-even pricing*. A common belief among some retailers is that a price should only end in an odd number (usually a 5, 7, or 9) *or* an even number (typically an 8). Furthermore, whenever possible, it is recommended that the odd or even number be part of an overall price set just below a round number. For example, the strategy is based on the premise that $1.98 will be perceived to be more than 2¢ less than $2.00 or that 49¢ will be taken to be greater than a penny below 50¢. When should one use an odd or an even price? No research exists and the logic is unclear, but it may be that an even price has the advantage of being both aesthetically pleasing and unobtrusive while an odd price is more dissonant and eye-catching. Hence, the choice of one tactic over the other involves trade-offs and is largely a matter of opinion or trial and error.

Still another variant of charm pricing is what one might call *representational pricing*. Here the seller selects a price for a product on the basis of the symbolic meaning of the number as reflected in another object, event, or behavior associated with that number. For instance, pieces of furniture will sometimes be priced at $1,776, souvenirs will be offered at $7 or $11, and drinks in a nightclub at special times such as "the happy hour" will be sold at 69¢. Can you guess what these numbers might mean *and* why they are used in these specific cases? Overall, the practitioner of representational pricing hopes that the affect or feelings connected with a number will transfer to his or her product and perhaps be remembered more readily.

Price Lining. Price lining is the tactic of offering a number of variations of a type of product with each variation priced at a different level. Generally, three different versions of a product will be displayed at three different prices. The three product versions are known as a "price line." The practice is nearly universal in the retail trade: fast-food chains such as A & W offer three sizes of hamburgers (papa, mama, and teen burgers); appliance stores sell inexpensive, medium-priced, and high-priced brands of radios and TVs; and supermarkets provide inexpensive dealer brands and moderate- and high-priced national brands of the same products.

The goal of price lining is multifaceted and intimately related to the overall strategy of market segmentation. Because consumers differ considerably in both their tastes and financial resources, a wide variety in the quality of the same product type is demanded by the public. In an attempt to appeal to as broad a spectrum as possible, sellers provide a wide range of products to conform to the diverse tastes and incomes of their clientele. In addition, the ability to offer a price line gives the merchant considerable leverage to entice buyers to seek a product just above their normal price and quality level. This practice is termed *trading up* and is, of course, notoriously practiced by the automobile industry, among other sellers. Car salespeople constantly attempt to persuade customers who show an initial preference for a compact car with few options, say, to purchase an intermediate-sized car with more luxurious accessories. The seller is motivated to persuade customers to trade up because the higher priced versions of a brand are generally more profitable. The buyer is tempted to "move up" because the product is usually perceptibly of higher quality and at the same time the increase in price is deceptively low when compared to the overall price that one would have to pay for the low-priced model. For example, a recent ad for men's suits in a discount store offered three options: "good" ($99), "better" ($119), and "best" ($149). A person finding the $99 suit attractive, for instance, might well change his mind after seeing what "only $20 more" could buy. In fact, marketers will sometimes offer more than three price lines to reduce the gap between levels.

Furthermore, for each product version at each price level, accessories are sometimes offered in a way that increases the total price above the one for the next highest level. This, in turn, may lead the consumer to reevaluate his or her needs and resources and jump to the next level.

One danger with price lining is that it may be confusing and make the consumer's task more difficult. Too many alternatives and options may be costly to produce, stock, and maintain, as well. Then, too, if some consumers originally willing to pay a higher price find that the lower priced model is satisfactory, the seller may even experience less revenue.

Price Reductions. Consumers will sometimes refrain from making a purchase because they perceive the price to be "just a little too much" for the quality of the product offered and/or for what they think they can afford. This common resistance to buying can be overcome sometimes through the judicious use of two price changing tactics: (1) the use of "sales" or "specials" and (2) discount pricing. The major appeal of a *sale* (i.e., a temporary decrease in price) is that consumers believe they are getting a product that is worth more than its price and/or are better able to afford the product and will be able to purchase more of other goods with the savings. The use of a sale allows the seller not only to dispose of slow-moving goods to make way for new styles or products but also, in the process, to win a class of purchasers that might not have ever entered the market in the absence of a sale.

Another alleged advantage to the retailer is that sales of certain items draw people into the store and the consumers then either trade up and/or purchase other goods that capture their attention. Supermarkets, for example, will advertise milk, bread, or other staples at very low prices hoping that once the customer is in the store, he or she will buy numerous more profitable items.

The low-priced goods, which might even be sold below cost, are called "loss leaders" in the trade. Periodic sales sometimes create excitement among consumers, who look forward to sales and comb the newspapers, travel from store to store on "bargain hunts," and generally anticipate and plan to take advantage of the "steals." In this way, the sales-conscious consumer has taken over some of the functions normally performed by the seller: namely, communicating one's wares and getting them to the consumer. Finally, the whole notion of a sale for some buyers is an opportunity to express one's astuteness or self-image. Certain individuals even find the search for and apparent inconvenience of a sale as a challenge or adventure. For others, however, sales are strictly utilitarian.

Sales have drawbacks, of course. Aside from the increased expense of signs and advertising, a sale can cease to be a novelty. Although difficult to estimate, firms may experience lost revenues to the extent that customers refrain from buying unless or until an anticipated future sale occurs. At the same time, all sellers risk cheapening the image of their brands by placing them on sale.

Discounts function in a way similar to sales: the buyer is believed to interpret the reduction as a means of getting more for less. Typically, discounts are more or less constant price reductions offered to the public and sold in an establishment (i.e., a "discount store") identified as dealing in reduced-price merchandise.

For consumer goods, the use of sales and discounts varies from country to country. In West Germany, for example, one seldom sees a discount store, and sales generally occur only in February of each year.

For industrial buying discounts are offered as a matter of course. Typically, discounts are given for three reasons. One is that it is thought that they serve as an inducement for purchase much as occurs in consumer buying during sales. A second is that they are used to meet the competition. The third belief is that buyers expect the discount and to fail to meet this expectation risks inducing an imbalance in the quid pro quo inherent in such exchanges. In general, there are three types of discounts offered in the industrial trade: cash, functional, and quantity discounts.[2] Each is briefly described below.

Cash Discounts. A cash discount is a price reduction offered the buyer under the condition that the discounted price be paid within a certain period of time; otherwise the full price must be paid. The most common terms are 2/10, net 30. This means that a 2 percent discount is provided if the bill is paid within 10 days, but if the option is not taken, then the full price is due within 30 days. For example, assume that a buyer agreed on a purchase price of $6,000 and was offered 2/10, net 30. Then, if the bill were paid within 10 days, $5,880 would be due, otherwise the full $6,000 would be payable within 30 days. Other cash discounts are of course offered such as 3/10, net 30, for instance.

From a buyer's standpoint, cash discounts represent a cost savings and in this way function as incentives. From the seller's viewpoint, cash discounts are believed to encourage prompt payment and to build goodwill. However, cash discounts incur risks for both parties in that sellers and buyers still must weigh the opportunity costs of engaging in the exchange. As with all of the forms of discounts discussed herein, virtually no research exists as to their true effects.

Functional Trade Discounts. Functional discounts are allowances a seller offers to a buyer for services rendered. Although this might entail outright payments, more often it consists of reductions in the purchase price of goods. Generally, the amount of discount varies depending on the type of buyer and functions performed. For example, a manufacturer of soap selling to a full-service wholesaler might offer a 25 percent discount to cover services performed by buyers in the general category of distributors, plus an additional 10 percent discount for conducting specific promotions. The same seller, assuming no laws are violated, might offer a grocery store only a 15 percent discount for the services it performs plus a 5 percent promotion allowance. The grocery store presumably gets less of a discount than the distributor because it performs less services. The schedule of discounts might even be more complex such as "25, 10, 5, and 2/10, net 30." What this means is that for a quantity of goods selling at a list price of $2,000, say, the buyer can deduct 25 percent of $2,000 for a category discount, yielding an effective price of $1,500. Then, 10 percent of this total is subject to a discount for a particular service rendered (e.g., advertising), leaving $1,350. And for a second specific service (e.g., providing credit), $67.50 is allowed (i.e., 5 percent of $1,350). If payment is made within 10 days, only $1,256.85 is due, otherwise $1,282.50 must be paid within 30 days.

From the seller's perspective, the functional discount is the price one must pay to obtain the services of marketing intermediaries. As discussed in the chapter on channels of distribution, intermediaries can assume much of the marketing burden including that related to storage, shipping, promotion, extending credit, and other functions. Functional discounts are also a means to stimulate sales from otherwise reluctant buyers.

Quantity Discounts. Price reductions based on how much a buyer purchases are termed quantity discounts. Two types exist. A cumulative quantity discount is based on the total amount purchased over a period of time. A noncumulative quantity discount is based on the amount purchased at a single point in time. A quantity discount might be set on the criterion of units bought (e.g., $2.00 per unit for 1 to 99 units, $1.95 per unit for 100 to 499 units, and $1.90 per unit for 500 or more units) or the dollar value of the purchase (e.g., a 5 percent discount for orders over $3,000 and up to and including $10,000 and an 8 percent discount for orders over $10,000). Because of legal constraints (e.g., the Robinson-Patman Act), quantity discounts must reflect cost savings due, for example, to a savings in billing or shipping.

What are the effects of quantity discounts? Aside from the obvious financial motivations on the part of buyers and demand stimulation motives on the part of sellers, there is the possibility that quantity purchases could alter the balance of power between buyer and seller. To the extent that quantity discounts induce large purchases and result in buyers concentrating their orders from one or a few sellers, the vulnerability of either party can be affected, depending on the importance and magnitude of the sale for the parties and the alternatives available to each. Switching costs will be incurred as a function of the substitutability of one seller to another for the buyer, the critical nature of the resources to both buyer and seller, and the level of the resources exchanged. These issues will be elaborated upon in Chapter 14 and again in Chapter 16.

Price/Quality Pricing. The final stimulus-response tactic that we will examine is price/quality pricing. Consumers base their decisions, in part, on the quality of product offerings. But quality is an intangible, subjective property that is only partly dependent on the physical attributes of the product. One factor affecting the perception of product quality is thought to be the price of the product itself. That is, as the price of a product rises, or as one compares higher priced brands to lower priced brands, the perception of product quality is believed to be enhanced.[3] This would seem to imply that price (P) influences the perception of quality (Q) in a positive way:

$$P \xrightarrow{+} Q.$$

A somewhat different and expanded view is suggested by Monroe, who feels that consumers might be more fundamentally concerned with the *overall value* of a product where value is *defined* to equal the ratio of perceived quality to price:

$$\text{value} \stackrel{d}{=} \frac{\textbf{perceived quality}}{\textbf{price}}$$

and perceived quality is itself believed to be a function of price.[4] You can see in this equation that as quality increases value will increase, and as price goes up value will decrease.

If we take Monroe's model one step further and hypothesize that value is a conceptually distinct inference—not defined by perceived quality and price, but rather influenced by perceived quality and price—then we might propose a simple price-quality-value model such as the one shown in Figure 12-2. Notice first that price ultimately has two opposite effects on the decision to purchase. One is a negative effect that represents the costs that a higher price entails. Not only will a high price be costly in and of itself, but it will reflect opportunity costs. Both factors are reflected in the negative arrow from price to the decision to purchase in Figure 12-2. On the other hand, price is often a cue or signal as to the quality of a product. Perhaps a consumer will consciously (or subconsciously) feel that higher prices represent finer workmanship, more product features, better materials, and so on. Hence, as price rises, so does the perception of higher quality. Quality judgments in turn might influence the perception of the overall value of the product (where value is taken here to represent a subjective judgment and not the ratio of quality to price as defined earlier). At a minimum, quality and price are inputs to the evaluation process the consumer uses in decision making, a process we will have more to say about shortly.

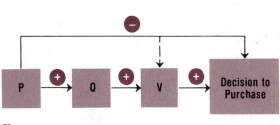

Key

P = perceived price
Q = perceived quality
V = inferred value
(+, −) = hypothesized polarity of influence

Figure 12-2. A simple price-quality-value model and its hypothesized effect on the decision to purchase

Finally, as shown in Figure 12-2, the inferred value of the entire product offering as reflected in its price and quality is shown as a determinant of the purchase decision itself. The greater the judged value, the higher the probability of a favorable decision and subsequent purchase, all other things being equal. Figure 12-2 is an oversimplification, and we have omitted other determinants in the decision process. For instance, the decision to purchase is not only a function of perceived price, quality, and value. The availability of substitutes from competitors, one's budget constraints, and family pressure are but a few of the forces left out of the model shown in Figure 12-2. But the model makes important points worth repeating; namely, price has opposing effects, operates complexly, and interacts with judgments about product quality and the overall value of the product to the consumer.

Figure 12-3 summarizes alternative ways in which prices might function. We might think of each submodel in the figure as constituting possible representations of how price as a stimulus influences the final decision. Each submodel might be appropriate for only a limited range of products, people, or societies. Unfortunately, very little research has been performed to tell us when one submodel or the other might be appropriate. The SOR submodel of Figure 12-3 represents an outline of probably the most realistic portrayal of price effects. Any price will harbor both negative and positive meanings that must be integrated in the decision process.

A final caveat to stress is that the hypothesized polarity of effects in Figures 12-2 and 12-3 are suggested as generalizations holding perhaps in only a majority of situations. There will always be exceptions to the rule. For example, under certain perhaps infrequent conditions, a high price might lead to an inference of no change in product quality or even reduced product quality on the part of a buyer. The former might result if a consumer believes that a higher price merely reflects extra costs for advertising, while the latter might reflect a judgment that the manufacturer is trying to cover up real deficiencies in a product by creating an image of exclusivity. In any event, the point to note is that it is not so much the stimulus itself (e.g., price) that influences behavior but rather the *meaning* of the stimulus for the person. And you are probably well aware, to model meaning and better predict choices, we must look deeper into the feelings and decision processes of consumers.

A Stimulus-Organism-Response View

As discussed in earlier chapters, it is necessary to consider what goes on inside the mind and body of the consumer if we are to gain a better understanding of why consumers buy what they buy. The exact reaction a person has to price—its meaning—will depend on how the person acts on the information reflected in the price and how the person feels about the price in emotional and social senses. At a simple level of description, we might depict the psychological processes intervening between price (stimulus) and purchase (response) as shown in Figure 12-4.

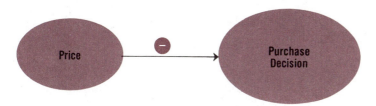

A. Common sense model

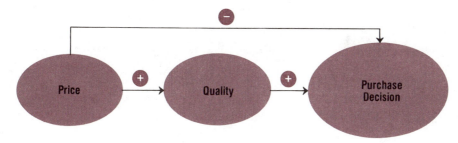

B. Price/Quality model

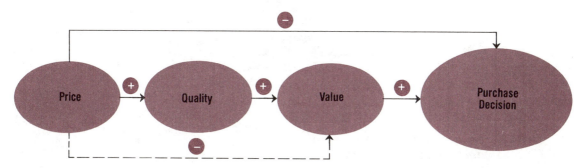

C. Price/Quality/Value model

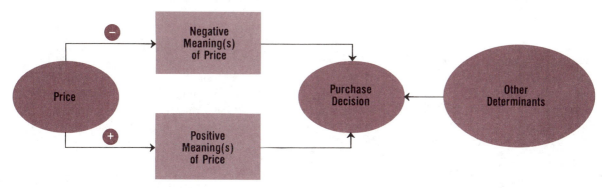

D. Outline of an S-O-R model

Figure 12-3. A summary of four models of how price as a stimulus might ultimately influence a decision to purchase

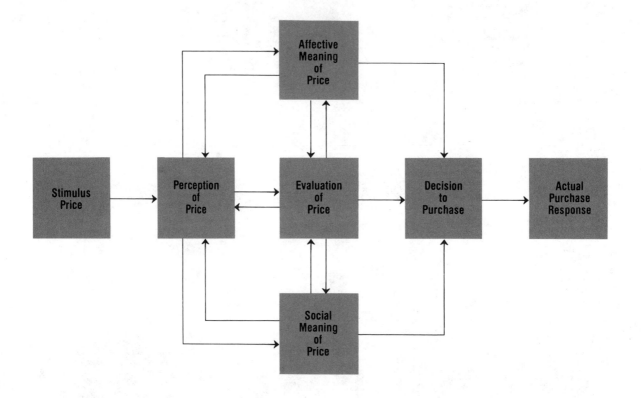

Figure 12-4. An overview of the S-O-R model of consumer reaction to price

The first stage begins with the consumer's perception of the level of the price. This is not as straightforward a process as one might think. What we see, what we perceive, is influenced not only by the physical characteristics of the medium communicating price but also by the psychology of the person. We actually construct the image of that which we see psychologically. You have probably often heard old sayings such as "Beauty is in the eyes of the beholder" or "We see what we want to see." These maxims reflect the reality that our needs, past experiences, and expectations sometimes shape and even distort our perceptions of the world. For example, when we are hungry, we might misread a price on an advertising product display board to be lower than what it really is. Psychologists have long known that our emotions and physiological states influence our perceptions. Figure 12-5 summarizes some of the forces affecting our perception of price. The stimuli and symbols shown in Figure 12-5 work through the processes indicated in the center of Figure 12-4. That is, they shape the consumer's emotional, cognitive (evaluative), and social reactions and these, in turn, feed back upon perception as shown in the figure.

Figure 12-5. Factors influencing the perception of price

Despite the central role of perception in the overall process, the most important psychological activities occur after perception, when the perceived price is transferred to working memory for further processing, where the information is acted upon and given affective, rational, and social meaning.

And in these stages the information and meaning of price are integrated with other information and thoughts and feelings of the consumer concerning possible purchase. The final decision to purchase is a function of all of these forces (plus external factors not shown in Figure 12-4 for simplicity).

For purchase decisions that require information processing and decision making, we can think of the role of price as being contingent on three possible situations: routinized response buying (RRB), limited problem solving (LPS), and extensive problem solving (EPS) contexts.[5]

In RRB, the consumer requires very little information to make a decision. The product might be inexpensive and therefore not require much deliberation and/or the consumer might have purchased it so many times that the next purchase demands little thinking. The purchase of milk or coffee in the supermarket often falls under these categories, as does, for instance, the ordering of paper clips or rubber bands by a small business. In either case, the role of price in the decision process is typically treated in a relatively simple way. The buyer might merely check the price to see if it is "not too high" or "the same as I paid last time." Price in this sense is regarded cognitively as a binary signal: it is either okay or it is too high. This is to be contrasted to the role of price in obviously more complex decisions such as the purchase of a television or a piece of machinery. In these situations, price is an input to a decision process perhaps involving cost benefit analyses, many comparisons to the competition, and other calculations. A final point to note is that price in RRB might at times encompass wide ranges of latitude or fuzzy ranges such as, "I will purchase a dozen donuts from store X if the price is no greater than about $4 to $5." The point is that, in RRB contexts, price is taken into account in the decision process but it is done quickly and with the use of a simple decision rule.

For more involved decisions where (a) the use or benefits of a product are not clear or are intricate and numerous, (b) the cost and risk associated with the product are high, and/or (c) the product is important to the buyer, price is usually evaluated more thoroughly and is integrated with other information in more complex ways. Imagine the implicit decision rules people might follow when deciding to purchase a pocket calculator—an LPS decision.

One individual might follow a lexicographic rule. He or she might begin by searching for "a high quality calculator—either a Hewlett Packard or a Texas Instruments model." Thus, the decision process is initiated with a search for two brands and elimination of other manufacturers. Next, after finding the focal brands, the consumer might employ a second lexicographic criterion: "examine only those calculators that have the full range of scientific functions." A third step in the decision process might then be to "select the brand that has the full range of functions, costs under $200 and/or offers the best value for the price, and is superior on most other secondary criteria such as overall appearance and size." This latter decision is an instance of the conjunctive rule.

A second consumer might weigh each of a set of criteria—e.g., price, perceived quality, warranty, number of functions provided—in such a way as to decide to choose the one brand that scores the highest on each criterion and allowing high scores on some criteria to compensate for low scores on others (a form of a linear compensatory rule).

Many other rules are possible, depending on the person and situation. For even more complex and involving decisions, more complex formal rules and procedures might be followed. The points to be stressed here are that price is but one of a number of criteria, its incorporation in the decision process increases in complexity and importance as one moves from RRB to LPS to EPS, and we can begin to understand the process by examining possible rules and criteria used by consumers in their decision making.

As a point of information, we should acknowledge that price often plays a minor role in some contexts. In addition to the case of wealthy consumers engaging in conspicuous consumption, we should note that impulse buying contexts often do not involve pricing decisions or if they do they are minimal such as in RRB. Typically, impulse buying is initiated by arousing stimuli that activate learned or reflex actions. Cognitive processing such as price comparisons are kept to a minimum in such situations.

From the viewpoint of the psychology of the buyer, we might represent the decision process in a simple model. To begin with, it is useful to define two broad categories of reactions that consumers have to prices: cognitive and emotional (or evaluative). An early reaction is often a cognitive one. The consumer perceives the price and compares it to his or her expectations and perhaps to the competition. This involves thinking processes, retrieval from memory, and active processing in short-term memory. Much of the activity is rational in the sense that information processing entails judgments about matters of fact and conceived means-ends relations. But cognitive processes are only half the story. The consumer also reacts emotionally or evaluatively. Affect and good/bad connotations are attached to the price, the product, the communication, the implications of purchase and product use, and so on. Then the consumer somehow organizes the collection of thoughts and feelings into an overall attitude, judgment, or preference. The integration, in turn, leads to a decision to purchase or not. Sometimes no immediate decision is made, except perhaps for an interim plan to acquire new information or to later weigh other factors.

How might a marketing researcher measure and represent this part of the decision process? One way is to use an expectancy-value model, a rule for the integration of cognitions and evaluations, and a rule for action. The researcher measures the reactions of consumers, hypothesizes plausible rules, and sees how well they predict behavior. For example, the following model is a popular simplified representation of the process:

$$A_j = \sum_{i=1}^{n} B_i\, a_i$$

R = choose brand with highest attitudinal score

where A_j is the consumer's attitude toward brand j and assumed to be formed as the product (i.e., integration) of n beliefs (B) times n evaluations (a). Presumably one belief and one evaluation would be for prices. Given that a consumer forms an attitude toward each of a set of four brands, say, we would predict, based on decision rule R, that he or she would decide to purchase the brand with the highest attitudinal score.

One can check the model by measuring a number of people's beliefs and evaluations of n attributes of the four brands and then seeing how well intentions to purchase or actual purchase are predicted. Many other functional forms for information integration can be used in addition to the summation of products of beliefs and evaluations—other decision rules are applicable, but we will not discuss them here. The simple representation in equation (1) illustrates the principles applying to even more complicated models. That is, attitudes (A_j) toward brands, products, or purchase acts are a function of beliefs and evaluations of product characteristics and/or consequences of product use and these in turn determine choice through a decision rule. We are only now beginning to understand these processes through research.

Price at the Macro Level

So far, we have seen that prices constitute one of a number of pieces of information that managers attach to their products and that consumers evaluate and weigh in their decision processes. This is perhaps the most easily understood meaning of price, for it is closest to the actual way we experience it as managers or consumers. However, it is also possible to study prices at a more abstract and aggregate level. We may examine prices, for example, as industrywide patterns, as they serve to bring supply and demand into equilibrium in the marketplace, and as they affect and are affected by social forces. Why might we desire to look at price at a macro level? First of all, prices at the aggregate level influence the well-being of society as a whole. To understand the health of the economy, we must examine the workings of pricing mechanisms, among other factors. Second, to influence economic conditions, public policy makers and others also need to know how prices operate. Indeed, the control of pricing practices is a major target of public policy. Finally, the study of prices at the macro level helps the manager understand how the firm relates to other firms and society as a whole.

Actually, although we have divided this chapter on pricing into two parts—a micro and a macro—both dimensions are mutually related. Moreover, they interact with managerial considerations, a topic discussed at length in Chapter 13. To see this, take a look at Figure 12-6. This figure shows the central elements of price at the macro level but, at the same time, includes micro and managerial elements as some of its component parts. Notice first at the right that there are three broad *outcomes* that prices influence: societal, organizational, and individual consumer outcomes. These outcomes are, of course, shaped by many other forces. But prices play an important role. At the societal level, prices can be seen to regulate the allocation and use of scarce resources and to insure that goods are produced at more or less reasonable levels of efficiency. Prices also indirectly affect the level of employment and interact with inflationary and other economic forces. And, although the relationship is not well understood, prices are connected to the distribution of income, producing or thwarting social equity depending on their ebb and flow. At the level of the firm, the prices that an organization sets and the prices set by other firms can often influence the profitability and market share and growth of these firms. Finally, prices have an obviously important impact on the well-being of consumers. The prices we pay ultimately shape our level of satisfaction and overall standard of living.

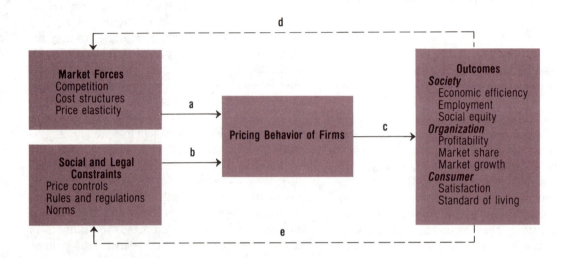

Figure 12-6. A macro view of price

All these outcomes—societal, organizational, and personal—are shown in Figure 12-6 to be affected by *pricing behavior*. We will have more to say about the nature of pricing behavior at the managerial level in the following chapter. For now, we note that firms devote considerable time and money in the determination of what level of prices to set for their products. The levels they set can often be interpreted in relation to competitors (e.g., price leadership or following) and consumers (e.g., price discrimination, skimming, penetration).

In general, at the macro level, we can explain pricing behavior as a function of two factors: *market forces* and *social and legal constraints*. If prices were set entirely on the basis of market forces (arrow a in Figure 12-6), then we would have the ideal-type market economy. For example, under pure competition the firm has little freedom to set the level of its price, while under oligopolistic conditions, the firm has more leeway. If prices were set entirely on the basis of social and legal forces, in contrast, then we would have the ideal-type of a planned economy (arrow b in Figure 12-6). In reality, no society in the world today is either a perfect market economy or a perfect planned economy. All systems involve a mixture of market forces and social and legal constraints in the determination of price (and output). The United States tends to emphasize a market system, but laws and regulations govern pricing behavior in important instances. Similarly, the Soviet Union is largely a centrally planned system, yet managers sometimes have some freedom to set prices in response to market forces. Thus, it is important to consider both paths a and b in Figure 12-6 if we are to comprehend price at a macro level.[6] We begin now with an analysis of market forces and social and legal constraints as they apply to price.

Market Forces

From an economic standpoint, we know that price plays a fundamental role. At the micro level, consumers are presumed to maximize utility and firms are assumed to maximize profits. Both do this subject to their budget constraints: i.e., their income and the prices of desired goods and services. When we aggregate up to the level of groups of consumers (e.g., a market) or groups of firms (e.g., an industry), we can see that consumers and producers respond to prices set as a consequence of supply and demand forces in the marketplace. Moreover, the prices that both set—consumers for their labor, firms for their goods—is dependent on market forces. We will discuss three of the more important ones herein: competition, cost structures, and price elasticity.

Competition. Typically (to take the viewpoint of the seller) we may identify three structural conditions under which organizations function. (See Table 12-1.)

Under pure competition, the number of sellers of the *same product* is large, and the firm has little freedom to determine what price to set for its product. As we shall see, it "chooses" a price equal to the market price for all sellers. (A slightly different condition is monopolistic competition, in which many sellers market somewhat differentiated products or services.)

TABLE 12-1
Three Basic Economic Structures Faced by a Seller

Structure Type	Description
Pure Competition	Many sellers market essentially the same product or service.
Monopolistic Competition	Many sellers market somewhat differentiated products or services.
Homogeneous Oligopoly	A small number of firms market basically the same product or service.
Differentiated Oligopoly	A small number of firms market somewhat differentiated products or services.
Monopoly	A single seller exists with no close substitutes.

Under an oligopoly, a few sellers of the same product (the *homogeneous* oligopoly) or similar products (the *differentiated* oligopoly) exist, and each has some freedom to set its price at a level different from the others. Nevertheless, the firms in an oligopoly usually discover that their freedom is limited by demand, costs, and the actions of their rivals.

Finally, under a monopoly, a single seller has considerable freedom to set its price. Yet, even here, demand and cost factors constrain that freedom somewhat, as we shall see.

In sum, then, the proposition is that at least a part of pricing behavior (e.g., the price level) is determined by competitive market forces embodied in structures of pure competition, oligopoly, or monopoly faced by the seller. To simplify our discussion of these forces, it should be noted that we will limit the presentation below to the case of relatively homogeneous products. The more important, but complicated, case of product differentiation is described in Chapter 13 within the context of managerial views of price. In Chapter 13 the topics of monopolistic competition and differentiated oligopoly are considered.

Pure Competition. To see the influence of pure competition on prices, let us look at Figure 12-7. We begin with the market before equilibrium (case A in Figure 12-7) where the numerous firms in the industry face a short-run supply, S_1. The interaction of industry supply and market demand (D_I) yields a (short-run) equilibrium price of $P_{1,I}$ (r in the figure). This is the price *taken as a given*, at least temporarily, by the firm represented at the left of Figure 12-7A. With this price ($P_{1,F}$), the firm is motivated to produce $q_{1,F}$, since this will maximize profits. That is, when marginal cost (MC) equals $P_{1,F}$, the profit will equal $x - y$ (as calculated from average total cost (ATC), quantity, and price considerations). The presence of profits, however, will motivate new firms to enter the market, and we will eventually experience a corresponding shift in industry supply to S_2 (see case B in Figure 12-7). This, in turn, will reduce the price towards an equilibrium value, $P_{2,I}$ (see path r → s). The firm will thus face a new price, and pressures will force the output of a new quantity, $q_{2,F}$, where $ATC = MC = P_{2,F}$. Here, no profits are realized and only total costs are recovered (see path x→z in Figure 12-7).

In short, firms competing under pure competition are forced to operate efficiently in the sense that the average costs per unit are at a minimum. Consumers benefit by having to pay a lower price than they would under other structures. Firms presumably make just enough (i.e., a "nominal" profit) to motivate them to remain in the market (indeed they can sell all they produce and at a satisfactory price) but perhaps not enough to innovate in the long run. In any event, pure competition determines the long-run price for the market ($P_{2,I} = P_{2,F}$). Although no flawless examples of perfect competition exist, agricultural crops approximate this situation. But even here, government actions in the form of price supports or outright purchases change the situation somewhat. One can readily understand why farmers, who continually face pressures to sell at a relatively low price and not make a profit, lobby for government intervention to subsidize higher prices.

In sum, under pure competition, firms cannot really control their pricing but must accept the going rate. They face little or no strategic choices with respect to pricing. The firm's demand curve is horizontal.

Monopoly. Before we discuss the more common case of oligopoly, let us consider the rather rare case of a monopoly (see Figure 12-8). Notice first that monopolies (and oligopolies) face downward-sloping demand curves. Different quantities of the firm's product will be demanded at different prices. It therefore is able to make strategic choices with respect to the pricing decision.

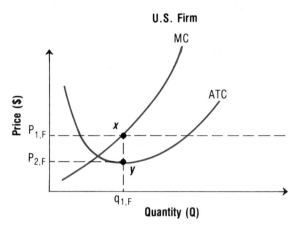

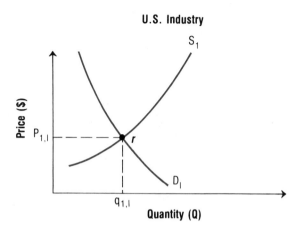

A. Before equilibrium

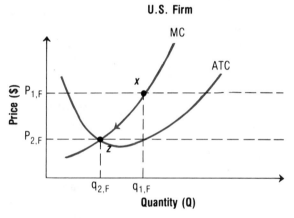

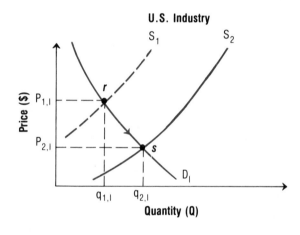

B. At equilibrium

$q_{2,F} < q_{1,F}$ $q_{2,I} > q_{1,I}$

$p_{2,F} < p_{1,F}$ $p_{2,I} < p_{1,I}$

Figure 12-7. Pricing under pure competition

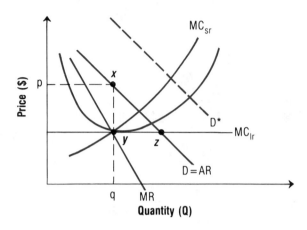

Figure 12-8. Pricing under a pure monopoly

A downward sloping demand curve has two important implications. First, a firm facing such a demand function knows that the quantity sold will be a function of the price it sets, and, therefore, care must be taken to determine the price best meeting the firm's goals. We call the movement along a particular demand curve arising from a change in price the *price elasticity of demand*. The important aspects of this will be discussed in the next section of this chapter. For now, note that price elasticity of demand refers to the buyer's sensitivity to changes in the price of one's product. It does not change the demand curve but rather exploits its properties.

The second implication of a downward-sloping demand curve to note is the concept of *demand shifts*. An example is shown in Figure 12-8, where the existing demand curve, *D*, is shown parallel to a potential new demand function *D** (shown as dashed lines). Demand actually increases from *D* to *D** to produce more units sold at a given price. Of course, the demand curve might shift to the left (i.e., decrease). A shift in demand might

occur as a consequence of an increase or decrease in the purchasing power of consumers or a change in the price of a substitute for the product in question. It is important to recognize the distinction between price elasticity and shifts of demand. The phenomena have different causes and different implications for society, management, and the consumer, as developed below.

To return to pricing under a monopoly, we can see in Figure 12-8 that when *MC* equals *MR*, the firm will charge *p* and sell *q*. Notice that *p* is greater than *MC* here, whereas $p = MC$ under pure competition. Let us look at the implications of *p* for a monopoly and compare these to pure competition. First, unlike the profitless pure competitor, the monopolist usually achieves a profit: profit $= (x - y)q$. Indeed, its freedom to set a price within at least a narrow to moderate range almost assures this outcome. Second, whereas the pure competitor produces efficiently (i.e., at the minimum total cost per unit of output), the monopolist need not necessarily. However, it should be acknowledged that it is possible for a monopolist to produce efficiently and/or fail to make a profit. That is, nothing within economic theory prevents this from happening. On the other hand, given economic theory, pure competition must ultimately result in no profit and efficiency of production. These implications of the theories should be kept in mind for they show that, in the sense of profits and productive efficiency of a firm, pure competition and monopoly need not differ, although they often do in practice. About the only differentiating point we can definitely make is that the price for a pure competitor will always equal marginal costs whereas the price of a monopolist must be greater than marginal cost. Without demonstrating this here, one can show that the price a monopolist sets restricts output and results in less total consumer satisfaction in the market than had the firm set $p = MC$. Thus, in this sense, the price set by a monopolist is detrimental to social welfare.

The concept of a monopoly as a solitary seller does not exist in the United States except perhaps for relatively small firms in isolated geographical areas or for new products for a short time in their introductory stages. Some examples of large firms in the U.S. approaching a monopoly include Campbell Soup with about 85 percent of the canned soup market and (up until deregulation) Western Electric with about 85 percent of the telephone equipment market. But in recent years, even these firms have been losing market share as new competitors enter the market.

Oligopoly. An oligopoly occurs when there are a few sellers, and each has some effect on market price and possibly on the pricing practices of others in the industry. But how many sellers is "a few"? One author suggests that an oligopoly occurs when the leading four firms in an industry control at least 40 percent of the market.[7] By this rule-of-thumb, it is estimated that more than half of the firms in the U.S. operate in oligopolistic markets. Leading examples are the producers of beer, automobiles, ready-to-eat cereals, gasoline, refrigerators, computers, and copy machines.

Let us examine a typical oligopoly. In Figure 12-9, we display the conditions faced by a two-firm oligopoly (i.e., a duopoly). For simplicity, we assume that the two firms have the same MR function and face demand D. However, Firm A has higher marginal costs than does Firm B (i.e., $MC_A > MC_B$). Under these conditions, Firm A will prefer to set its price at P_A, while Firm B will desire to set its price at P_B. Although not shown in the figure, one can easily calculate that the respective prices resulting from equating $MR = MC$ for firms A and B are optimum for each; and if one firm were forced to accept the price set by the other, then profits would be lower. Therefore, the firms face a dilemma of what price to set. They must take into account the potential pricing behavior of their rival since the market will not support two different prices in the long run.

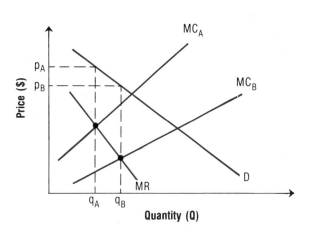

Figure 12-9. Pricing under a two-firm oligopoly

We know that the price each sets will most likely be somewhere between P_A and P_B, inclusive. But how will the firms decide on their price level? One way might involve direct contact and a negotiated price between P_A and P_B. However, one or both firms may prefer not to do this to maintain a perceived competitive edge. Also it may violate a law against collusive agreements. A second manner of resolution might entail a decision process wherein each firm takes into account its best guess as to the action or reaction of the other firm before setting its own price. For example, Firm B might decide, because it is in the better cost position, to take the lead and set a price slightly above P_B. In this way, it attains profits close to its optimum, but at the same time, does not threaten Firm A as much as if P_B were set. Thus, the potential for a pricing war is reduced. Nevertheless, this is not a very well-defined rationale to tell us exactly what price will be set.

Economists have developed theories for predicting price in an oligopolistic situation. These include explanations based on game theory, the theory of kinked demand functions, and other frameworks.[8] We will limit discussion here to kinked demand curves, for simplicity.[9] Figure 12-10 illustrates a typical case. Consider the kinked (i.e., bent) demand curve CKB faced by firms in an oligopolistic industry. This curve reflects the believed situation arising from decisions performed by rivals in the industry. Based on their judgments, the firms decide to price at p. Their logic is something like the following. For prices greater than p, the quantity sold will decrease rapidly because of the relatively flat portion of the demand curve CK. Therefore, no firm will be motivated to raise prices, as its profitability will be reduced (assuming other firms retain the lower price). This rationale rests on the assumption that, should one or two firms, say, raise their prices, then other firms can increase production and meet the excess demand, yet remain at their old price p. For prices less than p, in contrast, the quantity sold increases less

rapidly than it might under nonkinked conditions. Thus, firms are not motivated to lower prices, as this too results in less profitability.

The kinked demand curve CKB can be derived from two demand curves implicitly faced by a decision maker. Demand curve AKB in Figure 12-10 is the situation wherein the decision maker assumes that rivals will act so as to match any move of the decision maker. Demand curve CKD is the situation wherein the decision maker assumes that rivals will hold their price constant at p no matter what the decision maker does. In the kinked demand theory, it is presumed that a decision maker acts as if he or she anticipates that a rival will opt for the least favorable option in response to a price change. That is, if a decision maker decides to raise his or her price, then it is assumed that rivals will stand pat. Similarly, if a decision maker decides to lower his or her price, then it is presumed that rivals will follow suit. The combination of these strategies yields the kinked demand curve shown in Figure 12-10.

The important aspects of oligopolistic pricing are the following. First, firms have some leeway in setting prices. Second, nevertheless, they are interdependent with other firms, and this dependence, in addition to that provided by restrictions resulting from cost and demand factors, constrains their actions. Third, based on kinked demand theory, firms tend to reject price cutting as a viable strategy. Fourth, firms also face pressures to hold prices constant even in the face of moderate cost increases and shifts in the demand function. Nevertheless, two limitations of kinked demand theory deserve mention.[10] First, empirical data has not always corresponded to the theory. Second, the theory does not accurately specify what exact level p will be achieved. A final dimension of oligopolistic pricing to note is that the theory applies strongest for homogeneous products. Product differentiation tends to lessen the need for firms to take each other's actions into account, although it does not eliminate interdependencies among rivals for a share of the market.

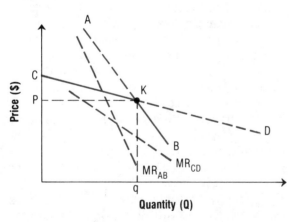

A-B Overall demand for industry

C-D Demand for focal firm, assuming all firms use same price

Figure 12-10. Price setting in an oligopoly: a kinked-demand explanation

Critique of Economic Theories of Price. Although economic theories represent useful frameworks for viewing price, they pose some drawbacks that need mentioning. Perhaps the most significant shortcoming concerns the assumptions upon which most models are based. Consumers are assumed to have perfect knowledge (e.g., to be aware of all brands and prices) and to maximize utility. To the extent that they are ignorant of alternative brands and use decision rules other than utility maximization, the theory will be in error. At the same time, economic theories presume that the manager has knowledge of costs and demand, but considerable error can exist here as well. Further, economic theories have not as yet fully integrated other decision requisites with the pricing decision. In fact, most economic theories assume that product, communication, and distribution decisions have already been made or do not interact with the pricing decision. Finally, the economic theories omit determinants of price such as power and conflict within the firm over goals and resources, social and political constraints, competitive responses, and unknown or unforeseen economic shocks.

Cost Structures. Pricing behavior is obviously influenced by costs. But the nature and extent of the effects are not well understood. In the long run, it can be asserted that costs provide a lower bound on what prices a firm sets. However, everyday price setting is guided more by short-run considerations with costs only suggesting rough guidelines. We might think of the pricing behavior of firms as being influenced by many forces: competition, costs, demand, social/legal constraints, and strategic managerial considerations related to goals of profitability, market share, growth, and marketing mix interactions. Each of these forces might, on occasion, have a separate effect on pricing behavior, while at other times only one or a few forces are determinative. We focus in this section on cost forces. But it should be remembered that cost is only one input.

Break-even Analysis. One of the most basic cost concepts is break-even analysis. To understand this idea, let us begin with the problem faced by a small retailer of automotive accessories. The retailer has been approached by a salesperson who is selling ice scrapers for cars. The wholesale price offer to the retailer is $1.50 for this deluxe, all-purpose scraper. This, then, is the variable cost (*VC*) to the retailer. The retailer estimates that sales of ice scrapers will entail a fixed cost (*FC*) of about $600 for the year, and that, based on past experience, he or she can expect to sell about 400 to local residents. What price must be charged to recover fixed and variable costs at this estimated sales volume (q_E)?

The break-even price can be calculated from the following formula:

$$P = \frac{FC + VC \times q_E}{q_E}$$
$$= \frac{\$600 + \$1.50 \times 400}{400}$$
$$= \$3.00$$

This is the price under which sales volume exactly covers fixed plus variable costs. A price less than $3.00 would result in a loss; a price greater than $3.00 would produce a profit.

Actually, the retailer's problem could have been reformulated in slightly different terms. That is, given *VC* and estimated *FC*, the retailer might have felt that the price he or she would have to charge (as a result of market forces) was "about $3.00." His or her problem is then: What quantity will I have to sell to break even? The break-even quantity can be calculated from the above formula, rearranged as follows:

$$q_{BE} = \frac{FC}{P - VC}$$

Substitution into this equation yields q_{BE} = 400. Figure 12-11 presents a graphic representation of the concepts in break-even analysis.

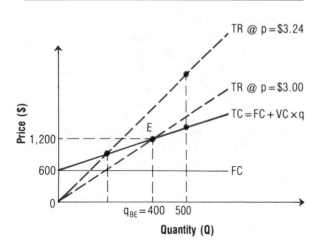

Figure 12-11. A break-even analysis

Break-even analysis is often a useful tool for making decisions. It formally introduces costs constraints into the decision-making process. However, it has a fundamental limitation. To calculate a break-even price, one must estimate demand. Conversely, to calculate a break-even quantity, one must estimate a viable price. Hence, the value of the approach is limited by the means and accuracy of demand or price estimation procedures. Perhaps more disconcerting, whichever way one applies the formula—either to determine price or to determine demand—one must assume that either demand or price is given. In other words, the theory assumes that, if we use the formula to compute price, we have no influence over demand (and vice versa). In reality, depending on the market structure, price influences demand, and demand influences price. So in this sense, the theory is based on a false assumption. Moreover, the theory assumes that costs can be validly divided into fixed and variable components. While true in the short run, this is definitely not true in the long run since most costs are effectively variable. Another problematic assumption is linearity in costs—nonlinearities may be the rule.

Nevertheless, in practice, managers have found that break-even analyses provide useful guidelines and occasionally are accurate. Sometimes, because of information limitations, break-even analyses are the only procedures that can be applied. A final point to note is that break-even analyses have been used also to estimate the price needed to yield a *target rate of return.* To see this usage, let us return to Figure 12-11. Suppose the retailer of ice scrapers again estimates $FC = \$600$ and $VC = \$1.50$, and further suppose that the salesperson, as an incentive, offers to pay for an advertisement in the local newspaper for each of the first four weeks in late fall. The retailer might predict that, with the free advertising, he or she would be able to sell 500 scrapers.

Assuming that the retailer normally aspires to make a 20 percent profit above total costs, what price must be charged to realize this goal? Using the formula

$$P = \frac{FC + VC \times q_E}{q_E},$$

we can calculate the price as

$$P = \frac{(\$600 + \$1.50 \times 500) + .2(\$600 + \$1.50 \times 500)}{500}$$

$$= \$3.24.$$

At this price, profits will amount to $270. The retailer must decide whether this price is reasonable to stimulate the required demand. He or she might feel that it is somewhat too high and psychologically unattractive. Perhaps $3.19 would be more unobtrusive. With an estimated demand of 500, $3.19 would still be profitable, as the break-even price is $2.70 at this volume.

Economies of Scale and Experience Curves. Break-even analyses provide a rough guide for how costs constrain prices. But the analyses are static. They do not take into account dynamic factors related to changes in production costs over time, size of an organization, its technology and production functions, and other factors. Two important cost-related forces shaping price are economies of scale and experience curve effects. Economies of scale refer to decreases in the costs of producing a product per unit as the volume of production increases over time. This results from more efficiently using inputs and spreading fixed costs over a greater volume. Actually, it is possible to achieve economies of scale in nearly every phase of an organization's operations, from manufacturing, to purchasing, marketing, and research and development, for example. Economies of scale are important market forces allowing firms producing at high volumes to set relatively lower prices than smaller firms.

Experience curves refer to the phenomenon of declines in unit costs as a firm accrues experience over time in the production of a product.[11] It has been observed in many companies that costs decline by a constant amount each time the *cumulative* output doubles. (By cumulative we mean that past output is added to present output at each point in time to yield a new total, termed *cumulative output*. The idea is that past experience should result in some learning and that a measure of this can be gained by adding past output to present output at each point in time.) Figure 12-12 illustrates the principle: it can be seen that, as cumulative output increases, costs decline by a constant amount given by the slope of the line.

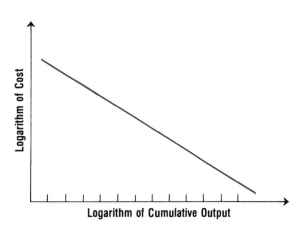

Figure 12-12. A typical experience curve

Why should costs decline? Presumably, the firm "learns" over time to better coordinate production, increase the productivity of machinery and equipment, and so on. Workers also are believed to better learn how to perform their tasks over time. Thus, costs decline over time.

Notice that the experience curve phenomenon is different from the cost savings resulting from economies of scale. Economies of scale depend on the size of the firm and can be achieved even in the short run. Learning from experience requires time and occurs to a certain extent for all firms, even smaller ones. The phenomena described by experience curves and economies of scale arise from different determinants of costs.

A last point to stress is that, as with economies of scale, when experience accures and costs decline, a basis exists for setting a relatively lower price. Figure 12-13 shows how this happened for the Ford Model T automobile in the first quarter of the century. Notice that the price dropped from nearly $4,000 in 1909 to about $1,000 in 1923. Much of this drop was due to both experience effects and economies of scale. We will consider experience curve effects again in the final chapter.

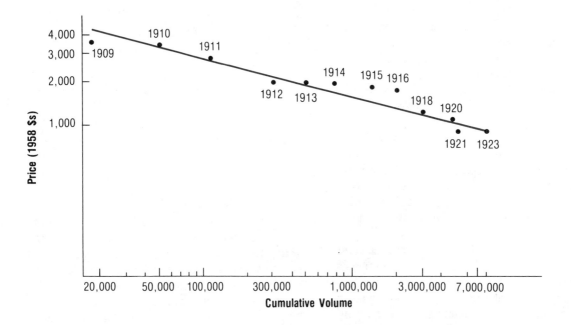

Figure 12-13. The experience curve for the Ford Model T, 1909–23

SOURCE: William J. Abernathy and Kenneth Wayne, "Limits of the Learning Curve," *Harvard Business Review* 52 (September–October 1974): 111. Copyright © 1974, by the President and Fellows of Harvard College; all rights reserved.

Other Cost Considerations. Costs depend on many other factors, but because of space limitations, we can do little more than list them here. One factor depends on the bargaining power of the firm, which, in turn, will be a function of the availability of substitute goods, the number and size of suppliers, the size of the focal firm and its purchase amount, and other factors. Similarly, the nature of the firm's accounting and costing procedures will affect computed costs and, hence, prices. Finally, a whole host of economic/technical forces within and without the firm will shape costs also.

Price Elasticity. We have seen how competitive forces in the market influence prices and how costs serve as constraints as well. But there is one additional important determinant: the demand for the product. One cannot charge too much for a product or no one will buy it. Similarly, if too little is charged, the firm may lose money. In between these extremes lie many potential price levels, each promising different levels of sales. One way to formally tie the level of demand to price is through the price elasticity of demand (e_p), which can be defined as

$$e_p = \frac{\% \text{ change in quantity demanded}}{\% \text{ change in price}}$$

$$= \frac{\dfrac{\Delta q}{q}}{\dfrac{\Delta p}{p}}$$

This equation shows how much of a change in sales we can expect if we change price by a particular amount. Three possible values for e_p deserve mention. First, consider $e_p < -1$. Here the percentage change in quantity demanded is greater than the percentage change in price. For example, if price decreases from \$5 to \$4 and sales go from 2,000 to 3,000 units, then $e_p = -2.5$. It can be shown that total revenue will increase if $e_p < -1$. We say that demand is therefore elastic (see Figure 12-14A). If $e_p = -1$, then the percentage change in demand equals the percentage change in price. Here no change in revenues will result from a price change. This is called unity elasticity. Finally, if $0 > e_p > -1$, then the percentage change in quantity demanded will be less than a percentage change in price. Total revenues will decrease with a price cut. We say that demand is thus inelastic (see Figure 12-14B). Generally, for the vast majority of products, e_p will be negative.

The concept of elasticity is useful as a tool for showing how revenues will change if we change prices. By doing a sensitivity analysis, one can determine the range of prices producing a corresponding range in revenues. Of course, management is often more

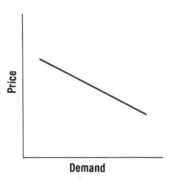

A. Elastic demand

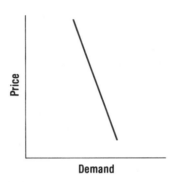

B. Inelastic demand

Figure 12-14. Examples of demand elasticity

concerned with the effect of price on profits. Consequently, one needs to take into account costs as well as revenue when considering elasticity effects. From economic theory considerations,[12] it can be shown that profits will be maximized when

$$\% \text{ markup} = \frac{-1}{1 + e_p} \times 100\%.$$

For example, for $e_p = -2$, the percent of markup on costs needed to maximize profit is 100 percent. Thus, if one has information on the elasticity of a market (e.g., through historical data), then the optimum price can be calculated. The above equation works best for retail organizations and then only imperfectly. Perhaps the best way to use elasticities is to compute profits under different price options and ranges. This, in turn, requires that demand, VC, and FC be taken into account. The important point to realize is that an optimal price will be complexly determined by demand, cost, and competitive forces.

Note further that, if price influences perceived quality, the elasticity coefficient might need to be altered. Within certain ranges or for certain market segments, a small price rise (drop) might lead to increased (decreased) demand because consumers infer more (less) quality. Thus, one should not view the elasticity coefficient as inevitably reflecting only classic economic notions of price/quantity effects but rather consumer psychological forces may also be at work. Indeed, when considering a price rise or cut, managers must take into account a whole host of economic, psychological, social, and firm-related considerations. These topics are discussed in the following chapter.

Social and Legal Constraints

The final topic we wish to discuss in regard to price at the macro level is the influence that environmental forces have over and above market factors and managerial leeway. The most prevalent and powerful forces occur through governmental actions. In general, governmental restrictions can arise from three sources: the Antitrust Division of the Justice Department, the Federal Trade Commission, and the president.[13]

The Antitrust Division. The Antitrust Division of the Justice Department has responsibility for enforcing antitrust laws. It shares this responsibility with the Federal Trade Commis-

sion. The Antitrust Division's activities are divided between the investigation of violations of laws and the initiation of court action against alleged violators. Court action occurs in cases adjudicated before one of the federal district courts. Although both the FTC and Antitrust Division can initiate civil actions against violators of antitrust laws, only the latter can engage in criminal complaints. Table 12-2 summarizes the more important antitrust legislation since its inception with the Sherman Act of 1890.

With respect to pricing, the most important aspects of legislation applies to price fixing, price discrimination, and deceptive pricing. Let us briefly define and comment on these.

Price Fixing. Price fixing is any agreement among firms to set prices at levels in concert with each other. It is illegal in the United States but is allowed in many parts of the world in one form or another. The rationale for the legislation is basically that price fixing is a restraint of trade and lessens competition. The Justice Division generally seeks criminal prosecution of price fixers under Section 1 of the Sherman Act. The penalties for conviction now may include personal fines of $100,000 and corporate fines of $1 million per count and/or prison sentences up to three years. The Justice Division can, of course, institute civil suits that may result in court injunctions to cease and desist from the illegal practices. Further, the Clayton Act permits persons injured by antitrust violators to sue for three times the amount of damages (called treble damages). To give one a picture of the extent of legal action, it should be noted that by the early 1980s corporate fines often totaled $11 million yearly; as many as 30 people per year were sentenced to an average of 100 days per person; and private antitrust suits per year often totaled more than 1,500. This tends to understate the impact of the law, as the threat of legal action often results in out-of-court settlements. The law also serves as a deterrent forcing firms to carefully weigh their actions.

TABLE 12-2
A Summary of Some Important Legal Developments Affecting Pricing Behavior

Date	Development	Description
1890	Sherman Act	Section 1: "Every contract, combination in the form of trust or otherwise, or conspiracy, in restraint of trade ... is ... illegal." Section 2: "Every person who shall monopolize, or attempt to monopolize ... any part of trade ... shall be deemed guilty ..." and penalized by imprisonment and/or fine. Section 4: Attorney General empowered to initiate suits. Section 7: Injured private persons can sue for recovery of three times the amount of damage.
1903	Antitrust Division of Justice Department	Created to enforce Sherman Act
1914	Clayton Act	Section 2: "... it shall be unlawful ... to discriminate in price between different purchasers ... when the effect of such discrimination may be to substantially lessen competition or tend to create a monopoly. ... Provided that nothing ... shall prevent discrimination in price ... on account of differences in the grade, quality or quantity of the commodity sold, or ... for differences in the cost of selling or transportation, or ... to meet competition ..."
1914	Federal Trade Commission Act	Section 5: Outlawed "unfair methods of competition." Set up an agency to enforce Clayton Act, investigate business practices, perform research, and conduct conferences.
1936	Robinson-Patman Act	Section 2a: "... it is unlawful ... to discriminate in price between different purchasers for commodities of like grade and quality ... where the effect ... may be substantially to lessen competition or tend to create a monopoly ..." But discrimination may be permitted to dispose of perishable, obsolescent, or seasonal goods; to make due allowances for differences in "the cost of manufacture, sale, or delivery"; or "in good faith to meet an equally low price of a competitor."
1938	Wheeler-Lea Amendment to FTC Act	Broadened FTC's jurisdiction to include practices that injure the public broadly and not merely those that directly injure a competitor. For example: deceptive advertising.
1974	Federal Antitrust Statute	Makes it a felony to violate federal antitrust laws; increases fines for individuals up to $100,000, for corporations up to $1,000,000 per count; and for violation of the Sherman Act, extends upper limit of prison sentences to three years.
1983	*Fall City Industries, Inc.,* v. *Vanco Beverage, Inc.* (51 LW 4275)	Clarifies and amplifies the "marketing competition" defense of Robinson-Patman Act by permitting seller to offer price differentials when a competitor has lower prices in a general area of selling.

Price Discrimination. Price discrimination occurs whenever there are unjustified price differences for the same product sold by a single seller. The Clayton Act directly forbids it (as does its amendment, the Robinson-Patman Act). However, discrimination is permitted (1) if cost differences exist in manufacture, selling, or delivery; (2) if the price is needed to meet lawful competition; or (3) if the price reflects different uses for the product, distribution in different markets, or sales at different points in time. (Other conditions apply, but are too numerous to mention here).

The rationale for legislation against price discrimination again rests with the belief that its practice restrains trade and lessens competition. Indeed, some economists feel that price discrimination additionally influences the distribution of income and allocative efficiency in detrimental ways. On the other hand, the interpretation of the law has sometimes been so difficult that some firms have refrained from using price as a stimulus but rather have resorted to nonprice competition out of fear of possible infringement. Whether this has enhanced or thwarted overall competition is difficult to judge. Moreover, although the original logic behind legislation was to protect small businesses, the vast majority of enforcement procedures has occurred against small businesses rather than their larger rivals. Nevertheless, since the early 1960s, when the number of price discrimination complaints was about 74 per year, activity has subsided considerably to less than an average of 6 per year in the last decade or so.

Deceptive Pricing. Deceptive pricing is an umbrella term used to capture a variety of practices (see also the discussion in Chapter 9). One form of deceptive pricing concerns false claims as to the amount of discount offered the public. For example, some furniture retailers have been known to claim a huge discount on a new piece of furniture where the undiscounted price has been inflated considerably. Another form of price deception occurs when the seller overcharges on numerous options associated with a base product. The automobile industry has been an alleged perpetrator of this practice, although the 1958 Automobile Information Disclosure Act makes this somewhat more difficult to do. Still another form of deceptive pricing is the presence of hidden charges or other costs. In the area of consumer credit services, for example, the 1969 Truth in Lending Law requires upfront disclosure of all finance charges and the actual interest rate charged on an annual basis. Unfortunately, there are so many ways to deceptively present prices in the marketplace that one cannot hope to rely on a law for each. Although the Federal Trade Commission is active through prosecution and the setting of guidelines for sellers, one must, in the end, rely perhaps more on a combination of trust in the seller and vigilance on the part of the buyer.

The Federal Trade Commission. The Federal Trade Commission is a federal agency charged with performing both investigatory and adjudicative functions related to business practices. It is responsible for enforcing compliance to the same legislation as under the charge of the Antitrust Division of the Justice Department. It does this through the issue of decrees (a direct communication to a violator) or formal complaints issued in court. In addition, the FTC (1) holds trade practices conferences where industries participate in reviews of their practices with the FTC; (2) conducts research on economic, marketing, or financial matters related to unfair competition or deceptive practices; and (3) investigates complaints initiated by others. An important aspect of the FTC is the investigation and adjudication of deceptive practices such as false or misleading advertising, as well as the pricing irregularities noted above. Much of its powers and responsibilities stem from the 1914 FTC Act and the 1938 Wheeler-Lea Amendment to the FTC Act (see Table 12-2).

The President. The final environmental constraints we consider are directives originating from the president and other officials in the executive branch of the federal government.

Although usually reserved for grave emergencies such as wartime, the president has occasionally issued controls in "normal times." In 1971, for example, President Nixon instituted a three-month wage and price freeze. Further controls were instituted in 1972 and 1973, but were eliminated in 1974 after numerous problems arose with shortages of such products as fertilizers, steel, petroleum, and food. The reason the shortages came about can perhaps be best seen in the case of the petroleum industry. The president froze heating oil prices at the level of prices in August 1971, a low point for the year. In normal times, manufacturers begin in late summer to produce heating oil in anticipation of the coming winter. However, the low price set during the 1971 freeze discouraged this, so they switched to the production of more gasoline, which was fixed at a very high price, because of the time of year. The net result was a shortage of heating oil in the winter. The problem was compounded further by a simultaneous high worldwide demand for petroleum (precipitated by economic boom times nearly everywhere) and OPEC's price increases.

Because of the impossibility of achieving adequate and equitable controls, the president obviously prefers not to contemplate their application. As an alternative, jawboning or "moral suasion" is often employed. Presidents Kennedy, Johnson, and Carter resorted to persuasive attempts to induce sellers to voluntarily restrain wage and price increases. Predictably, this resulted in mixed success at best. It is a very difficult task to control prices, and both market and planned economies have found that attempts to do so often backfire. President Reagan's tenure has been marked by a reluctance to influence business practices through any form of controls.

Summary

In this chapter, we introduced the idea of price and pricing from the perspective of the individual consumer and the vantage point of the larger economy and government. Although the price of a product and service is but one of many forces influencing demand, it is a very general and powerful factor.

Perhaps the simplest way to construe a price is as a stimulus designed to induce a response on the part of consumers. Very little research exists regarding the stimulus value of a price. Yet practitioners, through tradition or common folklore, employ a whole host of rules of thumb in this regard. Some of the more common practices include customary pricing, charm pricing (including conspicuous consumption, odd-even, and representational pricing), price lining, price reductions (i.e., sales, discounts), and price/quality pricing. Because of space limitations, we will only describe the last phenomenon, so you might wish to reread the discussion in the beginning of the chapter for comments on the others.

Price/quality pricing refers to the effect of price on the perception of the quality of a product. A high price, in and of itself, may lead a consumer to infer that the ingredients, materials, workmanship, or other aspects of a product are superior. Moreover, some consumers may view a high price as a signal of the rareness or exclusivity of the product. They may purchase the product precisely because it has a high price in the expectation that others will think well of them. Or such a purchase may simply be an expression of one's self-image. Alternatively, a low price might in fact communicate an image of cheapness, inferior quality, or the like. Notice that such effects run counter to that predicted by economic theory, which maintains that low prices result in an increase and high prices a decrease in demand. Review Figure 12-3 for a comparison of four conceptualizations of the effect of price on the consumer's purchase decision.

As an alternative to stimulus-response ideas of price effects, a stimulus-organism-response model was proposed (see Figure 12-4). Here price was hypothesized to affect decisions, depending on the nature and magnitude of psychological reactions. Any price was said to potentially convey emotional, rational, and social meanings. Thus, it is essential to consider the information-processing and affective responses of consumers to prices if we are to effectively estimate demand.

Howard's distinctions of routinized response buying, limited problem solving, and extensive problem solving were shown to represent one way to develop a stimulus-organism-response model of consumer reactions. Attitude and decision models are others. No matter what model one uses, it is important to study how consumers will react to the absolute price level as well as any anticipated changes up or down. Psychological reactions mediate the effect of any price as a stimulus, and it is crucial to get an indication of the scope and range of reactions. Indeed, knowledge of consumer reactions will not only help in the estimate of demand, but it will guide where and how information on pricing is communicated and even suggest whether product design or distribution changes need to be considered.

The final half of the chapter dealt with price at the macro level. We began with an analysis of economic issues. Little leeway is afforded in setting prices in purely competitive industries, and even monopolies have less flexibility than one might imagine. Oligopolies, the more common market conditions, have more flexibility. Although economic theory predicts prices fairly well under the ideal forms of competition (i.e., when products are undifferentiated), it has little to say for the cases where product differentiation exists. These more interesting and realistic situations pose special strategic issues for firms, and we will consider some of the problems and solutions in the next chapter.

Another topic that we discussed in the present chapter was break-even analysis. The following formula summarizes the relationship between quantity (q) and price (p):

$$q = \frac{FC}{p - VC},$$

where $FC =$ fixed costs and $VC =$ variable costs. Thus, given the price, one can estimate demand; or alternatively, given an estimate of demand, one can compute the price to break even.

The break-even analysis is an intuitive, easy-to-apply concept. It is useful when one has no knowledge of the specific responses of consumers. However, its effectiveness depends on how well one can estimate demand or on what the market will bear in pricing. Further, it assumes that costs can be broken down into fixed and variable components, an assumption that flies in the face of the tendency of most costs to become variable in the long run. Still another problem is that costs are assumed linear, when in fact this is seldom so. Finally, break-even analysis puts one in the position of taking demand as a given. Yet, successful marketing is predicated on a belief that management can, in effect, influence demand through strategic pricing. Nevertheless, break-even analysis does properly remind one that costs ultimately need to be considered when pricing.

Two factors affecting costs, and therefore pricing, are economies of scale and the experience curve effect. The former refers to the phenomenon whereby the costs of producing and marketing a product typically decline per unit as the *actual volume* goes up. The latter describes the observation that, as *cumulative volume* increases, costs decline by a constant amount. Economies of scale occur primarily in the purchasing of materials, use of labor, shipping, and advertising. Experience curve effects are reflected in the learning of skills and managerial know-how.

The final economic concept we presented was price elasticity. It is defined as

$$e_p = \frac{\% \text{ change in quantity demanded}}{\% \text{ change in price}}.$$

This shows how much of a change in sales one can expect if the price is changed by a specific amount. Although useful in forecasting and planning up to a point, we should remember that it applies when everything else is held constant (a notion difficult to implement), and it neglects some potentially counteracting elements such as those embodied in price/quality effects. That is, it is a coarse-grained tool overlooking many consumer psychology and competitive forces occurring at a finer-grained level.

The chapter closed with consideration of social and legal constraints. Three were presented: the Antitrust Division of the Justice Department, the Federal Trade Commission, and the president. The notions of price fixing, price discrimination, and deceptive pricing were introduced as well.

Managerial aspects of pricing are considered in the next chapter. Focus will be placed on strategic and tactical concerns.

Questions and Problems for Discussion

1 Customary pricing and charm pricing constitute two very old approaches to the pricing problem. Briefly describe these.

2 What is price lining and why is it practiced?

3 Discuss the various forms of price reductions including their pros and cons.

4 What is the relationship between price and quality from the perspective of the buyer?

5 Discuss the effect of prices on consumers from the viewpoint of the stimulus-organism-response model presented in the chapter.

6 According to economic theory, how are prices set under conditions of pure competition?

7 According to economic theory, what price will be set under monopolistic conditions?

8 According to economic theory, how are prices set in oligopolistic industries?

9 What are the main problems with economic theories of price setting?

10 What role does break-even analysis play in the setting of prices?

11 What effects do economies of scale and learning have on price setting?

12 What is price elasticity and what implications does it have for management?

13 What role does the Antitrust Division play in pricing?

14 What role does the Federal Trade Commission play in pricing?

15 What role does the president play in pricing?

NOTES

1. For discussions of these and others related to them, see Eli Ginzberg, "Customary Prices," *American Economic Review* 26 (June 1936): 296; Kent B. Monroe, "Buyers' Subjective Perceptions of Price," *Journal of Marketing Research* 10 (February 1973): 70-80; Benjamin P. Shapiro, "The Psychology of Pricing," *Harvard Business Review* 46 (July-August 1968): 14-25, 160. The price reduction category has not generally been treated in the literature but nevertheless reflects common practice in the retail trade. Similarly, the representational pricing tactic is a neglected topic.

2. For a fuller discussion of these than that presented here, see Kent B. Monroe, *Pricing: Making Profitable Decisions* (New York: McGraw-Hill, 1979).

3. Some research into the price/quality relationship has been conducted and can be found in H. J. Leavitt, "A Note on Some Experimental Findings about the Meaning of Price," *Journal of Business* 27 (July 1954): 205-210; D. S. Tull, R. A. Boring, and M. H. Gonsier, "A Note on the Relationship of Price and Imputed Quality," *Journal of Business* 37 (April 1964): 186-191; J. D. McConnell, "The Price-Quality Relationship in an Experimental Setting," *Journal of Marketing Research* 5 (August 1968): 300-303; Kent B. Monroe, "Buyers' Subjective Perceptions of Price," *Journal of Marketing Research* 10 (February 1973): 70-80; John J. Wheatley and John S. Y. Chiu, "The Effects of Price, Store Image, and Product and Respondent Characteristics on Perceptions of Quality," *Journal of Marketing Research* 14 (May 1977): 181-186.

4. Monroe, *Pricing*, p. 38.

5. The names for these situations—RRB, LPS, and EPS— were first suggested in John A. Howard, *Consumer Behavior: Application of Theory*, (New York: McGraw-Hill, 1977). For additional information on a cognitive view of price in consumer behavior, see Jacob Jacoby and Jerry Olson, "Consumer Response to Price: An Attitudinal Information Processing Perspective," in Y. Wind and M. E. Greenberg, eds., *Moving Ahead with Attitude Research* (Chicago: American Marketing Association, 1977), pp. 73-86.

6. We will omit discussion of feedback effects from outcomes to market forces and to social and legal constraints (paths *d* and *e*, respectively), for simplicity. The study of how the economy coordinates production activities with society's demand for goods and services can be found in the economic subfield of industrial organization. For relevant treatments of this subject matter see, for example, F. M. Scherer, *Industrial Market Structure and Economic Performance*, 2nd ed. (Chicago: Rand McNally, 1980).

7. See, for example, Scherer, *Industrial Market Structure and Economic Performance*, p. 67.

8. For a discussion of some of the frameworks, see Jack Hirschleifer, *Price Theory* (Englewood Cliffs, N.J.: Prentice-Hall, 1976).

9. Interesting treatments of kinked demand curves can be found in Walter J. Primeaux, Jr., and Mark R. Bomball, "A Reexamination of the Kinky Oligopoly Demand Curve," *Journal of Political Economy* 82 (July-August 1974): 851-62; Walter J. Primeaux, Jr., and Mickey C. Smith, "Pricing Patterns and the Kinky Demand Curve," *Journal of Law and Economics* 19 (April 1976): 189-99; Julian L. Simon, "A Further Test of the Kinky Oligopoly Demand Curve," *American Economic Review* 59 (December 1969): 971-75. A phenomenon not considered at this point is price leadership. This occurs when one firm in the industry initiates price changes and others follow suit. The price leader often is the market leader in terms of sales, technology, or other factors. In addition to the constraints provided by supply and demand, a market leader must typically look out for the interests of all in the industry as well as its own. Thus, price setting even in this case is partly determined from outside pressures.

10. See Hirshleifer, *Price Theory*; Primeaux and Smith, "Pricing Patterns and the Kinky Demand Curve."

11. Useful references are Bruce D. Henderson, *Perspectives on Experience* (Boston: Boston Consulting Group, 1970); William J. Abernathy and Kenneth Wayne, "Limits of the Learning Curve," *Harvard Business Review* 52 (September-October 1974): 109-19; C. Carl Pegels, "Startup of Learning Curves—Some New Approaches," *Decision Sciences* 7 (October 1976): 700-13; B. D. Henderson, *Henderson on Corporate Strategy* (Cambridge, Mass.: Abt Books, 1979).

12. See George Stigler, *The Theory of Price*, rev. ed. (New York: Macmillan, 1952), p. 38.

13. Local and state laws can be a factor, too, but will not be discussed here in the interest of brevity.

GLOSSARY

Antitrust Division. A part of the U.S. Justice Department responsible for enforcing antitrust laws. The responsibility is shared with the Federal Trade Commission in certain respects.

Break-Even Analysis. A method for determining a quantity of goods to produce, given the price and fixed and variable costs. The break-even formula reads

$$q = \frac{FC}{p - VC}$$

where q = break-even quantity, p = price, FC = fixed costs, and VC = variable costs.

Cash Discounts. A price reduction offered the buyer under the condition that the discounted price be paid within a certain period of time, otherwise the full price must be paid. For example, the 2/10, net 30 cash discount specifies that a 2 percent discount in price will be provided if the bill is paid within 10 days, otherwise the full price is due within 30 days.

Charm Pricing. The general process of setting prices on the basis of the psychological meaning of the numbers used to express the prices. There are three types of charm pricing: *conspicuous consumption pricing, odd-or-even pricing, and representational pricing.*

Clayton Act. *See* Table 12-2.

Conspicuous Consumption Pricing. The practice of setting a high price in the hope that buyers will perceive the product to be unique, consist of special ingredients or materials, or reflect exemplary workmanship.

Customary Pricing. The practice of using the same price for an extended period of time so as not to shock or induce resentment in the buyer.

Deceptive Pricing. A broad term used to describe such practices as false claims as to discounts offered, overcharges on product options, hidden charges, and so on.

Discount Pricing. *See* price reductions.

Economies of Scale. Decreases in the cost of producing a product per unit as a result of increased production. It results from more efficient use of inputs and the spreading of costs over a greater volume. Economies of scale not only occur in production but also in purchasing, marketing, and other areas. *See* experience curve.

Experience Curve. The decline in unit costs as a firm produces more in a cumulative sense. It is believed to be a consequence of "learning" in the sense that, as production increases cumulatively over time, firms learn to better coordinate production with other activities, increase productivity of machinery and equipment, and gain from the increased know-how of employees. *See* economies of scale.

Extensive Problem Solving. A decision situation faced by a buyer wherein considerable information is required. It applies to new products involving significant risk or to any complex product. Many product attributes are typically considered, and decision rules may be complicated in form and execution. Comparisons to alternative brands are the rule. *See* routinized response buying, limited problem solving.

Federal Antitrust Statute. See Table 12-2.

Federal Trade Commission (FTC). A federal agency responsible for investigating and adjudicating business practices. *See* Antitrust Division.

Federal Trade Commission Act. See Table 12-2.

Functional Trade Discounts. Allowances a seller offers to a buyer for services rendered. The allowance might entail an outright payment or more frequently a reduction in the purchase price of goods. Services include, among others, advertising, promotion, provision of credit, market research, storage, and delivery or pickup.

Limited Problem Solving (LPS). A decision situation faced by a buyer wherein a moderate amount of information is required. It applies to new products involving a moderate amount of risk or to products purchased infrequently which are moderately complex in attributes or use. Price is evaluated more thoroughly than in routinized response buying cases, and more complex decision rules are entailed. Further, a few to moderate number of product attributes may be evaluated in an LPS decision. Comparisons to a few alternative brands is possible. *See* routinized response buying, extensive problem solving.

Monopolistic Competition. An ideal-type form of organization characterized by many firms selling products that are at least partially differentiated. *See* pure competition, monopoly, oligopoly.

Monopoly. An ideal-type form of organization characterized by a single seller of a product or service that has no close substitutes. *See* pure competition, monopolistic competition, oligopoly.

Odd-or-Even Pricing. The practice of setting prices so that they end in either an odd number (e.g., 5, 7, or 9) or an even number (e.g., 6 or 8), usually just below a round number. For example, $1.98 may be used because it is believed that it will attract attention and lead the consumer to perceive that the price is somewhat less than 2¢ below $2.

Oligopoly. An ideal form of organization characterized by a small number of sellers wherein each has some effect on market price and possibly the pricing practices of others in the industry. If firms sell relatively homogeneous products or services, they are termed homogeneous oligopolies. If firms sell differentiated products, they are termed differentiated oligopolies. *See* pure competition, monopolistic competition, monopoly.

Price. The amount of money demanded by a seller in exchange for giving a product or services to a buyer.

Price Discrimination. Occurs whenever there are differences in price for the same product sold by a single seller that are not justified by (1) cost differences in manufacture, selling, or delivery, (2) a need to meet lawful competition, and (3) a set of other conditions.

Price Elasticity. The ratio of the percent change in quantity demanded to the percent change in price:

$$e_p = \frac{\%\ \textbf{change in quantity demanded}}{\%\ \textbf{change in price}}$$

The price elasticity coefficient shows how much of a change in sales one can expect if the price is changed by some particular amount.

Price Fixing. An agreement among competing firms to set prices at levels in relation to each other. Price fixing is illegal in the U.S. but allowed in some parts of the world.

Price Lining. The tactic of offering a number of variations of a product with each variation priced at a different level. A common practice is to offer three brands at three different prices.

Price/Quality Relationship. The phenomenon wherein the absolute level of a price or a price change leads a consumer to infer something about the quality of the product itself. A price can have positive *and* negative effects on a consumer's perception. Prices generally have emotional, rational, and social meanings as well. *See* value.

Price Reductions. A term used to identify two tactics for lowering prices: (1) sales (or specials) and (2) discount pricing. A sale is a temporary decrease in price designed to entice buyers. The consumer feels that he or she is better able to afford the product and at the same time have money left over for other uses. The seller sees a sale as a demand-inducing stimulus allowing one to dispose of slow-moving items and to win over consumers who might not otherwise have made a purchase. Discount pricing (as opposed to the different term, cash discounts) is the tactic of offering a product at "below retail" on a more-or-less ongoing basis. This is done most often by discount stores, catalog showrooms, and some small retailers. Sales, in contrast, tend to be a one-time or seasonal practice.

Pure Competition. An ideal form of organization characterized by a large number of firms selling essentially the same product or service. The product or service is relatively homogeneous. *See* monopolistic competition, monopoly, oligopoly.

Quantity Discounts. A price reduction based on how much a buyer purchases. A cumulative quantity discount is based on the total amount purchased over time. A noncumulative discount is based on the amount purchased at a single point in time.

Representational Pricing. The selection of a price on the basis of the presumed symbolic meaning of the numbers. For instance, a price of $7 or $7.77 may be perceived as both lucky and eye-catching.

Robinson-Patman Act. See Table 12-2.

Routinized Response Buying (RRB). A decision situation faced by a buyer wherein little information is required. Typically, it applies to inexpensive, standardized, or frequently purchased products. Few product attributes are considered in RRB decisions, with price and availability often the most important. Decision rules are generally simple such as the binary requirement "Is the price above my cutoff or not?" *See* limited problem solving, extensive problem solving.

Sales. *See* price reductions.

Sherman Act. See Table 12-2.

Specials. *See* price reductions.

Trading Up. The phenomenon of a consumer purchasing a higher priced brand from a seller after considering a lower priced brand from the same seller. The seller often tries to influence the consumer to do so because greater profits typically result. Consumers are sometimes vulnerable to such efforts, as the costs of trading up can appear deceptively lower than they are.

Value. Defined as the ratio of perceived quality to price.

Wheeler-Lea Amendment. See Table 12-2.

CHAPTER
THIRTEEN

The value, or WORTH of a man is, as of all things, his price; that is to say, so much would be given for the use of his power. And as in other things, so in men, not the seller, but the buyer, determines the price.
—— Thomas Hobbes (1588–1679)

PRICE: MANAGERIAL CONSIDERATIONS

Introduction

The discussion of price in Chapter 12 focused on the meaning of price at the micro level (i.e., the level of the psychology of the consumer) and at the macro level (i.e., the level of society as reflected in economic and legal viewpoints). We have discussed managerial aspects of price only as they have directly related to micro and macro considerations. Now we will develop the meaning of price more fully from the perspective of the organization. In one sense, the managerial viewpoint is an intermediate one bridging the micro and the macro. The successful functioning of any organization depends on how well it interprets the needs of its customers and adjusts the operations of the firm to meet those needs. At the same time, it must do this within the context of the larger social and economic environment which shapes its actions. Modern organizations have developed sophisticated procedures for coping with the opportunities and constraints they face.

Let us look more deeply into that aspect of the organization concerned with pricing. Figure 13-1 outlines the central components and their interrelationships. Notice first that a pricing program begins with *overall organization goals*. These are the ultimate ends and objectives necessary for the survival of the firm and the effective implementation of its mission. The goals are typically formulated as targets related to profitability, return on investment, meeting customer needs, being socially responsible in terms of employment and pollution practices, and so on. The important point to note is that these central goals influence and constrain the means required to meet the goals. Broadly speaking, the means encompass production, personnel, marketing, R & D, financial, accounting, and other programs. Each of these, in turn, has its own subgoals, which we term objectives. Only *marketing objectives* are displayed in Figure 13-1, but it should be remembered that the objectives of the other programs interact with these. Marketing objectives reflect goals for sales, market share, market growth, product line profitability, brand image, and so on. Although the line between marketing objectives and the goals of the firm is often a fine one, the former are derived from the latter and are more specific and/or serve as intermediate steps in the pursuit of the latter. Similarly, *pricing objectives* are even more specific and focused than marketing objectives. They typically serve as substeps needed to achieve the marketing objectives.

The most important pricing objective is the desired target market and its response: that is, what is the target market, how does it behave, and what response do we desire from it with what price strategy? The objective might be to attract a particular segment, to penetrate a market, to generate as much revenue as possible in the short run, or to smooth out seasonal fluctuations in demand, for example. Similarly, specific goals for trial and repeat buying in particular markets or segments may be specified. Somewhat less important, but nevertheless essential, are goals related to other products in the firm and to competitive rivals. For instance, the firm might have a policy that the price set for a new product should enhance the quality image of the company, should not compete or conflict with the prices of other products, and should not cannibalize their sales, as well. Similarly, with respect to rivals, the policy might be to meet competition, to act as a price leader, or to undercut the largest market shareholder, among other possibilities. There are other pricing objectives, but the aforementioned are the most fundamental.

An important point to emphasize in Figure 13-1 is that pricing objectives are not merely derivatives of marketing objectives and organizational goals. In fact, pricing objectives are also strongly influenced by market forces, social and legal constraints, and marketing mix considerations. Consider,

first, the role of market forces. Pricing objectives depend on the size and nature of the potential market. The psychology of consumers is a factor, as is the availability of substitute sources of satisfaction through completely different products. Suppliers play a role largely through the bargaining relationship they have with the focal firm and the effect this has on the latter's costs. And when setting pricing objectives, the firm must consider not only the reactions of existing rivals but the potential for new entrants. A low price, for example, risks retaliation from an old rival, while a high price invites the entry of a new one. Next, social and legal constraints provide direct guidelines that need to be taken into account in any pricing program. We have already discussed these in the previous chapter. Finally, marketing mix considerations constitute perhaps the most complex interactions. Indeed, any response of a market will depend upon the pattern of pricing, promotion, product, and distribution stimuli. Each of the marketing mix stimuli has the potential to complement or interfere with the others, depending on the circumstances. Hence, the firm must thoughtfully coordinate its marketing tactics if it is to obtain the desired response.

After a firm has set sound pricing objectives, it is in a position to implement them through *pricing tactics* (see Figure 13-1). Pricing tactics refer to the specific actions the firm takes as reflected in the price levels it sets, price differentials, product line pricing, new product pricing, dynamic pricing (i.e., pricing over time), and other actions. These actions, in turn, feed back upon marketing forces, the marketing mix, social and legal constraints, marketing objectives, and goals of the firm. We begin now with a discussion of some of the dynamics of the processes noted in Figure 13-1.

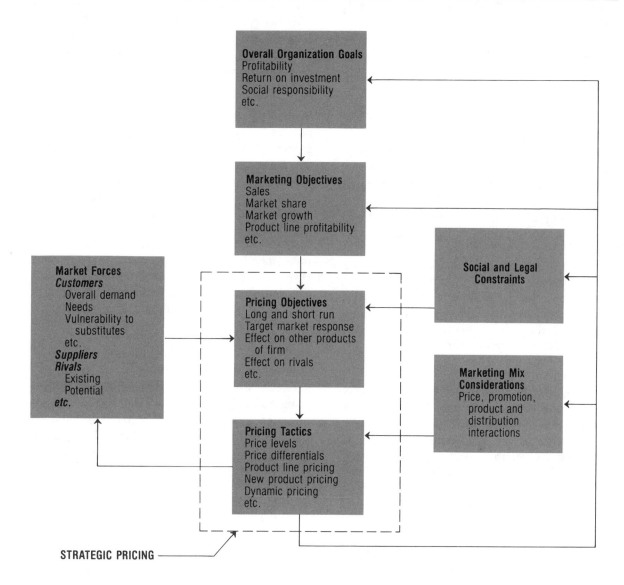

Figure 13-1. An overview of the role of
pricing in marketing management

Traditional Managerial Approaches to Pricing

Although most firms perform break-even analyses of one form or another, only a minority go much beyond this to take into account criteria such as noted in Figure 13-1. Even for these latter firms, activities are often limited to a specification of one objective and its relation to a single tactic. For example, some firms set the prices for their products based on the criterion of short-run profit maximization. It will prove informative to briefly examine a few of the more frequently applied approaches in order to discover their assets and shortcomings and point the way to needed developments.

Profit Maximization

Many firms state that profit maximization is their goal and follow formal procedures for working toward this end. One approach is to rely on the normative implications of economic theory. To see how economic theory might be used as a price setting tool, let us consider the recent experiences of a husband and wife company making two-piece jogging suits. The company is called Stayfit. The daughter of the owners has completed a marketing course, and being eager to both apply her knowledge and help her parents, has prepared an economic analysis designed to maximize short-run profitability of the firm. Her reasoning and calculations follow.

First, based on two years' experience in the Atlantic Seaboard states, Stayfit's costs were estimated as $20,000 fixed and $20 variable per suit. Thus, a cost equation could be written as

$$TC = 20,000 + 20q$$

where TC = total cost and q = quantity. The next problem was to determine an equation for predicting demand as a function of price. The owners of Stayfit saw a market niche for moderately priced jogging suits in New England, because at that time, only inexpensive (under $40) or expensive (over $100) suits sold there at retail. Through years of tinkering in the garage, one of the owners had developed an innovative and inexpensive machine for sewing fabric, while the other owner had designed a simple, but functional, outfit. In addition, the owners had astutely made purchases over time of odd-lot quantities of a high-quality synthetic fabric at very low prices. Indeed, Stayfit's suits had the look and feel of suits costing $100 or more. Hence, the owners believed that they had both the ability to make the suits as well as a differential advantage over the competition.

Their estimate of demand as a function of price was pieced together through data from a trade publication, their own sales experience with similar products in other areas of the country, and conversations with a friend of the family who worked for the purchasing department of a large clothing chain. From this information they forecast that the New England market could absorb about 8,000 jogging suits at a retail price of approximately $40 and only about 1,300 at a retail price of close to $100. Somewhere between these limits was an optimum price for them to charge to maximize their profits. The daughter of the owners used a simple straight-line estimate of demand as a function of price by connecting the points provided in the above forecast. Figure 13-2A shows the demand curve, where wholesale prices (about 50 percent of retail) are shown. The equation for this curve is

$$q = 12,480 - 224p$$

where p = price. This seemed like a good guess, as marketing texts almost universally illustrate profit maximization with a linear demand function. Notice that, as our intuition tells us, market demand falls as prices increase.

The final step in the analysis was to compute a price that maximizes profit. We can do this by first computing total revenue (*TR*):

$$TR = pq = 12{,}480p - 224p^2$$

Then, profit (P) equals $TR - TC$:

$$
\begin{aligned}
P &= 12{,}480p - 224p^2 - 20{,}000 - 20q \\
&= 12{,}480p - 224p^2 - 20{,}000 - \\
&\quad 20(12{,}480 - 224p) \\
&= -224p^2 + 16{,}960p - 249{,}600
\end{aligned}
$$

This profit equation can be solved graphically, by trial and error, or with the calculus, to show that $p = \$38$ yields the greatest profit. At $p = \$38$, P = \$71,424 and $q = 3{,}968$ suits. Overall, a wholesale price of \$38 would seem to allow the retailer the opportunity to charge about \$80, and the projected profit for Stayfit is impressive. Everyone was, in fact, enthusiastic about the prospects.

Before proceeding, however, the principals decided to get the opinion of a neutral party, a marketing professor. The professor was impressed with most phases of the analysis but felt that the demand curve was unrealistic. Although the end points used to estimate it seemed valid, given the information provided, the linear shape appeared to misrepresent consumer reactions. Consumers are often more resistant to price increases for certain ranges of prices than the linear function reveals, and they are less receptive to price decreases for some price ranges as well. Moreover, the absolute level of predicted quantity demanded appeared somewhat too high at most price levels to the professor. As a consequence, he recommended the price-quantity demand function shown in Figure 13-2B. The equation for this function is

$$q = 3.2\ (10^6)\ p^{-2}$$

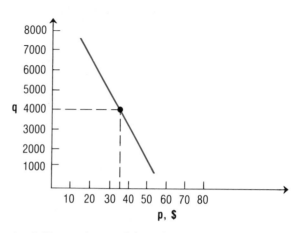

A. A linear demand function

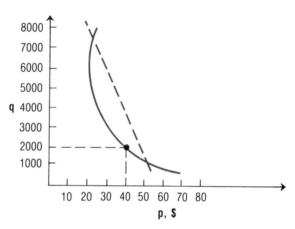

B. A nonlinear demand function

Figure 13-2. A profit maximization example

Quantity sold again decreases as price increases, but the rate and level better match intuition. Following the procedure outlined above, one can see that the optimal price for profit maximization is $p = \$40$ with a predicted profit of $P = \$20,000$ at a quantity demanded of $q = 2,000$. Although the computed price is not too far from that arising from the linear analysis, notice how much lower profits and sales are.

Assuming that the nonlinear curve is closer to reality, let us briefly look at the implications of the analyses. A first point to note is that had Stayfit followed the linear analysis and chosen to sell the jogging suits at $38, it would have sold about 2,217. Unfortunately, it would have produced 3,968 suits. With only $84,246 in revenues and total costs of $99,360, it would have operated at a loss. Perhaps Stayfit could have sold the 1,751 remaining suits later at a lower price to offset the losses, but clearly the forecast profit of $71,424 was way out of line.

A second issue to examine concerns what action to take based on the more realistic nonlinear analysis. Table 13-1 presents a sensitivity analysis showing the effects of choosing different price levels on expected profits and quantity demanded. Notice that the break-even price is $23.43 with a break-even quantity of 5,829. Notice further that profits do not vary much from about a price of $30 all the way up to about $50 or more. On the other hand, once the price falls below $30, profits drop off dramatically. Given their desire to fill the intermediate price niche of the market between $40 and $100 suits, Stayfit felt that the retailers might accept a price of no higher than $30–$35 so that they could, in turn, sell the suits in the $60–$70 range. This tactic, however, gives Stayfit only a sure profit of $15,556. Because they had another business opportunity promising a profit of $50,000, Stayfit decided not to produce the suits and enter the New England market. Had they followed the linear analysis implications, they would have entered the market. The outcome? Well, five months after making their decision, the bottom fell out of the jogging suit market, and retailers who had been selling suits at around $100 were forced to put them on sale for $50 or less to get rid of their stock. Stayfit would not have fared well. In contrast, the venture that they did enter, children's formal suits, was relatively profitable, yielding about $40,000 above costs in the first year.

TABLE 13-1

A Sensitivity Analysis of Profits and Quantity Demanded to Changes in Price for the Profit Maximization Example

Price p	20	23.43	25	30	40	50	60
Quantity q	8,000	5,829	5,120	3,556	2,000	1,280	889
Profits P	−20,000	0	5,600	15,556	20,000	18,400	15,556

Before we discuss other pricing strategies, let us mention some shortcomings of the profit maximization approach. The biggest hang-up is that its accuracy rests on how well one can estimate costs and demand.[1] Demand is very difficult to estimate, and cost estimates usually contain considerable errors in measurement as well. Second, the goal of profit maximization tends to obscure the value of other goals. Perhaps the firm would be willing to accept less than maximum profits if it needed to do so to gain a foothold in a market, for example. Third, profit maximization as described above does not explicitly take into account the reactions of rivals. Fourth, it ignores the influence of social and legal forces. Fifth, it is short-run oriented and fails to take into account long-run objectives and changing contingencies. Finally, profit maximization fails to incorporate the role of other marketing mix decisions. For these reasons, firms often pursue other approaches when setting prices.

Some Frequently Applied Alternatives

Six of the more common strategic alternatives to profit maximization include revenue maximization, cost minimization, market share leadership, market skimming, market penetration, and differentiation. Let us look at each of these.

Revenue Maximization. Some firms use sales maximization as their criterion. The motivation is simple. Often not enough cost data are available to compute a profit maximization price, and profit maximization's numerous other flaws make it problematic. On the other hand, the most visible and direct measure of the success of a firm is its sales. Measures of sales are easily obtained, and indeed, management tends to use sales as a barometer of the health of the business, as a criterion for promotion and bonuses, and as a guide for planning in production and other areas of operations. Given further that sales are correlated with profits, one can see that this goal has many attractions. However, one still must be able to estimate demand as a function of price. Although one avoids the problems with making accurate cost estimates, the need for good demand estimates has the same problems as does the profit maximization procedure. Also, because the correlation of sales with profits is usually less than perfect, the tactic frequently results in suboptimum performance. For example, with $TR = 12,480p - 224p^2$ for the linear analysis of the Stayfit Corporation, one can calculate the revenue maximization price as $p = \$27.86$. This price, however, yields $P = \$49,042$ for the linear analysis and $P = \$12,405$ for the nonlinear analysis. Both numbers are significantly under the maximum levels.

Cost Minimization. Another frequently practiced strategy is to strive to keep costs at a minimum. Porter terms this the strategy of "overall cost leadership" and notes that its successful implementation "requires aggressive construction of efficient-scale facilities, vigorous pursuit of cost reductions from experience [curve effects], tight cost and overhead control, avoidance of marginal customer accounts, and cost minimization in areas like R & D, service, sales force, advertising, and so on.[2] The motivation for a cost minimization approach might stem from a number of sources. First, the firm might only have accurate estimates of costs and at the same time feel it is impossible to specify a demand function. Second, a cost minimization strategy usually permits the firm to set a low price and thereby gain a competitive advantage over rivals. Finally, the cost minimization strategy is a deterrent to new entries in the market as potential rivals know that they face an uphill battle requiring large losses in the beginning and continued stiff competition throughout the product life cycle. For a firm to successfully employ a cost minimization strategy, it is believed that it must have a relatively high market share, bargaining power over suppliers, or other advantages.[3]

One might think that all firms strive to keep costs down and that such a strategy does not differentiate one firm from another. However, this is not necessarily the case, as other goals often take priority. Some firms, for example, aim for the quality-conscious segment of the market. This forces them to pay relatively more for product ingredients, workmanship, and/or advertising. Hence, for some firms, a lexicographic rule is followed such that costs have a lower priority than product quality. Hewlett Packard consistently followed this pattern for many years by pricing its small computers at the top of the line. Nevertheless, many firms such as Texas Instruments, Black & Decker, and Beaird Poulon (maker of chain saws) practice a cost minimization strategy to advantage. This allows them to set a relatively low price. Other firms, such as DuPont, watch costs closely yet price above market average somewhat as part of their pricing strategies.

Price setting under the larger goal of overall cost leadership operates primarily on a *cost-plus* basis. That is, a final price is set as a particular increase above costs.

The increase may be set as a function of historical practice, industry norms, or to achieve a certain goal such as sales or profitability. Notice that price setting can, and in fact often does, entail employing combinations of objectives. General Motors, for example, sets its prices as cost per unit plus an additional amount needed to achieve a return on capital of about 15 percent (after taxes). The cost per unit and total revenue, of course, are based on estimates of demand, and if these are in error, so will be the anticipated return. In addition to costs and desired return, General Motors and other firms using such an approach may adjust the final price on the basis of consumer price sensitivity, competition, and other considerations. Thus, it can be seen that price setting is a complex process that is part art and part science.

Market Share Leadership. Still another popular approach for some firms is to work for market share leadership. The belief is that this not only is required for survival but that it also leads directly to higher profits.[4] Price, of course, plays a very important role. Sometimes this means setting a price as low as possible to win the most sales. At other times, conditions are such that one must set a relatively higher price to create an image of product superiority and recoup high promotion and other costs. In either case, the company fine-tunes its price—either up or down—to achieve a particular market share. Pricing to achieve a market share is even done by firms below the market leader. These firms attempt to adjust their tactics to maintain their market position or perhaps move up a slot or two. Because of company goals or other constraints, however, they may not be able ever to achieve the top spot and they price accordingly. A firm that sets prices in order to maintain or achieve a particular market share must, of course, have a marketing information system attuned to the marketplace if it is to be successful. This means placing special emphasis on data gathering, statistical modeling, and simulations.

Market Skimming. An old approach to pricing new products is known as market skimming.[5] Here the firm sets its price at a high level with the aim of either leaving the market at a later predetermined point in time or lowering its price systematically over time. The strategy is based on the premise that potential customers will be relatively insensitive to price and eagerly purchase the product at a relatively high level. This will be possible to the extent that the product satisfies a genuine need and no substitutes exist in the market. Also, from the firm's standpoint, a high price tends to generate greater profits when it most needs them, and it keeps demand down to a manageable level until it can increase productive capacity. Many producers of toys and novelty items use this approach to pricing before the Christmas holidays when they introduce new products. After the holidays and throughout the following year they gradually lower the price to draw in those more price-sensitive patrons.

One drawback to the skimming policies in general is that it tends to entice other producers into the market, as these firms view the high price conditions as an opportunity for growth and profitability. Another point against the approach is that, depending on the product and public's reaction, skimming may be viewed as an exploitive ploy. Further, some people may withhold purchases from a firm because they know that they can wait and "the price will eventually fall." A few years ago, a large group of consumers anticipated that hand calculator prices would drop and therefore waited a year until they fell from $150 to $29.95 in one case. Thus, firms that regularly apply a skimming policy may find that it backfires because people are "onto their game."

Market Penetration. The opposite of marketing skimming is market penetration pricing, where a low price is set for a new product with the hope that it will quickly lead to high sales and gain a foothold in the market. It is a demand stimulation tactic based on the assumption that consumers are price sensitive. Its major disadvantages are that it often takes longer to make a profit than with a higher pricing policy and it makes it difficult to later raise prices, should conditions call for it. On the other hand, penetration pricing tends to discourage new entrants because they know that they will have to price low and fight it out with the existing competitors. Overall, we know very little about what exact price to set for new products, and market skimming and penetration guidelines are very rough rules-of-thumb at best. For this reason, firms are increasingly turning to simulation, experimentation, and other more formal procedures as aids in decision making.

Market Differentiation. The strategy of *market differentiation* attempts to create an offering that is perceived to be unique by a target market. This is done in one or both of two ways. First, uniqueness is achieved through the entire offering bundle. That is, one achieves a unique offering by varying the characteristics of the product, its package, its price, its promotional image, its distribution, or combinations of these. Notice that this dimension is broader than the usual concept of product differentiation, which is limited to changes in the physical product. We can attain uniqueness through an orchestration of the entire marketing mix. Second, uniqueness is achieved through selection of a target market. That is, who one markets to and where they are located define a second dimension of uniqueness. Table 13-2 presents a categorization of the kinds of differentiation arising from the crossing of market offering with target market. For simplicity, we have used product as the market offering dimension, but it should be remembered that the concept of market offering is broader.

TABLE 13-2
A Taxonomy for Market Differentiation Cases

TARGET MARKET	MARKET OFFERING (e.g., PRODUCT)	
	One Homogeneous Offering	*Heterogeneous Offerings*
One Specific Market	I Quasi differentiation	III Concentrated differentiation
A Few Specific Markets	II Focused differentiation	IV Multi-differentiation
No Specific Market (i.e., everyone)	V Undifferentiated marketing	

When the marketer attempts to sell to everyone rather than people in a well-defined target market, we say this is undifferentiated marketing (Case V in Table 13-2). If, at the other extreme, the marketer has a single homogeneous offering (e.g., one version or model of can opener) and sells this to one specific customer (e.g., a nationwide retailer), then we term this quasi differentiation (Case I). It is quasi in the sense that the seller most likely achieved the differentiation by default. Focused differentiation, Case II, occurs when one homogeneous offering is marketed in a few specific markets. For example, some small farmers in the South grow only oranges but market a portion of their crop to small retailers, a portion to schools, and a portion directly to the public in roadside fruit stands. Another instance of differentiation (concentrated differentiation) occurs when a producer has heterogeneous offerings and sells these to one specific market (Case III). This occurs, for instance, in the real estate business. Some agencies market only to the very wealthy but offer them a product line consisting of luxury homes and condominiums, investment properties, vacation villas, or time-sharing arrangements. Finally, multidifferentiation (Case IV) happens when heterogeneous offerings are sold to a few specific markets. Some large retailers fit this category in that they sell a wide product line but sometimes have ongoing bargain basements along with their main stores. Cases II and IV, of course, apply to situations where more than "a few" specific target markets are sold to.

The major advantage of a differentiation strategy is that it permits the firm greater price flexibility and the potential for higher profits. At the same time, it strengthens one's position vis-à-vis rivals. One disadvantage is that, in the course of achieving differentiation, the opportunity to achieve large volumes of sales or a high market share is sometimes traded off. Differentiation tends to produce an increase in market share within some target groups but can result in overall decreases in sales among an entire market or the subset formed by all of the focal targets. So we often see a redistribution of sales after a differentiation strategy is employed. Typically, it is hoped that an increase in profitability will compensate for the overall decrease in sales if it occurs. Of course, if the firm is highly successful in the new markets, net sales may not decrease and could conceivably even rise. Another disadvantage of differentiation is that costs often rise disproportionately. This happens because it is expensive to achieve differentiation due to research, product development, and promotional expenditures.

We have spoken of differentiation in a broad sense as if it were achieved through target market specification and marketing mix orchestrations. Differentia-

tion can also be achieved through pricing alone (in combination with target markets). This is known as *price discrimination*, and, in addition to the legal sanctions against it, it can be morally undesirable as well. Nevertheless, economists have identified three prerequisites where price discrimination works profitably. First, the seller must have at least a moderate amount of control over the price. This means that market forces and social and legal restrictions play a relatively minor role. Thus, price discrimination is more frequently performed in oligopolistic than in competitive industries. Second, the price discriminator must be able to choose target markets such that each has different price elasticities. Third, the opportunity for buyers to resell in another market must be negligible or limited.

A final issue concerning market differentiation is *product line pricing*. Every firm with two or more products to sell faces this problem. The problem occurs especially when offerings in the product line are related to each other. That is, pricing becomes difficult when the price of one good influences the demand for another and vice versa. This happens in two ways. First, products might be *substitutes*. Retailers of tires, for example, face a pricing problem because each car owner can only be sold different grades of the same size tire and because often a few different sizes of tires will fit on the same car. Moreover, the retailer might sell two or three different brands of tires. Under these conditions, the sales of all tires are highly interrelated in that a customer will usually only purchase one option while excluding the others. Thus, from the retailer's perspective, a price increase in one brand, grade, or size of tire will result in the increase in the demand for another.

Similarly, when products are *complements*, pricing is complicated. An interesting example occurs in the muffler installation trade. Mufflers, tail pipes, and exhaust pipes typically wear out within a short time of each other. Retailers competing for the repair business advertise lifetime guarantees on the mufflers even though few, if any, will actually last to live that long. The catch is that the muffler is priced very low, at about $20–$25, but tail and exhaust pipes, which are not guaranteed, are priced very high. Thus, the retailer still makes a hefty profit on later sales of pipes despite having to provide worn-out mufflers "free." In this example, the prices of the muffler and pipes are highly interrelated complements, and a decrease in the price of the former (i.e., it's free) results in an increase in the sale of the latter for the retailer offering the deal.

The task facing a firm with a product line is to set prices for the entire line so as to maximize the achievement of the goals of the firm. One procedure for determining an optimal price is to examine the industry and cross-elasticities for the offerings in a product line to ascertain the range of sales for changes in price. This can be done in a simulation.[6] Next, one can observe changes in costs as prices and revenue change. The ultimate goal is to compute the effects on profits so that an optimum strategy can be found.

Managing Prices

Price setting involves balancing constraints against objectives. Figure 13-3 shows the most important factors in this regard. Notice, first, that the manager's final decision involves the determination of at least four things:

1 the level of the price to set

2 the optimum time to reveal the price and contingencies for making changes in the future

3 the means for operationalizing the price

4 the manner of communicating the price.

The price might be set at a high, low, or moderate level. It might be revealed early or late in an introductory ad campaign. It will need to be integrated with the product life cycle and anticipated competitive responses over time, as well. A price can be actualized entirely as a monetary cost to the customer, or it might be expressed through a combination of deals, credits, trade-ins, or other complex arrangements. Finally, it can be communicated in a variety of ways: in the media, on the product, on the wall or a display, verbally, by letter, and so on. Each of these decision outcomes depends on the manager's decision process whereby the firm's constraints and goals are balanced. This, in turn, may be guided by organization policy, past practice, and formal models and simulations designed to arrive at quantitative goals.

Notice in Figure 13-3 that many constraints need to be considered. These reside in economic, legal, government, social, and firm restrictions. Because these have been described both in this and Chapter 12, nothing more will be said about them at this time. Notice also in Figure 13-3 that many goals will enter the decision process (e.g., return on investment, market share). These, too, have been considered at length heretofore and will not be mentioned again. You might review the list and examples at the left of Figure 13-3 to gain insight into the forces pushing and pulling at the manager when prices must be set.

Let us turn now to some of the considerations taken into account when balancing constraints and goals (see Figure 13-3). For purposes of discussion, we will divide the decision-making task into pricing new products and pricing throughout the remainder of the product life cycle.

Pricing New Products

New product pricing will vary depending upon the degree of "newness." Different issues arise for products entirely new to the market as compared to the introduction of a new brand in a market already containing more-or-less similar offerings.

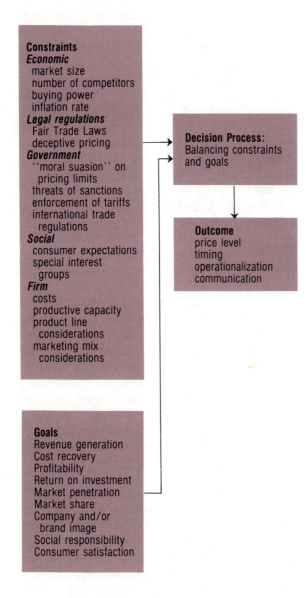

Constraints
Economic
  market size
  number of competitors
  buying power
  inflation rate
Legal regulations
  Fair Trade Laws
  deceptive pricing
Government
  "moral suasion" on
    pricing limits
  threats of sanctions
  enforcement of tariffs
  international trade
    regulations
Social
  consumer expectations
  special interest
    groups
Firm
  costs
  productive capacity
  product line
    considerations
  marketing mix
    considerations

Decision Process:
Balancing constraints
and goals

Outcome
price level
timing
operationalization
communication

Goals
Revenue generation
Cost recovery
Profitability
Return on investment
Market penetration
Market share
Company and/or
  brand image
Social responsibility
Consumer satisfaction

Figure 13-3. Setting prices from the manager's perspective

For entirely new products, the objective is to entice people to buy the product if only on a trial basis. What price should the manager set? This will depend on a number of factors.

One, of course, is the buyer. The price one sets may be perceived as a barrier or an attraction, depending on the buyer's resources and tastes. At the same time, the manager must realize a price sometimes signals other things to the buyer, such as quality. A low price might be an attraction, but depending on the product, might suggest inferior materials or a mass-produced article that everyone will eventually own. High prices might have any of several effects, depending on their meaning to customers.

Still another buyer reaction to price to consider is the anticipation of future price changes. The initial price in and of itself or in combination with other information might stimulate an early sale or conversely lead to postponement. Some buyers expect prices to rise due to cost increases, whereas others anticipate systematic price cuts due to competitive and other pressures.

A final buyer-related issue to consider is the role of incentives. The monetary price may only be part of the actual cost to a buyer. Coupons, credit, deals, transportation, storage, service, and guarantees constitute factors either interacting with the price or actually raising or lowering it. Obviously, expectations depend on the type of product (e.g., its complexity, patent protection, etc.), but it is important for managers to consider buyer reactions in any given situation.

At least two approaches for forecasting buyer reactions to prices should be considered. Conjoint analysis provides a quantitative indication of buyer reactions to price and the trade-offs among other product attributes. Another methodology to attend to is qualitative analysis. Through depth interviews, focus groups, or other techniques, it is possible to discover subtle and often counterintuitive reactions of potential buyers.

Conjoint analysis and qualitative methodologies are described in Chapter 7. They are essential inputs to the decision process.

The pricing of entirely new products will be influenced also by the firm's estimate of the life cycle of the product, the likely entrance of competitors, and financial goals (e.g., the need for cash, desired return on investment). Two options are usually contrasted: a penetration (i.e., low price) strategy or a skimming (i.e., high price) strategy. The former is taken when a long product life is anticipated, competitors might be attracted later into the market by profit attractions, and/or the firm has considerable cash on hand to pay for the intense communication and distribution efforts typically required for new products. The latter is taken when the life of a product is unknown or thought to be short, competitors are expected to enter soon, and/or cash for market introduction is in short supply.

When introducing a new brand into a market in which competition exists, pricing poses special problems. Some of the same considerations discussed heretofore with respect to buyer reactions toward entirely new products must be addressed, too. For example, the ability of people to afford the product, along with their perceptions of quality and their willingness to trade price for product attributes, must be assessed. In addition, however, management must evaluate the buyer's reaction to price in the light of prices of likely competitors. Because a new entrant to an ongoing market hopes to both attract nonusers of the product class and buyers of rival brands, it must set a price that, in combination with other features of its brand, gives it a differential advantage. This, in turn, means that brand positioning and marketing research will be essential (see Chapters 4, 5, 6, and 7).

Generally, if the firm strives for mass market appeal, it will set its price to meet the competition or score somewhat below it. On the other hand, if it goes after market niches, it may price high, especially if it has a strongly differentiated product. How high or how low must be within the bounds of buyer acceptability. The firm's degree of departure from the norm will additionally be governed by product life cycle and internal constraints. Thus, a price above or below the norm or the competition might be set in response to a declining or growing market or the return on investment or other financial needs of the firm.

Pricing over the Product Life Cycle

Price setting does not end with the introduction of a new product or brand. As time passes, managers must continually evaluate the necessity to revise prices either upward or downward. Again, the characteristics of buyers are a central concern. In addition to tracking buyer tastes, the firm must devote efforts to analysis of special classes of buyers. For example, the firm should regularly analyze its current buyers, former buyers who no longer purchase the product, former buyers who purchase from the competition, buyers loyal to rivals, switchers, and nonbuyers. This is necessary so that the firm can retain its present clientele, bring back old friends, entice buyers from the competitors, and induce trial from nonusers. Indeed, an understanding of buyer behavior might even lead to increased consumption from regular customers. In any case, it is important to analyze the differential effects of the current price and potential changes on various classes of buyers.

At the same time, price alterations might be necessitated by changes in product design, distribution, and communication tactics. For instance, the manufacturer of Brand X raisin bran cereal might add more raisins per box, switch from the use of wholesalers to direct delivery in its own trucks, or decrease its advertising and promotion budgets. Each of these changes would have an effect on sales that must be coordinated with price in an overall program.

Then, too, as the prices of supplies, labor, and raw materials change, so, too, do the costs of producing a product. This might require a price change to bring revenue and other financial goals into line.

Finally, even if buyer behavior, marketing mix, and costs were to remain constant, the firm might have to change prices simply in response to competitive pressures. This implies that the firm must monitor competitive moves and have a model for estimating the effects of any price changes on its own sales. Indeed, management must consider competitive conditions along all dimensions of the marketing mix and not merely price. We will have more to say about this near the end of the chapter.

New Developments and Future Directions in Pricing

Price Response Analysis[7]

An important consideration in the determination of what price to set is the timing and magnitude of the response of sales to a change in price. The so-called "law of demand" asserts that as price rises demand falls. But it does not specify the exact path that the inverse relation takes.

Figure 13-4 summarizes four possibilities in a *static* sense. Each shows that, as price increases, sales tend to decrease but at different rates. We have already seen the linear and multiplicative models in an earlier example. The curves represented in Figures 13-4A and 13-4B can be written in mathematical form, respectively, as $q = a - bp$ and $q = ap^b$, where a and b are parameters and are different in each equation. Notice that in the linear relation, as price changes by a fixed amount, quantity demanded will also change by a fixed amount at all points on the curve. A price increase (decrease) of one unit will result in a decrease (increase) of b units in demand at all levels of price. For the multiplicative relation, in contrast, the amount of increase or decrease in demand will depend on what price level one is at. For instance, at p_1 in Figure 13-4B, a small increase in price will result in a greater drop in demand than a comparable increase at p_2. Moreover, a small increase in price at p_1 will result in more of a decrease in demand than had the curve been a linear one.

The attraction relation shown in Figure 13-4C allows other possibilities to happen. For example, at p_1, a small increase in price will result in a decrease in demand at a rate less than the decrease in either the multiplicative or linear cases. At p_2, small changes produce effects similar to those found in the multiplicative case. The Gutenberg relation (Figure 13-4D), in contrast, shows somewhat similar reactions to price changes at p as does the multiplicative case, but at p_2, a small increase in price will produce more of a drop in demand than a comparable change under the multiplicative or linear models. In sum, the four response curves shown in Figure 13-4 permit the manager to make a wide range of predictions for changes in price. The task for the manager is to perform simulations and/or historical analyses to discover which curve best reflects his or her organization's situation. To focus on only the linear curve so often used in decision making is most likely an invalid practice in a majority of situations.[8] Indeed, as shown in Figure 13-4, the predictions made by the other curves are often at variance with the linear function.

Another way to take into account the effects of price changes on demand is through *dynamic modeling*. The relations shown in Figure 13-4 apply only if the price/quantity relationship remains constant over time. If the relation is known to change over time, then one might want to apply an approach which represents these changes. Consider the relations shown in Figure 13-5. Here we represent quantity demanded and price as functions of time and show them together to indicate their parallel changes. In the left-hand portion of Figure 13-5A, a price decrease results in an increase in demand with a rise at a decreasing rate to a saturation level. The right-hand portion of Figure 13-5A, in contrast, shows an increase in demand followed by a decrease to the saturation level. Figure 13-5B illustrates the parallel effects of a price increase. In addition to the time paths shown in Figure 13-5, we might envision situations where the path to saturation first rises (declines) at an increasing (decreasing) rate and then at a decreasing (increasing) rate. Other paths are possible, too. The points to stress are that price changes have different ultimate effects, proceed there at different rates, and take diverse paths, depending on the circumstances. Management scientists are only now beginning to study these effects.

The final time-related response issue concerns the product life cycle. Generally, it has been assumed that price elasticity increases during the introduction and growth stages, reaches a maximum during maturity, and thereafter begins to fall during the downturn in sales. Simon, however, argues that price elasticity is maximum at the introduction and decline stages and minimum during maturity.[9] Thus, two completely opposite views exist. We really do not know the true relationship of these opposites because the topic has not been researched much to date. The issue is important because the change in price elasticity over time has implications for the levels of sales and profits that the firm can expect. Hopefully, in the future marketers will study pricing and product life cycle interactions in more depth.

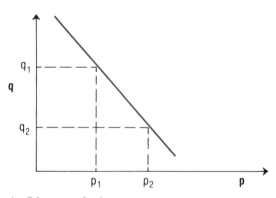

A. Linear relation $\qquad q = a - bp.$

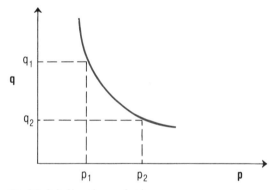

B. Multiplicative relation $\qquad q = ap^b, b < 0.$

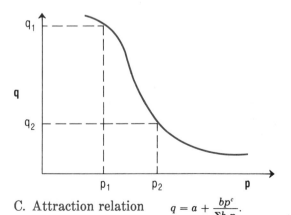

C. Attraction relation $\qquad q = a + \dfrac{bp^c}{\Sigma b_i p_i}.$

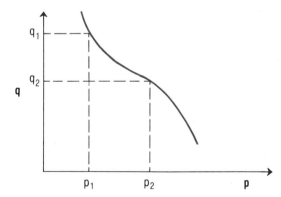

D. Gutenberg relation $\qquad q = a - bp + c\,sinh(dp).$

Figure 13-4. Four forms for the response of demand (q) to price (p)

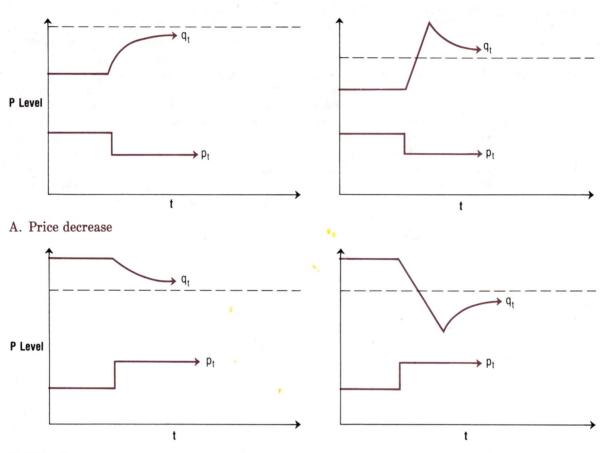

A. Price decrease

B. Price increase

Figure 13-5. Two common dynamic reactions to price

Marketing Mix Considerations

Marketers have long recognized that there are close relationships among the elements of the marketing mix. This is perhaps most evident when we casually observe the association between price and advertising of consumer goods in the marketplace. Firms that charge a premium price for their products generally spend more on advertising than do lower-priced rivals. Heinz Ketchup, for example, regularly sells at wholesale from 10 to 20 percent above the competition and at the same time spends more money on advertising. As the president of Heinz, Richard B. Patton, describes the situation (see p. 556, top):

EXHIBIT 13-1

The Role of Rebates as a Pricing Mechanism in Modern Economies

Under the dual pressures of inflation and sagging sales, consumer products firms are increasingly turning to rebates as an alternative or auxiliary pricing tool. By rebate is meant a refund of a portion of the purchase price to the purchaser from the manufacturer. In the typical application, a consumer buys a product from a retailer, the retailer then informs the manufacturer, who, in turn, sends a predetermined check for part of the purchase price back to the consumer. In this way, the purchase price has been reduced. The use of rebates is somewhat similar in intent and effect as discounts or sales. They are used by the sellers of small appliances (e.g., electric mixers, coffee makers, and radios) as well as by the sellers of consumer durables (e.g., washing machines, automobiles).

What are its effects? At the level of the individual buyer, rebates often serve as an incentive to make a purchase. However, it is questionable whether it really stimulates new demand and expansion of the market or whether people merely time their purchases to coincide with the rebate programs. In addition, people tend to both anticipate the rebates and become habituated to its effects. An automobile dealer recently described its impact on the consumer thusly:

All we are doing is borrowing sales from the coming months without making the market any bigger. In the process we are conditioning people like Pavlov's dogs to only come out when the rebate bell rings. It is going to be very difficult to deprogram them.[1]

From top management's standpoint, however, it is believed that rebates provide needed cash flows, remove inventory, and maintain fully operating factories. At the same time, it is claimed that rebates are necessary to meet the competition and to protect market share. Nevertheless, as one automotive executive noted:

Rebating is the last thing you want to do as far as marketing is concerned. It is a means of fleshing out inventory and maintaining market share. It is not looked upon as a way of generating higher total revenue, since you are effectively giving away money.[2]

A difficult managerial problem is to decide whether to offer rebates or not and, if so, at what level and for how long. Chrysler chose to maintain rebates for over a year, while the other automotive companies preferred shorter periods of two months or so. In any case, the use of rebates appears to be a last-ditch effort in bad times.

From a societal perspective, we need to ask if everyone is really better off when firms practice rebating. Or does the practice merely play on people's vulnerabilities, postpone the inevitable decline of industries, or deflect the energies of firms away from measures needed to make fundamental changes.

1. Quoted in Thomas L. Friedman, "U.S. Car Dealers See Rebates as Scant Help," *International Herald Tribune*, February 13–14, 1982.

2. Ibid.

Our goal is to blend advertising and pricing to produce optimum market share and profit margins. Our feeling is that consistency in advertising and pricing strategies is important to the success of any consumer product.[10]

Consistency typically means setting advertising and prices in relation to one another. Those that set higher prices generally spend relatively more on advertising.

The rationale for a correlation between pricing and advertising is a multifaceted one and has numerous and sometimes conflicting interpretations.[11] One idea is that once a firm has gained a foothold in the market through differentiation, it can charge higher prices than newer or less successfully differentiated brands. To maintain its lead, however, it must continue to outspend the competition in advertising. Lesser rivals, in turn, rely relatively more on pricing to gain a share of the market and thus set a lower price with relatively less spent on advertising. Still another explanation is that advertising makes consumers more price sensitive. For example, advertising might first stimulate the consumer's awareness of the advertised brands. Then, when shopping, the consumer compares these brands on price, while ignoring the unadvertised brands, which presumably set lower prices. Because the advertised brands have higher costs and aim for higher profits, we see a positive correlation between price and advertising across all products in a class. A final explanation is really a nonexplanation: it is maintained that it is so difficult to measure price and advertising that any relation can be found. Prices and costs vary across rival brands and across wholesalers and retailers, complicating the determination of price effects. Similarly, omitted variables such as product quality or systematic consumer differences confound things further. In addition, high advertising expenditures are sometimes associated with high costs (and high prices), but occasionally, they indirectly lower costs through economies of scale and other effects resulting from increased demand. So, for these and other reasons, the price relation is difficult to foretell.

Nevertheless, Farris and Reibstein report a strong positive relationship between relative advertising and average relative price for a sample of 227 consumer goods businesses.[12] The greater the advertising, the higher the price. In their survey, the authors measured relative advertising with a question asking each business to compare its advertising budget as a percentage of sales with the budgets of its leading competitors. This was measured on a scale ranging from spending "much less," to "somewhat less," to "about the same," to "somewhat more," to "much more." Similarly, relative price was measured by asking firms to compare their average factory selling price with those of their leading competitors. The question was answered with a quantitative response in percentages (e.g., +4 percent higher than competitors, −2 percent lower, etc.). Farris and Reibstein also found that the positive relationship between advertising and pricing held for variations in product quality, whether one was in the maturity or decline stages of the product life cycle (but not the introduction stage), whether the product was inexpensive (less than $10) or expensive (greater than $10), or whether the market was stable in terms of changes in competitors' sales. The relationship held to a greater extent for high market—as opposed to low market—share businesses, however. Finally, firms that were more consistent in their pricing and advertising policies tended to have greater return on investments. It should be noted that, in a larger study on the same data where more variables were statistically controlled, relative price and relative advertising were positively related for industrial goods firms but *not* for consumer businesses.[13]

Therefore, the nature of the relationship between advertising and pricing should be regarded as tentative. Certainly, we need to learn in detail about the nature of the relationship and the conditions under which it operates.

What about other marketing mix interactions with price? Unfortunately, we know very little about how pricing varies with product quality, distribution, or nonadvertising promotions. What is needed, further, is not only research establishing presence of such relations but a rationale and guidelines for managers on how to set prices optimally in the face of such interactions. Overall, the subfield of marketing dealing with pricing is in its early growth stage, and it remains a frontier for future study.

Summary

We began this chapter with an overview of the role of pricing in marketing management (see Figure 13-1). Everything begins with overall organization goals (e.g., return on investment), which sets the tone for further refinement in the decision process. Organizational goals shape marketing objectives (e.g., levels of sales, market share, market growth, product line profitability). Marketing objectives, in turn, influence pricing objectives. The latter include, among others, long- and short-run effects of prices (e.g., on earnings), specific target market responses (e.g., rate of trial, adoption, repeat purchasing), effects on other products in the firm (e.g., on company or brand image), and effects on rivals (e.g., the initiation of a price war).

Once we have specific pricing objectives in mind, tactics can be chosen to implement them. Managers use prices to generate sales and do so by skillfully setting the level of price and price differentials vis-à-vis the competition and one's own brands. This, of course, is an ongoing activity that must be done in the light of changing costs, consumer needs, and competitive pressures. In addition, social and legal constraints and input from other dimensions of the marketing mix indi-rectly determine price through their influence on pricing objectives (see Figure 13-1).

A number of traditional managerial approaches to pricing were then considered. Using classical microeconomic theory, we showed first how prices might be set to *maximize profits*. This requires knowledge of cost and demand equations. Because these are difficult to estimate and contain error, profit maximization pricing is infrequently done in practice. At the same time, the approach fails to take into account competitive, long-run, and other factors.

Given the practical and theoretical problems with profit maximization, some firms strive to *maximize revenue*. This still requires accurate estimates of demand, however. Moreover, even with good demand estimates, the price determined by using the method will generally not be the profit maximizing price. Still, the approach has its place in certain contexts.

Still another method is to set prices so as to *minimize costs*. Although one does not need accurate estimates of demand, reasonable data on costs are essential. To the extent that such data are lacking, however, the approach is problematic. Nevertheless, many firms use a modification such as *cost-plus pricing* or *overall cost leadership*.

Market share leadership pricing is also done on occasion. Here the hope is that a chosen price will attract a large share of consumers relative to competitors. The premise is that market share leads to profitability. Whether this is true or not is still a controversial and largely unproven issue.

When a firm employs different prices for different customers, we term the tactic *market differentiation pricing*. Such an approach is generally illegal except under certain conditions (see Chapter 12).

For *new products*, either *market skimming* or *market penetration* are the most common options. Under the former tactic, the firm sets its price at a high level with the aim of either leaving the market at a later time or lowering its price systematically over time. Under the latter tactic, a low price is set with the hope that it will quickly lead to increased sales and gain a foothold in the market.

The chapter then turned to a discussion of *product-line pricing* where the firm sets prices of its related products or brands in order to achieve goals such as maximum total profits, maximum revenues, or the minimization of cannibalization. The firm must consider the effects of the prices of individual brands on the sales of its complements and substitutes.

Next, the chapter considered pricing from the individual decision maker's perspective (see Figure 13-3). Four outputs must be determined: (1) the level of price to set, (2) the optimal time to reveal the price and determination of price contingencies over time, (3) the means for operationalizing the price, and (4) the manner of communicating the price.

For pricing *new products*, a key factor is the need to size up the buyer. This means researching the customer's rational and subjective reactions to the price as well as his or her judgments about where the price will be in the future. Similarly, the buyer's likely reactions to incentives must be assessed as these closely interact with price effects. New product pricing also must include product life cycle, potential competition, and financial considerations.

Price revisions constitute another activity essential for successful marketing. Here the firm must estimate the effects of prices on its current buyers, nonbuyers of the product class, brand switchers, people loyal to competitors' brands, and previous buyers of the firm's brand who now buy other brands. At the same time, price alterations must be evaluated in the light of changes in costs, product design, distribution, and marketing communication programs.

The chapter closed with a look at new developments and future directions in pricing. One set of concepts, *price response analysis*, focused on the relationship between price and demand. A set of quantitative relations was examined in both static and dynamic senses. This is a promising area now being explored by management scientists in marketing. Finally, recent research on the relationship between pricing and other marketing mix variables was examined.

Questions and Problems for Discussion

1 How do pricing decisions fit within the broader marketing management decision process?

2 Discuss the profit maximization approach to price setting and consider its pros and cons.

3 Revenue maximization, cost minimization, and market share leadership are three other approaches to setting prices. Briefly discuss these and note their assets and liabilities.

4 What are market skimming and market penetration strategies, when are they used, and what benefits and liabilities do they offer?

5 In any price setting program, four broad decisions must be made. Name these and discuss their relationship to marketing/organization goals and constraints.

6 What are some of the key factors to consider when pricing new products?

7 Discuss the issues surrounding the pricing of products over the product life cycle.

8 What is price response analysis and how can it help the manager?

9 What is the relationship of price with other decisions in the marketing mix?

NOTES

1. For a nice discussion of cost estimation issues, see Kent B. Monroe, *Pricing: Making Profitable Decisions* (New York: McGraw-Hill, 1979). Early operational demand procedures are discussed in Edgar A. Pessemier, "An Experimental Method for Estimating Demand," *Journal of Business* 33 (1960): 373–83; Edgar A. Pessemier and Richard D. Teach, "Pricing Experiments, Scaling Consumer Preferences, and Predicting Purchase Behavior," *Proceedings of the 1966 Marketing Educator's Conference* (Chicago: American Marketing Association, 1966), pp. 541–57; R. G. Stout, "Developing Data to Estimate Price-Quantity Relationships," *Journal of Marketing* 3 (April 1969): 34–36; John R. Nevin, "Laboratory Experiments for Estimating Consumer Demand: A Validation Study," *Journal of Marketing Research* 11 (August 1974): 261–68; John R. Nevin, "Using Experimental Data to Suggest and Evaluate Alternative Marketing Strategies," in S. C. Jain, ed., *Proceedings of the Educator's Conference* (Chicago: American Marketing Association, 1978).

2. Michael E. Porter, *Competitive Strategy: Techniques for Analyzing Industries and Competitors* (New York: The Free Press, 1980), p. 35.

3. Porter, *Competitive Strategy*, p. 36.

4. Robert D. Buzzell, Bradley T. Gale, and Ralph G. M. Sultan, "Market Share—A Key to Profitability," *Harvard Business Review* 53 (January-February 1975): 97–106.

5. For an early discussion of market skimming see Joel Dean, "Pricing Policies for New Products," *Harvard Business Review* 28 (November-December 1950): 28–36; and for an update, see Joel Dean, "Pricing Policies for New Products," *Harvard Business Review* 54 (November-December 1976): 141–53.

6. See David B. Montgomery and Glen L. Urban, *Management Science in Marketing* (Englewood Cliffs, N.J.: Prentice-Hall, 1969). Glen L. Urban, "A Mathematical Modeling Approach to Product Line Decisions," *Journal of Marketing Research* 6 (February 1969): 40–47.

7. Some of the material presented in this section was stimulated by discussions the author had with Professor Hermann Simon at the University of Bielefeld, West Germany, and in a seminar held at his university with his research fellows.

8. For a presentation of many common functional forms, see Philippe A. Naert and Peter S. H. Leeflang, *Building Implementable Marketing Models* (Boston: Martinus Nijhoff, 1978), ch. 5.

9. Personal communication with Professor Hermann Simon.

10. Quoted in Paul W. Farris and David J. Reibstein, "How Prices, Ad Expenditures, and Profits Are Linked," *Harvard Business Review* 57 (November-December 1979): 173–84.

11. See Farris and Reibstein, "How Prices, Ad Expenditures and Profits Are Linked"; Robert L. Steiner, "Does Advertising Lower Consumer Prices?" *Journal of Marketing* 37 (October 1973); Robert L. Steiner, "Marketing Productivity in Consumer Goods Industries—A Vertical Perspective," *Journal of Marketing* 42 (January 1978): 60–70; Dick R. Wittink, "Advertising Increases Sensitivity to Price," *Journal of Advertising Research* 17 (April 1977): 39–42; John F. Cady, "An Estimate of the Price Effects of Restriction on Drug Price Advertising," *Economic Inquiry* 14 (December 1976): 493–510.

12. Farris and Reibstein, "How Prices, Ad Expenditures, and Profits Are Linked."

13. See Paul W. Farris and Robert D. Buzzell, "Why Advertising and Promotional Costs Vary: Some Cross-Sectional Analyses," *Journal of Marketing* 43 (Fall 1979): 112–22.

GLOSSARY

Cost Minimizing Pricing. The price tactic whereby a price is chosen either (a) to minimize costs or (b) to be a percentage above costs (termed *cost-plus pricing*). Sometimes firms pursue an *overall cost leadership* strategy whereby costs are kept at a minimum and, given this constraint, prices are set according to other goals such as meeting the competition, pricing slightly above the norm, revenue maximization, and so on. *See* pricing tactics.

Cost-Plus Pricing. A pricing tactic whereby a price is set as a percentage increase over costs. For example, given costs, a firm may set a price as costs plus an increment believed necessary to generate a desired profit. Cost-plus pricing is sometimes called *markup pricing*. *See* pricing tactics.

Market Differentiation Pricing. The use of price as a means to differentiate the product from the competition. Although usually illegal and unethical, it might be justified under certain conditions (e.g., to reflect differences in distribution costs). *See* pricing tactics.

Market Penetration. A new product pricing tactic whereby a low price is set with the hope that it will quickly lead to sales and gain a foothold in the market. Such a tactic is believed to discourage new entrants. *See* market skimming, pricing tactics.

Market Share Leadership Pricing. The tactic whereby price is chosen so as to increase or maintain a particular market share. Such a tactic is believed to lead to profitability although this has not been proven conclusively. *See* pricing tactics.

Market Skimming. A new product pricing tactic whereby a high price is set with the aim of either leaving the market at a later time (and thereby hoping to generate high profits in the interim) or lowering the price systematically over time (and thereby continually drawing new customers as time passes). *See* market penetration, pricing tactics.

Markup Pricing. *See* cost-plus pricing.

New Product Pricing. *See* market skimming, market penetration.

Overall Cost Leadership. A term used to describe the firm's strategy consisting of minimizing costs in order to achieve a pricing or other marketing mix advantage over the competition. *See* pricing tactics.

Price Response Analysis. An analytical procedure usually based on simulations, managerial judgment, or actual historical data whereby sales can be estimated on the basis of changes in one's price.

Pricing Objectives. Goals related to the setting of prices and designed to serve as a means for achieving larger marketing objectives (see Figure 13-1). The goals concern short- versus long-run aims (e.g., early cash recovery versus market penetration), desired target market responses (e.g., trial and repeat buying), product line considerations, and induced competitive responses. *See* pricing tactics.

Pricing Tactics. The means needed to implement pricing objectives. The output consists of price levels, timing issues, price revision contingencies, monetary and nonmonetary operationalizations, and the communication of prices. Specific tactics include skimming, market penetration, profit maximization, revenue maximization, cost minimization, market share leadership, and market differentiation pricing.

Product Line Pricing. The practice of choosing prices for each item in a product line so as to achieve some goal or goals. The objective may be to minimize cannibalization, maximize profits or revenue, and so on. *See* pricing tactics.

Profit Maximization Pricing. The price tactic whereby a price is chosen so as to maximize profits. The approach is based upon classical microeconomic theory and requires estimates of cost and demand equations. Despite its appeal, many drawbacks exist with its use, as noted in the text. *See also* pricing tactics.

Rebates. A refund of a portion of the purchase price to the purchaser from the manufacturer. This is done to stimulate sales by providing a price-reducing incentive. See Exhibit 13-1.

Revenue Maximization Pricing. The price tactic whereby a price is chosen to maximize sales. This procedure depends on the accuracy of demand estimates in relation to possible prices. *See* pricing tactics.

Pricing Opportunities: Present and Future

Kent B. Monroe
Virginia Polytechnic
University

The pricing decisions for a modern organization are complex and important. Traditionally, these decisions have been determined by following the pricing practices of another organization or by following pricing practices established in the past. Today, environmental pressures are forcing new pricing approaches and strategies. However, careful analysis and research for pricing decisions have not been traditional policy of American businesses. Hence, many firms have not been prepared to change pricing strategies, and many of the popular pricing strategies discussed in the contemporary literature are often simplistic reactions that may produce unanticipated consequences.

The pricing literature has produced few new insights or approaches that would stimulate most businesses to change their methods of setting prices. While there may be many reasons for this lack of creative development of new approaches to pricing problems, two reasons are illustrative: (1) the economists' theory of price has dominated despite the obvious lack of realism; and (2) until recently, the seller's problem was primarily demand stimulation using promotional activities. Thus, there was little "payoff" in studying how buyers respond to prices and price changes, nor how to determine a set of prices that would lead to a better profit position for the firm.

The ability of firms to adapt to these environmental pressures will require new attitudes towards the price decision *and* the establishment of price research programs to provide better information on: (1) the buyers' use of price as a purchase decision variable, (2) cost, volume, and profit implications of alternative price decisions, (3) the integration of price in product life cycle strategies, and (4) organizing and administering the pricing function. We turn now to outlining first some behavioral aspects of such a research program, and then to some decision areas needing more research efforts.

Behavioral Responses to Price

During the past few years, consumer researchers have considered the effect of situational variables on consumer behavior. Within the area of price research there have been a number of papers pointing to the influence of variables other than the specific price variable on price perception.

Even though some multi-cue price-quality studies have not discovered significant price-quality relationships, there is little doubt that, absent perfect information, quality is perceived to be positively related to price. What the multi-cue studies have shown is that often product attributes play a more dominant role in quality perception than does price. Thus, the research questions that need more attention are:

1 How do buyers use price information in purchase decisions?

2 How are buyers' price perceptions affected or altered by the situation surrounding their purchase decisions?

Implication of Situational Variables for Price Perception. Extending the concept of situational variables to the question of price perception is worthwhile because it has been established that people judge prices and products differently depending on the context or background prevailing at the time of the judgment. Further, it has been also shown that similar prices have been perceived differently when these prices have been judged in different contexts. The primary objective of the recent price perception research has been on what may be termed physical aspects of the price stimuli. That is, the research question has been: "What happens to price perceptions when price structure of prices to be judged are varied?" Moreover, other studies have considered the more subjective frame of reference the buyer brings to the purchase situation.

Price Structure. Within a normal purchasing decision the buyer must choose from an array of alternative brands and sizes. Each of these choice alternatives has a price that, potentially, must be evaluated before a decision can be made. This array or set of prices that forms the evaluation set is called the *price structure*. Previous psychological studies have shown that judgments vary depending on the stimulus range, the frequency distribution of stimuli, the stimulus judged medium, and the end stimuli values. Each of these four parameters describes the stimulus structure. Hence, with prices as the stimuli, the price structure is described by the range of prices, the frequency distribution of prices, the price judged medium, and the lowest and highest prices in the price set.

It has been confirmed that presenting prices for judgment in order of increasing magnitude produce significantly higher categories of judgment than when the price series are presented in decreasing order of magnitude. These results suggest that subjects' frames of reference are sensitive to the contextual effect of order of presentation.

Frame of Reference. Recognizing that subsequent judgments are comparative in nature, then if the frame of reference changes, it is likely that the judgment may also change. In most situations, the buyer brings to the purchase problem some notion of past prices paid, or an expected or fair price to pay. Moreover, the buyer usually has an image of the store he is shopping in as well as an image of the brands available for purchase. Each of these variables form part of the background of the eventual purchase decision and, therefore, are contextual.

Summary. The purpose of this section of the paper has been to explore the contextual or frame of reference effects on buyer judgments. Focusing on the price variable, it has been demonstrated that the physical characteristics of the prices the buyer compares and evaluates affect judgments. Moreover, it has been demonstrated that subjective frames of reference also exist for the buyer and that these also affect buyers' judgments. It has also been demonstrated that these contextual effects can be experimentally tested and verified. It has demonstrated quite clearly the necessity for including contextual effects within the analysis of pricing experiments. The question of how judgment of a physical stimulus depends on other stimuli has been of considerable concern to psychologists for some time. It is now time for researchers to include contextual effects within their research paradigms, particularly those researchers exploring the role price plays in the purchase decision process.

Price Decision Research

As observed earlier, little research has been conducted that would help the decision maker analyze alternative pricing decisions. In particular, the cost-volume-profit impact is generally not known before a decision nor has relevant research been done on improving the pricing of products over their life cycles or on the administration of the pricing function. We now turn to reviewing some of these concerns.

Pricing over the Product Life Cycle. It is a premise of this paper that the management of a multiproduct firm should be concerned with managing products over their products' life cycles. Management, therefore, must develop plans that consider the life cycles of sales, total contribution, separable fixed costs, and separable assets employed with the different products. Moreover, management must control production and marketing costs and must control for the level of common costs and common assets employed. Indeed, as product sales grow, the experience curve phenomenon suggests costs and prices decline, but not automatically.

New Product Prices. One of the most challenging decision problems is that of determining the price of a new product. New product pricing decisions are usually made with very little information on demand, costs, competition and other variables that may affect success. The difficulty in pricing a new product depends on the relative "newness" of the product. Some products are new in the sense that a commodity which already exists in the market is offered by a company that is new to the industry. Other new products are new both to the company and to the market, but they are functionally competitive with established products.

The most difficult new product pricing problem occurs when the product is unique, i.e., functionally dissimilar to any other product. Essentially, demand is unknown and not all potential uses of the product are known. There are no comparable market experiences—no existing channels of distribution, no existing markups, no production and marketing cost experiences. Potential customers will be uncertain about the product in terms of its functioning, its reliability or its durability.

No comprehensive model has specifically focused on the new product pricing problem, perhaps because of the uncertainties surrounding this decision area. Several more generalized models have some character-istics which are capable of accommodating essential elements of the situation and can, therefore, be applied to new product pricing decisions. Typically, they are based on the foundations of marginal analysis and are only relevant to a single product situation.

Pricing a Mature Product. As the life of a product progresses, it becomes necessary to review past pricing decisions and to determine the desirability of a price change. With expanded sales, unit costs can decrease due to efficient productive changes and the ability to spread fixed costs of production and marketing over a greater volume. In addition, as a product moves into maturity, replacement sales constitute an increasing proportion of the demand for the product. Competition from substitute brands and private-label brands also tends to increase. Market conditions during this period rarely justify a price increase, hence, the pricing decision is usually one of reducing price or standing pat.

As in the area of new product pricing, no comprehensive price change model exists specifically for the mature product situation. Several efforts which address specific factors relevant to the decision area do exist. However, these are basically extensions of analytical aids relevant to the decision problem rather than a comprehensive price change model for mature products.

Factors which influence consideration of a price reduction are price elasticity of demand and unit cost reductions brought about by increased volume. Since a price decrease often will be followed by competitors, for a price reduction to be profitable, three conditions are necessary: (1) industry demand must be price elastic; (2) the firm's demand must be price elastic; and (3) revenues gained from the price reduction must be greater than the costs of producing and selling the additional units. For example, it can easily be demonstrated that even under conditions of price elasticity, a price reduction can result in a decrease in profits unless unit variable costs also decline.

The above discussion indicates caution in applying elasticity concepts to price reduction decisions. Competitors' reactions and market elasticity of demand must be considered. It must also be determined whether variable costs per unit may change thereby requiring reformulation of functional relationships. As a consequence of these complexities, a break-even analysis often is suggested to evaluate price changes. The percentage increase in volume (for various price reductions) necessary to maintain current profit levels may be computed. Management can then assess the likelihood that a lower price will produce a change in volume sufficient to meet and exceed this level.

Product Line Pricing. Most firms sell a variety of products requiring a set of different marketing strategies. Generally, the firm has several product lines—a group of products that are closely related either because they are used together, satisfy the same general needs, or are marketed together. Within a product line, there are usually some products that are functional substitutes for each other, and there are usually some products that are functionally complementary to each other. Because of the demand and cost interrelationships inherent within a product line, and because there are usually several price-market targets, the product-line pricing problem is one of the major challenges facing a marketing executive.

In contrast, today's multiproduct firm sells its products in markets that are not completely separable, and it becomes intuitively obvious that the level of sales of any one item in a product line may be influenced by the price of other items in the line. Thus, the variation of price for any given product may or may not produce the desired result unless prices of the other products in the line are also varied.

It has been shown that buyers are likely to have a range of acceptable prices for a product, and if the desired product is priced within this price range, the buyer may be favorably disposed to complete the purchase. Extending the concept of a price range to a product line provides an acceptable range of product line prices. In effect, then, the existence of high and low price limits represents a price-decision constraint. If some products are priced outside the acceptable price range, and some products are priced within the acceptable price range, there would seem to be a smaller probability a buyer would buy any product than if all products in the line were priced within the acceptable price range. In such a situation, the price-setter seemingly would want to constrain his pricing flexibility to those prices lying within the price range with highest probability of being accepted.

Of interest in the situation of determining price differentials is the concept of a constant proportion between just noticeably different (JND) stimuli. Or, stating the situation in reverse, the prices of two products should not be different unless the products themselves are perceived by buyers as being different.

Price Administration. We now turn to consider the problem of administering base prices throughout the channels of distribution and the markets in which the products are sold. Price administration deals with price adjustments for sales made under different conditions, such as:

1 sales made in different quantities

2 sales made to different types of middlemen performing different functions

3 sales made to buyers in different geographic locations

4 sales made with different credit and collection policies.

So far, the discussion on pricing has been oriented toward determining what may be called a base or list price. It is this price, or some reasonable deviation therefrom, that buyers normally encounter. However, there is another vital dimension to prices called price structure. Price structure involves determining:

1 the time and conditions of payment

2 the nature of discounts to be allowed the buyer

3 where and when title is to be taken by the buyer.

In establishing a price structure, there are many possibilities of antagonizing distributors and even incurring legal liability. Thus, it is necessary to avoid these dangers while, at the same time, using the price structure to achieve the desired profit objective.

Conclusion

The need for correct pricing decisions is becoming more important as today's pricing environment places increasing pressure for better, faster, and more frequent pricing decisions. Marketing researchers have not yet responded to this need by developing pricing models useful for pragmatic pricing decisions. A basic factor retarding such developments appears to be the dearth of research information characterizing competitive and especially market responses to prices and price changes. Within the firm, this lack of response information may be due to the relative managerial difficulty in justifying research budgets for the non expense-incurring area of pricing as compared to advertising which can consume a considerable proportion of company resources.

Happily, recent research developments, particularly in the areas of buyers' acceptable price ranges and price-quality perceptions, have stimulated some increased business and academic research in pricing. There have been some promising modeling efforts in product line pricing and the determination of optimal price discounts. Given the environmental pressures on pricing decisions, it is an appropriate time to develop significant pricing models. Hopefully, pricing researchers and pricing administrators have been stimulated to cooperate more fully toward that end.

CHAPTER FOURTEEN

The matter I allude to is the exorbitant price exacted by the merchants and vendors of goods for every necessary they dispose of. I am sensible the trouble and risk in importing give the adventurers a right to a generous price, and that such, from the motives of policy, should be paid; but yet I cannot conceive that they, in direct violation of every principle of generosity, of reason and of justice, should be allowed, if it is possible to restrain 'em, to avail themselves of the difficulties of the times, and to amass fortunes upon the public ruin.

——George Washington (1732–1799)

A marketing channel is essentially a method of organizing the work that has to be done to move goods from producers to consumers. The purpose of the work is to overcome various gaps that separate the goods and services from those who would use them.

The use of middlemen boils down largely to their superior efficiency in making goods widely available and accessible to target markets. Marketing intermediaries, through their experience, their specialization, their contacts, and their scale, offer the firm more than it can usually achieve on its own.

——Philip Kotler[1]

CHANNELS OF DISTRIBUTION

Introduction

A *channel of distribution* is the set of people and organizations concerned with the flow of products from producer to consumer. Sometimes a producer will sell directly to final customers by making contact through its own salespeople, manufacturer's representatives, advertisements, telephone, or mail. Actual flow of goods will occur via the post office, customer pickup, common carriers, or special delivery services. More often than not, intermediaries will be used. This may mean establishing one's own warehouses and retail outlets or cooperating with independent distributors and retailers. Whatever the system used, the managerial decisions and options can be quite numerous and complex.

By way of introduction, let us consider the example of a New England–based manufacturer of men's work shoes.[2] Figure 14-1 shows that the firm markets its shoes through six channels. Some shoes are sold by full- or part-time salespeople who travel to factories, construction sites, and other locations. The salesperson takes orders, and the manufacturer later ships the shoes directly to customers. A second route is by direct mail. Fliers are sent to prospective buyers, and subsequent orders are again shipped directly to customers. Shoemobile trucks are used on a limited scale to reach certain large industrial accounts through a third channel. Although each vehicle carries some shoes, most sales via this means also are filled through direct shipment from the factory to customer. About 20 shoemobiles are currently in operation. The fourth path shown in Figure 14-1 is through company-owned retail outlets. The firm owns more than 100 stores across the country that operate much the same as traditional shoe stores. Approximately 50 independently owned franchise stores comprise a fifth channel.

These, too, function along the lines of traditional shoe stores. Finally, the manufacturer sells its shoes to Sears, which markets them under its own brand name. Other options are open to the manufacturer such as selling to distributors, independent retail chains, the government, or overseas brokers. You can readily see how complex it can be to bring one's goods to market.

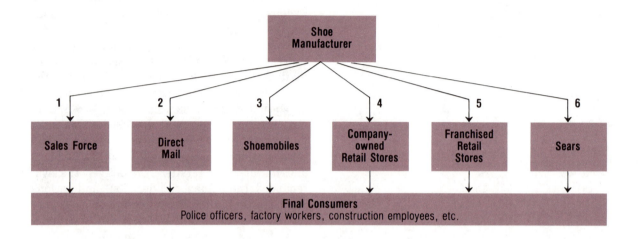

Figure 14-1. Channels of distribution used by a New England-based shoe manufacturer

SOURCE: Drawn from a discussion in Hirotaka J. Takeuchi, "Strategic Issues in Distribution," Harvard Business School Case Services, Boston, 1980, pp. 1–2.

The goal of this chapter will be to introduce you to the workings of channels of distribution and the decisions faced by firms choosing or, once chosen, managing channel systems. The chapter begins with a discussion of the role of channels of distribution. Consideration is given to the rationale underlying any channel, the functions performed, the types of channels, and a brief history of the evolution of channels. Next, an overview of the channel management process is provided. An attempt is made to show what are the key channel decisions and how they relate to other forces within and without the firm. The specific issues concerned with the design of the channel are then presented. These entail planning, assessment, and selection of alternatives, as well as ongoing system evaluation and channel modification decisions. The chapter then turns to operational decisions. Motivation, conflict management, evaluation and control, and communication are the central topics. Finally, the chapter closes with a discussion of legal concerns and physical distribution issues.

The Role of Channels of Distribution in Marketing

Why Are Channels Needed?

Imagine what it would be like if only producers and consumers existed and no intermediaries of any kind could be found. Either consumers would have to contact producers directly or vice versa, and one party or the other would have to physically transport the goods or alternatively use the postal system or common carriers.

The consumer could no longer go to the supermarket, say, to purchase eggs, fish, produce, canned goods, and napkins. Rather, he or she would have to separately contact a dairy farmer, a fisherman, a fruit and vegetable grower, a food processor, and a paper products manufacturer. Moreover, the consumer might find that it is necessary to contact multiple dairy farmers, fishermen, etc., to get one's money's worth. Indeed, considerable expense in phone calls, time, and transportation costs might be required to obtain one's food needs. Multiply this effort by the efforts needed to acquire the vast number of clothing, furniture, household supply, entertainment, and other products purchased by the typical family and we can see how overwhelmingly difficult it would be to live our lives in the way we are now accustomed.

The producer's activities would be equally difficult without the help of intermediaries. Consider the case of a publisher of books. How would the publisher sell its products? Would it have to go door-to-door? How many customers would travel to the factory to purchase an $8 paperback? If you think about it a minute, you will soon realize that the cost of a sales call, the probability that a person would buy a book, the dollar amount of a likely sale, and the cost to deliver a single book, which is the most likely purchase size, all point to formidable, if not insurmountable, obstacles for the publisher.

To see the problem in another light, let us focus on the simplified market systems shown in Figure 14-2. In panel A at the top, we see the case with no intermediaries. Here 3 businesspeople—a fisherman, a food processor, and a paper products manufacturer—market directly to 10 consumers. Whether the seller goes to the buyer or the buyer goes to the seller, we observe that a total of 30 contacts are made in this system. Contrast this to the situation shown in panel B where a single retailer fulfills an intermediary role. Now we find that only 13 contacts are required, for the businesspeople contact the retailer directly and each customer then shops at the retailer.

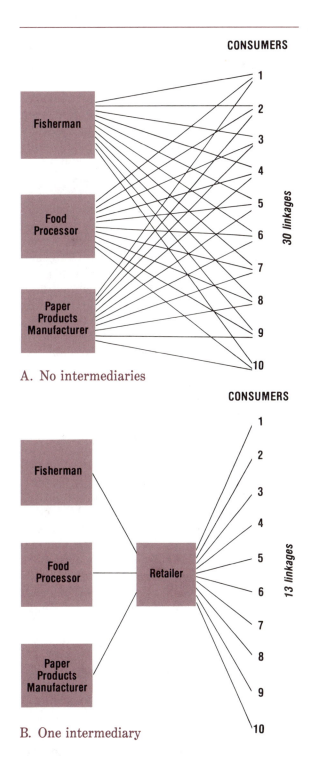

A. No intermediaries

B. One intermediary

Figure 14-2. A simple comparison of direct and indirect marketing systems

As revealed in Figure 14-2, the introduction of an intermediary simplifies the marketing process. Not only are the number of communication links reduced, but the number and length of transportation paths are lessened as well. The simplification even goes beyond that suggested in the figure when one realizes that each producer typically sells to many more customers than 10, and many more nonconsummated contacts occur than consummated ones.

Of course, the addition of an intermediary adds costs since increased effort, expenses, and risk must be paid. Nevertheless, in many cases, systems with intermediaries are often more efficient and sell products at lower prices than systems without them.

Two forces underlie the need for intermediaries: the *discrepancy of quantity* and the *discrepancy of assortment.*[3] Consider first the discrepancy of quantity. In order to take advantage of economies of scale and learning curve effects, most manufacturers must produce in very large quantities. Buyers, of course, purchase only a fraction of the seller's output. For some products (e.g., automobiles), manufacturers organize production to produce huge quantities of certain models in a particular time period, or for only a portion of the year, but buyers purchase the models over the entire year. For other products (e.g., air conditioners), manufacturers must, for various reasons, stretch out production over much of the year, yet customers buy predominantly in short time periods (e.g., summer). The result is that differences exist in the timing of supply and demand. Some goods must be stored in inventory and/or rushed to market to meet the temporarily divergent needs of buyers and sellers. This is what is known as the discrepancy of quantity.

Wholesalers, retailers, and other intermediaries reconcile discrepancies in quantity through the services they provide. For example, many small producers such as family farms or artisans do not have the time, knowledge, or resources to market all of their wares. Instead, they sell to intermediaries who buy from similar suppliers. The intermediaries, in turn, achieve economies of scale and other benefits not open to the small producers. This role of intermediaries has been termed *accumulation.* Producers often do not have the capital and human resources to perform the accumulation function themselves. Conversely, very large producers often sell in great quantities to intermediaries, who in turn have special expertise or advantage in subdividing the large quantities into smaller ones for customers demanding it. This role is known as the *breaking of bulk.* For instance, some wholesalers buy salt in bulk but put it in smaller packages for sale to retailers.

The discrepancy of assortment is the second force pressing for intermediaries. Most producers make only one or a limited number of products. Customers, on the other hand, desire a vast number of varied products and services. It is simply not feasible for consumers to meet all their needs by going to individual producers. A discrepancy exists between the range of goods desired by any particular consumer and what any specific producer makes. Somehow goods must be brought together in one or a few places to make the task of the consumer easier and provide an outlet for different producers.

The discrepancy of assortment is reconciled through intermediaries who perform two roles. One is termed *sorting.* Here the wholesaler or retailer divides products into different grades or qualities in order to reach target groups with different needs. Some food distributors, for example, purchase fruits and vegetables en masse from farmers. The quality will of course vary somewhat from farmer to farmer and even within the crop supplied by a single farmer. Restaurants, some supermarket chains, and specialty sellers desire relatively high-quality produce, whereas farmer's markets, institutions, and other supermarkets will opt for acceptable, but lower-quality, produce. The distributor sorts the produce by grade and sells it to suit. The second role is known as *assorting*. Here the intermediary accumulates a wide selection of products for the time-conscious consumer. The rise of department stores, shopping centers, and supermarkets reflects this customer need and role for intermediaries.

In sum, we can see that intermediaries exist, in part, because they satisfy the needs of manufacturers and consumers. The marketing system is simply more efficient with than without intermediaries. At least this appears to be true in many, if not most, instances. Another reason that intermediaries exist is because of historical precedent and/or the power they have once created. We will explore this argument at the end of this section when we discuss evolutionary considerations. For now, let us investigate some of the specific functions carried out by intermediaries.

The Functions Performed

Channels of distribution supply what economists term *place utility*. That is, a channel closes the gap that exists between manufacturer and customer by making goods available where and when they are needed and under the appropriate terms of trade.

Many functions are provided by channels of distribution. These occur for the benefit of producer, consumer, or both. Because the functions vary by type of intermediary, we will discuss them separately for retailers and for wholesalers. A *retailer* may be defined as an organization selling goods or services to final consumers. A *wholesaler* is an organization selling goods or services to retailers or to other organizations either for their own use or for resale. We will have more to say about the types of, and activities performed by, retailers and wholesalers later in the chapter. For now, let us examine the functions performed by each. In general, *retailers* fulfill one or more of the following functions:

- *Variety.* A collection of varied product lines, multiple grades, sizes, etc., is provided.

- *Location.* Goods are made available in places close to consumers.

- *Risk.* Retailers assume risks normally borne by producers related to lost, damaged, or stolen goods, insufficient demand, etc. Retailers reduce the risk of buyers by providing continuity, reputation for trust, involvement in the local community, etc.

- *Service.* Many services may be performed for customers such as financial assistance, provision of credit, guarantees, delivery, babysitting, repair, parking, transportation, restrooms, and so on. For producers, transportation, storage, market research, and other activities are carried out.

- *Personal Contact.* Through salespeople, information is supplied on product quality, use and maintenance of products, etc. Indeed, the nature of the relationship with a salesperson can be more important than the product itself on occasion.

- *Promotion.* Retailers advertise, participate in manufacturer promotions, and in other ways promote sales of the goods from producers.

- *Atmosphere.* Store image and ambiance reinforce product attributes and may be sought out as an end in and of itself.

- *Value.* Goods of particular qualities are provided at various prices to match the needs of customers to availability.

- *Social Role.* Retailers provide jobs, lessen the discrepancies of quantity and assortment, and often help reduce total costs of distribution. They also support the local community in other ways such as by giving money to charitable causes or providing a place for community functions (e.g., shopping centers permit concerts and school activities to use their premises).

Overall, retailers meet the needs of both producers and consumers.

Wholesalers also perform functions benefitting producer and consumer. The more important include:

For Producers:

- *Transportation.* Wholesalers deliver and sometimes even pick up goods. Producers can ship in bulk.

- *Storage.* Wholesalers carry inventory and thus reduce the manufacturer's need to store its products in company-owned warehouses.

- *Personal Selling.* Wholesalers approach producers and often have their own sales forces to call on retailers and industrial customers. This reduces the need for a producer to have a large sales force and to estimate demand at each individual local level.

- *Risk.* Wholesalers assume risks that would normally be borne by manufacturers (e.g., for damaged goods, failure of customers to pay).

- *Cash.* Because wholesalers usually purchase goods from producers and later resell them, producers are provided needed cash earlier and in larger amounts than might be forthcoming when dealing direct.

- *Services.* Wholesalers sometimes extend credit to producers, provide a convenient route for returned goods, perform market research, cooperate in advertising and promotion, and so on.

For Retailers and Other Customers:

- *Transportation.* Wholesalers deliver directly to retailers and other customers.

- *Storage.* The inventory carried by wholesalers can reduce the costs of carrying stock by the retailer.

- *Risk.* Wholesalers absorb some risk which might otherwise need to be borne by the retailer. For instance, a downturn in the market need not be devastating to a retailer who relies on a wholesaler to supply goods on demand, whereas a retailer dealing direct with a manufacturer and carrying large stocks might be hurt badly by market changes.

- *Place Utility.* Wholesalers provide goods where and when they are needed and in the desired quantity because they are closer to retailers and have the assortments required. Retailers do not need to contact as many suppliers.

- *Services.* Wholesalers grant credit to retailers, give advice on pricing and selling, share in promotion costs, pick up unsold merchandise, and so on.

The Types of Channels of Distribution

There are three basic systems used to reach a market. Figure 14-3 summarizes the options. Any firm will use one or more of these alternatives.

Direct Marketing. Direct marketing involves selling to customers primarily through mass communication media. Telephone and unsolicited orders are other forms of direct marketing. Outside sales forces and marketing intermediaries are not employed. We have already considered advertising in previous chapters. A person buying in response to an ad would typically contact the seller by phone or mail under the direct marketing option. The telephone is frequently used by firms, especially to sell newspaper subscriptions, insurance and financial services, and local community business offerings. Direct marketing by mail is also done extensively. Letters, brochures, fliers, and "foldouts" are sent in the hope that people will read them and order from the sender. Finally, catalogs comprise an effective direct marketing tactic, particularly for the time-conscious consumer. In each form of direct marketing, the seller contacts prospects (via advertisements, mail, phone, etc.), the buyer places an order (usually by phone or letter), and the seller then sends the goods (by mail or common carrier).

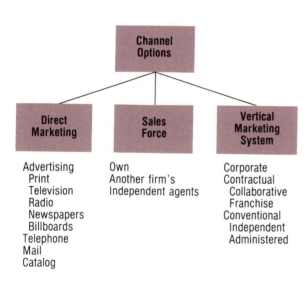

Figure 14-3. Three generic channels of distribution

Sales Force. The second option is to sell through a sales force (see Figure 14-3). We considered personal selling at length in two previous chapters. A firm might form its own sales force, utilize the services of someone else's, or hire independent agents such as manufacturer's representatives.

Vertical Marketing Systems. Marketing can be conducted through use of intermediaries in what is known as a vertical marketing system. A vertical marketing system is the set of organizations between producer and consumer directing the flow of goods and services.[4] It entails hierarchical and/or nonhierarchical relations among firms. As shown in Figure 14-3, there are three types of vertical marketing systems: corporate, contractual, and conventional. Let us examine each.

Corporate Systems. A corporate vertical marketing system consists of successive stages of production and distribution under single ownership. For example, the Firestone Tire & Rubber Company not only makes tires but owns and operates retail stores which sell automotive parts and equipment and make repairs on cars. Similarly, Sherwin-Williams (paints), Hart, Schaffner and Marx (men's clothing), Goodyear (tires), Florsheim (shoes), and Winchell's (donuts) operate corporate vertical marketing systems.

Contractual Systems. Under a contractual vertical marketing system, producers and intermediaries enter into an agreement to deal with each other. Neither party owns the other outright. Rather, they retain freedom of ownership but agree to certain limitations (e.g., to deal only with each other in a specified area) for mutual gain. A formal written contract is usually the rule.

The two most common types of contractual systems are the collaborative and franchise arrangements (see Figure 14-3). Under *collaborative agreements*, separate organizations share resources and/or agree to make joint purchases. They typically also expand operations up or down the length of the channel. Three collaborative agreements (sometimes also known as cooperatives) are worth noting.

In *producer-sponsored arrangements*, producers organize to market their wares. A good example is California Canners and Grocers, which markets canned fruits and vegetables worldwide. A group of farmers joined together to set up their own factory and sell their own products rather than go through independent wholesalers or large food processors.

In *wholesaler-sponsored arrangements*, a wholesaler organizes a group of producers or retailers for mutual cooperation. Probably the best examples of such "voluntaries" as they are also known are I.G.A. Grocers or Associated Grocers. These were started by wholesalers who succeeded in getting many small independent retailers to agree to purchase primarily from the wholesalers. Retailers get lower prices among other benefits. The wholesalers obtain guaranteed markets that aid in planning, reduce the need for large numbers of salespeople, and so on.

In *retailer-sponsored arrangements*, retailers organize to purchase or set up a common wholesaler. The system is similar to the wholesaler-sponsored arrangement. Piggly Wiggly is an example. Note that it is possible for collaborative systems to expand into all levels of channel operations from production through retail.

Franchise arrangements comprise the other type of contractual vertical marketing system.[5] Under a franchise agreement, a seller (the franchiser) gives an intermediary (the franchisee) certain services and exclusive rights to market the seller's product or service. In return, the intermediary agrees to follow certain procedures and not to purchase from others or to sell competing products or services. It is interesting to note that franchising is literally big business in that it allegedly accounts for about one-third of all retail sales in the United States.[6]

Two types of franchises dominate the scene: (1) *product or trade-name franchising* and (2) *business franchising*. Under the former, the franchiser gives the franchisee exclusive rights to market the franchiser's products. Although the franchisee might sell other products, he or she agrees not to sell competing ones. Examples include Jantzen bathing suits, Ford cars and trucks, Pepsi-Cola bottlers, Chevron gasoline service stations, and Florsheim shoes. Business franchising is similar to product franchising but is more integrative and restrictive. Here the franchisee deals only with the franchiser's products or services. Examples include H & R Block (accounting/tax services), Hertz Rent-a-Car, Kentucky Fried Chicken, McDonald's, Rexall Drug, 7-Eleven, Holiday Inn, and Century 21 Realty.

Franchise systems differ considerably from other forms of business relationships. For one thing, the failure rate for franchises is only about 4 percent by the end of the first five years, whereas approximately 65 percent of all new businesses fail in the same initial period. To start a franchise, a franchisee typically must pay up-front costs for capital and other requirements. This can be as low as $1,500 in the case of an H & R Block tax preparation office or as much as $7 million in the case of a Sheraton hotel. To open a Burger King franchise, the franchisee must pay more than $300,000 for the franchise and working capital, and perhaps an additional $350,000 or more for land and building costs.[7]

Conventional Systems. These consist of autonomous producers and intermediaries who enter into business relationships with each other in order to meet their own organization objectives. Two types exist: independent and administered. In the *independent system*, producers and intermediaries engage in low levels of cooperation, limited primarily to that surrounding the buying and selling of the goods in question. In the *administered system*, greater cooperation is achieved in the form of more diligent and aggressive selling. The greater cooperation is based upon the influence of one of the organizations in the vertical marketing system. This influence, in turn, might consist of one or more of the following factors: reward or coercive power, persuasive ability, bargaining or negotiation skills, expertise, information control, referent power, charisma, or intangible leadership attributes. The organization achieving an influential position is sometimes informally called the *channel captain.* It is best to think of independent and administered conventional channels as end points on a continuum ranging from nearly total independence to strong influence. Examples of firms engaged in conventional systems include General Electric, Procter & Gamble, Kraft, Newsweek, and many smaller and medium-size firms too numerous to mention.

Horizontal Marketing Systems. A final point to note with respect to types of channels systems is that horizontal arrangements occasionally exist. Horizontal arrangements are of two kinds. *Horizontal integration* occurs when two or more organizations at the same function level merge or join forces through acquisition. For example, large retail chains find that internal expansion is not sufficient and that acquisitions of existing outlets or chains are attractive. The other horizontal arrangement has been called *symbiotic marketing.*[8] Here two or more autonomous organizations at the same level of the channel cooperate in some way. For instance, Pillsbury makes refrigerated dough but uses Kraft to distribute and sell it through its sales force. Pillsbury still handles its own advertising, however. As another example, Xerox sells Apple Computers in Central and South America.

Evolutionary Considerations

Intermediaries have arisen in the so-called free enterprise and developing countries largely as a consequence of the willingness of entrepreneurs to take risks and pursue profits. Individual businesspeople saw that the needs of producers and/or consumers were not being met and that they could perform a facilitating role and be paid handsomely. At times, governments encourage the rise and operations of intermediaries through use of incentives and tax and tariff policies.

In the more centrally planned economies, most intermediaries are confined to warehouses, distribution centers, and local retailers under the management of the state. Social policies and logistical considerations take precedent over the independent inclinations of the people and organizations involved. Occasionally, informal or loosely regulated intermediaries such as farmer's markets, craftsmen's cooperatives, and family shops or restaurants are permitted in the planned economies.

An important point to stress in both free enterprise and planned systems is that social and political processes play a central role. These processes occur among the institutions and people engaged in cooperative activities to sell goods and between these entities and other organizations who would regulate or influence their conduct in some way. Thus, once established, marketing systems with intermediaries achieve a certain degree of power, resist certain changes, and attempt to protect or enhance their positions in the economy in various ways (e.g., through lobbying, threats, bribery, reason, acquisitions, contracts, etc.). This occurs because people's jobs are at stake, because every person and intermediary has certain rights and responsibilities under the political system within which they operate, and because individual and group goals sometimes come into conflict.

As a consequence, we can see that at any one particular point in time it is misleading to assert that the existence of intermediaries is due solely to their greater efficiency in performing the services needed to bring goods from producer to consumer. Sometimes the presence of particular intermediaries increases efficiency over what it would be without them. In other cases, it does not. Efficiency resulting from competitive dynamics certainly plays a role. But so too do historical processes and the social and political activities interlacing any system. We can readily recognize that the role of intermediaries in any marketing system is a complex mixture of economic, psychological, and sociological forces.

Scholars have formally studied the evolution of intermediaries. Most of these investigations have been descriptive endeavors of individual institutional types and have occurred primarily in the nonplanned economies.[9] For example, Table 14-1 depicts when various retailing entities first started in the United States. Interestingly, each institutional type has gone through a life cycle of introduction, growth, maturity, and (sometimes) decline. For instance, sales as a percentage of all retail sales and/or profits reached their zenith or declined for department stores in the 1950s, for supermarkets in the 1960s, and for discount outlets in the 1970s. From inception until maturity or decline, we see a shrinking of the retail institution life cycle. Thus, while department stores flourished for 80 years or more and supermarkets for about 35 years, discount outlets (20 years) and home improvement centers (15 years), among others, have witnessed more transient periods of prosperity.[10]

TABLE 14-1
The Emergence of Retail Institutions in the United States

Retail Institutions	Period When First Observed and/or Early Growth Began
Department Stores	1860s
Mail-order Houses	1870s and 1880s
Chain Stores	1920s
Supermarkets	1930s
Planned Shopping Centers	1940s
Discount Houses	1950s
Fast-Food Outlets	1960s
Convenience Stores	1960s
Catalog Showrooms	1970s
Hypermarkets	1970s
Value-Added Resellers	1980s

SOURCE: Adapted in part from a discussion in Philip Kotler, *Marketing Management*, 4th ed. (Englewood Cliffs, N.J.: Prentice-Hall, 1980), p. 421.

One of the earliest and more interesting theories of evolution is the *wheel of retailing hypothesis.*[11] This theory asserts that retail institutions emerge as low-price, low-margin operations. This positions them in relation to established retailers who have a tendency to bureacratize, grow unwieldly, carry large overheads, and offer expensive services and thus become vulnerable. The new retailer is therefore given the opportunity to gain a foothold in the market. However, as time passes, the newcomer, too, finds that operations get out of hand and costs rise, necessitating price increases. But this, in turn, makes the situation ripe for the entry of still other new entrants, and we find that the process has come full circle.

The wheel of retailing hypothesis is roughly descriptive of the evolution of department and chain stores. It does not, however, validly describe developments in convenience store outlets, some shopping centers, and vending machine distributors where the rule has generally been higher prices and margins throughout the life cycle. Another point to note is that individual firms over a long period of time upgrade or downgrade their images, services, and prices. Hence, the wheel of retailing neither necessarily turns in one direction nor fails to reverse direction. Sears, for example, has both raised and lowered the quality of its offerings over the course of its life cycle. It currently functions somewhere in the middle between such lower priced chains as Mervyn's and higher priced chains such as Neiman Marcus. Exhibit 14-1 describes new developments in J.C. Penney's stores.

EXHIBIT 14-1

Life Cycle Changes in Retailing: The Case of the J.C. Penney Co.

J.C. Penney's is now in the throes of an image change. Starting in 1983, it began remodeling its 1,600-store empire in a calculated move to shift away from its long-standing working and middle class positioning in order to appeal to "moderately upscale customers." So far about 500 stores have gone through the transformation which is expected to take until 1990 for completion.

The repositioning effort has been extensive. Building exteriors have gotten facelifts. Interiors have been rejuvenated with new lighting, plush carpeting, angled walls, strategically placed mirrors, wall dividers between adjacent areas, and other enhancements. Significantly, the merchandise is the center of the change and has been upgraded. Along with wide assortments and grades of clothing, for example, designer clothes now achieve special emphasis. The new overall store mix typically includes 75 percent soft goods and 25 percent hard goods. Particular consideration is given to women and to home furnishings such as giftware. Store imagery is reinforced through periodic use of themes carried throughout the store and through creation of intimate nooks and crannies within departments. An attempt has been made to adjust to local conditions. For example, only about 50 percent of any store's holdings are purchased centrally with the rest secured with strong regional and local inputs.

It is difficult to forecast whether Penney's efforts at change will be successful. But one can say with a reasonable degree of confidence that no attempt at change risks certain failure. Success hinges on a corporation's ability to anticipate fundamental changes in the marketplace and respond to them. At the same time, companies can accelerate or shape impending changes through the actions they take. This requires innovative product/service design, pricing, promotion, and channel of distribution program implementation.

SOURCE: Drawn in part from Janet Key, "J.C. Penney's Changing Its Polyester Image," *Times Tribune*, December 21, 1984.

Another theory worth noting is the *accordion hypothesis.* [12] Here it is maintained that retailers cycle back and forth between general line merchants with wide assortments of goods to specialized merchants with narrow lines. The cycle is driven, in part, by changes in buying habits and cost and profit factors. Although descriptive of some behavior in the marketplace, the accordion hypothesis does not go very far and should be regarded as suggestive.

Very little is known about the evolution of wholesale institutions.[13] In a certain sense, wholesalers also cycle through alternations between low-price–low-margin and high-price–high-margin operations. But, in general, wholesalers have been less quick to innovate than retailers and have not fared as well in terms of growth and profitability. Nevertheless, it should be acknowledged that some wholesalers have been successful through efforts to upgrade their sales forces, methods of selecting and retaining customers, services provided, and other practices.

Overview of Channel Management

Management of the channel of distribution should be viewed as one way for affecting the performance of the organization. Figure 14-4 outlines the role of channel managment in the firm and points out the key decisions that must be made. Channel of distribution objectives are derivatives of, and/or a means to achieve, larger marketing objectives and overall organization goals. They do this by facilitating the delivery of products or services meeting customer needs and doing so better than the competition.

More specifically, the channel of distribution must be seen as a means to manage market growth, market share, return on investment, achievement of social goals, and other ends. The most important operational objectives of any channel managment program are:

1 To provide a product or service when and where it is needed, at the desired price and quality, and with the needed services. These represent goals related to market coverage and satisfaction of customer needs.

2 To meet organization goals related to cost management and performance such as product line growth, profitability, and market share. These are outputs depending on internal practices, external actions, and competitive dynamics.

As shown in Figure 14-4, the channel objectives translate into two fundamental decisions: the channel design decision and the channel management decision. Before we review these, let us consider two additional forces shaping channel objectives.

Notice in Figure 14-4 that *environmental forces* and *marketing mix considerations* also interact with channel of distribution objectives. Consider first the environment. Geographic factors affect logistical requirements, as do the location of factors of production and the concentration and dispersion of customers. Another environmental element is the economy. Inflation, the availability of credit, the prices of goods, supplies, and labor, and other economic criteria serve as a backdrop facilitating or inhibiting the actions of producers and intermediaries alike. Related to this is the competitive environment. The number of competitors and their actions obviously affect channel of distribution objectives. Sometimes one has little choice but to match the competition; in other instances, an advantage can be gained through selection of a different channel than that used by leading competitors. Finally, the legal environment is an important determinant of channel objectives. Distribution practices must not restrain trade or tend to create a monopoly.

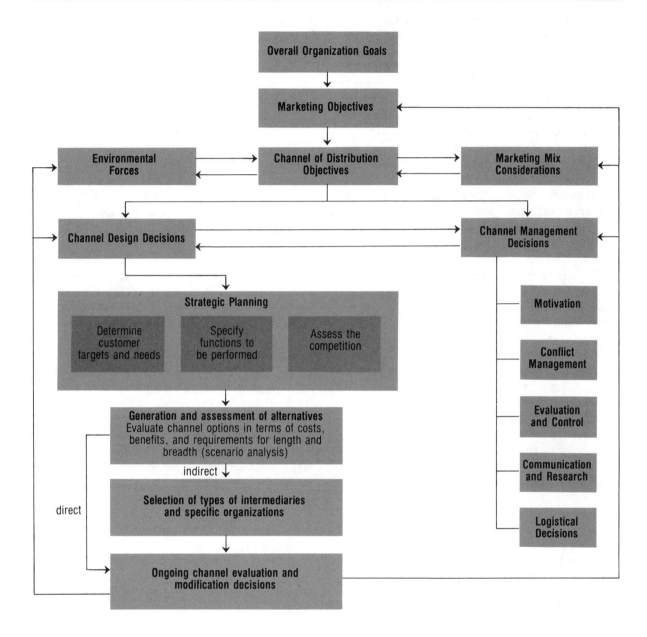

Figure 14-4. Overview of the channel-
of-distribution management process

Channel objectives cannot be divorced from other marketing mix decisions. Ideally, one would like to simultaneously optimize the product management, new product development, marketing communication, pricing, and distribution programs. Frequently, however, it is not possible to do so, and one or more programs must be specified first. For example, products are initially designed and the channel of distribution is chosen before pricing and promotion options are considered in many real-world situations. Thus, some producers decide first on whether to market direct or use wholesalers, and the outcome of the decision dictates whether a final consumer price is set or whether a markup must be taken into account. In other instances, marketing mix decisions are considered in pairs or small combinations. For instance, a channel option consisting of company-owned stores and extensive advertising might be weighed against a plan to sell to independent wholesalers and retailers with a large promotion program complementing a smaller advertising budget. Whatever the context, it is important to recognize that the setting of channel objectives does not occur in isolation but must somehow take into account the characteristics of the rest of the marketing mix.

A key decision is the *choice of a channel of distribution system* (see *Channel Design* in Figure 14-4). Given general channel objectives, three strategic planning tasks must be performed. The first begins with the customer. Management must clearly specify the target market(s) and understand customer needs. A key subdecision entails determination of the hoped-for intensity of market coverage. That is, the number of desired retail outlets per geographic area must be ascertained. This will be a consideration even if one decides to sell directly to independent wholesalers, for desired coverage of the final market is a goal constraining all choices open to management.

The second planning activity is specification of functions to be performed. Here management must consider both the final customer (whether consumer or industrial firm) and possible intermediaries. With respect to customers, the trade-offs between push and pull strategies should be addressed. With respect to intermediaries, desired services outputs must be delineated. Among others, these include delivery, credit, lot size, product quality, variety, selling support, return policies, repair, information gathering, and advertising.

The final strategic planning task is to assess the competition. This must be done under each channel alternative. The goal is to estimate relative product quality, prices, advertising, and promotion and to anticipate competitive moves.

Following planning, a set of scenarios consisting of channel alternatives should be generated and compared (see Figure 14-4). Here each channel option is evaluated in terms of costs and benefits. Intensity of market coverage and channel length are scrutinized closely. A key output at this stage is the decision whether to market direct or to use intermediaries.

As shown in Figure 14-4, if one decides on the indirect route to use intermediaries, the next task is to select the type of intermediary and the particular organizations with whom to cooperate. After selection of intermediaries or deciding to go direct, the final channel design decisions involve ongoing evaluation of performance and modification of practices and procedures.

Figure 14-4 also illustrates a second set of strategic choices, termed *channel management decisions*. These encompass everyday management processes. People and institutions must be motivated. Conflict must be resolved. Ongoing evaluation and control activities must be instituted. Communication must be facilitated and research performed. Finally, the logistical side of the distribution function must be managed.

Choosing Distribution Channels

The choice of a channel of distribution is a critical decision having far-reaching consequences and involving considerable risk. Unlike communication and pricing decisions, the channel design decision takes a long time to implement and typically binds the organization to a long-term commitment. Hence, once a channel is chosen, the firm loses a certain degree of freedom and might be forced to accept relatively lower levels of performance from intermediaries than it might desire. At the same time, large sums of money are generally required to start up or switch channels. This, too, makes changes difficult and the firm vulnerable. Lastly, one's distribution system can be a key determinant of the performance of the firm. Not only will the choice of design for the channel affect the selection and operation of the remaining elements of the marketing mix, but it will directly contribute to customer satisfaction and constrain or enhance the competitive and investment strategies of the firm. Therefore, proper channel design is crucial.

The strategic design decisions facing a producer are the following:

1 What intensity of market coverage is required and how can it be achieved?

2 Should we market directly to customers or indirectly via intermediaries? If we choose an indirect system, how long a channel should be employed and should multiple systems be employed?

3 Given an established channel arrangement, when should the intensity, length, or composition of channel systems be altered? That is, when should particular organizations be added or dropped in our existing system and when should we alter the structure of the system and develop new systems?

Let us now consider these decisions in detail.

Intensity of Coverage

A key decision is to ascertain the number of retail outlets per geographic area. This is sometimes called the *channel breadth* decision. There are basically three options: intensive, selective, or exclusive distribution. These are shown symbolically in Figure 14-5, where San Francisco and 10 of its shopping areas are depicted. A manufacturer of high-priced stereo equipment is faced with the problem of deciding how broad a coverage of the city should be pursued.

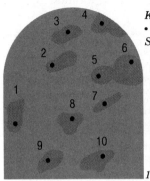

Key
• *Retail Outlet*
Shopping District:
  1. *Sunset*
  2. *Richmond*
  3. *Marina and Pacific Heights*
  4. *Fisherman's Wharf*
  5. *Union Square*
  6. *Embarcadero*
  7. *Market Street*
  8. *Mission*
  9. *Twin Peaks*
  10. *Visitacion Valley*

A. *Intensive distribution:* Many retail outlets per geographical territory

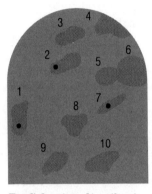

B. *Selective distribution:* Several retail outlets per geographical territory

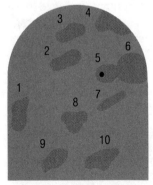

C. *Exclusive distribution:* One retail outlet per geographical territory

Figure 14-5. Three options for covering geographic areas: intensive, selective, and exclusive distribution

Intensive distribution consists of establishment of retail outlets in many locations within a geographical area. Thus, the stereo manufacturer might wish to have its line sold in each of the 10 shopping districts noted in Figure 14-5 in order to reach into every corner of the city. Alternatively, *selective distribution*, consisting of sales through several outlets, might be considered. In San Francisco, this could be accomplished through, for example, three strategically placed sites (see Figure 14-5). Finally, the stereo manufacturer might opt for *exclusive distribution* where only a single outlet per geographical area is chosen. Union Square in San Francisco (see Figure 14-5) might be appropriate since it is a convenient, well-traveled area by up-scale shoppers.

We should stress that intensive and selective distribution are relative terms depending on the nature of the product and customer behavior. For an expensive stereo manufacturer selling in San Francisco, intensive distribution might mean only 10 outlets. But for Coca-Cola, intensive distribution means literally thousands of outlets ranging from restaurants, to theaters, to grocery stores and supermarkets, to vending machines throughout the city.

As a general rule, convenience, shopping, and specialty consumer goods tend to be marketed through intensive, selective, and exclusive distribution systems, respectively. But there are exceptions. Similarly, for industrial goods, low-priced and/or standardized products tend to be sold intensively, whereas high-priced and/or custom made goods tend to be sold either directly or under selective or exclusive arrangements.

What are the factors governing how broad a market coverage to seek? These reside in product characteristics, customer behavior, required services, competitive factors, and the desired control over selling activities. We turn now to consideration of the issues involved.

Intensive Distribution. Under intensive distribution, the producer wishes to market his or her product in as many outlets as possible within a geographic area. This is especially appropriate for low-priced goods purchased in small quantities such as candy, toothpaste, coffee, soft drinks, and magazines. Such goods are bought frequently, often with little thought, and demand little effort on the part of the customer. Because the buyer purchases out of habit or impulse, convenience and availability are important considerations. Hence, numerous locations are required. Another type of product suited to intensive distribution is the low-priced emergency good such as pain remedies and light bulbs. Excedrin and other headache remedies can be purchased nearly everywhere: supermarkets, grocery stores, drugstores, department stores, mass merchandising outlets, hotels, newsstands, airports, and restaurants.

If a producer hopes to have a convenience or emergency good available when and where the customer needs it, intensive distribution is a must. However, it is not always possible to achieve as extensive distribution as one would like. For example, shelf space in the supermarket is limited, and fierce competition exists among producers for this scarce resource. Supermarkets generally do not carry every brand possible. Indeed, even if one is permitted to sell in the store, only a portion of the breadth or depth of one's product line may be permitted. Lipton Herb teas are made in six or more flavors, but some retailers will stock only three or four. Similarly, restaurants and fast food outlets tend to carry a limited line of soft drinks largely because of the space, maintenance, and inventory problems involved.

A number of advantages are associated with intensive distribution. Obviously, it stimulates sales volume because more people are exposed to the brand and may be induced to try it for the first time. In addition, because people generally will not shop for certain items, intensive distribution ensures that regular buyers will tend to repeat. Intensive distribution reinforces the brand name as well, since it is simply more visible.

On the other hand, certain disadvantages should be noted. The low price and small purchase size aspects of intensively distributed goods, coupled with strong competition, sometimes make margins low and profits thin. At the same time, retailers typically devote small amounts of selling effort to such goods because of the sheer numbers of products they must sell and the small contributions of each to profits.

Selective Distribution. Selective distribution is in one sense a compromise between intensive and exclusive distribution. Rather than selling to many or one outlet per geographic area, the producer sells to a few in the hope that sufficient market coverage and retailer effort will be achieved. Shopping and specialty goods frequently are marketed through selective distribution arrangements. Here the customer is willing to do comparison shopping among rival outlets or to seek a particular store because of the large purchase price, perceived risk, or product complexity. The retailer must be knowledgeable about the product and must often provide technical advice, credit, or other services.

Selective distribution is employed by many producers such as RCA in televisions, Yamaha in stereo equipment, Schwinn in bicycles, and Glidden in paints. Sometimes use of a few outlets per geographic area is motivated by image considerations. Although Anheuser-Busch uses intensive distribution to market its premium beer, Budweiser, it utilizes selective distribution to sell Michelob in order to create a high-quality, high-brow image for this super premium beer. Only select restaurants, liquor stores, taverns, and other outlets are sought. Positioning and competitive factors also play a role in market coverage. For example, Hartmann Luggage, maker of high-quality suitcases and bags, chooses to sell through particular department stores and luggage stores; this is a selective distribution decision. This was done, in part, to contrast with lower-quality products sold by American Tourister, Samsonite, and others who sell intensely through department stores, luggage stores, catalog showrooms, and mass merchandisers.[14]

The advantages of selective distribution are manifold. First, the producer can select retailers who are financially sound, respected in the community, and knowledgeable about the product and customer behavior. This means that the best image and grass roots marketing effort can be achieved. Second, selective distribution permits greater control than intensive distribution over pricing, selling, and other marketing functions. Producers provide more support to outlets, and outlets tend to cooperate more and sell more aggressively. Third, selective distribution often results in the use of fewer wholesalers and/or shorter channels. Along with this, interchannel conflict and competition may be reduced.

The primary disadvantage of selective distribution is that some missed sales may occur, since it provides less exposure than intensive distribution. Further, there is somewhat less control over retailers than with exclusive arrangements.

Exclusive Distribution. This strategy is especially appropriate for high-priced shopping and some specialty goods. The retailer is granted exclusive rights to sell the producer's product in a specified area. In return, the retailer usually agrees to refrain from selling competitors' brands and/or to make certain purchases from the producer.

Under exclusive distribution, the brand image for a product is maximized, especially for prestige items, and higher margins result for the retailer. At the same time, competition with other retailers selling the same brand is reduced. These factors lead to higher effort on the part of retailers than with other market coverage options. Further,

exclusive distribution permits the greatest amount of control over pricing, merchandising, and other practices. Its disadvantages include the weakest market coverage, the granting of relatively more power to retailers, somewhat less flexibility to alter the channel, and somewhat more vulnerability to economic conditions and changes in consumer behavior than with intensive or selective distribution.

Exclusive distribution arrangements can be found in a number of areas. Caterpillar tractors are sold through exclusive dealerships, as are Rolls-Royce automobiles. Similarly, McDonald's restaurants, Century 21 real estate, and Baskin-Robbins ice cream shops constitute exclusive distribution coverage.

It can be seen that the determination of channel breadth is a complicated affair. One must determine the trade-offs involved for each option and make comparisons across alternatives. Importantly, the channel breadth decision must be made along with the channel length decision.

Determination of Channel Length

The length of the channel of distribution refers to the number of levels of intermediaries between producer and final customer. Two basic decisions must be made: (1) should one market direct or use intermediaries? and (2) given this choice, how should one execute the decision? That is, how should one market directly or what kind of indirect channel system should one employ?

Direct or Indirect Marketing?[15] Although a firm may do some of both, a fundamental decision must be made whether to use direct or indirect marketing channels. A direct channel will consist of telephone, mass media, and/or face-to-face selling. An indirect channel will be made up of company-owned and/or independent intermediaries.

For industrial products, the choice is usually between use of a sales force to sell direct or use of intermediaries. A direct system may be favored when one or more of the following conditions are met: (1) the product is complex, (2) the product is costly, (3) few unit sales are made and/or orders are placed intermittently or for large quantities, (4) considerable service and support is needed, and (5) transportation costs are small, relative to the price of the product. Under these conditions, salespeople familiar with the product and how to use it are needed, and the greater cost over indirect systems is often justified. An indirect system tends to be favored for industrial products when one or more of the following criteria are met: (1) the product is simple or standardized, (2) the product is low in price, (3) customers are numerous and dispersed, (4) orders are placed frequently and in small quantities, (5) little or no service is required, and (6) transportation costs are high, relative to the price of the product. Here intermediaries can more efficiently perform the functions needed.

For consumer goods, the factors favoring a direct or indirect approach are much less clear. Indeed, successful direct selling has been found to occur for convenience goods (Amway, Fuller Brush), shopping/specialty goods (Avon, Mary Kay), and even consumer durables (Electrolux, encyclopedias). The vast number of consumers and the competitive environment permit alternative forms of marketing for the same products and make any general rules problematic. Nevertheless, it is safe to say that direct marketing for consumer goods is less important than it is for industrial goods. Less than 3 percent of all retail sales occur via direct marketing, whereas about 60 percent of industrial sales are made through this method.[16]

In general, direct channels permit maximum control over pricing, delivery, sales support, selling, and other marketing and distribution functions. They also allow for greater adjustment to customer needs and yield more information on the market. On the other hand, direct marketing is usually the most expensive mode of operation.

The aforementioned comments on direct versus indirect marketing are meant to be taken only as gross descriptions of the factors involved. In any real-world decision, one must examine all viable options and assess the pros and cons before making a choice. We have already covered some of the issues related to use of a sales force in previous chapters. Next we will consider the concerns surrounding determination of what type of channel to select.

Choice of a Channel System. Given that a firm has opted to market through intermediaries, one must choose either a corporate, contractual, or conventional vertical marketing system (see Figure 14-3). Each alternative has assets and liabilities.

Before we examine the individual pros and cons, let us consider some general ideas. The length of a distribution channel is partly dictated by the nature of the product sold and customer behavior. Convenience goods typically require quite long channels because of the number, dispersion, and buying habits of customers and because of logistical and economic considerations. Shopping goods demand somewhat shorter channels, and specialty items shorter channels yet. However, consumer goods seldom see very short channels, and the shortest generally occur for durables. Industrial goods run the gamut from long channels (standardized parts, maintenance materials) to short (custom-designed machinery).

An overriding concern in the determination of channel length is the amount of trade-off between costs and control a producer is willing to tolerate. Broadly speaking, the longer a channel, the lower the costs but the less the control over pricing, selling, merchandising, and general distribution functions. The shorter the channel, the greater the control but the higher the cost. Management must investigate each vertical marketing alternative in the light of product characteristics, buyer behavior, logistical requirements, costs, and the amount of control desired.

Consider first the corporate vertical marketing system. Outright ownership of intermediaries typically leads to a number of advantages. The manufacturer can exercise the maximum control over prices, personal selling, in-store services, advertising and promotion, store image, and market information gathering. The possibility that the retailer will favor a competitor's line or emphasize other products thought to be more profitable is, of course, eliminated. Corporate vertical marketing systems are also believed to exhibit economies of scale in certain circumstances, although this is not the rule.

Offsetting the advantages to corporate systems are several disadvantages. First and foremost, corporate systems are expensive. Considerable sums of money are needed to purchase buildings, land, and equipment; to hire and train personnel; and to transport, store, and advertise one's products. Many corporations simply do not have the financial wherewithal to initiate a corporate system. Some find it necessary to institute an approach consisting of independent intermediaries, company-owned stores, and franchises, among other "dual or multiple distribution systems." We will consider the issues surrounding the latter approach shortly. A second disadvantage is that manufacturers relinquish a certain degree of flexibility under the corporate vertical marketing system. For example, one expert observes

In the early 1970s Sherwin-Williams [which had its own outlets] could not capitalize on the growth of paint sales through do-it-yourself home centers and discount stores. Du Pont, which sold its Lucite paint through a conventional system, was in a much better position to take advantage of this new opportunity.[17]

The likelihood that some company store sales would be siphoned away and that store operators would be alienated if Sherwin-Williams sought other independent retailers made such a move undesirable. A third drawback with a vertical marketing system is that it represents a potential legal liability. A firm contemplating a merger or acquisition in order to expand vertically will find that the Federal Trade Commission or the Department of Justice may frown upon such actions if they threaten to lessen competition and/or tend to create a monopoly. Finally, in addition to high startup costs, corporate vertical marketing systems often are more expensive to operate on an ongoing basis than other approaches.

Conventional vertical marketing systems are strong where corporate systems are weak and weak where corporate systems are strong. That is, they tend to sacrifice control for a gain in efficiency. More specifically, conventional systems are the least expensive arrangements to set up and to maintain; they provide a wide range of functions and do so with a considerable degree of expertise; they permit the greatest amount of freedom to make additions or deletions in intermediaries and thereby respond to changing market conditions; and they shift some of the risk of doing business to the intermediary who most often purchases the manufacturer's products and in the process becomes vulnerable to fluctuating economic conditions and changing buying habits.

Conventional systems, conversely, are the least easy to control. Channel members typically carry multiple product lines and even competing brands. They emphasize the clear leaders in sales or profits from their own perspective, and many manufacturers find that the selling effort is less than desirable. Finally, the overall quality of intermediaries shows greater variation than other modes of distribution and more volatility in terms of turnover, profitability, and inter-channel conflict.

Somewhere in the middle lies the contractual vertical marketing system. Indeed, contractual systems frequently offer the best of both worlds in terms of control and costs. On the plus side, collaborative and franchise operations exhibit the highest levels of motivation and personal commitment to one's products and services of any system. This is especially so for franchises where the franchisee is more or less an independent business person with an exclusive product and territory. The contractual system also scores moderately well on control in that formal documents spell out rights and responsibilities, and the dependence of the intermediary on the manufacturer results in some power and influence over marketing practices. Lastly, because franchisees assume capital and operational expenses, agree to make purchases from the manufacturer, and pay up-front fees and continuing royalties, the manufacturer experiences less of a financial burden and at the same time has the resources to expand operations or outlets if desired.

All of this does not come without costs, however. The balance of power between franchiser and franchisee, for example, can sometimes result in coercive and exploitive relations. When this does occur, it is usually at the expense of the franchisee since he or she is small in comparison to, and strongly dependent upon, the franchiser. Cases where franchisers charged high prices for supplies and/or forced the franchisee to make unneeded purchases have sometimes occurred.

Some less reputable franchisers have grossly overestimated sales and misled prospective franchisees, as well. Such actions can lead to poor morale, undermotivated intermediaries, and even dysfunctional conflict. A less likely, but nevertheless quite disruptive, possibility is the formation of groups of franchisees under common ownership. For instance, 350 Burger King restaurants out of a total of about 2,700 are owned by Chart House. The countervailing power thus formed resulted in refusal by Chart House to institute certain practices that the franchiser required.[18] Such arrangements obviously lessen the control and flexibility of the franchiser and show that the balance of power between franchiser and franchisee can ebb and flow.

Evaluation of Alternatives. Consideration of channel length and breadth issues leaves the decision maker with a set of options from which to choose. How is one to select the appropriate system of distribution? Sometimes the "choice" is predetermined such as when the nature of buyer behavior and economic/logistic factors dictate that one use the same route as the competition. More often than not, however, several alternatives exist, and one must make an informed choice.

One way to do so is to (1) generate a set of attributes and consequences desired for any channel alternative, (2) rank or rate the importance of the attributes and consequences, (3) score each alternative on the attributes and consequences, and then (4) apply a computational rule such as the expectancy-value model. Other computational rules such as conjunctive, disjunctive, or lexicographic models might be appropriate, depending on the circumstances.

Table 14-2 presents a hypothetical example applied to the choice of a channel system. In this illustration, nine attributes/consequences were deemed desirable by management, and five different options were compared. The importance weights (W_i) for attributes/consequences reflect managerial consensus as to relative saliences. The scores of each alternative on the attributes/consequences (A_i) also constitute judgments made by management. Given the assessments made in the table, we can apply a computational rule to compare the options. The computational rule should combine relative importances and scores in a way that best relates to ultimate performance objectives of the firm. That is, one would like the computational rule to point to the channel alternative with the highest chance of success for profitability, growth, market share, or some other goal of the firm. This, too, involves subjective judgments on the part of management, but hopefully simulations and empirical data over time can aid in the decision process.

TABLE 14-2
Evaluation of Alternative Modes of Distribution

DESIRED ATTRIBUTES AND/OR CONSEQUENCES	IMPORTANCE WEIGHT (Wi)[a]	CHANNEL ALTERNATIVES AND THEIR SCORES ON ATTRIBUTES/CONSEQUENCES (A_{ij})[b]				
		Direct	Corporate	Franchise	Conventional #1	Conventional #2
Control over:						
prices	.5	10	10	7	2	2
selling	.5	10	8	7	2	4
image	.4	9	8	7	2	2
Coverage	.9	4	5	6	8	9
Costs (operating)	.7	8	4	7	8	8
Costs (start-up)	.2	6	1	3	4	3
Flexibility	.6	7	1	4	9	8
Competitive position	.8	3	2	1	6	8
Provision of services	.7	4	3	5	5	6

[a]The higher the fraction, the more important the attribute/consequence.
[b]The higher the number, the better the channel alternative scores on the respective attribute/consequence.

Let us assume that management believes that the simple expectancy-value model will provide satisfactory results. That is, the computational rule to use is

$$E_j = \sum_{i=1}^{n} W_i A_{ij},$$

where E_j is the evaluation total of channel option j, W_i is the weight for attribute/consequence i, and A_{ij} is the assessment of option j on attribute/consequence i. Application of this formula to the data on Table 14-2 yields:

$$E_1 = .5(10) + .5(10) + .4(9) + .9(4)$$
$$+ .7(8) + .2(6) + .6(7)$$
$$+ .8(3) + .7(4) = 33.4$$
$$E_2 = 24.0$$
$$E_3 = 27.4$$
$$E_4 = 30.1$$
$$E_5 = 33.5.$$

Thus, we see that a slight advantage is given to conventional channel 2. With no further information, this would be the alternative to choose.

After one has chosen a type of channel system, particular institutional members must be selected. Table 14-3 shows one way to do this where the problem is to select two independent wholesalers from the seven displayed. Here seven key attributes/consequences are noted. Application of the expectancy-value model to this decision gives: $E_A = 24.7$, $E_B = 28.2$, $E_C = 22.9$, $E_D = 25.4$, $E_E = 20.5$, $E_F = 27.7$, $E_G = 25.1$. Hence, wholesalers B and F rate the highest and should be chosen, given the assumptions made.

TABLE 14-3
Evaluation of Individual Wholesalers

Desired Attributes and/or Consequences	Importance Weight (Wi)[a]	Wholesaler Score on Attributes/ Consequences (A_{ij})[b]						
		A	B	C	D	E	F	G
Quality of Sales Force	.8	6	7	4	8	7	7	6
Inventory Capability	.5	8	8	7	5	5	9	4
Delivery and Pick-up Capabilities	.5	7	6	8	4	4	6	6
Location	.6	5	9	4	4	6	8	7
Credit Services	.6	6	8	4	9	4	5	7
Information Gathering Ability	.4	4	3	8	8	4	3	5
Relative Importance of Product to Wholesaler	.7	6	6	6	5	5	9	4

[a]The higher the fraction, the more important the attribute/consequence.
[b]The higher the number, the better the channel alternative scores on the respective attribute/consequence.

Before leaving the topic of channel evaluation, we should note a number of caveats. First, measurement issues must be given attention. Some computational rules require ratio scale measures, whereas others can be based on interval or ordinal scales. Second, the expectancy-value formula is a compensatory model in that low scores on some attributes can be balanced by high scores on others. To the extent that all attributes are important or that minimum thresholds are desired, different models may be required. Finally, it is important that the inputs to, and the validity of, any evaluation procedure be continually addressed. This means making improvements in the sources of data, training executives in judgment processes, and relating any model to performance criteria through statistical and simulation analyses.

Multiple Systems? Sometimes it is necessary to use alternative channels in parallel in order to reach a market. We saw in Figure 14-1, for instance, that the shoe manufacturer used six distinct routes to market its goods. The decision to use multiple systems or not hinges on desired market coverage, buying habits, and likely interchannel conflict.

Even though multiple channels are frequently used, one should be mindful of the drawbacks. At one time, some makers of automobiles such as Pontiac had their own company-owned dealer outlets. This caused hard feelings among independent dealers, and the practice has since stopped. Similar conflicts arose between major oil companies and independent service dealers. During the oil crisis of the 1970s, some independents allegedly were given second priority in favor of company-owned dealers. Still another consideration is the threat of antitrust suits, if one were to contemplate adding a new channel system to established ones. B. F. Goodrich was accused of fixing prices and restraint of trade when it sold tires in some states through both company-owned and franchised dealers.[19]

Channel Modification Decisions

Establishment of a channel of distribution is an expensive endeavor, involves considerable risk, and typically entails long-term commitments. For these reasons, changes are made less frequently than for product, price, and communication programs. Nevertheless, changes are made on occasion in order to pursue new opportunities, respond to market conditions, or prune unproductive channel members.

Consider recent developments in the computer industry.[20] At one time, Apple used manufacturer's representatives to sell to retail dealers but now relies on its own sales force which is comprised of 300 salespeople. As Lotus shifts from use of salespeople to reach corporate accounts to dealers in order to sell its software, smaller producers are moving to direct mail and ads in trade magazines. The sale of personal computers to businesses is becoming less one of selling direct by company sales forces and more one of selling through retail computer stores. Prior to 1984, for example, less than 30 percent of such sales occurred through computer stores, whereas more than 50 percent have been made since 1984. Buyers of computers are becoming more sophisticated. Price is less a factor than in the past, and comparison shopping for solutions to specific problems is the rule. This tends to favor retail outlets with multiple product lines and demonstration-oriented showroom floors. New methods of distribution are emerging such as Informat in Dallas which opened in 1985 and consists of 1.5 million square feet of space for more than 350 hardware, software, and service companies. Still another development is the value-added reseller (VAR) who purchases components and software from various manufacturers and puts them together or enhances them in certain ways for resale to users with specialized needs. So changes do occur in channels.

In general, any firm will consider one or more of three changes to make in its distribution policies. The simplest and most frequently made change is the addition or deletion of particular members of the channel. One might want to add a wholesaler or retailer to enter a new geographic region, to cover an existing one more thoroughly, or to reach a new type of buyer in an old market area. A more involved change would be to introduce or remove an entire channel network from producer to consumer. Thus, for example, a firm might augment its company store channel by selling also to a large retail chain that markets the product under its own house brand name. Alternatively, a firm might retrench from selling through a dual distribution network to use of a single channel. Finally, a manufacturer might decide to invent an entirely new form of distribution for itself. Sarah Coventry, the seller of jewelry, recently discontinued the use of home parties. Beginning in 1985, it sold through retail stores.

The actual decision to change one's distribution policies should be done carefully and in the light of a number of factors. Comparisons of sales, costs, profits, etc., among alternatives should be conducted. Competitive differences must also be taken into account. Of course, no change should be undertaken without investigation of the likely qualitative, as well as quantitative, responses of customers. Finally, one's responsibilities to intermediaries and their employees and social and ethical concerns must be weighed.

Management of Intermediary Relations

Once a channel of distribution has been established, considerable effort must be expended to see to it that operations run smoothly. One might think that mutual concern for profitability in contractual and conventional systems would be sufficient to manage the channel. After all, most intermediaries are responsible, independent businesspeople with a vested interest in generating sales. In reality, intermediaries handle products for many firms and therefore face decisions for allocating their time and effort. Moreover, conflicts over policies and procedures and over rights and responsibilities often produce differences of opinion on how one should conduct the business. These conflicts occur in corporate systems as well. As a consequence, the manufacturer or channel captain must give special consideration to the problems of motivation and control of channel member behavior, conflict management, and communication enhancement. These activities serve to promote cooperation and/or facilitate the initiation of influence. A healthy dose of behavioral science and management know-how is required.[21] Let us consider these activities further.

Motivation and Control[22]

Motivation and control can be viewed as two activities management performs in order to increase the effectiveness and efficiency of its distribution programs. By *motivation of channel members*, we mean the stimulation of enthusiastic and aggressive marketing on the part of intermediaries. *Channel control* is a related function and refers to the monitoring of performance and correction of improper actions or practices by channel members. Motivation is a positive action designed to provide rewards and create self-monitored behavior in the pursuit of desired goals. Control is a measurement and corrective action also designed to guide the channel towards goal attainment. The tactics used to motivate or control frequently overlap.

Motivation is accomplished in a number of ways. Design of an attractive product and creation of a unique brand image are necessary parts of the process, for intermediaries will be more enthusiastic about brands with differential advantages over the competition. But this is rarely enough because other producers add incentives and services making up for their product deficiencies. One of the most potent incentives is the margin the manufacturer gives its intermediaries. A *margin* (sometimes also termed *gross margin*

or *trade discount*) is the difference between the selling price an intermediary applies and the price it paid for the goods it handles. Obviously, the higher the margin on a sale, the greater the profit of the intermediary, other things being equal. Manufacturers typically base their prices of goods sold to intermediaries on the price the final customer will accept and the margin the intermediary can live with. Because intermediaries put forth efforts in proportion to margins received, the manufacturer should view the margin supplied as a motivational lever. At the same time, it is essential to take into account final customer sensitivity to price, manufacturer's costs, and the margins provided by competitor brands should the intermediary carry them. Sometimes too high a margin can result in high prices and dampen customer demand, while a retailer may find that a lower-margin competitor brand generates more profits than the higher-margin brand because of the greater volume generated. Thus, the high-margin brand can be at a disadvantage under certain conditions.

Other incentives are at the disposal of manufacturers or channel captains. Promotional discounts are sometimes given to an intermediary in the hope that it will induce cooperation. A *promotional discount* is a reduction in the price of goods sold to an intermediary and/or an outright grant in exchange for purchase of local advertising, increased shelf space, or other enhancement of the selling effort. A danger in the use of promotional or trade discounts is that the intermediary will merely absorb the incentives as increased profit and in the process not perform any extra services. Then, too, the effects of incentive discounts are often short-lived, since competitors eventually match or counter them. Nevertheless, when done in a timely and thoughtful way, discounts have their place.

Still another incentive of sorts is the *provision of services* to the intermediary. For example, Hoover, the manufacturer of vacuum cleaners, hires demonstration salespeople and supplies them to department stores such as Macy's as a demand stimulation service. The department store then has an added incentive to stock the full product line, whereas in the absence of the "free" sales help, it might not. Manufacturers provide other services to intermediaries such as advice on inventory management, merchandise displays, or store layout; training of sales personnel; and even stocking help.

Incentives may also be given on a "one-time" or periodic basis. For instance, *contests*, *prizes*, or *bonuses* are frequently used to stimulate effort.

So far, the incentives considered have consisted largely of tangible rewards. Threats, warnings, and punishments could also be applied, but these tend to create negative reactions in the long run, require closer monitoring, and produce fewer results than positive incentives.

A freqently overlooked motivator is the subtle use of *leadership* and *human relation skills*. Persuasion, friendly advice, concern for the intermediary's welfare, mutual goal setting, a positive attitude, enthusiasm, setting a good example, charm, showing pride and fairness in one's dealings, displaying objectivity when called for, and administering praise when deserved can each contribute to the motivation of channel members. Yet another intangible is the granting of responsibilities to intermediaries. This tends to generate high levels of commitment because it involves the intermediary and leads to internalization and even at times co-optation of goals.

A *formal control program* goes hand in hand with motivational activities. This is one place where a marketing information system can be put to advantage. Data must be collected regularly on costs, sales, special problems, and other information. Sound qualitative and quantitative research must be applied to assess the data, perform analyses, and interpret results. Budgets and performance standards must be designed and continually monitored. Alternative motivational, compensation, and promotion scenarios should be constructed and compared. For example, different balances between push (i.e., dealer promotion and discounts) and pull (i.e., packaging, advertising, couponing, dealing) strategies must be evaluated. Wherever and whenever appropriate, corrective action must be taken. This might entail issuance of persuasive memos, changes in motivational practices, reminders as to contractual responsibilities, legal action, adding or dropping channel members, or changing the organization or design of the channel itself.

A final point to note with respect to control is that *informal mechanisms* should not be ignored. Through ongoing personal and phone contact, subtle pressure is applied, and the opportunity is afforded for question asking and the mutual adjustments and accommodations that such encounters frequently permit. Similarly, friendships are maintained, and indirect, nonverbal communication is fostered. Rather than using directives or overreacting to drops in performance, informal control attempts sometimes are effective and avoid unnecessary conflicts. For an interesting example of motivation and control in a modern organization, see Exhibit 14-2.

Conflict Management[23]

Conflicts occur among intermediaries and between manufacturers and their channel members. Examples of the former include badmouthing, malicious rumor spreading, vandalism, and other injurious acts between competing retailers or competing wholesalers. Conflict between institutions within a channel of distribution take one or more of five forms.

Differences of opinion or diverging interests are probably the most common type of intrachannel conflict. These may reside in conflicting preferences over objectives, strategies, or tactics. For example, a manufacturer might desire that a high price be

EXHIBIT 14-2

Achieving High Motivation and Control in the Channel of Distribution without Formal Contracts

Contracts play an important role in the motivation and control of channel member behavior. However, formal contracts are not always used and may even be avoided as a matter of policy. Consider the case of the Benetton Corporation, an Italian manufacturer and marketer of clothing. From modest beginnings in 1965 as a family-run enterprise, Benetton today has grown to a network of over 2,500 retail establishments worldwide.

Its success rests primarily on its attractive products and unique distribution system. Benetton makes its own knitwear but waits until the last minute to dye the clothing to match fickle consumer tastes. Its consumer information system is predicated upon upward feedback from sales representatives and retailers coupled with the uncanny sense of its founders for style and consumer tastes. Unlike its competitors, Benetton does not sell to distributors, department stores, or full-line clothiers. Rather, it markets knitwear through company-owned and franchise-like stores, each only about 450 sq. ft. in area. Imaginative store location, distinctive clothing displays, and efficient inventory management are key elements in Benetton's merchandising success. But perhaps of even greater importance is its highly motivated, knowledgeable retail staff. The typical scenario consists of careful selection of an entrepreneur to run an outlet followed by provision of support in startup operations. However, each entrepreneur provides 51 percent or more of the initial investment, and Benetton extracts no fees or royalties. Indeed, if a store does well, the retailer is allowed to buy out Benetton's holdings at a price equal to the original Benetton investment. This further reinforces aggressive selling. At the same time, store owners are encouraged to expand outward and open new outlets with Benetton's help. The net result is an entrepreneurial spirit producing exploding sales for the company and accelerated wealth for individual shop owners. All of this has been accomplished without the need for formal contracts in many instances. Instead, a handshake, trust, and the sense of partnership drives the company onward.

SOURCE: Based in part on conversations with Professor Gianni Lorenzoni, University of Bologna, 1985.

maintained as part of a long-run product quality and image policy, whereas a retailer might believe that price cutting is necessary to stimulate demand. Conflicts of interest might occur simply because a wholesaler cannot devote as much attention to a brand that the manufacturer would like because a large product line requires that time and resources be spread among many brands.

A second kind of conflict is manifest in disagreements as to just division of profits between manufacturer and intermediary or the allocation of support and other resources among intermediaries in a particular channel. The perception that a manufacturer favors one or more other intermediaries at one's expense is a special case. Such instances might result in resentment, verbal abuse, suboptimal selling efforts, and even dissolution of the relationship.

The use of coercion, threats, or warnings sometimes is the seed of still another type of conflict. Hard feelings are likely to occur and develop into destructive conflict if such tactics are carried too far.

The fourth class of conficts arises from neglect of interfirm relations, a failure to fulfill obligations or promises, or subpar performance. These, too, cause resentment and might lead to acts injurious to one another.

A final form of channel conflict concerns interpersonal relations across organizational boundaries. Personality conflicts, jealousies, and disagreements over style and substance sometimes thwart the workings of business relations.

Before we discuss the ways that conflict can be resolved, we should acknowledge that conflict is not necessarily undesirable. Some amount of conflict can be functional when it serves as an arousal mechanism and forces one not to become habituated to the status quo or to take things for granted.

Some types of conflict, if they do not get out of hand, may even be necessary to create the proper motivational climate for aggressively conducting one's operations. And conflict between organizations can lead to greater cohesion and cooperation among groups within an organization as well as functional restructuring of tasks and formal relations. Unfortunately, we know very little if anything about the positive effects of conflict in the channel of distribution. The line between when to tolerate and when to thwart conflict is thin.

In general, conflict can be managed to advantage through use of one or more of the following mechanisms: superordinate goals, channel diplomats, exchange of persons, co-optation, joint membership in trade associations, mediation, channel reorganization, and the administration of power.[24] Under superordinate goals, the manufacturer or channel captain establishes objectives beneficial to all parties. The hope is that the intermediary will come to identify with the manufacturer and/or see that it is in one's own best interests to pursue certain policies. Channel diplomacy consists of the use of boundary-spanning personnel to build cohesive relations and to serve as ambassadors of goodwill.

Under the exchange-of-persons program, personnel temporarily switch roles across organizations or at least act as observers for periods of time. The goal is to build greater understanding of channel operations and promote empathy and positive affect among people who must deal with each other in everyday matters. Co-optation refers to the establishment of groups and the appointment of some members to the group from channel member organizations. For example, a manufacturer might form dealer councils to advise on policies and procedures and include among its members managers from intermediaries. An executive from an intermediary might even be appointed to the board of directors of the manufacturer. Co-optation results in the transference or creation of shared goals and interests. Joint membership in trade associations is still another conflict resolution mechanism with obvious cooperative aims. Mediation by an outside party can be used especially when impasses are met. Arbitration is an example. Some conflicts might be so intransigent that a reorganization or dissolution of ongoing relations must be contemplated. Finally, in certain instances, a powerful manufacturer or channel captain might be forced to use its resources to correct conflicts. This might mean the application of threats, warnings, promises, mendations, rewards, punishments, legal action, legitimate authority, or other modes of influence.[25]

Communication[26]

Communication serves three functions.

Information Function. Interpersonal and interorganizational relationships for everyday operations must be facilitated. Policies must be conveyed, points of clarification made, problems solved, and a whole host of other information exchanged. Much of this occurs formally via personal visits by salespeople, telephone conversations, seminars, memos, and letters. Some occurs informally through unplanned contacts at professional meetings, social gatherings, and other occasions. All members in the channel must give special consideration to the facilitation of communication. This means paying attention to communication patterns and flow rates to ascertain if information is conveyed accurately and quickly and is of the content needed to run the operations efficiently. Communication skills must be fostered, and the best vehicles must be employed to transmit, receive, and interpret messages. In addition, certain structural aspects of communication deserve scrutiny, such as the location and role of gatekeepers, communication facilitators, and critical paths and contingencies. Finally, efforts to succinctly and clearly communicate needs and directives must be implemented on an ongoing basis.

Research. Data must be gathered, internally analyzed, and interpreted. Recommendations must be instituted. Before this can happen, the needs of the parties must be clearly assessed and the research problem(s) defined. Although research is typically conducted and communicated in formal terms, considerable room for ambiguity exists. Moreover, research usually has political implications which further exacerbates the communication process. Yet, if firms are to learn about opportunities and problems and do something about them, they must perform sound research. It is essential that the firm's marketing information system monitor the operations of the channel and conduct research into its functioning. Firms now rely heavily on the information provided by checkout scanners, surveys, and panel studies, for example. Further, special thought must be given to the dissemination and use of things learned. Research reports and formal presentations are two activities in this regard.

Influence Function. In addition to gathering and conveying information, communication also serves as an instigator of action. The application of persuasion or power, for example, occurs through the medium of communication. Thus, motivation and control rest on the appropriate use of communication. We have already covered the influence side of communication in earlier chapters. Interpersonal processes and organization design are the heart of influence.

Legal Issues in Distribution[27]

The most important legal issues for discussion are those related to restraint of trade. Such practices are covered under the Clayton Act among others and have been interpreted further in a number of subsequent court cases. We will only briefly review some of the major legal concerns herein.

Tying agreements, in which a seller requires that a buyer make purchases of goods or services in addition to the ones desired are prohibited by the Clayton Act when they can be shown to lead to monopolistic behavior. The imposition of tying sales can be irritating and costly to a small buyer and has been most recently a problem in franchising.[28] Certain franchisees have found that some supplies that they are required to buy from the franchiser are not needed or can be purchased less expensively from other sources. This obviously causes hard feelings and can result in lower profits for all if no true economies of scale result from such arrangements.

Closely related to tying agreements is the practice known as *reciprocity*.[29] Broadly speaking, reciprocity occurs when two organizations agree to purchase one another's products or services or in some other way help each other as a condition for doing business. Over the years, the Federal Trade Commission and the Department of Justice have opposed such practices on the grounds that they are anticompetitive. A number of consent decrees disbanding reciprocal purchasing relations have occurred as a result.[30] Although formal reciprocal agreements are relatively easy to detect in large organizations, informal or friendly reciprocity is not.

Reciprocity is as much a cultural and psychological phenomenon as it is a legal or moral one. As a matter of fact, in some parts of the world, reciprocity is a necessary, expected, and legal way of doing business. As with the case of bribery, we see that reciprocity depends on one's viewpoint and values. Social norms of reciprocity operate in most cultures, including our own, as witnessed in such sayings as "Do unto others as you would have them do unto you," "We like to do business with our friends or with local vendors," and "You scratch my back and I'll scratch yours." The social and psychological pressures for which these sayings are symptoms pervade even the most formal business relations and must be understood and dealt with according to individual, organization, and societal codes of conduct.

A final legal issue is the *exclusive relationship*. Here a manufacturer requires that intermediaries carry no competing brands.

Perhaps the best way to understand the problem is to consider the case of Arnold, Schwinn & Co., the well-known maker of bicycles. In the 1960s, Schwinn bicycles were marketed through approximately 15,000 small and general merchandise stores across the country. About this time, competition became keen from Japanese and other overseas companies who sold much cheaper bicycles and often in the same outlets. To combat the threat, Schwinn decided to sell primarily through franchised dealers under exclusive relationships. About 3,000 franchisees were envisioned. In 1967, the Department of Justice sued Schwinn on the basis of restraint of trade. It was eventually ruled that Schwinn could use the franchise system only if it retained ownership of the bicycles sold by the dealers. This ruling was challenged but later upheld by the Supreme Court. In 1977, in another Supreme Court decision (*Continental TV* v. *Sylvania*), it was further ruled that vertical restrictions such as exclusive relationships are not illegal per se. Rather, such arrangements must be shown to restrain trade in an unreasonable way. This is the so-called "rule of reason" clause. One can readily see that things are still ambiguous and open to multiple interpretations. Nevertheless, especially when making major changes from one distribution system to another as Schwinn did, firms must consider the competitive and injurious effects of such moves.

Management of Logistics

Actual physical distribution or *logistics* is concerned with such activities as "freight transportation, warehousing, material handling, protective packaging, inventory control, plant and warehouse site selection, order processing, market forecasting, and customer service."[31] The costs of these activities comprise approximately 14 percent of sales for manufacturing firms and 26 percent of sales for intermediaries such as wholesalers and retailers.[32] Thus, a savings in logistics can be an important part of overall cost management. At the same time, effective logistics can give an organization an edge over the competition to the extent that it provides unique services or simply does traditional things better than others.

We might think of logistics management as a parallel, yet interrelated, function along with marketing, manufacturing, accounting/finance, and other subareas of the firm. The logistics function is best represented as a *system* of physical flows of goods, title, and information bound together through formal transportation, storage, planning, and communication activities within and between each institution in the channel of distribution. Figure 14-6 depicts the elements of the *logistics system* common to most organizations in this sense.

Suppliers provide raw materials, parts, equipment, and general supplies needed by the manufacturer. The purchasing department processes the orders and procures these inputs. Sometimes suppliers contact the firm first in order to make a sale. In other instances, the purchasing department initiates the contact. In any event, the purchasing department consults with manufacturing, finance, and marketing to guide its decisions. Needed supplies arrive by truck, train, or other medium and are received and stored temporarily in a warehouse. Internal movement of supplies and partially finished and completely finished goods is managed by the materials handling department (see Figure 14-6). This department also coordinates receiving, income warehousing, in-process storage, packing, outgoing warehousing, general inventory control, and shipping. The manufacturing department plans its activities in response to demand forecasts made by marketing and in turn supplies

purchasing with production plans so that materials, supplies, equipment, and other factors of production will be available as needed. The focal manufacturing firm represented in Figure 14-6 sells directly only to wholesalers who in turn sell directly to retailers. Notice that the intermediaries perform similar logistic functions as the manufacturer: materials handling, storage, order processing, sales negotiation, planning, customer services, and so on. Notice further the omnipresent role of transportation from beginning to end.

It is essential that management view the entire system of functions, flows, and relations shown in Figure 14-6 in an integrated way. This means running efficient warehousing and materials handling operations, managing inventories to reduce costs yet deliver a product when and where it is needed, and in general providing the services needed by final customers and cooperating institutions. In addition, special effort is required to coordinate the vast network of activities and do so mindful of the competition, environmental factors (e.g., geographic, climatic, labor, cultural, etc., considerations), and legal and ethical concerns.

In a simplified way, management's logistic decisions can be construed as a joint maximization problem. That is, one must balance the needs of customers for convenience, maximum information, fast delivery, etc., versus the costs of providing these functions. The costs reside in warehousing, materials handling, transportation, packing, order processing, inventory control, and related activities. Giving up some on customer demands to keep costs down means a certain amount of lost sales. Figure 14-7 shows the classic trade-off between management of transportation costs and lost sales by making customers wait different periods of time. In any real application, formal models and managerial judgment are needed to ascertain where to draw the line because more is involved than merely transportation costs and lost sales. Competition, for example, is a key consideration.

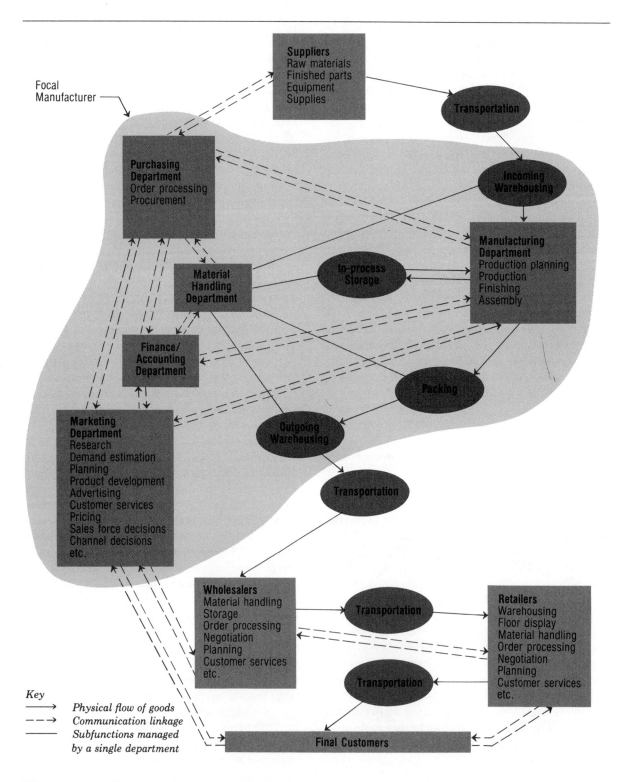

Figure 14-6. A representative logistics system

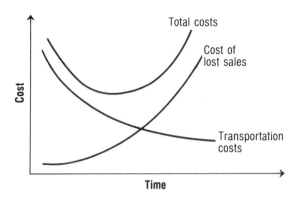

Figure 14-7. Minimization of total distribution costs as a function of transportation and delivery delay

We will briefly describe three basic management decisions in the logistic function: design of the logistic system, warehouse/inventory management, and transportation management. There are other decision areas in logistics, but discussion of these is beyond the scope of this text.

Design of the Logistics System[33]

Two basic decisions are faced by any firm in the design of its logistics system. The first concerns the location and number of production facilities and warehouses. The second resides in choices among transportation modes. Both decisions are obviously interrelated and depend additionally on the larger decision to market directly or through intermediaries.

If the firm decides to market directly to final customers, it will be faced primarily with the choice of what transportation system to employ.[34] Should it use the mail, its own delivery trucks, common carriers,

private parcel services, and/or the so-called contract carriers (i.e., specialized, independent shippers working under contract and often exempt from federal regulations governing common carriers and other modes of transportation)? We will touch upon transportation decisions at the end of this chapter. For now, note that transportation costs (monetary, time, damage, etc.) are the principal choice criteria once one has decided to market directly.

At the same time, we should stress that firms may still be faced with the decision to set up additional production/assembly facilities and/or warehouses even if they decide to market directly. For example, if after placing orders, customers require receipt of the goods in two days or less, mail, rail, or truck delivery may be insufficient for certain market areas distant from the manufacturer. If air or special delivery services are too expensive, the firm might benefit from establishment of regional production or warehouse facilities closer to the distant markets. Costs and likely demand must be weighed against each other when evaluating such options.

If the firm decides to market through intermediaries, it must decide (1) whether to set up additional production facilities and/or warehouses and (2) what type of transportation to use to and from plants and/or warehouses. Notice that these decisions must be made in addition to the problem of intermediary selection. Moreover, such decisions will be faced even if one uses a corporate or contractual channel system. The remainder of the chapter considers these issues.

Warehouse Management

Warehouses perform at least four functions: reception/delivery, breaking bulk, assembly, and storage. In addition, warehouses serve a financial role in that documentation attesting to the existence of goods can be used as collateral for loans.

Over the years, particular kinds of warehouses have emerged. Private warehouses are facilities owned by a firm for its own use. Public warehouses are facilities offered to any organization on a lease basis. Some warehouses specialize by goods or services. Most tend to be general merchandise warehouses and carry a vast array of goods. Similarly, some warehouses serve primarily as waystations in that goods are held for short periods of time, whereas others emphasize the storage function and stock goods for lengthy periods. The term *distribution center* has sometimes been used to designate warehouses employed in the waystation sense.

Two principal warehouse decisions facing the firm are (1) should private and/or public warehouses be used and (2) where should the warehouses be located? The choice between private and public warehouses depends first on the differences in costs for the functions performed. But beyond this, a number of other factors must be considered. Although private warehouses tend to cost more than public ones, they offer greater control of operations. Private warehouses are used at times simply because special handling and storage requirements cannot be met by others. On the other hand, public warehouses become the choice when warehouse documentation is desired for financial reasons, many locations and/or large storage spaces are needed and cannot be internally financed, and production or demand is intermittent, thereby resulting in only a periodic need for warehouse services.[35]

Warehouse site selection depends on customer coverage, timing, and cost considerations. Formal models and computer simulations have been developed to handle the design of warehouse locations.[36] However, discussion of the approaches are beyond the scope of this text.

Inventory Management[37]

Closely related to warehousing decisions is inventory management. A firm must decide how many goods to order for inventory and when to do so.

A rough rule-of-thumb guiding how much to order is the economic order quantity (EOQ) formula:

$$EOQ = \left[\frac{2DC_o}{C_u C_c} \right]^{\frac{1}{2}}$$

where D = annual demand, C_o = cost of placing a single order, C_u = cost per unit, and C_c = inventory carrying cost percentage. This formula yields the number of units to order at one particular point in time. It should be regarded as a rough estimate because of its dependence on demand and cost estimates and its neglect of exogenous factors such as manufacturing, transportation, and buying habit peculiarities.

Along with the decision on order quantity, the timing of orders must be ascertained. A crude rule-of-thumb that can be used in this regard is the so-called order point (OP) formula:

$$OP = L\overline{D} + LN_\sigma \sigma$$

where L = lead time needed to make a delivery, $\overline{D}$ = average demand during L, N_σ = number of standard deviations for demand needed to cover a desired percentage of demand, and σ = standard deviation of demand. This formula gives the point in units of inventory at which an order should be placed. Again, it rests on one's ability to estimate demand.

Warehouse / inventory decisions should be viewed as interrelated problems. Further, production, channel design, customer service, and other marketing mix elements should also be taken into account. It is not possible to do justice to the topic herein, and the reader interested in deeper coverage should consult the references provided at the end of the chapter.

Transportation Management

Five basic modes of transportation exist: railroads, trucking, air, pipelines, and shipping. Bus lines also carry goods, but they represent a very small percentage of total transportation of goods in the United States and most foreign countries. In 1980, the approximate percentage of intercity freight movement in the United States for each mode of transportation was railroads (37 percent), trucking (23 percent), air (less than 1 percent), pipelines (23 percent), and shipping on inland waterways (16 percent).[38]

The selection of one or more modes of transportation depends on a variety of factors. Cost is obviously a key constraint. Each mode varies considerably in this regard. Another consideration is the service desired. Some transporters have better facilities for pickup, delivery, credit, packing, and so on than others. Still another issue is risk.

Lost, damaged, stolen, or delayed shipments occur with different frequencies across the five modes of transport. In addition, the availability and flexibility of transporters might be a factor in making a choice. Some are more accommodating than others. Finally, the degree of control or influence over transporters varies from one mode to another, from one provider to another.

Each firm must identify the attributes it desires in a transportation service, assess the relative importance of each attribute to its operations, score each alternative transportation mode or provider on each attribute, and then apply a computational rule to integrate the data and judgments. Table 14-4 presents a simplified example for comparing the five different types of transportation. A real application would be more detailed. In addition, it should be realized that many products cannot be shipped by all alternatives.

TABLE 14-4
Comparison of Modes of Transportation on Key Attributes

ATTRIBUTE	ATTRIBUTE IMPORTANCE	SCORES OF TRANSPORTATION MODES ON ATTRIBUTES[b]				
		Railroads	Trucking	Air	Pipelines	Shipping
Speed of operation	—[a]	5	6	10	3	4
Frequency of service	—	5	8	9	9	4
Cost per unit of weight	—	7	6	2	9	10
Dependability of service	—	5	7	5	8	6
Extent of reach	—	7	10	5	2	3
Flexibility	—	6	5	3	1	7

[a]Depends on one's individual business situation.
[b]Based on a 1 to 10 point scale. The higher the number, the better the mode scores on the respective attribute. The numbers expressed here are rough judgments made by the author.

Summary

This chapter examined the marketing subarea known as channels of distribution. A channel of distribution is the set of people and organizations concerned with the flow of products from producer to customer.

Channels of distribution play a pivotal role in modern marketing practice. In its broadest sense, any channel reconciles the discrepancies of quantity and assortment of goods existing between manufacturer and final consumer. Indeed, it is generally recognized that the emergence of channels has resulted in greater efficiency in bringing goods to market.

The intermediaries between producer and consumer perform a variety of functions. Retailers make goods available when and where they are needed, at the proper quality, and in the desired assortment. They also absorb certain risks, handle personal selling and promotion, add concrete and intangible value to products, and supply services such as provision of credit, delivery, guarantees, repair, parking, and so on. Wholesalers deliver and pick up goods, store inventory, assume risk, engage in personal selling, and supply such services as granting credit, training, and advertising and promotion. In addition to the aforementioned functions, it is important to recognize that intermediaries represent a competitive tool. A differential advantage can be secured through the skillful choice and implementation of a distribution strategy.

Any firm will use one or more of three ways to bring its goods to market (see Figure 14-3). It can engage in direct marketing and sell by mail, catalogs, telephone, and advertising. It can sell through a sales force, either its own, another firm's, or via independent agents. Or it can utilize marketing intermediaries. When it chooses the latter, we say that it employs a *vertical marketing system.*

Three types of vertical marketing systems exist. The *corporate vertical marketing system* consists of successive stages of production and distribution under single ownership. Under the *contractual vertical marketing system*, producers and intermediaries enter into an agreement to deal with each other. Although the organizations retain their independence, they formally agree to certain responsibilities in exchange for benefits received. Collaborative (i.e., cooperative) arrangements and franchise arrangements are the two principal forms of contractual systems.

The third system is the *conventional vertical marketing system*. Here autonomous producers and intermediaries enter into business exchanges involving the buying and selling of goods. In addition to vertical marketing systems, we briefly considered *horizontal relationships* where firms at the same functional level cooperate in some way.

Many steps must be carried out in channel management decisions. You might want to review Figure 14-4 again to gain an overall perspective.

A key activity is the *choice of a distribution channel* which entails determination of *intensity* of market coverage, channel *length*, and channel *modification* decisions. The intensity or breadth decision addresses the required number of retail outlets per geographic area. Here the options are threefold: intensive, selective, or exclusive distribution. We described and illustrated each of these in the text and included a discussion of pros and cons.

The channel length decision is a fundamental one designed to answer two questions: (1) should we market direct or use intermediaries and (2) given either choice, how should we implement it. The advantages and disadvantages of the two options were addressed. And an extensive presentation was done of the assets and liabilities of alternative vertical marketing systems. Included in the discussion was an illustration of the use of the expectancy-value model in channel selection.

Channel modification decisions concern when particular channel members should be added or deleted, when whole networks of intermediaries should be introduced or removed, or when entirely new forms of distribution should be considered. These decisions are made in response to poor performance, changing market conditions or buying habits, competitive threats, or the identification of new opportunities.

Another major step in channel management is the everyday guidance of intermediary relations. Specifically, attention must be given to the following activities: *motivation and control of channel members, conflict management,* and *communication enhancement.* We cannot summarize the many activities here, so you are encouraged to briefly thumb through the appropriate pages in the text and review the central principles.

The chapter then turned to important *legal issues* in distribution management. Tying agreements, reciprocity, and exclusive relationships were scrutinized. Each was shown to violate legal rules when it resulted in restraint of trade or tended to create a monopoly.

Management of *logistics* was the final topic treated in the chapter. We discussed certain design issues related to plant and warehouse location and selection, inventory management, and transportation.

Questions and Problems for Discussion

1 Are wholesalers, retailers, and intermediaries really needed? What functions do they perform?

2 When deciding to market its goods, what three options does a manager generally have to get the goods to market? Discuss the differences and similarities.

3 Compare and contrast the corporate, contractual, and conventional vertical marketing systems.

4 To what does the term *horizontal marketing system* refer?

5 Describe the central features of the channel-of-distribution management process.

6 Market coverage can be accomplished through intensive, selective, or exclusive distribution. Define each of these and discuss their key advantages and disadvantages. What type of product is best suited for each strategy?

7 Discuss the issues surrounding the choice of a channel of distribution.

8 How might one evaluate the various alternative channels of distribution?

9 Under what conditions should an organization employ multiple channel systems to bring its goods to market?

10 What kinds of changes should any organization consider in its ongoing management of its channel(s)?

11 Discuss the ways a firm can motivate and control individuals and institutions in its channel of distribution.

12 What form does conflict take in the channel of distribution and how can it be managed?

13 What function does communication play in the channel of distribution and how can it be administered effectively?

14 What are tying agreements, reciprocity, and exclusive relationships?

15 Discuss the key decisions that must be made for logistics programs.

NOTES

1. Philip Kotler, *Marketing Management*, 4th ed. (Englewood Cliffs, N.J.: Prentice-Hall, 1984), pp. 417, 418–19.

2. This illustration is drawn from Hirotaka J. Takeuchi, "Strategic Issues in Distribution Channels," Harvard Business School Case Services, Boston, Mass., 1980.

3. See Wroe Alderson, "Factors Governing the Development of Marketing Channels," in Richard M. Clewett, ed., *Marketing Channels for Manufactured Goods* (Homewood, Ill.: Richard D. Irwin, 1954), pp. 5–34; R. Cox, C. S. Goodman, and T. C. Fichandler, *Distribution in a High Level Economy* (Englewood Cliffs, N.J.: Prentice-Hall, 1965); Wroe Alderson and Michael H. Halbert, *Men, Motives and Markets* (Englewood Cliffs, N.J.: Prentice-Hall, 1968).

4. This definition is broader than that proposed by some authors. For instance, one author defines vertical marketing systems as "professionally managed and centrally programmed networks, pre-engineered to achieve operating economies and maximum market impact." See Bert C. McCammon, Jr., "Perspectives for Distribution Programming," in L. P. Bucklin, ed., *Vertical Marketing Systems* (Glenview, Ill.: Scott, Foresman & Co., 1970), p. 43. This definition encompasses corporate, contractual, and administered marketing systems, but not independent systems. Our definition covers all of these (See Figure 14-3). The distinctions—corporate, contractual, and administered—are due to McCammon.

5. See Shelby D. Hunt and John R. Nevin, "Tying Agreements in Franchising," *Journal of Marketing* 39 (July 1975): 20–26; B. J. Lender and W. Lucas, "The Nature of Franchising: Part 1: Its History," *Atlantic Economic Review* (October 1969): 12–14; W. Lucas and B. J. Lender, "The Nature of Franchising: Part 2: Legal Difficulties," *Atlantic Economic Review* (November 1969): 18–21.

6. United States Department of Commerce, *Franchising in the Economy* (Washington, D.C.: U.S. Government Printing Office, 1979).

7. *Business Week*, June 7, 1982, p. 120.

8. Lee Adler, "Symbiotic Marketing," *Harvard Business Review* 43 (1966): 59–71.

9. Malcolm P. McNair, "Significant Trends and Developments in the Postwar Period," in A. B. Smith, ed., *Competitive Distribution in a Free, High-Level Economy and Its Implications for the University* (Pittsburgh: University of Pittsburgh Press, 1958), pp. 1–25; W. R. Davidson, "Changes in Distributive Institutions," *Journal of Marketing* 34 (January 1970); 7–10; Ralph F. Breyer, "Some Observations on 'Structural' Formation and the Growth of Marketing Channels," in Reavis Cox, Wroe Alderson, and Stanley J. Shapiro, eds., *Theory in Marketing* (Homewood, Ill.: Richard D. Irwin, Inc., 1964), pp. 163–75; William J. Reagan, "The Stages of Retail Development," in Cox, Alderson, and Shapiro, *Theory in Marketing*, pp. 139–53; Reavis Cox, *Distribution in a High Level Economy* (Englewood Cliffs, N.J.: Prentice-Hall, 1965), pp. 17–24; Wroe Alderson, "Factors Governing the Development of Marketing Channels," in R. M. Clewett, ed., *Marketing Channels* (Homewood, Ill.: Richard D. Irwin, Inc., 1954), pp. 5–34; Joseph P. Guiltinan, "Planned and Evolutionary Changes in Distribution Channels," *Journal of Retailing* 50 (Summer 1974): 79–91, 103.

10. W. R. Davidson; A. D. Bates, and S. J. Bass, "The Retail Life Cycle," *Harvard Business Review* 53 (November-December 1976): 94.

11. Stanley C. Hollander, "The Wheel of Retailing," *Journal of Marketing* 24 (July 1960): 37–42. See also Malcolm P. McNair, "Significant Trends and Developments in the Postwar Period"; and Bert C. McCammon, Jr., "Alternative Explanations of Institutional Change and Channel Evolution," in Stephen A. Greyser, ed., *Toward Scientific Marketing* (Chicago: American Marketing Association, 1963): 477–90.

12. Stanley C. Hollander, "Notes on the Retail Accordion," *Journal of Retailing* 42 (Summer 1966): 29–40, 54.

13. For some descriptive insights, see David A. Revzan, *Wholesaling in Marketing Organization* (New York: John Wiley & Sons, 1961); Theodore N. Beckman, "Changes in Wholesaling Structure and Performance," in Peter D. Bennet, ed., *Marketing and Economic Development* (Chicago: American Marketing Association, 1965), pp. 603–18.

14. Takeuchi, "Strategic Issues in Distribution Channels," pp. 12–13.

15. For some background on direct marketing, see Bob Stone, *Successful Direct Marketing Methods*, 2nd ed. (Chicago: Crain Books, 1979); Michael Granfield and Alfred Nicols, "Economic and Marketing Aspects of the Direct Selling Industry," *Journal of Retailing* 51 (1975): 35–50. See also, Larry J. Rosenberg and Elizabeth C. Hirschman, "Retailing without Stores," *Harvard Business Review* 57 (July–August, 1980): 103–12.

16. *Statistical Abstract of the United States* (Washington, D.C.: U.S. Government Printing Office, 1981), p. 818.

17. Takeuchi, "Strategic Issues in Distribution Channels," p. 5.

18. "Burger King Puts Down Its Duke," *Fortune*, June 16, 1980, cited in Takeuchi, "Strategic Issues in Distribution Channels," pp. 8–9.

19. *Business Week*, July 7, 1980, cited in Takeuchi, "Strategic Issues in Distribution Channels," p. 15.

20. These examples are drawn from Jim Mitchell, "Hardware, Software Makers Seek Innovative Ways to Sell," *Times Tribune* (Palo Alto, California), December 16, 1984, pp. c-10 & c-11.

21. For insights into the behavioral science side of channel management, see Louis W. Stern, ed., *Distribution Channels: Behavioral Dimensions* (Boston: Houghton Mifflin, 1969).

22. Important research on motivation and control can be found in Louis W. Stern, "The Concept of Channel Control," *Journal of Retailing* 43 (Summer 1967): 14–20; Louis P. Bucklin, "A Theory of Channel Control," *Journal of Marketing* 37 (January 1973): 39–47; Adel I. El-Ansary and Robert A. Robicheaux, "A Theory of Channel Control: Revisited," *Journal of Marketing* 38 (January 1974): 2–7; Michael J. Etgar, "Selection of an Effective Channel Control Mix," *Journal of Marketing* 42 (July 1978): 53–58; Harper W. Boyd, Jr., and Sydney J. Levy, *Promotion: A Behavioral View* (Englewood Cliffs, N.J.: Prentice-Hall, Inc., 1967).

23. Stern, *Distribution Channels;* Louis W. Stern, Brian Sternthal, and C. Samuel Craig, "Managing Conflict in Distribution Channels: A Laboratory Study," *Journal of Marketing Research* 10 (May 1973): 169–79; Shelby D. Hunt and John R. Nevin, "Power in a Channel of Distribution: Sources and Consequences," *Journal of Marketing Research* 11 (May 1974): 188–93; Robert F. Lusch, "Sources of Power: Their Impact on Intrachannel Conflict," *Journal of Marketing Research* 13 (November 1976): 382–90; Michael J. Etgar, "Intrachannel Conflict and Use of Power," *Journal of Marketing Research* 15 (May 1978): 273–74; Robert F. Lusch, "Intrachannel Conflict and Use of Power: A Reply, *Journal of Marketing Research* 15 (May 1978): 275–76; Jack Kasulis and Robert E. Spekman, "A Framework for the Use of Power," *European Journal of Marketing* 14 (1980): 180–91; Gary Frazier, "On the Measurement of Interfirm Power in Channels of Distribution," *Journal of Marketing Research* 20 (May 1983): 158–66; Michael J. Etgar, "Sources and Types of Intrachannel Conflict," *Journal of Retailing* 55 (Spring 1979): 61–78; James C. Anderson and James A. Narus, "A Model of the Distributor's Perspective of Distributor-Manufacturer Working Relationships," *Journal of Marketing* 48 (Fall 1984): 62–74; Louis W. Stern and Adel I. El-Ansary, *Marketing Channels* (Englewood Cliffs, N.J.: Prentice-Hall, 1977), ch. 7.

24. See Stern and El-Ansary, *Marketing Channels*, ch. 7; discussions with Professor Lynn W. Phillips proved valuable here also.

25. John F. Gaski, "The Theory of Power and Conflict in Channels of Distribution," *Journal of Marketing* 48 (Summer 1984): 9–29.

26. Reinhard Angelmar and Louis W. Stern, "Development of a Content Analytic System for Analysis of Bargaining Communication in Marketing," *Journal of Marketing Research* 15 (February 1978): 93–102; John R. Grabner, Jr., and Larry J. Rosenberg, "Communications in Distribution Channel Systems," in Louis W. Stern, ed., *Distribution Channels;* J. L. Loomis, "Communication and the Development of Trust and Cooperative Behavior," *Human Relations* 12 (1959): 108–18.

27. Ray O. Werner, "Marketing and the U.S. Supreme Court, 1968, 1974," *Journal of Marketing* 41 (1977): 32–43; Ray O. Werner, "Marketing and the United States Supreme Court," *Journal of Marketing* 46 (Spring 1982): 73–81; Richard A. Posner, "The Rule of Reason and the Economic Approach: Reflections on the *Sylvania* Decision," *University of Chicago Law Review* 45 (1977): 1–20.

28. Shelby D. Hunt and John R. Nevin, "Tying Agreements and Franchising," *Journal of Marketing* 39 (July 1975): 20–26.

29. F. Robert Finney, "Reciprocity: Gone but Not Forgotten," *Journal of Marketing* 42 (1978): 54–59.

30. Martin T. Farris, "Purchasing Reciprocity and Antitrust," *Journal of Purchasing* 9 (1973): 5–14.

31. This definition is based on an official statement by the National Council of Physical Distribution Management. See, for example, Donald J. Bowersox, *Logistical Management* (New York: Macmillan, 1974), p. 1. See also Ronald H. Ballou, *Basic Business Logistics* (Englewood Cliffs, N.J.: Prentice-Hall, 1978); James L. Heskett, "Logistics— Essential to Strategy," *Harvard Business Review* 54 (1977): 85–96; Donald J. Bowersox, M. Bixby Cooper, Douglas M. Lambert, and Donald A. Taylor, *Management in Marketing Channels* (New York: McGraw-Hill, 1980).

32. B. J. LaLonde and P. H. Zinszer, *Customer Service: Meaning and Measurement* (Chicago: National Council of Physical Distribution Management, 1976).

33. See Note 31. See also Joseph C. Clawson, "Fitting Branch Locations, Performance Standards, and Marketing Strategies to Local Conditions," *Journal of Marketing* 38 (January 1974): 8–15. For an interesting case history, see Kenneth W. Hessler, "Assignment—Design and Phase-in a New Distribution System," *Transportation and Distribution Management* (January 1965): 35–43.

34. The decision to market direct or through intermediaries will usually depend also on the costs of alternative modes of transportation as well as on the other factors noted earlier in the chapter. We do not mean to imply that the decision to market direct or through intermediaries is always or even frequently made before taking transportation costs into account. Ideally, one would like to consider all factors simultaneously. In our discussion in this part of the chapter, we have assumed a sequential decision process for ease of exposition.

35. For further discussion on differences between private and public warehousing, see Stern and El-Ansary, *Marketing Channels*, p. 150.

36. Arthur M. Geoffrion, "Better Distribution Planning with Computer Models," *Harvard Business Review* 53 (1976): 92–99; Kenneth B. Ackerman and Bernard J. LaLonde. "Making Warehousing More Efficient," *Harvard Business Review* 57 (1980): 94–102.

37. Stephen F. Love, *Inventory Control: Mathematical Models* (New York: McGraw-Hill, 1979).

38. *Statistical Abstract of the United States, 1982–1983.* (Washington, D.C.: U.S. Government Printing Office, 1984).

GLOSSARY

Accordion Hypothesis. A theory asserting that retailers cycle back and forth over time between general line merchants with wide assortments of goods to specialized merchants with narrow lines. *See* wheel of retailing hypothesis.

Accumulation. *See* discrepancy of quantity.

Assorting. *See* discrepancy of assortment.

Breaking of Bulk. *See* discrepancy of quantity.

Business Franchising. *See* franchise arrangements.

Channel Breadth. *See* intensity of market coverage.

Channel Captain. An organization in the channel system that assumes a leadership or directive role in selling goods or services. The channel captain might be a producer, manufacturer, wholesaler, distributor, or retailer.

Channel Communication. The one-way transference or two-way exchange of information and/or affect among channel members. Communication functions to obtain or provide data, transmit or implement research findings, and/or influence another channel member.

Channel Conflict. Opposition between two or more institutions across channels of distribution or between two or more members within a vertical marketing system. Interchannel conflict consists of injurious acts such as bad mouthing, malicious rumor spreading, vandalism, and stink bombing. Intrachannel conflict takes one or more of five forms: (1) differences of opinion or diverging interests, (2) disagreements over the sharing of profits or allocation of support and resources, (3) negative reactions to the application of coercion, threats, or warnings, (4) neglect of interorganization relations, failure to fulfill obligations or promises, or subpar performance, and (5) interpersonal disagreements such as personality conflicts, jealousies, and quarrels over style and substance. Conflict involves the application of an injurious act or the withholding of actions or resources that become injurious. Note that conflict differs from competition which entails no intent to injure or no direct injury. *See* conflict resolution.

Channel Control. The monitoring of channel performance and correction of improper or less desirable actions and practices on the part of intermediaries. Performed by the manufacturer or channel captain. Channel control goes hand in hand with the motivation of channel members.

Channel Diplomacy. Use of boundary-spanning personnel to build cohesion and generally serve as ambassadors of goodwill. A mechanism for managing channel conflict.

Channel Length. The number of levels of intermediaries between producer and final customer. *See* intensity of market coverage.

Channel of Distribution. The set of people and organizations concerned with the flow of products from producer to customer. *See* vertical marketing system, marketing intermediaries.

Collaborative Agreements. A form of contractual vertical marketing system wherein separate organizations share resources and/or agree to make joint purchases. Sometimes termed cooperatives. *See* vertical marketing system. Three forms exist:

Producer-Sponsored Arrangements. Here producers organize to market their goods through establishment of one or more intermediaries.

Wholesaler-Sponsored Arrangements. A wholesaler organizes a group of producers or retailers for mutual cooperation. Sometimes termed *voluntaries*.

Retailer-Sponsored Arrangements. Retailers organize to purchase or set up a common wholesaler.

Common Carriers. Transportation companies that move people and/or goods according to regular schedules. They accept orders from any person or organization. A formal contract is usually not employed. *See* contract carriers.

Conflict Resolution (in the channel). The management of dysfunctional conflict in the channel through application of one or more of the following tactics: superordinate goal setting, use of channel diplomats, exchange of persons, co-optation, joint membership in trade associations, mediation, channel reorganization, and the administration of power. *See* channel conflict.

Contract Carriers. Transportation companies that move goods and operate under a formal contract. Unlike common carriers, they frequently work under contract to a single or small number of shippers and do so for relatively long periods of time. Also, they provide more specialized services than common carriers. *See* common carriers.

Cooperatives. *See* collaborative agreements.

Co-optation. Establishment of groups and appointment of members from other channel organizations as well as one's own to the group. This conflict management tool is designed to induce shared goals and common interests among organizations in the channel.

Direct Marketing. Selling to customers without the use of marketing intermediaries. Rather, mail, telephone, and advertising are the principal direct marketing mechanisms.

Discrepancy of Assortment. The differences between the range of goods desired by final users and what particular producers make. *See* discrepancy of quantity. The discrepancy of assortment is resolved through two processes:

Sorting. The division of products into different grades or qualities in order to more effectively reach target markets.

Assorting. The accumulation of a wide selection of products for the convenience of buyers.

Discrepancy of Quantity. The difference between the amount of goods a producer makes and the amount desired by a final user. *See* discrepancy of assortment. The discrepancy of quantity is resolved through two processes:

Accumulation. An activity performed by intermediaries whereby the offerings of many producers are acquired, aggregated, and then resold.

Breaking of Bulk. An activity performed by intermediaries whereby the output of producers is acquired, subdivided, and then resold.

Distribution Center. A special type of warehouse used to temporarily store goods in transit.

Distributor. *See* wholesaler.

Dual Distribution. Use of two or more different channels of distribution to reach a market. The different channels may or may not be in direct competition with each other.

Economic Order Quantity (EOQ). The amount of goods to order to have a sufficient stock on hand. This amount depends on annual demand estimates, the cost of placing a single order, the inventory carrying cost percentage, and the cost per unit. A formula for computing the EOQ is provided in the text. Effective inventory management requires that the optimum EOQ be ascertained along with the order point.

Exchange of Persons. A conflict management mechanism in the channel consisting of the switching of personnel across organizations for short periods of time. The goal is to build greater understanding and promote empathy and positive attitudes among people who directly or indirectly deal with each other.

Exclusive Distribution. *See* intensity of market coverage.

Exclusive Relationships. A requirement by a manufacturer that an intermediary carry no competitive brands. Although not illegal per se, if a manufacturer contemplates switching channel systems from nonexclusive to exclusive relationships, such a move may be forbidden to the extent that it lessens trade and is injurious.

Franchise Arrangements. A form of contractual vertical marketing system whereby a seller (the franchiser) gives an intermediary (the franchisee) certain services and exclusive rights to market the seller's product or service and the intermediary, in turn, agrees to follow certain procedures and not to purchase from others or to sell competing products or services. *See* vertical marketing system. Two types occur:

Product or Trade-Name Franchising. The franchiser gives the franchisee exclusive rights to market the franchiser's products. Although the franchisee might also sell other products, he or she agrees not to sell competing ones.

Business Franchising. The franchiser gives the franchisee exclusive rights to market the franchiser's products, and the franchisee deals only or primarily with the franchiser and no other suppliers.

Horizontal Arrangements. The establishment of relationships between organizations at the same function level in the channel of distribution. There are two types:

Horizontal Integration. Two or more organizations at the same functional level merge or join forces through acquisition.

Symbiotic Marketing. Two or more organizations at the same functional level cooperate to aid one another in marketing.

Intensity of Market Coverage. The number of retail outlets per geographic area. Sometimes termed *channel breadth. Compare* channel length. Three forms occur:

Intensive Distribution. The establishment of retail outlets in many locations within a geographic area.

Selective Distribution. The establishment of retail outlets in a few locations within a geographic area.

Exclusive Distribution. The establishment of a single outlet within a geographic area.

Intermediaries. *See* marketing intermediaries.

Inventory. Goods stored in a warehouse, retail outlet, wholesaler, or on the premises of a manufacturer.

Jobber. *See* wholesaler.

Joint Memberships. A conflict management mechanism in the channel consisting of common participation in third-party groups such as trade associations. Designed to provide an opportunity for a common dialogue and to emphasize the mutual goals of channel members.

Logistics. The set of activities concerned with the physical movement of goods and auxillary services. These include freight transportation, warehousing, materials handling, protective packaging, inventory control, plant and warehouse site selection, order processing, market forecasting, and customer service.

Margin. The difference between the selling price of an intermediary's product and the price paid to acquire it. Also sometimes termed a *trade discount.*

Market Coverage. *See* intensity of market coverage.

Marketing Intermediaries. People and institutions facilitating the sale and/or transport of goods and services from producer to final customer. *See* vertical marketing system, channels of distribution, wholesalers, retailers.

Mediation. Third-party input to the resolution of conflict between channel members. Arbitration is one example.

Motivation of Channel Members. The stimulation of enthusiastic and aggressive marketing on the part of intermediaries by a manufacturer or channel captain. *See* channel control.

Multiple Channels. *See* dual distribution.

Order Point (OP). The point in units of inventory at which an order should be placed. This timing criterion depends on the lead time needed to make a delivery, average demand during the lead time, the standard deviation of demand, and the number of standard deviations needed to cover a preset coverage goal. A formula for computing the OP is provided in the text. Effective inventory management requires that the optimum OP be determined along with the economic order quantity.

Physical Distribution. *See* logistics.

Producer-Sponsored Arrangements. *See* collaborative agreements.

Promotional Discount. A reduction in the price of goods sold to an intermediary and/or outright monetary grant in exchange for purchase of local advertising, increased shelf space, or other enhancement of the selling effort.

Reciprocity. An agreement between two organizations to purchase one another's products or services or in some other way help each other as a condition for doing business. Reciprocity is generally regarded by the Federal Trade Commission and the Department of Justice as anticompetitive behavior and therefore subject to control.

Retailer. An organization selling goods or services to final consumers. *Compare* wholesaler.

Retailer-Sponsored Arrangements. *See* collaborative arrangements.

Selective Distribution. *See* intensity of market coverage.

Sorting. *See* discrepancy of assortment.

Superordinate Goals. Channel objectives established by a manufacturer or channel captain and valued by all channel members. Used as a motivator and mechanism for managing channel conflict.

Symbiotic Marketing. *See* horizontal arrangements.

Trade Discount. *See* margin.

Tying Agreements. The requirement by a seller that a buyer make purchases in addition to the ones desired as part of the terms of trade. If they can lead to monopolistic behavior or restrain trade, they are illegal.

Value-Added Reseller (VAR). An intermediary who purchases goods and puts them together or in some other way alters or enhances them for resale.

Vertical Marketing System. The set of organizations between producer and customer that direct the flow of goods and services. *See* channel of distribution and horizontal arrangements. There are three types of vertical marketing systems:

Corporate Vertical Marketing Systems. Successive stages of production and distribution under single ownership.

Contractual Vertical Marketing System. An organization of independent producers and intermediaries who enter into a formal agreement to deal with each other. Two broad types include collaborative agreements and franchise arrangements.

Conventional Vertical Marketing System. Autonomous producers and intermediaries who enter into business relations to buy and sell between themselves. Two types exist: independent and administered.

Voluntaries. A wholesaler-sponsored arrangement whereby producers or retailers organize for mutual cooperation. *See* collaborative agreements.

Warehousing. Logistic activities consisting of the reception of goods, breaking bulk, assembly, storage, and delivery. In addition, public warehouses provide documentation attesting to the existence of goods which can be used to obtain loans. Private warehouses are facilities owned by a firm for its own use. Public warehouses are facilities offered to any organization on a lease basis.

Wheel of Retailing Hypothesis. A theory maintaining that retail institutions emerge as low-price, low-margin operations and eventually evolve to higher-price, high-margin operations. *See* accordion hypothesis.

Wholesaler. An organization selling goods or services to retailers or to other organizations either for their own use or for resale. Sometimes termed a distributor or jobber. *Compare* retailer.

Wholesaler-Sponsored Arrangements. *See* collaborative agreements.

Channels of Distribution: Where the Field Is Today and Where It Is Going Tomorrow

Louis W. Stern
Northwestern University

A goal in studying the field of distribution channels is answering the following question: How can profit and not-for-profit enterprises go about the task of making goods and services *available* to industrial, household, and commercial customers as efficiently and effectively as possible? The answer to this question requires an in-depth analysis of the relationships among the various actors in distribution systems who, through a massive division of labor, are responsible for moving goods and services from points of production to points of consumption. These actors may include such well-known industrial institutions as retailers, wholesalers, and manufacturers. They may also include banks, advertising agencies, public warehouses, food brokers, grain elevators, and a host of other institutions and agencies that play a direct or indirect role in the process of generating availability.

Combining the efforts and energies and resources of these widely diverse actors is no simple task. In fact, the coordination mechanisms generally employed have both economic and political aspects. Terms of trade (prices, delivery dates, inventory levels, financial arrangements, payment schedules, and the like) have to be established among the actors in order for the work of a channel to be accomplished. The exact terms of trade arrived at within a marketing channel are strongly influenced by the amount of power that each actor brings to the "bargaining table." For example, bargaining with Sears or with General Motors over prices or delivery dates is different from bargaining with smaller companies, mainly because of the power that these giant firms wield in their respective marketing channels.

Understanding this fact about the relationship among the various actors in a channel of distribution is very important because, if resources are to be employed effectively and efficiently, it is necessary that a locus of power be present to organize the marketing channel's efforts. Sometimes the firm that has the greatest amount of power acts only in its own interests and uses its power to extract monopoly profits from others with which it interacts. This use of power is likely to bring about chaos and conflict within the channel over time, as the actors against whom the power is being used begin to move away from or against the firm seeking to manipulate them. Often such channels eventually lose marketplace impact, because they have lost sight of the fact that the only way in which they could serve the best interests of consumers is to coordinate their efforts and cooperate in the task of distribution rather than to suboptimize the entire distribution system. More and more attention is being placed on how to manage marketing channels in order to deliver appropriate service outputs to consumers and thereby to enhance customer satisfaction.

If a firm's product is not one that meets consumer needs, there is nothing the marketing channel can do to assure its success. On the other hand, if a product is really worthwhile, as perceived at least by a small segment of consumers, then what the actors in the marketing channel can do is make certain that consumers can purchase the product in the desired lot size, obtain the required delivery and localized backup necessary for the product, and find suitable outlets. Indeed, channel management involves making certain that the required service outputs are attached to each and every product marketed by the firm.

The field of distribution channels has now begun to focus directly on this issue of channel management. This is a significant change. Not too long ago, emphasis was strictly on the institutions themselves (retailers or wholesalers) and not on the relationships among the institutions. Because marketing channels represent such an enormous division of labor, it is absolutely essential to look at the task of making goods and services available from a managerial perspective if the task is going to be accomplished at all. Concern used to focus on such exciting and eye-popping issues as isolating the twenty-seven functions of the rack jobber or studying what the main differences are between one- and two-story warehouses. Now, attention is on the "flesh and blood" of what it means to get a set of very diverse actors to cooperate with one another in moving products and services from points of production to points of consumption.

Even as I am writing this short description, there is a tremendous shift in power taking place in distribution, especially in the marketing channels for consumer goods. Retailers are beginning to call the shots, and manufacturers are beginning to adapt to what the retailers want. For example, in the marketing channels for packaged goods that are sold through supermarket chains, companies such as Safeway and Kroger are rapidly adopting front-end scanners that read the Universal Product Codes off packages as they pass through checkout areas. While scanners were originally thought to be mainly useful for straightforward productivity reasons (no price marking necessary, faster movement through the checkout area, no misrings, etc.), supermarkets are quickly finding that the information they can generate is even more important than the initial productivity and that, in actuality, the information is permitting further improvements. For example, supermarkets that have scanners can now tell which items are selling in which stores in which locations and in which time periods (morning, evening). They can assess the worth of aisle-end displays, of increasing the amount of shelf space given to an item, or of a promotion run by a manufacturer. This all means that a retailer can begin to suggest strategy moves to the manufacturer, rather than waiting for the manufacturer to develop a strategy for the retailer. This significance of this is profound.

Companies like Procter & Gamble and General Foods will have to listen very, very attentively to what retailers are telling them and will have to show evidence of having acted upon the retailers' suggestions. Similar phenomena are taking place in other branches of retailing, although the supermarket has generally tended to lead such changes. (Remember that self-service and central checkouts were innovations of supermarkets, and those innovations then diffused to discount stores, bookstores, home improvement centers, and the like.)

Immediately over the horizon is the great age of data transmission. Increased emphasis will be placed on computer-to-computer interactions. The likely effect for marketing channels can only be conjectured, but there is no doubt that, with greater and greater frequency, order taking, billing, and even payments will become routinized as computer-to-computer interactions, especially for frequently purchased products of relatively low unit value. Within the marketing channel, manufacturers' computers will talk to wholesalers' and vice versa. The ultimate will happen when the consumer, through a home computer and a television set, will be able to communicate to the entire channel simultaneously, so that immediate adjustments can be made in response to consumer demands. Salesmen and purchasing agents will find their time freed up for more complex tasks, and the selling/buying function within companies will become upgraded to a more strategic level. Indeed, we will increasingly find that channel tasks will be divided into those susceptible to "high tech," where technology will replace effort, and those requiring "high touch," where personal attention will still be a significant factor in decision making. The question that remains is whether marketing channel members can convert high-touch activities to high tech (where increased efficiencies are possible), or whether they can move high tech to high touch, thereby differentiating their offerings in the market and adding value to consumers. It is likely that segmenting markets along these dimensions will be a critical task for marketers in the 1990s and beyond and that marketing channels will evolve and change structure according to the modes required. In fact, it is possible that what happens in marketing channels will be the key in determining whether the effort to gain efficiencies and/or meaningful differentiation succeeds.

CHAPTER FIFTEEN

Travel, in the younger sort, is a part of education; in the elder, a part of experience.
———*Francis Bacon (1561–1626)*

A man travels the world over in search of what he needs and returns home to find it.
———*George Moore (1852–1933)*

I am a citizen, not of Athens or Greece, but of the world.
———*Socrates (469?–399 B.C.)*

Except for editorial changes and additions, this chapter was prepared by Professor Kam-Hon Lee, of the Chinese University of Hong Kong.

INTERNATIONAL MARKETING: ENVIRONMENTAL FACTORS AND MANAGERIAL PERSPECTIVES

Introduction

International marketing has long been regarded as a stepchild of marketing. In comparison with other subareas of marketing, such as consumer behavior or marketing communication, international marketing is much less developed. We simply know very little about how to go about marketing across international and cross-cultural boundaries.

Yet, in the future, the importance of an international focus is sure to grow for at least two reasons. The first arises as a result of forces within the nation that a firm operates. As markets dry up and/or competition increases, firms need to look to foreign markets for opportunities for growth. In France and Italy, for example, domestic demand for wine has slowed considerably and even flattened out. This has occurred largely because population growth has been small and the wine-drinking market has become saturated. Tastes seem to be changing, too, away from alcoholic beverages to bottled water, soft drinks, and juices. In addition, cheaper wines from Spain, Rumania, and Bulgaria have driven down prices all over Western Europe. To avoid being squeezed between rising costs and falling profits, many French and Italian firms have successfully entered the United States market where a much smaller proportion of a very large population regularly drinks wine and, therefore, provides an untapped potential. Stagnation in economic growth, increased internal competition, and less viable markets within a home nation thus force many firms to pursue a *multinational marketing posture* to an ever-increasing degree.

A second reason that international marketing is certain to expand in importance is what has been termed the *globalization of markets*.[1] Modernization and technological changes have resulted in an explosion of demand for consumer and industrial goods on a worldwide basis. Firms cannot afford to miss the opportunities to market on a mass scale and thereby generate needed capital and take advantage of economies of scale in production and marketing. Indeed, to compete effectively with aggressive foreign and domestic concerns, corporations must either take advantage of cost economies afforded by giant homogeneous markets throughout the world and sell standardized products or else selectively seek multiple market niches around the four corners of the world through product differentiation or market focus strategies. International marketing is surely the next frontier for marketers to conquer.[2]

The single most important variable differentiating international marketing from domestic marketing is the heterogeneous and multifaceted macroenvironment for international marketing. There are many ways to think of environmental variables. This author prefers a three-fold classification, including *culture, economics,* and *politics.* Perhaps you have felt the impact of cultural differences as a tourist. The effect of culture is actually broader and deeper than this, of course. Significant cultural variables would certainly include differences in language, religion, values, attitudes, and social organization. The impact of economic differences is much better documented in the literature, borrowing heavily from the research results of international economics and economic development. Differences in the economic environment especially affect the profitability of going international. In comparison with culture and economics, the political dimension is perhaps even more significant. Political ideology and political relationships often produce inseparable bonds or insurmountable hurdles between nations. Political risks (e.g., political instability) are omnipresent. In addition, government policies guide company actions much as valleys direct the courses of great rivers. Many times,

the best laid plans of firms or individuals are thwarted by unforeseen political vagaries. Half of this chapter will be devoted to the study of these environmental variables and their relationships.

International marketing activities typically originate from within the firm yet are carried out often far away from the firm. In a free market economy, all of the above-mentioned environmental differences may be integrated and unified into one concept: the *perceived psychological distance* between management and a specific foreign market. When the distance is short, management has a strong inclination to go into that foreign market. When it is wide, management may be hesitant and opportunities will be missed. In international marketing, as in domestic marketing, effective management requires a strategic assembly of the marketing elements—of product design, channels of distribution, communication, pricing, and market planning. However, threats, opportunities, and emphases among these elements are quite different when operating in the international setting. The second half of this chapter will be devoted to the study of these managerial topics.

Environmental Factors

Culture

There are many kinds of cultural variables. In fact, in the broadest sense, even economics and politics can be deemed cultural variables. However, since they carry significant and unique impacts, which are quite different from other variables, we single them out in this chapter and give separate treatments. However, it should be noted that what we introduce here does not constitute a comprehensive coverage but rather should be viewed as illustrative cases. Nevertheless, behind these examples, there is a common thread which may be best conveyed through two well-known concepts.

The first concept is the so-called *self-reference criterion* (SRC).[3] The unconscious reference from one's own culture has been deemed the root cause of many problems in international marketing. The author has a friend who is a professor of international business in a business school in the United Kingdom. The professor's teenage son is full of the entrepreneurial spirit. Yet, recently he was surprised to learn that there are many people in this world who do not know English! Ignorance of the rest of the world and interpretation of it strictly from one's own viewpoint are all too often the context in which marketing gets done. Such cultural insensitivity, however, must be overcome if one hopes to compete effectively in an ever-shrinking world.

The second concept is the *insider's doctrine*.[4] When people talk about cultural differences, there is a tendency to exaggerate the difficulty of cross-cultural understanding. If it is carried too far, people may assume that only Chinese can understand the Chinese, only men can understand other men, and even only children can understand other children! The fallacy of this doctrine is quite obvious. If it is carried too far, we would be led to a dead end because only one person and no others can understand oneself! Marketers must value the insights from outsiders as well as from insiders. If the views of both parties point to similar conclusions, we will deem the results closer to the truth and say that there is covergent validity. Therefore, the objective of talking about culture is to sensitize one to the need to be cautious of one's own cultural biases and to be open to external information sources. Let us examine the main facets of culture in greater detail.

Language. Language is perhaps the most obvious aspect of culture. When two people get together and speak two different languages and neither is bilingual, we can immediately see the problem. Even nonverbal communication may be of little help. Cross-cultural exchanges often utilize interpreters and translators to facilitate communication. Consider how communication of a written message might be facilitated through use of a procedure known as *successive backward translation*.[5] For example, if we want to translate an English message into Chinese, we would ask a translator to translate the original English document into Chinese. Then we would ask still another translator to translate the Chinese document back into English. The sender of the message would compare the original English document with the translated English version to see if there were any errors. If there were, then these would be corrected and the procedure repeated until a mutual understanding was achieved. Anyone involved in translation work knows that there is seldom a one-to-one correspondence in meaning between two languages. For example, there are many terms describing "rice" in Chinese, but there is only one general term in English. On the other hand, there are many kinds of salad dressing in America, but there is only one such term in Chinese, and even that term is a "borrowed" phonetic translation of the English. Language differences such as these make it difficult for the Chinese to export rice to the English-speaking world and equally difficult for Americans to market salad dressing to China. When we add onto this all of the other cultural and technical problems, one can readily appreciate the difficulties in international marketing. See Exhibit 15-1 for an interesting illustration of the problems involved.

Sometimes, people believe that if one is bilingual, language is no longer a problem in communication. Such is not the case. In cross-cultural psychology, scholars have discovered that there is an effect known as *ethnic affirmation*. A bilingual Chinese may respond differently to the English and the Chinese versions of the very same message.[6] Therefore, if we take language as a medium of communication, the use of different languages interacts differently with a person's thinking pattern and causes problems in communication that must be resolved before there can be a meeting of the minds.

Moreover, cultural values are woven into every language. In Asia, silence does not mean consent as it often does in the West. A famous case occurred when British Leyland announced a joint venture with Toyota and later discovered that the Japanese did not share the same understanding of the terms of trade.[7] The Japanese reluctance to disagree openly with the "guest" even at the negotiation table was mistaken as a signal of acceptance. A language conveys the philosophy of life and underlying values of those people who speak that language and this may differ significantly from the philosophy and values of the opposite party in a cross-cultural exchange.

In addition, language carries the burden of history. In a British colony, the ability to speak English often becomes a symbol of prestige. However, this fact reminds the indigenous residents about the painful reality of occupation and dominance. Sometimes, the impact might become even more significant when the countries become independent. The Philippines, most people are surprised to learn, has the fourth-largest English-speaking population in the world. Although there is a national language, Filipino, English is also an official language. Moreover, English is in fact commonly used in practice and is powerful in business and everyday exchanges. It reminds the Filipinos about the American occupation, however, and the significance of American power even after independence. This can cause resentment and resistance to imported goods from the United States. Language can convey much more than people normally care to hear.

Religion. For the purposes of this discussion, we consider religion to be one's understanding of God and God's relationship with humans, with all the implications for life style entailed. Religion is closely related to our perception of the universe and the meaning of life. Because the influence of Christianity has appeared to wane in the West, Westerners have a tendency to ignore the significance of religion in business and international trade. This discussion will provide some examples of the dangers in discounting religious values in international trade among Eastern and Middle Eastern peoples, and also show very briefly in passing how religious values have a greater potential impact on international marketing in the West than we as insiders may recognize. In any case, whatever the extent of religion's influence in any particular culture, marketers should recognize that religious values influence the way people behave both as consumers and as entrepreneurs.[8]

General Effects of Religion. Whatever the beliefs of the marketer, religious values shape the behavior of others with whom business is conducted. Days and hours of operation may restrict business activity: in many Islamic countries businesses must be closed during prayer times and on certain holidays; even in the West, Christian holidays (and even Sundays in some areas) restrict business activities. What consumers will buy is also influenced by religious values: pork products cannot be marketed to Moslems or Jews, and in Christian areas of the West retailers find it advantageous to provide for an increase in seafood sales on Fridays even today.

Ethical values as well are attributable to religious values to a greater or lesser extent in different areas of the world, the fact that ethics is not restricted to religious believers notwithstanding. The practice of bribery varies in different parts of the world partly because of differences in religious world views.

EXHIBIT 15-1

Language Differences Are More Than a Matter of Translation

The Coca-Cola Company has experienced phenomenal success in marketing Coke throughout the world. But its achievements have not always come about smoothly. Cultural and language differences have posed special problems. To take but one particular example, consider the problem of producing advertising posters in a foreign land.

When the company first began marketing in China, it provided local retailers with signs printed in English. The retailers, of course, translated the signs into Chinese using their own characters. The translation chosen, however, was pronounced "Kĕ Cōū Kĕ lă," which unfortunately means "eat the wax tadpole." Although the crispness, cadence, and alliteration of Coca-Cola was captured, the translation was hardly flattering and foretold a certain depression in sales.

Faced with an inappropriate representation of Coca-Cola, researchers went to work to find an alternative. This was no easy task, and only after searching through many thousands of characters were they able to discover a suitable alternative. The characters finally chosen are pronounced "Kĕō Cōū Cŏ lĕă" and mean "may the mouth rejoice."

For Christians influenced by a recent and growing movement to live "in freedom and simplicity," consumption itself is an ethical decision.[9] In Islamic countries, charging or receiving interest on borrowed money is forbidden.

Religion is at the heart of human activities in much of the world. Its impact is far more penetrating than recognition of certain holidays (such as Christmas or Islamic Ramadan) or the existence of certain religious products (church buildings or mosques or religious goods)—although these are already quite significant from the marketing perspective.

Six Specific Examples. If we segment the world by religious beliefs, we have primarily Christianity, Islam, Hinduism, and Buddhism.[10] The dominant religion in a particular country often influences government policy and in other ways molds the macro environment in which a business operates. The first three examples below are taken from Christianity, on the assumption that most readers will have been exposed to them.

Take the example of the movement in Christianity to live simply in an affluent society, alluded to above. For those subscribing to these values, the New Testament concept of stewardship is applied by avoiding luxuries and diverting capital instead to social relief foundations, such as those responding to the needs of the famine-stricken in the Sahel and East Africa. The more such a movement has an influence on buying behavior, the more of a market there will be for necessities and the less of a market there will be for luxuries.

A recent exposition given by Schumacher[11] summarized the values of the "Protestant ethic," another set of Christian values, as recognizing three purposes of human work: (1) to provide necessary and useful goods and services, (2) to enable every one of us to use and thereby perfect our talents and abilities, and (3) to do so in service to, and in cooperation with, others so as to liberate ourselves from our inborn egocentricity. The implications for promotions aimed at groups espousing these values can be inferred.

Many Christians (and for that matter, many people in the West who have been influenced by Christianity, perhaps without knowing it) respond to economic cycles as signs of spiritual well-being or its opposite.[12] Large groups of people adjusting their consumption and managerial lives according to such assumptions about economic cycles in a country can lead to a self-fulfilling prophecy, reinforcing the behavior and disguising the existence of more purely economic factors.[13]

People in the West have become more aware of the influence of Islamic values on doing business in the Middle East, with the rise in power of oil-exporting countries there.[14] In Saudi Arabia, the government has a commitment to bringing business and Islamic values together, making Islamic religious values a significant factor in doing business in that country. Its impact can be institutionalized in surprising ways, as in the case of Islamic banking practices. In Islam, interest is forbidden and is viewed as usury. An Islamic bank does not pay interest, but instead offers a profit-sharing system to depositors. An Islamic bank may not charge interest either. Loans are interest-free, but are subject to service charges calculated by a system that does not resemble interest charges. Most of the deposits are channeled to profit-making investments. The investments themselves are restricted by Islamic values: the Kuwait Finance House (the state's bank) attempted to cut down the costs of consumer goods for Kuwaiti citizens in 1981 by increasing its investments in imports. To put more houses and apartments on the market and reduce the costs of housing, it expanded its real-estate activities.[15] The effect of religion on the practices of business, in general, and banking, in particular, has a long history in the West, going back at least to the Middle Ages.

Religion can be socialized in fundamental ways. The caste system of India is a case in point. Members of each caste have specific occupational and social roles. Companies operating in India may feel the impact of caste distinctions on personnel and staffing policies as well as on buying and selling practices. The castes also act as market segments, each requiring separate marketing strategies.[16] The caste system is disappearing to some extent as India's government implements modernization policies, but insofar as the policies' effects depend on religious acceptance, a true picture of the strength of Hindu caste values is important to the certainty of business planning there, even in the short term.

Religion can have an effect on one's whole economic outlook, as in the example of Buddhism.[17] The keynote to Buddhist economics is simplicity and nonviolence. In this framework, the analysis of standards of living is at odds with that of Western economists. Western economists measure standards of living by the amount of annual consumption and assume that those who consume more are better off than those who consume less. In contrast, the goal of Buddhist economics is to obtain the maximum well-being with the minimum of consumption. The measures used and the results obtained are thus quite different from those a Westerner would use; this raises questions about the appropriateness of standards that might be applied in evaluating stages of economic development in Buddhist countries.

In summary, religious beliefs often serve as conduits for the development of broader values and attitudes, topics we now turn to.

Values and Attitudes. Values and attitudes are at the core of the human psyche and help direct the way one evaluates objects and situations. If we want to make a differentiation, *values* tend to be more central than attitudes. According to Rokeach, values take two forms: terminal values and instrumental values. Terminal values are the end-stages of existence (for example, salvation, a world at peace) that are personally and socially worth striving for. Instrumental values refer to modes of conduct (for example, honesty, courage) that are personally and socially preferable in all situations with respect to all objects.[18] Once a person has internalized a value, it will become a standard for guiding action, for developing and maintaining attitudes towards relevant objects and situations, for justifying one's own and others' actions and attitudes, for morally judging self and others, and for comparing self and others. Values are very much influenced and formed by the religious beliefs one holds. At the same time, one's values are also influenced and formed by the values of the surrounding culture (i.e., the values inherited from generation to generation and from one's peers). Note that values often shape our behavior without our necessarily being aware of the process.

In comparison with values, *attitudes* are not so central. However, they are closer to the context of action. Attitudes refer to the predisposition to respond towards an object or a situation in an evaluative way. An attitude is persistent over time, carrying cognitive, affective, and conative elements. At the same time, attitudes convey a sense of direction and a degree of intensity. When we talk about attitudes, we usually have a specific object (for example, time, work, holiday) or a specific situation (for example, social gatherings) in mind. However, if we talk about the impact of our values towards work and our attitude towards work, it is less meaningful if not impossible to make a fine distinction. We saw in earlier chapters how attitudes relate to consumption. These attitudes can be thought to be based on our fundamental values.

To take a specific example, Howard used Rokeach's framework of values to explain the buying behavior of instant coffee purchasers.[19] When first introduced in the late 1940s, instant coffee carried the symbol of being a "lazy person" product.

Many people knew little about the product and wondered whether they should adopt it. Considerable information was needed in their decision making, and they were said to be in a state of *extensive problem solving* (EPS). Here, terminal values can be seen to bear on their decision (e.g., Am I a good person?). When people in principle accepted instant coffee as a viable consumption alternative but were not sure which brand of instant coffee to buy, they were characterized as being in a state of *limited problem solving* (LPS). In this situation, the instrumental values they held would bear significance in their decision (e.g., How much should I spend on coffee versus other foods?). When people become loyal to a particular brand, they are said to be in a state of *routinized response behavior* (RRB), and little deliberation takes place. They might only check whether the brand is available and whether the price is "right." In this case, the decision does not involve any personal values to speak of. Since Rokeach's framework was developed in the United States, the framework might not be applicable in other cultural contexts.[20] However, we can still expect values of different sorts unique to a particular culture to influence acceptance of different products and brands in that culture.

With respect to the values of managers, both England and Hofstede have performed extensive research from an international perspective.[21] England tried to discover the basic value orientations of managers from five different countries. He discovered that managers in the United States, Japan, and Korea tended to hold a pragmatic orientation, with stress placed on business performance. Managers in Australia, on the other hand, tended to hold a moral orientation, with stress placed on ethical principles in running a business. Hofstede collected data on values from 40 countries. This included data from employees of subsidiaries of one large multinational corporation, people who performed the same tasks, had similar education levels, had different nationalities, and worked in their respective home countries. Hofstede discovered that four dimensions could be used to explain a large portion of the value differences across the countries. The unexplained differences tended to be country specific. The four more-or-less universal dimensions were: (1) individualism versus collectivism (looking after one's own interest and the interest of one's immediate family, or looking after one's in-groups such as one's extended family); (2) power distance (the extent to which the less powerful persons in a society accept inequality in power and consider it as normal); (3) uncertainty avoidance (the extent to which people within that culture were made nervous by situations which they considered unstructured, unclear, or unpredictable, and the extent to which they tried to avoid such situations); and (4) masculinity versus femininity (stressing material success and assertiveness, or stressing quality of life and welfare for the needy). According to Hofstede, managers in the United States were more individualistic than managers in Japan, who were in turn more individualistic than managers in Hong Kong (a Chinese society). In terms of power distance, the reverse order resulted. These two findings may be expected by readers familiar with Japanese culture and the fact that it originally was heavily influenced by China. However, today Japan is more modern than Hong Kong. Thus, Japan stands between Hong Kong and the United States on the individualistic and power dimensions. However, managers in Japan had a much stronger tendency to avoid uncertainty and a much more masculine orientation than managers in the United States, while Hong Kong had the weakest tendency to avoid uncertainty among the three countries and less of a masculine orientation than the others. The findings showed also that the United States stood between Japan and Hong Kong on the dimensions of avoidance of uncertainty and masculinity, somewhat contrary to general impressions, perhaps.

If we subscribe to Hofstede's results, we would expect that managers in the United States tend to hold the principle of management by objectives, while managers in Japan tend to hold the principle of management by consensus. Also, we would expect that managers in the United States tend to deal with each other on a relatively more equal basis, whereas managers in Hong Kong are less egalitarian, and their relationships are more vertical (i.e., hierarchical). Following the same logic, because of a stronger tendency to avoid uncertainty, managers in Japan tend to be more deliberate and thorough in decision making than managers in the United States. Finally, because of the stronger masculine orientation, managers in Japan have an aggressive spirit and a greater desire "to knock out the competitors." This rationale carries significant implications for marketing strategy and implementation.

From the above discussion on values and the impact of values on consumers and managers, you should appreciate that there has been considerable research devoted to the area of values. However, these research efforts tend to be independent of each other, and there exists no coherent theory to unify them. The area of attitude study is somewhat different. In general, scholars subscribe to the view that attitude is a universal concept and consists of cognitive, affective, and conative components (see also Chapter 2). Also when we consider attitudes it is possible to be more concrete and specific than with values. For example, we could talk about attitudes toward Coca-Cola, giving blood, or Ronald Reagan.

The discussion of attitudes toward different objects in different cultures studies the *tradition-modernity dichotomy* perhaps more than any other concept.[22] Ironically, tradition and modernity represent two distinct sets of values that mold people's attitudes towards different objects. The most frequently studied and perhaps most central attitude objects include time, work, wealth, and change. Modernity is symbolized by industrialization, urbanization, rational thinking, specialization and division of labor, and a general emphasis on achievement. The impact of these forces on attitudes in economically advanced countries can be contrasted to the situation in economically less developed countries, where people have a different set of living principles. Because it is thought that more general attitudes toward time, work, wealth, and change trickle down to influence more specific attitudes toward products and even brands, we will focus on these general attitudes at this time. Chapter 2 and other parts of the text have already considered the effects of attitudes on consumption.

In the traditional view of time, the pattern is thought to be a cycle, which may come from people's perception of the regular rotations of the four seasons. In the modern view of time, the pattern is linear, which is perhaps stimulated by our notions of progress, technological development, and the seemingly ever-increasing quality of life. This is reinforced further by the use of watches and clocks, by our interdependence with different people and institutions, and by the working schedule nearly every person must observe. On the consumption side, we see an increasing role for such products as fast foods, microwave ovens, and instant coffee. On the side of business operations, we see photocopying machines, computers, and management techniques such as PERT (Program Evaluation and Review Technique) or CPP (Critical Path Planning). Similar discussions can be extended to the topics of work, wealth, change, and others. Each witnesses strong differences for people in modern as opposed to traditional societies.

McClelland performed a famous study on the impact of achievement motivation (one type of fundamental attitude) on economic development.[23] He drew upon Weber's hypothesis of Protestantism and the spirit of capitalism, and Winterbottom's work on the relationship between independence of parents and their child-rearing practices and motivation in their offspring. McClelland proposed the framework shown in Figure 15-1. The framework summarizes how general values and attitudes reinforced in a Protestant environment lead to the more specific values and attitudes associated with "the spirit of capitalism."

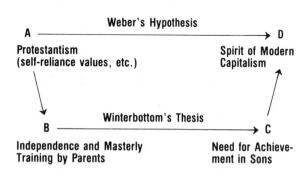

Figure 15-1. McClelland's integrative framework

SOURCE: Derived from David McClelland, *The Achieving Society* (New York: The Free Press), 1961, p. 47. Reprinted with the permission of the publisher.

McClelland's framework fits into our discussion very well and demonstrates the interrelationships among religion, values, attitudes, and business activities. Protestantism is a religion, which imparts the value of self-reliance and is related to the parents' child-rearing values like independence and mastery training. In turn, these child-rearing values impart achievement motivation in children which, in turn, induces a positive attitude toward work and the enterprising spirit. This positive attitude carries significant impact on all kinds of business activities as it serves as a motivating force for individuals and an incentive/control mechanism for managers.

In other cultures, less individualistic and more group-based values might serve as the underlying forces governing economic and business practices.

Social Organizations. In every society, language, religion, values, and attitudes must be preserved, promoted, or changed through some social mechanisms. In this regard, religious organizations, schools, social groups, and families function as the pillars of society.

The family is usually the most significant social organization for developing values and channeling social change in an Oriental society. Chinese society is an example. Religion, education, production, consumption, and even recreation were at one time all performed within the family.[24] The extended family (i.e., several generations and branches of related people with the same last name) would live together and thus become a factor for stability in society. However, when we look at the situation of Hong Kong, a modern Chinese society, we can see that there is significant deviation from the traditional mode. Most inhabitants in Hong Kong came from mainland China, carrying with them traditional Chinese values. However, in the course of time, the nuclear family (mother, father, and children) came to supplant the extended family. From 1960 to 1973, the percentage of nuclear families in Hong Kong rose from 63 percent to 73.5 percent. During the same period, the percentage of extended families declined from 14 percent to 2.5 percent.[25] This change was accelerated by the housing policies of the Hong Kong Government, who only recognized the immediate family as legitimate members of the family. Thus, as more and more people moved into public housing (at present, more than 50 percent of the population), the nuclear family firmly became the mode. Education, of course, was provided by public and private schools rather than the family. Further, in the course of time, there were more schools using English instead of Chinese as the medium of teaching. In the 1950s, the ratio between English-speaking and Chinese-speaking secondary schools was about 1 to 3. At present, the ratio has drastically reversed to about 10 to 1.

Since more than half of the secondary schools have a Christian affiliation, religion plays a significant role in Hong Kong. This tends to get multiplied as one moves up the education ladder. For instance, a study reported in 1974 shows that among women who received university education, 72 percent were Protestants and Catholics. However, among women who only received a primary education, the percentage was only 12.4 percent. With all of the above changes in social organization for Hong Kong, it should not be surprising to discover that the prevalent values in Hong Kong were very different from the traditional Chinese values along the tradition-modernity attitude scale.

Japan is another prominent example. The structure of the Japanese society has grown up around the structure and values of the Japanese family.[26] As with traditional Chinese values, the Japanese stress reverence for ancestors, the obligation to continue the unbroken family line, loyalty, and filial piety. By learning their place in the family, the Japanese learn their place in society. Up to the age of about five, the child receives considerable affection and indulgence. However, from five years on, children face the threat of being rejected by their parents if they do not conform to the parents' standards of behavior. The Japanese learn to depend on the group for their self-esteem. The fear of rejection and the need for approval and affection encourage a high standard of achievement. The education system in Japan also reflects the values of the traditional family. Students feel strong competitive pressures at all levels in Japanese education. Graduates of top universities occupy important posts in government and industry. Graduates of top secondary schools have a better chance to get into the top universities. The pressures can be felt even down to the kindergarten level, where written entrance examinations are often employed. In the schools and the universities, students learn to develop a social identity, and concepts of group loyalty and power take root.

America, too, feels the impact of social forces. For instance, values inherited from the founding fathers continue to be preserved and transmitted through churches, schools, government, and the larger culture. Despite cracks in the edifice, these values find their way into the everyday lives of most Americans.[27] Moreover, we see examples of purposeful attention given to certain values. For instance, McClelland and his colleagues launched the Harvard Entrepreneurial Motivation Project, which was carried out even in India.[28] Such programs mold the values of people and affect the way business is done. Of course, one must consider the appropriateness of any efforts to import or export one culture's value system to another's.

Economics

Economics has perhaps always been a significant factor in business studies. Even today, many people consider economics as a synonym for business. From the viewpoint of a business person involved in international marketing, international economics (especially international trade) provides a theoretical framework for interpreting the direction and initiation of international marketing activities. Much of modern economics is built on the foundation of the so-called rational man. As long as the profit-making motive remains the dominant driving force of business activities, economics remains a powerful perspective to interpret business behavior. At the same time, since economics is relatively more developed than other social science disciplines, it is easier to trace the stream of theoretical attempts to explain and predict the international marketing phenomenon.

According to traditional economic theory, there are two kinds of markets: product markets and money markets. For the sake of simplicity, we will limit our discussion to the "pure" theory of international trade (excluding "monetary" theory), although we fully recognize the significance and the impact of changing monetary policy on international trade. When we discuss the political environment, we will touch upon issues related to monetary policy. For an authoritative documentation of this group of theories, see Bhagwati.[29]

Managers in charge of international marketing activities need to understand and predict the future direction of international trade so that they can more effectively plan and exploit business opportunities. Let us consider some of the central economic forces in this regard.

Comparative Advantages/Costs. Adam Smith considered the significance of foreign trade more than 200 years ago.[30] He noticed that the land and labor of England produced generally more corn, woollens, and hardware than the home market demanded. The surplus part had to be sent abroad and exchanged for something for which a demand existed at home. Scholars in international trade call this the concept of *absolute advantages*. Because of specialization and the division of labor, nations can exchange a commodity for which they have an edge in production for a commodity for which they do not have an edge. This can be demonstrated easily in Table 15-1. Country A can use one unit of factor input (e.g., labor, land, capital) to produce 10 units of Product X, while Country B can only produce 5 units. On the other hand, Country B can use one unit of factor input to produce 10 units of Product Y, while Country A can only produce 5 units. When there is no specialization and division of labor, and when each country has 20 units of factor input and evenly allocates the factor inputs to two kinds of production activities, Country A will get 100 units of Product X and 50 units of Product Y, while Country B will get 50 units of Product X and 100 units of Product Y. However, if there is specialization and division of labor *between* nations, Country A can produce 200 units of Product X and Country B can produce 200 units of Product Y. If the two countries trade with each other, Country A gives 80 units of Product X to Country B and takes back 80 units of Product Y, and both countries are better off than before when there was no specialization and division of labor between nations. This advantage can only be realized through international trade.

TABLE 15-1
International Trade and Absolute Advantages

| | PRODUCTIVITY PATTERN | | NO SPECIALIZATION AND DIVISION OF LABOR, AND EVEN ALLOCATION OF 20 UNITS OF FACTOR INPUTS | | SPECIALIZATION AND DIVISION OF LABOR | | | |
| | | | | | Complete Specialization, and before Trading | | After Trading, 80 Units of Product X for 80 Units of Product Y | |
	Product X	Product Y	Product X	Product Y	Product X	Product Y	Product X	Product Y
Country A	10	5	100	50	200	0	120	80
Country B	5	10	50	100	0	200	80	120

David Ricardo proposed an even more general theory, the theory of *comparative advantage*, to explain and predict the pattern of trade across nations.[31] Ricardo assumed a two product–one factor input (labor) model, constant returns to scale, and the pretrade product/price ratio as a function exclusively of the output factor ratios contained in the production functions. (The same assumptions were implicitly made in the Adam Smith illustration.) Ricardo claimed that if a_x and a_y were the output factor ratios for Country A and b_x and b_y for Country B in production activities X and Y, respectively, Country A would export Product X and import Product Y if $a_x/a_y > b_x/b_y$. This can be easily demonstrated in the example shown in Table 15-2. Country A can use one unit of factor input to produce either 120 units of Product X or 100 units of Product Y, while Country B can use one unit of factor input to produce either 80 units of Product X or 90 units of Product Y. It seems that there is no need for Country A to trade with Country B. However, according to the Ricardian hypothesis, since $120/100 > 80/90$, it would be good for Country A to export some Product X and import some Product Y. If both countries have 20 units of factor inputs, both evenly allocate them to two production activities, and there is no trade, Country A will have 1,200 units of Product X and 1,000 units of Product Y, while Country B will have 800 units of Product X and 900 units of Product Y. However, if the countries decide to undergo specialization and a division of labor, and to depend on trade, they both can benefit. Country A may allocate 18 units of factor inputs to produce Product X and 2 units to produce Product Y, while Country B may allocate all 20 units to produce Product Y. If the two countries then trade with each other, Country A will be willing to use 880 units of Product X to exchange for 850 units of Product Y from Country B. After trading, Country A will have 1,280 units of Product X and 1,050 units of Product Y, while Country B will have 880 units of Product X and 950 units of Product Y. Again, both countries are better off than when there was no trade and no specialization and division of labor. The concept of absolute advantage is a special case of the notion of comparative advantage.

TABLE 15-2
International Trade and Comparative Advantages

	PRODUCTIVITY PATTERN		NO SPECIALIZATION AND DIVISION OF LABOR, AND EVEN ALLOCATION OF 20 UNITS OF FACTOR INPUTS		SPECIALIZATION AND DIVISION OF LABOR			
					Country A Allocates 18 Units of Factor Inputs for Product X and 2 Units for Product Y, While Country B Allocates All to Product Y		After Trading 880 Units of Product X for 850 Units of Product Y	
	Product X	Product Y	Product X	Product Y	Product X	Product Y	Product X	Product Y
Country A	120	100	1,200	1,000	2,160	200	1,280	1,050
Country B	80	90	800	900	0	1,800	880	950

The Ricardian hypothesis was proposed in the mid-1800s. There have been many subsequent elaborations, refinements, empirical testings, and discussions. However, this basic concept is still relevant and applicable today. Based on the "strong" (original) hypothesis, we can derive a weaker proposition, which can, however, explain a broader range of phenomena: There will be a hierarchy in which all products are ranked in terms of their comparative factor-productivity ratios such that it will always be true that each of a country's exports will have a higher factor-productivity ratio than each of its imports. This proposition corresponds well with the trade pattern in the United States.[32]

Factor Endowment. The Ricardian hypothesis makes the factor supply irrelevant in determining the trade pattern. Heckscher and Ohlin present an alternative way to explain the trade pattern and claim that international differences in factor endowments are the crucial elements determining comparative advantages.[33] The Heckscher-Ohlin theorem states that a country's exports intensively use the country's abundant factors. This concept introduces a two-factor model incorporating capital and labor as the basic factors of production. Thus, according to the theory, economically advanced countries will tend to export products for which a heavy capital commitment is required to produce. Less developed countries will tend to export products that are labor intensive. The factor endowment theory is considered an explanation of the effects of comparative advantages, since the rationale is logically consistent with Ricardo's theory. Yet, the new theorem enables us to understand even more about international trade.

Leontief attempted to ascertain the factor intensities of the average exports and competitive imports in the United States. His research revealed the startling result that exports are labor intensive while competitive imports are capital intensive.[34] The phenomenon is called the Leontief Paradox,

and it is reproduced in Table 15-3. Leontief used the 1947 and 1951 import and export data of the United States and specified the requirements of capital and labor for the import/export data in these two years. If we take k as the capital/labor ratio, k_{imp} and k_{exp} as the capital-labor ratios for import and export product categories, respectively, one would expect that $k_{imp}/k_{exp} < 1$ in both years. However, as we can see from Table 15-3, the capital/labor ratio for import items over export items was greater than 1 in both 1947 and 1951.

TABLE 15-3

Leontief's Data for U.S. Trade Statistics after World War II: Domestic Capital and Labor Requirements per Million Dollars of U.S. Exports and Competitive Import Replacement of Average 1947 and 1951 Composition

	1947		1951	
	Exported	*Imported*	*Exported*	*Imported*
Capital (1947 U.S.$)	2,550,780	3,091,339	2,256,800	2,303,400
Labor (man-year)	182.31	170.00	173.91	167.81

k: capital-labor ratio 1947 $k_{imp}/k_{exp} = 1.30$
1951 $k_{imp}/k_{exp} = 1.106$

Since the United States is considered capital abundant by any measure, the above pattern seems to contradict the Heckscher-Ohlin theorem. One explanation for the paradox given by Leontief was to claim that labor embodied (human) capital. Thus, it changes the pattern of factor abundance and factor intensities. When Leontief separated labor into agricultural and nonagricultural labor (the latter being an indicator of human capital), he discovered that the agricultural labor over nonagricultural labor ratio was lower in export items and higher in import replacement items. Thus, the ideas of comparative advantage and factor endowment remain as dominant explanatory concepts in international trade.

There have been subsequent attempts to explain international patterns. One significant proposal has been made by Linder.[35] He differentiated trade in primary products from trade in manufactures. Trade in primary products is determined by natural resource intensity. Trade in manufactures, on the other hand, is determined by technological superiority, managerial skills, and economies of scale. Thus, although the concept of comparative advantages is relevant, and comparative advantages are determined by factor endowments, this differentiation opened up the possibility of changing factor endowments, and thus, changing comparative advantages, which is especially significant in the trade of manufactures. This becomes even more significant when one realizes that the terms of trade for manufactures, in comparison with the terms of trade for primary products, is better for sellers, in terms of higher prices and better price stability. For less developed countries who desire to industrialize, the distinction between primary products and manufactures can be used to gain changes in comparative advantages in their favor.

Changing Patterns of International Competitiveness. Keesing examined a broad group of manufacturers and discovered that the pattern of trade is determined principally by the relative abundance of skilled and unskilled labor. Comparative advantages in the United States center in industries exhibiting a high percentage of professional labor and a low percentage of unskilled labor.[36] Keesing argued that differences in labor skills are sufficient to induce a persistent pattern of trade among nations because of historical differences in the supply of skilled labor (e.g., a need for skilled workers to train another generation of skilled workers), cultural differences in the desire and aptitude for the acquisition of skills, unequal incomes (a high correlation exists, for example, between income and education opportunity and skill acquisition), selective migration policies (rich countries typically accept only highly skilled labor from poor countries), and the previous trading pattern due to the division of labor (there is less of a chance for skill development in poorer countries). Keesing also pointed out that the situation could be changed by manipulating education, language, and migration policies in order to alter the relative endowment of skilled labor within and between countries.

Another study examined 19 industries in the United States and looked at research and development and the export performance of these industries.[37] It was concluded that there is a positive relationship between emphasis on research and development and export performance. Therefore, research advancement and technological know-how constitute a determining factor for export performance in manufacturing industries.

One researcher noticed that the competitiveness of production in a particular industry changes in the course of time.[38] The product life cycle concept was used to explain the changing relative competitiveness among the United States, advanced countries, and less developed countries. For new products, only the United States tended to possess the required technology and the market potential sufficiently large to sustain supply. Other advanced countries had much less demand for new products, although this tended to grow and eventually justify local production. For mature products, certain advanced countries tended to pick up the technology and produce at a lower cost. This would be accompanied by a decline in production activities in the United States and an increase in production activities in still other advanced countries. At the same time, less developed countries would experience a growing demand for the mature products, and this would eventually justify some local production. For standardized products, less developed countries would often pick up the technology and enjoy the best competitive advantages. When this happens, the United States became a net importer, and production activities in other advanced countries began to decline. In sum, competitiveness in a particular industry tends to occur first within the United States, then in other advanced countries, and finally in less developed countries, as a product progresses from introduction to maturity and finally to standardization. Of course, exceptions to this pattern frequently occur and more research is required to identify all the forces going on.

Based on the above discussion, one can see that a prerequisite for successful exporting in a particular industry is the possession of technology and low cost and skilled labor. However, competitive changes are not always unidirectional. One researcher investigated the case of electronic calculators and found a two-way competition between the United States and Japan from 1967 to 1977.[39] The relative shares of major producers in world calculator production are reported in Table 15-4. Notice that market share shifts seem to occur in three distinct phases. From 1967 to 1971, the Japanese share of the calculator market increased from 14 percent to 54 percent while the United States share fell from 25 percent to 3 percent! From 1971 to 1974, the United States regrouped and gained a share of 30 percent, while the Japanese fell to 44 percent. From 1974 to 1977, Japan again became dominant, achieving a 51 percent share to the United States' 21 percent. The Japanese success in the first phase can be explained by (1) the proportion of labor cost in production (30 percent of total production cost) and the cost of labor (one fifth of the rate in the United

States), (2) the ability to replace several thousand discrete components with less than 100 integrated circuits, and (3) a willingness to build the electromechanical calculator market and push electronic calculators. The American dominance in the second phase can be explained by the ability to integrate all the necessary circuit functions in a single, small chip. At that time, the cost of components and materials increased from 56 percent to 68 percent, while labor costs were reduced to 10 percent of the total cost of production. Also the wage rate in the United States as a percentage of the Japanese wage rate dropped from 500 percent to about 200 percent. Japanese dominance in the third phase can be explained by an innovation known as the "calculator on a substate" (COS), which made the assembly of electronic calculators even simpler than in the past. This example shows that whoever controls the technology and the necessary skills controls the secret of international competitiveness. It also shows the significance of technology transfer, innovation, and research and development in the overall productivity equation.

TABLE 15-4
Relative Shares of Major Producers in World Calculator Production

YEAR	WORLD PRODUCTION IN PERCENTAGES	SHARES OF INDIVIDUAL COUNTRIES IN PERCENTAGES			
		United States	Japan	West Germany	Italy
1967	100	25	14	13	21
1968	100	22	40	13	20
1969	100	21	28	13	16
1970	100	14	41	10	16
1971	100	3	54	7	4
1972	100	20	50	5	7
1973	100	29	48	2	4
1974	100	30	44	2	2
1975	100	19	52	1	1
1976	100	19	56	1	0
1977	100	21	51	1	0

SOURCE: Badiul A. Majumdar, ''Technology Transfers and International Competitiveness: The Case of Electronic Calculators,'' *Journal of International Business Studies* (Fall 1980): 104. Reprinted with the permission of the publisher.

Politics

As an academic discipline, politics is perhaps not as highly developed as economics. However, the political environment can have a profound impact on international marketing activities. As with the discussion of environmental variables, we will take the nation as the basic unit of analysis.[40] This is a natural perspective to take since it is implied in the term *international marketing*. In this section of the chapter, we consider the role that a government plays in international marketing, political stability, cross-national organizations related to international trade, and the trading networks among nations.

The Role of Government. Political ideology is a starting point for defining a nation. Capitalist countries place primary emphasis on exchange as the guiding principle for handling economic activities. By preserving freedom of choice and incorporating available alternatives, individuals are believed to achieve the highest welfare under the market-based system. A respect for individual rights becomes the foundation of social operations. Communist countries place relatively more emphasis on command as the guiding principle for handling economic activities. By centralizing decision-making power, governments are thought to best act on behalf of all people and assure social justice. A respect for collective survival becomes the foundation of social operations. The clash of ideologies subtly puts trade barriers between nations with differing ideologies. East-West trade, by and large, remains a growing but undeveloped potential. Moreover, the trade that does exist is often at the mercy of political struggles. The act of trading with the so-called enemy often becomes a "political football."[41] However, political ideologies are not static. U.S.-China trade is an example. A few years ago, the United States placed an embargo on trade with China because of the Korean War. Then in the 1970s, the ice was broken largely through the efforts of the Nixon administration. China, in the post–Gang of Four period (since 1971), launched four modernization plans with emphasis placed on international trade development. Despite ups and downs, trade between China and the United States has shown a steady upward trend. Neither country has changed its respective political ideology in a fundamental way. However, both "partners" changed how they implemented their policies and thereby helped the thaw in relations between them. China, in particular, has undergone a revolution of sorts in the way it now approaches economic and business practices.

The role of a government is not, of course, restricted to the preservation of a political ideology. There are many other ways to regulate trading activities. Fiscal policy, monetary policy, and trading policies are additional levers for affecting trade. *Fiscal policy* refers to government participation in buying and selling in product markets. Governments have enormous purchasing powers even in free market economies. Through bidding policies and specification formulation, for example, governments can show favoritism to domestic or international firms. Whenever political considerations become important, economic competitiveness often takes a back seat.

Monetary policy refers to government intervention in the money market. This is particularly relevant in international trade. Whenever a government exercises exchange control, international trading activities are at the mercy of bureaucrats. Firms that want to import into a country must be on the favored list in order to get needed supplies of materials and equipment. On the other hand, firms that want to export to a country must also be on the favored list in order to sell their products there. Moreover, even if one operates exclusively within a particular foreign country, the firm will find it difficult to remit profits to the home country because of scarcity of foreign exchange.

Firms operating under an exchange control system sometimes find ways to get around the problem, however. For example, Firm A in Country X may have generous grants in buying necessity items (e.g., food products), and limited grants in buying luxury items (e.g., cosmetics). Firm A may ask Firm B in Country Y, which sells necessity items, to raise the list price. On the surface, Firm A pays all currencies for the necessity items. In reality, Firm B agrees to credit the "surplus" amount to Firm B's account in Country Y. Firm A can import the desired amount of luxury items from Firm C in Country Y at a much lower list price and pay with a limited amount of foreign exchange grants. Firm C, in reality, gets the other portion of the actual payment from Firm A's bank account in Country Y. Thus Firm A can get around the exchange control. Firm B and Firm C agree to do so because they want to get the orders from Firm A. This allegedly unethical if not illegal practice has been known to occur frequently.

Another impact of monetary policy is related to the fluctuations of *exchange rates*. When a government devalues its currency, there will be a disturbance in international trading activities. In general, when a nation devalues its currency, the government is able to encourage exports and discourage imports. However, even for the export trade of the country devaluing its currency, the shape is like a J curve. The export amount in the short run will decline before it will increase. From the viewpoint of a firm in the country experiencing a devaluation, exchange rate fluctuations produce uncertainty in future business activities and discourage commitments to international marketing (little or no effect is typically felt on the firm's domestic marketing activities). Still another impact of monetary policy is related to the *interest rate* that the central bank in a country fixes. Interest rates in different countries determine the directions of money flows among nations, which in turn influences demand and supply of various currencies and affects exchange rates among different currencies in the exchange market. An export manager who obtained a profitable sales order may find himself later suffering a loss when he or she converts the earned foreign currency back into the currency of his or her home country.

The *trading policy* of a country is most directly related to international marketing activities. *Tariffs* are a special tax on imported products and thus affect their competitiveness in the market. This will influence the relative market share between imported products and domestic products. At the same time, different tariff scales may be imposed on different kinds of products (e.g., high tariffs for luxury items and low or no tariffs for necessities). Further, different tariff scales may be imposed on the same kind of products from different countries of origin (e.g., commonwealth countries favor each other while discriminating against noncommonwealth countries). Thus, trading policies also affect the relative competitiveness among products from different countries.

A *quota* is a restriction on the quantity of a product exported or imported. The impact is absolute. The most famous example in world trade is the MFA (Multi-Fibre Arrangement), which will be discussed later in the chapter. In general, a quota restriction encourages exporting countries to develop higher-quality products.

Perhaps the most basic trading policy a country has to make is whether it wants to take an export-led or import-substitution posture. Even among countries adopting free market systems, different strategies may be chosen for economic growth. For example, in the 1950s, Hong Kong adopted an outward-looking (i.e., export-led) policy. Hong Kong is not a country and lacks many of the conditions needed for economic self-sufficiency. It is natural for her to gravitate to an export-led policy. Taiwan and South Korea, on the other hand, have large national defense burdens, yet are relatively self-sufficient in an economic sense. An import-substitution policy might be to either of their advantages. As their economies have strengthened further, they have changed their trading policy to an export-led orientation in order to speed up economic progress. This accounts for their somewhat later adoption of an outward focus than Hong Kong.

Governments have varied rationales and constraints with respect to setting national policies. Some decisions that may be viewed as unwise from an economic perspective may be viewed as quite appropriate when one takes into account national priorities and beliefs in social welfare. Firms involved in international marketing activities have to work with these givens, avoid the unfavorable impacts, and exploit the opportunities.

Political Instability. The previous section discussed various aspects of government and assumed that it will continue to function more or less as it always has. What if the government falls? Between perfect stability and complete chaos, there is a wide range of threatening order such as general strikes, riots, martial law, or even civil war. Events of this type are generally beyond the coverage of export credit insurance. They pose special problems for firms operating in foreign countries and not merely exporting to them. Political scientists have developed measures of political instability that are applicable as inputs to some international marketing decisions.[42]

The Russett Measure counts the number of deaths per one million population that occurred as a result of political violence. The Banks and Textor Measure classifies a country into one of the four categories: (1) government generally stable since World War I, (2) government generally stable since World War II, (3) government moderately stable since World War II, and (4) government unstable since World War II. The Feierabend and Feierabend Index is a 7-point scale of political instability based upon the number and intensity of political activities of a nation. A total of 30 types of events have been identified and assigned different weights for measurement purposes in this index.

Obviously, a straight application of any single index of instability will not provide a definitive measure of political activity. In general, such paper-and-pencil exercises serve to help identify trouble spots but cannot provide an in-depth indication of political conditions. One study considered a number of approaches and presented an example of the assessment of the political instability of Indonesia.[43] The approaches included "grand tour," "old hands," Delphi techniques, and quantitative methods. In the grand tour method, a firm dispatches an executive or a team of people on an inspection tour. Some first-hand experience of the political environment often helps decision makers understand the more obvious problems. The "old hands" technique consists of solicitation of opinions from seasoned educators, diplomats, journalists, or business people. In the Delphi method, experts are again queried but in a different way. People are brought together and a moderator poses questions to the experts until a consensus is reached. Quantitative techniques in political risk assessment are based on historical and current information to describe more fully the underlying relationships affecting a nation state. Mathematical and/or statistical models are usually employed. The measures of political instability mentioned earlier are cases in point. Usually, firms use more than one approach to achieve a cross-check. If findings from different approaches agree with each other, the conclusion has more credibility.

International Organizations. When one talks about the political environment, it is essential to consider the situation beyond the national level. This is especially relevant for international marketing since transactions will be affected by the relationships between the foreign country and the home country as well as by other third-party arrangements. There are many relevant international organizations to consider. Because of space limitations, we will introduce only the most significant ones here.

The General Agreement on Tariffs and Trade (GATT) is probably the most relevant international organization regulating international trade. Since each nation is sovereign in setting its own trading policies, there is always the possibility of unilateral and arbitrary actions that pose conflicts of interest and incompatibilities, thereby minimizing international trade. The GATT can be said to be largely a product of the influence of the United States and reflects certain views that dominated the thinking on trading matters of U.S. diplomats in the 1940s.[44] These officials originally sought to establish a much grander institution, which was to be called the International Trade Organization. The idea first appeared in a pamphlet entitled *Proposals for Expansion of World Trade and Employment,* which was amended in successive conferences from 1946 to 1948 in London, New York, Geneva, and Havana. The final version was known as the Havana Charter, but was never approved.

Meanwhile, the General Agreement drawn up in Geneva in October 1947 and designed to record the results of a tariff conference, became the founding document for GATT. *The GATT arrangement strives to encourage free trade among all participating nations for the sake of global welfare.* Among other goals, GATT tries to abolish quota restrictions, to reduce tariffs, and to operate on a principle of nondiscrimination. Another aspect of GATT is known as the concept for consultation. When trade disputes arise, GATT provides a forum for consultation and peaceful settlement. In general, one may say that GATT contributed considerably to international trade expansion in the post–World War II period.

However, power politics sometimes continues to function. The Multi-Fibre Arrangement represents a case falling outside the governing spirit of GATT. The MFA served to protect developed nations at the expense of less developed nations who hoped to export their clothing wares.[45]

The United Nations Conference on Trade and Development (UNCTAD) is another potentially important international organizational directly related to world trade. Its aim is to seek fair prices for primary products through commodity agreements. Developed countries usually export manufactured goods, and less developed countries usually export primary products. In general, the terms of trade for primary products is less favorable than for manufactured goods. UNCTAD tries to set right the imbalance. To date, however, it has been largely unsuccessful. The only primary product that sells at a premium price is oil. But this resulted more through the efforts of the oil exporting countries and OPEC (the Organization of Petroleum Exporting Countries) than any influence of UNCTAD.[46]

Perhaps the most influential international organization indirectly related to world trade is the International Monetary Fund (IMF), which was established at Bretton Woods in 1944. The aim of the IMF is to gain stability of exchange rates. For many years, member countries self-declared an explicit value for their respective currencies and saw to it that it did not vary by more than one percent in either direction. Moreover, member countries agreed not to make any large changes without going through the prescribed procedures set by the IMF.[47] Such a commitment served to reduce risks related to fluctuating exchange rates. At present, all major industrial countries let their currencies "float" according to the demand and supply forces in the exchange market. However, the IMF still lends money to help countries with balance of payment problems, and it still presents a forum for international monetary cooperation. A stable exchange rate removes uncertainty in international trade and encourages international marketing activities.

Various regional economic associations play an important role in international trade. Two key ones in this regard are the European Economic Community (EEC) and the Association of East Asian nations (ASEAN). The EEC is a significant political and economic power in its own right. At present, there are 12 members: Belgium, the Netherlands, Luxemburg, West Germany, France, Italy, the United Kingdom, the Republic of Ireland, Denmark, Greece, Spain, and Portugal. The first 6 in the list were the founding members. Together, their political and economic power is comparable with that of the United States. The ASEAN is much less powerful in comparison with the EEC. Members of ASEAN include Indonesia, Malaysia, the Philippines, Singapore, and Thailand. As an interested nonmember, Japan invests heavily in these countries.[48] Moreover, the Asian Pacific Basin is one of the most rapidly developing regions in the world today and therefore should grow in its influence and importance. In general, we may note that regional economic associations encourage systematic reductions of trade barriers among member nations but at the same time pose barriers to trade for nonmember nations.

Trading Networks among Nations. The interlocking relationship among nations is usually more complicated than it appears. A case in point can be seen in a recent study of trading relationships among nations in the world.[49] Countries were organized in a hierarchical structure based on their direct and indirect trading relationships. Four reference points were chosen: 1951, 1961, 1971, and 1976. A country is viewed as dependent on another country and in the latter's trading framework when the former's largest export market is with the latter country. When two countries have each other as their largest export market, the country that exports the greater amount to the other country is termed the dependent country and is in the other country's trading network. The results of the study are summarized in Figures 15-2 through 15-5 where the dependent countries are shown listed below their respective dominant trading partners.

Based on Figures 15-2 to 15-5, we can make the following observations:

1 The U.S.S.R. and the other communist countries form a block of their own with the U.S.S.R. heading up the hierarchy. A significant change occurred when China left this block in 1971 and joined the U.S. block through Hong Kong.

2 The U.S. heads up the largest block. The main trading network for the U.S. is with the Latin American countries, although connections with Canada, Japan, and the United Kingdom are important.

(Text continues on p. 644.)

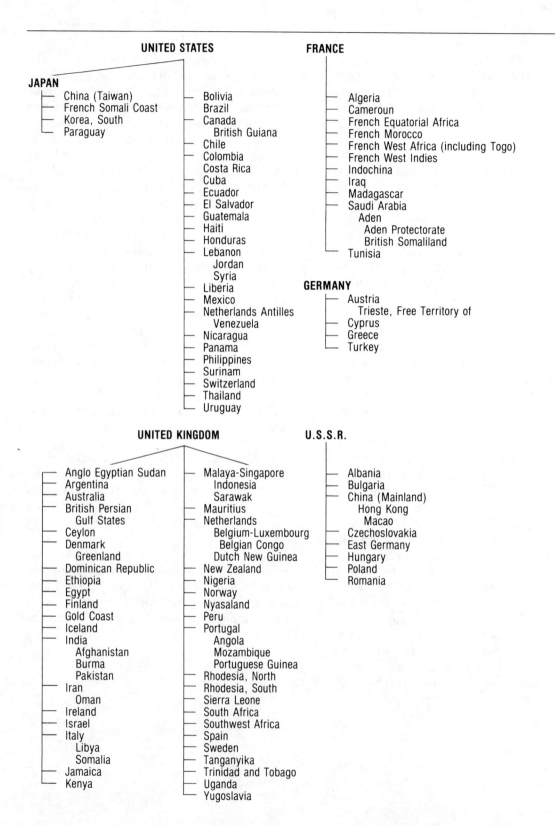

UNITED STATES

JAPAN
- China (Taiwan)
- French Somali Coast
- Korea, South
- Paraguay

- Bolivia
- Brazil
- Canada
  - British Guiana
- Chile
- Colombia
- Costa Rica
- Cuba
- Ecuador
- El Salvador
- Guatemala
- Haiti
- Honduras
- Lebanon
  - Jordan
  - Syria
- Liberia
- Mexico
- Netherlands Antilles
  - Venezuela
- Nicaragua
- Panama
- Philippines
- Surinam
- Switzerland
- Thailand
- Uruguay

FRANCE
- Algeria
- Cameroun
- French Equatorial Africa
- French Morocco
- French West Africa (including Togo)
- French West Indies
- Indochina
- Iraq
- Madagascar
- Saudi Arabia
  - Aden
    - Aden Protectorate
    - British Somaliland
- Tunisia

GERMANY
- Austria
  - Trieste, Free Territory of
- Cyprus
- Greece
- Turkey

UNITED KINGDOM
- Anglo Egyptian Sudan
- Argentina
- Australia
- British Persian
  - Gulf States
- Ceylon
- Denmark
  - Greenland
- Dominican Republic
- Ethiopia
- Egypt
- Finland
- Gold Coast
- Iceland
- India
  - Afghanistan
  - Burma
  - Pakistan
- Iran
  - Oman
- Ireland
- Israel
- Italy
  - Libya
  - Somalia
- Jamaica
- Kenya

- Malaya-Singapore
  - Indonesia
  - Sarawak
- Mauritius
- Netherlands
  - Belgium-Luxembourg
  - Belgian Congo
  - Dutch New Guinea
- New Zealand
- Nigeria
- Norway
- Nyasaland
- Peru
- Portugal
  - Angola
  - Mozambique
  - Portuguese Guinea
- Rhodesia, North
- Rhodesia, South
- Sierra Leone
- South Africa
- Southwest Africa
- Spain
- Sweden
- Tanganyika
- Trinidad and Tobago
- Uganda
- Yugoslavia

U.S.S.R.
- Albania
- Bulgaria
- China (Mainland)
  - Hong Kong
  - Macao
- Czechoslovakia
- East Germany
- Hungary
- Poland
- Romania

Figure 15-2. World trading networks: 1951

Source: Drawn from Robert Green and James Lutz, *The United States and World Trade: Changing Patterns and Dimensions* (New York: Praeger Publishers, 1978).

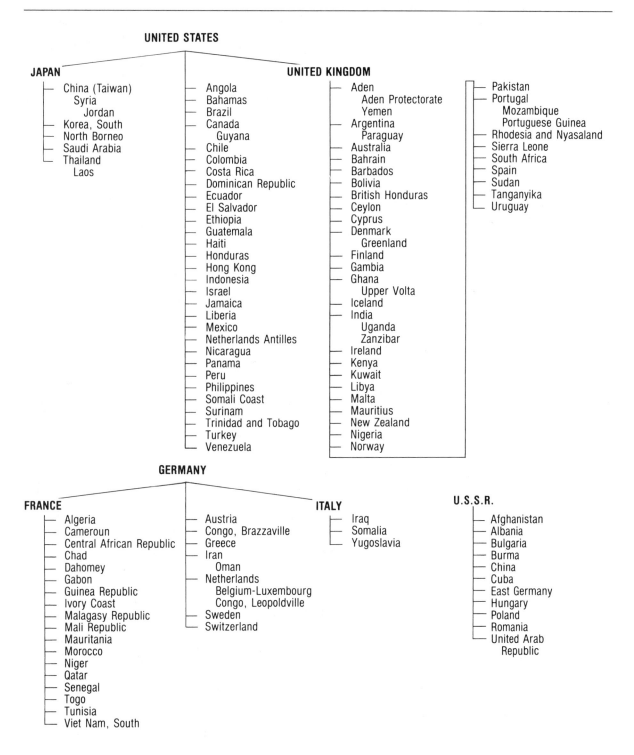

UNITED STATES

JAPAN
- China (Taiwan)
  - Syria
  - Jordan
- Korea, South
- North Borneo
- Saudi Arabia
- Thailand
  - Laos

UNITED KINGDOM
- Angola
- Bahamas
- Brazil
- Canada
  - Guyana
- Chile
- Colombia
- Costa Rica
- Dominican Republic
- Ecuador
- El Salvador
- Ethiopia
- Guatemala
- Haiti
- Honduras
- Hong Kong
- Indonesia
- Israel
- Jamaica
- Liberia
- Mexico
- Netherlands Antilles
- Nicaragua
- Panama
- Peru
- Philippines
- Somali Coast
- Surinam
- Trinidad and Tobago
- Turkey
- Venezuela

- Aden
  - Aden Protectorate
  - Yemen
- Argentina
  - Paraguay
- Australia
- Bahrain
- Barbados
- Bolivia
- British Honduras
- Ceylon
- Cyprus
- Denmark
  - Greenland
- Finland
- Gambia
- Ghana
  - Upper Volta
- Iceland
- India
  - Uganda
  - Zanzibar
- Ireland
- Kenya
- Kuwait
- Libya
- Malta
- Mauritius
- New Zealand
- Nigeria
- Norway

- Pakistan
- Portugal
  - Mozambique
  - Portuguese Guinea
- Rhodesia and Nyasaland
- Sierra Leone
- South Africa
- Spain
- Sudan
- Tanganyika
- Uruguay

GERMANY

FRANCE
- Algeria
- Cameroun
- Central African Republic
- Chad
- Dahomey
- Gabon
- Guinea Republic
- Ivory Coast
- Malagasy Republic
- Mali Republic
- Mauritania
- Morocco
- Niger
- Qatar
- Senegal
- Togo
- Tunisia
- Viet Nam, South

- Austria
- Congo, Brazzaville
- Greece
- Iran
  - Oman
- Netherlands
  - Belgium-Luxembourg
  - Congo, Leopoldville
- Sweden
- Switzerland

ITALY
- Iraq
- Somalia
- Yugoslavia

U.S.S.R.
- Afghanistan
- Albania
- Bulgaria
- Burma
- China
- Cuba
- East Germany
- Hungary
- Poland
- Romania
- United Arab
  Republic

Figure 15-3. World trading networks: 1961

SOURCE: Drawn from Robert Green and James Lutz, *The United States and World Trade: Changing Patterns and Dimensions* (New York: Praeger Publishers, 1978).

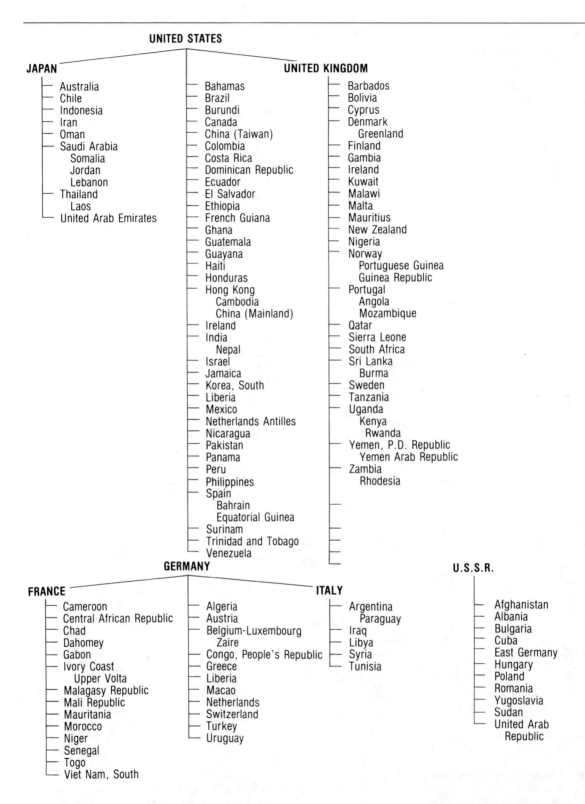

Figure 15-4. World trading networks: 1971

SOURCE: Drawn from Robert Green and James Lutz, *The United States and World Trade: Changing Patterns and Dimensions* (New York: Praeger Publishers, 1978).

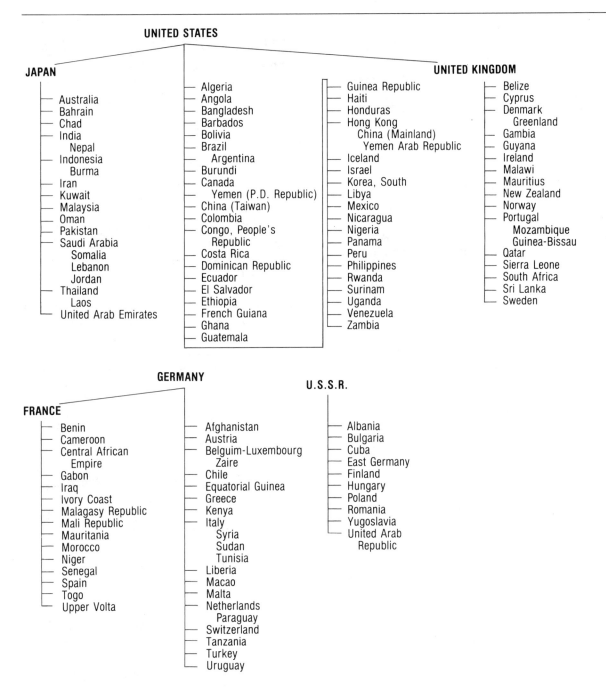

UNITED STATES

JAPAN
- Australia
- Bahrain
- Chad
- India
  - Nepal
- Indonesia
  - Burma
- Iran
- Kuwait
- Malaysia
- Oman
- Pakistan
- Saudi Arabia
  - Somalia
  - Lebanon
  - Jordan
- Thailand
  - Laos
- United Arab Emirates

- Algeria
- Angola
- Bangladesh
- Barbados
- Bolivia
- Brazil
  - Argentina
- Burundi
- Canada
  - Yemen (P.D. Republic)
- China (Taiwan)
- Colombia
- Congo, People's
  - Republic
- Costa Rica
- Dominican Republic
- Ecuador
- El Salvador
- Ethiopia
- French Guiana
- Ghana
- Guatemala

- Guinea Republic
- Haiti
- Honduras
- Hong Kong
  - China (Mainland)
  - Yemen Arab Republic
- Iceland
- Israel
- Korea, South
- Libya
- Mexico
- Nicaragua
- Nigeria
- Panama
- Peru
- Philippines
- Rwanda
- Surinam
- Uganda
- Venezuela
- Zambia

UNITED KINGDOM
- Belize
- Cyprus
- Denmark
  - Greenland
- Gambia
- Guyana
- Ireland
- Malawi
- Mauritius
- New Zealand
- Norway
- Portugal
  - Mozambique
  - Guinea-Bissau
- Qatar
- Sierra Leone
- South Africa
- Sri Lanka
- Sweden

GERMANY

FRANCE
- Benin
- Cameroon
- Central African
  - Empire
- Gabon
- Iraq
- Ivory Coast
- Malagasy Republic
- Mali Republic
- Mauritania
- Morocco
- Niger
- Senegal
- Spain
- Togo
- Upper Volta

- Afghanistan
- Austria
- Belguim-Luxembourg
  - Zaire
- Chile
- Equatorial Guinea
- Greece
- Kenya
- Italy
  - Syria
  - Sudan
  - Tunisia
- Liberia
- Macao
- Malta
- Netherlands
  - Paraguay
- Switzerland
- Tanzania
- Turkey
- Uruguay

U.S.S.R.
- Albania
- Bulgaria
- Cuba
- East Germany
- Finland
- Hungary
- Poland
- Romania
- Yugoslavia
- United Arab
  - Republic

Figure 15-5. World trading networks: 1976

Source: Drawn from Robert Green and James Lutz, *The United States and World Trade: Changing Patterns and Dimensions* (New York: Praeger Publishers, 1978).

3 West Germany forms a significant block in Europe. This is sustained by the EEC connection. France lost her own block but managed to occupy a significant position within the West Germany block. Countries within the French influence are largely former French colonies.

4 The UK declined in terms of influence and became a part of the U.S. block. Countries within the UK influence are largely former British colonies.

5 Japan is emerging as a leader of its own block. Through the years, Japan has become an economic power managing to include various oil exporting and Asian countries in its subblock.

6 Based on the patterns shown in the four figures, one can see that political influence is a key factor. Communist countries always form a block of their own. Some departures from this have occurred in recent years but not to a very large extent (e.g., Hungary, Rumania, Yugoslavia, and other Eastern European countries have pursued more trade with the West). Both the UK and France maintain strong influence over their previous colonies. Another factor to note is, of course, economic power. The U.S., with the greatest purchasing power, heads up the largest hierarchy. The UK's economy was declining, while Japan's was growing, throughout the period. Thus the UK subblock became smaller and the Japan subblock became larger. Cultural variables such as language also play a role. Former British colonies shifted to the U.S., while former French colonies, who had no alternative French-speaking buying power to turn to, stayed in the French subblock.

A Managerial Perspective

The major difference between international marketing and domestic marketing stems from complications in the environment. Many marketing concepts have been presented in the previous chapters. They are, by and large, equally applicable in the international marketing setting. The second half of this chapter focuses upon marketing concepts that are relatively unique to international marketing and are needed to overcome environmental obstacles.

The Initial Involvement Decision

Not all firms are (or should be) involved in export marketing. In the United States, approximately 88 percent of manufacturing firms are nonexporters.[50] In contrast, in the export led economy of Hong Kong, close to 90 percent of the manufacturing output is for exports with most manufacturers serving as subcontractors who sell their production capacities to import/export firms. From their perspective, these manufacturers feel that they are doing domestic rather than international marketing, although they full well know that their sales are subject to changes in the export markets.[51]

One recent case study revealed that decision makers who initiate exporting travel widely, display attitudes of complete unconcern about national boundaries, and in general reflect innovative outlooks.[52] Let us turn to some ways to view the innovation process in the international context.

The Internationalization Process. New product adoption is a process. Similarly, the internationalization of business can be viewed as a series of stages. Studies conducted in America, Australia, and Sweden show that the process is one of gradual involvement.[53] One way to represent the process is shown in Figure 15-6.[54] A firm in the beginning stage sells solely in the home market with no involvement in international marketing. Gradually, because of external and/or internal pressures, the firm attempts to evaluate export markets as a potentially fruitful direction for development.

With sufficient promise and resources, the firm may be ready to actively initiate an expansion into the international market. Eventually, the firm makes a long-term commitment to international marketing as part of its central corporate goals.

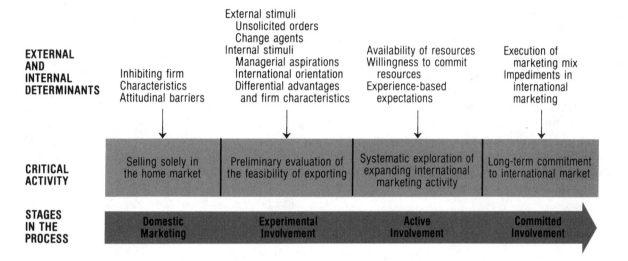

Figure 15-6. A model of the incremental internationalization process of a firm

SOURCE: S. Tamer Cavusgil and John R. Nevin, "A Conceptualization of the Initial Involvement in International Marketing," in Charles W. Lamb, Jr., and Patrick M. Dunne (eds.), *Theoretical Developments in Marketing* (Chicago: American Marketing Assn. Proceedings, 1980), p. 69. Reprinted with the permission of the American Marketing Association.

Determinants of Involvement in Internationalization. If the picture of initial exporting as an instance of the adoption of an innovation is correct, the tools consumer behavior researchers use to differentiate innovators from noninnovators may be worth examining. One survey of small and medium-sized manufacturers in Wisconsin revealed that differences do exist between heavy exporters and nonexporters.[55] Heavy exporters were very much concerned with the development of new products. They saw their products as being unique and price competitive. Further, they viewed themselves as being technologically advanced. On the other hand, nonexporters were generally not as interested in developing new products and at the same time construed technology as being only moderately important.

In another survey of manufacturing executives located in three Southeastern states, it was discovered that nonexporters and indirect exporters shared similar attitudes but differed from direct exporters.[56] On the one hand, all executives believed that direct exporting would offer more control over marketing programs, provide more information about foreign markets, and require more documentation and paperwork. On the other hand, only executives involved in direct exporting considered control of distribution activities to be important, thought that information about the foreign markets was essential, and tended not to mind the increased paperwork associated with foreign trade. Although much work needs to be done with respect to the adoption of an international outlook, the above studies suggest areas where innovators and noninnovators differ and point the way to what sense attitudes must be changed.

Product Decisions

Two aspects of any product play a key role in the success or failure of firms in the international market. One concerns standardization versus adaptation to the needs of foreign markets. Another is the idea of the international product life cycle hypothesis (IPLC), which is different from the usual PLC concept in terms of its management implications.

Standardization versus Adaptation. A standardized product enjoys economies of scale in production, in product research and development, in marketing, and in winning the loyalty of mobile consumers in domestic as well as foreign markets. For products requiring a particular technical specification, or when the foreign market is very small, it may not be feasible or desirable to develop a tailor-made product for every country. Moreover, because people rarely see products from a foreign land, it is sometimes effective to merely market the same product in various nations. Some products have such a strong sense of novelty, prestige, or quality that it would be foolish and uneconomical to change them for the foreign market. In Hong Kong, McDonald's Hamburgers capitalized on its "100% American components" image, which communicated something positive about its quality. Similarly, although joint agreements to produce or license jeans have been made in certain parts of the world, real American-made jeans are still a sought-after status symbol in most parts of the world.

In some instances, it is better to adapt a product to a foreign market. Consider the effect of climate. Oil-based facial creams sell well in Northern Europe, but do not sell well in warmer climates such as those found in Malaysia. Water-based facial creams that are stored in the refrigerator are more appropriate for tropical areas and cheaper to produce as well. Similarly, products stressing the importance of "freshness" might be better produced locally and sold with a local image. Beer is such an example. San Miguel is a Filipino beer. But it is produced and sold in Hong Kong with a distinctive local image rather than being shipped from the Philippines. Because people buy beer in part on the basis of subjective inferences, the locally produced "import" is perceived to be fresher and perhaps cheaper than would a true import. On the other hand, San Miguel is shipped to the United States and has achieved a foothold as a premium quality beer. To produce it in the United States would most likely not be justified by its small volume and the likely reactions buyers would have to another domestically produced beer among many others.

The International Product Life Cycle. The IPLC concept was first introduced by Wells.[57] According to the author, products in the U.S. have followed a pattern divided into four stages: (1) U.S. export strength, (2) foreign production starts, (3) foreign production begins to be competitive in certain export markets, and (4) import substitution in the U.S. begins. Implicitly, this hypothesis assumes that product innovation begins in the U.S., and in the course of time, the comparative advantage of production shifts to other countries, with the U.S.

even later importing from these sellers. Assuming that the IPLC is valid, U.S. firms may follow two strategies for survival: (1) continual product rollover by shifting resources to new products more suited to the unique demands of the American market and (2) manufacturing abroad to take advantage of lower production costs and to save tariffs and transportation costs.

A good example of life cycle changes has occurred in Sweden. For a long time, the Swedes produced high-quality machinery and other capital equipment, and experienced considerable success on the world market. As other developed and less-developed countries entered the market, however, the Swedes found that head-to-head competition became impossible. Very high labor and social costs threatened to drive them out of the international market.

Instead of abandoning their products, the Swedes shifted competition to a new plane by selling entire systems (e.g., assembly lines) and even factories. Many of their old products became subcomponents of these new products. A piece of machinery is now just as likely to be sold along with other capital equipment it complements as it is to be sold alone.

The Swedes' managerial know-how, combined with good products, permitted them to participate again with success in international trade.

Business practices in Japan necessitate a modification in the IPLC concept. Some products are developed in Japan for sale in market segments in advanced countries such as the U.S. For example, Japanese manufacturers produced color televisions for export to the U.S. five years before they also sold them to Japanese consumers.[58]

The case of Israel also reveals a need to modify the IPLC concept. Rather than following the U.S. in innovation, Israel is sometimes the market leader. One way this happens is through a tie-in strategy with advanced countries, serving as the latter's subcontractor for certain products. A small home market need not be a disadvantage, and a firm can even capitalize on experience curve effects through skillful international marketing. Thus, specialization can be an important determinant of success. Despite a number of exceptions to the IPLC, however, many products roughly follow the pattern in a variety of countries.[59]

Channel Decisions

International marketing poses different distribution problems from domestic issues. Geographic diversity is a key source of the differences. In general, a firm may employ indirect exporting, direct exporting, and direct production in foreign markets. The guiding economic principle is often to choose a channel with the lowest total distribution cost for the entire channel. Of course, behavioral and cultural factors will normally also need to be considered.[60] Let us explore the three channel options in greater detail.

Indirect Exporting. When a firm sells in its domestic market with open distribution, visitors who may also be retailers in a foreign country may make purchases for resale in their home country. For example, the author discovered that about half of the retail sales of watches by a leading brand in Hong Kong were bought by retailers from Southeast Asian countries who happened to travel to Hong Kong. A similar phenomenon also takes place in the toy industry. If a firm is aware of the situation but does not intervene, it nevertheless is involved in indirect exporting. Because this can represent a significant share of business and/or have implications for relationships with intermediaries in foreign countries, the firm should estimate and respond to such demand thoughtfully.

The normal way to conduct indirect exporting is to use the services of a trading company. Small manufacturers usually send sales representatives to various trading firms and solicit "orders" for production. Alternatively, trading firms search for dependable manufacturers to fulfill orders on hand. Established trading firms sometimes assemble manufacturers and give them various kinds of managerial support. A considerable portion of successful marketing by Hong Kong and Japanese firms rests with trading companies.

Direct Exporting. If a firm desires to explore international markets more aggressively and systematically, it may utilize a number of foreign dealers or appoint a sole agent to handle its business in a foreign country. Here, the firm takes greater initiative and gains more control over the foreign markets through the dealers and/or the sole agent. Usually, the firm must provide different kinds of support to the dealers or agent, including fees and trading allowances for promotions among others. In return, the dealers or agent may be asked to attain a quota. Further, in the case of sole agents, they may be asked not to handle any products of competitors.

As the demand for one's products grows, firms often establish overseas marketing subsidiaries. Usually, there are two basic motivations for this. One is to exercise tighter control over the channel of distribution and provide protection for one's products and brand names. Nevertheless, foreign dealers sometimes try to establish their own brand or, through certain practices, obscure the recognition of foreign brands. For example, consider the case of toys. Foreign dealers typically display toys from various sources according to age groups and/or price levels, rather than by manufacturers or specific brands. Consumers tend to recognize the dealer's name but not the names of the exporting firms and their brands.

Another basic motivation for having a foreign market subsidiary is to solicit market information. Since it is closer to the market, the firm will be able to monitor changes more effectively. In addition to getting a better pulse of consumer demand, the firm can study competitors. The foreign marketing subsidiary may be used to solicit quotations or even import products from various competitors. Since marketing effectiveness is determined, in part, by the amount and quality of market information, in so doing, one's competitive position can be enhanced.

Direct Production in Foreign Markets. *Licensing* is perhaps the easiest way to start production in a foreign market. The licensor (the international firm) may give the licensee (the national firm) various kinds of support: patent rights, trademark rights, and/or know-how in production. Licensing generally reduces transportation costs, increases the ability of the firm to respond to market demand, and expands the firm's production capacities. Sometimes, both the licensor and the licensee may be wary that consumers in the foreign market may fail to accept locally produced products as "authentic." One way to get around the problem is by having a 50/50 supply/source mix. That is, the licensee produces half of the supply in the foreign market, while the licensor sends half of the supply from production in the home country. In so doing, consumers have a chance to "compare" products from the two sources of supply and build confidence in the production expertise of the foreign market. This is especially significant in products related to fashion such as clothing or jewelry.

The *joint venture* is a more aggressive form of direct production. In the joint venture, a firm invests in foreign production and holds greater authority to guide the operation. For example, McDonald's operates under a 50 percent joint venture arrangement in Hong Kong. Local managers are provided with strong incentives, and at the same time, McDonald's maintains considerable influence on how to run the operations. Joint ventures take many forms and are similar to franchise operations.

A third option is the *wholly-owned production* arrangement. This, of course, provides the greatest protection of technology and production secrets. Also, for sophisticated items such as industrial materials, no foreign firm may be qualified and/or willing to invest in its own or a joint venture. The wholly-owned operation is sometimes preferred when significant growth is anticipated. At the same time, establishment of production capacity in a foreign market may enable the firm to supply nearby foreign markets. In the case of industrial raw materials, and supplies such as chemicals, local production can yield the needed competitive edge for the firm. It does this by ensuring supplies and a dependable delivery schedule, two factors helping to keep costs low and thereby permitting effective price moves.

Communication: Standardization in International Advertising

The key difference between international and domestic marketing communication lies in standardization. In domestic marketing, at least for advertising, the firm typically faces an "advertise big or not at all" decision. It is both very difficult and uneconomical to maintain significant regional differences in marketing promotion. But in international marketing communication, tailor-made programs are often a necessity because of language and cultural differences. Let us look at some examples.

Standardization in advertising should not be confused with standardization of products. Even if one markets the same product internationally, different selling appeals will sometimes be needed to reach different groups of people. Consider the example of Hong Kong as a tourist area. For tourists from the U.S. and Western Europe, the Hong Kong Tourist Association advertises Hong Kong as an Oriental city and a stepping stone for visiting China. For tourists from different parts of Asia, the Hong Kong Tourist association presents Hong Kong as a Westernized city and a shopping center for products from different countries in the world.[61]

Some marketers assume that people from different parts of the world are basically the same and perceive products homogeneously. Moreover, they believe that a standardized strategy will lead to a universally recognized company and brand image, as well as economies of scale. A well-known example is Coca-Cola. Several years ago, in a worldwide search for common and basic human needs, the Coca-Cola Company discovered that people from various parts of the world shared a desire to be competitive and achieve more than others. For example, when people run, they want to run faster than others. On the basis of the research, Coca-Cola developed the slogan "Coke Adds Life" as a reflection of this universal need.[62] Obviously, not all products lend themselves to such a universal approach. Indeed, even in the case of soft drinks, one may argue that a strategy of standardization should not automatically be pursued. One study showed, for instance, that college students in the U.S., France, India, and Brazil desire different product attributes. In relation to France and India, the U.S. sample placed greater emphasis on the more subjective and less functional product attributes. The Brazilian sample was even more concerned with subjective attributes than the U.S. sample.[63]

One study summarizes what we know about international advertising along the following lines:[64]

1 It is useful to make a distinction between the standardization of the "buying proposal" and the standardization of the "creative presentation." Buying proposals (i.e., the selling points) are more easily transferred across countries than creative executions of ads. For the case of "Coke Adds Life," both the buying proposal and creative presentation were standardized. For the case of Hong Kong as a tourist area, both the buying proposal and the creative presentation were different. In other cases, one may use different kinds of reference persons in different countries to present the same product benefits.

2 A significant factor influencing the transferability of advertising is the skill with which translation is done. It is believed that a idiomatic language is essential for good results.

3 The effect of cultural factors is significant. A culturally specific product is a poor candidate for a standardized advertising campaign.

4 Standardization can be expected to have varying success, depending on how product attributes are viewed by consumers from one country to another. Hence, research is needed to determine key product attributes desired by people within a foreign market. Matters of taste, socialization, and culture sometimes differ in a fundamental way.

5 Country of origin effects do have an influence. For example, U.S. students in one study had more favorable attitudes towards advertised products that were associated with Americans rather than with Egyptians. The opposite effect can of course occur such as when the use of foreign models suggests exotic, exclusive, and in other ways desirable characteristics, for instance.

Pricing

Pricing is significantly different in international marketing in comparison with domestic marketing. Let us elaborate on the issues below.

Differences between Pricing for Domestic and Pricing for Export Markets. The major differences in pricing in domestic and foreign markets are summarized in Table 15-5.[65] Read the nine points of difference before proceeding. A manager involved in export pricing faces professional buyers with considerable knowledge of cross-border sourcing. Price is determined on an ad hoc basis, because pricing can vary from one order to another. In most domestic pricing situations, a price once set has long-term carryover effects. Price is relatively more negotiable in foreign markets. The bargaining power on price levels depends typically on the order size. When the order size is large, the export price tends to be lower. For export pricing, cost factors are often taken as the base line for negotiation. Since goods will be delivered to a buyer, inventory costs for finished goods are low. Also, market feedback is much faster from the export market, unlike in domestic marketing where it takes longer to learn through intermediaries or feedback from sales personnel or records.

TABLE 15-5
Major Differences between Export and Domestic Pricing

Areas of Difference	Export Pricing	Domestic Pricing
Prime consideration	Cost factors	Consumer demand and competitive environment
Type of buyers	Professional buyers with knowledge of cross-border sourcing	a. Local wholesaler/retailer b. Ultimate consumer
Price setting	Price is determined on an ad-hoc basis	Price is fixed on a long-term basis
Retail price	Manufacturer has no control	Possible control by manufacturer
Flexibility	Price is negotiable	Price is not negotiable
Attitude toward price	Buyer keen on bargaining for cheaper prices	Seldom bargain, may shift to other brand if price is considered to be high
Bargaining power	Depends on order size	Buyer has no bargaining power
Feedback	Immediate from buyers	Through intermediaries or sales records
Finished goods inventory cost	Not considered	Considered in setting base prices

SOURCE: Ho-Fuk Lau, ''Pricing for the Domestic Market—A Briefing for the Export-oriented Manufacturers in Hong Kong,'' *The Hong Kong Manager*, April 1983, p. 19.

Export Pricing for a Firm with Domestic Operations. When a manager involved in export marketing tries to relate his or her export pricing decision to the domestic marketing operation, either a direct costing approach (when export activities do not require expansion of fixed cost facilities) or an incremental costing approach (when export activities require expansion of fixed costs facilities) may be used. Also, a firm from a developing country with exchange control may want to emphasize that there is a net yield of foreign currency as well as profit making. The various considerations are summarized in Table 15-6.[66] Case 1 presents the situation where no expansion of facilities is required. Case 2 presents the situation where expansion of facilities is required. Case 1 uses the variable cost standard, while Case 2 uses the incremental cost standard. When the impact of the export decision is positive on both net profit and yield of foreign currency, the appropriate decision is to export. When the impact of the export decision is negative on both net profit and yield of foreign currency, no exporting should be done. When the impact of the export decision is negative on net profit but positive on yield of foreign currency (or vice versa), the decision depends on the trade-off between these two aspects.

TABLE 15-6
Impact of the Foreign Cost Component on Export Pricing

		IMPACT OF DECISION ON	
CONDITION	DECISION	Net Profit	Yield of Foreign Currency
Case 1: No change in existing condition[a]			
1.1 Revenue realized in foreign currency is equal to or exceeds variable cost.	Export	Positive	Positive
1.2 Revenue realized in foreign currency is less than total variable cost and also less than the foreign portion of variable cost.	Don't Export	Positive	Positive
1.3 Revenue realized in foreign currency is less than total variable cost, but greater than its foreign components.	Export	Negative	Positive
	Don't Export	Positive	Negative
Case 2: Assuming expansion in facilities[b]			
2.1 Revenue realized in foreign currency is equal to or exceeds total incremental cost.	Export	Positive	Positive
2.2 Revenue realized in foreign currency is less than the total incremental cost and also less than the foreign components of incremental cost.	Don't Export	Positive	Positive
2.3 Revenue realized in foreign currency is less than the total incremental cost, but greater than its foreign components.	Export	Negative	Positive
	Don't Export	Positive	Negative

[a]Short-run analysis assuming no alternative use for excess capacity and thus no opportunity cost.
[b]Assuming no alternative use for excess capacity and thus no opportunity cost.

Source: Exhibit 2 of Mohamed E. Moustafa, ''Pricing Strategy for Export Activity in Developing Nations,'' *Journal of International Business Studies* (Spring/Summer 1978): 95–102. Reprinted with the permission of the publisher.

Transfer Pricing. Any time a company begins foreign production, transfer pricing becomes a significant issue. A high transfer price will make the outlook of the domestic operation appear better, while the outlook of the foreign subsidiary will appear inferior. A low transfer price has the reverse effect. Transfer pricing is a very complicated issue, and many factors are involved. Herein, we will only be able to summarize some of the more central considerations found in the literature:

1 Tax considerations: There is always a motivation to set the transfer price at a level that enables the company to maximize the global after-tax earnings.

2 Restriction of profit repatriation: Even if a country has a low corporate profit tax rate, it makes little sense to accumulate profits in the foreign country if they cannot be remitted to the parent company.

3 Fear of devaluation: No company would like to put more "eggs" in a "shaky" basket, because unexpected devaluations could lead to heavy losses.

4 Sound management practices: The way a transfer price is set up may affect the outlook of relative performances in different subsidiaries. It may have significant impact on the morale of employees, and it may affect the fairness of performance evaluations.

5 Consistency and external pressure: Tax authorities of different countries may want to exert pressures and demand international uniformity in accounting practices. Once a certain accounting system is set up, the firm may find it difficult to make subsequent changes in order to benefit the company as a whole when the environment changes.

6 Management loyalty to different countries: The directors may want to favor a particular country to pay more taxes to one than another and thereby enhance earnings.

Marketing planning in international marketing is not very different from marketing planning in domestic marketing. However, three points should be stressed:

1 Marketing research activities, in comparison with other marketing functions, should be more ethnocentric than geocentric. In other words, marketing research should be conducted in a localized fashion.[67] Therefore, research for international markets might be thought of as a coordinated sum of research for a number of domestic markets. This is not to say that such problems as equivalence of concepts and comparability of data are not present. It only says that if all "domestic" marketing research activities are properly carried out in the local context, the information has a chance of effectively aiding decision making.

2 Portfolio analysis of one's products in relation to market share, growth, and profitability is a must. It is up to the planner to assemble the product/market mix to maximize expected returns and minimize risks.[68]

3 In general, a firm can follow either a diversification or a concentration strategy in expanding into the international market. It is recommended that a firm follow the *concentration strategy* (emphasis on resources in a few markets and gradual expansion into new territories) when the sales response function is an S curve, when the growth rate of each market is high, when sales stability in each market is high, when the competitive lead time is long, when market spillover effects are low, when the need for product adaptation is high, when the need for communication adaptation is high, when economies of scale in distribution are high, when program control requirements are high, and when the extent of constraints is high.

On the other hand, a firm may want to follow the *diversification strategy* (fast penetration into a large number of markets and diffusion of efforts among them) when the situation is reversed.[69]

Summary

International marketing is an important (although relatively young) and rapidly growing subject area. The single most fundamental variable differentiating international marketing from domestic marketing is its heterogeneous and multifaceted macro environment. One way to study the impact of the international macro environment is to use a three-category classification including *cultural, economic,* and *political environments.*

The *cultural environment* forms the basis of communication among nations. A person engaged in international marketing should not refer exclusively to his or her own culture when attempting to understand other cultures. On the other hand, it is wrong to assume that one cannot understand cultures other than the one to which one belongs. Language, religion, values, and attitudes, among others, form the main dimensions of any cultural environment. They are preserved and transmitted through social organizations such as schools, families, religious bodies, and formal groups (e.g., the Girl Scouts, the Democratic Party, the Veterans of Foreign Wars).

The *economic environment* constitutes the setting for profit opportunities in trading among nations. Factor endowments in different countries determine the direction of specialization and the division of labor. From a static perspective, countries tend to develop industries in which they have an edge in production. On the other hand, from a dynamic perspective, countries may want to create a situation so that they can enhance their technological levels, and thus, productivity levels, in industries they may want to pursue in the future.

The *political environment* poses still another powerful set of forces constraining or facilitating international trade. Fiscal, monetary, and trading policies are the manifest ways governments thwart or encourage trade. Also, the political stability of a country shapes international trade in fundamental ways.

The major difference between international and domestic marketing lies in the complexity of the environment. Some managerial tools are equally relevant in domestic and international markets. However, there are many relatively unique management concepts and principles that deserve special attention.

With respect to products, a firm must consider the issue of "standardization versus adaptation." A standard product for all countries may carry a "foreign" appeal, while an adapted product may be geared to the particular needs of a country. With respect to product development, one has to be aware of the international product life cycle concept. The application of marketing tools varies from stage to stage, and continual vigilance is needed during all stages from new product development through exporting, importing, and decline.

With respect to channels of distribution, a firm may employ indirect exporting, direct exporting, and/or direct production in foreign markets. Direct production in foreign markets takes the form of licensing, joint venture, and/or wholly-owned production operations.

With respect to communication, a firm must consider the issue of standardization in international advertising. In general, it is advisable to standardize the selling points (i.e., product attributes and benefits) but not the creative executions. However, exceptions abound, and firms must do research whenever possible. Also, standardization is less likely when we have a culture-specific product and when we lack the skills for effective translation. The selection and training of sales personnel are also important considerations, as consummation of a sale often depends on the nature and quality of face-to-face interactions.

With respect to pricing, export pricing is significantly different from domestic pricing. Among other differences, export pricing is typically determined on a rather ad hoc basis, primarily based on cost factors. Also, when a firm operates in two or more countries, it must deal with the issue of transfer pricing for internal transactions across countries.

With respect to marketing planning, a firm must consider whether it should penetrate quickly into a large number of markets or concentrate its resources in a few markets with gradual expansion into new territories.

International marketing is a new and largely unknown area. We have but touched on some of the issues. Yet, the future of all countries will more and more be dependent on how well firms practice marketing in the ever-shrinking global context.

Questions and Problems for Discussion

1 Over the years, companies such as Pepsico have followed an international marketing policy wherein the same product and advertising program have been used in each country. Discuss the advantages and disadvantages of such a practice.

2 What do we mean by culture and in what ways does it affect international marketing?

3 Describe the economic forces at work in the international environment and point out how they affect marketing.

4 What political variables influence marketing in the international context and how do they do so?

5 What is the international product life cycle concept and what relevance does it have for the conduct of marketing?

6 Discuss the three channel-of-distribution options open to any marketer in the international context.

7 How does the pricing decision in domestic and export marketing differ?

8 Contrast the concentration strategy with the diversification strategy when expanding into the international market.

9 What overall marketing strategy in general and channel-of-distribution strategy in particular would you recommend for the following firms contemplating marketing internationally?

a Firm XYZ experiences highly uneven demand for its lawn furniture, which results in underutilization of its production capacity.

b Acme Enterprises makes motors for air conditioning and refrigerator systems. Its motors employ a new technology and offer increased reliability and durability for users in hot climates. However, likely markets in countries in South America, Africa, and the Far East typically have trade practices making export prohibitive.

c Tarolli Pizzas, Inc., has developed an inexpensive yet tasty dried pizza line. Its production process results in the maximum preservation of the vitamin, mineral, and protein content of the pizza ingredients. Mr. Andreolli, the owner, feels that Third World countries would benefit from the product, as laboratory tests reveal that it provides an inexpensive, balanced meal. However, Tarolli Pizzas is a small operation limited to a single plant in a large Midwestern city.

NOTES

1. Theodore Levitt, *The Marketing Imagination* (New York: The Free Press, 1983), Chapter 2.

2. In the United States, the need for greater emphasis on international marketing can be seen in the directive by the American Assembly of Collegiate Schools of Business (AACSB) that recommends that international content be explicitly incorporated in all areas of the business curriculum. The AACSB has also sponsored seminars and workshops for faculty and published monographs to guide universities in internationalizing their programs. See also Ivan R. Vernon ed., *Academy of International Business Newsletter*, March 19, 1982, pp. 11 and 13, and *Academy of International Business Newsletter*, December 1, 1981, p. 5; and John U. Farley and Jerry Wind, "International Marketing: The Neglect Continues," *Journal of Marketing* 44 (Summer 1980): 5-6.

3. James A. Lee, "Cultural Analysis in Overseas Operations," *Harvard Business Review* 44 (March–April 1966): 106-14.

4. Robert K. Merton, "Insiders and Outsiders: A Chapter in the Sociology of Knowledge," *American Journal of Sociology* 78 (July 1972): 9-47.

5. Oswald Werner and Donald T. Campbell, "Translating, Working through Interpreters, and the Problems of Decentering," in Raoul Naroll and Ronald Cohen, ed., *A Handbook of Method in Cultural Anthropology* (New York: Columbia University Press, 1970), pp. 398-420.

6. Michael H. Bond and Kuo-Shu Yang, "Ethnic Affirmation versus Cross-Cultural Accommodation: The Variable Impact of Questionnaire Language on Chinese Bilinguals in Hong Kong," *Journal of Cross Cultural Psychology* (June 1982): 169-85. For additional insights into the role of language in marketing, see Sue E. Berryman, et al., *Foreign Language and International Studies Specialists: The Market Place and National Policy* (Santa Monica, Cal.: The Rand Corporation, 1979); Paul Simon, *The Tongue-Tied American Confronting the Foreign Language Crisis* (New York: Continuum, 1980); Toivo S. Aijo, "The Most Important Language in International Business Is That of Your Customer—or Isn't?" *Der Markt* 89 (1984): 7-17.

7. Paddy Bowie, "When Silence Doesn't Mean Consent," *Euro-Asia Business Review* 1, 1 (1982): 32-34.

8. Vern Terpstra, *The Cultural Environment of International Business* (Cincinnati, Oh.: South-Western Publishing Co., 1978), p. 20.

9. Richard Foster, *The Freedom of Simplicity* (London: Triangle, 1981).

10. Ralph Winter, *Penetrating the Last Frontiers* (Pasadena, Cal.: U.S. Center for World Mission, 1978). J. N. D. Anderson, ed., *The World's Religions* (London: Inter-Varsity Fellowship, 1951).

11. E. F. Schumacher, *Good Work* (London: Abacus, 1980).

12. Allan Cheek, *Practical Christian Management* (London: B. A. Check, 1973).

13. Marion E. Wade and Glenn D. Kittler, *Meet Mr. Service Master* (Chicago: Moody Press, 1969).

14. John Harbron, "With the Saudi Manager, Business and Culture Must Intermingle," *Business Quarterly* 41 (Summer 1976): 17-19.

15. "Islamic Banking," *Arabia, The Islamic World Review*, June 1982, pp. 56-57.

16. Vern Terpstra, *International Marketing*, 2d ed. (Hinsdale, Ill.: The Dryden Press, 1978), pp. 103-10.

17. E. F. Schumacher, *Small Is Beautiful* (London: Abacus, 1974), pp. 51-60.

18. M. Rokeach, *The Nature of Human Values* (New York: McGraw-Hill, Inc., 1977).

19. John Howard, *Consumer Behavior: Application of Theory* (New York: McGraw-Hill, 1977).

20. Kam-Hon Lee, "The Rokeach Inventory of Personal Values as a Measurement Tool in Cross Cultural Consumer Research," in *Proceedings of 1983 Academy of Marketing Science Annual Conference*, 1983, pp. 427-29.

21. G. England, *The Manager and His Values: An International Perspective* (Cambridge, Mass.: Ballinger Publishing Co., 1975); G. Hofstede, *Culture's Consequences*, Russell Sage Publishers, 1980.

22. Ambrose Y. C. King, *From Tradition to Modernity* (Taipei, Taiwan: Shih Pao Book Series, 1978). (In Chinese.)

23. David McClelland, *The Achieving Society* (New York: The Free Press, 1961).

24. C. K. Yang, *Religion in Chinese Society* (Berkeley and Los Angeles: University of California Press, 1961).

25. Kam-Hon Lee, "Social and Cultural Environment," in K. C. Mun, K. H. Lee, H. M. Yau, and K. C. Tse, eds., *Marketing Management* (Hong Kong: Commercial Press, 1982), pp. 32–48. (In Chinese.)

26. Arnold H. De Graaf, Jean Olthuis, and Anne Tuiningen, *Japan, A Way of Life* (Toronto: Joy in Learning Curriculum Development and Training Centre, 1980).

27. "Battered Pillars of the American System," *Fortune*, April 1975, pp. 133–35, 138–50.

28. David C. McClelland and David G. Winter, *Motivating Economic Achievement* (New York: The Free Press, 1969).

29. Jagdish Bhagwati, "The Pure Theory of International Trade: A Survey," *The Economic Journal* (March 1964): 1–84.

30. Adam Smith, *The Wealth of Nations, Books I–III* (Middlesex, England: Penguin Books Ltd., 1970), pp. 472–75.

31. This is based on Bhagwati, "The Pure Theory of International Trade."

32. Vern Terpstra, *International Marketing*, 2d ed. (Hinsdale, Ill.: The Dryden Press, 1978), p. 28.

33. F. Heckscher, "The Effect of Foreign Trade on the Distribution of Income," in H. S. Ellis and L. A. Metzler, eds., *Readings in the Theory of International Trade* (Philadelphia: Blakiston for American Economic Association, 1949); B. Ohlin, *Interregional and International Trade* (Cambridge, Mass.: Harvard University Press, Harvard Economic Studies, Vol. 39, 1933).

34. W. Leontief, "Domestic Production and Foreign Trade: The American Capital Position Re-examined," *Proceedings of the American Philosophical Society*, September 1953. W. Leontief, "Factor Proportions and Structure of American Trade, Further Theoretical and Empirical Analysis," *Review of Economics and Statistics* (November 1956): 386–407.

35. S. Linder, *An Essay on Trades and Transformation* (New York: John Wiley & Sons, 1961).

36. Donald Keesing, "Labor Skills and Comparative Advantages," *American Economic Review* 56 (May 1966): 249–58.

37. William Gruber, Dileep Mehta, and Raymond Vernon, "The R & D Factor in International Trade and International Investment of United States Industries," *Journal of Political Economy* 75 (February 1967): 20–37.

38. Raymond Vernon, "International Investment and International Trade in the Produce Cycle," *Quarterly Journal of Economics* 80 (May 1966): 190–207.

39. Badiul A. Majumdar, "Technology Transfers and International Competitiveness: The Case of Electronic Calculators," *Journal of International Business Studies* 11 (Fall 1980): 103–11.

40. Liander, et al., *Comparative Analysis for International Marketing* (Boston: Allyn & Bacon, 1967).

41. Vern Terpstra, *The Cultural Environment of International Business* (Cincinnati, Oh.: South-Western Publishing Co., 1978), pp. 231–32.

42. Robert Green and Christopher Korth, "Political Instability and the Foreign Investor," *California Management Review* 16 (Fall 1974): 23–31.

43. R. J. Rummel and David A. Heenan, "How Multinationals Analyze Political Risk," *Harvard Business Review* 56 (January–February 1978): 67–76.

44. This is based on Kenneth W. Dam, *The GATT Law and International Economic Organization* (Chicago: The University of Chicago Press, 1970).

45. Donald B. Keesing and Martin Wolf, *Textile Quotas against Developing Countries* (London: Trade Policy Research Centre, 1980).

46. Peter R. O'Dell, *Oil and World Power*, 6th ed. (Middlesex, England: Penguin Books Ltd., 1981).

47. Raymond Vernon, *The Economic Environment of International Business* (Englewood Cliffs, N.J.: Prentice-Hall, 1972), pp. 15–17.

48. Peng-Lim Chee, "International Rivalry: U.S.–Japanese Competition in the ASEAN Countries," (Seattle, Wash.: University of Washington, Pacific Rim Project Working Paper, 1981).

49. This is based on Robert Green and James Lutz, *The United States and World Trade, Changing Patterns and Dimensions* (New York: Praeger Publishers, 1978).

50. S. Tamer Cavusgil and John R. Nevin, "A Conceptualization of the Initial Involvement in International Marketing," in Charles W. Lamb, Jr., and Patrick M. Dunne, eds., *Theoretical Developments in Marketing* (Chicago: American Marketing Association Proceedings, 1980), pp. 68–71.

51. Kam-Hon Lee, "Development of Hong Kong's Place in International Trade," *The World Economy*, September 1982, pp. 187–200.

52. Kenneth Simmonds and H. Smith, "The First Export Order: A Marketing Innovation," *British Journal of Marketing* (Summer 1968): 93–100.

53. Warren J. Bilkey and George Tesar, "The Export Behavior of Smaller Sized Wisconsin Manufacturing Firms," *Journal of International Business Studies* 8 (Spring–Summer 1977): 93–98. Finn Wiedersheim-Paul, H. D. Olson, and L. S. Welch, "Pre-Export Activity: The First Step in Internationalization," *Journal of International Business Studies* 9 (Spring–Summer 1978): 47–58. J. Johanson and F. Wiedersheim-Paul, "The Internationalization of the Firm—Four Swedish Case Studies," *The Journal of Management Studies* 12 (October 1975): 305–22.

54. Cavusgil and Nevin, "A Conceptualization of the Initial Involvement in International Marketing."

55. George Tesar, "Identification of Planning, Attitudinal, and Operational Differences Among Types of Exporters," *American Journal of Small Business* (October 1977): 16–21; S. Tamer Cavusgil and John R. Nevin, "Internal Determinants of Export Marketing Behavior: An Empirical Investigation," *Journal of Marketing Research* 18 (February 1981): 114–19.

56. Donald L. Brady and William O. Bearden, "The Effect of Managerial Attitudes on Alternative Exporting Methods," *Journal of International Business Studies* 10 (Winter 1979): 79–84.

57. Louis T. Wells, Jr., "A Product Life Cycle for International Trade?" *Journal of Marketing* 32 (July 1968): 1–6.

58. Yoshi Tsurumi, "Japanese Multinational Firms," in Kappor, ed., *Asian Business and Environment in Transition* (Princeton, N.J.: The Darwin Press, 1976), pp. 403–19.

59. Igal Ayal, "International Product Life Cycle: A Reassessment and Product Policy Implications," *Journal of Marketing* 45 (Fall 1981): 91–96.

60. Louis P. Bucklin, *Competition and Evolution in Distributive Trades* (Englewood Cliffs, N.J.: Prentice-Hall, 1972). Examples of behavior research in international marketing channels are A. Ahmed, "Channel Control in International Markets," *European Journal of Marketing* 11 (1977): 327–36. Phillip J. Rosson and I. D. Ford, "Stake, Conflict, and Performance in Export Marketing Channels," *Management International Review* 20 (1980): 31–37.

61. Personal communication with the Far East Regional Director of Hong Kong Tourist Association.

62. Personal communication with the account executive in charge of the Coca-Cola account in Hong Kong.

63. Robert T. Green, William H. Cunningham, and Isabella Cunningham, "The Effectiveness of Standardized Global Advertising," *Journal of Advertising* 4 (Summer 1975): 25–30.

64. S. Tamar Cavusgil and John R. Nevin, "State-of-the-Art in International Marketing: An Assessment," in Ben Enis and Kenneth Roering, ed., *Review of Marketing 1981* (Chicago: American Marketing Association, 1981), p. 204.

65. Ho-Fuk Lau, "Pricing for the Domestic Market—A Briefing for the Export-led Manufacturers in Hong Kong," *The Hong Kong Manager*, April 1983, pp. 17–22.

66. Mohamed E. Moustafa, "Pricing Strategy for Export Activity in Developing Nations," *Journal of International Business Studies* 9 (Spring–Summer 1978): 95–102.

67. Y. Wind, S. Douglas, and H. Perlmutter, "Guidelines for Developing International Marketing Strategy," *Journal of Marketing* 37 (April 1973): 14–23.

68. Y. Wind, "Research for Multinational Product Policy," in Warren Keegan and Charles Myer, eds., *Multinational Product Management* (Chicago: American Marketing Association Proceedings, 1977), pp. 165–84; Jean-Claude Larreche, "The International Product-Market Portfolio," in Subhash C. Jain, ed., *Research Frontiers in Marketing: Dialogues and Direction* (Chicago: American Marketing Association, 1978), pp. 276–81.

69. Igal Ayal and Jehiel Zif, "Market Expansion Strategies in Multinational Marketing," *Journal of Marketing* 43 (Spring 1979): 84–94.

GLOSSARY

Absolute Advantages/Costs. The phenomenon in international trade wherein nations can exchange something with which they have an edge in production for something with which they do not and both may be better off. Specialization and the division of labor makes this possible. *See* comparative advantages/costs.

Attitudes. A predisposition to respond towards an object, act, or situation in an evaluative way. An attitude is persistent over time, carrying cognitive (knowledge), affective (emotion), and conative (intention) elements. It also exhibits directionality and intensity. See Chapter 2.

Backward Translation Procedure. A research method recommended in cross-cultural studies whereby a message (e.g., a questionnaire) is translated back and forth between the original language and the translated language using different bilingual translators until the backward translated version (in the original language) is virtually the same as the original version. By use of this procedure, one can insure that the intended message is indeed transmitted.

Comparative Advantages/Costs. A concept used to explain trade across nations. If a_x and a_y are the output-factor ratios for country A and b_x and b_y for Country B in production activities X and Y, respectively, Country A will export Product X and import Product Y if $a_x/a_y > b_x/b_y$. *See* absolute advantages/costs.

Export-Led Trading Policy. A policy advocating that a country should develop industries with a promise for success in export markets.

GATT. The General Agreement on Tariffs and Trade. This is an international organization whose mission is to encourage free trade among all participating nations for the sake of global welfare.

IMF. The International Monetary Fund. This is an international organization whose mission is to encourage international monetary cooperation and see stability of exchange rates among nations.

Import-Substitution Trading Policy. A policy advocating that a country should develop industries in the local market so that it need not import such products in the future.

Insider's Doctrine. The belief that cross-cultural understanding is very difficult if not impossible for an outsider. It contends that one must belong to a culture in order to understand that culture; for example, only blacks can understand blacks, whites can understand whites, etc.

International Marketing. The subject area of marketing exploring marketing activities in an international setting.

International Product Life Cycle (IPLC). A model hypothesizing that products follow a pattern divided into four stages: (1) U.S. exports are strong, (2) foreign production starts, (3) foreign production becomes competitive in export markets, and (4) import substitution begins.

Joint Venture. A type of involvement in a foreign market. The firm invests in foreign production and has authority to guide the operations along with the national partner.

Licensing. An arrangement whereby a firm produces in a foreign market. The licensor (the international firm) may give the licensee (the national firm) various kinds of support: e.g., patent rights, trademark rights, and/or know-how in production.

Religion. The understanding of God and God's relationship with men and women. It is also a social institution with profound effects on values, attitudes, behavior, and business practices.

Self-Reference Criterion. A natural human tendency, often unconscious, to see another culture only from one's own cultural perspective.

Transfer Pricing. The price charged to a unit of a company in one country by another unit of the same company in another country for the sake of products and/or services rendered by the latter to the former.

UNCTAD. The United Nations Conference on Trade and Development. This is an international organization whose goal is to seek improvement in pricing of primary products through commodity agreements.

Values. Central mental reactions of human beings. They provide a standard for guiding action, for developing and maintaining attitudes toward relevant objects and situations, for justifying one's own and others' actions and attitudes, and for morally judging and comparing self with others. Values indirectly affect what products people seek and like or dislike, how they interpret ads, how they go about buying and selling, and so forth.

International Marketing: Where It Is Today, Where It Will Be Tomorrow

John L. Graham
University of
Southern California

America is now selling more of its goods and services overseas than ever before—some $350 billion in 1983. This export trade accounted for more than 5 million jobs in the United States. During the 1980s we have exported more than 10 percent of our gross national product. Despite the growth and importance of international trade, the United States has been losing ground steadily to its international competitors. West Germany, Japan, and Great Britain export on the average almost 20 percent of their GNPs. The United States' share of world trade has dropped from roughly 18 percent to 13 percent since 1960. From 1891 to 1970, America had an unbroken string of trade surpluses. Since 1970 we've had deficits in every year save two.

The competition is tough. General Motors, RCA, Caterpillar Tractors and all the other giants of American industry are feeling the pressure of high-quality, low-cost, aggressively promoted, and efficiently distributed foreign products and services, both in domestic and international markets. It's a healthy competition, pushing American industry to work harder at production *and marketing.*

Today's environment for international marketing is dynamic indeed. Developing countries comprise fast-growing markets for a wide variety of goods and services. And often the only way to keep pace with foreign competitors is to confront them in their own home markets. Many U.S. companies are meeting the challenges. But many are not. The Commerce Department suggests that there are 18,000 firms that could export but do not. These latter companies should be the focus of our attention in the future.

The barriers facing firms inexperienced in international marketing are substantial, but not insurmountable. These barriers can roughly be organized into four categories—financial, legal, cultural, and psychological. Financial and legal barriers to trade, although often of critical importance, are perhaps the easiest with which to cope because their effects can be readily identified and measured. That is, tariff schedules and advertising laws are a matter of public record. Alternatively, cultural and psychological barriers to trade are much more difficult to manage. Nationalism, differing styles of negotiation, prejudice or risk aversion are more subtle barriers to international marketing. Even when clearly identified, the impact of cultural and psychological barriers may be very difficult, if not impossible, to translate into an item on an income statement. Each of the four barriers will be discussed with consideration given to management implications and future trends.

Financial Barriers

Trans-oceanic shipping costs are perhaps the most obvious barriers to exporting. However, the trend is toward industry deregulation and increased efficiency, and these costs will become less important as time passes.

Tariffs can have substantial effects on exporters' income statements. Tariff schedules are complex and ever-changing, but during the last few years tariff barriers have been generally reduced through on-going international trade negotiations. Five management options for dealing with tariff barriers are: (1) pay it; (2) protest unfavorable classification and/or valuation decisions; (3) lobby for lowered tariffs through international trade negotiations; (4) use free trade zones; or (5) smuggling. The establishment and use of free trade zones is becoming much more common. Smuggling is the oldest management option, but it is by no means recommended. However, international marketers should be aware that competitors may use such tactics and thereby gain an illegal competitive advantage.

Communication and transportation systems in the United States are the most efficient in the world. Thus, American firms should plan for increased costs of promotion and distribution in foreign markets.

Product homologation costs are perhaps the most important financial barriers facing international marketers. That is, products must be changed to coincide with the tastes and legal requirements of foreign markets. As examples, smaller capacity refrigerators are preferred in many foreign countries; or machine tools may have to be converted to metric specifications.

A final financial barrier to exporting pertains to the various credit and currency risks associated with international transactions. Bankers' fees for letters of credit, foreign credit extension, and currency hedging must be considered.

These several financial barriers can consume the profits of international transactions very quickly. The most important management implication stemming from these barriers is that American firms must take a long-term view toward export markets. Hurdling the extra promotional, distribution, and product homologation costs is best accomplished through volume and long production runs and associated economies of scale.

Legal Barriers

Protectionism tends to vary with national economic performance. Thus, as the world economy recedes, protectionist trade barriers grow. Indeed, during the last few years we have witnessed widespread adoption of quotas, boycotts, subsidies, and even some increased tariffs. Moreover, a longer list of more subtle forms of protectionism makes international marketing more difficult—counter-trade requirements, customs and product approval procedures, administrative guidance, and other discriminatory government and company policies. Individual firms can influence (and have influenced) the effects of these legal barriers best through voicing complaints to the U.S. trade representative.

Laws constraining marketing decisions in foreign countries are sometimes more strict and sometimes more lenient than those in the United States. For example, tying agreements or price fixing may be permitted in some foreign countries. Alternatively, comparative advertising or puffery may be illegal. Firms wishing to export will have to continue to consider the impact of such laws on their marketing operations.

Companies marketing products abroad should anticipate foreign government interference and participation in business transactions. In many developing countries and in countries with planned economies the government may indeed be *the* buyer.

Home country governments both restrict and promote foreign trade. The U.S. government promotes trade in several ways. The Commerce and Agriculture Departments provide an array of marketing and financial services. The U.S. Trade Representative continuously participates in efforts to reduce foreign protectionism as cited above. The Export-Import Bank provides a series of financial services. Finally, the government provides tax incentives for firms whose revenues are primarily derived from exports.

U.S. antitrust laws have been viewed as an obstacle to U.S. firms wishing to export and compete internationally. However, in recent months legislation has been passed easing restrictions of the formation of trading companies and research and development consortia. U.S. personal income tax laws are considered to be a substantial barrier to America's participation in international markets. That is, the United States is the only country to tax personal income made in foreign countries. Such laws make it much more economical to hire indigenous or third-country nationals to represent American firms in foreign countries. Foreign representatives are less likely to specify American equipment for ancillary purposes, and they are less likely to report important competitive developments to American headquarters. Many American executives identify the Foreign Corrupt Practices Act as an important disincentive to trade. That is, foreign competitors are "free" to bribe foreign government officials and decision makers, and therefore enjoy a competitive advantage over American firms. However, analysis of America's trade performance since the passage of the FCPA does not support such industry claims. Further, it appears that recent attempts in Congress to change or eliminate the law have been put aside. Finally, the federal government restricts exporting of several kinds of high-tech products for security purposes and other political reasons. The Reagan administration has taken a particularly strong stance in this regard.

Cultural Barriers

Nationalism will remain an important, albeit difficult to measure, barrier to trade. "Buy French" or "Buy Japanese" can be strong influences on industrial and consumer purchases.

Cultural differences have pervasive implications for marketing research in other countries. Statistical data may not be available—no census in the People's Republic of China; primary research may not be possible—illiteracy or privacy customs may preclude mail surveys; and comparable samples for cross-cultural comparisons may be difficult to implement.

Business relationships and practices vary across cultures. Selling processes, negotiation styles, and expectations about agreements are usually very different in other countries. The person or approach which works best in the United States may not work at all in a foreign country. Because the American educational system has deemphasized language training and associated overseas study during the 1970s and 1980s, this problem will only get worse in the immediate future.

Obviously advertising across cultures is very difficult. Language and symbols are culture bound, and much has been written about the myriad "very large" mistakes that even the largest multinational companies have made over the years. A recent trend toward joint ventures among advertising agencies may help in this regard.

The structure of distribution systems also varies across cultures. As an example, interorganizational ties in Japanese channels of distribution are stronger and longer-lasting than in the United States. These ties are composed of equity ownership, loans, formal and informal reciprocity agreements, and exchange of personnel. Such strong relationships are precluded in the United States by antitrust laws *and* custom. Such strong interorganizational relationships in Japan virtually eliminate opportunities for foreign suppliers of component parts. But other kinds of foreign goods may be sold in Japan, such as capital equipment, where long-standing commercial relationships are not as pervasive.

The cultural barriers are the most difficult to deal with. Little research is available upon which to base prescriptions. Knowledge about a particular culture doesn't help very much in understanding others. For example, one might expect Japanese and Korean bargaining styles to be similar. However, having observed both Japanese and Korean businessmen in bargaining situations, we would be hard-pressed to find two negotiation styles that are more different! It is dangerous from a marketing standpoint to try to "categorize" cultures.

Psychological Barriers

The last set of barriers to international marketing, the psychological ones, are the least obvious from the manager's point of view. Little has been written about them because they are very difficult to research. We cannot ask executives about decision factors about which they are unaware or loath to reveal. Nonetheless they deserve mention. Ethnocentrism, a belief in the superiority or importance of one's group, causes us to ignore the importance of learning about and understanding our foreign clients. Racial and ethnic prejudices, often vestiges of World War II,

hamper sound business judgment. Risk aversion is another problem. Secretary of Commerce Malcolm Baldrige suggests that some American executives are "afraid to export." Finally, focus on short-term performance criteria also constrains a firm's ability to enter international markets. International markets take time to develop. Profits are generally derived from volume realized in the long run. This requires establishment of long-term business relationships based on mutual trust and goals. Appropriately designed products, tailored promotional strategies, and efficient distribution systems all take time to develop in a foreign environment.

The foregoing barriers to successful market penetration abroad are especially important for smaller businesses and entrepreneurs. Capital and other resources are often very limited, and "tripping" on any of the financial, legal, cultural, or psychological barriers discussed above may prove to be a fatal mistake for a smaller company. Yet the future "more global marketplace" holds much promise for knowledgeable marketers in all sizes and types of American companies.

MARKETING: RETROSPECTIVE AND PROSPECTIVE

The Centrality of Marketing

Marketing is a management function whose popularity seems to ebb and flow with the times. In the 1970s, every firm of course did its share of marketing, but as inflation raged or shortages became the rule, financial considerations, procurement, and production took center stage. Today, and for the rest of the 1980s, it is forecasted that marketing will be "the new priority" that no organization can afford to ignore.[1] What are we to make of the changing emphasis on marketing? Is it as important as contemporary observers make it out to be?

Actually, one should not pay too much attention to the apparent rise and fall of the marketing function, at least not in the short run. For beneath the surface of its swings in popularity lies a fundamental trend that is transforming the role of marketing dramatically. Marketing is moving from a separate, parallel function among production, finance, personnel, R & D, and other areas to an *integrative function* that not only binds the separate areas of the firm together but serves as the primary means for *responding to and influencing the environment* to advantage. Indeed, marketing is no longer synonymous with advertising or selling but consists of a variety of tasks, each attuned to the constraints within the firm and the opportunities and vicissitudes of the marketplace. Marketing is no longer solely a task for specialists but is shared also by managers traditionally concerned with other operating and planning tasks in the firm. Overall, marketing concepts and methods pervade the organization from boardroom to assembly line.

Before we describe the emerging role of marketing and the new forms it is taking, let us briefly sketch the forces producing the changes. The forces are phenomena with which you are familiar, but you probably have not realized just how far-reaching their effects have been.

The most important changes concern the *customer*. At the micro level, individual tastes are becoming more numerous, more refined, and more fickle. The result has been a proliferation of distinct market segments that demand unique products and services and new ways to reach them. At the same time, there has been a continual shift in aggregate markets. Some emerge overnight. Some persist a long time and either experience a rebirth or die. Others grow slowly. Still others expand by leaps and bounds. Obviously, if it is to satisfy market segments and profitably reap the rewards of volatile markets, the firm must adjust and readjust its marketing programs on an ever more frequent basis.

The adjustment process also becomes a new imperative because of a second factor: the *competitor*. In recent years, more aggressive and more sophisticated rivals have been vying for the same markets as those served by our brands. Advances in product and production technologies, market monitoring techniques, and strategic managerial know-how have raised the level of competition to a new plane. To compound matters, legal and regulatory bodies, which have always been procompetition, now seem to push free enterprise with an evangelistic fervor. Although this is most evident in the deregulation of the airline, trucking, banking, and telecommunications industries, it has been felt throughout the business community in forms ranging from antitrust and deceptive advertising regulations by the FTC to confrontation in the courts. Increased competition puts new burdens on marketing, since it is primarily through product design, pricing, promotion, advertising, and distribution that competitive effects are mitigated or overcome.

A third force influencing the nature and importance of marketing is the *economy*. Except during deep recessions or depressions, which tended to be few and far between, heretofore managers could count on a growing population, ever-increasing disposable incomes, low credit terms, tax incentives, and in general a favorable business climate. But mild recessions have occurred more frequently, thus increasing competitive pressures and putting new strains on marketing. Even in inflationary times, marketing must be pursued with a new urgency as people feel the impulse to spend in new ways and marketers scramble to uncover the ever-budding market segments. No longer can managers expect prosperity to continue unabated. Rather, we seem to face a never-ending alternation of turmoil and calm for indeterminate periods of time. Marketing tools are an essential means to adapt to these fluctuations.

As the consumer, the competitor, and the economic environments change, marketers increasingly realize that it is not enough merely to respond to the forces around them. New advances in marketing strategy and tactics make it possible to influence consumer choices, the competitive climate, and economic conditions to a certain extent. This chapter introduces you to the most important concepts and methods of marketing management. We begin with a discussion of two broad objectives that guide any marketing effort: satisfying buyer needs and achieving a competitive advantage. We then turn to planning and implementing the marketing effort. Overall marketing strategy and market selection comprise the planning topics. Implementation is concerned with such tactical issues as product management and new product development, marketing communication (i.e., advertising, promotion, publicity, and personal selling), pricing, and channels of distribution.

Two Guiding Principles

In much the same way that individual behavior is driven by one's fundamental values and social behavior is governed by norms and laws, marketing efforts

MARKETING: RETROSPECTIVE AND PROSPECTIVE

The Centrality of Marketing

Marketing is a management function whose popularity seems to ebb and flow with the times. In the 1970s, every firm of course did its share of marketing, but as inflation raged or shortages became the rule, financial considerations, procurement, and production took center stage. Today, and for the rest of the 1980s, it is forecasted that marketing will be "the new priority" that no organization can afford to ignore.[1] What are we to make of the changing emphasis on marketing? Is it as important as contemporary observers make it out to be?

Actually, one should not pay too much attention to the apparent rise and fall of the marketing function, at least not in the short run. For beneath the surface of its swings in popularity lies a fundamental trend that is transforming the role of marketing dramatically. Marketing is moving from a separate, parallel function among production, finance, personnel, R & D, and other areas to an *integrative function* that not only binds the separate areas of the firm together but serves as the primary means for *responding to and influencing the environment* to advantage. Indeed, marketing is no longer synonymous with advertising or selling but consists of a variety of tasks, each attuned to the constraints within the firm and the opportunities and vicissitudes of the marketplace. Marketing is no longer solely a task for specialists but is shared also by managers traditionally concerned with other operating and planning tasks in the firm. Overall, marketing concepts and methods pervade the organization from boardroom to assembly line.

Before we describe the emerging role of marketing and the new forms it is taking, let us briefly sketch the forces producing the changes. The forces are phenomena with which you are familiar, but you probably have not realized just how far-reaching their effects have been.

The most important changes concern the *customer*. At the micro level, individual tastes are becoming more numerous, more refined, and more fickle. The result has been a proliferation of distinct market segments that demand unique products and services and new ways to reach them. At the same time, there has been a continual shift in aggregate markets. Some emerge overnight. Some persist a long time and either experience a rebirth or die. Others grow slowly. Still others expand by leaps and bounds. Obviously, if it is to satisfy market segments and profitably reap the rewards of volatile markets, the firm must adjust and readjust its marketing programs on an ever more frequent basis.

The adjustment process also becomes a new imperative because of a second factor: the *competitor*. In recent years, more aggressive and more sophisticated rivals have been vying for the same markets as those served by our brands. Advances in product and production technologies, market monitoring techniques, and strategic managerial know-how have raised the level of competition to a new plane. To compound matters, legal and regulatory bodies, which have always been procompetition, now seem to push free enterprise with an evangelistic fervor. Although this is most evident in the deregulation of the airline, trucking, banking, and telecommunications industries, it has been felt throughout the business community in forms ranging from antitrust and deceptive advertising regulations by the FTC to confrontation in the courts. Increased competition puts new burdens on marketing, since it is primarily through product design, pricing, promotion, advertising, and distribution that competitive effects are mitigated or overcome.

A third force influencing the nature and importance of marketing is the *economy*. Except during deep recessions or depressions, which tended to be few and far between, heretofore managers could count on a growing population, ever-increasing disposable incomes, low credit terms, tax incentives, and in general a favorable business climate. But mild recessions have occurred more frequently, thus increasing competitive pressures and putting new strains on marketing. Even in inflationary times, marketing must be pursued with a new urgency as people feel the impulse to spend in new ways and marketers scramble to uncover the ever-budding market segments. No longer can managers expect prosperity to continue unabated. Rather, we seem to face a never-ending alternation of turmoil and calm for indeterminate periods of time. Marketing tools are an essential means to adapt to these fluctuations.

As the consumer, the competitor, and the economic environments change, marketers increasingly realize that it is not enough merely to respond to the forces around them. New advances in marketing strategy and tactics make it possible to influence consumer choices, the competitive climate, and economic conditions to a certain extent. This chapter introduces you to the most important concepts and methods of marketing management. We begin with a discussion of two broad objectives that guide any marketing effort: satisfying buyer needs and achieving a competitive advantage. We then turn to planning and implementing the marketing effort. Overall marketing strategy and market selection comprise the planning topics. Implementation is concerned with such tactical issues as product management and new product development, marketing communication (i.e., advertising, promotion, publicity, and personal selling), pricing, and channels of distribution.

Two Guiding Principles

In much the same way that individual behavior is driven by one's fundamental values and social behavior is governed by norms and laws, marketing efforts

CHAPTER
SIXTEEN

He lives doubly who also enjoys the past.
    —— *Marcus Valerius Martial*
            (A.D. 40?–104?)

Let us not go over the old ground, let us rather prepare for what is to come.
    —— *Marcus Tullius Cicero*
            (106–43 B.C.)

I. The Centrality of Marketing
II. Two Guiding Principles
    A. **Customer Analysis**
    B. **Competitive Analysis**
       1. **Product Differentiation: The Case of 7-Up**
       2. **Overall Cost Leadership: From Computers to Chain Saws**
       3. **Special Market Focus: Lipton Herbal Teas**
III. Planning and Implementing the Marketing Effort
    A. **Overall Marketing Strategy**
       1. **Industry Analysis**
       2. **The Product Portfolio**
       3. **Strategic Group Analysis**
    B. **Market Selection**
       1. **Consumer Behavior**
       2. **Market Segmentation**
       3. **Market Monitoring and Decision Support Systems**
    C. **Product Decisions**
       1. **New Product Development**
       2. **Perceptual Maps and Product Positioning**
       3. **Managing the Product through Its Life Cycle**
    D. **Communication Decisions**
       1. **A Communication Model**
       2. **Advertising**
       3. **Promotion**
       4. **Personal Selling**
    E. **Price Decisions**
       1. **Goals and Constraints in Pricing**
       2. **Pricing Tactics**

are—or should be—motivated by two principles. Specifically, marketing strives to (1) meet customer needs and (2) provide a product or service superior to that offered by the competition.

As simple as these principles might seem, they are difficult to sustain in practice, and each year the failures regularly outnumber the successes. Let us examine some of these failures and successes to gain a perspective before we turn to an examination of the key functional areas of marketing.

Customer Analysis

In order to meet customer needs, firms spend a lot of time and money on research. A common strategy is to concentrate one's efforts on new product development. The rationale is that consumers are satisfied through products, so it behooves one to begin here.

Consider the case of Frost 8/80, a "dry white" whiskey introduced by Brown-Forman Distillers in the early 1970s.[2] After much fanfare and a reported $6.5 million investment, Brown-Forman withdrew the brand from the market, less than two years after its introduction. The reason given was that sales were simply too low. Estimates of the losses extend beyond the $2 million mark.

The Frost 8/80 case is noteworthy because Brown-Forman appeared to have done all the right things prior to launch. The brand was targeted at a unique niche in the market. Management thought that a large enough segment of consumers would welcome a clear whiskey, just as many buyers had earlier accepted the concept of a light whiskey. Unlike the latter, which was amber in color and considered a less strong-tasting whiskey intended to be drunken straight or with water, Frost 8/80 was positioned as a versatile mixer. The product seemed destined for success, given industry statistics showing a shift in drinking preferences from the harsher bourbons and whiskeys toward the softer liquors such as vodka, gin, or scotch. Moreover, women and young people increasingly were turning to the latter, preferring sweeter, less alcoholic mixed drinks. Since Frost 8/80 was basically a filtered whiskey, Brown-Forman hoped that sufficient sales here would forestall the effects of slow growth and eventual decline in the demand for its traditional whiskey brands.

Before deciding to market Frost 8/80, Brown-Forman performed a series of activities quite typical of modern companies. First, a concept study was conducted to get an idea of people's receptivity to a dry, white whiskey. Favorable reactions led to interviews and surveys to discover how people might consume the product and what their feelings were toward it. A third step was a taste test which tended to show that people liked the product. Fourth, outside experts were consulted in the choosing of a name, bottle, and label. Consumer panels were utilized to obtain still more information in a fifth step. The final stage consisted of heavy advertising to inform the public of the brand and its uses.

With such a textbook program, why did Frost 8/80 fail? Industry watchers offered many reasons, including an insufficient market base, neglect to test market, and a reluctance of management to stick it out until a customer franchise could be built. The most likely explanations, however, lay in Brown-Forman's failure to perform a proper customer analysis. Essentially, the company did not carry its research deep enough into how consumers make choices and how they would respond to Frost 8/80.

As we will explore in more depth later in the chapter, one objective of customer research is to first discover which product attributes are important to consumers and only then design a product to meet the consumer's needs. Following a more or less armchair approach, Brown-Forman turned the process on its head by assuming that a white whiskey would meet needs similar to those filled by the traditional clear liquors. They began with a product and then hoped to prove that a need existed.

More importantly, the research performed by Brown-Forman did not get to the heart of customer decision making but rather only revealed surface symptoms of consumer behavior. Contemporary research over a wide range of products and services shows that key activities in the decision process concern how consumers make inferences as to product attributes, how they then organize the information so gleaned, and how finally the structure of information in memory influences consumer choices. The process proceeds something like the following:

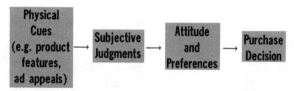

That is, objective information communicated through actual physical product attributes or ads is perceived by the consumer who, in turn, makes abstractions from the "hard" information to form subjective judgments. The inferred data need not be directly related to the physical cues but can be connected to other thoughts and feelings which may even be at odds with the intended communication. Next, the subjective information is integrated into an attitude, which then influences one's decision to make a purchase or not.

Consider how the process works for a hypothetical consumer, Tom R. Tom R. bought a bottle of Frost 8/80 at the suggestion of the retail clerk at his local liquor store. A dealer promotion made the purchase attractive in that it was a full dollar below the regular price and the price of existing liquors. Later at home, Tom R. poured a small amount of Frost 8/80 in a glass, just to see how it tasted. But Tom R. could not decide whether he liked or disliked Frost 8/80. The physical cues—the clear liquid, the lack of a strong odor, the advertising—suggested to him that the product would be tasteless. But once he tried it, he found something quite different: a strong whiskey taste. In effect, his expectations were violated, and the dissonance produced confusion. Had he tried first to mix Frost 8/80 with 7-Up or Coke, he may never have had the ambivalent reaction. But the initial, undiluted taste created a first impression that remained with him and generated uncertainties. His doubts were raised as to the purity of Frost 8/80 as well. After all, vodka is colorless and supposedly made of "pure" potatoes. But Tom R. wondered what exactly was the new taste. Perhaps, artificial ingredients were added to make the drink a synthetic concoction. Equally disconcerting was the thought that other people would have a similar reaction. The safe decision would be not to risk social embarrassment and to forgo serving it to guests. As a consequence of such reactions, repeat sales never reached desirable levels in the market.

It is easy to see how such negative inferences, both conscious and nonconscious, could arise in response to the physical cues. In addition, such negative attributions can easily lead to unfavorable attitudes and a decision not to buy the brand again. If decision making is construed as an attempt to gain knowledge and confidence about the world around us, then the uncertainty engendered by Frost 8/80 was an impediment to the process of consumer choice. It is interesting to note, too, that Brown-Forman compounded the uncertainty by switching ad agencies during the first year. The resulting change in themes only led to more confusion. This would be expected to affect the rate of first-time, as well as repeat, purchasing. What consumers needed was a way to "learn" about the product under favorable circumstances. Free tastings of mixed drinks in stores (where legal) or taverns where the seller could control the consumer's initial introduction to the product, advertising that prepared prospective customers for what they would experience when they tried the product, and other tactics might have been more fruitful. But even more basic than this, Brown-Forman never demonstrated that Frost 8/80 satisfied a genuine need and that a sufficiently large market existed.

The point of the Frost 8/80 example is to stress the importance of performing a sound customer analysis. This means discovering what consumers' needs are; which product attributes satisfy these needs; how customers will search for, evaluate, and consume the product; and how the tools under the control of the marketer can be used to facilitate the customer decision process.

Competitive Analysis

Even if one has developed a product that meets consumers' needs, success may not be forthcoming if competitors get the upper hand. Therefore, analysis of the competition is as important as study of the consumer. The goal is to meet customer needs with a product or service that achieves a differential advantage over the competition. The differential advantage might be superior product quality, a lower price, greater availability, more favorable credit terms, better service, a unique brand image, and so on.

Typically, to overcome competitive threats, one of three broad approaches can be taken: product differentiation, overall cost leadership, or special market focus.[3] Let us consider each through an illustration.

Product Differentiation: The Case of 7-Up. 7-Up was introduced in 1929 and quickly established itself as a popular drink, despite the presence of literally hundreds of competitors that tasted much the same. Nevertheless, its market share was small, and most people purchased it as either a good mixer (especially with bootlegged whiskey in those Prohibition years) or a remedy for headache and other minor ills. Indeed, a key promotion advocated 7-Up "for home and hospital use." In 1942, the J. Walter Thompson ad agency took over the account and stressed the product's fresh taste along with the old image of "you like it, it likes you." Although it eventually became the third leading soft drink behind Coca-Cola and Pepsi, it lagged far behind the two leaders. Moreover, sales growth in the mid 1960s was considerably below the industry average, and four new competitors were threatening 7-Up: Coca-Cola's Sprite, Pepsi Cola's Teem, Canada Dry's Wink, and Royal Crown's Upper-10.

Something had to be done, and the first step was consumer research. The findings were surprising. Management had believed that consumers thought of 7-Up as one of a number of soft drinks. Therefore, they had also believed that the brand would at least enter the set of possible thirst-quenching alternatives when consumers needed to choose a drink. But what they found was quite different. When asked to list what they thought of when the words "soft drink" came to mind, most people listed Coke, Pepsi, Dr Pepper, or another cola. In the minds of consumers, "soft drink" was equated with "cola." 7-Up either never entered their thoughts or tended to be considered only as a mixer or health aid. So when consumers made up a shopping list, went to a restaurant, or were offered a soft drink at the home of a friend, most of them never really considered 7-Up.

The problem can thus be seen to be one of brand image, consumer knowledge, and the strength and entrenchment of the competition. Yet the solution was not straightforward. One might think that the expenditure of more money on advertising or promotion was called for; but, nevertheless, examination of the competition suggested a caution.

In 1967, Pepsi spent approximately $55 million on advertising and Coke about $44 million. This was about four times as much as 7-Up's $12 million. To make matters worse, Sprite and Teem spent $10 million and $9 million, respectively, on advertising. Clearly, more advertising dollars would be expensive and problematic in effect. 7-Up had to get many consumers who happened to be cola drinkers to try 7-Up—and it had to do so without raising costs excessively or initiating a price/advertising/promotion war with the leaders, who had greater resources.

The solution pursued was the now famous "Uncola" campaign by the J. Walter Thompson agency. 7-Up changed its advertising to introduce 7-Up as an alternative to cola drinks. Some ads emphasized that 7-Up has a "fresh, clean taste," and is "wet ... wild, never too sweet ... (with) no aftertaste." Other ads called attention to the occasions one might want a 7-Up: at the restaurant, with a hamburger, on a picnic, with snacks, etc. Still other ads made direct comparisons to colas, stressing, for example, the "fresh, clean," and "alive" ingredients of 7-Up (i.e., lemons and limes) versus the dark, shriveled, and dead-looking contents of colas (i.e., cola nuts). Promotions included free 7-Up glasses in the shape of the famous Coca-Cola glass, but upside down. In short, consumers were forced to consider 7-Up uniquely and in a new comparative light.

The campaign worked. In the three years following introduction of the Uncola campaign, 7-Up's sales increased an average of nearly 20 percent per year compared with only about 14 percent for the industry. The three prior years had shown a 3 percent per year average gain for 7-Up, but a 10 percent yearly average for the industry.[4]

The 7-Up case is a classic example of a (pure) *product differentiation* competitive strategy. The firm's brand was positioned relative to the competition, and consumers perceived it in a unique way. This was done on a marketwide basis, in contrast to the alternative strategy of product differentiation for specific segments, which is a special case of the market focus strategy that we will consider shortly. Product differentiation creates a distinctive image for a brand, and, if done properly, meets a genuine need and increases the loyalty of customers. It can make consumers less price-sensitive and vulnerable to the offerings of competitors. Although 7-Up created differentiation primarily through its new advertising and secondarily through its product formulation, product differentiation can also be produced by pricing, distribution, packaging, auxiliary services, or other marketing tactics. Product differentiation must be based on things perceived by the consumer as real benefits or else repeat sales will not materialize. Also, it can be expensive to create, and it can be imitated by the competitors in the long run. Therefore, more than other strategies, it demands constant injections of new ideas. And money.

Overall Cost Leadership: From Computers to Chain Saws. The goal in overall cost leadership is to keep manufacturing, material, and/or other costs to a minimum and in so doing increase demand through the expected effect that a relatively low industry price will have. The increased volume, in turn, leads to absolute economies of scale and experience curve effects (discussed later) which then feedback lowering costs still further. The hoped-for ultimate effect, as with product differentiation, is a large market share. Indeed, cost leadership seems to work best for firms that already have a high relative market share. Furthermore, overall cost leadership entails a never-ending vigil of stringent cost and overhead control and the weeding out of marginal customers and product variations. Like the (pure) product differentiation strategy, overall cost leadership is a marketwide competitive strategy.

A number of firms follow an overall cost leadership approach. This is perhaps most obvious in the home computer industry. Let us briefly focus on Texas Instruments. Its president, J. Fred Bucy, has identified four strategic components as central to

Texas Instruments' success.[5] The first is the *experience curve* concept.[6] As shown in Figure 16-1, the average cost per unit of an item typically decreases as cumulative output increases. In fact, the Boston Consulting Group asserts that the costs of most items will decline about 20 percent to 30 percent for each doubling of cumulative production. Why? Because with the passage of time, labor becomes more efficient, innovations arise in manufacturing, products are redesigned to take advantage of material and other savings, and other learning occurs. This is especially so within the solid-state electronics industry where it is not uncommon to experience a doubling and even redoubling of cumulative production in the first two or three years. Obviously, firms that ride the crest of the experience curve phenomenon, such as Texas Instruments, can charge relatively lower prices and capture larger market shares. Notice, too, that experience curve effects are not limited to production costs but may apply to marketing costs as well.

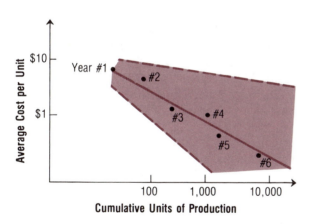

Figure 16-1. The experience curve phenomenon: a hypothetical example

The line plotted through the datum points is typical; the shaded area indicates that the slopes of actual experience curves vary considerably according to the nature of the product and other variables.

A second component of Texas Instruments' overall cost leadership approach is the *importance of being first* to develop a new market. Although not a necessary component for success, being first typically permits an early capitalization on the experience curve, leads to a favorable brand image and the building of a customer base, and results in higher profit margins. Being first can be risky, however, if market acceptance is slower than expected and competitors wait in the wings to take advantage of the learning and primary demand investment of the market pioneer. In Texas Instruments' case, being first was a decided advantage.

Accumulated units of production with products related to a focal product is a third component of Texas Instruments' strategy and is termed *shared experience*. Thus, Texas Instruments finds similar uses for its semiconductors in hand calculators, minicomputers, digital watches, and computer terminals. This permits a reduction in costs by parceling them out among products, and the shared experience then enhances the overall cost leadership of individual products still further.

Finally, Texas Instruments follows a philosophy of *design to cost*. In the words of its president, "[T]his involves deciding today what the selling price and performance of a given product must be years in the future and designing the product and the equipment for producing it to meet both cost and performance goals."[7] Primary emphasis is thus placed on cost; the secondary objective is "to avoid designing into a product more performance than the market is willing to buy."[8]

Overall cost leadership is thus at odds with the product differentiation strategy. It is not so much that firms such as Texas Instruments do not differentiate their products. Indeed, they do this to some extent through product design, advertising, market segmentation, and distribution policies. Nevertheless, low costs are given the highest priority, and product differentiation is emphasized to a lesser extent than it is by firms that pursue a (pure) product differentiation posture. Similarly, the product differentiator is not unconcerned with costs. Rather, goals for superior product quality, brand image, or other factors are met first. This generally entails spending more; hence the inherent trade-off. In rare instances (for example, the components businesses), it is in fact possible to find both high product quality and overall cost leadership.[9] But this is the exception rather than the rule.

Overall cost leadership is a powerful strategy, but it can be dangerous in the long run. We have already mentioned the possibility of slow consumer adoption of the product. Another potential problem is that price competition, the primary demand stimulation tool, is easily copied by others. Still another threat is the possibility that competitors will develop new technologies and modify the product significantly to advantage or even create a substitute. Then, too, even if consumers are initially enthusiastic, tastes may change, and the firm will be left with an unfulfilled recovery of its investment.

For Texas Instruments, the home computer market proved damaging in the long run. The introduction of its Model 99/4A in 1979 led to a market share of 26 percent by 1982. However, competition based primarily on price by Commodore, Radio Shack, Atari, and Timex forced Texas Instruments to lower its price from a high of $1,000 in 1979 to less than $250 in 1982. Further intensification of competition in 1983 saw the price of Model 99/4A plummet to less than $89 with a rebate. Market share slipped to 19 percent in 1983 as well. Although the overall size of the market doubled between 1982 and 1983, Texas Instruments could not profitably compete in the home computer market and therefore withdrew. Not only the price wars but also consumer shifts in tastes took their toll as buyers became more sophisticated and demanded value and certain benefits as the primary product attributes.

Price became relatively less important. Such is the pitfall of relying too heavily on an overall cost leadership strategy over time.

As a final comment on the overall cost leadership strategy, we note that each industry typically witnesses a variety of strategies, and one or more firms frequently find overall cost leadership viable. In the chain saw industry, for example, we see that one market leader in 1973, McCulloch (with 27 percent of the market), pursued an overall cost leadership approach, whereas the other market leader, Homelite (with 28 percent of the market), followed a product differentiation strategy based on high quality and a network of servicing dealers.[10] These firms and the industry as a whole tended to sell large, high-priced chain saws, most of which were bought by professional woodsmen and farmers. Then, beginning about 1973, Beaird-Poulan began marketing very low-priced, smaller chain saws for casual users. Its market share then was about 8 percent. With other firms soon following suit, the market exploded as a consequence of the new mass market appeal of chain saws. By 1977, the market shares of Homelite, Beaird-Poulan, and McCulloch were approximately 23 percent, 22 percent, and 20 percent, respectively, and the market for casual users increased from about 430,000 units in 1972 to 1,750,000 in 1977. The casual user segment was now about 70 percent of a $1.15 billion market.

Notice that the market leaders employed the two generic strategies we have discussed so far. Notice also that, contrary to Texas Instruments' experience, price rivalry had not harmed the position of the original overall cost leader, McCulloch. And further, notice the dramatic rise of Beaird-Poulan, the other practitioner of overall cost leadership. The chain saw industry also illustrates the possibility of other strategic approaches. For example, the German company,

Stihl, uses a product differentiation strategy but directs its brand to a particular market segment: professional users. Its product is of even higher quality (and price) than Homelite's, and it finds that a place exists for it in the market, too. In fact, it maintained a market share of 7 or 8 percent from 1972 until 1980. Other firms in the industry with no or ill-defined competitive strategies (for example Remington or Roper) have fared less well. Later in the chapter we will discuss other strategic concepts that help to explain why different approaches flourish in some cases but fail in others. Now we introduce the third generic strategy.

Special Market Focus: Lipton Herbal Teas. Whereas the product differentiation and overall cost leadership strategies strive to dominate—or at least survive in—entire markets, the market focus strategy aims for a particular segment or small number of segments of a larger market. Once such a segment is found, the firm employs either a product differentiation or overall cost leadership approach to attack it. In this sense, the special market focus strategy can be considered a subset of the previous two.

A good example of a market focus strategy is the case of Lipton Herbal Teas. Prior to 1978, the market for herb teas in the U.S. was minuscule, perhaps only 2 or 3 percent of the entire black tea market. In Germany and other parts of Europe, in contrast, herb teas were thought to account for 40 to 45 percent of the entire market for tea. Therefore, it was thought the U.S. might well represent a large, untapped market. (Note that herb teas are not teas, strictly speaking, and are caffeine-free.)

In 1979–1980, Lipton launched its entries into the herb tea market which at that time was pursued primarily by Celestial Seasonings and by Bigelow. Its alleged goal was sales of at least 5 percent of the black tea market in the first year or so. Lipton hoped also to achieve economies of scale in production and reduce overhead, since it was already making regular tea. This should give Lipton a cost advantage over its smaller competitors including Celestial Seasonings. Nevertheless, its principal strategy was one of product differentiation, for reasons we will mention shortly.

The target audience was defined as women aged 25–49, with middle to upper incomes, and who were average to heavy black tea drinkers. Herbal tea drinkers were, of course, also sought. In addition, the psychographic profile of the target consumer was "an independent woman, with strong convictions, and who feels comfortable making decisions."[11] As a consequence, a very specific and relatively small market segment was sought.

Differentiation from regular tea was accomplished through a variety of tactics. The product was made with high-quality, natural ingredients and, as noted, no caffeine. Originally, five flavors were offered: orange, spice, chamomile, hibiscus, and almond. Later a sixth was added: citrus sunset, which contains the davana herb from India. Print ads stressed "naturally delicious" and "no caffeine." They contained colorful pictures of the tea boxes and very little copy. A cents-off coupon worth as much as 25¢ on a box of 16 bags was often part of the ad. One TV ad emphasized the quality of life, another natural settings. The theme of romance was discernible in most ads as well. Dealer promotions such as "2 free with 10" and "no payment for 6 months" were tried to gain retail acceptance. Finally, although the familiar rectangular box was used, the package was made more exotic, feminine, and flowery than traditional styles. Further, the rectangular box was designed so that the largest side caught the eye of the consumer, rather than the end as is usually the case. This not only provided a larger shelf facing, but it minimized overhead, since more boxes could be stacked advantageously to reduce space.

Lipton thus pursued a small segment of the market and used a product differentiation strategy. It explicitly strove to create "maximum differentiation" from its regular and flavored teas. This was done in order not to cannibalize sales. Also, Lipton was concerned that a "no caffeine" selling point might backfire on its other products, which, with sales in the hundreds of millions of dollars and heavy in caffeine, could be hurt if the same consumers were pursued. Finally, Lipton's marketing people believed that many American consumers would find the cost of herbal tea excessive (about 10¢ more per box), the idea of drinking "flowers" repugnant, the image of an herb tea drinker as too hip or exotic and not in keeping with the regular tea-drinker's self-image, or drinking herb tea dangerous (some people believe that herbs are upsetting or potentially toxic). Hence, product differentiation was called for to protect Lipton's existing products and to reach the proper market segment.

The market focus strategy is not applied only by giants such as Lipton. As a matter of fact, many small and medium-sized firms find the strategy the only way to survive against their larger rivals. In other words, they find it essential to go after market niches. We see the market focus strategy being applied with increasing frequency, too, as a consequence of the ever-greater splintering of consumer markets. In certain ways, a market focus orientation even requires more marketing than other strategies. Segments are difficult to find and reach. They must be of a sufficient size and/or the product and a marketing campaign must be altered to make a profit. And they are more sensitive to competition and changes in consumer tastes, thereby requiring closer monitoring and more frequent changes in marketing programs.

This completes our discussion of the two guiding principles of modern marketing: customer analysis and competitive analysis. Implicit in the presentation was a third activity: *analysis of the constraints, power, and liabilities of the firm.* This, in turn, implies taking into account the goals of the firm, its financial and human resources, its production capabilities, its organization structure, the economic environment, the social-political-legal environment, and other factors. Each of these must be considered from a marketing perspective. However, because discussion of these topics is beyond the scope of this text, nothing more will be said about them here. We turn now to the marketing tools managers have at their disposal to respond to or influence their markets.

Planning and Implementing the Marketing Effort

Overall Marketing Strategy

Industry Analysis. Nowhere is the integrative function of marketing more evident than in its role as the lever regulating a firm's place in its industry. An industry may be viewed as having two attributes or consequences for the firm. The first is called a *shirt-tail effect.* To a certain extent, as the industry goes, so goes the firm. There are forces underlying every industry that more or less affect all firms equally. Thus all firms face, among other forces, an actual and a potential market; a particular economic, technological, and human environment with common assets and liabilities; and a set of competitive and legal rules governing conduct. Although these forces constraint or facilitate a firm's operations, they do not, by themselves, determine its performance. Rather, it is through the *boot-strap effect* that a firm controls its destiny. By boot-strap effect we mean the actions taken by a firm to respond to or influence the competitive pressures it feels as a member of an industry. Obviously, some firms are better able to do this than others. The competitive threats and ways to combat them serve as one basis for marketing strategy.

Any firm will face five classes of competitive threats in an industry.[12] These are (1) threats of new entrants, (2) rivalry among existing firms, (3) threats of substitute products, (4) bargaining power of suppliers, and (5) bargaining power of customers. The essence of marketing strategy with respect to these threats is to maximize the relative power of the firm vis-à-vis the sources of each threat.

Threats of New Entrants. Firms within an industry often resist the entry of new firms. The rationale is that there is only so much business to go around and a new seller simply means less for all. In general, entrance to an industry is controlled by two factors. One consists of the specific actions taken by existing firms.

A case in point is the experience of Southwest Airlines. Claiming that the Texas market could not support another airline, Braniff, Trans Texas, and Continental Airlines asked for a restraining order prohibiting issuance of a license to Southwest in 1968. Only after Southwest appealed to the State Supreme Court was it allowed to fly in 1970. However, the company had no planes, pilots, or supporting staff. To raise capital, Southwest decided to sell stock. But just as the stock was to go public, Braniff and Trans Texas (now Texas International) again attempted to block the venture on the grounds that Southwest's proposal would violate certain intrastate exclusivity requirements. This claim, too, was found later to be groundless. Finally, Southwest began to fly in 1971, four years after incorporation. In the ensuing year, however, three more major law suits, two going all the way to the U.S. Supreme Court, nearly broke the back of Southwest.

But these were not the only roadblocks faced by Southwest. Braniff, in particular, allegedly tried to block the entrance of Southwest through numerous price-cutting, scheduling, and other competitive marketing moves. Throughout the turmoil, Southwest persevered by following an overall cost leadership strategy aimed at a special market segment: people flying between large cities over short to medium hauls. Today Southwest has revenues approaching $400 million and regularly attains the highest profit margins among all domestic carriers.

The other force controlling entry to a market consists of natural barriers. These include high capital requirements, inherent economies of scale, special product differentiation (e.g., high advertising needed to build a brand image), impediments to distribution, established cost disadvantages, and certain government policies.[13]

From a marketing perspective, any firm must consider the strength of another's potential entry, what effects it would have on the firm and market, and what if any actions to take. Barriers to entry, either natural or initiated by competing firms, tend to promote industry concentration over time. Some firms may want to increase the barriers and resist the entry of newcomers; the market leader invariably finds itself in this position. On occasion, firms may wish to reduce entry barriers or at least not resist a newcomer. For example, a firm that has a small share of the market and uses a market focus strategy based on product differentiation may welcome the entry of a firm that would compete with the low-cost market leader on the basis of price. Such battles tend to lower the quality of the low-cost firms' products or at least allow the high-quality marketer a chance to siphon off disenchanted buyers from the price-oriented combatants. In any case, the threat of a new entrant in an industry should cause the existing firms to reassess their pricing, product quality, advertising, and other marketing tactics, as well as their capital requirements, economies of scale, and government policies.

Rivalry among Existing Firms. This is the classic notion of competition. The strategic alternatives include product differentiation, cost leadership, and market focus. The means to compete reside in product, price, communication, and/or distribution tactics. Specific choices of strategy and implementation are governed, in part, by market share, growth, and the nature of overlap of strategies among firms within the industry. We will discuss the managerial guidelines in these respects below when we consider portfolio and strategic group analysis.

For now, the only rivalry-based concept we shall mention is that of *exit barriers* to firms in an industry. Firms find it difficult to leave an industry when their investments in land, labor, and capital are great within the industry or when government regulations forbid them to do so. In addition, entangling relationships with other products and departments within the firm, intangible commitments to employees and communities, and inertia and outright fear sometimes play a role. Exit barriers thwart the movement of excess capacity, intensify intra-industry competition, and in the extreme damage the profitability of an industry. Firms are forced into head-to-head confrontations and respond in kind (for example imitative price cutting) or to even injure competitors. This is especially so when market growth slows or when competitors are numerous. While the ideal situation for a competitor often is where exit barriers are low and entry barriers are high, firms have little influence over their situation in this regard. Product differentiation and market segmentation may be key marketing options in the effort to reduce the harmful effects of high exit barriers.

Threats of Substitutes.
Competition occurs at many levels even when we limit consideration to the needs of consumers. People buy products because of the needs that the products satisfy. But needs are not always the obvious entities we sometimes believe them to be.

Imagine that you are the brand manager for Pringle's Potato Chips. What need does Pringle's satisfy and with what does it compete? Obviously, Pringle's satisfies a general hunger need or a specific craving for starch, salt, and bulk. And it competes with Frito-Lay, among other brands of potato chips. But behind the obvious we can see that the competition here is among similar firms and for a relatively circumscribed need. Competition among regular, ruffled, low-calorie, cheese, or barbecue flavored potato chips—all of which address similar needs—involves basically the same class of competitors. However, this is only part of the picture.

At the same time, Pringle's competes with other snack foods—peanuts, pretzels, crackers, candy, hors d'oeuvres, even fresh cauliflower. To be sure, such competition is further removed from the Pringle's–Frito-Lay encounter. But a similar need is involved, and at least some of the time Pringle's competes with each of these or some other snack food. Actually, consumer needs may even be more complex than this. Pringle's may be consumed, not because of an urge for salt or bulk, but out of habit, or on an impulse, in a quest for variety, or as a social gesture so as to please a guest or not offend a host.

Then, too, we sometimes view consumption too narrowly. The decision to buy Pringle's is seldom an isolated choice. Rather, it fits within a larger pattern of consumption or expresses a part of one's personality or life style: the elderly buy Pringle's because of its long shelf life, the wealthy because of its novelty. Construed in this sense, Pringle's competes with other ideas (dieting, health consciousness), and activities (saving for a special gift), as well as in the traditional senses. We thus begin to see that any product competes in a generic sense with a wide spectrum of brands, products, and "things" that threaten to become substitutes.

What this means for a firm is that it must not view its offerings parochially. Competition from substitutes places constraints on price, product and package design, distribution, and even advertising. A firm must identify and take into account the larger competitive network. The study of competition in a generic sense also opens up new opportunities if a firm can discover new uses for its products. Thus, Arm and Hammer markets baking soda not only for traditional uses but for odor absorption in the refrigerator or in cat litter boxes, and for cleaning teeth. Chex is now promoted as a party snack as well as a crunchy cereal. And reflecting the changing times, as well as a very competitive gift-giving market, the diamond industry has progressed from an undifferentiated selling approach to specific emphasis of engagements and weddings in its ads ("Diamonds are Forever"), and most recently to highlighting anniversaries of all sorts as appropriate occasions for giving a diamond throughout one's life.

The threat of competition from substitutes again points up the crucial role of customer analysis. A firm must do research to look deeply into the consumer's psyche as well as to explore the larger life space that surrounds the act of consumption. Of equal importance, the firm must view itself not as a producer of a specific product but as the provider of the means to satisfy particular needs. This forces the firm to open up its operations and compete at both deeper and broader levels. The National Cash Register Company for a long time perceived its mission too narrowly: it saw itself a seller of cash registers (and rather slow and unadaptable ones at that). When competitors offered new electronic systems that satisfied a wide spectrum of needs including information storage and processing, NCR belatedly followed suit. The IBM corporation is not so much in the computer business as it is in the business of satisfying the information processing needs of firms. Canon does not sell copy machines, per se, but rather is concerned with helping firms improve office productivity. The firm that purposefully considers threats of substitutes builds its programs around the broader functions that its products satisfy and in the process enhances its chances for success in the long run.

Bargaining Power of Suppliers. The firms in an industry receive their resources from suppliers (i.e., the sellers of materials, service, and other things needed to produce one's offerings). Because suppliers to a certain extent control the prices and quality of their goods and services, they indirectly influence the performance of firms which are its customers. Although companies can pass along cost increases to the ultimate consumer, the market can bear only so much, and excessive costs at the supply end can damage the profitability and growth of an entire industry.

The exact terms of trade depend on the relative power between suppliers and firms in the industry. Power lies in the bargaining abilities of the parties, the availability of alternatives, and the importance of the things exchanged. Five factors have been identified in this regard. A supplier group will be more powerful, vis-à-vis an industry customer, to the extent that (1) it is dominated by a few companies and is more concentrated than the industry it sells to; (2) it is not obliged to contend with other substitute products for sale to the industry; (3) the industry is not an important customer of the supplier group; (4) the supplier group's products are differentiated or it has built up *switching costs* (the costs that any one of its customers would incur in switching to another supplier); and (5) the supplier group poses a credible threat of forward integration (e.g., expansion into manufacturing in direct competition with its customers).[14]

To ensure success, a firm must overcome any dependence on its suppliers. Often its options may be limited, however, because many of the imbalances are external to the firm. Nevertheless, to the extent that a firm can purchase a large portion of a seller's goods (yet retain alternative sources in the wings), confine purchases to standardized items, threaten to backward integrate, and/or reduce its switching costs in some way, it can lessen its dependence on the supplier. From a marketing standpoint, control over suppliers is essential to maintain product quality, pricing, and distribution programs. Moreover, as Coleco's experience shows with its introduction of the Cabbage Patch Kids dolls, a bottleneck at the supplier end can result in enormous numbers of missed sales, the loss of goodwill with retailer and consumer alike, and the opportunity for rivals to enter the still unsaturated market.

Bargaining Power of Customers. A parallel competitive threat to a firm lies in the relative power of its customers. A powerful buyer can command lower prices, more service, special product features, and other concessions: witness the clout that Sears and other giant retailers have in their dealings with some manufacturers of appliances, furniture, and housewares. A buyer group will be powerful in relation to a seller if (1) it is concentrated or purchases large volumes relative to seller's sales, (2) the products it purchases from the industry represent a significant fraction of the customer's costs or purchases, (3) the products it purchases from the industry are standard or undifferentiated, (4) it faces few switching costs, (5) it earns low profits and therefore places special emphasis on paying a low price, (6) buyers pose a credible threat of backward integration, and (7) the industry's product is unimportant to the quality of the buyers' products or services.[15]

A nice illustration of the bargaining power of customers and what it means for marketing can be seen in the example of the U.S. apparel industry. With annual sales in the $20 billion range as of the mid-1980s, U.S. apparel makers face a life and death threat from importers. Whereas imports were a relatively minor consideration in the 1960s, when they represented only 10 to 12 percent of domestic production, today 50 percent or more of all clothing sales in the U.S. originates overseas. The squeeze on domestic firms has forced them to compete on product differentiation terms, since the cheaper wages of manufacturers overseas make overall cost leadership impossible. As a consequence, domestic producers

have been pushing so-called "designer goods" at an unheard-of pace. But anyone can play the designer-goods game, and imitators quickly joined in. This in turn has forced large retailers to demand that they too carry designer clothes so as not to be outdone by boutique shops, and even discount stores have managed to procure some designer brands. The result has been a decline in sales for many clothing manufacturers and retailers.

To compound matters, large retailers have been flexing their muscles in still another way, to the consternation of producers: they now market their own private-label clothing along with name brands. In this way, chains such as Neiman-Marcus, Saks Fifth Avenue, Lord & Taylor, and even J. C. Penney can offer "exclusive" merchandise and charge the prices necessary to make a profit. Given their buying power and the fact that private-label brands do not carry the overhead of a designer brand, retailers can demand favorable terms from the manufacturer. Indeed, the retailer can threaten to purchase more goods from importers because its merchandise is made to its own specifications and U.S. makers offer no special expertise. In short, the power of retail buyers constitutes a threat to U.S. clothing manufacturers that is matched only by the threat of foreign rivalry. With labor costs higher here, U.S. clothing makers are caught in the middle, and their future looks bleak.

Generally, however, a firm faced by a powerful buyer has a number of marketing remedies. Perhaps the most far-ranging and fundamental remedy is the product(s) the firm has to offer. Through product design, a brand image, service, exclusive or selective distribution, or other marketing tactics, sellers must create a distinctive offering. However, because this edge is typically short-lived, the firm must put considerable investment into the monitoring of consumer tastes and new product development, topics we will turn to shortly. Moreover, the firm must give special emphasis to market selection, for survival may hinge on finding the right niches in the marketplace. Finally, either through outright vertical integration or through closer cooperation with intermediaries, the firm can seek to extend its power over consumer pricing, selling, consumer monitoring, and other marketing decisions. In Italy, a renaissance of sorts in the clothing industry has begun where "vertical disintegration" and the formation of "constellations" of firms has replaced both vertically integrated and totally independent enterprises.[16]

This completes our discussion of industry analysis. Along with the ideas noted earlier under competitive analysis, these principles provide the backdrop to the more micro topics in strategy that we will consider next. Successful marketing requires that a firm understand its position in an industry so that it can make choices which not only meet consumer needs but also overcome the five competitive threats noted earlier. This means taking special care to position a firm in relation to its customers, suppliers, rivals, and its own internal capabilities. It means also an ability to plan, monitor, and forecast changes in the environment. All of this takes place, of course, within a legal and ethical environment that constrains choices still further.

The Product Portfolio. Nearly every business markets a number of product classes or brands within a product class. However, seldom do all these products or brands perform equally well, and different strategies may be required for each to accomplish the larger goals of the organization. One way to manage the strategy of all products is to view them together (i.e., as the product portfolio) according to a small number of fundamental criteria. We will scrutinize one such scheme developed by the Boston Consulting Group (BCG).[17] However, it should be noted that other frameworks exist such as General Electric's strategic business screen,[18] Shell's directional policy matrix,[19] or McKinsey's integrated method.

The BCG product portfolio approach to corporate strategy is illustrated in Figure 16-2. Market growth and relative market share (i.e., the ratio of a firm's sales to that of the largest competitor) are used to classify a firm's products or brands. The choice of these two criteria is based on the supposition that market growth reflects both the vitality of the market and the stage a product is in its life cycle, whereas relative market share reveals the competitive position of a firm. Because market growth is only indirectly and partially influenceable by a firm, the primary strategic decision is thought to reside in choices to improve market share. This, in turn, requires application of specific marketing tactics such as advertising or price changes. Moreover, it is believed that high market share will lead to profitability.[20] However, every firm must decide for itself the strength of the relationship and whether it is truly causal or not.

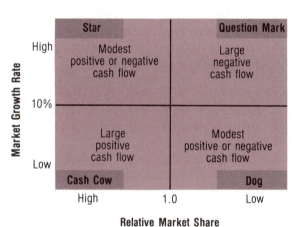

Figure 16-2. A summary of the Boston Consulting Group approach to corporate strategy

Notice in Figure 16-2 that the division of market growth and relative market share into high and low categories results in a four-fold classification. A 10 percent market growth rate and a 1.0 relative market share are used as arbitrary divisions of the two dimensions. A firm's products might then be plotted anywhere in the matrix. So plotted, a product will be labeled either a cash cow, a star, a question mark, or a dog:

- A *cash cow* is a product with low growth but high market share. It generates high amounts of cash and a profit. But because of poor prospects for growth and relative ease in maintaining share, not all the cash can or should be reinvested in the cash cow (by investment is meant spending on product development, advertising, promotion, distribution, or other marketing tactics). Rather BCG maintains that the generated cash should optimally be used to invest in a question mark product.

- *Stars* are high-growth and high-market-share products. To maintain share will require relatively more investment than for a cash cow. Although handsome profits typically occur for stars, the cash flow will be small and may even be negative (i.e., requiring support from a cash cow or outside help). Eventually, as market growth slows, stars become cash cows.

- High growth and low market share define a *question mark*. Not only does a question mark not generate a cash flow, but it draws cash from other products or sources (ideally from a cash cow). The cash is needed to maintain or gain share. Generally, profits will be low or nonexistent here. With no cash infusion, a question mark may become a dog. But with the proper investment, it can become a star. A strategic choice must be made with a question mark product.

- A *dog* consists of a low-growth and low–market-share product. It either does not generate much cash or does not require much. To extricate a dog from the category is either impossible or very expensive. The options open to a firm here typically involve harvesting (i.e., milking the product until it fails completely), sale of the product, or outright abandonment. Dogs, of course, are losing propositions and, given the cash drain, are often disposed of quickly.

The BCG product portfolio is designed to help a firm manage its products over time. A "success sequence" would be an investment from a cash cow to a question mark, in order to move the latter to star status and eventually to a cash cow. "Disaster sequences" include the star→question mark→dog ordering (or some subset of the progression) and the cash cow→dog sequence. At the same time, a firm must maintain a mixture and balance between products so as to ensure that some will generate cash and others will use it to advantage. The product portfolio is designed for long-run decisions of about five years or more.

To take the example of Texas Instruments again, we see that its home computer business was a question mark by 1983. To make it a star, considerable investment would have been necessary, especially given the very high market growth rate, the intensity of competition, and the much greater share by Commodore. Further, the rapidly declining price of home computers meant that less cash would be generated. All in all, Texas Instruments made the decision to disinvest its home computer business before it became a dog.

The Boston Consulting Group asserts that any firm should strive to create an internal balance of products based on the following "ideal" distribution in the product portfolio:

Products with the largest sales . . . should appear either as "stars" or "cash cows." Few products should appear in the "question marks" quadrant: they require heavy cash commitment to transform them into "stars" and can be major losers if something goes wrong. The majority of products should be positioned as "cash cows" . . . since these underwrite the remaining products . . . Few products should appear as "dogs" since these are "cash traps." . . . [21]

Further, as a competitive tool, the BCG product portfolio can be used in a number of ways. First, estimates of product portfolios for competitors should be made. These can be studied and compared among themselves and with the focal firm's to anticipate the effects of attempts to gain share or to divest, and to forecast possible moves by the competitors.

As an example, consider again the chain saw industry, especially the position of McCulloch. McCulloch's market share dropped from about 27 percent in 1973 to 20 percent in 1977. Worse, from a position where it and Homelite shared roles as the market leaders in 1973, it saw its ranking drop to third as Beaird-Poulan skyrocketed from relative obscurity to more than match the leaders. In terms of the BCG matrix, McCulloch was a question mark in 1973 but near the threshold of star status. What might have McCulloch, or rather its parent firm Black & Decker, done to preserve McCulloch's market share? Well, Black & Decker had two cash cows at this time: its U.S. Power Tools and International Power Tools divisions, which together accounted for about 85 percent of its total business. Given the mushrooming casual user segment of the chain saw market, Black & Decker might have invested in McCulloch to make it a star. It might also have pursued more aggressively the high-profit professional user market. Instead, partly in response to an antitrust challenge of Black & Decker's acquisition of McCulloch by the Justice Department in early 1974, Black & Decker kept its businesses separate. By the time the case was settled in Black & Decker's favor in

November 1976, it had missed its opportunity to become the market leader. Indeed, earnings for McCulloch dropped sharply in the late 1970s and into the 1980s, as the chain saw market matured. Black & Decker then divested itself of McCulloch. Whether investment could have made it a star in the casual user and pro markets is difficult to say. But it might well have enhanced its earnings in the short run and reaped more revenue from sale of a stronger McCulloch. Although still in third place, McCulloch's market share is now below 20 percent.

The BCG matrix can also be used to forecast trends. Portfolios of the focal firm and competitors can be prepared for the previous five-year period, the present, and an anticipated future period to gain insight into changing market, product life cycle, and competitive conditions. In fact, analyses over time are essential because a static application of the portfolio matrix can be misleading. For example, a small-share company in a low-growth market may do well over time if it succeeds in increasing its share significantly at the expense of its rivals.

It is important to realize that portfolio analysis, or any other such framework, provides only a partial picture of the health of a firm's products. Any particular firm may find that market growth and market share considerations are less important than other factors, given its unique situation. For example, government regulations, the nature of technology, or any one of the many threats to competition in industries that we mentioned earlier might be the dominant factor. Then, too, care must be taken to fashion a program to implement any strategy chosen. The soundest strategy may fall flat if the wrong marketing tactics are pursued. We turn now to the final strategic tool, one that is intermediate between industry analysis and the product portfolio approach.

Strategic Group Analysis. A vast array of marketing tactics is available to firms for implementing their strategic choices. The product can vary in features, quality, and packaging. Price can vary by quantity bought or time period. Service, credit, and warranties can be added as enticements. Different advertising messages can be employed along with varied media and scheduling alternatives. Dealer and customer promotions can augment the marketing effort. Sales forces permit forceful, face-to-face selling. Options in physical distribution and in retailing and wholesaling permit a tailoring of availability and selling at the grass roots level. And so on.

Despite the many possible combinations of tactics that might be chosen, in practice an industry is usually characterized by a small number of fundamental tactics common to all or most participants. The particular combination of tactics chosen constitutes the firm's strategy, and firms' strategies differ in their relative emphasis on the various tactics. Typically, two or three tactics are sufficient to define an industry. Moreover, a cross-classification of tactics generally finds well-defined clusters of emphasis whereby firms within a cluster can be seen to compete among themselves, each firm using a combination of options common to its cluster but different than combinations found in other clusters.

In one study of 64 companies in 8 different industries, it was discovered that the following two goals described the strategic groups:

1 Achieve the lowest delivered cost position relative to competition, coupled with both an acceptable delivered quality and a pricing policy to gain profitable volume and market share growth (or)

2 Achieve the highest product/service/quality differentiation position relative to competition, coupled with both an acceptable delivered cost structure and a pricing policy to gain margins sufficient to fund reinvestment in product/service differentiation.[22]

The most successful companies scored high on one of these two dimensions *and* moderately high on the other. To score low on one dimension (for example, achieving a high-delivered cost) or moderately high on both generally meant inferior performances. Success thus entails making a commitment to one of the dimensions while maintaining secondary emphasis on the other. Apparently only three of these firms were able to pursue both dimensions at a high level: Caterpillar in the heavy equipment industry, Philip Morris in cigarettes, and Daimler-Benz in truck manufacturing. It was also found that in each of the eight industries the firm that offered the lowest delivered cost tended to grow slowly and have a lower sales turnover, whereas the differentiated position leader grew faster and had a higher sales turnover. In addition, contrary to the Boston Consulting Group's advice, cash cows were used more for internal reinvestment than for support of question marks. And overall cost leadership was practiced successfully by lower, as well as higher, market share firms, contrary to earlier conventional wisdom. Overall, companies succeeded best when they strove for a leadership position in either low delivered cost or product differentiation.

Strategic group analyses are important planning aids and can explain why some firms in an industry are more profitable than others.[23] In practice, every industry will have its own unique dimensions that define the groups. Typical dimensions include product differentiation, degree of vertical integration, overall cost leadership, type of distribution channel, and mix of communication strategies. Figure 16-3 presents an example of a strategic group analysis applied to the chain saw industry in the early 1970s. Notice that quality brand image and mix of distribution channels define three primary strategic groups: the professional, branded mass market, and private label groups (Skil, a small producer, is off by itself, though close to two groups). Notice further that Homelite and McCulloch, the market leaders, offer moderately high-quality brands distributed through hardware, farm, and department stores. Beaird-Poulan sells primarily under private labels to specialty and department stores and as a consequence has a lower-quality brand image. With its subsequent marketing of small, low-priced saws in the mid to late 1970s, however, it had begun to sell both branded and private label saws through nearly all channel options. In the process, it was able to function in two strategic groups. Finally, Stihl and the other members of the pro group market high-quality products through dealers. Of special note is the fact that the three groups permit relatively independent marketing strategies without much competition between groups.

To return to the case of McCulloch, we see that it failed to differentiate itself sufficiently from Homelite and at the same time was joined in the branded mass market group by Beaird-Poulan. One option for McCulloch might have been sale of a higher-quality saw created for the professional market (and for the casual users who might trade

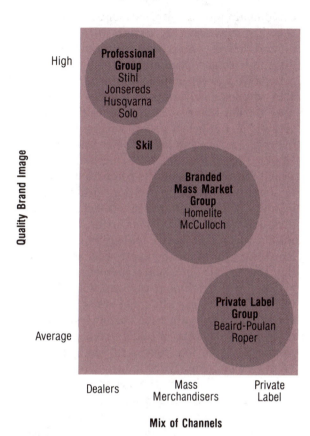

Figure 16-3. An example of a strategic group map applied to the chain saw industry

Source: Michael E. Porter, *Competitive Strategy: Techniques for Analyzing Industries and Competitors* (New York: The Free Press, 1980), p. 153. Reprinted with the permission of The Free Press, a division of Macmillan, Inc. Copyright © 1980, The Free Press.

up), but sold through certain strategically located chain stores. Alternatively, it could have used regional servicing dealers with free pick-up and delivery. As it was, McCulloch chose to fight in both the branded and the private label groups with lower and moderately priced saws. This worked fairly well as long as the casual user market was growing. But once this growth slowed, McCulloch was left with a depressed, narrow position and increased competition.

A firm must decide which strategic group(s) to compete in and how to achieve a leadership position within it. Profitability of a particular firm will depend on the strategic group it functions in as well as its ability to implement its strategy in that group. Strategic groups can compete with each other, but they generally isolate competitors across groups. Membership in a group will differentially affect a firm's ability to resist entry into the industry, bargain with customers and suppliers, and combat inroads from substitute products. Then, too, each strategic group will have its own mobility inhibitors across groups, market potential, growth rate, and intensity of competition within the group.

In sum, successful marketing requires three strategic activities. First, a firm must combat the five competitive threats in its industry. Although all rivals face these threats, each should strive to attain a differential advantage over competitors by enhancing its own power position vis-à-vis the threats. Second, a firm must choose a strategic group and adjust its activities accordingly. The competition within and between strategic groups provides both unique opportunities and constraints for the firm that demand consideration. Finally, a firm must analyze the position of its products in terms of a portfolio wherein growth, market share, cash flow, and profitability considerations are managed for all its offerings. From a marketing stance, each strategic level of analysis reaches fruition through careful market selection and careful implementation of product, communication, price, and distribution decisions. Let us look at these tactical choices now.

Market Selection

The choice of what market(s) to serve is perhaps the most crucial decision faced by a firm because not only do all other marketing decisions follow from this choice but the ultimate success of the firm depends on the acceptance of its products. It is not enough to assume that a market exists or that once a product is made marketing can invariably sell it. Rather, one must begin with assessment of customer needs. Given that the product fills a need and (it is hoped) achieves a competitive advantage, one can then evaluate the size of the market and begin to plan and carry through the tactical activities needed to reach it.

Consumer Behavior. A key activity in market selection is the analysis of customer behavior. Earlier we presented a simplified model and said that the consumer decision process begins by exposure to physical cues. The consumer then perceives these as subjective attributes, benefits, etc., and somehow organizes them in memory to form an attitude toward the product offering. Finally, attitude is thought to influence the decision process one way or the other.

In reality, of course, the decision process is much more complex than this. As a matter of fact, marketers have developed a number of theories that break down the process into many psychological and social psychological components. It is beyond the scope of this chapter to consider these (references to some leading treatments appear at the end). We will, however, briefly describe the central elements that cut across many of the theories and indicate how these are used in practice.

Thinking Processes.

The dominant consideration in virtually all theories of consumer choice is how consumers process information. One way to represent information processing is in terms of the beliefs consumers have and the organization of these beliefs in their memory. Beliefs are subjective judgments as to which attributes a product has (for instance its weight, durability, or cost) and how much of each attribute the product possesses (for instance heavy, highly durable, or moderately expensive). A belief might consist also of a judgment about the consequences of purchase or product use (for example "Brand X will keep my floors clean for two weeks"). Beliefs are used by consumers to make choices among alternative brands or among broad consumption options.

Marketers have developed many models to depict how beliefs are formed, grouped, and used in decision making. Obviously, from a managerial perspective, if we know what beliefs a consumer has toward our brand, we can better decide how to communicate its attributes; change, add, or remove attributes; influence beliefs and decision making; and so on. In addition, we can see how consumers view our brand and the competitors' brands in order to discover our relative advantage or disadvantage and help determine what, if anything, we must do to further improve the situation. Thinking processes constitute the more or less rational side of consumption decisions. They dominate industrial buying and play an important role in everyday consumer choice as well.

Feeling Processes.

It is also important to understand the emotional reactions of consumers to our products. These reactions harbor needs and motives for buying, as well as evaluations of the utility or importance of specific product attributes. Together with beliefs, our feelings determine our attitudes and thus indirectly influence choice. A firm's knowledge of the feelings of consumers about its products (and the products of its competitors) contributes to the design of its products, packages, persuasive communications, promotions and deals; to its pricing; and even to its distribution decisions. Like beliefs, feelings toward our brand and rival brands need to be considered in order to assess the strength of our competitive position. Emotional considerations obviously pervade everyday consumer decision making, yet they can be salient factors in industrial buying, too, despite efforts to focus on economic and other supposedly rational criteria.

Social Processes.

Buying is not strictly a psychological process. Social processes shape consumption, too. This takes many forms such as the influence of norms, peer pressure, family decision-making activities, organizational buying processes, and bargaining and negotiation, among others. Knowledge of the role of social factors in choice is especially helpful in the design of advertising and other marketing communications.

A Model.

In order to gain insight into how consumers make choices, marketers have developed representations, or models, of the processes. These imperfect models represent the causes of decisions or of actual choice outcomes. Sometimes this modeling is done in laboratory experiments; at other times naturalistic surveys are employed. One model that has proved useful in forecasting as well as in product design and advertising is the attitude model. In simplified form, this model can be written as:

$$P \text{ or } I = f(B, F, S)$$

That is, actual purchase behaviors (P) or intentions to buy (I) are hypothesized to be a function of one's beliefs (B), feelings (F), and social pressures (S). More complicated models are used to represent choices among alternative brands and to account for the full range of psychological and social determinants. The literature is filled with specific examples. Although most of these models employ quantitative methods, qualitative research serves as an essential complement in most real-world applications.

Market Segmentation. Customer analysis is primarily an activity directed at the study of consumers as individuals. It thus focuses on micro phenomena. Although this helps in product design and other tactical decisions, it does not provide information on the size and composition of markets or how groups of consumers will respond to product offerings. Knowledge of the macro side of consumption is essential because for most firms it is impossible to make and deliver a unique product to each and every consumer. Trade-offs must be made between the ideal of fully satisfying everyone's needs and the capabilities of firms to meet these needs. In practice, well-defined markets or market segments must be identified so that some standardization and accompanying efficiencies can be taken advantage of. The process for doing so has come to be known as *market segmentation.*

Market segmentation is the activity of identifying subgroups of the population as potential customers. Segmentation should yield a group of people with favorable attitudes toward—and it is to be hoped, intentions to buy—one's product. In addition, the segment should be of a sufficient size to warrant pursuit, reachable, and not overly competitive. The following criteria represent typical bases for market segmentaton in that tastes of people classified into each category vary and represent differential opportunities for marketing that must be assessed:

- *Demographic.* Age, sex, income, occupation, family size, education, religious affiliation, marital status, race.

- *Geographic.* Section of country; urban, rural, or suburban.

- *Psychological.* Personality, attitudes, life style.

- *Social.* Social class, group affiliation.

- *Behavioral.* Benefits sought, typical consumption amount, end use, consumption status (e.g., nonuser, first time, repeat).

One of the most fruitful means of segmentation is known as *benefit segmentation.* Consumers are grouped according to the product attributes they desire most or the consequences of product use they value most highly. Notice that this procedure begins with criteria that are clearly related to consumer needs. Indeed, the objective is to discover relatively homogeneous clusters of buyers with similar needs. After consumers have been grouped in this way, correlates of people within segments are sought. For instance, key demographic and psychological attributes of people are often recorded, as are actual behaviors (previous purchases, statements of preferences, activities, and so on). This gives management a picture of the key benefits people seek in the product it offers, how many people prefer each benefit, and what characteristics describe the people in each benefit segment. Such information can be used in decisions about product design, advertising, pricing and distribution. Table 16-1 provides an example applied to the market for bank services. Notice that five distinct groups of consumers emerge, each varying in size and benefit sought. Notice further how the consumers differ by segment and how they perceive the various banks. A particular bank could use these data to see if it is serving who it thinks it is and determine if an untapped market exists. The picture thus provided could also help the bank in tailoring services and communicating with customers.

Market segmentation can be a useful strategic tool. Consider the case of the copy machine business.[24] For years, Xerox owned the copy machine market. Its marketing was based on products that used a dry toner and parts unique to each model of machine. Xerox manufactured and assembled most of its components. This permitted the manufacture of a high-quality, durable machine suitable for customers who wanted high quality, high-volume production, or both. Of course, the price of the machine was high, too.

TABLE 16-1

An Example of Benefit Segmentation

SEGMENT	1	2	3	4	5
NAME	*Front runners*	*Loan seekers*	*Representative subgroup*	*Value seekers*	*One-stop bankers*
Principal benefits sought	Large Bank for all Good advertising	Good reputation Loans easily available Low loan interest	No differences (about average on all benefits sought)	High savings interest Quick service Low loan interest Plenty of parking	Wide variety of services Convenient hours Quick service Encourage financial responsibility Convenient branch
Banks favored	Commercial Bank A	Commercial B Savings X	Commercial A Commercial B	Savings Y Savings Z	Commercial A Commercial B
Demographic	Young Rent home	More transient More blue collar		Tend to save more	Older
Life-style characteristics[a]	High ability to manage money	Liberal about use of credit Positive about bank loans		Conservative overall life-style Conservative about use of credit Low propensity toward risk taking	Conservative about use of credit Positive toward checking account
Size (n)	8 (2%)	51 (15%)	118 (34%)	89 (26%)	78 (23%)

[a]Dimensions represent factor scores of all 196 general and banking-specific life-style items.

SOURCE: Roger J. Calatone and Alan G. Sawyer, "The Stability of Benefit Segments," *Journal of Marketing Research* 15 (August 1978): 400. Reprinted with the permission of the American Marketing Association.

The company had its own sales force and service personnel. During this period, customers had to lease the machines from Xerox. Its high-quality machines regularly captured 70 percent or more of the market.

Enter the competition. Savin saw an opportunity to go after the low-price, infrequent-user market. To do this, it used the cheaper liquid toner technology and employed interchangeable parts across its line of machines. Although the speed and quality of its copies could not match Xerox's, the target market accepted this trade-off to get a much lower price. A side benefit was somewhat better reliability. To reach the more fragmented market, Savin used a dealer system and sold its machines rather than leasing them. This was not only necessary but cheaper. Service was provided by the dealers; a simpler machine made this possible, and Savin provided support to the dealer. Finally, Savin purchased all its parts, and assembled them in Japan; this gave it further cost advantage. The result was that Savin succeeded in finding an unfulfilled market segment and providing a product that would satisfy consumers in that segment. Today, many competitors pursue the low and high end of the copy-machine market, and Xerox has been forced to more actively segment and alter its marketing tactics to meet this competition.

Market Monitoring and Decision Support Systems. A key factor in market selection, as well as in the management of the entire marketing program, is the collection, analysis, and use of information. Modern marketing organizations are increasingly establishing separate departments for this function, which goes by such names as *management information systems* or *decision support systems.* Just as frequently, firms perform the information function through closer coordination of their many separate departments. Discussion of this important topic is beyond the scope of this chapter. At the risk of understatement, we simply note that special attention must be given to consumer research, data analysis and storage (for example statistical modeling, establishment of an archive), normative support systems (such as mathematical models and interactive computer support programs), and new ways of disseminating and using the information.

Product Decisions

New Product Development. Changing consumer tastes and evolving economic and competitive conditions make product innovation a necessity for maintenance of a healthy business. Today's leading companies no longer leave things to chance or the inventive genius of a founder; they rely on a purposeful program of new product development. To be sure, the program is part art and part science. But the large expenditures involved, together with the sobering realization that failure rates are high, make it imperative that efforts be made to meld art and science and do so well before the product is launched. It is estimated that the cost of designing, developing, and introducing a new industrial product averages more than $2 million, while expenditures for a new consumer product average about $6 million. The chance for success at the design stage is given as about 30 percent for industrial and 20 percent for consumer goods.[25]

Many activities must be coordinated to bring a product successfully to market. The most important fall within the following five stages:

Creative Phase ⟶ Design and Development Phase ⟶ Testing Phase ⟶ Launch ⟶ Ongoing Management

In the *creative phase,* new ideas are generated. These may arise from secondary sources, consumer research (for example, interviews), the R & D department, feedback from salespeople, consumer suggestions or complaints, employee contributions, and even the competition. Some firms use separate creative groups or executive brainstorming sessions. Brand managers generally provide important input here. Occasionally, outside agencies or individuals are consulted. Once a new idea is generated, its utility must be assessed. This is usually done by means of subjective judgments, perhaps aided by rules-of-thumb and ranking or rating methods. Criteria considered at this early stage include estimates of the cost of development, potential receptivity of consumers, ease and cost of manufacture and marketing, profitability, degree of probable competition, and likelihood of success at each of the remaining four stages of the new product development process.

The *design and development* stage is in many ways the most crucial. It is here that the product takes shape conceptually and physically, that marketing plans are first formulated, and that a realistic assessment of costs and expected sales and profits is made. A particularly critical activity is customer analysis and market segmentation. This is done, in part, through a technique termed *perceptual mapping,* which we will describe in a moment. At the same time, the new product must be analyzed vis-à-vis the competition. This also can be done, in part, through perceptual mapping in a process termed *product positioning.* Finally, in the case of most consumer goods, the design will be given its toughest evaluation through mock pretests in which consumers evaluate the product and ads and express their preferences in simulated purchase environments. Various models and rules-of-thumb have been developed to aid in the interpretation of the data thus obtained. The Assessor model or BBDO's NEWS model are two leading examples.[26] The goal is to get feedback on the attractiveness of product attributes and communication tactics and to estimate trial and repeat purchasing. The design and development phase is a particularly sensitive one, as managers have vested interests, and the firm wants to avoid rejecting potentially fruitful products or approving losers. Yet considerable uncertainty persists at this stage.

The third stage, *testing*, is designed to reduce uncertainty and provide more feedback. Typically, the product is given to one or a few users if it is an industrial product or introduced into one or a handful of cities if it is a consumer good. Test marketing is expensive, generally $1 to $1.5 million. However, the information it provides for the fine-tuning of the entire marketing effort is more valid than that supplied by most pretests because testing is done under more naturalistic conditions and with larger, more representative samples. The information sought includes awareness of the brand, knowledge of product attributes, attitudes and preferences, intentions to try the product, and actual trial and repeat purchase rates. In addition, panel diaries of consumers are sometimes used, as are store audits, consumer intercepts at the time of purchase, and post-trial interviews. Demographic, psychographic, life style, and media exposure data may also be monitored. As with pretest data, the information gained from test marketing may be used in formal models to forecast trial and repeat purchasing behaviors after the product is put on the market. The drawbacks of test marketing, in addition to high cost, are that rollout and national introduction may be delayed. This permits the competition to learn at the firm's expense and to catch up. Some companies even sabotage the test marketing of their competitors by changing their own pricing, advertising, and promotion programs in the public test market. For these reasons, many firms by-pass test marketing, despite the loss in information that entails. Some companies, such as manufacturers of durable goods or industrial goods, find it impractical to test market in any event.

Product launch is the fourth step. Here the product is introduced to the public, either nation-wide or on a market-by-market basis to coordinate with production or other constraints. Special care is given to the monitoring of consumer adoptions, reactions by competitors, and problems in distribution. Invariably there are bugs in the coordination of the entire marketing effort, and these require immediate attention. Planning, monitoring, and a resilient, fast acting management control system are essential at this stage.

Finally, the new product development process "ends" with *ongoing management*. We will discuss this activity shortly when we consider managing the product through its life cycle.

Perceptual Maps and Product Positioning. Most products and services have many physical and intangible attributes with varied consequences for a would-be purchaser. An automobile is not merely "an automobile." Rather, for a consumer, it is a bundle of objectives and subjective characteristics (size, color, ease of handling, roominess, comfort, price, etc.) and consequences (such as feelings of pride, power, or prestige). The marketer's task is a difficult one for he or she must decide how many attributes to build into the product, how much quality to include in each attribute, and how to put the attributes together to gain a competitive advantage. Fortunately, due largely to implicit coping strategies employed by consumers in everyday decision making, only a few product attributes are important in any actual choice process. Indeed, two or three key attributes are often sufficient to predict consumer choices. As products become more complex and consumers become more sophisticated, however, more attributes need to be taken into account.

The conjunction of key product attributes and consumer perceptions (or beliefs) can be fruitfully represented in a *perceptual map*. Figure 16-4 presents one consumer's perception of beers for sale in Northern California. Perceptual maps can also be prepared for groups of consumers and market segments. The dots show the perceived positions of different beers (disregard the circles for the moment). The two most common methodologies used to produce perceptual maps are multidimensional scaling and factor analysis, but we will not discuss these procedures here.

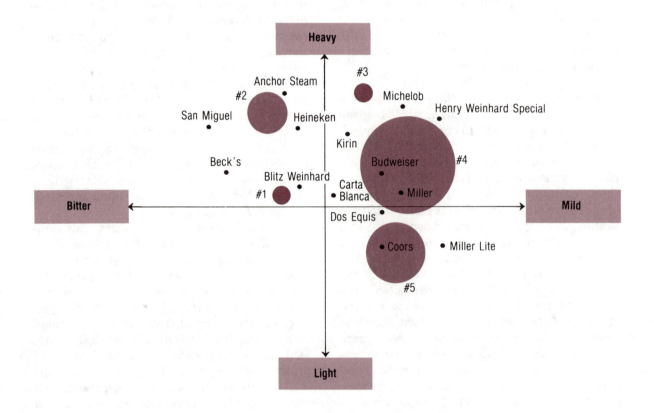

Figure 16-4. A perceptual map of the beer market in Northern California according to one beer drinker, with centroids of consumer preferences

The dots represent the positions of brands as perceived by one beer drinker. The circles superimposed on this particular map represent centroids of consumer preferences; the size of a circle indicates an estimate of the number of people (or share of the market) preferring that particular combination of the heavy-light and bitter-mild attributes.

Notice first in Figure 16-4 that this consumer uses two attributes to describe beers: heavy-light and bitter-mild. Some people employ more attributes and different ones (for instance, gaseousness and calorie content), but these two are quite common across the population. Notice further that the brands cover much of the map. This indicates that the consumer believes that brands differ on the two dimensions to a considerable degree. San Miguel is perceived as a rather heavy, bitter beer, for example, whereas Miller Lite is seen as a very mild, moderately light beer.

What can one learn from perceptual maps? First, they indicate what are the most important attributes in consumer decision making. These attributes then can become the focal ones in product design and advertising decisions. Second, perceptual maps show where one's own brand and those of the competition score in the minds of consumers on each salient attribute. Management thus obtains an indication of where it is strong or weak and who its primary rivals are. Third, perceptual maps suggest possible opportunities in the market. In Figure 16-4, for example, we see that no beer is perceived by this particular consumer to be both bitter and light. This suggests a potential entry point for a new product or an alternative strategy for a beer on the border of the bitter-light quadrant (e.g., Beck's). Of course, whether this unfilled niche is really a viable market or not will depend on (1) the firm's ability to produce and market a light, bitter beer (and/or to convincingly advertise it as such) and—of first importance—(2) the number of people who would prefer such a beer and would be willing to try it.

This brings us to the related and important concept of *product (or brand) positioning*. The goal here is to use perceptual maps to suggest the best competitive tactics to pursue in market selection, product design (or redesign), and communication,

pricing, and distribution decisions. Study of a product's position relative to that of its competitors on a perceptual map serves as a starting point for exploring competitive moves and their implications.

To take an example, let us assume the perspective of Carta Blanca. In Figure 16-4, we have presented estimates of the sizes of consumer groups preferring various combinations of heavy-light and bitter-mild attributes in a beer. The circles represent centroids of consumer preferences; the size of the circle indicates the number of people (or percentage of the market) preferring the respective combinations of heavy-light and bitter-mild beer attributes. For purposes of discussion, we will assume that the perceptions of everyone surveyed can be represented as shown. We will further assume that Carta Blanca is losing market share and feels a need to respond accordingly.

Carta Blanca has three options. First, it can compete with Blitz-Weinhard and go after preference group 1. To do this, it might use advertising to stress that it is neither too heavy nor too light, too bitter nor too mild. Rather, it is "the best of balanced beers," say. Comparative ads with Blitz-Weinhard might be considered as well. In addition, a reformulation of the brewing process or ingredients might be called for to make Carta Blanca somewhat more bitter. Consumer research would show if this is necessary. Whether pursuit of preference group 1 is viable or not depends on the number of people in this group, their current brand preferences, the cost of going after these people, and the attractiveness of the remaining two preference group options.

Carta Blanca's second option is to take on Budweiser and Miller, who "own" preference group 4, the largest market segment. This probably is not viable, given that Carta Blanca is an imported beer that appeals to small numbers of beer drinkers, whereas Budweiser and Miller are domestic products with well entrenched popular images. Budweiser and Miller also have cost advantages and greater marketing resources.

Carta Blanca's third option would be to go after preference group 5. This large segment desires a mild, light beer and currently has only three competitors. Here, Carta Blanca must consider the costs of changing its image, the costs of reformulating its product, and the size and receptivity of the preference group.

Whatever option is chosen, it is important to consider also the likely responses of competitors. For example, Blitz-Weinhard would be likely to counter any threat by Carta Blanca. It could do this by cutting its price (since it has a distribution advantage), by advertising, or by doing both. A long-shot option for Carta Blanca might be to create a new market and pursue a slightly bitter, slightly light position in the hope of changing people's taste preferences or winning new adherents in the empty quadrant. Many other competitive issues are suggested by perceptual maps, but we cannot examine them here.

Before we consider the ongoing management of products, we should mention a recently developed tool that is proving to be especially useful in the design phase. *Conjoint analysis* is an analytical technique that permits management to compare alternative product or service designs on the basis of consumer reactions. The procedure provides measures of consumer utility for attributes of products and enables management to select product versions with maximum appeal.

Managing the Product through Its Life Cycle. All products pass through life cycles. An ideal sequence of sales might be represented as follows:

introduction ⟶ rapid growth ⟶
slow growth ⟶ leveling off ⟶ decline

Of course, some products never make it past introduction, others skip a stage or two, and still others continue on indefinitely as if renewed from time to time. Whatever the pattern of sales, management must orchestrate the application of marketing tactics throughout the life cycle of a product. In this sense, the product life cycle is at least partially controllable by management. Each stage in the life cycle of a product will require a different balance among marketing tactics. Resources must be allocated to advertising, promotions, personal selling, distribution, and pricing in a way that meets the goals of the firm. During the *product introduction phase,* profits are nonexistent and the objective typically is to increase consumers' product awareness and trial purchases (and stimulation of a healthy repurchase rate in the case of frequently purchased products). Advertising will be heavy in order to inform people. Promotions will be used to motivate dealers and consumers. The sales force will concentrate its efforts on building distribution. The price may be set low to take advantage of experience curve effects and forestall competition. Or it may be set high to reap early rewards (more on this shortly).

During periods of *rapid growth,* adjustments must be made. These should, in turn, be guided by market research, including so-called tracking studies of awareness, attitudes, intentions, trial purchase, and repeat purchase rates. Market share may become a critical barometer, too. Fine-tuning and shifts in emphasis from one marketing tactic to another invariably take place. Normative managerial models and simulations may be used to aid in decision making here also. Advertising will shift from information presentations to persuasion and may be reduced somewhat from initially high introductory levels. Promotion, too, will be reduced and shifted from trial-inducing tactics such as sampling to repeat purchase teasers such as couponing or cents-off deals. The sales force will work to cement dealer relationships and ensure that deliveries, product quality, etc., will be fulfilled. Prices may be lowered somewhat to meet the competition.

Slow growth and leveling off periods demand still other responses. Here the firm must assess its own growth in relation to market growth and take into account its market share as well. A change in product design may be required to meet the demanding tastes of people slow to try the product or to compete effectively with a new entrant. Advertising and promotion may have to be changed again to combat wearout (i.e., a decline in ad effectiveness over time) or meet the competition. Prices may have to be lowered still further. Market segmentation takes on a special urgency as a means of survival and furthering of the goals of the firm.

As the *decline phase* approaches, difficult decisions must be faced. Should the firm harvest, disinvest, or reinvest? Again, growth and market share must be weighed against goals and capabilities of the firm and the nature of the market and competition. An outcome to avoid is the self-fulfilling prophecy whereby an "apparent" decline is accelerated by a withdrawal of marketing support, and a potentially viable product is brought to a premature end. If the firm decides to harvest, then most expenditures on marketing will be reduced, and the product will be left to die on its own. If the firm chooses instead to reinvest, it may have to do so across the board, with major product design innovations, repositioning, and renewed expenditures on advertising, promotion, selling, and distribution.

A final set of product decisions concern *product line planning*. The firm must decide whether to have a product line and, if so, what its composition should be. Consumer needs, the location of market segments, competition, market growth, market share, cannibalization, and profitability are important inputs to the decision process. Creating a well-designed product line entails looking not only at the health of each brand but also at the synergy among brands. The image and profitability of brands may be enhanced by careful design of the entire line, since cross-fertilization often occurs. The role of the product line also changes over time with the leveling-off phase of the product life cycle revealing the product line's maximum contribution. The product portfolio and strategic group frameworks are especially useful in product line decisions. Given the decision to employ product lines, the marketer must view his or her task as allocating marketing expenditures to the support of tactics that will best meet the firm's goals for profitability, market share, and growth.

Communication Decisions

A Communication Model. Communication tactics are one of the most important and flexible links between an organization and its markets. Unlike product, price, and distribution tactics, which are more difficult to change and which remain relatively stable over time, communication is often the first and most effective lever an organization has to respond to or influence its markets. The range of communication tactics includes advertising, promotion, publicity, and personal selling. The goal of communication is to inform, educate, persuade, and/or influence behavior directly.

In simplified form, the communication process is as follows:

communicator $\longrightarrow$ message $\longrightarrow$ medium $\longrightarrow$ receiver
$\lfloor$_____ feedback _____$\rfloor$

That is, a communicator sends a message through some medium to a receiver who processes the message and responds with feedback. Of course, communicator and receiver often change roles in rapid succession, and instead of a one-way sequence, the process is very much one of mutual exchanges. Nevertheless, in analyzing and designing communication tactics, it is useful to consider the process of communication as being a relatively unilateral one.

Figure 16-5 outlines the main variables and processes underlying communication in marketing. Let us begin with a description of the processes going on within the consumer (i.e. receiver) after receipt of a message (see bottom of figure). Exposure to an ad, sales pitch, or other marketing communication leads first to perceptual processes. These may or may not occur at the level of awareness or involve conscious allocation of attention. In any case, perceived information may have one or both of two effects (see *a* and *b* in Figure 16-5). One is to influence the consumer's needs or motives and induce affective responses. For example, physiological responses might be stimulated, along with felt positive emotions, and the desire for a product actuated. This, in turn, might lead to thoughts about the brand, how to acquire it, and so forth (*d*). Alternatively, perceived information might lead directly (*b*) to message comprehension and further cognitive responses (for example, generation of support for or counter arguments against, the core selling point). The resulting "information processing" might stimulate feelings about the message, brand, etc., as well (*c*). Information (*e*) and affective reactions (*f*) then are organized and integrated, and an attitude toward the brand and/or communication is formed (*g*). The output of this stage serves as input to mental decision-making activities in which the consumer activates old preferences or develops new ones. This may lead further (*h*) to intentions to buy and, eventually, to purchase. Postpurchase experiences finally result in satisfaction/dissatisfaction and feedback upon the consumer's needs, motives, and feelings (*i*) and/or knowledge (*j*).

The value of examining how consumers process messages lies in its use in the design of communications. Each stage shown in the bottom of Figure 16-5 will be affected differently by different communication tactics. For instance, humorous ads can be effective in stimulating attention, creating desired emotional responses, and at times inducing yielding to a persuasive appeal. But they are less useful in conveying information and aiding directly in decision making. Rational appeals, in contrast, excel in developing understanding, promoting effective information integration, and generally enhancing decision making. But they are less effective in influencing emotions. One goal in the study of how consumers process messages is to select the most appropriate communication tactic, given the product, consumer characteristics, competition, and stage the product is in in its life cycle. Notice also that the ultimate choice to buy or not will be a differential function of the nature of communications and how they are processed at various stages leading up to choice. Only by considering the differential mental and emotional effects of messages at each stage can managers select the best communication options. This, in turn, requires that consumer research be performed along with the design of communication programs.

The top half of Figure 16-5 presents the three primary levers that managers have to influence the communication process: communicator variables, message variables, and media variables. The options noted for each, individually and in combination, compose the communication mix. Let us briefly consider these.

The effect of a message can be augmented through the choice of characteristics of *the communicator*. To the extent that a spokesperson is perceived as being more expert, trustworthy, or attractive, the message will be believed to a stronger degree. Similarly, the more that a communicator is perceived to directly or indirectly provide him or her with rewards (monetary, psychic, or social outcomes), the greater the likelihood that a communication will have its intended effect. Note that communicator variables are separate elements under the control of management and work along with other determinants to influence consumers. Skillful choice of a communicator can lead to the development of a unique brand image (Karl Malden for American Express) and can influence special target markets (Mr. T in antidrug ads).

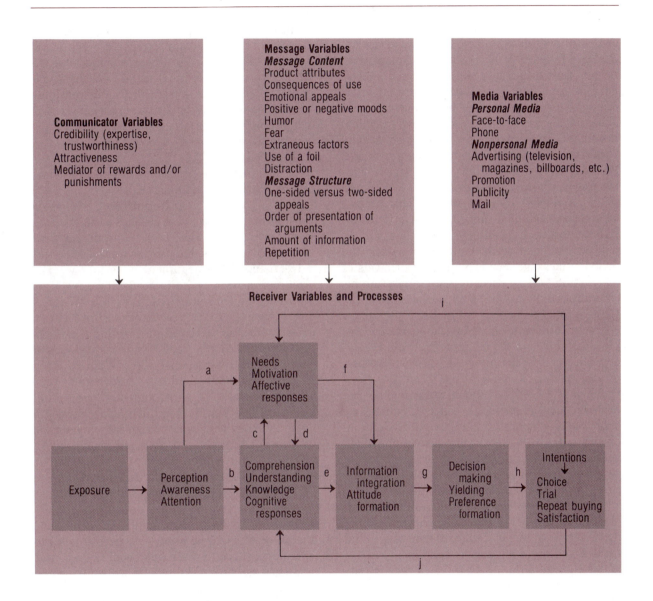

Figure 16-5. Communication processes in marketing

Perhaps the most effective means of influence lie in *the message* itself (see Figure 16-5). Here managers must give special attention to what is said (message content) and how it is said (message structure).

Two basic choices underlie the *message content* decision. Should rational or emotional appeals be used? A product with distinct attributes and benefits for a consumer or one that has utilitarian overtones lends itself to a rational approach. Ads for drain cleaners, motor oil, and investments generally follow this approach. Products whose appeal lie in psychic or social consequences or brands that differ only slightly from the competition find emotional appeals more effective. We see this in cosmetics, beer, and cigarette advertisements. Of course, sometimes rational arguments and mood or other nonrational stimulants are combined into a single message. Witness Mercedes-Benz ads, which stress engineering yet also appeal to desires for luxury, status, and even excitement. Although difficult to execute, such dual tactics can be quite effective. In addition, seemingly extraneous content will be included occasionally along with the primary message. For example, small levels of distraction will be used to temporarily inhibit counterargumentation by an audience until the focal selling point can be made. Many ploys common to novels, plays, or the opera are employed: the use of a foil, fantasy, drama, comedy, slice-of-life, testimonials, satire, suspense, or storytelling, to name a few.

Equally critical is the organization of message content, which we term *message structure* in Figure 16-5. Here decisions must be made as to the use of one-sided versus two-sided appeals (i.e., presentation of only positive or positive and negative information), order of presentation of arguments (i.e., whether to place the strongest argument first, in the middle, or at the end), the amount of information to convey in any one message, and the scheduling of messages over time.

A third lever in the communication mix is *media selection.* This is an important problem area, not only because of its obvious role in reaching customers and in market selection, but because different media are more persuasive than others, depending on the needs of consumers, and the characteristics of the focal product and the competition. Personal media (i.e., salespeople) are particularly effective for expensive products, prolonged negotiations, custom designing of the product, influencing intermediaries, and closing sales.

Nonpersonal media such as advertising, promotion, publicity, or catalog and mail marketing have the advantages of extensive reach capabilities, low cost per prospect reached, and the ability to stimulate trial use or purchase, remind people about availability, and reinforce other modes of selling (for example advertising can prepare and soften up a prospect before the encounter with a retailer or salesperson).

Advertising. Three special concerns of advertising include repetition, message execution, and operations management.

Repetition. What is the optimal number of exposures of an ad? One researcher claims that three exposures are all that are needed to achieve the desired effects of advertising.[27] The argument is as follows. The first exposure to an ad is needed to attract attention. The consumer reacts with a "What is it?" response. A later, second exposure has two effects. One is a recognition reaction (i.e., "Ah, ha, I've seen this before!"), whereas the second is an evaluative response (i.e., "What of it?"). Beyond this point, no deeper information processing occurs. The third and each succeeding exposure are simply reminder ads calling up from memory that which is already known (or believed). According to this argument, more than three exposures is not only wasteful but leads to disengagement of audience interest. This is the so-called *wearout phenomenon.*

One operational objective of advertising, then, might be to produce as many repetitions as are needed to achieve three exposures for as many people in a target audience as is feasible. Inevitably, some people will become overexposed, and as time passes the message will have less and less effectiveness. This might be indicated by a leveling off in awareness measures or even sales. What can be done to overcome wearout? One solution is to change the content or structure of the message. New communicators (spokespersons) or new humorous executions might be tried, for instance. Or new media might be explored in an effort to reach previously inaccessible consumers. Still another tactic is to introduce new product attributes not advertised before.

Message Execution.
How should one design and implement an advertisement? At least three issues must be addressed here. One is *media involvement*. Each medium has its own characteristics, which are more or less interesting to a target customer. For example, television is generally considered a low-involvement medium in that viewers tend to sit passively, let their minds drift, or even tune out commercials. Magazines, on the other hand, are more involving and permit exposure to ads to occur at more active and deeper levels. Obviously, every advertiser attempts to make its ads alluring, whatever the medium chosen. However, product characteristics, consumer media habits, and other considerations suggest that the marketer should carefully match his or her offering to the advertising medium and the target audience. Different media pose different problems and offer different opportunities.

A related issue is *product involvement*. Just as consumers are involved to different degrees with different media, so too do they find products to be important in varying degrees. For products of lesser salience to a consumer, information processing may occur in a shallow way, encompass few product attributes, and proceed quickly. Habit and impulse frequently play a role as well. More salient products encourage deeper information processing and over a wider spectrum of attributes, with much comparison among brands. Television ads for Panasonic video cameras convey about a dozen product attributes, whereas Trident gum ads seldom stress more than one or two. This, too, will affect the choice of media, the type of messages constructed, the scheduling of repetitions, and so on. Note also that *brand involvement* can be a factor.

Finally, message execution should take into account how consumers will react to a message and the processes that they will go through as they react. Marketers have found that the following sequences occur most frequently in real world decision making:[28]

1 learn ⟶ feel ⟶ do,

2 feel ⟶ learn ⟶ do,

3 do ⟶ learn ⟶ feel, or

4 do ⟶ feel ⟶ learn.

By "learn" is meant the comprehension, information integration, and decision making activities of Figure 16-5. "Feel" refers to needs, motives, affective responses, attitude and preference formation. "Do" stands for actual trial or repeat buying activities or other behaviors: shopping, examination of independent reports, talking to a salesperson, making a purchase, and so on.

Sequence 1 applies when products are complex, risky, expensive, and/or are considered important by the consumer. Here considerable information is first scrutinized and weighed before feelings develop and a decision to act or not is made. The purchase of a home computer would be an example. Sequence 2 also occurs in instances where consumers find the product to be important to them, but where the nature of the product or message is such as to first induce affective reactions. These reactions, in turn, generate thinking processes that lead to action. The purchase of clothing often fits this pattern. Sequence 3 figures in the purchase of everyday items such as dishwashing detergent, coffee, or milk. Either through habit or impulse or because a product is so simple or uninvolving, it is purchased with little or no forethought. Its subsequent use or contemplation, however, leads to thoughts about the brand ("For small loads of dishes, I'll try half a capful") and, finally, affective reactions (e.g., "I really like brand X detergent"). Sequence 4 is similar to 3, but here feelings follow action directly and then lead to thoughts. For instance, at mid-morning, a vaguely perceived hunger pang might stimulate purchase of a candy bar from a vending machine. Biting into the bar triggers pleasurable feelings and elicits such thoughts as "This is a good buy" and "I think I'll get another."

If advertisers have sound information about how consumers react to messages and the processes they go through in decision making, they can create more effective ads. For example, products falling within sequence 1 typically require a demonstration of the product's use and benefits and detailed information—which requires considerable ad copy. More involving media, such as magazines or direct mail, may dominate. Products in sequence 2 require emotional appeals to involve an audience and make use of appeals to the ego or to self-esteem. Magazine ads and strong TV executions may be needed here. Those products which elicit sequence 3 demand executions that induce trial purchases or remind consumers of an offering. Radio or TV spots might work well; so might magazine ads with coupons. Sequence 4 products suggest ads that arouse emotions. Magazine or strong TV commercials are a possibility. Point-of-purchase displays are options for products in sequences 3 and 4, as well.

The above considerations are of course only rough guidelines. In the final analysis, any ad will reflect the particular philosophy, history, and style of the ad agency that creates it. Thus a marketer must not only know his or her own product, customers, and competitors well but must also carefully evaluate alternative agencies and ad executions to arrive at a proper fit. These are largely subjective decisions.

Operations Management. Finally, *the advertising effort must be well managed.* Two critical concerns here are copy testing and budgeting. *Copy testing* refers to measurement of the effectiveness of advertising. Although statistical and mathematical modeling can be used to establish the relationship between advertising expenditures and sales (or market share), more frequently the effects of ads are determined by gauging their impact on intermediate variables, such as consumers' awareness, knowledge, recall, or recognition of the ad; their beliefs about the product's attributes; their interest in the product; and their intentions to buy or not to buy. Such indirect measurement is employed because it is easier, cheaper, and yet thought to be reasonably valid. Many independent companies offer copy testing services to advertisers.

Advertising budgets are set in a variety of ways. Sometimes a budget is made on the basis of subjective judgments by executives. A second method is simply to peg the budget to that of the competition: to meet the competitor's ad budget, exceed it, or fall below it by some percentage. Usually, however, budgets are set as a percentage of sales (for example last quarter's or this quarter's expectations). Unfortunately, each of the aforementioned tactics tends to be a hit-or-miss affair. A better way is to set ad budgets at levels needed to achieve some desired goal. The *objective and task method* attempts to do just this. The organization first defines a specific goal to be achieved—say "60 percent awareness of our new brand in Market Y by next year." Next, the tasks—number of repetitions, media selection, spokesperson, etc.—are designed to reach the goal. The budget is then set on the basis of the tasks needed to reach the goal. Experimentation, statistical modeling, normative models, and market monitoring may be used in trying to meet the goals.

Promotion. Promotions are incentives directed at consumers or dealers to get them to buy one's brand. Whereas advertising is most often designed to induce a psychological response prior to action, promotions are attempts to stimulate actions directly. The most common consumer promotions are coupons, free samples, premiums, cents-off deals, contests, games, and prizes. *Speciality advertising* is really a type of promotion whereby free gifts in the form of a pen, calendar, coffee mug, or other item are given to a consumer. The gift serves as a reward for performing the desired action (patronizing Dry Cleaner X, buying Magazine Y) and usually bears the name and telephone number of the sponsor as a constant reminder. Typical dealer promotions include point-of-purchase (POP) displays, cash allowances, credit, gifts, bonuses, "2 for 1" deals, contests, prizes, and free advice or information.

An important point to stress is that the communication mix tactics are interdependent and sometimes mutually reinforcing. This is nowhere more evident than with advertising and promotion. One study, for example, showed that advertising and promotion work together to produce a multiplier effect such that sales were much greater when both were used than when either one alone was employed. This study found, for example, that sales of coffee were 0.6 purchases per 100 shoppers when no ads or POP displays were used, 2.5 purchases per 100 when only POP displays were used, 1.9 per 100 with only ads, but 8.1 per 100 when *both* ads and POP displays were used.[29] Note, too, that many promotions only reach consumers through ads.

The question management faces, then, is not so much whether to promote or to advertise but rather what proportion of each to employ. In practice, a wide range of advertising to promotion budget ratios are used. One consumer product firm sets its ratio at 70:30, for example. What factors govern the balance? One is buyer behavior. If, for example, most prospective purchasers of a certain product decide to buy (or not) before they enter the store, then the ratio should be more heavily in favor of advertising. But if most prospects make up their minds at the shelf, then the ratio should favor promotion—specifically, POP promotion. Competition is a second factor. A small competitor cannot hope to emulate a large one, but it may gain a competitive edge by using a vastly different advertising-to-promotion ratio than the competition uses. Still another consideration is the stage a product is in in its life cycle. Introduction, growth, leveling-off, and decline require different tactics. Many other considerations including market share, strategic group position, and firm constraints may enter the picture.

Personal Selling. Face-to-face communication, while expensive, is the most compelling medium available to a seller. Personal contact permits a dynamic adjustment of needs and offerings on the part of both buyer and seller, and it facilitates the gaining of a commitment. Moreover, salespeople smooth out problems subsequent to the sale (for instance, late delivery), provide feedback about the market, and generate new business. In an age where everything and everyone seems to get lost in the crowd, personal selling lets the firm tailor its offerings, reach the right customer, communicate complex benefits and terms, and push control deeper into the channel of distribution. Although more expensive on a per customer basis than advertising, personal selling frequently costs less in absolute terms when the number of customers is small, the items are high-priced, or both.

For decades, researchers and practitioners have searched in vain for the magical profile of the "ideal" salesperson. At one time or another, he or she was thought to need money more than achievement, high ego strength, empathy, verbal skills, aggressiveness, an aloof attitude, unusual levels of drive, to be loved, and so on. Eventually the ideal salesperson could be described by any and all attributes, and no one—or everyone—could fit the bill.

There is no such thing as the ideal salesperson. But within the past few years, research has identified a small number of fundamental attributes or abilities common to most successful outside salespeople. First and foremost, motivation is required. Salespeople must both value the intrinsic and extrinsic rewards associated with selling and believe that working hard will earn them these rewards. Second, leading salespeople tend to have high levels of self-confidence and self-esteem, especially in relation to the specific job at hand. To the extent that attaining high levels of sales is consistent with their task-specific self-image, salespeople are motivated to work hard to achieve at a level in concert with that self-image. Third, the ability to learn from feedback and supervision is crucial, especially as it serves to promote and reinforce job satisfaction. Fourth, successful salespeople generally cope better with ambiguity on the job. (Ambiguity arises from lack of certainty as to what the supervisor, customer, and others expect of one.) Fifth, salespeople must be able to deal with conflict, tension, and strain. These aspects of the job are consequences of organizational boundary-spanning activities and differences in interests, points of view, and job pressures. Finally, effective selling requires an ability to analyze customer needs and plan and adjust one's activities and communication tactics to advantage. In personal selling, interpersonal skills reign supreme.

The management of a company's personal selling effort entails several key decisions. After goals for sales and profitability are set, one of the manager's first tasks is to determine the size of the sales force. This might be done by estimating the desired productivity of salespeople and taking into account the number of total customers (actual plus potential) as well as geographic, economic, and other considerations. At the same time, the manager must decide how to organize the sales force (by geographic territory, customer type, product category, brand, or whatever). This done, the manager can determine the size of each territory or the number of accounts and/or products that each salesperson will have. These decisions should, if possible, be based at least partly on target sales or profit figures. A recruitment, selection, and training program must be designed as well. Finally, supervision, compensation, work standards (for instance, call norms), and general planning, management, and control mechanisms must be set in place. Many of the above issues can be approached through various normative models that have been proposed by marketers to aid in planning and decision making. Job design, leadership, and career development principles are important, too.

Just as advertising and promotion are mutually reinforcing activities, so too may personal selling interact with other modes in the communication mix to more effectively generate sales. A key decision is whether to pursue a *push*, a *pull*, or a *push-pull* strategy. That is, should the firm place major emphasis on selling to intermediaries (the push strategy), to final customers (the pull strategy), or both? The push strategy requires a vigorous sales force, dealer promotions, and relatively high margin pricing. The pull strategy rests largely on advertising with perhaps some consumer promotions. Most firms use a push-pull strategy, yet industrial goods sellers rely relatively more on a push mode, whereas the strategies of consumer goods sellers are more balanced or lean toward a pull mode. The choice of balance between push and pull depends on how and where consumers make decisions, the size of the market, what consumer media habits are, the nature and complexity of the product, the competition, market growth, market share, and so forth.

Price Decisions

Goals and Constraints in Pricing. Long gone are the days when prices were set haphazardly as an automatic and more-or-less fixed markup over costs. Today, price is viewed in an active and not merely reactive sense as one way to stimulate demand, compete effectively, or both. As a tactical tool, price offers a number of benefits to the firm. First, unlike most communication, product, or distribution tactics that entail up-front costs as well as involved plans and procedures for their implementation, price moves do not require costly expenditures and can be instituted easily. Second, consumers find appeals based on price easier to understand and respond to than the more indirect and abstract effects of advertising, product attribute, and distribution-based (e.g., location) appeals. Finally, even when other tactics such as personal selling or image advertising are the primary concern, price can be a valuable and readily applied adjunct, reinforcing the effects of other marketing tools. On the other hand, price cutting can be perceived as a threat by competitors and lead to price wars in which all companies suffer. Also, price cuts can lead to negative inferences about product quality.

The pricing process begins with the goals of the firm and the objectives for the brand in question. Common options are to view price as a means to achieve or maintain market share, stimulate primary and secondary demand, increase short- or long-run profitability, signal competitors that one means business or alternatively wishes to avoid a price war, discourage new entrants, strengthen and reward intermediaries (for example by providing them with healthy margins), communicate value to consumers, stay within the law, or simply act in a socially responsible way. Most of these ends require that the firm conduct research to determine the relationship between price and sales. This may mean conducting experiments, running statistical analyses of data, performing simulations, or employing normative models based on managerial judgments and other data.[30]

With rare exceptions, prices are constrained to fall within a relatively narrow range. At the bottom end, costs provide a floor below which the firm cannot survive for long. At the top end, prices are constrained by competitive undercutting or by a ceiling on what consumers can afford or what they feel gives them value. In between lies the degrees of freedom open to a firm.

Taking a proactive stance, we can think of the pricing problem as one of maximizing profits or some other goal. For example, we know that profits (z) can be written as a function of price (p), costs (c), and quantity sold (q), $z = (p-c)q$. Our objective is to arrive at the highest level of z through an optimal choice of p. However, p is constrained by consumer preferences, the competition, and

government regulations. Further, z can be influenced by keeping c low, which, in turn, depends on q, experience curve effects, and shared experience and costs with other products (see earlier discussion on overall cost leadership and learning curve effects). Moreover, q, itself, is at least partially influenceable through p and the remaining marketing mix tools. Thus, z can be increased indirectly by stimulating demand. We find, therefore, that the maximization of z is a complex endeavor. Nevertheless, once we have an idea of the determinants of constraints for p, c, and q, we can use calculus or simulations to arrive at a maximum z. The task thus depends on arriving at realistic functions for p, c, and q. It is beyond the scope of this chapter to cover the many recent developments in this area.[31] We will, however, briefly sketch some of the qualitative considerations.

Consider first the constraints on price and the implications of setting various price levels. To satisfy consumer needs, price should reflect, and be set on the basis of, perceived benefits to consumers. But how can this be done? One way is to use conjoint analysis and treat price as a product attribute along with other attributes. In a survey, the consumer then must choose a product with a bundle of attributes producing his or her highest utility. Conjoint analysis yields the consumer's judged disutility of specific price options and shows the trade-offs between various prices and product attributes. The price suggested by a conjoint analysis is of course constrained further by what competitors are offering and what is legally permissible. Product differentiation and careful market selection can lessen the impact of these constraints, however. A last point to note is that price elasticities—especially those which are a function of product life cycle stage—must be taken into account in planning.

The determinants of costs must also be scrutinized. Fixed costs that are large relative to variable costs often dictate low pricing in order to increase capacity utilization. On the other hand, large variable costs relative to fixed costs sometimes force up the price. In either case, however, efforts will be made to drive down both fixed and variable costs. Economies of scale, experience curve, shared learning, and product line considerations play a role here. Moreover, overall strategic goals must be taken into account. An overall cost leadership orientation will result in lower prices than will a product differentiation approach, for example.

Pricing must be coordinated with all the tactics used in implementing the marketing mix. This is so not only because the various tactics interact and can thwart or augment each other but also because profits and other goals are proportional to the magnitude of marketing mix expenditures which stimulate demand, as suggested by the profit formula discussed earlier. Therefore, the effects on demand of *all* the marketing tactics including price must be ascertained when determining price.

Pricing Tactics. Prices come in various forms; they are not limited to a single "purchase price." Quantity discounts, "2 for 1" deals, promotion allowances, coupons, and other gambits widen the scope of pricing tactics. Let us explore the options open to a marketer.

For a new product, either a price skimming or penetration pricing tactic is warranted. With *price skimming*, a high price is set. The hope is that enough customers exist who will be willing to pay a premium for the brand. As this market dries up, prices will be reduced gradually to draw in other customers. Price skimming is used when one wants to create an image of high product quality, when rivals will be slow to enter the market, when buyers value the product highly and demand is inelastic, or when fixed and variable costs either benefit little from experience curve effects or fail to achieve significant economies of scale. Hewlett-Packard, Polaroid, and DuPont have been known to practice price skimming.

Penetration pricing is the tactic of introducing a product at a low price, perhaps in anticipation of future cost declines and a burgeoning market. Over time, the price may or may not be raised. It is frequently employed as part of a market share strategy, as well as a means to generate primary demand. Unlike skimming, penetration pricing tends to discourage new entrants in that it signals strong price competition and relatively low profits. Penetration pricing works best when production and distribution channels are in place, consumers are price sensitive, either the adoption process is fast or the product is a frequently purchased good, and sufficient economies of scale and experience curve effects are forthcoming. Texas Instruments, Japanese auto makers, and Beaird-Poulan have used this approach.

The prices of industrial goods are strongly influenced by costs and competition. Indeed, many such goods are sold through competitive bidding arrangements. Alternatively, contracts are employed which focus on cost-plus or target-incentive considerations. Functionality and value are, of course, central concerns. In the selling of industrial goods, much negotiating of terms and tailoring of the product to the individual customer is done. This tends to make price not so much a decision variable, set independently by the seller and presented to the buyer in a take it or leave it fashion, as it is a mutually constructed accommodation that is constrained by factors that face both seller and buyer.

By contrast, pricing of consumer goods necessarily is done much more on the basis of company needs and before presentation to the consumer. Although market research is performed, so many buyers are involved, with all their different tastes and resources, that an "average" price must be set. In addition, the manufacturer must often take wholesalers and retailers into account when setting prices. Intermediaries require incentives and compensation for their efforts. This complicates the price-setting task and introduces an additional set of constraints. Industrial goods sold through distributors or manufacturers' representatives exhibit similar problems.

Pricing decisions must be made throughout the life cycle of a product. Price elasticities typically decline as the product moves from the introduction phase, through the growth phase, to the leveling-off phase. They increase, however, in the decline phase. Moreover, increases in competition throughout the product life cycle drive prices downward. At the same time, variations in growth, market share, and profitability across brands in a product line interact complexly with price decisions and must be watched carefully.

Distribution Decisions

Designing the Channel. The *channel of distribution* is the system of institutions used to deliver goods to the final consumer. The intermediaries who make up a given channel might include brokers, manufacturers' representatives, distributors, wholesalers, and retailers. Some or all might be wholly owned by the manufacturer or even by one of the intermediaries. Alternatively, the system might consist of independent businesses that buy and sell the goods of producers or act as the producers' agents through contractual agreements. Still another possibility is that a manufacturer might sell directly to its customers without going through intermediaries. For instance, direct mail, a sales force coupled with delivery through common carriers, or mobile company stores might be used. No matter what system is employed to bring the goods to market, certain *functions* must be fulfilled: transportation, storage, transfer of title, provision of credit or other special services, assortment, selling, delivery, receipt of funds, and so on.

Channel decisions must be considered carefully for several reasons. First, and most obviously, the channel of distribution is an essential link, a gatekeeper to the market. Shelf space in the supermarket or an account with an aggressive distributor is not only a necessity but tends to function as a self-fulfilling prophecy. That is, the channel stimulates demand, just as advertising, product design, and price cuts do. Second, it is very expensive and time consuming to set up and maintain a distribution channel. The commitment risks are great, and there is little room for error. Moreover, it is difficult to make changes in a channel once the channel has been set in place. Third, the channel of distribution may provide the competitive edge over rivals. This edge may be a unique location, efficient delivery and inventory practices, special selling skills, market monitoring services, or some other advantage. Finally, the selection of a channel will constrain or facilitate the choice and implementation of other marketing tactics. For example, retailers often require assistance from manufacturers in the form of promotions and business advice and at the same time expect the manufacturer to conduct advertising and other demand-stimulating activities. Different channel options imply different balances of power, influence, and control between manufacturer and intermediary as well.

The design of the channel depends on how consumers make decisions about the particular product, the number and dispersion of consumers, the amount of goods to be sold and their value, the costs of various channel options, the tasks that must be performed (e.g., service, credit provision, market research), and competitive practices. For example, when purchasing clothing most people like to compare many styles, colors, and brands, try on alternatives, receive a certain amount of help from salespeople, and make use of tailoring services. These factors, in turn, make clothing stores or store departments the dominant form of distribution. Nevertheless, for a few people who have neither the time nor the inclination to shop, catalog shopping is attractive, despite the uncertainties of fit and the absence of service.

We can view the *channel design* process as follows. First, the firm must decide whether *to sell direct or to work through intermediaries*. This, in turn, depends upon (1) how well each channel option can perform the aforementioned distribution functions for the firm, (2) the costs of reaching consumers, and (3) the degree of control the firm desires in managing the distribution of its goods. Selling direct provides the maximum control but is more expensive and less flexible in providing certain functions. Management must, therefore, weigh the gains against the costs to determine what is best in its own particular situation. Most consumer goods manufacturers find that it is easier and cheaper to go through independent wholesalers or distributors than it is to sell to retailers. But there are exceptions. Gallo Wine, for example, is large enough to do much of its own distribution directly to retailers. Industrial goods firms sometimes sell through distributors, yet in many cases they find direct selling possible.

If management decides to sell through intermediaries, then it must choose the *breadth of coverage* needed to reach consumers. Three possibilities exist. One is an *intensive distribution* system, in which the producer seeks as many outlets for its wares as possible in a market area. This option is most appropriate for selling to the mass market, particularly by producers of convenience consumer goods (for instance, breakfast cereal or paper napkins) or undifferentiated industrial goods (for instance, nuts and bolts). Buyers of these goods do little shopping around, purchase with a minimal amount of deliberation, and value convenience more than anything else. Intensive distribution also lends itself to products whose costs per unit to store, display, or sell are low. Pepsi Cola, Johnson's Wax, and Kellogg's Raisin Bran employ intensive distribution.

A second breadth of coverage option is *exclusive distribution*. This is the polar extreme of intensive distribution in that only a single outlet per market area is utilized. The producer hopes to create a unique image for its product, to obtain more vigorous selling efforts, and to extend its control over certain practices of the distributor or retailer (for instance in pricing, quality control, or market monitoring). In exchange, the intermediary receives the right to be the sole seller for the producer's goods and thereby gains special services and a competitive advantage in the market area. Most automotive companies, some manufacturers of expensive china, and certain appliance makers use exclusive distribution arrangements.

Selective distribution is the third option for achieving breadth of coverage. Here the firm seeks more than one, but considerably fewer than all, outlets in a market in the hope of obtaining many of the advantages of exclusive distribution while at the same time reaching further into the market. However, being a compromise tactic, it shares some disadvantages of both polar extremes. Selective distribution is especially appropriate for medium to moderately high-priced shopping, specialty, or industrial goods where personal selling is required. For example, Calvin Klein clothes, Hartmann Luggage, and Pioneer Electronics use what is essentially a selective distribution approach.

In addition to choosing a breadth of coverage option, the user of intermediaries also must decide upon the vertical *length of the channel system*. Here, too, at least three possibilities exist: corporate, contractual, or independent (also termed conventional or administered) systems.

The *corporate marketing channel* is one in which all stages from manufacture through distribution come under single ownership. Leading examples include Goodyear tires, Sherwin-Williams paints, and Shell oil and gas services. The advantages of a corporate system include lower costs (through standardization and other economies of scale) and greater control than with the other options. In particular, a firm can achieve more influence over hiring, pricing, promotion and selling, provision of service, and even product quality with a corporate system than it can with a contractual or an independent system. On the other hand, corporate systems require very large capital investments, are risky both financially and legally (i.e., they may invite antitrust actions), and tend to be less adaptive to changing market and competitive conditions. It should be noted that some firms employ a modified corporate channel system by vertically integrating partway into distribution.

Contractual channel systems consist of collections of more-or-less independent companies bound by legal agreements akin to exclusive distribution, yet going further. The most common contractual systems are *franchises*, but retail cooperatives and voluntary chains organized by wholesalers are also examples. Here we will focus on franchising which accounts for about one-third of all retail sales in the U.S.

Under franchising, the franchisor provides the franchisee with materials, a product, financial know-how, and other services. An exclusive right to sell the franchisor's product or service in a market area is also provided. The franchisee, in turn, agrees to abide by certain requirements and procedures dealing with selling, product or service quality, and other marketing functions, and perhaps also to pay a fee and/or percentage of revenues. Soft drink producers such as Coca-Cola, for example, sell the right to use their names and market their products in a market area and provide syrup concentrate to bottlers (i.e., franchised wholesalers) in exchange for finished production and marketing services. Another type of franchise operation is exemplified by Burger King, which provides land, equipment, supplies, technical and managerial advice, marketing plans, advertising support, and other services to a franchisee who pays an up-front investment fee, makes periodic royalty payments, and manages the business.

Franchising has pros and cons for franchisor and franchisee alike. On the plus side, franchisors obtain capital, a highly motivated distributor/retailer, and some economies of scale through purchases of supplies, manufacture, advertising, and promotion. Moreover, although franchising affords less control than does a corporate channel system, a strong degree of influence over marketing practice is still possible. Franchisees benefit in that they receive considerable amounts of money and support to get started in their own business, "instant" brand recognition and reputation, and ongoing managerial advice. On the negative side, however, the franchisor loses some control over, and is even dependent on, the franchisees. Uneven quality control by one or a few franchisees can hurt the industry-wide image of the franchisor's business, and legal encounters sometimes mar ongoing relationships with franchisees as well. Further, franchisees occasionally find that their freedom is restricted and that they must purchase supplies or services they do not want or which they could procure at less cost elsewhere. The initial investment for a franchise can be heavy, too, reaching into the hundreds of thousands of dollars or more.

Independent channel systems—the third vertical option—consist of loose associations of separate private enterprises that cooperate with each other for mutual gain. Typically, an independent wholesaler or distributor handles the goods for many producers and manufacturers. The services that independent intermediaries provide include such functions as storage and inventory control, delivery to retailers, provision of credit to buyers, a sales force, transfer of title, and information gathering on the marketplace. The intermediary usually buys goods from a manufacturer at a discount and resells them to retailers at a profit. Consignment selling or the right to return unsold merchandise are also frequent practices.

Independent channel systems offer producers the advantage of obtaining marketing services at a cost less than they could provide. Moreover, with an independent system the producer gains more flexibility and incurs less risk than it would with a corporate or contractual system. One may more easily switch to other independent intermediaries or set up an entirely new system in response to a changing market or competitive threats. Still another benefit is the expertise and market monitoring services provided. Unlike a contractual or franchise system, independents deal with competitors and sometimes are closer to the market. On the negative side, producers lose considerable control and at times pay higher margins. Procter & Gamble and General Electric are two well-known users of independent channels of distribution.

Managing Channel Relationships. Distribution decisions do not end with the design and establishment of the channel. Rather, choices must be made continuously with regard to channel modifications and ongoing management. Consumer tastes and purchase habits change, competitors invent new products and ways of marketing, and intermediaries' loyalties and levels of performance shift over time. The firm must evaluate the effectiveness of its current channel relations and alter them as necessary. This might mean adding or deleting wholesalers or retailers to change the breadth of coverage. More fundamentally, it might even mean introducing or bypassing a level in the length of the channel or exploring entirely new ways of bringing goods to the market. Which of these options is chosen will depend on the discovery of new markets or evolutions in old ones, competitive moves by rivals, or inadequacies in the existing arrangements.

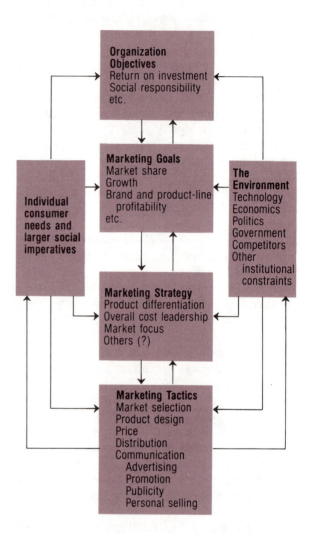

Figure 16-6. A summary of marketing management

Ongoing management of channel relationships, which may well constitute the producer's largest commitment in time and energy, can be the key to achievement of a competitive edge. A central concern here is motivation. The success of a firm rests, in part, on the productivity of individuals over whom it may have limited control. Healthy margins, attractive compensation, credit, contests, promotional allowances, point-of-purchase displays, various services, and other facets of the terms of trade can boost individual efforts to the producer's advantage. In addition, the intangible side of management—leadership and the everyday dealings in human contact—deserve attention. Formal and informal lines of communication facilitate the implementation of influence and accommodations that must be made in both directions if the channel is to compete effectively.

Also important is the management of conflict among members of the channel. Misunderstandings, conflicts of interest, and tension and strain are endemic to interpersonal and interfirm relationships. To cope with these, an attempt must be made to reduce ambiguity in expectations, rights, and responsibilities. A climate of cooperation and fairness must be fostered. These can be accomplished, in part, by establishing clear rules and procedures, making communications explicit, and engaging in joint decision making where appropriate.

Finally, a firm must establish managerial controls over channel operations. This means formulating appropriate goals, monitoring performance, administering rewards or corrective actions, and adjusting the functions of the channel to the other marketing tools.

Conclusion

Marketing is both the glue that binds the functional areas of the firm together and the bridge to the outer environment that leads to consumer satisfaction and, ultimately, the firm's survival. We have provided but a sketch of the many parts of modern marketing management. It is our hope that this chapter will motivate you to probe deeper into the marketing literature, develop a greater understanding of marketing, and eventually become a better manager in whatever area you may function. A summary of the major topics of the chapter appears in Figure 16-6.

NOTES

1. "Marketing: The New Priority," *Business Week*, November 21, 1983, pp. 96–99, 102–104, 106; "To Market, to Market," *Newsweek*, January 9, 1984, pp. 70–72.

2. Some of the facts of this case are drawn from Frederick C. Klein, "How a New Product Was Brought to Market Only to Flop Miserably," *The Wall Street Journal*, January 5, 1973, pp. 1, 19.

3. The three approaches are described in Michael E. Porter, *Competitive Strategy: Techniques for Analyzing Industries and Competitors* (New York: The Free Press, 1980). See also William K. Hall, "Survival Strategies in a Hostile Environment," *Harvard Business Review* 58 (September–October, 1980): 75–85.

4. In later years, after the 1978 acquisition of 7-Up by Philip Morris and a switch in ad agencies to N W Ayer, and into the 1980s, 7-Up seems to have lost some of its earlier hard-won successes. It is still far behind the market leaders—Coke and Pepsi—who have over 40 percent of the market, and with less than 6 percent market share is being pushed by Dr. Pepper and others. Perhaps 7-Up has reached a watershed in consumer acceptance or else the competition is too powerful to overcome.

5. J. Fred Bucy, "Marketing in a Goal-Oriented Organization: The Texas Instruments Approach," in J. Backman and J. Czepiel, eds., *Changing Marketing Strategy in a New Economy* (Indianapolis, Ind.: Bobbs Merrill, 1977).

6. "Note on the Use of Experience Curves in Competitive Decision Making" (Boston: Harvard Business School, Intercollegiate Case Clearing House, 9-175-174, 1975).

7. J. Fred Bucy, "Marketing in a Goal-Oriented Organization," 1977.

8. J. Fred Bucy, "Marketing in a Goal-Oriented Organization," 1977.

9. Lynn W. Phillips, Dae R. Chang, and Robert D. Buzzell, "Product Quality, Cost Position and Business Performance: A Test of Some Key Hypotheses," *Journal of Marketing* 47 (Spring 1983): 26–43.

10. The data quoted for the firms in the chain saw industry came from personal communication with Professor Michael E. Porter, as well as two cases he wrote: "The Chain Saw Industry in 1974" (Boston: Harvard Business School, Intercollegiate Case Clearing House, 9-379-157); and "The Chain Saw Industry in 1978" (Boston: Harvard Business School, Intercollegiate Case Clearing House, 9-379-176, 1979).

11. Much of the information presented here on Lipton Herbal Teas is drawn from a presentation by, and subsequent personal communications with, John W. Sullivan, who at the time of the case was president of Kelly, Nason, the ad agency for Lipton Herbal Teas.

12. Porter, *Competitive Strategy*.

13. See Porter, *Competitive Strategy*.

14. Michael E. Porter, "Notes on the Structural Analysis of Industries" (Boston, Mass.: Harvard Business School, No. 376-054, 1975).

15. Porter, "Notes on the Structural Analysis of Industries."

16. Gianni Lorenzoni, "From Vertical Integration to Vertical Disintegration: A Case of Successful Turnaround," unpublished working paper, University of Bologna, Italy, 1984.

17. "A Note on the Boston Consulting Group Concept of Competitive Analysis and Corporate Strategy" (Boston, Mass.: Harvard Business School, Intercollegiate Case Clearing House, No. 9-175-175, 1975); George S. Day, "Diagnosing the Product Portfolio," *Journal of Marketing* 41 (April 1977): 29–38.

18. Charles W. Hofer and Dan Schendel, *Strategy Formulation: Analytical Concepts* (St. Paul, Minn.: West Publishing Co., 1978).

19. S. J. Q. Robinson, R. E. Hichens, and D. P. Wade, "The Directional Policy Matrix-Tool for Strategic Planning," *Long-Range Planning* (June 1978): 8–15; D. E. Hussey, "Portfolio Analysis: Practical Experience with the Directional Policy Matrix," *Long-Range Planning* (August 1978): 2–8.

20. Robert D. Buzzell, Bradley T. Gale, and Ralph G. M. Sultan, "Market Share—A Key to Profitability," *Harvard Business Review* 53 (January–February 1975): 97–106.

21. George S. Day, "A Note on the Boston Consulting Group," p. 7.

22. Hall, "Survival Strategies in a Hostile Environment," pp. 78–79.

23. Porter, *Competitive Strategy*, Chapter 7.

24. This example is taken from a presentation to one of my MBA classes given by Mr. Elliot B. Ross of McKinsey and Company, Inc.

25. The estimated costs and failure rates are derived from Glen L. Urban and John R. Hauser, *Design and Marketing of New Products* (Englewood Cliffs, N.J.: Prentice-Hall, 1980), Ch. 2.

26. Alvin J. Silk and Glen L. Urban, "Pre-test Market Evaluation of New Packaged Goods: A Model and Measurement Methodology," *Journal of Marketing Research* 15 (May 1978): 171-91.

27. Herbert E. Krugman, "Why Three Exposures May Be Enough," *Journal of Advertising Research* 12 (December 1972): 11-14.

28. Richard Vaughn, "How Advertising Works: A Planning Model," *Journal of Advertising Research* 20 (1980): 27-33.

29. Point-of-Purchase Advertising Institute, 1978, quoted in D. I. Hawkins, R. J. Best, and K. A. Coney, *Consumer Behavior: Implications for Marketing Strategy* (Plano, Tex.: Business Publications, 1983), p. 563.

30. Kent B. Monroe and Albert J. Della Bitta, "Models for Pricing Decisions," *Journal of Marketing Research* 15 (August 1978): 413-28.

31. Robert J. Dolan and Abel P. Jeuland, "Experience Curves and Dynamic Demand Models: Implications for Optimal Pricing Strategies," *Journal of Marketing* 18 (Winter 1981): 52-73; C. D. Fogg and K. H. Kohnken, "Price-Cost Planning," *Journal of Marketing* 15 (April 1978): 97-106; Hermann Simon, "Dynamics of Price Elasticity and Brand Life Cycles: An Empirical Study," *Journal of Marketing Research* 16 (November 1979): 439-52; Frank M. Bass and Alain V. Bultez, "A Note on Optimal Strategic Pricing of Technological Innovations," *Marketing Science* 1 (Fall 1982): 371-78; B. Robinson and C. Lakhani, "Dynamic Price Models for New-Product Planning," *Management Science* 21 (1975): 1113-22.

Strategic Marketing — The Search for a Sustainable Competitive Advantage

David A. Aaker
University of California
at Berkeley

Strategic market management includes the product market investment decision which specifies the product markets in which the firm is to compete and the associated level of investment. Investment alternatives usually include divestment, milking, and holding strategies in addition to growth investment options. A second element of a business strategy is the development or maintenance of sustainable competitive advantages (SCAs) that will provide the entrepreneurial thrusts of the business.

The product market investment decision was in part stimulated by portfolio model and has absorbed considerable interest during the past two decades. However, attention is now shifting to the ability to compete, that is, to the development of sustainable competitive advantages. The challenge is to identify a source of a sustainable competitive advantage that exists or can be developed, a difficult task that will require new insights, structures, and methods. The search for SCAs suggests several issues and questions that business units will need to address during the coming decades.

What Skill or Asset Will Underlie the SCA?

A viable SCA usually is based upon one or more *business skills* or *assets*, which must be assessed relative to competitors and the environment and must be projected to a time when the key success factors of an industry may change. The difficulty of assessing the relevance and adequacy of a distinctive competence is illustrated by the decision of Coca-Cola to first enter the wine business in 1977 only to exit six years later. The relevance of their marketing and distribution competence was possibly overvalued in the light of the complexities of the wine market and the intensity of the competition.

Can a Preemptive Move Work?

A second source of a sustainable competitive advantage is a preemptive move. For example, a hospital supply firm made substantial inroads against a dominant, established firm by offering to place computer terminals in hospitals to facilitate ordering those items needed for emergencies. The terminals, of course, ultimately were used to order routine as well as emergency orders. Since hospitals had a need for only one such terminal, the established firm found its belated effort to duplicate the service frustrated—they had been preempted. However, successful preemptive moves are difficult to identify and risky to implement. The question is not only whether it will be successful and what investment will be required but whether competitors really will find it difficult to duplicate the innovation. Preemptive moves are similar to the so-called first-mover effect wherein a firm that enters a market first often enjoys learning curve, brand image, or other advantages over latecomers.

Can Synergy Be Created?

A third source of an SCA is an exploitable synergy. Synergy means that two or more business units operating together will be superior to the same business units operating independently. Generally the synergy will be caused by some commonality in the two operations such as distribution, brand image, sales or advertising effort, R & D effort, or manufacturing. As a result of synergy, the combined businesses will either have (1) increased revenues, (2) decreased operating costs, or (3) reduced investment.

Arm & Hammer, for example, capitalized on a 97 percent name recognition by successfully introducing a heavy-duty laundry detergent, an oven cleaner, and a liquid detergent. Because synergistic advantages are unique to an organization, they are difficult for competitors to imitate. The issue is usually to determine whether potential synergy will be realized. The Arm & Hammer name also spawned two failures—a spray underarm deodorant, for which the Arm & Hammer name may have had the wrong connotations (e.g., "too coarse"), and a spray disinfectant.

Is a Global Strategy Needed?

As illustrated by companies from Boeing to McDonald's, the ability to conceive and execute a global business strategy can provide the basis for an SCA. The ability to distribute operations across countries can be crucial in avoiding trade barriers. Mexico, for example, requires that 60 percent of automobiles sold in the country be made locally. Huge-scale economies are potentially available to those that can offer standardized consumer products, such as VCRs or automobiles, to multiple countries. In some industries, however, the need is to be able to adapt products and services to local conditions and markets. One obstacle to the development of global strategies is to effectively analyze the international environment of the business. The projection of the policies and strategies of competitors and governments of foreign countries can be critical but extremely difficult. The strategy employed by a foreign competitor, a policy change by a key government, the financial difficulty of a major country, or a worldwide shortage of some raw material may have a dramatic impact on an organization's strategy.

Will a Low-Cost Strategy Work?

One way to compete successfully is to have a low-cost strategy based upon economies of scale and experience curve effects caused by high volume, a cost-driven product design, manufacturing efficiencies, low overhead, efficient distribution, a government subsidy, purchasing assets of competitors below replacement cost, or by offering a "no-frills" product. The latter, simply to remove all frills and extras from the product or service, can be effective. Thus, warehouse furniture stores and legal services clinics can operate at a low cost and do so over long periods of time since the competition cannot easily stop offering the service that their customers are accustomed to and which is often built into their facilities.

Can the Strategy Be Implemented?

Too often strategy is developed without taking implementation issues into consideration. There are financial considerations. Are there enough resources to see through the strategy development phase even if competitors respond more aggressively than forecasts suggest or if the market is more difficult to impact than first thought? Perhaps more serious are organizational considerations. Does the strategy fit the people, culture, reward systems, and structure of the organization? A seemingly appropriate marketing strategy can fail if the organization setting is wrong. A distribution company with control over space for gum and candy in supermarkets decided to add a similar product that had been previously distributed primarily through drug stores. The obvious synergy never lived up to expectations because the incentive structure was inadequate to motivate the route people to actually push the new product.

Looking Ahead

The development of SCAs requires vision supported by a thorough understanding of the customer and potential customer. Thus, it seems clear that marketing tools and concepts will play a growing role in the process.

FOR FURTHER READING

I. Strategy

Michael E. Porter, *Competitive Strategy: Techniques for Analyzing Industries and Competitors*. New York: The Free Press, 1980.

Michael E. Porter, *Competitive Strategy*. New York: The Free Press, 1985.

II. General Marketing

Philip Kotler, *Marketing Management: Analysis, Planning, and Control*, 5th ed. Englewood Cliffs, N.J.: Prentice-Hall, 1984.

Joseph P. Guiltinan and Gordon W. Paul, *Marketing Management: Strategies and Programs*, 2nd ed. New York: McGraw-Hill, 1985.

III. Consumer Behavior

James R. Bettman, *An Information Processing Theory of Consumer Choice*. Reading, Mass.: Addison-Wesley, 1979.

Brian A. Sternthal and C. Samuel Craig, *Consumer Behavior: An Information Processing Perspective*. Englewood Cliffs, N.J.: Prentice-Hall, 1981.

John A. Howard, *Consumer Behavior: Application of Theory*. New York: McGraw-Hill, 1977.

IV. Product Decisions

Glen L. Urban and John R. Hauser, *Design and Marketing of New Products*. Englewood Cliffs, N.J.: Prentice-Hall, 1980.

Yoram J. Wind, *Product Policy: Concepts, Methods, and Strategy*. Reading, Mass.: Addison-Wesley, 1982.

V. Communication Decisions

David A. Aaker and John G. Myers, *Advertising Management*, 2nd ed. Englewood Cliffs, N.J.: Prentice-Hall, 1982.

Michael L. Ray, *Advertising and Communication Management*. Englewood Cliffs, N.J.: Prentice-Hall, 1982.

G. David Hughes and Charles H. Singler, *Strategic Sales Management*. Reading, Mass.: Addison-Wesley, 1983.

VI. Price Decisions

Kent B. Monroe, *Pricing: Making Profitable Decisions*. New York: McGraw-Hill, 1979.

VII. Distribution Decisions

Louis W. Stern and Adel I. El-Ansary, *Marketing Channels*, 2nd ed. Englewood Cliffs, N.J.: Prentice-Hall, 1982.

VIII. Marketing Research and Modeling

Paul E. Green and Donald S. Tull, *Research for Marketing Decisions*, 4th ed. Englewood Cliffs, N.J.: Prentice-Hall, 1978.

Gary L. Lilien and Philip Kotler, *Marketing Decision Making: A Model-Building Approach*. New York: Harper & Row, 1983.

IX. Miscellaneous

Theodore Levitt, *The Marketing Imagination*. New York: The Free Press, 1983.

Jagdish N. Sheth, *Winning Back Your Market*. New York: John Wiley & Sons, 1985.

Regis McKenna, *The Regis Touch*. Reading, Mass.: Addison-Wesley, 1985.

EPILOGUE: FINAL THOUGHTS

If you have built castles in the air,
your work need not be lost;
that is where they should be.
Now put foundations under them.
——Henry David Thoreau
(1817–1862)

You now have been exposed to the scope and complexities of marketing. My hope is that you have gained an *understanding* of the art and science of marketing and have developed an *intuition* for approaching marketing problems. It is also my hope that your interest in further study of marketing has been whetted and that you will be inspired to approach your everyday consumption activities and your work-related tasks with enthusiasm and high spirits. Marketing is so much a part of our lives that a basic grounding in its principles is sure to enrich your life experience.

But knowledge and a positive attitude are not enough. You must take the first step to turn that which you have learned into practice and fulfill the promise of performance, self-actualization, and social gain upon which higher education rests.

INDEX
